THE LITERATURE OF MEDIEVAL ENGLAND

THE LITERATURE OF MEDIEVAL ENGLAND

Edited by

D. W. ROBERTSON, JR.

Princeton University

*Sapientiam omnium antiquorum
exquiret sapiens.*

McGRAW-HILL BOOK COMPANY   *New York   St. Louis
San Francisco   Düsseldorf   London   Mexico   Panama   Sydney   Toronto*

This book was set in Bembo by William Clowes & Sons Ltd.
and printed on permanent paper and bound by Von Hoffmann Press,
Inc. The designer was Joan O'Connor; the drawings were done
by BMA Associates, Inc. The editors were Robert Fry and
Helen Greenberg. Les Kaplan supervised the production.

THE LITERATURE OF MEDIEVAL ENGLAND

Library of Congress Catalog Card Number 75–95827
53158
1234567890VHVH79876543210

ACKNOWLEDGMENTS

1 "A Pastourelle," "The Abandoned Hunt," and "As I Went on Yole Day" from *Early English Lyrics* by Chambers and Sidgewick. Reprinted by permission of Sidgewick and Jackson, Ltd.

2 "A Garland of Peacock's Feathers," "A Nun Whose Face Alone He Saw," "Aubade," "The Poet Talks with a Gray Friar," "The Poet Finds Other Things Than Love in an Inn," "The Ladies of Llanbadarn," and "May and January" from *Dafydd Ap Gwilym: Fifty Poems, Y Cymmrodor, XLVII*, by Bell and Bell. 1942. Reprinted by permission of the Honourable Society of Cymmrodorion.

3 *Sir Gawain and the Green Knight*, translated by Theodore Howard Banks, Jr. © 1929, 1957. Reprinted by permission of Appleton-Century-Crofts, Educational Division, Meredith Corporation.

From: Examples of Music Before 1400, selected and edited by Harold Gleason. Copyright 1942, Meredith Corporation. Reprinted by permission of Appleton-Century-Crofts.

From: The Statesman's Book of John Salisbury, translated and edited by John Dickinson. © 1927, 1955. Reprinted by permission of Appleton-Century-Crofts, Educational Division, Meredith Corporation.

4 "The Battle of Maldon" from *An Anthology of Old English Poetry*, translated by Charles W. Kennedy. © 1960 by Oxford University Press, Inc. Reprinted by permission.

"A Dream of the Cross" from *Early English Christian Poetry*, translated by Charles W. Kennedy. Oxford University Press, 1952. Reprinted by permission.

Beowulf: The Oldest English Epic, translated by Charles W. Kennedy. © 1940 by Oxford University Press, Inc. Renewed 1968 by Charles W. Kennedy. Reprinted by permission.

5 "Mactacio Abel," "Secunda Pastorum" from the *Wakefield Pageants in the Towneley Plays* by A. C. Cowley. Reprinted by permission of Manchester University Press.

6 "I and Pangur Ban My Cat" from *The Irish Tradition* by Robin Flower. Reprinted by permission of Clarendon Press, Oxford.

"Accessus to Can Grande della Scala" from *The Letters of Dante*, ed. Paget Toynbee, 2/e. Reprinted by permission of Clarendon Press, Oxford.

"Prologue," "Knight's Tale," "Prologue to the Miller's Tale," "Miller's Tale," "Wife of Bath's Prologue and Tale," "Words to Pardoner," and "Pardoner's Prologue and Tale" from *The Works of Geoffry Chaucer*, ed. W. W. Skeat. Reprinted by permission of Clarendon Press, Oxford.

"The Fair Maid of Astolat" from *The Works of Sir Thomas Malory*, ed. by Eugene Vinaver, 2/e. Reprinted by permission of Clarendon Press, Oxford.

7 Selection from *Piers the Ploughman*, translated by J. L. Goodridge. Reprinted by permission of Penguin Books, Ltd.

8 "The Epistle of Valerius to Ruffinus" from *Courtier's Trifles*, by Walter Map. Reprinted by permission of Chatto and Windus, Ltd.

9 "The Wanderer" from *Old English Elegies* by Charles W. Kennedy. Reprinted by permission of C. W. Kennedy.

10 "Everyman" from *Chief Pre-Shakespearean Drama* by John Q. Adams. Reprinted by permission of Houghton Mifflin Company.

11 "Boniface Advises Nithard to Continue His Studies," "Bishop Daniel of Winchester Advises Boniface on the Method of Converting the Heathen," "Boniface Askes Abbess Eadburga to Make Him a Copy of the Epistle of St. Peter in Letters of Gold," and "Boniface Asks Abbot Huetbert of Wearmouth to Send Him the Works of Bede" from *The Anglo-Saxon Missionaries in Germany* by C. H. Talbot. Reprinted by permission of Sheed and Ward, Inc., New York and London.

12   Chapter V, Chapter IX, Chapter X, Chapter XII from *Boccaccio on Poetry* by Charles G. Osgood, © 1956, by the Liberal Arts Press, Inc. Reprinted by permission of the Bobbs-Merrill Company, Inc.

13   Selection from musical score from *Early Medieval Music* by Huges, 1955. Reprinted by permission of Oxford University Press, London.

   Musical Score for "Angelus Ad Virginem" from *Ars Nova and the Renaissance, the New Oxford History of Music*, Vol. III, 1960. Reprinted by permission of Oxford University Press, London.

14   Selection from *Adam, a Religious Play of the Twelfth Century* by Stone. Reprinted by permission of the University of Washington Press.

15   Selections from *John of Salisbury's Frivolities of Courtiers and Footprints of Philosophers*, translated by Joseph B. Pike. Reprinted by permission of University of Minnesota Press, Minneapolis. © 1938 University of Minnesota.

16   "Culhwch and Olwen" from the book *The Mabinogion*. Translated by Gwyn Jones and Thomas Jones. Everyman's Library Edition, 1949. Reprinted by permission of E. P. Dutton and Company, Inc.

The author wishes to acknowledge those who provided the photographs and drawings in this book.

Text Art

Figure 1a   Photographie Giraudon.
Figure 1b   Photographie Giraudon.
Figure 2   By courtesy of the Trustees of the British Museum.
Figure 3   Diagram supplied by Chauncey Wood.
Figure 4   Diagram supplied by Chauncey Wood.
Figure 5   Diagram supplied by Chauncey Wood.
Figure 6   Copyright Museum of the History of Science, Oxford.
Figure 7a   Diagram supplied by Chauncey Wood.
Figure 7b   Diagram supplied by Chauncey Wood.
Figure 8   Cambridge University Press, Oxford.
Figure 9   Peterhouse College, Cambridge.
Figure 10   Diagram supplied by Chauncey Wood.
Figure 11   Art Reference Bureau.
Figure 12   Photographie Giraudon.
Figure 13   National Museum, Dublin.
Figure 14   National Museum of Wales.
Figure 15   Photographie Giraudon.
Figure 16   By courtesy of the Trustees of the British Museum.
Figure 17   By courtesy of the Trustees of the British Museum.
Figure 18   By courtesy of the Trustees of the British Museum.

Figure 19   By courtesy of the Trustees of the British Museum.
Figure 20   National Monuments Record. Crown Copyright.
Figure 21   Photographie Giraudon.
Figure 22   Photographie Giraudon.
Figure 23   Victoria and Albert Museum. Crown Copyright.
Figure 24   By courtesy of the Trustees of the British Museum.
Figure 25   From the Bayeux Tapestry, Edited by Sir Frank Stenton, Published by Phaidon Press, London, and Frederick A. Praeger, Inc., New York.
Figure 26   National Buildings Record, London.
Figure 27   By courtesy of the Trustees of the British Museum.
Figure 28   National Buildings Record, London.
Figure 29   Bodleian Library, Oxford.
Figure 30   Victoria and Albert Museum, London.
Figure 31   By courtesy of the Trustees of the British Museum.
Figure 32   By courtesy of the Trustees of the British Museum.
Figure 33   By courtesy of the Trustees of the British Museum.
Figure 34   Reproduced by courtesy of the Trustees, The National Gallery, London.
Figure 35   By courtesy of the Trustees of the British Museum.
Figure 36   By courtesy of the Trustees of the British Museum.
Figure 37   Princeton University Library.
Figure 38   Princeton University Library.
Figure 39   By courtesy of the Trustees of the British Museum.
Figure 40   By courtesy of the Trustees of the British Museum.
Figure 41   Princeton University Library

Chapter-opening Art

General Introduction   Photographie Giraudon.
Chapter I   By courtesy of the Trustees of the British Museum.
Chapter II   By courtesy of the Trustees of the British Museum.
Chapter III   Universitetets Oldsaksamling, Oslo.
Chapter IV   Photographie Giraudon.
Chapter V   University of London.
Chapter VI   Bodleian Library, Oxford.
Chapter VII   By courtesy of the Trustees of the British Museum
Chapter VIII   Bodleian Library, Oxford.
Chapter IX   By courtesy of the Trustees of the British Museum.
Chapter X   Bodleian Library, Oxford.
Chapter XI   Photographie Giraudon.
Chapter XII   Bodleian Library, Oxford.

PREFACE

The present volume is designed to provide an introduction to the literature produced in the British Isles during the Middle Ages. Selections from literature in Irish, Welsh, Latin, and French, as well as in Old and Middle English, are included. Except for some material in late Middle English, these selections appear in translations or modernizations. Irish and Welsh were not, in the Middle Ages, English; and Irishmen and Welshmen still maintain their distinct cultures. Nevertheless, the literature written in these languages had considerable influence on the development of English literature and deserves the careful attention of students of English. Latin was a literary language in England throughout the Middle Ages, so that Anglo-Latin literature has a legitimate place in English literary history. The tendency to relegate it to a vague realm of cultural background seldom brought into direct focus has no justification. For many years French was the language of the English royal court. There is little excuse for assigning literature written in French under English patronage to the literary history of France. It is to be hoped that students of English literature will in the future extend their horizons to include works by Englishmen who happened to write in French or Latin, and even to Continental writers who worked under English royal patronage. The authors of such literature usually had no intention of alienating themselves from the cultural traditions of England, and some of them produced work of great merit, now either neglected except by specialists or treated only in histories of French literature. In only one section of this volume, that devoted to literary theory, are works included by writers not specifically associated with England. Sophisticated literary culture during the Middle Ages was genuinely international, so that it is difficult to represent a single general subject of this kind without drawing upon writers of various nationalities.

In general, the editorial apparatus is arranged to afford minimum assistance to the general reader and preliminary guidance for the student. The bibliographies, which are elementary and highly selective, do not include articles in learned journals, since the general reader has no easy access to them, and the student may well find that his instructor wishes to make his own selections from the enormous mass of material available in this form. Critical opinions vary sharply concerning some of the more important texts. Where extensive annotation has been considered necessary among the selections here included, the editor has not sought to be eclectic, but has expressed his own views, with the full realization, however, that other views are possible. The opinions expressed will at least serve as a point of departure for the reader.

The principles of selection considered in the compilation of a volume of this kind are extremely complex, involving, as they do, matters of availability, the comparative merits of translations, the space available, and so on. A few translations by the editor appear. These were made for very mundane reasons, not because the editor especially wished to write translations. They include selections from Alcuin, John the Scot, Sedulius Scotus, St. Ethelred, Richard de Bury, Marie de France, Bernart of Ventadour, one poem by Froissart, and some excerpts from the mythographers. New translations were very generously supplied for this volume by the late H. V. M. Dennis, by L. A. Muinzer, by William O. Rogers, III, and by F. X. Newman. The section on cosmology in the General Introduction was provided by Professor Chauncey Wood. The editor is well aware of the fact that he who seeks to please everyone may well please no one. But at the very least there is sufficient variety in the present volume to provide those who may use it an opportunity to make their own selections from it.

D. W. Robertson, Jr.

CONTENTS

VI. Medieval Literary Theory   *263*

VIII. *Middle English Literature:* *Songs and Short Poems*   345

IX. *Middle English Literature: Romance*   *367*

X. *Middle English Literature: Piers the Ploughman*   *423*

XI. *Middle English Literature: Chaucer*   *467*

XII. *Middle English Literature: Early Drama in England*   *571*

THE
LITERATURE
OF MEDIEVAL
ENGLAND

GENERAL INTRODUCTION

I. Medieval Life and Ideals

The period of European history extending from the last days of classical antiquity to the Renaissance of the fifteenth century is known as "the Middle Ages"—the ages in between—as though these ages constituted a kind of interregnum between the classical world and what is thought of as a revival of classical traditions in modern times. Thus the philosopher Hegel characterized the period as one of "infinite falsehood" marked by the isolation and subservience of the individual and by the gradual "secularization" of the Church. In a more popular sense, the word *medieval* is still used frequently to describe harsh, oppressive, or superstitious practices. Most of us are therefore prepared to assume offhand that the Middle Ages marked an unproductive period

Facing page: Très riches heures du Duc de Berry. *A warm hearth in February.*

from which humanity is fortunate to have escaped. However, recent historians have begun to discover that the break between antiquity and the Middle Ages, especially in intellectual and cultural development, was not so sharp as was once thought and that, moreover, the decisive beginnings of the modern world are to be found, not in the Renaissance, but in the mid-eighteenth century. With these newer perspectives there has come a revival of interest in medieval culture, an interest inspired not so much by the romantic nostalgia that made knights and their ladies favorite subjects of nineteenth-century romance, but by a genuine desire for understanding.

However we may characterize them, the thousand years of the Middle Ages form a rich and varied chapter in human history. The unsettled social conditions of the early years of the period, marked by the gradual economic and political collapse of the Roman Empire and by the success of barbarian invasions, left the task of maintaining cultural traditions to the Church. Monastic centers were islands of civilization in a chaotic world of economic collapse and warfare. As time passed, a new form of social organization, known as feudalism, gradually developed to replace the family, tribal, and warrior groups of the barbarians. During the eleventh and twelfth centuries feudal society rapidly developed its own ideals, consistent with the hierarchical patterns of Patristic theology and reinforced by the ethical doctrines of late classical philosophy, especially as those doctrines were found explicitly in the writings of Cicero and Seneca and implicitly in the writings of Virgil, Horace, and Ovid. Among philosophical writings, *The Consolation of Philosophy* of Boethius exerted a profound and continuous influence. The Church gradually spread its civilizing disciplines beyond the monasteries, which began to be replaced as centers of learning by cathedral schools. Some of these schools became universities, and one of them, at Paris, became the center of European culture. Toward the close of the period, feudal ideals came to be supplemented by a more nationalistic spirit, trade and commerce contributed to the rapid growth and relative prosperity of cities, and, by the fifteenth century, the merchant classes were beginning to assert a culture of their own, still basically religious in outlook, but nevertheless different in taste and attitude from the more aristocratic culture of the past. The break with the aristocratic traditions of the past was not completed,

however, until the French Revolution, and we should not seek modern attitudes toward the individual or toward society in medieval writings. There is some truth in the assertion that the rococo style marks the last flowering of a tradition that extends from antiquity without fundamental upheaval throughout the Middle Ages and the Renaissance. In any event, the Middle Ages can hardly be called a period of stagnation, a mere lapse between Athens and Washington.

From a sociological point of view, medieval men tended to bond themselves together in small, tightly knit groups, most of which preserved the hierarchical structure of the patriarchal family. To a certain extent, this development may be said to have begun in late antiquity, when the country villas of wealthy Romans throughout the empire, having been cut off by inflation and heavy taxation from the cities, frequently became independent and self-supporting. The Germanic barbarians, meanwhile, formed themselves into small military units somewhat resembling the *comitatus* described by Tacitus in the *Germania*. These groups were originally bound by blood relationships, but in the course of time military leaders began to acquire followers from alien families bound to them by personal contractual obligations designed to perpetuate the kind of integrity that rested originally on family ties. Later on, feudal holdings supported groups bound by ties of homage and fidelity to a noble overlord. When merchants began to flourish in urban centers, they formed guilds or confraternities, which were not trade unions in the modern sense, but groups of men, some poor and some wealthy, banded together in a restricted area by virtue of a common interest in a trade or craft. Typically, such guilds originally developed from parish fraternities centered in local parish churches. Meanwhile, there were fraternities of other kinds, not associated with any special trade, and in the country the parish church frequently served as a center for community life. The prosperous craftsman in the city might have living in his house a number of servants, journeymen, or apprentices, who, like his own wife and children, formed a part of his *familia* or household, and to whom he acted as a father as well as a master. For the most part, industrial work was carried on in households of this kind. The master's house was his shop; his workers sat at his table and slept under his roof.

This fragmentation of society into small units, largely familial in structure, constitutes what Hegel called "isolation"; but, as modern sociologists inform us, although small groups may be isolated to a certain extent from one another and may come into conflict at times, they serve to prevent the isolation of the individual who belongs to them. During the Middle Ages, most men, except during dislocations arising from war or pestilence, enjoyed a more or less natural place in their communities. Young boys could readily see their elders at work, knew what they did, and were not puzzled about their own identity as members of the community. In this situation a man's interests were naturally centered on the welfare of his group, which was, in effect, a part of his own identity. The behavior of the other members of the group to which he belonged was a matter of vital interest to him, since the effects of that behavior on his own welfare were immediately apparent. Group behavior, however, is a moral rather than a psychological problem. It was natural, therefore, that medieval men should think in moral terms, whereas we today, as members of large amorphous groups not based on close personal relationships, are likely to think of our problems as being personal or psychological.

However isolated medieval social groups may have been from one another, and however frequently they may have come in conflict with each other, in feudal warfare, in clashes among guilds, or in other ways, they were united by a common set of Christian beliefs and by a common interest in the larger community of the Church. Here they shared not only a mutual respect for the Word of God, but also, especially after the end of the twelfth century, a mutual participation in the sacraments. The fact that men were professed Christians, however, did not mean that they were necessarily moral in their behavior, nor that they were hypocrites or pagans if they were not moral. Medieval Christian doctrine readily acknowledged that Christ came for the benefit of sinners, not for the sake of the virtuous. No man was thought to be free from the stain of sin. One of the decrees of the great Lateran Council of 1215 stipulated that every individual among the adult faithful should go to confession before his parish priest at least once a year, the assumption being that he would have need to reveal a considerable number of "deadly" sins accumulated during a year's time, no matter how virtuous he might be. The whole point of the New Law, or the message of the New Testament, was felt to be that mercy is available through Christ to all those who are truly penitent. The Old Law, it was said, told men what not to do, but offered no relief from the almost impossible task of obeying all its admonitions. The New Law provided an opportunity to love God and one's fellow man in such a way that contrition might follow violation of the moral law. Medieval Christianity was a religion of love, not of righteousness.

At the same time, however, the "love of one's neighbor" had nothing in common with "the brotherhood of man," an ideal popularized both by Christian thinkers and by secular philosophers during the nineteenth century. The fact of humanity was not regarded as an excuse for errant behavior, nor as a predicament beset by ambiguity and potential irrationality. It implied, on the contrary, an obligation to act reasonably. Medieval society, as it developed, became hierarchical in structure, and it was widely recognized that some men were more lovable, or more reasonable, than others. Vicious men were not thought of as being merely bestial, but as worse than bestial, since a beast has no reason to corrupt. We should not, therefore, expect democratic or humanitarian sentiments among medieval authors. Such sentiments were not promulgated by medieval theologians and would certainly have found small sympathy among the medieval nobility.

It cannot be emphasized too strongly, however, that the New Law, frequently expressed as "justice tempered with mercy," or as the love of "common profit," as contrasted with self-love or malice, was a social and political as well as a theological ideal. King Alfred introduced his laws with the Ten Commandments followed by the two Precepts of Charity, feudal lords of all ranks were urged to temper justice with mercy in the treatment of their subjects, vassals were admonished to love their overlords, university colleges were theoretically unified in charity, and even Italian cities were described as communities held together by a bond of charity. The problem of whether or not this ideal was observed, as in the nature of things it frequently was not, was of urgent practical importance to men in all walks of life. Tyranny and oppression in any medieval community, from the hierarchy of the kingdom to the domestic hierarchy of the family, were associated with the Old Law, the malice of which was considered natural to fallen man. It is hardly surprising, therefore, that contrasts between the Old Law and the New should have been one of the most characteristic

Figure 1a *The Church. Strassbourg Cathedral.*

Law was thought of as a fulfillment of the Old, and charitable love was simply love directed toward "the invisible things of God" that lay beyond, but implicit in, the visible things of creation. When we see figures of the Church and the Synagogue on Gothic portals (Figure 1); we should recall that these figures do not represent a contrast between Christianity and Judaism literally; they exemplify, from a medieval point of view, determining factors in the behavior of any individual and in the structure of any community. The Synagogue stands with the broken staff of worldly dominion or tyranny in one hand and the tables of the Mosaic law drooping toward the earth in the other. Her blindfold indicates her inability to see spiritual realities beneath the surfaces of the visible and tangible. On the other side, the Church holds the Cross, the symbol of victory through penance, in one hand and the chalice of the grace of the New Law in the other. Among the throngs who enter the church between these two figures, there are those still bound in the spirit of the Synagogue by desire for self-satisfaction through things that may be seen or touched. Their hearts are set on wealth, power, fame, or the pleasures of the flesh. These are men who seek to dominate and exploit the communities to which they belong for their own selfish purposes, driven by that worst ingredient of what were called vices, or evil habits of the soul, malice. Beside them walk the more charitable, penitent for their transgressions, their hearts set on God, the supreme exemplar of justice, wisdom, and mercy. Perhaps some walked in one way on one day and in another on the next, but the charitable were those capable of the civilized restraints and daily sacrifices that make life in a community possible. At the same time, there was thought to be something of the Church and something of the Synagogue in every man. No one extricates himself completely from worldly concern, no matter how hard he may try to do so.

It should be emphasized that the attitudes of men of all kinds in this congregation are basically practical and not at all sentimental. It was felt that devotion to God was extremely reasonable and that those who pursued selfish ends were foolish and that their actions were self-defeating. The transitory world of the tangible was said to produce merely transient satisfactions leading to inevitable frustration. Creation was thought of as a grand hierarchy, but beyond the hierarchy of nature was a hierarchy of values that alone could satisfy a reasonable

themes of medieval art and literature. The theme is by no means theoretical or academic in the context of medieval life. If a man's neighbors in his community were selfish and malicious, the day-to-day consequences of that fact might be very distressing to him; on the other hand, if he acted out of malice himself, the result would be an uncomfortable isolation from the group that furnished his identity and made his own achievements meaningful.

The two laws or loves were not opposites; the New

creature. The two statues thus stand as exemplifications of what we should call political, social, and psychological realities—realities that confront everyone daily in the ordinary conduct of life.

Until the last years of the Middle Ages men did not ordinarily think in what we would call political, social, and psychological terms. They easily identified their own interests with those of their communities, so that we should not be surprised to find, in medieval texts, problems of these three types all discussed in terms of morality. With reference to the last especially, it is significant that the word *personality*, used to mean the peculiar qualities of a given individual, did not come into current use until the eighteenth century, and that ideas like "the force of personality," or "the depths of personality," are peculiar to the nineteenth and twentieth centuries. Some recent theologians have, indeed, sought to locate God in the depths of the personality, and human personality has become a primary concern of modern literature and art. But such ideas, and the profound interest in psychology that accompanies them, are the products of an industrial civilization in which individuals find themselves more or less isolated in their efforts to achieve meaningful life as members of large, loosely formed groups. Medieval men were likely to think of their problems as community problems and of their own behavior in moral rather than in psychological terms. It is a mistake, therefore, to seek psychological profundity in medieval art or to expect characters in medieval literature to display personality in the modern sense of the word. There is no reason why this fact should be disappointing. The same shortcoming, if we wish to call it that, characterizes most classical literature and art as well. The better able we are to refrain from reading our own conventions into earlier literature and art, the better we shall be able to understand and, actually, to appreciate that literature and art and to understand the peculiar appeal of the literature and art of our own time.

During the Middle Ages human behavior was most often analyzed in terms of virtues and vices (Figure 2). We have been taught by the nineteenth century to think of morality as being a dull subject, the concern of stuffy and hypocritical persons who are likely to seek to oppress our innocent natural inclinations so that we become even more unhappy than we already are. Concerning nineteenth-century morality all this may be true, for the Christianity of the period is characteristic-

Figure 1b   *The Synagogue. Strassbourg Cathedral.*

ally a religion of literal-minded righteousness rather than of love, frequently much closer in spirit to what medieval men called the Synagogue than to what they called the Church. Medieval morality was a different sort of thing entirely, embracing, as it did, much of the best ethical content of late classical thought. It was founded squarely on the principle that human behavior is ultimately a matter of love. The Christian conception of grace developed from the conviction that if men could be led to love properly, that is, to love intelligible

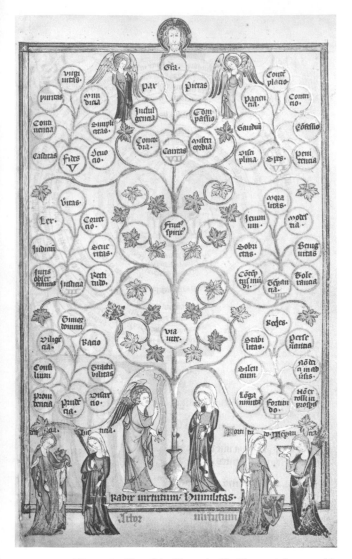

Figure 2 *Tree of the Virtues (14C). The tree is here rooted in Humility, typified by the Blessed Virgin Mary at the Annunciation. Its fruits are the Cardinal Virtues numbered I through IV, each with seven attendant virtues, and the Theological Virtues, numbered V through VII, each also with seven attendant virtues. The figures at the bottom represent the Cardinal Virtues once more. From left to right they are Prudence, Justice, Fortitude, and Temperance.*

tween prosperity and adversity, or changes in Fortune, as they were called, would not affect them deeply. A virtuous man could, to paraphrase St. Augustine, love and do what he wished to do, satisfying his own desires and at the same time contributing to the welfare of his fellow men.

The vices that men were taught to avoid were described as essentially selfish habits of the soul springing from misdirected love. Such habits led to actions called sins, or actions contrary to reason. In accordance with the most popular classification developed during the Middle Ages, especially relevant to confession and penance, there were said to be seven such vices: pride (or vainglory), covetousness (or avarice), wrath, envy, sloth, gluttony, and lechery. The first five of these were usually thought of as being spiritual, and the last two as being physical, although the fifth, sloth, might have both physical and spiritual manifestations. Since the physical vices could manifest themselves without any very great element of malice, they were somewhat less serious than the first five. A man habitually inclined toward any one of them was said to be "vicious," his actions in manifesting them were called "sins," or, if they were especially grave, "crimes." Sins were said to be of two kinds: "venial" and "mortal." Venial sins, inadvertent rather than deliberate manifestations of the vices, were thought to be characteristic of ordinary human behavior. A sincere daily recitation of the Paternoster was considered a sufficient remedy for them, and no one was required to mention them at confession. But deliberate manifestations of the vices involving the full consent of the reason were "deadly" sins. Under the Old Law they incurred almost automatic damnation, but under the New Law the stains they left on the soul could be at least partially removed through contrition of heart, confession to a priest, and satisfaction, or the performance of acts of charity and self-denial.

From a practical point of view, a vicious person in these terms would be a disruptive element in his community, and the more elevated his station in the community hierarchy, the more dangerous his actions would become to its welfare. At the same time, it is not difficult to see that any of the vices might lead to what we would call alienation and frustration. Medieval men expressed a similar idea by saying that the vicious man was a slave to his own desires. The problem of sin was thus a very practical matter in daily life and not simply

rather than tangible realities, they could live together in harmony and be freed from the burdens of social oppression and personal frustration. Fluctuations be-a manifestation of what is sometimes mistakenly assumed to be a characteristic medieval concentration on the afterlife.

The virtues commended by the medieval Church were subject to a variety of classifications, depending on the context in which they were being discussed. A virtue, like a vice, was described as a habit of the soul having its origin in love. That is, love directed toward creatures for their own sakes, or cupidity, led to vices. Love directed toward God, who was frequently described as the epitome of power, wisdom, and love, or toward the intelligible, led to virtue. Using a distinction found in Cicero, medieval writers insisted that a virtue has two parts: an "office," or form of behavior, and an "end," or goal toward which the virtuous action is directed. A kind of behavior usually considered to be virtuous but motivated by selfish interests had the office of a virtue, but not its end. Such action was said to represent "false virtue," or "vice masquerading as virtue." For example, chastity had long been considered a virtue under certain circumstances in antiquity, and it was still regarded as a virtue in the Middle Ages. But chastity for a selfish end, like worldly reputation, was actually the manifestation of a vice. St. Gregory, for example, called such chastity "fornication of the spirit." It is obvious that persons who, either because they are misguided or because they are deliberately malicious, disguise their vices as virtues may be even more dangerous to their communities than overtly vicious persons. It was often said that when Antichrist came, he would come not as a pagan but as a hypocrite.

Among the virtues most frequently mentioned are the "theological" virtues and the "cardinal" virtues. The theological virtues—faith, hope, and charity—are perhaps the most difficult to describe in modern terms. Today we have a great deal of what might be called scientific faith. That is, the scientist who performs certain operations in his laboratory has faith that similar materials under similarly controlled conditions will always behave in the same way. Even when he confesses that the laws he discovers are merely descriptions based on arbitrary classifications, he maintains his faith in their validity. Laymen are readily led to place even greater confidence in them, since they may result in better communications systems, foods, medicines, weapons, and so on. Medieval men, frequently to the disgust of modern historians of science, placed far less faith in "knowledge by experiment upon things seen."

Their technology, although it grew considerably during the later Middle Ages, was comparatively underdeveloped. However, we should remember that technology depends for its development on the general structure of society; it grows to meet needs largely created by itself. Medieval men were more concerned with the values used to make human relationships meaningful, and to them the first requisite of such meaningful relationships was faith, not in the validity of natural law, but in God.

God has meant a great many different things to different people in the course of history, and the general concept of God has undergone changes over the centuries concomitant with changes in society. Medieval men tended to think in terms of hierarchies, and to them God represented the apex in the hierarchy of being. God was not, strictly speaking, the apex of the hierarchy of physical being, but the apex of the hierarchy of intelligible being. During the seventeenth and eighteenth centuries these two hierarchies became confused, so that the intelligible became a kind of upper extension of the visible. Once placed there, it became more and more remote, since it was clearly not subject to the same sort of analysis as was the visible hierarchy. The romantics still looked for it in the visible world, seeking God in nature, or transformed it into a transcendent infinite. Today, it has become increasingly difficult to comprehend the idea of an external reality of the intelligible, so that we seek various kinds of subjective reality to replace it. But we shall have difficulty understanding medieval art and literature unless we can imagine that men once believed firmly in an external realm of the intelligible readily accessible to the reason. To medieval men, God was something that existed outside of the world of space and time, except, that is, in His Incarnation. However, He permeated the physical world, through which He might be understood partly as in a mirror. He was also the source of the virtues. To believe in God was, among other things, to believe in the reality and efficacy of virtue. Faith was conventionally described as "belief in things unseen," and those things unseen supplied the necessary motivation for the kind of conduct that was thought to make life on earth satisfying and bearable. It was often said that God is love, and love was, as we have seen, the binding force of community life.

To the medieval mind, if a man had no faith, he could not be expected to be virtuous except when an appearance of virtue suited his selfish interests. A faithless man was therefore regarded as an untrustworthy man. In medieval society, at least in the northern parts of Europe, contracts between lord and vassal were verbal rather than written. Their terms depended upon remembered custom, and their efficacy was a function of the integrity of the parties. In a feudal kingdom a bond of fidelity extended by degrees from the serf on the manor to the king, and the king, theoretically at least, owed fealty to God for his holdings. The faith a man owed his fellows was felt to be an aspect of his faith in God. Faith placed in a temporal object for its own sake—in a man, in a woman, or in wealth or position—was regarded as false faith, in the nature of things inevitably frustrating and disappointing. Men, women, possessions, and worldly acquisitions of all kinds are subject to the whims of Fortune. He who has faith in them subjects himself to those whims also.

Hope, the second of the theological virtues, is first of all the hope that men of goodwill may have for an eternal reward. But hope is not always a virtue, and whether it is virtuous or not, it is a matter of daily concern. The covetous man hopes that new wealth may be his, the lecherous man hopes for the favors of many ladies, and so on. The virtuous man hopes for a certain inner peace that comes with spontaneously virtuous inclinations, for fortitude to bear his afflictions, and for the peace and goodwill of his fellow men. Hope for temporal satisfaction was thought of as false hope dependent on Fortune. This does not mean that men could not hope to improve their lot. So long as such hope was consistent with common profit rather than centered on immediate personal satisfactions, it was thought to be virtuous.

The last of the theological virtues, often called the greatest of them, was charity, or love. All men, it was said, love, for without love a man would die, since he would have no interest in preserving himself or in perpetuating his species. Love, that is, was regarded as the source of all human motivation. Theologians explained that before the Fall Adam and Eve loved as they should, without concupiscence. After the Fall, in which both reason and love were impaired, man acquired the concupiscence that had formerly been proper only to the beasts, for without it he would not have protected himself and would have had no inclination to perpetuate his species. Human beings are said to inherit this concupiscence, so that all who are born in

the world naturally love first of all those things that can be seen and touched. Through grace, however, provided by the example and teachings of Christ and by the Holy Spirit (or that aspect of the Trinity whose function is love), men may be contented with a sufficiency appropriate to their station and may direct their love toward the intelligible. That is, charity, combined with a reason restored at least partially to its original condition, removed malice from the heart and allowed men to function pleasurably as useful members of their communities. The idea that man should love God and his neighbors for the sake of God had profound social and political as well as psychological implications.

The cardinal virtues, actually an inheritance from antiquity, were justice, prudence, temperance, and fortitude. Allied with them were a host of other virtues, some gleaned from classical and Patristic authorities, and some, like courtesy and chivalry, derived from peculiarly medieval social needs. A special set of virtues, seven in number, was associated with the Gifts of the Holy Spirit and together these virtues were regarded as remedies for the seven principal vices.[1] Thus the gift of the fear of God is effective against pride and conducive to the virtue of humility. The gift of piety is effective against envy and produces the virtue of benignity or friendship. Similarly, through the gift of knowledge, temperance replaces wrath; through the gift of fortitude, prowess replaces sloth; through the gift of counsel, mercy replaces avarice; through the gift of understanding, sobriety replaces gluttony; and through the gift of wisdom, chastity replaces lechery. The vices here have somewhat different connotations from those with the same names in the ordinary lists made for confessional purposes. It is clear, for example, that lechery, which here requires the highest gift of wisdom for its eradication, is not simply a matter of casual physical lapses and that gluttony is something more than a peasant's occasional drunkenness. The fear of God was, on scriptural authority, regarded as the "beginning of wisdom," and the various steps beginning with humility and ending in wisdom represent an upward progress. If we look at the list as a whole, it becomes clear that virtue not only involves some sort of self-denial; it also entails positive and forceful effort for the sake of others. No man was expected to be altogether virtuous, but all men were encouraged to love virtue, which was, as Cicero had long ago pointed out in his treatise on friendship, the only satisfying source of amicable human relationships. One was urged to love his fellow man, not because he was accidentally human, but because he was either virtuous or potentially virtuous. The saints, the philosophers of antiquity, and the heroes of both ancient and medieval times were revered for their virtues.

Without virtue, it was felt, the communities of medieval society would have become stale, dull, and conducive to perpetual fear and suspicion. Ruskin regarded sin as a terrible and perpetual burden, and Cardinal Newman did not wish to encumber liberal education with the burden of virtue. But to the medieval mind, sin ceased to become a necessary burden with the New Law, and although all men were thought to be sinners, most could find some virtues suited to their station that they could regard with genuine reverence and even enthusiasm.

Whatever we may think of the Church today, or of Christianity generally, we should be careful not to confuse modern conditions with medieval conditions. During the Middle Ages the Church was responsible for the establishment and maintenance of civilized life in Western Europe. The literary monuments of Latin antiquity are for the most part available to us today only by virtue of the fact that they were copied by medieval scribes, typically in monasteries. We may say that the Church controlled medieval education, but the only reason it did so was that it established and maintained educational institutions. Until the late Middle Ages no one was especially anxious to relieve the Church of this

responsibility, and very few thought that the Church was oppressive or blindly authoritarian in doctrine. Members of the ecclesiastical hierarchy were, like everyone else, human. Some of them were notorious sinners, and some were ignorant, selfish, and locally oppressive. Churchmen participated freely in the life of the times. A bishop might be a great feudal lord, an abbot might profit considerably in the wool trade, and high ecclesiastics frequently held major positions in royal governments. In country parishes, the parson or vicar shared in the agricultural pursuits of his community. In a given country the ecclesiastical hierarchy was affected by the general health of the realm. Thus during the last quarter of the fourteenth century in England, the decay of political institutions was accompanied by a decay in ecclesiastical institutions. In general, when reform movements arose, their aim was not the establishment of a new secular morality, but the restoration of what were regarded as good ancient and traditional customs, based on a thoroughly Christian ideology. We should bear in mind that the revolt against Christianity that permeated much nineteenth-century and early-twentieth-century thought was a revolt against Christianity as it was conceived at the time, not as it was conceived in earlier times. Medieval authors lacked the avid pursuit of the new and different and the general rebelliousness that characterize modern authors. Their interests were still, generally, centered on their communities rather than on personal feelings and private problems.

Note

1   For an excellent account of these virtues and their significance, see Rosemond Tuve, *Allegorical Imagery*, Princeton University Press, Princeton, N.J., 1966, chap. 2.

II. *Medieval Astronomy and Astrology*[1]

In this day of clocks, calendars, and television weather forecasts, the daily and annual apparent motions of the heavens have less utility than they at one time possessed and are as a consequence virtually unknown in any detail. To be sure, the universe is still studied, and the philosophical implications of these observations are considered, but because of our present conceptions about the nature and functioning of the universe, this study is carried on in a rarefied atmosphere of advanced mathematics and is in general divorced from our daily experience. Of course, both amateur and professional sailors are often well informed about the moon's phases and the tides, while a great many people have developed an interest in celestial mechanics recently because of the dramatic space program. However, insofar as we may say that medieval man had a vision of the world that was an operative part of his thought and art, we may more accurately say that we today have no vision of the world at all than to say that ours is different. Unhappily we have fared in quite another manner on a lesser level, for the practice of selling astrological information, a practice that we tend to relegate to the supposedly superstitious Middle Ages, is now carried on in more efficient media than ever before, such as magazines and the radio, and as a result such messages undoubtedly reach larger numbers of people today than in theoretically less enlightened times.[2]

There are other, less obtrusive, ways in which astronomy and astrology still have a role in our society —ways that are often little known. For example, the appropriate Sunday for Easter is determined now as it was in the Middle Ages by a certain relationship between the vernal equinox and the full moon; and our language bears the imprint of centuries of concern for astrology in such adjectives as *saturnine, jovial, mercurial, martial,* and even *venereal,* while *lunatic* and *disaster* owe their origins to the Latin *luna,* the moon, and *astrum,* a star. Finally, in a lighter vein, there is a curious vogue at the moment for decorations involving armillary spheres (from the Latin *armilla,* meaning bracelet), which have appeared as statuary, lamp bases, and designs for Christmas cards. In more basic ways, however, not only is the so-called Ptolemaic or geocentric

cosmology no longer with us, but no true successor has taken its place. Christianity formerly linked cosmology with religious philosophy so that the image of the universe reached out to every aspect of human thought, but the grand, predictable turnings of the heavens that figured forth the order and harmony of the universe, which Marlowe called "the wondrous architecture of the world," have found no heirs in modern cosmology, which is ultimately dependent upon random events.

The very differentness of the medieval universe from our own invites our study of it, for we cannot fully appreciate the world we live in until we contrast it with a different *Weltanschauung,* or "world picture," and the older cosmology is indeed very unlike our own. For example, C. S. Lewis has pointed out that where our universe is thought to be dark, the other one was presumed to be illuminated; and while Pascal could be disturbed by the silence of the vast spaces between the stars, the universe was formerly thought to produce the "music of the spheres" that only the wise man could hear. Furthermore, the often-heard charge that the earth-centered universe of former times was the product of man's sense of self-importance is questionable, for we may observe in a medieval poet and philosopher like Dante that although the spheres are first described as surrounding earth, they are then more properly seen in an inverted order surrounding God, so that God, not man, is at the center.[3] This, of course, may be contrasted to our contemporary cosmology, which has no spiritual center and which is fleeing its physical center (if it has one) rather than "dancing" or "singing" around it. This last is important, for our universe comprises galaxies that flee from each other at paradoxically increasing speeds, perhaps caused by some cosmic explosion; movement in the older world was caused by an attraction for something higher, and this attraction was invariably called love.[4]

The older universe, then, was ordered where ours is random, harmonious where ours is explosive, and spiritually directed where ours has neither physical nor spiritual goal. Ours is running down, it might be added, while the older one was moved by divine love, a power source not subject to decay. The former world, then, is not only a different place, but also a very attractive one, one that man's mind could perceive as relating to himself both physically and spiritually, while our present concept is of a universe operating blindly according to laws in which man plays no conceivable part. Order, harmony, and purpose characterize the old cosmology, in which everything is linked and graduated. Thus St. Bonaventura in his *Itinerarium Mentis in Deum* could say that earth and its inhabitants, being terrestrial bodies, were mutable and corrupt, while celestial bodies such as planets were mutable and incorruptible, and super-celestial bodies such as the souls in heaven were immutable and incorruptible. In this way, the heavens are seen not as cutting us off from the rest of the universe but linking us as a tertium quid (a necessary third thing in the middle) with God. The link was rational, too, for the movements of the stars and planets were complex but predictable, and it was reason that was brought to bear upon both the physical and the spiritual implications of celestial motions. Interestingly, this was approximately the same view held by non-Christians, and it is worthwhile remarking that Ovid, a Roman poet of about the time of Christ, resolves problems on earth by the literary and mythic device of catasterism (literally "catapulting to the stars"), in which the protagonists of his stories are changed by metamorphosis into constellations in the heavens, where there is no more strife.[5] Mythology and astronomy were not divorced in Ovid's day, we see, and they remained symbolic counterparts of one another throughout the Middle Ages.

This universe, both comforting and awe-inspiring, was more useful on every level than our own is, and philosophers and theologians commented on the implications of its apparent motions while these same motions were both clock and calendar to the common man. He planted his crops by the sign of the zodiac and the phase of the moon, divided the Church's daily offices of worship by a seasonally variable clock dependent on the length of the day, and sometimes debased the theologian's belief that some events had been signaled by unusual celestial phenomena (such as the star of Bethlehem) into a superstitious confidence in horoscopes. Thus, in Chaucer the observation of the heavens runs the gamut from the Host's time-telling to Troilus's listening to the music of the spheres, and determinism ranges from God's turning the heavens with a "ravishing sway" in Chaucer's translation of Boethius to Nicholas's intentionally false prophecy in

the Miller's Tale of a second Noah's Flood, which he claims to have seen in his astronomy. Thus, for Chaucer even the failings of popular astrology have a part in his comic and successful vision of an ordered, graduated world.

In spite of the attractiveness of the old cosmology from a philosophical point of view, many students are reluctant to devote their study to a system that is "false" when they might better study the "true" universe that we know today. However, that our present conception of celestial mechanics is different from those advanced in previous centuries, many of which are grouped under the heading Ptolemaic, should not be a bar to our study. The very existence of different cosmologies across the ages makes one wonder whether man's observation of the heavens determines his view of himself so much as his conception of himself determines his observation of the heavens.[6] In other words, philosophy can influence science at least as much as science can influence philosophy, and we take too much of an evolutionary view of things when we consider the state of knowledge to proceed from error to truth, and we take too little an evolutionary view when we assume that truth has arrived now rather than that it may arrive tomorrow.[7] Scientific ideas, like most ideas, have a way of going out of vogue, and this is probably as true for today's scientific truths as it was for what was considered an adequate explanation of observable phenomena in an earlier day. We need only to consider how many facts were made fiction by Einstein's work to realize that the rule for judging the science of an earlier day should be "Judge not, that ye be not judged."

It follows, then, that whether or not a previous idea is now maintained has nothing to do with the intrinsic worth of the idea or system. The Ptolemaic universe, for example, was not at all unsophisticated; it permitted quite accurate predictions. And because the general state of astronomical knowledge in the second century A.D. was not very accomplished, one might argue that Ptolemy went further beyond his contemporaries than did Copernicus or Galileo in the sixteenth and seventeenth centuries. Indeed, it has been suggested by Owen Barfield that the real difference between Ptolemy and Copernicus's successor, Galileo, is not that one system is true and the other false (a heliocentric universe had been suggested as early as the third century A.D.) but that there was a change in the theory of theory; and while Ptolemy's system had been taught as a hypothesis that would explain phenomena, Galileo had argued that the heliocentric hypothesis was literally and physically true.[8] Because the Copernican, heliocentric theory accounted for the celestial motions better than the Ptolemaic, geocentric system, people indeed began to believe it to be more than a theory, so that it is worthwhile to point out that it is *not* perfect: the motions of Mercury are not completely accounted for by it, and only now can they be explained by reference to Einstein's work. Moreover, it should be remembered that in contradiction to both Ptolemy and Copernicus, no one seriously maintains today that either the sun or the earth is at the center of anything more than our local solar system. Our system is rather far out from the center of a certain spiral nebula, which exists in turn along with many others. Thus the continual advances in "knowledge" indicate that some day our own knowledge of the laws of the universe may be studied more for what it tells about us than for what it tells about the way things really are.

The necessity for a system to explain the motions of the stars stems from the predictable but uneven and swerving motion of the planets, which get their names from the Greek word for wanderer. We should remark here that while there is quite a difference between a star and a planet, the sun was treated as a planet in the Middle Ages because of its motion and in spite of its obvious disparity in brilliance. People in the Middle Ages also distinguished between "pure" astronomy and "judicial" astronomy, the latter being the casting of horoscopes, predicting of the future, and so forth, but they used the words *astronomy* and *astrology* interchangeably. In pure astronomy, then, we are basically concerned with the simple motions of the stars and the rather more complex motions of the planets. Both the stars and the planets, like the sun, move from east to west continually, so that were we to mark the position of the sun at different times of day or of a particular star at different times of night, we should note that both moved from east to west, and the stars and planets, again like the sun, complete a revolution in a day's time. More accurately, however, the sun *almost* completes a revolution, falling short by about 1 degree out of the 360 in a circle. Thus, if we noted the constellation visible on the eastern horizon just before the sun rose and then looked for that same group of stars some weeks or months later, we should find it to be no longer just on the horizon before dawn but slightly elevated. This process would continue, so that six months later our constellation would be in the west at sunrise and in a year's time it would once again be visible back in the east at dawn.

We could look at this fact in another way. Instead of saying that the various star groups moved we could say that the sun did not move as fast as the star sphere, to use the medieval concept, and that it dropped backward at the rate of about 1 degree per day. Yet another way of expressing this phenomenon would be to say that the sun had two motions, a daily one from east to west, and a yearly one from west to east. Because of the importance of both the daily and the yearly course of the sun to agriculture, people took note of the various star groups that the sun had as a kind of invisible backdrop (invisible because of the sun's brightness) and gave many of them the names of animals, because of fancied resemblances in form. The twelve constellations form, of course, the zodiac, which gets its name from the same Greek word that is the root of *zoo*. The sun's course, traced against this path of constellations in the fixed stars, which, unlike the planets, are static in relation to one another, inscribes a circle called the "ecliptic."

Figures 3 and 4 illustrate the sun's two motions. In Figure 3 we see the sun at sunrise in the first degree of Aries, which is the vernal equinox, or beginning of spring. The exact moment of the beginning of spring comes when the yearly course of the sun along the ecliptic intersects the celestial equator or equinoctial. If we were standing on earth looking south, the sun would rise on our left, and if the celestial equator were a visible line, we should see the sun run along its arc, revolving on the same axis. As the whole universe rotates from east to west, the band of the zodiac is carried along at an angle to the celestial equator and may be said to swivel around daily as a wheel would if lying propped up at its center on the ground. When the sun is halfway between the extremities of this wheel, the sun revolves along the celestial equator, but in its annual motion it is like a fly crawling along the zodiac wheel in the opposite direction from the wheel's daily, swiveling motion. Thus, as the sun goes "higher" on the zodiac wheel, it revolves higher than the celestial equator, and we have spring and summer; and when it creeps down the zodiac to its nadir, we have winter. The product of these two motions, of course, is a spiral—one with $182\frac{1}{2}$ turns from top to bottom and the same number back the other way, giving us 365 days in a year.

If we remember that the daily motion of the zodiac is east to west along with everything else, but that it is at an angle to the axis of daily rotation, much confusion will be avoided. Figure 5 shows one way of regarding the sun's two motions: as motions around two poles. Its daily course we understand, and here we see that it moves along the ecliptic on another axis 1 degree per day in the opposite direction from the daily motion and in a different plane. Because the plane is different, the sun's annual motion seems to be upward and then downward. This motion, of course, is what we see when the sun passes higher every day toward midsummer and then slightly lower each day until the winter solstice (literally the standing still of the sun). Its highest daily path is on the day it enters the first degree of Cancer, so that a line designating that path is called the Tropic of Cancer, and its lowest path is known as the Tropic of Capricorn. Thus, in a famous metaphor, Dante described the two motions of the sun as resulting in a spiral motion now up, now down, like the turning screw of a great press.

Once the two motions of the sun are understood, the other apparent motions of the heavens are not difficult to determine. The other planets known in the Middle Ages (Saturn, Jupiter, Mars, Venus, Mercury, and the moon) were like the sun in that they had both a daily and an annual motion, but they were unlike the sun in that their annual motion was more complex. Thus, while the sun moves steadily contrary to its daily motion in its annual course, the other planets at times turn away from their usual annual motion and move in the opposite direction. This turning against the usual annual motion was called "retrograde motion." In addition to retrograde motion the planets by no means proceed evenly in their direct or retrograde movements, and there are variations in their motion and wide variations in the time it takes to complete a cycle of the zodiac. Thus the moon, moving swiftly along, manages to sweep around the zodiac from west to east in about a month, while Mars takes about two and a half years and Saturn takes thirty years.

The spheres of the planets, we should be reminded, were not considered as tangible entities in the Middle Ages, but were simply hypothetical constructs created for the sake of making the theory easily understood. In addition to the sphere for each planet there were several other spheres in the later Middle Ages that, while not strictly Ptolemaic, were needed to account for still

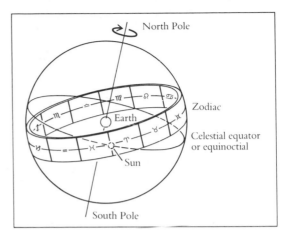

Figure 3 *Sunrise at the vernal equinox.*

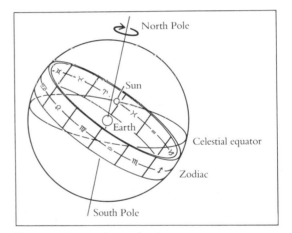

Figure 4 *Sunset at the vernal equinox.*

other motions of the heavens. There was an outermost sphere called the *primum mobile*, or "first-moving," which moved all other spheres in their daily courses; and then there was a crystalline sphere, which accounted for calendrical precession, that slow decrease in the date of the vernal equinox by about 3 days each 400 years. This we now plan for in our calendars by omitting leap year at the end of the century—except when the year is evenly divisible by 400, as with 1600 or 2000. Finally, the sphere of the fixed stars, which contained the zodiac, was also thought to have a very slow annual motion that accounted for the precession of the

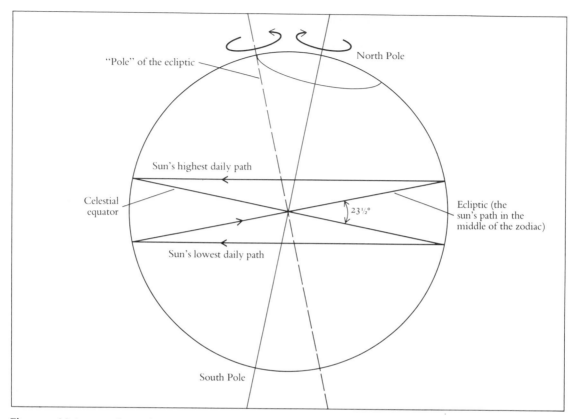

Figure 5 *Motions around two poles.*

equinoxes, that is, the fact that the first degree of Aries is retrogressing through the fixed stars a fraction of a degree each year. The later astronomers thought that this movement did not proceed steadily in one direction but was sporadic, and they gave it the name "trepidation."

To explain these many different motions of the stars and the planets was the goal of many of the ancient philosophies, for men not only were inquisitive about the world around them, but also desired to find in it both order and harmony. The wandering motion of the planets was felt to undermine the simplicity and regularity of the philosophical systems that were being expounded to explain the workings of the world. Indeed, the impetus for early astronomical theories seems to have been the desire to explain the apparently uneven and irregular motions of the heavens in such a way that regular motion would lie behind irregular

appearance. The theory of spheres that nestled one inside the other like the layers of an onion was agreed by all to be the basic arrangement of the world, but the precise positioning and operation of the spheres needed to account for the observable phenomena were the subject of some debate.

Aristotle taught that the spheres were concentric, with the earth as the common center, but his system was not adequate for predicting the observed courses of the planets, and other philosophers soon turned from *concentric* spheres to *eccentric* ones, that is, spheres turning around a center located somewhere other than at the earth in the middle. When Ptolemy came along in the second century A.D., he summed up and modified some previous systems, and his own theories received various modifications later. Thus the adjective *Ptolemaic* used generically to describe the geocentric cosmology extant before Copernicus is very misleading. Moreover, representations of the pre-Copernican world usually show a series of concentric circles rather than of eccentric spheres, and although this scheme makes things simpler for the student, it too is very misleading. The illustration in Figure 6 of a Ptolemaic universe gives some idea of the beautiful and complex cosmology envisioned in the Middle Ages, but a model taking in all the details would be vastly more complicated still. In a final instance of this sort of thing we may remark that Ptolemy's eccentric spheres did not in fact suit everyone in the later Middle Ages, and an Arab named Alpetragius offered a system involving both concentric spheres and motion around different poles. Although there is at present a good deal of discussion over the extent of his influence, it is probable that Dante believed in this system, and certainly his very existence is a reminder to us to beware of generalizations about the Ptolemaic universe.

The way in which the Ptolemaic system accounts for the several motions of the planets, and for the inequalities of these motions, varies for different planets, but its bases are the "eccentric," the "equant," and the "epicycle." The eccentric sphere, or circle if we want to keep our discussion in two dimensions, is called the "deferent." The motion of a point on the deferent, moving at an equal speed around the center, would be uneven in speed when viewed from the earth, but while the deferent was a step in the right direction, it was not sufficient to explain all the problems of motion. The first modification of the system is the assumption that our arbitrary moving point on the circumference of the deferent moved at an even speed not when viewed from the center of its own deferent but when viewed from a different point, called the equant, twice the distance from the earth as the center of the deferent, along what was called the line of the aux. (See Figure 7a.) For the sun this is sufficient, but for the other planets it was necessary to use a further modification, the epicycle, which was imagined as the circular path of a planet around a point on the circumference of the deferent circle. (See Figure 7b.) For the planet Mercury it was necessary to introduce a deferent center that revolved in a circle, and for the moon, both a revolving center of the deferent and a revolving equant.

Thus far we have been discussing pure as opposed to judicial astronomy, but we should not neglect these more or less practical applications of the observations of the heavenly movements to the world around us. From the obvious effects on earthly things of the sun's

Figure 6 *Ptolemaic universe.*

daily passage across the sky, and the pronounced change in the seasons that comes as the sun passes nearer to or farther from the celestial equator, an ability to affect earthly things was extended to other celestial bodies, and the planets were thought to be able to affect not only physical things like the leafing of the trees when the sun was in certain parts of the zodiac, but also mental and emotional conditions in people. The influence of astral configurations on character was thought to come mainly at the moment of birth, and so astrologers studied a person's horoscope, the positions of the stars at birth, in order to determine his character and probable future. No one likes to believe in *complete* astral determinism, however, and so one's horoscope led one to try to mitigate fate by elections, the choosing of propitious times for doing things, and questions, a sort of formal attempt to discover the unknown. People wanted to know the future not in order to accede to it but in order to evade it, however contradictory that may seem to us.

In order that the casting of horoscopes, the elections of times, and the asking of questions not be infringed

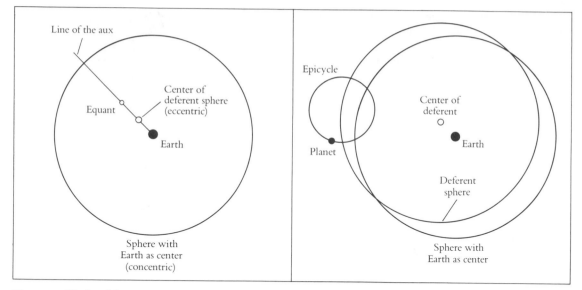

Figure 7a *The line of the aux.*

Figure 7b *The epicycle.*

upon by amateurs, astrologers were concerned with a bewildering variety of relationships, all of which needed to be calculated by reference to tables, and these relationships were subject to various interpretations of *meaning* once determined in fact. The sign in the ascendant, that is, rising in the east at the moment of birth, was extremely important in horoscopes, and it should be remarked that this involves some precise calculation, for all twelve signs move across the eastern horizon every day in their east-to-west motion. Today the very simplified horoscopes of newspapers and radio depend upon the sign the sun is in during the *month* of one's birth, so that all people born between July 21 and August 21 are said to be under the sign of Leo, while those born between December 21 and January 21 are said to be under the sign of Capricorn. Not so in the Middle Ages, when the important thing was not the sun sign, but the ascendant, which changed every few hours. Thus it was necessary to know the day, hour, and minute of birth and to compute the ascendant sign accordingly. In addition to the signs, the planets are of great importance in judicial astrology, and they were studied in terms of where they were in regard to the signs, where they were in regard to each other, and where they were in regard to the twelve houses of the heavens.

The word *house* is very confusing because it refers to two things. First of all, the planets were thought to have particular relationships to certain signs, so that each planet had two houses, that is, two signs of the zodiac in which its influence would be very strong, the exceptions being the sun and the moon, which have only one house each. This does not mean that the planets are always in certain signs, but rather that when they are there they are particularly powerful. The other houses are arbitrary divisions of the whole heaven into twelve equal or unequal parts, depending on the system, which then are enumerated counterclockwise and said to have to do with certain things such as death, marriage, travel, and so forth. One approach simply divided the heavens into equal 30-degree sections going counterclockwise from the eastern horizon; but the other, more common method, divided the zodiac by great circles calculated from a point directly overhead, from which point the zodiac appears as an ellipse rather than a circle, and the resultant division was into unequal parts. These houses were studied for what planets were in them and for what planets were in what geometrical aspects to them just as the signs were. Indeed, there are times when it is difficult to tell whether an astrologer is referring to these projected, divisional houses or to the houses in the signs. The divisional houses were most often charted in a square rather than in a circle, and the twelve houses were successively given the names "angle," "succedent," and "cadent," and this was repeated around the chart. The lines dividing these houses were called "cusps." Figure 8 shows one way of relating the divisional houses and the zodiac. Here the equal divisions are used and a circle has been employed for clarity. Figure 9 shows a typical medieval rendering of a horoscope.

With either system the position of the planets was all important. If a planet was in a sign or in a house it was significant, while if it was in opposition to the sign or house, that is, diametrically opposed to it, that could be important too. Furthermore, the relationships of the planets to each other was thought to be very important, so that if two planets were in conjunction (located in the same degree of the zodiac), or in triune opposition to some other planets, or in any one of a half dozen other aspects, the astrologer would duly note it. Finally, while the projected houses had assigned concerns such as death and marriage and a corresponding set of assigned values (a planet in the house would be fortunate or unfortunate), the signs of the zodiac employed more elaborate rules. In addition to the houses of the planets in the signs, each sign was the "exaltation" of a planet, the "debility" of a planet, and the "fall" of a planet. Furthermore, the exact internal location of a planet was important, for the planet could be weakened or strengthened in its influence by being in a division of the sign that was arbitrarily assigned to one of the planets. There were threefold divisions of the signs called "decans" from the fact that each one had 10 degrees, and fivefold divisions called "terms," which were unequal in the number of degrees they contained.

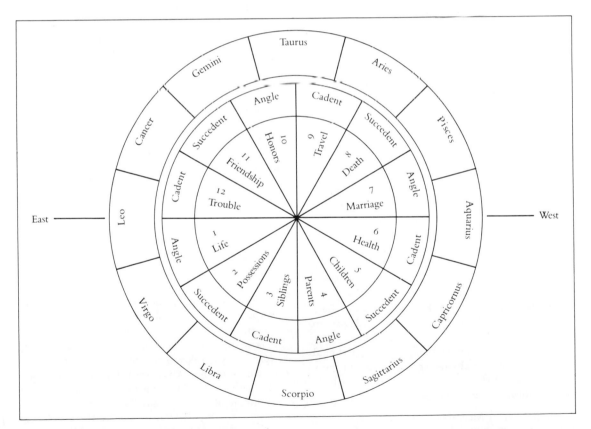

Figure 8 *The divisional houses and the zodiac.*

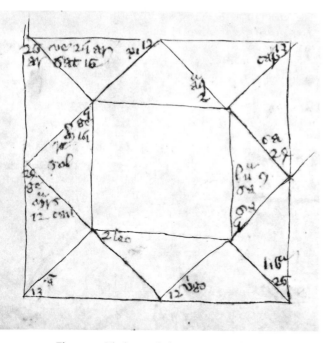

Figure 9 *The houses of a horoscope arranged in a square.*

Thus, at a particular moment the planet Jupiter would be in a specific term and decan of a sign in which he might be very powerful or very weak and in a house in which his presence was customarily thought to be bad or good. (See Figure 10.)

All this, then, is not simple but is at least discoverable; and while it is one thing to cast a horoscope or ask a question, it is quite another to supply answers or agree on meanings. The extraordinary complication of astrology attracted some and repelled others, but Chaucer, typically, was amused by it. Chaucer noted, for example, that the exaltations and falls of the planets in various signs are suspiciously symmetrical in the astrologers' manuals, and so he has the Wife of Bath speciously conclude that this astrological pattern "causes" men and women to be in "opposition" when they cannot be in "conjunction." Note the technical accuracy accompanied by rather coarse sexual imagery otherwise. This lack of harmony in tone gives the lie to any presumed harmony in content:

> The children of Mercurie and of Venus
> Been in hir wirking ful contrarius;

Mercurie loveth wisdom and science,
And Venus loveth ryot and dispence.
And, for hir diverse disposicioun,
Ech falleth in otheres exaltacioun;
And thus, god woot! Mercurie is desolat
In Pisces, wher Venus is exaltat;
And Venus falleth ther Mercurie is reysed.
Therfore no womman of no clerk is preysed.
The clerk, whan he is old, and may noght do
Of Venus werkes worth his olde sho,
Thanne sit he doun, and writ in his dotage
That wommen can nat kepe hir mariage!

[ll. 697–710]

The real reason that clerks write about women's lack of faithfulness stems from a rhetorical convention in which marriage was scorned in contrast to virginity, so that the Wife's ascription of the cause to astrological influence on two kinds of people is far from the mark, and she herself gives it the lie by adding a second explanation: that clerks scorn women because of their own sexual impotence. The humor of the passage, however, is fully understood only when we remark that Chaucer himself, poet and scholar, is obviously to be included with the ranks of the children of Mercury. Chaucer brings in some astrological imagery here only to make mirth with it and fun of it.

The Wife of Bath has a horoscope, too, albeit a much-abbreviated one, and its operation in the poem is much like that of the passage we have just studied. The Wife's horoscope does not by any means tell us the position of each planet, but is reduced to the simplest form, which is the most useful artistically and the least useful astrologically. She says, "Myn ascendent was Taur, and Mars therinne." The discovery of Mars in the ascending sign Taurus would have meant something to an astrologer, but he would have modified the significance of that planet in that sign by filling out the description of character by reference to the other planets and signs involved and would perhaps even change his original conclusions if the other planets seemed to overrule the importance of Mars in the ascendant. The discovery of Mars in the ascendant sign Taurus was commonly explained by astrologers as an indication that the person for whom the horoscope was being cast (often called the "native") would be unchaste, and the Ellesmere manuscript of *The Canterbury Tales* contains a marginal notation to that effect from one of the astrologers, copied in by a scribe. Chaucer is again *using* astrology,

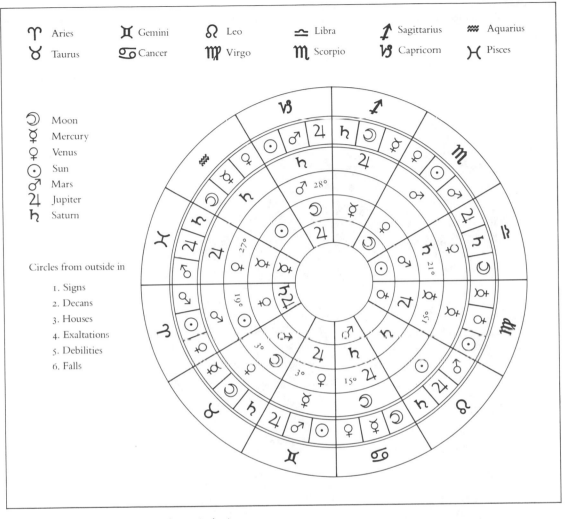

| ♈ Aries | ♊ Gemini | ♌ Leo | ♎ Libra | ♐ Sagittarius | ♒ Aquarius |
| ♉ Taurus | ♋ Cancer | ♍ Virgo | ♏ Scorpio | ♑ Capricorn | ♓ Pisces |

☽ Moon
☿ Mercury
♀ Venus
☉ Sun
♂ Mars
♃ Jupiter
♄ Saturn

Circles from outside in

1. Signs
2. Decans
3. Houses
4. Exaltations
5. Debilities
6. Falls

Figure 10 *Planetary strengths and weaknesses in the signs.*

for not only is the horoscope too abbreviated from a technical point of view, but also we must remark that it does not tell us anything about the Wife that we do not already know. In view of the fact that the Wife has had five husbands, "Withouten oother compaignye in youthe," there is little question about her chastity, so that Chaucer is certainly not using the horoscope per se in order to tell us something about her character that we didn't already know. Rather, it is the Wife's comment on her horoscope ("Allas! allas! that ever love was synne!") that tells us something new about her:

namely, that she believes she has been condemned to be as she is by astral decree. The fact that Chaucer uses the reaction to a horoscope rather than the horoscope itself in his development of character is a typical instance of his employment of astrological imagery for emphasis and explanation rather than as a controlling factor in his writing.

Much the same sort of situation is found in the famous first paragraph of *The Canterbury Tales*. There Chaucer says that the sun has run its half course in the Ram, but since he also says that the month is April, most scholars have assumed that he is circuitously and amusingly saying that the sun has run both its first and its second half course in the Ram, for the first one is entirely in March. In other words, the sun has completed its course in the Ram and is now rising and setting against the backdrop of Taurus. The Wife of Bath's horoscope was involved with this same sign of Taurus. This sign seems to have been associated regularly with sensual behavior, probably because of its connection with Venus, one of whose houses is located there. A picture of this sign (Figure 11), a fresco dating from about a half century after Chaucer's death, shows the Bull and the sun in the center of the middle band, indicating that the sun, in its annual course, is in Taurus. The three figures

Figure 11 *Fresco from Palazzo Schifanoia.*

in that same middle band are of the three rulers of the decans. In the top band we see Venus herself, with Mars chained to her chair. On our left we see a couple embracing in the foreground, while to our right there are some ladies playing musical instruments while rabbits hop about underfoot. Venus and the embracing couple furnish the key to the rest of the figures, which are not hard to interpret. The procreative facility of rabbits was as well known in the Middle Ages as it is today, and music is used suggestively several times by Chaucer; for example, in the General Prologue, where it is the activity of birds that are not sleeping at night, and again in the Miller's Tale, where the "melodye" is a good deal more specific. Indeed the month of April itself was often derived from Aphrodite, an alternative name for Venus, and behind Chaucer's superficially noncommittal statement of the time of the year, there is a wealth of suggestion connected with the sign of Taurus.

Chaucer frequently uses astrological imagery when dealing with time, which is a reminder to us that he *uses* astrology for poetic purposes and probably did not believe in it to any great extent. We all believe that the sun's motion causes the day and the seasons, and Chaucer would surely have believed that there was more celestial influence than that. However, he would not have gone very far toward judicial astrology in his beliefs. In his *Treatise on the Astrolabe* (an astrolabe being an instrument for determining the positions of stars), he expressly rejects judicial astronomy's three main fields—nativities, elections, and questions—as being "rites of pagans" in which his spirit "has no faith."

There is a clear precedent for the use of things astrological without a concomitant belief in them in the labors of the months on the medieval cathedrals. (See Figure 12.) The signs of the zodiac were used to show the divisions of the year, and each was accompanied by an illustration of some agricultural task that was appropriate to the season. These are astrological in a sense, but they are also ecclesiastical, in that the necessity for

Figure 12 *Labors of the months: March, April, and May. Amiens Cathedral.*

tilling the soil was visited upon man as a punishment for the fall of Adam. The images of the signs of the zodiac did not imply astral but rather divine influence, and the orderly progression of labors would remind man of a more profound order, which in turn could lead him to reflect that while condemned to labor, he did not labor without hope. Astrological imagery, then, could be put to good use by a Church that steadfastly denied any truth in judicial astrology throughout the Middle Ages. We should not forget that a part of the medieval interest in astronomy arose from the necessity for computing the date for Easter. Chaucer's astrolabe had the dates of various saints' days around its rim.

Pagan myth was employed in much the same way as astrology; that is to say, it was employed for what worth it might bring through exploitation rather than admired for any intrinsic value. Ovid's translation of figures in these stories to the heavens, which we have already mentioned, reminds us that in late antiquity pagan gods and planets were confused, which is to say that the thinkers of that day saw no good reason to talk about Mars the planet in a different way from Mars the god of war. When Christianity triumphed in the Western world, the literary successors of Ovid lumped gods and planets under the heading of "possibly instructive errors," and once more they went without distinction, although perhaps now for a different reason. At all events, by the time of the later Middle Ages it was possible for the author of the anonymous *Ovide Moralisé* to tell an Ovidian tale such as the story of the adultery of Mars and Venus as a story of gods, as a story of famous people, and as an astronomical phenomenon, without much distinction among the several ap-

proaches. Clearly Mars and Venus are not important as gods or planets, but rather are flexible symbols to serve the poet's poetic intentions. Thus in the Knight's Tale Chaucer describes Venus, Mars, and Diana as gods and goddesses, and Saturn as a planet or planetary god, but this doesn't mean that he has lost control of his material or that he has confused planets and gods or that the tale is essentially deterministic in tone. Rather we should see a different emphasis, an emphasis on the fact that if one puts one's trust in the lust of Venus, the anger of Mars, the self-serving chastity of Diana, and the revenge of Saturn, there is a certain determination of the future that does not depend on either planets or gods but rather on logical probabilities.

For Chaucer, then, the stars could be used to obtain wisdom or abused to obtain false wisdom, so that all depends on the individual's choice of perspective. The stars are ordered; it is man who is sometimes erratic. From this it follows that all that was not *judicial* astronomy was held in the highest esteem by Chaucer and other medieval humanists; and in the famous and influential *Consolation of Philosophy* by Boethius, which Chaucer translated, the first picture we receive of a philosopher is that of an astronomer who lifts his head towards the stars to study their motions and their causes. Thus, when Chaucer brings into the Miller's Tale the oft-told story of an astrologer who walked along looking at the stars and consequently fell into a marlpit, neither Chaucer nor his audience would confuse the two ways of looking upward at the stars. For Chaucer the real importance of the stars lies beyond them.

Notes

1   The editor is grateful to Prof. Chauncey Wood for providing this introduction to medieval cosmology.

2   For more details on the remarkable popularity of astrology today, see chap. I of Louis Macneice's *Astrology*, New York, 1964, and *Newsweek*, Sept. 14, 1964, p. 56, where it is reported that in France more than $650 million is spent on astrology annually.

3   C. S. Lewis, *The Discarded Image*, Cambridge, 1964, pp. 111–112, 116. It must be emphasized that one of the most important factors in theorizing about cosmology is the knowledge of both the nature and origin of previous cosmological hypotheses. Without this, as Professor Burtt has observed, new theories will be nothing more than "the objectification of the mood of an age." Edwin Arthur Burtt, *The Metaphysical Foundations of Modern Physical Science*, rev. ed., reprinted in Doubleday Anchor Books, Garden City, N.Y., n.d., p. 304.

4 In a felicitous phrase Prof. Sherman Hawkins has described the difference between current and former beliefs about the causality of motion as ". . . the difference between a physics of push and a metaphysics of pull." [Sherman Hawkins, "Mutabilitie and the Cycle of the Months," in *Form and Convention in the Poetry of Edmund Spenser*, ed. by William Nelson, New York and London, 1961, p. 78.] This turnabout is one of the most important watersheds in Western intellectual history. In the seventeenth century Galileo argued that God was more a creator than an attractor—an efficient cause rather than a final cause—and the idea of the world as a perfect machine soon followed in Huyghens and Leibniz, and with it the concept of God as a species of engineer. See Burtt, *Metaphysical Foundations*, pp. 98–101, and Carl L. Becker, *The Heavenly City of the Eighteenth Century Philosophers*, New Haven, Conn., 1932.

5 That most medieval of modern poets, T. S. Eliot, refers to this concept of celestial reconciliation in "Burnt Norton."

6 C. S. Lewis has argued that a cosmology reflects the psychology of an age as much as it does the knowledge of an age. (*The Discarded Image*, p. 222.) We should also note that the truth of our contemporary cosmology depends upon a theory that deals with particles that are in fact treated more metaphysically than physically. As the great physicist Werner Heisenberg has observed, "The natural laws formulated mathematically in quantum theory no longer deal with the elementary particles themselves but with our knowledge of them. Nor is it possible to ask whether or not these particles exist in space and time objectively, since the only processes we can refer to as taking place are those which represent the interplay of particles with some other system, e.g., a measuring instrument." From this astute observation Heisenberg draws the brilliant and startling conclusion that "*The scientific world-view has ceased to be a scientific view in the true sense of the word.*" Werner Heisenberg, *The Physicist's Conception of Nature*, London, 1958, pp. 15, 29.

7 The history of the idea of progress itself is too complex to be discussed here, but we may ponder the implications of the suggestion that modern ideas of progress owe something to the fact that Christianity had provided a meaning for history by holding that Christ came "in the fullness of time" to "fulfill the scriptures." The idea of *human* progress, then, may represent the secularization of an attitude that was originally religious and had to do with divine intervention. (See H. Butterfield, *The Origins of Modern Science: 1300 1800*, New York, 1951, p. 166.) Moreover, whether we agree with the conclusions of one cosmological theory or another, we should note that good scientific method forms the basis of more than one world view. Plato's Pythagorean friend Archytas, for example, proved his theory of mathematical harmony in the celestial bodies just like a modern scientist. (See Leo Spitzer, *Classical and Christian Ideas of World Harmony*, ed. by Anna Granville Hatcher, Baltimore, 1963, pp. 10–11.) As Burtt has observed, contemporary empiricists, had they lived in the sixteenth century, would have scoffed at Copernicus on empirical (experiential) grounds, for there were definite objections to the new theory according to the science of the time, which could not *then* be answered. See Burtt, *Metaphysical Foundations*, p. 37.

8 Owen Barfield, *Saving the Appearances*, London, 1957, pp. 50–51. In the middle of the sixteenth century, when Copernicus advanced his theory that the sun and not the earth was at the center of the universe, his *main* concern was not whether or not the earth *actually* moved but merely whether or not his theory accounted for the observable facts more simply than did Ptolemy's. He did, however, affirm that if the shift of point of reference resulted in a simpler expression of the facts, it was legitimate to make the shift. Kepler and Galileo, less than a century later, were much more emphatic in arguing that the new concepts gave a true picture of the real world. See Burtt, *Metaphysical Foundations*, pp. 52–98.

III. The Medieval Bible

Since the Bible was the central text of the medieval educational system and is frequently reflected in literature, there are many references to it in this book. Unless there is some indication to the contrary, these references are to the Douay-Reims translation, which is much closer to the Latin texts familiar during the Middle Ages than either the King James Bible or any of the newer translations. The Douay Bible differs from the usual modern editions of the King James Bible, which omit some material in the original King James Version, in a number of significant respects. In the first place, the Old Testament contains seven books not included in the current King James standard editions:

1 Tobias
2 Judith
3 Wisdom
4 Ecclesiasticus
5 Baruch
6 1 Machabees
7 2 Machabees

Among these, Wisdom and Ecclesiasticus were highly regarded during the Middle Ages for their moral content. The books of Machabees were favored by the feudal nobility, who found in them an inspiration to chivalric enterprise. There are a number of minor differences as well. Thus 1 and 2 Samuel in the King James Bible are 1 and 2 Kings in the Douay. The third and fourth books of Kings in the latter correspond with the first and second books of Kings in the King James text.

There are also specific differences in translation, some of which are of considerable theological significance. For example, Luke 2:14 appears in the Vulgate, in the Douay Bible, and in the King James Version in the following forms:

Vulgate: *Gloria in altissimis Deo*
          et in terra pax hominibus bonae
              voluntatis.
Douay: Glory to God in the highest;
          and on earth peace to men of good
              will.

King James: Glory to God in the highest,
          and on earth peace, good will toward
              men.

It will be observed that the Vulgate and the Douay distribute peace somewhat more restrictively than the King James. Again, Psalm 14:1–2 (King James: Ps. 15:1–2) appears as follows in the three texts:

Vulgate: *Domine, quis habitabit in tabernaculo tuo,*
          aut quis requiescat in monte sancto tuo?
          Qui ingreditur sine macula et operatur
              iustitiam.
Douay: Lord, who shall dwell in thy tabernacle?
          or who shall rest in thy holy hill?
          He that walketh without blemish, and
              worketh justice.
King James: Lord, who shall abide in thy tabernacle?
          who shall dwell in thy holy hill?
          He that walketh uprightly and worketh
              righteousness. . . .

The Vulgate phrase *sine macula* ("without blemish") appears elsewhere and was regarded during the Middle Ages as an equivalent for the virtue of innocence (or freedom from the stain of sin), but this idea is hardly conveyed by the King James phrase "walketh uprightly." Readers of the Middle English poem "Pearl" who are familiar only with the King James Bible are likely to miss some of the connotations of the poet's insistence that the pearl was "without spot." One further illustration will serve to emphasize the fact that the figurative language of the Vulgate, frequently reflected both in the medieval visual arts and in literary texts, is often altered beyond recognition in the King James Version. The text here is Proverbs 23:33–34:

Vulgate: *Oculi tui videbunt extraneas*
              et cor tuum loquetur perversa,
          et eris sicut dormiens in medio mari
              et quasi sopitus gubernator, amisso clavo.
Douay: Thy eyes shall behold strange women,
          and thy heart shall utter perverse
              things.

And thou shalt be as one sleeping in the
midst of the sea,
and as a pilot fast asleep, when the
stern is lost.

King James: Thine eyes shall behold strange women,
and thine heart shall utter perverse
things.
Yea, thou shalt be as he that lieth down
in the midst of the sea,
or as he that lieth upon the top of a
mast.

Those familiar only with the somewhat puzzling situation described in the King James Bible will recognize with difficulty the echo of these verses that appears in Chaucer's *Troilus*, where Troilus laments, after seeing Criseyde for the first time,

Al steerles withinne a boot am I
Amydde the see. . . .

Many similar examples could be cited. Although it is true that the biblical texts quoted by St. Augustine sometimes differ slightly from the Vulgate and that there were textual differences among Latin Bibles in use during the Middle Ages, the Vulgate text is far more useful to students of medieval literature than any other text now in print. A convenient and inexpensive edition is published by La Editorial Catolica of Madrid.

To return, however, to the differences between the King James Version and the Douay. There is some variation in nomenclature, some of which is of minor importance:

King James	Douay
1 and 2 Chronicles	1 and 2 Paralipomenon
Song of Solomon	Canticle of Canticles
Isaiah	Isaias
Jeremiah	Jeremias
Ezekiel	Ezechiel
Hosea	Osee
Obadiah	Abdias
Jonah	Jonas
Micah	Micheas
Habakkuk	Habacuc
Zephaniah	Sophonias
Haggai	Aggeus
Zechariah	Zacharias
Malachi	Malachias
Revelation	Apocalypse

The two versions also display considerable variation in the spelling of proper names in the text. It is especially important to notice that the Psalms in the Douay text are not numbered as they are in the King James text, and that individual psalms are not divided into verses in the same way in the two versions. There are other differences in addition to those indicated above, but these should be sufficient to alert the reader, so that he will not be confused at the outset.

Modern writers often allege that during the Middle Ages the Church kept the Bible away from laymen, imposing the authority of its doctrine on the unsuspecting public without reference to the text. Several considerations should be kept in mind, however, when we weigh this allegation. In the first place, the Bible appeared as a very large and expensive manuscript that few persons could afford to own. Again, less well-educated persons were not generally inclined to question traditional interpretations of the text, which were largely based on Patristic authority. Finally, educated men rightly thought that the Old Testament, which is not Christian on the surface, could be very misleading to the unlearned; and, as Chaucer's Wife of Bath demonstrates, even the New Testament could be readily misunderstood by the unwary. Much that proved offensive and self-destructive in nineteenth-century Christianity arose from literal-minded, Old Testament-oriented attitudes that led to profound misunderstandings of the New Testament as well, especially of the Epistles of St. Paul. These considerations aside, medieval sermons were usually devoted to explanations of the Scriptures, which were liberally quoted in them, so that even illiterate persons might in the course of time acquire a considerable knowledge of the Bible. We should not forget that persons who do not read, or who read only a little, are likely to have extremely good verbal memories.

During the later Middle Ages, Latin manuscript texts of the Bible often appeared with glosses. These were of various types, but the two most important were the interlinear gloss and the ordinary gloss. The former, as its name indicates, was a gloss between the lines containing explanations of difficult words in the text. The ordinary gloss surrounded the text in the margins of the page. It was made up largely of explanations and interpretations derived from the Fathers of the Church. These explanations were used both by students of the Bible in schools and by preachers in the composition of sermons. Whether one learned about the Bible in sermons, therefore, or by studying it in school, or by reading it alone, it was almost always accompanied by some kind of interpretation. Some knowledge of the ordinary gloss, therefore, and of the more influential Patristic and medieval exegetical writings is essential if we are to understand the significance of scriptural texts as they are quoted, paraphrased, or echoed in literary works. The exegetes also introduce us to a conceptual world or "universe of discourse" familiar to literate persons throughout the Middle Ages but very different from our habitual modes of thought today.[1]

Patristic exegesis emphasized what was called the "spirit" beneath the "letter" of the text. The Old Testament especially was thought to be confusing, contradictory, and misleading on the surface. It could be understood only in the light of the teachings of Christ in the New Testament. The basic theory and some examples of this kind of interpretation were furnished by St. Paul, whose exegetical principles were elaborated and applied to the Bible as a whole by the Fathers of the Church. An excellent brief introduction to the theory of Patristic exegesis may be found in St. Augustine's *On Christian Doctrine*, now available in several English translations. Medieval exegesis generally carried on and elaborated the techniques described in this work.

A simplified conception of the nature of the medieval approach to the Scriptures is furnished by the twelfth-century *Didascalicon* of Hugh of St. Victor, a book widely used in the universities during the later Middle Ages.[2] Hugh tells us that the scriptural text should be approached first with reference to the "letter," or, that is, as it may be analyzed with such tools as grammar and lexicography. Next the "sense," or obvious meaning, of the text is considered. If the sense is clear and unambiguous, no further analysis is required, and further exposition is not necessary. However, the sense often leaves the philosophical or doctrinal implication of the text unexplained, and then one must look for its "sentence," or full implication. Where the Bible was concerned, the sentence frequently involved the spiritual meaning. Since St. Paul had used the word *allegory* in this connection (Gal. 4:22ff.) and since the spiritual meaning was often implied rather than stated, it was often called the allegorical meaning. The word *allegory* here does not mean "extended metaphor" or metaphor of any kind; it means that the text says one thing but implies something else.

The allegory of the text was said to arise first of all because the words used in it might be "signs" of something else. Thus, for example, the word *Jerusalem* was the name of a city, but it was also said to mean "vision of peace." This sort of verbal allegory is common to writings of many kinds, sacred or profane, and it appears (in forms like significant proper names) in works that are not otherwise allegorical in any way. However, the scriptural text specifically, which was thought to have been inspired throughout by the Holy Spirit, was said to mention "things" or "things done" in such a way that they also were signs of other things. This does not mean that the things done were not considered to be literally true. A fable or parable describes things that exist only in imagination and things done that never took place, and a fable or parable is an allegory. But the things and things done in the Bible were thought of as being literally true and signs of something else at the same time. For example, the Ark was said to have been built by Noah (Douay: "Noe"), and no one denied the literal truth of this action; but the Ark was also thought of as a sign of the Church.

The sentence of the Biblical text was thus frequently based on the idea that its spiritual meaning was also an allegorical meaning. It had long been obvious that spiritual understanding involves various kinds of application. Either the state of the Church generally, or that of the individual, or the character of the afterlife and the implications of actions with regard to it, may be involved. In the thirteenth century, applications of these kinds came to be described with a more or less conventional terminology. That is, spiritual meanings that refer to the Church are called "allegorical," those that refer to the individual are called "tropological," and those that refer to the afterlife are called "anagogical." Since the Church, the individual, and the abodes of the afterlife were all thought of as hierarchies operating on similar principles, analogies among them were very easy to construct. The city of Jerusalem, for example, as distinct from the word *Jerusalem*, was said to imply *allegorically* the Church of the faithful praising God; *tropologically* the heart of the faithful Christian praising God; and *anagogically* the celestial city of heaven. Insofar as things and things done were concerned generally, they were sometimes said to have significance in one of these ways, sometimes in two, and sometimes in all three. Since the tropological application affected the life of the individual, it was frequently considered to be the most important of these kinds of relevance. Ideas about the nature of the Church or of the afterlife were useful and instructive, but ideas about the individual were immediately practical and had a direct bearing on the conduct of life.

It should be emphasized that the spiritual interpretation of the Bible was thought to be eminently reasonable. Spiritual exposition had as its goal "wisdom," or the knowledge of things human and divine; and wisdom was the fruit of the higher part of the reason that distinguishes human beings from animals. Accuracy in the literal interpretation of the Bible was insisted upon, even though medieval men lacked modern philological and historical techniques. However, once the literal meaning was established, it was considered a Christian duty to discover spiritual significance wherever that significance was not evident in the sense of the text. To adhere to the sense, or the letter, when it did imply spiritual understanding was thought to indicate a fleshly, or bestial, attitude toward the text. The letter read without understanding, as St. Paul says, "kills." In order for the Scriptures to give life, the veil must be removed. During the thirteenth century, rationalistic tendencies began to appear in medieval thought. As they developed, those who fostered them found spiritual understanding more and more mystical in nature, so that in academic circles especially a conflict began to arise between faith on the one hand and reason on the other. However, late medieval humanistic thought, as contrasted with academic or scholastic thought, maintained the ancient concept of wisdom more or less intact.

From a modern point of view, the specific results of spiritual interpretation are sometimes rather startling. It is true that no single spiritual meaning for any scriptural text was thought of as being definitive. That is, a given text might suggest a large number of equally valid spiritual meanings. However, a great many interpretations, especially those of Patristic origin, tended to become more or less standard and were very widely known. The modern student who wishes to familiarize himself with the traditions of medieval exegesis has no real alternative to a study of the texts themselves, many of which remain untranslated. A good beginning can be made by reading the commentaries of the Fathers, especially those of Augustine, Gregory, and Bede. In no instance is it wise to assume that ideas appearing in modern sermons or commentaries resemble medieval ideas about the scriptural text. The medieval Bible was not our Bible, and the assumption that we know what a quotation, citation, or echo from the Bible means simply because we can read it will often lead us astray.

Notes

1   The only reliable work devoted specifically to this subject is not at present available in English: Henri de Lubac, *Exégèse médiévale*, Paris, 1961–1964.

2   There is a translation by Jerome Taylor, Columbia University Press, New York, 1961.

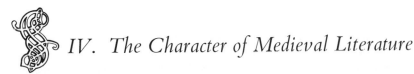 *IV.   The Character of Medieval Literature*

The arts in the Middle Ages were essentially different from those of modern times. Art as a thing in itself, with its own laws and its own independent development, is largely a product of the general fragmentation of culture into separate and self-conscious disciplines that began to take place in a decisive way during the eighteenth century. No one during the Middle Ages would have pursued art for its own sake, or regarded art as a kind of religion permitting one to achieve fulfillment in escape from the frustrations of daily life. Medieval men tended, as we have seen, to organize themselves into tightly knit groups. Their artistic expression was typically a functional part of community life, ordinarily the product of deliberate patronage by members in the upper scale of the group hierarchy and frequently promoted for the purpose of having a salutary effect on the group as a whole. Among the kinds of groups engaged in literary patronage throughout the Middle Ages are the court and the monastery. To these may be added, during the latter part of the period, the cathedral, the friary, and the fraternity, or guild.

This situation implies, first of all, that medieval literature does not often reflect the peculiar personal feeling of the author. It reflects instead the attitudes of the group for which it is written, or an idealization of those attitudes, or a criticism, frequently humorous, of the group itself or of rival groups in society as a whole. Further, the characters in medieval narrative are not fashioned as free personalities inviting us to share vicariously their experiences. They are, rather, representative of ideas or attitudes designed to serve either as good or bad examples for the literary audience. Even where the lyric is concerned, the feelings expressed are usually those that may be attributed to an individual in a given situation—a lover, a worshiper, or a warrior—and not the personal feelings of the author. Unlike modern literature, medieval literature is seldom either directly or indirectly autobiographical. The artist was not a man isolated from his social group. He was, instead, a craftsman working in fairly close harmony with his immediate associates. If he wished to criticize his patrons or the members of his group, he did so not from a feeling of rebelliousness, but from a desire to restore lost or decayed ideals. Medieval art and literature are, in this sense, typically conservative. None of this implies any special restrictions on the freedom of the artist. Some artists were much better than other artists, either because they were talented or because they understood the conceptions with which they dealt in a more profound way than their fellows. They did not refrain from being revolutionaries and social outcasts because they lacked freedom; for the most part they were genuinely interested in the welfare of the groups of which they were a part. The artist as a social outcast, more aware than the masses whom he transcended in sensitivity and understanding, was unknown in the Middle Ages. There were no masses to transcend, and no one assumed that artists had special privileges by virtue of the sanctity of art.

Since the groups that made up medieval society were, as we have seen, united by a common religious interest, no matter how much they might conflict with one another in other ways, the basic philosophy that dominates medieval literature is Christian. In this connection, however, we should remember that there were urgent practical reasons in the conduct of daily affairs that made a Christian attitude desirable and, moreover, that Christian attitudes then might differ radically from Christian attitudes today. Severe and outspoken criticism of the ecclesiastical hierarchy or facetious treatment of the conventional rituals of Christian worship did not then imply a lack of Christian belief. As we have seen, Antichrist was associated with hypocrisy; and religious organizations, like the orders of friars or the papal Curia, might suffer extremely severe criticism from persons of unquestionable piety when there was reason for suspecting hypocrisy in the conduct of their affairs. Again, no one felt that Christianity incurred any obligation to be solemn and serious, except, that is, for certain reformers and for a number of friars during the later Middle Ages who wished to convey a public image of intense piety. Religious or semireligious festivities might be very jovial and convivial, even shocking (or psychologically revealing) to modern taste, without detriment to what we would call their sincerity. The last-mentioned quality, incidentally, did not become a literary virtue until the eighteenth century. Finally, medieval men generally did not consider reticence about ordinary physiological functions—sexual intercourse, urination, or defecation—to be an aspect of the Christian outlook. The Bible itself is quite outspoken about these matters, and in any event, medieval life did not afford sufficient privacy to make them obscene. Women and children were not sheltered from direct social contact with them, either in fact or in conversation. The medieval arts, therefore, should not be considered pagan or anti-Christian because they may be humorous or because they may contain references to what we characterize as the facts of life.

Courtly literature especially is likely to be witty and humorous. Early Irish prose literature is sometimes marked by that outrageous humorous exaggeration that still typifies the Celtic temperament. After the middle of the twelfth century, an interest in the poetry of Ovid not only enriched considerably the vocabulary of medieval iconography but also contributed markedly to its humor. It is true that a great deal of literature was written for courtly audiences that is hardly distinguishable in surface piety from monastic literature. On the other hand, court poets might produce political propaganda or invective against feudal opponents that is hardly very pious. And troubadours could produce popular songs not much different in theme from popular songs at any other time. William IX of Aquitaine, the earliest of the troubadours whose work has survived, had an enormous reputation for being able to entertain his followers on crusade. His military subordinates clearly displayed the same kind of interests that military men isolated from the company of women may be expected to have at any time. But these interests imply neither a lack of religious integrity nor an inclination toward paganism. More serious courtly literature might be entertaining and instructive at the same time, more or less in the fashion recommended by Horace in the *Ars poetica*. Poets like Chrétien de Troyes, who wrote the earliest Arthurian romances, or Jean de Meun, or Chaucer used narrative materials from a wide variety of sources to produce poems that were at once entertaining and instructive.

The instructive or philosophical content of medieval poetry with an entertaining surface was frequently achieved by what was called allegory (i.e., by saying one thing to mean another). In late antiquity it became an established conviction among educated persons that poetic fables, as distinct from histories, descriptions, or philosophical expositions in verse, concealed an inner philosophical truth. This conventional attitude persisted throughout the Middle Ages, so that we find writers from Patristic times to the age of Boccaccio and Salutati insisting that poetry is by nature allegorical; for example, a fable in which animals talk, show human desires and attitudes, and so on, is not actually about animals. It says one thing and implies something else, so that it is, in medieval terms, allegorical. Generally, the figurative materials in medieval literature are not designed to convey nondiscursive emotional attitudes; instead, they convey ideas.

Allegorical poetic effects could be achieved in two ways: either by the use of exemplary narrative or by the use of specific allegorical devices like irony, personified abstraction, or signs of various kinds. These methods were frequently combined. That is, a poem might contain personified abstractions, exemplary narrative, and signs, or words, things, and actions, signifying something else. The personified abstraction was capable

of great variation in that it could be presented as a more or less bare abstract quality, clothed in attributes or conventionalized significant characteristics, or finally, given human attributes with a considerable degree of verisimilitude. The difference between a personified abstraction and a character that exemplifies some abstract quality is thus a difference in verisimilitude rather than in kind. Among the signs ordinarily used in medieval poetry, the pagan deities of antiquity appear very frequently. That is, Venus may indicate either sexual pleasure or sexual love. Most signs could appear "in a good sense" or "in an evil sense." Thus Venus could also indicate celestial love or legitimate love. These alternatives, incidentally, are classical as well as medieval, as readers of Lucretius are aware. The deities are not essentially different from personified abstractions. They may be used in a very abstract way, clothed in attributes (e.g., roses, rabbits, doves, where Venus is concerned), or made to look human. Where mythology and astrology overlap, astrological materials could be mingled with mythological materials, and astrological configurations generally might be used as signs. Such use did not, as we have seen, imply belief in astrology any more than the use of the pagan gods and goddesses implied belief in paganism.

Medieval poets, especially during the latter half of the Middle Ages, had a wide variety of conventional signs at their disposal. In the first place, Gothic art developed a highly sophisticated language of signs and attributes,[1] much of which could be used by poets. As a matter of fact, some of the materials of this kind that appear in art had a literary origin, so that it is sometimes difficult to determine whether a poet derived a given convention from something he had read or from something he had seen. Again, conventionally significant imagery derived from the Scriptures or from the traditions of scriptural exegesis, as well as significant action derived from the same sources, was frequently used by poets. As we have seen, the spiritual interpretation of Scripture implied a kind of "sacramental universe," so that a great many things not mentioned in the Scriptures came to have conventional significations that might be utilized by poets.

In view of the functional and practical nature of most medieval poetry, its association with group interests, and its lack of any specific concern for psychology, we should endeavor as best we can to discover its implications for its immediate audience if we wish to understand it; that is, the interpretation of its allegory is essential to any real appreciation for it. The nineteenth century developed a taste for fantasy, for fictional realms that were "worlds in themselves" apart from everyday reality. Readers were urged to approach poetic fictions with "a willing suspension of disbelief." During the twentieth century a further taste has developed for "inner realities" and highly intense emotional stimuli in poetry. Medieval literary audiences of any sophistication did not ordinarily enjoy fantasy for its own sake, and they were more interested in the external reality of the intelligible as it was applicable to practical affairs than they were in either golden realms of imagined experiences or in intense emotional excitement. It follows that we should seek to translate what happens in sophisticated medieval poetry in conceptual and practical terms. In this respect, medieval literature is, from an anthropological point of view, more primitive than modern literature. That is, it is the product of a highly integrated culture in which the arts have an immediate functional relevance to the culture as a whole.

Note

1   An excellent introduction to this subject, only partially outdated, is E. Mâle, *The Gothic Image*, Harper & Row, Publishers, Incorporated, New York, 1958.

V. The Literature of Medieval England

During the Middle Ages literature was produced in the British Isles in a number of languages, the most important of which are English, Latin, Irish, Welsh, French, and Provençal. These languages all belong to what is called the Indo-European family, consisting of a large number of related languages that may be classified in ten groups:

1	Indo-Iranian	6	Celtic
2	Armenian	7	Germanic
3	Greek	8	Balto-Slavic
4	Albanian	9	Tocharian
5	Italic	10	Hittite (?)
	(Latin and related dialects)		

English is a member of the Germanic group, which may be divided as follows:

1   East Germanic (Gothic)
2   North Germanic (Icelandic, Norwegian, Swedish, Danish)
3   West Germanic (English, Frisian, Saxon, Dutch, German)

The English language as it was spoken in the British Isles from the seventh century to around 1100 is called Old English (or Anglo-Saxon). During the eleventh and early twelfth centuries the gradual changes in the language gave it a recognizably new character, so that we call English spoken between 1100 and 1500 Middle English. In the course of its history medieval English was subjected to strong influences from Latin, from the North Germanic languages, and from French.

Latin was the learned language of England throughout the medieval period. It was employed in the liturgy of the Church, in official documents, and in the keeping of accounts. It has been estimated that about 40 percent of the male lay population of London during the late fourteenth and early fifteenth centuries could read some Latin. Medieval Latin was a functional (rather than an artificial) language, and it frequently differs from classical Latin. The vocabulary was adapted to the needs of the clergy and of the merchants, and the syntax sometimes shows strong vernacular influences. A few writers throughout the period, like John of Salisbury in the twelfth century, could write excellent Latin in the classical manner. Medieval Latin, however, should not be judged by classical standards, any more than Modern (New) English should be judged by Old English standards. The Latin of St. Bernard is very different from that of Cicero, but it could produce kinds of eloquence of which Cicero would have been incapable. Latin exerted its strongest influence on the English language during the early Renaissance, when it ceased to be a living language and writers began to use the vernacular for subjects that had formerly been treated in Latin.

When Julius Caesar invaded Britain in 54 B.C., he was resisted by a Celtic population with a distinctive culture of its own. After the Roman settlement in England under Claudius, a Romano-British culture was established. This culture gradually decayed with the breakup of the empire, and England was overrun by Germanic tribesmen in the course of the fifth century. However, the Celtic population maintained its language in Ireland, Scotland, Cornwall, and the Isle of Man. In all these areas except Cornwall there are Celtic-speaking peoples today. The Celtic languages are divided into two major groups: Continental Celtic and Insular Celtic. Continental Celtic survives only in a few inscriptions and in some reflections in Classical authors. Insular Celtic may be divided into two major families:

1 Gaelic (Irish, Scottish Gaelic, and Manx)
2 Britannic (Welsh, Cornish, Breton, and Pictish)

During the Middle Ages, Irish and Welsh were important literary languages. Irish spoken before A.D. 900 is called Old Irish, and that spoken between 900 and the beginning of the seventeenth century is called Middle Irish. Welsh spoken before the end of the eighth century is called Early Welsh, that spoken between A.D. 800 and about 1100 is called Old Welsh, and that spoken from about 1100 to about 1400 is called Medieval Welsh. The Welsh consider Dafydd ap Gwilym, a fourteenth-century poet, to be the father of Modern Welsh.

Between A.D. 700 and 1100 the Latin spoken by uneducated people in Europe gradually developed in the direction of the various romance languages. In the general area of France, Vulgar Latin, or common spoken Latin, became identifiable as Old French around 1100. Changes in Old French were great enough so that we call the language spoken between around 1300 to about 1515 Middle French. Meanwhile, the Norman conquerors of England in 1066 made French the language of the English aristocracy. A special dialect, called Anglo-Norman, became the language of the court and of the law, as well as a literary language of some importance.[1] It was the official language of Parliament until 1363. At about the time Anglo-Norman ceased to be spoken naturally, an interest developed in the artificial cultivation of French, and Englishmen became conscious of a distinction between the decaying native dialect and the more elegant French of Paris. Chaucer's contemporary, John Gower, produced literary works in English, French, and Latin. Meanwhile, in the twelfth century the English court occasionally patronized poets who wrote in Provençal, a dialect that developed in the south of France and became for a time an international literary language.

Since this anthology contains selections from the literature of the British Isles during the Middle Ages, it includes translations from Latin, French, Provençal, Irish, and Welsh, as well as selections from literature written in Old and Middle English. Each of these literatures has its peculiar traditions and characteristics and thoroughly merits study. The earliest literary monuments produced in the British Isles are in Irish. Early Irish culture remains largely mysterious. The mythological backgrounds of Irish literature are obscure, and Irish Christianity, introduced by St. Patrick, has special peculiarities of its own. The prose narratives that contain clear evidence of an Old Irish origin survive in late manuscripts, so that they are difficult to date precisely. However, the most famous of these, the *Táin Bó Cúalnge* ("Cattle Raid of Cooley"), seems to reflect a late Iron Age culture modified somewhat by Christian and learned elements.[2] It may have been written down in the seventh century. Early Irish poetry frequently displays a high degree of technical competence. It is notable for its interest in nature. Welsh literature as it survives is much more distinctly provincial than Irish literature. The prose narratives of the *Mabinogion* that are not clear imitations of French sources demonstrate the Celtic love for exaggeration and color. They also reveal an obscure mythological background to which Welsh scholars have recently devoted a great deal of attention. Both Irish and Welsh traditions contributed narrative motifs to the Arthurian romances that developed in France during the second half of the twelfth century. It is doubtful, however, that the more sophisticated authors of French romances had any interest at all in the transmission of Celtic traditions for themselves. Celtic narrative materials were used rather as vehicles for the expression of ideas that were immediately relevant to courtly audiences. Irish and Welsh poetry, meanwhile, seem to have had little influence on poetic traditions in other languages, with some exceptions in Latin.

Much more literature was produced in Latin during the Middle Ages than had been produced in antiquity. Meanwhile, classical literature itself continued to be read in the schools and imitated by medieval writers, who regarded it as a natural part of their cultural heritage and not as something from a remote past to be artificially cultivated. In other words, the world of the Latin classics was not set off from the medieval world by a sense of historical distance of a kind that developed during the Renaissance. Classical literature was thought of as a source of eloquence on the one hand and of wisdom on the other, so that medieval interest in it was practical rather than purely aesthetic. The British Isles produced influential writings in Latin of a wide variety of types, extending from theological and historical works by authors like Pelagius, Bede, John the Scot, St. Ethelred, or Bishop Grosseteste, to humanistic writings by men like John of Salisbury or Richard de Bury. Meanwhile, British or English writers also produced a considerable body of Latin poetry.[3]

As we have seen, after the Norman Conquest, French became the language of the English aristocracy. Literary works in French were produced for the English nobility both by writers in England proper and by those in areas on the Continent under English domination.[4] Writers seem to have been especially concerned during the twelfth and thirteenth centuries to produce works in French for the benefit of noblemen who could not read Latin with ease. These works ranged from adaptations of standard theological texts to purely literary productions like the *Lais* of Marie de France. The new rulers of England were especially interested in histories, both of their own traditions and of the traditions of the English and British peoples they had conquered. Under Henry II some troubadour poetry was written at the English court, a fact that has some influence on the subsequent development of the English lyric.

The major periods of literary activity in English are, first of all, the period from the seventh century to the Norman Conquest, when literature was produced in Old English, and second, the fourteenth century, when English again became the natural language of the English aristocracy. However, it should not be assumed that English died out altogether as a literary language during the intervening years. English prose has a fairly continuous history throughout the Middle Ages, and some of the finest lyrics in Middle English survive from the thirteenth century. Native poetic traditions were kept alive, especially in provincial areas isolated from the more sophisticated French tastes of the royal court. With these facts in mind, it is safe to say that Old English literature is characteristically Germanic in its outward form. The verse form of *Beowulf*, for example, as well as much of its poetic diction, reflects the traditions of popular Germanic heroic poetry. Middle English literature, on the other hand, tends to show a strong French influence superimposed to a greater or lesser extent on native Germanic conventions. Insofar as the content of both Old and Middle English literature is concerned, however, the dominant influence is clearly that of Christian-Latin culture. It is this underlying content that gives Old and Middle English literature a fundamental unity. The impression frequently encountered that Old English is essentially Germanic and hence outside the mainstream of English literature generally arises from too great a concentration on its form, language, and diction and insufficient attention to its content and to its immediate cultural environment.

Notes

1   See M. Dominica Legge, *Anglo-Norman Literature and Its Background*, Clarendon Press, Oxford, 1963.

2   See Kenneth Hurlstone Jackson, *The Oldest Irish Tradition: A Window on the Iron Age*, Cambridge University Press, London, 1964. For a general account with summaries of the more important prose works and some translations from the poetry, see Myles Dillon, *Early Irish Literature*, The University of Chicago Press, Chicago, 1948.

3 For Latin literature in England before the Norman Conquest, see W. F. Bolton, *A History of Anglo-Latin Literature*, vol. I, Princeton University Press, Princeton, N.J., 1967. Vol. II of this work is now in preparation. It contains an excellent bibliography.

4 For an interesting account of one of these, the poet Wace, see Urban T. Holmes, "Norman Literature and Wace," in William Matthews, *Medieval Secular Literature*, University of California Press, Berkeley, 1965, pp. 46–47.

I

EARLY CELTIC LITERATURE IN BRITAIN

Though we know that there were poets among the Celts on the Continent, the earliest Celtic literature that survives comes from the British Isles. It is written in Irish or Welsh, and of these the Irish is the older and, on the whole, more important.

Early Irish poetry is extraordinarily clear, simple, and vivid. Its form is strict, elaborate, and of great importance. If the Irish poet's thought is usually simple and his vision direct, his metrical technique is for the most part formal, intricate, and oblique. The Roman legions never reached Ireland, which remained a world apart from the mainstream of European civilization until the Christian missionaries of the fifth century, led by the Briton, St. Patrick, arrived in the island.

Facing page: Decorative page from the Lindisfarne Gospels.

A. Poetry[1]

In the following translations an attempt is made to imitate, or at least to suggest, the form of the original. A pleasant and informative introduction to Old Irish poetry may be found in Robin Flower, The Irish Tradition, *Clarendon Press, Oxford, 1947. The best anthology, which contains texts, translations, a good introduction, and extensive notes, is Gerard Murphy,* Early Irish Lyrics, *Clarendon Press, Oxford, 1956. For early Welsh poetry, not represented in these selections, see H. J. Bell,* The Development of Welsh Poetry, *Clarendon Press, Oxford, 1936.*

Note

1   The introduction to this section and all translations except number 27 were generously supplied by the late Mr. H. V. M. Dennis, whose enthusiasm for Old Irish literature and intimate knowledge of its peculiarities were the envy of all his friends. The text of number 27 is from *The Irish Tradition* by Robin Flower, here reprinted through the courtesy of the Clarendon Press.

1
Little bell,
Sweetly struck on windy night;
Better is a tryst with thee
Than to be with woman light.

2
From Torach to Chodhna fair,
A woman who gold ring bare,
In brave, bright-side Brian's day
Erin round made lone her way.

3
Ah, merl, thou art satisfied
With thy nest in brake remote:
Hermit that no bell dost beat,
Soft, sweet, peaceful is thy note.

4
I have heard:
He for poems does not give steeds,
Does with what fits him endow: cow.

5
Hollow mount, wolves' haunt, rough, dark—
The wind wails around its glens,
Wolves howl in its deep ravines,
The dun-brown deer now bold bawl,
Autumn over all descends,   5
Above its crags the crane screams.

6
The small bird
Has notes poured
From beak-point
      Bright yellow.
He flings glee   5
O'er Lake Lee,
Merl on tree
      In meadow.

7
Here look forth
East by north,
O'er sea, vast,
      Teeming,

Seal's abode,
Splendid, wild,
With flood-tide
　　Brimming.

8

O'er me reaches woodland wall,
Merl-song sounds round—this I tell—
O'er the lines my book filling
Birds their trilling chorus swell.

Chants clear cuckoo well—sweet joy— *5*
Bush atop in garment grey,
God's Doom! May the Lord save me,
Well write I 'neath shady spray.

9

My small cell by Túam's cove,
Mansion would not be more fit:
With the stars I love above,
With sun, with moon over it.

The Smith there his craft did ply— *5*
And that ye be told the truth—
My heart's darling, God on high,
Was the roofer of its roof.

House on which no rain descends,
Place where none fears pointed spear, *10*
Bright as garden which extends
With no wall of wattles near.

10

The wind is bitter tonight,
The wide sea's hair it whirls white;
I fear not o'er clear sea course
From Lothland men fetched by force.

11

Ciarnad Cormac's maid with quern
For a hundred ground the corn.
Daily grinding of ten bags
Was not work of one who lags.

The noble King met with her— *5*
They alone in her house were—
She in secret pregnant grew,
Then much grinding could not do.

5 Then Conn's grandson her to save,
Millwright brought o'er the wild wave; *10*
Cormac the son of Art had
The first mill—it helped Ciarnad.

12

Heart is he,
Oak-seed is;
Young is he,
Him I kiss.

13

I am Eve, great Adam's wife:
I wronged Jesus long ago;
I of Heaven robbed my race,
To the tree 'twas mine to go.

Pleasant was my Kingly house, *5*
Ill my choice that brought me shame,
Ill the counsel whence I pine,
Alas! my hand is profane.

'Twas I plucked the apple down
From the bough above and ate, *10*
Folly, while they stay alive,
Women never will forsake.

Ice would not be anywhere,
Wind-bright water would not be,
Hell would not, sorrow would not, *15*
Fear'd not be, but for me.

14

Hither, yon, the yellow bee,
Nimble, in the sun fares wide:
Boldly o'er the great plain flits,
Safe, his fellows joins in hive.

15

My beloved little crane,
Glory of my goodly home,
Best companion of them all,
Noble is, although a thrall.

16

Waves of the sea, very bright,
And the sand have o'er them gone;
In his small, weak wicker boat
Coning they have leaped upon.

The woman cast her white hair
In the boat on Coning there—
Hateful is the laugh that she
Laughs today at Torta's Tree.

17

Good is peaceful summertime,
Still the tall and stately wood
Which no whistling winds disturb,
Shady groves are plumed with green,
Ripples on the rivers run,
   Warmth in turf is good.

18

Fare to Rome:
Much vexation, small gain got!
The King whom thou seekest here,
Not with thee brought, thou findest not.

19

"Whence cometh reading's son?"
"From blessed Clon I come
And now my reading done,
I go down to swords."
"Of Clon the tidings tell."
"What I have heard I will:
By fresh graves foxes dwell
   And on entrails gorge."

20

I would have for King of Kings
   A great pool of ale;
I would have Heaven's folk
   In drinking never fail.

I would have food of faith
   And blessed innocence;
I would have in my house
   Flails of penitence.

I would have the angels
   In my house with me;
I would have for their use
   Vats of constancy.

I would have in flagons
   Charity to share;
I would have in beakers
   Kindness for those there.

I would have them drinking
   With cheerfulness;
I would have Jesus Himself
   Present to bless.

I would have three Marys—
   Honored, renowned;
I would have Heaven's folk
   On all sides around.

I would have for myself
   The Lord's liege to be,
That in trouble His blessing
   Might comfort me.

21

Bird on willow-tree I hear,
Fair small beak whose call is clear,
Sweet bright bill of chap smart, stout,
Merry notes, merl's voice, ring out.

22

Had bright gold the brown leaf been
   Which the wood drops down,
Had the white wave silver been—
   Lavished it had Finn.

23

To reap a field ere it is ripe,
Is it right, O stars' High King?
It is eating ere the hour
Flower of hazel, white with spring.

24

Blackbirds to swans, an ounce to great weight,
Forms of slave-women, to forms of the great;
Kings to Domnall, noise to notes played,
Rushlight to candle, blades to my blade.

25

Fish-filled main,
Fertile plain,
Flood of fish,
Fish in waves,
Flight of birds,
Ocean rough,
Hailstones white,
Salmon run,

Mighty whale,
Sailing song,   10
Flood of fish.

26
Pleasureless
Is the deed which I have done:
I caused him I love distress.

Mad was I
Not to yield me to his will—   5
But for fear of King on high.

Not unwise
Was the way he chose to go
Past Hell's pains to Paradise.

Slight the thing   10
That from me tore Curithir—
Great my kindness was to him.

I am she,
Liadan who loved Curithir:
True the tale they tell of me.   15

Short the time
That I spent with Curithir.
Sweet did I our converse find.

Woodland song
Sang to me with Curithir—   20
With the dark sea's voice along.

Would that none
Had from me torn Curithir,
Of the things that I have done.

Do not hide   25
That 'twas he was my heart's love,
Whatso'er I love beside.

Raging fire
Has run through this heart of mine,
Which without him must expire.   30

27
I and Pangur Bán my cat,
'Tis a like task we are at:
Hunting mice is his delight,
Hunting words I sit all night.

Better far than praise of men   5
'Tis to sit with book and pen;
Pangur bears me no ill will,
He too plies his simple skill.

'Tis a merry thing to see
At our tasks how glad are we,   10
When at home we sit and find
Entertainment to our mind.

Oftentimes a mouse will stray
In the hero Pangur's way;
Oftentimes my keen thought set   15
Takes a meaning in its net.

'Gainst the wall he sets his eye
Full and fierce and sharp and sly;
'Gainst the wall of knowledge I
All my little wisdom try.   20

When a mouse darts from its den
O how glad is Pangur then!
O what gladness do I prove
When I solve the doubts I love!

So in peace our tasks we ply,   25
Pangur Bán, my cat, and I;
In our arts we find our bliss,
I have mine and he has his.

Practice every day has made
Pangur perfect in his trade;   30
I get wisdom day and night
Turning darkness into light.

B. Prose

From a literary point of view, the most interesting prose works in Old Irish are the narrative cycles or series of stories centering around the adventures of an outstanding hero. Of these cycles the earliest and most important is the Ulster Cycle, whose heroes belong to the Ulaid, or people of northeastern Ireland. Their king was Conchobar (Conor), who held court at Emain Macha near modern Armagh. Their chief hero was Cú Chulainn (Cuchulain) who, in the long epic narrative Táin Bó Cúalnge *("Cattle Raid of Cooley") defended his people when, during a time that they were helpless as a result of a curse, they were attacked by an army from Connacht.*

Although the manuscripts containing the stories of the Ulaid are late, it is generally assumed on linguistic and other grounds that the tales themselves, which purport to describe events which took place near the time of the birth of Christ, are quite early. Thus the Táin *may have been put in writing for the first time as early as the seventh century, when, presumably, it had already enjoyed a long history in oral tradition.*

The tales are terse, abrupt, and frequently humorous. Narrative patterns in them sometimes appear later in the literature of France and England.

The best general introduction to the narrative material of early Ireland is Myles Dillon, Early Irish Literature, *The University of Chicago Press, Chicago, 1948. For some of the complex problems involved in the interpretation of this material, see T. F. O'Rahilly,* Early Irish History and Mythology, *The Dublin Institute for Advanced Studies, Dublin, 1946.*

"THE EXILE OF THE SONS OF USNACH"[1]

In the house of Feidlimid, the son of Dall, even he who was the narrator of stories to Conor the king, the men of Ulster sat at their ale; and before the men, in order to attend upon them, stood the wife of Feidlimid, and she was great with child. Round about the board went drinking-horns, and portions of food; and the revellers shouted in their drunken mirth. And when the men desired to lay themselves down to sleep, the woman also went to her couch; and, as she passed through the midst of the house, the child cried out in her womb, so that its shriek was heard throughout the whole house, and throughout the outer court that lay about it. And upon that shriek, all the men sprang up; and, head closely packed by head, they thronged together in the house, whereupon Sencha, the son of Ailill, rebuked them: "Let none of you stir!" cried he, "and let the woman be brought before us, that we may learn what is the meaning of that cry." Then they brought the woman before them, and thus spoke to her Feidlimid, her spouse:

What is that, of all cries far the fiercest,
  In thy womb raging loudly and long?
Through all ears with that clamour thou piercest;
  With that scream, from sides swollen and strong:

Of great woe, for that cry, is foreboding my heart;
That is torn through with terror, and sore with the
  smart.

Then the woman turned her, and she approached Cathbad the Druid, for he was a man of knowledge, and thus she spoke to him:

Give thou ear to me, Cathbad, thou fair one of face,
Thou great crown of our honour, and royal in race;
Let the man so exalted still higher be set,
Let the Druid draw knowledge, that Druids can get.
For I want words of wisdom, and none can I fetch;
Nor to Felim a torch of sure knowledge can stretch:
As no wit of a woman can wot what she bears,
I know naught of that cry from within me that tears.

And then said Cathbad:

'Tis a maid who screamed wildly so lately,
  Fair and curling shall locks round her flow,
And her eyes be blue-centred and stately;
  And her cheeks, like the foxglove, shall glow.
For the tint of her skin, we commend her,
  In its whiteness, like snow newly shed;
And her teeth are all faultless in splendour;
  And her lips, like to coral, are red:

A fair woman is she, for whom heroes, that fight
In their chariots for Ulster, to death shall be dight.

'Tis a woman that shriek who hath given,
    Golden-haired, with long tresses, and tall;
For whose love many chiefs shall have striven,
    And great kings for her favours shall call.
To the west she shall hasten, beguiling
    A great host, that from Ulster shall steal:
Red as coral, her lips shall be smiling,
    As her teeth, white as pearls, they reveal:
Aye, that woman is fair, and great queens shall be fain
Of her form, that is faultless, unflawed by a stain.

Then Cathbad laid his hand upon the body of the woman; and the little child moved beneath his hand: "Aye, indeed," he said, "it is a woman child who is here: Deirdre shall be her name, and evil woe shall be upon her."

Now some days after that came the girl child into the world; and then thus sang Cathbad:

O Deirdre! of ruin great cause thou art;
    Though famous, and fair, and pale:
Ere that Félim's hid daughter from life shall part,
    All Ulster her deeds shall wail.

Aye, mischief shall come, in the after-time,
    Thou fair shining maid, for thee;
Hear ye this: Usna's sons, the three chiefs sublime,
    To banishment forced shall be.

While thou art in life, shall a fierce wild deed
    In Emain, though late, be done:
Later yet, it shall mourn it refused to heed
    The guard of Róg's powerful son.

O lady of worth! 'tis to thee we owe
    That Fergus to exile flies;
That a son of king Conor we hail in woe,
    When Fiachna is hurt, and dies.

O lady of worth! 'tis all thine the guilt!
    Gerrc, Illadan's son, is slain;
And when Eogan mac Doorha's great life is spilt,
    Not less shall be found our pain.

Grim deed shalt thou do, and in wrath shalt rave
    Against glorious Ulster's king:

In that spot shall men dig thee thy tiny grave;
    Of Deirdre they long shall sing.

"Let that maiden be slain!" cried out the young men of Ulster; but "Not so!" said Conor; "she shall in the morning be brought to me, and shall be reared according to my will, and she shall be my wife, and in my companionship shall she dwell."

The men of Ulster were not so hardy as to turn him from his purpose, and thus it was done. The maiden was reared in a house that belonged to Conor, and she grew up to be the fairest maid in all Ireland. She was brought up at a distance from the king's court; so that none of the men of Ulster might see her till the time came when she was to share the royal couch: none of mankind was permitted to enter the house where she was reared, save only her foster-father, and her foster-mother; and in addition to these Levorcham, to whom naught could any refuse, for she was a witch.

Now once it chanced upon a certain day in the time of winter that the foster-father of Deirdre had employed himself in skinning a calf upon the snow, in order to prepare a roast for her, and the blood of the calf lay upon the snow, and she saw a black raven who came down to drink it. And "Levorcham," said Deirdre, "that man only will I love, who hath the three colours that I see here, his hair as black as the raven, his cheeks red like the blood, and his body as white as the snow." "Dignity and good fortune to thee!" said Levorcham; "that man is not far away. Yonder is he in the burg which is nigh; and the name of him is Naisi, the son of Usnach." "I shall never be in good health again," said Deirdre, "until the time come when I may see him."

It befell that Naisi was upon a certain day alone upon the rampart of the burg of Emain, and he sent his warrior-cry with music abroad: well did the musical cry ring out that was raised by the sons of Usnach. Each cow and every beast that heard them, gave of milk two-thirds more than its wont; and each man by whom that cry was heard deemed it to be fully joyous, and a dear pleasure to him. Goodly moreover was the play that these men made with their weapons; if the whole province of Ulster had been assembled together against them in one place, and they three only had been able to set their backs against one another, the men of Ulster would not have borne away victory from those three: so well were they skilled in parry and defence. And they were swift of foot when they hunted the game, and with them it was the custom to chase the quarry to its death.

Now when this Naisi found himself alone on the plain, Deirdre also soon escaped outside her house to him, and she ran past him, and at first he knew not who she might be.

"Fair is the young heifer that springs past me!" he cried.

"Well may the young heifers be great," she said, "in a place where none may find a bull."

"Thou hast, as thy bull," said he, "the bull of the whole province of Ulster, even Conor the king of Ulster."

"I would choose between you two," she said, "and I would take for myself a younger bull, even such as thou art."

"Not so, indeed," said Naisi, "for I fear the prophecy of Cathbad."

"Sayest thou this, as meaning to refuse me?" said she.

"Yea indeed," he said; and she sprang upon him, and she seized him by his two ears. "Two ears of shame and of mockery shalt thou have," she cried, "if thou take me not with thee."

"Release me, O my wife!" said he.

"That will I."

Then Naisi raised his musical warrior-cry, and the men of Ulster heard it, and each of them one after another sprang up: and the sons of Usnach hurried out in order to hold back their brother.

"What is it," they said, "that thou dost? let it not be by any fault of thine that war is stirred up between us and the men of Ulster."

Then he told them all that had been done; and "There shall evil come on thee from this," said they; "moreover thou shalt lie under the reproach of shame so long as thou dost live; and we will go with her into another land, for there is no king in all Ireland who will refuse us welcome if we come to him."

Then they took counsel together, and that same night they departed, three times fifty warriors, and the same number of women, and dogs, and servants, and Deirdre went with them. And for a long time they wandered about Ireland, in homage to this man or that; and often Conor sought to slay them, either by ambuscade or by treachery; from round about Assaroe, near to Bally-shannon in the west, they journeyed, and they turned them back to Benn Etar, in the north-east, which men to-day call the Mountain of Howth. Nevertheless the men of Ulster drave them from the land, and they came to the land of Alba, and in its wildernesses they dwelled. And when the chase of the wild beasts of the mountains failed them, they made foray upon the cattle of the men of Alba, and took them for themselves; and the men of Alba gathered themselves together with intent to destroy them. Then they took shelter with the king of Alba, and the king took them into his following, and they served him in war. And they made for themselves houses of their own in the meadows by the king's burg: it was on account of Deirdre that these houses were made, for they feared that men might see her, and that on her account they might be slain.

Now one day the high-steward of the king went out in the early morning, and he made a cast about Naisi's house, and saw those two sleeping therein, and he hurried back to the king, and awaked him: "We have," said he, "up to this day found no wife for thee of like dignity to thyself. Naisi the son of Usnach hath a wife of worth sufficient for the emperor of the western world! Let Naisi be slain, and let his wife share thy couch."

"Not so!" said the king, "but do thou prepare thyself to go each day to her house, and woo her for me secretly."

Thus was it done; but Deirdre, whatsoever the steward told her, was accustomed straightway to recount it each even to her spouse; and since nothing was obtained from her, the sons of Usnach were sent into dangers, and into wars, and into strifes that thereby they might be overcome. Nevertheless they showed themselves to be stout in every strife, so that no advantage did the king gain from them by such attempts as these.

The men of Alba were gathered together to destroy the sons of Usnach, and this also was told to Deirdre. And she told her news to Naisi: "Depart hence!" said she, "for if ye depart not this night, upon the morrow ye shall be slain!" And they marched away that night, and they betook themselves to an island of the sea.

Now the news of what had passed was brought to the men of Ulster. "'Tis pity, O Conor!" said they, "that the sons of Usnach should die in the land of foes, for the sake of an evil woman. It is better that they should come under thy protection, and that the (fated) slaying should be done here, and that they should come into their own land, rather than that they should fall at the hands of foes." "Let them come to us then," said Conor, "and let men go as securities to them." The news was brought to them.

"This is welcome news for us," they said; "we will indeed come, and let Fergus come as our surety, and Dubhtach, and Cormac the son of Conor." These then went to them, and they moved them to pass over the sea.

But at the contrivance of Conor, Fergus was pressed to join in an ale-feast, while the sons of Usnach were pledged to eat no food in Erin, until they had eaten the food of Conor. So Fergus tarried behind with Dubhtach and Cormac; and the sons of Usnach went on, accompanied by Fiacha, Fergus' son; until they came to the meadows around Emain.

Now at that time Eogan the son of Durthacht had come to Emain to make his peace with Conor, for they had for a long time been at enmity; and to him, and to the warmen of Conor, the charge was given that they should slay the sons of Usnach, in order that they should not come before the king. The sons of Usnach stood upon the level part of the meadows, and the women sat upon the ramparts of Emain. And Eogan came with his warriors across the meadow, and the son of Fergus took his place by Naisi's side. And Eogan greeted them with a mighty thrust of his spear, and the spear brake Naisi's back in sunder, and passed through it. The son of Fergus made a spring, and he threw both arms around Naisi, and he brought him beneath himself to shelter him, while he threw himself down above him; and it was thus that Naisi was slain, through the body of the son of Fergus. Then there began a murder throughout the meadow, so that none escaped who did not fall by the points of the spears, or the edge of the sword, and Deirdre was brought to Conor to be in his power, and her arms were bound behind her back.

Now the sureties who had remained behind, heard what had been done, even Fergus and Dubhtach, and Cormac. And thereon they hastened forward, and they forthwith performed great deeds. Dubhtach slew, with the one thrust of his spear, Mane a son of Conor, and Fiachna the son of Feidelm, Conor's daughter; and Fergus struck down Traigthren, the son of Traiglethan, and his brother. And Conor was wroth at this, and he came to the fight with them; so that upon that day three hundred of the men of Ulster fell. And Dubhtach slew the women of Ulster; and, ere the day dawned, Fergus set Emain on fire. Then they went away into exile, and betook them to the land of Connaught to find shelter with Ailill and Maev, for they knew that that royal pair would give them good entertainment. To the men of Ulster the exiles showed no love: three thousand stout men went with them; and for sixteen years never did they allow cries of lamentation and of fear among the Ulstermen to cease: each night their vengeful forays caused men to quake, and to wail.

Deirdre lived on for a year in the household of Conor; and during all that time she smiled no smile of laughter; she satisfied not herself with food or with sleep, and she raised not her head from her knee. And if any one brought before her people of mirth, she used to speak thus:

Though eager troops, and fair to see,
    May home return, though these ye wait:
When Usna's sons came home to me,
    They came with more heroic state.

With hazel mead, my Naisi stood:
    And near our fire his bath I'd pour;
On Aindle's stately back the wood;
    On Ardan's ox, or goodly boar.

Though sweet that goodly mead ye think
    That warlike Conor drinks in hall,
I oft have known a sweeter drink,
    Where leaps in foam the waterfall:

Our board was spread beneath the tree,
    And Naisi raised the cooking flame:
More sweet than honey-sauced to me
    Was meat, prepared from Naisi's game.

Though well your horns may music blow,
    Though sweet each month your pipes may sound,
I fearless say, that well I know
    A sweeter strain I oft have found.

Though horns and pipes be sounding clear,
    Though Conor's mind in these rejoice,
More magic strain, more sweet, more dear
    Was Usna's Children's noble voice.

Like sound of wave, rolled Naisi's bass;
    We'd hear him long, so sweet he sang:
And Ardan's voice took middle place;
    And clearly Aindle's tenor rang.

Now Naisi lies within his tomb:
  A sorry guard his friends supplied;
His kindred poured his cup of doom,
  That poisoned cup, by which he died.

Ah! Berthan dear! thy lands are fair;
  Thy men are proud, though hills be stern:
Alas! to-day I rise not there
  To wait for Usna's sons' return.

That firm, just mind, so loved, alas!
  The dear shy youth, with touch of scorn,
I loved with him through woods to pass,
  And girding in the early morn.

When bent on foes, they boded ill,
  Those dear grey eyes, that maids adored;
When, spent with toil, his troops lay still,
  Through Irish woods his tenor soared.

For this it is, no more I sleep;
  No more my nails with pink I stain:
No joy can break the watch I keep;
  For Usna's sons come not again.

For half the night no sleep I find;
  No couch can me to rest beguile:
'Mid crowds of thoughts still strays my mind;
  I find no time to eat or smile.

In eastern Emain's proud array
  No time to joy is left for me;
For gorgeous house, and garments gay,
  Nor peace, nor joy, nor rest can be.

  And when Conor sought to soothe her, thus Deirdre
would answer him:

Ah Conor! what of thee? I naught can do?
  Lament and sorrow on my life have passed:
The ill you fashioned lives my whole life through;
  A little time your love for me would last.

The man to me most fair beneath the sky,
  The man I loved, in death away you tore:
The crime you did was great; for, till I die,
  That face I loved I never shall see more.

That he is gone is all my sorrow still;
  Before me looms the shape of Usna's son;
Though o'er his body white is yon dark hill,
  There's much I'd lavish, if but him I won.

I see his cheeks, with meadow's blush they glow;
  Black as a beetle, runs his eyebrows' line;
His lips are red; and, white as noble snow
  I see his teeth, like pearls they seem to shine.

Well have I known the splendid garb he bears,
  Oft among Alba's warriors seen of old:
A crimson mantle, such as courtier wears,
  And edged with border wrought of ruddy gold.

Of silk his tunic; great its costly price;
  For full one hundred pearls thereon are sewn;
Stitched with *findruine*,[2] bright with strange device,
  Full fifty ounces weighed those threads alone.

Gold-hilted in his hand I see his sword;
  Two spears he holds, with spear-heads grim and
      green;
Around his shield the yellow gold is poured,
  And in its midst a silver boss is seen.

Fair Fergus ruin on us all hath brought!
  We crossed the ocean, and to him gave heed:
His honour by a cup of ale was bought;
  From him hath passed the fame of each high deed.

If Ulster on this plain were gathered here
  Before king Conor; and those troops he'd give,
I'd lose them all, nor think the bargain dear,
  If I with Naisi, Usna's son, could live.

Break not, O king, my heart to-day in me;
  For soon, though young, I come my grave unto:
My grief is stronger than the strength of sea;
  Thou, Conor, knowest well my word is true.

  "Whom dost thou hate the most," said Conor, "of
these whom thou now seest?"
  "Thee thyself," she answered, "and with thee Eogan
the son of Durthacht."

  "Then," said Conor, "thou shalt dwell with Eogan
for a year;" and he gave Deirdre over into Eogan's
hand.

Now upon the morrow they went away over the festal plain of Macha, and Deirdre sat behind Eogan in the chariot; and the two who were with her were the two men whom she would never willingly have seen together upon the earth, and as she looked upon them, "Ha, Deirdre," said Conor, "it is the same glance that a ewe gives when between two rams that thou sharest now between me and Eogan!" Now there was a great rock of stone in front of them, and Deirdre struck her head upon that stone, and she shattered her head, and so she died.

This then is the tale of the exile of the sons of Usnach, and of the Exile of Fergus, and of the death of Deirdre.

From the
TÁIN BÓ CÚALNGE
" The Boyhood Deeds of Cuchulain "[3]

[*The* Táin *opens with an argument between King Ailill and Queen Medb of Connacht as they lie in bed together. At issue is the question of who was better provided at the time of their marriage. It appears that Medb had as much as Ailill except that a great white bull of hers, Whitehorn, had gone into Ailill's herd because it did not wish to be owned by a woman. To make up for its loss, Medb sought to borrow a bull from the cantred of Cúalnge in Ulster. When this attempt failed, she determined to get the bull by force. With the aid of Fergus son of Roech, and Cormac son of Conchobar, who were in exile from Ulster, she set out northward with an army. Meanwhile, the Ulaid, except for Cuchulain and his father Sualtam, were under a curse and unable to fight. Cuchulain defended Ulster single-handed. After some initial successes on Cuchulain's part, Fergus identified him to Medb and began the account of his boyhood deeds that follows.*]

"Now this lad was reared in the house of his father and mother at Dairgthech ['the Oak House' (?)], namely, in the plain of Murthemne, and the tales of the youths of Emain were told to him. For there are always thrice fifty boys at play there," said Fergus. "Forasmuch as in this wise Conchobar passed his reign ever since he, the king, assumed his sovereignty, to wit: As soon as he arose, forthwith in settling the cares and affairs of the province; thereafter, the day he divided in three: first, the first third he spent a-watching the youths play games of skill and of hurling; the next third of the day, a-playing draughts and chess, and the last

third a-feasting on meat and a-quaffing ale, till sleep possessed them all, the while minstrels and harpers lulled him to sleep. For all that I am a long time in banishment because of him, I give my word," said Fergus, "there is not in Erin nor in Alba a warrior the like of Conchobar."

"And the lad was told the tales of the boys and the boy-troop in Emain; and the child said to his mother, he would go to have part in the games on the play-field of Emain. 'It is too soon for thee, little son,' said his mother; 'wait till there go with thee a champion of the champions of Ulster, or some of the attendants of Conchobar to enjoin thy protection and thy safety on the boy-troop.' 'I think it too long for that, my mother,' the little lad answered, 'I will not wait for it. But do thou show me what place lies Emain Macha.' 'Northwards, there; it is far away from thee,' said his mother, 'the place wherein it lies, and the way is hard. Sliab Fuait lies between thee and Emain.' 'At all hazards, I will essay it,' he answered.

"The boy fared forth and took his playthings with him. His little lath-shield he took, and his hurley of bronze and his ball of silver; and he took his little javelin for throwing; and his toy-staff he took with its fire hardened butt-end, and he began to shorten the length of his journey with them. He would give the ball a stroke with the hurl-bat, so that he sent it a long distance from him. Then with a second throw he would cast his hurley so that it went a distance no shorter than the first throw. He would hurl his little darts, and let fly his toy-staff, and make a wild chase after them. Then he would catch up his hurl-bat and pick up the ball and snatch up the dart, and the stock of the toy-staff had not touched the ground when he caught its tip which was in the air.

"He went his way to the mound-seat of Emain, where was the boy-troop. Thrice fifty youths were with Folloman, Conchobar's son, at their games on the fair-green of Emain.

"The little lad went on to the play-field into the midst of the boys, and he whipped the ball between his two legs away from them, nor did he suffer it to travel higher up than the top of his knee, nor did he let it lower down than his ankle, and he drove it and held it between his two legs and not one of the boys was able to get a prod nor a stroke nor a blow nor a shot at it, so that he carried it over the brink of the goal away from them. Then he goes to the youths without binding them to protect him. For no one used to approach them on their play-field without first securing from them a pledge of protection. He was weetless thereof.

"Then they all gazed upon him. They wondered and marvelled. 'Come, boys!' cried Folloman, Conchobar's son, 'the urchin insults us. Throw yourselves all on yon fellow, and his death shall come at my hands; for it is geis among you for any youth to come into your game, without first entrusting his safety to you. And do you all attack him together, for we know that yon wight is some one of the heroes of Ulster; and they shall not make it their wont to break into your sports without first entrusting their safety and protection to you.'

"Thereupon they all set upon him together. They cast their thrice fifty hurl-bats at the poll of the boy's head. He raises his single toy-staff and wards off the thrice fifty hurlies, so that they neither hurt him nor harm him, and he takes a load of them on his back. Then they throw their thrice fifty balls at the lad. He raises his upper arm and his forearm and the palms of his hands against them and parries the thrice fifty balls, and he catches them, each single ball in his bosom. They throw at him the thrice fifty play-spears charred at the end. The boy raises his little lath-shield against them and fends off the thrice fifty play-staffs, and they all remain stuck in his lath-shield. Thereupon contortions took hold of him. Thou wouldst have weened it was a hammering wherewith each hair was hammered into his head, with such an uprising it rose. Thou wouldst have weened it was a spark of fire that was on every single hair there. He closed one of his eyes so that it was no wider than the eye of a needle. He opened the other wide so that it was as big as the mouth of a mead-cup. He stretched his mouth from his jaw-bones to his ears; he opened his mouth wide to his jaw so that his gullet was seen. The champion's light rose up from his crown.

"It was then he ran in among them. He scattered fifty king's sons of them over the ground underneath him before they got to the gate of Emain. Five of them," Fergus continued, "dashed headlong between me and Conchobar, where we were playing chess, even on Cennchaem ['Fairhead'] the chessboard of Conchobar, on the mound-seat of Emain. The little boy pursued them to cut them off. Then he sprang over the chess-board after the nine. Conchobar seized the little lad by the wrists. 'Hold, little boy. I see 'tis not gently thou dealest with the boy-band.' 'Good reason I have,' quoth the little lad. 'From home, from mother and father I came to play with them, and they have not been good to me. I had not a guest's honour at the hands of the boy-troop on my arrival, for all that I came from far-away lands.' 'How is that? Who art thou, and what is thy name?' asked Conchobar. 'Little Setanta am I, son of Sualtaim. Son am I to Dechtirè, thine own sister; and not through thee did I expect to be thus aggrieved.' 'How so, little one?' said Conchobar. 'Knewest thou not that it is forbidden among the boy-troop, that it is geis for them for any boy to approach them in their land without first claiming his protection from them?' 'I knew it not,' said the lad. 'Had I known it, I would have been on my guard against them.' 'Good, now, ye boys,' Conchobar cried; 'take ye upon you the protection of the little lad.' 'We grant it, indeed,' they made answer.

"The little lad went into the game again under the protection of the boy-troop. Thereupon they loosed hands from him, and once more he rushed amongst them throughout the house. He laid low fifty of their princes on the ground under him. Their fathers thought it was death he had given them. That was it not, but stunned they were with front-blows and mid-blows and long-blows. 'Hold!' cried Conchobar. 'Why art thou yet at them?' 'I swear by my gods whom I worship' (said the boy) 'they shall all come under my protection and shielding, as I have put myself under their protection and shielding. Otherwise I shall not lighten my hands off them until I have brought them all to earth.' 'Well, little lad, take thou upon thee the protection of the boy-troop.' 'I grant it, indeed,' said the lad. Thereupon the boy-troop went under his protection and shielding.

"Then they all went back to the play-field, and the boys whom he had overthrown there arose. Their nurses and tutors helped them.

"Now, once upon a time," continued Fergus, "when he was a gilla, he slept not in Emain Macha till morning. 'Tell me,' Conchobar said to him, 'why sleepest thou not in Emain Macha, Cuchulain?' 'I sleep not, unless it be equally high at my head and my feet.' Then Conchobar had a pillar-stone set up at his head and another at his feet, and between them a bed apart was made for him.

"Another time a certain man went to wake him, and the lad struck him with his fist in the neck or in the forehead, so that it drove in the front of his forehead on to his brain and he overthrew the pillar-stone with his forearm. 'It is known,' exclaimed Ailill, 'that that was the fist of a champion and the arm of a hero.' And from that time," continued Fergus, "no one durst wake him, so that he used to wake of himself.

"Then, another time, he played ball on the play-field east of Emain, and he was alone on one side against the thrice fifty boys. He always worsted in every game in the east [?] in this way. Thereafter the lad began to use his fists on them, so that fifty boys of them died thereof. He took to flight then, till he took refuge under the cushion of Conchobar's couch. The Ulstermen sprang up all around him. I, too, sprang up, and Conchobar, threat. The lad himself rose up under the couch, so that he hove up the couch and the thirty warriors that were on it withal, so that he bore it into the middle of the house. Straightway the Ulstermen sat around him in the house. We settled it then," continued Fergus, "and reconciled the boy-troop to him afterwards.

"The broil of war arose between Ulster and Eogan son of Durthacht. The Ulstermen go forth to the war. The lad Setanta is left behind asleep. The men of Ulster are beaten. Conchobar and Cuscraid Menn ['the Stammerer'] of Macha are left on the field and many besides them. Their groans awaken the lad. Thereat he stretches himself, so that the two stones are snapped that are near him This took place in the presence of Bricriu yonder," Fergus added. "Then he gets up. I meet him at the door of the liss, I being severely wounded. 'Hey, God keep thy life, O Fergus my master,' says he; 'where is Conchobar?' 'I know not,' I answer. Thereupon he goes out. The night is dark. He makes for the battlefield, until he sees before him a man and half his head on him and half of another man on his back. 'Help me, Cuchulain,' he cries; 'I have been stricken, and I bear on my back half of my brother. Carry it for me a while.' 'I will not carry it,' says he. Thereupon the man throws the load at him. Cuchulain throws it back from him. They grapple with one another. Cuchulain is overthrown. Then I heard something. It was Badb from the corpses: 'Ill the stuff of a warrior that is there under the feet of a phantom.' Thereat Cuchulain arises from underneath him, and he strikes off his head with his playing-stick and proceeds to drive the ball before him over the field of battle.

"'Is my master Conchobar on this battle-field?' That one makes answer. He goes towards him, to where he espies him in a ditch and the earth piled around him on both sides to hide him. 'Wherefore art thou come to the battle-field?' Conchobar asks; 'is it that thou mightst see mortal terror there?' Then Cuchulain lifts him out of the ditch. The six strong men of Ulster that were with us could not have lifted him out more bravely. 'Get thee before us to yonder house,' says Conchobar, 'to make me a fire there.' He kindles a great fire for him. 'Good now,' quoth Conchobar, 'if one would bring me a roast pig, I would live.' 'I will go fetch it,' says Cuchulain. Thereupon he sallies out, when he sees a man at a cooking-pit in the heart of the wood. One of his hands holds his weapons therein, the other roasts the pork. Ill-favoured, indeed, is the man. For the which, Cuchulain attacks him and takes his head and his pig with him. Conchobar eats the pig then. 'Let us go to our house,' says Conchobar. They meet Cuscraid son of Conchobar and there were heavy wounds on him. Cuchulain carries him on his back. The three then proceed to Emain Macha.

"Another time the Ulstermen were in their 'Pains.' Now, there was no 'Pains' amongst us," Fergus continued, "in women or boys, nor in any one outside the borders of Ulster, nor in Cuchulain and his father. It was for this reason no one dared shed the blood of the men of Ulster, for that the 'Pains' fell on the one that wounded them. There came thrice nine men from the Isles of Faiche. They pass over our rear fort, the whiles we are in our 'Pains.' The women scream in the fort. The youths are in the play-field. They come at the cry. When the boys catch sight of the swarthy men, they all take to flight save Cuchulain alone. He hurls the hand-stones and his playing-staff at them. He slays nine of them and they leave fifty wounds on him and proceed thence on their journey.

"A youngster did that deed," Fergus continued, "at the close of five years after his birth, when he overthrew the sons of champions and warriors at the very door of their liss and dûn. No need is there of wonder or surprise, if he should do great deeds, if he should come to the confines of the land, if he should cut off the four-pronged fork, if he should slay one man or two men or three men or four men, when there are seventeen full years of him now on the Cattle-lifting of Cualnge. 'In sooth, then, we know that youth,' spoke out Conall Cernach ["the Victorious"], 'and it is all the better we should know him, for he is a fosterling of our own.'

Then it was that Cormac Conlongas son of Conchobar spake: "Again that little lad performed a second deed in the following year." "What deed was that?" asked Ailill.

"A goodly smith there was in the land of Ulster, Culann the Smith, by name. He made ready a feast for Conchobar and set out for Emain to invite him. He made known to him that only a few should come with him, that he should bring none but a true guest along, forasmuch as it was not a domain or lands of his own that he had, but the fruit of his two hands, his sledges and anvils, his fists and his tongs. Conchobar replied that only a few would go to him.

"Culann went back to the smithy to prepare and make ready meat and drink in readiness for the king. Conchobar sat in Emain till it was time to set out for the feast, till came the close of the day. The king put his fine, light travelling apparel about him, and went with fifty chariot-chiefs of those that were noblest and most illustrious of the heroes, and betook him to the boys before starting, to bid them farewell. It was always his custom to visit and revisit them when going and coming, to seek his blessing of the boys. Conchobar came on to the fair-green, and he saw a thing that astounded him: Thrice fifty boys at one end of the green and a single boy at the other, and the single boy won the victory at the goal and at hurling from the thrice fifty boys. When it was at hole-play they were— a game of hole that used to be played on the fair-green of Emain—and it was their turn to drive and his to keep

Figure 13 *Tara brooch.*

guard, he would catch the thrice fifty balls just outside of the hole, and not one went by him into the hole. When it was their turn to keep guard and his to drive, he would send the thrice fifty balls into the hole without fail, and the boys were unable to ward them off. When it was at tearing off each other's garments they played, he would strip off them their thrice fifty suits so that they were quite naked, and they were not able all of them to take as much as the brooch from his mantle. When it was at wrestling they were, he would throw those same thrice fifty boys to the ground under him, and they did not succeed all of them around him in lifting him up. Conchobar looked with wonder at the little lad. 'O, ye youths,' cried Conchobar. 'Hail to the land whence cometh the lad ye see, if the deeds of his manhood shall be such as are those of his boyhood!' ''Tis not just to speak thus,' exclaimed Fergus; 'e'en as the little lad grows, so will his deeds of manhood grow with him.' 'The little lad shall be called to us, that he may come with us to enjoy the feast to which we go.' The little lad was summoned to Conchobar. 'Good, my lad,' said Conchobar. 'Come thou with us to enjoy the feast whereto we go, for thou art a guest.' 'Nay, but I will not go,' the little boy answered. 'How so?' asked Conchobar. 'Forasmuch as the boys have not yet had their fill of games and of sport, and I will not leave them till they have had enough play.' 'It is too long for us to await thee till then, little boy, and by no means shall we wait.' 'Go then before us,' said the little boy, 'and I will follow after ye.' 'Thou knowest naught of the way, little boy,' said Conchobar. 'I will follow the trail of the company and of the horses and chariots.'

"Thereafter Conchobar came to the house of Culann the Smith. The king was waited upon and all were shown honour, as befitted their rank and calling and privileges, nobility and gentle accomplishment. Straw and fresh rushes were spread out under them. They commenced to carouse and make merry. Culann inquired of Conchobar: 'Hast thou, O king, appointed any to come after thee this night to this dûn?' 'No, I appointed no one,' replied Conchobar, for he had forgotten the little lad whom he had charged to come after him. 'Why so?' asked Conchobar. 'An excellent blood-hound have I, that was brought from Spain. There are three chains upon him, and three men at each chain. Because of our goods and our cattle he is slipped and the liss is closed. When his dog-chain is loosed from him, no one dares approach the same cantred with him to make a course or a circuit, and he knows no one but myself. The power of hundreds is in him for strength.' Then spake Conchobar, 'Let the dûn be opened for the ban-dog, that he may guard the cantred.' The dog-chain is taken off the ban-dog, and he makes a swift round of the cantred. And he comes to the mound whereon he was wont to keep guard of the stead, and there he was, his head couched on his paws, and wild, untameable, furious, savage, ferocious, ready for fight was the dog that was there.

"As for the boys: They were in Emain until the time came for them to disperse. Each of them went to the house of his father and mother, of his foster-mother and foster-father. Then the little lad went on the trail of the party, till he reached the house of Culann the Smith. He began to shorten the way as he went with his play-things. He threw his ball and threw his club after it, so that it hit the ball. The one throw was no greater than the other. Then he threw his staff after them both, so that it reached the ball and the club before ever they fell. Soon the lad came up. When he was nigh to the green of the fort wherein were Culann and Conchobar, he threw all his play-things before him except only the ball. The watch-dog descried the lad and bayed at him, so that in all the countryside was heard the howl of the watch-hound. And not a division of feasting was what he was inclined to make of him, but to swallow him down at one gulp past the cavity of his chest and the width of his throat and the pipe of his breast. And it interfered not with the lad's play, although the hound made for him. And the lad had not with him any means of defence, but he hurled an unerring cast of the ball, so that it passed through the gullet of the watch-dog's neck and carried the guts within him out through his back door, and he laid hold of the hound by the two legs and dashed him against a pillar-stone that was near him, so that every limb of him sprang apart, so that he broke into bits all over the ground. Conchobar heard the yelp of the ban-dog. Conchobar and his people could not move; they weened they would not find the lad alive before them. 'Alas, O warriors,' cried Conchobar; 'in no good luck have we come to enjoy this feast.' 'How so?' asked all. 'The little lad who has come to meet me, my sister's son, Setanta son of Sualtaim, is undone through the hound.' As one man, arose all the renowned men of Ulster. Though a door of the hostel was thrown wide open, they all rushed in the other direction out over the palings of the fortress. But fast as they all got

there, faster than all arrived Fergus, and he lifted the little lad from the ground on the slope of his shoulder and bore him into the presence of Conchobar. They put him on Conchobar's knee. A great alarm arose amongst them that the king's sister's son should have been all but killed. And Culann came out, and he saw his slaughter-hound in many pieces. He felt his heart beating against his breast. Whereupon he went into the dûn. 'Welcome thy coming, little lad,' said Culann, 'because of thy mother and father, but not welcome is thy coming for thine own sake. Yet would that I had not made a feast.' 'What hast thou against the lad?' queried Conchobar. 'Not luckily for me hast thou come to quaff my ale and to eat my food; for my substance is now a wealth gone to waste, and my livelihood is a livelihood lost now after my dog. He hath kept honor and life for me. Good was the friend thou hast robbed me of, even my dog, in that he tended my herds and flocks and stock for me; he was the protection of all our cattle, both afield and at home.' 'Be not angered thereat, O Culann my master,' said the little boy. 'It is no great matter, for I will pass a just judgment upon it.' 'What judgment thereon wilt thou pass, lad?' Conchobar asked. 'If there is a whelp of the breed of that dog in Erin, he shall be reared by me till he be fit to do business as was his sire. Till then myself will be the hound to protect his flocks and his cattle and his land and even himself in the meanwhile. And I will safeguard the whole plain of Murthemne, and no one will carry off flock nor herd without that I know it.'

"'Well hast thou given judgment, little lad,' said Conchobar. 'In sooth, we ourselves could not give one that would be better,' said Cathba. 'Why should it not be from this that thou shouldst take the name Cuchulain ["Wolfhound of Culann"]?' 'Nay, then,' answered the lad; 'dearer to me mine own name, Setanta son of Sualtaim.' 'Say not so, lad,' Cathba continued; 'for the men of Erin and Alba shall hear that name and the mouths of the men of Erin and Alba shall be full of that name!' 'It pleaseth me so, whatever the name that is given me,' quoth the little lad. Hence the famous name that stuck to him, namely Cuchulain, after he had killed the hound that was Culann's the Smith's.

"'A little lad did that deed,' added Cormac Conlongas son of Conchobar, 'when he had completed six years after his birth, when he slew the watch-dog that hosts nor companies dared not approach in the same cantred. No need would there be of wonder or of surprise if he should come to the edge of the marches, if he should cut off the four-pronged fork, if he should slay one man or two men or three men or four men, now when his seventeen years are completed on the Cattle-driving of Cualnge!'

"The little lad performed a third deed in the following year," said Fiachu son of Firaba. "What deed performed he?" asked Ailill.

"Cathba the druid was with his son, namely Conchobar son of Ness, imparting learning to his pupils in the north-east of Emain, and eight eager pupils in the class of druidic cunning were with him. That is the number that Cathba instructed. One of them questioned his teacher, what fortune and presage might there be for the day they were in, whether it was good or whether it was ill. Then spake Cathba: 'The little boy that takes arms this day shall be splendid and renowned for deeds of arms above the youths of Erin and the tales of his high deeds shall be told forever, but he shall be short-lived and fleeting.' Cuchulain overheard what he said, though far off at his play-feats south-west of Emain; and he threw away all his play-things and hastened to Conchobar's sleep-room to ask for arms. 'All good attend thee, O king of the Fenè!' cried the little lad. 'This greeting is the speech of one soliciting something of some one. What wouldst thou, lad?' said Conchobar. 'To take arms,' the lad made answer. 'Who hath advised thee, little boy?' asked Conchobar. 'Cathba the druid,' said the lad. 'He would not deceive thee, little boy,' said Conchobar. Conchobar gave him two spears and a sword and a shield. The little boy shook and brandished the arms in the middle of the house so that he made small pieces and fragments of them. Conchobar gave him other two spears and a shield and a sword. He shook and brandished, flourished and poised them, so that he shivered them into small pieces and fragments. There where were the fourteen suits of arms which Conchobar had in Emain, in reserve in case of breaking of weapons or for equipping the youths and the boys—to the end that whatever boy assumed arms, it might be Conchobar that gave him the equipment of battle, and the victory of cunning would be his thenceforward—even so, this little boy made splinters and fragments of them all.

"'Truly these arms here are not good, O Conchobar my master,' the stripling cried. 'Herefrom cometh not what is worthy of me.' Conchobar gave him his own

two spears and his shield and his sword. He shook and he brandished, he bent and he poised them so that tip touched butt, and he brake not the arms and they bore up against him, and he saluted the king whose arms they were. 'Truly, these arms are good,' said the little boy; 'they are suited to me. Hail to the king whose arms and equipment these are. Hail to the land whereout he is come!'

"Then Cathba the druid chanced to come into the tent, and what he said was, 'Hath he yonder taken arms?' Cathba asked. 'Aye, then, it must be,' Conchobar answered. 'Not by his mother's son would I wish them to be taken this day,' said Cathba. 'How so? Was it not thyself advised him?' Conchobar asked. 'Not I, in faith,' replied Cathba. 'What mean'st thou, bewitched elf-man?' cried Conchobar to Cuchulain. 'Is it a lie thou hast told us?' 'But be not wroth thereat, O my master Conchobar,' said the little boy. 'No lie have I told; for yet is it he that advised me, when he taught his other pupils this morning. For his pupil asked him what luck might lie in the day, and he said: The youth that took arms on this day would be illustrious and famous, that his name would be over the men of Erin for ever, and that no evil result would be on him thereafter, except that he would be fleeting and short-lived. To the south of Emain I heard him, and then I came to thee.' 'That I avow to be true,' spake Cathba. 'Good indeed is the day, glorious and renowned shalt thou be, the one that taketh arms, yet passing and short-lived!' 'Noble the gift!' cried Cuchulain. 'Little it recks me, though I should be but one day and one night in the world, if only the fame of me and of my deeds live after me!'

"Another day one of them asked of the druids for what that day would be propitious. 'The one that mounts a chariot to-day,' Cathba answered, 'his name will be renowned over Erin for ever.' Now Cuchulain heard that. He went to Conchobar and said to him, 'O Conchobar my master, give me a chariot!' He gave him a chariot. 'Come, lad, mount the chariot, for this is the next thing for thee.'

"He mounted the chariot. He put his hands between the two poles of the chariot, and the first chariot he mounted withal he shook and tossed about him till he reduced it to splinters and fragments. He mounted the second chariot, so that he made small pieces and fragments of it in like manner. Further he made pieces of the third chariot. There where were the seventeen

Figure 14 *Celtic chariot.*

chariots which Conchobar kept for the boy-troop and youths in Emain, the lad made small pieces and fragments of them and they did not withstand him. 'These chariots here are not good, O my master Conchobar,' said the little boy; 'my merit cometh not from them.' 'Where is Ibar son of Riangabair?' asked Conchobar. 'Here, in sooth, am I,' Ibar answered. 'Take with thee mine own two steeds for him yonder, and yoke my chariot.' Thereupon the charioteer took the horses and yoked the chariot. Then the little boy mounted the chariot and Conchobar's charioteer with him. He shook the chariot about him, and it withstood him, and he broke it not. 'Truly this chariot is good,' cried the lad, 'and this chariot is suited to me.' The charioteer turned the chariot under him. 'Prithee, little boy,' said Ibar, 'come out of the chariot now and let the horses out on their pasture.' 'It is yet too soon, O Ibar,' the lad answered. 'The horses are fair. I, too, am fair, their little lad. Only let us go on a circuit of Emain to-day and thou shalt have a reward therefor, to-day being my first day of taking arms, to the end that it be a victory of cunning for me.'

"Thrice they made the circuit of Emain. 'Leave the horses now to their grazing, O little boy,' said Ibar. 'It is yet too soon, O Ibar,' the little lad answered; 'let us keep on, that the boys may give me a blessing to-day the first day of my taking arms.' They kept their course to the place where the boys were. 'Is it arms he yonder has taken?' each one asked. 'Of a truth, are they.' 'May it be for victory, for first wounding and triumph. But we deem it too soon for thee to take arms, because thou departest from us at the game-feats.' 'By no means will I leave ye, but for luck I took arms this day.' 'Now, little boy, leave the horses to their grazing,' said Ibar. 'It is still too soon for that, O Ibar,' the lad answered. 'Ply the goad on the horses,' said he. 'What way, then?' the charioteer asked. 'As far as the road shall lead,' answered Cuchulain. 'And this great road winding by us, what way leads it?' the lad asked. 'What is that to thee?' Ibar answered. 'But thou art a pleasant wight, I trow, little lad,' quoth Ibar. 'I wish, fellow, to inquire about the high-road of the province, what stretch it goes?' 'To Áth na Foraire ["the Ford of Watching"] in Sliab Fuait it goes,' Ibar answered. 'Wherefore is it called "the Ford of Watching," knowest thou?' 'Yea, I know it well,' Ibar made answer. 'A stout warrior of Ulster is on watch and on guard there every day, so that there come no strange youths into Ulster to challenge them to battle, and he is a champion to give battle in behalf of the whole province. Likewise if men of song leave the Ulstermen and the province in dudgeon, he is there to soothe them by proffering treasures and valuables, and so to save the honour of the province. Again, if men of song enter the land, he is the man that is their surety that they win the favour of Conchobar, so that songs and lays made for him will be the first to be sung after their arrival in Emain.' 'Knowest thou who is at the ford to-day?' 'Yea, I know,' Ibar answered; 'Conall Cernach ["the Triumphant"], the heroic, warlike son of Amargin, royal champion of Erin,' Ibar answered. 'Thither guide us, fellow, that so we reach the ford.'

"Onwards they drove into sight of the ford where was Conall. Now it fell to Conall Cernach to guard the province that day. For each champion of Ulster spent his day on Sliab Fuait to protect him that came with a lay or to fight with a warrior, so that some one would be there to meet him, in order that none might come to Emain unperceived. 'Are those arms he yonder has taken?' asked Conall. 'Of a truth, are they,' Ibar made answer. 'May it be for victory and for triumph and first wounding,' said Conall; 'but we think it too soon for thee to take arms, because thou art not yet capable of deeds. Were it surety he needed, he that should come hither,' he continued, 'so wouldst thou furnish a perfect warrant amongst the Ulstermen, and the nobles of the province would rise up to support thee in the contest.' 'What dost thou here, O Conall my master?' asked the lad. 'Watch and ward of the province, lad, I keep here,' Conall made answer. 'Do thou go home now, O master Conall,' said the lad, 'and leave me the watch and guard of the province to keep here.' 'Say not so, little son,' replied Conall; ''twould be enough, were it to protect one that came with a song; were it to fight with a man, however, that is still too soon for thee; thou art not yet able to cope with a goodly warrior.' 'Then, will I keep on to the south,' said the little boy, 'to Fertas ["the Bank"] of Loch Echtrann for a while; champions are wont to take stand there; perchance I may redden my hands on friend or on foe this day.' 'I will go, little boy,' said Conall, 'to save thee, that thou go not alone into peril on the border.' 'Not so,' said the lad. 'But I will go,' said Conall; 'for the men of Ulster will blame me for leaving thee to go alone on the border.'

"Conall's horses were caught for him and his chariot was yoked and he set out to protect the little boy. When Conall came up abreast of him, Cuchulain felt certain that, even though a chance came to him, Conall would not permit him to use it. He picked up a hand-stone from the ground which was the full of his grasp. He

hurled it from him from his sling the length of a stone-shot at the yoke of Conall's chariot, so that he broke the chariot-collar in two and thereby Conall fell to the ground, so that the nape of his neck went out from his shoulder. 'What have we here, boy?' asked Conall; 'why threwest thou the stone?' 'It is I threw it to see if my cast be straight, or how I cast at all, or if I have the stuff of a warrior in me.' 'A bane on thy cast and a bane on thyself as well. E'en though thou leavest thy head this time with thine enemies, I will go no further to protect thee.' ''Twas what I craved of thee,' answered he; 'for it is geis amongst you men of Ulster to proceed, after a mishap has befallen your chariots. Go back to Emain, O Conall, and leave me here to keep watch.' 'That pleaseth me well,' replied Conall. Conall turned back northwards again to the Ford of Watching. Thereafter Conall Cernach went not past that place.

"As for the little boy, he fared southwards to Fertas Locha Echtrann. He remained there till the end of the day and they found no one there before them. 'If we dared tell thee, little boy,' spoke Ibar, 'it were time for us to return to Emain now; for dealing and carving and dispensing of food is long since begun in Emain, and there is a place assigned for thee there. Every day it is appointed thee to sit between Conchobar's feet, while for me there is naught but to tarry among the hostlers and tumblers of Conchobar's household. For that reason, methinks it is time to have a scramble among them.' 'Fetch then the horses for us.' The charioteer fetched the horses and the lad mounted the chariot. 'But, O Ibar, what hill is that there now, the hill to the north?' the lad asked. 'Now, that is Sliab Moduirn,' Ibar answered. 'Let us go and get there,' said Cuchulain. Then they go on till they reach it. When they reached the mountain, Cuchulain asked, 'And what is that white cairn yonder on the height of the mountain?' 'And that is Finncharn ["the White Cairn"] of Sliab Moduirn,' Ibar answered. 'But yonder cairn is beautiful,' exclaimed the lad. 'It surely is beautiful,' Ibar answered. 'Lead on, fellow, till we reach yonder cairn.' 'Well, but thou art both a pleasant and tedious inquisitor, I see,' exclaimed Ibar; 'but this is my first journey and my first time with thee. It shall be my last time till the very day of doom, if once I get back to Emain.'

"Howbeit they went to the top of the hill. 'It is pleasant here, O Ibar,' the little boy exclaimed. 'Point out to me Ulster on every side, for I am no wise acquainted with the land of my master Conchobar.'

The horseman pointed him out Ulster all around him. He pointed him out the hills and the fields and the mounts of the province on every side. He pointed him out the plains and the dûns and the strongholds of the province. ''Tis a goodly sight, O Ibar,' exclaimed the little lad. 'What is that indented, angular, bordered and glenny plain to the south of us?' 'Mag Breg,' replied Ibar. 'Tell thou to me the buildings and forts of that plain.' The gilla taught him the name of every chief dûn between Temair and Cenannas, Temair and Taltiu, Cletech and Cnogba and Brug ["the Fort"] of Mac ind Oc. He pointed out to him then the dûn of the three sons of Necht Scenè ["the Fierce"]: Foill and Fandall and Tuachall, their names; Fer Ulli son of Lugaid was their father, and Necht from the mouth of the Scenè was their mother. Now the Ulstermen had slain their father; it was for that reason they were at war with Ulster. 'But are those not Necht's sons, that boast that not more of the Ulstermen are alive than have fallen at their hands?' 'The same, in sooth,' answered the gilla. 'On with us to the dûn of the macNechta,' cried the little boy. 'Alas, in truth, that thou sayest so,' quoth Ibar; ''tis a peril for us.' 'Truly, not to avoid it do we go,' answered Cuchulain. 'We know it is an act of great folly for us to say so, but whoever may go,' said Ibar, 'it will not be myself.' 'Living or dead, go there thou shalt,' the little boy cried. ''Tis alive I shall go to the south,' answered Ibar, 'and dead I shall be left at the dûn, I know, even at the dûn of the macNechta.'

"They push on to the dûn and they unharness their horses in the place where the bog and the river meet south of the dûn of the macNechta. And the little boy sprang out of the chariot onto the green. Thus was the green of the dûn, with a pillar-stone upon it and an iron band around that, and a band for prowess it was, and there was a writing in ogam at its joint, and this is the writing it bore: 'Whoever should come to the green, if he be a champion, it is geis for him to depart from the green without giving challenge to single combat.' The lad deciphered the writing and put his two arms around the pillar-stone. Just as the pillar-stone was with its ring, he flung it with a cast of his hand into the moat, so that a wave passed over it. 'Methinks,' spake Ibar, 'it is no better now than to be where it was. And we know thou shalt now get on this green the thing thou desirest, even the token of death, yea, of doom and destruction!' For it was the violation of a geis of the sons of Necht Scenè to do that thing. 'Good, O Ibar, spread the chariot-coverings and its skins for me that I may snatch a little sleep.' 'Woe is me, that thou sayest so,' answered the gilla; 'for a foeman's land is this and not a green for diversion.' And Cuchulain said to the gilla, 'Do not awaken me for a few but awaken me for many.' The gilla arranged the chariot-coverings and its skins under Cuchulain, and the lad fell asleep on the green.

"Then came one of the macNechta on to the fair-green, to wit, Foill son of Necht. Then was the charioteer sore afraid, for he durst not waken him, for Cuchulain had told him at first not to waken him for a few. 'Unyoke not the horses, gilla,' cried Foill. 'I am not fain to, at all,' answered Ibar; 'the reins and the lines are still in my hand.' 'Whose horses are those, then?' Foill asked. 'Two of Conchobar's horses,' answered the gilla; 'the two of the dappled heads.' 'That is the knowledge I have of them. And what hath brought these steeds here to the borders?' 'A tender youth that has assumed arms amongst us to-day for luck and good omen,' the horseboy answered, 'is come to the edges of the marshes to display his comeliness.' 'May it not be for victory nor for triumph, his first-taking of arms,' exclaimed Foill. 'Let him not stop in our land and let the horses not graze here any longer. If I knew he was fit for deeds, it is dead he should go back northwards to Emain and not alive!' 'In good sooth, he is not fit for deeds,' Ibar answered; 'it is by no means right to say it of him; it is the seventh year since he was taken from the crib. Think not to earn enmity,' Ibar said further to the warrior; 'and moreover the child sleepeth.'

"The little lad raised his face from the ground and drew his hand over his face, and he became as one crimson wheelball from his crown to the ground. 'Not a child am I, at all, but it is to seek battle with a man that this child here is come. Aye, but I am fit for deeds!' the lad cried. 'That pleaseth me well,' said the champion; 'but more like than what thou sayest, meseemeth, thou art not fit for deeds.' 'Thou wilt know that better if we go to the ford. But, go fetch thy weapons, for I see it is in the guise of a churl thou art come, and I slay nor charioteers nor grooms nor folk without arms.' The man went apace after his arms. 'Now thou shouldst have a care for us against yonder man that comes to meet thee, little lad,' said Ibar. 'And why so?' asked the lad. 'Foill son of Necht is the man thou seest. Neither points nor edges of weapons can harm him.' 'Not before me shouldst thou say that, O Ibar,' quoth the lad. 'I will put my hand to the lath-trick for him, namely, to the apple of twice-melted iron, and it will light upon the disc of his shield and on the flat of his forehead, and it will carry away the size of an apple of his brain out through the back of his head, so that it will make a sieve-hole outside of his head, till the light of the sky will be visible through his head.'

"Foill son of Necht came forth. Cuchulain took the lath-trick in hand for him and threw it from him the length of his cast, so that it lighted on the flat of his shield and on the front of his forehead and carried away the bulk of an apple of his brain out through the back of his head, so that it made a sieve-hole thereof outside of his head, till the light of the sky might be seen through his head. He went to him then and struck off the head from the trunk. Thereafter he bore away his spoils and his head with him.

"Then came the second son out on the green, his name Tuachall ["the Cunning"] son of Necht. 'Aha, I see thou wouldst boast of this deed,' quoth Tuachall. 'In the first place I deem it no cause to boast for slaying one champion,' said Cuchulain; 'thou shalt not boast of it this time, for thou shalt fall by my hand.' 'Off with thee for thine arms, then, for 'tis not as a warrior thou art come.' The man rushed after his arms. 'Thou shouldst have a care for us against yon man, lad,' said Ibar. 'How so?' the lad asked. 'Tuachall son of Necht is the man thou beholdest. And he is nowise mis-named, for he falls not by arms at all. Unless thou worstest him with the first blow or with the first shot or with the first touch, thou wilt not worst him ever, because of his craftiness and the skill wherewith he plays round the points of the weapons.' 'That should not be said before me, O Ibar,' cried the lad. 'I swear by the god by whom my people swear, he shall never again ply his skill on the men of Ulster. I will put my hand on Conchobar's well-tempered lance, on the Craisech Nemè ["the Venomous Lance"]. It will be an outlaw's hand to him. It will light on the shield over his belly, and it will crush through his ribs on the farther side after piercing his heart in his breast. That would be the smiting cast of an enemy and not the friendliness of a fellow countryman! From me he shall not get sick-nursing or care till the brink of doom.'

"Tuachall son of Necht came forth on the green, and the lad laid his hand on Conchobar's lance against him, and it struck the shield above his belly and broke through the ribs on the farther side after piercing his

heart within his breast. He struck off his head or ever it reached the ground. Thereafter Cuchulain carried off his head and his spoils with him to his own charioteer.

"Then came the youngest of the sons forth on the green, namely, Fandall son of Necht. 'Fools were the folk who fought with thee here,' cried Fandall. 'How, now!' cried the lad. 'Come down to the pool, where thy foot findeth not bottom.' Fandall rushed on to the pool. 'Thou shouldst be wary for us of him, little boy,' said Ibar. 'Why should I then?' asked the lad. 'Fandall son of Necht is the man whom thou seest. For this he bears the name Fandall ["the Swallow"]: like a swallow or weasel he courseth the sea; the swimmers of the world cannot reach him.' 'Thou shouldst not speak thus before me, O Ibar,' said the lad. 'I swear, never again will he ply that feat on the men of Ulster. Thou knowest the river that is in our land, in Emain, the Callann. When the boys frequent it with their games of sport and when the water is not beneath them, if the surface is not reached by them all, I do carry a boy over it on either of my palms and a boy on either of my shoulders, and I myself do not even wet my ankles under the weight of them.'

"They met upon the water and they engaged in wrestling upon it, and the little boy closed his arms over Fandall, so that the sea came up even with him, and he gave him a deft blow with Conchobar's sword and chopped off his head from the trunk, and left the body to go down with the stream, and he carried off the head and the spoils with him.

"Thereupon Cuchulain went into the dûn and pillaged the place and burned it so that its buildings were no higher than its walls. And they turned on their way to Sliab Fuait and carried the three heads of Necht's sons with them. Soon Cuchulain heard the cry of their mother after them, of Necht Scenè, namely. 'Now I will not give over my spoils,' cried Cuchulain, 'till I reach Emain Macha.' Thereupon Cuchulain and Ibar set out for Emain Macha with their spoils. It was then Cuchulain spoke to his charioteer: 'Thou didst promise us a good run,' said Cuchulain, 'and we need it now because of the storm and pursuit that is after us.' Forthwith they hasten to Sliab Fuait. Such was the speed of the course they held over Breg, after the urging of the charioteer, that the horses of the chariot overtook the wind and the birds in their flight and Cuchulain caught the throw he had cast from his sling or ever it reached the ground.

"When they came to Sliab Fuait they espied a herd of wild deer before them. 'What are those many cattle, O Ibar, those nimble ones yonder?' asked the lad; 'are they tame or are they other deer?' 'They are real wild deer, indeed,' Ibar answered; 'herds of wild deer that haunt the wastes of Sliab Fuait.' 'Which,' asked Cuchulain, 'would the men of Ulster deem best, to bring them dead or alive?' 'More wonderful, alive,' answered the charioteer; 'not every one can do it so; but dead, there is none of them cannot do it. Thou canst not do this, carry off any of them alive.' 'Truly I can,' said Cuchulain. 'Ply the goad for us on the horses into the bog, to see can we take some of them.' The charioteer drove a goad into the horses. It was beyond the power of the king's overfat steeds to keep up with the deer. Soon the horses stuck in the marsh. The lad got down from the chariot and as the fruit of his run and his race, in the morass which was around him, he caught two of the swift, stout deer. He fastened them to the back poles and the bows and the thongs of the chariot.

"They continued their way to the mound-seat of Emain, where they saw flocks of white swans flying by them. 'What are those birds there, O Ibar?' the lad asked; 'are yonder birds tame or are they other birds?' 'Indeed, they are real wild birds,' Ibar answered; 'flocks of swans are they that come from the rocks and crags and islands of the great sea without, to feed on the plains and smooth spots of Erin.' 'Which would be stranger to the Ulstermen, O Ibar, for them to be fetched alive to Emain or dead?' asked the lad. 'Stranger far, alive,' Ibar answered, 'for not every one succeeds in taking the birds alive, while they are many that take them dead.' Then did the lad perform one of his lesser feats upon them: he put a small stone in his sling, so that he brought down eight of the birds; and then he performed a greater feat: he threw a large stone at them and he brought down sixteen of their number. With his return stroke all that was done. He fastened them to the hind poles and the bows and the thongs and the ropes and the traces of the chariot.

" 'Take the birds along with thee, O Ibar,' cried the lad to his charioteer. 'If I myself go to take them,' he added, 'the wild deer will spring upon thee.' 'I am in sore straits,' answered Ibar; 'I find it not easy to go.' 'What may it be?' asked the lad. 'Great cause have I. The horses have become wild, so that I cannot go by them. If I stir at all from where I am, the chariot's iron wheels will cut me down because of their sharpness and because of the strength and the power and the might of the career of the horses. If I make any move, the horns of the deer will pierce and gore me, for the horns of the stag have filled the whole space between the two shafts of the chariot.' 'Ah, no true champion art thou any longer, O Ibar,' said the lad; 'step thus from his horn. I swear by the god by whom the Ulstermen swear, because of the look I shall give at the horses they will not depart from the straight way; at the look I shall give at the deer they will bend their heads in fear and awe of me; they will not dare move, and it will be safe for thee e'en though thou goest in front of their horns.' And so it was done. Cuchulain fastened the reins. Then the charioteer went and collected the birds, and he bound them to the hind poles and to the thongs and the traces of the chariot. Thus it was that he proceeded to Emain Macha: the wild deer behind his chariot, and the flock of swans flying over the same, and the three heads of the sons of Necht Scenè and the jewels, treasures and wealth of their enemies arranged in his chariot.

"Thereupon they went on till bravely, boldly, battle-victoriously, boastingly, blade-redded, they reached the fair plain of Emain. It was then Lebarcham, the watch in Emain Macha, came forth and discerned them, she, the daughter of Aue ["Ear"] and of Adarc ["Horn"] and she hastened to Conchobar's house, her eye restless in her head and her tongue faltering in her jaw. 'A single chariot-fighter is here, coming towards Emain Macha,' cried Lebarcham, 'and his coming is fearful. The heads of his foes all red in his chariot with him. Beautiful, all-white birds he has hovering around in the chariot. With him are wild, untamed deer, bound and fettered, shackled and pinioned. And I give my word, if he be not attended to this night, blood will flow over Conchobar's province by him and the youths of Ulster will fall by his hand.' 'We know him, that chariot-fighter,' spake Conchobar; 'belike it is the little gilla, my sister's son, who went to the edge of the marches at the beginning of the day, who has reddened his hands and is still unsated of combat, and unless he be attended to, all the youths of Emain will fall by his hand.' Soon he turned the left side of his chariot towards Emain, and this was geis for Emain. And Cuchulain cried, 'I swear by the god by whom the Ulstermen swear, if a man be not found to engage with me, I will spill the blood of every one in the dûn!'

"And this was the counsel they agreed to follow: to let out the womenfolk to meet the youth, namely, thrice fifty women, even ten and seven-score bold, stark-naked women, at one and the same time, and their chieftainess, Scannlach ["the Wanton"] before them, to discover their persons and their shame to him. 'Let the young women go,' said Conchobar, 'and bare their paps and their breasts and their swelling bosoms, and if he be a true warrior he will not withstand being bound, and he shall be placed in a vat of cold water until his anger go from him.' Thereupon the young women all arose and marched out, and these are the names of those queens: Sgamalus and Sgannlach and Sgiathan, Feidlim and Deigtini Finnchas, and Finngheal and Fidniam and Niam, daughter of Celtchar son of Uthechar; and they discovered their nakedness and all their shame to him. 'These are the warriors that will meet thee to-day,' quoth Mugain, wife of Conchobar son of Ness. The lad hid his face from them and turned his gaze on the chariot, that he might not see the nakedness or the shame of the women. Then the lad was lifted out of the chariot. He was placed in three vats of cold water to extinguish his wrath; and the first vat into which he was put burst its staves and its hoops like the cracking of nuts around him. The next vat into which he went boiled with bubbles as big as fists therefrom. The third vat into which he went, some men might endure it and others might not. Then the boy's wrath went down.

"Thereupon he came out, and his festive garments were put on him by Mugain the queen. His comeliness appeared on him and he made a crimson wheel-ball of himself from his crown to the ground. A shout was raised at the bluish purple about him. Beautiful then was the lad that was raised up in view. Seven toes he had to each of his two feet, and seven fingers to each of his two hands, and seven pupils to each of his two kingly eyes, and seven gems of the brilliance of the eye was each separate pupil. Four spots of down on either of his two cheeks: a blue spot, a purple spot, a green spot, a yellow spot. Fifty strands of bright-yellow hair from one ear to the other, like to a comb of birch twigs or like to a brooch of pale gold in the face of the sun. A clear, white, shorn spot was upon him, as if a cow had licked it. A fair, laced green mantle about him; a silver pin therein over his white breast, so that the eyes of men could not look at it for its gleam and its brightness. A hooded tunic of thread of gold about him. A magnificent, fair-coloured, dark purple shield he bore. Two hard, five-pointed spears in his hand. A diadem of gold

round his head. And the lad was seated between the two feet of Conchobar, and that was his couch ever after, and the king began to stroke his close-shorn hair.

"A mere lad accomplished these deeds at the end of seven years after his birth," continued Fiachu son of Fiarba; "for he overcame heroes and battle-champions at whose hands two-thirds of the men of Ulster had fallen, and these had not got their revenge on them until that scion rose up for them. No need then is there of wonder or of surprise, though he came to the border, though he slew one man or two men or three men or four men, though he cut off the four-headed pole with one cut and one blow of his shining sword when now are fulfilled his seventeen years at the time of the Táin Bó Cúalnge."

Albeit gladness, joy and happiness was the part of the men of Ulster for that sorrow, grief and unhappiness was the part of the men of Erin, for they knew that the little lad that had done those deeds in the time of his boyhood, it would be no wonder if he should do great deeds of valour in the time of his manhood.

From
THE FEAST OF BRICRIU[4]

[*Bricriu "of the poisonous tongue" made a great feast for Conchobar and the Ulstermen where he deviously managed to create an enormous dissension among the warriors and among their wives as to which warrior deserved the hero's portion. After a number of tests, Cuchulain finally proved his superiority in the manner following.*]

Once upon a time as the Ultonians were in Emain, fatigued after the gathering and the games, Conchobar and Fergus mac Rōig, with Ultonia's nobles as well, proceeded from the sporting field outside and gat seated in the Royal Court [*lit.* Red Branch] of Conchobar. Neither Cuchulainn nor Conall the Victorious nor Logaire the Triumphant were there that night. But the hosts of Ultonia's valiant heroes were there. As they were seated, it being eventide, and the day drawing towards the close, they saw a big uncouth fellow of exceeding ugliness drawing nigh them into the hall. To them it seemed as if none of the Ultonians would reach half his height. Horrible and ugly was the carle's guise. Next his skin he wore an old hide with a dark dun mantle around him, and over him a great spreading club-tree [branch] the size of a winter-shed, under which thirty bullocks could find shelter. Ravenous yellow eyes he had, protruding from his head, each of the twain the size of an ox-vat. Each finger as thick as another person's wrist. In his left hand a stock, a burden for twenty yoke of oxen. In his right hand an axe weighing thrice fifty glowing molten masses [of metal]. Its handle would require a plough-team [a yoke of six] to move it. Its sharpness such that it would lop off hairs, the wind blowing them against its edge.

In that guise he went and stood by the fork-beam beside the fire. "Is the hall lacking in room for you," quoth Duach of the Chafer Tongue to the uncouth clodhopper, "that ye find no other place than by the fork-beam, unless ye wish to be domestic luminary?— only sooner will a blaze be to the house than brightness to the household." "What property soever may be mine, sooth ye will agree, no matter how big I am, that the household as a whole will be enlightened, while the hall will not be burnt.

"That, however, is not my sole function; I have others as well. But neither in Erin nor in Alba nor in Europe nor in Africa nor in Asia, including Greece, Scythia, the Isles of Gades, the Pillars of Hercules, and Bregon's Tower (Brigantium), have I found the quest on which I have come, nor a man to do me fairplay regarding it. Since ye Ultonians have excelled all the folks of those lands in strength, prowess, valor; in rank, magnanimity, dignity; in truth, generosity and worth, get ye one among you to give me the boon I crave."

"In sooth it is not just that the honour of a province be carried off," quoth Fergus mac Rōich, "because of one man who fails in keeping his word of honour. Death, certainly, is not a whit nearer to him than to you." "Not that I shun it," quoth he. "Make thy quest known to us then," quoth Fergus mac Rōich. "If but fairplay be vouchsafed me, I will tell it." "It is right also to give fairplay," quoth Sencha, son of Ailill, "for it beseemeth not a great clannish folk to break a mutual covenant over any unknown individual. To us too it seemeth likely, if at long last you find such a person, you will find here one worthy of you." "Conchobar I put aside," he quoth, "for sake of his sovranty, and Fergus mac Rōich also on account of his like privilege. These two excepted, come whosoever of you that may venture, that I may cut off his head to-night, he mine to-morrow night."

"Sure then there is no warrior here," quoth Duach,

Figure 15 Très riches heures de Jean de France. *The sun in the Ram in March.*

"after these two." "By my troth there will be this moment," quoth Fat-Neck, son of Short Head, as he sprang on to the floor of the hall. The strength then of yon Fat-Neck was as the strength of a hundred warriors, each arm having the might of a hundred "centaurs." "Bend down, bachlach," quoth Fat-Neck, "that I may cut your head off to-night, you to cut off mine to-morrow night." "Were that my quest, I could have got it anywhere," quoth the bachlach. "Let us act according to our covenant," he quoth, "I to cut off your head to-night, you to avenge it to-morrow night." "By my people's god," quoth Duach of the Chafer Tongue, "death is thus for thee no pleasant prospect should the man killed to-night attack thee on the morrow. It is given to you alone if you have the power, being killed night after night [*lit.* to be killed every night], to avenge it next day." "Truly I will carry out what you all as a body agree upon by way of counsel, strange as it may seem to you," quoth the bachlach. He then pledged the other to keep his troth in this contention as to fulfilling his tryst on the morrow.

With that Fat-Neck took the axe from out of the bachlach's hand. Seven feet apart were its two angles. Then did the bachlach put his neck across the block. Fat-Neck dealt a blow across it with the axe till it stuck in the block underneath, cutting off the head till it lay by the base of the fork-beam, the house being filled with the blood. Straightway the bachlach rose, recovered himself, clasped his head, block and axe to his breast, thus made his exit from the hall with blood streaming from his neck. It filled the Red Branch on every side. Great was the folk's horror, wondering at the marvel that had appeared to them. "By my people's god," quoth Duach of the Chafer Tongue, "if the bachlach, having been killed to-night, come back to-morrow, he will not leave a man alive in Ultonia." The following night, however, he returned, and Fat-Neck shirked him. Then began the bachlach to urge his pact with Fat-Neck. "Sooth it is not right for Fat-Neck not to fulfil his covenant with me."

That night, however, Loigaire the Triumphant was present. "Who of the warriors that contest Ultonia's Champion's Portion will carry out a covenant to-night with me? Where is Loigaire the Triumphant?" quoth he. "Here," said Loigaire. He pledged him too, yet Loigaire kept not his tryst. The bachlach returned on the morrow and similarly pledged Conall Cernach, who came not as he had sworn.

The fourth night the bachlach returned, and fierce and furious was he. All the ladies of Ultonia came that night to see the strange marvel that had come into the Red Branch. That night Cuchulainn was there also. Then the fellow began to upbraid them. "Ye men of Ultonia, your valor and your prowess are gone. Your warriors greatly covet the Champion's Portion, yet are unable to contest it. Where is yon poor mad wight that is hight Cuchulainn? Fain would I know if *his* word be

better than the others'." "No covenant do I desire with you," quoth Cuchulainn. "Likely is that, you wretched fly[5]; greatly thou dost fear to die." Whereupon Cuchulainn sprang towards him and dealt him a blow with the axe, hurling his head to the top rafter of the Red Branch till the whole hall shook. Cuchulainn again caught up the head and gave it a blow with the axe and smashed it. Thereafter the bachlach rose up.

On the morrow the Ultonians were watching Cuchulainn to see whether he would shirk the bachlach as the other heroes had done. As Cuchulainn was awaiting the bachlach, they saw that great dejection seized him. It had been fitting had they sung his dirge. They felt sure his life would last only till the bachlach came. Then quoth Cuchulainn with shame to Conchobar: "Thou shall not go until my pledge to the bachlach is fulfilled; for death awaits me, and I would rather have death with honor."

They were there as the day was closing when they saw the bachlach approaching. "Where is Cuchulainn?" he quoth. "Here am I," he answered. "You're dull of speech to-night, unhappy one; greatly you fear to die. Yet, though great your fear, death you have not shirked." Thereafter Cuchulainn went up to him and stretched his neck across the block, which was of such size that his neck reached but half-way. "Stretch out your neck, you wretch," the bachlach quoth. "You keep me in torment," quoth Cuchulainn. "Despatch me quickly; last night, by my troth, I tormented you not. Verily I swear if you torment me, I shall make myself as long as a crane above you." "I cannot slay you," quoth the bachlach, "what with the size of the block and the shortness of your neck and of your side" [*sic!*].

Then Cuchulainn stretched out his neck so that a warrior's full-grown foot would have fitted between any two of his ribs; his neck he distended till it reached the other side of the block. The bachlach raised his axe till it reached the roof-tree of the hall. The creaking of the old hide that was about the fellow and the crashing of the axe—both his arms being raised aloft with all his might—were as the loud noise of a wood tempest-tossed in a night of storm. Down it came then . . . on his neck, its blunt side below—all the nobles of Ultonia gazing upon them.

"O Cuchulainn, arise! . . . Of the warriors of Ultonia and Erin, no matter their mettle, none is found to be compared with thee in valour, bravery and truthfulness. The sovranty of the heroes of Erin to thee from this hour forth and the Champion's Portion undisputed, and to thy lady the precedence alway of the ladies of Ultonia in the Mead Hall. And whosoever shall lay wager against thee from now, as my folks swear I swear, while on life he will be in [sore scathe]." Then the bachlach vanished. It was Curoi mac Dairi who in that guise had come to fulfill the promise he had given to Cuchulainn.

Notes

1 From A. H. Leahy, *Heroic Romances of Ireland*, David Nutt, London, 1905, vol. I, pp. 91–102.

2 Usually translated "white bronze." Cf. the "bridle of findrinny" in Yeats, "The Wanderings of Oisin."

3 From Joseph Dunn, *The Ancient Irish Epic Tale Táin Bó Cúalnge*, David Nutt, London, 1914, pp. 41–79.

4 Translated by George Henderson, David Nutt, Early Irish Texts Society, London, 1899, pp. 117–129.

5 The word for *fly* in the original is *cuil*, which forms a pun on Cuchulain's name.

II

EARLY ANGLO-LATIN LITERATURE

The very extensive and varied Latin literature produced in Britain before the Norman Conquest has not received the attention it deserves, both for its own sake and for the light it sheds on the vernacular literature of the period. The authors include one of the world's great historians, Bede; a famous and important scholar, Alcuin; and one of the most influential theologians of the early Middle Ages, John the Scot.

For the period down to A.D. 740 the first volume of W. F. Bolton, *A History of Anglo-Latin Literature*, Princeton University Press, Princeton, N.J., 1967, is now available. Much valuable material may be found in Eleanor S. Duckett, *Anglo-Saxon Saints and Scholars*, The Macmillan Company, New York, 1947, and in M. L. W. Laistner, *Thought and Letters in Western Europe*,

Facing page: Roman Bacchic plate found in Britain.

61

second edition, Methuen and Co., Ltd., London, 1957. There is a chapter on Latin Literature in George K.

Anderson, *The Literature of the Anglo-Saxons*, Princeton University Press, Princeton, N.J., 1949.

A. Gildas

Gildas composed a history, On the Destruction and Conquest of Britain, *perhaps shortly before* A.D. *548. He was himself a Briton who deeply resented the conduct of his countrymen; most of his book is, in fact, a diatribe against their iniquity couched in scriptural terms. The historical part of his treatise, printed below, contains interesting information in spite of some inaccuracies. Among other things, he tells us about a battle at* Mons Badonicus *after which there was an extended period of peace. This battle is also mentioned by Nennius, who says it took place at* Mons Badonis. *We do not know where "Mons Badonicus" or "Mons Badonis" is, but it is interesting that Nennius thought of it as the site of Arthur's final victory. The fact that Gildas does not mention Arthur has caused many scholars to think that he never existed.*

For some account of Gildas and for modern accounts of the events he describes, see R. G. Collingwood and J. N. L. Myres, Roman Britain and the English Settlements, *second edition, Clarendon Press, Oxford, 1937. A good, brief discussion will also be found in Peter Hunter Blair,* An Introduction to Anglo-Saxon England, *Cambridge University Press, London, 1956. For the Arthurian problem especially, see Kenneth H. Jackson, "The Arthur of History," in R. S. Loomis,* Arthurian Literature in the Middle Ages, *Clarendon Press, Oxford, 1959, pages 1–11.*

From
ON THE DESTRUCTION AND CONQUEST OF BRITAIN[1]

The island of Britain, situated on almost the utmost border of the earth, towards the south and west, and poised in the divine balance, as it is said, which supports the whole world, stretches out from the south-west towards the north pole, and is eight hundred miles long and two hundred broad, except where the headlands of sundry promontories stretch farther into the sea. It is surrounded by the ocean, which forms winding bays, and is strongly defended by this ample, and, if I may so call it, impassable barrier, save on the south side, where the narrow sea affords a passage to Belgic Gaul. It is enriched by the mouths of two noble rivers, the Thames and the Severn, as it were two arms, by which foreign luxuries were of old imported, and by other streams of less importance. It is famous for eight and twenty cities, and is embellished by certain castles, with walls, towers, well barred gates, and houses with threatening battlements built on high, and provided with all requisite instruments of defence. Its plains are spacious, its hills are pleasantly situated, adapted for superior tillage, and its mountains are admirably calculated for the alternate pasturage of cattle, where flowers of various colors, trodden by the feet of man, give it the appearance of a lovely picture. It is decked, like a man's chosen bride, with divers jewels, with lucid fountains and abundant brooks wandering over the snow white sands; with transparent rivers, flowing in gentle murmurs, and offering a sweet pledge of slumber to those who recline upon their banks, whilst it is irrigated by abundant lakes, which pour forth cool torrents of refreshing water.

This island, stiff-necked and stubborn-minded, from the time of its being first inhabited, ungratefully rebels, sometimes against God, sometimes against her own citizens, and frequently, also, against foreign kings and their subjects. For what can there either be, or be committed, more disgraceful or more unrighteous in human affairs, than to refuse to show fear to God or affection to one's own countrymen, and (without detriment to one's faith) to refuse due honor to those of higher

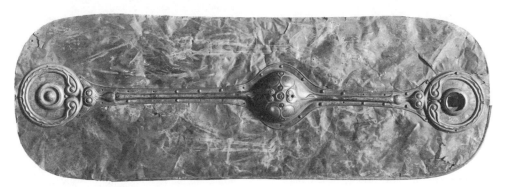

Figure 16 *British shield.*

dignity, to cast off all regard to reason, human and divine, and, in contempt of heaven and earth, to be guided by one's own sensual inventions? I shall, therefore, omit those ancient errors common to all the nations of the earth, in which, before Christ came in the flesh, all mankind were bound; nor shall I enumerate those diabolical idols of my country, which almost surpassed in number those of Egypt, and of which we still see some mouldering away within or without the deserted temples, with stiff and deformed features as was customary. Nor will I call out upon the mountains, fountains, or hills, or upon the rivers, which now are subservient to the use of men, but once were an abomination and destruction to them, and to which the blind people paid divine honor. I shall also pass over the bygone times of our cruel tyrants, whose notoriety was spread over to far distant countries; so that Porphyry, that dog who in the east was always so fierce against the church, in his mad and vain style added this also, that "Britain is a land fertile in tyrants." I will only endeavor to relate the evils which Britain suffered in the times of the Roman emperors, and also those which she caused to distant states; but so far as lies in my power, I shall not follow the writings and records of my own country, which (if there ever were any of them) have been consumed in the fires of the enemy, or have accompanied my exiled countrymen into distant lands, but guided by the relations of foreign writers, which, being broken and interrupted in many places, are therefore by no means clear.

For when the rulers of Rome had obtained the empire of the world, subdued all the neighboring nations and islands towards the east, and strengthened their renown by the first peace which they made with the Parthians, who border on India, there was a general cessation from war throughout the whole world; the fierce flame which they kindled could not be extinguished or checked by the Western Ocean, but passing beyond the sea, imposed submission upon our island without resistance, and entirely reduced to obedience its unwarlike but faithless people, not so much by fire and sword and warlike engines, like other nations, but threats alone, and menaces of judgments frowning on their countenance, whilst terror penetrated to their hearts.

When afterwards they returned to Rome, for want of pay, as is said, and had no suspicion of an approaching rebellion, that deceitful lioness (Boadicea)[2] put to death the rulers who had been left among them, to unfold more fully and to confirm the enterprises of the Romans. When the report of these things reached the senate, and they with a speedy army made haste to take vengeance on the crafty foxes as they called them, there was no bold navy on the sea to fight bravely for the country; by land there was no marshalled army, no right wing of battle, nor other preparation for resistance; but their backs were their shields against their vanquishers, and they presented their necks to their swords, whilst chill terror ran through every limb, and they stretched out their hands to be bound, like women; so that it has become a proverb far and wide, that the Britons are neither brave in war nor faithful in time of peace.

The Romans, therefore, having slain many of the rebels, and reserved others for slaves, that the land might not be entirely reduced to desolation, left the island, destitute as it was of wine and oil, and returned to Italy, leaving behind them taskmasters, to scourge the shoulders of the natives, to reduce their necks to the yoke, and their soil to the vassalage of a Roman province; to chastise the crafty race, not with warlike weapons, but with rods, and if necessary to gird upon their sides the naked sword, so that it was no longer thought to be Britain, but a Roman island; and all their money, whether of copper, gold, or silver, was stamped with Cæsar's image.

Meanwhile these islands, stiff with cold and frost, and in a distant region of the world, remote from the visible sun, received the beams of light, that is, the holy precepts of Christ, the true Sun, showing to the whole world his splendour, not only from the temporal firmament, but from the height of heaven, which surpasses every thing temporal, at the latter part, as we know, of the reign of Tiberius Cæsar, by whom his religion was propagated without impediment, and death threatened to those who interfered with its professors.

These rays of light were received with lukewarm minds by the inhabitants, but they nevertheless took root among some of them in a greater or less degree, until the nine years' persecution of the tyrant Diocletian, when the churches throughout the whole world were overthrown, all the copies of the Holy Scriptures which could be found burned in the streets, and the chosen pastors of God's flock butchered, together with their innocent sheep, in order that not a vestige, if possible, might remain in some provinces of Christ's religion. What disgraceful flights then took place—what slaughter and death inflicted by way of punishment in divers shapes—what dreadful apostacies from religion; and on the contrary, what glorious crowns of martyrdom then were won—what raving fury was displayed by the persecutors, and patience on the part of the suffering saints, ecclesiastical history informs us; for the whole church were crowding in a body, to leave behind them the dark things of this world, and to make the best of their way to the happy mansions of heaven, as if to their proper home.

God, therefore, who wishes all men to be saved, and who calls sinners no less than those who think themselves righteous, magnified his mercy towards us, and, as we know, during the above-named persecution, that Britain might not totally be enveloped in the dark shades of night, he, of his own free gift, kindled up among us bright luminaries of holy martyrs, whose places of burial and of martyrdom, had they not for our manifold crimes been interfered with and destroyed by the barbarians, would have still kindled in the minds of the beholders no small fire of divine charity. Such were St. Alban of Verulam, Aaron and Julius, citizens of Carlisle, and the rest, of both sexes, who in different places stood their ground in the Christian contest.

The first of these martyrs, St. Alban, for charity's sake saved another confessor who was pursued by his persecutors, and was on the point of being seized, by hiding him in his house, and then by changing clothes with him, imitating in this the example of Christ, who laid down his life for his sheep, and exposing himself in the other's clothes to be pursued in his stead. So pleasing to God was this conduct, that between his confession and martyrdom, he was honored with the performance of wonderful miracles in presence of the impious blasphemers who were carrying the Roman standards, and like the Israelites of old, who trod dry-foot an unfrequented path whilst the ark of the covenant stood some time on the sands in the midst of Jordan; so also the martyr, with a thousand others, opened a path across the noble river Thames, whose waters stood abrupt like precipices on either side; and seeing this, the first of his executors was stricken with awe, and from a wolf became a lamb; so that he thirsted for martyrdom, and boldly underwent that for which he thirsted. The other holy martyrs were tormented with divers sufferings, and their limbs were racked in such unheard of ways, that they, without delay, erected the trophies of their glorious martyrdom even in the gates of the city of Jerusalem. For those who survived hid themselves in woods and deserts, and secret caves, waiting until God, who is the righteous judge of all, should reward their persecutors with judgment, and themselves with protection of their lives.

In less than ten years, therefore, of the above-named persecution, and when these bloody decrees began to fail in consequence of the death of their authors, all Christ's young disciples, after so long and wintry a night, begin to behold the genial light of heaven. They rebuild the churches, which had been levelled to the ground; they found, erect, and finish churches to the holy martyrs, and everywhere show their ensigns as token of their victory; festivals are celebrated and sacraments received with clean hearts and lips, and all the church's sons rejoice as it were in the fostering bosom of a mother. For this holy union remained between Christ their head and the members of his church, until the Arian treason, fatal as a serpent, and vomiting its poison from beyond the sea, caused deadly dissension between brothers inhabiting the same house, and thus, as if a road were made across the sea, like wild beasts of all descriptions, and darting the poison of every heresy from their jaws, they inflicted dreadful wounds upon their country, which is ever desirous to hear something new, and remains constant long to nothing.

At length also, new races of tyrants sprang up, in terrific numbers, and the island, still bearing its Roman name, but casting off her institutes and laws, sent forth among the Gauls that bitter scion of her own planting Maximus, with a great number of followers, and the ensigns of royalty, which he bore without decency and without lawful right, but in a tyrannical manner, and amid the disturbances of the seditious soldiery. He, by cunning arts rather than by valour, attaching to his rule, by perjury and falsehood, all the neighboring towns and provinces, against the Roman state, extended one of his wings to Spain, the other to Italy, fixed the seat of his unholy government at Treves, and so furiously pushed his rebellion against his lawful emperors that he drove one of them out of Rome, and caused the other to terminate his most holy life. Trusting to these successful attempts, he not long after lost his accursed head before the walls of Aquileia, whereas he had before cut off the crowned heads of almost all the world.

After this, Britain is left deprived of all her soldiery and armed bands, of her cruel governors, and of the flower of her youth, who went with Maximus, but never again returned; and utterly ignorant as she was of the art of war, groaned in amazement for many years under the cruelty of two foreign nations—the Scots from the north-west, and the Picts from the north.

The Britons, impatient at the assaults of the Scots and Picts, their hostilities and dreadful oppressions, send ambassadors to Rome with letters, entreating in piteous terms the assistance of an armed band to protect them, and offering loyal and ready submission to the authority of Rome, if they only would expel their invading foes. A legion is immediately sent, forgetting their past rebellion, and provided sufficiently with arms. When they had crossed over the sea and landed, they came at once to close conflict with their cruel enemies, and slew great numbers of them. All of them were driven beyond the borders, and the humiliated natives rescued from the bloody slavery which awaited them. By the advice of their protectors, they now built a wall across the island from one sea to the other, which being manned with a proper force, might be a terror to the foes whom it was intended to repel, and a protection to their friends whom it covered. But this wall, being made of turf instead of stone, was of no use to that foolish people, who had no head to guide them.

The Roman legion had no sooner returned home in joy and triumph, than their former foes, like hungry and ravening wolves, rushing with greedy jaws upon the fold which is left without a shepherd, and wafted both by the strength of oarsmen and the blowing wind, break through the boundaries, and spread slaughter on every side, and like mowers cutting down the ripe corn, they cut up, tread under foot, and overrun the whole country.

And now again they send suppliant ambassadors, with their garments rent and their heads covered with ashes, imploring assistance from the Romans, and like timorous chickens, crowding under the protecting wings of their parents, that their wretched country might not altogether be destroyed, and that the Roman name, which now was but an empty sound to fill the ear, might not become a reproach even to distant nations. Upon this, the Romans, moved with compassion, as far as human nature can be, at the relations of such horrors, send forward, like eagles in their flight, their unexpected bands of cavalry by land and mariners by sea, and planting their terrible swords upon the shoulders of their enemies, they mow them down like leaves which fall at the destined period; and as a mountain-torrent swelled with numerous streams, and bursting its banks with roaring noise, with foaming crest and yeasty wave rising to the stars, by whose eddying currents our eyes are as it were dazzled, does with one of its billows overwhelm every obstacle in its way, so did our illustrious defenders vigorously drive our enemies' band beyond the sea, if any could so escape them; for it was beyond those same seas that they transported, year after year, the plunder which they had gained, no one daring to resist them.

The Romans, therefore, left the country, giving notice that they could no longer be harassed by such laborious expeditions, nor suffer the Roman standards, with so large and brave an army, to be worn out by sea and land by fighting against these unwarlike, plundering vagabonds; but that the islanders, inuring themselves to warlike weapons, and bravely fighting, should valiantly protect their country, their property, wives and children, and, what is dearer than these, their liberty and lives; that they should not suffer their hands to be tied behind their backs by a nation which, unless they were enervated by idleness and sloth, was not more powerful than themselves, but that they should arm those hands with buckler, sword, and spear, ready for the field of battle; and, because they thought this also of advantage to the people they were about to leave, they, with the help of the miserable natives, built a wall different from the former, by public and private contributions, and of the same structure as walls generally, extending in a straight line from sea to sea, between some cities, which, from fear of their enemies, had there by chance been built. They then give energetic counsel to the timorous natives, and leave them patterns by which to manufacture arms. Moreover, on the south coast where their vessels lay, as there was some apprehension lest the barbarians might land, they erected towers at stated intervals, commanding a prospect of the sea; and then left the island never to return.

No sooner were they gone, than the Picts and Scots, like worms which in the heat of mid-day come forth from their holes, hastily land again from their canoes, in which they had been carried beyond the Cichican valley, differing one from another in manners, but inspired with the same avidity for blood, and all more eager to shroud their villainous faces in bushy hair than to cover with decent clothing those parts of their body which required it. Moreover, having heard of the departure of our friends, and their resolution never to return, they seized with greater boldness than before on all the country towards the extreme north as far as the wall. To oppose them there was placed on the heights a garrison equally slow to fight and ill adapted to run away, a useless and panic-struck company, who slumbered away days and nights on their unprofitable watch. Meanwhile the hooked weapons of their enemies were not idle, and our wretched countrymen were dragged from the wall and dashed against the ground. Such premature death, however, painful as it was, saved them from seeing the miserable sufferings of their brothers and children. But why should I say more? They left their cities, abandoned the protection of the wall, and dispersed themselves in flight more desperately than before. The enemy, on the other hand, pursued them with more unrelenting cruelty than before, and butchered our countrymen like sheep, so that their habitations were like those of savage beasts; for they turned their arms upon each other, and for the sake of a little sustenance, imbrued their hands in the blood of their fellow countrymen. Thus foreign calamities were augmented by domestic feuds; so that the whole country was entirely destitute of provisions, save such as could be procured in the chase.

Again, therefore, the wretched remnant, sending to Ætius, a powerful Roman citizen, address him as follows: "To Ætius, now consul for the third time: the groans of the Britons." And again a little further, thus: "The barbarians drive us to the sea; the sea throws us back on the barbarians: thus two modes of death await us, we are either slain or drowned." The Romans, however, could not assist them, and in the meantime the discomfited people, wandering in the woods, began to feel the effects of a severe famine, which compelled many of them without delay to yield themselves up to their cruel persecutors, to obtain subsistence: others of them, however, lying hid in mountains, caves, and woods, continually sallied out from thence to renew the war. And then it was, for the first time, that they overthrew their enemies, who had for so many years been living in their country; for their trust was not in man, but in God; according to the maxim of Philo, "We must have divine assistance, when that of man fails." The boldness of the enemy was for a while checked, but not the wickedness of our countrymen: the enemy left our people, but the people did not leave their sins.

For it has always been a custom with our nation, as it is at present, to be impotent in repelling foreign foes, but bold and invincible in raising civil war, and bearing the burdens of their offences; they are impotent, I say, in following the standard of peace and truth, but bold in wickedness and falsehood. The audacious invaders therefore return to their winter quarters, determined before long again to return and plunder. And then, too, the Picts for the first time seated themselves at the extremity of the island, where they afterwards continued, occasionally plundering and wasting the country. During these truces, the wounds of the distressed people are healed, but another sore, still more venomous, broke out. No sooner were the ravages of the enemy checked, than the island was deluged with a most extraordinary plenty of all things, greater than was before known, and with it grew up every kind of luxury and licentiousness. It grew with so firm a root, that one might truly say of it, "Such fornication is heard of among you, as never was known the like among the Gentiles." But besides this vice, there arose also every other, to which human nature is liable, and in particular that hatred of truth, together with her supporters, which still at present destroys every thing good in the island; the love of falsehood, together with its inventors, the reception of crime in the place of virtue, the respect shown to wickedness rather than goodness, the love of darkness instead of the sun, the admission of Satan as an angel of light. Kings were anointed, not according to God's ordinance, but such as showed themselves more cruel than the rest; and soon after, they were put to death by those who had elected them, without any inquiry into their merits, but because others still more cruel were chosen to succeed them. If any one of these was of a milder nature than the rest, or in any way more regardful of the truth, he was looked upon as the ruiner of the country, every body cast a dart at him, and they valued things alike whether pleasing or displeasing to God, unless it so happened that what displeased him was pleasing to themselves. So that the words of the prophet, addressed to the people of old, might well be applied to our own countrymen: "Children without a law, have ye left God and provoked to anger the holy one of Israel? Why will ye still inquire, adding iniquity? Every head is languid and every heart is sad; from the sole of the foot to the crown, there is no health in him." And thus they did all things contrary to their salvation, as if no remedy could be applied to the world by the true Physician of all men. And not only the laity did so, but our Lord's own flock and its shepherds, who ought to have been an example to the people, slumbered away their time in drunkenness, as if they had been dipped in wine; whilst the swellings of pride, the jar of strife, the griping talons of envy, and the confused estimate of right and wrong, got such entire possession of them, that there seemed to be poured out (and the same still continueth) contempt upon princes, and to be made by their vanities to wander astray and not in the way.

Meanwhile, God being willing to purify his family who were infected by so deep a stain of woe, and at the hearing only of their calamities to amend them; a vague rumour suddenly as if on wings reaches the ears of all, that their inveterate foes were rapidly approaching to destroy the whole country, and to take possession of it, as of old, from one end to the other. But yet they derived no advantage from this intelligence; for, like frantic beasts, taking the bit of reason between their teeth, they abandoned the safe and narrow road, and rushed forward upon the broad downward path of vice, which leads to death. Whilst, therefore, as Solomon says, the stubborn servant is not cured by words, the fool is scourged and feels it not: a pestilential disease mortally affected the foolish people, which, without the sword, cut off so large a number of persons, that the living were not able to bury them. But even this was no warning to them, that in them also might be fulfilled the words of Isaiah the prophet, "And God hath called his people to lamentation, to baldness, and to the girdle of sackcloth; behold they begin to kill calves, and to slay rams, to eat, to drink, and to say, 'We will eat and drink, for to-morrow we shall die.'" For the time was approaching, when all their iniquities, as formerly those of the Amorrhæans, should be fulfilled. For a council was called to settle what was best and most expedient to be done, in order to repel such frequent and fatal irruptions and plunderings of the above-named nations.

Then all the councillors, together with that proud tyrant Gurthrigern [Vortigern], the British king, were so blinded, that, as a protection to their country, they sealed its doom by inviting in among them (like wolves into the sheep-fold), the fierce and impious Saxons, a race hateful both to God and men, to repel the invasions of the northern nations. Nothing was ever so pernicious to our country, nothing was ever so unlucky. What palpable darkness must have enveloped their minds—darkness desperate and cruel! Those very people whom, when absent, they dreaded more than death itself, were invited to reside, as one may say, under the selfsame roof. Foolish are the princes, as it is said, of Thafneos, giving counsel to unwise Pharaoh. A multitude of whelps came forth from the lair of this barbaric lioness, in three cyuls, as they call them, that is, in three ships of war, with their sails wafted by the wind and with omens and prophecies favorable, for it was foretold by a certain soothsayer among them, that they should occupy the country to which they were sailing three hundred years, and half of that time, a hundred and fifty years, should plunder and despoil the same. They first landed on the eastern side of the island, by the invitation of the unlucky king, and there fixed their sharp talons, apparently to fight in favor of the island, but alas! more truly against it. Their mother-land, finding her first brood thus successful, sends forth a larger company of her wolfish offspring, which sailing over, join themselves to their bastard-born comrades. From that time the germ of iniquity and the root of contention planted their poison amongst us, as we deserved, and shot forth into leaves and branches. The barbarians being thus introduced as soldiers into the island, to encounter, as they falsely said, any dangers in defence of their hospitable entertainers, obtain an allowance of provisions, which, for some time being plentifully bestowed, stopped their doggish mouths. Yet they complain that their monthly supplies are not furnished in sufficient abundance, and they industriously aggravate each occasion of quarrel, saying that unless more liberality is shown them, they will break the treaty and plunder the whole island. In a short time, they follow up their threats with deeds.

For the fire of vengeance, justly kindled by former crimes, spread from sea to sea, fed by the hands of our foes in the east, and did not cease, until, destroying the neighbouring towns and lands, it reached the other side of the island, and dipped its red and savage tongue in the western ocean. In these assaults, therefore, not unlike that of the Assyrian upon Judea, was fulfilled in our case what the prophet describes in words of lamentation: "They have burned with fire the sanctuary; they have polluted on earth the tabernacle of thy name." And again, "O God, the gentiles have come into thine inheritance; thy holy temple have they defiled," &c. So that all the columns were levelled with the ground by the frequent strokes of the battering-ram, all the husbandmen routed, together with their bishops, priests, and people, whilst the sword gleamed, and the flames crackled around them on every side. Lamentable to behold, in the midst of the streets lay the tops of lofty towers, tumbled to the ground, stones of high walls, holy altars, fragments of human bodies, covered with livid clots of coagulated blood, looking as if they had been squeezed together in a press; and with no chance of being buried, save in the ruins of the houses, or in the ravening bellies of wild beasts and birds; with reverence be it spoken for their blessed souls, if, indeed, there were many found who were carried, at that time, into the high heaven by the holy angels. So entirely had the vintage, once so fine, degenerated and become bitter,

that, in the words of the prophet, there was hardly a grape or ear of corn to be seen where the husbandman had turned his back.

Some, therefore, of the miserable remnant, being taken in the mountains, were murdered in great numbers; others, constrained by famine, came and yielded themselves to be slaves for ever to their foes, running the risk of being instantly slain, which truly was the greatest favour that could be offered them: some others passed beyond the seas with loud lamentations instead of the voice of exhortation. "Thou hast given us as sheep to be slaughtered, and among the Gentiles hast thou dispersed us." Others, committing the safeguard of their lives, which were in continual jeopardy, to the mountains, precipices, thickly wooded forests, and to the rocks of the seas (albeit with trembling hearts), remained still in their country. But in the meanwhile, an opportunity happening, when these most cruel robbers were returned home, the poor remnants of our nation (to whom flocked from divers places round about our miserable countrymen as fast as bees to their hives, for fear of an ensuing storm), being strengthened by God, calling upon him with all their hearts, as the poet says, "With their unnumbered vows they burden heaven," that they might not be brought to utter destruction, took arms under the conduct of Ambrosius Aurelianus, a modest man, who of all the Roman nation was then alone in the confusion of this troubled period by chance left alive. His parents, who for their merit were adorned with the purple, had been slain in these same broils, and now his progeny in these our days, although shamefully degenerated from the worthiness of their ancestors, provoke to battle their cruel conquerors, and by the goodness of our Lord obtain the victory.

After this, sometimes our countrymen, sometimes the enemy, won the field, to the end that our Lord might in this land try after his accustomed manner these his Israelites, whether they loved him or not, until the year of the siege of Bath-hill,[3] when took place also the last almost, though not the least slaughter of our cruel foes, which was (as I am sure) forty-four years and one month after the landing of the Saxons, and also the time of my own nativity. And yet neither to this day are the cities of our country inhabited as before, but being forsaken and overthrown, still lie desolate; our foreign wars having ceased, but our civil troubles still remaining. For as well the remembrance of such a terrible desolation of the island, as also of the unexpected recovery of the same, remained in the minds of those who were eye-witnesses of the wonderful events of both, and in regard thereof, kings, public magistrates, and private persons, with priests and clergymen, did all and every one of them live orderly according to their several vocations. But when these had departed out of this world, and a new race succeeded, who were ignorant of this troublesome time, and had only experience of the present prosperity, all the laws of truth and justice were so shaken and subverted, that not so much as a vestige or remembrance of these virtues remained among the above-named orders of men, except among a very few who, compared with the great multitude which were daily rushing headlong down to hell, are accounted so small a number, that our reverend mother, the church, scarcely beholds them, her only true children, reposing in her bosom; whose worthy lives, being a pattern to all men, and beloved of God, inasmuch as by their holy prayers, as by certain pillars and most profitable supporters, our infirmity is sustained up, that it may not utterly be broken down, I would have no one suppose I intended to reprove, if forced by the increasing multitude of offences, I have freely, aye, with anguish, not so much declared as bewailed the wickedness of those who are become servants, not only to their bellies, but also to the devil rather than to Christ, who is our blessed God, world without end.

For why shall their countrymen conceal what foreign nations round about now not only know, but also continually are casting in their teeth?

Notes

1   The translation is that of J. A. Giles in *Six Old English Chronicles*, George Bell and Sons, London, 1891.

2   Boudicca, wife of Prasutagus, King of the Iceni. When Prasutagus died (A.D. 61), the Emperor Nero's procurator, Decianus Catus, confiscated the property of the Icenian nobles. Boudicca was flogged and her daughters raped. But the Iceni and other Britons who were resentful of Roman policy rallied around Boudicca, who led them against their Roman enemies with great vigor.

3   "Bath-hill" here represents the "Mons Badonicus" of the original.

B. St. Bede

St. Bede the Venerable, who lived from about A.D. 673 to about 735, entered the monastery of Benedict Biscop at Wearmouth at the age of seven. In A.D. 682 he was transferred to the monastery at Jarrow under Abbot Ceolfrid, where he spent the remainder of his life. Among his many writings, which include a number of commentaries on the Bible that were influential throughout the Middle Ages, the most famous is The Ecclesiastical History of the English Nation, *from which some selections appear following. This work, which shows remarkable care in the gathering and organization of historical material, was completed in A.D. 731. It has remained to this day one of the Classics of the English-speaking world.*

There is a good chapter on Bede and an extensive bibliography in W. F. Bolton, A History of Anglo-Latin Literature, *Princeton University Press, Princeton, N.J., 1967.*

From
THE ECCLESIASTICAL HISTORY
OF THE ENGLISH NATION[1]

Preface   To The Most Glorious King Ceolwulph, Bede The Servant of Christ, and Priest

I formerly, at your request, most readily transmitted to you the Ecclesiastical History of the English Nation, which I had newly published, for you to read, and give it your approbation; and I now send it again to be transcribed, and more fully considered at your leisure. And I cannot but commend the sincerity and zeal, with which you not only diligently give ear to hear the words of the Holy Scripture, but also industriously take care to become acquainted with the actions and sayings of former men of renown, especially of our own nation. For if history relates good things of good men, the attentive hearer is excited to imitate that which is good; or if it mentions ill things of wicked persons, nevertheless the religious and pious hearer or reader, shunning that which is hurtful and perverse, is the more earnestly excited to perform those things which he knows to be good, and worthy of God. Of which you also being deeply sensible, are desirous that the said history should be more fully made familiar to yourself, and to those over whom the Divine Authority has appointed you governor, from your great regard to their general welfare. But to the end that I may remove all occasion of doubting what I have written, both from yourself and other readers or hearers of this history, I will take care briefly to intimate from what authors I chiefly learned the same.

My principal authority and aid in this work was the learned and reverend Abbot Albinus; who, educated in the Church of Canterbury by those venerable and learned men, Archbishop Theodore[2] of blessed memory, and the Abbot Adrian,[3] transmitted to me by Nothelmus, the pious priest of the Church of London, either in writing, or by word of mouth of the same Nothelmus, all that he thought worthy of memory, that had been done in the province of Kent, or the adjacent parts, by the disciples of the blessed Pope Gregory, as he had learned the same either from written records, or the traditions of his ancestors. The same Nothelmus, afterwards going to Rome, having, with leave of the present Pope Gregory, searched into the archives of the holy Roman Church, found there

some epistles of the blessed Pope Gregory, and other popes; and returning home, by the advice of the aforesaid most reverend father Albinus, brought them to me, to be inserted in my history. Thus, from the beginning of this volume to the time when the English nation received the faith of Christ, have we collected the writings of our predecessors, and from them gathered matter for our history; but from that time till the present, what was transacted in the Church of Canterbury, by the disciples of St. Gregory or their successors, and under what kings the same happened, has been conveyed to us by Nothelmus through the industry of the aforesaid Abbot Albinus. They also partly informed me by what bishops and under what kings the provinces of the East and West Saxons, as also of the East Angles, and of the Northumbrians, received the faith of Christ. In short, I was chiefly encouraged to undertake this work by the persuasions of the same Albinus. In like manner, Daniel, the most reverend Bishop of the West Saxons, who is still living, communicated to me in writing some things relating to the Ecclesiastical History of that province, and the next adjoining to it of the South Saxons, as also of the Isle of Wight. But how, by the pious ministry of Cedd and Ceadda, the province of the Mercians was brought to the faith of Christ, which they knew not before, and how that of the East Saxons recovered the same, after having expelled it, and how those fathers lived and died, we learned from the brethren of the monastery, which was built by them, and is called Lestingæ. What ecclesiastical transactions took place in the province of the East Angles, was partly made known to us from the writings and tradition of our ancestors, and partly by relation of the most reverend Abbot Esius. What was done towards promoting the faith, and what was the sacerdotal succession in the province of Lindsey, we had either from the letters of the most reverend Prelate Cynebert, or by word of mouth from other persons of good credit. But what was done in the Church throughout the province of the Northumbrians, from the time when they received the faith of Christ till this present, I received not from any particular author, but by the faithful testimony of innumerable witnesses, who might know or remember the same; besides what I had of my own knowledge. Wherein it is to be observed, that what I have written concerning our most holy father, and Bishop Cuthbert, either in this volume, or in my treatise on his life and actions, I partly took, and faithfully copied from what I found written of him by the brethren of the Church of Lindisfarn; but at the same time took care to add such things as I could myself have knowledge of by the faithful testimony of such as knew him. And I humbly entreat the reader, that if he shall in this that we have written find any thing not delivered according to the truth, he will not impute the same to me, who, as the true rule of history requires, have labored sincerely to commit to writing such things as I could gather from common report, for the instruction of posterity.

Moreover I beseech all men who shall hear or read this history of our nation, that for my manifold infirmities both of mind and body, they will offer up frequent supplications to the throne of Grace. And I further pray, that in recompense for the labor wherewith I have recorded in the several countries and cities those events which were most worthy of note, and most grateful to the ears of their inhabitants, I may for my reward have the benefit of their pious prayers.

Book I

Chapter I   Of the Situation of Britain and Ireland, and of Their Ancient Inhabitants

Britain, an island in the ocean, formerly called Albion, lies at a considerable distance to the north and west from the three largest countries in Europe—Germany, France and Spain. It extends 800 miles in length towards the north, and is 200 miles in breadth, excepting only the greater distances of several promontories; by which its compass is made to be 3675 miles. To the south, as you pass along the nearest shore of the Belgic Gaul, the first place in Britain which opens to the eye, is the city of Rutubi Portus, which is by the English corrupted into Reptacestir.[4] The distance from hence across the sea to Gessoriacum,[5] the nearest shore of the Morini, is 50 miles, or as some writers say, 450 furlongs. On the back of the island, where it opens to the immense ocean, it has the islands called Orcades. Britain excels for grain and trees, and is fit for feeding cattle and beasts of burden. It also produces vines in some places, and has plenty of land and water fowls of several sorts; and is remarkable for rivers abounding in fish, and plentiful springs. It has the greatest plenty of salmon and eels; seals are also frequently taken, and dolphins, as also

whales; besides many sorts of shellfish, among which are mussels, in which are often found excellent pearls of all colors, red, purple, violet and green, but mostly white. There is also great store of cockles, of which the scarlet dye is made; a most beautiful color, which never fades with the heat of the sun or the washing of rain; but the older it is, the more beautiful it becomes. It has salt springs, and hot springs, and from them flow rivers which furnish hot baths, proper for all ages and sexes, in several places, as is requisite for every one. For water, as St. Basil says, receives the heating quality, when it runs along certain metals, and becomes not only hot but scalding. Britain has also many veins of metals, as copper, iron, lead and silver; it has likewise much and excellent jet, which is black and sparkling, glittering at the fire, and being heated, drives away serpents; being warmed with rubbing, it holds fast whatever is applied to it, like amber. The island was formerly embellished with twenty-eight most noble cities, besides innumerable castles, which were all strongly secured with walls, towers, gates and locks. And, in regard that it lies almost under the North Pole, the nights are light in summer, so that at midnight the beholders are often in doubt whether the evening twilight still continues, or that of the morning is come on; for the sun, which, during the night, is not long under the earth, returns to the east in the morning by the northern regions. For which reason the days are of a great length in summer, as on the contrary, the nights are in winter, the sun then withdrawing into the southern parts, so that they are eighteen hours long. Thus the nights are extraordinarily short in summer, and the days in winter, that is, of only six equinoctial hours. Whereas, in Armenia, Macedon, Italy, and other countries of the same latitude, the longest day or night extends but to fifteen hours, and the shortest to nine.

This island at present, following the number of the books in which the Divine law was written, contains five nations, the English, Britons, Scots, Picts and Latins, each in its own peculiar dialect cultivating the sublime study of Divine truth. The Latin tongue is, by the study of the Scriptures, become common to all the rest. At first this island had no other inhabitants but the Britons, from whom it derived its name, and who coming over into Britain, as is reported, from Armorica, possessed themselves of the southern parts thereof. When they, beginning at the south, had made themselves masters of the greatest part of the island, it happened, that the nation of the Picts coming into the ocean from Scythia, as is reported, in a few tall ships, were driven by the winds beyond the shores of Britain, and arrived off Ireland, on the northern coasts, where, finding the nation of the Scots, they requested to be allowed to settle among them, but could not succeed in obtaining their request. Ireland is the greatest island next to Britain, and seated to the westward of it; but as it is shorter than Britain to the north, so running out far beyond it to the south, it is opposite to the northern parts of Spain, though a spacious sea lies between them. The Picts, as has been said, arriving in this island by sea, desired they might have a place to settle and inhabit granted them. The Scots answered, that the island could not contain them both; but "we can give you good advice," said they, "what to do; we know there is another island, not far from ours, to the eastward, which we often see at a distance, when the days are clear. If you will repair thither, you may be able to obtain settlements; or if they should oppose you, you may make use of us as auxiliaries." The Picts accordingly sailing over into Britain, began to inhabit the northern parts thereof, for the Britons were possessed of the southern. Now the Picts having no wives, and asking them of the Scots, they would not consent to grant them upon any other terms, than that when any difficulty should arise, they should rather choose themselves a king from the female royal race than from the male: which custom, as is well known, has been observed among the Picts to this day. In process of time, Britain, besides the Britons and the Picts, received a third nation, the Scots, who, departing out of Ireland under their leader Reuda, either by fair means, or by force of arms, secured to themselves those settlements among the Picts which they still possess. From the name of their commander, they are to this day called Dalreudins; for in their language Dal signifies a part.

Ireland, in breadth, and for wholesomeness and serene air, far surpasses Britain; for the snow scarcely ever lies there above three days: no man makes hay in the summer for winter's provision, or builds stables for his beasts of burden. No reptiles are found there, and no snake can live there; for, though often carried thither out of Britain, as soon as the ship comes near the shore, and the scent of the air reaches them, they die. On the contrary, almost all things in the island are good against poison. In short, we have known that when some persons have been bitten by serpents, the scrapings of leaves of books that were brought out of Ireland, being put into water, and given them to drink, have immediately expelled the spreading poison, and assuaged the swelling. The island abounds in milk and honey, nor is there any want of vines, fish or fowl; and it is remarkable for deer and goats. It is properly the country of the Scots, who, migrating from thence, as has been said, added a third nation in Britain to the Britons and the Picts. There is a very large gulf of the sea, which formerly divided the nation of the Picts from the Britons; which gulf runs from the west very far into the land, where, to this day, stands the strong city of the Britons, called Alcluith.[6] The Scots arriving on the north side of this bay, settled themselves there.

Chapter II   Caius Julius Caesar, the First Roman That Came into Britain

Britain had never been visited by the Romans, and was, indeed, entirely unknown to them before the time of Caius Julius Caesar, who, in the year 693 after the building of Rome, but the sixtieth year before the incarnation of our Lord, being consul with Lucius Bibulus, whilst he made war upon the Germans and the Gauls, which were divided only by the river Rhine, came into the province of the Morini, from whence is the nearest and shortest passage into Britain. Here, having provided about eighty ships of burden and vessels with oars, he sailed over into Britain; where, being first roughly handled in a battle, and then meeting with a violent storm, he lost a considerable part of his fleet, no small number of soldiers, and almost all his horse. Returning into Gaul, he put his legions into winter quarters, and gave orders for building six hundred sail of both sorts. With these he passed over early in the spring into Britain, but, whilst he was marching with a large army towards the enemy, the ships riding at anchor, were by a tempest either dashed one against another, or driven upon the sands and wrecked. Forty of them perished, the rest were, with much difficulty, repaired. Caesar's cavalry was at the first charge defeated by the Britons, and Labienus, the tribune, slain. In the second engagement, he, with great hazard to his men, put the Britons to flight. Thence he proceeded to the river Thames, where an immense multitude of the enemy had posted themselves on the farthest side of the river, under the command of

Cassibelan, and fenced the bank of the river and almost all the ford under water with sharp stakes: the remains of these are to be seen to this day, apparently about the thickness of a man's thigh, and being cased with lead, remain fixed immovably in the bottom of the river. This being perceived and avoided by the Romans, the barbarians, not able to stand the shock of the legions, hid themselves in the woods, whence they grievously galled the Romans with repeated sallies. In the mean time, the strong city of the Trinobantes, with its commander Androgius, surrendered to Caesar, giving him forty hostages. Many other cities, following their example, made a treaty with the Romans. By their assistance, Caesar at length, with much difficulty, took Cassibelan's town, situated between two marshes, fortified by the adjacent woods, and plentifully furnished with all necessaries. After this Caesar returned into Gaul, but he had no sooner put his legions into winter quarters, than he was suddenly beset and distracted with wars and tumults raised against him on every side.

Chapter III   Claudius, the Second of the Romans Who Came into Britain, Brought the Islands Orcades into Subjection to the Roman Empire; and Vespasian, Sent by Him, Reduced the Isle of Wight under Their Dominion

In the year of Rome, 798, the Emperor Claudius, the fourth from Augustas, being desirous to approve himself a beneficial prince to the republic, and eagerly bent upon war and conquest, undertook an expedition into Britain, which seemed to be stirred up to rebellion by the refusal of the Romans to give up certain deserters. He was the only one, either before or after Julius Caesar, who had dared to land upon the island; yet, within a very few days, without any fight or bloodshed, the greatest part of the island was surrendered into his hands. He also added to the Roman empire the Orcades, which lie in the ocean beyond Britain, and then returning to Rome the sixth month after his departure, he gave his son the title of Britannicus. This war he concluded in the fourth year of his empire, which is the forty-sixth from the incarnation of our Lord. In which year there happened a most grievous famine in Syria, which, in the Acts of the Apostles, is recorded to have been foretold by the prophet Agabus. Vespasian, who

came to be emperor after Nero, being sent into Britain by the same Claudius, brought also under the Roman dominion the Isle of Wight, which is next to Britain on the south, and is about thirty miles in length from east to west, and twelve from north to south; being six miles distant from the southern coast of Britain at the east end, and three only at the west. Nero, succeeding Claudius in the empire, attempted nothing in martial affairs; and therefore, among innumerable other detriments brought upon the Roman state, he almost lost Britain; for under him two most noble towns were there taken and destroyed.

Chapter X   How in the Reign of Arcadius, Pelagius, a Briton, Insolently Impugned the Grace of God

In the year of our Lord 394, Arcadius, the son of Theodosius, the forty-third from Augustus, taking the empire upon him, with his brother Honorius, held it thirteen years. In his time, Pelagius, a Briton, spread far and near the infection of his perfidious doctrine against the assistance of the Divine grace, being seconded therein by his associate, Julianus of Campania, whose anger was kindled by the loss of his bishopric, of which he had been just deprived. St. Augustin, and the other orthodox fathers, quoted many thousand catholic opinions against them, yet they would not correct their madness; but, on the contrary, their folly was rather increased by contradiction, and they refused to embrace the truth; which Prosper, the rhetorician, has beautifully expressed thus in heroic verse:

Contra Augustinum narratur serpere quidam
  Scriptor, quem dudum livor adurit edax.
Qui caput obscuris contectum utcunque cavernis
  Tollere humo miserum protulit anguiculum.
Aut hunc fruge sua aequorei pavere Britanni,
  Aut huic Campano gramine corda tument.

An insect scribbler durst 'gainst Austin write,
Whose very heart was scorch'd with hellish spite.
Presumptuous serpent! from what midnight den,
Durst thou to crawl on earth and look at men?
Sure thou at first wast fed on Britain's plains,
Or in thy breast Vesuvian sulphur reigns.

Chapter XXII   The Britons, Being for a Time Delivered from Foreign Invasions, Wasted Themselves by Civil Wars, and Then Gave Themselves Up to More Heinous Crimes

In the meantime, in Britain, there was some respite from foreign, but not from civil war. There still remained the ruins of cities destroyed by the enemy and abandoned; and the natives, who had escaped the enemy, now fought against each other. However, the kings, priests, private men, and the nobility, still remembering the late calamities and slaughters, in some measure kept within bounds; but when these died, and another generation succeeded, which knew nothing of those times, and was only acquainted with the present peaceable state of things, all the bonds of sincerity and justice were so entirely broken, that there was not only no trace of them remaining, but few persons seemed to be aware that such virtues had ever existed. Among other most wicked actions, not to be expressed, which their own historian, Gildas, mournfully takes notice of, they added this, that they never preached the faith to the Saxons, or English, who dwelt amongst them; however, the goodness of God did not forsake his people, whom he foreknew, but sent to the aforesaid nation much more worthy preachers, to bring it to the faith.

Chapter XXIII   How Pope Gregory Sent Augustine, with Other Monks, to Preach to the English, and Encouraged Them by a Letter of Exhortation, Not to Cease from Their Labor

In the year of our Lord 582, Maurice, the fifty-fourth from Augustus, ascended the throne, and reigned twenty-one years. In the tenth year of his reign, Gregory, a man renowned for learning and behavior, was promoted to the apostolical see of Rome, and presided over it thirteen years, six months, and ten days. He, being moved by Divine inspiration, in the fourteenth year of the same emperor, and about the one hundred and fiftieth after the coming of the English into Britain, sent the servant of God, Augustine, and with him, several other monks, who feared the Lord, to preach the word of God to the English nation. They

having, in obedience to the pope's commands, undertaken that work, were, on their journey, seized with a sudden fear, and began to think of returning home, rather than proceed to a barbarous, fierce, and unbelieving nation, to whose very language they were strangers; and this they unanimously agreed was the safest course. In short, they sent back Augustine, whom he had appointed to be consecrated bishop, in case they were received by the English, that he might, by humble entreaty, obtain of the holy Gregory, that they should not be compelled to undertake so dangerous, toilsome, and uncertain a journey. The pope, in reply, sent them a hortatory epistle, persuading them to proceed in the work of the Divine word, and rely on the assistance of the Almighty. The purport of which letter was as follows:

> Gregory, the servant of the servants of God, to the servants of our Lord. Forasmuch as it had been better not to begin a good work, than to think of desisting from that which has been begun, it behoves you (most beloved sons) to fulfill the good work, which, by the help of our Lord, you have undertaken. Let not, therefore, the toil of the journey, nor the tongues of evil speaking men, deter you; but with all possible earnestness and zeal perform that which, by God's direction, you have undertaken; being assured, that much labor is followed by an eternal reward. When Augustine, your chief, returns, whom we also constitute your abbot, humbly obey him in all things; knowing, that whatsoever you shall do by his direction, will, in all respects, be available to your souls. Almighty God protect you with his grace, and grant that I may, in the heavenly country, see the fruits of your labor. Inasmuch as, though I cannot labor with you, I shall partake in the joy of the reward, because I am willing to labor. God keep you in safety, my most beloved sons. Dated the 10th of the kalends of August, in the fourteenth year of the reign of our pious and most august lord, Mauritius Tiberius, the thirteenth year after the consulship of our said lord.[7] The fourteenth indiction.

Chapter XXIV   How He Wrote to the Bishop of Arles to Entertain Them

The same venerable pope also sent a letter to Etherius, Bishop of Arles, exhorting him to give favorable entertainment to Augustine on his way to Britain; which letter was in these words:

To our most reverend and holy brother, Etherius, fellow bishop, Gregory, the servant of the servants of God. Although religious men stand in need of no recommendation with priests who have the charity which is pleasing to God; yet, as a proper opportunity is offered to write, we have thought fit to send you our letter, to inform you, that we have directed thither, for the good of souls, the bearer of these presents, Augustine, the servant of God, of whose industry we are assured, with other servants of God, whom it is requisite that your holiness assist with priestly affection, and afford him all the comfort in your power. And to the end that you may be the more ready in your assistance, we have enjoined him particularly to inform you of the occasion of his coming; knowing, that when you are acquainted with it, you will, as the matter requires, for the sake of God, zealously afford him your relief. We also in all things recommend to your charity, Candidus, the priest, our common son, whom we have transferred to the government of a small patrimony in our church. God keep you in safety, most reverend brother. Dated the 10th of the kalends of August, in the fourteenth year of the reign of our most pious and august lord, Mauritius Tiberius, the thirteenth year after the consulship of our said lord. The fourteenth indiction.

Chapter XXV   *Augustine, Coming into Britain, First Preached in the Isle of Thanet to the King of Kent, and Having Obtained Licence, Entered That County in Order to Preach Therein*

Augustine, being strengthened by the confirmation of the blessed Father Gregory, returned to the work of the word of God, with the servants of Christ, and arrived in Britain. Ethelbert was at that time the most powerful king of Kent,[8] who had extended his dominions as far as the great river Humber, by which the Southern-Saxons are divided from the Northern. On the east of Kent is the large Isle of Thanet, containing, according to the English way of reckoning, 600 families, divided from the other land by the river Wantsumu, which is about three furlongs over, and fordable only in two places, for both ends of it run into the sea. In this island landed the servant of our Lord, Augustine, and his companions, being as is reported nearly forty men. They had, by order of the blessed

Pope Gregory, taken interpreters of the nation of the Franks, and sending to Ethelbert, signified that they were come from Rome, and brought a joyful message, which most undoubtedly assured all that took advantage of it everlasting joys in heaven, and a kingdom that would never end, with the living and true God. The king, having heard this, ordered them to stay in that island where they had landed, and that they should be furnished with all necessaries, till he should consider what to do with them. For he had before heard of the Christian religion, having a Christian wife of the royal family of the Franks, called Berta; whom he had received from her parents, upon condition that she should be permitted to practise her religion with the Bishop Luidhard, who was sent with her to preserve her faith. Some days after, the king came into the island, and sitting in the open air, ordered Augustine and his companions to be brought into his presence. For he had taken precaution that they should not come to him in any house, lest, according to an ancient superstition, if they practiced any magical arts, they might impose upon him, and so get the better of him. But they came furnished with Divine, not with magic virtue, bearing a silver cross for their banner, and the image of our Lord and Saviour painted on a board; and singing the litany, they offered up their prayers to the Lord for the eternal salvation both of themselves and of those to whom they were come. Having, pursuant to the king's commands, sat down, and preached to him and all his attendants there present, the word of life, the king answered thus:

> Your words and promises are very fair, but as they are new to us, and of uncertain import, I cannot approve of them, forsaking that which I have so long followed with the whole English nation. But because you are come from far into my kingdom, and, as I conceive, are desirous to impart to us those things which you believe to be true, and most beneficial, we will not molest you, but give you favorable entertainment, and take care to supply you with your necessary sustenance; nor do we forbid you by preaching to gain as many as you can to your religion.

Accordingly he permitted them to reside in the city of Canterbury, which was the metropolis of all his dominions, and, pursuant to his promise, besides allowing them sustenance, did not refuse them liberty to preach. It is reported that, as they drew near to the city, after their manner, with the holy cross, and the image of our sovereign Lord and King, Jesus Christ, they, in consort, sung this litany: " We beseech thee, O Lord, in all thy mercy, that thy anger and wrath be turned away from this city, and from thy holy house, because we have sinned. Hallelujah."

Chapter XXVI St. Augustine in Kent Followed the Doctrine and Manner of Living of the Primitive Church, and Settled His Episcopal See in the Royal City

As soon as they entered the dwelling-place assigned them, they began to imitate the course of life practiced in the primitive church; applying themselves to frequent prayer, watching and fasting; preaching the word of life to as many as they could; despising all worldly things, as not belonging to them; receiving only their necessary food from those they taught; living themselves in all respects comfortable to what they prescribed to others, and being always disposed to suffer any adversity, and even to die for that truth which they preached. In short, several believed and were baptized, admiring the simplicity of their innocent life, and the sweetness of their heavenly doctrine. There was on the east side of the city, a church dedicated to the honor of St. Martin, built whilst the Romans were still in the island, wherein the queen, who, as has been said before, was a Christian, used to pray. In this, they first began to meet, to sing, to pray, to say mass, to preach, and to baptize, till the king, being converted to the faith, granted them leave to preach openly, and build or repair churches in all places. When he, among the rest, induced by the unspotted life of these holy men, and their delightful promises, which, by many miracles, they proved to be most certain, believed and was baptized, greater numbers began daily to flock together to hear the word, and, forsaking their heathen rites, to associate themselves, by believing, to the unity of the church of Christ. Their conversion the king so far encouraged, as that he compelled none to embrace Christianity, but only showed more affection to the believers, as to his fellow-citizens in the heavenly kingdom. For he had learned from his instructors and leaders to salvation, that the service of Christ ought to be voluntary, not by compulsion. Nor was it long before he gave his teachers a settled place in his metropolis of Canterbury, with such possessions of different kinds as were necessary for their subsistence.

Chapter XXVII St. Augustine, Being Made Bishop, Sends to Acquaint Pope Gregory with What Had Been Done, and Receives His Answer to the Doubts He Had Proposed to Him[9]

In the meantime, Augustine, the man of God, repaired to Arles, and, pursuant to the orders received from the holy Father Gregory, was ordained archbishop of the English nation, by Etherius, archbishop of that city. Then returning into Britain, he sent Laurentius, the priest, and Peter, the monk, to Rome, to acquaint Pope Gregory, that the nation of the English had received the faith of Christ, and that he was himself made their bishop. At the same time, he desired his solution of some doubts that occurred to him. He soon received proper answers to his questions, which we have also thought fit to insert in this our history:

The First Question of Augustine, Bishop of the Church of Canterbury

Concerning bishops, how they are to behave themselves toward their clergy, or into how many portions the things given by the faithful to the altar are to be divided; and how the bishop is to act in the church?

Gregory, Pope of the City of Rome, Answers

Holy writ, which no doubt you are well versed in, testifies, and particularly St. Paul's Epistle to Timothy, wherein he endeavors to instruct him how he should behave himself in the house of God; but it is the custom of the apostolic see to prescribe rules to bishops newly ordained, that all emoluments which accrue, are to be divided into four portions—one for the bishop and his family, because of hospitality and entertainments; another for the clergy; a third for the poor; and the fourth for the repair of churches. But in regard that you, my brother, being brought up under monastic rules, are not to live apart from your clergy in the English church, which, by God's assistance, has been lately brought to the faith; you are to follow that course of life which our forefathers did in the time of the primitive church, when none of them said any thing that he possessed was his own, but all things were in common among them. But if there are any clerks not received into holy orders, who cannot live continent, they are to take wives, and receive their stipends abroad; because we know it is written by the same fathers above-mentioned, that a distribution was made to each of them according to every one's wants. Care is also to be taken of their stipends, and provision to be made, and they are to be kept under ecclesiastical rules, that they may live orderly, and attend to singing of psalms, and by the help of God, preserve their hearts and tongues and bodies from all that is unlawful. But as for those that live in common, why need we say any thing of making portions, or keeping hospitality and exhibiting mercy? inasmuch as all that can be spared is to be spent in pious and religious works, according to the commands of Him who is the Lord and Master of all, "Give alms of such things as you have, and behold all things are clean unto you."

Augustine's Second Question

Whereas the faith is one and the same, why are there different customs in different churches; and why is one custom of masses observed in the holy Roman Church, and another in the Gallican Church?

Pope Gregory Answers

You know, my brother, the custom of the Roman Church in which you remember you were bred up. But it pleases me, that if you have found any thing, either in the Roman, or the Gallican, or any other church, which may be more acceptable to Almighty God, you carefully make choice of the same, and sedulously teach the church of the English, which as yet is new in the faith, whatsoever you can gather from the several churches. "For things are not to be loved for the sake of places, but places for the sake of good things." Choose, therefore, from every church those things that are pious, religious and upright, and having, as it were, made them up in one mass, let the minds of the English be accustomed thereto.

Augustine's Third Question

I beseech you to inform me, what punishment must be inflicted, if any one shall take any thing by stealth from the church?

Gregory Answers

You may judge, my brother, by the person of the thief, in what manner he is to be corrected. For there are some, who, having substance, commit theft; and there are others, who transgress in this point through want. Wherefore it is requisite, that some be punished in their purses, others with stripes; some with more severity, and some more mildly. And when the severity is more, it is to proceed from charity, not from passion; because this is done to him who is corrected, that he may not be delivered up to hell-fire. For it behoves us to maintain discipline among the faithful, as good parents do with their carnal children, whom they punish with stripes for their faults, and yet design to make those their heirs whom they chastise; and they preserve what they possess for those whom they seem in anger to persecute. This charity is, therefore, to be kept in mind, and it dictates the measure of the punishment, so that the mind may do nothing beyond the rule of reason. You may add, that they are to restore those things which they have stolen from the church. But, God forbid, that the church should make profit from those earthly things which it seems to lose, or seek gain out of such vanities.

Augustine's Fourth Question

Whether two brothers may marry two sisters, which are of a family far removed from them?

Gregory Answers

This may lawfully be done; for nothing is found in holy writ that seems to contradict it.

Augustine's Fifth Question

To what degree may the faithful marry with their kindred; and whether it is lawful for men to marry their step-mothers, and relations?

Gregory Answers

A certain worldly law in the Roman commonwealth allows, that the son and daughter of a brother and sister, or of two brothers, or two sisters, may be joined in matrimony; but we have found by experience, that no offspring can come of such wedlock; and the Divine law prohibits "to uncover the nakedness of kindred." Hence of necessity it must be the third or fourth generation of the faithful, that can be lawfully joined in matrimony; for the second, which we have mentioned, must altogether abstain from one another. To have to do with one's stepmother is a heinous crime, because it is written in the law, "Thou shalt not uncover the nakedness of thy father;" now the son, indeed, cannot uncover his father's nakedness, but in regard that it is written, "They shall be two in one flesh;" he that presumes to uncover the nakedness of his stepmother, who was one flesh with his father, certainly uncovers the nakedness of his father. It is also prohibited to have to do with a sister-in-law, because by the former union she is become the brother's flesh. For which thing also John the Baptist was beheaded, and ended his life in holy martyrdom. For though he was not ordered to deny Christ, and indeed was killed for confessing Christ, yet in regard that the same Jesus Christ, our Lord, said, "I am the Truth," because John was killed for the truth, he also shed his blood for Christ. But forasmuch as there are many of the English, who, whilst they were still in infidelity, are said to have been joined in this execrable matrimony, when they come to the faith they are to be admonished to abstain, and be made to know that this is a grievous sin. Let them fear the dreadful judgment of God, lest, for the gratification of their carnal appetites, they incur the torments of eternal punishment. Yet they are not on this account to be deprived of the communion of the body and blood of Christ, lest they seem to be punished for those things which they did through ignorance before they had received baptism. For at this time the holy Church chastises some things through zeal, and tolerates some through meekness, and connives at some things through discretion, that so she may often, by this forbearance and connivance, suppress the evil which she disapproves. But all that come to the faith are to be admonished not to do such things. And if any shall be guilty of them, they are to be excluded from the communion of the body and blood of Christ. For as the offense is, in some measure, to be tolerated in those who did it through ignorance, so it is to be strenuously prosecuted in those who do not fear to sin knowingly.

Augustine's Sixth Question

Whether a bishop may be ordained without other bishops being present, in case there be so great a distance between them, that they cannot easily come together?

Gregory Answers

As for the Church of England, in which you are as yet the only bishop, you can not otherwise ordain a bishop than in the absence of other bishops; for when do any bishops ever come from France, that they may be present as witnesses to you in ordaining a bishop? But we would have you, my brother, to ordain bishops in such a manner, that the said bishops may not be far asunder, to the end, that when a new bishop is to be ordained, there be no difficulty, but that the other bishops, whose presence is necessary, may easily come together. Thus, when, by the help of God, bishops shall be so constituted in places everywhere near to one another, no ordination of a bishop is to be performed without assembling three or four bishops. For, even in spiritual affairs, we may take example by the temporal, that they may be wisely and discreetly conducted. It is certain, that when marriages are celebrated in the world, some married persons are assembled, that those who went before in the way of matrimony, may also partake in the joy of the succeeding couple. Why then, at this spiritual ordination, wherein, by means of the sacred ministry, man is joined to God, should not such persons be assembled, as may either rejoice in the advancement of the new bishop, or jointly pour forth their prayers to Almighty God for his preservation?

Augustine's Seventh Question

How are we to deal with the bishops of France and Britain?

Gregory Answers

We give you no authority over the bishops of France, because the Bishop of Arles received the pall in ancient times from my predecessor, and we are not to deprive him of the authority he has received. If it shall therefore happen, my brother, that you go over into the province of France, you are to concert with the said Bishop of Arles, how, if there be any faults among the bishops, they may be amended. And if he shall be lukewarm in keeping up discipline, he is to be corrected by your zeal; to whom we have also written, that when your holiness shall be in France, he may also use all his endeavors to assist you, and put away from the behavior of the bishops all that shall be opposite to the command of our Creator. But you of your own authority shall not have power to judge the bishops of

France, but by persuading, soothing, and showing good works for them to imitate; you shall reform the minds of wicked men to the pursuit of holiness; for it is written in the law, "When thou comest into the standing corn of thy neighbors, then thou mayest pluck the ears with thine hand; but thou shalt not move a sickle unto thy neighbor's standing corn." For thou mayest not apply the sickle of judgment in that harvest, which seems to have been committed to another; but by the effect of good works thou shalt clear the Lord's wheat of the chaff of their vices, and convert them into the body of the Church, as it were, by eating. But whatsoever is to be done by authority, must be transacted with the aforesaid Bishop of Arles, lest that should be omitted, which the ancient institution of the fathers has appointed. But as for all the bishops of Britain, we commit them to your care, that the unlearned may be taught, the weak strengthened by persuasion, and the perverse corrected by authority.

Augustine's Eighth Question

Whether a woman with child ought to be baptized? Or how long after she has brought forth, may she come into the church? As also, after how many days the infant born may be baptized, lest he be prevented by death? Or how long after her husband may have carnal copulation with her? Or whether it be lawful for her to come into the church when she has her courses? Or to receive the holy sacrament of communion? Or whether a man, who has had to do with his wife, may come into the church before he has washed with water? Or approach to receive the mystery of the holy communion? All which things are requisite to be known by the rude nation of the English.

Gregory Answers

I do not doubt but that these questions have been put to you, my brother, and I think I have already answered you therein. But I believe you would wish the opinion which you yourself might give to be confirmed by mine also. Why should not a woman with child be baptized, since the fruitfulness of the flesh is no offense in the eyes of Almighty God? For when our first parents sinned in Paradise, they forfeited the immortality which they had received, by the just judgment of God. Because, therefore, Almighty God would not for their fault wholly destroy the human race, he

both deprived man of immortality for his sin, and, at the same time, of his great goodness, reserved to him the power of propagating his race after him. On what account then can that which is preserved to the human race, by the free gift of Almighty God, be excluded from the privilege of baptism? For it is very foolish to imagine that the gift of grace opposes that mystery in which all sin is blotted out. When a woman is delivered, after how many days she may come into the church, you have been informed by reading the Old Testament, viz. that she is to abstain for a male child thirty-three days, and sixty-six for a female. Now you must know that this is to be taken in a mystery; for if she enters the church the very hour that she is delivered, to return thanks, she is not guilty of any sin; because the pleasure of the flesh is in the fault, and not the pain; but the pleasure is in the copulation of the flesh, whereas there is pain in bringing forth the child. Wherefore it is said to the first mother of all, "In sorrow shalt thou bring forth children." If, therefore, we forbid a woman that has brought forth, to enter the church, we make a crime of her very punishment. To baptize either a woman who has brought forth, if there be danger of death, even the very hour that she brings forth, or that which she has brought forth the very hour it is born, is in no way prohibited, because, as the grace of the holy mystery is to be with much discretion provided for the living and understanding, so is it to be without any delay offered to the dying; lest, while a further time is sought to confer the mystery of redemption, a small delay intervening, the person that is to be redeemed is dead and gone. Her husband is not to have to do with her, till the infant born be weaned. A bad custom is sprung up in the behavior of married people, that is, that women disdain to suckle the children which they bring forth, and give them to other women to suckle; which seems to have been invented on no other account but incontinency; because as they will not be continent, they will not suckle the children which they bear. Those women, therefore, who, from bad custom, give their children to others to bring up, must not have to do with their husbands till the time of purification is past. For even when there has been no childbirth, women are forbidden to have to do with their husbands, whilst they have their monthly courses, insomuch that the law condemns to death any man that "shall approach unto a woman during her uncleanness." Yet the woman, nevertheless, must not be forbidden to come into the church whilst she has her monthly courses; because the superfluity of nature cannot be imputed to her as a crime; and it is not just that she should be refused admittance into the church, for that which she suffers against her will. For we know, that the woman who had the issue of blood, humbly approaching behind our Lord's back, touched the hem of his garment, and her distemper immediately departed from her. If, therefore, she that had an issue of blood, might commendably touch the garment of our Lord, why may not she, who has the monthly courses, lawfully enter into the church of God? But you may say, her distemper compelled her, whereas these we speak of are bound by custom. Consider then, most dear brother, that all we suffer in this mortal flesh, through the infirmity of our nature, is ordained by the just judgment of God after the fall; for to hunger, to thirst, to be hot, to be cold, to be weary, is from the infirmity of our nature; and what else is it to seek food against hunger, drink against thirst, air against heat, clothes against cold, rest against weariness, than to procure a remedy against distempers? Thus to a woman her monthly courses are a distemper. If, therefore, it was a commendable boldness in her, who in her disease touched our Lord's garment, why may not that which is allowed to one infirm person, be granted to all women, who, through the fault of their nature, are distempered? It must not, therefore, be forbidden to receive the mystery of the holy communion during those days. But if any one out of profound respect does not presume to do it, she is to be commended; yet if she receives it, she is not to be judged. For it is the part of noble minds in some manner to acknowledge their faults, even where there is no offense; because very often that is done without a fault, which, nevertheless, proceeded from a fault. Therefore, when we are hungry, it is no crime to eat; yet our being hungry proceeds from the sin of the first man. The monthly courses are no crime in women, because they naturally happen; however, because our nature itself is so depraved, that it appears to be so without the concurrence of the will, the fault proceeds from sin, and thereby human nature may herself know what she is become by judgment. And let man, who wilfully committed the offense, bear the guilt of that offense. And, therefore, let women consider with themselves, and if they do not presume, during their monthly courses, to approach the sacrament of the body and blood of our Lord, they are to be commended for their praiseworthy consideration; but

when they are carried away with love of the same mystery to receive it out of the usual custom of religious life, they are not to be restrained, as we said before. For as in the Old Testament the outward works are observed, so in the New Testament, that which is outwardly done, is not so diligently regarded as that which is inwardly thought, in order to punish it by a discerning judgment. For whereas the law forbids the eating of many things as unclean, yet our Lord says in the Gospel, "Not that which goeth into the mouth defileth a man; but that which cometh out of the mouth, this defileth a man." And presently after he added, expounding the same, "Out of the heart proceedeth evil thoughts." Where it is sufficiently shown, that that is declared by Almighty God to be polluted in fact, which proceeds from the root of a polluted thought. Whence also Paul the apostle says, "Unto the pure all things are pure, but unto them that are defiled and unbelieving, nothing is pure." And presently after, declaring the cause of that defilement, he adds, "For even their mind and conscience is defiled." If, therefore, meat is not unclean to him who has a clean mind, why shall that which a clean woman suffers according to nature, be imputed to her as uncleanness? A man lying with his own wife is not to enter the church unless washed with water, nor is he to enter immediately although washed. The law prescribed to the ancient people, that a man who had had to do with a woman, should be washed with water, and not enter into the church before the setting of the sun. Which, nevertheless, may be understood spiritually, because a man has to do with a woman when the mind is led by the imagination to unlawful concupiscence; for unless the fire of concupiscence be first driven from his mind, he is not to think himself worthy of the congregation of the brethren, whilst he thus indulges an unlawful passion. For though several nations have different opinions concerning this affair, and seem to observe different rules, it was always the custom of the Romans from ancient times, after having to do with a man's own wife, to be cleansed by washing, and for some time respectfully to forbear entering the church. Nor do we, in so saying, assign matrimony to be a fault, but forasmuch as lawful intercourse with one's wife cannot be had without the pleasure of the flesh, it is proper to forbear entering the holy place, because the pleasure itself cannot be without a fault. For he was not born of adultery or fornication, but of lawful marriage, who said, "Behold I was conceived in iniquity, and in sin my mother brought me forth." For he who knew himself to have been conceived in iniquity, lamented that he was born from sin, because the tree in its bough bears the moisture it drew from the root. In which words, however, he does not call the copulation of the married couple iniquity, but the pleasure of the copulation. For there are many things which are proved to be lawful, and yet we are somewhat defiled in doing them. As very often by being angry we correct faults, and at the same time disturb our own peace of mind; and though that which we do is right, yet it is not to be approved that our mind should be discomposed. For he who said, "My eye was disturbed with anger," had been angry at the vices of those who had offended. Now, in regard that only a sedate mind can apply itself to contemplation, he grieved that his eye was disturbed with anger; because whilst he was correcting evil actions below, he was obliged to be withdrawn and disturbed from the contemplation of things above. Anger against vice is, therefore, commendable, and yet painful to a man, because he thinks that by his mind being agitated, he has incurred some guilt. The lawful carnal copulation must, therefore, be for the sake of children, not of pleasure; and fleshly commerce must be to procure offspring, not to satisfy vices. But if any man makes use of his wife, not led by the desire of pleasure, but only for the sake of getting children, such a man is certainly to be left to his own judgment, either as to entering the church, or as to receiving the mystery of the body and blood of our Lord, which he, who being placed in the fire cannot burn, is not to be forbidden by us to receive. But when, not the love of getting children, but pleasure prevails in the work of copulation, the pair have cause to lament their having to do with one another. For this the holy preaching allows them, and yet fills the mind with dread of the very allowance. For when Paul the apostle said, "Let him that cannot contain, have his wife;" he presently took care to subjoin, "But this I say by way of indulgence, not by way of command." For that is not granted by way of indulgence which is lawful, because it is just; and, therefore, that which he said he indulged, he showed to be an offense. It is seriously to be considered, that when God was to speak to the people on Mount Sinai, he first commanded them to abstain from women. And if so much cleanness of body was there required, where God spoke to the people by the means of a subject creature, that those who were to hear the words of God, should

not have had to do with women, how much more ought women, who receive the body of Almighty God, to preserve themselves in cleanness of flesh, lest they be burdened with the very greatness of that unutterable mystery? For this reason it was said to David, concerning his men, by the priest, that if they were clean from women, they should receive the shewbread, which they would not have received at all, had not David first declared them to be clean from women. Then the man, who, after having had to do with his wife, has been washed with water, is also capable of receiving the mystery of the holy communion, when it is lawful for him, according to what has been before declared, to enter the church.

Augustine's Ninth Question

Whether, after an illusion, such as happens in a dream, any man may receive the body of our Lord, or if he be a priest, celebrate the Divine mysteries?

Gregory Answers

The testament of the old law, as has been said already in the article above, calls such a man polluted, and allows him not to enter into the church till the evening after being washed with water. Which, nevertheless, spiritual people, taking in another sense, will understand in the same manner as above; because he is imposed upon as it were in a dream, who, being tempted with filthiness, is defiled by real representations in thought, and he is to be washed with water, that he may cleanse away the sins of thought with tears; and unless the fire of temptation depart before, may know himself to be guilty as it were until the evening. But discretion is very necessary in that illusion, that one may seriously consider what causes it to happen in the mind of the person sleeping; for sometimes it proceeds from excess of eating or drinking; sometimes from the superfluity or infirmity of nature, and sometimes from the thoughts. And when it happens, either through superfluity or infirmity of nature, such an illusion is not to be feared, because it is rather to be lamented, that the mind of the person, who knew nothing of it, suffers the same, than that he occasioned it. But when the appetite of gluttony commits excess in food, and thereupon the receptacles of the humors are oppressed, the mind from thence contracts some guilt; yet not so much as to obstruct the receiving of the holy mystery, or celebrating mass, when a holy-day requires it, or necessity obliges the sacrament to be administered, because there is no other priest in the place; for if there be others who can perform the ministry, the illusion proceeding from overeating is not to exclude a man from receiving the sacred mystery; but I am of opinion, he ought humbly to abstain from offering the sacrifice of the mystery; but not from receiving it, unless the mind of the person sleeping has been filled with some foul imagination. For there are some, who for the most part so suffer the illusion, that their mind, even during the sleep of the body, is not defiled with filthy thoughts. In which case, one thing is evident, that the mind is guilty even in its own judgment, for though it does not remember to have seen any thing whilst the body was sleeping, yet it calls to mind that when waking it fell into bodily gluttony. But if the sleeping illusion proceeds from evil thoughts when waking, then the guilt is manifest to the mind; for the man perceives from whence that filth sprung, because what he had knowingly thought of, that he afterward suffered unwittingly. But it is to be considered, whether that thought was no more than a suggestion, or proceeded to enjoyment, or, which is still more criminal, consented to sin. For all sin is fulfilled in three ways, viz. by suggestion, by delight, and by consent. Suggestion is occasioned by the devil, delight is from the flesh, and consent from the mind. For the serpent suggested the first offense, and Eve, as flesh, was delighted with it, but Adam consented, as the spirit, or mind. And much discretion is requisite for the mind to sit as judge between suggestion and delight, and between delight and consent. For if the evil spirit suggest a sin to the mind, if there ensue no delight in the sin, the sin is in no way committed; but when the flesh begins to be delighted, then sin begins to grow. But if it deliberately consents, then the sin is known to be perfected. The beginning, therefore, of sin is in the suggestion, the nourishing of it in delight, but in the consent is its perfection. And it often happens that what the evil spirit sows in thought, the flesh draws to delight, and yet the soul does not consent to that delight. And whereas the flesh cannot be delighted without the soul, yet the mind struggling against the pleasures of the flesh, is somewhat unwillingly tied down by the carnal delight, so that through reason it contradicts, and does not consent, yet being influenced by delight, it grievously laments its being so bound. Wherefore that principal soldier of our Lord's host, sighing, said, "I see another law in my members warring against the law of my mind, and bringing me into captivity to the law of sin, which is in my members." Now if he was a captive, he did not fight; but he did fight, therefore he was not a captive; he therefore fought by the law of the mind, which the law that is in the members opposed; if he fought so, he was no captive. Thus, then, man is, as I may say, a captive and yet free. Free on account of justice, which he loves, a captive by the delight which he unwillingly bears within him.[10]

Book II

Chapter I Of the Death of the Blessed Pope Gregory

At this time, that is, in the year of our Lord 605, the blessed Pope Gregory, after having most gloriously governed the Roman apostolic see thirteen years six months and ten days, died, and was translated to the eternal see of the heavenly kingdom. Of whom, in regard that he by his zeal converted our nation, the English, from the power of Satan to the faith of Christ, it behoves us to discourse more at large in our Ecclesiastical History, for we may and ought rightly to call him our apostle; because, whereas he bore the pontifical power over all the world, and was placed over the churches already reduced to the faith of truth, he made our nation, till then given up to idols, the church of Christ, so that we may be allowed thus to attribute to him the character of an apostle; for though he is not an apostle to others, yet he is so to us; for we are the seal of his apostleship in our Lord. He was by nation a Roman, son to Gordian, deducing his race from ancestors that were not only noble, but religious. And Felix, once bishop of the same apostolical see, a man of great honor in Christ and his church, was his great-grandfather. Nor did he exercise the nobility of religion with less virtue of devotion than his parents and kindred. But that worldly nobility which he seemed to have, by the help of the Divine grace, he entirely used to gain the honor of eternal dignity; for soon quitting his secular habit, he repaired to a monastery, wherein he began to behave himself with so much grace of perfection, that (as he was afterwards wont with tears to testify) his mind was above all transitory things; that he despised all that is subject to change; that he used to think of nothing but what was heavenly; that whilst detained by the body, he by contemplation broke through the bonds of the flesh; and that he loved death, which is a terror to almost all men, as the entrance into life, and the reward of his labors. This he said of himself, not to boast of his progress in virtue, but rather to bewail the decay which, as he was wont to declare, he imagined he sustained through the pastoral care. In short, when he was, one day, in private, discoursing with Peter, his deacon, after having enumerated the former virtues of his mind, he with grief added, "But now, on account of the pastoral care, it is entangled with the affairs of laymen, and after so beautiful an appearance of repose, is defiled with the dust of earthly action. And after having wasted itself by condescending to many, when it desires the inward things, it returns to them less qualified to enjoy them. I therefore consider what I endure, I consider what I have lost, and when I behold that loss, what I bear appears the more grievous." This the holy man said out of the excess of his humility. But it becomes us to believe that he lost nothing of his monastic perfection by his pastoral care, but rather that he improved the more through the labor of the conversion of many, than by the former repose of his conversation, and chiefly because, whilst exercising the pontifical function, he provided to have his house made a monastery. And when first drawn from the monastery, ordained to the ministry of the altar, and sent legate to Constantinople from the apostolic see, though he conversed with the people of the palace, yet he intermitted not his former heavenly life; for some of the brethren of his monastery, having out of brotherly charity followed him to the royal city, he kept them for the better following of regular observances, viz. that at all times by their example, as he writes himself, he might be held fast to the calm shore of prayer, as it were with the cable of an anchor, whilst he should be tossed up and down by the continual waves of worldly affairs; and daily among them, by the intercourse of studious reading, strengthen his mind whilst it was shaken with temporal concerns. By their company he was not only guarded against earthly assaults, but more and more inflamed in the exercises of a heavenly life. For they persuaded him to give a mystical exposition of the book of holy Job, which is involved in great obscurity; nor could he refuse to undertake that work, which brotherly affection imposed on him for the future benefit of many; but in a wonderful manner, by five-and-thirty books of exposition, taught how that same book is to be understood literally; how to be referred to the mysteries of Christ and the church; and in what sense it is to be adapted to every one of the faithful.[11] This work he began when legate in the royal city, but finished it at Rome after being made pope.[12] Whilst he was in the royal city, he, by the assistance of the Divine grace of Catholic truth, crushed in its first rise a heresy newly started, concerning the state of our resurrection. For Eutychius, bishop of that city, taught, that our body, in that glory of resurrection, would be impalpable, and more subtile than the wind and air; which he hearing, proved by force of truth, and by the instance of the resurrection of our Lord, that this doctrine was every way opposite to the Christian faith. For the Catholic faith is that our body, sublimed in the glory of immortality, is rendered subtile by the effect of the spiritual power, but palpable by the reality of nature; according to the example of our Lord's body, of which, when risen from the dead, he himself says to his disciples, "Handle me and see, for a spirit hath not flesh and bones, as ye see me have." In asserting which faith, the venerable Father Gregory so earnestly labored against the rising heresy, and by the assistance of the most pious emperor, Tiberius Constantine, so fully suppressed it, that none has been since found to revive it. He likewise composed another notable book, called "Liber Pastoralis," wherein he manifestly showed what sort of persons ought to be preferred to govern the church; how such rulers ought to live; with how much discretion to instruct every one of their hearers, and how seriously to reflect every day on their own frailty.[13] He also wrote forty homilies on the gospel, which he equally divided into two volumes;[14] and composed four books of dialogues, into which, at the request of Peter, his deacon, he collected the miracles of the saints whom he either knew, or had heard to be most renowned in Italy, for an example to posterity to lead their lives; to the end that, as in his books of expositions, what virtues ought to be labored for, so by describing the miracles of saints, he might make known the glory of those virtues.[15] He further, in twenty-two homilies, discovered how much light there is concealed in the first and last parts of the prophet Ezekiel, which seemed the most obscure. Besides which, he wrote the "Book of Answers," to the questions of Augustine, the first bishop of the English nation, as we have shown above, inserting the same book entire in his history; besides the useful little "Synodical Book," which he composed with the bishops of Italy on the necessary affairs of the church; and also familiar letters to certain persons. And it is the more wonderful that he could write so many and such large volumes, in regard that almost all the time of his youth, to use his own words, he was often tormented with pains in his bowels, and a weakness of his stomach, whilst he was continually suffering from slow fever. But whereas at the same time he carefully reflected that, as the Scripture testifies, "Every son that is received is scourged," the more he labored and was depressed under those present evils, the more he assured himself of his eternal salvation. Thus much is said of his immortal genius, which could not be restrained by such severe bodily pains; for other popes applied themselves to building, or adorning of churches with gold and silver, but Gregory was entirely intent upon gaining souls. Whatsoever money he had, he diligently took care to distribute and give to the poor, that "his righteousness might endure for ever, and his horn be exalted with honor;" so that what blessed Job said might be truly said of him, "When the ear heard me, then it blessed me; and when the eye saw me, it gave witness to me: because I delivered the poor that cried, and the fatherless, and him that had none to help him. The blessing of him that was ready to perish came upon me, and I caused the widow's heart to sing for joy. I put on righteousness, and it clothed me; my judgment was as a robe and a diadem. I was the eye to the blind, and feet was I to the lame. I was father to the poor; and the cause which I knew not, I searched out. And I brake the jaws of the wicked, and plucked the spoil out of his teeth." And a little after: "If I have withheld," says he, "the poor from their desire; or have caused the eye of the widow to fail; or have eaten my morsel myself alone, and the fatherless hath not eaten thereof. For of my youth compassion grew up with me, and from my mother's womb it came forth with me." To the works of his piety and righteousness this also appertains, that he withdrew our nation, by the preachers he sent hither, from the teeth of the old enemy, and made it partaker of eternal liberty; in whose faith and salvation rejoicing, and worthily commending the same, he in his exposition on holy Job, says, "Behold, a tongue of Britain, which only knew how to utter barbarous language, has long since begun to resound the Hebrew Hallelujah! Behold, the once swelling ocean now serves prostrate

at the feet of the saints; and its barbarous motions, which earthly princes could not subdue with the sword, are now, through the fear of God, bound by the mouths of priests with words only; and he that stood not in awe of the fighting troops of the infidels, now fears the faithful tongues of the humble! For by reason that the virtue of the Divine knowledge is infused into it by precepts, heavenly words, and conspicuous miracles, it is curbed by the dread of the same Divinity, so as to fear to act wickedly, and bends all its desires to arrive at eternal glory." In which words holy Gregory declares this also, that St. Augustine and his companions brought the English to receive the truth, not only by the preaching of words, but also by showing of heavenly signs. The holy Pope Gregory, among other things, caused masses to be celebrated in the churches of the apostles, Peter and Paul, over their bodies. And in the celebration of masses, he added three words full of great goodness and perfection: "And dispose our days in thy peace, and preserve us from eternal damnation, and rank us in the number of thy elect, through Christ our Lord."

He governed the church in the days of the emperors Mauritius and Phocas, but passing out of this life in the second year of the same Phocas, he departed to the true life which is in heaven. His body was buried in the church of St. Peter the Apostle, before the sacristy, on the 4th day of the Ides of March, to rise one day in the same body in glory with the rest of the holy pastors of the church. On his tomb was written this epitaph:

Suscipe, terra, tuo corpus de corpore sumptum,
   Reddere quod valeas, vivificante Deo.
Spiritus astra petit, lethi nil jura nocebunt,
   Cui vitae alterius mors magis ipsa via est.
Pontificis summi hoc clauduntur membra sepulchro,
   Qui innumeris semper vivit ubique bonis.
Esuriem dapibus superavit, frigora veste,
   Atque animas monitis texit ab hoste sacris.
Implebatque actu, quicquid sermone docebat,
   Esset ut exemplum, mystica verba loquens.
Ad Christum Anglos convertit pietate magistra,
   Acquirens fidei agmina gente nova.
Hic labor, hoc studium, haec tibi cura, hoc pastor agebas,
   Ut Domino offerres plurima lucra gregis.
Hisque Dei Consul factus, laetare triumphis,
   Nam mercedem operum jam sine fine tenes.

In English, thus:

Earth! take that body which at first you gave,
Till God again shall raise it from the grave.
His soul amidst the stars finds heavenly day:
In vain the gates of night can make essay
On him whose death but leads to life the way.
To this dark tomb, this prelate, though decreed,
Lives in all places by his pious deed.
Before his bounteous board pale Hunger fled;
To warm the poor he fleecy garments spread;
And to secure their souls from Satan's power,
He taught by sacred precepts every hour.
Nor only taught; but first th' example led,
Liv'd o'er his rules, and acted what he said.
To English Saxons Christian truth he taught,
And a believing flock to heaven he brought.
This was thy work and study, this thy care,
Offerings to thy Redeemer to prepare.
For these to heavenly honors raised on high,
Where thy reward of labors ne'er shall die.

Nor is the account of St. Gregory, which has been handed down to us by the tradition of our ancestors, to be passed by in silence, in relation to his motives for taking such care of the salvation of our nation. It is reported, that some merchants having just arrived at Rome on a certain day, many things were to be sold in the marketplace, and abundance of people resorted thither to buy: Gregory himself went with the rest, and, among other things, some boys were set to sale, their bodies white, their countenances beautiful, and their hair very fine. Having viewed them, he asked, as is said, from what country or nation they were brought? and was told, from the Island of Britain, whose inhabitants were of such personable appearance. He again inquired, whether those islanders were Christians, or still involved in the errors of Paganism? and was informed that they were Pagans. Then fetching a deep sigh from the bottom of his heart, "Alas! what pity," said he, " that the author of darkness is possessed of men of such fair countenances; and that being remarkable for such graceful aspects, their minds should be void of inward grace." He therefore again asked, what was the name of that nation? and was answered, that they were called Angles. "Right," said he, "for they have an angelic face, and it becomes such to be coheirs with the angels in heaven. What is the name," proceeded he,

"of the province from which they are brought?" It was replied, that the natives of that province were called Deiri. "Truly are they *De iri*," said he, "withdrawn from wrath, and called to the mercy of Christ. How is the king of that province called?" They told him his name was Ælla; and he, alluding to the name, said, "Allelujah, the praise of God the Creator must be sung in those parts." Then repairing to the bishop of the Roman apostolical see (for he was not himself then made pope), he entreated him to send some ministers of the word into Britain to the nation of the English, by whom it might be converted to Christ; declaring himself ready to undertake that work, by the assistance of God, if the apostolic pope should think fit to have it so done. Which not being then able to perform, because, though the pope was willing to grant his request, yet the citizens of Rome could not be brought to consent that so noble, so renowned, and so learned a man should depart the city; as soon as he was himself made pope, he perfected the long-desired work, sending other preachers, but himself by his prayers and exhortations assisting the preaching, that it might be successful. This account, as we have received it from the ancients, we have thought fit to insert in our Ecclesiastical History.

Book III

Chapter III   The Same King Oswald, Asking a Bishop of the Scottish Nation, Had Aidan Sent Him, and Granted Him an Episcopal See in the Isle of Lindisfarn

The same Oswald, as soon as he ascended the throne, being desirous that all his nation should receive the Christian faith, whereof he had found happy experience in vanquishing the barbarians, sent to the elders of the Scots, among whom himself and his followers, when in banishment, had received the sacrament of baptism, desiring they would send him a bishop, by whose instruction and ministry the English nation, which he governed, might be taught the advantages, and receive the sacraments of the Christian faith. Nor were they slow in granting his request; but sent him Bishop Aidan,[16] a man of singular meekness, piety, and moderation; zealous in the cause of God, though not altogether according to knowledge; for he was wont

Figure 17 *Opening of the Gospel of St. Mark from the Lindis-farne Gospels (A.D. 721). The text, which is deliberately obscure, reads:* Initium Euangelii Iesu Christi Filii Dei Sicut Scriptum Est In Esaia Propheta. *The interlinear gloss is in Old English.*

he desired. Which place, as the tide flows and ebbs twice a day, is enclosed by the waves of the sea like an island; and again, twice in the day, when the shore is left dry, becomes contiguous to the land. The king also humbly and willingly in all cases giving ear to his admonitions, industriously applied himself to build and extend the church of Christ in his kingdom; wherein, when the bishop, who was not skilful in the English tongue, preached the gospel, it was most delightful to see the king himself interpreting the word of God to his commanders and ministers, for he had perfectly learned the language of the Scots during his long banishment. From that time many of the Scots came daily into Britain, and with great devotion preached the word to those provinces of the English, over which King Oswald reigned, and those among them that had received priest's orders, administered to them the grace of baptism. Churches were built in several places; the people joyfully flocked together to hear the word; money and lands were given of the king's bounty to build monasteries; the English, great and small, were, by their Scottish masters, instructed in the rules and observance of regular discipline; for most of them that came to preach were monks. Bishop Aidan was him-self a monk of the island called Hii, whose monastery was for a long time the chief of almost all those of the northern Scots, and all those of the Picts, and had the direction of their people. That island belongs to Britain, being divided from it by a small arm of the sea, but had been long since given by the Picts, who inhabit those parts of Britain, to the Scottish monks, because they had received the faith of Christ through their preaching.

Book IV

Chapter XXIII   Of the Life and Death of the Abbess Hilda

In the year of the incarnation of our Lord 680, the most religious servant of Christ, Hilda, abbess of the monas-tery that is called Streaneshalh, as above-mentioned, after having performed many heavenly works on earth, passed from thence to receive the rewards of the heavenly life, on the 15th day of the kalends of December, at the age of sixty-six years; the first thirty-three of which she spent living most nobly in the secular habit; and more nobly dedicated the remaining

to keep Easter Sunday according to the custom of his country, which we have before so often mentioned, from the fourteenth to the twentieth moon; the northern province of the Scots, and all the nation of the Picts, celebrating Easter then after that manner, and believing that they therein followed the writings of the holy and praiseworthy Father Anatolius; the truth of which every skilful person can discern. But the Scots which dwelt in the south of Ireland had long since, by the admonition of the bishop of the apostolic see, learned to observe Easter according to the canonical custom. On the arrival of the bishop, the king appointed him his episcopal see in the isle of Lindisfarn, as half to our Lord in a monastic life. For she was nobly born, being the daughter of Hereric, nephew to King Edwin, with which king she also embraced the faith and mysteries of Christ, at the preaching of Paulinus, the first bishop of the Northumbrians, of blessed memory, and preserved the same undefiled till she obtained the full enjoyment thereof in heaven. Resolving to quit the secular habit, and to serve him alone, she withdrew into the province of the East Angles, for she was allied to the king; being desirous to pass over from thence into France, to forsake her native country and all she had, and so live a stranger for our Lord in the monastery of Cale, that she might with more ease attain to the eternal kingdom in heaven; because her sister Heresuit, mother to Aldulf, king of the East Angles, at that time living in the same monastery, under regular discipline, was waiting for her eternal reward. Being led by her example, she continued a whole year in the aforesaid province, with the design of going abroad; afterwards, Bishop Aidan being recalled home, he gave her the land of one family on the north side of the river Wire; where she also led a monastic life a year, with very few companions. After which she was made abbess in the monastery called Heortheu, which monastery had been founded, not long before, by the religious servant of Christ, Heru, who is said to have been the first woman that in the province of the Northumbrians took upon her the habit and life of a nun, being consecrated by Bishop Aidan; but she, soon after she had founded that monastery, went away to the city of Kalcaceaster, and there fixed her dwelling. Hilda, the servant of Christ, being set over that monastery, began immediately to reduce all things to a regular system, according as she had been instructed by learned men; for Bishop Aidan, and other religious men that knew her and loved her, frequently visited and diligently instructed her, because of her innate wisdom and inclination to the service of God. When she had for some years governed this monastery, wholly intent upon establishing a regular life, it happened that she also undertook either to build or to arrange a monastery in the place called Streaneshalh, which work she industriously performed; for she put this monastery under the same regular discipline as she had done the former; and taught there the strict observance of justice, piety, chastity, and other virtues, and particularly of peace and charity; so that, after the example of the primitive church, no person was there rich, and none poor, all

being in common to all, and none having any property. Her prudence was so great, that not only indifferent persons, but even kings and princes, as occasion offered, asked and received her advice; she obliged those who were under her direction to attend so much to reading of the holy scriptures, and to exercise themselves so much in works of justice, that many might be there found fit for the ecclesiastical degree, that is, to serve at the altar: in short, we afterwards saw five bishops taken out of that monastery, and all of them men of singular merit and sanctity, whose names were Bosa, Aetla, Oftfor, John, and Wilfrid. We have above taken notice, that the first of them was consecrated bishop at York; of the second, it is to be observed that he was appointed Bishop of Dorchester. Of the two last we shall speak hereafter, as they were consecrated: the first was Bishop of Hagulstad, the second of the church of York; of the third we will here take notice, that having applied himself to the reading and observation of the scriptures, in both the monasteries of Hilda, at length being desirous to attain to greater perfection, he went into Kent, to Archbishop Theodore, of blessed memory; where, having spent some more time in sacred studies, he also resolved to go to Rome, which, in those days, was reckoned of great moment: returning thence into Britain, he took his way into the province of Wiccii, where King Osric then ruled, and continued there a long time, preaching the word of faith, and making himself an example of good life to all that saw and heard him. At that time, Bosel, the bishop of that province, labored under such weakness of body, that he could not himself perform the episcopal functions; for which reason, this Oftfor was, by universal consent, chosen bishop in his stead, and by order of King Ethelred, consecrated by Bishop Wilfrid, of blessed memory, who was then bishop of the Midland Angles, because Archbishop Theodore was dead, and no other bishop ordained in his place. Before the aforesaid man of God, Bosel, Tatfrith, a most learned and industrious man, and of excellent ability, had been chosen bishop there, from the same abbess's monastery, but had been snatched away by an untimely death, before he could be ordained. Thus this servant of Christ, Abbess Hilda, whom all that knew her called mother, for her singular piety and grace, was not only an example of good life to those that lived in her monastery, but afforded occasion of amendment and salvation to many who lived at a distance, to whom the fame was brought of her industry and virtue; for it was necessary that the dream which her mother, Bregusuit, had, during her infancy, should be fulfilled. At the time that her husband, Hereric, lived in banishment, under Cerdic, king of the Britons, where he was also poisoned, she fancied, in a dream, that she was seeking for him, most carefully, and could find no sign of him any where; but, after having used all her industry to seek him, she found a most precious jewel under her garment, which, whilst she was looking on it very attentively, cast such a light as spread itself throughout all Britain; which dream was brought to pass in her daughter that we speak of, whose life was a bright example, not only to herself, but to all who desired to live well. When she had governed this monastery many years, it pleased Him who has made such merciful provision for our salvation, to give her holy soul the trial of a long sickness, to the end that, according to the apostle's example, her virtue might be perfected in infirmity. Falling into a fever, she fell into a violent heat, and was afflicted with the same for six years continually; during all which time she never failed either to return thanks to her Maker, or publicly and privately to instruct the flock committed to her charge; for by her own example she admonished all persons to serve God dutifully in perfect health, and always to return thanks to him in adversity, or bodily infirmity. In the seventh year of her sickness, the distemper turning inwards, she approached her last day, and about cock-crowing, having received the holy communion to further her on her way, and called together the servants of Christ that were within the same monastery, she admonished them to preserve evangelical peace among themselves, and with all others; and as she was making her speech, she joyfully saw death approaching, or if I may speak in the words of our Lord, passed from death to life. That same night it pleased Almighty God, by a manifest vision, to make known her death in another monastery, at a distance from hers, which she had built that same year, and is called Hakenes. There was in that monastery a certain nun called Begu, who, having dedicated her virginity to God, had served him upwards of thirty years in monastical conversation. This nun being then in the dormitory of the sisters, on a sudden heard the well-known sound of a bell in the air, which used to awake

and call them to prayers, when any one of them was taken out of this world, and opening her eyes, as she thought, she saw the top of the house open, and a strong light pour in from above; looking earnestly upon that light, she saw the soul of the aforesaid servant of God in that same light, attended and conducted to heaven by angels. Then awaking, and seeing the other sisters lying round about her, she perceived that what she had seen was either in a dream or a vision; and rising immediately in a great fright, she ran to the virgin who then presided in the monastery instead of the abbess, and whose name was Frigyth, and with many tears and sighs, told her that the Abbess Hilda, mother of them all, had departed this life, and had in her sight ascended to eternal bliss, and to the company of the inhabitants of heaven, with a great light, and with angels conducting her. Frigyth having heard it, awoke all the sisters, and calling them to the church, admonished them to pray and sing psalms for her soul; which they did during the remainder of the night; and at break of day, the brothers came with news of her death, from the place where she had died. They answered that they knew it before, and then related how and when they had heard it, by which it appeared that her death had been revealed to them in a vision the very same hour that the others said she had died. Thus it was by heaven happily ordained, that when some saw her departure out of this world, the others should be acquainted with her admittance into the spiritual life which is eternal. These monasteries are about thirteen miles distant from each other. It is also reported, that her death was, in a vision, made known to one of the holy virgins who loved her most passionately, in the same monastery where the said servant of God died. This nun saw her soul ascend to heaven in the company of angels; and this she declared, the very same hour that it happened, to those servants of Christ that were with her; and awakened them to pray for her soul, even before the rest of the congregation had heard of her death. The truth of which was known to the whole monastery in the morning. This same nun was at that time with some other servant of Christ, in the remotest part of the monastery, where the women newly converted were wont to be upon trial, till they were regularly instructed, and taken into the society of the congregation.

Chapter XXIV There Was in the Said Abbess's Monastery a Brother, on Whom the Gift of Writing Verses Was Bestowed by Heaven

There was in this abbess's monastery a certain brother, particularly remarkable for the grace of God, who was wont to make pious and religious verses, so that whatever was interpreted to him out of scripture, he soon after put the same into poetical expressions of much sweetness and humility, in English, which was his native language. By his verses the minds of many were often excited to despise the world, and to aspire to heaven. Others after him attempted, in the English nation, to compose religious poems, but none could ever compare with him, for he did not learn the art of poetry from men, but from God; for which reason he never could compose any trivial or vain poem, but only those which relate to religion suited his religious tongue; for having lived in a secular habit till he was well advanced in years, he had never learned any thing of versifying; for which reason being sometimes at entertainments, when it was agreed for the sake of mirth that all present should sing in their turns, when he saw the instrument come towards him, he rose up from table and returned home. Having done so at a certain time, and gone out of the house where the entertainment was, to the stable, where he had to take care of the horses that night, he there composed himself to rest at the proper time; a person appeared to him in his sleep, and saluting him by his name, said, "Cedmon, sing some song to me." He answered, "I cannot sing; for that was the reason why I left the entertainment, and retired to this place, because I could not sing." The other who talked to him, replied, "However you shall sing." "What shall I sing?" rejoined he. "Sing the beginning of created beings," said the other. Hereupon he presently began to sing verses to the praise of God, which he had never heard, the purport whereof was thus: We are now to praise the Maker of the heavenly kingdom, the power of the Creator and his counsel, the deeds of the Father of glory. How he, being the eternal God, became the author of all miracles, who first, as almighty preserver of the human race, created heaven for the sons of men as the roof of the house, and next the earth.[17] This is the sense, but not the words in order as he sang them in his sleep; for verses, though never so well composed, cannot be literally translated out of one language into another, without losing much of their beauty and loftiness. Awaking from his sleep, he remembered all that he had sung in his dream, and soon added much more to the same effect in verse worthy of the Deity. In the morning he came to the steward, his superior; he acquainted him with the gift he had received; and being conducted to the abbess, he was ordered, in the presence of many learned men, to tell his dream, and repeat the verses, that they might give all their judgment what it was, and whence his verse proceeded. They all concluded, that heavenly grace had been conferred on him by our Lord. They expounded to him a passage in holy writ, either historical, or doctrinal, ordering him, if he could, to put the same into verse. Having undertaken it, he went away, and returning the next morning, gave it to them composed in most excellent verse; whereupon the abbess, embracing the grace of God in the man, instructed him to quit the secular habit, and take upon him the monastic life; which being accordingly done, she associated him to the rest of the brethren in her monastery, and ordered that he should be taught the whole series of sacred history. Thus Cedmon, keeping in mind all he heard, and as it were chewing the cud, converted the same into most harmonious verse; and sweetly repeating the same, made his masters in their turn his hearers. He sang the creation of the world, the origin of man, and all the history of Genesis; and made many verses on the departure of the children of Israel out of Egypt, and their entering into the land of promise, with many other histories from holy writ; the incarnation, passion, resurrection of our Lord, and his ascension into heaven; the coming of the Holy Ghost, and the preaching of the apostles; also the terror of future judgment, the horror of the pains of hell, and the delights of heaven; besides many more about the Divine benefits and judgments, by which he endeavored to turn away all men from the love of vice, and to excite in them the love of, and application to, good actions; for he was a very religious man, and humbly submissive to regular discipline, but full of zeal against those who behaved themselves otherwise; for which reason he ended his life happily. For when the time of his departure drew near, he labored for the space of fourteen days under a bodily infirmity which seemed to prepare the way, yet so moderate that he could talk and walk the whole time. In his neighborhood was the house to which those that were sick, and like shortly to die, were carried. He desired the person that attended him, in the evening, as the night came on in which he was to depart this life, to make ready a place there for him to take his rest. This person, wondering why he should desire it, because there was as yet no sign of his dying soon, did what he had ordered. He accordingly went there, and conversing pleasantly in a joyful manner with the rest that were in the house before, when it was past midnight, he asked them, whether they had the Eucharist there? They answered, "What need of the Eucharist? for you are not likely to die, since you talk so merrily with us, as if you were in perfect health." "However," said he, "bring me the Eucharist." Having received the same into his hand, he asked, whether they were all in charity with him, and without any enmity or rancor? They answered, that they were all in perfect charity, and free from anger; and in their turn asked him, whether he was in the same mind toward them? He answered, "I am in charity, my children, with all the servants of God." Then strengthening himself with the heavenly viaticum, he prepared for the entrance into another life, and asked, how near the time was when the brothers were to be awakened to sing the nocturnal praises of our Lord? They answered, "It is not far off." Then he said, "Well, let us wait that hour;" and signing himself with the sign of the cross, he laid his head on the pillow, and falling into a slumber, ended his life so in silence. Thus it came to pass, that as he had served God with a simple and pure mind, and undisturbed devotion, so he now departed to his presence, leaving the world by a quiet death; and that tongue, which had composed so many holy words in praise of the Creator, uttered its last words whilst he was in the act of signing himself with the cross, and recommending himself into his hands, and by what has been here said, he seems to have had foreknowledge of his death.

Conclusion

Thus much of the Ecclesiastical History of the Britons, and more especially of the English nation, as far as I could learn either from the writings of the ancients, or the tradition of our ancestors, or of my own knowledge, has, with the help of God, been digested by me, Bede, the servant of God, and priest of the monastery of the blessed apostles, Peter and Paul, which is at Wiremuth and Gyrwum; who being born in the territory of that same monastery, was given, at seven years of age, to be educated by the most reverend Abbot Benedict, and afterward by Ceolfrid; and spending all the remaining time of my life in that monastery, I wholly applied myself to the study of Scripture, and amidst the observance of regular discipline, and the daily care of singing in the church, I always took delight in learning, teaching, and writing. In the nineteenth year of my age, I received deacon's orders; in the thirtieth, those of the priesthood, both of them by the ministry of the most reverend Bishop John, and by order of the Abbot Ceolfrid. From which time, till the fifty-ninth year of my age, I have made it my business, for the use of me and mine, to compile out of the works of the venerable Fathers, and to interpret and explain according to their meaning these following pieces:

On the Beginning of Genesis, to the Birth of Isaac, the Election of Israel, and the Reprobation of Ismael, three books.

Of the Tabernacle and its Vessels, and of the Priestly Vestments, three books.

On the first Part of Samuel, to the Death of Saul, four books.

Of the Building of the Temple, of Allegorical Exposition, like the rest, two books.

Item, on Kings, a Book of thirty Questions.

On Solomon's Proverbs, three books.

On the Canticles, six books.

On Isaiah, Daniel, the twelve Prophets, and Part of Jeremy, Distinctions of Chapters, collected out of St. Jerom's Treatise.

On Esdras and Nehemiah, three books.

On the Song of Habacuc, one book.

On the Book of the blessed Father Tobias, one Book of Allegorical Exposition concerning Christ and the Church.

Also, Chapters of Readings on Moses's Pentateuch, Joshua, and Judges.

On the Books of Kings and Chronicles.

On the Book of the blessed Father Job.

On the Parables, Ecclesiastes, and Canticles.

On the Prophets Isaiah, Esdras, and Nehemiah.

On the Gospel of Mark, four books.

On the Gospel of Luke, six books.

Of Homilies on the Gospel, two books.

On the Apostle, I have carefully transcribed in order all that I have found in St. Augustine's Works.

On the Acts of the Apostles, two books.

On the seven Catholic Epistles, a book on each.

On the Revelation of St. John, three books.

Also, Chapters of Readings on all the New Testament, except the Gospel.

Also a book of Epistles to different Persons, of which one is of the Six Ages of the World; one of the Mansions of the Children of Israel; one on the Words of Isaiah, "And they shall be shut up in the prison, and after many days shall they be visited;" one of the Reason of the Bissextile, or Leap Year, and of the Equinox, according to Anatolius.

Also, of the Histories of Saints. I translated the Book of the Life and Passion of St. Felix, Confessor, from Paulinus's Work in metre, into prose.

The Book of the Life and Passion of St. Anastasius, which was ill translated from the Greek, and worse amended by some unskillful person, I have corrected as to the sense.

I have written the Life of the Holy Father Cuthbert, who was both monk and prelate, first in heroic verse, and then in prose.

The History of the Abbots of this Monastery, in which I rejoice to serve the Divine Goodness, viz. Benedict, Ceolfrid, and Huetberht, in two books.

The Ecclesiastical History of our Island and Nation, in five books.

The Martyrology of the Birth-Days of the Holy Martyrs, in which I have carefully endeavored to set down all that I could find, and not only on what day, but also by what sort of combat, or under what prince they overcame the world.

A Book of Hymns in several sorts of metre, or rhyme.

A Book of Epigrams in heroic or elegiac verse.

Of the Nature of Things, and of the Times, one book of each.

Also, of the Times, one larger book.

A Book of Orthography digested in Alphabetical Order.

Also a Book of the Art of Poetry, and to it I have added another little Book of Tropes and Figures; that is, of the Figures and Manners of Speaking in which the Holy Scriptures are written.

And now I beseech thee, good Jesus, that to whom thou hast graciously granted sweetly to partake of the words of thy wisdom and knowledge, thou wilt also vouchsafe that he may some time or other come to thee the fountain of all wisdom, and always appear before thy face. Amen.

Notes

1   The translation is by J. A. Giles, E. Lumley, London, 1840.

2   For an account of Theodore of Tarsus and his work in England, see F. M. Stenton, *Anglo-Saxon England*, Clarendon Press, Oxford, 1947, chap. V. Theodore is best known for his influence in transferring certain features of the Irish penitential system to the Western Church.

3   Now usually spelled Hadrian.

4   Richborough.

5   Boulogne.

6   Dumbarton.

7   A.D. 596.

8   St. Augustine (not to be confused with the Bishop of Hippo) arrived in A.D. 597. After his conversion Ethelbert founded St. Paul's Cathedral in London. He also issued the earliest set of laws in any Germanic language.

9   The following questions and answers give us an unusual glimpse of the problems confronting early missionaries in Britain.

10   The idea that all sin involves three steps—suggestion, delight, and consent—which are related respectively to the activities of the serpent, Eve, and Adam as they are described in Genesis—became a commonplace of medieval thought. It appears, for example, in Chaucer's Parson's Tale.

11   That is, in the language of the later scholastics, literally, allegorically, and tropologically. The allegorical meaning of a biblical text is that which shows its application to "the mysteries of Christ and

the Church," and its tropological meaning shows "in what sense it is to be adapted to every one of the faithful." The logic of this process is clear: Gregory wished to show first the specifically Christian significance of the Old Testament passage and then its relevance to the life of the individual Christian. If the first step were omitted, the Old Testament would remain simply a Hebrew (not a Christian) document, and if the second step were omitted, it would have no relevance to the life of the individual Christian reader. Gregory's method became a model for spiritual interpretation during the later Middle Ages.

12   The work in question is the celebrated *Moralia* on the Book of Job, which was often copied in medieval scriptoria. It is a rich source for biblical symbolism as well as being a work remarkable for genuine and uncomplicated devotion. It was among the favorite books of John of Salisbury.

13   The *Pastoral Care*, which was translated into English by King Alfred, became a standard manual on the conduct of the priesthood.

14   Gregory's homilies on the Gospels as well as those on Ezechiel circulated widely in the early Middle Ages.

15   The narratives of the *Dialogues* contributed to the growing medieval taste for legends of the saints.

16   For an account of Aidan and some of his contemporaries, see Eleanor Duckett, *The Wandering Saints of the Early Middle Ages*, W. W. Norton & Company, Inc., New York, 1959, chap. VI.

17   A careful and sympathetic account of this poem appears in B. F. Huppé, *Doctrine and Poetry*, State University of New York Press, New York, 1959, chap. IV.

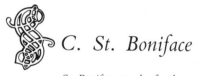 C. *St. Boniface*

St. Boniface was by far the most important English missionary to the Continent during the eighth century. He reorganized the Frankish Church, spread English learning to the Continent, and paved the way for the Carolingian Renaissance. His correspondence forms an extremely important source of historical information about the period.

For a brief account of St. Boniface and other English missionaries, see F. M. Stenton, Anglo-Saxon England, *second edition, Clarendon Press, Oxford, 1947. A good introduction appears in Eleanor S. Duckett,* Anglo-Saxon Saints and Scholars, *The Macmillan Company, New York, 1947. For collections of the letters in English, see E. Emerton,* The Letters of Saint Boniface, *Columbia University Press, New York, 1940; and C. H. Talbot,* The Anglo-Saxon Missionaries in Germany, *Sheed & Ward, Inc., New York, 1954. These selections are from the latter collection.*

BONIFACE ADVISES NITHARD TO CONTINUE HIS STUDIES
[A.D. 716–719]

To my dear friend and companion, who was drawn to me not by gifts of perishable gold nor by the smooth tongue of flattery but by the similarity of our ideals and the bonds of unfailing love, Wynfrith, a suppliant, sends greetings for eternal welfare in Jesus Christ.

Lowly as I am, noble youth, I beg you not to disregard the words of Solomon the wise: "In all thy works remember thy last end and thou shalt never sin." Walk whilst you have the light lest the darkness of death come upon you. Temporal things pass swiftly away, but the eternal that never fade will soon be upon us. All the treasures of this world, such as gold, silver, precious stones of every hue, succulent and dainty food and costly garments, melt away like shadows, vanish like smoke, dissolve like foam on the sea. The psalmist uttered the truth when he said: "Man's days are like grass: like the flower of the field he flourishes." And again: "My days are like a shadow that declineth and I am withered like grass."

Men who wallow in luxury are said in Holy Scripture to pass sleepless nights through anxiety, spinning their fragile webs that catch only dust or a breath of wind, for as the psalmist says: "They gather together treasure and know not for whom they gather it." And at the moment when death, the minion of baneful Pluto, barks at the door, foaming at the mouth and gnashing his teeth, they faint with fear; then, deprived of heavenly consolation, they lose in an instant both their precious souls and the deceitful gains for which they have slaved like misers night and day. Finally, they are snatched by the claws of fiends and borne off to the gloomy caverns of Erebus, there to suffer everlasting torments.

There is no doubting the truth of this. In all earnestness and affection I beg you to consider this matter very carefully. Give rein to your natural gifts and abilities; do not stifle your literary talents and your keen spiritual understanding with gross pleasures of the flesh. Keep in mind the words of the psalmist: "His delight is in the words of the law of the Lord; in his law he meditates day and night": and elsewhere: "O how I love thy law, it is my meditation all the day." Call to mind also the words of Moses: "This book of the law shall not depart out of thy mouth, but thou shalt meditate therein day and night." Put aside all harmful obstacles; strive with unflagging zest to pursue your study of the scriptures and thereby acquire that nobility of mind which is divine wisdom. It is more precious than gold, more beautiful than silver, more lustrous than onyx, clearer than crystal, more costly than topaz,[1] and, according to the opinion of the Preacher, all things that may be desired are not to be compared with it.[2]

Can there be a more fitting pursuit in youth or a more valuable possession in old age than a knowledge of Holy Writ? In the midst of storms it will preserve you from the dangers of shipwreck and guide you to the shore of an enchanting paradise and the everlasting bliss of the angels. Of it the same wise man has remarked: "Wisdom overcometh evil: it stretches from end to end mightily and disposes all things sweetly. Her have I loved from my youth and have become enamored of her form."[3]

If God allows me to return home, for such is my intention, I promise to remain steadfast at your side, helping you in your study of Sacred Scripture to the best of my ability.

BISHOP DANIEL OF WINCHESTER ADVISES BONIFACE ON THE METHOD OF CONVERTING THE HEATHEN
[A.D. 723–724]

To Boniface, honored and beloved leader, Daniel, servant of the people of God.

Great is my joy, brother and colleague in the episcopate, that your good work has received its reward. Supported by your deep faith and great courage, you have embarked upon the conversion of heathens whose hearts have hitherto been stony and barren; and with the Gospel as your ploughshare you have labored tirelessly day after day to transform them into harvest-bearing fields. Well may the words of the prophet be applied to you: "A voice of one crying in the wilderness, etc."

Yet not less deserving of reward are they who give what help they can to such a good and deserving work by relieving the poverty of the laborers, so that they may pursue unhampered the task of preaching and begetting children to Christ. And so, moved by affection and good will, I am taking the liberty of making a few suggestions, in order to show you how, in my opinion, you may overcome with the least possible trouble the resistance of this barbarous people.

Do not begin by arguing with them about the genealogies of their false gods. Accept their statement that they were begotten by other gods through the intercourse of male and female and then you will be able to prove that, as these gods and goddesses did not exist before, and were born like men, they must be men and not gods. When they have been forced to admit that their gods had a beginning, since they were begotten by others, they should be asked whether the world had a beginning or was always in existence. There is no doubt that before the universe was created there was no place in which these created gods could have subsisted or dwelt. And by "universe" I mean not merely heaven and earth which we see with our eyes but the whole extent of space which even the heathens can grasp in their imagination. If they maintain that the universe had no beginning, try to refute their arguments and bring forward convincing proofs; and if they persist in arguing, ask them, Who ruled it? How did the gods bring under their sway a universe that existed before them? Whence or by whom or when was the first god or goddess begotten? Do they believe that gods and goddesses still beget other gods and goddesses? If they do not, when did they cease and why? If they do, the number of gods must be infinite. In such a case, who is the most powerful among these different gods? Surely no mortal man can know. Yet man must take care not to offend this god who is more powerful than the rest. Do they think the gods should be worshipped for the sake of temporal and transitory benefits or for eternal and future reward? If for temporal benefit let them say in what respect the heathens are better off than the Christians. What do the heathen gods gain from the sacrifices if they already possess everything? Or why do the gods leave it to the whim of their subjects to decide what kind of tribute shall be paid? If they need such sacrifices, why do they not choose more suitable ones? If they do not need them, then the people are wrong in thinking that they can placate the gods with such offerings and victims.

These and similar questions, and many others that it would be tedious to mention, should be put to them, not in an offensive and irritating way but calmly and with great moderation. From time to time their superstitions should be compared with our Christian dogmas and touched upon indirectly, so that the heathens, more out of confusion than exasperation, may be ashamed of their absurd opinions and may recognize that their disgusting rites and legends have not escaped our notice.

This conclusion also must be drawn: If the gods are omnipotent, beneficent and just, they must reward their devotees and punish those who despise them. Why then, if they act thus in temporal affairs, do they spare the Christians who cast down their idols and turn away from their worship the inhabitants of practically the entire globe? And whilst the Christians are allowed to possess the countries that are rich in oil and wine and other commodities, why have they left to the heathens the frozen lands of the north, where the gods, banished from the rest of the world, are falsely supposed to dwell?

The heathens are frequently to be reminded of the supremacy of the Christian world and of the fact that they who still cling to outworn beliefs are in a very small minority.

If they boast that the gods have held undisputed sway over these people from the beginning, point out to them that formerly the whole world was given over to the worship of idols until, by the grace of Christ and through the knowledge of one God, its Almighty Creator and Ruler, it was enlightened, vivified and reconciled to God. For what does the baptizing of the children of Christian parents signify if not the purification of each one from the uncleanness of the guilt of heathenism in which the entire human race was involved?

It has given me great pleasure, brother, for the love I bear you, to bring these matters to your notice. Afflicted though I am with bodily infirmities, I may well say with the psalmist: "I know, O Lord, that thy judgment is just and that in truth thou hast afflicted me." For this reason, I earnestly entreat Your Reverence and those with you who serve Christ in the spirit to pray for me that the Lord who made me taste of the wine of compunction may quickly aid me unto mercy, that as He has punished me justly, so He may graciously pardon and mercifully enable me to sing in gratitude the words of the prophet: "According to the number of my sorrows, thy consolations have comforted my soul."

I pray for your welfare in Christ, my very dear colleague, and beg you to remember me.

BONIFACE ASKS ABBESS EADBURGA TO MAKE HIM A COPY OF THE EPISTLE OF ST. PETER IN LETTERS OF GOLD
[A.D. 735]

To the most reverend and beloved sister, Abbess Eadburga, Boniface, least of the servants of God, loving greetings.

I pray Almighty God, the Rewarder of all good works, that when you reach the heavenly mansions and the everlasting tents He will repay you for all the generosity you have shown to me. For, many times, by your useful gifts of books and vestments, you have consoled and relieved me in my distress. And so I beg you to continue the good work you have begun by copying out for me in letters of gold the epistles of my lord, St. Peter, that a reverence and love of the Holy

Scriptures may be impressed on the minds of the heathens to whom I preach, and that I may ever have before my gaze the words of him who guided me along this path.

The materials [gold] needed for the copy I am sending by the priest Eoban.

Deal, then, my dear sister, with this my request as you have so generously dealt with them in the past, so that here on earth your deeds may shine in letters of gold to the glory of our Father who is in heaven.

For your well-being in Christ and for your continual progress in virtue I offer my prayers.

BONIFACE ASKS ABBOT HUETBERT[4] OF WEARMOUTH TO SEND HIM THE WORKS OF BEDE
[A.D. 746–747]

To his very dear and revered brother Abbot Huetbert, and to all the brethren of his holy community, Boniface, a humble servant of the servants of God, sends greeting of brotherly love in Christ.

We earnestly beseech you, kind brother, to assist us with your holy prayers in our labors among the rude and savage people of Germany, where we are sowing the seed of the Gospel. Pray that we may not be scorched by the fiery furnace of the Babylonians, but rather that the seed strewn in the furrows may germinate and grow an abundant harvest. For, in the words of the Apostle, "neither he that planteth nor he that watereth is of any account, but only God who giveth the increase."

Meanwhile, I beg you to be so kind as to copy and send me the treatises of the monk Bede, that profound student of the Scriptures, who, as we have heard, lately shone in your midst like a light of the Church.

If it would not give you too much trouble, pray send me also a cloak—it would be of great comfort to me in my journeys.

As a token of my deep affection for you I am sending you a coverlet, as they call them here, made of goat's hair. I beg you to accept it, trifling though it is, as a reminder of me.

May the Blessed Trinity, one God, guard you and prosper you in health and every holy virtue in this life, and glorify and reward you in future blessedness among the shining cohorts of the angels.

Notes

1 Job 28:17, 19.

2 Prov. 8:11.

3 Wisd. 8:1.

4 After pursuing his studies in Rome, Huetbert became Abbot of Wearmouth and Jarrow in A.D. 716.

D. Alcuin

Alcuin (A.D. 735–804) was educated at York, where, in A.D. 767, he became master of the school. While returning from a journey to Rome in A.D. 780 he met Charlemagne, who invited him to come to his court. Alcuin accepted the invitation and became head of the Palace School. In A.D. 796 Charlemagne gave him the Abbey of St. Martin at Tours, where he worked until his death. Alcuin is best remembered as an educator and organizer of studies. He is the author of some poems, a number of doctrinal and theological works, and a series of letters which cast a great deal of light on his period.

For an introduction to Alcuin, see Eleanor S. Duckett, Alcuin, Friend of Charlemagne, *The Macmillan Company, New York, 1951. The poetry is discussed by F. J. E. Raby,* A History of Christian Latin Poetry from the Beginnings to the Close of the Middle Ages, *Clarendon Press, Oxford, 1927.*

"THE STRIFE BETWEEN WINTER AND SPRING"[1]

Quickly the shepherds from the high mountains
Sought the Spring light, green under trees,
Gathered together to praise the light Muses.
There came young Daphnis and old Palemon:
All made ready to sing in praise of the cuckoo. 5
Thither came Spring draped in a garland,
And cold, icy Winter shaggy and stiff.
Among them was great strife, in song, of the
 cuckoo.
Spring played first, warbling three verses:

"Most beloved of birds, come to me, cuckoo! 10
A most welcome guest to everyone's rooftop,
Gushing sweet songs from a bright shining beak!"

Then Winter responded with harsh words of
 disdain,
"May the cuckoo not come, but sleep in black
 caves;
For whenever he comes, he always brings hunger." 15

Spring
"Come to me, cuckoo! bring tender buds!
Old friend of the sun, thrust away frost!
The sun loves the cuckoo as his calm light
 increases."

Winter
"May the cuckoo not come, for he causes hard
 labor,

Sets men at war, breaks blessed peace, 20
Disturbs the whole world: sea and earth struggle."

Spring
"Why do you, slow Winter, heap blame on the
 cuckoo
Who lie stupid and foul in your shadowy caverns
After revels to Venus and riots to Bacchus?"

Winter
"Riches are mine, gay feasting is mine, 25
Sleeping is sweet, the hearthside is warm.
Of these the cuckoo knows nothing, but only
 makes mischief."

Spring
"The cuckoo brings flowers, fosters the honey,
Builds himself nests, flies over calm seas,
Generates little ones, clothes all the green fields." 30

Winter
"These things annoy me, though they're happy to
 you.
I like to count gold, stored away in my chests,
To stuff myself always, and always to rest."

Spring
"Who for you, lazy Winter, ever sodden and
 sleeping,
Would gather up wealth, or store away treasure, 35
If Spring and bright Summer did not labor before
 you?"

Winter

"You say very truly: since they work for me
    always,
They are my servants under my lordship,
Serving me as a lord, working hard for my
    welfare."

Spring

"You're no lord of theirs, but a proud pauper,   40
Unable to nourish yourself on your own,
Unless the cuckoo who comes brings sustenance
for you."

Then old Palemon spoke from above,
And Daphnis as well, and all the good shepherds:

"Say no more, Winter, old glutton of things.   45
Come to us, cuckoo, sweet friend of the shepherds,
And let the new buds burst forth on our hillsides!
May there be food for our beasts and sweet rest in
    the fields!
And may green branches bring shade for men
    who are weary,
May goats have full udders when they come to   50
    the milking,
May birds vary their notes in praise of the sun.
Bring us these, O cuckoo! Come to us quickly!
For you are sweet love, guest welcome to all.
All things await thee—sea, earth and sky.
Hail! sweet beauty. Hail! cuckoo. Hail to thee   55
    always!"

"THE LOST NIGHTINGALE"

The hand that snatched you from the copse,
    O Nightingale!
    Envied all the joy you brought to me.
You overwhelmed my heart with surging melody
    And lightened all my sadness with your song.
May all the birds from everywhere now join   5
    with me
    To sing a dirge for you, O Nightingale!
Your color was but dull, not dull your harmony,
    A great voice from a tiny throat.
Your varied melodies had but a single theme—
    The praise of your Creator from your heart.   10
You never faltered in the shadows of the night,
    Praising mysteries, O noble bird!

With thundering tones the Cherubim praise
    always,
    But your voice could praise forever too.

"FAREWELL TO HIS CELL"

O my cell, sweet dwelling, beloved,
    Forever, o cell, farewell!
Girdled with sighing limbs of trees,
    A wood laughing with flowers,
Thy fields offer sweetest herbs,   5
    Remedies for the ill.
Girdled with streams where happy anglers
    Cast nets from flowery banks,
Thy cloisters smell of apple blossoms,
    Mingled lilies and roses.   10
Birds of all kinds sing matins there,
    Praising their Creator.
Once the master's holy voice
    Spoke wisdom from books.
In holy praise the hours were sung   15
    Peaceful in voice and heart.
For thee, my cell, I sing in tears,
    And groan at your misfortune
For thou hast fled the poet's song,
    A strange hand now sways thee.   20
No more will Flaccus nor sage Homer,
    Nor youths fill thee with song.
So the world's beauty passes,
    And all is swept away.
Nothing lasts, nothing remains,   25
    Night usurps the day.
Winter crushes lovely flowers,
    Rough winds stir the sea.
The youth who once pursued the stags
    Now leans upon a staff.   30
Why do we fools so love thee, world
    That falls away in flight?
Flee! Let us love Christ.
    May God sway our hearts.
He will defend His own from foes,   35
    Snatching our hearts to Heaven.
Let our hearts love and praise Him—
    Our Fame, our Life, our Haven.

21 Flaccus nor sage Homer Flaccus was an
epithet for Alcuin himself, and he called one of his
pupils "Homer."

From a
LETTER TO HIGBALD, BISHOP OF LINDISFARNE, *written in* A.D. 797

By all means have in your household a prudent steward who will carefully provide for the care of the poor. It is better that paupers should eat at your table than that you should feed minstrels or voluptuous persons of any kind. As St. Jerome says, those who cultivate drunkenness have strayed, as it were, into the pit of Hell. Drunkenness embodies two evils: first, it is to act against the precept of God, who said, "And take heed to yourselves, lest perhaps your hearts be overcharged with surfeiting and drunkenness" [Luke 21:34]; the second evil is that one is tempted to seek praise for drunkenness when one ought to do penance for it. "Blessed is the man . . . who hath not had regard to vanities and lying follies" [Ps. 39:5]. Lying follies are ostentatious clothing and assiduous rioting in drink. For the Prophet says, "Woe to you that are mighty to drink wine, and stout men at drunkenness" [Isa. 5:22]. As Solomon says, "Whoever is delighted therewith shall not be wise" [Prov. 20:1]. And indeed you should be an example of all soberness and continence.

Let the Word of God be heard at the meals of the brethren. There it is proper to hear a reader, not a harper, the sermons of the Fathers, not the songs of the pagans. What has Ingeld to do with Christ?[2] The house is narrow; it cannot hold both of them. The Celestial King did not wish you to have communion with pagan and profligate rulers in name only; for He is an Eternal King who rules in Heaven, while the other, an abandoned pagan, laments in Hell. Hear the voices of readers in your house, not those of laughing crowds in the public squares.

Notes

1   The ascription of these lines to Alcuin has been disputed. "Verses," as Bede said, "cannot be literally translated out of one language into another without losing much of their beauty and loftiness." The editor is indebted to his friend and colleague Robert Fagles for criticisms of the first versions of these translations. The student who can read Latin should by all means consult the originals.

2   This is an echo of St. Paul's admonitions to the Corinthians (2 Cor. 6:14–16): "Bear not the yoke with unbelievers. For what participation hath justice with injustice? Or what fellowship has light with darkness? And what concord hath Christ with Belial? Or what part hath the faithful with the unbeliever? And what agreement hath the temple of God with idols?" Alcuin probably had in mind St. Jerome's elaboration of this passage in his famous letter to Eustochium written in A.D. 384. After citing the above passage, Jerome adds, "What has Horace to do with the Psalter? Or Vergil with the Gospels? Or Cicero with the Apostle?" He goes on to describe his own errant taste for pagan letters at a time when he should have been occupied with sacred texts.

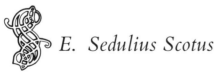 E.   *Sedulius Scotus*

Sedulius Scotus (d. A.D. 860) is the author of a treatise on the government of princes, some scriptural commentaries, and a number of poems. He was one of numerous Irishmen who established themselves on the Continent in the ninth century. Primarily, Scotus seems to have been a grammarian. His poems are frequently addressed to rulers or bishops. One of these in a lighter vein is translated below. See F. J. E. Raby, A History of Christian Latin Poetry, *Clarendon Press, Oxford, 1927 for a discussion of his poetry.*

"COMPLAINT TO BISHOP HARTGAR"

Now the fields turn green, now the flowers bloom,
Now the vines all swell in the sweetest time of
   year.
Now the bright-winged birds soften the air with
   song,
Now sea, now earth, now stars and planets smile.

But no force enlivens water, sorry stuff.   5
When mead, when beer, when wine are all drunk
   up,

O how that substance dwindles in the mingled
   flesh
Which earth most kindly fosters with the dewy
   air!

I say I am a poet, perhaps an Orpheus,
An "ox that treadeth out the corn" on your   10
   behalf;
I'm your knight in battle with the arms of wisdom.
Now go, my Muse, beg some vigor for us both.

    10 **"ox that treadeth out the corn"** Cf. Deut. 25:4 ("Thou shalt not muzzle the ox that treadeth out the corn") and the uses made of this verse in 1 Cor. 9:9; 1 Tim. 5:18.

 # F. Johannes Scotus Erigena

John the Scot (ca. A.D. 800–870) was an Irishman who became master of the Palace School under Charles the Bald (ca. A.D. 850). He is the author of a commentary on the Gospel of St. John and a translation of Pseudo-Dionysius On the Celestial Hierarchy. His great original work, from which a brief selection appears, is On the Division of Nature, which was condemned as heretical in 1225. Meanwhile, however, many of the ideas in it and in the translation of Pseudo-Dionysius had become an integral part of the medieval intellectual tradition.

   For John's philosophy, see Henry Bett, Johannes Scotus Erigena, *Cambridge University Press, London, 1925. Interested students who read French should consult M. Cappuyns,* Jean Scot Erigène, *Louvain and Paris, 1933.*

From
ON THE DIVISION OF NATURE,
Book IV, Chapter 16, "Paradise"

[*The first part of this chapter is devoted to an analysis of quotations and citations from St. Augustine, St. Ambrose, St. Gregory of Nyssa, and Origen to make two general points: (1) the narrative of the creation of man and the establishment of paradise in the first two chapters of Genesis may be interpreted spiritually as well as literally; (2) the spiritual interpretation may involve parallels between certain external features of paradise and certain internal features of human nature. In the latter part of the chapter, translated below, the principal details are drawn from the authorities quoted. The exposition is in the form of a dialogue between a master and his disciple.*]

Master

Whoever examines carefully the words of the theologians quoted above will discover, I believe, the opinion that the word *Paradise* in the Holy Scriptures signifies, when taken as a figurative expression, nothing other than human nature made in the Image of God. For truly the plantation of God is this very nature, which He created in His own Image and Likeness [Gen. 1:27], or, that is, in an Image wholly like Himself, except, as we have said, for that part of man subjected to the reason. He created this nature in Eden, or, that is, in the delights of eternal felicity and the blessedness of the Divine Image, greater and better than anything else in the whole tangible world, not in size, but in dignity. The fertile earth of this Paradise was the essential body of man, potentially immortal. For the natural body is said to die when it seems to die together with what is added to it, while it remains immortal in itself. For it is drawn back so that what is added to it [i.e., its sinful nature] suffers. In a way, then, it can die, and in another way it can not. The body of the first man, as St. Augustine says, could avoid death, and indeed would not have died if it had not been corrupted by the poison of man's prevarication. But it would have flourished with the beauty of spiritual flowers and not grown old with the passage of time. The water of this garden represents the senses of the incorruptible body capable of perceiving forms of sensible things without any deception of false phantasies.[1] Its air was the Divine Wisdom illuminated with the rays of reason, which knew the natures of all things. Its aether was the soul, in accordance with the Divine Nature in an eternal and unerring motion immutable but mutably revolved being fixed, with other characteristics attributed to the Divine Image but which, since they may not be understood, should be revered in silence. In this Paradise, as the holy Scripture testifies, the Fountain of Life has its place, and in it four virtues figured by the four principal rivers of the world [Gen. 2:10–14] have their source: prudence, temperance, fortitude, and justice.[2] These streams, flowing from Divine Wisdom, which is the fountain and virtue of all life, irrigate the surface of human nature. Welling first in the secret recesses of humanity, as if in the most secret imaginable pores of the earth, the waters surge into invisible virtues and then scatter into the effects of overt good actions, producing innumerable kinds of virtuous behavior. From them all virtuous actions proceed, and to them they return; for virtues arise from wisdom and return to it.

The great Gregory of Nyssa, whom we have quoted, explains that in this Paradise there are two trees, "of which one," as he says, "is called *pan*," or, that is, "all," and the other *gnostón*, which means "the knowable." However, that we may more easily understand the meaning of the latter tree, let us call it "mixed."[3] What is this *pan* or "all," whose fruit man is enjoined to eat as food? *Pan* is that tree of which the Scripture says, "And the Lord God brought forth from the ground *omne lignum*[4] fair to behold and pleasant to eat of, the tree of life also in the midst of Paradise" [Gen. 1:9]. Notice how one and the same tree is spoken of in two ways in the prophetic text. First it is called the "all" tree "fair

to behold and pleasant to eat of," and then "the tree of life also in the midst of paradise." And a little after it is said, "Of *omni ligno* of paradise thou shalt eat" [Gen. 2:16], calling one tree "all" tree. No one following the teaching of Gregory will think there to be in Paradise many trees of diverse forms and diverse fruits, like a forest full of trees, but only two trees, one *pan*, and the other *gnostón*. And *pan xylon*, or *omne lignum* [i.e., the "all" tree] is the Word, the Wisdom of the Father, Our Lord Jesus Christ, who is the fruitful "all" tree planted in the midst of our human nature. We may understand this in two ways: first, He is planted there in accordance with His divinity, by which our nature was created, contained, nourished, vivified, illuminated, deified, moved, and made to be, for "in him we move and live and are" [Acts 17:28]; second, in that He annexed our nature to His own in a unified substance that it might be saved and recalled to its first condition, so that He existed in two natures, divine and human. And that is what the Scripture says—He "brought forth from the ground," that is, from the material of our nature, "*omne lignum*," that is, the Incarnate Word, in which and through which all things are made, and who is all. He alone is substantial good. For other things which are said to be good are not good in themselves but only in their participation in His good, and He is of Himself truly existing, and every good and happiness, the fountain and origin of every good and happiness, the cause and the beginning, the end and the perfection, the motion and the quiet, the mean and the extremity, the neighborhood and the place, whose fruit is eternal life, whose eating is joy and happiness and ineffable delight, whose aspect is beauty. He is beauty and the beauty of all beauty, the cause and plenitude of beauty whose taste knows no satiety. By so much as He is consumed, by so much he who consumes Him is urged by desire to consume more. The first men were commanded to eat of the fruit of this "all" tree, of this plenitude of good things, and still all men are commanded to live by its nourishment. But since the first parents did not wish to consume this food, preferring the mortal fruit which was prohibited to them, not only they, but indeed also the whole race which was propagated by them, were by the most just divine judgment expelled to death. Do you not see what the expression "all" tree was intended to signify figuratively by the holy Prophet, or, rather, by the Holy Spirit through the Prophet?

I see clearly, and it signifies nothing else, as I understand it, than God the Lord made man, the whole good of all Paradise, or, that is to say, of our nature. And to subsist on this tree, to eat of it, or, that is, to see it with pious understanding or to believe in it faithfully, is eternal life and incorruptible health. To ignore it or deny it, however, is eternal death and infinite corruption.

Master
It remains, then, to speak of *gnostón*, or of the Tree of Knowledge of Good and Evil. We have said that the word *gnostón* is easier to understand if translated from sense to sense rather than from word to word, and may be said to mean "mixed." And *gnostón* is, according to the master whose interpretation we both follow and gratefully summarize as it casts light on obscurity, malice[5] colored with a phantasy of good insinuated into the corporal senses. This tree is entirely contrary to the first one, *pan*. Just as we should imagine all good in the first one, and that it is, in fact, all good, so in this one we should think of the whole universe of evil. The first, therefore, is every good subsisting in truth, the second every evil seducing the evil with a phantasy. Why these two trees, that is, the "all" tree called the Tree of Life, and the other tree of Knowledge of Good and Evil are said to have been placed in the midst of Paradise is not an idle question. It may, I think, be answered this way.

If, in the first place, Paradise embraces all human nature visible and invisible, exterior and interior,[6] made according to the Image of God and added to later because of sin,[7] we may see if we follow Gregory's treatise *On the Image* carefully that this nature thus divided generally may be divided specifically into six parts. But first it falls into two major parts, one to which corporal things are attributed, the other consisting of the mind. And those things which are to be attributed to the body, or, that is, to the exterior man, may be reasonably divided into three parts. Of these the first is the body itself as it is formed and constituted of matter, of which it is only to be said that nothing inferior to it is to be found in human nature. The second part is the next upward, which can be and is called by various names. It is called "nutritive" or "growth-promoting," because it nourishes the body and causes it to grow in one whole lest it should dissolve and perish. It is also called the "vital force," not without reason, for it not only

preserves the life of the body, but also moves it from place to place in space, or through both spatial and temporal intervals. It is moved through spatial intervals by the agency of the members and through temporal intervals as it increases in age and perfection. The third part is that part in which the five senses are located. And this part, indeed, receives phantasies of all sensible things external to man and conveys them to the memory. The whole of the exterior man is made up of these three parts.

The interior man, which subsists in the mind and is made in the Image of God, is also tripartite. It has an interior sense by means of which the mind receives phantasies of sensible things which are captured by the bodily senses and passes judgment upon them. The next part is reason which investigates the reasonable ordering of all things either sensed or understood. The highest part of man is the soul, above which there is nothing superior in human nature. It has two proper functions: to control the other parts inferior to it,[8] and to contemplate that which is above it, its God, and to study those things which are either in it or exterior to it nearby with a view to determining how they may be allowed to ascend toward God. Do you understand, then, the sexpartite division of human nature? A human being lives, senses things within the body and outside the body, reasons, and understands. But those three parts which make up the inferior part of human nature are corruptible and subject to dissolution. Meanwhile, the three upper parts, which are constituted in the mind alone, are incorruptible, insoluble, and justly eternal. For the Image of Divine Nature is expressed in them. Among the Greeks, as we have taught in earlier books, this triune part of human nature is said to consist of *ousia*, *dynamis*, and *energia*, which, according to the opinion of St. Dionysius,[9] cannot pass away, be corrupted, nor in any way perish.

Thus the extremities of human nature may be considered as the two ends of Paradise, below and above, aside from which there is no created human nature. For beyond the soul there is only God above, and beneath the material substance which makes up the body there is nothing, not that nothing which exists through the contrasting excellency of nature, but that nothing which is called nothing and is nothing through the privation of nature.[10] We find, then, unless I err, that the soul occupies the topmost place in human nature, the body the lowest place. Look in the midst of these natures and you find an area beneath the soul and the reason but above the vital force of the body which nourishes life. Here in the middle part of human nature as if in the midst of Paradise are two senses, one exterior, adhering to the vital motion of the body, and one interior, joined inseparably and consubstantially with the reason and the soul. In these two senses, as if in two places within the Paradise of human nature, are those two intelligible trees, *pan* and *gnostón*, the former in the interior sense, the latter in the exterior. In the interior man dwells Truth and all good, which is the Word of God, Our Lord Jesus Christ, beyond whom nothing is good since He is all true and substantial good and blessedness. To Him evil and malice are opposed in various ways. And since no evil is either found in the nature of things or proceeds causally from natural things, if we consider it in itself it is nothing else than an irrational, perverse, and imperfect motion of the rational nature; and it occupies no other place in nature than that place where falsity presides. The proper realm of falsity, however, is the realm of the corporal senses. For no other part of human nature receives error of falsity except the exterior sense, so that by this sense the interior sense and the reason—even the understanding itself—are frequently deceived. Thus in the place of falsity and vain phantasies, that is, in the corporal sense, which in Greek is called *aesthesis*, and which is represented in the figure of the woman,[11] the tree *gnostón*, or the Tree of Knowledge of Good and Evil, is located. Its fruit is mixed or confused knowledge, malice covered by a phantasy of good, or evil formed to appear good, or, to speak simply, false good, or evil lurking under the figure of good. The external sense is confounded, then, by a lurking evil glossed over with an appearance of good and seduced by it. Within this sense there is, as it were, a woman unable to discern malice which lies under an appearance of good. Malice in itself is a kind of deformity and an abominable evil. If the erring sense were able to perceive it in itself, it would never pursue it nor delight in it, but rather flee and abhor it. Thus the foolish sense errs, and is deceived, thinking that to be beautiful and pleasant to use which is actually evil.

To use an example, when a phantasy of gold or of some sensible material is imprinted on the corporal sense, it seems to it to be beautiful and attractive, for it is taken from external creation, which is good. But the woman, or the carnal sense, is deceived and delighted, not discerning the malice or *philargyria*[12] "which is the root of all evil" [I Tim. 6:10] hiding under this false and phantastic beauty. Our Lord says, "Whosoever shall look on a woman to lust after her, hath already committed adultery with her in his heart" [Matt. 5:28].[13] But if He had spoken more openly, He might have said, "He who receives a phantasy of feminine beauty in his carnal sense has already committed adultery in his thought, desiring the evil of libido, which secretly attracts him beneath the false imagination of the beauty of the woman."

There is, as we have said, a Tree of Knowledge of Good and Evil proffering a pernicious malice in the figure of good; and that tree, as if within a woman, is implanted in the carnal sense, which it deceives. If the soul consents to this woman, the integrity of human nature is corrupted altogether. For if the most excellent part of human nature prevaricates, what remains for the salvation of the inferior parts? The fruit of this tree is mixed knowledge of good and evil, that is, an indiscreet appetite, love, concupiscence, and delight centered on an evil imagined to be good, by which, as if by a certain serpent, the ancient enemy seduced our first parents to lie, so that death was added to human nature. Just as the soul deserted God, the body was deserted by the soul. However, in this place "knowledge" does not mean disciplined knowledge and judgment concerning nature, but an illicit motion and a confused appetite leading to a concupiscence for evil, or, in other words, a sin produced by a false appearance of the good colored with attractiveness. But perhaps you wish to inquire whether God planted this tree, whose fruit is a mixed and confused appetite for good and evil, and whose nature is evil colored over with a phantasy of good, in the Paradise of human nature?

Disciple

Indeed I do ask, and I think not idly. For if God created it, He must be considered as a Creator of evil and a cause of death, and it is most impious to say this of the Author of all good, and much worse to believe it or even to think it. If it was not planted by God, how did it come to be placed in human nature?

Master

We should first consult the holy Scripture, which without hesitation says that *pan* belongs to the divine plantation, saying, "And the Lord God brought forth the 'all' tree, fair to behold and pleasant to eat of" [Gen. 2:9], and as if to explain the quality of this tree called "all," adds, "the tree of life also in the midst of paradise." But to say these things more plainly, that tree is not only all good and all beauty and all suave and spiritual food, but also the Tree of Life by which this Paradise, which is human nature, lives, and in whose midst it is placed. That which follows, however, "and the tree of knowledge of good and evil," does not sufficiently explain whether this tree also was supplied from above, so that we should read, "And He produced the Tree of Knowledge of Good and Evil in Paradise, just as He produced the Tree of Life," or whether what is here introduced is absolute, "and the tree of knowledge of good and evil," so that we do not think it to have been produced by God, but consider it only as something contrary or opposed to the first tree, so that just as that one is all good and a cause of life to the living, this one is all evil and the cause of death to the dying. But should we not think rather that since the Knowledge of Good and Evil is a tree, in so far as it is surrounded by the appearance of good, it is from God, who is the Cause of all beauty and attractiveness, whether this beauty or attractiveness is sensed or understood in a substance or in a phantasy of sensible matter located in the corporal sense for transference to the interior sense? And further, should we not think that in that this evil surrounded by the appearance of good is in itself an unrecognized and formless evil, it is neither from God nor from any certain and definite cause? For evil, which is not found substantially in the nature of things, is variable and uncaused. In so far as that tree is evil, then, it is not to be referred to a cause because it is nothing at all. But in so far as it is made good so that it deceives the incautious, whose phantasies are formed from its material, it was made by the Creator of all good and is in itself good and not evil at all. The beauty, then, by which evil seduces those whom it kills is good, for it is a phantasy of a certain good. But the evil is altogether evil and not created by a good, since it is contrary to all good. Thus if anyone scrutinizes closely the nature of phantasies in which evil is colored over because, being unformed, deformed, unattractive, and uncaused, it could not appear in itself, he will find that nature to be altogether good.

In order to make this argument clear, let us suppose two men, one wise and neither titillated nor stimulated by avarice, and the other stupid, avaricious, and every-where pricked and lacerated by the thorns of perverse cupidity. Placing these two men together, let there be brought a vase of refined gold decorated with most precious stones, fit for royal use. Both the wise man and the avaricious man look upon it, both receive a phantasy of the vase in their corporal sense, place it in the memory, and consider it in thought. The wise man refers the beauty of this vase, whose phantasy he considers within himself, altogether to the praise of the Creator of all natures. No evil of cupidity arises in him, no poison of *philargyria* infects the intention of his pure mind, no libido contaminates him. Unfortunately, the avaricious man works in a contrary way. As soon as he drinks in the phantasy of the vase, he glows with the flame of cupidity, he is consumed, contaminated, killed, referring the beauty of the phantasy not to Him who said, "the silver is mine, and the gold is mine" [Aggeus 2:9], but plunging himself into a most foul pool of cupidity and gulping it down. Do you not see that the phantasy of a single vase was in both men good and beautiful? But in the sense of the wise man it was simple and natural, with no malice in it, while in the sense of the avaricious man the phantasy was double, mixed by the contrary evil of cupidity which mingled with it. The phantasy shaped and colored over this malice so that it seemed to be good, when it was, as a matter of fact, a most poisonous evil. Thus evil was not planted in man; it is made by a perverse and irrational action of the free and rational will.[14] And this action is not something within nature, but outside of it, and may be seen to arise from bestial intemperance;[15] it is mixed, however, with good, a good tinctured by the counsel and astuteness of the Ancient Enemy to the end that the carnal senses may be deceived by libidinous emotions and thus destroyed by death.

Nor do I say this in order to refute those who say that the aforementioned Tree of Knowledge of Good and Evil is altogether good, and that it was, historically, made in Paradise, and that its fruit is knowledge, or knowledge by experience of good and evil.[16] For if the first men had abstained from the touch and taste of this tree, as they were commanded to do, they would have achieved eternal life and perpetual beatitude without any intervening death. But, consenting to diabolic guile, in their miserable intemperance they illicitly consumed the fruit of this deadly tree, falling into eternal death and infelicity.

May he who does not think that these things which

we have said between us are worthy of being read and diligently studied select from the opinions of the Fathers we have quoted those things which he thinks should be approved. May he take care, however, not to condemn us hastily, thinking what we have said to be fortified by no authority but only something contrived contrary to Patristic tradition. You have, I think, a brief and open exposition of Paradise in so far as our powers and labors suffice for it.

Notes

1 The word *phantasy* here means a sense impression which may be lodged in the memory and considered in thought.

2 St. Ambrose is cited in the first part of the chapter to show that "The Phison, which according to the Greeks is the Ganges, is called prudence; the Gehon, which is the Nile, is called temperance; the Tigris, named for the velocity of its current, is called fortitude; and the Euphrates is justice." This interpretation of the rivers became a medieval commonplace.

3 Gregory's thought shows a strong Platonic influence. He is quoted earlier in the chapter as saying, "The most universal and highest reason holds that the form of all good is intrinsically a whole, and is single." The word *mixed* thus has pejorative connotations.

4 The Latin *omne lignum* is translated in the Douay version "all manner of trees," and this became the usual interpretation of the text. However, the Latin word *omne* and the Greek word *pan* modify words for tree in the singular form. John adopts Gregory's rendering for the purposes of the present argument, but he uses it as a tool by means of which to arrive at something else, not an end in itself.

5 The Latin word *malitia* ("malice") had a much broader meaning than modern *malice*. It implied not only ill will, but also the various implications of corrupted will: cupidity, lust, wrath, envy, and so on.

6 The distinction between the exterior man and the interior man is derived from 2 Cor. 4:16: "Our exterior man is corrupted, yet the interior man is renewed." This Pauline distinction played a large part in medieval thought.

7 In the earlier part of the chapter, the theory of the two creations of man is introduced. One was said to take place outside of paradise (Gen. 1:26–27; 2:7) and one inside (Gen. 2:18ff.). According to one interpretation, man was first made in the image and likeness of God and later placed in paradise (Gen. 2:15). Here woman was added (Gen. 2:18). Gregory of Nyssa held that the feminine element was added because of foreknown original sin.

8 In scriptural contexts and generally in medieval thought the soul was thought to supervise and control the other elements in human nature.

9 John the Scot translated *The Celestial Hierarchy* and wrote a commentary on it. The author, one Dionysius, was thought to be Dionysius the Areopagite (Acts 17:34), who became patron saint of France. *The Celestial Hierarchy* exerted an enormous influence on medieval thought.

10 According to accepted Christian doctrine, evil is not an entity in itself, but a privation of the good.

11 St. Ambrose is quoted in the first part of the chapter to the effect that the motion of the senses (*aesthesis*) is represented by Eve in the narrative of the Fall. Throughout the Middle Ages, to be manly was to be strong and virtuous, there being an obvious relationship between Latin *vir* ("man") and the word *virtus*. To be effeminate on the other hand was to be weak, soft, and prone to vice. This is a figurative contrast, however; actual women were thought to be quite capable of virtue. A great deal of the "anti-feminist" literature of the Middle Ages reflects the figurative distinction.

12 The Greek word *philargyria* is here used as a synonym for the Latin *cupiditas* of the Vulgate text. The word *cupiditas* ("cupidity") now variously translated "lust" or "desire for money" implies a love for any creature for its own sake.

13 John explains elsewhere that the word *woman* in this passage implies the beauty of the sensible world in any form and that the word *adultery* implies any sort of turning away from God. For a similar explanation together with an exposition which has important analogies with this whole discussion, see St. Augustine, *Our Lord's Sermon on the Mount*, chap. XII. The relevant passage may be found in the translation by the Rev. William Findlay, T. and T. Clark, Edinburgh, 1873, pp. 26–30.

14 This conclusion is harmonious with the orthodox medieval view. Evil was not created and does not exist. What we call evil is a privation or disordering of the good made possible by the free will of man, which, although it is in itself a good, gives him an opportunity to abuse the good things of creation. Notice that this doctrine places the responsibility for evil squarely on the individual.

15 The beasts have no reason and hence cannot be vicious. However, at the Fall man took on bestial characteristics which are, in him, vices. Thus, for example, guile is a good thing in a fox because it contributes to his survival. However, it is an evil in a man, since a man should be reasonable. Hence the adjective *bestial* when applied to a man implies a disordered or vicious nature.

16 For example, St. Augustine. Earlier in the chapter John says, "We simply compare the conclusions of the Fathers among ourselves, but it is not our intention to decide which one should be believed. Each one abounds in lessons, and may those who come after choose which they will, leaving contentions aside."

 # G. Asser

Asser (d. A.D. 910) was a priest of St. David's in Wales who befriended King Alfred and became Bishop of Sherborne. His only surviving work is his Life of King Alfred, *written in A.D. 893. A great deal of his book is made up of a chronicle of the times, but he does include some interesting material on the life and aspirations of Alfred. The account of the King's career breaks off at the time when he was learning Latin.*

The fullest treatment of Asser's work appears in the introduction to the edition by W. H. Stevenson, Clarendon Press, Oxford, 1904.

From LIFE OF KING ALFRED

In the year of our Lord's incarnation 849, was born Alfred, king of the Anglo-Saxons, at the royal village of Wanating, in Berkshire, which country has its name from the wood of Berroc, where the box-tree grows most abundantly. His genealogy is traced in the following order. King Alfred was the son of king Ethelwulf, who was the son of Egbert, who was the son of Elmund, the son of Eafa, who was the son of Eoppa, who was the son of Ingild. Ingild, and Ina, the famous king of the West-Saxons, were two brothers. Ina went to Rome, and there ending this life honorably, entered the heavenly kingdom, to reign there for ever with Christ. Ingild and Ina were the sons of Coenred, who was the son of Ceolwald, who was the son of Cudam, who was the son of Cuthwin, who was the son of Ceawlin, who was the son of Cynric, who was the son of Creoda, who was the son of Cerdic, who was the son of Elesa, who was the son of Gewis, from whom the Britons name all that nation Gegwis, who was the son of Brond, who was the son of Beldeg, who was the son of Woden, who was the son of Frithowald, who was the son of Frealaf, who was the son of Frithuwulf, who was the son of Finn of Godwulf, who was the son of Geat, which Geat the pagans long worshipped as a god. Sedulius[1] makes mention of him in his metrical Paschal poem, as follows:

When gentile poets with their fictions vain,
In tragic language and bombastic strain,
To their god Geat, comic deity,
    Loud praises sing, &c.

Geat was the son of Tætwa, who was the son of Beaw, who was the son of Sceldi, who was the son of Heremod, who was the son of Itermon, who was the son of Hathra, who was the son of Guala, who was the son of Bedwig, who was the son of Shem, who was the son of Noah, who was the son of Lamech, who was the son of Methusalem, who was the son of Enoch, who was the son of Malaleel, who was the son of Cainian, who was the son of Enos, who was the son of Seth, who was the son of Adam.

The mother of Alfred was named Osburga, a religious woman, noble both by birth and by nature; she was daughter of Oslac, the famous butler of king Ethelwulf, which Oslac was a Goth by nation, descended from the Goths and Jutes, of the seed, namely, of Stuf and Whitgar, two brothers and counts; who, having received possession of the Isle of Wight from their uncle, king Cerdic, and his son Cynric their cousin, slew the few British inhabitants whom they could find in that island, at a place called Gwihtgaraburgh; for the other inhabitants of the island had either been slain or escaped into exile.

In the year of our Lord's incarnation 851, which was the third after the birth of king Alfred, Ceorl, earl of Devon, fought with the men of Devon against the pagans at a place called Wicgambeorg; and the Christians gained the victory; and that same year the pagans first wintered in the island called Sheppey, which means the Sheep-isle, and is situated in the river Thames between Essex and Kent, but is nearer to Kent than to Essex; it has in it a fine monastery.

The same year also a great army of the pagans came with three hundred and fifty ships to the mouth of the river Thames, and sacked Dorobernia, which is the city of the Cantuarians, and also the city of London, which lies on the north bank of the river Thames, on the confines of Essex and Middlesex; but yet that city belongs in truth to Essex; and they put to flight Berthwulf, king of Mercia, with all the army, which he had led out to oppose them.

After these things, the aforesaid pagan host went into Surrey, which is a district situated on the south bank of the river Thames, and to the west of Kent. And Ethelwulf, king of the West-Saxons, and his son Ethelbald, with all their army, fought a long time against them at a place called Ac-lea, i.e. the Oak-plain, and there, after a lengthened battle, which was fought with much bravery on both sides, the greater part of the pagan multitude was destroyed and cut to pieces, so that we never heard of their being so defeated, either before or since, in any country, in one day; and the Christians gained an honorable victory, and were triumphant over their graves.

In the same year king Athelstan, son of king Ethelwulf, and earl Ealhere slew a large army of pagans in Kent, at a place called Sandwich, and took nine ships of their fleet; the others escaped by flight.

In the year of our Lord's incarnation 853, which was the fifth of king Alfred, Burhred, king of the Mercians, sent messengers, and prayed Ethelwulf, king of the West-Saxons, to come and help him in reducing the midland Britons, who dwell between Mercia and the western sea, and who struggled against him most immoderately. So without delay, king Ethelwulf, having received the embassy, moved his army, and advanced with king Burhred against Britain, and immediately, on entering that country, he began to ravage it; and having reduced it under subjection to king Burhred, he returned home.

In the same year, king Ethelwulf sent his son Alfred, above-named, to Rome, with an honorable escort both of nobles and commoners. Pope Leo [the fourth] at that time presided over the apostolic see, and he anointed for king the aforesaid Alfred, and adopted him as his spiritual son. The same year also, earl Ealhere, with the men of Kent, and Huda with the men of Surrey, fought bravely and resolutely against an army of the pagans, in the island, which is called in the Saxon tongue, Tenet, but Ruim in the British language. The battle lasted a long time, and many fell on both sides, and also were drowned in the water; and both the earls were there slain. In the same year also, after Easter, Ethelwulf, king of the West-Saxons, gave his daughter to Burhred, king of the Mercians, and the marriage was celebrated royally at the royal vill of Chippenham. . . .

In the year of our Lord's incarnation 866, which was the eighteenth of king Alfred, Ethelred, brother of Ethelbert, king of the West-Saxons, undertook the government of the kingdom for five years; and the same year a large fleet of pagans came to Britain from the Danube, and wintered in the kingdom of the Eastern-Saxons, which is called in Saxon East-Anglia; and there they became principally an army of cavalry. But, to speak in nautical phrase, I will no longer commit my vessel to the power of the waves and of its sails, or keeping off from land steer my round-about course through so many calamities of wars and series of years, but will return to that which first prompted me to this task; that is to say, I think it right in this place briefly to relate as much as has come to my knowledge about the character of my revered lord Alfred, king of the Anglo-Saxons, during the years that he was an infant and a boy.

He was loved by his father and mother, and even by all the people, above all his brothers, and was educated altogether at the court of the king. As he advanced through the years of infancy and youth, his form appeared more comely than that of his brothers; in look, in speech, and in manners he was more graceful than they. His noble nature implanted in him from his cradle a love of wisdom above all things; but, with shame be it spoken, by the unworthy neglect of his parents and nurses, he remained illiterate even till he was twelve years old or more; but he listened with serious attention to the Saxon poems which he often heard recited, and easily retained them in his docile memory. He was a zealous practiser of hunting in all its branches, and hunted with great assiduity and success; for skill and good fortune in this art, as in all others, are among the gifts of God, as we also have often witnessed.

On a certain day, therefore, his mother was showing him and his brother a Saxon book of poetry, which she held in her hand, and said, "Whichever of you shall the soonest learn this volume shall have it for his own." Stimulated by these words, or rather by the Divine inspiration, and allured by the beautifully illuminated letter at the beginning of the volume, he spoke before all his brothers, who, though his seniors in age, were not so in grace, and answered, "Will you really give that book to one of us, that is to say, to him who can first understand and repeat it to you?" At this his mother smiled with satisfaction, and confirmed what she had before said. Upon which the boy took the book out of her hand, and went to his master to read it, and in due time brought it to his mother and recited it.

After this he learned the daily course, that is, the celebration of the hours, and afterwards certain psalms, and several prayers, contained in a certain book which he kept day and night in his bosom, as we ourselves have seen, and carried about with him to assist his prayers, amid all the bustle and business of this present life. But, sad to say, he could not gratify his most ardent wish to learn the liberal arts, because, as he said, there were no good readers at that time in all the kingdom of the West-Saxons.

This he confessed, with many lamentations and sighs, to have been one of his greatest difficulties and impediments in this life, namely, that when he was young and had the capacity for learning, he could not find teachers; but, when he was more advanced in life, he was harassed by so many diseases unknown to all the physicians of this island, as well as by internal and external anxieties of sovereignty, and by continual invasions of the pagans, and had his teachers and writers also so much disturbed, that there was no time for reading. But yet among the impediments of this present life, from infancy up to the present time, and, as I believe, even until his death, he continued to feel the same insatiable desire of knowledge, and still aspires after it. . . .

The same year, after Easter, the aforesaid king Ethelred, having bravely, honorably, and with good repute, governed his kingdom five years, through much tribulation, went the way of all flesh, and was buried in Wimborne Minster, where he awaits the coming of the Lord, and the first resurrection with the just.

The same year, the aforesaid Alfred, who had been up to that time only of secondary rank, whilst his brothers were alive, now, by God's permission, undertook the government of the whole kingdom, amid the acclamations of all the people; and if he had chosen, he might have done so before, whilst his brother above-named was still alive; for in wisdom and other qualities he surpassed all his brothers, and moreover, was warlike and victorious in all his wars. And when he had reigned one month, almost against his will, for he did not think he could alone sustain the multitude and ferocity of the pagans, though even during his brothers' lives, he had borne the woes of many,—he fought a battle with a few men, and on very unequal terms, against all the army of the pagans, at a hill called Wilton, on the south bank of the river Wily, from which river the whole of that district is named, and after a long and fierce engagement, the pagans, seeing the danger they were in, and no longer able to bear the attack of their enemies, turned their backs and fled. But, oh, shame to say, they deceived their too audacious pursuers, and again rallying, gained the victory. Let no one be surprised that the Christians had but a small number of men, for the Saxons had been worn out by eight battles in one year, against the pagans, of whom they had slain one king, nine dukes, and innumerable troops of soldiers, besides endless skirmishes, both by night and by day, in which the oft-named Alfred, and all his chieftains, with their men, and several of his ministers, were engaged without rest or cessation against the pagans. How many thousand pagans fell in these numberless skirmishes God alone knows, over and above those who were slain in the eight battles above-mentioned. In the same year the Saxons made peace with the pagans, on condition that they should take their departure, and they did so. . . .

At the same time the above-named Alfred, king of the West-Saxons, with a few of his nobles, and certain soldiers and vassals, used to lead an unquiet life among the woodlands of the county of Somerset, in great tribulation; for he had none of the necessaries of life, except what he could forage openly or stealthily, by frequent sallies, from the pagans, or even from the Christians who had submitted to the rule of the pagans, and as we read in the Life of St. Neot, at the house of one of his cowherds.

But it happened on a certain day, that the country-woman, wife of the cowherd, was preparing some loaves to bake, and the king, sitting at the hearth, made ready his bow and arrows and other warlike instruments. The unlucky woman espying the cakes burning at the fire, ran up to remove them, and rebuking the brave king, exclaimed:

Ca'sn thee mind the ke-aks, man, an' doossen zee 'em
    burn?
I'm boun thee's eat 'em vast enough, az zoon az 'tiz
    the turn.

The blundering woman little thought that it was king Alfred, who had fought so many battles against the pagans, and gained so many victories over them.

But the Almighty not only granted to the same glorious king victories over his enemies, but also permitted him to be harassed by them, to be sunk down by adversities, and depressed by the low estate of his followers, to the end that he might learn that there is one Lord of all things, to whom every knee doth bow, and in whose hand are the hearts of kings; who puts down the mighty from their seat and exalteth the humble; who suffers his servants when they are elevated at the summit of prosperity to be touched by the rod of adversity, that in their humility they may not despair of God's mercy, and in their prosperity they may not boast of their honors, but may also know, to whom they owe all the things which they possess.

We may believe that the calamity was brought upon the king aforesaid, because, in the beginning of his reign, when he was a youth, and influenced by youthful feelings, he would not listen to the petitions which his subjects made to him for help in their necessities, or for relief from those who oppressed them; but he repulsed them from him, and paid no heed to their requests. This particular gave much annoyance to the holy man St. Neot, who was his relation, and often foretold to him, in the spirit of prophecy, that he would suffer great adversity on this account; but Alfred neither attended to the reproof of the man of God, nor listened to his true prediction. Wherefore, seeing that a man's sins must be corrected either in this world or the next, the true and righteous Judge was willing that his sin should not go unpunished in this world, to the end that he might spare him in the world to come. From this cause, therefore, the aforesaid Alfred often fell into such great misery, that sometimes none of his subjects knew where he was or what had become of him. . . .

Wherefore, to return to that from which I digressed, that I may not be compelled by my long navigation to abandon the port of rest which I was making for, I propose, as far as my knowledge will enable me, to speak of the life and character and just conduct of my lord Alfred, king of the Anglo-Saxons, after he married the above named respected lady of Mercian race, his wife; and, with God's blessing, I will despatch it succinctly and briefly, as I promised, that I may not offend the delicate minds of my readers by prolixity in relating each new event.

His nuptials were honorably celebrated in Mercia, among innumerable multitudes of people of both sexes; and after continual feasts, both by night and by day, he was immediately seized, in presence of all the people, by sudden and overwhelming pain, as yet unknown to all the physicians; for it was unknown to all who were then present, and even to those who daily see him up to the present time—which, sad to say! is the worst of all, that he should have protracted it so long from the twentieth to the fortieth year of his life, and even more than that through the space of so many years—from what cause so great a malady arose. For many thought that this was occasioned by the favour and fascination of the people who surrounded him; others, by some spite of the devil, who is ever jealous of the good; others, from an unusual kind of fever. He had this sort of severe disease from his childhood; but once, divine

Providence so ordered it, that when he was on a visit to Cornwall for the sake of hunting, and had turned out of the road to pray in a certain chapel, in which rests the body of Saint Guerir, and now also St. Neot rests there —for king Alfred was always from his infancy a frequent visitor of holy places for the sake of prayer and almsgiving—he prostrated himself for private devotion, and, after some time spent therein, he entreated of God's mercy, that in his boundless clemency he would exchange the torments of the malady which then afflicted him for some other lighter disease; but with this condition, that such disease should not show itself outwardly in his body, lest he should be an object of contempt, and less able to benefit mankind; for he had great dread of leprosy or blindness, or any such complaint, as makes men useless or contemptible when it afflicts them. When he had finished his prayers, he proceeded on his journey, and not long after he felt within him that by the hand of the Almighty he was healed, according to his request, of his disorder, and that it was entirely eradicated, although he had first had even this complaint in the flower of his youth, by his devout and pious prayers and supplications to Almighty God. For if I may be allowed to speak briefly, but in a somewhat preposterous order, of his zealous piety to God, in the flower of his youth, before he entered the marriage state, he wished to strengthen his mind in the observance of God's commandments, for he perceived that he could with difficulty abstain from gratifying his carnal desires; and, because he feared the anger of God, if he should do anything contrary to his will, he used often to rise in the morning at the cock-crow, and go to pray in the churches and at the relics of the saints. There he prostrated himself on the ground, and prayed that God in his mercy would strengthen his mind still more in his service by some infirmity such as he might bear, but not such as would render him imbecile and contemptible in his worldly duties; and when he had often prayed with much devotion to this effect, after an interval of some time, Providence vouchsafed to afflict him with the above-named disease, which he bore long and painfully for many years, and even despaired of life, until he entirely got rid of it by his prayers; but, sad to say! it was replaced, as we have said, at his marriage by another which incessantly tormented him, night and day, from the twentieth to the forty-fourth year of his life. But if ever, by God's mercy, he was relieved from this infirmity for a single day or night,

yet the fear and dread of that dreadful malady never left him, but rendered him almost useless, as he thought, for every duty, whether human or divine.

The sons and daughters, which he had by his wife above mentioned were Ethelfled the eldest, after whom came Edward, then Ethelgiva, then Ethelswitha, and Ethelwerd, besides those who died in their infancy, one of whom was Edmund. Ethelfled, when she arrived at a marriageable age, was united to Ethered, earl of Mercia; Ethelgiva also was dedicated to God, and submitted to the rules of a monastic life. Ethelwerd the youngest, by the divine counsels and the admirable prudence of the king, was consigned to the schools of learning, where, with the children of almost all the nobility of the country, and many also who were not noble, he prospered under the diligent care of his teachers. Books in both languages, namely, Latin and Saxon, were both read in the school. They also learned to write; so that before they were of an age to practice manly arts, namely, hunting and such pursuits as befit noblemen, they became studious and clever in the liberal arts. Edward and Ethelswitha were bred up in the king's court and received great attention from their attendants and nurses; nay, they continue to this day, with the love of all about them, and showing affability, and even gentleness toward all, both natives and foreigners, and in complete subjection to their father; nor, among their other studies which appertain to this life and are fit for noble youths, are they suffered to pass their time idly and unprofitably without learning the liberal arts; for they have carefully learned the Psalms and Saxon books, especially the Saxon poems, and are continually in the habit of making use of books.

In the meantime, the king, during the frequent wars and other trammels of this present life, the invasions of the pagans, and his own daily infirmities of body, continued to carry on the government, and to exercise hunting in all its branches; to teach his workers in gold and artificers of all kinds, his falconers, hawkers and dog-keepers; to build houses, majestic and good, beyond all the precedents of his ancestors, by his new mechanical inventions; to recite the Saxon books, and especially to learn by heart the Saxon poems, and to make others learn them; and he alone never desisted from studying, most diligently, to the best of his ability; he attended the mass and other daily services of religion; he was frequent in psalm-singing and prayer, at the hours both of the day and the night. He also went to the churches, as we have already said, in the night-time to pray, secretly, and unknown to his courtiers; he bestowed alms and largesses on both natives and foreigners of all countries; he was affable and pleasant to all, and curiously eager to investigate things unknown. Many Franks, Frisons, Gauls, pagans, Britons, Scots, and Armoricans, noble and ignoble, submitted voluntarily to his dominion; and all of them, according to their nation and deserving, were ruled, loved, honored, and enriched with money and power. Moreover, the king was in the habit of hearing the divine scriptures read by his own countrymen, or, if by any chance it so happened, in company with foreigners, and he attended to it with sedulity and solicitude. His bishops, too, and all ecclesiastics, his earls and nobles, ministers and friends, were loved by him with wonderful affection, and their sons, who were bred up in the royal household, were no less dear to him than his own; he had them instructed in all kinds of good morals, and among other things, never ceased to teach them letters night and day; but as if he had no consolation in all these things, and suffered no other annoyance either from within or without, yet he was harassed by daily and nightly affliction, that he complained to God, and to all who were admitted to his familiar love, that Almighty God had made him ignorant of divine wisdom, and of the liberal arts; in this emulating the pious, the wise, and wealthy Solomon, king of the Hebrews, who at first, despising all present glory and riches, asked wisdom of God, and found both, namely, wisdom and worldly glory; as it is written, "Seek first the kingdom of God and his righteousness, and all these things shall be added unto you." But God, who is always the inspector of the thoughts of the mind within, and the instigator of all good intentions, and a most plentiful aider, that good desires may be formed—for he would not instigate a man to good intentions, unless he also amply supplied that which the man justly and properly wishes to have—instigated the king's mind within; as it is written, "I will hearken what the Lord God will say concerning me." He would avail himself of every opportunity to procure coadjutors in his good designs, to aid him in his strivings after wisdom, that he might attain to what he aimed at; and, like a prudent bird, which rising in summer with the early morning from her beloved nest, steers her rapid flight through the uncertain tracks of ether, and descends on the manifold and varied flowers of grasses, herbs, and shrubs, essaying

that which pleases most, that she may bear it to her home, so did he direct his eyes afar, and seek without, that which he had not within, namely, in his own kingdom.

But God at that time, as some consolation to the king's benevolence, yielding to his complaint, sent certain lights to illuminate him, namely, Werefrith, bishop of the church of Worcester, a man well versed in divine scripture, who, by the king's command, first turned the books of the Dialogues of pope Gregory and Peter, his disciple, from Latin into Saxon, and sometimes putting sense for sense, interpreted them with clearness and elegance. After him was Plegmund, a Mercian by birth, archbishop of the church of Canterbury, a venerable man, and endowed with wisdom; Ethelstan also, and Werewulf, his priests and chaplains, Mercians by birth, and erudite. These four had been invited out of Mercia by king Alfred, who exalted them with many honors and powers in the kingdom of the West-Saxons, besides the privileges which archbishop Plegmund and bishop Werefrith enjoyed in Mercia. By their teaching and wisdom the king's desires increased unceasingly, and were gratified. Night and day, whenever he had leisure, he commanded such men as these to read books to him; for he never suffered himself to be without one of them, wherefore he possessed a knowledge of every book, though of himself he could not yet understand anything of books, for he had not yet learned to read any thing.

But the king's commendable avarice could not be gratified even in this; wherefore he sent messengers beyond the sea to Gaul, to procure teachers, and he invited from thence Grimbald, priest and monk, a venerable man, and good singer, adorned with every kind of ecclesiastical discipline and good morals, and most learned in holy scripture. He also obtained from thence John, also priest and monk, a man of most energetic talents, and learned in all kinds of literary science, and skilled in many other arts. By the teaching of these men the king's mind was much enlarged, and he enriched and honoured them with much influence. . . .

In the same year also Alfred, king of the Anglo-Saxons, so often before mentioned, by divine inspiration, began, on one and the same day, to read and to interpret; but that I may explain this more fully to those who are ignorant, I will relate the cause of this long delay in beginning.

On a certain day we were both of us sitting in the king's chamber, talking on all kinds of subjects, as usual, and it happened that I read to him a quotation out of a certain book. He heard it attentively with both his ears, and addressed me with a thoughtful mind, showing me at the same moment a book which he carried in his bosom, wherein the daily courses and psalms, and prayers which he had read in his youth, were written, and he commanded me to write the same quotation in that book. Hearing this, and perceiving his ingenuous benevolence, and devout desire of studying the words of divine wisdom, I gave, though in secret, boundless thanks to Almighty God, who had implanted such a love of wisdom in the king's heart. But I could not find any empty space in that book wherein to write the quotation, for it was already full of various matters; wherefore I made a little delay, principally that I might stir up the bright intellect of the king to a higher acquaintance with the divine testimonies. Upon his urging me to make haste and write it quickly, I said to him, "Are you willing that I should write that quotation on some leaf apart? For it is not certain whether we shall not find one or more other such extracts which will please you; and if that should so happen, we shall be glad that we have kept them apart." "Your plan is good," said he, and I gladly made haste to get ready a sheet, in the beginning of which I wrote what he bade me; and on that same day, I wrote therein, as I had anticipated, no less than three other quotations which pleased him; and from that time we daily talked together, and found out other quotations which pleased him, so that the sheet became full, and deservedly so; according as it is written, "The just man builds upon a moderate foundation, and by degrees passes to greater things." Thus, like a most productive bee, he flew here and there, asking questions, as he went, until he had eagerly and unceasingly collected many various flowers of divine Scriptures, with which he thickly stored the cells of his mind.

Now when that first quotation was copied, he was eager at once to read, and to interpret in Saxon, and then to teach others; even as we read of that happy robber, who recognized his Lord, aye, the Lord of all men, as he was hanging on the blessed cross, and, saluting him with his bodily eyes only, because elsewhere he was all pierced with nails, cried, "Lord, remember me when thou comest into thy kingdom!" for it was only at the end of his life that he began to learn the rudiments of the Christian faith. But the king, inspired by God, began to study the rudiments of divine Scripture on the sacred solemnity of St. Martin [Nov. 11], and he continued to learn the flowers collected by certain masters, and to reduce them into the form of one book, as he was then able, although mixed one with another, until it became almost as large as a psalter. This book he called his Enchiridion or Manual, because he carefully kept it at hand day and night, and found, as he told me, no small consolation therein.

Note

1   This is not Sedulius Scotus but a poet of the fifth century.

 H. St. Ethelwold of Winchester

St. Ethelwold (d. A.D. 984) was one of the great leaders of the tenth-century monastic reform in England. His significance for students of literature rests on the fact that one of his accomplishments was the compilation of an Agreement Concerning the Rule *which sought to establish a standard for monastic observances in England. This* Agreement *contains what is perhaps the earliest known example of a drama performed at Easter matins.*
    The medieval liturgical drama apparently developed from what was called a "trope." Originally, a trope was a melismatic melody (i.e., a melody without words) used in addition to the standard melismatic melodies of the

Gregorian chant. The chant as it was established allowed no room for development, but enthusiasm for the music during the ninth century led to the addition of these melodies which were new and whose use was optional. When such melodies were added to the Alleluia of the mass, they were called "sequences." Tropes generally and the special type known as sequences were thus optional additions to the musical repertory of the liturgy. But melismatic melodies are difficult to remember, and during the ninth century words were composed to be used in singing them, first for the special tropes called sequences. But the practice spread to other tropes as well, so that in the course of time the words sequence and trope could be applied either to the melodies themselves or to the words composed to accompany them. Some very beautiful poems were composed as sequences during the eleventh and twelfth centuries.

Among the various tropes, one in particular was of special significance for the development of the drama. This one, which was used before the Introit of the Easter mass, consists of a dialogue:

"Whom do you seek in the sepulchre, O followers of Christ?"
"Jesus of Nazareth crucified, O celestial one."[1]
"He is not here. He arose as He foretold. Go, announce that he arose from the sepulchre."

Below is the Latin text together with a transcription of the music used in the tenth century at St. Gall.[2]

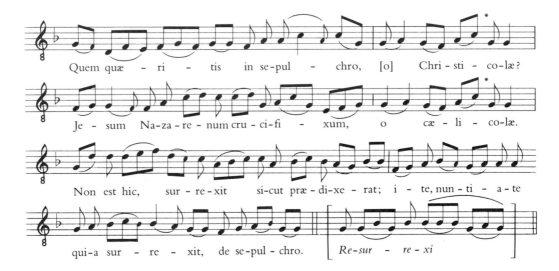

The trope did not achieve dramatic form, however, until it became attached to the last canticle of matins on Easter morning, just before the Te Deum laudamus ("We praise thee, O Lord!"). This position was natural, since the Te Deum was sung just at sunrise, an event regarded as being symbolic of the Resurrection. Once there, the trope was "troped," or elaborated, and given its dramatic form. To understand the little play which follows, it is necessary to know something of the services that preceded it.

The Agreement Concerning the Rule describes a special service of adoration for the Cross to be performed on Good Friday. After this Adoratio, the deacons who have been carrying the Cross wrap it in a cloth and place it in a sepulchre, in this instance a part of the altar closed off with a veil. There it is guarded by two or three brothers singing psalms until the eve of the Resurrection. Sometime before matins on Easter morning, the Cross is removed to prepare for the ceremony described below. During the later Middle Ages a special Easter sepulchre was frequently built as a permanent fixture in churches for use in ceremonies of this type.

On the monastic reform of the tenth century and the part played by St. Ethelwold in it, see F. M. Stenton, Anglo-Saxon England, second edition, Clarendon Press, Oxford, 1947, chap. XIII. There is a good discussion of tropes and of the rise of the liturgical drama in Dom Anselm Hughes, editor, Early Medieval Music, Oxford University Press, London, 1955. The standard work on the liturgical drama is Karl Young, The Drama of the Medieval Church, Clarendon Press, Oxford, 1933. A good, brief introduction will be found in Hardin Craig,

English Religious Drama of the Middle Ages, *Clarendon Press, Oxford, 1955. Many traditional assumptions about the liturgical drama are questioned in the recent and stimulating study by O. B. Hardison, Jr.,* Christian Rite and Christian Drama in the Middle Ages, *The Johns Hopkins Press, Baltimore, 1965.* The Agreement Concerning the Rule *has been edited in translation by Thomas Symonds, Thomas Nelson & Sons, New York, 1953.*

From
THE AGREEMENT CONCERNING THE RULE

While the third lesson is being chanted, let four brethren vest themselves. Let one of these dressed in an alb enter, but as if for some other purpose, and secretly approach the place of the sepulchre. And there let him sit quietly holding a palm frond in his hand. While the third responsory is being celebrated, let the other three brethren follow, all dressed in copes and carrying thuribles filled with incense; and let them come before the sepulchre all walking slowly and gesturing with the thuribles as if searching for something. These things are done to imitate the Angel sitting in the tomb and the women approaching with spices to anoint the body of Jesus. But when the brother who waits sees those who wander as if in search of something approach him, let him begin to sing in a sweet medium voice:

Whom do you seek in the sepulchre, O followers of Christ?

When he has sung this to the end, let the other three respond as if with one voice:

Jesus of Nazareth crucified, O celestial one.

To which let him reply:

He is not here. He arose as He foretold. Go, announce that He arose from the dead.

At his command, let the three turn themselves to the choir, saying:

Alleluia! The Lord has arisen! Today the strong lion, Christ the Son of God has arisen from the dead!

When this has been said, let the one seated chant the antiphon as if recalling the other three:

Come and see the place where the Lord was laid. Alleluia!

Saying these words, let him arise and lifting the veil show the place of the Cross empty except for the cloth in which the Cross had been wrapped. Having seen this, let the other three put down the thuribles which they had carried into the sepulchre, take the cloth and extend it before the clergy as if to show that the Lord had arisen and was not wrapped in it, meanwhile singing this antiphon:

The Lord who was hung on the Tree of the Cross has arisen from the dead!

And let them place the cloth upon the altar. When the antiphon has been concluded, let the Prior, rejoicing with them at the triumph of Our Lord in that He cast off death and arose, begin the hymn:

We praise thee, O Lord!

And when this has been begun, let all the bells ring together.

Notes

1 Many texts of this dialogue, like the Latin one below, make this expression plural. In the dramatic presentation there were often two angels at the tomb rather than one as specified by St. Ethelwold.

2 The word *Resurrexi* at the end together with the melody accompanying it belongs to the beginning of the Introit of the mass. The musical score is reprinted from Hughes, *Early Medieval Music*, Oxford University Press, London, 1955.

OLD ENGLISH LITERATURE

The surviving monuments of Old English literature probably represent only a small part of a much larger body of writings. This is especially true of the poetry. Bede tells us that other poets imitated Caedmon, and we know from Asser's *Life* that King Alfred was especially fond of poems in English. The name of one poet, Cynewulf, survives; but we know even less about him as a person than we know about Caedmon. Of the surviving poetry, the greatest portion is clearly of Christian inspiration and reflects only indirectly the traditions of the pagan Germanic past. In some instances, notably where the most famous of the poems, *Beowulf*, is concerned, scholars are still disputing the relative importance of pagan and Christian ideals as sources of literary inspiration. The problem is complicated by the fact that the Christianity of the period embodied

Facing page: Aseberg ship.

many attitudes that appear strange to us today and by the further fact that our knowledge of Germanic paganism is fragmentary. It is clear that what is called "the code of the *comitatus*" described by Tacitus plays, in a modified form, a large part in some of the poems. This is especially true of *The Battle of Maldon*. But it is not at all clear that this code was felt to be at variance with the Christian ideals of the day.

For a general survey of Old English literature, see George K. Anderson, *The Literature of the Anglo-Saxons*, Princeton University Press, Princeton, N.J., 1949. The question of the exact nature of Old English versification is still not settled, but a sensitive and useful analysis is provided by John C. Pope, *The Rhythm of Beowulf*, Yale University Press, New Haven, Conn., 1942. The Christianity of the period and its influence on the poetry are discussed by Bernard F. Huppé, *Doctrine and Poetry*, State University of New York Press, New York, 1959. Representative selections from the specifically Christian poetry of the period in excellent Modern English translations may be found in Charles W. Kennedy,

Early English Christian Poetry, Oxford University Press, New York, 1963. The same author's *The Earliest English Poetry*, Oxford University Press, New York, 1943, contains balanced critical accounts of the poems. A convenient survey of recent criticism is afforded by Stanley Greenfield, *A Critical History of Old English Literature*, New York University Press, New York, 1965. The serious student who wishes to explore Old English cultural backgrounds should consult Dorothy Whitelock's lecture, *Changing Currents in Anglo-Saxon Studies*, Cambridge University Press, London, 1958.

There are a number of good books that supply historical background. Perhaps the most attractive is R. H. Hodgkin, *History of the Anglo-Saxons*, second edition, Oxford University Press, London, 1939. The standard history is now F. M. Stenton, *Anglo-Saxon England*, second edition, Clarendon Press, Oxford, 1947. A readable brief survey is Peter Hunter Blair, *An Introduction to Anglo-Saxon England*, Cambridge University Press, London, 1956.

 ## A. *Beowulf*[1]

We do not know exactly when Beowulf *was composed, and we know nothing about the author. A great deal has been written about the poem, and attitudes toward it have changed considerably in recent years. For a general introduction the student should consult F. Klaeber's edition of the original text, D. C. Heath and Company, Boston, 1950, which contains in addition to a long and careful introduction extensive notes and a full bibliography. A standard work is R. W. Chambers,* Beowulf, *Cambridge University Press, London, 1959, a book that includes much useful material. Some notion of the character of more recent criticism may be obtained by consulting Lewis E. Nicholson,* An Anthology of Beowulf Criticism, *University of Notre Dame Press, Notre Dame, Ind., 1963. More conservative attitudes toward the poem have recently been restated by Kenneth Sisam,* The Structure of Beowulf, *Clarendon Press, Oxford, 1965.*

Note

1   The translation is by Charles W. Kennedy, reprinted by permission of the Oxford University Press.

BEOWULF

[The Danish Court and the Raids of Grendel]

Lo! we have listened to many a lay
Of the Spear-Danes' fame, their splendor of old,
Their mighty princes, and martial deeds!
Many a mead-hall Scyld, son of Sceaf,
Snatched from the forces of savage foes.
From a friendless foundling, feeble and wretched,
He grew to a terror as time brought change.
He throve under heaven in power and pride
Till alien peoples beyond the ocean
Paid toll and tribute. A good king he!
　To him thereafter an heir was born,
A son of his house, whom God had given
As stay to the people; God saw the distress
The leaderless nation had long endured.
The Giver of glory, the Lord of life,
Showered fame on the son of Scyld;
His name was honored, Beowulf known,
To the farthest dwellings in Danish lands.
So must a young man strive for good
With gracious gifts from his father's store,
That in later seasons, if war shall scourge,
A willing people may serve him well.
'Tis by earning honor a man must rise
In every state. Then his hour struck,
And Scyld passed on to the peace of God.
　As their leader had bidden, whose word was law
In the Scylding realm which he long had ruled,
His loving comrades carried him down
To the shore of ocean; a ring-prowed ship,
Straining at anchor and sheeted with ice,
Rode in the harbor, a prince's pride.
Therein they laid him, their well-loved lord,
Their ring-bestower, in the ship's embrace,
The mighty prince at the foot of the mast
Amid much treasure and many a gem
From far-off lands. No lordlier ship
Have I ever heard of, with weapons heaped,
With battle-armor, with bills and byrnies.
On the ruler's breast lay a royal treasure
As the ship put out on the unknown deep.
With no less adornment they dressed him round,
Or gift of treasure, than once they gave
Who launched him first on the lonely sea
While still but a child. A golden standard

They raised above him, high over head,
Let the wave take him on trackless seas.
Mournful their mood and heavy their hearts;
Nor wise man nor warrior knows for a truth
Unto what haven that cargo came.
　Then Beowulf ruled o'er the Scylding realm,
Beloved and famous, for many a year—
The prince, his father, had passed away—
Till, firm in wisdom and fierce in war,
The mighty Healfdene held the reign,
Ruled, while he lived, the lordly Scyldings.
Four sons and daughters were seed of his line,
Heorogar and Hrothgar, leaders of hosts,
And Halga, the good. I have also heard
A daughter was Onela's consort and queen,
The fair bed-mate of the Battle-Scylfing.
　To Hrothgar was granted glory in war,
Success in battle; retainers bold
Obeyed him gladly; his band increased
To a mighty host. Then his mind was moved
To have men fashion a high-built hall,
A mightier mead-hall than man had known,
Wherein to portion to old and young
All goodly treasure that God had given,
Save only the folk-land, and lives of men.
His word was published to many a people
Far and wide o'er the ways of earth
To rear a folk-stead richly adorned;
The task was speeded, the time soon came
That the famous mead-hall was finished and done.
To distant nations its name was known,
The Hall of the Hart; and the king kept well
His pledge and promise to deal out gifts,
Rings at the banquet. The great hall rose
High and horn-gabled, holding its place
Till the battle-surge of consuming flame
Should swallow it up; the hour was near
That the deadly hate of a daughter's husband
Should kindle to fury and savage feud.
　Then an evil spirit who dwelt in the darkness
Endured it ill that he heard each day
The din of revelry ring through the hall,
The sound of the harp, and the scop's sweet song.
A skillful bard sang the ancient story
Of man's creation; how the Maker wrought
The shining earth with its circling waters;
In splendor established the sun and moon
As lights to illumine the land of men;

Fairly adorning the fields of earth
With leaves and branches; creating life
In every creature that breathes and moves.
So the lordly warriors lived in gladness,
At ease and happy, till a fiend from hell
Began a series of savage crimes.
They called him Grendel, a demon grim
Haunting the fen-lands, holding the moors,
Ranging the wastes, where the wretched wight
Made his lair with the monster kin;
He bore the curse of the seed of Cain
Whereby God punished the grievous guilt
Of Abel's murder. Nor ever had Cain
Cause to boast of that deed of blood;
God banished him far from the fields of men;
Of his blood was begotten an evil brood,
Marauding monsters and menacing trolls,
Goblins and giants who battled with God
A long time. Grimly He gave them reward!
    Then at the nightfall the fiend drew near
Where the timbered mead-hall towered on high,
To spy how the Danes fared after the feast.
Within the wine-hall he found the warriors
Fast in slumber, forgetting grief,
Forgetting the woe of the world of men.
Grim and greedy the gruesome monster,
Fierce and furious, launched attack,
Slew thirty spearmen asleep in the hall,
Sped away gloating, gripping the spoil,
Dragging the dead men home to his den.
Then in the dawn with the coming of daybreak
The war-might of Grendel was widely known.
Mirth was stilled by the sound of weeping;
The wail of the mourner awoke with day.
And the peerless hero, the honored prince,
Weighed down with woe and heavy of heart,
Sat sorely grieving for slaughtered thanes,
As they traced the track of the cursed monster.
From that day onward the deadly feud
Was a long-enduring and loathsome strife.
    Not longer was it than one night later
The fiend returning renewed attack
With heart firm-fixed in the hateful war,
Feeling no rue for the grievous wrong.
'Twas easy thereafter to mark the men
Who sought their slumber elsewhere afar,
Found beds in the bowers, since Grendel's hate
Was so badly blazoned in baleful signs.

He held himself at a safer distance
Who escaped the clutch of the demon's claw.
So Grendel raided and ravaged the realm,
One against all, in an evil war
Till the best of buildings was empty and still.
'Twas a weary while! Twelve winters' time
The lord of the Scyldings had suffered woe,
Sore affliction and deep distress.
And the malice of Grendel, in mournful lays,
Was widely sung by the sons of men,
The hateful feud that he fought with Hrothgar—
Year after year of struggle and strife,
An endless scourging, a scorning of peace
With any man of the Danish might.
No strength could move him to stay his hand,
Or pay for his murders; the wise knew well
They could hope for no halting of savage assault.
Like a dark death-shadow the ravaging demon,
Night-long prowling the misty moors,
Ensnared the warriors, wary or weak.
No man can say how these shades of hell
Come and go on their grisly rounds.
    With many an outrage, many a crime,
The fierce lone-goer, the foe of man,
Stained the seats of the high-built house,
Haunting the hall in the hateful dark.
But throne or treasure he might not touch,
Finding no favor or grace with God.
Great was the grief of the Scylding leader,
His spirit shaken, while many a lord
Gathered in council considering long
In what way brave men best could struggle
Against these terrors of sudden attack.
From time to time in their heathen temples
Paying homage they offered prayer
That the Slayer of souls would send them succor
From all the torment that troubled the folk.
Such was the fashion and such the faith
Of their heathen hearts that they looked to hell,
Not knowing the Maker, the mighty Judge,
Nor how to worship the Wielder of glory,
The Lord of heaven, the God of hosts.
Woe unto him who in fierce affliction
Shall plunge his soul in the fiery pit
With no hope of mercy or healing change;
But well with the soul that at death seeks God,
And finds his peace in his Father's bosom.
    The son of Healfdene was heavy-hearted,

Sorrowfully brooding in sore distress,
Finding no help in a hopeless strife;
Too bitter the struggle that stunned the people,
The long oppression, loathsome and grim.

[The Coming of Beowulf]

Then tales of the terrible deeds of Grendel
Reached Hygelac's thane in his home with the
    Geats;
Of living strong men he was the strongest,
Fearless and gallant and great of heart.
He gave command for a goodly vessel
Fitted and furnished; he fain would sail
Over the swan-road to seek the king
Who suffered so sorely for need of men.
And his bold retainers found little to blame
In his daring venture, dear though he was;
They viewed the omens, and urged him on.
Brave was the band he had gathered about him,
Fourteen stalwarts seasoned and bold,
Seeking the shore where the ship lay waiting,
A sea-skilled mariner sighting the landmarks.
Came the hour of boarding; the boat was riding
The waves of the harbor under the hill.
The eager mariners mounted the prow;
Billows were breaking, sea against sand.
In the ship's hold snugly they stowed their
    trappings,
Gleaming armor and battle-gear;
Launched the vessel, the well-braced bark,
Seaward bound on a joyous journey.
Over breaking billows, with bellying sail
And foamy beak, like a flying bird
The ship sped on, till the next day's sun
Showed sea-cliffs shining, towering hills
And stretching headlands. The sea was crossed,
The voyage ended, the vessel moored.
And the Weder people waded ashore
With clatter of trappings and coats of mail;
Gave thanks to God that His grace had granted
Sea-paths safe for their ocean-journey.
    Then the Scylding coast-guard watched from
      the sea-cliff
Warriors bearing their shining shields,
Their gleaming war-gear, ashore from the ship.
His mind was puzzled, he wondered much

What men they were. On his good horse
    mounted,
Hrothgar's thane made haste to the beach,
Boldly brandished his mighty spear
With manful challenge: "What men are you,
Carrying weapons and clad in steel,
Who thus come driving across the deep
On the ocean-lanes in your lofty ship?
Long have I served as the Scylding outpost,
Held watch and ward at the ocean's edge
Lest foreign foemen with hostile fleet
Should come to harry our Danish home,
And never more openly sailed to these shores
Men without password, or leave to land.
I have never laid eyes upon earl on earth
More stalwart and sturdy than one of your troop,
A hero in armor; no hall-thane he
Tricked out with weapons, unless looks belie him,
And noble bearing. But now I must know
Your birth and breeding, nor may you come
In cunning stealth upon Danish soil.
You distant-dwellers, you far sea-farers,
Hearken, and ponder words that are plain:
'Tis best you hasten to have me know
Who your kindred and whence you come,"
    The lord of the seamen gave swift reply,
The prince of the Weders unlocked his
      word-hoard:
"We are sprung of a strain of the Geatish stock,
Hygelac's comrades and hearth-companions.
My father was famous in many a folk-land,
A leader noble, Ecgtheow his name!
Many a winter went over his head
Before death took him from home and tribe;
Well nigh every wise man remembers him well
Far and wide on the ways of earth.
With loyal purpose we seek your lord,
The prince of your people, great Healfdene's son.
Be kindly of counsel; weighty the cause
That leads us to visit the lord of the Danes;
Nor need it be secret, as far as I know!
You know if it's true, as we've heard it told,
That among the Scyldings some secret scather,
Some stealthy demon in dead of night,
With grisly horror and fiendish hate
Is spreading unheard-of havoc and death.
Mayhap I can counsel the good, old king
What way he can master the merciless fiend,

If his coil of evil is ever to end
And feverish care grow cooler and fade—
Or else ever after his doom shall be
Distress and sorrow while still there stands
This best of halls on its lofty height."
   Then from the saddle the coast-guard spoke,
The fearless sentry: "A seasoned warrior
Must know the difference between words and
     deeds,
If his wits are with him. I take your word
That your band is loyal to the lord of the
     Scyldings.
Now go your way with your weapons and
     armor,
And I will guide you; I'll give command
That my good retainers may guard your ship,
Your fresh-tarred floater, from every foe,
And hold it safe in its sandy berth,
Till the curving prow once again shall carry
The loved man home to the land of the Geat.
To hero so gallant shall surely be granted
To come from the swordplay sound and safe."
   Then the Geats marched on; behind at her
     mooring,
Fastened at anchor, their broad-beamed boat
Safely rode on her swinging cable.
Boar-heads glittered on glistening helmets
Above their cheek-guards, gleaming with gold;
Bright and fire-hardened the boar held watch
Over the column of marching men.
Onward they hurried in eager haste
Till their eyes caught sight of the high-built hall,
Splendid with gold, the seat of the king,
Most stately of structures under the sun;
Its light shone out over many a land.
The coast-guard showed them the shining hall,
The home of heroes; made plain the path;
Turned his horse; gave tongue to words:
"It is time to leave you! The mighty Lord
In His mercy shield you and hold you safe
In your bold adventure. I'll back to the sea
And hold my watch against hostile horde."

[Beowulf's Welcome at Hrothgar's Court]

The street had paving of colored stone;
The path was plain to the marching men.
Bright were their byrnies, hard and hand-linked;

In their shining armor the chain-mail sang
As the troop in their war-gear tramped to the hall.
The sea-weary sailors set down their shields,
Their wide, bright bucklers along the wall,
And sank to the bench. Their byrnies rang.
Their stout spears stood in a stack together
Shod with iron and shaped of ash.
'Twas a well-armed troop! Then a stately warrior
Questioned the strangers about their kin:
"Whence come you bearing your burnished
     shields,
Your steel-gray harness and visored helms,
Your heap of spears? I am Hrothgar's herald,
His servant-thane. I have never seen strangers,
So great a number, of nobler mien.
Not exiles, I ween, but high-minded heroes
In greatness of heart have you sought out
     Hrothgar."
Then bold under helmet the hero made answer,
The lord of the Weders, manful of mood,
Mighty of heart: "We are Hygelac's men,
His board-companions; Beowulf is my name.
I will state my mission to Healfdene's son,
The noble leader, your lordly prince,
If he will grant approach to his gracious
     presence."
And Wulfgar answered, the Wendel prince,
Renowned for merit in many a land,
For war-might and wisdom: "I will learn the
     wish
Of the Scylding leader, the lord of the Danes,
Our honored ruler and giver of rings,
Concerning your mission, and soon report
The answer our leader thinks good to give."
   He swiftly strode to where Hrothgar sat
Old and gray with his earls about him;
Crossed the floor and stood face to face
With the Danish king; he knew courtly custom.
Wulfgar saluted his lord and friend:
"Men from afar have fared to our land
Over ocean's margin—men of the Geats,
Their leader called Beowulf—seeking a boon,
The holding of parley, my prince, with thee.
O gracious Hrothgar, refuse not the favor!
In their splendid war-gear they merit well
The esteem of earls; he's a stalwart leader
Who led this troop to the land of the Danes."
   Hrothgar spoke, the lord of the Scyldings:

"Their leader I knew when he still was a lad.
His father was Ecgtheow; Hrethel the Geat
Gave him in wedlock his only daughter.
Now is their son come, keen for adventure,
Finding his way to a faithful friend.
Sea-faring men who have voyaged to Geatland
With gifts of treasure as token of peace,
Say that his hand-grip has thirty men's strength.
God, in His mercy, has sent him to save us—
So springs my hope—from Grendel's assaults.
For his gallant courage I'll load him with gifts!
Make haste now, marshal the men to the hall,
And give them welcome to Danish ground."

Then to the door went the well-known
    warrior,
Spoke from the threshold welcoming words:
"The Danish leader, my lord, declares
That he knows your kinship; right welcome
    you come,
You stout sea-rovers, to Danish soil.
Enter now, in your shining armor
And vizored helmets, to Hrothgar's hall.
But leave your shields and the shafts of slaughter
To wait the issue and weighing of words."

Then the bold one rose with his band around
    him,
A splendid massing of mighty thanes;
A few stood guard as the Geat gave bidding
Over the weapons stacked by the wall.
They followed in haste on the heels of their leader
Under Heorot's roof. Full ready and bold
The helmeted warrior strode to the hearth;
Beowulf spoke; his byrny glittered,
His war-net woven by cunning of smith:
"Hail! King Hrothgar! I am Hygelac's thane,
Hygelac's kinsman. Many a deed
Of honor and daring I've done in my youth.
This business of Grendel was brought to my ears
On my native soil. The sea-farers say
This best of buildings, this boasted hall,
Stands dark and deserted when sun is set,
When darkening shadows gather with dusk.
The best of my people, prudent and brave,
Urged me, King Hrothgar, to seek you out;
They had in remembrance my courage and
    might.
Many had seen me come safe from the conflict,
Bloody from battle; five foes I bound

Of the giant kindred, and crushed their clan.
Hard-driven in danger and darkness of night
I slew the nicors that swam the sea,
Avenged the woe they had caused the Weders,
And ended their evil—they needed the lesson!
And now with Grendel, the fearful fiend,
Single-handed I'll settle the strife!
Prince of the Danes, protector of Scyldings,
Lord of nations, and leader of men,
I beg one favor—refuse me not,
Since I come thus faring from far-off lands—
That I may alone with my loyal earls,
With this hardy company, cleanse Hart-Hall.
I have heard that the demon in proud disdain
Spurns all weapons; and I too scorn—
May Hygelac's heart have joy of the deed—
To bear my sword, or sheltering shield,
Or yellow buckler, to battle the fiend.
With hand-grip only I'll grapple with Grendel;
Foe against foe I'll fight to the death,
And the one who is taken must trust to God's
    grace!
The dèmon, I doubt not, is minded to feast
In the hall unaffrighted, as often before,
On the force of the Hrethmen, the folk of the
    Geats.
No need then to bury the body he mangles!
If death shall call me, he'll carry away
My gory flesh to his fen-retreat
To gorge at leisure and gulp me down,
Soiling the marshes with stains of blood.
There'll be little need longer to care for my body!
If the battle slays me, to Hygelac send
This best of corselets that covers my breast,
Heirloom of Hrethel, and Wayland's work,
Finest of byrnies. Fate goes as Fate must!"

Hrothgar spoke, the lord of the Scyldings:
"Deed of daring and dream of honor
Bring you, friend Beowulf, knowing our need!
Your father once fought the greatest of feuds,
Laid Heatholaf low, of the Wylfing line;
And the folk of the Weders refused him shelter
For fear of revenge. Then he fled to the South-
    Danes,
The Honor-Scyldings beyond the sea.
I was then first governing Danish ground,
As a young lad ruling the spacious realm,
The home-land of warriors. Heorogar was dead,

The son of Healfdene no longer living,
My older brother, and better than I!
Thereafter by payment composing the feud,
O'er the water's ridge I sent to the Wylfing
Ancient treasure; he swore me oaths!
It is sorrow sore to recite to another
The wrongs that Grendel has wrought in the hall,
His savage hatred and sudden assaults.
My war-troop is weakened, my hall-band is
    wasted;
Fate swept them away into Grendel's grip.
But God may easily bring to an end
The ruinous deeds of the ravaging foe.
Full often my warriors over their ale-cups
Boldly boasted, when drunk with beer,
They would bide in the beer-hall the coming of
    battle,
The fury of Grendel, with flashing swords.
Then in the dawn, when the daylight
    strengthened,
The hall stood reddened and reeking with gore,
Bench-boards wet with the blood of battle;
And I had the fewer of faithful fighters,
Beloved retainers, whom Death had taken.
Sit now at the banquet, unbend your mood,
Speak of great deeds as your heart may spur
    you!"
    Then in the beer-hall were benches made ready
For the Geatish heroes. Noble of heart,
Proud and stalwart, they sat them down
And a beer-thane served them; bore in his hands
The patterned ale-cup, pouring the mead,
While the scop's sweet singing was heard in the
    hall.
There was joy of heroes, a host at ease,
A welcome meeting of Weder and Dane.

[Unferth Taunts Beowulf]

Then out spoke Unferth, Ecglaf's son,
Who sat at the feet of the Scylding lord,
Picking a quarrel—for Beowulf's quest,
His bold sea-voyaging, irked him sore;
He bore it ill that any man other
In all the earth should ever achieve
More fame under heaven than he himself:
"Are you the Beowulf that strove with Breca

In a swimming match in the open sea,
Both of you wantonly tempting the waves,
Risking your lives on the lonely deep
For a silly boast? No man could dissuade you,
Nor friend nor foe, from the foolhardy venture
Of ocean-swimming; with outstretched arms
You clasped the sea-stream, measured her streets,
With plowing shoulders parted the waves.
The sea-flood boiled with its wintry surges,
Seven nights you toiled in the tossing sea;
His strength was the greater, his swimming the
    stronger!
The waves upbore you at break of day
To the stretching beach of the Battle-Ræmas;
And Breca departed, beloved of his people,
To the land of the Brondings, the beauteous
    home,
The stronghold fair, where he governed the folk,
The city and treasure; Beanstan's son
Made good his boast to the full against you!
Therefore, I ween, worse fate shall befall,
Stout as you are in the struggle of war,
In deeds of battle, if you dare to abide
Encounter with Grendel at coming of night."
    Beowulf spoke, the son of Ecgtheow:
"My good friend Unferth, addled with beer
Much have you made of the deeds of Breca!
I count it true that I had more courage,
More strength in swimming than any other man.
In our youth we boasted—we were both of us
    boys—
We would risk our lives in the raging sea.
And we made it good! We gripped in our hands
Naked swords, as we swam in the waves,
Guarding us well from the whales' assault.
In the breaking seas he could not outstrip me,
Nor would I leave him. For five nights long
Side by side we strove in the waters
Till racing combers wrenched us apart,
Freezing squalls, and the falling night,
And a bitter north wind's icy blast.
Rough were the waves; the wrath of the sea-fish
Was fiercely roused; but my firm-linked byrny,
The gold-adorned corselet that covered my
    breast,
Gave firm defense from the clutching foe.
Down to the bottom a savage sea-beast
Fiercely dragged me and held me fast

In a deadly grip; none the less it was granted me
To pierce the monster with point of steel.
Death swept it away with the swing of my sword.
   "The grisly sea-beasts again and again
Beset me sore; but I served them home
With my faithful blade as was well-befitting.
They failed of their pleasure to feast their fill
Crowding round my corpse on the ocean-
     bottom!
Bloody with wounds, at the break of day,
They lay on the sea-beach slain with the sword.
No more would they cumber the mariner's
     course
On the ocean deep. From the east came the sun,
Bright beacon of God, and the seas subsided;
I beheld the headlands, the windy walls.
Fate often delivers an undoomed earl
If his spirit be gallant! And so I was granted
To slay with the sword-edge nine of the nicors.
I have never heard tell of more terrible strife
Under dome of heaven in darkness of night,
Nor of man harder pressed on the paths of ocean.
But I freed my life from the grip of the foe
Though spent with the struggle. The billows
     bore me,
The swirling currents and surging seas,
To the land of the Finns. And little I've heard
Of any such valiant adventures from you!
Neither Breca nor you in the press of battle
Ever showed such daring with dripping swords—
Though I boast not of it! But you stained your
     blade
With blood of your brothers, your closest of kin;
And for that you'll endure damnation in hell,
Sharp as you are! I say for a truth,
Son of Ecglaf, never had Grendel
Wrought such havoc and woe in the hall,
That horrid demon so harried your king,
If your heart were as brave as you'd have men
     think!
But Grendel has found that he never need fear
Revenge from your people, or valiant attack
From the Victor-Scyldings; he takes his toll,
Sparing none of the Danish stock.
He slays and slaughters and works his will
Fearing no hurt at the hands of the Danes!
But soon will I show him the stuff of the Geats,
Their courage in battle and strength in the strife;

Then let him who may go bold to the mead-hall
When the next day dawns on the dwellings of
     men,
And the sun in splendor shines warm from the
     south."
Glad of heart was the giver of treasure,
Hoary-headed and hardy in war;
The lordly leader had hope of help
As he listened to Beowulf's bold resolve.
   There was revel of heroes and high carouse,
Their speech was happy; and Hrothgar's queen,
Of gentle manners, in jewelled splendor
Gave courtly greeting to all the guests.
The high-born lady first bore the beaker
To the Danish leader, lord of the land,
Bade him be blithe at the drinking of beer;
Beloved of his people, the peerless king
Joined in the feasting, had joy of the cup.
Then to all alike went the Helming lady
Bearing the beaker to old and young,
Till the jewelled queen with courtly grace
Paused before Beowulf, proffered the mead.
She greeted the Geat and to God gave thanks,
Wise of word, that her wish was granted;
At last she could look to a hero for help,
Comfort in evil. He took the cup,
The hardy warrior, at Wealhtheow's hand
And, eager for battle, uttered his boast;
Beowulf spoke, the son of Ecgtheow:
"I had firm resolve when I set to sea
With my band of earls in my ocean-ship,
Fully to work the will of your people
Or fall in the struggle slain by the foe.
I shall either perform deeds fitting an earl
Or meet in this mead-hall the coming of death!"
Then the woman was pleased with the words he
     uttered,
The Geat-lord's boast; the gold-decked queen
Went in state to sit by her lord.

[Beowulf Slays Grendel]

In the hall as of old were brave words spoken,
There was noise of revel; happy the host
Till the son of Healfdene would go to his rest.
He knew that the monster would meet in the hall
Relentless struggle when light of the sun

Was dusky with gloom of the gathering night,
And shadow-shapes crept in the covering dark,
Dim under heaven. The host arose.
Hrothgar graciously greeted his guest,
Gave rule of the wine-hall, and wished him well,
Praised the warrior in parting words:
"Never to any man, early or late,
Since first I could brandish buckler and sword,
Have I trusted this ale-hall save only to you!
Be mindful of glory, show forth your strength,
Keep watch against foe! No wish of your heart
Shall go unfulfilled if you live through the fight."
  Then Hrothgar withdrew with his host of
    retainers,
The prince of the Scyldings, seeking his queen,
The bed of his consort. The King of Glory
Had stablished a hall-watch, a guard against
    Grendel,
Dutifully serving the Danish lord,
The land defending from loathsome fiend.
The Geatish hero put all his hope
In his fearless might and the mercy of God!
He stripped from his shoulders the byrny of steel,
Doffed helmet from head; into hand of thane
Gave inlaid iron, the best of blades;
Bade him keep well the weapons of war.
Beowulf uttered a gallant boast,
The stalwart Geat, ere he sought his bed:
"I count myself nowise weaker in war
Or grapple of battle than Grendel himself.
Therefore I scorn to slay him with sword,
Deal deadly wound, as I well might do!
Nothing he knows of a noble fighting,
Of thrusting and hewing and hacking of shield,
Fierce as he is in the fury of war.
In the shades of darkness we'll spurn the sword
If he dares without weapon to do or to die.
And God in His wisdom shall glory assign,
The ruling Lord, as He deems it right."
Then the bold in battle bowed down to his rest,
Cheek pressed pillow; the peerless thanes
Were stretched in slumber around their lord.
Not one had hope of return to his home,
To the stronghold or land where he lived as a boy.
For they knew how death had befallen the Danes,
How many were slain as they slept in the wine-
    hall.

But the wise Lord wove them fortune in war,
Gave strong support to the Weder people;
They slew their foe by the single strength
Of a hero's courage. The truth is clear,
God rules forever the race of men.
  Then through the shades of enshrouding night
The fiend came stealing; the archers slept
Whose duty was holding the horn-decked hall—
Though one was watching—full well they knew
No evil demon could drag them down
To shades under ground if God were not willing.
But the hero watched awaiting the foe,
Abiding in anger the issue of war.
  From the stretching moors, from the misty
    hollows,
Grendel came creeping, accursed of God,
A murderous ravager minded to snare
Spoil of heroes in high-built hall.
Under clouded heavens he held his way
Till there rose before him the high-roofed house,
Wine-hall of warriors gleaming with gold.
Nor was it the first of his fierce assaults
On the home of Hrothgar; but never before
Had he found worse fate or hardier hall-thanes!
Storming the building he burst the portal,
Though fastened of iron, with fiendish strength;
Forced open the entrance in savage fury
And rushed in rage o'er the shining floor.
A baleful glare from his eyes was gleaming
Most like to a flame. He found in the hall
Many a warrior sealed in slumber,
A host of kinsmen. His heart rejoiced;
The savage monster was minded to sever
Lives from bodies ere break of day,
To feast his fill of the flesh of men.
But he was not fated to glut his greed
With more of mankind when the night was
    ended!
  The hardy kinsman of Hygelac waited
To see how the monster would make his attack.
The demon delayed not, but quickly clutched
A sleeping thane in his swift assault,
Tore him in pieces, bit through the bones,
Gulped the blood, and gobbled the flesh,
Greedily gorged on the lifeless corpse,
The hands and the feet. Then the fiend stepped
    nearer,

Sprang on the Sea-Geat lying outstretched,
Clasping him close with his monstrous claw.
But Beowulf grappled and gripped him hard,
Struggled up on his elbow; the shepherd of sins
Soon found that never before had he felt
In any man other in all the earth
A mightier hand-grip; his mood was humbled,
His courage fled; but he found no escape!
He was fain to be gone; he would flee to the
    darkness,
The fellowship of devils. Far different his fate
From that which befell him in former days!
The hardy hero, Hygelac's kinsman,
Remembered the boast he had made at the
    banquet;
He sprang to his feet, clutched Grendel fast,
Though fingers were cracking, the fiend pulling
    free.
The earl pressed after; the monster was minded
To win his freedom and flee to the fens.
He knew that his fingers were fast in the grip
Of a savage foe. Sorry the venture,
The raid that the ravager made on the hall.
    There was din in Heorot. For all the Danes,
The city-dwellers, the stalwart Scyldings,
That was a bitter spilling of beer!
The walls resounded, the fight was fierce,
Savage the strife as the warriors struggled.
The wonder was that the lofty wine-hall
Withstood the struggle, nor crashed to earth,
The house so fair; it was firmly fastened
Within and without with iron bands
Cunningly smithied; though men have said
That many a mead-bench gleaming with gold
Sprang from its sill as the warriors strove.
The Scylding wise men had never weened
That any ravage could wreck the building,
Firmly fashioned and finished with bone,
Or any cunning compass its fall,
Till the time when the swelter and surge of fire
Should swallow it up in a swirl of flame.
    Continuous tumult filled the hall;
A terror fell on the Danish folk
As they heard through the wall the horrible
    wailing,
The groans of Grendel, the foe of God
Howling his hideous hymn of pain,

The hell-thane shrieking in sore defeat.
He was fast in the grip of the man who was
    greatest
Of mortal men in the strength of his might,
Who would never rest while the wretch was
    living,
Counting his life-days a menace to man.
    Many an earl of Beowulf brandished
His ancient iron to guard his lord,
To shelter safely the peerless prince.
They had no knowledge, those daring thanes,
When they drew their weapons to hack and hew,
To thrust to the heart, that the sharpest sword,
The choicest iron in all the world,
Could work no harm to the hideous foe.
On every sword he had laid a spell,
On every blade; but a bitter death
Was to be his fate; far was the journey
The monster made to the home of fiends.
    Then he who had wrought such wrong to men,
With grim delight as he warred with God,
Soon found that his strength was feeble and
    failing
In the crushing hold of Hygelac's thane.
Each loathed the other while life should last!
There Grendel suffered a grievous hurt,
A wound in the shoulder, gaping and wide;
Sinews snapped and bone-joints broke,
And Beowulf gained the glory of battle.
Grendel, fated, fled to the fens,
To his joyless dwelling, sick unto death.
He knew in his heart that his hours were
    numbered,
His days at an end. For all the Danes
Their wish was fulfilled in the fall of Grendel.
The stranger from far, the stalwart and strong,
Had purged of evil the hall of Hrothgar,
And cleansed of crime; the heart of the hero
Joyed in the deed his daring had done.
The lord of the Geats made good to the East-
    Danes
The boast he had uttered; he ended their ill,
And all the sorrow they suffered long
And needs must suffer—a foul offense.
The token was clear when the bold in battle
Laid down the shoulder and dripping claw—
Grendel's arm—in the gabled hall!

[The Joy of the Danes and the Lay of Sigemund]

When morning came, as they tell the tale,
Many a warrior hastened to hall,
Folk-leaders faring from far and near
Over wide-running ways, to gaze at the wonder,
The trail of the demon. Nor seemed his death
A matter of sorrow to any man
Who viewed the tracks of the vanquished
    monster
As he slunk weary-hearted away from the hall,
Doomed and defeated and marking his flight
With bloody prints to the nicors' pool.
The crimson currents bubbled and heaved
In eddying reaches reddened with gore;
The surges boiled with the fiery blood.
But the monster had sunk from the sight of men.
In that fenny covert the cursed fiend
Not long thereafter laid down his life,
His heathen spirit; and hell received him.

   Then all the comrades, the old and young,
The brave of heart, in a blithesome band
Came riding their horses home from the mere.
Beowulf's prowess was praised in song;
And many men stated that south or north,
Over all the world, or between the seas,
Or under the heaven, no hero was greater,
More worthy of rule. But no whit they slighted
The gracious Hrothgar, their good old king.
Time and again they galloped their horses,
Racing their roans where the roads seemed
    fairest;
Time and again a gleeman chanted,
A minstrel mindful of saga and lay.
He wove his words in a winsome pattern,
Hymning the burden of Beowulf's feat,
Clothing the story in skillful verse.

   All tales he had ever heard told he sang of
    Sigemund's glory,
Deeds of the Wælsing forgotten, his weary roving
   and wars,
Feuds and fighting unknown to men, save Fitela only,
Tales told by uncle to nephew when the two were
   companions,
What time they were bosom-comrades in battle and
   bitter strife.
Many of monster blood these two had slain with the
   sword-edge;

Great glory Sigemund gained that lingered long after
   death,
When he daringly slew the dragon that guarded the
   hoard of gold.
Under the ancient rock the warrior ventured alone,
No Fitela fighting beside him; but still it befell
That his firm steel pierced the worm, the point stood
   fast in the wall;
The dragon had died the death! And the hero's daring
Had won the treasure to have and to hold as his heart
   might wish.
Then the Wælsing loaded his sea-boat, laid in the
   breast of the ship
Wondrous and shining treasure; the worm dissolved
   in the heat.
Sigemund was strongest of men in his deeds of daring,
Warrior's shield and defender, most famous in days
   of old
After Heremod's might diminished, his valor and
   vigor in war,
Betrayed in the land of the Jutes to the hands of his
   foemen, and slain.
Too long the surges of sorrow swept over his soul;
   in the end
His life was a lingering woe to people and princes.
In former days his fate was mourned by many a warrior
Who had trusted his lord for protection from terror
   and woe,
Had hoped that the prince would prosper, wielding
   his father's wealth,
Ruling the tribe and the treasure, the Scylding city
   and home.
Hygelac's kinsman had favor and friendship of all
   mankind,
But the stain of sin sank deep into Heremod's heart.

   Time and again on their galloping steeds
Over yellow roads they measured the mile-paths;
Morning sun mounted the shining sky
And many a hero strode to the hall,
Stout of heart, to behold the wonder.
The worthy ruler, the warder of treasure,
Set out from the bowers with stately train;
The queen with her maidens paced over the
    mead-path.
   Then spoke Hrothgar; hasting to hall
He stood at the steps, stared up at the roof
High and gold-gleaming; saw Grendel's hand:

"Thanks be to God for this glorious sight!
I have suffered much evil, much outrage from
    Grendel,
But the God of glory works wonder on wonder.
I had no hope of a haven from sorrow
While this best of houses stood badged with
    blood,
A woe far-reaching for all the wise
Who weened that they never could hold the hall
Against the assaults of devils and demons.
But now with God's help this hero has compassed
A deed our cunning could no way contrive.
Surely that woman may say with truth,
Who bore this son, if she still be living,
Our ancient God showed favor and grace
On her bringing-forth! O best of men,
I will keep you, Beowulf, close to my heart
In firm affection; as son to father
Hold fast henceforth to this foster-kinship.
You shall know not want of treasure or wealth
Or goodly gift that your wish may crave,
While I have power. For poorer deeds
I have granted guerdon, and graced with honor
Weaker warriors, feebler in fight.
You have done such deeds that your fame shall
    flourish
Through all the ages! God grant you still
All goodly grace as He gave before."
    Beowulf spoke, the son of Ecgtheow:
"By the favor of God we won the fight,
Did the deed of valor, and boldly dared
The might of the monster. I would you could see
The fiend himself lying dead before you!
I thought to grip him in stubborn grasp
And bind him down on the bed of death,
There to lie straining in struggle for life,
While I gripped him fast lest he vanish away.
But I might not hold him or hinder his going
For God did not grant it, my fingers failed.
Too savage the strain of his fiendish strength!
To save his life he left shoulder and claw,
The arm of the monster, to mark his track.
But he bought no comfort; no whit thereby
Shall the wretched ravager racked with sin,
The loathsome spoiler, prolong his life.
A deep wound holds him in deadly grip,
In baleful bondage; and black with crime
The demon shall wait for the day of doom

When the God of glory shall give decree."
    Then slower of speech was the son of Ecglaf,
More wary of boasting of warlike deeds,
While the nobles gazed at the grisly claw,
The fiend's hand fastened by hero's might
On the lofty roof. Most like to steel
Were the hardened nails, the heathen's hand-
    spurs,
Horrible, monstrous; and many men said
No tempered sword, no excellent iron,
Could have harmed the monster or hacked away
The demon's battle-claw dripping with blood.

[The Feast and the Lay of Finnsburg]

In joyful haste was Heorot decked
And a willing host of women and men
Gaily dressed and adorned the guest-hall.
Splendid hangings with sheen of gold
Shone on the walls, a glorious sight
To eyes that delight to behold such wonders.
The shining building was wholly shattered
Though braced and fastened with iron bands;
Hinges were riven; the roof alone
Remained unharmed when the horrid monster,
Foul with evil, slunk off in flight,
Hopeless of life. It is hard to flee
The touch of death, let him try who will;
Necessity urges the sons of men,
The dwellers on earth, to their destined place
Where the body, bound in its narrow bed,
After the feasting is fast in slumber.
    Soon was the time when the son of Healfdene
Went to the wine-hall; he fain would join
With happy heart in the joy of feasting.
I never have heard of a mightier muster
Of proud retainers around their prince.
All at ease they bent to the benches,
Had joy of the banquet; their kinsmen bold,
Hrothgar and Hrothulf, happy of heart,
In the high-built hall drank many a mead-cup.
The hall of Hrothgar was filled with friends;
No treachery yet had troubled the Scyldings.
Upon Beowulf, then, as a token of triumph,
Hrothgar bestowed a standard of gold,
A banner embroidered, a byrny and helm.
In sight of many, a costly sword

Before the hero was borne on high;
Beowulf drank of many a bowl.
No need for shame in the sight of heroes
For gifts so gracious! I never have heard
Of many men dealing in friendlier fashion,
To others on ale-bench, richer rewards,
Four such treasures fretted with gold!
On the crest of the helmet a crowning wreath,
Woven of wire-work, warded the head
Lest tempered swordblade, sharp from the file,
Deal deadly wound when the shielded warrior
Went forth to battle against the foe.
Eight horses also with plated headstalls
The lord of heroes bade lead into hall;
On one was a saddle skillfully fashioned
And set with jewels, the battle-seat
Of the king himself, when the son of Healfdene
Would fain take part in the play of swords;
Never in fray had his valor failed,
His kingly courage, when corpses were falling.
And the prince of the Ingwines gave all these gifts
To the hand of Beowulf, horses and armor;
Bade him enjoy them! With generous heart
The noble leader, the lord of heroes,
Rewarded the struggle with steeds and with
    treasure,
So that none can belittle, and none can blame,
Who tells the tale as it truly happened.
    Then on the ale-bench to each of the earls
Who embarked with Beowulf, sailing the sea-
    paths,
The lord of princes dealt ancient heirlooms,
Gift of treasure, and guerdon of gold
To requite his slaughter whom Grendel slew,
As he would have slain others, but all-wise God
And the hero's courage had conquered Fate.
The Lord ruled over the lives of men
As He rules them still. Therefore understanding
And a prudent spirit are surely best!
He must suffer much of both weal and woe
Who dwells here long in these days of strife.
    Then song and revelry rose in the hall;
Before Healfdene's leader the harp was struck
And hall-joy wakened; the song was sung,
Hrothgar's gleeman rehearsed the lay
Of the sons of Finn when the terror befell them:

*Hnæf of the Scyldings, the Half-Dane, fell in the
    Frisian slaughter;*

*Nor had Hildeburh cause to acclaim the faith of the
    Jutish folk,*
*Blameless, bereft of her brothers in battle, and
    stripped of her sons*
*Who fell overcome by their fate and wounded with
    spears!*
*Not for nothing Hoc's daughter bewailed death's
    bitter decree,*
*In the dawn under morning skies, when she saw the
    slaughter of kinsmen*
*In the place where her days had been filled with the
    fairest delights of the world.*
Finn's thanes were slain in the fight, save only a few;
*Nor could he do battle with Hengest or harry his
    shattered host;*
*And the Frisians made terms with the Danes, a
    truce, a hall for their dwelling,*
*A throne, and a sharing of rights with the sons of the
    Jutes,*
*And that Finn, the son of Folcwalda, each day
    would honor the Danes,*
*The host of Hengest, with gifts, with rings and
    guerdon of gold,*
*Such portion of plated treasure as he dealt to the
    Frisian folk*
*When he gladdened their hearts in the hall. So both
    were bound by the truce.*
*And Finn swore Hengest with oaths that were
    forceful and firm*
*He would rightfully rule his remnant, follow his
    council's decree,*
*And that no man should break the truce, or breach it
    by word or by will,*
*Nor the lordless in malice lament they were fated to
    follow*
*The man who had murdered their liege; and, if ever a
    Frisian*
*Fanned the feud with insolent speech, the sword
    should avenge it.*
    *Then a funeral pyre was prepared, and gold was
    drawn from the hoard,*
The best of the Scylding leaders was laid on the bier;
*In the burning pile was a gleaming of blood-stained
    byrnies,*
*The gilded swine and the boar-helm hard from the
    hammer,*
Many a warrior fated with wounds and fallen in battle.
*And Hildeburh bade that her son be laid on the bier
    of Hnæf,*

His body consumed in the surging flame at his uncle's
   shoulder.
Beside it the lady lamented, singing her mournful dirge.
The hero was placed on the pyre; the greatest of
   funeral flames
Rolled with a roar to the skies at the burial barrow.
Heads melted and gashes gaped, the mortal wounds
   of the body,
Blood poured out in the flames; the fire, most greedy
   of spirits,
Swallowed up all whom battle had taken of both
   their peoples.
Their glory was gone! The warriors went to their
   homes,
Bereft of their friends, returning to Friesland, to city
   and stronghold.
   Then Hengest abode with Finn all the slaughter-
      stained winter,
But his heart longed ever for home, though he could
   not launch on the sea
His ring-stemmed ship, for the billows boiled with
   the storm,
Strove with the wind, and the winter locked ocean in
   bonds of ice;
Till a new Spring shone once more on the dwellings
   of men,
The sunny and shining days which ever observe their
   season.
The winter was banished afar, and fair the bosom of
   earth.
Then the exile longed to be gone, the guest from his
   dwelling,
But his thoughts were more on revenge than on
   voyaging over the wave,
Plotting assault on the Jutes, renewal of war with
   the sword.
So he spurned not the naked hint when Hunlafing
   laid in his lap
The battle-flasher, the best of blades, well known to
   the Jutes!
In his own home death by the sword befell Finn,
   the fierce-hearted,
When Guthlaf and Oslaf requited the grim attack,
The woe encountered beyond the sea, the sorrow they
   suffered,
Nor could bridle the restive spirits within their
   breasts!
   Then the hall was reddened with blood and bodies
      of foemen,

Finn killed in the midst of his men, and the fair
   queen taken.
The Scylding warriors bore to their ships all treasure
   and wealth,
Such store as they found in the home of Finn of
   jewels and gems.
And the noble queen they carried across the sea-paths,
Brought her back to the Danes, to her own dear
   people.

So the song was sung, the lay recited,
The sound of revelry rose in the hall.
Stewards poured wine from wondrous vessels;
And Wealhtheow, wearing a golden crown,
Came forth in state where the two were sitting,
Courteous comrades, uncle and nephew,
Each true to the other in ties of peace.
Unferth, the orator, sat at the feet
Of the lord of the Scyldings; and both showed
   trust
In his noble mind, though he had no mercy
On kinsmen in swordplay; the Scylding queen
   spoke:
"My sovereign lord, dispenser of treasure,
Drink now of this flagon, have joy of the feast!
Speak to the Geats, O gold-friend of men,
In winning words as is well-befitting;
Be kind to the Geat-men and mindful of gifts
From the gold you have garnered from near
   and far.
You have taken as son, so many have told me,
This hardy hero. Heorot is cleansed,
The gleaming gift-hall. Rejoice while you may
In lavish bounty, and leave to your kin
People and kingdom when time shall come,
Your destined hour, to look on death.
I know the heart of my gracious Hrothulf,
That he'll safely shelter and shield our sons
When you leave this world, if he still is living.
I know he will favor with gracious gifts
These boys of ours, if he bears in mind
The many honors and marks of love
We bestowed upon him while he still was a boy."
   She turned to the bench where her boys were
      sitting,
Hrethric and Hrothmund, the sons of heroes,
The youth together; there the good man sat,
Beowulf of the Geats, beside the two brothers.
Then the cup was offered with gracious greeting,

And seemly presents of spiraled gold,
A corselet, and rings, and the goodliest collar
Of all that ever were known on earth.
I have never heard tell of a worthier treasure
In the hoarding of heroes beneath the sky
Since Hama bore off to the shining city
The Brosings' jewel, setting and gems,
Fled from Eormenric's cruel craft
And sought the grace of eternal glory.
Hygelac, the Geat, grandson of Swerting
Wore the ring in the last of his raids,
Guarding the spoil under banner in battle,
Defending the treasure. Overtaken by Fate,
In the flush of pride he fought with the Frisians
And met disaster. The mighty prince
Carried the ring o'er the cup of the waves,
The precious jewel, and sank under shield.
Then his body fell into Frankish hands,
His woven corselet and jewelled collar,
And weaker warriors plundered the dead
After the carnage and welter of war.
The field of battle was covered with corpses
Of Geats who had fallen, slain by the sword.
    The sound of revelry rose in the hall;
Wealhtheow spoke to the warrior host:
"Take, dear Beowulf, collar and corselet,
Wear these treasures with right good will!
Thrive and prosper and prove your might!
Befriend my boys with your kindly counsel;
I will remember and I will repay.
You have earned the undying honor of heroes
In regions reaching as far and wide
As the windy walls that the sea encircles.
May Fate show favor while life shall last!
I wish you wealth to your heart's content;
In your days of glory be good to my sons!
Here each hero is true to other,
Gentle of spirit, loyal to lord,
Friendly thanes and a folk united,
Wine-cheered warriors who do my will."

[The Troll-wife Avenges Grendel]

Then she went to her seat. At the fairest of feasts
Men drank of the wine-cup, knowing not Fate,
Nor the fearful doom that befell the earls
When darkness gathered, and gracious Hrothgar

Sought his dwelling and sank to rest.
A host of heroes guarded the hall
As they oft had done in the days of old.
They stripped the benches and spread the floor
With beds and bolsters. But one of the beer-
        thanes
Bowed to his hall-rest doomed to death.
They set at their heads their shining shields,
Their battle-bucklers; and there on the bench
Above each hero his towering helmet,
His spear and corselet hung close at hand.
It was ever their wont to be ready for war
At home or in field, as it ever befell
That their lord had need. 'Twas a noble race!
    Then they sank to slumber. But one paid dear
For his evening rest, as had often happened
When Grendel haunted the lordly hall
And wrought such ruin, till his end was come,
Death for his sins; it was easily seen,
Though the monster was slain, an avenger
        survived
Prolonging the feud, though the fiend had
        perished.
The mother of Grendel, a monstrous hag,
Brooded over her misery, doomed to dwell
In evil waters and icy streams
From ancient ages when Cain had killed
His only brother, his father's son.
Banished and branded with marks of murder
Cain fled far from the joys of men,
Haunting the barrens, begetting a brood
Of grisly monsters; and Grendel was one,
The fiendish ogre who found in the hall
A hero on watch, and awaiting the fray.
The monster grappled; the Geat took thought
Of the strength of his might, that marvelous gift
Which the Lord had given; in God he trusted
For help and succor and strong support,
Whereby he humbled the fiend from hell,
Destroyed the demon; and Grendel fled,
Harrowed in heart and hateful to man,
Deprived of joy, to the place of death.
But rabid and raging his mother resolved
On a dreadful revenge for the death of her son!
    She stole to the hall where the Danes were
        sleeping,
And horror fell on the host of earls
When the dam of Grendel burst in the door.

But the terror was less as the war-craft is weaker,
A woman's strength, than the might of a man
When the hilted sword, well shaped by the
    hammer,
The blood-stained iron of tempered edge,
Hews the boar from the foeman's helmet.
Then in the hall was the hard-edged blade,
The stout steel, brandished above the benches;
Seizing their shields men stayed not for helmet
Or ample byrny, when fear befell.
As soon as discovered, the hag was in haste
To fly to the open, to flee for her life.
One of the warriors she swiftly seized,
Clutched him fast and made off to the fens.
He was of heroes the dearest to Hrothgar,
The best of comrades between two seas;
The warrior brave, the stout-hearted spearman,
She slew in his sleep. Nor was Beowulf there;
But after the banquet another abode
Had been assigned to the glorious Geat.
There was tumult in Heorot. She tore from its
    place
The blood-stained claw. Care was renewed!
It was no good bargain when both in turn
Must pay the price with the lives of friends!
    Then the white-haired warrior, the aged king,
Was numb with sorrow, knowing his thane
No longer was living, his dearest man dead.
Beowulf, the brave, was speedily summoned,
Brought to the bower; the noble prince
Came with his comrades at dawn of day
Where the wise king awaited if God would
    award
Some happier turn in these tidings of woe.
The hero came tramping into the hall
With his chosen band—the boards resounded—
Greeted the leader, the Ingwine lord,
And asked if the night had been peaceful and
    pleasant.
    Hrothgar spoke, the lord of the Scyldings:
"Ask not of pleasure; pain is renewed
For the Danish people. Æschere is dead!
Dead is Yrmenlaf's elder brother!
He was my comrade, closest of counsellors,
My shoulder-companion as side by side
We fought for our lives in the welter of war,
In the shock of battle when boar-helms crashed.
As an earl should be, a prince without peer,

Such was Æschere, slain in the hall
By the wandering demon! I know not whither
She fled to shelter, proud of her spoil,
Gorged to the full. She avenged the feud
Wherein yesternight you grappled with Grendel
And savagely slew him because so long
He had hunted and harried the men of my folk.
He fell in the battle and paid with his life.
But now another fierce ravager rises
Avenging her kinsman, and carries it far,
As it seems to many a saddened thane
Who grieves in his heart for his treasure-giver.
This woe weighs heavy! The hand lies still
That once was lavish of all delights.
    "Oft in the hall I have heard my people,
Comrades and counsellors, telling a tale
Of evil spirits their eyes have sighted,
Two mighty marauders who haunt the moors.
One shape, as clearly as men could see,
Seemed woman's likeness, and one seemed man,
An outcast wretch of another world,
And huger far than a human form.
Grendel my countrymen called him, not
    knowing
What monster-brood spawned him, what sire
    begot.
Wild and lonely the land they live in,
Wind-swept ridges and wolf-retreats,
Dread tracts of fen where the falling torrent
Downward dips into gloom and shadow
Under the dusk of the darkening cliff.
Not far in miles lies the lonely mere
Where trees firm-rooted and hung with frost
Overshroud the wave with shadowing gloom.
And there a portent appears each night,
A flame in the water; no man so wise
Who knows the bound of its bottomless depth.
The heather-stepper, the horned stag,
The antlered hart hard driven by hounds,
Invading that forest in flight from afar
Will turn at bay and die on the brink
Ere ever he'll plunge in that haunted pool.
'Tis an eerie spot! Its tossing spray
Mounts dark to heaven when high winds stir
The driving storm, and the sky is murky,
And with foul weather the heavens weep.
On your arm only rests all our hope!
Not yet have you tempted those terrible reaches

The region that shelters that sinful wight.
Go if you dare! I will give requital
With ancient treasure and twisted gold,
As I formerly gave in guerdon of battle,
If out of that combat you come alive."
   Beowulf spoke, the son of Ecgtheow:
"Sorrow not, brave one! Better for man
To avenge a friend than much to mourn.
All men must die; let him who may
Win glory ere death. That guerdon is best
For a noble man when his name survives him.
Then let us rise up, O ward of the realm,
And haste us forth to behold the track
Of Grendel's dam. And I give you pledge
She shall not in safety escape to cover,
To earthy cavern, or forest fastness,
Or gulf of ocean, go where she may.
This day with patience endure the burden
Of every woe, as I know you will."
Up sprang the ancient, gave thanks to God
For the heartening words the hero had spoken.

[Beowulf Slays the Troll-Wife]

Quickly a horse was bridled for Hrothgar,
A mettlesome charger with braided mane;
In royal splendor the king rode forth
Mid the trampling tread of a troop of shieldmen.
The tracks lay clear where the fiend had fared
Over plain and bottom and woodland path,
Through murky moorland making her way
With the lifeless body, the best of thanes
Who of old with Hrothgar had guarded the hall.
By a narrow path the king pressed on
Through rocky upland and rugged ravine,
A lonely journey, past looming headlands,
The lair of monster and lurking troll.
Tried retainers, a trusty few,
Advanced with Hrothgar to view the ground.
Sudden they came on a dismal covert
Of trees that hung over hoary stone,
Over churning water and blood-stained wave.
Then for the Danes was the woe the deeper,
The sorrow sharper for Scylding earls,
When they first caught sight, on the rocky
    sea-cliff,
Of slaughtered Æschere's severed head.

The water boiled in a bloody swirling
With seething gore as the spearmen gazed.
The trumpet sounded a martial strain;
The shield-troop halted. Their eyes beheld
The swimming forms of strange sea-dragons,
Dim serpent shapes in the watery depths,
Sea-beasts sunning on headland slopes;
Snakelike monsters that oft at sunrise
On evil errands scour the sea.
Startled by tumult and trumpet's blare,
Enraged and savage, they swam away;
But one the lord of the Geats brought low,
Stripped of his sea-strength, despoiled of life,
As the bitter bow-bolt pierced his heart.
His watery-speed grew slower, and ceased,
And he floated, caught in the clutch of death.
Then they hauled him in with sharp-hooked
    boar-spears,
By sheer strength grappled and dragged him
    ashore,
A wondrous wave-beast; and all the array
Gathered to gaze at the grisly guest.
   Beowulf donned his armor for battle,
Heeded not danger; the hand-braided byrny,
Broad of shoulder and richly bedecked,
Must stand the ordeal of the watery depths.
Well could that corselet defend the frame
Lest hostile thrust should pierce to the heart.
Or blows of battle beat down the life.
A gleaming helmet guarded his head
As he planned his plunge to the depths of the
    pool
Through the heaving waters—a helm adorned
With lavish inlay and lordly chains,
Ancient work of the weapon-smith
Skilfully fashioned, beset with the boar,
That no blade of battle might bite it through.
Not the least or the worst of his war-equipment
Was the sword the herald of Hrothgar loaned
In his hour of need—Hrunting its name—
An ancient heirloom, trusty and tried;
Its blade was iron, with etched design,
Tempered in blood of many a battle.
Never in fight had it failed the hand
That drew it daring the perils of war,
The rush of the foe. Not the first time then
That its edge must venture on valiant deeds.
But Ecglaf's stalwart son was unmindful

Of words he had spoken while heated with wine,
When he loaned the blade to a better swordsman.
He himself dared not hazard his life
In deeds of note in the watery depths;
And thereby he forfeited honor and fame.
Not so with that other undaunted spirit
After he donned his armor for battle.
Beowulf spoke, the son of Ecgtheow:
"O gracious ruler, gold-giver to men,
As I now set forth to attempt this feat,
Great son of Healfdene, hold well in mind
The solemn pledge we plighted of old,
That if doing your service I meet my death
You will mark my fall with a father's love.
Protect my kinsmen, my trusty comrades,
If battle take me. And all the treasure
You have heaped on me bestow upon Hygelac,
Hrothgar beloved! The lord of the Geats,
The son of Hrethel, shall see the proof,
Shall know as he gazes on jewels and gold,
That I found an unsparing dispenser of bounty,
And joyed, while I lived, in his generous gifts.
Give back to Unferth the ancient blade,
The sword-edge splendid with curving scrolls,
For either with Hrunting I'll reap rich harvest
Of glorious deeds, or death shall take me."
    After these words the prince of the Weders
Awaited no answer, but turned to the task,
Straightway plunged in the swirling pool.
Nigh unto a day he endured the depths
Ere he first had view of the vast sea-bottom.
Soon she found, who had haunted the flood,
A ravening hag, for a hundred half-years,
Greedy and grim, that a man was groping
In daring search through the sea-troll's home.
Swift she grappled and grasped the warrior
With horrid grip, but could work no harm,
No hurt to his body; the ring-locked byrny
Cloaked his life from her clutching claw;
Nor could she tear through the tempered mail
With her savage fingers. The she-wolf bore
The ring-prince down through the watery depths
To her den at the bottom; nor could Beowulf
    draw
His blade for battle, though brave his mood.
Many a sea-beast, strange sea-monsters,
Tasked him hard with their menacing tusks,
Broke his byrny and smote him sore.

Then he found himself in a fearsome hall
Where water came not to work him hurt,
But the flood was stayed by the sheltering roof.
There in the glow of firelight gleaming
The hero had view of the huge sea-troll.
He swung his war-sword with all his strength,
Withheld not the blow, and the savage blade
Sang on her head its hymn of hate.
But the bold one found that the battle-flasher
Would bite no longer, nor harm her life.
The sword-edge failed at his sorest need.
Often of old with ease it had suffered
The clash of battle, cleaving the helm,
The fated warrior's woven mail.
That time was first for the treasured blade
That its glory failed in the press of the fray.
But fixed of purpose and firm of mood
Hygelac's earl was mindful of honor;
In wrath, undaunted, he dashed to earth
The jewelled sword with its scrolled design,
The blade of steel; staked all on strength,
On the might of his hand, as a man must do
Who thinks to win in the welter of battle
Enduring glory; he fears not death.
The Geat-prince joyed in the straining struggle,
Stalwart-hearted and stirred to wrath,
Gripped the shoulder of Grendel's dam
And headlong hurled the hag to the ground.
But she quickly clutched him and drew him close,
Countered the onset with savage claw.
The warrior staggered, for all his strength,
Dismayed and shaken and borne to earth.
She knelt upon him and drew her dagger,
With broad bright blade, to avenge her son,
Her only issue. But the corselet's steel
Shielded his breast and sheltered his life
Withstanding entrance of point and edge.
    Then the prince of the Geats would have
        gone his journey,
The son of Ecgtheow, under the ground;
But his sturdy breast-net, his battle-corselet,
Gave him succor, and holy God,
The Lord all-wise, awarded the mastery;
Heaven's Ruler gave right decree.
    Swift the hero sprang to his feet;
Saw mid the war-gear a stately sword,
An ancient war-brand of biting edge,
Choicest of weapons worthy and strong,

The work of giants, a warrior's joy,
So heavy no hand but his own could hold it,
Bear to battle or wield in war.
Then the Scylding warrior, savage and grim,
Seized the ring-hilt and swung the sword,
Struck with fury, despairing of life,
Thrust at the throat, broke through the bone-
        rings;
The stout blade stabbed through her fated flesh.
She sank in death; the sword was bloody;
The hero joyed in the work of his hand.
The gleaming radiance shimmered and shone
As the candle of heaven shines clear from the sky.
Wrathful and resolute Hygelac's thane
Surveyed the span of the spacious hall;
Grimly gripping the hilted sword
With upraised weapon he turned to the wall.
The blade had failed not the battle-prince;
A full requital he firmly planned
For all the injury Grendel had done
In numberless raids on the Danish race,
When he slew the hearth-companions of
        Hrothgar,
Devoured fifteen of the Danish folk
Clasped in slumber, and carried away
As many more spearmen, a hideous spoil.
All this the stout-heart had stern requited;
And there before him bereft of life
He saw the broken body of Grendel
Stilled in battle, and stretched in death,
As the struggle in Heorot smote him down.
The corpse sprang wide as he struck the blow,
The hard sword-stroke that severed the head.
    Then the tried retainers, who there with
        Hrothgar
Watched the face of the foaming pool,
Saw that the churning reaches were reddened,
The eddying surges stained with blood.
And the gray, old spearmen spoke of the hero,
Having no hope he would ever return
Crowned with triumph and cheered with spoil.
Many were sure that the savage sea-wolf
Had slain their leader. At last came noon.
The stalwart Scyldings forsook the headland;
Their proud gold-giver departed home.
But the Geats sat grieving and sick in spirit,
Stared at the water with longing eyes,
Having no hope they would ever behold

Their gracious leader and lord again.
    Then the great sword, eaten with blood of
        battle,
Began to soften and waste away
In iron icicles, wonder of wonders,
Melting away most like to ice
When the Father looses the fetters of frost,
Slackens the bondage that binds the wave,
Strong in power of times and seasons;
He is true God! Of the goodly treasures
From the sea-cave Beowulf took but two,
The monster's head and the precious hilt
Blazing with gems; but the blade had melted,
The sword dissolved, in the deadly heat,
The venomous blood of the fallen fiend.

[Beowulf Returns to Heorot]

Then he who had compassed the fall of his foes
Came swimming up through the swirling surge.
Cleansed were the currents, the boundless abyss,
Where the evil monster had died the death
And looked her last on this fleeting world.
With sturdy strokes the lord of the seamen
To land came swimming, rejoiced in his spoil,
Had joy of the burden he brought from the
        depths.
And his mighty thanes came forward to meet
        him,
Gave thanks to God they were granted to see
Their well-loved leader both sound and safe.
From the stalwart hero his helmet and byrny
Were quickly loosened; the lake lay still,
Its motionless reaches reddened with blood.
Fain of heart men fared o'er the footpaths,
Measured the ways and the well-known roads.
From the sea-cliff's brim the warriors bore
The head of Grendel, with heavy toil;
Four of the stoutest, with all their strength,
Could hardly carry on swaying spear
Grendel's head to the gold-decked hall.
Swift they strode, the daring and dauntless,
Fourteen Geats, to the Hall of the Hart;
And proud in the midst of his marching men
Their leader measured the path to the mead-hall.
The hero entered, the hardy in battle,
The great in glory, to greet the king;
And Grendel's head by the hair was carried

Across the floor where the feasters drank—
A terrible sight for lord and for lady—
A gruesome vision whereon men gazed!
 Beowulf spoke, the son of Ecgtheow:
"O son of Healfdene, lord of the Scyldings!
This sea-spoil wondrous, whereon you stare,
We joyously bring you in token of triumph!
Barely with life surviving the battle,
The war under water, I wrought the deed
Weary and spent; and death had been swift
Had God not granted His sheltering strength.
My strong-edged Hrunting, stoutest of blades,
Availed me nothing. But God revealed—
Often His arm has aided the friendless—
The fairest of weapons hanging on wall,
An ancient broadsword; I seized the blade,
Slew in the struggle, as fortune availed,
The cavern-warders. But the war-brand old,
The battle-blade with its scrolled design,
Dissolved in the gush of the venomous gore;
The hilt alone I brought from the battle.
The record of ruin, and slaughter of Danes,
These wrongs I avenged, as was fitting and right.
Now I can promise you, prince of the Scyldings,
Henceforth in Heorot rest without rue
For you and your nobles; nor need you dread
Slaughter of follower, stalwart or stripling,
Or death of earl, as of old you did."
Into the hand of the aged leader,
The gray-haired hero, he gave the hilt,
The work of giants, the wonder of gold.
At the death of the demons the Danish lord
Took in his keeping the cunning craft,
The wondrous marvel, of mighty smiths;
When the world was freed of the ravaging fiend,
The foe of God, and his fearful dam
Marked with murder and badged with blood,
The bound hilt passed to the best of kings
Who ever held sceptre beside two seas,
And dealt out treasure in Danish land!
 Hrothgar spoke, beholding the hilt,
The ancient relic whereon was etched
An olden record of struggle and strife,
The flood that ravaged the giant race,
The rushing deluge of ruin and death.
That evil kindred were alien to God,
But the Ruler avenged with the wrath of the
 deep!

On the hilt-guards, likewise, of gleaming gold
Was rightly carven in cunning runes,
Set forth and blazoned, for whom that blade,
With spiral tooling and twisted hilt,
That fairest of swords, was fashioned and
 smithied.
Then out spoke Hrothgar, Healfdene's son,
And all the retainers were silent and still:
"Well may he say, whose judgment is just,
Recalling to memory men of the past,
That this earl was born of a better stock!
Your fame, friend Beowulf, is blazoned abroad
Over all wide ways, and to every people.
In manful fashion have you showed your
 strength,
Your might and wisdom. My word I will keep,
The plighted friendship we formerly pledged.
Long shall you stand as a stay to your people,
A help to heroes, as Heremod was not
To the Honor-Scyldings, to Ecgwela's sons!
Not joy to kindred, but carnage and death,
He wrought as he ruled o'er the race of the Danes.
In savage anger he slew his comrades,
His table-companions, till, lawless and lone,
An odious outcast, he fled from men.
Though God had graced him with gifts of
 strength,
Over all men exalting him, still in his breast
A bloodthirsty spirit was rooted and strong.
He dealt not rings to the Danes for glory;
His lot was eternal torment of woe,
And lasting affliction. Learn from his fate!
Strive for virtue! I speak for your good;
In the wisdom of age I have told the tale.
 "'Tis a wondrous marvel how mighty God
In gracious spirit bestows on men
The gift of wisdom, and goodly lands,
And princely power! He rules over all!
He suffers a man of lordly line
To set his heart on his own desires,
Awards him fullness of wordly joy,
A fair home-land, and the sway of cities,
The wide dominion of many a realm,
An ample kingdom, till, cursed with folly,
The thoughts of his heart take no heed of his end.
He lives in luxury, knowing not want,
Knowing no shadow of sickness or age;
No haunting sorrow darkens his spirit,

No hatred or discord deepens to war;
The world is sweet, to his every desire,
And evil assails not—until in his heart
Pride overpowering gathers and grows!
The warder slumbers, the guard of his spirit;
Too sound is that sleep, too sluggish the weight
Of worldly affairs, too pressing the Foe,
The Archer who looses the arrows of sin.
   "Then is his heart pierced, under his helm,
His soul in his bosom, with bitter dart.
He has no defense for the fierce assaults
Of the loathsome Fiend. What he long has
    cherished
Seems all too little! In anger and greed
He gives no guerdon of plated rings.
Since God has granted him glory and wealth
He forgets the future, unmindful of Fate.
But it comes to pass in the day appointed
His feeble body withers and fails;
Death descends, and another seizes
His hoarded riches and rashly spends
The princely treasure, imprudent of heart.
Beloved Beowulf, best of warriors,
Avoid such evil and seek the good,
The heavenly wisdom. Beware of pride!
Now for a time you shall feel the fullness
And know the glory of strength, but soon
Sickness or sword shall strip you of might,
Or clutch of fire, or clasp of flood,
Or flight of arrow, or bite of blade,
Or relentless age; or the light of the eye
Shall darken and dim, and death on a sudden,
O lordly ruler, shall lay you low.
   "A hundred half-years I've been head of the
    Ring-Danes,
Defending the folk against many a tribe
With spear-point and sword in the surges of
    battle
Till not one was hostile 'neath heaven's expanse.
But a loathsome change swept over the land,
Grief after gladness, when Grendel came,
That evil invader, that ancient foe!
Great sorrow of soul from his malice I suffered;
But thanks be to God who has spared me to see
His bloody head at the battle's end!
Join now in the banquet; have joy of the feast,
O mighty in battle! And the morrow shall bring
Exchange of treasure in ample store."

Happy of heart the Geat leader hastened,
Took seat at the board as the good king bade.
Once more, as of old, brave heroes made merry
And tumult of revelry rose in the hall.
   Then dark over men the night shadows
    deepened;
The host all arose, for Hrothgar was minded,
The gray, old Scylding, to go to his rest.
On Beowulf too, after labor of battle,
Came limitless longing and craving for sleep.
A hall-thane graciously guided the hero,
Weary and worn, to the place prepared,
Serving his wishes and every want
As befitted a mariner come from afar.
The stout-hearted warrior sank to his rest;
The lofty building, splendid and spacious,
Towered above him. His sleep was sound
Till the black-coated raven, blithesome of spirit,
Hailed the coming of Heaven's bliss.

[The Parting of Beowulf and Hrothgar]

Then over the shadows uprose the sun.
The Geats were in haste, and eager of heart
To depart to their people. Beowulf longed
To embark in his boat, to set sail for his home.
The hero tendered the good sword Hrunting
To the son of Ecglaf, bidding him bear
The lovely blade; gave thanks for the loan,
Called it a faithful friend in the fray,
Bitter in battle. The greathearted hero
Spoke no word in blame of the blade!
Arrayed in war-gear, and ready for sea,
The warriors bestirred them; and, dear to the
    Danes,
Beowulf sought the high seat of the king.
The gallant in war gave greeting to Hrothgar;
Beowulf spoke, the son of Ecgtheow:
"It is time at last to tell of our longing!
Our homes are far, and our hearts are fain
To seek again Hygelac over the sea.
You have welcomed us royally, harbored us well
As a man could wish; if I ever can win
Your affection more fully, O leader of heroes,
Swift shall you find me to serve you again!
If ever I learn, o'er the levels of ocean,
That neighboring nations beset you sore,

As in former days when foemen oppressed,
With thanes by the thousand I will hasten to help.
For I know that Hygelac, lord of the Geats,
Prince of the people, though young in years,
Will favor and further by word and deed
That my arm may aid you, and do you honor,
With stout ash-spear and succor of strength
In the press of need. And if princely Hrethric
Shall purpose to come to the court of the Geats,
He will find there a legion of loyal friends.
That man fares best to a foreign country
Who himself is stalwart and stout of heart."
    Hrothgar addressed him, uttered his answer:
"Truly, these words has the Lord of wisdom
Set in your heart, for I never have harkened
To speech so sage from a man so young.
You have strength, and prudence, and wisdom
    of word!
I count it true if it come to pass
That point of spear in the press of battle,
Or deadly sickness, or stroke of sword,
Shall slay your leader, the son of Hrethel,
The prince of your people, and you still live,
The Sea-Geats could have no happier choice
If you would be willing to rule the realm,
As king to hold guard o'er the hoard and the
    heroes.
The longer I know you, the better I like you,
Beloved Beowulf! You have brought it to pass
That between our peoples a lasting peace
Shall bind the Geats to the Danish-born;
And strife shall vanish, and war shall cease,
And former feuds, while I rule this realm.
And many a man, in the sharing of treasure,
Shall greet another with goodly gifts
O'er the gannet's bath. And the ring-stemmed
    ship
Shall bear over ocean bountiful riches
In pledge of friendship. Our peoples, I know,
Shall be firm united toward foe and friend,
Faultless in all things, in fashion of old."
    Then the son of Healfdene, shelter of earls,
Bestowed twelve gifts on the hero in hall,
Bade him in safety with bounty of treasure
Seek his dear people, and soon return.
The peerless leader, the Scylding lord,
Kissed the good thane and clasped to his bosom
While tears welled fast from the old man's eyes.

Both chances he weighed in his wise, old heart,
But greatly doubted if ever again
They should meet at council or drinking of
    mead.
Nor could Hrothgar master—so dear was the
    man—
His swelling sorrow; a yearning love
For the dauntless hero, deep in his heart,
Burned through his blood. Beowulf, the brave,
Prizing his treasure and proud of the gold,
Turned away, treading the grassy plain.
The ring-stemmed sea-goer, riding at anchor,
Awaited her lord. There was loud acclaim
Of Hrothgar's gifts, as they went their way.
He was a king without failing or fault,
Till old age, master of all mankind,
Stripped him of power and pride of strength.

[Beowulf Returns to Geatland]

Then down to the sea came the band of the brave,
The host of young heroes in harness of war,
In their woven mail; and the coast-warden
    viewed
The heroes' return, as he heeded their coming!
No uncivil greeting he gave from the sea-cliff
As they strode to ship in their glistening steel;
But rode toward them and called their return
A welcome sight for their Weder kin.
There on the sand the ring-stemmed ship,
The broad-bosomed bark, was loaded with
    war-gear,
With horses and treasure; the mast towered high
Over the riches of Hrothgar's hoard.
A battle-sword Beowulf gave to the boatwarden
Hilted with gold; and thereafter in hall
He had the more honor because of the heirloom,
The shining treasure. The ship was launched.
Cleaving the combers of open sea
They dropped the shoreline of Denmark astern.
A stretching sea-cloth, a bellying sail,
Was bent on the mast; there was groaning of
    timbers;
A gale was blowing; the boat drove on.
The foamy-necked plunger plowed through the
    billows,
The ring-stemmed ship through the breaking
    seas,

Till at last they sighted the sea-cliffs of Geatland,
The well-known headlands; and, whipped by
    the wind,
The boat drove shoreward and beached on the
    sand.
  Straightway the harbor-watch strode to the
    seashore;
Long had he watched for the well-loved men,
Scanning the ocean with eager eyes!
The broad-bosomed boat he bound to the shingle
With anchor ropes, lest the rip of the tide
Should wrench from its mooring the comely
    craft.
  From the good ship Beowulf bade them bear
The precious jewels and plated gold,
The princely treasure. Not long was the path
That led to where Hygelac, son of Hrethel,
The giver of treasure, abode in his home
Hard by the sea-wall, hedged by his thanes.
Spacious the castle, splendid the king
On his high hall-seat; youthful was Hygd,
Wise and well-born—though winters but few
Hæreth's daughter had dwelt at court.
She was noble of spirit, not sparing in gifts
Of princely treasure to the people of the Geats.

  *Of the pride of Thryth, and her crimes, the fair
    folk-queen was free;*
*Thryth, of whose liegemen none dared by day, save
    only her lord,*
*Lift up his eyes to her face, lest his fate be a mortal
    bondage,*
*Seizure and fetters and sword, a blow of the
    patterned blade*
*Declaring his doom, and proclaiming the coming of
    death.*
That is no way of a queen, nor custom of lovely lady,
*Though peerless her beauty and proud, that a weaver
    of peace*
*Should send a dear man to his death for a feigned
    affront.*
*But the kinsman of Hemming at last made an end of
    her evil.*
For men at the drinking of mead tell tale of a change,
*How she wrought less ruin and wrong when, given
    in marriage*
*Gleaming with jewels and gold, to the high-born
    hero and young,*
Over the fallow flood she sailed, at her father's bidding

Seeking the land of Offa, and there while she lived,
Famed for goodness, fulfilled her fate on the throne.
She held high love for her lord, the leader of heroes,
*The best, I have heard, of mankind or the children
    of men*
*Between the two seas; for Offa, the stalwart, was
    honored*
*For his gifts and his greatness in war. With wisdom
    he governed;*
*And from him Eomær descended, Hemming's
    kinsman, grandson of Garmund,*
Stalwart and strong in war, and the helper of heroes.

  Then the hero strode with his stalwart band
Across the stretches of sandy beach,
The wide sea-shingle. The world-candle shone,
The hot sun hasting on high from the south.
Marching together they made their way
To where in his stronghold the stout young king,
Ongentheow's slayer, protector of earls,
Dispensed his treasure. Soon Hygelac heard
Of the landing of Beowulf, bulwark of men,
That his shoulder-companion had come to his
    court
Sound and safe from the strife of battle.
  The hall was prepared, as the prince gave
    bidding,
Places made ready for much travelled men.
And he who came safe from the surges of battle
Sat by the side of the king himself,
Kinsman by kinsman; in courtly speech
His liege lord greeted the loyal thane
With hearty welcome. And Hæreth's daughter
Passed through the hall-building pouring the
    mead,
With courtesy greeting the gathered host,
Bearing the cup to the hands of the heroes.
In friendly fashion in high-built hall
Hygelac questioned his comrade and thane;
For an eager longing burned in his breast
To hear from the Sea-Geats the tale of their
    travels.
"How did you fare in your far sea-roving,
Beloved Beowulf, in your swift resolve
To sail to the conflict, the combat in Heorot,
Across the salt waves? Did you soften at all
The sorrows of Hrothgar, the weight of his woe?
Deeply I brooded with burden of care
For I had no faith in this far sea-venture

For one so beloved. Long I implored
That you go not against the murderous monster,
But let the South Danes settle the feud
Themselves with Grendel. To God be thanks
That my eyes behold you unharmed and
    unhurt."
    Beowulf spoke, the son of Ecgtheow:
"My dear lord Hygelac, many have heard
Of that famous grapple 'twixt Grendel and me,
The bitter struggle and strife in the hall
Where he formerly wrought such ruin and
    wrong,
Such lasting sorrow for Scylding men!
All that I avenged! Not any on earth
Who longest lives of that loathsome brood,
No kin of Grendel cloaked in his crime,
Has cause to boast of that battle by night!
First, in that country, I fared to the hall
With greeting for Hrothgar; Healfdene's
    kinsman
Learned all my purpose, assigned me a place
Beside his own son. 'Twas a happy host!
I never have seen under span of heaven
More mirth of heroes sitting at mead!
The peerless queen, the peace-pledge of peoples,
Passed on her round through the princely hall;
There was spurring of revels, dispensing of rings,
Ere the noble woman went to her seat.
    "At times in the host the daughter of Hrothgar
Offered the beaker to earls in turn;
Freawaru men called her, the feasters in hall,
As she held out to heroes the well-wrought cup.
Youthful and gleaming with jewels of gold
To the fair son of Froda the maiden is plighted.
For the Scylding leader, the lord of the land,
Deems it wise counsel, accounting it gain,
To settle by marriage the murderous feud,
The bloody slaughter! But seldom for long
Does the spear go ungrasped when a prince has
    perished,
Though the bride in her beauty be peerless and
    proud!
Ill may it please the Heathobard prince
And all his thanes, when he leads his lady
Into the hall, that a Danish noble
Should be welcomed there by the Heathobard
    host.
For on him shall flash their forefathers' heirlooms,
Hard-edged, ring-hilted, the Heathobards' hoard

When of old they had war-might, nor wasted in
    battle
Their lives and the lives of their well-loved
    thanes.
    "Then an aged spearman shall speak at the
    beer-feast,
The treasure beholding with sorrow of heart,
Remembering sadly the slaughter of men,
Grimly goading the young hero's spirit,
Spurring to battle, speaking this word:
'Do you see, my lord, the sword of your father,
The blade he bore to the last of his fights,
The pride of his heart as, under his helmet,
The Scyldings slew him, the savage Danes,
When Withergyld fell, and after the slaughter,
The fall of heroes, they held the field?
And now a son of those bloody butchers,
Proud in his trappings, tramps into hall
And boasts of the killing, clothed with the
    treasure
That is yours by your birthright to have and to
    hold?'
    "Over and over the old man will urge him,
With cutting reminders recalling the past
Till it comes at last that the lady's thane,
For the deeds of his father, shall forfeit his life
In a bloody slaughter, slain by the sword,
While the slayer goes scatheless knowing the
    land.
On both sides then shall sword-oaths be broken
When hate boils up within Ingeld's heart,
And his love of his lady grows cooler and lessens
Because of his troubles. I count not true
Heathobard faith, nor their part in the peace,
Nor their friendship firm to the Danish folk.
    "I must now speak on, dispenser of treasure,
Further of Grendel, till fully you know
How we fared in that fierce and furious fight!
When the jewel of heaven had journeyed o'er
    earth,
The wrathful demon, the deadly foe,
Stole through the darkness spying us out
Where still unharmed we guarded the gold-hall.
But doom in battle and bitter death
Were Handscio's fate! He was first to perish
Though girded with weapon and famous in war.
Grendel murdered him, mangled his body,
Bolted the dear man's bloody corpse.
No sooner for that would the slaughterous spirit,

Bloody of tooth and brooding on evil,
Turn empty-handed away from the hall!
The mighty monster made trial of my strength
Clutching me close with his ready claw.
Wide and wondrous his huge pouch hung
Cunningly fastened, and fashioned with skill
From skin of dragon by devil's craft.
Therein the monster was minded to thrust me
Sinless and blameless, and many beside.
But it might not be, when I rose in wrath,
And fronted the hell-fiend face to face.
Too long is the tale how I took requital
On the cursed foe for his every crime,
But the deeds I did were a lasting honor,
Beloved prince, to your people's name.
He fled away, and a fleeting while
Possessed his life and the world's delights;
But he left in Heorot his severed hand,
A bloody reminder to mark his track.
Humbled in spirit and wretched in heart
Down he sank to the depths of the pool.
  "When the morrow fell, and we feasted
    together,
The Scylding ruler rewarded me well
For the bloody strife, in guerdon bestowing
Goodly treasure of beaten gold.
There was song and revel. The aged Scylding
From well-stored mind spoke much of the past.
A warrior sang to the strains of the glee-wood,
Sometimes melodies mirthful and joyous,
Sometimes lays that were tragic and true.
And the great-hearted ruler at times would tell
A tale of wonder in fitting words.
Heavy with years the white-haired warrior
Grieved for his youth and the strength that was
    gone;
And his heart was moved by the weight of his
    winters
And many a memory out of the past.
All the long day we made merry together
Till another night came to the children of men,
And quickly the mother of Grendel was minded
To wreak her vengeance; raging with grief
She came to the hall where the hate of the
    Weders
Had slain her son. But the hideous hag
Avenged his killing; with furious clutch
She seized a warrior—the soul of Æschere,

Wise and aged, went forth from the flesh!
Not at all could the Danes, when the morrow
    dawned,
Set brand to his body or burn on the bale
Their well-loved comrade. With fiendish clasp
She carried his corpse through the fall of the
    force.
That was to Hrothgar, prince of the people,
Sorest of sorrows that ever befell!
For your sake the sad-hearted hero implored me
To prove my valor and, venturing life,
To win renown in the watery depths.
He promised reward. Full well is it known
How I humbled the horrible guard of the gulf.
Hand to hand for a space we struggled
Till the swirling eddies were stained with blood;
With cleaving sword-edge I severed the head
Of Grendel's hag in that hall of strife.
Not easily thence did I issue alive,
But my death was not fated; not yet was I
    doomed!
  "Then the son of Healfdene, the shelter of
    earls,
Gave many a treasure to mark the deed.
The good king governed with courtly custom;
In no least way did I lose reward,
The meed of my might; but he gave me treasure,
Healfdene's son, to my heart's desire.
These riches I bring you, ruler of heroes,
And warmly tender with right good will.
Save for you, King Hygelac, few are my
    kinsmen,
Few are the favors but come from you."
  Then he bade men bring the boar-crested
    headpiece,
The towering helmet, and steel-gray sark,
The splendid war-sword, and spoke this word:
"The good king Hrothgar gave me this gift,
This battle-armor, and first to you
Bade tell the tale of his friendly favor.
He said King Heorogar, lord of the Scyldings,
Long had worn it, but had no wish
To leave the mail to his manful son,
The dauntless Heoroweard, dear though he was!
Well may you wear it! Have joy of it all."
As I've heard the tale, he followed the trappings
With four bay horses, matched and swift,
Graciously granting possession of both,

The steeds and the wealth. 'Tis the way of a
    kinsman,
Not weaving in secret the wiles of malice
Nor plotting the fall of a faithful friend.
To his kinsman Hygelac, hardy in war,
The heart of the nephew was trusty and true;
Dear to each was the other's good!
To Hygd, as I've heard, he presented three horses
Gaily saddled, slender and sleek,
And the gleaming necklace Wealhtheow gave,
A peerless gift from a prince's daughter.
With the gracious guerdon, the goodly jewel,
Her breast thereafter was well bedecked.

    So the son of Ecgtheow bore himself bravely,
Known for his courage and courteous deeds,
Strove after honor, slew not his comrades
In drunken brawling; nor brutal his mood.
But the bountiful gifts which the Lord God
    gave him
He held with a power supreme among men.
He had long been scorned, when the sons of the
    Geats
Accounted him worthless; the Weder lord
Held him not high among heroes in hall.
Laggard they deemed him, slothful and slack.
But time brought solace for all his ills!

    Then the battle-bold king, the bulwark of
        heroes,
Bade bring a battle-sword banded with gold,
The heirloom of Hrethel; no sharper steel,
No lovelier treasure, belonged to the Geats.
He laid the war-blade on Beowulf's lap,
Gave him a hall and a stately seat
And hides seven thousand. Inherited lands
Both held by birth-fee, home and estate.
But one held rule o'er the spacious realm,
And higher therein his order and rank.

[The Fire-Dragon and the Treasure]

It later befell in the years that followed
After Hygelac sank in the surges of war,
And the sword slew Heardred under his shield
When the Battle-Scylfings, those bitter fighters,
Invaded the land of the victor-folk
Overwhelming Hereric's nephew in war,
That the kingdom came into Beowulf's hand.

For fifty winters he governed it well,
Aged and wise with the wisdom of years,
Till a fire-drake flying in darkness of night
Began to ravage and work his will.
On the upland heath he guarded a hoard,
A stone barrow lofty. Under it lay
A path concealed from the sight of men.
There a thief broke in on the heathen treasure,
Laid hand on a flagon all fretted with gold,
As the dragon discovered, though cozened in
    sleep
By the pilferer's cunning. The people soon found
That the mood of the dragon was roused to
    wrath!

    Not at all with intent, of his own free will,
Did he ravish the hoard, who committed the
    wrong;
But in dire distress the thrall of a thane,
A guilty fugitive fleeing the lash,
Forced his way in. There a horror befell him!
Yet the wretched exile escaped from the dragon,
Swift in retreat when the terror arose.
A flagon he took. There, many such treasures
Lay heaped in that earth-hall where the owner
    of old
Had carefully hidden the precious hoard,
The countless wealth of a princely clan.
Death came upon them in days gone by
And he who lived longest, the last of his line,
Guarding the treasure and grieving for friend,
Deemed it his lot that a little while only
He too might hold that ancient hoard.
A barrow new-built near the ocean billows
Stood cunningly fashioned beneath the cliff;
Into the barrow the ring-warden bore
The princely treasure, the precious trove
Of golden wealth, and these words he spoke:
"Keep thou, O Earth, what men could not
    keep—
This costly treasure—it came from thee!
Baleful slaughter has swept away,
Death in battle, the last of my blood;
They have lived their lives; they have left the
    mead-hall.
Now I have no one to wield the sword,
No one to polish the plated cup,
The precious flagon—the host is fled.
The hard-forged helmet fretted with gold

Shall be stripped of its inlay; the burnishers sleep
Whose charge was to brighten the battle-masks.
Likewise the corselet that countered in war
Mid clashing of bucklers the bite of the sword—
Corselet and warrior decay into dust;
Mailed coat and hero are moveless and still.
No mirth of gleewood, no music of harp,
No good hawk swinging in flight through the
    hall;
No swift steed stamps in the castle yard;
Death has ravished an ancient race."
So sad of mood he bemoaned his sorrow,
Lonely and sole survivor of all,
Restless by day and wretched by night
Till the clutch of death caught at his heart.
Then the goodly treasure was found unguarded
By the venomous dragon enveloped in flame,
The old naked night-foe flying in darkness,
Haunting the barrows; a bane that brings
A fearful dread to the dwellers of earth.
His wont is to hunt out a hoard under ground
And guard heathen gold, growing old with the
    years.
But no whit for that is his fortune more fair!
    For three hundred winters this waster of
        peoples
Held the huge treasure-hall under the earth
Till the robber aroused him to anger and rage,
Stole the rich beaker and bore to his master,
Imploring his lord for a compact of peace.
So the hoard was robbed and its riches
    plundered;
To the wretch was granted the boon that he
    begged;
And his liege-lord first had view of the treasure,
The ancient work of the men of old.
Then the worm awakened and war was kindled,
The rush of the monster along the rock,
When the fierce one found the tracks of the foe;
He had stepped too close in his stealthy cunning
To the dragon's head. But a man undoomed
May endure with ease disaster and woe
If he has His favor who wields the world.
Swiftly the fire-drake sought through the plain
The man who wrought him this wrong in his
    sleep.
Inflamed and savage he circled the mound,
But the waste was deserted—no man was in sight.

The worm's mood was kindled to battle and war;
Time and again he returned to the barrow
Seeking the treasure-cup. Soon he was sure
That a man had plundered the precious gold.
Enraged and restless the hoard-warden waited
The gloom of evening. The guard of the mound
Was swollen with anger; the fierce one resolved
To requite with fire the theft of the cup.
Then the day was sped as the worm desired;
Lurking no longer within his wall
He sallied forth surrounded with fire,
Encircled with flame. For the folk of the land
The beginning was dread as the ending was
    grievous
That came so quickly upon their lord.
    Then the baleful stranger belched fire and
        flame,
Burned the bright dwellings—the glow of the
    blaze
Filled hearts with horror. The hostile flier
Was minded to leave there nothing alive.
From near and from far the war of the dragon,
The might of the monster, was widely revealed
So that all could see how the ravaging scather
Hated and humbled the Geatish folk.
Then he hastened back ere the break of dawn
To his secret den and the spoil of gold.
He had compassed the land with a flame of fire,
A blaze of burning; he trusted the wall,
The sheltering mound, and the strength of his
    might—
But his trust betrayed him! The terrible news
Was brought to Beowulf, told for a truth,
That his home was consumed in the surges of fire,
The goodly dwelling and throne of the Geats.
The heart of the hero was heavy with anguish,
The greatest of sorrows; in his wisdom he
    weened
He had grievously angered the Lord Everlasting,
Blamefully broken the ancient law.
Dark thoughts stirred in his surging bosom,
Welled in his breast, as was not his wont.
The flame of the dragon had levelled the fortress,
The people's stronghold washed by the wave.
But the king of warriors, prince of the Weders,
Exacted an ample revenge for it all.
The lord of warriors and leader of earls
Bade work him of iron a wondrous shield,

Knowing full well that wood could not serve him
Nor linden defend him against the flame.
The stalwart hero was doomed to suffer
The destined end of his days on earth;
Likewise the worm, though for many a winter
He had held his watch o'er the wealth of the
    hoard.
The ring-prince scorned to assault the dragon
With a mighty army, or host of men.
He feared not the combat, nor counted of worth
The might of the worm, his courage and craft,
Since often aforetime, beset in the fray,
He had safely issued from many an onset,
Many a combat and, crowned with success,
Purged of evil the hall of Hrothgar
And crushed out Grendel's loathsome kin.

   Nor was that the least of his grim engagements
When Hygelac fell, great Hrethel's son;
When the lord of the people, the prince of the
    Geats,
Died of his wounds in the welter of battle,
Perished in Friesland, smitten with swords.
Thence Beowulf came by his strength in
    swimming;
Thirty sets of armor he bore on his back
As he hasted to ocean. The Hetware men
Had no cause to boast of their prowess in battle
When they gathered against him with linden
    shields.
But few of them ever escaped his assault
Or came back alive to the homes they had left;
So the son of Ecgtheow swam the sea-stretches,
Lonely and sad, to the land of his kin.
Hygd then tendered him kingdom and treasure,
Wealth of riches and royal throne,
For she had no hope with Hygelac dead
That her son could defend the seat of his fathers
From foreign foemen. But even in need,
No whit the more could they move the hero
To be Heardred's liege, or lord of the land.
But he fostered Heardred with friendly counsel,
With honor and favor among the folk,
Till he came of age and governed the Geats.
Then the sons of Ohthere fleeing in exile
Sought out Heardred over the sea.
They had risen against the lord of the Scylfings,
Best of the sea-kings, bestower of rings,
An illustrious prince in the land of the Swedes.

So Heardred fell. For harboring exiles
The son of Hygelac died by the sword.
Ongentheow's son, after Heardred was slain,
Returned to his home, and Beowulf held
The princely power and governed the Geats.
He was a good king, grimly requiting
In later days the death of his prince.
Crossing the sea with a swarming host
He befriended Eadgils, Ohthere's son,
In his woe and affliction, with weapons and men;
He took revenge in a savage assault,
And slew the king. So Ecgtheow's son
Had come in safety through all his battles,
His bitter struggles and savage strife,
To the day when he fought with the deadly
    worm.
With eleven comrades, kindled to rage
The Geat lord went to gaze on the dragon.
Full well he knew how the feud arose,
The fearful affliction; for into his hold
From hand of finder the flagon had come.
The thirteenth man in the hurrying throng
Was the sorrowful captive who caused the feud.
With woeful spirit and all unwilling
Needs must he guide them, for he only knew
Where the earth-hall stood near the breaking
    billows
Filled with jewels and beaten gold.
The monstrous warden, waiting for battle,
Watched and guarded the hoarded wealth.
No easy bargain for any of men
To seize that treasure! The stalwart king,
Gold-friend of Geats, took seat on the headland,
Hailed his comrades and wished them well.
Sad was his spirit, restless and ready,
And the march of Fate immeasurably near;
Fate that would strike, seek his soul's treasure,
And deal asunder the spirit and flesh.
Not long was his life encased in the body!
   Beowulf spoke, the son of Ecgtheow:
"Many an ordeal I endured in youth,
And many a battle. I remember it all.
I was seven winters old when the prince of the
    people,
The lord of the treasure-hoard, Hrethel the king,
From the hand of my father had me and held me,
Recalling our kinship with treasure and feast.
As long as he lived I was no less beloved,

As thane in his hall, than the sons of his house,
Herebeald and Hæthcyn and Hygelac, my lord.
For the eldest brother the bed of death
Was foully fashioned by brother's deed
When Hæthcyn let fly a bolt from his horn-bow,
Missed the mark, and murdered his lord;
Brother slew brother with bloody shaft—
A tragic deed and beyond atonement,
A foul offense to sicken the heart!
Yet none the less was the lot of the prince
To lay down his soul and his life, unavenged.
   "Even so sad and sorrowful is it,
And bitter to bear, to an old man's heart,
Seeing his young son swing on the gallows.
He wails his dirge and his wild lament
While his son hangs high, a spoil to the raven;
His aged heart can contrive no help.
Each dawn brings grief for the son that is gone
And his heart has no hope of another heir,
Seeing the one has gone to his grave.
In the house of his son he gazes in sorrow
On wine-hall deserted and swept by the wind,
Empty of joy. The horsemen and heroes
Sleep in the grave. No sound of the harp,
No welcoming revels as often of old!
He goes to his bed with his burden of grief;
To his spirit it seems that dwelling and land
Are empty and lonely, lacking his son.
   "So the helm of the Weders yearned after
      Herebeald
And welling sadness surged in his heart.
He could not avenge the feud on the slayer
Nor punish the prince for the loathsome deed,
Though he loved him no longer, nor held him
      dear.
Because of this sorrow that sore befell
He left life's joys for the heavenly light,
Granting his sons, as a good man will,
Cities and land, when he went from the world.
   "Then across the wide water was conflict and
      war,
A striving and struggle of Swedes and Geats,
A bitter hatred, when Hrethel died.
Ongentheow's sons were dauntless and daring,
Cared not for keeping of peace overseas;
But often around Hreosnabeorh slaughtered and
      slew.
My kinsmen avenged the feud and the evil,

As many have heard, though one of the Weders
Paid with his life—a bargain full bitter!
Hæthcyn's fate was to fall in the fight.
It is often recounted, a kinsman with sword-edge
Avenged in the morning the murderer's deed
When Ongentheow met Eofor. Helm split
      asunder;
The aged Scylfing sank down to his death.
The hand that felled him remembered the feud
And drew not back from the deadly blow.
   "For all the rich gifts that Hygelac gave me
I repaid him in battle with shining sword,
As chance was given. He granted me land,
A gracious dwelling and goodly estate.
Nor needed he seek of the Gifths, or the Spear-
      Danes,
Or in Swedish land, a lesser in war
To fight for pay; in the press of battle
I was always before him alone in the van.
So shall I bear me while life-days last,
While the sword holds out that has served me
      well
Early and late since I slew Dæghrefn,
The Frankish hero, before the host.
He brought no spoil from the field of battle,
No corselet of mail to the Frisian king.
Not by the sword the warden of standards,
The stalwart warrior, fell in the fight.
My battle-grip shattered the bones of his body
And silenced the heart-beat. But now with the
      sword,
With hand and hard blade, I must fight for the
      treasure."

[Beowulf and Wiglaf Slay the Dragon]

For the last time Beowulf uttered his boast:
"I came in safety through many a conflict
In the days of my youth; and now even yet,
Old as I am, I will fight this feud,
Do manful deeds, if the dire destroyer
Will come from his cavern to meet my sword."
The king for the last time greeted his comrades,
Bold helmet-bearers and faithful friends:
"I would bear no sword nor weapon to battle
With the evil worm, if I knew how else
I could close with the fiend, as I grappled with
      Grendel.

From the worm I look for a welling of fire,
A belching of venom, and therefore I bear
Shield and byrny. Not one foot's space
Will I flee from the monster, the ward of the
    mound.
It shall fare with us both in the fight at the wall
As Fate shall allot, the lord of mankind.
Though bold in spirit, I make no boast
As I go to fight with the flying serpent.
Clad in your corselets and trappings of war,
By the side of the barrow abide you to see
Which of us twain may best after battle
Survive his wounds. Not yours the adventure,
Nor the mission of any, save mine alone,
To measure his strength with the monstrous
    dragon
And play the part of a valiant carl.
By deeds of daring I'll gain the gold
Or death in battle shall break your lord."
    Then the stalwart rose with his shield upon
        him,
Bold under helmet, bearing his sark
Under the stone-cliff; he trusted the strength
Of his single might. Not so does a coward!
He who survived through many a struggle,
Many a combat and crashing of troops,
Saw where a stone-arch stood by the wall
And a gushing stream broke out from the barrow.
Hot with fire was the flow of its surge,
Nor could any abide near the hoard unburned,
Nor endure its depths, for the flame of the
    dragon.
Then the lord of the Geats in the grip of his fury
Gave shout of defiance; the strong-heart stormed.
His voice rang out with the rage of battle,
Resounding under the hoary stone.
Hate was aroused; the hoard-warden knew
'Twas the voice of a man. No more was there
    time
To sue for peace; the breath of the serpent,
A blast of venom, burst from the rock.
The ground resounded; the lord of the Geats
Under the barrow swung up his shield
To face the dragon; the coiling foe
Was gathered to strike in the deadly strife.
The stalwart hero had drawn his sword,
His ancient heirloom of tempered edge;
In the heart of each was fear of the other!

The shelter of kinsmen stood stout of heart
Under towering shield as the great worm coiled;
Clad in his war-gear he waited the rush.
In twisting folds the flame-breathing dragon
Sped to its fate. The shield of the prince
For a lesser while guarded his life and his body
Than heart had hoped. For the first time then
It was not his portion to prosper in war;
Fate did not grant him glory in battle!
Then lifted his arm the lord of the Geats
And smote the worm with his ancient sword
But the brown edge failed as it fell on bone,
And cut less deep than the king had need
In his sore distress. Savage in mood
The ward of the barrow countered the blow
With a blast of fire; wide sprang the flame.
The ruler of Geats had no reason to boast;
His unsheathed iron, his excellent sword,
Had weakened as it should not, had failed in the
    fight.
It was no easy journey for Ecgtheow's son
To leave this world and against his will
Find elsewhere a dwelling! So every man shall
In the end give over this fleeting life.
    Not long was the lull. Swiftly the battlers
Renewed their grapple. The guard of the hoard
Grew fiercer in fury. His venomous breath
Beat in his breast. Enveloped in flame
The folk-leader suffered a sore distress.
No succoring band of shoulder-companions,
No sons of warriors aided him then
By valor in battle. They fled to the forest
To save their lives; but a sorrowful spirit
Welled in the breast of one of the band.
The call of kinship can never be stilled
In the heart of a man who is trusty and true.
    His name was Wiglaf, Weohstan's son,
A prince of the Scylfings, a peerless thane,
Ælfhere's kinsman; he saw his king
Under his helmet smitten with heat.
He thought of the gifts which his lord had given,
The wealth and the land of the Wægmunding
    line
And all the folk-rights his father had owned;
Nor could he hold back, but snatched up his
    buckler,
His linden shield and his ancient sword,
Heirloom of Eanmund, Ohthere's son,

Figure 18 *Purse lid from Sutton Hoo ship.*

Whom Weohstan slew with the sword in battle,
Wretched and friendless and far from home.
The brown-hewed helmet he bore to his kinsmen,
The ancient blade and the byrny of rings.
These Onela gave him—his nephew's arms—
Nor called for vengeance, nor fought the feud,
Though Weohstan had slaughtered his brother's
    son.
He held the treasures for many half-years,
The byrny and sword, till his son was of age
For manful deeds, as his father before him.
Among the Geats he gave him of war-gear
Countless numbers of every kind;
Then, full of winters, he left the world,
Gave over this life. And Wiglaf, the lad,
Was to face with his lord the first of his battles,
The hazard of war. But his heart did not fail
Nor the blade of his kinsman weaken in war,
As the worm soon found when they met in the
    fight!
  Wiglaf spoke in sorrow of soul,
With bitter reproach rebuking his comrades:
"I remember the time, as we drank in the
    mead-hall,
When we swore to our lord who bestowed
    these rings

That we would repay for the war-gear and
    armor,
The hard swords and helmets, if need like this
Should ever befall him. He chose us out
From all the host for this high adventure,
Deemed us worthy of glorious deeds,
Gave me these treasures, regarded us all
As high-hearted bearers of helmet and spear—
Though our lord himself, the shield of his
    people,
Thought single-handed to finish this feat,
Since of mortal men his measure was most
Of feats of daring and deeds of fame.
Now is the day that our lord has need
Of the strength and courage of stalwart men.
Let us haste to succor his sore distress
In the horrible heat and the merciless flame.
God knows I had rather the fire should enfold
My body and limbs with my gold-friend and
    lord.
Shameful it seems that we carry our shields
Back to our homes ere we harry the foe
And ward the life of the Weder king.
Full well I know it is not his due
That he alone, of the host of the Geats,
Should suffer affliction and fall in the fight.

One helmet and sword, one byrny and shield,
Shall serve for us both in the storm of strife."
Then Wiglaf dashed through the deadly reek
In his battle-helmet to help his lord.
Brief were his words: "Beloved Beowulf,
Summon your strength, remember the vow
You made of old in the years of youth
Not to allow your glory to lessen
As long as you lived. With resolute heart,
And dauntless daring, defend your life
With all your force. I fight at your side!"
   Once again the worm, when the words were
     spoken,
The hideous foe in a horror of flame,
Rushed in rage at the hated men.
Wiglaf's buckler was burned to the boss
In the billows of fire; his byrny of mail
Gave the young hero no help or defense.
But he stoutly pressed on under shield of his
     kinsman
When his own was consumed in the scorching
     flame.
Then the king once more was mindful of glory,
Swung his great sword-blade with all his might
And drove it home on the dragon's head.
But Nægling broke, it failed in the battle,
The blade of Beowulf, ancient and gray.
It was not his lot that edges of iron
Could help him in battle; his hand was too
     strong,
Overtaxed, I am told, every blade with its blow.
Though he bore a wondrous hard weapon to
     war,
No whit the better was he thereby!
   A third time then the terrible scather,
The monstrous dragon inflamed with the feud,
Rushed on the king when the opening offered,
Fierce and flaming; fastened its fangs
In Beowulf's throat; he was bloodied with gore;
His life-blood streamed from the welling wound.
   As they tell the tale, in the king's sore need
His shoulder-companion showed forth his valor,
His craft and courage, and native strength.
To the head of the dragon he paid no heed,
Though his hand was burned as he helped his
     king.
A little lower the stalwart struck
At the evil beast, and his blade drove home

Plated and gleaming. The fire began
To lessen and wane. The king of the Weders
Summoned his wits; he drew the dagger
He wore on his corselet, cutting and keen,
And slit asunder the worm with the blow.
So they felled the foe and wrought their revenge;
The kinsmen together had killed the dragon.
So a man should be when the need is bitter!
That was the last fight Beowulf fought;
That was the end of his work in the world.

[Beowulf's Death]

The wound which the dragon had dealt him
     began
To swell and burn; and soon he could feel
The baneful venom inflaming his breast.
The wise, old warrior sank down by the wall
And stared at the work of the giants of old,
The arches of stone and the standing columns
Upholding the ancient earth-hall within.
His loyal thane, the kindest of comrades,
Saw Beowulf bloody and broken in war;
In his hands bore water and bathed his leader,
And loosened the helm from his dear lord's head.
   Beowulf spoke, though his hurt was sore,
The wounds of battle grievous and grim.
Full well he weened that his life was ended,
And all the joy of his years on earth;
That his days were done, and Death most near;
"My armor and sword I would leave to my son
Had Fate but granted, born of my body,
An heir to follow me after I'm gone.
For fifty winters I've ruled this realm,
And never a lord of a neighboring land
Dared strike with terror or seek with sword.
In my life I abode by the lot assigned,
Kept well what was mine, courted no quarrels,
Swore no false oaths. And now for all this
Though my hurt is grievous, my heart is glad.
When life leaves body, the Lord of mankind
Cannot lay to my charge the killing of kinsmen!
Go quickly, dear Wiglaf, to gaze on the gold
Beneath the hoar stone. The dragon lies still
In the slumber of death, despoiled of his hoard.
Make haste that my eyes may behold the treasure,
The gleaming jewels, the goodly store,

And, glad of the gold, more peacefully leave
The life and the realm I have ruled so long."
   Then Weohstan's son, as they tell the tale,
Clad in his corselet and trappings of war,
Hearkened at once to his wounded lord.
Under roof of the barrow he broke his way.
Proud in triumph he stood by the seat,
Saw glittering jewels and gold on the ground,
The den of the dragon, the old dawn-flier,
And all the wonders along the walls.
Great bowls and flagons of bygone men
Lay all unburnished and barren of gems,
Many a helmet ancient and rusted,
Many an arm-ring cunningly wrought.
Treasure and gold, though hid in the ground,
Override man's wishes, hide them who will!
High o'er the hoard he beheld a banner,
Greatest of wonders, woven with skill,
All wrought of gold; its radiance lighted
The vasty ground and the glittering gems.
But no sign of the worm! The sword-edge had
   slain him.
As I've heard the tale, the hero unaided
Rifled those riches of giants of old,
The hoard in the barrow, and heaped in his arms
Beakers and platters, picked what he would
And took the banner, the brightest of signs.
The ancient sword with its edge of iron
Had slain the worm who watched o'er the
   wealth,
In the midnight flaming, with menace of fire
Protecting the treasure for many a year
Till he died the death. Then Wiglaf departed
In haste returning enriched with spoil.
He feared, and wondered if still he would find
The lord of the Weders alive on the plain,
Broken and weary and smitten with wounds.
With his freight of treasure he found the prince,
His dear lord, bloody and nigh unto death.
With water he bathed him till words broke forth
From the hoard of his heart and, aged and sad,
Beowulf spoke, as he gazed on the gold:
"For this goodly treasure whereon I gaze
I give my thanks to the Lord of all,
To the Prince of glory, Eternal God,
Who granted me grace to gain for my people
Such dower of riches before my death.
I gave my life for this golden hoard.
Heed well the wants, the need of my people;

My hour is come, and my end is near.
Bid warriors build, when they burn my body,
A stately barrow on the headland's height.
It shall be for remembrance among my people
As it towers high on the Cape of the Whale,
And sailors shall know it as Beowulf's Barrow,
Sea-faring mariners driving their ships
Through fogs of ocean from far countries."
Then the great-hearted king unclasped from his
   throat
A collar of gold, and gave to his thane;
Gave the young hero his gold-decked helmet,
His ring and his byrny, and wished him well.
"You are the last of the Wægmunding line.
All my kinsmen, earls in their glory,
Fate has sent to their final doom,
And I must follow." These words were the last
The old king spoke ere the pyre received him,
The leaping flames of the funeral blaze,
And his breath went forth from his bosom, his
   soul
Went forth from the flesh, to the joys of the just.
   Then bitter it was for Beowulf's thane
To behold his loved one lying on earth
Suffering sore at the end of life.
The monster that slew him, the dreadful dragon,
Likewise lay broken and brought to his death.
The worm no longer could rule the hoard,
But the hard, sharp sword, the work of the
   hammer,
Had laid him low; and the winged dragon
Lay stretched near the barrow, broken and still.
No more in the midnight he soared in air,
Disclosing his presence, and proud of his gold;
For he sank to earth by the sword of the king.
But few of mankind, if the tales be true,
Has it prospered much, though mighty in war
And daring in deed, to encounter the breath
Of the venomous worm or plunder his wealth
When the ward of the barrow held watch o'er
   the mound.
Beowulf bartered his life for the treasure;
Both foes had finished this fleeting life.
   Not long was it then till the laggards in battle
Came forth from the forest, ten craven in fight,
Who had dared not face the attack of the foe
In their lord's great need. The shirkers in shame
Came wearing their bucklers and trappings of
   war

Where the old man lay. They looked upon
  Wiglaf.
Weary he sat by the side of his leader
Attempting with water to waken his lord.
It availed him little; the wish was vain!
He could not stay his soul upon earth,
Nor one whit alter the will of God.
The Lord ruled over the lives of men
As He rules them still. With a stern rebuke
He reproached the cowards whose courage had
  failed.
Wiglaf addressed them, Weohstan's son;
Gazed sad of heart on the hateful men:
"Lo! he may say who would speak the truth
That the lord who gave you these goodly rings,
This warlike armor wherein you stand—
When oft on the ale-bench he dealt to his hall-
  men
Helmet and byrny, endowing his thanes
With the fairest he found from near or from far—
That he grievously wasted these trappings of war
When battle befell him. The king of the folk
Had no need to boast of his friends in the fight.
But the God of victory granted him strength
To avenge himself with the edge of the sword
When he needed valor. Of little avail
The help I brought in the bitter battle!
Yet still I strove, though beyond my strength,
To aid my kinsman. And ever the weaker
The savage foe when I struck with my sword;
Ever the weaker the welling flame!
Too few defenders surrounded our ruler
When the hour of evil and terror befell.
Now granting of treasure and giving of swords,
Inherited land-right and joy of the home,
Shall cease from your kindred. And each of
  your clan
Shall fail of his birthright when men from afar
Hear tell of your flight and your dastardly deed.
Death is better for every earl
Than life besmirched with the brand of shame!"

[The Messenger Foretells the Doom of the Geats]

Than Wiglaf bade tell the tidings of battle
Up over the cliff in the camp of the host
Where the linden-bearers all morning long
Sat wretched in spirit, and ready for both,

The return, or the death, of their dear-loved lord.
Not long did he hide, who rode up the headland,
The news of their sorrow, but spoke before all:
"Our leader lies low, the lord of the Weders,
The king of the Geats, on the couch of death.
He sleeps his last sleep by the deeds of the worm.
The dreadful dragon is stretched beside him
Slain with dagger-wounds. Not by the sword
Could he quell the monster or lay him low.
And Wiglaf is sitting, Weohstan's son,
Bent over Beowulf, living by dead.
Death watch he keeps in sorrow of spirit
Over the bodies of friend and foe.

  *Now comes peril of war when this news is
    rumored abroad,*
*The fall of our king known afar among Frisians and
    Franks!*
*For a fierce feud rose with the Franks when
    Hygelac's warlike host*
*Invaded the Frisian fields, and the Hetware
    vanquished the Geats,*
*Overcame with the weight of their hordes, and
    Hygelac fell in the fray;*
It was not his lot to live on dispensing the spoils of war.
*And never since then of the Franks had we favor or
    friend.*
  *And I harbor no hope of peace or faith from the
    Swedish folk,*
*For well is it known of men that Ongentheow slew
    with the sword*
*Hæthcyn, the son of Hrethel, near Ravenswood, in
    the fight*
*When the Swedish people in pride swept down on
    the Geats.*
And Ohthere's aged father, old and a terror in battle,
*Made onslaught, killing their king, and rescued his
    queen,*
Ohthere's mother and Onela's, aged, bereft of her gold.
He followed the flying foe till, lordless and lorn,
*They barely escaped into Ravenswood. There he
    beset them,*
A wretched remnant of war, and weary with wounds.
*And all the long hours of the night he thundered his
    threats*
*That some on the morrow he would slay with the
    edge of the sword,*
*And some should swing on the gallows for food for
    the fowls!*

But hope returned with the dawn to the heavy-hearted
When they heard the sound of the trumpets and
     Hygelac's horn,
As the good king came with his troops marching up
     on their track.
    Then was a gory meeting of Swedes and Geats;
On all sides carnage and slaughter, savage and grim,
As the struggling foemen grappled and swayed in the
     fight.
And the old earl Ongentheow, crestfallen and cowed,
Fled with his men to a fastness, withdrew to the hills.
He had tasted Hygelac's strength, the skill of the
     hero in war,
And he had no hope to resist or strive with the sea-men,
To save his hoard from their hands, or his children,
     or wife.
So the old king fled to his fortress; but over the plain
Hygelac's banners swept on in pursuit of the Swedes,
Stormed to the stronghold's defenses, and old
     Ongentheow
Was brought to bay with the sword, and subject to
     Eofor's will!
Wulf, son of Wonred, in wrath then struck with his
     sword,
And the blood in streams burst forth from under the
     old man's hair.
Yet the aged Scylfing was all undaunted and
     answered the stroke
With a bitter exchange in the battle; and Wonred's
     brave son
Could not requite the blow, for the hero had cleft his
     helmet,
And, covered with blood, he was forced to bow; he
     fell to the earth.
But his death was not doomed, and he rallied,
     though the wound was deep.
Then Hygelac's hardy thane, when his brother lay
     low,
Struck with his ancient blade, a sturdy sword of the
     giants,
Cut through the shield-wall, cleaving the helmet.
     The king,
The folk-defender, sank down. He was hurt unto
     death.
Then were many that bound Wulf's wounds when
     the fight was won,
When the Geats held the ground of battle; as booty
     of war

Eofor stripped Ongentheow of iron byrny and helm,
Of sword-blade hilted and hard, and bore unto
     Hygelac
The old man's trappings of war. And Hygelac took
     the treasures,
Promising fair rewards, and this he fulfilled.
The son of Hrethel, the king of the Geats, when he
     came to his home,
Repaid with princely treasure the prowess of Eofor
     and Wulf;
Gave each an hundred thousand of land and linked
     rings,
And none could belittle or blame. They had won the
     honor in war.
He gave to Eofor also the hand of his only daughter
To be a pledge of good will, and the pride of his home.

This is the fighting and this the feud,
The bitter hatred, that breeds the dread
Lest the Swedish people should swarm against us
Learning our lord lies lifeless and still.
His was the hand that defended the hoard,
Heroes, and realm against ravaging foe,
By noble counsel and dauntless deed.
Let us go quickly to look on the king
Who brought us treasure, and bear his corpse
To the funeral pyre. The precious hoard
Shall burn with the hero. There lies the heap
Of untold treasure so grimly gained,
Jewels and gems he bought with his blood
At the end of life. All these at the last
The flames shall veil and the brands devour.
No man for remembrance shall take from the
     treasure,
Nor beauteous maiden adorn her breast
With gleaming jewel; bereft of gold
And tragic-hearted many shall tread
A foreign soil, now their lord has ceased
From laughter and revel and rapture of joy.
Many a spear in the cold of morning
Shall be borne in hand uplifted on high.
No sound of harp shall waken the warrior,
But the dusky raven despoiling the dead
Shall clamor and cry and call to the eagle
What fare he found at the carrion-feast
The while with the wolf he worried the corpses."
    So the stalwart hero had told his tidings,
His fateful message; nor spoke amiss

As to truth or telling. The host arose;
On their woeful way to the Eagles' Ness
They went with tears to behold the wonder.
They found the friend, who had dealt them
    treasure
In former days, on the bed of death,
Stretched out lifeless upon the sand.
The last of the good king's days was gone;
Wondrous the death of the Weder prince!
They had sighted first, where it lay outstretched,
The monstrous wonder, the loathsome worm,
The horrible fire-drake, hideous-hued,
Scorched with the flame. The spread of its length
Was fifty foot-measures! Oft in the night
It sported in air, then sinking to earth
Returned to its den. Now moveless in death
It had seen the last of its earthly lair.
Beside the dragon were bowls and beakers,
Platters lying, and precious swords
Eaten with rust, where the hoard had rested
A thousand winters in the womb of earth.
That boundless treasure of bygone men,
The golden dower, was girt with a spell
So that never a man might ravage the ring-hall
Save as God himself, the Giver of victory—
He is the Shelter and Shield of men—
Might allow such man as seemed to Him meet,
Might grant whom He would, to gather the
    treasure.
    His way of life, who had wickedly hoarded
The wealth of treasure beneath the wall,
Had an evil end, as was widely seen.
Many the dragon had sent to death,
But in fearful fashion the feud was avenged!
'Tis a wondrous thing when a warlike earl
Comes to the close of his destined days,
When he may no longer among his kinsmen
Feast in the mead-hall. So Beowulf fared
When he sought the dragon in deadly battle!
Himself he knew not what fate was in store
Nor the coming end of his earthly life.
The lordly princes who placed the treasure
Had cursed it deep to the day of doom,
That the man who plundered and gathered the
    gold
Might pay for the evil imprisoned in hell,
Shackled in torment and punished with pain,
Except the invader should first be favored

With the loving grace of the Lord of all!
    Then spoke Wiglaf, Weohstan's son:
"Often for one man many must sorrow
As has now befallen the folk of the Geats.
We could not persuade the king by our counsel,
Our well-loved leader, to shun assault
On the dreadful dragon guarding the gold;
To let him lie where he long had lurked
In his secret lair till the world shall end.
But Beowulf, dauntless, pressed to his doom.
The hoard was uncovered; heavy the cost;
Too strong the fate that constrained the king!
I entered the barrow, beholding the hoard
And all the treasure throughout the hall;
In fearful fashion the way was opened,
An entrance under the wall of earth.
Of the hoarded treasure I heaped in my arms
A weighty burden, and bore to my king.
He yet was living; his wits were clear.
Much the old man said in his sorrow;
Sent you greeting, and bade you build
In the place of burning a lofty barrow,
Proud and peerless, to mark his deeds;
For he was of all men the worthiest warrior
In all the earth, while he still might rule
And wield the wealth of his lordly land.
Let us haste once more to behold the treasure,
The gleaming wonders beneath the wall.
I will show the way that you all may see
And closely scan the rings and the gold.
Let the bier be ready, the pyre prepared,
When we come again to carry our lord,
Our leader beloved, where long he shall lie
In the kindly care of the Lord of all."

[Beowulf's Funeral]

Then the son of Weohstan, stalwart in war,
Bade send command to the heads of homes
To bring from afar the wood for the burning
Where the good king lay: "Now glede shall
    devour,
As dark flame waxes, the warrior prince
Who has often withstood the shower of steel
When the storm of arrows, sped from the string,
Broke over shield, and shaft did service,
With feather-fittings guiding the barb."

Then the wise son of Weohstan chose from
    the host
Seven thanes of the king, the best of the band;
Eight heroes together they hied to the barrow
In under the roof of the fearful foe;
One of the warriors leading the way
Bore in his hand a burning brand.
They cast no lots who should loot the treasure
When they saw unguarded the gold in the hall
Lying there useless; little they scrupled
As quickly they plundered the precious store.
Over the sea-cliff into the ocean
They tumbled the dragon, the deadly worm,
Let the sea-tide swallow the guarder of gold.
Then a wagon was loaded with well-wrought
    treasure,
A countless number of every kind;
And the aged warrior, the white-haired king,
Was borne on high to the Cape of the Whale.

    The Geat folk fashioned a peerless pyre
Hung round with helmets and battle-boards,
With gleaming byrnies as Beowulf bade.
In sorrow of soul they laid on the pyre
Their mighty leader, their well-loved lord.
The warriors kindled the bale on the barrow,
Wakened the greatest of funeral fires.
Dark o'er the blaze the wood-smoke mounted;
The winds were still, and the sound of weeping
Rose with the roar of the surging flame
Till the heat of the fire had broken the body.
With hearts that were heavy they chanted their
    sorrow,

Singing a dirge for the death of their lord;
And an aged woman with upbound locks
Lamented for Beowulf, wailing in woe.
Over and over she uttered her dread
Of sorrow to come, of bloodshed and slaughter,
Terror of battle, and bondage, and shame.
The smoke of the bale-fire rose to the sky!

    The men of the Weder folk fashioned a mound
Broad and high on the brow of the cliff,
Seen from afar by seafaring men.
Ten days they worked on the warrior's barrow
Inclosing the ash of the funeral flame
With a wall as worthy as wisdom could shape.
They bore to the barrow the rings and the gems,
The wealth of the hoard the heroes had
    plundered.
The olden treasure they gave to the earth,
The gold to the ground, where it still remains
As useless to men as it was of yore.
Then round the mound rode the brave in battle,
The sons of warriors, twelve in a band,
Bemoaning their sorrow and mourning their
    king.
They sang their dirge and spoke of the hero
Vaunting his valor and venturous deeds.
So is it proper a man should praise
His friendly lord with a loving heart,
When his soul must forth from the fleeting flesh.
So the folk of the Geats, the friends of his hearth,
Bemoaned the fall of their mighty lord;
Said he was kindest of worldly kings,
Mildest, most gentle, most eager for fame.

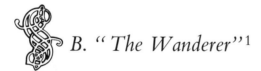

B. "The Wanderer"[1]

Oft to the Wanderer, weary of exile,
Cometh God's pity, compassionate love,
Though woefully toiling on wintry seas
With churning oar in the icy wave,
Homeless and helpless he fled from Fate.   5
Thus saith the Wanderer mindful of misery,
Grievous disasters, and death of kin:

"Oft when the day broke, oft at the dawning,
Lonely and wretched I wailed my woe.
No man is living, no comrade left,   10
To whom I dare fully unlock my heart.
I have learned truly the mark of a man
Is keeping his counsel and locking his lips,
Let him think what he will! For, woe of heart

Withstandeth not Fate; a failing spirit 15
Earneth no help. Men eager for honor
Bury their sorrow deep in the breast.
So have I also, often, in wretchedness
Fettered my feelings, far from my kin,
Homeless and hapless, since days of old, 20
When the dark earth covered my dear lord's face,
And I sailed away with sorrowful heart,
Over wintry seas, seeking a gold-lord,
If far or near lived one to befriend me
With gift in the mead-hall and comfort for grief. 25
Who bears it, knows what a bitter companion,
Shoulder to shoulder, sorrow can be,
When friends are no more. His fortune is exile,
Not gifts of fine gold; a heart that is frozen,
Earth's winsomeness dead. And he dreams of the
    hallmen,
The dealing of treasure, the days of his youth, 30
When his lord bade welcome to wassail and feast.
But gone is that gladness, and never again
Shall come the loved counsel of comrade and
    king.
Even in slumber his sorrow assaileth, 35
And, dreaming, he claspeth his dear lord again,
Head on knee, hand on knee, loyally laying,
Pledging his liege as in days long past.
Then from his slumber he starts lonely-hearted,
Beholding gray stretches of tossing sea, 40
Sea-birds bathing, with wings outspread,
While hail-storms darken, and driving snow.
Bitterer then is the bane of his wretchedness,
The longing for loved one: his grief is renewed.
The forms of his kinsmen take shape in the
    silence;
In rapture he greets them; in gladness he scans 45
Old comrades remembered. But they melt into air
With no word of greeting to gladden his heart.
Then again surges his sorrow upon him;
And grimly he spurs on his weary soul 50
Once more to the toil of the tossing sea.
No wonder therefore, in all the world,
If a shadow darkens upon my spirit
When I reflect on the fates of men—
How one by one proud warriors vanish 55
From the halls that knew them, and day by day
All this earth ages and droops unto death.
No man may know wisdom till many a winter
Has been his portion. A wise man is patient,

Not swift to anger, nor hasty of speech, 60
Neither too weak, nor too reckless, in war,
Neither fearful nor fain, nor too wishful of wealth,
Nor too eager in vow—ere he know the event.
A brave man must bide when he speaketh his
    boast
Until he know surely the goal of his spirit. 65
A wise man will ponder how dread is that doom
When all this world's wealth shall be scattered
    and waste—
As now, over all, through the regions of earth,
Walls stand rime-covered and swept by the winds.
The battlements crumble, the wine-halls decay; 70
Joyless and silent the heroes are sleeping
Where the proud host fell by the wall they
    defended.
Some battle launched on their long, last journey;
One a bird bore o'er the billowing sea;
One the gray wolf slew; one a grieving earl 75
Sadly gave to the grave's embrace.
The Warden of men hath wasted this world
Till the sound of music and revel is stilled,
And these giant-built structures stand empty of
    life.
He who shall muse on these moldering ruins, 80
And deeply ponder this darkling life,
Must brood on old legends of battle and
    bloodshed,
And heavy the mood that troubles his heart:
'Where now is the warrior? Where is the war-
    horse?
Bestowal of treasure, and sharing of feast? 85
Alas! the bright ale-cup, the byrny-clad warrior,
The prince in his splendor—those days are long
    sped
In the night of the past, as if they never had been!'
And now remains only, for warriors' memorial,
A wall wondrous high with serpent shapes carved. 90
Storms of ash-spears have smitten the earls,
Carnage of weapon, and conquering Fate.
Storms now batter these ramparts of stone;
Blowing snow and the blast of winter
Enfold the earth; night-shadows fall 95
Darkly lowering, from the north driving
Raging hail in wrath upon men.
Wretchedness fills the realm of earth,
And Fate's decrees transform the world.
Here wealth is fleeting, friends are fleeting, 100

Man is fleeting, maid is fleeting;
All the foundation of earth shall fail!"
Thus spake the sage in solitude pondering.
Good man is he who guardeth his faith.
He must never too quickly unburden his breast   105

Of its sorrow, but eagerly strive for redress;
And happy the man who seeketh for mercy
From his heavenly Father, our Fortress and
   Strength.

Note

1   Translated by Charles W. Kennedy. Reprinted from *Old English Elegies*, Princeton University Press, Princeton, N.J., 1936, by permission of the publisher.

C. *"The Soul's Voyage"*[1]

The Seafarer

Let me tell you the truth of myself,
Tell of my travels, my times of torment,
The agonized hours that often I lived through;
I have borne in my breast a bitter pain.

I have known my ship as a cell of pain   5
On a sharp, choppy sea. Often my stand
Was the bow of the boat in the black night watches
While we courted the cliffs. Clamped in cold
My feet were frozen. But fiery the pain was—
Hot in my heart—where a hunger tore through   10
My shoal-weary spirit.

No man can know
To whom, on farmland, Fortune smiles fairly,
How sore I suffered on the ice-choked channels,
Suffered the winter on the exiles' byway,   15
Torn from my tribe.

Ice hung from me. Hail showers flayed me.
I heard there only the howl of the sea,
The ice-cluttered course. My hearth-song
   comfort?
The swan's squawk. Gannet's scream   20
And yell of gull served me for laughter of men.

The mourning mew was my cheering mead-drink.
Storms shook the cliffs there. Shrilly shouted
The ice feathered tern, spray feathered eagle.

My spirit was helpless to seek out its home,   25
Its own tribe's Protector.

He knows but little who lives in pleasure,
Who crowds in the city, seldom in peril,
Haughty and wine-happy, how I have awaited
With weary frustration my free sea voyage.   30

Night blackened. North snow blew.
Ice gripped the ground. The cold grains,
Hail from heaven, hissed on the heath.

Therefore my broodings break on my breast:
That I might go, know the open ocean,   35
The salt waves' motion, mighty sea swell.
Every moment my spirit demands
That forth I fare, that far from here
I hunt my home at a Stranger's hearth.
There is no man on earth so tough of temper,   40
So free in giving, so valiant in youth,
So daring in doing nor dear to his lord,

Who has no fear of his own sea-faring
Nor of where his Lord has set the course.
No heed has he then for the thrum of the harp,   45
Giving of wealth or warmth of women
Nor anything else but the wide surging sea
Which he burns to embark on.

      Trees flower. Towns shine fresh.
      Meadows are merry. Earth makes haste.   50

These things drive the daring spirit
To launch its sea voyage, set sail on its highway.

The cuckoo chides me—a cry of sadness.
He sings, summer's sentry, a song of warning
Chill to the spirit: 55

    "No man of this world, no, none whatsoever
    Knows, in his ease, how sore a man suffers
    Who travels the broad sea trail of exile."

And yet springs my spirit out of its cell,
Flies unfettered over the sea flood,   60
Swings wild and wide above the whale's home,
The world's wide sweep; wings then back to me,
Eager and hungry, a screaming lone flyer;
Soars over the seaway, a spirit free,
Circling the sea-paths.   65

      Warmer to me are delights of the Lord
      Than the death of this life,
      This moment on shore.

      I cannot believe
      That the ground's good fruit will always
        grow.   70

Three things always threaten a man;
Sickness or age or the shock of quick death
Will snatch the soul from the strongest warrior.
Thus has he need, who treasures his name,
The praise of his people after his parting,   75
To daunt the devil before his departing,
Do well on earth and worthily conquer.
Then will his children chant his praises,
And ever after the angels will praise him,
Eternally, endlessly doing him honor.   80

For the age of earthly honor has passed us.
Gone are the heroes of earth's great houses.
No more are there kings or chieftains or wealth-
    givers,
Who, of all men, did greatest deeds
And lived most honorably, noble heroes.   85
Mirth has gone from us. Glory has left us.
The meek have inherited. They manage the world
And sweat to enjoy it. Grandeur is servile.
The world, disgraced, grows old and withers.

Likewise each man. Age comes upon him.   90
He laments his gray locks, his lost companions,
Children of chieftains chill in graves.
He cannot inhabit the house of his flesh
When life has left it; nor swallow sweetness;
Nor shout in pain; nor stir his hand;   95
Nor think; nor feel. Friends and brothers
Will find the grave with his golden treasures,
Drop gold in with him to purchase his passage.

But gold secreted, cached in coffers,
Cannot buy back a blackened soul,   100
Ransom it from the wrath of Judgment.

Great is the terror when God turns his face away
    from the world,
The world He fashioned, the earth's far corners,
The high roofed heavens.

Stupid the man who scorns the Almighty.   105
    Death is an ambush.
Happy is he who is humbled: Heaven awaits
    him.
God upholds him who lives in His hands.

      Steer your will well. Keep it on course.
      Keep faith with your fellows.
      Follow wisdom.   110
      Love those who love Him. Hate His enemies.
      Until you be placed on the funeral pyre
      Your comrades have made you.

      God's scheme is stricter,
      The Mover mightier than men can imagine.   115

Let us think where we have a haven;
Consider the course which will carry us there;
Bravely strike out toward bliss unbounded,
With hope, toward Heaven
Where life is limitless, loving the Lord.   120

He has exalted us, seaman and soarer,
He, King of Glory, God Eternal,
To Whom be thanks for ever and ever
World without end. Amen.

Note

1 The editor is grateful to William O. Rogers III for allowing him to use this very vigorous translation of the Old English poem.

 D. *"A Dream of the Cross"*[1]

The influence of this poem is attested by the fact that a passage from it appears carved in runes on the Ruthwell Cross, a stone monument probably dating from the late seventh century. A further inscription on the Brussels Cross, which dates probably from the late tenth or early eleventh century, may be a reminiscence of the poem. For a description of the crosses, see the introduction to the Old English text by Bruce Dickens and Alan S. C. Ross, second edition, Methuen & Co., Ltd., London, 1945. The date of the Ruthwell Cross and its iconographic program are discussed by F. Saxl, "The Ruthwell Cross," in England and the Mediterranean Tradition, *Oxford University Press, London, 1945.*

"A DREAM OF THE CROSS"[1]
(Dream of the Rood)

   Lo! I will tell   the dearest of dreams
That I dreamed in the midnight   when mortal
      men
Were sunk in slumber.   Me-seemed I saw
A wondrous Tree   towering in air,
Most shining of crosses   compassed with light.   5
Brightly that beacon   was gilded with gold;
Jewels adorned it   fair at the foot,
Five on the shoulder-beam,   blazing in splendor.
Through all creation   the angels of God
Beheld it shining—   no cross of shame!   10
Holy spirits   gazed on its gleaming,
Men upon earth   and all this great creation.
   Wondrous that Tree,   that Token of triumph,
And I a transgressor   soiled with my sins!
I gazed on the Rood   arrayed in glory,   15
Shining in beauty   and gilded with gold,

The Cross of the Savior   beset with gems.
But through the gold-work   outgleamed a token
Of the ancient evil   of sinful men
Where the Rood on its right side   once sweat
      blood.   20
Saddened and rueful,   smitten with terror
At the wondrous Vision,   I saw the Cross
Swiftly varying   vesture and hue,
Now wet and stained   with the Blood outwelling,
Now fairly jewelled   with gold and gems.   25
   Then, as I lay there,   long I gazed
In rue and sadness   on my Savior's Tree,
Till I heard in dream   how the Cross addressed
      me,
Of all woods worthiest,   speaking these words:
   "Long years ago   (well yet I remember)   30
They hewed me down   on the edge of the holt,
Severed my trunk;   strong foemen took me,
For a spectacle wrought me,   a gallows for rogues.
High on their shoulders   they bore me to hilltop,

Fastened me firmly,   an army of foes! 35
    "Then I saw the King   of all mankind
In brave mood hasting   to mount upon me.
Refuse I dared not,   nor bow nor break,
Though I felt earth's confines   shudder in fear;
All foes I might fell,   yet still I stood fast. 40
    "Then the young Warrior,   God, the All-
        Wielder,
Put off His raiment,   steadfast and strong;
With lordly mood   in the sight of many
He mounted the Cross   to redeem mankind.
When the Hero clasped me   I trembled in terror, 45
But I dared not bow me   nor bend to earth;
I must needs stand fast.   Upraised as the Rood
I held the High King,   the Lord of heaven.
I dared not bow!   With black nails driven
Those sinners pierced me;   the prints are clear, 50
The open wounds.   I dared injure none.
They mocked us both.   I was wet with blood
From the Hero's side   when He sent forth His
        spirit.
    "Many a bale   I bore on that hill-side
Seeing the Lord   in agony outstretched. 55
Black darkness covered   with clouds God's body,
That radiant splendor   Shadow went forth
Wan under heaven;   all creation wept
Bewailing the King's death.   Christ was on the
        Cross.
    "Then many came quickly,   faring from far, 60
Hurrying to the Prince.   I beheld it all.
Sorely smitten with sorrow   in meekness I bowed
To the hands of men.   From His heavy and bitter
        pain
They lifted Almighty God.   Those warriors left
        me
Standing bespattered with blood;   I was
        wounded with spears. 65
Limb-weary they laid Him down;   they stood at
        His head,
Looked on the Lord of heaven   as He lay there
        at rest
From His bitter ordeal all forspent.   In sight of
        His slayers
They made Him a sepulchre   carved from the
        shining stone;
Therein laid the Lord of triumph.   At evening tide 70
Sadly they sang their dirges   and wearily turned
        away

From their lordly Prince;   there He lay all still
        and alone.
    "There at our station   a long time we stood
Sorrowfully weeping   after the wailing of men
Had died away.   The corpse grew cold, 75
The fair life-dwelling.   Down to earth
Men hacked and felled us,   a grievous fate!
They dug a pit   and buried us deep.
But there God's friends   and followers found me
And graced me with treasure   of silver and gold. 80
    "Now may you learn,   O man beloved,
The bitter sorrows   that I have borne,
The work of caitiffs.   But the time is come
That men upon earth   and through all creation
Show me honor   and bow to this sign. 85
On me a while   God's Son once suffered;
Now I tower under heaven   in glory attired
With healing for all   that hold me in awe.
Of old I was once   the most woeful of tortures,
Most hateful to all men,   till I opened for them 90
The true Way of life.   Lo! the Lord of glory,
The Warden of heaven,   above all wood
Has glorified me   as Almighty God
Has honored His Mother,   even Mary herself,
Over all womankind   in the eyes of men. 95
    "Now I give you bidding,   O man beloved,
Reveal this Vision   to the sons of men,
And clearly tell   of the Tree of glory
Whereon God suffered   for man's many sins
And the evil that Adam   once wrought of old. 100
    "Death He suffered,   but our Savior rose
By virtue of His great might   as a help to men.
He ascended to heaven.   But hither again
He shall come unto earth   to seek mankind,
The Lord Himself   on the Day of Doom, 105
Almighty God   with His angel hosts.
And then will He judge,   Who has power of
        judgment,
To each man according   as here on earth
In this fleeting life   he shall win reward.
    "Nor there may any   be free from fear 110
Hearing the words   which the Wielder shall utter.
He shall ask before many: Where is the man
Who would taste bitter death   as He did on the
        Tree?
And all shall be fearful   and few shall know
What to say unto Christ.   But none at His
        Coming 115

Shall need to fear if he bears in his breast
This best of symbols; and every soul
From the ways of earth through the Cross shall
   come
To heavenly glory, who would dwell with God."
    Then with ardent spirit and earnest zeal,   120
Companionless, lonely, I prayed to the Cross.
My soul was fain of death. I had endured
Many an hour of longing. It is my life's hope
That I may turn to this Token of triumph,
I above all men, and revere it well.   125
    This is my heart's desire, and all my hope
Waits on the Cross. In this world now
I have few powerful friends; they have fared
   hence
Away from these earthly gauds seeking the
   King of glory,
Dwelling now with the High Father in heaven
   above,   130
Abiding in rapture. Each day I dream
Of the hour when the Cross of my Lord, whereof
   here on earth
I once had vision, from this fleeting life may
   fetch me

And bring me where is great gladness and
   heavenly bliss,
Where the people of God are planted and
   stablished for ever   135
In joy everlasting. There may it lodge me
Where I may abide in glory knowing bliss with
   the saints.
    May the Lord befriend me who on earth of old
Once suffered on the Cross for the sins of men.
He redeemed us, endowed us with life and a
   heavenly home.   140
Therein was hope renewed with blessing and bliss
For those who endured the burning. In that
   great deed
God's Son was triumphant, possessing power
   and strength!
Almighty, Sole-Ruling He came to the
   kingdom of God
Bringing a host of souls to angelic bliss,   145
To join the saints who abode in the splendor
   of glory,
When the Lord, Almighty God, came again to
   His throne.

Note

1   Translated by Charles W. Kennedy. Reprinted from *Early English Christian Poetry*, Oxford University Press, New York, 1963, by permission of the publisher.

 ## E. *The Battle of Maldon*[1]

The Battle of Maldon was fought on August 11, A.D. 991, between Viking raiders from Norway and the men of Essex led by Byrhtnoth and his household companions. The English prevented the invaders from crossing the River Blackwater at a ford or causeway which was passable at low tide. But Byrhtnoth allowed them to cross in order to do battle. He was defeated in the subsequent engagement. Byrhtnoth was himself a leader famous not only for his valor but also for his piety and for the protection he gave to monasteries. We lack the beginning and the end of the poem, but the portion that survives seems to be a remarkably accurate description of the actual events.

    An excellent introduction to the poem appears in the edition by E. V. Gordon, second edition, Methuen & Co., Ltd., London, 1949.

THE BATTLE OF MALDON

. . . was broken.
He bade a warrior   abandon his horse
And hurry forward   to join the fighters,
Take thought to his hands   and a stout heart.
Then Offa's kinsmen   knew that the eorl   5
Would never suffer   weakness or fear;
And he let from hand   his beloved hawk
Fly to the forest,   and made haste to the front;
By which one could know   the lad would never
Weaken in war   when he seized a sword.   10
   Eadric also   stood by his lord,
His prince, in the battle;   forward he bore
His spear to the fight;   he had firm resolve
While he could hold   in hard hand-grip
Broad sword and buckler;   he made good his
      boast   15
That he would battle   beside his lord.
   Byrhtnoth began   to hearten his fighters;
He rode and gave counsel,   instructing the men
How they should stand   and defend the spot.
He bade that they hold   their bucklers aright   20
Firm in their hands,   and be not afraid.
When he had fairly   mustered the folk
He lighted down   where it liked him well,
Where he knew his retainers   were truest and best.
   Then stood on the strand   and boldly shouted   25
The Viking herald,   boastfully hurled
To the eorl on the shore   the shipmen's message:
"These dauntless seamen   have sent me to you,
Bade me say   you must quickly send
Riches for ransom;   better for you   30
That you buy off with tribute   a battle of spears
Than that we should wage   hard war against you.
Nor need we waste strength   if you will consent;
But we for the gold   will confirm a peace.
If you will agree,   who are greatest here,   35
To ransom your people   and promise to pay
On their own terms   unto the shipmen
Gold for goodwill,   and have peace at our hands,
We with the treasure   will take to our ships,
Put to sea,   and observe the peace."   40
   Byrhtnoth addressed him; brandished his shield;
Shook pliant ash-spear;   speaking with words
Enraged and resolute,   gave him answer:
"Hear you, sea-rover,   what my people say?
The tribute they'll send you   is tribute of spears,   45

Ancient sword-edge   and poisoned point,
Weapons availing you   little in war!
Pirate messenger,   publish this answer,
Proclaim to your people   tidings more grim:
Here stands no ignoble   eorl with his army   50
Guarding my lord Æthelred's   country and coast,
His land and his folk.   The heathen shall fall
In the clash of battle.   Too shameful it seems
That you with our tribute   should take to your
      ships
Unfought, when thus far   you've invaded our
      land.   55
You shall not so easily   take our treasure,
But sword-edge and spear-point   first shall
      decide,
The grim play of battle,   ere tribute is granted."
   Then he bade bear buckler,   warriors advance
And form their ranks   on the river's edge;   60
Not yet, for the tide,   could either attack.
The flood-tide was flowing   after the ebb,
And the currents locked.   Too long it seemed
Till men to battle   might bear their spears.
Near Panta River   in proud array   65
Stood the East Saxon host   and the Viking horde;
Nor could either army   do harm to the other
Except who through arrow-flight   found his
      death.
   Then the flood-tide ebbed;   the raiders stood
      ready,
The pirate army   eager for war.   70
The lord commanded   a war-hardened man
To defend the ford,   Wulfstan his name,
Brave among kinsmen,   Ceola's son.
He wounded with weapon   the foremost man
Who first there fiercely   set foot on the ford.   75
At Wulfstan's shoulder   stood fearless fighters,
Ælfere and Maccus,   a mighty pair.
Never would such   take flight at the ford!
But they bravely defended   against the foe
What time they were able   to wield their
      weapons.   80
   When the pirates perceived   and clearly saw
That they had been met   by bitter bridge-
      wardens,
The Viking shipmen   began to dissemble,
Asked for permission   to make approach,
To fare over ford   and take their troops.   85
It was then the eorl   disdainfully granted

Too much ground   to the hostile host.
Across cold water   Byrhthelm's son
Shouted reply,   and the shipmen hearkened:
"Now way is made open, come quickly to us,   90
Warriors to the onset;   God only knows
Who shall hold sway   on the field of slaughter."
   The war-wolves advanced,   heeded not water,
West across Panta; the Viking host
Over shining water   carried their shields.   95
Among his warriors   Byrhtnoth stood bold
Against the grim foe;   bade form with shields
The war-hedge for battle,   hold firm the folk
Against the foemen.   Then fighting was near,
Honor in battle.   The hour was come   100
Doomed men must fall.   A din arose.
Raven and eagle   were eager for carnage;
There was uproar on earth.   Men let from their
      hands
File-hard darts   and sharp spears fly.
Bows were busy,   shield stopped point,   105
Bitter was the battle-rush.   Warriors fell
In both the armies.   Young men lay dead.
Wulfmær was wounded;   Byrhtnoth's kin,
His sister's son,   was savagely butchered
Choosing the slaughter-bed,   slain with the
      sword.   110
   Then to the seamen   requital was made.
I have heard that Eadweard   slew one with sword,
Withheld not the blow;   the fated fighter
Fell at his feet.   And for that the prince
Thanked his retainer   when later was time.   115
So resisted   the stout of heart,
Young men in battle;   boldly strove
Who first with spear,   warrior with weapon,
Could visit death   on life that was doomed.
There was slaughter on earth; steadfast they
      stood,   120
And Byrhtnoth heartened them,   bidding each
      man
Take thought to the war   who would win from
      the Danes.
   The battle-hard brandished   his weapon for
      war,
His shield for defense,   and stormed at the foe;
Even so bold   went eorl against churl.   125
Both purposed evil,   each for the other.
Then the shipman cast   a southern spear
And the lord of warriors   suffered a wound.

He thrust with his shield   so the shaft was
      shattered,
The lance was broken,   the parts fell back.   130
The prince was angered; he stung with his spear
The arrogant Viking   who gave him the wound.
He fought with skill   driving his dart
Through the pirate's throat;   he thrust with hand
So he touched the life   of the savage foe.   135
Then most quickly   he cast another
And the byrny burst.   He was wounded in breast
Through his woven mail,   and the poisoned point
Bit at his heart.   The eorl was the blither;
The proud man laughed,   gave thanks to God   140
For that day's work   which the Lord had
      granted.
   But one of the shipmen   hurled from his hand
A flying spear;   and the speeding dart
Pierced through Æthelred's   princely thane.
A stripling lad   stood at his shoulder,   145
A boy in the battle,   who bravely drew
The bloody spear   from the warrior's side,
Wulmær the youthful,   Wulfstan's son.
Back he hurled   the battle-hard dart;
The point pierced in   and he sank to earth   150
Whose hand had given   the grievous hurt.
   Then a pirate warrior   went to the eorl;
Soon would he seize   his jewels and gems,
His armor of rings,   and his well-wrought sword.
But Byrhtnoth snatched   his sword from the
      sheath,   155
Broad and brown-edged,   and struck at his byrny.
Too speedily one   of the shipmen hindered,
Striking aside   the arm of the eorl;
And the gold-hilted sword   fell to the ground,
Nor might he hold longer   the hard blade,   160
Or wield his weapon.   Once more he spoke;
The aged ruler   rallied his men,
Bade them go forward   and bear them well.
No more could he stand   firm on his feet,
But he looked to heaven. . . .   165
   "I give Thee thanks,   O God of men,
For all the joys   I have had on earth.
O Lord of mercy,   I have most need
That now Thou wilt grant me   good to my soul,
That my spirit may come   into Thy kingdom,   170
O Prince of angels,   departing in peace
Into Thy power.   To Thee I pray
No fiend of hell   may have hold upon me."

Then the heathen scoundrels hacked him down
And both the fighters who stood at his side.   175
Ælfnoth and Wulmær both were fallen;
They laid down their lives beside their lord.
    Then fled from the battle who feared to be
        there:
The sons of Odda were first in flight,
Godric from battle, leaving his lord   180
Who had given him many a goodly steed;
He leaped on the horse that belonged to his
        leader,
Rode in the trappings that were not his right,
And his brothers with him both galloped off.
Godrinc and Godwig recked not of war,   185
But turned from the fighting, took to the wood,
Fled to the fastness, and saved their lives;
And more of men than was any way right
If they had remembered the many gifts
Their lord had given them to their good.   190
As Offa once said, at an earlier time
In the meeting-place when he held assembly,
That many were there making brave boasts
Who would never hold out in the hour of need.
Then was fallen the lord of the folk,   195
Æthelred's eorl; and his hearth-companions
All beheld that their lord lay dead.
    Forward they pressed, the proud retainers,
Fiercely charged those fearless thanes.
Each of them wished one thing of two: 200
To avenge his leader or lose his life.
Ælfric's son spurred them to battle,
A warrior young; in words that were bold
Ælfwine spoke, undaunted of spirit:
    "Take thought of the times when we talked
        at mead,   205
Seated on benches making our boasts,
Warriors in hall, concerning hard battle.
Now comes the test who truly is bold!
I purpose to prove my lineage to all men:
That in Mercia I come of a mighty clan;   210
Ealhelm the name of my aged father,
A powerful caldorman wealthy and wise.
None shall reproach me among that people
That I was willing to slink from the strife,
Hastening home when my lord lies dead,   215
Slain in the battle. Of all disasters
That to me is the greatest of griefs,
For he was my kinsman; he was my lord."

Then he dashed forward, took thought of the
        feud;
One of the shipmen he stabbed with spear   220
Among the folk, and he fell to earth
Slain with weapon. He encouraged his comrades,
Friends and companions to press to the front.
    Offa spoke and brandished his ash-spear:
"Now hast thou, Ælfwine, heartened us all   225
In the hour of need. Now our lord lies dead,
Our eorl on earth, there is need that we all,
Each of us here embolden the others,
Warriors to combat, while hand may bear
Good sword and spear, and hold hard blade.   230
This sneaking Godric, Odda's son,
Has betrayed us all; for when he rode off
Sitting on horse, on our lord's proud steed,
Many men weened that it was our lord.
On the field of fate now the folk is divided,   235
The shield-hedge is shattered; cursed be his deed
That he caused so many to flee from the fight."
    Leofsunu spoke, lifted his buckler,
His board for protection, making his boast:
"I promise you here I will never turn hence   240
Or flee one foot, but I'll fight in the front,
In the bitter strife, and avenge my lord.
Steadfast warriors by the River Stour
Shall never have need of words to reproach me,
Now my lord is fallen, that lordless I fled,   245
Turned back from the battle and went to my
        home;
But weapon shall take me, sword-edge and
        spear."
Then in rage he rushed to the fighting
Despising to flee.
                    Dunnere shook spear,   250
The aged churl, called out to them all,
Bidding take vengeance for Byrhtnoth's fall:
"He may not weaken who thinks to avenge
His lord on this folk, nor fear for his life."
Then they rushed forward, recked not of life,   255
Household-retainers fierce in the fight,
Bitter spear-bearers beseeching God
They might work revenge for their friendly lord
In death and destruction upon the foe.
    Then a hostage began to give them help,   260
Of Northumbrian race and hardy kin,
A son of Ecglaf, Æscferth his name.
He wavered not in the midst of the war-play

But forward pressed   to the arrow-flight,
Now shooting on shield,   now piercing a
   shipman,   265
But oft and often   dealing a wound,
While he could wield   his weapon in war.
   In front line still   stood Eadweard the long,
Skillful and eager;   he spoke his boast:
That he would not flee   foot-measure of ground   270
Nor turn from the battle   where his better lay
   dead.
He shattered the shield-wall   and fought with
   the Danes.
Upon the shipmen   he stoutly avenged
His gracious lord   ere he sank in the slaughter.
So did Ætheric,   excellent comrade,   275
Sibyrht's brother;   he boldly strove
Eager and ready;   and many another
Stood their ground   and shattered the shields.
Bucklers broke,   and byrnies sang
A song of terror.   Then Offa smote   280
One of the shipmen   and laid him low;
But Gadd's kinsman also   fell in the fight.
Quickly in battle   was Offa cut down.
But he had performed   what he promised his
   lord,
When he made his boast   to his bracelet-
   bestower,   285
That both unharmed   they would ride to the
   borough,
Back to their homes,   or fall in the fight
And perish of wounds   in the place of slaughter.
Thane-like he lay   beside his lord.

Then was breaking of bucklers,   shipmen
   advanced   290
Bold to the battle;   sharp spears pierced
Life-house of doomed men.   Wistan hastened,
Thurstan's son,   and strove with the Danes.
Three he slew   in the stress of battle
Ere Wiglin's son   was slain in the war.   295
The strife was stern,   warriors were steadfast,
Bold in battle;   fighters fell
Weary with wounds.   Death covered earth.
Oswold and Ealdwald   all the while,
Both the brothers,   marshalled their men;   300
Bade friend and kinsman   endure in combat
And never weaken,   but wield the sword.
   Byrhtwold encouraged them,   brandishing
   buckler,
Aged companion   shaking ash-spear;
Stout were the words   he spoke to his men: 305
   "Heart must be braver,   courage the bolder,
Mood the stouter   as our strength grows less!
Here on the ground   my good lord lies
Gory with wounds.   Always will he regret it
Who now from this battle   thinks to turn back.   310
I am old in years;   I will never yield,
But here at the last   beside my lord,
By the leader I love   I think to lie."
   And Godric to battle   heartened them all;
Æthelgar's son   hurled many a spear   315
At the Viking horde.   First in the front
He hacked and hewed   till he fell in the
   slaughter.
He was not the Godric   who fled from the
   fight. . . .

Note

1   Translated by Charles W. Kennedy and reprinted from *An Anthology of Old English Poetry*, Oxford University Press, New York, 1960, by permission of the publishers.

F. King Alfred

King Alfred (A.D. 849–899) was the greatest of the early English kings. In addition to his prowess as a warrior, his genius as an administrator, and his wisdom as a legislator, King Alfred displayed a considerable desire for learning. He did much to encourage literacy in his kingdom. He translated, or had translated, a number of important books. The series begins with the Dialogues of Pope Gregory the Great translated by Werferth, Bishop of Winchester. Alfred then translated the Cura Pastoralis by the same author; the preface is printed here. This work remained for centuries, in one form or another, a standard manual on the conduct of the priesthood. Two historical works occupied Alfred's attention: the history of Orosius and the Ecclesiastical History of Bede. The former is an annalistic account of ancient history to which Alfred added a great deal of material based on his own observation. He then turned to The Consolation of Philosophy of Boethius. Alfred's translation "sense for sense" constitutes a kind of commentary on the original which was still being quoted in the fourteenth century by Nicholas Trivet. Finally, Alfred translated the Soliloquies of St. Augustine.

For a biography of Alfred, see Eleanor S. Duckett, Alfred the Great, The University of Chicago Press, Chicago, 1956. The historical works mentioned in the general introduction to this section all contain material on Alfred and furnish additional bibliography. A modern translation of Gregory's Cura Pastoralis has been made by Henry Davis, The Newman Press, Westminster, Md., 1950.

Preface to the
CURA PASTORALIS [1]

King Alfred greets Bishop Waerferth in a fond and friendly manner, and I say to you that I very often recall what wise men there were throughout England in former times of both religious and secular station. And I recall how happy the times were then throughout England, and how the kings who ruled the people in those days obeyed God and his messengers, and how they maintained their peace and their customs and their power within their borders, and also extended their territory. And I recall how they flourished both in war and in wisdom, and moreover how zealous those of religious station were in teaching and learning and in all the services they owed to God, and how people from abroad sought wisdom and learning in this land, and how we should be obliged to find these elsewhere now if we had to have them. Learning declined so completely in England that there came to be very few on this side of the Humber who could understand their mass book in English or even translate a letter from Latin into English; and I think there were not many beyond the Humber who could do so. There were so few that I cannot recall even a single person south of the Thames who could do so when I became king.

Thanks be to Almighty God that we have any supply of teachers now! And therefore I bid you to do what I believe you desire: I bid you to free yourself from worldly matters as often as you can, so that you may apply wherever possible the knowledge which God gave you. Consider what punishments then came to us on account of this world, when we neither loved knowledge ourselves nor permitted other men to do so: we loved only the name "Christian," and very few loved the virtues.

When I remembered all this, I remembered also how I saw, before our land was all laid waste and burned, that the churches throughout all England stood filled with treasures and books, and that there was a great throng of God's servants, and that those servants gained very little benefit from the books because they could not understand a bit of them, as they were not written in their own language. It was as if they said, "Our predecessors who formerly occupied these places loved learning, and through that they obtained riches and left them to us. Here one may yet see their footprints, but we cannot follow after them, and therefore we have now lost both the wealth and the wisdom, because we would not bow our minds to the trail." When I remembered all this, I marvelled exceedingly that the good wise men who lived formerly throughout

England, and who had learned all those books perfectly, would not translate any portion of them into their own language. But I soon answered myself and said, "They did not suppose that men would ever become so careless, and that learning would decline to such an extent; because they desired learning to flourish, they neglected translation and desired that the more languages we knew, the greater the wisdom might be in our land."

Then I remembered how the Law of God was first composed in the Hebrew language, and how afterwards the Greeks, when they had learned it, translated it all into their own language and also all other books of the Bible. And later in similar fashion the Romans, after they had learned the Scriptures, had wise translators render them all into their own language. Therefore it seems better to me, if it seems so to you, that we also translate certain books which are most necessary for all men to know—translate them into the language which we all may understand, and bring it about, as we very easily may with God's help if we have peace, that all the free-born English youths who have sufficient wealth to apply themselves to learning be set to that task while they cannot be employed otherwise, until such a time as they can read English well. Afterwards let us teach Latin to those whom we desire to instruct further and to raise to a higher station.

When I remembered how the learning of Latin had previously declined throughout England, and how nevertheless many could read English, I began, among various and other concerns of this kingdom, to translate into English the book that is called in Latin *Pastoralis* and in English "Shepherd-Book," sometimes word by word, sometimes meaning by meaning, just as I learned it from Plegmund my archbishop, from Asser my bishop, from Grimbold my mass-priest, and from John my mass-priest. After I had learned it, I translated it into English, just as I understood it and just as I might recount it most intelligibly. And to each bishopric in my kingdom I wish to send a copy; and in each will be a bookmark which is worth fifty marcuses. And I command in God's name that no one remove the bookmark from the book nor the book from the minster. It is not known how long there may be such learned bishops as now, thank God, are everywhere. Therefore I should like the book and bookmark always to be kept at their appointed place, unless the bishop desires to have them with him, or his copy is somewhere on loan, or someone is making another copy.

Note

1   The editor wishes to thank his friend L. A. Muinzer for this translation.

 G. Aelfric

Aelfric (ca. A.D. 955– ca. 1020) became Abbot of Eynsham, Oxfordshire, in 1005. He is remembered for his homilies, for his Lives of the Saints, *for some translations of the Bible, and for miscellaneous religious writings. He exhibited considerable facility in the composition of rhythmic prose in English. He also composed a Latin abridgment of the* Agreement Concerning the Rule *of St. Ethelwold.*

The following selections illustrate some of the problems involved in interpreting the Bible for the uninstructed. Although the method of the homily may seem strange, it is based firmly on Patristic sources.

Figure 19 *The Franks Casket. The casket is named for the British antiquarian Sir A. W. Franks. On the left is a scene from the saga of Wayland, and on the right is a representation of the Adoration of the Magi. The runic inscription is in the Northumbrian dialect of Old English.*

PREFACE TO GENESIS [1]

Aelfric the monk humbly greets Aldorman Aethelward. You asked me, beloved one, to translate for you the Book of Genesis from Latin into English; at the time it seemed to me oppressive to do this for you, and you said that I need translate the book only up to the part about Isaac, Abraham's son, because some other person had translated the book from the part about Isaac to the end. Now it seems to me, beloved one, that the work is very hazardous for me or for any man to undertake, because I fear that if some foolish person reads this book or hears it read, he will suppose that he may live now in the era of the New Law just as our forefathers lived in the time before the Old Law was established, or as men lived under the Law of Moses. Once I observed that a certain mass-priest, who was my teacher at the time and who knew some Latin, had the book of Genesis in his possession; he said that the patriarch Jacob had four wives, two sisters and their two handmaidens. He spoke very truly, but he did not know—nor I yet at that time—how great a difference there is between the Old Law and the New. At the beginning of this world, a brother took his sister as a wife, and sometimes a father even begat on his own daughter, and many a man had a number of wives in order to increase the race; and in the earliest times a man might not marry anyone but a relative. If anyone desires to live after the coming of Christ as men lived before or under the Law of Moses, that man is not a Christian, nor is he even worthy to have any Christian person eat with him. If the ignorant priests understand any little bit in the Latin books, then they immediately think that they can be great teachers; but they do not understand, however, the spiritual meaning therein and that the Old Law was a betokening of things to come, or that the New Testament after Christ's Incarnation was a fulfillment of all those things which the Old Testament signified beforehand about Christ and His chosen ones. Also, they often quote Paul and ask why they may not have a wife as the Apostle Peter had, and they are unwilling to hear or to understand that the blessed Peter lived according to the Law of Moses until the time when Christ came to men and began to preach

His holy Gospel and chose Peter as His first companion. Then Peter immediately left his wife, and all the twelve apostles who had wives left both wives and possessions and followed Christ's teaching to the New Law and chastity which He Himself then established. Priests are appointed teachers to the lay folk: it would befit them now to understand the spiritual meaning of the Old Law and what Christ Himself and His apostles taught in the New Testament, so that they could successfully guide the people to God's faith and set an example for them which would be conducive to good works.

We also declare ahead of time that the book is very difficult to understand spiritually, and that we have written no more than the bare narrative. It will therefore seem to the ignorant that all the meaning is locked in the simple narrative, but that is very far from true. The book is called "Genesis," that is, "The Book of Generation," because it is the first book of the Bible and tells of the origin of each thing, although it does not tell of the creation of the angels. It begins thus: *In principio creavit deus celum et terram*, which is in English, "In the beginning God created heaven and earth." It was truly so brought about that Almighty God made in the beginning those things which He desired to create. However, according to the spiritual meaning the beginning is Christ, as He Himself said to the Jews, "I am the beginning who speak to you." Through this Beginning God the Father made heaven and earth, for He shaped all created things through the Son, who was the Wisdom of the Father which was constantly brought forth from Him. After that, *Spiritus dei ferebatur super aquas* appears in the first verse of the book; that is in English, "And God's spirit was borne over the waters." God's Spirit is the Holy Ghost, through whom the Father gave life to all those creatures which He shaped through the Son, and the Holy Ghost travels through the hearts of men and bestows upon us forgiveness of our sins, first through water in baptism and afterward through penance; and if anyone rejects the forgiveness which the Holy Ghost bestows, then his sin is unpardonable through all eternity. The Holy Trinity is revealed later in this book, as it is in the words which God utters: "Let us make man in our image." Because He said, "Let *us* make," the Trinity is betokened; because He said, "in our *image*," the true oneness of God is proclaimed: He did not utter the plural "in our images," but the singular "in our image." Later, three angels came to Abraham, and he spoke to all three as if to one.

And how did Abel's blood cry out to God except as the evil deeds of each man accuse him before God without words? By these little touches, one may understand how deep the book is in spiritual meaning, though it is written in clear words. In a later part of the book, Joseph, who was given over to the Egyptians, and who delivered that race from the great famine, symbolized Christ, who was given over to death for our sake and who delivered us from the eternal famine of hellish torment. That great tabernacle which Moses made with wonderful skill in the desert as God Himself directed him symbolized God's church, which He Himself established through His apostles, complete with numerous ornaments and beautiful customs. The people brought gold and silver and precious gems and many glorious things for that structure; some also brought goat hair as God had commanded. The gold symbolized our faith and our good intention, which we must offer to God; the silver symbolized God's words and the holy teachings which we must have in order to do God's work; the gems symbolized various beauties in God's people; the goat hair symbolized the firm repentance of those men who feel sorrow for their sins. People also offered cattle of many kinds to God as a sacrifice within the tabernacle, concerning which the symbolism is very complex, and it was commanded that at the offering the tail should always be whole on the beast to symbolize that God desires us always to act properly until the end of our life: then the tail is offered in our works.

Now, the aforesaid book is written very narrowly in many places and nevertheless very deeply with regard to spiritual meaning, and it is arranged just as God Himself dictated it to the writer Moses, and we dare write no more in English than the Latin has, nor change the arrangement of the words except in those places alone in which Latin and English usage do not have a common idiom. He who makes a translation from Latin into English, or who turns Latin into English in his teaching must always so arrange the wording that the English is set forth in its own idiom: otherwise it will be very misleading for the reader who does not understand the idiom of the Latin. It is also to be kept in mind that there were certain heretics who wished to reject the Old Law and certain others who wished to retain the Old and reject the New, just as the Jews do; but Christ Himself and His apostles taught us both to observe the Old Law spiritually and the New truly through our actions. God created for us two eyes and two ears, two nostrils and two lips, two hands and two feet, and He desired also to have two Testaments written in this world, the Old and the New, because He does as He pleases, and He has no councillor and no one need ask Him, "Why do you thus?" We must turn our will to His decrees, and we cannot bend His decrees to our pleasure.

I say now that I neither dare nor desire to translate any book from Latin into English after this one, and I beseech you, beloved aldorman, no longer to ask that of me, lest I be disobedient if I don't do as you request, or fall into error if I do. May God be merciful to you forever and ever. I ask now in God's name that if anyone desires to copy this book, he check his text thoroughly against the original, because I shall have no control over the text though someone corrupt it through the employment of inaccurate scribes—and it is his worry then, not mine. Great mischief does the bad copyist if he is unwilling to correct his mistakes.

HOMILY FOR MID-LENT SUNDAY[2]

Abiit Jesus trans mare Galileæ: et reliqua.[3]

"Jesus went over the sea of Galilee, which is called of Tiberias, and a great multitude followed him, because they had seen the miracles which he had wrought on the diseased men. Then Jesus went up into a mountain, and there sat with his disciples, and the holy Easter-tide was then very nigh. Jesus then looked up, and saw that there was a great multitude coming, and said to one of his disciples, who was called Philip, With what can we buy bread for this people? This he said to prove the disciple: himself knew what he would do. Then Philip answered, Though two hundred pennyworth of bread were bought, yet could not every one of them get a morsel. Then said one of his disciples, who was called Andrew, Peter's brother, Here beareth a lad five barley loaves, and two fishes, but what is that for so great a multitude? Then said Jesus, Make the people sit. And there was much grass on the place pleasant to sit on: and they then all sat, about five thousand men. Then Jesus took the five loaves, and blessed, and brake, and divided them among those sitting: in like manner also he divided the fishes; and they all had enough. When they all were full, Jesus said to his disciples, Gather the remainder, and let it not be lost, and they gathered the fragments, and filled twelve baskets with the remainder. The people, who saw this miracle, said that Christ was the true prophet who was to come to this world."

The sea which Jesus passed over betokeneth this present world, which Christ came to and passed over; that is he came to this world in human nature, and passed over this life; he came to death, and from death arose; and went up on a mountain, and there sat with his disciples, for he ascended to heaven, and there sits now with his saints. Rightly is the sea compared to this world, for it is sometimes serene and pleasant to navigate on, sometimes also very rough and terrible to be on. So is this world; sometimes it is desirable and pleasant to dwell in, sometimes also it is very rugged, and mingled with divers things, so that it is too often very unpleasant to inhabit. Sometimes we are hale, sometimes sick; now joyful, and again in great affliction; therefore is this life, as we before said, compared to the sea.

When Jesus was sitting on the mountain, he lifted up his eyes, and saw that there was a great multitude coming. All those who come to him, that is those who incline to the right faith, Jesus sees, and on them he has pity, and enlightens their understanding with his grace, that they may come to him without error, and to these he gives ghostly food, that they may not faint by the way. When he asked Philip, whence they could buy bread for the people, he showed Philip's ignorance. Well Christ knew what he would do, and he knew that Philip knew not. Then said Andrew, that a lad there bare five barley loaves and two fishes. Then said Jesus, "Make the people sit," and so on, as we have before repeated it to you. Jesus saw the hungry people, and he compassionately fed them, both by his goodness and by his might. What could his goodness alone have done, unless there had been might with that goodness? His disciples would also have fed the people, but they had not wherewithal. Jesus had the good will to nourish them, and the power to execute it.

God hath wrought many miracles and daily works; but those miracles are much weakened in the sight of men, because they are very usual. A greater miracle it is that God Almighty every day feeds all the world, and directs the good, than that miracle was, that he filled five thousand men with five loaves: but men wondered at this, not because it was a greater miracle, but because it was unusual. Who now gives fruit to our fields, and multiplies the harvest from a few grains of corn, but he who multiplied the five loaves? The might was there in Christ's hands, and the five loaves were, as it were, seed, not sown in the earth, but multiplied by him who created the earth.

This miracle is very great, and deep in its significations. Often some one sees fair characters written, then praises he the writer and the characters, but knows not what they mean. He who understands the art of writing praises their fairness, and reads the characters, and comprehends their meaning. In one way we look at a picture, and in another at characters. Nothing more is necessary for a picture than that you see and praise it: but it is not enough to look at characters without, at the same time, reading them, and understanding their signification. So also it is with regard to the miracle which God wrought with the five loaves: it is not enough that we wonder at the miracle, or praise God on account of it, without also understanding its spiritual sense.

The five loaves which the lad bare, betoken the five books which the leader Moses appointed in the old law. The lad who bare them, and tasted not of them, was the Jewish people, who read the five books, and knew therein no spiritual signification, before Christ came, and opened the books, and disclosed their spiritual sense to his disciples, and they afterwards to all christian people. We cannot now enumerate to you all the five books, but we will tell you that God himself dictated them, and that Moses wrote them, for the guidance and instruction of the ancient people of Israel, and of us also in a spiritual sense. These books were written concerning Christ, but the spiritual sense was hidden from the people, until Christ came himself to men, and opened the secrets of the books, according to the spiritual sense.

Alii evangelistæ ferunt, quia panes et pisces Dominus discipulis distribuisset, discipuli autem ministraverunt turbis. He brake the five loaves and gave to his disciples, and bade them bear them to the people; for he taught them the heavenly lore: and they went throughout all the world, and preached, as Christ himself had taught. When he had broken the loaves then were they multiplied, and grew in his hands; for the five books were spiritually devised, and wise doctors expounded them, and founded on those books many other books; and we with the doctrine of those books are daily spiritually fed.

The loaves were of barley. Barley is very difficult to prepare, and, nevertheless, feeds a man when it is prepared. So was the old law very difficult and obscure to understand; but, nevertheless, when we come to the flour, that is to the signification, then it feeds and strengthens our mind with the hidden lore. There were five loaves, and there were five thousand men fed; because the Jewish people was subject to God's law, which stood written in five books. When Christ asked Philip, and proved him, as we before read, by that asking he betokened the people's ignorance, who were under that law, and knew not the spiritual sense which was concealed in that law.

The two fishes betokened the Psalms and the sayings of the prophets. The one of these announced and proclaimed Christ's advent with psalm-singing, and the other with prophecy, as if they were meat to the five barley loaves, that is, to the five legal books. The people, who were there fed, sat on the grass. The grass betokened fleshly desire, as the prophet said, "Every flesh is grass, and the glory of the flesh is as the blossom of plants." Now should everyone who will sit at God's refection, and partake of spiritual instruction, tread and press down the grass, that is, he should overpower his fleshly lusts, and ever dispose his body to the service of God.

There were counted at that refection five thousand males; because those men who belong to the spiritual refection should be manfully made, as the apostle said; he said, "Be watchful, and stand on faith, and undertake manfully, and be bold." Though if a woman be manly by nature, and strong to God's will, she will be counted among the men who sit at the table of God. Thousand is a perfect number, and no number extends beyond it. With that number is betokened the perfection of those men who nourish their souls with God's precepts.

"Jesus then bade the remainder to be gathered, that it might not be lost; and they filled twelve baskets with the fragments." The remainder of the refection, that is the depth of the doctrine, which secular men may not understand, that should our teachers gather, that it may not be lost, and preserve in their scrips, that is, in their hearts, and have ever ready to draw forth the wisdom and doctrine both of the old law and of the new. They gathered then twelve baskets full of the fragments. The twelvefold number betokened the twelve apostles; because they received the mysteries of the doctrine, which the lay folk could not understand.

"The people, who saw that miracle, said of Christ, that he was the true prophet who was to come." In one sense they said the truth: he was a prophet, for he knew all future things, and also prophesied many things which will, without doubt, be fulfilled. He is a prophet, and he is the prophecy of all prophets, for all the prophets have prophesied of him, and Christ has fulfilled the prophecies of them all. The people saw the miracle, and they greatly wondered at it. That miracle is recorded, and we have heard it. What their eyes did in them, that does our faith in us. They saw it, and we believe it, who saw it not; and we are therefore accounted the better, as Jesus, in another place, said of us, "Blessed are they who see me not, and, nevertheless, believe in me, and celebrate my miracles."

The people said of Christ, that he was a true prophet. Now we say of Christ, that he is Son of the Living God, who was to come to redeem the whole world from the power of the devil, and from hell-torment. The people knew not of those benefits, that they might have said that he was God, but they said that he was a prophet. We say now, with full belief, that Christ is a true prophet, and Prophet of all prophets, and that he is truly Son of the Almighty God, as mighty as his Father, with whom he liveth and reigneth in unity of the Holy Ghost, ever without end to eternity. Amen.

Notes

1   The selection was translated especially for this collection by L. A. Muinzer.
2   From Benjamin Thorpe, *The Homilies of the Anglo-Saxon Church*, Aelfric Society, London, 1844.
3   John 6:1ff.

LATER CELTIC
LITERATURE IN BRITAIN

During the later Middle Ages, Ireland continued to produce poetry of a high order. In prose, the Fenian Cycle of tales centering around the hero Finn mac Cumaill became popular. However, students of English have usually been more interested in the Welsh literature of the period. First of all, a collection of Welsh tales called, somewhat inaccurately, *The Mabinogion*, was produced which contains some interesting early material about King Arthur. Again, the Welsh poet Dafydd ap Gwilym has been widely hailed as the greatest poet who ever wrote in a Celtic language.

For the Irish literature of the period, see Robin Flower, *The Irish Tradition*, Clarendon Press, Oxford, 1947. Irish narratives are described and summarized by Myles Dillon, *Early Irish*

Facing page: Très riches heures de Jean de France. *The sun entering Libra in September.*

Literature, The University of Chicago Press, Chicago, 1948. There are introductions to Welsh poetry by H. I. Bell, *The Development of Welsh Poetry*, Clarendon Press, Oxford, 1936; and, more recently, by Gwyn Williams, *An Introduction to Welsh Poetry*, Faber & Faber, Ltd., London, 1953.

A. The Mabinogion

The Mabinogion *properly so-called consists of four tales or "branches" which were originally devoted to stories concerning the youthful deeds of Welsh traditional heroes. However, the title has come to be applied to a collection containing these tales and seven others of miscellaneous character and date. The seven others include four independent native tales, of which "Culhwch and Olwen" is the most important, and three romances probably based ultimately on the work of the great French poet Chrétien de Troyes. "Culhwch and Olwen" is now usually said to have been composed at some time during the later eleventh century, although some scholars prefer a later date.*

A great deal has been written about The Mabinogion, *but for a statement of currently accepted opinion concerning the tale which follows, see Idris Llewelyn Foster, "Culhwch and Olwen and Rhonabwy's Dream," in R. S. Loomis,* Arthurian Literature in the Middle Ages, *Clarendon Press, Oxford, 1959. This text is reprinted from* The Mabinogion, *translated by Gwyn Jones and Thomas Jones, E. P. Dutton & Co., Inc., New York, 1949, by permission of the publishers.*

"CULHWCH AND OLWEN"

Cilydd son of Cyleddon Wledig wished for a wife as wellborn as himself. The wife that he took was Goleuddydd daughter of Anlawdd Wledig. After his stay with her the country went to prayers whether they might have offspring, and they got a son through the prayers of the country. But from the time she grew with child, she went mad, without coming near a dwelling. When her time came upon her, her right sense came back to her; it came in a place where a swineherd was keeping a herd of swine, and through terror of the swine the queen was delivered. And the swineherd took the boy until he came to the court. And the boy was baptized, and the name Culhwch given to him because he was found in a pig-run.[1] Nonetheless the boy was of gentle lineage: he was first cousin to Arthur. And the boy was put out to nurse.

And after that the boy's mother, Goleuddydd daughter of Anlawdd Wledig, grew sick. She called her husband to her, and quoth she to him, "I am going to die of this sickness, and thou wilt wish for another wife. And these days wives are the dispensers of gifts, but it is wrong for thee to despoil thy son. I ask of thee

that thou take no wife till thou see a two-headed briar on my grave." That he promised her. She summoned her preceptor to her and bade him strip the grave each year, so that nothing might grow on it. The queen died. The king would send an attendant every morning to see whether anything was growing on the grave. At the end of seven years the preceptor neglected that which he had promised the queen. One day when the king was hunting, he drew near the graveyard; he wanted to see the grave whereby he was to take a wife. He saw the briar. And when he saw it the king took counsel where he might get a wife. Quoth one of the counsellors, "I could tell of a woman would suit thee well. She is the wife of king Doged." They decided to seek her out. And they slew the king, and his wife they brought home with them, and an only daughter she had along with her; and they took possession of the king's lands.

Upon a day as the good lady went walking abroad, she came to the house of an old crone who was in the town, without a tooth in her head. Quoth the queen: "Crone, wilt thou for God's sake tell me what I ask of thee? Where are the children of the man who has carried me off by force?" Quoth the crone: "He has no children." Quoth the queen: "Woe is me that I should have come to a childless man!" Said the crone: "Thou needst not say that. It is prophesied that he shall have offspring. 'Tis by thee he shall have it, since he has not had it by another. Besides, be not unhappy, he has one son."

The good lady returned home joyfully, and quoth she to her husband, "What reason hast thou to hide thy child from me?" Quoth the king, "I will hide him no longer." Messengers were sent after the boy, and he came to the court. His stepmother said to him, "It were well for thee to take a wife, son, and I have a daughter meet for any nobleman in the world." Quoth the boy, "I am not yet of an age to take a wife." Said she in reply: "I will swear a destiny upon thee, that thy side shall never strike against woman till thou win Olwen daughter of Ysbaddaden Chief Giant." The boy colored, and love of the maiden entered into every limb of him, although he had never seen her. Quoth his father to him, "How, son, why dost thou color? What ails thee?" "My stepmother has sworn on me that I shall never win a wife until I win Olwen daughter of Ysbaddaden Chief Giant." "It is easy for thee to achieve that, son," said his father to him. "Arthur is thy first cousin. Go then to Arthur to trim thy hair, and ask that of him as his gift to thee."

Off went the boy on a steed with light-gray head, four winters old, with well-knit fork, shell-hoofed, and a gold tubular bridle-bit in its mouth. And under him a precious gold saddle, and in his hand two whetted spears of silver. A battle-axe in his hand, the forearm's length of a full grown man from ridge to edge. It would draw blood from the wind; it would be swifter than the swiftest dewdrop from the stalk to the ground, when the dew would be heaviest in the month of June. A gold-hilted sword on his thigh, and the blade of it gold, and a gold-chased buckler upon him, with the hue of heaven's lightning therein, and an ivory boss therein. And two greyhounds, whitebreasted, brindled, in front of him, with a collar of red gold about the neck of either, from shoulder-swell to ear. The one that was on the left side would be on the right, and the one that was on the right side would be on the left, like two sea-swallows sporting around him. Four clods the four hoofs of his steed would cut, like four swallows in the air over his head, now before him, now behind him. A four-cornered mantle of purple upon him, and an apple of red gold in each of its corners, a hundred kine was the worth of each apple. The worth of three hundred kine in precious gold was there in his foot gear and his stirrups, from the top of his thigh to the tip of his toe. Never a hair-tip stirred upon him, so exceeding light his steed's canter under him on his way to the gate of Arthur's court.

Quoth the youth, "Is there a porter?" "There is. And thou, may thy head not be thine, that thou dost ask! I am porter to Arthur each first day of January, but my deputies for the year save then, none other than Huandaw and Gogigwr and Llaesgymyn, and Penpingion who goes upon his head to spare his feet, neither heavenwards nor earthwards, but like a rolling stone on a court floor." "Open the gate." "I will not." "Why wilt thou not open it?" "Knife has gone into meat, and drink into horn, and a thronging in Arthur's hall. Save the son of a king of a rightful dominion, or a craftsman who brings his craft, none may enter. Meat for thy dogs and corn for thy horse, and hot peppered chops for thyself, and wine brimming over, and delectable songs before thee. Food for fifty men shall come to thee in the hospice; there men from afar take their meat, and the scions of other countries who do not proffer a craft in Arthur's court. It will be no worse for thee there than for Arthur in the court: a woman to sleep with thee, and delectable songs before thee. To-morrow at tierce, when the gate is opened for the host that came here to-day, for thee shall the gate be opened first, and thou shalt sit wherever thou wilt in Arthur's hall, from its upper end to its lower." The youth said, "I will do nothing of that. If thou open the gate, it is well. If thou open it not, I will bring dishonor upon thy lord and ill report upon thee. And I will raise three shouts at the entrance of this gate, so that it shall not be less audible on the top of Pengwaedd in Cornwall and in the depths of Dinsel in the North, and in Esgeir Oerfel in Ireland. And every woman with child that is in this court shall miscarry, and such of them as are not with child their wombs shall turn to a burden within them, so that they may never bear child from this day forth." Quoth Glewlwyd Mighty-grasp, "Shout as much as thou wilt about the laws of Arthur's court, thou shalt not be let in till first I go and have word with Arthur."

And Glewlwyd came into the hall. Quoth Arthur to him, "Thou hast news from the gate?" "I have. Two-thirds of my life are past, and two-thirds of thine own. I was of old in Caer Se and Asse, in Sach and Salach, in Lotor and Ffotor. I was of old in India the Great and

India the Lesser. I was of old in the contest between the two Ynyrs, when the twelve hostages were brought from Llychlyn. And of old I was in Egrop, and in Africa was I, and in the islands of Corsica, and in Caer Brythwch and Brythach, and Nerthach. I was there of old when thou didst slay the war-band of Gleis son of Merin, when thou didst slay Mil the Black, son of Dugum; I was there of old when thou didst conquer Greece unto the east. I was of old in Caer Oeth and Anoeth, and in Caer Nefenhyr Nine-teeth. Fair kingly men saw we there, but never saw I a man so comely as this who is even now at the entrance to the gate." Quoth Arthur, "If thou didst enter walking go thou out running. And he that looks upon the light, and opens his eye and shuts it, an injunction upon him. And let some serve with golden drinking horns, and others with hot peppered chops, so that there be ample meat and drink for him. A shameful thing it is to leave in wind and rain a man such as thou tellest of." Quoth Cei: "By the hand of my friend, if my counsel were acted upon, the laws of court would not be broken for his sake." "Not so, fair Cei. We are noble men so long as we are resorted to. The greater the bounty we show, all the greater will be our nobility and our fame and our glory."

And Glewlwyd came to the gate and opened the gate to him. And what every man did, to dismount at the gate on the horse-block, he did not do; but on his steed he came inside. Quoth Culhwch, "Hail, sovereign prince of this Island! Be it no worse unto the lower half of the house than unto the upper. Be this greeting equally to thy nobles, and thy retinue, and thy leaders of hosts. May there be none without his share of it. Even as I gave thee full greeting, may thy grace and thy faith and thy glory be in this Island." "God's truth, so be it, chieftain! Greeting to thee too. Sit thou between two of the warriors, and delectable song before thee, and the privilege of an atheling for thee, an heir to a throne, for as long as thou shalt be here. And when I dispense my gifts to guests and men from afar, it shall be at thy hand that I so begin in this court." Quoth the youth: "I have not come here to wheedle meat and drink. But if I obtain my boon, I will repay it, and I will praise it. If I obtain it not, I will bear hence thine honor as far as thy renown was farthest in the four corners of the world." Quoth Arthur, "Though thou bide not here, chieftain, thou shalt obtain the boon thy head and thy tongue shall name, as far as wind dries, as far as rain

wets, as far as sun runs, as far as sea stretches, as far as earth extends, save only my ship and my mantle, and Caledfwlch my sword, and Rhongomyniad my spear, and Wynebgwrthucher my shield, and Carnwennan my dagger, and Gwenhwyfar my wife." "God's truth thereon?" "Thou shalt have it gladly. Name what thou wilt." "I will. I would have my hair trimmed." "That thou shalt have." Arthur took a golden comb and shears with loops of silver, and he combed his head.

And he asked who he was. Quoth Arthur: "My heart grows tender towards thee: I know thou art sprung from my blood. Declare who thou art." "I will: Culhwch son of Cilydd son of Cyleddon Wledig, by Goleuddydd daughter of Anlawdd Wledig, my mother." Quoth Arthur: "True it is. Thou art then my first cousin. Name what thou wilt, and thou shalt have it, whatever thy mouth and thy tongue shall name." "God's truth thereon to me, and the truth of thy kingdom?" "Thou shalt have it gladly." "My claim on thee is that thou get me Olwen daughter of Ysbaddaden Chief Giant. And I invoke her in the name of thy warriors."

He invoked his boon in the name of Cei and Bedwyr, and Greidawl Gallddofydd, and Gwythyr son of Greidawl, and Greid son of Eri, and Cynddylig the Guide, and Tathal Frank-deceit, and Maelwys son of Baeddan, and Cnychwr son of Nes, and Cubert son of Daere, and Fercos son of Roch, and Lluber Beuthach, and Corfil Berfach, and Gwyn son of Esni, and Gwyn son of Nwyfre, and Gwyn son of Nudd, and Edern son of Nudd, and Adwy son of Gereint, and Fflewdwr Fflam Wledig. . . . [There follows a long list of heroes.] The gentle gold-torqued maidens of this Island: in addition to Gwenhwyfar, the first lady of this Island, and Gwenhwyach her sister, and Rathtyen the only daughter of Clememyl—Celemon daughter of Cei, and Tangwen daughter of Gweir Dathar the Servitor, Gwen Alarch[2] daughter of Cynwal Hundred-hogs, Eurneid daughter of Clydno Eidin, Eneuawg daughter of Bedwyr, Enrhydreg daughter of Tuduathar, Gwenwledyr daughter of Gwaredur Bow-back, Erdudfyl daughter of Tryffin, Eurolwyn daughter of Gwdolwyn the Dwarf, Teleri daughter of Peul, Indeg daughter of Garwy the Tall, Morfudd daughter of Urien Rheged, fair Gwenlliant the magnanimous maiden, Creiddylad daughter of Lludd Silver-hand (the maiden of most majesty that was ever in the Island of Britain and its three adjacent islands. And for her Gwythyr son of

Greidawl and Gwyn son of Nudd fight for ever each May-calends till the day of doom), Ellylw daughter of Neol Hang-cock (and she lived three generations), Esyllt Whiteneck and Esyllt Slenderneck—in the name of all these did Culhwch son of Cilydd invoke his boon.

Arthur said, "Ah, chieftain, I have never heard tell of the maiden thou tellest of, nor of her parents. I will gladly send messengers to seek her." From that night till the same night at the end of a year the messengers were a-wandering. At the end of the year, when Arthur's messengers had found nothing, said the chieftain, "Every one has obtained his boon, yet am I still lacking. I will away and take thine honor with me." Said Cei, "Ah, chieftain, overmuch dost thou asperse Arthur. Come thou with us. Till thou shalt say she exists not in the world, or till we find her, we will not be parted from thee."

Then Cei arose. Cei had this peculiarity, nine nights and nine days his breath lasted under water, nine nights and nine days would he be without sleep. A wound from Cei's sword no physician might heal. A wondrous gift had Cei: when it pleased him he would be as tall as the tallest tree in the forest. Another peculiarity had he: when the rain was heaviest, a handbreadth before his hand and another behind his hand what would be in his hand would be dry, by reason of the greatness of his heat; and when the cold was hardest on his comrades, that would be to them kindling to light a fire.

Arthur called on Bedwyr, who never shrank from an enterprise upon which Cei was bound. It was thus with Bedwyr, that none was so handsome as he in this Island, save Arthur and Drych son of Cibddar, and this too, that though he was one-handed no three warriors drew blood in the same field faster than he. Another strange quality was his; one thrust would there be of his spear, and nine counter-thrusts.

Arthur called on Cynddylig the Guide. "Go thou for me upon this enterprise along with the chieftain." He was no worse a guide in the land he had never seen than in his own land.

He called Gwrhyr Interpreter of Tongues: he knew all tongues.

He called Gwalchmei son of Gwyar, because he never came home without the quest he had gone to seek. He was the best of walkers and the best of riders. He was Arthur's nephew, his sister's son, and his first cousin.

Arthur called on Menw son of Teirgwaedd, for should they come to a heathen land he might cast a spell over them, so that none might see them and they see every one.

Away they went till they came to a wide open plain and saw a fort, the greatest of forts in the world. That day they journeyed. When they thought they were near to the fort they were no nearer than at first. And the second and the third day they journeyed, and with difficulty did they get thereto. However, as they were coming to the same plain as it, they could see a great flock of sheep without limit or end to it, and a shepherd tending the sheep on top of a mound, and a jerkin of skins upon him, and at his side a shaggy mastiff which was bigger than a nine year old stallion. It was the way of him that never a lamb had he lost, much less a grown beast. No company had ever fared past him that he did not do it harm or deadly hurt; every dead tree and bush that was on the plain, his breath would burn them to the very ground.

Quoth Cei: "Gwrhyr Interpreter of Tongues, go and have word with yonder man." "Cei, I made no promise to go save as far as thou thyself wouldst go." "Then let us go there together." Quoth Menw son of Teirgwaedd: "Have no qualms to go thither. I will cast a spell over the dog, so that he shall do harm to none."

They came to where the shepherd was. Quoth they, "Things are well with thee, shepherd." "May things never be better with you than with me." "Yea, by God, for thou art chief." "There is no affliction to do me harm save my wife." "Whose are the sheep thou tendest, or whose is the fort?" "Fools of men that you are! Throughout the world it is known that this is the fort of Ysbaddaden Chief Giant." "And thou, who art thou?" "Custennin son of Mynwyedig am I, and because of my wife Ysbaddaden Chief Giant has wrought my ruin. You too, who are you?" "Messengers of Arthur are here, to seek Olwen." "Whew, men! God protect you! For all the world, do not that. Never a one has come to make that request that went away with his life."

The shepherd arose. As he arose Culhwch gave him a ring of gold. He sought to put on the ring, but it would not go on him, and he placed it in the finger of his glove and went home and gave the glove to his wife. And she took the ring from the glove. "Whence came this ring to thee, husband? 'Twas not often that thou hast had treasure-trove." "I went to the sea, to find sea-food. Lo! I saw a body coming in on the tide. Never saw I body so beautiful as that, and on its finger I found this ring." "Alas, husband, since sea does not tolerate a dead man's jewel therein, show me that body." "Wife, the one whose body that is, thou shalt see him here presently." "Who is that?" the woman asked. "Culhwch son of Cilydd son of Cyleddon Wledig, by Goleuddydd daughter of Anlawdd Wledig, his mother, who is come to seek Olwen." Two feelings possessed her: she was glad that her nephew, her sister's son, was coming to her; and she was sad because she had never seen any depart with his life that had come to make that request.

They came forward to the gate of the shepherd Custennin's court. She heard the noise of their coming. She ran with joy to meet them. Cei snatched a log out of the wood-pile, and she came to meet them, to try and throw her arms about their necks. Cei thrust a stake between her two hands. She squeezed the stake so that it became a twisted withe. Quoth Cei, "Woman, had it been I thou didst squeeze in this wise, there were no need for another to love me ever. An ill love, that!"

They came into the house and their needs were supplied. After a while, when all were letting themselves be busied, the woman opened a coffer alongside the hearth, and out of it arose a lad with curly yellow hair. Quoth Gwrhyr, "'Twere pity to hide a lad like this. I know that it is no fault of his own that is visited upon him." Quoth the woman, "He is all that is left. Three-and-twenty sons of mine has Ysbaddaden Chief Giant slain, and I have no more hope of this one than of the others." Quoth Cei, "Let him keep company with me, and we shall not be slain save together."

They ate. Quoth the woman, "On what errand are you come hither?" "We are come to seek Olwen." "For God's sake, since none from the fort has yet seen you, get you back!" "God knows we will not get us back till we have seen the maiden. Will she come to where she may be seen?" "She comes hither every Saturday to wash her head; and in the bowl where she washes she leaves all her rings. Neither she nor her messenger ever comes for them." "Will she come hither if she is sent for?" "God knows I will not slay my soul. I will not betray the one who trusts in me. But if you pledge your word you will do her no harm, I will send for her." "We pledge it," said they.

She was sent for. And she came, with a robe of flame-red silk about her, and around the maiden's neck a torque of red gold, and precious pearls thereon and rubies. Yellower was her head than the flower of the broom, whiter was her flesh than the foam of the wave; whiter were her palms and her fingers than the shoots of the marsh trefoil from amidst the fine gravel of a welling spring. Neither the eye of the mewed hawk, nor the eye of the thrice-mewed falcon, not an eye was there fairer than hers. Whiter were her breasts than the breast of the white swan, redder were her cheeks than the reddest foxgloves. Whoso beheld her would be filled with love of her. Four white trefoils sprang up behind her wherever she went; and for that reason was she called Olwen.[3]

She entered the house and sat between Culhwch and the high seat, and even as he saw her he knew her. Said Culhwch to her, "Ah maiden, 'tis thou I have loved. And come thou with me." "Lest sin be charged to thee and me, that I may not do at all. My father has sought a pledge of me that I go not without his counsel, for he shall live only until I go with a husband. There is, however, counsel I will give thee, if thou wilt take it. Go ask me of my father. And however much he demand of thee, do thou promise to get it, and me too shalt thou get. But if he have cause to doubt at all, get me thou shalt not, and 'tis well for thee if thou escape with thy life." "I promise all that, and will obtain it," said he.

She went to her chamber. They then arose to go after her to the fort, and slew nine gatemen who were at nine gates without a man crying out, and nine mastiffs without one squealing. And they went forward to the hall.

Quoth they, "In the name of God and man, greeting unto thee, Ysbaddaden Chief Giant." "And you, where are you going?" "We are going to seek Olwen thy daughter for Culhwch son of Cilydd." "Where are those rascal servants and those ruffians of mine?" said he. "Raise up the forks under my two eyelids that I may see my future son-in-law." That was done. "Come hither to-morrow. I will give you some answer."

They rose, and Ysbaddaden Chief Giant snatched at one of the three poisoned stone-spears which were by his hand and hurled it after them. And Bedwyr caught it and hurled it back at him, and pierced Ysbaddaden Chief Giant right through the ball of his knee. Quoth he, "Thou cursed savage son-in-law! I shall walk the worse up a slope. Like the sting of a gadfly the poisoned iron has pained me. Cursed be the smith who fashioned it, and the anvil on which it was wrought, so painful it is!"

That night they lodged in the house of Custennin.

And on the morrow with pomp and with brave combs set in their hair they came into the hall. They said, "Ysbaddaden Chief Giant, give us thy daughter in return for her portion and her maiden fee to thee and her two kinswomen. And unless thou give her, thou shalt meet thy death because of her." "She and her four great-grandmothers and her four great-grandfathers are yet alive. I must needs take counsel with them." "So be it with thee," said they. "Let us go to our meat." As they arose he took hold of the second stone-spear which was by his hand and hurled it after them. And Menw son of Teirgwaedd caught it and hurled it back at him, and pierced him in the middle of his breast, so that it came out in the small of his back. "Thou cursed savage son-in-law! Like the bite of a big-headed leech the hard iron has pained me. Cursed be the forge wherein it was heated. When I go uphill, I shall have tightness of chest, and belly-ache, and a frequent loathing of meat." They went to their meat.

And the third day they came to court. Quoth they, "Ysbaddaden Chief Giant, shoot at us no more. Seek not thy harm and deadly hurt and death." "Where are my servants? Raise up the forks—my eyelids have fallen over the balls of my eyes—so that I may take a look at my future son-in-law." They arose, and as they arose he took the third poisoned stone-spear and hurled it after them. And Culhwch caught it and hurled it back, even as he wished, and pierced him through the ball of the eye, so that it came out through the nape of the neck. "Thou cursed savage son-in-law! So long as I am left alive, the sight of my eyes will be the worse. When I go against the wind they will water, a headache I shall have, and a giddiness each new moon. Cursed be the forge wherein it was heated. Like the bite of a mad dog to me the way the poisoned iron has pierced me." They went to their meat.

On the morrow they came to court. Quoth they, "Shoot not at us. Seek not the harm and deadly hurt and martyrdom that are upon thee, or what may be worse, if such be thy wish. Give us thy daughter." "Where is he who is told to seek my daughter?" "'Tis I who seek her, Culhwch son of Cilydd." "Come hither where I may see thee." A chair was placed under him, face to face with him.

Said Ysbaddaden Chief Giant, "Is it thou that seekest my daughter?" "'Tis I who seek her." "Thy pledge would I have that thou wilt not do worse by me than is just." "Thou shalt have it." "When I have myself gotten that which I shall name to thee, then thou shalt get my daughter." "Name what thou wouldst name."

"I will," said he. "Dost see the great thicket yonder?" "I see." "I must have it uprooted out of the earth and burnt on the face of the ground so that the cinders and ashes thereof be its manure; and that it be ploughed and sown so that it be ripe in the morning against the drying of the dew, in order that it may be made into meat and drink for thy wedding guests and my daughter's. And all that I must have done in one day."

"It is easy for me to get that, though thou think it is not easy."

"Though thou get that, there is that thou wilt not get. A husbandman to till and prepare that land, other than Amaethon son of Dôn. He will not come with thee of his own free will, nor canst thou compel him."

"It is easy for me to get that, though thou think it is not easy."

"Though thou get that, there is that thou wilt not get. Gofannon son of Dôn to come to the headland to set the irons. He will not do work of his own free will, save for a king in his own right, nor canst thou compel him."

"It is easy for me to get that, though thou think it is not easy."

"Though thou get that, there is that thou wilt not get. The two oxen of Gwlwlydd Wineu, both yoked together to plough well the rough ground yonder. He will not give them of his own free will, nor canst thou compel him."

"It is easy for me to get that, though thou think it is not easy."

"Though thou get that, there is that thou wilt not get. The Melyn Gwanwyn and the Ych Brych,[4] both yoked together, must I have."

"It is easy for me to get that, though thou think it is not easy."

"Though thou get that, there is that thou wilt not get. The two horned oxen, one of which is beyond Mynydd Bannawg,[5] and the other this side—and to fetch them together in the one plough. Nyniaw and Peibiaw are they, whom God transformed into oxen for their sins."

"It is easy for me to get that, though thou think it is not easy."

"Though thou get that, there is that thou wilt not get. Dost see the hoed tilth yonder?" "I see." "When first I met the mother of that maiden, nine hestors of flax seed were sown therein; neither black nor white has come out of it yet, and I have that measure still. I must have that in the new-broken ground yonder, so that it may be a white veil for my daughter's head on the day of thy wedding-feast."

"It is easy for me to get that, though thou think it is not easy."

"Though thou get that, there is that thou wilt not get. Honey that will be nine times sweeter than the honey of a virgin swarm, without drones and without bees, to make bragget for the feast."

"It is easy for me to get that, though thou think it is not easy."

"Though thou get that, there is that thou wilt not get. The cup of Llwyr son of Llwyrion, in which is the best of all drink; for there is no vessel in the world which can hold that strong drink, save it. Thou shalt not have it of his own free will, nor canst thou compel him."

"It is easy for me to get that, though thou think it is not easy."

"Though thou get that, there is that thou wilt not get. The hamper of Gwyddneu Long-shank: if the whole world should come around it, thrice nine men at a time, the meat that every one wished for he would find therein, to his liking. I must eat therefrom the night my daughter sleeps with thee. He will give it to no one of his own free will, nor canst thou compel him."

"It is easy for me to get that, though thou think it is not easy."

"Though thou get that, there is that thou wilt not get. The horn of Gwlgawd Gododdin to pour out for us that night. He will not give it of his own free will, nor canst thou compel him."

"It is easy for me to get that, though thou think it is not easy."

"Though thou get that, there is that thou wilt not get. The harp of Teirtu to entertain me that night. When a man pleases, it will play of itself; when one would have it so, it will be silent. He will not give it of his own free will, nor canst thou compel him."

"It is easy for me to get that, though thou think it is not easy."

"Though thou get that, there is that thou wilt not get. The birds of Rhiannon, they that wake the dead and lull the living to sleep, must I have to entertain me that night."

"It is easy for me to get that, though thou think it is not easy."

"Though thou get that, there is that thou wilt not get. The cauldron of Diwrnach the Irishman, the overseer of Odgar son of Aedd king of Ireland, to boil meat for thy wedding guests."

"It is easy for me to get that, though thou think it is not easy."

"Though thou get that, there is that thou wilt not get. I must needs wash my head and shave my beard. The tusk of Ysgithyrwyn Chief Boar I must have, wherewith to shave myself. I shall be none the better for that unless it be plucked from his head while alive."

"It is easy for me to get that, though thou think it is not easy."

"Though thou get that, there is that thou wilt not get. There is no one in the world can pluck it from his head save Odgar son of Aedd king of Ireland."

"It is easy for me to get that, though thou think it is not easy."

"Though thou get that, there is that thou wilt not get. I will not entrust the keeping of the tusk to any save Cadw of Prydein.[6] The threescore cantrefs of Prydein are under him. He will not come out of his kingdom of his own free will, nor can he be compelled."

"It is easy for me to get that, though thou think it is not easy."

"Though thou get that, there is that thou wilt not get. I must needs dress my beard for me to be shaved. It will never settle unless the blood of the Black Witch be obtained, daughter of the White Witch, from the head of the Valley of Grief in the uplands of Hell."

"It is easy for me to get that, though thou think it is not easy."

"Though thou get that, there is that thou wilt not get. The blood will be of no use unless it be obtained while warm. There is no vessel in the world will keep heat in the liquid that is put therein save the bottles of Gwyddolwyn the Dwarf, which keep their heat from the time when the liquid is put into them in the east till one reaches the west. He will not give them of his own free will, nor canst thou compel him."

"It is easy for me to get that, though thou think it is not easy."

"Though thou get that, there is that thou wilt not get. Some will wish for milk, but there will be no way to get milk for every one until the bottles of Rhynnon Stiff-beard are obtained. In them no liquid ever turns sour. He will not give them of his own free will, nor can he be compelled."

"It is easy for me to get that, though thou think it is not easy."

"Though thou get that, there is that thou wilt not get. There is no comb and shears in the world wherewith my hair may be dressed, so exceeding stiff it is, save the comb and shears that are between the two ears of Twrch Trwyth son of Taredd Wledig. He will not give them of his own free will, nor canst thou compel him."

"It is easy for me to get that, though thou think it is not easy."

"Though thou get that, there is that thou wilt not get. Twrch Trwyth will not be hunted till Drudwyn be obtained, the whelp of Greid son of Eri."

"It is easy for me to get that, though thou think it is not easy."

"Though thou get that, there is that thou wilt not get. There is no leash in the world may hold on him, save the leash of Cors Hundred-claws."

"It is easy for me to get that, though thou think it is not easy."

"Though thou get that, there is that thou wilt not get. There is no collar in the world can hold the leash, save the collar of Canhastyr Hundred-hands."

"It is easy for me to get that, though thou think it is not easy."

"Though thou get that, there is that thou wilt not get. The chain of Cilydd Hundred-holds to hold the collar along with the leash."

"It is easy for me to get that, though thou think it is not easy."

"Though thou get that, there is that thou wilt not get. There is no huntsman in the world can act as houndsman to that hound, save Mabon son of Modron, who was taken away when three nights old from his mother. Where he is is unknown, or what his state is, whether alive or dead."

"It is easy for me to get that, though thou think it is not easy."

"Though thou get that, there is that thou wilt not get. Gwyn Dun-mane, the steed of Gweddw (as swift as the wave is he!), under Mabon to hunt Twrch Trwyth. He will not give him of his own free will, nor canst thou compel him."

"It is easy for me to get that, though thou think it is not easy."

"Though thou get that, there is that thou wilt not get. Mabon will never be obtained, where he is is un-known, till his kinsman Eidoel son of Aer be first obtained; for he will be untiring in quest of him. He is his first cousin."

"It is easy for me to get that, though thou think it is not easy."

"Though thou get that, there is that thou wilt not get. Garselit the Irishman, chief huntsman of Ireland is he. Twrch Trwyth will never be hunted without him."

"It is easy for me to get that, though thou think it is not easy."

"Though thou get that, there is that thou wilt not get. A leash from the beard of Dillus the Bearded, for save that there is nothing will hold those two whelps. And no use can be made of it unless it be twitched out of his beard while he is alive, and he be plucked with wooden tweezers. He will not allow any one to do that to him while he lives, but it will be useless if dead, for it will be brittle."

"It is easy for me to get that, though thou think it is not easy."

"Though thou get that, there is that thou wilt not get. There is no huntsman in the world will hold those two whelps, save Cynedyr the Wild son of Hetwn the Leper. Nine times wilder is he than the wildest wild beast on the mountain. Him wilt thou never get, nor wilt thou get my daughter."

"It is easy for me to get that, though thou think it is not easy."

"Though thou get that, there is that thou wilt not get. Thou wilt not hunt Twrch Trwyth until Gwyn son of Nudd be obtained, in whom God has set the spirit of the demons of Annwn, lest this world be destroyed. He will not be spared thence."

"It is easy for me to get that, though thou think it is not easy."

"Though thou get that, there is that thou wilt not get. There is no horse in the world that will avail Gwyn to hunt Twrch Trwyth, save Du[7] the horse of Moro Oerfeddawg."

"It is easy for me to get that, though thou think it is not easy."

"Though thou get that, there is that thou wilt not get. Until Gwilenhin king of France come, Twrch Trwyth will never be hunted without him. It is improper for him to leave his kingdom, and he will never come hither."

"It is easy for me to get that, though thou think it is not easy."

"Though thou get that, there is that thou wilt not get. Twrch Trwyth will never be hunted without the son of Alun Dyfed be obtained. A good unleasher is he."

"It is easy for me to get that, though thou think it is not easy."

"Though thou get that, there is that thou wilt not get. Twrch Trwyth will never be hunted until Aned and Aethlem be obtained. Swift as a gust of wind would they be; never were they unleashed on a beast they did not kill."

"It is easy for me to get that, though thou think it is not easy."

"Though thou get that, there is that thou wilt not get. Arthur and his huntsmen to hunt Twrch Trwyth. A man of might is he, and he will not come with thee—the reason is that he is a man of mine."

"It is easy for me to get that, though thou think it is not easy."

"Though thou get that, there is that thou wilt not get. Twrch Trwyth can never be hunted until Bwlch and Cyfwlch and Syfwlch be obtained, sons of Cilydd Cyfwlch, grandsons of Cleddyf Difwlch. Three gleaming glitterers their three shields; three pointed piercers their three spears; three keen carvers their three swords; Glas, Glesig, Gleisad, their three dogs; Call, Cuall, Cafall, their three horses; Hwyrddyddwg and Drwgddyddwg and Llwyrddyddwg, their three wives; Och and Garym and Diasbad, their three witches; Lluched and Neued and Eisywed, their three daughters; Drwg and Gwaeth and Gwaethaf Oll, their three maidservants. The three men shall wind their horns, and all the others will come to make outcry, till none would care though the sky should fall to earth."

"It is easy for me to get that, though thou think it is not easy."

"Though thou get that, there is that thou wilt not get. The sword of Wrnach the Giant; never can he be slain save with that. He will not give it to any one, neither for price nor for favor, nor canst thou compel him."

"It is easy for me to get that, though thou think it is not easy."

"Though thou get that, there is that thou wilt not get. Wakefulness without sleep at night shalt thou have in seeking those things. And thou wilt not get them, nor wilt thou get my daughter."

"Horses shall I have and horsemen, and my lord and kinsman Arthur will get me all those things. And I shall win thy daughter, and thou shalt lose thy life."

"Set forward now. Thou shalt not be answerable for food or raiment for my daughter. Seek those things. And when those things are won, my daughter too thou shalt win."

That day they journeyed till evening, until there was seen a great fort of mortared stone, the greatest of forts in the world. Lo, they saw coming from the fort a black man, bigger than three men of this world. Quoth they to him: "Whence comest thou, fellow?" "From the fort you see yonder." "Whose is the fort?" "Fools of men that you are! There is none in the world does not know whose fort this is. It belongs to Wrnach the Giant." "What usage is there for a guest and far-comer alighting at this fort?" "Ah, chieftain, God protect you! No guest has ever come thence with his life. None is permitted therein save him who brings his craft."

They made their way to the gate. Quoth Gwrhyr Interpreter of Tongues, "Is there a porter?" "There is. And thou, may thy head not be thine, that thou dost ask!" "Open the gate." "I will not." "Why wilt thou not open it?" "Knife has gone into meat, and drink into horn, and a thronging in Wrnach's hall. Save for a craftsman who brings his craft, it will not be opened again this night." Quoth Cei, "Porter, I have a craft." "What craft hast thou?" "I am the best furbisher of swords in the world." "I will go and tell that to Wrnach the Giant and will bring thee an answer."

The porter came inside. Said Wrnach the Giant, "Thou hast news from the gate?" "I have. There is a company at the entrance to the gate who would like to come in." "Didst thou ask if they had a craft with them?" "I did, and one of them declared he knew how to furbish swords." "I had need of him. For some time I have been seeking one who should polish my sword, but I found him not. Let that man in, since he had a craft."

The porter came and opened the gate, and Cei came inside all alone. And he greeted Wrnach the Giant. A chair was placed under him. Said Wrnach, "Why, man, is this true which is reported of thee, that thou knowest how to furbish swords?" "I do that," said Cei. The sword was brought to him. Cei took a striped whetstone from under his arm. "Which dost thou prefer upon it, white-haft or dark-haft?" "Do with it what pleases thee, as though it were thine own." He cleaned half of one side of the blade for him and put it in his hand. "Does that content thee?" "I would rather than all that is in my dominions that the whole of it were like this. It is a shame a man as good as thou should be without a fellow." "Oia, good sir, I have a fellow, though he does not practise this craft." "Who is he?" "Let the porter go forth, and I will tell his tokens: the head of his spear will leave its shaft, and it will draw blood from the wind, and settle upon the shaft again." The gate was opened and Bedwyr entered in. Said Cei, "A wondrous gift has Bedwyr, though he does not practise this craft."

And there was great debate concerning the entry of Cei and Bedwyr betwixt those men outside, and a young lad who came in with them, the shepherd Custennin's only son. He and his comrades with him, as though it were nothing out of the way, crossed the three baileys until they came inside the fort. Quoth his comrades of Custennin's son, "Best of men is he." From then on he was called Goreu son of Custennin.[8] They dispersed to their lodgings that they might slay those who lodged them, without the Giant knowing.

The furbishing the sword was done, and Cei gave it into the hand of Wrnach the Giant, as though to see whether the work was to his satisfaction. Said the giant, "The work is good, and I am content with it." Quoth Cei, "It is thy scabbard has damaged thy sword. Give it to me to take out the wooden side-pieces, and let me make new ones for it." And he took the scabbard, and the sword in the other hand. He came and stood over the giant, as if he would put the sword into the scabbard. He sank it into the giant's head and took off his head at a blow. They laid waste the fort and took away what treasures they would. To the very day at the end of a year they came to Arthur's court, and the sword of Wrnach the Giant with them.

They told Arthur how it had gone with them. Arthur said, "Which of those marvels will it be best to seek first?" "It will be best," said they, "to seek Mabon son of Modron, and there is no getting him until his kinsman Eidoel son of Aer is got first." Arthur rose up, and the warriors of the Island of Britain with him, to seek for Eidoel; and they came to Glini's outer wall, to where Eidoel was in prison. Glini stood on the rampart of the fort, and he said, "Arthur, what wouldst thou have of me, since thou wilt not leave me alone on this crag? I have no good herein and no pleasure, neither wheat nor oats have I, without thee too seeking to do me harm." Arthur said, "Not to thy hurt have I come

hither, but to seek out the prisoner that is with thee." "I will give thee the prisoner, though I had not bargained to give him up to any one. And besides this, my aid and my backing thou shalt have."

The men said to Arthur, "Lord, get thee home. Thou canst not proceed with thy host to seek things so petty as these." Arthur said, "Gwrhyr Interpreter of Tongues, it is right for thee to go on this quest. All tongues hast thou, and thou canst speak with some of the birds and the beasts. Eidoel, it is right for thee to go along with my men to seek him—he is thy first cousin. Cei and Bedwyr, I have hope that whatever you go to seek will be obtained. Go then for me on this quest."

They went on their way as far as the Ouzel of Cilgwri. "For God's sake," Gwrhyr asked her, "knowest thou aught of Mabon son of Modron, who was taken when three nights old from betwixt his mother and the wall?" The Ouzel said, "When first I came hither, there was a smith's anvil here, and as for me I was a young bird. No work has been done upon it save whilst my beak was thereon every evening. To-day there is not so much of it as a nut not worn away. God's vengeance on me if I have heard aught of the man you are asking after. Nevertheless, that which it is right and proper for me to do for Arthur's messengers, I will do. There is a kind of creature God made before me; I will go along as your guide thither."

They came to the place where the Stag of Rhedynfre was. "Stag of Rhedynfre, here we have come to thee, Arthur's messengers, since we know of no animal older than thou. Say, knowest thou aught of Mabon son of Modron, who was taken away from his mother when three nights old?" The Stag said, "When first I came hither, there was but one tine on either side of my head, and there were no trees here save a single oak-sapling, and that grew into an oak with a hundred branches, and the oak thereafter fell, and to-day there is naught of it save a red stump; from that day to this I have been here. I have heard naught of him you are asking after. Nevertheless I will be your guide, since you are Arthur's messengers, to the place where there is an animal God made before me."

They came to the place where the Owl of Cwm Cawlwyd was. "Owl of Cwm Cawlwyd, here are Arthur's messengers. Knowest thou aught of Mabon son of Modron, who was taken away from his mother when three nights old?" "If I knew it, I would tell it. When first I came hither, the great valley you see was a wooded glen, and a race of men came thereto and it was laid waste. And the second wood grew up therein, and this wood is the third. And as for me, why! the roots of my wings are mere stumps. From that day to this I have heard naught of the man you are asking after. Nevertheless I will be a guide to Arthur's messengers until you come to the place where is the oldest creature that is in this world, and he that has fared furthest afield, the Eagle of Gwernabwy.''

Gwrhyr said, "Eagle of Gwernabwy, we have come to thee, Arthur's messengers, to ask whether thou knowest aught of Mabon son of Modron who was taken away from his mother when three nights old?" The Eagle said, "I came here a long time ago, and when first I came hither I had a stone, and from its top I pecked at the stars each evening; now it is not a hand-breadth in height. From that day to this I have been here, but have heard naught of him you are asking after. Save that at one faring I went to seek my meat as far as Llyn Llyw, and when I came there I sank my claws into a salmon, thinking he would be meat for me many a long day, and he drew me down into the depths, so that it was with difficulty I got away. from him. And my whole kindred and I went after him, to seek to destroy him. But he sent messengers to make peace with me, and came to me in person to have fifty tridents taken out of his back. Unless he knows something of what you seek, I know none who may. Nevertheless, I will be your guide to the place where he is.''

They came to the place where he was. The Eagle said, "Salmon of Llyn Llyw, I have come to thee with Arthur's messengers to ask whether thou knowest aught of Mabon son of Modron who was taken away from his mother when three nights old?" "As much as I know, I will tell. With every tide I go up along the river till I come to the bend of the wall of Caer Loyw; and there I found such distress that I never found its equal in all my life; and, that you may believe, let one of you come here on my two shoulders." And Cei and Gwrhyr Interpreter of Tongues went upon the salmon's two shoulders, and they journeyed until they came to the far side of the wall from the prisoner, and they could hear wailing and lamentation on the far side of the wall from them. Gwrhyr said, "What man laments in this house of stone?" "Alas, man, there is cause for him who is here to lament. Mabon son of Modron is here in prison; and none was ever so cruelly imprisoned in a prison house as I; neither the imprisonment of Lludd

Silver-hand nor the imprisonment of Greid son of Eri." "Hast thou hope of getting thy release for gold or for silver or for worldly wealth, or by battle and fighting?" "What is got of me, will be got by fighting.''

They returned thence and came to where Arthur was. They told where Mabon son of Modron was in prison. Arthur summoned the warriors of this Island and went to Caer Loyw where Mabon was in prison. Cei and Bedwyr went upon the two shoulders of the fish. Whilst Arthur's warriors assaulted the fort, Cei broke through the wall and took the prisoner on his back; and still he fought with the men. Arthur came home and Mabon with him, a free man.

Arthur said, "Which of the marvels is it now best to seek first?" "It is best to seek for the two whelps of the bitch Rhymhi." "Is it known where she is?" asked Arthur. "She is," said one, "at Aber Deu Gleddyf." Arthur came to the house of Tringad in Aber Cleddyf and asked him, "Hast thou heard of her in these parts? In what shape is she?" "In the shape of a she-wolf," answered he, "and she goes about with her two whelps. Often has she slain my stock, and she is down in Aber Cleddyf in a cave.''

Arthur went to sea in his ship Prydwen, and others by land to hunt the bitch, and in this wise they surrounded her and her two whelps, and God changed them back into their own semblance for Arthur. Arthur's host dispersed, one by one, two by two.

And as Gwythyr son of Greidawl was one day journeying over a mountain, he heard a wailing and a grievous lamentation, and these were a horrid noise to hear. He sprang forward in that direction, and when he came there he drew his sword and smote off the anthill level with the ground, and so saved them from the fire. And they said to him, "Take thou God's blessing and ours, and that which no man can ever recover, we will come and recover it for thee." It was they thereafter who came with the nine hestors of flax seed which Ysbaddaden Chief Giant had named to Culhwch, in full measure, with none of it wanting save for a single flax seed. And the lame ant brought that in before night.

As Cei and Bedwyr were sitting on top of Pumlumon on Carn Gwylathyr, in the highest wind in the world, they looked about them and they could see a great smoke towards the south, far off from them, and not blowing across with the wind. And then Cei said, "By the hand of my friend, see yonder the fire of a warrior." They hastened toward the smoke and approached thither, watching from afar as Dillus the Bearded was singeing a wild boar. Now, he was the mightiest warrior that ever fled from Arthur. Then Bedwyr said to Cei, "Dost know him?" "I know him," said Cei; "that is Dillus the Bearded. There is no leash in the world may hold Drudwyn the whelp of Greid son of Eri, save a leash from the beard of him thou seest yonder. And that too will be of no use unless it be plucked alive with wooden tweezers from his beard; for it will be brittle, dead." "What is our counsel concerning that?" asked Bedwyr. "Let us suffer him," said Cei, "to eat his fill of meat and after that he will fall asleep." Whilst he was about this, they busied themselves making tweezers. When Cei knew for certain that he was asleep, he dug a pit under his feet, the biggest in the world, and he struck him a blow mighty past telling, and pressed him down in the pit until they had entirely twitched out his beard with the tweezers; and after that they slew him outright.

And then the two of them went to Celli Wig in Cornwall, and a leash from Dillus the Bearded's beard with them. And Cei gave it into Arthur's hand, and thereupon Arthur sang this englyn:

Cei made a leash
From Dillus' beard, son of Furei.
Were he alive, thy death he'd be.

And because of this Cei grew angry, so that it was with difficulty the warriors of this Island made peace between Cei and Arthur. But nevertheless, neither for Arthur's lack of help, nor for the slaying of his men, did Cei have aught to do with him in his hour of need from that time forward.

And then Arthur said, "Which of the marvels will it now be best to seek?" "It will be best to seek Drudwyn the whelp of Greid son of Eri."

A short while before this Creiddylad daughter of Lludd Silver-hand went with Gwythyr son of Greidawl; and before he had slept with her there came Gwyn son of Nudd and carried her off by force. Gwythyr son of Greidawl gathered a host, and he came to fight with Gwyn son of Nudd. And Gwyn prevailed, and he took prisoner Greid son of Eri, Glinneu son of Taran, and Gwrgwst the Half-naked and Dyfnarth his son. And he took prisoner Pen son of Nethawg, and Nwython, and Cyledyr the Wild his son, and he slew Nwython and took out his heart, and compelled Cyledyr to eat his father's heart; and because of this

Cyledyr went mad. Arthur heard tell of this, and he came into the North and summoned to him Gwyn son of Nudd and set free his noblemen from his prison, and peace was made between Gwyn son of Nudd and Gwythyr son of Greidawl. This is the peace that was made: the maiden should remain in her father's house, unmolested by either side, and there should be battle between Gwyn and Gwythyr each May-calends for ever and ever, from that day till doomsday; and the one of them that should be victor on doomsday, let him have the maiden.

And when those lords had been thus reconciled, Arthur obtained Dun-mane the steed of Gweddw, and the leash of Cors Hundred-claws.

After that Arthur made his way to Llydaw, and with him Mabon son of Mellt and Gware Golden-hair, to seek the two dogs of Glythfyr Ledewig. And when he had obtained them, Arthur went to the west of Ireland to seek out Gwrgi Seferi, and Odgar son of Aedd king of Ireland along with him. And after that Arthur went into the North and caught Cyledyr the Wild; and he went after Ysgithyrwyn Chief Boar. And Mabon son of Mellt went, and the two dogs of Glythfyr Ledewig in his hand, and Drudwyn the whelp of Greid son of Eri. And Arthur himself took his place in the hunt, and Cafall, Arthur's dog, in his hand. And Cadw of Prydein mounted Llamrei, Arthur's mare, and he was the first to bring the boar to bay. And then Cadw of Prydein armed him with a hatchet, and boldly and gallantly set upon the boar and split his head in two. And Cadw took the tusk. It was not the dogs which Ysbaddaden had named to Culhwch which killed the boar, but Cafall, Arthur's own dog.

And after Ysgithyrwyn Chief Boar was slain, Arthur and his host went to Celli Wig in Cornwall; and thence he sent Menw son of Teirgwaedd to see whether the treasures were between the two ears of Twrch Trwyth —so mean a thing would it be to go to fight with him, had he not those treasures. However, it was certain that he was there; he had already laid waste the third part of Ireland. Menw went to seek them out. He saw them in Esgeir Oerfel in Ireland. And Menw transformed himself into the likeness of a bird and alighted over his lair and sought to snatch one of the treasures away from him. But for all that he got nothing save one of his bristles. The other arose in his might and shook himself so that some of his poison caught him. And after that Menw was never without scathe.

After that Arthur sent a messenger to Odgar son of Aedd king of Ireland, to ask for the cauldron of Diwrnach the Irishman, his overseer. Odgar besought him to give it. Said Diwrnach, "God knows, though he should be the better for getting one glimpse of it, he should not have it." And Arthur's messenger came back from Ireland with a nay. Arthur set out and a light force with him, and went in Prydwen his ship, and came to Ireland, and they made for the house of Diwrnach the Irishman. The hosts of Odgar took note of their strength; and after they had eaten and drunk their fill Arthur demanded the cauldron. He made answer that were he to give it to any one, he would have given it at the word of Odgar king of Ireland. When he had spoken them nay, Bedwyr arose and laid hold of the cauldron and put it on the back of Hygwydd, Arthur's servant; he was brother by the same mother to Cacamwri, Arthur's servant. His office was always to carry Arthur's cauldron and to kindle fire under it. Llenlleawg the Irishman seized Caledfwlch and swung it in a round and he slew Diwrnach the Irishman and all his host. The hosts of Ireland came and fought with them. And when the hosts were utterly routed Arthur and his men went on board ship before their very eyes, and with them the cauldron full of the treasures of Ireland. And they disembarked at the house of Llwydeu son of Cel Coed, at Porth Cerddin in Dyfed. And Mesur-y-Peir is there.[9]

And then Arthur gathered together what warriors there were in the Island of Britain and its three adjacent islands, and what there were in France and Brittany and Normandy and the Summer Country, and what there were of picked dogs and horses of renown. And with all those hosts he went to Ireland, and at his coming there was great fear and trembling in Ireland. And when Arthur had come to land, there came to him the saints of Ireland to ask his protection. And he granted them protection, and they gave him their blessing. The men of Ireland came to Arthur and gave him a tribute of victuals. Arthur came to Esgeir Oerfel in Ireland, to the place where Twrch Trwyth was, and his seven young pigs with him. Dogs were let loose at him from all sides. That day until evening the Irish fought with him; nevertheless he laid waste one of the five provinces of Ireland. And on the morrow Arthur's war-band fought with him: save for what evil they got from him, they got nothing good. The third day Arthur himself fought with him, nine nights and nine days: he slew of his pigs but one pigling. His men asked Arthur what was the history of that swine, and he told them: "He was a king, and for his wickedness God transformed him into a swine."

Arthur sent Gwrhyr Interpreter of Tongues to seek to have word with him. Gwrhyr went in the form of a bird and alighted above the lair of him and his seven young pigs. And Gwrhyr Interpreter of Tongues asked him, "For His sake who made thee in this shape, if you can speak, I beseech one of you to come and talk with Arthur." Grugyn Silver-bristle made answer. Like wings of silver were all his bristles; what way he went through wood and meadow one could discern from how his bristles glittered. This was the answer Grugyn gave: "By Him who made us in this shape, we will neither do nor say aught for Arthur. Harm enough hath God wrought us, to have made us in this shape, without you too coming to fight with us." "I tell you, Arthur will fight for the comb, the razor and the shears which are between the two ears of Twrch Trwyth." Said Grugyn, "Until first his life be taken, those treasures will not be taken. And to-morrow in the morning we will set out hence and go into Arthur's country, and there we will do all the mischief we can."

They set out by sea towards Wales; and Arthur and his hosts, his horses and his dogs, went aboard Prydwen, and in the twinkling of an eye they saw them. Twrch Trwyth came to land at Porth Cleis in Dyfed. That night Arthur came as far as Mynyw. On the morrow Arthur was told they had gone by, and he overtook him killing the cattle of Cynwas Cwryfagyl, after slaying what men and beasts were in Deu Gleddyf before the coming of Arthur.

From the time of Arthur's coming, Twrch Trwyth made off thence to Preseleu. Arthur and the hosts of the world came thither. Arthur sent his men to the hunt, Eli and Trachmyr, and Drudwyn the whelp of Greid son of Eri in his own hand; and Gwarthegydd son of Caw in another quarter, with the two dogs of Glythfyr Ledewig in his hand; and Bedwyr with Arthur's dog Cafall in his hand. And he ranged all the warriors on either side the Nyfer. There came the three sons of Cleddyf Difwlch, men who had won great fame at the slaying of Ysgithyrwyn Chief Boar. And then he set out from Glyn Nyfer and came to Cwm Cerwyn, and there he stood at bay. And he then slew four of Arthur's champions, Gwarthegydd son of Caw, Tarawg of Allt Clwyd, Rheiddwn son of Eli Adfer, and Isgofan the

Generous. And after he had slain those men, again he stood at bay against them there, and slew Gwydre son of Arthur, Garselit the Irishman, Glew son of Ysgawd, and Isgawyn son of Banon. And then he himself was wounded.

And the morrow's morn at point of day some of the men caught up with him. And then he slew Huandaw and Gogigwr and Penpingon, the three servants of Glewlwyd Mighty-grasp, so that God knows he had never a servant left to him in the world, save only Llaesgymyn,[10] a man for whom none was the better. And over and above those he slew many a man of the country, and Gwlyddyn the Craftsman, Arthur's chief builder. And then Arthur caught up with him at Peluniawg, and he then slew Madawg son of Teithion, and Gwyn son of Tringad son of Neued, and Eiriawn Penlloran. And thence he went to Aber Tywi. And there he stood at bay against them, and he then slew Cynlas son of Cynan and Gwilenhin king of France. Thereafter he went to Glyn Ystun, and then the men and dogs lost him.

Arthur summoned to him Gwyn son of Nudd and asked him whether he knew aught of Twrch Trwyth. He said he did not. Thereupon all the huntsmen went to hunt the pigs as far as Dyffryn Llychwr. And Grugyn Silver-bristle and Llwydawg the Hewer dashed into them and slew the huntsmen so that not a soul of them escaped alive, save one man only. So Arthur and his hosts came to the place where Grugyn and Llwydawg were. And then he let loose upon them all the dogs that had been named to this end. And at the clamor that was then raised, and the barking, Twrch Trwyth came up and defended them. And ever since they had crossed the Irish Sea, he had not set eyes on them till now. Then was he beset by men and dogs. With might and with main he went to Mynydd Amanw, and then a pigling was slain of his pigs. And then they joined with him life for life, and it was then Twrch Llawin was slain. And then another of his pigs was slain, Gwys was his name. And he then went to Dyffryn Amanw, and there Banw and Benwig were slain. Not one of his pigs went with him alive from that place, save Grugyn Silver-bristle and Llwydawg the Hewer.

From that place they went on to Llwch Ewin, and Arthur caught up with him there. Then he stood at bay. And then he slew Echel Big-hip, and Arwyli son of Gwyddawg Gwyr, and many a man and dog besides. And after that they went on to Llwch Tawy. Grugyn Silver-bristle then parted from them, and Grugyn thereafter made for Din Tywi. And he proceeded then into Ceredigiawn, and Eli and Trachmyr with him, and a multitude along with them besides. And he came as far as Garth Grugyn. And there Grugyn was slain in their midst, and he slew Rhuddfyw Rhys and many a man with him. And then Llwydawg went on to Ystrad Yw. And there the men of Llydaw met with him, and he then slew Hir Peisawg king of Llydaw, and Llygadrudd Emys and Gwrfoddw, Arthur's uncles, his mother's brothers. And there he himself was slain.

Twrch Trwyth went then between Tawy and Ewyas. Arthur summoned Cornwall and Devon to meet him at the mouth of the Severn. And Arthur said to the warriors of this Island: "Twrch Trwyth has slain many of my men. By the valor of men, not while I am alive shall he go into Cornwall. I will pursue him no further, but I will join with him life for life. You, do what you will." And by his counsel a body of horsemen was sent, and the dogs of the Island with them, as far as Ewyas, and they beat back thence to the Severn, and they waylaid him there with what tried warriors there were in this Island, and drove him by sheer force into Severn. And Mabon son of Modron went with him into Severn, on Gwyn Dun-mane the steed of Gweddw, and Goreu son of Custennin and Menw son of Teirgwaedd, between Llyn Lliwan and Aber Gwy. And Arthur fell upon him, and the champions of Britain along with him. Osla Big-knife drew near, and Manawydan son of Llŷr, and Cacamwri, Arthur's servant, and Gwyngelli, and closed in on him. And first they laid hold of his feet, and soused him in Severn till it was flooding over him. On the one side Mabon son of Modron spurred his horse and took the razor from him, and on the other Cyledyr the Wild, on another horse, plunged into Severn with him and took from him the shears. But or ever the comb could be taken he found land with his feet; and from the moment he found land neither dog nor man nor horse could keep up with him until he went into Cornwall. Whatever mischief was come by in seeking those treasures from him, worse was come by in seeking to save the two men from drowning. Cacamwri, as he was dragged forth, two quernstones dragged him into the depths. As Osla Big-knife was running after the boar, his knife fell out of its sheath and he lost it; and his sheath thereafter being full of water, as he was dragged forth, it dragged him back into the depths.

Then Arthur went with his hosts until he caught up with him in Cornwall. Whatever mischief was come by before that was play to what was come by then in seeking the comb. But from mischief to mischief the comb was won from him. And then he was forced out of Cornwall and driven straight forward into the sea. From that time forth never a one has known where he went, and Aned and Aethlem with him. And Arthur went thence to Celli Wig in Cornwall, to bathe himself and rid him of his weariness.

Said Arthur, "Is there any of the marvels still unobtained?" Said one of the men, "There is: the blood of the Black Witch, daughter of the White Witch, from the head of the Valley of Grief in the uplands of Hell." Arthur set out for the North and came to where the hag's cave was. And it was the counsel of Gwyn son of Nudd and Gwythyr son of Greidawl that Cacamwri and Hygwydd his brother be sent to fight with the hag. And as they came inside the cave the hag grabbed at them, and caught Hygwydd by the hair of his head and flung him to the floor beneath her. And Cacamwri seized her by the hair of her head, and dragged her to the ground off Hygwydd, but she then turned on Cacamwri and dressed them down both and disarmed them, and drove them out squealing and squalling. And Arthur was angered to see his two servants well nigh slain, and he sought to seize the cave. And then Gwyn and Gwythyr told him, "It is neither seemly nor pleasant for us to see thee scuffling with a hag. Send Long Amren and Long Eiddil into the cave." And they

went. But if ill was the plight of the first two, the plight of those two was worse, so that God knows not one of the whole four could have stirred from the place, but for the way they were all four loaded on Llamrei, Arthur's mare. And then Arthur seized the entrance to the cave, and from the entrance he took aim at the hag with Carnwennan his knife, and struck her across the middle until she was as two tubs. And Cadw of Prydein took the witch's blood and kept it with him.

And then Culhwch set forth, and Goreu son of Custennin with him, and every one that wished ill to Ysbaddaden Chief Giant, and those marvels with them to his court. And Cadw of Prydein came to shave his beard, flesh and skin to the bone, and his two ears outright. And Culhwch said, "Hast had thy shave, man?" "I have," said he. "And is thy daughter mine now?" "Thine," said he. "And thou needst not thank me for that, but thank Arthur who has secured her for thee. Of my own free will thou shouldst never have had her. And it is high time to take away my life." And then Goreu son of Custennin caught him by the hair of his head and dragged him behind him to the mound, and cut off his head, and set it on the bailey-stake. And he took possession of his fort and his dominions.

And that night Culhwch slept with Olwen, and she was his only wife so long as he lived. And the hosts of Arthur dispersed, every one to his country.

And in this wise did Culhwch win Olwen daughter of Ysbaddaden Chief Giant.

Glossary

1 Culhwch: pig-run. A fanciful explanation, from hwch: pig. 2 White Swan. 3 Olwen: White-track (charming but fanciful). 4 Yellow-Palewhite and the Speckled Ox. 5 A mountain in Scotland, possibly the Grampians. 6 Cadw of Prydein: Cadw of Pictland. Cadw: to keep. 7 Du: black. 8 Goreu: best. 9 Mesur-y-Peir. The place-name has apparently not survived. Its elements mean "Measure of the Cauldron," but the explanation is onomastic. 10 Llaesgymyn: Slack-hewer.

B. Dafydd Ap Gwilym

Dafydd ap Gwilym (ca. 1325–ca. 1380) was born at Bro Gynin in Cardiganshire into a family of the Norman-Welsh aristocracy of South Wales. His poetry shows the influence, probably indirect, of the troubadours, but he owes far more to native Welsh traditions. The Celtic love for nature is very evident in his work. The love poetry of Dafydd and his contemporaries should not be taken to represent the kind of intense personal feeling that results from actual involvement. The two favorite ladies in Dafydd's poems, Morfudd, who is fair, and Dyddgu, who is dark, are probably merely types. Again, some of the poems, in spite of their obvious emphasis on physical desire, may have been courtly compliments to noble ladies who had no personal interest in the poet at all.

For discussions of the poems, see the references at the beginning of this section and, further, H. Idris Bell and David Bell, Dafydd ap Gwilym: Fifty Poems, Y Cymmrodor, *XLVIII (1942). The selections below are reprinted by permission from this volume. The text of the poems has been edited by Thomas Parry,* Gwaith Dafydd ap Gwilym, *University of Wales, Cardiff, 1952.*

"A GARLAND OF PEACOCK'S FEATHERS"

Now, now is the time for love and delight:
To arise in the morning with the amorous light!
I arose with a passion of singing and went
To look for my lady by woodland and bent.
"Lady," I said, "will you weave for me, please,   5
A garland of leaves gleaned from the trees,
Will you gather and bind where the sap runs free
And make from the twigs a crown for me?
Suppose it," I said, "a token of grace."
But the lady looked in her poet's face.   10

"Dafydd," she said, "you speak your words well,
But here in the woods where the peacocks dwell
'Tis shame not to know how unhappy it were
To strip the birches and see them bare;
They have not too many nor leaves to spare   15
For one to come picking and pruning there.
Dafydd," she said, "you'll not find me ever
At binding of branches for you or another."

But yet she is kind and surely I have,
Long to delight me, the gift she gave.   20
It was made from the clothes the peacocks shed,
A gold-veil garland to grace my head.
Could garland of cambric be ever more bright,
Or the feathery blossoms which fall in the light?
They were plumes overlaid like the branches
   above,   25

The butterflies painted with God's own love;
A work such as kings or queens devise,
Wheels, towers, lanterns which blind the flies,
The full moon risen on sunset skies,
The hollow circle of dead men's eyes.   30
Oh, this magical ware from magician's chest
From delight of its giving shall never be lost.
My Gwen, you gave it as token and favor
To your poet, Dafydd, your minstrel lover!

From wings and feathers this she bound,   35
The darling achievement of skilled hand.
God had woven through and through it
The love of a lady for her dear poet.
There was pleasure in every feather and fold,
Bright tents of color, pavilions of gold.   40

D. B.[1]

"A NUN WHOSE FACE ALONE HE SAW"

One who was beautiful passed last night.
Oh, had she but lingered a little in sight!
My cheek was white, for love was upon me,
An aching heart for the face of Gwenonwy.
I think it were better had I been blind,   5
For her passing beauty but left behind,
In the eye of the mind to trouble me now,
An image of brightness, a noble brow.

The tailor who thus with enchantment for tool
Stitched at her raiment was worse than a fool,   10
To clothe in darkness one so bright
And hide her from sight, could it ever be right?
All but the face! O Father above!
That the face was concealed not, to break me
    with love!
The face, and above it temples and brow—   15
The pearls of deep seas, whole seas of snow.

This was the forehead which Jesus made:
The hair on her temples like murrey he laid;
He gave her two brows bent crescent-wise,
To bind with sable her stately eyes.   20
Her brows like the mid-summer leaves are sable,
Dark like the brows of the wild-eyed Sibyl.
So between temple and cheek were set
At the root of the nose those brows of jet,
As a blackbird is seen before a white wave,   25
As the blackest of mantles much brightness have.

Like sunlight playing in some deep well,
Her innocent eyes their hollows fill.
It seems is held in sunlight or glass,
Like sparks of light, the laughter she has.   30
Black on white parchment her eyelids dwell,
And lo, the sea swallow bestrides the sea swell!

With loveliness her cheek's inlaid,
Of golden crowns and apples made.
Roses she gathers and rose leaves,   35
And on her cheek some petals weaves.
Or seems on waxen cheeks the vine
As on white chalk its grapes to twine.
Red, ripe cherries they are when she blushes,
As coral the honeysuckle flushes;   40
Two drops of blood on snow congealed,
And lo, with red holly her cheeks are sealed.

My lady is lovely as I have said;
Her cheeks as the dawn in the east are red.
And her lips beneath them are lovely too,   45
That the petals of foxgloves they seem to you.
A dream I found on her lips to-day,
And her mouth was pensive as if to say
Some smooth, unurgent, distant thing,
The breath in her nostrils was harboring.   50

Her silver chin is a running tide,
Which washes the shore where her cheeks abide,
A silver chin on a silver throat,
A sight to write a poem about!

She stole my eyes with treachery,   55
My lighted candles she took from me.
Of a face and a running wave I speak,
Of a girl's head and a foxglove cheek.
Never in girlhood in its prime
Was beauty more sublime.   60

                                    D. B.

"AUBADE"

"O passing night, have pity," I said;
"She is most lovely who shares my bed."
But the brief night fled, and we, lover by lover,
Put a week in that night, and that all but over.

Who would not judge it quickly gone   5
Who lay as lover by such a one?
She shone in my arms like candleshine,
That the strength and ardor and love were mine
To take in place of sleep from night
The sleepless honor of her delight.   10
And when at height of ecstasy
I took her loveliness to me,
Behold the dawn, the morning light
Veiled in splendor the eastern night.

And then Gwen said: "My soul, arise,   15
Be not betrayed to morning eyes.
What profit in love now day is near?
For God's sake go; linger not here."

"Beautiful lady, the daylight were bitter,
But can it be true if the untruth is better?   20
It is only the moon and the darling light
Of an eddy of stars, God's gift to night;
And frankly to speak, most surely I'd say
It is but your fancy, an imagined day."

"Then for what, my soul, should call the crow   25
If not for the dawn in the meadows below?"

"It is only some bird the fleas are at;
They plague her, poor thing, and she croaks for
    that."

"But listen, my dear, in the homesteads near
The dogs are fighting and some bay clear."   30

"They scent from the copses the vixen's lair,
And trouble at midnight the still night air."

"My poet, be still; for shame to tease,
Sorrow will pay for a fool's ease.
Arise, my soul, with the feet of night,   35
Open the door, make heaviness light,
And run to the woods where the shadows linger;
The keen dogs watch with a watchdog's anger."

"We lie not far from the holt in the hollow;
I can run so swift no dog may follow,   40
And none can catch me, if spies there are none,
In the ways God's favor has made my own."

"My faithful poet, but tell me this;
Will you come again if a dark night there is?"

"If such a night comes, I shall not fail,   45
And you'll hear me coming, your nightingale."
                                        D. B.

"THE POET TALKS
    WITH A GRAY FRIAR"
——————————————————————

Oh, that the maiden all men praise,
Who keeps her court in the woodland ways,
Had heard the words that in my ear
The gray brother spoke of her
To-day when to his cell I'd gone   5
There to confess my sins each one.

"A poet," I confessed, "am I
Given up to idolatry,
And long have worshipped, I avow,
A snow-white lady black of brow,   10
But from my murderess I have had
No gift or grace to make me glad,
But love her yet and for her sake
Must still endure my long heart-ache

And bear her praise through all the land,   15
Yet lack her favors in the end,
Longing but to find her laid
Between the wall and me in my bed."

To this the brother straight replies:
"Son, I'll give you sage advice,   20
Since the foam-white maid so long
Has done your heart this piteous wrong.
Think rather on the day of Doom,
Saving your soul from pains to come;
Bid farewell to your idle rhymes   25
And to your paters fall betimes.
Not for *cywydd's* or *englyn's* sake
Did God for man atonement make.
There's nought in what you minstrels sing
But idle chatter and cozening.   30
Men and women you entice
To wantonness and many a vice.
Praise of the body is not well
If it lead the soul to hell."

Then I to all that I had heard   35
Answered the brother word for word:
"God is not so cruel, friend,
As old dotards would pretend.
He'll never damn a gallant lad
For love of matron or of maid.   40
Three things beloved of all there be—
Woman, fair weather, health, these three;
Of all the flowers in heaven that are,
Save God, a woman is fairest far,
And from a woman all men known   45
Received their life save three alone.
Should it then our wonder move
That maid and wife win men's love?
From heaven come mirth and jollity,
But out of hell all misery.   50
Pleasure grows from poet's song
For sick and whole, old and young.
We have equal warrant each,
I to write verses, you to preach;
As you your trade of begging ply,   55
So I my trade of minstrelsy.
Englyn and *awdl*—are not these
One with your hymns and sequences,
And the psalms of David that you love
Cywyddau writ for God above?   60

Not by one food or regimen
Does God nourish the life of men.
Times are given us for our food,
And times for prayer and solitude,
For preaching also there are times, 65
And so no less for shaping rhymes.
At every feast and junketing
To pleasure ladies poets sing;
Paters in church are sung that so
Our soul to Paradise may go. 70
Truly did Yscuthach say,
Carousing with his bards one day:
'Happy face prospers still,
Sour looks come to ill.'

Some men to piety are inclined, 75
For good cheer others have a mind.
The *cywydd* there are few to write
But paters all men can recite,
And therefore, brother, I opine
That song is not the greatest sin. 80
When all men love as much to hear
The pater as the harp-string clear
Or as the girls of Gwynedd long
To hear the wanton *cywydd* sung,
Why then, I swear, from morn to night 85
My punctual pater I'll recite;
Till then, if e'er a monk I make me
To mumble prayers, the devil take me!"

H. I. B.

Glossary

27 **cywydd, englyn** Welsh poetic measures. See the section on versification in Williams, *Introduction to Welsh Poetry*, pp. 232ff. **46 three alone** It has been suggested that Adam, Eve, and Melchisedech are intended. **71 Yscuthach** not identified.

"THE POET FINDS OTHER THINGS THAN LOVE IN AN INN"

I and my servant on travel came
To a city of good repute and name.
And since I am a Welshman bred
It seemed as for my pleasure made.
I took a lodging in the common inn 5
And straightway called to bring me wine.

But here in the house for my delight
I saw a lady, beautiful, bright
Like the morning sun, who could but move,
Being dainty and white, my heart to love. 10
I thought to boast with a banquet to her,
For her face was the aspect of gossamer.
And surely such tricks for young men are meet
To bring a shy lady across to their seat.

And then when the shyness and faint word were
gone— 15

And why should they tarry?—in the hall was
begun
A merry to-do, for a feast they laid
In honor before me to honor the maid,
As though 'twere the wedding that very day.
Attentive I was and so bold to say 20
Two words in her ear but never a third;
And no one caught a single word.

Love was busy that eve and I made
A tryst to come to the sprightly maid,
When folk were abed and quiet the house, 25
To sleep with her. Dark were her brows.
And when in bed the people slept,
All but the maid and I, I crept
From my bed in the darkness and sought to find
The bed of the girl—but Fate was unkind. 30

I came to where—damned chance!—were laid
Three English in a stinking bed,
And by them each was set his pack,

Figure 20 *Dolwyddelan Castle. It is said to have been the birthplace of Llywelyn the Great (d. 1240), who cultivated traditional Welsh literature in his court.*

Hicking and Jocking and Jack.
And then one foul-mouthed numskull spluttered,   35
And monstrous angry to the others muttered:
"There's a Welshman, I guess, in the darkness
    there.
If he's a Welshman then deceit is near.
He's a thief, I'll swear to you.
Look out and guard yourselves, you two."   40

Nimble I was not though great my need.
A noisy disgrace I brought on my head.
Unskillful in escaping, I stumbled and fell,
That the whole house echoed the sound of my
    fall.
I barked my shin against a stool   45
And bruised my ankle hard and true
(The ostler who put it there was a fool).
Not fools enough, the stool squeaked too.

Breathless in my haste I hit
Now this, now that, and free of it   50
I could not get for all my fumbling.
I caught my forehead in my tumbling,
And knocked the table trestles over.

Nothing then my flight could cover.
Down went the table, the basin then,   55
And a great resounding copper pan.
And far away into the night behind me
The clang re-echoed for all to find me,
And I helpless enough. Then all
The dogs began to bark and call   60
The ostler, who called the house from bed.
There was a bitter story indeed.
I could see their scowling faces round me,
Making a circle until they found me,
And I, a wild poet, grim with fright,   65
Keeping silence in the night.

Boldly then I knelt and prayed
In hiding with a heart afraid;
And by the grace of Jesus' name,
Because my prayer was strong, I came   70
Back to my sorry bed at last,
And that from the troubled night's unrest
Was the best I got, but the saints I'll praise—
And may the Lord God pardon my ways!

D. B.

"THE LADIES OF LLANBADARN"

My load's so heavy, I'm like to fall—
Plague o' the women, one and all!
Woo as I would, this many a year,
Not one among them would be my dear,
Were 't budding lass, but half-grown,   5
Or maid or matron or crabbed crone!

What fear, what malice can this be
That, young or old, they'll none of me?
For what whit worse were a fine-browed maid
To clasp me close in the wood's deep shade?   10
Never was day when I loved not;
So long bewitchment fell to my lot
As no man ever before me knew—
Each day I fancied a girl or two;
Yet ne'er a one but made such show   15
As I had been her deadliest foe.

Never was Sunday that passed by
But in Llanbadarn church was I,
My looks for the ladies, signalling love,
And the nape of my neck for God above;   20
And after I had gazed long
Over my feathers at the throng,
Says to her friend some saucy belle,
In lilting tones I heard too well:
"Yon pale lad with the languishing air,   25
His head bedecked with his sister's hair,
Why that fond look, that moonstruck gaze?
His eyes have learned love's evil ways."

"What can he hope? 'Tis all a show,"
Her friend beside her whispers low,   30
"Let him wait there till Doomsday wake him;
Fie on the fool, the Devil take him!"

From lips so lovely what cruel word—
For love's wild wonder an ill reward!
And I must bid adieu, it seems,   35
To the world's life and all my dreams,
Take me off to some lone glade
And there turn hermit, a villain's trade.
So many a backward look, alas,

I've given some dear disdainful lass   40
That head and neck awry have grown;
Yet still I tread my ways alone!

                        H. I. B.

"MAY AND JANUARY"

Hail, month of the greenwood choir,
May, month that I desire,
Strong knight, love's reward,
Of the wildwood tangle master and lord,
Love's companion, friend of the birds,   5
Whom lovers praise with loving words,
Herald of endless whisperings,
And prattle of sweet, secret things.
Mary, but my soul is fain
To welcome May's month again,   10
Hot his honors to maintain,
Conquering every green glen,
Weaving wondrously through warm days
A green web for the high-ways.
The bitter battle of frost is over,   15
And close-wove veils each thicket cover,
Green are the paths where April trod
Now May is here, and the woods are loud;
Every oak's high summit rings
With the young birds' lusty carollings,   20
And every copse is sweet with song,
And cuckoo calls, and the days are long,
And a white haze, when the wind dies,
Over the heart of the valley lies,
And evening skies are blue and clear,   25
And the trees ashimmer with gossamer,
And birds busy the woodland through,
And the boughs put on their leaves anew,
And within me, Morfudd, memories move
Waking the manifold moods of love.   30

But that black month, how unlike this,
Unmeet for love and lovers' kiss,
When days are short and the dull rain drips,
And the wild wind the woodland strips,
Month of fierce frost and scourging hail,   35
When the world wears an icy mail,
And torrents swell and the cold grips,
And a brown flood fills the brook to the lips,
And the rivers roar on their turbid way,

And dark and wrathful is the day,   40   May double share of ill, I pray,
And the sky is dull, heavy and cold,   Such surly churlishness repay.
And sullen clouds the moon enfold.

                                                                                    H. I. B.

Note

1   Poems signed "D. B." are translated by David Bell; those signed "H. I. B." are translated by
H. Idris Bell.

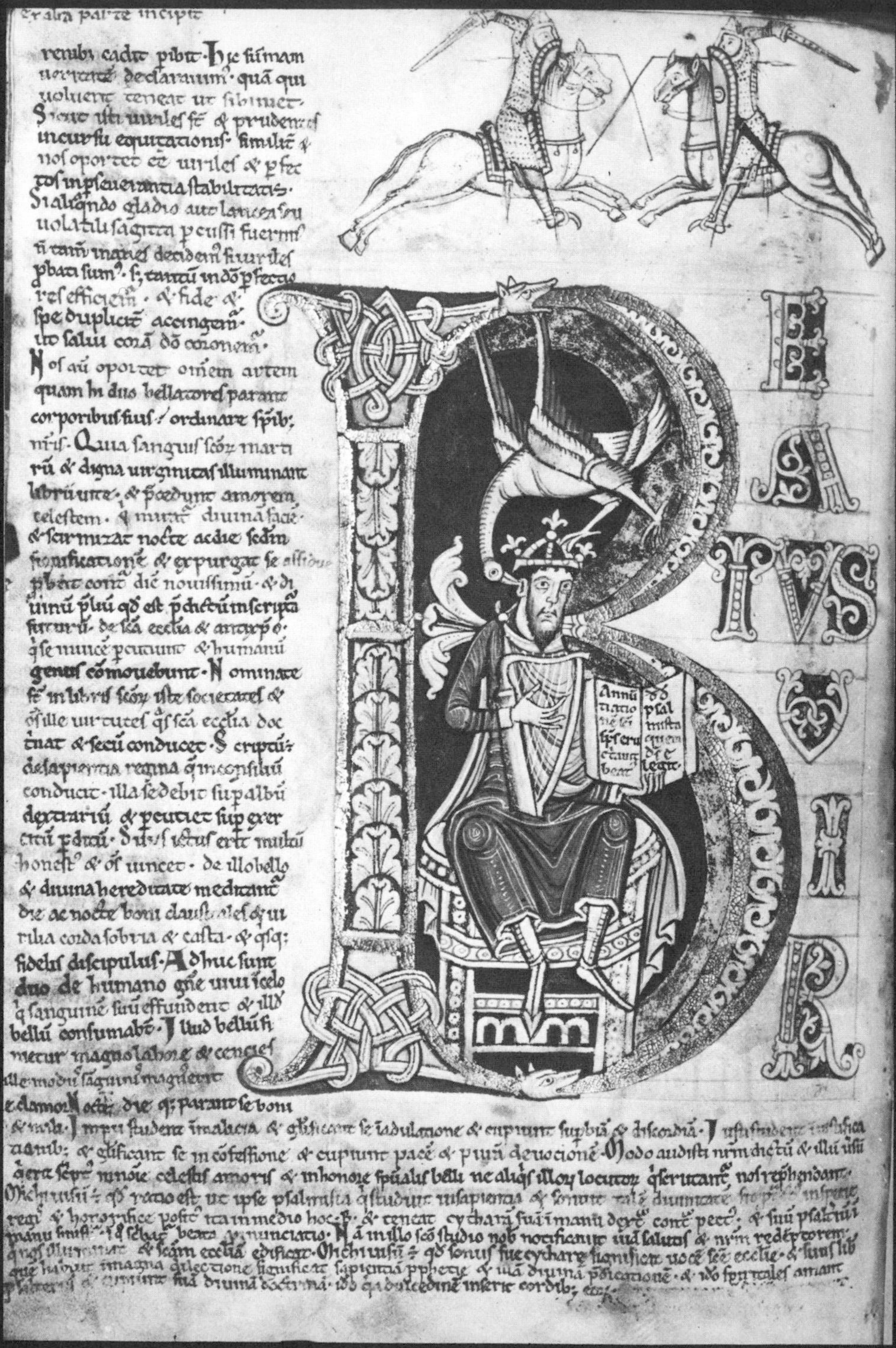
BEATUS VIR

V

LATER LATIN
LITERATURE IN BRITAIN

The twelfth century witnessed an enormous extension of interest in classical literature as well as an increase in the production of literary works in medieval Latin. The use of classical literature for doctrinal purposes became common. Ovid, Vergil, Horace, Juvenal, Terence, and other writers were frequently quoted or imitated; and there was a steadily growing tendency to use Cicero, Seneca, Apuleius, and other philosophical writers to support Christian teaching. During the thirteenth century the growth of Aristotelianism, especially in academic circles, tended to smother the humanistic attitudes developed earlier. One result was the growth of that scholastic Latin which seemed so barbarous to Petrarch, Erasmus, and to many writers of the Renaissance. However, humanism of the kind best represented in England by John of Salisbury continued

Facing page: Beatus page from the St. Alban's Psalter. Here the marginal gloss refers to the illustration in the right upper corner rather than to the text. It explains that the corporal struggle of the knights should be imitated spiritually.

to enjoy a life of its own, frequently appearing in vernacular sources.

The best introduction to twelfth-century humanism is C. H. Haskins, *The Renaissance of the Twelfth Century*, Harvard University Press, Cambridge, Mass., 1927. A lively picture of the life of the times is given by Urban Tigner Holmes, Jr., *Daily Living in the Twelfth Century*, The University of Wisconsin Press, Madison, 1952. An excellent and readable introduction in a convenient form is Doris Mary Stenton, *English Society in the Early Middle Ages*, Penguin Books, Inc., Baltimore, 1951. The best general history is A. L. Poole, *From Domesday Book to Magna Carta*, Clarendon Press, Oxford, 1951.

 # A. St. Ethelred[1] of Rievaulx

St. Ethelred (1110–1167) was born at Hexham of Saxon parentage. As a young man he became seneschal to David I of Scotland, but in 1133 he decided to enter the Cistercian Abbey of Rievaulx. On a journey to Rome in 1141 he became acquainted with St. Bernard of Clairvaux. Between 1142 and 1147 he was Abbot of Revesby in Lincolnshire, but in the latter year was elected Abbot of Rievaulx. His reputation and influence in England were considerable.

Among St. Ethelred's works are a number of historical writings which include A Genealogy of the Kings of England, On the Battle of the Standard, On the Saints of Hexham and their Miracles, The Life of St. Edward the Confessor, *and* The Life of St. Ninian. *He also wrote some sermons and miscellaneous pieces, but his most famous books are* The Mirror of Charity *and* On Spiritual Friendship. *These two works were combined into a sort of compendium by Peter of Blois under the title* On Christian Friendship. *On Spiritual Friendship was translated into French by Jean de Meun, author of the famous continuation of the* Roman de la rose. *We may assume that most educated persons during the later Middle Ages held ideas on friendship very similar to those expressed by St. Ethelred.*

For an introduction to St. Ethelred, see F. M. Powicke, Ailred of Rievaulx and His Biographer Walter Daniel, *University of Manchester Press, Manchester, 1922. There have been several modern translations of* On Spiritual Friendship *in various languages.*

ON SPIRITUAL FRIENDSHIP

Prologue

When I was still a boy in school and was much delighted by the pleasant company of my fellows, among the inclinations and vices to which that age is inclined my heart abandoned itself to affection and to love in such a way that I thought there to be nothing more sweet, joyful, and useful than to love and to be loved. Thus flitting among various loves and friendships, my heart was torn this way and that; and being ignorant of the law of true friendship, I was often deceived by what only appeared to be friendship. Finally one day there came to my attention that book which Cicero wrote concerning friendship.[2] It immediately struck me as being both useful for the gravity of its discourse and sweet for the pleasantness of its eloquence.[3] And although I did not think myself worthy of the kind of friendship it proposed, I was happy to have found an ideal of friendship according to which I could guide my loves and affections.

But when it pleased my good Master to correct my wanderings, to raise me from my earth-bound state, and to cleanse my leprosy with His life-giving touch, I abandoned the hope of the world and entered a monastery. At once I applied myself to the study of sacred letters, whereas before my squinting eyes, accustomed to carnal shadows, had been content only to touch their surfaces. Thenceforward the Holy Scriptures grew sweeter and that knowledge which the world had given me grew viler by comparison. I recalled what I had read in the aforementioned book on friendship, and I was astonished to find that it no longer appealed to me as it once had. For then nothing unflavored with the honey-sweetness of Jesus, nothing unseasoned with the salt of the Holy Scriptures could gain complete hold over my affections. And again and again reflecting upon it, I wondered whether Cicero's teaching might not be strengthened by Scriptural authority. When, moreover, I had read many things in the writings of the Fathers concerning friendship, wishing to love spiritually but being incapable, I determined to write something concerning spiritual friendship and to set forth rules by which I might experience a chaste and holy love.

Hence I have divided this little work into three books: the first showing what friendship is and its cause or origin, the second demonstrating the fruits and excellence of friendship, and the third explaining to the best of my ability how and among whom it may be preserved intact to the end.

If the reading of this work profits anyone, let him give thanks to God, and pray that Christ may have mercy on me for my sins. If, on the other hand, anyone finds what I have written superfluous, let him spare my infelicity in allowing my thoughts to be constrained along the lines of these meditations.

Book I   On the Nature and Origin of Friendship

Ethelred
Now I am here and you are here, and I hope that Christ may make a third between us. Here no one makes a noise or interrupts our friendly conversation; no voice or tumult disturbs our pleasant solitude. Now, beloved brother, open your heart and let the ears of your friend hear what you will. Let us not be ungrateful for the place, time, and leisure. For a little while ago I was seated among the brothers. When all were talking, one was questioning, one was disputing, this one was asking concerning the Scriptures, that one concerning vices, another concerning the virtues, but you alone were silent. Now and again you raised your head as if preparing to enter the conversation, but as though your voice were stuck in your throat, you lowered your head again and were silent. Again, you left us for a little

and returned with a sad face. All this led me to conclude that you wished to unburden your mind but were distrustful of the crowd and desired secrecy.

Yvo
So it was, indeed. And I am very grateful that you care for your pupil, not otherwise than if the spirit of charity had revealed what was in his heart to you. May your benevolence grant that whenever you come to visit your sons here[4] you let me converse with you alone and reveal the tempests in my heart!

Ethelred
I shall do so willingly. It is a joy to me that I do not find you inclined to vain and idle conversation, but that you always speak of something useful and necessary to your spiritual development. Speak therefore securely and share all your thoughts and cares with your friend so that you may learn and teach, give and receive, pour forth and drink.

Yvo
I am ready to learn, not to teach; not to give, but to receive; to drink, not to pour forth. For these things my age demands, my ignorance makes necessary, and my profession commands. But lest this time be used unwisely I wish you to teach me something of spiritual friendship. I should like to know what it is, what its usefulness may be, its beginning and its end, whether it may exist among all persons, and if not among all, among whom, and, moreover, how it may be continued unimpaired and concluded in holiness without any annoyance of dissension.

Ethelred
I am astonished that you think to ask me concerning these things when the most ancient and excellent teachers have treated them most thoroughly, especially since you have spent your youth studying them, and in particular have read the *De amicitia* of Cicero. That author discusses the question most fully in all of its aspects with a pleasing style and describes, as it were, the laws and precepts concerning it.

Yvo
I am not altogether ignorant of the book, and many things in it have delighted me. But since I have tasted the sweetness from the honeycomb of the sacred Scriptures[5] and the mellifluous name of Christ has overcome and liberated my affections, whatever I read

or hear that lacks the salt of the sacred letters and the spicy sweetness of His name, however subtly or eloquently it may be presented, seems neither palatable nor clear to me. Thus I wish to support with Scriptural authority those things which have been said by the ancients when they are consonant with reason and when they are useful in some way for an understanding of the subject we are discussing. And I wish you to teach me more fully how that friendship which ought to exist between us may have begun in Christ, may be maintained in Christ, and may have its utility and end referred to Christ.[6] It must be true that Cicero did not know the virtue of friendship, for he was completely ignorant of the beginning and end of friendship, that is, of Christ Himself.

Ethelred

That is true. I do not wish to teach you these things but rather to converse with you so that you speak without regard to my person or to my status. For you yourself have lighted the most splendid light which will illuminate us in our way, not permitting us to wander in byways but leading us by a sure path to a certain end in the question proposed. What more sublime may be said of friendship, what more true, what more useful, than that it begins in Christ, is maintained in Christ, and perfected in Christ! Now tell me. What must we consider concerning friendship first of all?

Yvo

First I think we must ascertain what friendship is. Otherwise our discussion will be futile because we shall not know what it is that we are talking about.

Ethelred

Does the definition of Cicero fail to satisfy you? "Friendship is an accord about things human and divine made with benevolence and charity."

Yvo

If you are satisfied with this definition it is enough for me.

Ethelred

Shall we say that those who have the same attitude toward things human and divine, who have the same will with benevolence and charity, have arrived at the perfection of friendship?

Yvo

Why not? Nevertheless, I do not see what a pagan would wish to signify by the words *benevolence* and *charity*.

Ethelred

Undoubtedly the word *charity* denotes an affection of the heart and *benevolence* denotes the effect of action. For one thing is equally desirable in both human and divine affairs; that is, that accord in the mind should be sweet and precious and that in exterior things action should be benevolent and joyful.

Yvo

I think that this definition would suffice for me except that it could apply equally well to pagans and Jews, not to mention wicked Christians. And I am persuaded that true friendship cannot exist among those who are without Christ.

Ethelred

What we have to say later on will show whether the definition is too narrow or embraces too much; then we can either reject it or adopt it as being sufficient and complete. Meanwhile, although this definition may seem to you less than perfect it will suffice for us to understand what friendship is.

Yvo

Let me not burden you to explain the insufficiencies of the definition; rather, I should like to have you explain the meaning of the word.

Ethelred

I shall try, but you must indulge my ignorance and not force me to teach what I do not know. The word *amicus* ["friend"] is derived, I believe, from the word *amor* ["love"], and the word *amicitia* ["friendship"] from the word *amicus*. Now *amor* is a certain affection of the rational soul through which it seeks something with desire and wishes to enjoy it. Through love the soul also enjoys the object with a certain inner pleasure, embraces it, and remains possessed of it. In our *Speculum caritatis*[7] which you know very well, we have attempted to explain this affection or emotion as clearly and diligently as possible. Now an *amicus* ["friend"] is said to be a "guardian of love," or, as some put it, "the guardian of the soul itself."[8] My friend, then, should be the guardian of my love, or the guardian of my soul, and he should preserve all its secrets in faithful silence. Whatever he finds there vicious he should seek to correct and tolerate to the best of his ability. He should share my soul's joys and sorrows, and he should feel all the concerns of his friend as though they were his own. Thus friendship is that virtue by which souls are joined together in a bond of love and pleasure so that they are made one instead of two. For this reason even worldly philosophers consider friendship to be not something fortuitous or ephemeral but to be among those virtues that are eternal. Solomon in Proverbs [17:17] seems to agree with them, for he says, "He that is a friend loveth at all times," manifestly declaring friendship to be eternal if it is true friendship. If friendship ceases, then it was not true friendship, although it seemed to be so.

Yvo

How is it then that we read of grave discords that arise sometimes between most loving friends?

Ethelred

We shall return to this matter, if God is willing, later on in the proper place. Meanwhile, I wish you to believe that no one is a true friend who could injure a person he has once received in friendship. Further, neither has anyone tasted the delights of true friendship who, being injured, ceases to love one whom he once loved. For he who is a true friend "loveth at all times." Let him be reproached, injured, cast in the flames, or crucified, he who is a friend "loveth at all times." As our Jerome says, "A friendship which can cease was never true."[9]

Yvo

Since there is such perfection in friendship, it is no wonder that antiquity has commemorated so few who were true friends. As Cicero says, fame celebrates hardly two or three pairs of friends in all the years past. If, then, in our Christian times friends are so rarely found, it is in vain that I study that virtue whose marvellous and astonishing sublimity I despair of attaining.

Ethelred

As someone once said, even the striving for great things is something great. Whence it is a characteristic of a great mind to pursue sublime and difficult tasks always, either to the end that the desired goal may be attained or that it may at least be understood, and, being known, desired. For he may be thought to have progressed not a little who from his knowledge of a virtue knows how far he is from it. Nevertheless, no Christian should despair of attaining any virtue, for he hears daily the divine Voice resounding from the Gospel [John 16:24]: "Ask and you shall receive," and so on. It is no wonder

that there were so few followers of true virtue among the pagans, for they did not know the giver and Lord of virtues, of whom it is written [Ps. 23:10], "The Lord of virtues, he is the King of Glory."[10] Among His faithful I could number not three or four but a thousand pairs of friends prepared to die for their companions, an act of a kind the pagans say or feign to be a great miracle in their tale of Pilades and Orestes. Did not they manifest the virtue of true friendship in accordance with the definition of Cicero of whom it is written [Acts 4:32], "And the multitude of believers had but one heart and one soul: neither did anyone say that aught of the things he possessed was his own; but all things were common to them"? Was there not a perfect "accord concerning things human and divine with charity and benevolence" among those whose hearts and souls were one? How many martyrs have given their lives for their brothers? How many of them spared neither expense, labor, nor bodily torture for them? I believe you have frequently read, and not without tears, of that maiden of Antioch, torn from the stews by the most praiseworthy ruse of a soldier, who suffered martyrdom with the one who had been the custodian of her honor in the house of prostitution?[11] I could give you many other examples, but I wish to avoid prolixity, and their very number suggests that it would be unnecessary Jesus Christ "declared and spoke" in the words of the Psalm concerning His works, "they are multiplied above number" [Ps. 39:6]. And He also said, "Greater love than this no man hath, that a man lay down his life for his friends" [John 15:13].

Yvo

Then we are not to discern any difference between friendship and charity?

Ethelred

Rather, there is a great difference. For divine authority sanctions that many more be embraced in charity than are accepted in friendship. We are compelled by the law of charity to receive into the bosom of our love not only our friends but also our enemies. But we call our friends only those to whom we are not afraid to commit our heart and whatever is in it; and they in turn are bound to us by the same law of faith and security.

Yvo

But many living according to the world and permitting themselves various vices join together in a similar bond, and hold that tie of friendship pleasant and sweet above all the delights of the world! I hope that it may not trouble you to set apart from so many kinds of friendship that friendship we call "spiritual" to distinguish it from others. For it is confused and obscured in a way by these others, and they, so to speak, attack and revile those seeking and desiring spiritual friendship and hinder their communion. A comparison among these kinds of friendship will make spiritual friendship a clearer and more desirable goal for us, and incite us to attain it.

Ethelred

Those among whom there is accord for the sake of vices falsely assume the illustrious name of friendship. But he who does not love is no friend. And he who loves iniquity does not love a man. For "he that loveth iniquity" does not love, but "hateth his own soul" [Ps. 10:6]. He who does not love his own soul can certainly not love the soul of anyone else. Whence it follows that such persons glory in the false name of friendship, unsupported by truth. Nevertheless, although in the kind of friendship which is either stained by libido, fouled by avarice, or soiled by lechery there may be experienced some degree of sweetness, it should be added that it is the sweeter the more honest it is, and also more secure, that the more chaste it is the more joyful it becomes, and that the more generous it is, the more happy it is. We must endure the fact that because of a certain similarity in the affections those friendships which are not true friendships may be called friendship. But that friendship which is spiritual, and therefore true, must be sharply distinguished from them.

We may speak of three kinds of friendship: carnal, worldly, and spiritual. An agreement concerning vices creates carnal friendship; the hope of gain creates worldly friendship; and a similarity in their lives, customs, and aspirations cements spiritual friendship between good men.

Carnal friendship takes its beginning from affection that like a whore spreads out its feet to all who pass, following them with indiscriminately fornicating ears and eyes. Through these entries an image of beautiful bodies or voluptuous pleasures is led into the mind, and the mind thinks it blessedness to enjoy these things at will. But it feels them to be less enjoyable without a companion. Then with gestures, nods, words, and flattery one mind is captured by another and they be-

come joined together as one, so that having entered into a miserable pact, one does and suffers to be done by the other whatever is criminal or sacrilegious. They think nothing sweeter or more just than this friendship. To them, to like the same thing and to dislike the same thing is to be governed by the laws of friendship. This kind of friendship is neither undertaken with deliberation, tested by judgment, nor ruled by reason; rather it is torn hither and thither by the impetus of affection. It serves no moderation, produces nothing honest, and has no eye to what is convenient or inconvenient. On the contrary, it approaches everything inconsiderately, indiscreetly, lightly, and without moderation. Thus, as if agitated by certain furies, it is either consumed by itself or destroyed by the same levity with which it was contracted.

Worldly friendship born of cupidity for temporal goods or things is always full of frauds and deceits; nothing is certain in it, nothing constant, nothing secure. Indeed, it changes with fortune and follows the purse. Whence it is is written [Ecclus. 6:8], "For there is a friend for his own occasion, and he will not abide in the day of thy trouble." Take away the hope of profit and at once he ceases to be a friend. A certain writer elegantly derides this friendship in verse:

He is no friend of a person, but of prosperity
Who in good fortune holds but flees in bad.

However, the beginning of this vicious friendship sometimes leads to a certain portion of true friendship; that is, those who enter an agreement out of a common desire for money during the time that they serve each other faithfully in their iniquitous desire for gain come to a pleasant concord at least in the realm of worldly things. Nevertheless, this friendship should never be called true friendship because it is undertaken and maintained through temporal concerns.

Spiritual friendship, which we have called true friendship, does not proceed from a consideration of any kind of worldly utility, nor from any extrinsic cause; rather it is desired on account of the real dignity of man and the feeling of the human breast, so that its fruit and its reward is nothing other than itself. Whence Our Lord says in the Gospel [John 15:16–17], "I have appointed you that you should go and bring forth fruit," that is, "that you love one another." For in this friendship is the way of perfection, and the fruit arises from a perception of the sweetness of this perfection.

Thus spiritual friendship arises among the good through a similarity of life, customs, and aspirations; and this is an accord in benevolence and charity. This definition seems to me sufficient to describe friendship so long as the word *charity* is taken in our sense,[12] so that all vice is eliminated from friendship, and the word *benevolence* is used to mean that sense of loving which is moved with a certain sweetness within us. Where such friendship exists, there also is that inclination to like the same thing and to dislike the same thing, the sweeter the more sincere, the more pleasant the more holy. Those who love in this way cannot like anything improper nor dislike anything proper. Prudence directs this friendship, justice rules it, fortitude protects it, temperance moderates it.[13] We shall speak of these virtues in their place. Now, however, to return to your initial question concerning what friendship is, do you feel that we have said enough?

Yvo
Those things which have been said suffice amply, and nothing further to ask about it occurs to me. But before we go on to other things, I wish to know how friendship takes its origin among mortals, that is, whether it arises from nature, by chance, by some necessity, or whether there is a law that implants it among men so that it becomes a custom, a custom, indeed, that makes it commendable?

Ethelred
It seems to me that nature first implants friendship in human hearts, then experience fortifies it, and the authority of the law regulates it. God the highest power and the highest good is sufficient to Himself, for He is His good, His glory, and His happiness. Nor is there anything which He requires outside Himself, neither man, nor angel, nor earth, nor sky, nor anything that is in these. To Him all creatures proclaim, "Thou art my God, for thou hast no need of my goods" [Ps. 15:2]. Not only is He sufficient to Himself, but He is also the sufficiency to all things, giving being to some, to others feeling as well, to others knowing also; for He is the cause of everything existing, the life of everything sentient, and the wisdom of everything having understanding. He is the highest nature who instituted all natures, ordered all things in their places, and distributed all things individually in their times.[14]

He wished, moreover, and His eternal Reason so decreed, that all His creatures establish peace and unite in society. In this way all things bear a trace of unity from Him who is the highest and purest unity. Thus it is that no individual thing of any kind remains solitary but joins together with other things in a certain society made up of many. To begin with insentient things, what soil or what river brings forth only one single stone of a single kind? What forest produces only one specimen of a single species of tree? Thus even among insensible creatures it is as if a certain love of society shines forth, for no one of them is solitary. Each creature is both created in and remains in a certain society of its kind.

And if we turn our attention to sentient things, we find that there the image of innumerable kinds of friendship and society and love shines forth. Although in other ways, they may be accused of behaving irrationally, certainly in this respect they imitate the human heart in such a way that they seem almost rational. Thus they follow one another, gather together, express their affections with motions and cries; so avidly and joyfully do they delight in mutual society that they seem to care for nothing more than the attractions of friendship.

In the same way also the divine Wisdom provided that not one lone angel was created but many, among whom there is a pleasing society, a most sweet love producing a single will and a single perfection. And the fact that one is superior and another inferior might give rise to envy if the charity of friendship did not intervene. Thus their multitude excludes solitude that their joy may be increased in the communion of charity among many.

Then, when God created man, that the good of society might be commended more highly He said, "It is not good for man to be alone; let us make him a help like unto himself" [Gen. 2:18]. Nor did the divine Virtue form this help from a similar or even from the same material. But as an express incentive to charity and friendship He created the woman from the substance of the man himself. Most aptly the second human being was taken from the side of the first so that nature might show them to be equal and as it were collateral, with neither superior nor inferior, as friendship demands.[15] Thus nature impressed the inclination toward charity and friendship in the human heart on account of its origin, an inclination that an inner feeling of loving soon increased with a taste of its sweetness.

But after the fall of the first human beings, when, as

charity grew cool and cupidity usurped its place, private good was placed before common profit and the splendor of friendship and love was corrupted by avarice so that the customs of men were depraved by contention, hatred, and suspicion, then good men distinguished between charity and friendship, concluding that although enemies and perverse persons should be loved, nevertheless there could not exist any communion of will or counsel between the good and the evil. Thus friendship, which at first, like charity, was common to all and followed by all, was restricted by a natural law to a few good persons who, seeing the sacred rights of faith and society violated by many, joined themselves in a stricter bond of love and friendship, finding rest in the peace of mutual charity in the midst of the evil persons they could see or from whose actions they suffered.[16]

But even those in whom impiety obliterated all feeling for virtue sought through reason, which could not be extinguished in them, to preserve the inclination toward friendship and society; for without companions neither the avaricious can enjoy his riches, nor the ambitious his fame, nor the lecherous his pleasure. Thus certain detestable bonds of society were established even among the worst men, which, glossed over with the most beautiful name of friendship, are distinguished by law and precept from true friendship, lest when the latter is sought, one may fall incautiously into one of them because of a specious resemblance. In this way friendship, which was instituted by nature and fortified by custom, is regulated by law.[17] It is therefore clear that friendship is natural, like virtue, wisdom, and other natural things, which, as natural goods, are both desired and preserved for their own sakes; and that all who have these things use them well and do not abuse them.[18]

Yvo
Do not many abuse wisdom in that they desire to please men by it, or are proud of the wisdom they have acquired? Or are there not those who make a business of it and think their profit in it piety?

Ethelred
Concerning this you should be satisfied by our Augustine who said, "Who pleases himself pleases a foolish man, for he is surely a foolish man who pleases himself."[19] And whoever is foolish is not wise; and whoever is not wise is not wise in that he has no wisdom. How can wisdom be ill-used by one who has no

wisdom? In the same way, proud chastity is no virtue; for pride, which is a vice, makes that which is thought to be a virtue conform to itself so that it is not a virtue but a vice.

Yvo
But if you will excuse my questioning what you have said, it does not seem just to join wisdom with friendship when there is no comparison between them.

Ethelred
Frequently one compares small things with greater, good things with better, feeble things with more powerful things, although they are not equated; and this is especially true among the virtues. For although they may differ in degree, they nevertheless have certain basic similarities. Thus widowhood is related to virginity, conjugal chastity to widowhood, and although there are great differences among these virtues, in so far as they are virtues they have a certain resemblance. For conjugal chastity is no less a virtue because it is excelled by the continence of widowhood; and although both of these are excelled by holy virginity, the last does not obliterate the grace of the other two. If you will examine well what we have said concerning friendship, you will see that it is related to wisdom or stuffed with it to such an extent that I might also say that friendship is nothing else than wisdom.[20]

Yvo
You astonish me, and I do not think you can easily persuade me.

Ethelred
Have you forgotten what the Scripture says, "He that is a friend loveth at all times"? And our Jerome says, as I remember, "Friendship which can cease was never true." Again, friendship cannot subsist without charity as we have already shown sufficiently. If, therefore, friendship thrives eternally, and truth illuminates it, and charity sweetens it, tell me, should you withhold the name of wisdom from these three?

Yvo
What is this? Would you say of friendship what John the friend of Jesus said of love, "God is friendship"?

Ethelred
Perhaps the expression is unusual and lacks Scriptural authority, but I do not hesitate to apply what follows

in the text concerning charity to friendship, for "he that abideth in friendship abideth in God, and God in him" [cf. 1 John 4:16]. You will see this more clearly when we begin to discuss the fruits or utility of friendship. Meanwhile, if you think we have said enough concerning what friendship is, in so far as the simplicity of our small ingenuity allows, let us reserve the explanation of other things that you wish to have clarified for another time.

Yvo
Although the delay is painful in view of my desire to learn, it is now not only time for dinner, which it is not permitted to miss, but also there are others to whom you owe attention waiting patiently for your presence.

Notes

1   The name appears frequently as *Ailred* or *Aelred*.

2   The *De amicitia*. In this work Cicero emphasized the idea that virtue is the only real basis for friendship. The book was a more or less standard educational text throughout the later Middle Ages and the Renaissance. It had a profound effect on Dante, as he tells in the *Convivio*, 1:12.

3   Books were customarily judged during the later Middle Ages for their wisdom and eloquence. These two virtues were also the goal of medieval education.

4   The dialogue is set in some monastery dependent on Rievaulx which St. Ethelred is visiting.

5   The figure of "honey from the honeycomb" was frequently applied to doctrine gleaned by exposition from the Bible.

6   During the twelfth century it was emphasized that any virtue has an "office" or pattern of behavior and an "end" toward which that behavior is directed. Except among certain scholastic philosophers who in this matter as in many others represent academic rather than common opinion, it was usually held that if the end of a pattern of behavior is not charity, or in other words, Christ, then that pattern does not constitute a virtue. Thus, for example, St. Gregory tells us that chastity maintained for the sake of worldly reputation is no virtue but a kind of "fornication of the spirit."

7   *The Mirror of Charity* is now available in a partial translation by Geoffrey Webb and Adrian Walker, A. R. Mowbray, London, 1962.

8   The definition in this sentence is from the *Etymologies* of Isidore of Seville, a standard medieval reference book.

9   *Letters*, 3:6.

10   The Douay Bible has "Lord of hosts" for the Vulgate *dominus virtutum*.

11   The story is told by St. Ambrose in his *Treatise Concerning Virgins*, 2:4.

12   *Charity* in medieval texts means "the love of God and of one's neighbor for the sake of God," not "almsgiving."

13   Prudence, justice, temperance, and fortitude are the four cardinal virtues.

14   Statements of this kind should not be neglected as so much rhetoric. St. Ethelred is emphasizing the reasonable order of Divine Providence. A firm belief in a providential order and a willingness to face the consequences of that belief are characteristic of medieval thought. The implications of this attitude are sometimes very difficult for the modern reader to grasp.

15   The idea that Eve was formed from the side of Adam to demonstrate her social equality is a medieval commonplace.

16   The theoretical basis for social unity during the Middle Ages was love. Thus the vassals of a feudal lord, the subjects of a prince, or the citizens of an Italian city were thought to be joined together in a bond of mutual love.

17   The law referred to is the New Law of charity.

18   The distinction between *use* and *abuse* is a commonplace derived ultimately from St. Augustine, who said (*On Christian Doctrine*, 1 :4, 4), "To use something . . . is to employ it in obtaining that which you love, provided that it is worthy of love. For an illicit use should rather be called a waste or an abuse."

19   *Sermons*, 47:9, 13.

20   The word *wisdom* usually has little meaning today, but medieval thinkers distinguished sharply between *scientia*, or knowledge of things seen, and *sapientia* (wisdom), or knowledge of things seen as they are related to things divine. To an age whose studies centered on the Bible "knowledge of things divine" had fairly definite connotations and very specific implications for the conduct of life.

B. *John of Salisbury*

John of Salisbury (ca. 1120–1180) was born in Old Sarum, probably into a family named Little. Beyond one unrevealing anecdote in The Policraticus *we know nothing about his early education. Concerning his later education we know considerably more. He went to France in 1136, where he studied for a time under Abelard, who was lecturing on the Mont Ste. Geneviève in Paris. Abelard gave up his lectures there in 1137, and John turned for instruction to Robert of Melun. Later he went to Chartres, where the humanistic tradition established by Bernard of Chartres was still flourishing. There he studied under William of Conches, author of an important commentary on the* Consolation *of Boethius, and the rhetorician Thierry of Chartres. He also pursued some studies in the quadrivium under Richard l'Evêque and became acquainted with the philosopher Gilbert de la Porré. Returning to Paris in 1140, John studied under Peter Helias, a rhetorician, and Adam du Petit Pont, who lectured in philosophy.*

Evidently John obtained a position in the papal retinue, for we find him attending the Council of Reims in 1148 and obtaining a letter of introduction from St. Bernard to Theobald of Canterbury, whose secretary he became in 1154. At Canterbury he wrote his two best known works, The Policraticus *and* The Metalogicon, *both of which he dedicated to Thomas Becket when the latter was Chancellor of England. After Thomas became Archbishop, John entered his service; but, having incurred the suspicions of King Henry, he was forced to leave England. He took refuge in Reims with an old friend, Peter of Celle, who was Abbot of St. Rémy there. When Archbishop Thomas was banished, John served him in France, always siding with the spiritual cause in the struggle between St. Thomas and King Henry, but at the same time seeking to moderate the demands of the Archbishop, who was a man of rather inflexible determination. John preceded Thomas to England and was probably with him on the day of his martyrdom. In 1176 John became Bishop of Chartres.*

John's principal works are The Policraticus *(from which some selections appear here) and* The Metalogicon, *a defense of the proper use of logic which incidentally contains a great deal of information about education in the twelfth century. Historians have frequently criticized* The Policraticus *for not giving us a descriptive view of English feudal society. What it provides instead is in some ways more important: an extremely literate and very learned exposition of the ideals of that society. For depth of learning, humanity, and a real command of the Latin language, John of Salisbury has few if any equals among English writers of any age.*

An excellent brief introduction to the life and works of John of Salisbury is Clement C. J. Webb, John of Salisbury, *Methuen & Co., Ltd., London, 1932. A translation of* The Metalogicon *by Daniel D. McGarry,* The University of California Press, Berkeley, 1962, *is available in a convenient paperback edition. A stimulating book is Hans Liebeschütz,* Mediaeval Humanism in the Life and Writings of John of Salisbury, *Warburg Institute, London, 1950. The Latin texts of* The Policraticus *and* The Metalogicon *have been presented in magnificent annotated editions by Clement C. J. Webb, Clarendon Press, Oxford, 1909 and 1929.*

Book I

*Chapter VI   Music, Instruments, Melodies,
Their Enjoyment and Proper Use*

One should not slander music by charging it with being
an ally of the frivolities of courtiers, although many
frivolous individuals endeavor by its help to advance
their own interests. Music is indeed one of the liberal
arts and it has an honorable origin whether it claims
Pythagoras, Moses, or Tubal,[2] the father of those who
play upon the harp, as the author of its being. Because
of the great power exercised by it, its many forms, and
the harmonies that serve it, it embraces the universe;
that is to say, it reconciles the clashing and dissonant
relations of all that exists and of all that is thought and
expressed in words by a sort of ever varying but still
harmonious law derived from its own symmetry. By it
the phenomena of the heavens are ruled and the activities
of the world and men are governed. Its instruments
form and fashion conduct and, by a kind of miracle of
nature, clothe with melodies and colorful forms of
rhymes and measures the tone of the voice, whether
expressed in words or not, and adorn them as with a
robe of beauty.

To add our own testimony, the Fathers of the Church
have highly praised music. Finally, by virtue of it the
violence of the evil spirit is controlled, and thanks to it
his power over his own subjects is weakened. For when
the evil spirit of the Lord took possession of Saul, David
sang, harp in hand, until the spirit ceased to trouble the
king.[3] Even though the spirit which is concealed in the
word be not yet revealed, it is most fitting that the soul,
thanks to a kindred element, calm itself and forget all
resentment when harmonies of like origin with itself
and mysteries of nature in her kindlier aspects are
revealed in sound.

The opinion or conviction is widespread that the soul
consists of musical harmonies. The prince of all philosophers, Plato[4] (if the Aristotelians will permit), since he
postulated a soul consisting of divisible and indivisible
elements and fashioned it of the same and divers nature,
believed that it could exist only if he united the divers
lines which in manifold division radiated from both
elements by portions consisting of half as much again,

of four thirds and nine eighths, due regard being given
to semitone and interval.[5] Consequently under a few
clear terms the variety, however great, of discordant
elements may be shown to be closely related to the soul
by reason of a harmony due to a similarity in their
kindred natures. Hence, by a kind of course through
concealed passages, it pervades the whole universe with
its own vital force. Sense harmonizing with reason
regulates and renders efficient the life of each nature
and substance by decree of divine disposition. The soul
therefore distributes nourishment to all things and
thrives in each of them in its own essence except insofar
as it is not submerged by the weight of corporeal mass
or as the confusion of external commotion does not
disturb the spirit's tranquility. When this assails it
nothing can be more wholesome than for the soul to
be recalled, so to speak, from the violence of tumult to
itself by nature's tones, which are its own. What, in fine,
can be more comparable to the spirit of man than tone?
When it is molded in him, passing through all that
surrounds it, with course as nimble as it is invisible, it
fills the ear, and with its being penetrates dense bodies
without impairing them; it, as it were, by touch influences the mind and at its bidding depresses or exalts
it. Although tone is by no means spirit, it certainly is a
type of conveyance of spirit and is the medium of spirit
—now human, now divine, and again prophetic. When
heard in its more delicately uttered strains, it captivates
with its beauty even austere minds and by the exhibi-
tion of a sort of charming gaiety drives gloom away. It
is potent to wipe away the swirling clouds of dust and
mist that have found lodgment in our minds.

Consequently the Christian Fathers, when they were
spreading reverence for the Church, held that not only
vocal but instrumental music should be turned to the
service of the Lord for the purpose of improving morals
and of turning men's minds to the love of God by inspiring a feeling of joy for goodness. If the authority of
the Church Militant appears insignificant to you, even
the Church Triumphant will not refrain from sounding
the praise of music. The son of thunder saw its elders
and revealed them to you and their voices were as the
voice of harpers harping with their harps.[6] But if you
have not yet heard them, listen to the King exulting and
desiring you to be a sharer in his kingdom and his
triumph, for he says: Take up psalm and bring hither
the timbrel, the pleasant psaltery with the harp.[7]
Wherefore? you say. That you may praise him with

the timbrel and choir. Praise him with strings and organs.[8]

This is the sole or principal use of music. The Phrygian mode and other corrupting types serve no purpose in wholesome training; rather develop the evil inherent in its devotee. Legitimate musical instruction grieves and laments its disfigurement by a vice that is not inherent in it and by the fact that a harlot's appearance is given to that which was wont to inspire virile minds with manly ideals. The singing of love songs in the presence of men of eminence was once considered in bad taste, but now it is considered praiseworthy for men of greater eminence to sing and play love songs which they themselves with greater propriety call *stulticinia*, follies.

The very service of the Church is defiled, in that before the face of the Lord, in the very sanctuary of sanctuaries, they, showing off as it were, strive with the effeminate dalliance of wanton tones and musical phrasing to astound, enervate, and dwarf simple souls. When one hears the excessively caressing melodies of voices beginning, chiming in, carrying the air, dying away, rising again, and dominating, he may well believe that it is the song of the sirens and not the sound of men's voices; he may marvel at the flexibility of tone which neither the nightingale, the parrot, or any bird with greater range than these can rival. Such indeed is the ease of running up or down the scale, such the dividing or doubling of the notes and the repetitions of the phrases and their incorporation one by one; the high and very high notes are so tempered with low or somewhat low that one's very ears lose the ability to discriminate, and the mind, soothed by such sweetness, no longer has power to pass judgment upon what it hears. When this type of music is carried to the extreme it is more likely to stir lascivious sensations in the loins than devotion in the heart. But if it be kept within reasonable limits it frees the mind from care, banishes worry about things temporal, and by imparting joy and peace and by inspiring a deep love for God draws souls to association with the angels.

But how may these reasonable limits be realized? "My lips shall greatly rejoice" says the psalmist "when I shall sing to thee."[9] If therefore out of the abundance of the heart your mouth sing the praise of the Lord,[10] if you make music with the spirit and the mind, if in fine you sing in wisdom,[11] even without the use of words, you possess the secret of true moderation and,

not so much with the rejoicing of the voice as with that of the mind, you soothe the ears of the Most High and wisely avert his wrath.

He who, however, expresses passion or vanity, who prostitutes the voice to his own desires, who makes music the medium of pandering, is indeed ignorant of the song of the Lord[12] and is revelling with Babylonian strains in a foreign land. Such as he gives greater delight; why I know not, unless it be that

> We strive for the forbidden ever,
> And long for the denied,[13]

and that stolen waters are sweeter and hidden bread is more pleasant.[14] The Phrygian mode, by decree of the philosophers, had long before been banished from the court of Greece, and all such melodies as lead to the abyss of lust and corruption.

Do you not recall that the mothers and wives of the Thracians poured out upon Orpheus all their indignation, even to the degree of arousing the ill will of the fates, because he had by his melodies rendered their males effeminate? (Granted that he moved the spirits of the nether world and appeased its stern lord and that thanks to his song, he won, though on ill-starred terms, his Eurydice's return.) Therefore plaints of men of his type can expect for the most part no happy outcome. Possibly the reason is that

> Base gain can have no happy end.[15]

However, influences that weaken the character and subvert morals are everywhere borrowed from our own age, for we concede that it is superabundantly supplied with vices of its own. If you notice that any one of those somewhat addicted to such faults is at the same time dignified, moderate, and modest, be sure to count him among the strong men of our day. He is indeed a *rara avis*.[16]

Consequently a certain venerable man,[17] the superior of some seven hundred nuns, imposed the law upon his convents that all the canticles be stripped entirely of their melodious vestments and rest content with the enunciation alone that expressed the meaning of the psalms and lauds.

The holy man was indeed suspicious of languishing tones as being related to voluptuousness, which is the parent of lust. Does not such music intensify day by day the evil of feasting? As though there can be no deadly poisons except those that are administered! Is it not folly to throw straw on the fire, oil on the hearth,[18] poison to the snake?

Though the wickedness of deeds be obscured by a veil of words whose fundamental meaning is the same, it makes no difference. The Greek word for banqueting signifies dining together or drinking together; we with greater propriety term it *convivium*, living together.[19] Do not feasts seem in themselves sufficiently inane unless enlivened with song? The Lord chid the custom, saying, Woe to you that arise up early in the morning to follow your drunkenness, to drink till the evening, to be inflamed with wine. The harp and the lyre, the timbrel and pipe, and wine are in your feasts. The work of the Lord you regard not, nor do you consider the works of his hands.[20] Was it not at a feast that the king of Babylon[21] saw the handwriting on the wall—Mene, Mene, Tekel—by which it was announced that his kingdom had been numbered, found wanting, and divided? By divine judgment, indeed, he who exposes the vessels of the Lord, that is human bodies, to the short-lived joys of passion and opens the chamber of the bridegroom to the foulness of the Evil Spirit is judged unworthy of his kingdom.

> Argus had a head surrounded with
> A hundred eyes,[22]

all of which were not so much lulled to sleep as put out by the charm of a single pipe. Who art thou to boast of being more circumspect than he?

Notes

1   The selections from books I and III are from *Frivolities of Courtiers and Footprints of Philosophers* translated by Joseph B. Pike, The University of Minnesota Press, Minneapolis, 1938. The selections from books IV, VI, and VIII are from *The Statesman's Book* translated by John Dickinson, Alfred A. Knopf, Inc., New York, 1927. The selections are reproduced by permission of the publishers.

2   See Gen. 6:21 and Paul E. Beichner, C.S.C., *The Medieval Representative of Music, Jubal or Tubal-cain?*, University of Notre Dame Press, Notre Dame, Ind., 1954.

3   I Kings 16:23.

4   *Timaeus*, 35A, B. In the Middle Ages, music was the study of harmonious proportions, wherever they might be found. Thus there was a "musical" relation between Christ and man, between the body and the soul, and so on. Musical principles were employed in establishing the proportions of churches and cathedrals. The proportions used in vocal and instrumental music were frequently used not so much to please the ear as to influence the mind.

5   For this rather technical matter, see Boethius, *De musica*, 2:28, 3; 3:4, 8. This was the standard text for the study of musical theory.

6   Apoc. 14:2; cf. Mark 3:17.

7   Ps. 80:2.

8   Ps. 90:4.

9   Ps. 70:23.

10   Matt. 22:2, 4; Luke 6:45.

11   Cf. 1 Cor. 14:15.

12   Ps. 136:4.

13   Ovid, *Amores*, 3:4, 17. The works of Ovid were widely used as school texts and were well known among the educated.

14   Prov. 9:17.

15   Ovid, *Amores*, 1:10, 48.

16   Juvenal, *Satires*, 6:165.

17   Gilbert of Sempringham. Robert Mannyng of Brunne, author of *Handlyng Synne*, a work famous for its exemplary stories, was a member of Gilbert's order.

18   Horace, *Satires*, 2:3, 321.

19 Cicero, *De senectute*, 45. This philosophical treatise on old age was frequently used as a school text.
20 Isa. 5:11, 12.
21 Dan. 5:24–28.
22 Ovid, *Metamorphoses*, 1:625.

Book III

Chapter VIII   The Comedy or Tragedy of This World[1]

Petronius does indeed employ an appropriate simile, because almost everything that takes place in the seething mob of the irreligious is more like comedy than real life. It has been said that the life of man on earth is a warfare.[2] If the spirit of the prophet had had any conception of our times, he would have been correct in saying that the life of man on earth is a comedy, where each forgetting his own plays another's role. Perhaps the oracular utterance of the prophet intended to teach that those not yet swallowed up by the earth wage continuous war; for, prisoners of their own vice, they are dragged to punishment like an ox to the altar. In pursuit of their own passions, although they are seen in body inhabiting the surface of the earth, in reality they have been swallowed up and are going down alive into hell.[3]

Using another figure of speech we may say that the earth is everywhere inhabited by those whose intercourse is not in the heavens,[4] nor are they aware that they possess anything in the sky; all they comprehend is what they see on the surface of the earth.

Constant warfare is also proclaimed for those (if we may return to fable) who know their water of Tantalus, vulture of Ticinum, wheel of Ixion, urn of Danaides, or stone of Sisyphus,[5] their worldly desires being impossible to satisfy as long as they are absent from God.[6] Their life is a warfare and assuredly a worry.

Now if this figure does not appeal to you, you may be taught by another interpretation, that life on earth is a trial;[7] and this, if we take the literal meaning of the word, usually implies evil. In this trial, at any rate, or warfare, although the Lord has reserved for himself seven thousand men,[8] almost the entire world, according to the opinion of our friend Petronius, is seen to play the part of actor to perfection, the actors gazing as it were upon their own comedy and what is worse, so absorbed in it that they are unable to return to reality when occasion demands. I have seen children imitate so long those afflicted with stuttering that even when they wished to they were unable to speak in the normal way; for usage, as someone has said,[9] is difficult to unlearn, and habit becomes second nature;[10]

> You pitch it forth with fork but it comes back Again.[11]

As a consequence the moralist wisely and indeed happily remarks "Accustom yourself from an early age to the best way to live; practice will make it agreeable to you."[12]

So this comedy of the age affects the thought of even great men. The different periods of time take on the character of shifts of scene. The individuals become subordinate to the acts as the play of mocking fortune unfolds itself in them; for what else can it be that invests at one moment some unknown upstart with wide flung power and raises him to a throne and again hurls another born to the purple from his imperial height down into chains, dooms him to captivity, and casts him forth into extreme misery? Or, and this is his usual fate, stains the blades of ignoble men or even vile slaves with the blood not merely of rulers but of princes.

> If fortune wills, she makes a consul teach;
> She wills again and lo! the teacher takes
> The consul's seat.[13]

The life of man appears to be a tragedy rather than a comedy in that the end is almost invariably sad; for all the sweetness of the world, however entrancing it may be, grows bitter, and mourning taketh hold of the end of joy [14] However prosperous the unjust may be in their lives, however enriched by association with the successful, and however much fortune is at their beck and call, at the end of their course she casts them down and she at length becomes as bitter as wormwood.[15] Job says

> Why then do the wicked live, are they advanced and
>   strengthened with riches?
> Their seed continueth before them, a multitude of
>   kinsmen and of children and of children's children
>   in their sight.

Their houses are secure and peaceable and the rod of
   God is not upon them.
Their cattle have conceived and failed not; their cow
   has calved and is not deprived of her fruit.
Their little ones go out like a flock and their children
   dance and play.
They take the timbrel and the harp and rejoice at the
   sound of the organ.
They spend their days in wealth and in a moment
   they go down to hell.[16]

What sadder exit to former joy! What unhappy end
of a happy life! This is the way of those who are not in
the labor of men[17] nor are they scourged like other
men. The counsel of God indeed casts them down[18]
while they were lifted up. All this is assuredly to be
ascribed to Him rather than to fortune, which is itself
from Him or, as I am inclined to believe, does not exist
at all;

Thou shouldst not deem the goddess fortune blind.
   There's no such being as she.[19]

Homer also,[20] in that masterpiece of his, disclaimed
any knowledge of fortune; in fact she is nowhere
named in that long poem. He preferred to commit the
control of the universe to God alone, whom he calls
moera, rather than to ascribe anything to the hazard of
fortune, which by general consent is regarded as no
goddess, and is furthermore called blind and is so represented in art. It is idle to accuse her of blindness since
she is nowhere to be found in the domain of nature.
   Consequently it is also proved that no such thing as
chance exists if one define it as an unforeseen occur-
rence, since nothing takes place without a proper cause
or reason preceding,[21] and since a trustworthy preacher
teaches us that nothing upon earth takes place without
a cause.[22] None the less, because some things happen
contrary to the purpose and to the expectation of those
interested in them, they are included in the term *chance*,
although they are just as truly foreseen in the mind of
the Dispenser as are those things which are seen by the
laws of nature to be confined by the bonds of necessity.[23] In like manner also it is apparent that these very
happenings are connected with the primal cause of all
things in such a way that all things are referred to it, and
in my opinion this cause itself necessarily follows by the
affirmation of all things that of necessity exist.
   Perhaps the more prudent will smile at my lack of
wisdom in agreeing that the existence of God is a corol-
lary of the existence of all things. It is the Peripatetics
who have taught me that cause is inferred, and with
probability, from effect. Furthermore the expounders
of our faith of necessity infer a cause deriving from all
things, of which, by which, and in which cause[24] are
all existing things, and without which nothing has been
created or can exist.
   The fact therefore that we are seen to ascribe some
event to fortune does not prejudge the case in her favor.
But since we are addressing men we use the words in
vogue among men, discussing with our dull wits,[25] as
before remarked, various questions, but giving no
profound explanation of any. Now if this be indulgently
conceded, what prevents our listening to what the
pagan philosophers have written for general edifica-
tion? It has been said "For what things soever were
written, were written for our learning,"[26] that through
patience and the comfort of the scriptures we may have
hope.
   As long as peace is absent from the sons of Adam,
who have been born to labor, prepared for flagellation,
conceived in sin, reared in toil, rushing rather than
traveling toward death, than which there is no sadder
sight, patience is necessary, an effective consolation
which, derived from the balm of joy in the conscience
and from the boundless clemency of God, fosters and
strengthens those pre-destined for life by inspiring
them with hope of the future. "O keeper of men" said
Job, expressing in his own person the calamities of
mankind, "why hast thou set me opposite to thee and
I am become burdensome to myself?"[27] There really
is no one who, when his faults begin to cry out within
him, does not find cause and matter for grief, since on
the testimony of Philosophy herself it is man's lot to
have what he does not want and to want what he does
not have.[28] Consequently the soul of the believer for
whom the joys of real beatitude are deferred, seeks the
upper with the nether watery ground.[29]
   To lend an attentive ear to the fantasies of the
gentiles, the end of all things is tragic, or if the name of
comedy be preferred I offer no objection, provided that
we are agreed that, as Petronius remarks,[30] almost all
the world is playing a part. A certain distinguished
author[31] of our own time, albeit in the language of the
unbelievers, has felicitously expressed the same thought;

Blind destiny allots his puny tasks
To man. Our age supplies amusement, nay,
Derision, to the gods.

It is surprising how nearly coextensive with the world is the stage on which this endless, marvelous, incomparable tragedy, or if you will comedy, can be played; its area is in fact that of the whole world.

It is most difficult for anyone excluded to be admitted, or admitted to be excluded, as long as he wears this muddy vesture of decay. To be thrown off it must be of such fine texture indeed that it can be passed through the eye of a needle[32] without touching it at all. Otherwise no one makes his exit intact, perhaps for the reason that the Styx,[33] nine times wound around, hems in this all so spacious stage. "I have seen" says Ecclesiastes "all things that are done under the sun, and behold, all is vanity";[34] and this is because all things that withdraw from the firm ground of truth become subject to the vanity which so graces our comedy; for not willingly was the creature made subject to vanity.[35]

Although this habitation of ours is entirely enclosed by nine circles, or rather spheres,[36] all of us must none the less make our exit, and inexorable Charon in that bark as decrepit as himself will ferry us across. Others will ever take our place, and thus ephemeral man abides in his kind just as, though water flows by, the river we know remains in its bed. It is written; Where are the princes of the nations knowing war from the beginning? And who take their diversions with the birds of the air and hoard up gold wherein men trust, joining house to house and field to field, even to the end of the place? And there is no end of their getting.[37] Straightway is added that of which all have been persuaded by unvarying experience: They have gone down to hell and others are risen up in their place.[38]

None the less those departing hence have been kindly dealt with in that they are not taken from this drama of fortune to be cast into exterior darkness,[39] where there shall be weeping and gnashing of teeth, nor do they have to pass from the snow waters which Job, the holy man, mentions to excessive heat.[40] Kindly have they been dealt with in that they await their Elysian Fields, which the sun of justice illumines with his light.[41] But why do my words exclude the Elysian Fields from the confines of things mutable? They are indeed, as far as possible, included, stretching away with the broadness of good souls to whom it has been granted by the Father of lights[42] to devote their entire energy to the knowledge and love of good. Hence the moralist addresses the restless man in search of an empty happiness outside himself;

Thou seekest that which lieth everywhere
In Ulubrae as well, if thou dost have
But a contented mind.[43]

Notes

1 Notice that both comedy and tragedy are regarded as representations of vicious persons. When the outcome of vice is sad rather than amusing, the result is tragedy. The attitude that vice is amusing because it is unreasonable and hence ludicrous forms the basis for much medieval humor, both in the visual arts and in literature. In both comedy and tragedy the vicious are figuratively said to subject themselves to Fortune. To understand this figure—for no one in the Middle Ages with any education at all believed either in the existence of a goddess called Fortune or in the possibility of fortuitous events—the reader is urged to study carefully *The Consolation of Philosophy* of Boethius. This was not only one of John of Salisbury's favorite books, but also one of the favorite books among educated persons throughout the Middle Ages and the Renaissance. A modern translation by Richard Green is available in a paperback edition, The Bobbs-Merrill Company, Inc., Indianapolis, 1962. Analyses of this work by modern specialists in philosophy should be avoided.

2 Job 7:1.

3 Num. 16:30.

4 Phil. 3:20.

5 These figures in Hades were taken to represent various kinds of worldly desire. Thus Tantalus was said to represent insatiable avarice, Ticius the avidity to know future events because of temporal concern, Ixion the tempestuous concern of men involved in a quest for worldly satisfaction, especially profit in business, and so on.

6   2 Cor. 5:6.

7   An alternative reading of the biblical text.

8   3 Kings 19:18.

9   Quintilian, *Institutes*, 1:1, 5.

10 Cicero, *De inventione*, 1:2, 3; *De finibus*, 5:25, 74.

11 Horace, *Epistles*, 1:10, 24.

12 Cicero, *Ad Herrenium*, 4:17, 24.

13 Juvenal, *Satires*, 7:197–198.

14 Prov. 14:30.

15 Prov. 5:4.

16 Job 21:7–13.

17 Ps. 72:5.

18 Ps. 72:18.

19 Cato, *Distichs*, 4:3.

20 Quoted from Macrobius, *Saturnalia*, 5:16, 18.

21 Plato, *Timaeus* (trans. by Chalcidius), 28A.

22 Job 5:6.

23 The argument here is similar to that in Boethius, *Consolation*, 5:1.

24 Rom. 11:36; John 1:3.

25 Cicero, *De amicitia*, 5:19.

26 Rom. 15:4. This was a favorite authority to sanction the use either of pagan letters or of fabulous narratives for Christian purposes. Chaucer uses it at the close of the Nun's Priest's Tale and in his Retractions.

27 Job 7:20.

28 Boethius, *Consolation*, 3:3.

29 Josh. 15:19.

30 *Satyricon*, 80.

31 Perhaps Bernard Silvestris.

32 Matt. 19:24; Mark 10:25; Luke 18:25. To understand what is meant here, it is necessary to know that the "muddy vesture" is not the literal flesh, but the "old man" which all Christians "put off" at baptism and are supposed to put off as often as necessary thereafter through penance.

33 Vergil, *Georgics*, 4:480; *Aeneid*, 6:439.

34 Eccles. 1:14.

35 Rom. 8:20.

36 Cicero, *The Dream of Scipio*, 4.

37 Bar. 3:16–18; Isa. 5:8.

38 Bar. 3:19.

39 Matt. 8:12.

40 Job 24:19.

41 Mal. 4:2.

42 James 1:17.

43 Horace, *Epistles*, 1:11, 29–30.

Book IV

Chapter III   That the Prince Is the Minister of the Priests and Inferior to Them; and of What Amounts to Faithful Performance of the Prince's Ministry

This sword, then, the prince receives from the hand of the Church, although she herself has no sword of blood at all.[1] Nevertheless she has this sword, but she uses it by the hand of the prince, upon whom she confers the power of bodily coercion, retaining to herself authority over spiritual things in the person of the pontiffs. The prince is, then, as it were, a minister of the priestly power, and one who exercises that side of the sacred offices which seems unworthy of the hands of the priesthood. For every office existing under, and concerned with the execution of, the sacred laws is really a religious office, but that is inferior which consists in punishing crimes, and which therefore seems to be typified in the person of the hangman. Wherefore Constantine, most faithful emperor of the Romans, when he had convoked the council of priests at Nicaea, neither dared to take the chief place for himself nor even to sit among the presbyters, but chose the hindmost seat.[2] Moreover, the decrees which he heard approved by them he reverenced as if he had seen them emanate from the judgment-seat of the divine majesty.[3] Even the rolls of petitions containing accusations against priests which they brought to him in a steady stream he took and placed in his bosom without opening them.[4] And after recalling them to charity and harmony, he said that it was not permissible for him, as a man, and one who was subject to the judgment of priests, to examine cases touching gods, who cannot be judged save by God alone. And the petitions which he had received he put into the fire without even looking at them, fearing to give publicity to accusations and censures against the fathers, and thereby incur the curse of Cham, the undutiful son, who did not hide his father's shame.[5] Wherefore he said, as is narrated in the writings of Nicholas the Roman pontiff, " Verily if with mine own eyes I had seen a priest of God, or any of those who wear the monastic garb, sinning, I would spread my cloak and hide him, that he might not be seen of any."[6] Also Theodosius, the great emperor, for a merited fault, though not so grave a one, was suspended by the priest of Milan from the exercise of his regal powers and from the insignia of his imperial office, and patiently and solemnly he performed the penance for homicide which was laid upon him.[7] Again, according to the testimony of the teacher of the gentiles, greater is he who blesses man than he who is blessed;[8] and so he in whose hands is the authority to confer a dignity excels in honor and the privileges of honor him upon whom the dignity itself is conferred. Further, by the reasoning of the law it is his right to refuse who has the power to grant, and he who can lawfully bestow can lawfully take away.[9] Did not Samuel pass sentence of deposition against Saul by reason of his disobedience, and supersede him on the pinnacle of kingly rule with the lowly son of Ysai?[10] But if one who has been appointed prince has performed duly and faithfully the ministry which he has undertaken, as great honor and reverence are to be shown to him as the head excels in honor all the members of the body. Now he performs his ministry faithfully when he is mindful of his true status, and remembers that he bears the person of the *universitas* of those subject to him; and when he is fully conscious that he owes his life not to himself and his own private ends, but to others, and allots it to them accordingly, with duly ordered charity and affection. Therefore he owes the whole of himself to God, most of himself to his country, much to his relatives and friends, very little to foreigners, but still somewhat. He has duties to the very wise and the very foolish, to little children and to the aged. Supervision over these classes of persons is common to all in authority, both those who have care over spiritual things and those who exercise temporal jurisdiction. Wherefore Melchisedech,[11] the earliest whom the Scripture introduces as both king and priest (to say nought at present concerning the mystery wherein he prefigures Christ, who was born in heaven without a mother and on earth without a father); of him, I say, we read that he had neither father nor mother, not because he was in fact without either, but because in the eyes of reason the kingly power and the priestly power are not born of flesh and blood, since in bestowing either, regard for ancestry ought not to prevail over merits and virtues, but only the wholesome wishes of faithful subjects should prevail; and when anyone has ascended to the supreme exercise of either power, he ought wholly to forget the affections of flesh and blood, and do only that which is demanded by the safety and welfare of his subjects. And so let him be both father and husband to his subjects, or, if he has known some affection more tender still, let him employ that; let him desire to be loved rather than feared, and show himself to them as such a man that they will out of devotion prefer his life to their own, and regard his preservation and safety as a kind of public life; and then all things will prosper well for him, and a small bodyguard will, in case of need, prevail by their loyalty against innumerable adversaries. For love is strong as death[12]; and the wedge[13] which is held together by strands of love is not easily broken.[14]

When the Dorians were about to fight against the Athenians they consulted the oracles regarding the outcome of the battle. The reply was that they would be victorious if they did not kill the king of the Athenians. When they went to war their soldiers were therefore enjoined above all else to care for the safety of the king. At that time the king of the Athenians was Codrus, who, learning of the response of the god and the precautions of the enemy, laid aside his royal garb and entered the camp of the enemy bearing faggots on his back. Men tried to bar his way and a disturbance arose in the course of which he was killed by a soldier whom he had struck with his pruning-hook. When the king's body was recognized, the Dorians returned home without fighting a battle. Thus the Athenians were delivered from the war by the valor of their leader, who[15] offered himself up to death for the safety of his country. Likewise Ligurgus in his reign established decrees which confirmed the people in obedience to their princes, and the princes in just principles of government; he abolished the use of gold and silver, which are the material of all wickedness, he gave to the senate guardianship over the laws and to the people the power of recruiting the senate; he decreed that virgins should be given in marriage without a dowry to the end that men might make choice of wives and not of money; he desired the greatest honor to be bestowed upon old men in proportion to their age; and verily nowhere else on earth does old age enjoy a more honored station. Then, in order to give perpetuity to his laws, he bound the city by an oath to change nothing of his laws until he should return again. He thereupon set out for Crete and lived there in perpetual exile; and when he died, he ordered his bones to be thrown into the sea for fear that if they should be taken back to Lacedaemon, they might regard themselves as absolved from the obligation of their oath in the matter of changing the laws.[16]

These examples I employ the more willingly because I find that the Apostle Paul also used them in preaching to the Athenians. That excellent preacher sought to win entrance for Jesus Christ and Him crucified into their minds by showing from the example of many gentiles that deliverance had come through the ignominy of a cross. And he argued that this was not wont to happen save by the blood of just men and of those who bear the magistracy of a people. Carrying forward this line of thought, there could be found none sufficient to deliver all nations, to wit both Jews and gentiles, save One to whom all nations were given for His inheritance, and all the earth foreordained to be His possession. But this, he asserted, could be none other than the Son of the all-powerful Father, since none except God holds sway over all nations and all lands. While he preached in this manner the ignominy of the cross to the end that the folly of the gentiles might gradually be removed, he little by little bore upward the word of faith and the tongue of his preaching till it rose to the word of God, and God's wisdom, and finally to the very throne of the divine majesty, and then, lest the virtue of the gospel, because it has revealed itself under the infirmity of the flesh, might be held cheap by the obstinacy of the Jews and the folly of the gentiles,[17] he explained to them the works of the Crucified One, which were further confirmed by the testimony of fame; since it was agreed among all that they could be done by none save God. But since fame frequently speaks untruth on opposite sides, fame itself was confirmed by the fact that His disciples were doing marvellous works; for at the shadow of a disciple those who were sick of any infirmity were healed. Why should I continue? The subtlety of Aristotle, the refinements of Crisippus, the snares of all the philosophers He confuted by rising from the dead.

How the Decii, Roman generals, devoted themselves to death for their armies, is a celebrated tale. Julius Cæsar also said, "A general who does not labor to be dear to his soldiers' hearts does not know how to furnish them with weapons; does not know that a general's humaneness to his troops takes the place of a host against the enemy." He never said to his soldiers, "Go thither," but always "Follow me"; he said this because toil which is shared by the leader always seems to the soldier to be less hard. We have also his authority for the opinion that bodily pleasure is to be avoided; for he said that if in war men's bodies are wounded with swords, in peace they are no less wounded with pleasures. He had perceived, conqueror of nations as he was, that pleasure cannot in any way be so easily conquered as by avoiding it, since he himself who had subdued many nations had been snared in the toils of Venus by a shameless woman.[18]

Notes

1 Cf. Luke 22:38.
2 See Cassiodorus, *Hist. Tripartita*, 2:5.
3 *Ibid.*, 2:14.
4 *Ibid.*, 2:2.
5 Gen. 9:22.
6 Nicholas I, *Epistles*, 86.
7 Ambrose, *On the Death of Theodosius*, 24.
8 Heb. 7:7.
9 *Digest*, 1:17, 3.
10 1 Kings 15:28; 16.
11 See Gen. 14:18; Heb:7.
12 Cant. 8:6.
13 Cf. Eccles. 4:12. The "wedge" is a battle wedge.
14 The idea that a prince should rule by fear rather than love was most forcibly stated by Machiavelli.
15 Justinus, *Epitome*, 3:3, 7–9.
16 *Ibid.*, 3:3, 11–12.
17 Cf. 1 Cor. 1:23.
18 Cleopatra. Notice the unromantic attitude toward Venus, who is here, as elsewhere in medieval texts, a figure of speech.

Book VI

Chapter VIII   That the Soldiery of Arms Is Necessarily Bound to Religion Like That Which Is Consecrated to Membership in the Clergy and the Service of God; and That the Name of Soldier Is One of Honor and Toil[1]

Turn over in your mind the words of the oath itself, and you will find that the soldiery of arms not less than the spiritual soldiery is bound by the requirements of its official duties to the sacred service and worship of God; for they owe obedience to the prince and ever-watchful service to the commonwealth, loyally and according to God. Wherefore, as I have said above, those who are neither selected nor sworn, although they may be reckoned as soldiers in name, are in reality no more soldiers than men are priests and clerics whom the Church has never called into orders. For the name of soldier is one of honor, as it is one of toil. And no man can take honor upon himself, but one who is called of God glories in the honor which is conferred upon him.[2]

Moyses and the leaders of the faithful people, whenever it became needful to fight the enemy, selected men who were brave and well-trained to war.[3] For these qualities are conditions prerequisite to selection. But the man who without being selected yet forces his way into the service, provokes against himself the sword which he usurps by his own rashness. For he runs against the everlasting decree that he who takes up the sword shall perish by the sword.[4] Indeed if we accept the authority of Cicero regarding such a man, he is rightly called not a soldier but an assassin.[5] For in the writings of the ancients men are called assassins and brigands who follow the profession of arms without a commission from the law. For the arms which the law does not itself use, can only be used against the law.

The sacred Gospel narrative bears witness that two

swords are enough for the Christian *imperium*,[6] all others belong to those who with swords and cudgels draw nigh to take Christ captive and seek to destroy His name.[7] For wherein do they partake of the character of the true soldier who, although they may have been called, yet do not obey the law according to their oath, but deem the glory of their military service to consist in bringing contempt upon the priesthood, in cheapening the authority of the Church, in so extending the kingdom of man as to narrow the empire of Christ, and in proclaiming their own praises and flattering and extolling themselves with false commendations, thus imitating the braggart soldier to the amusement of all who hear them?[8] Their valor shines forth chiefly in stabbing with swords or tongues the clergy and the unarmed soldiery. But what is the office of the duly ordained soldiery? To defend the Church, to assail infidelity, to venerate the priesthood, to protect the poor from injuries, to pacify the province, to pour out their blood for their brothers (as the formula of their oath instructs them), and, if need be, to lay down their lives.

The high praises of God are in their throat, and two-edged swords are in their hands to execute punishment on the nations and rebuke upon the peoples, and to bind their kings in chains and their nobles in links of iron.[9] But to what end? To the end that they may serve madness, vanity, avarice, or their own private self-will? By no means. Rather to the end that they may execute the judgment that is committed to them to execute; wherein each follows not his own will but the deliberate decision of God, the angels, and men, in accordance with equity and the public utility. I say "to the end that they may *execute*"; for as it is for judges to pronounce judgment, so it is for these to perform their office by executing it. Verily, "This honor have all His saints."[10] For soldiers that do these things are "saints," and are the more loyal to their prince in proportion as they more zealously keep the faith of God; and they advance the more successfully the honor of their own valor as they seek the more faithfully in all things the glory of their God.[11]

Notes

1 This chapter and the next constitute one of the most forceful statements available of the ideal underlying medieval knighthood.

2 Cf. Heb. 5:4.

3 Cf. Exod. 17:9.

4 Matt. 26:52.

5 Perhaps a citation from Cicero's lost *Republic*.

6 Cf. Luke 22:38.

7 Cf. Luke 22:52.

8 The best-known example is Thraso in *The Eunuch* of Terence.

9 Cf. Ps. 149:6–8.

10 Ps. 149:9.

11 The allegiance a knight owed his lord was considered to be an aspect of his allegiance to God. It was assumed that if he were not loyal to God, he had no reason to be loyal to anyone else.

Chapter IX   That the Faith Which Is Owed to God Is to Be Preferred before Any Man, Nor Can Man Be Served Unless God Is Served

It makes no difference whether a soldier serves one of the faithful or an infidel, so long as he serves without impairing or violating his own faith. For we read that men of the faith served Diocletian and Julian and other godless rulers as soldiers, and gave them loyalty and reverence as being princes engaged in the defence of the commonwealth. They fought against the enemies of the empire, but they kept the commandments of God; and if ever they were bidden to disobey the law, they preferred God before man. "Princes sat and accused them";[1] but they were practiced in the justifications of God, speaking firmly and doing His commandments without perplexity and with all loyalty. We also read that David served Achis, and observed toward him the loyalty and reverence of a soldier.[2]

This rule must be enjoined upon and fulfilled by every soldier, namely, that he shall keep inviolate the faith which he owes first to God and afterwards to the prince and to the commonwealth. And greater things always take precedence over lesser, so that faith is not to be kept to the commonwealth nor to the prince contrary to God, but according to God, as the formula of the military oath itself puts it. Wherefore I marvel greatly if any prince dares to put his trust in those whom he sees not keeping the faith which they owe to their God, to whom, without mentioning other obligations, they are bound even by their military oath. Under what disease of the reason must a prince be laboring who trusts that a man will show fidelity to himself who before his eyes reveals himself as corrupt and faithless toward Him to whom he is under the greatest of all obligations? It may be said in answer that such a man fears his prince; but surely if another and stronger prince shall appear upon the scene,[3] he will fear him more. Perchance he loves his prince; but if another, who is kinder and more generous, shall appear, he will doubtless love him with an even greater love. There is nought which the godless wretch will not stoop to do who prefers man before God. It is vain to expect one to be true to his secondary loyalty who holds his primary loyalty in no regard.

Notes

1 Ps. 118:23.
2 1 Kings 27:2ff.
3 Cf. Luke 11:22.

Chapter XIV That Military Discipline Is of the Greatest Use, and of What Chiefly Destroys Military Strength

Therefore military discipline is necessary, and I cannot easily say how great is the utility thereof. As has been said, discipline profited the Romans to the point that they subjected the whole world to their sway. Also Alexander of Macedon, who inherited from his father a small but well-trained army, after habituating it to service, attacked the world and overthrew countless hosts of foes. Xerses was checked at Termopilae by scarce three hundred Spartans, and after he had with difficulty destroyed them by his enormous force and at the cost of a large number of his men, he said that he had been thus trapped because, while he had many men, none of them were steadfast in discipline. And this was the truth, as was attested by their flight at Salamis, where shameful defeat came upon that king who led to war so many nations that even their leaders could scarce be numbered; and he escaped with barely a single ship. For it is said that his custom was to count the leaders of his army because of their multitude by taking a spear from each leader, so that from the number of the spears the number of the leaders might be ascertained. But a leader is utterly useless who does not maintain discipline among his men; and he hopes in vain for victory who does not assiduously train both the minds and hands of his soldiers. One who becomes a soldier suddenly, will desert his leader with like suddenness, nor will a soldier be steadfast to endure labor who has not been trained and practiced in labor continually. Cæsar was confident of heart because he found opposed to him an army of sudden soldiers and a superannuated leader who during the long repose of peace had unlearned the art of leadership.

Even when victory is despaired of, the heart may still be roused to courage by the hope of revenge. For at times

The only safety of the vanquished is to hope for no safety,[1]

and to regard themselves as victorious if none dies unavenged.[2] To sate revenge then comes to be looked upon as a great boon; and loss of life is well repaid by the consolation of vengeance. A man easily falls in with the necessity of fighting if he has difficulty in finding any way of escape. Men who are aggressors tend to dare too much, and often their opponents by desiring to die honorably and manfully have the good fortune to win the victory. For "fortune favors the brave"[3] and, when the crisis of the fight impends,

> The degenerate mind is disclosed by fear,[4]

than which nought is more disgraceful in those who profess the name and office of a soldier. For military law visits the cowardly with its greatest severities.

The leader in war must also use the utmost care

> That women and wine do not make soft the soldier's heart.[5]

For luxury always conquers, but only those whose strength it has first sapped; and it is to be avoided the more zealously for the greater fierceness with which it rages among its votaries. Antiochus formed an army of such luxury and extravagance that even the common soldiers made their boots of gold, and trod under foot the stuff for love whereof the peoples war. Also the Parthian nation is frequently vanquished because it is so luxurious. For

> As you advance toward the land of the dawn and the heat of the world,
> The mildness of the sky softens the nations.[6]

They are not wont to meet in the front and shock of battle hand to hand, but try so far as may be to injure the enemy from a distance. They do not know how to sit down before a city and win it by patience and strength. They fight mounted on horses which charge and then turn their backs, pretending flight. By ancient custom they give their signals not with the trumpet but with the timbrel; nor can they fight long, for they would be irresistible if their endurance equalled their onset. By nature silent, more ready to act than to speak, sparing of food, with no fidelity to word or promise, they obey their chiefs from fear, not from respect or duty. But a government which is corrupted by luxury, cannot long stand, or if it stands, will vomit forth under the pressure of God's judgment whatever it has drunk down with immoderate luxury. It does not know its own just measure, nor will it repress its intemperance before it has fallen into the last extremity of baseness through overindulgence in license.

Analyze the calamities of the Assyrians and you will be convinced by the testimony of history that luxury was the cause which overturned their kingdoms. Among other things Trogus tells that Sardanapallus, the last king of the Assyrians, was more feeble and corrupted than a woman. A prefect, who by the greatest effort had at last with difficulty obtained admission to his presence, a thing which had never before been permitted to any, found him among flocks of harlots spinning purple thread from a distaff, wearing the garb of a woman, and surpassing all the women in the softness of his body and the wantonness of his eyes, as he divided the threads among the virgins. Having seen these things, the prefect was indignant that such a might of men, handling steel and bearing arms, should be under subjection to this woman, and reported to his comrades the things which he had seen. He said that he for one refused to obey a ruler who chose to be a woman rather than a man. A conspiracy was therefore formed; upon hearing of which, the king retired to his royal hall, and building a great pyre, lighted it and consigned himself and all his riches to the flames; herein alone imitating a man.

And thus when the ruggedness of earlier kings is sapped by luxury, effeminacy increases among their successors as it were from step to step, until at last, when it reaches the final pitch of womanish weakness, there comes destruction and dissolution. The Roman empire was almost prostrated and rent asunder under Nero, who devoured all things by his gluttony, befouled them with his lust, drained them by his avarice, shattered them by his cowardice, sucked out their life by his luxury and pride. He never donned a garment twice, that there might be at least one point wherein he could outshine all others by a glory exclusive and peculiar to himself. So long as Rome permitted, he made the whole world inglorious; whatever the industry of others accumulated was wasted by his idleness.

Notes

1 Vergil, *Aeneid*, 2:354.
2 Cf. Horace, *Satires*, 2:8, 34.
3 Vergil, *Aeneid*, 10:284.
4 *Ibid.*, 4:13.

5   Ovid, *Fasti*, 1:301. The text reads "Venus and wine." Medieval (as opposed to modern) writers on chivalry almost unanimously insist that its ideals are inconsistent with lechery. In the fourteenth century Bishop Bradwardine attributed the defeat of the French at Crecy in part to the fact that they fought under the inspiration of Cupid and Venus.

6   Lucan, *Pharsalia*, 8:365–366.

Chapter XXII   *That Without Prudence and Watchfulness No Magistrate Can Remain in Safety and Vigor, and That a Commonwealth Does Not Flourish Whose Head Is Enfeebled*

Venerable communities likewise, if they follow in the footsteps of the bees, will set forth on the journey toward life by the shortest and quickest road. Read in Maro[1] of the foundation of Carthage, and from the comparison you will be led to admire the happy beginnings of that fortunate city. For you will see that all labored together in common, and none idled, and that their queen supplied aid for the structure of the city to rise; and if she did not join with her own hands in the labor of the lower orders, yet with her eyes she superintended the work and gave to it the undivided attention of her mind. For without prudence and constant watchfulness not only will a commonwealth not progress, but even the humblest household will not rest on a secure foundation. Wherefore in praising Ulysses Homer teaches that prudence, which according to the poetic convention he symbolizes under the name of Minerva, was his constant companion.[2] His imitator Maro, wishing to describe a man notable for feats of arms and for piety, and whom he deemed worthy to make the ancestor of the Romans, gave to him Acates as an associate in all his good undertakings, in token that prudent watchfulness is the surest way of advancing our undertakings,[3] and to signify that the affairs of a prudent man often succeed because he is not forestalled by the snares of schemers, but advancing as it were along an invisible path, and not publishing what he purposes, he thus attains to the goal of his intention. The poetic figure is apt because neither the work of warfare nor of piety can be successfully practised without watchfulness and prudence. It is a trustworthy combination when watchfulness is joined to prudence, because a keen mind is dulled by disuse, and on the other hand watchfulness is of no avail unless its exertions are founded on a rich vein of natural ability:

Each demands the aid and friendly coöperation of the other.[4]

But however correct the commencement of any work, it will not go forward successfully unless prudence, or Minerva, attends its course throughout. Recall the lines of the Mantuan poet, who under cover of fables expresses all the truths of philosophy.[5] Listen therefore to the diligence of the new citizens:

As bees in early summer ply their toil
In sunshine amid flowery meadows, training the while
The full-grown offspring of the hive; or store
The liquid honey and distend the comb with nectar sweet;
Or else receive the loads of incomers, or, formed in column,
Drive the drones, an idle throng, forth from the hives;
The work goes hotly forward and the fragrant honey smells strong of thyme;[6]

in the same way the citizens are held to their different tasks, and so long as the duties of each individual are performed with an eye to the welfare of the whole, so long, that is, as justice is practised, the sweetness of honey pervades the allotted sphere of all.

But the happiness of no body politic will be lasting unless the head is preserved in safety and vigor and looks out for the whole body.[7] If you did not know this, you might learn from the example of Dido. For with what careless and irresponsible levity did she admit Aeneas, what favor did she too quickly bestow on an unknown stranger, an exile, a fugitive, of whose plight and motives she was ignorant, and whose person was suspicious! With what curiosity did the ears of the chief men drink in the fabulous tales of a man who was striving to clear himself from blame, who was seeking his own glory and reaching out for something wherewith to captivate the minds of his hearers! And, so, smooth words led to the introduction of the man into the city, seductive flattery won for him the favor of hospitality, the captivated attentiveness of all spread an elaborate banquet, the banquet was followed by marvellous tales and accompanied by the frivolity of a hunt and various other wanton delights. These things brought forth fruit in fornication, in the burning down of the city and the desolation of its citizens, and bequeathed to future generations the seeds of undying enmity. This was the end of the effeminate rule of a woman, which, though it had a beginning and basis in virtue, could not find an issue into subsequent prosperity. It indicates lack of prudence to admit a man who, although the duty of hospitality forbade his exclusion, would none the less have been better allowed to enter as a stranger and not as a ruler.[8]

Notes

1   Vergil, *Aeneid*, 1:423ff.

2   John derived this information not from Homer but probably from Apuleius, *On the God of Socrates*, 24.

3   The great commentary on Vergil by Servius tells us that the name *Achates* is derived from a Greek word meaning solicitude, which, he says, always accompanies kings.

4   Horace, *Ars poetica*, 410–411.

5   It was generally held during the Middle Ages that poetic fables are instruments for the expression of philosophical ideas.

6   Vergil, *Aeneid*, 1:430–436.

7   John develops elsewhere the figure of the "body" politic, of which the prince is the "head." Students of English literature may recall the use of this figure in Shakespeare's *Coriolanus*, 1:1, where the head is significantly omitted.

8   Gen. 19:9.

Book VIII

Chapter XX   That by the Authority of the Divine Page It Is a Lawful and Glorious Act to Slay Public Tyrants, Provided That the Slayer Is Not Bound by Fealty to the Tyrant, or Does Not for Some Other Reason Sacrifice Justice and Honor Thereby

It would be a long and tedious task if I wished to bring down to our own times the series of gentile tyrants; a man with only one life will hardly be able to recall the list, for it eludes the mind and overpowers the tongue. My opinions on the subject of tyrants are, however, set forth more fully in my little work entitled "Of the Ends of Tyrants,"[1] a brief manual wherein I have carefully sought to avoid the tedium of prolixity and the obscurity of too great compression. But lest the authority of Roman history be held in small account because it has for the most part been written by infidels concerning infidels, let its lesson be confirmed by examples drawn from sacred and Christian history. For it is everywhere obvious that, in the words of Valerius, only that power is secure in the long run which places bounds to its own exercise.[2] And surely nought is so splendid or so magnificent that it does not need to be tempered by moderation. The earliest tyrant whom the divine page brings before us is Nembroth,[3] the mighty hunter before the Lord (who is also called Ninus in some histories, although this does not agree with the proper reckoning of dates); and I have already said above that he was a reprobate. For verily he desired to be lord in his own right and not under God, and it was in his time that the attempt to raise a tower to Heaven was made by frail mortality, destined in their blindness to be overthrown and scattered in confusion. Let us, therefore, advance to him[4] who was set over the people by the divine choice, which deserted him when he gave himself up to a wicked desire of ruling rather than of reigning, and in the end he was so utterly overthrown that in the anguish of his suffering he was compelled to put an end to himself.[5] For a right and wholesome assumption of the royal office is of no avail, or only of very little, if the later life of the ruler is at variance there-with, nor does a judge look wholly to the origin of things, but makes his judgment to depend upon their outcome and ending.

The well-known narrative of the Books of Kings and Chronicles shows, according to the authority of Jerome,[6] that Israel was oppressed by tyrants from the beginning and that Juda had none but wicked kings save only David, Josiah and Ezechiah. Yet I can easily believe that Salomon and perhaps some of the others in Juda recovered when God recalled them to the true way. And I will be readily persuaded that tyrants in-stead of legitimate princes were rightly deserved by a stiff-necked and stubborn people who always resisted the Holy Spirit, and by their gentile abominations pro-voked to wrath not Moyses only, the servant of the law, but God Himself, the Lord of the law.[7] For tyrants are demanded, introduced, and raised to power by sin, and are excluded, blotted out, and destroyed by repent-ance. And even before the time of their kings, as the Book of Judges relates, the children of Israel were time without number in bondage to tyrants, being visited with affliction on many different occasions in accord-ance with the dispensation of God, and then often, when they cried aloud to the Lord, they were delivered. And when the allotted time of their punishment was fulfilled, they were allowed to cast off the yoke from their necks by the slaughter of their tyrants; nor is blame attached to any of those by whose valor a peni-tent and humbled people was thus set free, but their memory is preserved in affection by posterity as servants of the Lord. This is clear from the subjoined examples.

"The people of Israel were in bondage to Eglon the king of Moab for eighteen years; and then they cried aloud to God, who raised up for them a savior called Aoth, the famous son of Iera, the son of Gemini, who used both hands with the same skill as the right hand. And the children of Israel sent presents to Eglon, the king of Moab, by him; and he made for himself a two-edged sword having in the midst a haft of the length of the palm of the hand, and girded himself therewith beneath his cloak on his right thigh, and presented the gifts to Eglon, the king of Moab. Now Eglon was exceeding fat; and when he had made an end of pre-senting the gifts, he went away after his companions who had come with him. But he himself turned back from Gilgal where the idols were, and said to the king, 'I have a secret word for thy ear, O king.' And the king

commanded silence. And all that were about him having gone forth, Aoth came unto him. And he was sitting alone in a cool upper room. And Aoth said, 'I have a word from God unto thee.' And the king forth-with rose up from his throne. And Aoth put forth his left hand and took the dagger from his right thigh, and thrust it into his belly with such force that the haft also went into the wound after the blade, and the fat closed over it. And he did not draw out the sword, but left it in the body where it had entered. And straightway by nature's secret passages, the excrements of his belly burst forth. But Aoth closed the doors carefully, and fastened them with the bolt and departed by a pos-tern."[8]

And elsewhere, "Sisara, fleeing, came to the tent of Jael the wife of Abner Cinei. For there was peace be-tween Jabin the king of Asor and the house of Abner Cinei. Therefore, Jael went forth to meet Sisara and said unto him, 'Come in to me, my lord, come in and fear not.' And he, having entered her tent and been covered by her with a cloak, said to her, 'Give me, I pray thee, a little water because I thirst greatly.' And she opened a skin of milk, and gave him to drink, and covered him. And Sisara said to her, 'Stand before the door of the tent and when any shall come inquiring of thee and shall say "Is there any man here?" thou shalt say, "No, there is none."' Then Jael, the wife of Abner, took a nail of the tent, and took likewise a hammer. And entering softly and silently, she put the nail upon the temple of his head, and striking it with the hammer, drove it through his brain fast into the ground. And thus passing from sleep into death he fainted away, and died."[9] Did she thereby win the praise or the censure of posterity? "Blessed among women shall be Jael the wife of Abner Cinei," says the Scripture, "and blessed shall she be in her tent. He asked for water, and she gave him milk and offered him butter in a princely dish. She put her left-hand to the nail, and her right-hand to the workmen's hammer, and she smote Sisara, seeking in his head a place for a wound, and piercing his temple forcefully."[10]

Let me prove by another story that it is just for public tyrants to be killed and the people thus set free for the service of God. This story shows that even priests of God repute the killing of tyrants as a pious act, and if it appears to wear the semblance of treachery, they say that it is consecrated to the Lord by a holy mystery. Thus Holofernes fell a victim not to the valor of the enemy but to his own vices by means of a sword in the hands of a woman; and he who had been terrible to strong men was vanquished by luxury and drink, and slain by a woman. Nor would the woman have gained access to the tyrant had she not piously dissimulated her hostile intention. For that is not treachery which serves the cause of the faith and fights in behalf of charity. For verily it was due to the woman's faith that she upbraided the priests because they had set a time-limit upon the divine mercy by agreeing with the enemy that they would surrender themselves and deliver up the city if the Lord should not come to their aid within five days. Likewise it was because of her charity that she shrank from no perils so long as she might deliver her brethren and the people of the Lord from the enemy. For this is shown by her words as she went forth to save them: "Bring to pass, Lord," she prayed, "that by his own sword his pride may be cut off, and that he may be caught in the net of his own eyes turned upon me, and do Thou destroy him, through the lips of my charity. Grant to me constancy of soul that I may despise him, and fortitude that I may destroy him. For it will be a glorious monument of Thy name when the hand of a woman shall strike him down."[11] "Then she called her maid, and, going down into her house, she took off her hair-cloth from her, and put away the garments of her widowhood, and bathed her body and anointed herself with the finest myrrh, and parted the hair of her head, and placed a mitre upon her head, and clothed herself with garments of gladness, binding sandals upon her feet, and donned her bracelets and lillies and ear-rings and finger-rings, and adorned herself with all her ornaments. And the Lord gave her more beauty because all this toilet was for the sake of virtue and not of lust. And therefore the Lord increased her beauty so that she appeared to the eyes of all men lovely beyond compare."[12] And thus arriving at her destination, and captivating the public enemy, "Judith spake unto Holofernes, saying: 'Receive the words of thy handmaid, for if thou wilt follow them, God will do a perfected work with thee. For Nebugodonosor, the king of the earth, liveth, and thy virtue liveth, which is in thee for the correction of all erring souls, since not men alone, but also the beasts of the field serve him through thee, and obey him. For the strength and industry of thy mind is heralded abroad to all the nations, and it has been told to the whole age that thou alone art mighty and good in all his kingdom, and thy

discipline is preached to all nations.'"[13] And in addition she said, "I will come and tell all things to thee, so that I may bring thee through the midst of Jerusalem, and thou shalt have all the people of Israel as sheep that have no shepherd; and not a single dog shall bark against thee, because these things are told to me by the providence of God."[14] What more insidious scheme, I ask you, could have been devised, what could have been said that would have been more seductive than this bestowal of mystic counsel? And so Holofernes said: "There is not another such woman upon the earth in look, in beauty, or in the sense of her words."[15] For his heart was sorely smitten and burned with desire of her. Then he said, "Drink now and lay thee down for jollity since thou hast found favor in my sight."[16] But she who had not come to wanton, used a borrowed wantonness as the instrument of her devotion and courage. And his cruelty she first lulled asleep by her blandishments, and then with the weapons of affection she slew him to deliver her people. Therefore she struck Holofernes upon the neck, and cut off his head, and handed it to her maid that it might be placed in a wallet to be carried back into the city which had been saved by the hand of a woman.

The histories teach, however, that none should undertake the death of a tyrant who is bound to him by an oath or by the obligation of fealty. For we read that Sedechias,[17] because he disregarded the sacred obligation of fealty, was led into captivity; and that in the case of another of the kings of Juda whose name escapes my memory, his eyes were plucked out because, falling into faithlessness, he did not keep before his sight God, to whom the oath is taken; since sureties for good behavior are justly given even to a tyrant.

But as for the use of poison, although I see it sometimes wrongfully adopted by infidels, I do not read that it is ever permitted by any law. Not that I do not believe that tyrants ought to be removed from our midst, but it should be done without loss of religion and honor. For David, the best of all kings that I have read of, and who, save in the incident of Urias Etheus,[18] walked blamelessly in all things, although he had to endure the most grievous tyrant,[19] and although he often had an opportunity of destroying him, yet preferred to spare him, trusting in the mercy of God, within whose power it was to set him free without sin. He therefore determined to abide in patience until the tyrant should either suffer a change of heart and be visited by God with return of charity, or else should fall in battle, or otherwise meet his end by the just judgment of God. How great was his patience can be discerned from the fact that when he had cut off the edge of Saul's robe in the cave, and again when, having entered the camp by night, he rebuked the negligence of the sentinels, in both cases he compelled the king to confess that David was acting the juster part. And surely the method of destroying tyrants which is the most useful and the safest, is for those who are oppressed to take refuge humbly in the protection of God's mercy, and lifting up undefiled hands to the Lord, to pray devoutly that the scourge wherewith they are afflicted may be turned aside from them. For the sins of transgressors are the strength of tyrants. Wherefore Achior, the captain of all the children of Amon, gave this most wholesome counsel to Holofernes: "Inquire diligently, my lord," said he, " whether there be any iniquity of the people in the sight of their God, and then let us go up to them, because their God will abandon them and deliver them to thee, and they shall be subdued beneath the yoke of thy power. But if there be no offence of this people in the sight of their God, we shall not be able to withstand them, because their God will defend them, and we shall be exposed to the reproach and scorn of all the earth."[20]

Notes

1 This work has not survived.
2 Valerius Maximus, 4:1, 8.
3 Gen. 10:8, 9.
4 Saul.
5 See 1 Kings 31:4.
6 *Commentary on Jeremiah*, 22:14.
7 See Exod. 32:9; Ezek. 2:4; Acts 7:51.
8 Judg. 3:14–24.
9 Judg. 4:17–21.
10 Judg. 5:24–26.
11 Jth. 9:12–15.
12 Jth. 10:2–4.
13 Jth. 11:4–6.
14 Jth. 11:15–16.
15 Jth. 11:19.
16 Jth. 12:17.
17 2 Par. 36:13.
18 2 Kings 11:2ff.
19 Saul. See 1 Kings 24:4ff.; 26:7ff.
20 Jth. 5:24–25.

C. Walter Map

Walter Map (1140–ca. 1210) was a Welshman of whose early life we know little beyond the fact that he studied with Gérard Pucelle at Paris. When he returned to England in 1162, he became attached to the court of Henry II, whom he served for a time as an itinerant justice. He was present at the Lateran Council in 1179. Some time before 1186 he became Chancellor at Lincoln, and in 1197 he was made Archdeacon of Oxford.

Formerly a great many Latin poems and some Arthurian romances were attributed to Map, but the only work now ascribed to him with certainty is his Courtier's Trifles, *a book of miscellaneous reflections on a variety of topics which displays a special animus against the Cistercians. The book itself was not extremely popular, but one section of it, the epistle of Valerius to Ruffinus, enjoyed a life of its own. It circulated widely in manuscript and even accumulated commentaries, one of which was written in the fourteenth century by the famous English Dominican scholar Nicholas Trivet. The epistle is usually described as a landmark in the history of antifeminist literature, but a careful reading will show that the remarks about women are for the most part jocular and that what the author wishes to do seriously is to castigate and satirize not women but those who seek through women to pursue pleasure rather than wisdom.*

There is a translation of Map's book by F. Tupper and M. B. Ogle, Chatto and Windus, London, 1924, from which this selection is reprinted.

From
COURTIER'S TRIFLES
The Epistle of Valerius to Ruffinus

The Advice of Valerius to Ruffinus the Philosopher not to Marry

I am forbidden to speak and yet I cannot be silent. I hate cranes and the voice of the owl, the bubo, and other birds who forebode with doleful cries the bitterness of a muddy winter, and so dost thou deride the prophecies of loss to come—true prophecies, too, if thou continuest in thy course. Hence I am forbidden to speak, being a prophet of truth, and not a diviner of my own desire.

I love the nightingale and the merle,[1] that herald with gentle harmony the delight of the soft air, and I love above all the swallow that filleth to the brim the season of coveted joy with a rich plenty of pleasures—nor am I wrong.

Thou lovest parasites and players who whisper of sugared baits to come, and especially Circe,[2] who doth cheat thee by pouring profusely sensual delights that are redolent of the aroma of sweetness long drawn out. For fear that thou be made swine or ass, I cannot hold my peace.

Ministering Babel pledgeth thee in the honeyed poison; it moveth itself aright,[3] and awakeneth delight in thee and leadeth thy spirit's force whither it will.[4] Hence I am forbidden to speak.

I know that "at the last, it will bite as a serpent,"[5] and will make a wound which will defy every antidote (treacle). Hence I cannot keep silent.

Thou hast many advocates of thy pleasures, most practised in pleading against thy well-being. Shall I be the only one to hold the tongue—I, who alone proclaim the bitter truth which thou loathest? Hence I am forbidden to speak.

The foolish "voice of the goose among swans,"[6] which are trained only to give pleasure, hath been blamed, yet the voice of the goose taught the senators to save the city from burning, their treasures from theft, themselves from the enemy's weapons. Perchance thou, too, wilt understand, with the senators, because thou art wise, that the swans chant death to you and the goose hisseth safety. Hence I cannot keep silent.

Thou art all aflame with thy desires, and, being ensnared by the beauty of a lovely person, thou knowest not, poor wretch, that what thou seekest is a chimera.[7] But thou art doomed to know that this triform monster, although it is beautified with the face of a noble lion, yet is blemished with the belly of a reeking kid and is beweaponed with the virulent tail of a viper. Therefore I am forbidden to speak.

Figure 21 *Aristotle and Phyllis. Lyon Cathedral. According to legend, Aristotle, in spite of his age and wisdom, became so besotted with passion for a mistress of King Alexander's that he allowed her to saddle and bridle him and ride on his back. The story, best told in the* Lai d'Aristote *of Henri d'Andeli, exemplifies the hierarchical inversion induced by Venus.*

Ulysses was enticed by the song of the sirens,[8] but because "he knew the voices of the sirens and the cups of Circe,"[9] he won for himself, by the fetters of virtue, the power of shunning the abyss. Moreover, I, trusting in the Lord, predict that thou wilt be the imitator of Ulysses, not of Empedocles, who, under the power of his philosophy, to say nothing of his melancholy, chose Etna as his tomb, and that thou wilt hearken to the parable which thou hearest; but of this I am afraid. Hence I cannot keep silent.

Finally, stronger is that flame of thine[10] by which a part of thee hath become the foe of thyself, than that flame in thee by which thou art kindled into love of me. Lest the greater draw the lesser to itself and I die, therefore I am forbidden to speak.

That I may speak with the spirit in which I am thine, let the fires be weighed in any scale, equal or unequal, and let whatever thou mayst do or decide result in the danger of my life. Thou must indulge me who, out of the impatience of my love, cannot keep silent.

The first wife of the first man (Adam) after the first creation of man, by the first sin, relieved her first hunger against God's direct command. Great hath been the spawn of Disobedience, which until the end of the world will never cease from assailing women and rendering them ever unwearied in carrying to the fell consequences their chief inheritance from their mother. O friend, a man's highest reproach is a disobedient wife. Beware!

The truth of God, which cannot err, saith of the

blessed David: "I have found a man after mine own heart."[11] Yet even he is a signal instance of descent, through the love of woman, from adultery to homicide,[12] that "offences may never come singly."[13] For every sin is rich in abundant company and surrendereth whatever home it entereth to the pollution of its fellow vices. O friend, Bathsheba spake not a word and maligned no man, yet she became the instigation of the overthrow of the perfect man and the dart of death to her innocent mate. Shall she be held guiltless who shall battle by her charm of speech as Samson's Delilah, and by her grace of form as Bathsheba, although her beauty alone may have triumphed without her will? If thou art not more after God's heart than David, doubt not that thou too mayst fall.

That sun of men, Solomon, treasure-house of the Lord's delights, chief dwelling-place of wisdom, was darkened by the inky blackness of shadows and lost the light of his soul, the fragrance of his fame, the glory of his home, by the witchery of women.[14] At the last, having bowed his knee to Baal,[15] he was degraded from a priest of the Lord to a limb of the devil, so that he seemed to be thrust over a yet greater precipice than Phoebus, who, after Phaeton's fall, was changed from the Apollo of Jove into the shepherd of Admetus[16] Friend, if thou art not wiser than Solomon—and no man is that—thou art not greater than he who can be bewitched by woman. "Open thine eyes and see."[17]

Even the very good woman, who is rarer than the phoenix, cannot be loved without the loathsome bitterness of fear and worry and constant unhappiness. But bad women, of whom the swarm is so large that no spot is without their malice, punish bitterly the bestowal of love, and devote themselves utterly to dealing distress, "to the division of soul and body."[18] O friend, a trite moral is, "Look to whom thou givest." True morality is, "Look to whom thou givest thyself."[19]

Lucretia and Penelope, as well as the Sabine women, have borne aloft the banners of modesty and they have brought back trophies with but few in their following. Friend, there is now no Lucretia, no Penelope, no Sabine woman. Fear all the sex.

Scylla, the daughter of Nisos,[20] and Myrrha,[21] the daughter of Cinyras, have opposed the Sabine battle-lines, and have led in their train great throngs attended by an army of all the vices, so that they dispense to their captives groanings and sighs, and, in the end, hell itself. My friend, lest thou become the prey of merciless pil-

lages, thou must not slumber while their army is passing.

Jupiter, king of earth, who was also called king of heaven on account of his matchless might of body and his peerless excellence of mind, compelled himself to bellow for Europa.[22] My friend, lo, him whom worth lifted above the heavens, a woman hath lowered to the level of brutes! A woman will have the power to compel thee to bellow unless thou art greater than Jupiter, to whose greatness no one else was equal.

Phoebus, who first environed the round of the whole world with the rays of his wisdom, so that he might rightly win the sole honor of the name of Sol, was infatuated with the love of Leucothoe, to his own disgrace and her destruction;[23] and, through the repeated change of the eclipse, he frequently came to lack his own light, of which the whole world felt the loss. My friend, "lest the light which is in thee be turned to darkness,"[24] flee Leucothoe.

Then there was Mars, who attained the name of "God of Battles" through the well-known number of victories, in which his ready valor stood him greatly in stead. Although he knew no fear for himself, he was bound with Venus by Vulcan in chains, invisible, to be sure, but tangible this too amid the mocking applause and the derision of the heavenly court.[25] My friend, meditate at least upon the chains which thou dost not see and yet already in part feel, and snatch thyself away while they are still breakable, lest that lame and loathsome smith whom "no god ever honored at his board nor goddess with her bed"[26] shall chain thee in his fashion to his Venus and shall make thee like unto himself, lame and loathsome, or, what I fear more, shall render thee club-footed; in such wise that thou canst not have the saving grace of a cloven hoof,[27] but, bound to Venus, thou wilt become the distress and laughing-stock of onlookers, while the blind[28] applaud thee and those with sight threaten.

Pallas was condemned by a false judge of goddesses,[29] since she promised to bestow not pleasure but profit. Friend, dost thou, too, ever judge in this wise?

I mark that thou, in growing disgust of spirit, art turning very rapidly the leaves before thee and art not attending to the meaning, but art awaiting the figures of rhetoric.[30] In vain "thou waitest for this muddy river"[31] to flow out or for these noisome floods to pass and to yield to currents of pure water; since all streams must be like their source, either muddy or clear. Thus the weakness of my speech expresseth the ignorance of my heart, and the swelling unevenness of my diction offendeth a delicate spirit. Conscious as I am of this weakness, I should have abandoned gladly this task of dissuasion; but, because I could not hold my peace, therefore I spake as well as I could. But if I possessed as much merit of style as zest of writing, I should send thee such fine words, mated in such noble union, that each of them apart and all of them together would seem to bless the author. But because thou owest to me everything that a lover as yet bare and unfruitful—I do not say barren—can deserve from all men, lend me meantime thine ear in patience while I unfold what I have enfolded. And do not exact from me the rouge and white lead of the orator, my ignorance of which I confess and bemourn, but accept the will of the writer and the truth of his page.

Julius Caesar, "for whose greatness the world was too narrow,"[32] on the day that too cruel Atropos dared to break the thread of his noble life, bent his ear humbly, at the doors of the Capitol, to Tongillus—a poor man, indeed, but a prophet—when he offered him tablets (of writing). Had he, instead, bent his mind to the warning, his murderers and not he would have paid the penalty. Thou indeed inclinest thine ear to me, the sender of this writing, as the asp to charmers[33]; but thou offerest thy mind as a boar to dogs. Thou art as soothed as the serpent, dipsas,[34] upon which the sun shone with equatorial rays. Thou art as thoughtful for thyself as was the betrayed Medea.[35] Thou pitiest thyself as the sea the shipwrecked. In that thou restrainest thy hand, it is out of reverence to the king's peace. O my friend, the conqueror of the world, although nearly perfect, bent himself humbly to his faithful servant, and he almost escaped because he almost obeyed; and he yielded to punishment because he did not yield full obedience. Much humility availed him naught, because it was not full humility. What will thy wild savagery and thy inflexible vigor and thy dreaded haughtiness avail thee, if thou voluntarily rushest unarmed into the snares of robbers? Humble thyself, prithee, to the measure of his humility, who humbled under himself the whole world, and listen to thy friend. And if thou thinkest that Caesar erred, not hearkening to counsel, listen and mark what hath happened to others, that their injury may be to thy profit. Without hurt is the chastening to which these patterns persuade thee. Thou art safe in some sanctuary or other, or thou languishest

in some asylum. Caesar looked upon the merciless traitors and did not turn back. If thou hast always evaded such self-discipline, thou hast found the pious impious (i.e. thou hast not been able to distinguish the pious from the impious).

King Phoroneus, who did not begrudge the transmission of treasures of law to his people,[36] but was the first of the Greeks to make such studies precious, on the day when he entered upon the way of all flesh,[37] said to Leontius his brother: "I should have lacked naught that tendeth to the highest happiness had I always lacked a wife." Leontius asked, "And how did a wife stand in your way?" And he replied, "All husbands know how." My friend, would that thou hadst marriage behind thee and not before, that thou mightest know what hindereth happiness.

When Emperor Valens—at eighty as chaste as a maid —heard, on the day of his death, that his triumphs, which had been numerous, were being proclaimed anew, he said that he gloried in only one victory; and when asked, "Which one?" replied, "The one in which I tamed my basest enemy, my flesh." My friend, this emperor would have gone ingloriously out of the world had he not bravely resisted that with which thou hast closely contracted.

Cicero, after the divorce of Terentia, was unwilling to marry, professing himself unable to give his attention at once to a wife and to philosophy. My friend, would that thy spirit would thus answer thee, or thy tongue me, and thou wouldst deign to imitate the master of eloquence at least in thy speech, in order to give me hope, even though it should prove vain!

Canius from Gades (the Columns of Hercules), a poet of light and pleasing style, was reproved thus by Livy of Aponus, the grave historian, who was a married man, for delighting in the love of many ladies: "Thou mayst not share our philosophy while thou art shared by so many; for Tityus doth not love Juno with that liver which many vultures rend into many pieces." And Canius answered: "If at any time I fall, I arise more careful; if I am somewhat bowed down to earth, I seek the upper air more briskly. The alternation of nights rendereth the days brighter, as an endless continuance of shadows is the likeness of hell. So the first lilies of spring, which are clarified by the warm rays of the sun, delight in a larger joy under the change of the northeast breeze and of the western zephyr, but are destroyed by one breath of the thunderous south wind. Hence

Mars, breaking his cords, reclineth in the company of the gods, at the heavenly table, while far away from this the uxorious Vulcan is bound by his own rope. Thus many threads bind more lightly than one chain; and philosophy bringeth to me delights and to thee a solace." My friend, I approve of the words of both of these, but of the life of neither. And yet, many maladies interrupted by the alternation of health are less painful than one illness which affecteth us with incurable pangs.

Pacuvius, in tears, said to his neighbour Arrius: "My friend, I have in my garden a barren tree on which my first wife hanged herself, and then my second, and just now my third." Arrius answered him: "I marvel that thou hast found cause for tears in such a run of good luck," and again, "Great heavens, what heavy costs to thee hang from that tree!" and thirdly, "My friend, give me of that tree some branches to plant." And I say to thee, my friend, I fear that thou too wilt have to beg branches of that tree at a time when thou wilt not be able to find them.

Sulpicius felt where his shoe pinched him, seeing that he divorced a high-born and chaste wife. My friend, beware of a pinching shoe which cannot be pulled off.

Cato of Utica said, "If the world could exist without women, our intercourse would not be without gods." My friend, Cato spoke only of what he had felt and known; nor doth any one curse the mockery of women unless tricked and tried by painful experiences. It is proper to trust such witnesses, because they speak with all truth: they know how enjoyment of love pleaseth and how it pricketh the beloved; they know that the flower of Venus is a rose, because under its crimson lurk many thorns.[38]

Metellus answered to Marius, whose daughter he would not marry, though she was of large dowry, great beauty, high birth, and fair fame: "I prefer to be mine own than hers." Marius replied to him: "Nay, she will be thine." Then said Metellus: "Not so, a man must needs belong to his wife, for it is true to logic that 'the predicates will be such as the subjects will permit.'" Thus Metellus' wit in words saved his back from burdens. My friend, if it is reasonable to marry, it is not expedient. May thy love be neither blind in the case nor on the basis of property, so that thou mayst choose the face of a wife, not her dress, and her soul, not her gold, and that a woman, not a dowry, may wed thee. Thus, if it is any way possible, thou wilt be able to *predicate* that thou art not making the *subject* envious.

Lais of Corinth, renowned for great beauty, deigned to accept the embraces only of kings and lords; she tried, however, to share the couch of Demosthenes the philosopher, so that, by solving the miracle of his far-famed chastity, she would be reputed to have moved stones with her lures as Amphion with his lyre; and she drew him sweetly into her arms, disarmed by her endearments. When his self-control was slackened by the charm of her bed, she craved of him, in return for her favor, one hundred talents. But he said, lifting eyes to heaven: "I buy not repentance at any such rate." My friend, would that thou, too, wouldst raise to heaven a keen mind, and escape that which must be redeemed with repentance.

Livia slew her husband, whom she hated overmuch; Lucilia hers, whom she overmuch loved. The one of her own will mixed aconite; the other by mistake mingled for her man a potion of madness, instead of a cup of love. My friend, they strive with opposite intent; neither, however, is cheated of the goal of women's wiles, that is, her own natural evil. Women journey by widely different ways, but by whatever windings they may wander, and through however many trackless regions they may travel, there is only one outlet, one goal of all their trails, one crown and common ground of all their differences—wickedness. Find a warning against them in the experience that a woman is bold for the gratification of all her love or hate and is an adept at hurting when she will, which is always. And frequently, when she is ready to assist, she hindereth, hence it cometh to pass that she doeth harm even against her own heart's wish. Thou art placed in a furnace: if thou art gold, thou wilt go forth gold.

Deianira dressed Tirynthius (Hercules) in a shirt, and she drew vengeance upon the mauler of the monsters through monsters' blood, and she concluded to her distress what she had conceived for her delight.[39] My friend, Thestias (Deianira) knew that Nessus was pierced by the dart of Hercules, indeed saw him with her own eyes, yet she believed Nessus against Hercules; and, as if with her own intent, she clothed in a shroud him whom she ought to have clothed in a shirt. The unbalanced woman of wrong head and rash spirit is ever willing to settle upon the sovereign thing which is her wish, not which is befitting; and, as she desireth, above all, to please, she is wont to place her own pleasure before everything. Hercules achieved twelve labors, more than mortal; by the thirteenth, which surpassed all immortals, he was consumed. Thus the bravest of men met death, in like measure lamented and lamenting, even he who without lament bore on his shoulders the arch of heaven.

Pray what woman among thousands of thousands ever hath saddened with perpetual repulse the persistently solicitous suitor? What woman doth repeatedly reject the prayer of the petitioner? Her response hath a savor of favor, and however hard she seemeth, she will always have in some corner or other of her words some hidden kindling for thy craving. However much she may deny, she denieth not altogether.[40]

Gold broke through the barriers of the tower of Acrisius, and melted the virginity of Danae,[41] which was guarded by many a rampart. My friend, thus the unchaste raineth from heaven upon the maiden whose chastity hath triumphed over earth; thus he from heaven overcometh her whom the lowly enticeth not, thus the north wind overturneth the tree which the west wind doth not budge.

Perictione (Pennutia), a virgin verging on old age, and renowned for her chastity, at length conceived "under the pressure of Apollo's phantom,"[42] and bore Plato. My friend, lo, an apparition in sleep hath deflowered her whom many watchings have preserved undefiled, as every rose garden is always robbed of its crimson by a whirlwind. But to a good purpose—if anything of the sort can be called good—because Plato waxed like unto his father in wisdom, and became the heir of both the name and fame of his mighty sire.

My friend, are you amazed or are you, the rather, affronted, because in my parallels I point out heathen as worthy of your imitation, idolatries to a Christian, wolves to a lamb, evil men to a good. I wish you to be like unto the fruitful bee, which draweth honey from the nettle, "so that you may suck honey from the stone and oil from the hardest rock."[43] I know the superstition of the heathen; but every one of God's creatures furnisheth some honorable illustration, whence He himself is called lion, or serpent, or ram.[44] The unbelieving perform very many things perversely; nevertheless they do some things which, although barren in their case, would in ours bring forth fruit abundantly. But if those who lived without hope, without faith, without charity, indeed without a preacher,[45] made coats of skins[46] (in human wise), and, if we should become asses or sows or brutes in some inhuman form,[47]

of what reward of faith, of charity, of hope should we be deemed worthy, although we might behold prophets, apostles, and chief of all, Him, the Lord of the pure heart,[48] whom only pure eyes are permitted to perceive? Or if they have wearied themselves in the pursuit of their own designs with no perception of future bliss, but only with the hope of avoiding ignorant minds, what shall we have in return for our neglect of the sacred page, whose end is truth and whose illumination is "a lamp unto the feet" and "a light unto the path"[49] to eternal light? Would that thou mayst select this sacred page, would that thou mayst peruse this, would that "thou mayst bring this into thy chamber,"[50] that "the king may bring thee unto his"![51] Thou hast already ploughed closely this field of Holy Writ for the flowers of thy spring, in this thy summer "He expecteth thee to make grapes"; to the hurt of this do not marry another lest, in the time of harvest, "thou wilt make wild grapes."[52] I do not wish thee to be the bridegroom of Venus, but of Pallas.[53] She will adorn thee with precious jewels; she will clothe thee in a marriage garment.[54] These nuptials will boast Apollo[55] as the attendant; the Fescennine verses chanted there will be taught[56] by the married Stilbon to the cedars of Lebanon. Devoutly but fearfully have I conceived the hope of this solemn union, which I so greatly desire; for this reason have I planned this whole reading; to this end, the whole discourse, albeit slowly, will hasten. With the firmness of this dissuasion is armed the whole man of me, whose dart, hardened with many a point of steel, thou dost now feel.

The Conclusion of the foregoing Epistle

Hard is the hand of the surgeon, but healing. "Hard is this speech also,"[57] but healthy; and may thou find it as useful as it is devoted. My friend, thou protestest that I inflict upon thee a narrow rule of living. So be it! For "narrow is the way which leadeth to life,"[58] nor is the path plain by which men proceed to a plenitude of joys. Nay, even to attain to moderate pleasures we must pass through rough places. Jason heard that he must voyage through a sea that up to this time had not been deflowered by ships or oars and must make his way by sulphur-breathing bulls and by the post of a poisonous serpent to the golden fleece. Employing a counsel that was sound but not sweet, he departed, and returned bringing the desired treasure. Thus humility of mind accepteth the wormwood of surly truth; dutiful care doth fertilize it, and persistent service bringeth it to fruit. Thus Auster, the south wind, cup-bearer of the rains, bringeth up the seed, Aquilo (from the north), sweeper of the ways, strengtheneth it, Zephyr, the creator of flowers, advanceth it to a rich yield. Thus stern beginnings are rewarded with a sweet ending, thus a strait path leadeth to stately mansions; thus a narrow road windeth to the land of the living.[59] But, to support belief in my words by the testimony of the ancients, read the *Aureolus* ("Little Golden Book") of

Theophrastus[60] and the story of Jason's Medea, and thou wilt find almost nothing impossible to a woman.

The End of the foregoing Epistle

My friend, may the omnipotent God grant thee power not to be deceived by the deceit of the omnipotent female, and may He illuminate thy heart, that thou wilt not, with eyes bespelled, continue on the way I fear. But, that I may not seem to thee the author of *Orestes*,[61] farewell!

Notes

1   The thrustlecock.

2   Medieval commentators held that the cup of Circe was filled with sensual delights that metamorphose men into beasts in a moral sense. The antidote, the herb *moly* used by Ulysses, is wisdom, which is here being offered by Valerius. For Circe, see Ovid, *Metamorphoses*, 14:223ff.

3   The phrase should read "it goeth in pleasantly," which is a quotation from the passage in Prov. 23:31–34: "Look not upon the wine when it is yellow, when the color thereof shineth in the glass: *it goeth in pleasantly*, but, *in the end, it will bite like a snake* and will spread abroad poison like a basilisk. Thy eyes shall behold strange women and thy heart shall utter perverse things. And thou shalt be as one sleeping in the midst of the sea, and as a pilot when the stern (rudder) is lost." Walter uses the phrases in italics.

4   An echo of Ezech. 1:12.

5   See n. 3.

6   Vergil, *Eclogues*, 9:36. The story is told by Livy.

7   The chimera was a conventional symbol for lechery. One authority has it that the lionlike head represents the fierceness of passion, the goatlike body its consummation, and the serpentine tail the contrition that follows the illicit act.

8   The sirens were usually said to represent the three temptations before which Adam fell and which were overcome by Christ in the wilderness: gluttony, vainglory, and avarice. The first of these represents all the temptations of the flesh generalized under the term *gluttony*.

9   Horace, *Epistles*, 1:2, 23.

10   The flame of lechery—which is here in question, not simply the desire to marry—is a commonplace in both scriptural and classical sources.

11   1 Kings 13:14; Acts 13:22.

12   See 2 Kings 11.

13   The Vulgate reads *scandala*, and so does Map's text. See Matt. 8:7.

14   Cf. 3 Kings 11.

15   Cf. 3 Kings 19:18.

16   See Ovid, *Metamorphoses*, 6:122–124.

17   Cf. 4 Kings 19:16.

18   Heb. 4:12.

19   Cf. *The Didache*, 1:6.

20   *Metamorphoses*, 8:11ff.

21   *Metamorphoses*, 10:312ff.

22 *Metamorphoses*, 2:846ff.

23 *Metamorphoses*, 4:190ff.

24 Luke 11:35.

25 *Metamorphoses*, 4:167ff.

26 Vergil, *Eclogues*, 4:63.

27 See Lev. 11:3. Traditionally the cloven hoof is said to indicate figuratively the ability among men to distinguish between good and evil.

28 That is, the morally blind.

29 Paris, who preferred Venus to either Pallas or Juno. Commonly Pallas was said to represent wisdom, Juno worldly prosperity, and Venus the pleasure of the flesh. The foolishness of Paris in selecting Venus is stressed in both classical and medieval sources.

30 A not infrequent complaint on the part of medieval authors who wish their readers to pay attention to their *sententias*, or meaningful ideas, and not to the ornaments of speech. That is, one should follow Pallas in reading rather than Venus. The word *sententias* is used in the text here.

31 Horace, *Epistles*, 1:2, 42.

32 Juvenal, *Satires*, 10:168ff.

33 That is, without hearing. See Ps. 57:5-6.

34 That is, not at all. The word *dipsas*, which is the name for a serpent, means "thirst."

35 The story of Medea is told by Ovid in *Metamorphoses*, 7.

36 Cf. St. Augustine, *City of God*, 18:3. The story that follows, however, is not in this source.

37 3 Kings 2:2.

38 The thorns of this rose ordinarily are said to represent the compunction or penance that follows the act of Venus.

39 See Ovid, *Metamorphoses*, 9:138ff.

40 Martial, 4:18.

41 See Ovid, *Metamorphoses*, 4:610ff., or *Ars amatoria*, 3:415-416.

42 From St. Jerome's epistle *Against Jovinian*.

43 Deut. 32:13, a verse frequently used to defend the use of pagan literature.

44 E.g., see Apoc. 5:5; Ps. 21:7; Deut. 5:17-18. To understand these passages as Map understood them it is necessary to read them spiritually.

45 Rom. 10:14.

46 Gen. 3:21. The phrase "in human wise" is irrelevant and not in the text.

47 That is, like the men transformed by Circe.

48 Matt. 5:8.

49 Ps. 118:105.

50 Cf. Gen. 24:67.

51 Cant. 1:3.

52 Isa. 5:2.

53 This sentence expresses the theme of the epistle.

54 Cf. Isa. 61:10. Here the wisdom of Pallas becomes the Wisdom of God, or Christ.

55 That is, truth.

56 The allusion is to the first book of Martianus Capella, *On the Marriage of Mercury and Philology*.

57 John 6:61.

58 Matt. 7:14.

59 Ps. 26:13.

60 This work is included in St. Jerome's epistle *Against Jovinian*.

61 Juvenal, *Satires*, 1:6.

D. Geoffrey of Monmouth

Geoffrey of Monmouth, or Geoffrey, son of Arthur (ca. 1098–1155), first appears in our records as a witness to the foundation charter of Osney Abbey. He was probably a teacher in an Oxford school. In 1152 he was ordained priest and later in the same year consecrated Bishop of St. Asaph.

Geoffrey's works consist of The Prophesies of Merlin, *a poetic* Life of Merlin, *and the famous* History of the Kings of Britain, *which contains the earliest full account of King Arthur. Geoffrey tells us that he based his book on a British history given to him by Walter, Archdeacon of Oxford. However, it is clear that a great deal of his narrative is his own. The work was produced for the Norman aristocracy with two principal ends in view: (1) to supply a moral warning, somewhat similar to that supplied by Gildas albeit in a much more restrained manner, concerning the dangers of civil dissensions, divisions, and lack of steadfast purpose resulting from moral weakness in the commonwealth; and (2) to provide in the person of King Arthur a basis for British* pietas, *or, that is, a revered and powerful British hero whose virtues would be an inspiration and whose conquests would set a precedent for the greatness of England. As feudal rulers, the Normans in England were deeply interested in the traditions and customs of their new country. Arthur provided a great ruler in the British line to match Alfred in the Anglo-Saxon line. From the point of view of literary history Geoffrey is important as the fountainhead of Arthurian legend employed as a basis for patriotic inspiration. His most important immediate successors were Wace, whose* Brut *presents material from the* History *in French verse, and Lawman (or Layamon), who composed an English poem employing the same source.*

The first romance proper on Arthurian themes was the Erec *of Chrétien de Troyes, who was interested neither in advising the Norman English about civil dangers nor in fostering the cult of a British hero. It is probable that he used an Arthurian setting to indicate that he was writing fabulous narratives and that his careful involvement of Arthurian characters in a twelfth-century environment was not without a certain amount of humor. He did not, however, altogether neglect Geoffrey's themes.*

For a brief account of Geoffrey and his work, see John Jay Parry and Robert A. Caldwell, "Geoffrey of Monmouth," in R. S. Loomis, Arthurian Literature in the Middle Ages, *Clarendon Press, Oxford, 1959. There is an enormous amount of useful factual information in J. S. P. Tatlock,* The Legendary History of Britain, *The University of California Press, Berkeley, 1950. A stimulating but conjectural discussion appears in the introduction to Acton Griscom,* The Historia Regum Britanniae of Geoffrey of Monmouth, *Longmans Green & Co., Inc., New York, 1929. Some of the most interesting recent work having a bearing on Geoffrey appears in two essays by Christopher Brooke, "The Archbishops of St David's, Llandaff and Caerlon-on-Usk," in* Studies in the Early British Church, *edited by Nora K. Chadwick, Cambridge University Press, London, 1958; and "St. Peter of Gloucester and St. Cadoc of Llancarfan," in* Celt and Saxon, *edited by Nora K. Chadwick, Cambridge University Press, London, 1963.*

The following translation is that of J. A. Giles.

From
THE HISTORY OF THE KINGS OF BRITAIN

Book VIII

Chapter XIX   *Uther, Falling in Love with Igerna, Enjoys Her by the Assistance of Merlin's Magical Operations*

After this victory Uther repaired to the city of Alclud, where he settled the affairs of that province, and restored peace everywhere. He also made a progress round all the countries of the Scots, and tamed the fierceness of that rebellious people, by such a strict administration of justice, as none of his predecessors had exercised before: so that in his time offenders were everywhere under great terror, since they were sure of being punished without mercy. At last, when he had established peace in the northern provinces, he went to London, and commanded Octa and Eosa to be kept in prison there. The Easter following he ordered all the nobility of the kingdom to meet at that city, in order to celebrate that great festival; in honor of which he designed to wear his crown. The summons was everywhere obeyed, and there was a great concourse from all cities to celebrate the day. So the king observed the festival with great solemnity, as he had designed, and very joyfully entertained his nobility, of whom there was a very great muster, with their wives and daughters, suitably to the magnificence of the banquet prepared for them. And having been received with joy by the king, they also expressed the same in their deportment before him. Among the rest was present Gorlois, duke of Cornwall, with his wife Igerna, the greatest beauty in all Britain. No sooner had the king cast his eyes upon her among the rest of the ladies, than he fell passionately in love with her, and little regarding the rest, made her the subject of all his thoughts. She was the only lady that he continually served with fresh dishes, and to whom he sent golden cups by his confidants; on her he bestowed all his smiles, and to her addressed all his discourse. The husband, discovering this, fell into a great rage, and retired from the court without taking leave: nor was there any body that could stop him, while he was under fear of losing the chief object of his delight. Uther, therefore, in great wrath commanded him to return back to court, to make him satisfaction for this affront.

But Gorlois refused to obey; upon which the king was highly incensed, and swore he would destroy his country, if he did not speedily compound for his offense. Accordingly, without delay, while their anger was hot against each other, the king got together a great army, and marched into Cornwall, the cities and towns whereof he set on fire. But Gorlois durst not engage with him, on account of the inferiority of his numbers; and thought it a wiser course to fortify his towns, till he could get succor from Ireland. And as he was under more concern for his wife than himself, he put her into the town of Tintagel, upon the seashore, which he looked upon as a place of great safety. But he himself entered the castle of Dimilioc, to prevent their being both at once involved in the same danger, if any should happen. The king, informed of this, went to the town where Gorlois was, which he besieged, and shut up all the avenues to it. A whole week was now past, when, retaining in mind his love to Igerna, he said to one of his confidants, named Ulfin de Ricaradoch: "My passion for Igerna is such, that I can neither have ease of mind, nor health of body, till I obtain her: and if you cannot assist me with your advice how to accomplish my desire, the inward torments I endure will kill me." "Who can advise you in this matter," said Ulfin, "when no force will enable us to have access to her in the town of Tintagel? For it is situated upon the sea, and on every side surrounded by it; and there is but one entrance into it, and that through a straight rock, which three men shall be able to defend against the whole power of the kingdom. Notwithstanding, if the prophet Merlin would in earnest set about this attempt, I am of opinion, you might with his advice obtain your wishes." The king readily believed what he was so well inclined to, and ordered Merlin, who was also come to the siege, to be called. Merlin, therefore, being introduced into the king's presence, was commanded to give his advice, how the king might accomplish his desire with respect to Igerna. And he, finding the great anguish of the king, was moved by such excessive love, and said, "To accomplish your desire, you must make use of such arts as have not been heard of in your time. I know how, by the force of my medicines, to give you the exact likeness of Gorlois, so that in all respects you shall seem to be no other than himself. If you will therefore obey my prescriptions, I will metamorphose you into the true semblance of Gorlois, and Ulfin into Jordan of Tintagel, his familiar friend; and I myself, being transformed into another shape, will make the third in the adventure; and in this disguise you may go safely to the town where Igerna is, and have admittance to her." The king complied with the proposal, and acted with great caution in this affair; and when he had committed the care of the siege to his intimate friends, underwent the medical applications of Merlin, by whom he was transformed into the likeness of Gorlois; as was Ulfin also into Jordan, and Merlin himself into Bricel; so that nobody could see any remains now of their former likeness. They then set forward on their way to Tintagel, at which they arrived in the evening twilight, and forthwith signified to the porter, that the consul was come; upon which the gates were opened, and the men let in. For what room could there be for suspicion, when Gorlois himself seemed to be there present? The king therefore stayed that night with Igerna, and had the full enjoyment of her, for she was deceived with the false disguise which he had put on, and the artful and amorous discourses wherewith he entertained her. He told her he had left his own place besieged, purely to provide for the safety of her dear self, and the town she was in; so that believing all that he said, she refused him nothing which he desired. The same night therefore she conceived of the most renowned Arthur, whose heroic and wonderful actions have justly rendered his name famous to posterity.

Chapter XX   Gorlois Being Killed, Uther Marries Igerna

In the meantime, as soon as the king's absence was discovered at the siege, his army unadvisedly made an assault upon the walls, and provoked the besieged count to a battle; who himself also, acting as inconsiderately as they, sallied forth with his men, thinking with such a small handful to oppose a powerful army; but happened to be killed in the very first brunt of the fight, and had all his men routed. The town also was taken; but all the riches of it were not shared equally among the besiegers, but every one greedily took what he could get, according as fortune or his own strength favored him. After this bold attempt, came messengers to Igerna, with the news both of the duke's death, and of the event of the siege. But when they saw the king in the likeness of the consul, sitting close by her, they were struck with shame and astonishment at his safe arrival there, whom they had left dead at the siege; for they were wholly ignorant of the miracles which Merlin had wrought with his medicines. The king therefore smiled at the news, and embracing the countess, said to her: "Your own eyes may convince you that I am not dead, but alive. But notwithstanding, the destruction of the town, and the slaughter of my men, is what very much grieves me; so that there is reason to fear the king's coming upon us, and taking us in this place. To prevent which, I will go out to meet him, and make my peace with him, for fear of a worse disaster." Accordingly, as soon as he was out of the town, he went to his army, and having put off the disguise of Gorlois, was now Uther Pendragon again. When he had a full relation made to him how matters had succeeded, he was sorry for the death of Gorlois, but rejoiced that Igerna was now at liberty to marry again. Then he returned to the town of Tintagel, which he took, and in it, what he impatiently wished for, Igerna herself. After this they continued to live together with much affection for each other, and had a son and daughter, whose names were Arthur and Anne.

Book IX

Chapter I   Arthur Succeeds Uther His Father in the Kingdom of Britain, and Besieges Colgrin

Uther Pendragon being dead, the nobility from several provinces assembled together at Silchester, and proposed to Dubricius, archbishop of Legions,[1] that he should consecrate Arthur, Uther's son, to be their king. For they were now in great straits, because, upon hearing of the king's death, the Saxons had invited over their countrymen from Germany, and, under the command of Colgrin, were attempting to exterminate the whole British race. They had also entirely subdued all that part of the island which extends from the Humber to the sea of Caithness. Dubricius, therefore, grieving for the calamities of his country, in conjunction with the other bishops, set the crown upon Arthur's head. Arthur was then fifteen years old, but a youth of such unparalleled courage and generosity, joined with that sweetness of temper and innate goodness, as gained him universal love. When his coronation was over, he, according to usual custom, showed his bounty and munificence to the people. And such a number of soldiers flocked to him upon it, that his treasury was not able to answer that vast expense. But such a spirit of generosity, joined with valor, can never long want means to support itself. Arthur, therefore, the better to keep up his munificence, resolved to make use of his courage, and to fall upon the Saxons, that he might enrich his followers with their wealth. To this he was also moved by the justice of the cause, since the entire monarchy of Britain belonged to him by hereditary right. Hereupon assembling the youth under his command, he marched to York, of which, when Colgrin had intelligence, he met him with a very great army, composed of Saxons, Scots, and Picts, by the river Duglas; where a battle happened, with the loss of the greater part of both armies. Notwithstanding, the victory fell to Arthur, who pursued Colgrin to York, and there besieged him. Baldulph, upon the news of his brother's flight, went towards the siege with a body of six thousand men, to his relief; for at the time of the battle he was upon the sea-coast, waiting the arrival of duke Cheldric with succors from Germany. And being now no more than ten miles distant from the city, his purpose was to make a speedy march in the night-time, and fall upon the enemy by way of surprise. But Arthur, having intelligence of his design, sent a detachment of six hundred horse, and three thousand foot, under the command of Cador, duke of Cornwall, to meet him the same night. Cador, therefore, falling into the same road along which the enemy was passing, made a sudden assault upon them, and entirely defeated the Saxons, and put them to flight. Baldulph was excessively grieved at this disappointment in the relief which he intended for his brother, and began to think of some other stratagem to gain access to him; in which if he could but succeed, he thought they might concert measures together for their safety. And since he had no other way for it, he shaved his head and beard, and put on the habit of a jester with a harp, and in this disguise walked up and down in the camp, playing upon his instrument as if he had been a harper. He thus passed unsuspected, and by a little and little went up to the walls of the city, where he was at last discovered by the besieged, who thereupon drew him up with cords, and conducted him to his brother. At this unexpected, though much desired meeting, they spent some time in joyfully embracing each other, and then began to consider various stratagems for their delivery. At last, just as they were considering their case desperate, the ambassadors returned from Germany, and brought with them to Albania a fleet of six hundred

sail, laden with brave soldiers, under the command of Cheldric. Upon this news, Arthur was dissuaded by his council from continuing the siege any longer, for fear of hazarding a battle with so powerful and numerous an army.

Chapter II   Hoel Sends Fifteen Thousand Men to Arthur's Assistance

Arthur complied with their advice, and made his retreat to London, where he called an assembly of all the clergy and nobility of the kingdom, to ask their advice, what course to take against the formidable power of the pagans. After some deliberation, it was agreed that ambassadors should be despatched into Armorica, to king Hoel, to represent to him the calamitous state of Britain. Hoel was the son of Arthur's sister by Dubricius, king of the Armorican Britons; so that, upon advice of the disturbances his uncle was threatened with, he ordered his fleet to be got ready, and, having assembled fifteen thousand men, he arrived with the first fair wind at Hamo's Port,[2] and was received with all suitable honor by Arthur, and most affectionately embraced by him.

Chapter III   Arthur Makes the Saxons His Tributaries

After a few days they went to relieve the city Kaerliudcoit,[3] that was besieged by the pagans; which being situated upon a mountain, between two rivers in the province of Lindisia, is called by another name Lindocolinum. As soon as they arrived there with all their forces, they fought with the Saxons, and made a grievous slaughter of them, to the number of six thousand; part of whom were drowned in the rivers, part fell by the hands of the Britons. The rest in a great consternation quitted the siege and fled, but were closely pursued by Arthur, till they came to the wood of Celidon, where they endeavored to form themselves into a body again, and make a stand. And here they again joined battle with the Britons, and made a brave defense, whilst the trees that were in the place secured them against the enemies' arrows. Arthur, seeing this, commanded the trees that were in that part of the wood to be cut down, and the trunks to be placed quite round them, so as to hinder their getting out; resolving to keep them pent up here till he could reduce them by famine. He then commanded his troops to besiege the wood, and continued three days in that place. The Saxons, having now no provisions to sustain them, and being just ready to starve with hunger, begged for leave to go out; in consideration whereof they offered to leave all their gold and silver behind them, and return back to Germany with nothing but their empty ships. They promised also that they would pay him tribute from Germany, and leave hostages with him. Arthur, after consultation, about it, granted their petition; allowing them only leave to depart, and retaining all their treasures, as also hostages for payment of the tribute. But as they were under sail on their return home, they repented of their bargain, and tacked about again towards Britain, and went on shore at Totness.[4] No sooner were they landed, than they made an utter devastation of the country as far as the Severn sea, and put all the peasants to the sword. From thence they pursued their furious march to the town of Bath, and laid siege to it. When the king had intelligence of it, he was beyond measure surprised at their proceedings, and immediately gave orders for the execution of the hostages. And desisting from an attempt which he had entered upon to reduce the Scots and Picts, he marched with the utmost expedition to raise the siege; but labored under very great difficulties, because he had left his nephew Hoel sick at Alclud.[5] At length, having entered the province of Somerset, and beheld how the siege was carried on, he addressed himself to his followers in these words: "Since these impious and detestable Saxons have disdained to keep faith with me, I, to keep faith with God, will endeavor to revenge the blood of my countrymen this day upon them. To arms, soldiers, to arms, and courageously fall upon the perfidious wretches, over whom we shall, with Christ assisting us, undoubtedly obtain the victory."

Chapter IV   Dubricius's Speech Against the Treacherous Saxons. Arthur with His Own Hand Kills Four Hundred and Seventy Saxons in One Battle. Colgrin and Baldulph Are Killed in the Same

When he had done speaking, St. Dubricius, archbishop of Legions, going to the top of a hill, cried out with a loud voice, "You that have the honor to profess the Christian faith, keep fixed in your minds the love which you owe to your country and fellow subjects, whose sufferings by the treachery of the pagans will be an ever-

lasting reproach to you, if you do not courageously defend them. It is your country which you fight for, and for which you should, when required, voluntarily suffer death; for that itself is victory and the cure of the soul. For he that shall die for his brethren, offers himself a living sacrifice to God, and has Christ for his example, who condescended to lay down his life for his brethren. If therefore any of you shall be killed in this war, that death itself, which is suffered in so glorious a cause, shall be to him for penance and absolution of all his sins."[6] At these words, all of them, encouraged with the benediction of the holy prelate, instantly armed themselves, and prepared to obey his orders. Also Arthur himself, having put on a coat of mail suitable to the grandeur of so powerful a king, placed a golden helmet upon his head, on which was engraven the figure of a dragon; and on his shoulders his shield called Priwen[7]; upon which the picture of the blessed Mary, mother of God, was painted, in order to put him frequently in mind of her. Then girding on his Caliburn, which was an excellent sword made in the isle of Avallon,[8] he graced his right hand with his lance, named Ron,[9] which was hard, broad, and fit for slaughter. After this, having placed his men in order, he boldly attacked the Saxons, who were drawn out in the shape of a wedge, as their manner was. And they, notwithstanding that the Britons fought with great eagerness, made a noble defense all that day; but at length, towards sunsetting, climbed up the next mountain, which served them for a camp: for they desired no larger extent of ground, since they confided very much in their numbers. The next morning Arthur, with his army, went up the mountain, but lost many of his men in the ascent, by the advantage which the Saxons had in their station on the top, from whence they could pour down upon him with much greater speed, than he was able to advance against them. Notwithstanding, after a very hard struggle, the Britons gained the summit of the hill, and quickly came to a close engagement with the enemy, who again gave them a warm reception, and made a vigorous defense. In this manner was a great part of that day also spent; whereupon Arthur, provoked to see the little advantage he had yet gained, and that victory still continued in suspense, drew out his Caliburn, and, calling upon the name of the blessed Virgin, rushed forward with great fury into the thickest of the enemy's ranks; of whom (such was the merit of his prayers) not one escaped alive that felt the fury of his sword; neither did he give over the fury of his assault until he had, with his Caliburn alone, killed four hundred and seventy men. The Britons, seeing this, followed their leader in great multitudes, and made slaughter on all sides; so that Colgrin, and Baldulph his brother, and many thousands more, fell before them. But Cheldric, in this imminent danger of his men, betook himself to flight.

Chapter V   The Saxons, After Their Leader Cheldric Was Killed, Are All Compelled by Cador to Surrender

The victory being thus gained, the king commanded Cador, duke of Cornwall, to pursue them, while he himself should hasten his march into Albania: from whence he had advice that the Scots and Picts were besieging Alclud, in which, as we said before, Hoel lay sick. Therefore he hastened to his assistance, for fear he might fall into the hands of the barbarians. In the meantime the duke of Cornwall, who had the command of ten thousand men, would not as yet pursue the Saxons in their flight, but speedily made himself master of their ships, to hinder their getting on board, and manned them with his best soldiers, who were to beat back the pagans in case they should flee thither: after this he hastily pursued the enemy, according to Arthur's command, and allowed no quarter to those he could overtake. So that they whose behavior before was so cruel and insolent, now with timorous hearts fled for shelter, sometimes to the coverts of the woods, sometimes to mountains and caves, to prolong a wretched life. At last, when none of these places could afford them a safe retreat, they entered the Isle of Thanet with their broken forces; but neither did they there get free from the duke of Cornwall's pursuit, for he still continued slaughtering them, and gave them no respite till he had killed Cheldric, and taken hostages for the surrender of the rest.

Chapter VI   Arthur Grants a Pardon to the Scots and Picts, Besieged at the Lake Lumond

Having therefore settled peace here, he directed his march to Alclud, which Arthur had relieved from the oppression of barbarians, and from thence conducted his army to Mureif, where the Scots and Picts were besieged; after three several battles with the king and his nephew, they had fled as far as this province, and entering upon the lake Lumond, sought for refuge in the islands that are upon it. This lake contains sixty islands, and receives sixty rivers into it which empty themselves into the sea by no more than one mouth. There is also an equal number of rocks in these islands, as also of eagles' nests in those rocks, which flocked together there every year, and, by the loud and general noise which they now made, foreboded some remarkable event that should happen to the kingdom. To these islands, therefore, had the enemy fled, thinking the lake would serve them instead of a fortification; but it proved of little advantage to them. For Arthur, having got together a fleet, sailed round the rivers, and besieged the enemy fifteen days together, by which they were so straitened with hunger, that they died by thousands. While he was harassing them in this manner Guillamurius, king of Ireland, came up in a fleet with a very great army of barbarians, in order to relieve the besieged. This obliged Arthur to raise the siege, and turn his arms against the Irish, whom he slew without mercy, and compelled the rest to return back to their country. After this victory, he proceeded in his first attempt, which was to extirpate the whole race of the Scots and Picts, and treated them with an unparalleled severity. And as he allowed quarter to none, the bishops of that miserable country, with all the inferior clergy, met together, and bearing the reliques of the saints and other consecrated things of the church before them, barefooted, came to implore the king's mercy for their people. As soon as they were admitted into his presence, they fell down upon their knees, and humbly besought him to have pity on their distressed country, since the sufferings which he had already made it undergo, were sufficient; nor was there any necessity to cut off the small remainder to a man; and that he would allow them the enjoyment of a small part of the country, since they were willing to bear the yoke which he should impose upon them. The king was moved at the manner of their delivering this petition, and could not forbear expressing his clemency to them with tears; and at the request of those holy men, granted them pardon.

Chapter VII   Arthur Relates the Wonderful Nature of Some Ponds

This affair being concluded, Hoel had the curiosity to view the situation of the lake, and wondered to find the number of the rivers, islands, rocks, and eagles' nests, so exactly correspond: and while he was reflecting upon it as something that appeared miraculous, Arthur came to him, and told him of another pond in the same province, which was yet more wonderful. For not far from thence was one whose length and breadth were each twenty feet, and depth five feet. But whether its square figure was natural or artificial, the wonder of it was, there were four different sorts of fishes in the four several corners of it, none of which were ever found in any other part of the pond but their own. He told him likewise of another pond in Wales, near the Severn, called by the country people Linligwan, into which when the sea flows, it receives it in the manner of a gulf, but so as to swallow up the tide, and never be filled, or have its banks covered by it. But at the ebbing of the sea, it throws out the waters which it had swallowed, as high as a mountain, and at last dashes and covers the banks with them. In the meantime, if all the people of that country should stand near with their faces toward it, and happened to have their clothes sprinkled with the dashing of the waves, they would hardly, if at all, escape being swallowed up by the pond. But with their backs towards it, they need not fear being dashed, though they stood upon the very banks.

Chapter VIII   Arthur Restores York to Its Ancient Beauty, Especially as to Its Churches

The king, after his general pardon granted to the Scots, went to York to celebrate the feast of Christ's nativity, which was now at hand. On entering the city, he beheld with grief the desolation of the churches; for upon the expulsion of the holy Archbishop Sanxo, and of all the clergy there, the temples which were half burned down, had no longer divine service performed in them: so much had the impious rage of the pagans prevailed. After this, in an assembly of the clergy and people, he appointed Pyramus his chaplain metropolitan of that see. The churches that lay level with the ground, he rebuilt, and (which was their chief ornament) saw them filled with assemblies of devout persons of both sexes. Also the nobility that were driven out by the disturbances of the Saxons, he restored to their country.

Chapter IX   Arthur Honors Angusel with the Scepter of the Scots; Urian with That of Mureif; and Lot with the Consulship of Londonesia

There were there three brothers of royal blood, viz. Lot, Urian, and Angusel, who, before the Saxons had

prevailed, held the government of those parts. Being willing therefore to bestow on these, as he did on others, the rights of their ancestors, he restored to Angusel the sovereignty over the Scots; his brother Urian he honored with the scepter of Mureif [10]; and Lot, who in time of Aurelius Ambrosius had married his sister, by whom he had two sons, Walgan and Modred, he reestablished in the consulship of Londonesia, and the other provinces belonging to him. At length, when the whole country was reduced by him to its ancient state, he took to wife Guanhumara,[11] descended from a noble family of Romans, who was educated under duke Cador, and in beauty surpassed all the women of the island.

Chapter X   Arthur Adds to His Government Ireland, Iceland, Gothland, and the Orkneys

The next summer he fitted out a fleet, and made an expedition into Ireland, which he was desirous to reduce. Upon landing there, he was met by king Guillamurius before mentioned, with a vast number of men, who came with a design to fight him; but at the very beginning of the battle, those naked and unarmed people were miserably routed, and fled to such places as lay open to them for shelter. Guillamurius also in a short time was taken prisoner, and forced to submit; as were also all the other princes of the country after the king's example, being under great consternation at what had happened. After an entire conquest of Ireland, he made a voyage with his fleet to Iceland, which he also subdued. And now a rumor spreading over the rest of the islands, that no country was able to withstand him, Doldavius, king of Gothland, and Gunfasius, king of the Orkneys, came voluntarily, and made their submission, on a promise of paying tribute. Then, as soon as winter was over, he returned back to Britain, where having established the kingdom, he resided in it for twelve years together in peace.

Chapter XI   Arthur Subdues Norway, Dacia, Aquitaine, and Gaul

After this, having invited over to him all persons whatsoever that were famous for valor in foreign nations, he began to augment the number of his domestics, and introduced such politeness into his court, as people of the remotest countries thought worthy of their imitation. So that there was not a nobleman who thought himself of any consideration, unless his clothes and arms were made in the same fashion as those of Arthur's knights. At length the fame of his munificence and valor spreading over the whole world, he became a terror to the kings of other countries, who grievously feared the loss of their dominions, if he should make any attempt upon them. Being much perplexed with these anxious cares, they repaired their cities and towers, and built towns in convenient places, the better to fortify themselves against any enterprise of Arthur, when occasion should require. Arthur, being informed of what they were doing, was delighted to find how much they stood in awe of him, and formed a design for the conquest of all Europe. Then having prepared his fleet, he first attempted Norway, that he might procure the crown of it for Lot, his sister's husband. This Lot was the nephew of Sichelin, king of the Norwegians, who being then dead, had appointed him his successor in the kingdom. But the Norwegians, disdaining to receive him, had advanced one Riculf to the sovereignty, and having fortified their cities, thought they were able to oppose Arthur. Walgan,[12] the son of Lot, was then a youth twelve years old, and was recommended by his uncle to the service of pope Supplicius, from whom he received arms. But to return to the history: as soon as Arthur arrived on the coast of Norway, king Riculf, attended with the whole power of that kingdom, met him, and gave him battle, in which, after a great loss of blood on both sides, the Britons at length had the advantage, and making a vigorous charge, killed Riculf and many others with him. Having thus defeated them, they set the cities on fire, dispersed the country people, and pursued the victory till they had reduced all Norway, as also Dacia, under the dominion of Arthur. After the conquest of these countries, and establishment of Lot upon the throne of Norway, Arthur made a voyage to Gaul, and dividing his army into several bodies, began to lay waste that country on all sides. The province of Gaul was then committed to Flollo, a Roman tribune, who held the government of it under the emperor Leo. Upon intelligence of Arthur's coming, he raised all the forces that were under his command, and made war against him, but without success. For Arthur was attended with the youth of all the islands that he had subdued; for which reason he was reported to have such an army as was thought invincible. And even the greater part of the Gallic army, encouraged by his bounty, came over to his service. Therefore Flollo, seeing the disadvantages he lay under, left his camp, and fled with a small number to Paris. There having recruited his army, he fortified the city, and resolved to stand another engagement with Arthur. But while he was thinking of strengthening himself with auxiliary forces in the neighboring countries, Arthur came upon him unawares, and besieged him in the city. When a month had passed, Flollo, with grief observing his people perish with hunger, sent a message to Arthur, that they two alone should decide the conquest for the kingdom in a duel: for being a person of great stature, boldness and courage, he gave this challenge in confidence of success. Arthur was extremely pleased at Flollo's proposal, and sent him word back again, that he would give him the meeting which he desired. A treaty, therefore, being on both sides agreed to, they met together in the island without the city, where the people waited to see the event. They were both gracefully armed, and mounted on admirably swift horses; and it was hard to tell which gave greater hopes of victory. When they had presented themselves against each other with their lances aloft, they put spurs to their horses, and began a fierce encounter. But Arthur, who handled his lance more warily, struck it into the upper part of Flollo's breast, and avoiding his enemy's weapon, laid him prostrate upon the ground, and was just going to despatch him with his drawn sword, when Flollo, starting up on a sudden, met him with his lance couched, wherewith he mortally stabbed the breast of Arthur's horse, and caused both him and his rider to fall. The Britons, when they saw their king lying on the ground, fearing he was killed, could hardly be restrained from breach of covenant, and falling with one consent upon the Gauls. But just as they were upon rushing into the lists, Arthur hastily got up, and guarding himself with his shield, advanced with speed against Flollo. And now they renewed the assault with great rage, eagerly bent upon one another's destruction. At length Flollo, watching his advantage, gave Arthur a blow upon the forehead, which might have proved mortal, had he not blunted the edge of his weapon against the helmet. When Arthur saw his coat of mail and shield red with blood, he was inflamed with still greater rage, and lifting up his Caliburn with his utmost strength struck it through the helmet into Flollo's head, and made a terrible gash. With this wound Flollo fell down, tearing the ground with his spurs, and expired. As soon as this news was spread through the army, the citizens ran together, and opening the gates, surrendered the city to Arthur. After the victory, he divided his army into two parts; one of which he committed to the conduct of Hoel, whom he ordered to march against Guitard, commander of the Pictavians[13]; while he with the other part should endeavor to reduce the other provinces. Hoel upon this entered Aquitaine, possessed himself of the cities of that country, and after distressing Guitard in several battles, forced him to surrender. He also destroyed Gascony with fire and sword, and subdued the princes of it. At the end of nine years, in which time all the parts of Gaul were entirely reduced, Arthur returned back to Paris, where he kept his court, and calling an assembly of the clergy and people, established peace and the just administration of the laws in that kingdom. Then he bestowed Neustria, now called Normandy, upon Bedver, his butler; the province of Andegavia[14] upon Caius,[15] his sewer;[16] and several other provinces upon his great men that attended him. Thus having settled the peace of the cities and countries there, he returned back in the beginning of spring to Britain.

Chapter XII   Arthur Summons a Great Many Kings, Princes, Archbishops, to a Solemn Assembly at the City of Legions

Upon the approach of the feast of Pentecost, Arthur, the better to demonstrate his joy after such triumphant success, and for the more solemn observation of that festival, and reconciling the minds of the princes that were now subject to him, resolved, during that season, to hold a magnificent court, to place the crown upon his head, and to invite all the kings and dukes under his subjection, to the solemnity. And when he had communicated his design to his familiar friends, he pitched upon the City of Legions as a proper place for his purpose. For besides its great wealth above the other cities, its situation, which was in Glamorganshire upon the river Uske, near the Severn sea, was most pleasant, and fit for so great a solemnity. For on one side it was washed by that noble river, so that the kings and princes from the countries beyond the seas might have the convenience of sailing up to it. On the other side, the beauty of the meadows and groves, and magnificence of the royal palaces with lofty gilded roofs that adorned it,

made it even rival the grandeur of Rome. It was also famous for two churches; whereof one was built in honor of the Martyr Julius, and adorned with a choir of virgins, who had devoted themselves wholly to the service of God; but the other, which was founded in memory of St. Aaron, his companion, and maintained a convent of canons, was the third metropolitan church of Britain. Besides, there was a college of two hundred philosophers, who, being learned in astronomy and the other arts, were diligent in observing the courses of the stars, and gave Arthur true predictions of the events that would happen at that time. In this place, therefore, which afforded such delights, were preparations made for the ensuing festival. Ambassadors were then sent into several kingdoms, to invite to court the princes both of Gaul and all the adjacent islands. Accordingly there came Angusel, king of Albania, now Scotland; Urian, king of Mureif; Cadwallo Lewirh, king of the Venedotians, now called the North Wales men; Sater, king of the Demetians, or South Wales men; Cador, king of Cornwall; also the archbishops of the three metropolitan sees, London, York, and Dubricius of the City of Legions. This prelate, who was primate of Britain, and legate of the apostolical see, was so eminent for his piety, that he could cure any sick person by his prayers. There came also the consuls of the principal cities, viz. Morvid, consul of Gloucester; Mauron, of Worcester; Anaraut, of Salisbury; Arthgal, of Cargueit or Warguit; Jugein, of Legecester; Cursalen, of Kaicester; Kinmare, duke of Dorobernia; Galluc, of Salisbury; Urgennius, of Bath; Jonathal, of Dorchester; Boso, of Ridoc, that is, Oxford. Besides the consuls, came the following worthies of no less dignity: Danaut, Map papo; Cheneus, Map coil; Peredur, Mab eridur; Guiful, Map Nogoit; Regin, Map claut; Eddelein, Map cledauc; Kincar, Mab bagan; Kimmare; Gorboroniam, Map goit; Clofaut, Rupmaneton; Kimbelim, Map trunat; Cathleus, Map catel; Kinlich, Map neton; and many others too tedious to enumerate. From the adjacent islands came Guillamurius, king of Ireland; Mulvasius, king of Iceland; Doldavius, king of Gothland; Gunfasius, king of the Orkneys; Lot, king of Norway; Aschillius, king of the Dacians. From the parts beyond the seas, came Holdin, king of Ruteni; Leodegarius, consul of Bolonia; Bedver, the butler, duke of Normandy; Borellus, of Cenomania; Caius, the sewer, duke of Andegavia; Guitard, of Pictavia; also the twelve peers of Gaul, whom Guerinus Carnotensis brought along with him: Hoel, duke of the Armorican Britons, and his nobility, who came with such a train of mules, horses, and rich furniture, as it is difficult to describe. Besides these, there remained no prince of any consideration on this side of Spain, who came not upon this invitation. And no wonder, when Arthur's munificence, which was celebrated over the whole world, made him beloved by all people.

Chapter XIII A Description of the Royal Pomp at the Coronation of Arthur

When all were assembled together in the city, upon the day of the solemnity, the archbishops were conducted to the palace, in order to place the crown upon the king's head. Therefore Dubricius, inasmuch as the court was kept in his diocese, made himself ready to celebrate the office, and undertook the ordering of whatever related to it. As soon as the king was invested with his royal habiliments, he was conducted in great pomp to the metropolitan church, supported on each side by two archbishops, and having four kings, viz. of Albania, Cornwall, Demetia, and Venedotia, whose right it was, bearing four golden swords before him. He was also attended with a concert of all sorts of music, which made most excellent harmony. On another part was the queen, dressed out in her richest ornaments, conducted by the archbishops and bishops to the Temple of Virgins; the four queens also of the kings last mentioned, bearing before her four white doves according to ancient custom; and after her there followed a retinue of women, making all imaginable demonstrations of joy. When the whole procession was ended, so transporting was the harmony of the musical instruments and voices, whereof there was a vast variety in both churches, that the knights who attended were in doubt which to prefer, and therefore crowded from the one to the other by turns, and were far from being tired with the solemnity, though the whole day had been spent in it.[17] At last, when divine service was over at both churches, the king and queen put off their crowns, and putting on their lighter ornaments, went to the banquet; he to one palace with the men, and she to another with the women. For the Britons still observed the ancient custom of Troy, by which the men and women used to celebrate their festivals apart. When they had all taken their seats according to precedence,

Caius the scwer, in rich robes of ermine, with a thousand young noblemen, all in like manner clothed with ermine, served up the dishes. From another part, Bedver the butler was followed with the same number of attendants, in various habits, who waited with all kinds of cups and drinking vessels. In the queen's palace were innumerable waiters, dressed with variety of ornaments, all performing their respective offices; which if I should describe particularly, I should draw out the history to a tedious length. For at that time Britain had arrived at such a pitch of grandeur, that in abundance of riches, luxury of ornaments, and politeness of inhabitants, it far surpassed all other kingdoms. The knights in it that were famous for feats of chivalry, wore their clothes and arms all of the same color and fashion: and the women also no less celebrated for their wit, wore all the same kind of apparel; and esteemed none worthy of their love, but such as had given a proof of their valor in three several battles. Thus was the valor of the men an encouragement for the women's chastity, and the love of the women a spur to the soldier's bravery.

Chapter XIV After a Variety of Sports at the Coronation, Arthur Amply Rewards His Servants

As soon as the banquets were over, they went into the fields without the city, to divert themselves with various sports. The military men composed a kind of diversion in imitation of a fight on horseback; and the ladies, placed on the top of the walls as spectators, in a sportive manner darted their amorous glances at the courtiers, the more to encourage them. Others spent the remainder of the day in other diversions, such as shooting with bows and arrows, tossing the pike, casting of heavy stones and rocks, playing at dice and the like, and all these inoffensively and without quarrelling. Whoever gained the victory in any of these sports, was rewarded with a rich prize by Arthur. In this manner were the first three days spent; and on the fourth, all who, upon account of their titles, bore any kind of office at this solemnity, were called together to receive honors and preferments in reward of their services, and to fill up the vacancies in the governments of cities and castles, archbishoprics, bishoprics, abbeys, and other posts of honor.

Chapter XV   A Letter from Lucius Tiberius, General of the Romans, to Arthur Being Read, They Consult about an Answer to It

But St. Dubricius, from a pious desire of leading a hermit's life, made a voluntary resignation of his archiepiscopal dignity; and in his room was consecrated David, the king's uncle, whose life was a perfect example of that goodness which by his doctrine he taught. In place of St. Samson, archbishop of Dole, was appointed, with the consent of Hoel, king of the Armorican Britons, Chelianus, [Kilian] a priest of Llandaff, a person highly recommended for his good life and character. The bishopric of Silchester was conferred upon Mauganius, that of Winchester upon Diwanius, and that of Alclud upon Eledanius. While he was disposing of these preferments upon them, it happened that twelve men of an advanced age, and venerable aspect, and bearing olive branches in their right hands, for a token that they were come upon an embassy, appeared before the king, moving towards him with a slow pace, and speaking with a soft voice; and after their compliments paid, presented him with a letter from Lucius Tiberius, in these words:—

"Lucius, procurator of the commonwealth, to Arthur, king of Britain, according to his desert. The insolence of your tyranny is what fills me with the highest admiration, and the injuries you have done to Rome still increase my wonder. But it is provoking to reflect, that you are grown so much above yourself, as wilfully to avoid seeing this: nor do you consider what it is to have offended by unjust deeds a senate, to whom you cannot be ignorant the whole world owes vassalage. For the tribute of Britain, which the senate had enjoined you to pay, and which used to be paid to the Roman emperors successively from the time of Julius Cæsar, you have had the presumption to withhold, in contempt of their imperial authority. You have seized upon the province of the Allobroges, and all the islands of the ocean, whose kings, while the Roman power prevailed in those parts, paid tribute to our ancestors. And because the senate have decreed to demand justice of you for such repeated injuries, I command you to appear at Rome before the middle of August the next year, there to make satisfaction to your masters, and undergo such sentence as they shall in justice pass upon you. Which if you refuse to do, I shall come to you, and endeavor to recover with my sword, what you in your madness have robbed us of."

As soon as the letter was read in the presence of the kings and consuls, Arthur withdrew with them into the Giant's Tower, which was at the entrance of the palace, to think what answer was fit to be returned to such an insolent message. As they were going up the stairs, Cador, duke of Cornwall, who was a man of a merry disposition, said to the king in a jocose manner: "I have been till now under fear, lest the easy life which the Britons lead, by enjoying a long peace, might make them cowards, and extinguish the fame of their gallantry, by which they have raised their name above all other nations. For where the exercise of arms is wanting, and the pleasures of women, dice, and other diversions take place, no doubt, what remains of virtue, honor, courage, and thirst of praise, will be tainted with the rust of idleness. For now almost five years have passed, since we have been abandoned to these delights, and have had no exercise of war. Therefore, to deliver us from sloth, God has stirred up this spirit of the Romans, to restore our military virtues to their ancient state." In this manner did he entertain them with discourse, till they were come to their seats, on which when they were all placed, Arthur spoke to them after this manner.

Chapter XVI   Arthur, Holding a Council with the Kings, Desires Every One of Them to Deliver Their Opinions

"My companions both in good and bad fortune, whose abilities both in counsel and war I have hitherto experienced; the present exigence of affairs, after the message which we have received, requires your careful deliberation and prudent resolutions; for whatever is wisely concerted, is easily executed. Therefore we shall be the better able to bear the annoyance which Lucius threatens to give us, if we unanimously apply ourselves to consider how to overcome it. In my opinion we have no great reason to fear him, when we reflect upon the unjust pretence on which he demands tribute of us. He says he has a right to it, because it was paid to Julius Cæsar, and his successors, who invaded Britain with an army at the invitation of the ancient Britons, when they were quarrelling among themselves, and by force reduced the country under their power, when weakened by civil dissension. And because they gained it in this manner, they had the injustice to take tribute of it.

For that can never be possessed justly, which is gained by force and violence. So that he has no reasonable grounds to pretend we are of right his tributaries. But since he has the presumption to make an unjust demand of us, we have certainly as good reason to demand of him tribute from Rome; let the longer sword therefore determine the right between us. For if Rome has decreed that tribute ought to be paid to it from Britain, on account of its having been formerly under the yoke of Julius Cæsar, and other Roman emperors; I for the same reason now decree, that Rome ought to pay tribute to me, because my predecessors formerly held the government of it. For Belinus, that glorious king of the Britons, with the assistance of his brother Brennus, duke of the Allobroges, after they had hanged up twenty noble Romans in the middle of the market-place, took their city, and kept possession of it a long time.[18] Likewise Constantine, the son of Helena, and Maximian [Maximus], who were both my kinsmen, and both wore the crown of Britain, gained the imperial throne of Rome. Do not you, therefore, think that we ought to demand tribute of the Romans? As for Gaul and the adjacent islands of the ocean, we have no occasion to return them any answer, since they did not defend them, when we attempted to free them from their power." As soon as he had done speaking to this effect, Hoel, king of the Armorican Britons, who had the precedence of the rest, made answer in these words.

Chapter XVII   The Opinion of Hoel, King of Armorica, Concerning a War with the Romans

"After the most profound deliberation that any of us shall be able to make, I think better advice cannot be given, than what your majesty in your great wisdom and policy now offers. Your speech, which is no less wise than eloquent, has superseded all consultation on our part; and nothing remains for us to do, but to admire and gratefully acknowledge your majesty's firmness of mind, and depth of policy, to which we owe such excellent advice. For if upon this motive you are pleased to make an expedition to Rome, I doubt not but it will be crowned with glorious success; since it will be undertaken for the defence of our liberties, and to demand justly of our enemies, what they have unjustly demanded of us. For that person who would rob another, deserves to lose his own by him against whom the attempt is made. And, therefore, since the Romans

threatened us with this injury, it will undoubtedly turn to their own loss, if we can have but an opportunity of engaging with them. This is what the Britons universally desire; this is what we have promised us in the Sibylline prophecies, which expressly declare, that the Roman empire shall be obtained by three persons, natives of Britain. The oracle is fulfilled in two of them, since it is manifest (as your majesty observed) that those two celebrated princes, Belinus and Constantine, governed the Roman empire: and now you are the third to whom this supreme dignity is promised. Make haste, therefore, to receive what God makes no delay to give you; to subdue those who are ready to receive your yoke; and to advance us all, who for your advancement will spare neither limbs nor life. And that you may accomplish this, I myself will attend you in person with ten thousand men."

Chapter XVIII   The Opinion of Angusel

When Hoel concluded his speech, Angusel, king of Albania, declared his good affection to the cause after this manner. "I am not able to express the joy that has transported me, since my lord has declared to us his designs. For we seem to have done nothing by all our past wars with so many and potent princes, if the Romans and Germans be suffered to enjoy peace, and we do not severely revenge on them the grievous oppressions which they formerly brought upon this country. But now, since we are at liberty to encounter them, I am overwhelmed with joy and eagerness of desire, to see a battle with them, when the blood of those cruel oppressors will be no less acceptable to me than a spring of water is to one who is parched with thirst. If I shall but live to see that day, how sweet will be the wounds which I shall then either receive or give? Nay, how sweet will be even death itself, when suffered in revenging the injuries done to our ancestors, in defending our liberties, and in promoting the glory of our king! Let us then begin with these poltroons, and spoil them of all their trophies, by making an entire conquest of them. And I for my share will add to the army two thousand horse, besides foot."

Chapter XIX   They Unanimously Agree upon a War with the Romans

To the same effect spoke all the rest, and promised each of them their full quota of forces; so that besides those promised by the duke of Armorica, the number of men from the island of Britain alone was sixty thousand, all completely armed. But the kings of the other islands, as they had not been accustomed to any cavalry, promised their quota of infantry; and, from the six provincial islands, viz. Ireland, Iceland, Gothland, the Orkneys, Norway, and Dacia, were reckoned a hundred and twenty thousand. From the duchies of Gaul, that is, of the Ruteni, the Portunians, the Estrusians, the Cenomanni, the Andegavians, and Pictavians, were eighty thousand. From the twelve consulships of those who came along with Guerinus Carnotensis, twelve hundred. All together made up a hundred and eighty-three thousand two hundred, besides foot which did not easily fall under number.

Chapter XX Arthur Prepares for a War, and Refuses to Pay Tribute to the Romans

King Arthur, seeing all unanimously ready for his service, ordered them to return back to their countries with speed, and get ready the forces which they had promised, and to hasten to the general rendezvous upon the kalends of August, at the mouth of the river Barba, that from thence they might advance with them to the borders of the Allobroges, to meet the Romans. Then he sent word to the emperors by their ambassadors; that as to paying them tribute, he would in no wise obey their commands; and that the journey he was about to make to Rome, was not to stand the award of their sentence, but to demand of them what they had judicially decreed to demand of him. With this answer the ambassadors departed; and at the same time also departed all the kings and noblemen, to perform with all expedition the orders that had been given them.

Book X

Chapter I Lucius Tiberius Calls Together the Eastern Kings against the Britons

Lucius Tiberius, on receiving this answer, by order of the senate published a decree, for the eastern kings to come with their forces, and assist in the conquest of Britain. In obedience to which there came in a very short time, Epistrophius, king of the Grecians; Musten-sar, king of the Africans; Alifantinam, king of Spain; Hirtacius, king of the Parthians; Boccus, of the Medes; Sertorius, of Libya; Teucer, king of Phrygia; Serses, king of the Itureans; Pandrasus, king of Egypt; Micipsa, king of Babylon; Polytetes, duke of Bithynia; Teucer, duke of Phrygia; Evander, of Syria; Æthion, of Bœotia; Hippolytus, of Crete, with the generals and nobility under them. Of the senatorian order also came, Lucius Catellus, Marius Lepidus, Caius Metellus Cotta, Quintus Milvius Catulus, Quintus Carutius, and as many others as made up the number of forty thousand one hundred and sixty.

Chapter II Arthur Commits to His Nephew Modred the Government of Britain. His Dream at Hamo's Port

After the necessary dispositions were made, upon the kalends of August, they began their march towards Britain, which when Arthur had intelligence of, he committed the government of the kingdom to his nephew Modred, and queen Guanhumara, and marched with his army to Hamo's Port, where the wind stood fair for him. But while he, surrounded with all his numerous fleet, was sailing joyfully with a brisk gale, it happened that about midnight he fell into a very sound sleep, and in a dream saw a bear flying in the air, at the noise of which all the shores trembled; also a terrible dragon flying from the west, which enlightened the country with the brightness of its eyes. When these two met, they began a dreadful fight; but the dragon with its fiery breath burned the bear which often assaulted him, and threw him down scorched to the ground. Arthur upon this awaking, related his dream to those that stood about him, who took upon them to interpret it, and told him that the dragon signified himself, but the bear, some giant that should encounter with him; and that the fight portended the duel that would be between them, and the dragon's victory the same that would happen to himself. But Arthur conjectured it portended something else, and that the vision was applicable to himself and the emperor. As soon as the morning after this night's sail appeared, they found themselves arrived at the mouth of the river Barba. And there they pitched their tents, to wait the arrival of the kings of the islands and the generals of the other provinces.

Chapter III   Arthur Kills a Spanish Giant Who Had Stolen Away Helena, the Niece of Hoel

In the meantime Arthur had news brought him, that a giant of monstrous size was come from the shores of Spain, and had forcibly taken away Helena, the niece of duke Hoel, from her guard, and fled with her to the top of that which is now called Michael's Mount; and that the soldiers of the country who pursued him were able to do nothing against him. For whether they attacked him by sea or land, he either overturned their ships with vast rocks, or killed them with several sorts of darts, besides many of them that he took and devoured half alive. The next night, therefore, at the second hour, Arthur, taking along with him Caius the sewer, and Bedver the butler, went out privately from the camp, and hastened towards the mountain. For being a man of undaunted courage, he did not care to lead his army against such monsters; both because he could in this manner animate his men by his own example, and also because he was alone sufficient to deal with them. As soon as they came near the mountain, they saw a fire burning upon the top of it, and another on a lesser mountain, that was not far from it. And being in doubt upon which of them the giant dwelt, they sent away Bedver to know the certainty of the matter. So he, finding a boat, sailed over in it first to the lesser mountain, to which he could in no other way have access, because it was situated in the sea. When he had begun to climb up to the top of it, he was at first frightened with a dismal howling cry of a woman from above, and imagined the monster to be there: but quickly rousing up his courage, he drew his sword, and having reached the top, found nothing but the fire which he had before seen at a distance. He discovered also a grave newly made, and an old woman weeping and howling by it, who at the sight of him instantly cried out in words interrupted with sighs, "O, unhappy man, what misfortune brings you to this place? O the inexpressible tortures of death that you must suffer! I pity you, I pity you, because the detestable monster will this night destroy the flower of your youth. For that most wicked and odious giant, who brought the duke's niece, whom I have just now buried here, and me, her nurse, along with her into this mountain, will come and immediately murder you in a most cruel manner. O deplorable fate! This most illustrious princess, sinking under the fear her tender heart conceived, while the foul monster would have embraced her, fainted away and expired. And when he could not satiate his brutish lust upon her, who was the very soul, joy, and happiness of my life, being enraged at the disappointment of his bestial desire, he forcibly committed a rape upon me, who (let God and my old age witness) abhorred his embraces. Fly, dear sir, fly, for fear he may come, as he usually does, to lie with me, and finding you here most barbarously butcher you." Bedver, moved at what she said, as much as it is possible for human nature to be, endeavored with kind words to assuage her grief, and to comfort her with the promise of speedy help: and then returned back to Arthur, and gave him an account of what he had met with. Arthur very much lamented the damsel's sad fate, and ordered his companions to leave him to deal with him alone; unless there was an absolute necessity, and then they were to come in boldly to his assistance. From hence they went directly to the next mountain, leaving their horses with their armor-bearers, and ascended to the top, Arthur leading the way. The deformed savage was then by the fire, with his face besmeared with the clotted blood of swine, part of which he already devoured, and was roasting the remainder upon spits by the fire. But at the sight of them, whose appearance was a surprise to him, he hastened to his club, which two strong men could hardly lift from the ground. Upon this the king drew his sword, and guarding himself with his shield, ran with all his speed to prevent his getting it. But the other, who was not ignorant of his design, had by this time snatched it up, and gave the king such a terrible blow upon his shield, that he made the shores ring with the noise, and perfectly stunned the king's ears with it. Arthur, fired with rage at this, lifted up his sword, and gave him a wound in the forehead, which was not indeed mortal, but yet such as made the blood gush out over his face and eyes, and so blinded him; for he had partly warded off the stroke from his forehead with his club, and prevented its being fatal. However, his loss of sight, by reason of the blood flowing over his eyes, made him exert himself with greater fury, and like an enraged boar against a hunting-spear, so did he rush in against Arthur's sword, and grasping him about the waist, forced him down upon his knees. But Arthur, nothing daunted, slipped out of his hands, and so exerted himself with his sword, that he gave the giant no respite till he had struck it up to the very back through his skull. At this the hideous monster raised a dreadful roar, and like an oak torn up from the roots by the winds, so did he make the ground resound with his fall. Arthur, bursting out into a fit of laughter at the sight, commanded Bedver to cut off his head, and give it to one of the armor-bearers, who was to carry it to the camp, and there expose it to public view, but with orders for the spectators of this combat to keep silence. He told them he had found none of so great strength, since he killed the giant Ritho, who had challenged him to fight, upon the mountain Aravius. This giant had made himself furs of the beards of kings he had killed, and had sent word to Arthur carefully to cut off his beard and send it to him; and then, out of respect to his pre-eminence over other kings, his beard should have the honor of the principal place. But if he refused to do it, he challenged him to a duel, with this offer, that the conqueror should have the furs, and also the beard of the vanquished for a trophy of his victory. In his conflict, therefore, Arthur proved victorious, and took the beard and spoils of the giant: and, as he said before, had met with none that could be compared to him for strength, till his last engagement. After this victory, they returned at the second watch of the night to the camp with the head; to see which there was a great concourse of people, all extolling this wonderful exploit of Arthur, by which he had freed the country from a most destructive and voracious monster. But Hoel, in great grief for the loss of his niece, commanded a mausoleum to be built over her body in the mountain where she was buried, which, taking the damsel's name, is called Helena's Tomb to this day.

Chapter IV Arthur's Ambassadors to Lucius Tiberius Deliver Petreius Cotta, Whom They Took Prisoner, to Arthur

As soon as all the forces were arrived which Arthur expected, he marched from thence to Augustodunum,[19] where he supposed the general was. But when he came to the river Alba, he had intelligence brought him of his having encamped not far off, and that he was come with so vast an army, that he would not be able to withstand it. However, this did not deter him from pursuing his enterprise; but he pitched his camp upon the bank of the river, to facilitate the bringing up of his forces, and to secure his retreat, if there should be occasion; and sent Boso the consul of Oxford, and Guerinus

Carnotensis,[20] with his nephew Walgan, to Lucius Tiberius, requiring him either to retire from the coasts of Gaul, or come the next day, that they might try their right to that country with their swords. The retinue of young courtiers that attended Walgan, highly rejoicing at this opportunity, were urgent with him to find some occasion for a quarrel in the commander's camp, that so they might engage the Romans. Accordingly they went to Lucius, and commanded him to retire out of Gaul, or hazard a battle the next day. But while he was answering them, that he was not come to retire, but to govern the country, there was present Caius Quintilianus, his nephew, who said, "That the Britons were better at boasting and threatening, than they were at fighting." Walgan immediately took fire at this, and ran upon him with his drawn sword, wherewith he cut off his head, and then retreated speedily with his companions to their horses. The Romans, both horse and foot, pursued to revenge the loss of their countryman upon the ambassadors, who fled with great precipitation. But Guerinus Carnotensis, just as one of them was come up to him, rallied on a sudden, and with his lance struck at once through his armor and the very middle of his body, and laid him prostrate on the ground. The sight of this noble exploit raised the emulation of Boso of Oxford, who, wheeling about his horse, struck his lance into the throat of the first man he met with, and dismounted him mortally wounded. In the meantime, Marcellus Mutius, with great eagerness to revenge Quintilian's death, was just upon the back of Walgan, and laid hold of him; which the other quickly obliged him to quit, by cleaving both his helmet and head to the breast with his sword. He also bade him, when he arrived at the infernal regions, tell the man he had killed in the camp, "That in this manner the Britons showed their boasting and threatening." Then having reassembled his men, he encouraged them to despatch every one his pursuer in the same manner as he had done; which accordingly they did not fail to accomplish. Notwithstanding, the Romans continued their pursuit with lances and swords, wherewith they annoyed the others, though without slaughter or taking any prisoners. But as they came near a certain wood, a party of six thousand Britons, who seeing the flight of the consuls, had hid themselves, to be in readiness for their assistance, sallied forth, and putting spurs to their horses, rent the air with their loud shouts, and being well fenced with their shields, assaulted the Romans suddenly, and forced them to fly. And now it was the Britons' turn to pursue, which they did with better success, for they dismounted, killed, or took several of the enemy. Petreius, the senator, upon this news, hastened to the assistance of his countrymen with ten thousand men, and compelled the Britons to retreat to the wood from whence they had sallied forth; though not without loss of his own men. For the Britons, being well acquainted with the ground, in their flight killed a great number of their pursuers. The Britons thus giving ground, Hider, with another reinforcement of five thousand men, advanced with speed to sustain them; so that they again faced those, upon whom they had turned their backs, and renewed the assault with great vigor. The Romans also stood their ground, and continued the fight with various success. The great fault of the Britons was, that though they had been very eager to begin the fight, yet when begun they were less careful of the hazard they ran. Whereas the Romans were under better discipline, and had the advantage of a prudent commander, Petreius Cotta, to tell them where to advance, and where to give ground, and by these means did great injury to the enemy. When Boso observed this, he drew off from the rest a large party of those whom he knew to be the stoutest men, and spoke to them after this manner: "Since we have begun this fight without Arthur's knowledge, we must take care that we be not defeated in the enterprise. For, if we should, we shall both very much endanger our men, and incur the king's high displeasure. Rouse up your courage, and follow me through the Roman squadrons, that with the favor of good fortune we may either kill or take Petreius prisoner." With this they put spurs to their horses, and piercing through the enemies' thickest ranks, reached the place where Petreius was giving his commands. Boso hastily ran in upon him, and grasping him about the neck, fell with him to the ground, as he had intended. The Romans hereupon ran to his delivery, as did the Britons to Boso's assistance; which occasioned on both sides great slaughter, noise, and confusion, while one party strove to rescue their leader, and the other to keep him prisoner. So that this proved the sharpest part of the whole fight, and wherein their spears, swords, and arrows had the fullest employment. At length, the Britons, joining in a close body, and sustaining patiently the assaults of the Romans, retired to the main body of their army with Petreius: which they had no sooner done, than they again attacked them,

being now deprived of their leader, very much weakened, dispirited, and just beginning to flee. They, therefore, eagerly pursued, beat down, and killed several of them, and as soon as they had plundered them, pursued the rest: but they took the greatest number of them prisoners, being desirous to present them to the king. When they had at last sufficiently harassed them, they returned with their plunder and prisoners to the camp; where they gave an account of what had happened, and presented Petreius Cotta with the other prisoners before Arthur, with great joy for the victory. Arthur congratulated them upon it, and promised them advancement to greater honors, for behaving themselves so gallantly when he was absent from them. Then he gave his command to some of his men, to conduct the prisoners the next day to Paris, and deliver them to be kept in custody there till further orders. The party that were to undertake this charge, he ordered to be conducted by Cador, Bedver, and the two consuls, Borellus and Richerius, with their servants, till they should be out of all fear of disturbance from the Romans.

Chapter V   The Romans Attack the Britons with a Very Great Force, but Are Put to Flight by Them

But the Romans, happening to get intelligence of their design, at the command of their general chose out fifteen thousand men, who that night were to get before the others in their march, and rescue their fellow soldiers out of their hands. They were to be commanded by Vulteius Catellus and Quintus Carutius, senators, as also Evander, king of Syria, and Sertorius, king of Libya. Accordingly they began their march that very night, and possessed themselves of a place convenient for lying in ambuscade, through which they supposed the others would pass. In the morning the Britons set forward along the same road with their prisoners, and were now approaching the place in perfect ignorance of the cunning stratagem of the enemy. No sooner had they entered it, than the Romans, to their great surprise, sprang forth and fell furiously upon them. Notwithstanding, the Britons, at length recovering from their consternation, assembled together, and prepared for a bold opposition, by appointing a party to guard the prisoners, and drawing out the rest in order of battle against the enemy. Richerius and Bedver had the command of the party that were set over the prisoners; but

Cador, duke of Cornwall, and Borellus headed the others. But all the Romans had made their sally without being placed in any order, and cared not to form themselves, that they might lose no time in the slaughter of the Britons, whom they saw busied in marshalling their troops, and preparing only for their defence. By this conduct the Britons were extremely weakened, and would have shamefully lost their prisoners, had not good fortune rendered them assistance. For Guitard, commander of the Pictavians, happened to get information of the designed stratagem, and was come up with three thousand men, by the help of which they at last got the advantage, and paid back the slaughter upon their insolent assailants. Nevertheless, the loss which they sustained at the beginning of this action was very considerable. For they lost Borellus, the famous consul of the Cenomanni, in an encounter with Evander, king of Syria, who stuck his lance into his throat; besides four noblemen, viz. Hirelgas Deperirus, Mauricius Cadorcanensis, Aliduc of Tintagel, and Hider his son, than whom braver men were hardly to be found. But yet neither did this loss dispirit the Britons, but rather made them more resolute to keep the prisoners, and kill the enemy. The Romans, now finding themselves unable to maintain the fight any longer, suddenly quitted the field, and made towards their camp; but were pursued with slaughter by the Britons, who also took many of them, and allowed them no respite till they had killed Vulteius Catellus and Evander, king of Syria, and wholly dispersed the rest. After which they sent away their former prisoners to Paris, whither they were to conduct them, and returned back with those newly taken to the king; to whom they gave great hopes of a complete conquest of their enemies, since very few of the great number that came against them had met with any success.

Chapter VI   Lucius Tiberius Goes to Lengriæ. Arthur, Designing to Vanquish Him, by a Stratagem Possesses Himself of the Valley of Suesia

These repeated disasters wrought no small disturbance in the mind of Lucius Tiberius, and made him hesitate whether to bring it to a general battle with Arthur, or to retire into Augustodunum, and stay till the emperor Leo with his forces could come to his assistance. At length, giving way to his fears, he entered Lengriæ with his army, intending to reach the other city the night following. Arthur, finding this, and being desirous to get before him in his march, left the city on the left hand, and the same night entered a certain valley called Suesia, through which Lucius was to pass. There he divided his men into several bodies, commanding one legion, over which Morvid, consul of Gloucester, was appointed general, to wait close by, that he might retreat to them if there should be occasion, and from thence rally his broken forces for a second battle. The rest he divided into seven parts, in each of which he placed five thousand five hundred and fifty-five men, all completely armed. He also appointed different stations to his horse and foot, and gave command that just as the foot should advance to the attack, the horse, keeping close together in their ranks, should at the same moment march up obliquely, and endeavor to put the enemy into disorder. The companies of foot were, after the British manner, drawn out into a square, with a right and left wing, under the command of Angusel, king of Albania, and Cador, duke of Cornwall; the one presiding over the right wing, the other over the left. Over another party were placed the two famous consuls, Guerinus of Chartres and Boso of Richiden, called in the Saxon tongue Oxineford; over a third were Aschillius, king of the Dacians, and Lot, king of the Norwegians; the fourth being commanded by Hoel, duke of the Armoricans, and Walgan, the king's nephew. After these were four other parties placed in the rear; the first commanded by Caius the sewer, and Bedver the butler; the second by Holdin, duke of the Ruteni, and Guitard of the Pictavians; the third by Vigenis of Legecester, Jonathal of Dorchester, and Cursalem of Caicester; the fourth by Urbgennius of Bath. Behind all these, Arthur, for himself and the legion, that was to attend near him, made choice of a place, where he set up a golden dragon for a standard, whither the wounded or fatigued might in case of necessity retreat, as into their camp. The legion that was with him consisted of six thousand six hundred and sixty-six men.

Chapter VII   Arthur's Exhortation to His Soldiers

After he had thus placed them all in their stations, he made the following speech to his soldiers: "My brave countrymen, who have made Britain the mistress of thirty kingdoms, I congratulate you upon your late noble exploit, which to me is a proof that your valor is so far from being impaired, that it is rather increased. Though you have been five years without exercise, wherein the softening pleasures of an easy life had a greater share of your time than the use of arms; yet all this has not made you degenerate from your natural bravery, which you have shown in forcing the Romans to flee. The pride of their leaders has animated them to attempt the invasion of your liberties. They have tried you in battle, with numbers superior to yours, and have not been able to stand before you; but have basely withdrawn themselves into that city, from which they are now ready to march out, and to pass through this valley in their way to Augustodunum; so that you may have an opportunity of falling upon them unawares like a flock of sheep. Certainly they expected to find in you the cowardice of the Eastern nations, when they thought to make your country tributary, and you their slaves. What, have they never heard of your wars, with the Dacians, Norwegians, and princes of the Gauls, whom you reduced under my power, and freed from their shameful yoke? We, then, that have had success in a greater war, need no doubt of it in a less, if we do but endeavor with the same spirit to vanquish these poltroons. You shall want no rewards of honor, if as faithful soldiers you do but strictly obey my commands. For as soon as we have routed them, we will march straight to Rome, and take it; and then all the gold, silver, palaces, towers, towns, cities, and other riches of the vanquished shall be yours." He had hardly done speaking before they all with one voice declared, that they were ready to suffer death, rather than quit the field while he had life.

Chapter VIII   Lucius Tiberius, Discovering Arthur's Design, in a Speech Animates His Followers to Fight

But Lucius Tiberius, discovering the designs that were formed against him, would not flee, as he had at first intended, but taking new courage, resolved to march to the same valley against them; and calling together his principal commanders, spoke to them in these words: "Venerable fathers, to whose empire both the Eastern and Western kingdoms owe obedience, remember the virtues of your ancestors, who were not afraid to shed their blood, when the vanquishing of the enemies of the commonwealth required it; but to leave an example of their courage and military virtues to their posterity, behaved themselves in all battles with that contempt of death, as if God had given them some security against it. By this conduct they often triumphed, and by triumphing escaped death. Such was the reward of their virtue from Divine Providence, which overrules all events. The increase of the commonwealth, and of their own valor was owing to this; and all those virtues that usually adorn the great, as integrity, honor, and munificence, flourishing a long time in them, raised them and their posterity to the empire of the whole world. Let their noble examples animate you: rouse up the spirit of the ancient Romans, and be not afraid to march out against our enemies that are lying in ambush before us in the valley, but boldly with your swords demand of them your just rights. Do not think that I retired into this city for fear of engaging with them; but I thought that, as their pursuit of us was rash and foolish, so we might hence on a sudden intercept them in it, and by dividing their main body make a great slaughter of them. But now, since they have altered the measures which we supposed they had taken, let us also alter ours. Let us go in quest of them and bravely fall upon them; or if they shall happen to have the advantage in the beginning of the battle, let us only stand our ground during the fury of their first assault, and the victory will undoubtedly be ours; for in many battles this manner of conduct has been attended with victory." As soon as he had made an end of speaking these and other things, they all declared their assent, promised with an oath to stand by him, and hastened to arm themselves. Which when they had done, they marched out of Lengriæ to the valley where Arthur had drawn out his forces in order of battle. Then they also began to marshal their army, which they divided into twelve companies, and according to the Roman manner of battle, drew out each company into the form of a wedge, consisting of six thousand six hundred and sixty-six men. Each company also had its respective leaders, who were to give direction when to advance, or when to be upon the defensive. One of them was headed by Lucius Catellus the senator, and Alifantinam, king of Spain; another by Hirtacius, king of the Parthians, and Marius Lepidus, a senator; a third by Boccus, king of the Medes, and Caius Metellus, a senator; a fourth by Sertorius, king of Libya, and Quintus Milvius, a senator. These four companies were placed in the front of the army. In the rear of these were four others, whereof one was commanded by Serses, king of the Itureans; another by Pandrasus, king of Egypt; a third by Polytetes, duke of Bithynia; a fourth by Teucer, duke of Phrygia. And again behind all these four others, whereof the commanders were Quintus Carucius, a senator, Lælius Ostiensis, Sulpitius Subuculus, and Mauricius Sylvanus. As for the general himself, he was sometimes in one place, sometimes another, to encourage and direct as there should be occasion. For a standard he ordered a golden eagle to be firmly set up in the center, for his men to repair to whenever they should happen to be separated from their company.

Chapter IX   A Battle between Arthur and Lucius Tiberius

And now the Britons and Romans stood presenting their arms at one another; when forthwith at the sound of the trumpets, the company that was headed by the king of Spain and Lucius Catellus, boldly rushed forward against that which the king of Scotland and duke of Cornwall led, but were not able to make the least breach in their firm ranks. So that while these stood their ground, up came Guerinus and Boso with a body of horse upon their full speed, broke through the party that began the assault, and met with another which the king of the Parthians was leading up against Aschillius, king of Dacia. After this first onset, there followed a general engagement of both armies with great violence, and several breaches were made on each side. The shouts, the slaughter, the quantity of blood spilled, and the agonies of the dying, made a dreadful scene of horror. At first, the Britons sustained a great loss, by having Bedver the butler killed, and Caius the sewer mortally wounded. For, as Bedver met Boccus, king of the Medes, he fell dead by a stab of his lance amidst the enemies' troops. And Caius, in endeavoring to revenge his death, was surrounded by the Median troops, and there received a mortal wound; yet as a brave soldier he opened himself a way with the wing which he led, killed and dispersed the Medes, and would have made a safe retreat with all his men, had he not met the king of Libya with the forces under him, who put his whole company into disorder; yet not so great, but that he was still able to get off with a few, and flee with Bedver's corps to the golden dragon. The Neustrians grievously lamented at the sight of their leader's mangled body;

and so did the Andegavians, when they beheld their consul wounded. But there was now no room for complaints, for the furious and bloody shocks of both armies made it necessary to provide for their own defense. Therefore Hireglas, the nephew of Bedver, being extremely enraged at his death, called up to him three hundred men, and like a wild boar amongst a pack of dogs, broke through the enemies' ranks with his horse, making towards the place where he had seen the standard of the king of the Medes; little regarding what might befall him, if he could but revenge the loss of his uncle. At length he reached the place, killed the king, brought off his body to his companions, and laid it by that of his uncle, where he mangled it in the same manner. Then calling with a loud voice to his countrymen, he animated their troops, and vehemently pressed them to exert themselves to the utmost, now that their spirits were raised, and the enemy disheartened; and especially as they had the advantage of them in being placed in better order, and so might the more grievously annoy them. Encouraged with this exhortation, they began a general assault upon the enemy, which was attended with a terrible slaughter on both sides. For on the part of the Romans, besides many others, fell Alifantinam, king of Spain, Micipsa of Babylon, as also Quintus Milvius and Marius Lepidus, senators. On the part of the Britons, Holdin, king of the Ruteni, Leodegarius of Bolonia, and three consuls of Britain, Cursalem of Caicester, Galluc of Salisbury, and Urbgennius of Bath. So that the troops which they commanded, being extremely weakened, retreated till they came to the army of the Armorican Britons, commanded by Hoel and Walgan. But these, being inflamed at the retreat of their friends, encouraged them to stand their ground, and caused them with the help of their own forces to put their pursuers to flight. While they continued this pursuit, they beat down and killed several of them, and gave them no respite, till they came to the general's troop; who, seeing the distress of his companions, hastened to their assistance.

Chapter X   Hoel and Walgan Signalize Their Valor in the Fight

And now in this latter encounter the Britons were worsted, with the loss of Kimarcoc, consul of Trigeria, and two thousand with him; besides three famous noblemen, Richomarcus, Bloccovius, and Jagivius of

Bodloan, who, had they but enjoyed the dignity of princes, would have been celebrated for their valor through all succeeding ages. For, during this assault which they made in conjunction with Hoel and Walgan, there was not an enemy within their reach that could escape the fury of their sword or lance. But upon their falling in among Lucius's party, they were surrounded by them, and suffered the same fate with the consul and the other men. The loss of these men made those matchless heroes, Hoel and Walgan, much more eager to assault the general's ranks, and to try on all sides where to make the greatest impression. But Walgan, whose valor was never to be foiled, endeavored to gain access to Lucius himself, that he might encounter him, and with this view beat down and killed all that stood in his way. And Hoel, not inferior to him, did no less service in another part, by spiriting up his men, and giving and receiving blows among the enemy with the same undaunted courage. It was hard to determine, which of them was the stoutest soldier.

Chapter XI   Lucius Tiberius Being Killed, the Britons Obtain the Victory

But Walgan, by forcing his way through the enemy's troops, as we said before, found at last (what he had wished for) access to the general, and immediately encountered him. Lucius, being then in the flower of his youth, and a person of great courage and vigor, desired nothing more than to engage with such a one as might put his strength to its full trial. Putting himself, therefore, into a posture of defense, he received Walgan with joy, and was not a little proud to try his courage with one of whom he had heard such great things. The fight continued between them a long time, with great force of blows, and no less dexterity in warding them off, each being resolved upon the other's destruction. During this sharp conflict between them, the Romans, on a sudden, recovering their courage, made an assault upon the Armoricans, and having relieved their general, repulsed Hoel and Walgan, with their troops, till they found themselves unawares met by Arthur and the forces under him. For he, hearing of the slaughter that was a little before made of his men, had speedily advanced with his legion, and drawing out his Caliburn, spoke to them, with a loud voice, after this manner: "What are you doing, soldiers? Will you suffer these effeminate wretches to escape? Let not one of them get

off alive. Remember the force of your arms, that have reduced thirty kingdoms under my subjection. Remember your ancestors, whom the Romans, when at the height of their power, made tributary. Remember your liberties, which these pitiful fellows, that are much your inferiors, attempt to deprive you of. Let none of them escape alive. What are you doing?" With these expostulations, he rushed upon the enemy, made terrible havoc among them, and not a man did he meet but at one blow he laid either him or his horse dead upon the ground. They, therefore, in astonishment fled from him, as a flock of sheep from a fierce lion, whom raging hunger provokes to devour whatever happens to come near him. Their arms were no manner of protection to them against the force with which this valiant prince wielded his Caliburn. Two kings, Sertorius of Libya, and Polytetes of Bithynia, unfortunately felt its fury, and had their heads cut off by it. The Britons, when they saw the king performing such wonders, took courage again. With one consent they assaulted the Romans, kept close together in their ranks, and while they assailed the foot in one part, endeavored to beat down and pierce through the horse in another. Notwithstanding, the Romans made a brave defense, and at the instigation of Lucius labored to pay back their slaughter upon the Britons. The eagerness and force that were now shown on both sides were as great as if it was the beginning of the battle. Arthur continued to do great execution with his own hand, and encouraged the Britons to maintain the fight; as Lucius Tiberius did the Romans, and made them perform many memorable exploits. He himself, in the meantime, was very active in going from place to place, and suffered none to escape with life that happened to come within the reach of his sword or lance. The slaughter that was now made on both sides was very dreadful, and the turns of fortune various, sometimes the Britons prevailing, sometimes the Romans. At last, while this sharp dispute continued, Morvid, consul of Gloucester with his legion, which, as we said before, was placed between the hills, came up with speed upon the rear of the enemy, and to their great surprise assaulted, broke through, and dispersed them with great slaughter. This last and decisive blow proved fatal to many thousands of Romans, and even to the general Lucius himself, who was killed among the crowds with a lance by an unknown hand. But the Britons, by long maintaining the fight, at last with great difficulty gained the victory.

Chapter XII   Part of the Romans Flee; the Rest, of Their Own Accord, Surrender Themselves for Slaves

The Romans, being now, therefore, dispersed, betook themselves through fear, some to the by-ways and woods, some to the cities and towns, and all other places, where they could be most safe; but were either killed or taken and plundered by the Britons who pursued: so that great part of them voluntarily and shamefully held forth their hands, to receive their chains, in order to prolong for a while a wretched life. In all which the justice of Divine Providence was very visible; considering how unjustly the ancestors of the Britons were formerly invaded and harassed by those of the Romans; and that these stood only in defense of that liberty, which the others would have deprived them of; and refused the tribute, which the others had no right to demand.

Chapter XIII   The Bodies of the Slain Are Decently Buried, Each in Their Respective Countries

Arthur, after he had completed his victory, gave orders for separating the bodies of his nobility from those of the enemy, and preparing a pompous funeral for them; and that, when ready, they should be carried to the abbeys of their respective countries, there to be honorably buried. But Bedver the butler was, with great lamentation of the Neustrians, carried to his own city Bajocæ,[21] which Bedver the first, his great grandfather, had built. There he was, with great solemnity, laid close by the wall, in a burying-place on the south side of the city. But Cheudo[22] was carried, grievously wounded to Camus,[23] a town which he had himself built, where in a short time he died of his wounds, and was buried, as became a duke of Andegavia, in a convent of hermits, which was in a wood not far from the town. Also Holdin, duke of Ruteni, was carried to Flanders, and buried in his own city Terivana.[24] The other consuls and noblemen were conveyed to the neighboring abbeys, according to Arthur's orders. Out of his great clemency, also, he ordered the country people to take care of the burial of the enemy, and to carry the body of Lucius to the senate, and tell them, that was the only tribute which Britain ought to pay them. After this he stayed in those parts till the next winter was over, and

employed his time in reducing the cities of the Allobroges. But at the beginning of the following summer, as he was on his march towards Rome and was beginning to pass the Alps, he had news brought him that his nephew Modred, to whose care he had entrusted Britain, had by tyrannical and treasonable practices set the crown upon his own head; and that queen Guanhumara, in violation of her first marriage, had wickedly married him.

Book XI

Chapter I   Modred Makes a Great Slaughter of Arthur's Men, but Is Beaten, and Flees to Winchester

Of the matter now to be treated of, most noble consul, Geoffrey of Monmouth shall be silent; but will, nevertheless, though in a mean style, briefly relate what he found in the British book above mentioned, and heard from that most learned historian, Walter, archdeacon of Oxford, concerning the wars which this renowned king, upon his return to Britain after this victory, waged against his nephew. As soon, therefore, as the report, of this flagrant wickedness reached him, he immediately desisted from his enterprise against Leo, king of the Romans; and having sent away Hoel, duke of the Armoricans, with the army of Gaul, to restore peace in those parts, returned back with speed to Britain, attended only by the kings of the islands, and their armies. But the wicked traitor, Modred, had sent Cheldric, the Saxon leader, into Germany, there to raise all the forces he could find, and return with all speed: and in consideration of this service, had promised him all that part of the island, which reaches from the Humber to Scotland, and whatever Hengist and Horsa had possessed of Kent in the time of Vortigern. So that he, in obedience to his commands, had arrived with eight hundred ships filled with pagan soldiers, and had entered into covenant to obey the traitor as his sovereign; who had also drawn to his assistance the Scots, Picts, Irish, and all others whom he knew to be enemies to his uncle. His whole army, taking pagans and Christians together, amounted to eighty thousand men; with the help of whom he met Arthur just after his landing at the port of Rutupi,[25] and joining battle with him, made a very great slaughter of his men. For the same day fell Angusel, king of Albania, and Walgan, the king's nephew, with innumerable others. Angusel was succeeded in his kingdom by Eventus, his brother Urian's son, who afterwards performed many famous exploits in those wars. After they had at last, with much difficulty, got ashore, they paid back the slaughter, and put Modred and his army to flight. For, by long practice in war, they had learned an excellent way of ordering their forces; which was so managed, that while their foot were employed either in an assault or upon the defensive, the horse would come in at full speed obliquely, break through the enemy's ranks, and so force them to flee. Nevertheless, this perjured usurper got his forces together again, and the night following entered Winchester. As soon as queen Guanhumara heard this, she immediately, despairing of success, fled from York to the City of Legions, where she resolved to lead a chaste life among the nuns in the church of Julius the Martyr, and entered herself one of their order.

Chapter II   Modred, after Being Twice Besieged and Routed, Is Killed. Arthur, Being Wounded, Gives Up the Kingdom to Constantine

But Arthur, whose anger was now much more inflamed, upon the loss of so many hundreds of his fellow soldiers, after he had buried his slain, went on the third day to the city, and there besieged the traitor, who, notwithstanding, was unwilling to desist from his enterprise, but used all methods to encourage his adherents, and marching out with his troops prepared to fight his uncle. In the battle that followed hereupon, great numbers lost their lives on both sides; but at last Modred's army suffered most, so that he was forced to quit the field shamefully. From hence he made a precipitate flight, and, without taking any care for the burial of his slain, marched in haste towards Cornwall. Arthur, being inwardly grieved that he should so often escape, forthwith pursued him into that country as far as the river Cambula, where the other was expecting his coming. And Modred, as he was the boldest of men, and always the quickest at making an attack, immediately placed his troops in order, resolving either to conquer or to die, rather than continue his flight any longer. He had yet remaining with him sixty thousand men, out of whom he composed three bodies, which contained each of them six thousand six hundred and

sixty-six men: but all the rest he joined in one body; and having assigned to each of the other parties their leaders, he took the command of this upon himself. After he had made this disposition of his forces, he endeavored to animate them, and promised them the estates of their enemies if they came off with victory. Arthur, on the other side, also marshalled his army, which he divided into nine square companies, with a right and left wing; and having appointed to each of them their commanders, exhorted them to make a total rout of those robbers and perjured villains, who, being brought over into the island from foreign countries at the instance of the arch-traitor, were attempting to rob them of all their honors. He likewise told them that a mixed army composed of barbarous people of so many different countries, and who were all raw soldiers and inexperienced in war, would never be able to stand against such brave veteran troops as they were, provided they did their duty. After this encouragement given by each general to his fellow soldiers, the battle on a sudden began with great fury; wherein it would be both grievous and tedious to relate the slaughter, the cruel havoc, and the excess of fury that was to be seen on both sides. In this manner they spent a good part of the day, till Arthur at last made a push with his company, consisting of six thousand six hundred and sixty-six men, against that in which he knew Modred was; and having opened a way with their swords, they pierced quite through it, and made a grievous slaughter. For in this assault fell the wicked traitor himself, and many thousands with him. But notwithstanding the loss of him, the rest did not flee, but running together from all parts of the field maintained their ground with undaunted courage. The fight now grew more furious than ever, and proved fatal to almost all the commanders and their forces. For on Modred's side fell Cheldric, Elasius, Egbrict, and Bunignus, Saxons; Gillapatric, Gillamor, Gistafel, and Gillarius, Irish; also the Scots and Picts, with almost all their leaders: on Arthur's side, Olbrict, king of Norway; Aschillius, king of Dacia; Cador Limenic Cassibellaun, with many thousands of others, as well Britons as foreigners, that he had brought with him. And even the renowned king Arthur himself was mortally wounded; and being carried thence to the isle of Avallon to be cured of his wounds, he gave up the crown of Britain to his kinsman Constantine, the son of Cador, duke of Cornwall, in the five hundred and forty-second year of our Lord's incarnation.

Notes

1 Caerlon.

2 Southampton.

3 Lincoln.

4 In south Devonshire.

5 Dumbarton.

6 Cf. the speech of Turpin in *Roland*, ll. 1124ff.

7 Priwen (Pridwen). This is a Welsh word whose meaning is not clear. It may mean something like "splendid white."

8 "Isle of Apples"? The location of this place is not clear. Later writers, for reasons of their own, associated it with Glastonbury.

9 *Ron* (Rhon) is Welsh for "lance."

10 Moray.

11 Guenevere.

12 Gawain.

13 Poitevins.

14 Anjou.

15 Kay.

16 That is, "seneschal."

17 This passage reflects twelfth-century enthusiasm for ecclesiastical music.

18 Brennus with his Gauls took Rome in the fourth century B.C.

19 Autun.

20 That is, "of Chartres."

21 Bayeux.

22 Kay

23 Chinon.

24 Thérouanne.

25 Richborough.

E. *"The Apocalypse of Golias"*[1]

"The Apocalypse of Golias the Bishop," although little known today, was a very popular and widely circulated poem in the Middle Ages. It was composed, in Latin, in the late twelfth or early thirteenth century, most probably in England, and its author is unknown (although early manuscripts attribute the poem to a number of writers, including Walter of Chatillon, Alanus de Insulis, Walter Map, John of Salisbury, and, more cautiously, "a certain not unlearned Englishman"). "Golias," the name traditionally attached to the poem, is neither the name of a person nor a pseudonym, but rather the name of a literary and social attitude, the personification of contempt for official hypocrisy. The writers who used the name copied it from the biblical giant Goliath, appropriately so, for Golias is the bitter enemy of those who are supposed to represent goodness and order. Irreverent, gross (the name is sometimes spelled "Gulias," punning on the word gula, *or gluttony), and outraged, Golias is the self-appointed scourge of the clergy's corruption and ignorance. His weapon is wit, a wit both learned and cheerfully coarse, sometimes more ingenious than clever, but usually brutally effective.*

In the "Apocalypse" itself, a parody of the last book of the Bible, the clergy is anatomized as the Book of Seven Seals is opened up, the successive seals arranged in hierarchical order, so that the survey works down from the pope and bishops, through archdeacons, deans, curial officials, parish priests, clerks, and concludes with the abbots and their monks. Animal images underline the satire throughout: the lay people of the Church are depicted as misled sheep or as hunted quarry, while the clergymen assume the shape of predators. It is interesting that this pattern breaks down in the case of the monks, the lowest and most degenerate of the clergy; their behavior is so gross that they are not compared to animals—they are animals.

The Latin original of the poem is in four-line, monorhymed stanzas. The translation preserves this form approximately, but limits rhyming to the second and fourth lines of each stanza. It is based on the edition of Karl Strecker, Die Apokalypse des Golias (Rome, 1928). There is an older edition of the poem in Thomas Wright's The Latin Poems Commonly Attributed to Walter Mapes, Camden Society, London, 1841. For further discussion of the poem consult the preface to Strecker's edition; F. J. E. Raby, A History of Secular Latin Poetry in the Middle Ages, second edition, Oxford, 1957, vol. II, 214ff.; and F. X. Newman, "The Structure of Vision in Apocalypsis Goliae," Mediaeval Studies, vol. 29, 1967.

Note

1   The editor wishes to thank Prof. F. X. Newman for the introduction to and translation of "The Apocalypse of Golias."

"THE APOCALYPSE OF GOLIAS THE BISHOP"

Apollo's lamp was burning in the Bull,   1
Its flaming darts were pouring from the air,
And so I sought the shadow of a wood,
In hopes of finding gentle Zephyr there.

At mid-day I was stretched out in the shade   2
Of Jove's own tree, when suddenly there rose
Before my eyes—Pythagoras! "In flesh,
Or not, I do not know: God knows."

I noticed that his body bore the signs   3
Of all the Arts that mankind knows.
(But if this revelation was "in flesh,
Or not, I do not know: God knows.")

Upon his forehead shone Astronomy;   4
The rows of teeth denoted Grammar's rules;
The tongue significant of Rhetoric;
The lips were Logic's animated tools.

The fingers acted for Arithmetic;   5
The throbbing pulse kept Music's rhythmic beat;
The eyes were figures of Geometry:
Each Liberal Art had found its proper seat.

Below these were the Practical: 6
With Ethics on his breast and even—look!—
Mechanics on his back, Pythagoras was
A man who could be read, a human book!

Then holding out the palm of his right hand,   7
The ancient sage commanded me to read.
The characters I saw there simply said:
"I am your guide; you follow where I lead."

He went, I followed, and—more quickly done   8
Than said—was whirled into an Other Land,
A place of wonders, where I saw a vast,
Unnumbered crowd, an almost endless band.

And while I stood there, wondering who they   9
    were,
I noticed each was marked upon the forehead.
The marks, I soon enough discerned, were names,
Engraved as if on flints or sheets of lead.

Here Master Priscian beats his pupil's palms,   10
And Aristotle beats the empty air;
There Tully's words make smooth what once
    was harsh,
And Ptolemy makes stars his special care.

Boethius is counting out his sums,   11
While Euclid thinks of all that space entails;
Pythagoras is pounding at a forge,
Discovering the first musician's scales.

Here Lucan leads a band of warlike men,   12
And Virgil tinkers with a brazen fly;
There Ovid entertains a mob with tales,
And Persius flays a fool and makes him cry.

Incomparable Statius stands apart,   13
A poet eloquent, but not verbose.
While Terence does a vulgar little jig,
Hippocrates gives boors a wormwood dose.

I stared and stared at all these learned men,   14
Until an angel with a face of light
Commanded, "Look up there, above the clouds!
Prepare to see an even greater sight!"

Immediately I looked into the sky,   15
And promptly found myself "in spiritu";
Then something drew me swiftly up and up,
Until the gate of Heaven loomed in view.

A blinding sheet of lightning filled the sky;   16
I couldn't see, the brilliance was so keen!
But soon the angel who had brought me said,
"Look up—and see what only John has seen.

"To seven Asian churches the Apostle   17
Sent description of his mystic visions;
To seven English churches you will do
The same—with one or two minute revisions."

From somewhere came a bursting, swelling roar,   18
So loud that I could hardly think or feel,
Like battle trumpets blaring out a charge,
Or like the thunder of a monstrous wheel.

The echo of the blast was barely gone,   19
When I perceived a man who in his hand
Held seven candlesticks and seven stars.
My Angel said, "Now see and understand!

"The candelabra mean the seven Churches,   20
The stars, the Bishops as they live today,
Or *should* live, for the light of grace is hidden
Under bushels, man has lost the Way."

The Angel then held up that mighty Book,   21
Whose mystic words were sealed with seven seals.
"Read carefully," he said, "what you find here,
For you must tell the world what it reveals.

"This Book is allegorical in style;   22
No other style could suit the subject more:
A Prelate is an allegory inside-out,
A handsome shell, but rotten at the core."

The seal on Chapter One was opened up,   23
And I beheld four fascinating beasts.
In shape the beasts were not at all alike;
In motion, like four dancers at a feast.

The first of them was very like a lion,   24
An ox and eagle next (or so it seemed),
And then a man. They flew, they whirled about,
And each was full of eyes that glared and gleamed.

I wondered what this odd quartet could be,   25
And when the clasping seal was all undone,
The mystery of their meaning was revealed.
Now here's the honest truth about each one.

The Lion is our holy Pope Voracious,   26
Who, when he's thirsty, trades his books for bocks
(His favorite "book" remains the golden Mark).
The Rock has put his Church upon the rocks.

The Ox is Bishop Avarus the Worst.   27
He likes to browse in pasture or in pen.
He gnaws and chews wherever he may be,
And stuffs himself with goods of other men.

The Eagle is Archdeacon Pilferpurse.   28
He soars the skies, a robber seeking prey,
And when he spies a victim down below,
He pounces, eats, and goes his pious way.

The human face belongs to the good Dean,   29
A master of refined duplicity.
He lies and cheats with such a pious air,
He's won himself a name for sanctity.

The four of them are fitted out with wings   30
(To help them fly around in search of prey);
They've eyes in front and even in their backs
(So they can spot a profit either way).

And each of them is spinning like a wheel 31
(The symbolism here is not inscrutable:
They change their minds with every passing
      whim;
Their values are completely mutable.)

When I had scanned this cover sign, I read 32
The chapter that was underneath the sign.
It told of Bishops, shepherds who mislead
Their flocks, by carelessness or by design.

The Bishop likes to make his sheep his prey; 33
He stabs them with the horns that crown his head.
This pastor is a kind of fearsome bull
Who feeds no flocks, but with his flock is fed.

The Bishop nurtures well his errant sheep, 34
That feeble, lame, and driven little flock.
Since they supply his milk and wool, he tries—
Good Shepherd—not to lose producing stock.

If he finds some faults among his lambs, 35
If any lapse of faith should greet his eye,
He shears them with the scissors of the law,
And wrings their udders (that is, purses) dry.

So errant flock is led by errant guide, 36
And neither one can see the way to go.
But once the lambs are fleeced, the Shepherd
      leaves
The bloody carcass to the wolf and crow.

His ring means that he's married to his people; 37
His staff, that he will lead them out of grief;
But badly wed and badly led are they
Whose Bishop is a tyrant and a thief.

When I had finished reading Chapter One, 38
The sky grew dark with clouds, the lightning
      flashed
And while a wheel of thunder crossed the sky,
I watched the second wondrous seal unclasped.

Archdeacon was discussed in Chapter Two, 39
That master thief who hides behind the laws.
Whatever juicy bits Lord Bishop drops,
Archdeacon snatches with his sharpened claws.

He sits at synod, as they say, "all eyes," 40
A two-faced Janus and a lynx-eyed sleuth.
He's quick as Argus at detecting crime,
But blind as Polyphemus to the truth.

Among the thousands of old laws, Archdeacon's 41
Sure to find one that will make you crawl;
Unless he gets his bribe, the rule is this:
"He Who Breaks One Law Has Broken All."

In court Archdeacon hears the evidence, 42
Then renders judgment like a canonist.
The verdict goes according to the bribe:
Archdeacon is a faithful Simonist.

He puts the Church's laws on public sale 43
And, like an auctioneer, he's very genial;
To those who say he's sinning, he replies,
His actions are not venal, merely venial.

From time to time his busy little spies 44
Will catch a whore who's working at her trade.
She won't escape, no matter how she tries,
Till both her fines—in court and bed—are paid.

A priest whose case is labeled "genitive," 45
Has recklessly imperiled his vocation;
A little bribe (or "dative") will not do,
Archdeacon's price amounts to an "ablation."

At this point sun and moon put out their light, 46
The air grew almost thick enough to feel.
I knew then that I'd soon see Chapter Three,
And in a flash, a hand broke off its seal.

"Read!" my Angel said, and so I did, 47
The story of a sportsman's life of crime.
This fellow loves to fish (for gold), to hunt
(In Venus' chase), to swim (in vice and slime).

The hunter is the Dean, in shape a man, 48
But really more a virus than a *vir*.
He poisons every honest man he meets,
But always manages to *look* sincere.

The Dean is the Archdeacon's little dog, 49
Whose barking is less painful than his bite.
This canine canonist is never full,
Although he gobbles gold from morn to night.

The Dean's a dog whose nose is very keen: 50
Let the quarry run and hide and sweat,
The Dean will sniff him out unerringly,
And drive him into the Archdeacon's net.

In court the Dean obeys these simple rules: 51
Frustrate the true and aid the lying cause;
Be certain only when the facts are vague;
And always seek to circumvent the laws.

He'll promise help to those who give him gold, 52
But after they have quenched his burning thirst,
He doesn't know them; suddenly he's cold.
Why work for what's already in his purse?

He has an awful itching in his palm, 53
He says, and asks if you can help him out.
But when you've oiled the hand with soothing
   gold,
He's suddenly afflicted with the gout!

Friend of wrong and enemy of right, 54
He yet will side with justice—for a price.
In love with Ticius when he's being watched,
He soon reverts, when he's alone, to vice.

A golden hand appeared out of the sky, 55
And with three fingers lifted up the Book,
Broke off the seal and vanished as it came;
But as it went it showed me where to look.

The Curia was exposed in Chapter Four. 56
The Bishop's bureaucrats are so debased,
The record of their crimes ran off the page:
To fit new sins, some old ones were erased.

The very earth is fearful of these men, 57
Who have become the terror of their time.
Their birth "amid the rocks of Rhodope"
Left them tough enough for any crime.

How could the pen of one untutored scribe 58
Record the mischief that the Curia's done?
What voice, what tongue is bold enough to speak
Of vice that any decent man would shun?

The piddling little faults of simple men 59
Are published far and wide for all to know;

The Curia's are hid from public view;
They rob and cheat and steal incognito.

Officials of the court are mighty hunters, 60
Can catch the wariest man at any time.
Fly, they shoot you; hide, they track you down.
The careless birds they net; the wise ones, lime.

The Bishop's vaults are heaped with shiny gold, 61
A thousand pieces squeezed from needy men,
But it is rumored that for every coin
The Bishop gets, the Bishop's men keep ten.

These huntsmen visit churches in their rounds, 62
And always want to know about their founding,
By which they do not mean some moldy saint,
But whether there's an income worth
   impounding.

The word *official* comes from *facere*, 63
Which means "to do," and *ob*, which means
   "against."
Thus etymology reveals the truth;
In one word is a way of life condensed.—

Soon winds and quakings filled the trembling air, 64
And then a voice resounded from the sky.
"Epheta!" it proclaimed; the seal flew off,
And Chapter Five lay open to the eye.

A preface named the topic: parish Priests, 65
Who so respect and love divinity,
That for a penny they would spit at Christ,
Or auction off the Holy Trinity.

The Priest is called by God to Holy Orders, 66
And is charged with care of sacred things,
But since he's almost always charged with wine,
He fouls the service, belching as he sings.

Sacerdos comes *sacer*, meaning "holy," 67
But *Presbyter* for Priest is somewhat better,
For *bibo* is "I drink" and *ter* is "triply;"
The Priest is of the spirits, not the letter.

The Priest has learned to sin with confidence. 68
He listens to confessions during Lent,
And when he finds out what the *people* do,
Decides that *he* has little to repent.

This hateful, bloody man abhors his flock;   69
He'd like to see them all go under grass.
He'd rather have one ample whore in bed,
Than eleven thousand virgins at his mass.

When mass is done, the Priest takes off his robes,   70
And finds a cheerful prostitute to plow;
In this he's just like Jupiter of old,
Who left Olympus to pursue a cow.

He warns the pretty women of his flock,   71
Not to forget that someday they'll be dead,
And tells them that no female can be saved,
Unless she's paid her body-tithe in bed.

So goes the little fox from hole to hole,   72
And leaves a crop of bastards where he's tilled,
Less out of lust than in the hope the souls
He breeds will make up for the ones he's killed.

At this the heavens opened to reveal   73
A noble woman dressed in rich array.
Her cheek glowed red; her hand seemed made of
   snow.
At her command the next seal fell away.

The page was dense with tiny, crowded strokes;   74
No scribe had ever done such tedious work;
A gloss filled up the space between the lines.
The subject? the excesses of the Clerk.

Sleepy, sloppy, dull, yet full of pride,   75
With low, disgusting tastes and high ambition,
He hides his sordid lusts and filthy deeds,
While scheming how to better his position.

The vicar-Clerk assumes the Parson's chore   76
Of caring for the flock's immortal souls.
The Parson merely keeps the benefice—
The profit from the livings he controls.

The Parson has so many parishes,   77
His function has become just ornamental;
He moves around so much, that if he's found
In his own church, it's merely accidental.

The Parson's humble cottage has a roof,   78
That's higher than the Church of All the Saints.

A dozen altars could be clothed for what
His mistress spends on dresses and on paints.

He built himself a hunting lodge and park,   79
Has money, rings, expensive clothes and more.
He's rich with all the riches of the Church,
While Christ is standing naked at his door.

The Vicar rules the souls assigned to him,   80
And cares for them the way he does his own—
Which means he leads the people into sin,
Until they're just as bad as he has grown.

The Clergy are the source of every sin,   81
The very Clerks who should be deep in prayer.
Business matters take up all their time;
For God or man they just have none to spare.

This one's master sends him overseas;   82
That one has no credit, but he buys;
Another plows his fields the summer long;
And each one turns his orders into lies.

This one keeps his tonsure out of sight;   83
Call that one "Doctor" and he smirks,
Although his "studies" keep him up all night.
It's hard to tell the laymen from the Clerks.

A swarm of Ethiopes quite suddenly   84
Popped up from caves and caused me some
   dismay.
They formed a kind of chorus, shouting out
In seven bursts, "Tu autem, Domine!"

My guiding Angel shook from head to foot;   85
The shouting seemed to shake the very heaven.
The Angel looked as if about to die,
When they broke off the seal of Chapter Seven.

The title of this chapter was "The Abbot."   86
The Abbot is the monks' own guide to Hell,
A cloisterer who's never in his place,
Except when he is sleeping in his cell.

A deep contempt for every worldly joy,   87
And harsh ascetic silence mark the Abbots.
They're also noted for their humble hearts,
Their threadbare, shabby cloaks—and matching
   habits.

Figure 22 Très riches heures de Jean de France. *The sun in Sagittarius in November.*

The Abbot knows the shabbier the cloak,   88
The better it conceals a lecher's tail.
He also knows that faces without beards
Are easier to shove in mugs of ale.

Contrition's tears forever dew his cheeks   89
(But he can grin when wine is passed around);
He piously refrains from using speech
(He slanders with a gesture, not a sound).

A dining Abbot's something to behold: 90
The eager teeth, the swiftly moving jaws,
The yawning throat, the gut a foaming sink,
The trembling fingers raking food like claws.

When Abbot and his brethren sit to feast,   91
They quickly pass the cups of wine along.
The Abbot lifts the cup above his head,
And makes the rafters echo with his song:

"How lovely is the vessel of the Lord!   92
Behold the chalice of inebriation!
O Bacchus, be the master of our board!
O Son of the Vine, be always our salvation!"

Then lifting up his cup again, he asks,   93
"This chalice I am now about to sup,
Can you too drink it?" Quickly all reply,
"We can! Just watch us! Bottoms up!"

The one thing that can spoil a pious feast,   94
Is a dispute about who's had the most.
The abbey therefore has a simple rule:
"The limit is a cup per monk per toast."

A second popular decree is this: 95
"A zealous monk will *never* leave a drop."
A third: "Since God abhors a vacuum,
Make sure your belly's stuffed before you stop."

The drunken monks are like demoniacs,   96
And chatter like a flock of noisy birds.
Their conversation seldom makes much sense,
Since Master Stomach teaches them the words.

They chew and chew until their jaws puff out;   97
Their huge, distended guts are even worse;
And, as a final touch, the wine they swill
Provokes a swelling in the "nether purse."

If only they knew etymology,   98
The Abbot says, his critics would keep shut:
For study shows that *work* derives from *shirk*,
And *wine* from *fine*, while *good* goes back to *gut*.

The Monk has many ways to break the Rule: 99
From lying fraud that violates a trust,
Through ignorance and aimlessness of soul,
To gluttony and solitary lust.

No devil is so grasping as the Monk,   100
Nor half so good at keeping what he gets.
Monks borrow gold, but never give it back;
Their vows, they claim, forbid them to pay debts.

The Monk is silent while he chews his meat;   101
He *concentrates* when he sits down to eat.
He never stands if he can find a seat;
His gut might be too heavy for his feet.

By day the monk performs a drunken jig;   102
By night he does an older dance in bed.
Such are the works of ardent piety,
By which he'll earn a halo for his head.

When I had heard and seen all this,   103
My guardian seized me until I cried for pain,
And then, with delicate, angelic skill,
He split my skull and opened up my brain.

He next took out a little piece of straw,   104
And, lest that I forget my wondrous vision,
Inscribed the whole thing on my tender brain,
Then carefully sewed up my odd incision.

I next was carried up above the clouds;   105
The third and highest Heaven lay revealed!
But what I saw there in that holy place,
Is so profound it must be kept concealed.

I saw the Highest Judge hold up His rod,   106
And silence all the millions round His throne.
I listened to the deep decrees of God,
Which can be understood by Him alone.

While all this passed before my dazzled eyes,   107
A pang of hunger made my stomach quiver.
I calmed it with a loaf of poppy-bread,
Washed down with water from the Lethe River.

That bread and water brought forgetfulness.   108
I've done what few or none have done before,
Seen sights undreamed of, heard amazing things,
I've flown as high as humankind can soar,

But now, another Cato, here I am,   109
Returned to earth, and nothing now remains

Of all I saw, except the little that
The Angel has engraved upon my brains.

The wonders and the mysteries I've seen!   110
Things you'll never know until you're dead.
I've seen God! the angels! Paradise!
And then forgot them when I ate some bread.

MEDIEVAL LITERARY THEORY

The following selections are designed to afford a brief introduction to the literary attitudes that were current during the Middle Ages. They are concerned, first of all, with the theoretical basis for medieval aesthetics, which placed much more emphasis on the intellectual value of poetry and far less emphasis on emotion for its own sake than does modern aesthetic theory. Again, medieval ideas of genre were neither those that we associate with Aristotle's *Poetics*, which was not well known in the Middle Ages and would not then have been appreciated, nor those which have been developed since the Renaissance. The selections also include some material that will serve as an introduction to the nature of medieval attitudes toward classical poetry and toward mythology. The Bible and the classics were the two most important sources of medieval poetic

Facing page: Jupiter, Mars, and Venus.

imagery. Limitations of space do not permit a formal introduction to the nature of conventional scriptural imagery here, but the selections do offer many clues that will be helpful indirectly. For the development of such imagery in late medieval art, which has many analogies with literature, see the very helpful book by Emile Mâle, *The Gothic Image*, Harper & Row, Publishers, Incorporated, New York, 1958. Although in some respects Mâle's study is out of date, every serious student of medieval culture should read it carefully. A general account of the significance of the materials in this section may be found in D. W. Robertson, Jr., *A Preface to Chaucer*, Princeton University Press, Princeton, N.J., 1962.

 A. *John of Salisbury*

For an introduction to John of Salisbury, see Section V. The following selections from The Policraticus *are reprinted by permission from Joseph B. Pike,* Frivolities of Courtiers and Footprints of Philosophers, *The University of Minnesota Press, Minneapolis, 1938.*

 The chapter on the Epicureans, although it is not primarily concerned with literary matters, illustrates how an interpretation of a classical poem might be used in philosophical discussion.

From
THE POLICRATICUS

Book VII

Chapter X All Writings Should Be Read; the Benediction That Was Given the Original People and the Sons of Noah; the Authority of No Gentile Should Outweigh Reason

It may be assumed that all writings[1] except those that have been disapproved should be read, since it is believed that all that has been written and all that has been done have been ordained for man's utility although at times he makes bad use of them.[2] For the angels too were, so to speak, ordained on account of the soul, but the corporeal world, according to the statement of the Fathers, for the use of the body.

 In the beginning God blessed man, saying: Increase and multiply and fill the earth and subdue it and rule over the fishes of the sea and the fowls of the air and all living creatures that move upon the earth. And in addition he conceded to them as their food every herb bearing seed and all trees according to their use[3] (for before the flood they are thought to have abstained

from flesh[4]). Those also whom the ark that foreshadowed the Church[5] rescued from the destruction of the flood he blessed, and laid down the law, saying: Increase and multiply and fill the earth. And let the fear and dread of you be upon all beasts of the earth and upon all the fowls of the air and all that move upon the earth; all the fishes of the sea are delivered into your hand. And everything that moveth and liveth shall be meat for you; even as the green herb have I delivered them all to you; saving that flesh with blood thou shalt not eat.[6]

 Behold! The same grace of benediction, the same authority of position, and the same favor of food was for the most part conferred upon the first born and upon the sons of Noah, for increase and multiplication express extension of grace; the domination of earth and the terror of beast indicate the privilege of power, and the universality of food that of liberty; all things are clean to the clean.[7]

 I do not recall that the privilege of this benediction was granted at any other period than at that when innocence was granted at creation or was recovered by the medium of the sacrament and repentance. For that reason perhaps it was said both to these immediately after the flood and to those who lived before sin came into the world, "Increase and multiply," that the increase and multiplication of that at any rate which God conferred through nature and restored by grace be attained. This is the order: to increase in themselves and, as it were, to multiply in their descendants; in themselves, for progress in merit; in their numerous descendants, by a kind of propagation of virtues. I do not remember that when nature is defiled by sin, any order is given to increase and multiply.

Although what has been previously said may be taken literally since all things are adapted to man's needs, and although those very things which seem to be deadly even to sight, smell, and hearing, not to mention touch and taste (which latter class are more dangerous), become food for man or are changed into food, nevertheless the investigator with mystic tendencies will be able to discover another meaning as well. The historical interpretation however is strengthened by the fact that we frequently see fish and wild beasts of sound health whose flesh is quite edible devouring poisonous reptiles, and by the fact that poisons themselves are used in medicaments by which mankind is not only preserved but its infirmities cured.

But since historical significance is to be examined first, any meaning that excels in forming for the mind faith and faith's works, that is to say good character, is the more desirable and clearly the more useful. The aim always to be sought in reading is that man should constantly surpass himself in virtue. But since the foregoing passage of Scripture can be directed effectively to many purposes, I agree that by grace derived from the blessing of God it can be adapted also to the task of inspiring free will for the increase and multiplication of virtue, and after virtues have been multiplied by grace, to the task of subduing the earth; for when man has subdued this within himself he attains dominion over self and over others, with the result that being favored above all living creatures, he inspires fear and terror in all that moves upon the earth.

Therefore all things serve as food for him because in all creatures the Lord speaks to him in words of his salvation.[8] It is clear that he is fed in all things by which the life of man profits for its own regulation and for that of character. For it is agreed that all building of character[9] is by the Lord, and when anyone either by work or by word or in any other way is instructed for virtue he is profitably fed by things granted him by the Lord. For all the instruction of salvation is, as it were,

the word of God, and true teaching by whomsoever offered must be accepted for the reason that truth is always uncorrupted and incorruptible.

Before and after the flood the use of all things was conceded, provided there was abstinence from the use of blood; and before and after baptism, provided he avoided sin, no one was anywhere prevented from receiving instruction. If the apostle is the odor of death unto death[10] for some, what hinders that the vessel of death be of advantage to another for life? When therefore it is said "Eat whatever you wish except blood" it is as if it were figuratively said "Provided you avoid sin, read what you wish." Just as in meat diet there are some kinds which are digested beneficially, some are turned into unassimilated humors, and others are, by an expulsive force, entirely ejected; there are some which if moderately indulged in are advantageous to those in good health but harmful to others threatened with illness; some are good for the feeble, but not so good for the sound and convalescent, for these in themselves do not strengthen; they give indeed little nourishment to the delicate, more to the common organs which require, so to speak, a richer diet.

Just so in books there is something profitable for everybody provided, be it understood the reading is done with discrimination and that only is selected which is edifying to faith and morals. There is matter which is of profit to stronger minds but is to be kept from the artless; there is that which an innately sound mind rejects; there is that which it digests for character building or perfecting eloquence; there is that which hardens the soul and causes spiritual indigestion in matters of faith and good works. There is scarcely a piece of writing in which something is not found either in meaning or expression that the discriminating reader will not reject. The safe and cautious thing to do is to read only Catholic books. It is somewhat dangerous to expose the unsophisticated to pagan literature; but a training in both is very useful to those safe in the faith, for accurate reading on a wide range of subjects makes the scholar; careful selection of the better makes the saint.

We ought as it were to imitate bees. We read in the book entitled *Saturnalia* and in the epistles of Seneca[11] to Lucilius: "Bees roam about and sip flowers, then arrange what they bring in, distribute it in combs, and by a mixing process and by their own peculiar scent change the taste of the various ingredients into one flavor. Whatever we have acquired by our varied reading [let us also turn to virtue's purpose, that all may combine into a category of things to be transacted by the directing force of reason]. For in the mind as well things are preserved better when kept separate, and this very separation, aided by a sort of leaven by which the whole is seasoned, mixes together the various samples to produce a single savor. The result is that even if the origin of the combination is apparent it appears to be something else than that from which we know it is derived. This is what we see nature doing in our body without any effort on our own part; the food which we receive, as long as it retains its own original quality and floats about intact, is an unwholesome weight on the stomach; but when it is changed from that which it was, then it is that it changes into tissue";[12] for blood is set apart by divine commandment for the avoidance of sin.[13]

The shepherd of the Church[14] was enjoined to kill and eat crawling and unclean things; now although this specifically applies to his summoning of the gentiles it may teach, by reason of the similarity of the case, that when we have slain our errors we have nothing to fear from the doctrines of the gentiles. As long as the Pythagoreans teach innocence, frugality, and contempt for the world they should be given a hearing; when they thrust souls which they have lifted to the sky back into bodies of beasts, even a Plato, if he be so taught, should be slain. In this particular he overreached himself in following Pythagoras, because he taught that as the dead are formed from the living, so the living from the dead and that they pass into various bodies according to their characters; consequently the lines:

Myself (for I remember well the fact)
Euphorbus was, the son of Panthoüs,
And in the Trojan war, the heavy spear
Of Menelaus lodged full in my
Left breast.[15]

Therefore let the pagan writers be read in a way that their authority be not prejudicial to reason; for the burning weed,[16] as the rose is plucked, sometimes burns the hand of him who touches it.

Wisdom is as it were a spring from which rivers go out[17] watering all the land, and its divine pages not only fill with delight the place of its birth but also make their way among the nations to such an extent that they are not entirely unknown even to the Ethiopians. It is from this source that the flowering, perfumed, fruitful works of the pagan world spring, and should perchance any artless reader enter their field let him keep in mind this quotation:

Flee hence, O ye who gather flowers
Or berries growing on the ground; the clammy
Snake is hiding in the grass.[18]

It is no sluggard who carries off the apples of the Hesperides guarded by the ever sleepless dragon,[19] nor one who reads as though not awake but drowsing and dreaming as if eager to reach the end of his task. It is certain that the pious and wise reader who spends time lovingly over his books always rejects errors and comes close to life in all things. Hence the saying of the teacher of teachers, Jerome: Love the knowledge of the Scriptures and you will not love the errors of the flesh.[20]

Notes

1   Cf. Rom. 15:4.
2   The contrast here is between *use* and *abuse* in the Augustinian sense. See *On Christian Doctrine*, 1:3, 4.
3   Gen. 1:28–29.
4   John may have seen this idea expressed in St. Jerome's treatise *Against Jovinian*.
5   Cf. 1 Peter 3:20, 21. This is a commonplace of Patristic and medieval exegesis.
6   Gen. 9:1–4.
7   Titus 1:15; cf. Rom. 14:20.
8   The "words" here are figurative. Hugh of St. Victor says that the things of the created world constitute the voice of God speaking to men. That is, spiritual meanings are to be derived from nature,

or from what came to be called "the Book of God's Work," as well as from the sacred text, or "the Book of God's Word." The "food" referred to is, of course, spiritual food.

9 Eph. 2:21.

10 2 Cor. 2:16.

11 *Epistles*, 84:5, 6.

12 From *Saturnalia*, 1.

13 Gen. 9:4.

14 St. Peter. See Acts 11:5ff.

15 Ovid, *Metamorphoses*, 15:160–162.

16 John here plays on the similarity of *urtica* and *uro*, a device borrowed from the *Etymologies* of Isidore of Seville. However, the meaning is simply "thorn."

17 Gen. 2:10ff.

18 Vergil, *Eclogues*, 3:92–93.

19 Macrobius, *Saturnalia*, 1:20, 3.

20 St. Jerome, *Epistles*, 125:11.

Chapter XI   What Constitutes True Philosophy; the Aim of All Writing

Herein lies true philosophy, and it is the most pleasant and salutary advantage that wide reading confers. Wisdom itself embraces a knowledge of all things, directs all things, and itself fixes the proper limit of deeds, words, and thoughts everywhere in the life of man. There is however that for which even she knows not how to fix a boundary; there is that for which she establishes a mode in the fact that it has no limit. Whatever wisdom does and whatever she says leads to the truth, that with true philosophers she has no limit; for her substance is of that which nowhere has an end. If indeed, according to Plato,[1] the philosopher is he who loves God, what else is philosophy if not the love of the divine? This is something that brooks no limit, otherwise philosophy herself would be restricted, and this is inexpedient; for that which is restricted also ceases to be, and if God's love be extinguished the word philosophy vanishes into thin air.

So also the Incarnate Wisdom of God, though He limits many things, enjoins that love for God be limitless; except that this mode is prescribed for charity, that God be loved with love that has no limits; for Jesus said "Thou shalt love thy neighbor as thyself."[2] He likewise had said before "Thou shalt love the Lord thy God with thy whole heart and with thy whole soul and with thy whole mind and with thy whole strength."[3] He also added "On these two words dependeth the whole law and the prophets."[4] If therefore all that has been written attends on the prophets and the law, that is to say, if all teaching has the aim of subjecting man to the law of God, who doubts that all things are accredited to the law of God; who doubts that all things are accredited to the realm of charity? Whoever then by the agency of philosophy acquires or spreads charity has attained his aim as a philosopher. Consequently this is the true and unvarying rule of philosophers, that each one busy himself in all that he reads or learns, does, or abstains from doing, with advancing the cause of charity. Charity is never meaningless and apart; it conducts honor, self-control, and sobriety, modesty, and the whole army of venerable virtues to man as to the temple of the Lord and dedicates him to piety.

All that has not this aim in the arts and in literature is not philosophic doctrine but the idle fable and pretext of those over whose impiety the wrath of God is revealed from heaven.[5] All their chattering seems flat, silly, and senseless to the true philosopher. Listen not to me but to the prophet speaking of such things: "The wicked have told me fables but not as thy law."[6] Therefore to give expression to truth and justice is common both to those who are philosophers and to those who are not; to tell the truth and lies, to teach good and evil, is not a characteristic of philosophers. It is only at times that the mere imitator of the philosopher teaches righteousness, but he who practices the righteousness which he teaches really is a philosopher.

Notes

1 John is here reflecting St. Augustine, *City of God*, 8:5.
2 Matt. 22:39.
3 Matt. 22:37.
4 Cf. Matt. 22:40.
5 Rom. 1:18.
6 Ps. 118:85.

Book VIII

Chapter XXIV   Epicureans Never Attain Their Goal

Unless a stubborn disputant dissemble that which reason does not allow to be dissembled, it is as clear as day that the Epicureans do not attain their end. Though they do indeed aspire to a tranquil life and to play the sage to sate their lust, nay, to play the fool (for no one sagely can satisfy evil desires), no one attains such aims through these rivers of Babylon.[1] I am also of the opinion that they who wish to do their own will are to be rated as Epicureans; for when actions become the slave of lust, affection changes to passion. If affection obey not affection, the more you wish the more you are tortured if, that is, there be lust in your will; if not, at times to wish for the unattainable is pleasurable and fruitful if perchance you hunger and thirst after justice,[2] toilsome as well. And so the world is filled with Epicureans for the reason that in its great multitude of men there are few who are not slaves to lust, that is to corrupt will, while there are either none or very few who are not entangled in the meshes of worry that will involves.

Man was excluded from the place of pleasure[3] from the moment that lust prevailed for the reason that life can be neither pleasing nor tranquil for one who has begun to be swayed by it. Man preferred to do what he pleased rather than what he was commanded and was cast out into the place of misery, into the land of labor, in order that the earth put forth, for him and his seed, thorns and thistles, and that he, who obedient in rectitude of desire might have had full pleasure with no difficulties and labor, should eat his bread by the sweat of his brow.[4] He had found all things prepared for his necessity and pleasure. (The word *vultus* [brow] according to those who have some interest in etymology is derived from the word *volendo* [wishing];[5] and its sweat suggests the labor and anxiety involved in corrupt will.)

If therefore there is sweating for that which strengthens man's heart and that gives him joy even in partaking,[6] what is there that mortal man should suppose conceded to him without labor? The soul recalls what sentence the Creator pronounced against the sinning mother of all of us. She therefore who brings forth[7] offspring of sin without labor brings forth in sorrow children of the virtues; for sinful nature is prone to evil and is corrupt from its youth, an age that is near to its origin, so that without labor or difficulty it can fall, and cannot be lifted up to goodness without labor, and when lifted up it cannot stand without difficulty and without grace. She therefore brings forth sins, daughters, not sons, without sorrow but indubitably for sorrow; on the other hand sons in sorrow, but assuredly for joy, not sorrow.

Therefore the Epicurean abides in sorrow and his life brings forth sons and daughters and he is ever groaning at troubles present or to come. For to omit all else, he either does not rejoice in the present or, if he is not blind, he takes the measure of events and mourns them as departing and fleeting. It is indeed denied joyful things to abide unless one finds his joy in those things that make happy or avail for eternal life. This world passeth[8] and all its desirable things; however much it flatters the unwary and pledges them the sweet allurements of its deception, its end is more bitter than any wormwood;[9] and because reason everywhere convinces that its present state is imperfect, it ever promises something substantial for the future, with the result that in the case of all its lovers and followers, it has from the very beginning brought not even one to perfection or satisfied his desires.

Hence it is that the miser hungers in the midst of wealth, that the one at the pinnacle of power is a slave, that the devotee of pleasure is tortured in the midst of luxury by the failure of his joy, and that the wooer of fame and favor in the towering pride of his vainglory is as nothing. A man to whom these facts are not manifest is indeed quite blind, since every one of those devoted to such interests confesses that he lacks what he is seeking.

There are however those whose eyes are blinded to such an extent that they are unable to see what is perfectly apparent in itself.[10] So sightless moles[11] are not acquainted with the blessing of light; enjoying the darkness natural to them they hate the purer air and are unable to survive if kept any length of time from the earth and their lurking places. Are not they who always abide in the ground, whose whole association is held down to the earth so that they are incapable of high or divine, nay, even of human thought, the very personification of the mole? And whose is the right to contemplate erect in the dignity of body and soul the heavens and what is in them, while other animals[12] are borne along with faces turned down to earth? They however as a result of their own mole-like nature are bent down.

He who is stained by guilt is assuredly worse than he who labors by nature's command. Nor should you believe that he is high minded who prefers to precede his fellow men not so much by virtue as by vice. But why in that drove of moles do I censure blindness except that it appears to be the source of other things? It is the source of rivers of vice so that you see converging as it were in one body the rapacity of the lion, the cruelty of the tiger, the gluttony of the wolf, the spots of the leopard, the cunning of the fox, the tenacity of the harpy, the filthiness of the sow, the wantonness of the he-goat, the pride of the horse, the stolidity of the mule, the venom of the hydra, the blackness of the crow, and whatever other perversity loathsome creation has been able to impose upon man.[13]

From such a source have flowed these universal calamities, as it promises a knowledge of good and evil and a similitude to God by means of rapine. Consequently the nature of man is prone to evil whose infancy of innocence, so to speak, continued as long as he abstained from communication perverted and perverting. Man spoke not[14] and remained innocent. A deep sleep was cast upon him and he fell asleep in innocence. He awoke, and recognizing a helpmate like unto himself which God had fashioned for him, he spoke the wonderful works of God.[15]

But from the day that he was given speech and led out through the door of curiosity, he had converse with the tempter. As if he had attained maturity after child-hood, he was swollen with the pride within him; and transgressing the command the keeping of which would have profited for his glory, he was corrupted, with the result that after the marvelous and inviolable law of the condition then imposed upon it, this union of flesh and spirit rebelled, so that in no way can the two be harmonized without the intervention of the grace of Him who hath made both one[16] and shall make flesh to be absorbed by spirit at the judgment of the elect.

If the words of the pagan may be employed by the Christian who believes that a nature divine and pleasing to God because of the grace inherent in it can belong to the elect alone (although I do not think that either the words or the thoughts of the pagans are to be shunned provided their errors are avoided), Virgil seems to have been by divine wisdom given a hint of this very fact. Under the cloak of poetic imagination in his *Eneid*[17] he subtly represents the six periods of life by the division of the work into six books. In these, in imitation of the *Odyssey*, he appears to have represented the origin and progress of man. The character he sets forth and develops he leads on and conducts down into the nether world. For Eneas who therein represents the soul, is so named for the reason that it is a dweller in the body, for *ennos*, according to the Greeks, is "dweller," and *demas* "body." The name Eneas is formed of these two elements to signify life dwelling, as it were, in a hut of flesh. In the same way Neptune is called *ennosigeus* because he is a dweller in Sigeum.

The first book of the *Aeneid* then, under the figure of a shipwreck, sets forth the manifest tribulations of childhood, which is shaken by its own tempests; and at the termination of the period the abundance of food and drink of manhood is in evidence at the gaiety of the banquet. On the confines of boyhood conversation facilitates the interchange of ideas, and its freedom from restraint leads to the narration of stories and the mingling of the true and the false for the reason that a multitude of words[18] cannot want sin. The third book sings the varied errors of youth which, as it were, belong to it because that age knows almost nothing but error; since indeed the moralist says

The beardless youth, at length his guard removed,
Exults in horses, hounds, and games upon
The sunlit field. Like wax he molds to vice;
Is rude to his advisers and slow to see
What's good for him. He's lavish with his cash.[19]

The first period, then, has its nurse; the second its guardian; the third, the freer it is the more easily it is led astray but not yet so far as to commit crime. The fourth period introduces illicit love and fans the flame unwisely lit within his heart, to kindle the pyre of the ill-fated queen; for reason, personified by Mercury, persuades that happiness is not ordained for forbidden love and teaches that he who, when he was a child,[20] understood as a child, spoke as a child, and acted as a child, after he had irrevocably taken to flight puts away the things of a child. Therefore let us return to the moralist quoted above:

> With other aims the age and spirit of
> The man seeks wealth and friends, becomes
> A slave to office and shuns to do
> That which it will straightway strive hard
> To change.[21]

Therefore mature manhood blushes at childish and youthful things, and if one has not power to weigh anchor and flee from perverted pleasure and impure love, he will sever the cable. Thus too the chaste son of the patriarch[22] left his garment in the hand of the adulteress that he might not be implicated in the crime of adultery.

The fifth period brings with it civic maturity and represents the period that is adjacent to old age, nay, that is already entering it. The protagonist reviews the honors held by his sires, venerates his ancestors, and, as if he were solemnizing games at the tomb of an Anchises, in them he recalls the misery of his exile. As he emerges from this he enters the sixth period and suffers the loss of Palinurus and Misenus, the pilot who fell asleep and who incited to rash battle. Since by now his emotions are numbed and his powers waning, he experiences not so much old age itself as its decay and, as it were, a descent to the lower world, to review there the errors of his past life, as though all his achievements had come to naught. He learns there that another way must be traveled by those who wish to attain the fond embraces of Lavinia and the destined kingdom of Italy as a sort of citadel of beatitude.

It is agreed by those who devote their activities to the investigation of the meaning of authors that Virgil has evinced his power in a double field by arraying the mysteries of philosophic moral perfection in the gossamer of poetic fancy. Although this statement is specifically made in connection with the first sin, it can with clarity and reason be demonstrated with regard to every step, that man's nature from youth on is prone to evil; so that from the moment he began to enjoy free will, though under limitation, he of his own accord fell into sin and then, as he deserved, plunged headlong into punishment. In no way can he be raised to goodness unless God in his grace places a supporting hand beneath him.

Broad therefore is the way[23] of the Epicureans, and it leadeth indubitably to death, through perils however, through error, through bitterness, and through all kinds of vanities, so that no one finds on it a joyful and tranquil condition of life or ever reaches such a state by following it; for that beatitude be grasped, its foundation must be planted upon true, not vain blessings. Vain blessings do indeed cast their votary into exterior darkness[24] where there is weeping of eyes and gnashing of teeth, tingling of ears,[25] the various tortures and afflictions of the damned, and where no order but everlasting horror dwelleth.[26]

Notes

1 Ps. 136:1. According to St. Augustine, the rivers of Babylon in this psalm "are all things which are loved in this world and which pass away."

2 Matt. 5:6.

3 Paradise.

4 Gen. 3:17ff.

5 The etymology is that of Isidore of Seville.

6 That is, bread. See Ps. 103:15.

7 Gen. 3:16.

8 1 Cor. 7:13.

9 Prov. 5:4.

10   Cf. Rom. 11:8; Matt. 13:14–15; John 12:40; Isa. 6:9–10. For the theme in art, see Erwin Panofsky, *Studies in Iconology*, Harper & Row, Publishers, Incorporated, New York, 1962, pp. 185ff.

11   Vergil, *Georgics*, 1:183.

12   Ovid, *Metamorphoses*, 1:84–86.

13   Comparisons such as this are responsible for many of the grotesques in medieval art.

14   Cf. Gen. 2:18ff.

15   Acts 2:11.

16   See Eph. 2:13–16 and Gal. 5:17. In connection with this last passage, St. Augustine explains (*On Christian Doctrine*, 1:24, 24–25) that there is no natural enmity between the flesh and the spirit. By "flesh" St. Paul means not the body but the evil habit of the flesh inherited from the Fall.

17   The following interpretation of *The Aeneid* is based on the commentary by Bernard Silvestris.

18   Prov. 10:19.

19   Horace, *Ars poetica*, 161–164.

20   I Cor. 13:11.

21   Horace, *Ars poetica*, 166–168.

22   That is, Joseph. See Gen. 39:12.

23   Matt. 7:13.

24   Matt. 8:12; 22:13; 25:30.

25   Jer. 19:3.

26   Job 10:22.

 # B. Dante

Dante Alighieri (1265–1321), the famous author of The Divine Comedy, *has left us a number of observations about poets and poetry. In some ways the easiest to understand are those which he wrote as an accessus or explanatory preface to his great poem for Can Grande della Scala.*

The medieval accessus is well discussed by Jean Leclercq, The Love of Learning and the Desire for God, *Fordham University Press, New York, 1961. The following selection is reprinted by permission from Paget Toynbee,* The Letters of Dante, *Clarendon Press, Oxford, 1920.*

ACCESSUS
to His Poem for Can Grande della Scala

To the magnificent and most victorious Lord, the Lord Can Grande della Scala, Vicar-General of the most holy principality of Caesar in the city of Verona, and town of Vicenza, his most devoted servant, Dante Alighieri, a Florentine by birth, not by disposition, prayeth long and happy life, and perpetual increase of the glory of his name.

The illustrious renown of your Magnificence, which wakeful Fame spreads abroad as she flies, affects divers persons in divers ways, so that some it uplifts with the hope of good fortune, while others it casts down with the dread of destruction. The report whereof, overtopping all deeds of recent times, I erstwhile did deem extravagant, as going beyond the appearance of truth. But that continued uncertainty might not keep me longer in suspense, even as the Queen of the South sought Jerusalem,[1] and as Pallas sought Helicon,[2] so did I seek Verona, in order to examine with my own trusty eyes the things of which I had heard. And there was I witness of your splendor, there was I witness and partaker of your bounty; and whereas I had formerly suspected the reports to be somewhat unmeasured, I afterwards recognized that it was the facts themselves that were beyond measure. Whence it came to pass that whereas through hearsay alone, with a certain subjection of mind, I had previously become well disposed towards you, at the first sight of you I became your most devoted servant and friend.

Nor do I think that in assuming the name of friend I shall lay myself open to a charge of presumption, as some perchance might object; inasmuch as unequals no less than equals are united by the sacred tie of friendship. For if one should examine friendships which have been pleasant and profitable, it will be evident that in many cases the bond has been between persons of superior station and their inferiors. And if our attention be directed to true friendship for its own sake, shall we not find that the friends of illustrious and mighty princes have many a time been men obscure in condition but of distinguished virtue? Why not? since even the friendship of God and man is in no wise impeded by the disparity between them. But if any man consider this assertion unseemly, let him hearken to the Holy Spirit when it declares that certain men have been partakers of its friendship. For in *Wisdom* we read, concerning wisdom: "For she is a treasure unto men that never faileth; which they that use are made partakers of the friendship of God."[3] But the common herd in their ignorance judge without discernment; and even as they imagine the sun to be a foot across, so they judge with regard to questions of conduct; and they are deceived by their foolish credulity with regard to both the one and the other matter. But it does not become us, to whom it has been given to know what is best in our nature, to follow in the footsteps of the common herd; nay, rather are we bound to oppose their errors. For those who have vigor of intellect and reason, being endowed with a certain divine liberty, are not restricted by precedent. Nor is this to be wondered at, for it is not they who receive direction from the laws, but rather the laws from them. It is manifest, therefore, that what I said above, namely that I was your most devoted servant and friend, in no wise savors of presumption.

Esteeming, then, your friendship as a most precious treasure, I desire to preserve it with assiduous forethought and anxious care. Therefore, since it is a doctrine of ethics that friendship is equalized and preserved by reciprocity, it is my wish to preserve due reciprocity in making a return for the bounty more than once conferred upon me. For which reason I have often and long examined such poor gifts as I can offer, and have set them out separately, and scrutinized each in turn, in order to decide which would be the most worthy and the most acceptable to you. And I have found nothing more suitable even for your exalted station than the sublime cantica of the *Comedy* which is adorned with the title of *Paradise*; this, then, dedicated to yourself, with the present letter to serve as its superscription, I inscribe, offer, and in fine commend to you.

Nor does the simple ardor of my affection permit me to pass over in silence the consideration that in this offering there may seem to be greater honor and fame conferred on the patron than on the gift; the rather that in the address I shall appear to such as read with attention to have given utterance to a forecast as to the increase of the glory of your name—and this of set purpose. But eagerness for your favor, for which I thirst, heedless of envy, will urge me forward to the goal which was my aim from the first. And so, having made an end of what I had to say in epistolary form, I will now in the capacity of commentator essay a few words by way of introduction to the work which is offered for your acceptance.

As the Philosopher says in the second book of the *Metaphysics*, "as a thing is in respect of being, so is it in respect of truth"[4]; the reason of which is, that the truth concerning a thing, which consists in the truth as in its subject, is the perfect likeness of the thing as it is. Now of things which exist, some are such as to have absolute being in themselves; while others are such as to have their being dependent upon something else, by virtue of a certain relation, as being in existence at the same time, or having respect to some other thing, as in the case of correlatives, such as father and son, master and servant, double and half, the whole and part, and other similar things, in so far as they are related. Inasmuch, then, as the being of such things depends upon something else, it follows that the truth of these things likewise depends upon something else; for if the half is unknown, its double cannot be known; and so of the rest.

If any one, therefore, is desirous of offering any sort of introduction to part of a work, it behoves him to furnish some notion of the whole of which it is a part. Wherefore I, too, being desirous of offering something by way of introduction to the above-mentioned part of the whole *Comedy*, thought it incumbent on me in the first place to say something concerning the work as a whole, in order that access to the part might be the easier and the more perfect. There are six points, then, as to which inquiry must be made at the beginning of every didactic work; namely, the subject, the author, the form, the aim, the title of the book, and the branch of philosophy to which it belongs. Now of these six points there are three in respect of which the part which I have had in mind to address to you differs from the whole work; namely, the subject, the form, and the title; whereas in respect of the others there is no difference, as is obvious to any one who considers the matter. Consequently, in an examination of the whole, these three points must be made the subject of a separate inquiry; which being done, the way will be sufficiently clear for the introduction to the part. Later we will examine the other three points, not only with reference to the whole work, but also with reference to the particular part which is offered to you.

For the elucidation, therefore, of what we have to say, it must be understood that the meaning of this work is not of one kind only; rather the work may be described as "polysemous," that is, having several meanings; for the first meaning is that which is conveyed by the letter, and the next is that which is conveyed by what the letter signifies; the former of which is called literal, while the latter is called allegorical, or mystical. And for the better illustration of this method of exposition we may apply it to the following verses: "When Israel went out of Egypt, the house of Jacob from a people of strange language; Judah was his sanctuary, and Israel his dominion."[5] For if we consider the letter alone, the thing signified to us is the going out of the children of Israel from Egypt in the time of Moses; if the allegory, our redemption through Christ is signified; if the moral sense, the conversion of the soul from the sorrow and misery of sin to a state of grace is signified; if the anagogical, the passing of the sanctified soul from the bondage of the corruption of this world to the liberty of everlasting glory is signified. And although these mystical meanings are called by various names, they may one and all in a general sense be termed allegorical, inasmuch as they are different (diversi) from the literal or historical; for the word "allegory" is so called from the Greek alleon, which in Latin is alienum (strange) or diversum (different).

This being understood, it is clear that the subject, with regard to which the alternative meanings are brought into play, must be twofold. And therefore the subject of this work must be considered in the first place from the point of view of the literal meaning, and next from that of the allegorical interpretation. The subject, then, of the whole work, taken in the literal sense only, is the state of souls after death, pure and simple. For on and about that the argument of the whole work turns. If, however, the work be regarded from the allegorical point of view, the subject is man according as by his merits or demerits in the exercise of his free will he is deserving of reward or punishment by justice.

And the form is twofold—the form of the treatise, and the form of the treatment. The form of the treatise is threefold, according to the threefold division. The first division is that whereby the whole work is divided into three cantiche; the second, whereby each cantica is divided into cantos; and the third, whereby each canto is divided into rhymed lines. The form or manner of treatment is poetic, fictive, descriptive, digressive, and figurative; and further, it is definitive, analytical, probative, refutative, and exemplificative.

The title of the book is "Here begins the *Comedy* of Dante Alighieri, A Florentine by birth, not by disposition." For the understanding of which it must be noted that "comedy" is so called from *comos*, a village, and *oda*, a song; whence comedy is as it were a "rustic song." Now comedy is a certain kind of poetical narration which differs from all others. It differs, then, from tragedy in its subject-matter, in that tragedy at the beginning is admirable and placid, but at the end or issue is foul and horrible. And tragedy is so called from *tragos*, a goat, and *oda*; as it were a "goat-song," that is to say foul like a goat, as appears from the tragedies of Seneca. Whereas comedy begins with sundry adverse conditions, but ends happily, as appears from the comedies of Terence. And for this reason it is the custom of some writers in their salutation to say by way of greeting: "a tragic beginning and a comic ending to you!" Tragedy and comedy differ likewise in their style of language; for that of tragedy is high-flown and sublime, while that of comedy is unstudied and lowly. And this is implied by Horace in the *Art of Poetry*, where he grants that the comedian may on occasion use the language of tragedy, and vice versa:

Yet sometimes comedy her voice will raise,
And angry Chremes scold with swelling phrase;
And prosy periods oft our ears assail
When Telephus and Peleus tell their tragic tale.[6]

And from this it is clear that the present work is to be described as a comedy. For if we consider the subject-matter, at the beginning it is horrible and foul, as being *Hell*; but at the close it is happy, desirable, and pleasing, as being *Paradise*. As regards the style of language, the style is unstudied and lowly, as being in the vulgar tongue, in which even women-folk hold their talk. And hence it is evident why the work is called a comedy. And there are other kinds of poetical narration, such as the pastoral poem, the elegy, the satire, and the votive song, as may also be gathered from Horace in the *Art of Poetry*; but of these we need say nothing at present.

It can now be shown in what manner the subject of the part offered to you is to be determined. For if the subject of the whole work taken in the literal sense is the state of souls after death, pure and simple, without limitation; it is evident that in this part the same state is the subject, but with a limitation, namely the state of blessed souls after death. And if the subject of the whole work from the allegorical point of view is man according as by his merits or demerits in the exercise of his free will he is deserving of reward or punishment by justice, it is evident that in this part this subject has a limitation, and that it is man according as by his merits he is deserving of reward by justice.

In like manner the form of the part is determined by that of the whole work. For if the form of the treatise as a whole is threefold, in this part it is twofold only, the division being that of the cantica and of the cantos.

The first division (into cantiche) cannot be applicable to the form of the part, since the cantica is itself a part under the first division.

The title of the book also is clear. For the title of the whole book is "Here begins the *Comedy*," &c., as above; but the title of the part is "Here begins the third cantica of the *Comedy* of Dante, which is called *Paradise*."

These three points, in which the part differs from the whole, having been examined, we may now turn our attention to the other three, in respect of which there is no difference between the part and the whole. The author, then, of the whole and of the part is the person mentioned above, who is seen to be such throughout.

The aim of the whole and of the part might be manifold; as, for instance, immediate and remote. But leaving aside any minute examination of this question, it may be stated briefly that the aim of the whole and of the part is to remove those living in this life from a state of misery, and to bring them to a state of happiness.

The branch of philosophy to which the work is subject, in the whole as in the part, is that of morals or ethics; inasmuch as the whole as well as the part was conceived, not for speculation, but with a practical object. For if in certain parts or passages the treatment is after the manner of speculative philosophy, that is not for the sake of speculation, but for a practical purpose; since, as the Philosopher says in the second book of the *Metaphysics*: "practical men occasionally speculate on things in their particular and temporal relations."[7]

Notes

1 Matt. 12:42; Luke 11:31.
2 Ovid, *Metamorphoses*, 5:254.
3 Wisd. 7:14.
4 Aristotle, *Metaphysics*, 2:1.
5 Ps. 113:1–2.
6 Horace, *Ars poetica*, 93–96.
7 *Metaphysics*, 2:1.

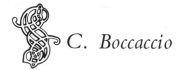

C. Boccaccio

Giovanni Boccaccio (1313–1375) is best known as the author of The Decameron, *a collection of tales which has won for its author an undeserved reputation for immorality and irreverence. Modern biographies of Boccaccio are frequently fictional in character, being based on a naïve acceptance of his early poems as evidence for his own life. Boccaccio's most ambitious work was not* The Decameron, *but a long Latin treatise* On the Genealogy of the Gentile Gods. *This work embodies a systematic account of the deities of pagan myth arranged in accordance with their family relationships. It also contains a great deal of allegorical interpretation of narratives concerning the gods. The* Genealogy *became a more or less standard manual for poets and painters. It was the last in a long series of medieval mythographic manuals beginning with the work of Fulgentius and, at the same time, the basis for similar manuals produced in the Renaissance. The fourteenth and fifteenth books of the* Genealogy *contain a spirited defense of poetry as it was understood during the Middle Ages.*

The best introduction to Boccaccio's views on poetry is Charles G. Osgood, Boccaccio on Poetry, *The Bobbs-Merrill Co., Inc., Indianapolis, 1956. The following selections are reprinted by permission from this source.*

From
THE GENEALOGY OF THE GENTILE GODS

Book XIV

V   Other Cavillers at the Poets and Their Imputations

There is also, O most serene of rulers, as you know far better than I, a kind of house established in this world by God's gift, in the image of a celestial council, and devoted only to sacred studies. Within, on a lofty throne, sits Philosophy,[1] messenger from the very bosom of God, mistress of all knowledge. Noble is her mien and radiant with godlike splendor. There she sits arrayed in royal robes and adorned with a golden crown, like the Empress of all the World. In her left hand she holds several books, with her right hand she wields a royal scepter, and in clear and fluent discourse she shows forth to such as will listen the truly praiseworthy ideals of human character, the forces of our Mother Nature, the true good, and the secrets[2] of heaven. If you enter you do not doubt that it is a sanctuary full worthy of all reverence; and if you look about, you will clearly see there every opportunity for the higher pursuits of the human mind, both speculation and knowledge, and will gaze with wonder till you regard it not merely as one all-inclusive household, but almost the very image of the divine mind. Among other

objects of great veneration there, behind the mistress of the household, are certain men seated in high places, few in number, of gentle aspect and utterance, who are so distinguished by their seriousness, honesty, and true humility, that you take them for gods not mortals. These men abound in the faith and doctrine of their mistress, and give freely to others of the fullness of their knowledge.

But there is also another group[3]—a noisy crowd—of all sorts and conditions. Some of these have resigned all pride, and live in watchful obedience to the injunctions of their superiors, in hopes that their obsequious zeal may gain them promotion. But others there are who grow so elated with what is virtually elementary knowledge, that they fall upon their great mistress' robes as it were with their talons, and in violent haste tear away a few shreds as samples; then don various titles which they often pick up for a price; and, as puffed up as if they knew the whole subject of divinity, they rush forth from the sacred house, setting such mischief afoot among ignorant people as only the wise can calculate. Yet these rascals are sworn conspirators against all high arts. First they try to counterfeit a good man; they exchange their natural expression for an anxious, careful one. They go about with downcast eye to appear inseparable from their thoughts. Their pace is slow to make the uneducated think that they stagger under an excessive weight of high speculation. They dress unpretentiously, not because they are really modest, but only to mask themselves with sanctity.

Their talk is little and serious. If you ask them a question they heave a sigh, pause a moment, raise their eyes to heaven, and at length deign to answer. They hope the bystanders will infer from this that their words rise slowly to their lips, not from any lack of eloquence, but because they are fetched from the remote sanctuary of heavenly secrets. They profess piety, sanctity, and justice, and often, forsooth, utter the words of the prophet, "The zeal of God's house hath eaten me up."[4]

Then they proceed to display their wonderful knowledge, and whatever they don't know they damn—to good effect too. This they do to avoid inquiry about subjects of which they are ignorant, or else to affect scorn and indifference in such matters as cheap, trivial, and obvious, while they have devoted themselves to things of greater importance. When they have caught inexperienced minds in traps of this sort, they proceed boldly to range about town, dabble in business, give advice, arrange marriages, appear at big dinners, dictate wills, act as executors of estates, and otherwise display arrogance unbecoming to a philosopher. Thus they blow up a huge cloud of popular reputation, and thereby so strut with vanity that, when they walk abroad, they want to have everybody's finger pointing them out, to overhear people saying that they are great masters of their subjects, and see how the grand folk rise to meet them in the squares of the city and call them "Rabbi,"[5] speak to them, invite them, give place and defer to them. Straightway they throw off all restraint and become bold enough for anything; they are not afraid to lay their own sickles to the harvest of another; and haply, while they are basely defiling other people's business, the talk may fall upon poetry and poets. At the sound of the word they blaze up in such a sudden fury that you would say their eyes were afire. They cannot stop; they go raging on by the very momentum of their wrath. Finally, like conspirators against a deadly enemy, in the schools, in public squares, in pulpits, with a lazy crowd, as a rule, for an audience, they break out into such mad denunciation of poets that the bystanders are afraid of the speakers themselves, let alone the harmless objects of attack.

They say poetry is absolutely of no account, and the making of poetry a useless and absurd craft; that poets are tale-mongers, or, in lower terms, liars; that they live in the country among the woods and mountains because they lack manners and polish. They say, besides, that their poems are false, obscure, lewd, and replete with absurd and silly tales of pagan gods, and that they make Jove, who was, in point of fact, an obscene and adulterous man, now the father of gods, now king of heaven, now fire, or air, or man, or bull, or eagle, or similar irrelevant things; in like manner poets exalt to fame Juno and infinite others under various names. Again and again they cry out that poets are seducers of the mind, prompters of crime, and, to make their foul charge, fouler, if possible, they say they are philosophers' apes, that it is a heinous crime to read or possess the books of poets; and then, without making any distinction, they prop themselves up, as they say, with Plato's authority to the effect that poets ought to be turned out-of-doors—nay, out of town, and that the Muses, their mumming mistresses, as Boethius says, being sweet with deadly sweetness, are detestable, and should be driven out with them and utterly rejected. But it would take too long to cite everything that their irritable spite and deadly hatred prompt these madmen to say. It is also before judges like these—so eminent, forsooth, so fair, so merciful, so well-inclined—that my work will appear, O glorious Prince; and I know full well they will gather about it like famished lions,[6] to seek what they may devour. Since my book has entirely to do with poetic material, I cannot look for a milder sentence from them than in their rage they thunder down upon poets. I am well aware that I offer my breast to the same missiles that their hatred has already employed; but I shall endeavor to ward them off.

O merciful God, meet now this foolish and ill-considered clamor of mad men, and oppose their rage. And thou, O best of kings, as I advance upon their line, support me with the strength of thy noble soul, and help me in my fight for thee; for courage and a stout heart must now be mine. Sharp and poisonous are their weapons, but weak withal. Foolish judges though they be, they are strong in other ways, and I tremble with fear before them, unless God, who deserteth not them that trust in Him, and thou, also, favor me. Slender is my strength and my mind weak, but great is my expectation of help; borne up by such hope, I shall rush upon them with justice at my right hand.

IX It Is Rather Useful than Damnable to Compose Stories

These fine cattle bellow still further to the effect that poets are tale-mongers, or, to use the lower and more hateful term which they sometimes employ in their resentment—liars. No doubt the ignorant will regard such an imputation as particularly objectionable. But I scorn it. The foul language of some men cannot infect the glorious name of the illustrious. Yet I grieve to see these revilers in a purple rage let themselves loose upon the innocent. If I conceded that poets deal in stories, in that they are composers of fiction, I think I hereby incur no further disgrace than a philosopher would in drawing up a syllogism. For if I show the nature of a fable or story, its various kinds, and which kinds these "liars" employ, I do not think the composers of fiction will appear guilty of so monstrous a crime as these gentlemen maintain. First of all, the word "fable" [7] (*fabula*) has an honorable origin in the verb *for, faris*, hence "conversation" (*confabulatio*), which means only "talking together" (*collocutio*). This is clearly shown by Luke [8] in his Gospel, where he is speaking of the two disciples who went to the village of Emmaus after the Passion. He says:

And they talked together of all these things which had happened.
And it came to pass, that, while they communed together, and reasoned, Jesus himself drew near, and went with them.

Hence, if it is a sin to compose stories, it is a sin to converse, which only the veriest fool would admit. For nature has not granted us the power of speech unless for purposes of conversation, and the exchange of ideas.

But, they may object, nature meant this gift for a useful purpose, not for idle nonsense; and fiction is just that—idle nonsense. True enough, if the poet had intended to compose a mere tale. But I have time and time again proved that the meaning of fiction is far from superficial. Wherefore, some writers have framed this definition of fiction (*fabula*): Fiction is a form of discourse, which, under guise of invention, illustrates or proves an idea; and, as its superficial aspect is removed, the meaning of the author is clear. If, then, sense is revealed from under the veil of fiction, the composition of fiction is not idle nonsense. Of fiction I distinguish four kinds: The first superficially lacks all appearance of truth; for example, when brutes or inanimate things converse. Aesop, an ancient Greek, grave and venerable, was past master in this form; and though it is a common and popular form both in city and country, yet Aristotle, [9] chief of the Peripatetics, and a man of

divine intellect, did not scorn to use it in his books. The second kind at times superficially mingles fiction with truth, as when we tell of the daughters of Minyas at their spinning, who, when they spurned the orgies of Bacchus, were turned to bats; or the mates of the sailor Acestes, [10] who for contriving the rape of the boy Bacchus, were turned to fish. This form has been employed from the beginning by the most ancient poets, whose object it has been to clothe in fiction divine and human matters alike; they who have followed the sublimer inventions of the poets have improved upon them; while some of the comic writers have perverted them, caring more for the approval of a licentious public than for honesty. The third kind is more like history than fiction, and famous poets have employed it in a variety of ways. For however much the heroic poets seem to be writing history—as Vergil in his description of Aeneas tossed by the storm, or Homer in his account of Ulysses bound to the mast to escape the lure of the Sirens' song—yet their hidden meaning is far other than appears on the surface. The better of the comic poets, Terence and Plautus, for example, have also employed this form, but they intend naught other than the literal meaning of their lines. Yet by their art they portray varieties of human nature and conversation, incidentally teaching the reader and putting him on his guard. If the events they describe have not actually taken place, yet since they are common, they could have occurred, or might at some time. My opponents need not be so squeamish—Christ, who is God, used this sort of fiction again and again in his parables!

The fourth kind contains no truth at all, either superficial or hidden, since it consists only of old wives' tales.

Now, if my eminent opponents condemn the first kind of fiction, then they must include the account in Holy Writ describing the conference of the trees [11] of the forest on choosing a king. If the second, then nearly the whole sacred body of the Old Testament will be rejected. God forbid, since the writings of the Old Testament and the writings of the poets seem as it were to keep step with each other, and that too in respect to the method of their composition. For where history is lacking, neither one concerns itself with the superficial possibility, but what the poet calls fable or fiction our theologians have named figure. The truth of this may be seen by fairer judges than my opponents, if they will but weigh in a true scale the outward literary semblance of the visions of Isaiah, Ezekiel, Daniel, and other sacred writers on the one hand, with the outward literary semblance of the fiction of poets on the other. If they find any real discrepancy in their methods, either of implication or exposition, I will accept their condemnation. If they condemn the third form of fiction, it is the same as condemning the form which our Savior Jesus Christ, the Son of God, often used when He was in the flesh, though Holy Writ does not call it "poetry," but "parable,"[12] some call it "exemplum," because it is used as such.

I count as naught their condemnation of the fourth form of fiction, since it proceeds from no consistent principle, nor is fortified by the reinforcement of any of the arts, nor carried logically to a conclusion. Fiction of this kind has nothing in common with the works of the poets, though I imagine these objectors think poetry differs from it in no respect.

I now ask whether they are going to call the Holy Spirit, or Christ, the very God, liars, who both in the same Godhead have uttered fictions. I hardly think so, if they are wise. I might show them, your Majesty, if there were time, that difference of names constitutes no objection where methods agree. But they may see for themselves. Fiction, which they scorn because of its mere name, has been the means, as we often read, of quelling minds aroused to a mad rage, and subduing them to their pristine gentleness. Thus, when the Roman plebs seceded from the senate, they were called back from the sacred mount to the city by Menenius Agrippa,[13] a man of great influence, all by means of a story. By fiction, too, the strength and spirits of great men worn out in the strain of serious crises, have been restored. This appears, not by ancient instance alone, but constantly. One knows of princes who have been deeply engaged in important matters, but after the noble and happy disposal of their affairs of state, obey, as it were, the warning of nature, and revive their spent forces by calling about them such men as will renew their weary minds with diverting stories and conversation. Fiction has, in some cases, sufficed to lift the oppressive weight of adversity and furnish consolation, as appears in Lucius Apuleius;[14] he tells how the highborn maiden Charis, while bewailing her unhappy condition as captive among thieves, was in some degree restored through hearing from an old woman the charming story of Psyche. Through fiction, it is well known, the mind that is slipping into inactivity is

recalled to a state of better and more vigorous fruition. Not to mention minor instances, such as my own, I once heard Giacopo Sanseverino, Count of Tricarico and Chiarmonti, say that he had heard his father tell of Robert, son of King Charles—himself in after time the famous King of Jerusalem and Sicily—how as a boy he was so dull that it took the utmost skill and patience of his master to teach him the mere elements of letters. When all his friends were nearly in despair of his doing anything, his master, by the most subtle skill, as it were, lured his mind with the fables of Aesop into so grand a passion for study and knowledge, that in a brief time he not only learned the Liberal Arts familiar to Italy, but entered with wonderful keenness of mind into the very inner mysteries of sacred philosophy. In short, he made of himself a king whose superior in learning men have not seen since Solomon.

Such then is the power of fiction that it pleases the unlearned by its external appearance, and exercises the minds of the learned with its hidden truth; and thus both are edified and delighted[15] with one and the same perusal. Then let not these disparagers raise their heads to vent their spleen in scornful words, and spew their ignorance upon poets! If they have any sense at all, let them look to their own speciousness before they try to dim the splendor of others with the cloud of their maledictions. Let them see, I pray, how pernicious are their jeers, fit to rouse the laughter only of girls. When they have made themselves clean, let them purify the tales of others, mindful of Christ's commandment[16] to the accusers of the woman taken in adultery, that he who was without sin should cast the first stone.

X   It Is a Fool's Notion That Poets Convey No Meaning beneath the Surface of Their Fictions

Some of the railers are bold enough to say, on their own authority, that only an utter fool would imagine the best poets to have hidden any meaning in their stories; rather, they have invented them just to display the great power of their eloquence, and show how easily such tales may bring the injudicious mind to take fiction for truth. O the injustice of men! O what absurd dunces! What clumsiness! While they are trying to put down others, they imagine in their ignorance that they are exalting themselves. Who but an ignoramus would dare to say that poets purposely make their inventions void and empty, trusting in the superficial appearance of their tales to show their eloquence? As who should say that truth and eloquence cannot go together. Surely they have missed Quintilian's saying; it was this great orator's opinion that real power of eloquence is inconsistent with falsehood. But this matter I will postpone that I may come to the immediate subject of this chapter. Let any man, then, read the line in Vergil's *Bucolics*:[17]

He sung the secret seeds of Nature's frame,

and what follows on the same matter: or in the *Georgics*:[18]

That bees have portions of ethereal thought
Endued with particles of heavenly fires.

with the relevant lines; or in the *Aeneid*:[19]

Know first that heaven and earth's compacted frame,
And flowing waters, and the starry frame, etc.

This is poetry from which the sap of philosophy runs pure. Then is any reader so muddled as not to see clearly that Vergil was a philosopher; or mad enough to think that he, with all his deep learning, would, merely for the sake of displaying his eloquence—in which his powers were indeed extraordinary—have led the shepherd Aristeus[20] into his mother Climene's presence in the depths of the earth, or brought Aeneas to see his father in Hades? Or can anyone believe he wrote such lines without some meaning or intention hidden beneath the superficial veil of myth? Again, let any man consider our own poet Dante as he often unties with amazingly skilful demonstration the hard knots of holy theology; will such a one be so insensible as not to perceive that Dante was a great theologian as well as philosopher? And, if this is clear, what intention does he seem to have had in presenting the picture of the griffon[21] with wings and legs, drawing the chariot on top of the austere mountain, together with the seven candlesticks, and the seven nymphs, and the rest of the triumphal procession? Was it merely to show his dexterity in composing metrical narrative? To mention another instance: that most distinguished Christian gentleman, Francis Petrarch, whose life and character we have, with our own eyes, beheld so laudable in all

sanctity—and by God's grace shall continue to behold for a long time; no one has saved and employed to better advantage—I will not say, his time, but every crumb of it, than he. Is there anyone sane enough to suppose that he devoted all those watches of the night, all those holy seasons of meditation, all those hours and days and years—which we have a right to assume that he did, considering the force and dignity of his bucolic verse, the exquisite beauty of his style and diction—I say, would he have taken such pains merely to represent Gallus begging Tyrrhenus[22] for his reeds, or Pamphilus and Mitio[23] in a squabble, or other like pastoral nonsense? No man in his right mind will agree that these were his final object; much less, if he considers his prose treatise on the solitary life, or the one which he calls *On the Remedies for all Fortunes*, not to mention many others. Herein all that is clear and holy in the bosom of moral philosophy is presented in so majestic a style, that nothing could be uttered for the instruction of mankind more replete, more beautified, more mature, nay, more holy. I would cite also my own eclogues,[24] of whose meaning I am, of course, fully aware; but I have decided not to, partly because I am not great enough to be associated with the most distinguished men, and partly because the discussion of one's attainments had better be left to others.

Then let the babblers stop their nonsense, and silence their pride if they can; for one can never escape the conviction that great men, nursed with the milk of the Muses, brought up in the very home of philosophy, and disciplined in sacred studies, have laid away the very deepest meaning in their poems; and not only this, but there was never a maundering old woman, sitting with others late of a winter's night at the home fireside, making up tales of Hell, the fates, ghosts, and the like—much of it pure invention—that she did not feel beneath the surface of her tale, as far as her limited mind allowed, at least some meaning—sometimes ridiculous no doubt—with which she tries to scare the little ones, or divert the young ladies, or amuse the old, or at least show the power of fortune.

XII   The Obscurity of Poetry Is Not Just Cause for Condemning It

These cavillers further object that poetry is often obscure, and that poets are to blame for it, since their end is to make an incomprehensible statement appear to be wrought with exquisite artistry; regardless of the old rule of the orators, that a speech must be simple and clear. Perverse notion! Who but a deceiver himself would have sunk low enough not merely to hate what he could not understand, but incriminate it, if he could? I admit that poets are at times obscure. At the same time will these accusers please answer me? Take those philosophers among whom they shamelessly intrude; do they always find their close reasoning as simple and clear as they say an oration should be? If they say yes, they lie; for the works of Plato and Aristotle, to go no further, abound in difficulties so tangled and involved that from their day to the present, though searched and pondered by many a man of keen insight, they have yielded no clear nor consistent meaning. But why do I talk of philosophers? There is the utterance of Holy Writ, of which they especially like to be thought expounders; though proceeding from the Holy Ghost, is it not full to overflowing with obscurities and ambiguities? It is indeed, and for all their denial, the truth will openly assert itself. Many are the witnesses, of whom let them be pleased to consult Augustine,[25] a man of great sanctity and learning, and of such intellectual power that, without a teacher, as he says himself, he learned many arts, besides all that the philosophers teach of the ten categories. Yet he did not blush to admit that he could not understand the beginning of Isaiah.[26] It seems that obscurities are not confined to poetry. Why then do they not criticize philosophers as well as poets? Why do they not say that the Holy Spirit wove obscure sayings into his works, just to give them an appearance of clever artistry? As if He were not the sublime Artificer of the Universe![27] I have no doubt they are bold enough to say such things, if they were not aware that philosophers already had their defenders, and did not remember the punishment[28] prepared for them that blaspheme against the Holy Ghost. So they pounce upon the poets because they seem defenseless, with the added reason that, where no punishment is imminent, no guilt is involved. They should have realized that when things perfectly clear seem obscure, it is the beholder's fault. To a half-blind man, even when the sun is shining its brightest, the sky looks cloudy. Some things are naturally so profound that not without difficulty can the most exceptional keenness in intellect sound their depths; like the sun's globe, by which, before they can clearly discern it, strong eyes are sometimes repelled. On the other hand,

some things, though naturally clear perhaps, are so veiled by the artist's skill that scarcely anyone could by mental effort derive sense from them; as the immense body of the sun when hidden in clouds cannot be exactly located by the eye of the most learned astronomer. That some of the prophetic poems are in this class, I do not deny.

Yet not by this token is it fair to condemn them; for surely it is not one of the poet's various functions to rip up and lay bare the meaning which lies hidden in his inventions. Rather where matters truly solemn and memorable are too much exposed, it is his office by every effort to protect as well as he can and remove them from the gaze of the irreverent, that they cheapen not by too common familiarity.[29] So when he discharges this duty and does it ingeniously, the poet earns commendation, not anathema.

Wherefore I again grant that poets are at times obscure, but invariably explicable if approached by a sane mind; for these cavillers view them with owl eyes, not human. Surely no one can believe that poets invidiously veil the truth with fiction, either to deprive the reader of the hidden sense, or to appear the more clever; but rather to make truths which would otherwise cheapen by exposure the object of strong intellectual effort and various interpretation, that in ultimate discovery they shall be more precious.[30] In a far higher degree is this the method of the Holy Spirit; nay, every right-minded man should be assured of it beyond any doubt. Besides it is established by Augustine in the *City of God*, Book Eleven, when he says:

The obscurity of the divine word has certainly this advantage, that it causes many opinions about the truth to be started and discussed, each reader seeing some fresh meaning in it.

Elsewhere he says of Psalm 126:

For perhaps the words are rather obscurely expressed for this reason, that they may call forth many understandings, and that men may go away the richer, because they have found that closed which might be opened in many ways, than if they could open and discover it by one interpretation.

To make further use of Augustine's testimony (which so far is adverse to these recalcitrants), to show them how I apply to the obscurities of poetry his advice on the right attitude toward the obscurities of Holy Writ, I will quote his comment on Psalm 146:

There is nothing in it contradictory: somewhat there is which is obscure, not in order that it may be denied thee, but that it may exercise him that shall afterward receive it, etc.

But enough of the testimony of holy men on this point, I will not bore my opponents by again urging them to regard the obscurities of poetry as Augustine regards the obscurities of Holy Writ. Rather I wish that they would wrinkle their brows a bit, and consider fairly and squarely, how, if this is true of sacred literature addressed to all nations, in far greater measure is it true of poetry, which is addressed to the few.

If by chance in condemning the difficulty of the text, they really mean its figures of diction and oratorical colors and the beauty which they fail to recognize in alien words, if on this account they pronounce poetry obscure—my only advice is for them to go back to the grammar schools, bow to the ferule, study, and learn what license ancient authority granted the poets in such matters, and give particular attention to such alien terms as are permissible beyond common and homely use. But why dwell so long upon the subject? I could have urged them in a sentence to put off the old mind,[31] and put on the new and noble; then will that which now seems to them obscure look familiar and open. Let them not trust to concealing their gross confusion of mind in the precepts of the old orators; for I am sure the poets were ever mindful of such. But let them observe that oratory is quite different, in arrangement of words, from fiction, and that fiction has been consigned to the discretion of the inventor as being the legitimate work of another art than oratory. "In poetic narrative above all, the poets maintain majesty of style and corresponding dignity." As saith Francis Petrarch in the Third Book of his *Invectives*, contrary to my opponents' supposition, "Such majesty and dignity are not intended to hinder those who wish to understand, but rather propose a delightful task, and are designed to enhance the reader's pleasure and support his memory. What we acquire with difficulty and keep with care is always the dearer to us;" so continues Petrarch.[32] In fine, if their minds are dull, let them not blame the poets but their own sloth. Let them not keep up a silly howl against those whose lives and actions contrast most favorably with their own. Nay, at the very outset they have taken fright at mere appearances, and bid fair to spend themselves for nothing. Then let them retire in good time, sooner than exhaust their torpid minds with the onset and suffer a violent repulse.

But I repeat my advice to those who would appreciate poetry, and unwind its difficult involutions. You must read, you must persevere, you must sit up nights, you must inquire, and exert the utmost power of your mind. If one way does not lead to the desired meaning, take another; if obstacles arise, then still another; until, if your strength holds out, you will find that clear which at first looked dark. For we are forbidden by divine command[33] to give that which is holy to dogs, or to cast pearls before swine.

Notes

1   This personification is basically the same lady who appears in *The Consolation of Philosophy* of Boethius, in the books of Wisdom and Ecclesiasticus in the Vulgate Bible, and in a number of medieval and Renaissance poems. She is, for example, the inspiration for Dante's Beatrice.

2   Ideals, forces, and secrets make up a conventional threefold division of theology.

3   That is, the friars.

4   Ps. 68:10; John 2:17. The foolish friar in St. Thomas More's *Utopia* repeats this verse.

5   See Matt. 23:1–14. The friars were frequently associated with the Pharisees by their enemies. Boccaccio is here echoing, indirectly, the attack on the friars in the thirteenth century by William of St. Amour. Chaucer does exactly the same thing when he calls his friar "maister."

6   Cf. 1 Peter 5:8.

7   Boccaccio here draws on the *Etymologies* of Isidore of Seville.

8   Luke 24:14–15.

9   E.g., *Rhetoric*, 2:20.

10   Ovid, *Metamorphoses*, 4:31–415; 3:582–686.

11 Judg. 9:8–15.

12 Boccaccio here echoes an argument advanced by Petrarch.

13 Livy 2:32.

14 *Metamorphoses*, 4:21.

15 The doctrine of "exercise and delight" is Augustinian.

16 John 8:7.

17 The reference is to *Eclogues*, 6:31–86.

18 *Georgics*, 4:219–227.

19 *Aeneid*, 6:724–751.

20 *Georgics*, 4:414ff. For *Climene* read *Cyrene*.

21 *Purgatorio*, 29:108ff.

22 Eclogue 4.

23 Eclogue 6. For Petrarch's attitude toward his eclogues, see *Familiari*, 10:4.

24 Boccaccio explains his eclogues in a letter to Martino de Signa.

25 See *Confessions*, 4:16.

26 The relevant passage occurs in a comment on Ps. 126. St. Augustine's commentary on the Psalms was among the favorite books of both Boccaccio and Petrarch. Boccaccio gave Petrarch a copy.

27 Wisd. 7:21–22.

28 Mark 3:29.

29 This is an echo of St. Augustine's defense of obscurity in the Scriptures.

30 The idea is again Augustinian.

31 Eph. 4:22–23; Col. 3:9. In other words, exactly the same clearness of vision is required to read poetry as is required to see the spiritual meaning of the Scriptures.

32 Again the idea is Augustinian.

33 Matt. 7:6.

D. *Richard de Bury*

Richard Aungervyle (1287–1345), known more familiarly as Richard de Bury, began his official career as tutor to Edward of Windsor. When Edward came to the throne Richard was made Cofferer, Keeper and Treasurer of the Wardrobe, and finally, Keeper of the Privy Seal. He held a number of preferments until he became Bishop of Durham in 1333. In 1334 he was Lord Chancellor of England. During his travels he met Petrarch, who called him, somewhat grudgingly, "a man of eager mind, not ignorant of letters, a man from his youth curious about little known things." While he was Bishop of Durham Richard gathered around him a group of distinguished men who were encouraged to dispute before him every day at dinner. Among them were Bradwardine, the author of a famous anti-Pelagian treatise; Burley, a translator of Aristotle; and Acton, the canonist. Richard's best-known work is the Philobiblon, *a treatise on the love of books.*

For Richard and his circle, see W. A. Pantin, The English Church in the Fourteenth Century, *Cambridge University Press, London, 1955. A translation of the* Philobiblon *is available,* The University of California Press, Berkeley, 1948. *There is an annotated edition of the original Latin by A. Altamura, Naples, 1954. The following selections have been translated by the editor.*

From the
PHILOBIBLION

Chapter VI   The Complaint of Books against the Mendicant Orders

Poor in spirit,[1] yet most rich in faith;[2] the offscouring of this world,[3] yet the salt of the earth;[4] despisers of the world, and fishers of men[5]—how blessed you are if in suffering poverty for the sake of Christ[6] you know how to possess your souls in patience! For it is neither need, the scourge of iniquity, nor the adverse fortune of your parents, nor any violent necessity that thus oppresses you with want, but a devoted will and a Christ-like choice by which you consider best that life which Omnipotent God made Man taught to be best, both in His preaching and by His example. Indeed, you are the newly born of the ever-fruitful Church, newly substituted for the patriarchs and prophets by divine power, that your sound may go forth unto all the earth,[7] and, trained in wholesome doctrines, you may proclaim before people and before kings the invincible faith of Christ.

Now the second chapter above sufficiently demonstrates that the faith of the fathers is chiefly enclosed in books, whence it follows most clearly that you should be lovers of books more than other Christians. We are commanded to sow upon all waters[8] because the Most High is not a respecter of persons,[9] nor does the Most Merciful who wished to die for sinners desire their death. But he desired to heal the contrite, to lift up the fallen, and to correct the perverse with a spirit of lenity. For this most salutary purpose nursing Mother Church planted you willingly, and once you were planted, she watered you with her favors,[10] and when you were watered, she raised you up with privileges so that you might be assistants to pastors and curates in procuring the salvation of faithful souls. Whence also the Constitutions of the Order of Preachers[11] say of them that they were principally instituted for the study of the sacred Scriptures and the salvation of their neighbors; and not only should they know themselves obligated to the love of books by the rule of their revered patron Augustine which commands that books be consulted daily, but indeed as soon as they read the Prologue of their constitutions, they will find it in the title.

But for shame! Not only these Preachers but others who follow their example have been withdrawn from the paternal care and study of books by a superfluous triple solicitude: that is, for the belly, for clothing, and for houses. Having neglected the Providence of the Savior, whom the Psalmist promises to be solicitous for the needy and the poor,[12] they are occupied with the needs of the failing body in order that their feasts may be splendid and their vestments rich in a manner contrary to the rule of their order, not to mention the fabric of their houses erected like fortified castles to a height hardly suited to the poverty they profess.[13] On account of these things we books, who have always sought their advancement and have conceded them seats of honor among the powerful and noble,[14] are now estranged from the affections of their hearts and rated as superfluous, except that they hold fast to certain quartos of little value from which they bring forth their Iberian laments and apocryphal ravings,[15] not as food for the refreshment of souls, but rather to tickle the ears of the listeners. Holy Scripture is not expounded, but altogether set aside, as though it were commonplace and already made known to all. Yet hardly any have touched its hem;[16] for such is the profundity of its words that it cannot be comprehended by the human understanding, even if it devotes its greatest effort and most profound study to it, as St. Augustine asserts.[17] He who gives himself to it assiduously, if only He who created the spirit of piety will open the door,[18] may extract from its nucleus a thousand lessons of moral discipline which will not only be powerful in most recent newness,[19] but will also refresh the understanding of the auditors with a most savory sweetness. Whence the first professors of evangelical poverty, after having paid their respects, as it were, to the secular sciences, calling upon all their ingenuity devoted themselves to labors on the Scriptures, meditating night and day on the Law of God. Whatever they could steal from a starving belly or tear from their half-clad bodies they thought to be of the greatest profit when they applied it to the repair and copying of books. . . .

Notes

1 Matt. 5:3.
2 James 2:5.
3 1 Cor. 4:13.
4 Matt. 5:13.
5 Matt. 4:19.
6 The mendicant orders subjected themselves to voluntary poverty.
7 Rom. 10:18 from Ps. 18:5.
8 Isa. 32:20.
9 Acts 10:34.
10 Cf. 1 Cor. 3:6ff.
11 The Dominicans.
12 Ps. 39:18. Cf. 9:10; 11:6; 21:27; etc.
13 In fourteenth-century England the friars, who professed poverty and begged for sustenance, were notorious for their feasting, for their splendid and very costly copes, and for their sumptuous houses. The strictures against them in *Piers the Plowman* and in Chaucer's Summoner's Tale are in part due to these evidences of hypocrisy.
14 The friars were accused of seeking the society of the wealthy and neglecting the poor.
15 Perhaps a reference in part to the work of Gerard de Borgo San Donnino.
16 Cf. Matt. 14:36.
17 See the letter to Volusianus in St. Augustine, *Letters*, translated by J. G. Cunningham, T. and T. Clark, Edinburgh, 1872, 1875, vol. II:178, 193.
18 Col. 4:3.
19 Cf. Rom. 7:6. This verse was often cited in connection with the spiritual interpretation, which found the New Law implied everywhere in the Bible.

Chapter XIII   Why We Have Not Altogether Neglected the Fables of the Poets

All the various missiles by means of which those who love only the naked truth attack the poets are to be warded off with a double shield, either by pointing out that in their obscene material a pleasing style of speech may be learned, or that where the material is feigned but a virtuous doctrine[1] is implied, a natural or historical truth is enclosed beneath the figurative eloquence of the fiction.[2]

Although almost all men by nature desire to know, not all of them are equally delighted by the process of learning; indeed, when the labor of study is tasted, and the fatigue of the senses is perceived, many throw away the nut unadvisedly before the shell is removed and the kernel obtained.[3] For a double love is inborn in man, that is, a love of liberty in his own guidance, and a certain pleasure in work. For this reason no one subjects himself to the rule of others or willingly pursues a labor which involves any effort. For pleasure perfects work, just as beauty perfects youth, as Aristotle most truly asserts in the tenth book of the *Ethics*. Concerning this matter the prudence of the Ancients devised a remedy by means of which the wanton will of man might be captured as if by a certain pious fraud, when they hid away Minerva in secret beneath the lascivious mask of pleasure.[4] We are accustomed to lure children with rewards so that they will wish to learn those things to which we force them, though unwilling, to apply themselves. For corrupted nature[5] does not migrate toward virtues with the same impetus with which it supinely thrusts itself toward vices. Horace tells us about this in a little verse, when he is speaking of the art of poetry, saying,

Poets wish either to teach or to delight.[6]

He implies the same thing in another verse of the same book more openly, writing,

He hits the mark who mingles the useful with the sweet.[7]

How many students of Euclid has the "Flight of the Wretched"[8] thrown back like a high and steep cliff which the aid of ladders could not help scale! "Hard," they say, "is this discourse. Who can hear it?" That son of Inconstancy who finally wished to be changed into an ass perhaps would not have dismissed the study of philosophy if it had appeared to him familiarly, dressed in a veil of pleasure. But soon stupefied by the chair of Crato and infinite questions, he saw no refuge but flight.

We adduce these arguments in defense of the poets. Now we wish to show that those who study them with the proper intention are also to be freed from blame. In the first place, as we have shown in the last chapter, the ignorance of a single word may impede the understanding of the longest sentence. Since, therefore, the sayings of the saints often allude to the fictions of the poets, it follows of necessity that if the poem introduced is not known, the whole intention of the author will be obscured. And certainly, as Cassiodorus says in his book, *The Institutes of Sacred Letters*, those things without which great things cannot stand are not to be considered small. It follows, therefore, that to be ignorant of the poets is to be ignorant of Jerome, Augustine, Boethius, Lactantius, Sidonius, and a great many others, a litany of whom could not be included in a long chapter.

The Venerable Bede has resolved this debate most clearly in a distinction as recorded by the distinguished compiler Gratian,[9] that repeater of many authors who was as confused in his form of presentation as he was eager in the compilation of material. For he writes thus in Distinction XXXVII called *Turbat acumen*: "Some read secular literature for pleasure, delighted by poetic and ornamented language; but some study these writings for purposes of instruction, in such a way that the errors of the pagans may be detested but that useful things found in them may be devoutly converted for the use of sacred learning. Such persons apply themselves to secular literature in a laudable way." These are the conclusions of Bede.

Admonished by this wholesome instruction, let the detractors of those who study the poets be silent henceforth; nor should those ignorant of these things desire companions in their ignorance, for this would be similar to the solace of the wretched.[10] Let anyone therefore institute in himself a pious intention, and, with any material whatsoever, the conditions of virtue being observed, he shall make a study pleasing to God; and if he may find profit in a poet, even as great Vergil says he did in Ennius, he will not go astray.

Notes

1 The Latin word here is *sententia*.

2 The two benefits to be derived from the study of poetry are thus eloquence and wisdom.

3 The most vivid use of this figure occurs in the proem to an anonymous commentary on the *Thebaid* of Statius, where a poem is said to be like a nut with a pretty shell. Boys, attracted by the shell, merely play with the nut. The more sophisticated open the shell (i.e., interpret the allegory) to obtain the inner nourishment.

4 That is, Minerva, or wisdom, is hidden (so to speak) beneath the mask of Venus, or pleasure.

5 That is, human nature after the Fall.

6 *Ars poetica*, 333.

7 *Ibid.*, 343.

8 The Fifth Proposition was called by this name during the Middle Ages.

9 Gratian produced in the middle of the twelfth century the first effective systematic presentation of canon law.

10 That is, "misery loves company."

E. Excerpts from the Mythographers and Commentators on the Classics

In order to understand the use made of mythological and astrological materials by poets like Dante or Chaucer, it is necessary to know something about the way in which classical poetry and the gods and goddesses who inhabit it were understood during the Middle Ages. We should recognize in the first place the fact that the underlying allegorical method of the medieval commentators has its origin in antiquity itself; it was not something invented in the Middle Ages. Even Plato thought poetry to be allegorical. It is true, however, that the medieval mythographers were sometimes more interested in what their material might mean to a Christian audience than in what it might have meant to the original authors. Their works thus contain a mixture of ideas that have a genuine basis in classical thought and theological interpretations which would have been impossible in antiquity. In considering this fact, however, we should remember that Christian thought as it was developed by the Fathers of the Church embraced many of the best ideas of classical philosophy, so that some of the " moral" interpretations of the Middle Ages are in fact often closer to classical thought than the " aesthetic" interpretations of modern scholars.

The following excerpts give only a brief indication of the nature of the material. The authors involved may be identified here very briefly. William of Conches taught at Chartres in the early twelfth century. He is the author of the most famous medieval commentary on The Consolation of Philosophy *of Boethius. Bernard Silvestris wrote a commentary on* The Aeneid *in the twelfth century that replaced the older commentary of Fulgentius and remained a standard work of reference throughout the Middle Ages. Alexander Neckam is best known as the author of an encyclopedia,* De naturis rerum, *which has been edited in modern times by Thomas Wright (London, 1863). He also wrote a long commentary on Martianus Capella containing a great deal of mythographic material. The " Third Vatican Mythographer" is the author of the last of three mythographic treatises preserved in a manuscript in the Vatican Library. He may have been one Albericus of London, or, perhaps, Alexander Neckam. Produced during the twelfth century, this work enjoyed a considerable reputation. Petrarch had a copy made for his own library. Arnulf of Orleans was the most famous of the medieval commentators on Ovid, carrying on the ancient tradition of literary studies at Orleans in the twelfth century. Radulfus de Longo Campo is the author of a commentary on the* Anticlaudianus *of Alanus de Insulis. Petrus Berchorius (Pierre Bersuire) wrote, in the fourteenth century, a commentary on Ovid, a commentary on the Bible, a moralized encyclopedia, a scriptural dictionary, and a translation of Livy. Nicholas Trivet, a fourteenth-century English Dominican, is the author of numerous commentaries, the best known of which is his comment on* The Consolation of Philosophy *of Boethius.*

For an introduction to these materials and others like them, see Jean Seznec, The Survival of the Pagan Gods, *Random House, Inc., New York, 1952.*

TYPES OF POETRY

Poetry is the discipline of enclosing grave and illustrious speech in meter or prose. There are three kinds of poetry: history, fable, and argument (or comedy). History is the narration of something that is either true or narrated with verisimilitude. A fable is a narration of something that is neither true nor narrated with verisimilitude. An argument [i.e., comedy] is a narration of something which is not true but which is told with verisimilitude. Under history are contained satire and tragedy. A satire is devoted completely to the extirpation of vice and the inculcation of virtue. A tragedy is altogether in contempt of fortune. Although fable and argument are fictitious, they are directed toward the contempt of vice and the appetite for virtue. Thus poetry expels vices and inspires virtue, sometimes through history, sometimes through fable, and sometimes through argument.

—Radulfus de Longo Campo

THE USE OF *THE AENEID*

Some poets write for utility, like the satirists, some for delight, like the comic poets, and some for both, like the historical poets. Whence Horace says,

Poets wish either to instruct or to delight,
Or to present the pleasing and virtuous together.[1]

A certain delight may be had in this poem [i.e., *The Aeneid*] both from the verbal ornament and figurative language and from the various adventures and deeds of men which are related in it. Indeed, if anyone exerts himself to imitate all these things, he may acquire the greatest skill in writing as well as inducements through example to pursue virtuous actions in the events narrated. It has, therefore, a double utility for the reader: first, skill in writing which may be acquired through imitation, and, second, prudence in right action which is acquired from the import of the events narrated.

—Bernard Silvestris

THE MEANING OF THE *METAMORPHOSES*

In this title (i.e., *Metamorphoses*) the material of the work is designated (i.e., mutation), and the work concerns mutation of three kinds: natural, magical, and spiritual. Natural mutation is that which is made by the combining or breaking up of elements. For example, elements are combined when a child develops from sperm or when a chicken develops from an egg; and elements are broken up when they are separated or dissolved in a given body, or reduced to powder by fire or by some other agency. Magical mutation is that performed by the skill of magicians, as in the stories of Lycaon and Io, who were changed not in mind but in body.[2] Spiritual metamorphosis is that which concerns the spirit, like the change from sanity to insanity or the reverse. Thus Agave and Antonoë were changed in spirit and not in body. It should also be noted that mutation may be made from one animate thing to another animate thing, as when Lycaon becomes a wolf; or from an inanimate thing to another inanimate thing, as when the house of Baucis becomes a temple; or from an inanimate thing to an animate thing, as when the statue of Pygmalion becomes a virgin; or from an animate thing to an inanimate thing, as when the dragon became a stone.

The intention of the work is to speak of mutation, not in such a way that we shall understand only that mutation which takes place externally among good or evil corporal things, but so that we may perceive also that mutation which takes place within, like that in the mind, to the end that we may be led from error to knowledge of the Creator in truth. There are two motions of the mind, one rational and one irrational. The rational motion is that which imitates the motion of the firmament, from east to west; and the irrational motion is that which imitates the motion of the planets, which are moved contrary to the firmament. God gave the soul reason by means of which the sensuality might be restrained, just as the motion of the seven planets is restrained by the motion of the firmament. But we, like the planets, neglecting the rational motion, are drawn away from our Creator. Seeing this, Ovid wished to show us by fabulous narration that motion of the mind which should be made within. Hence it is said, for example, that Io was changed into a cow because she sank down into vicious actions, and that she resumed her original form because she emerged from vices. Or, his intention is to call us back from too much love for temporal things to the single worship of our Creator by demonstrating the stability of celestial things and the mutability of earthly things. . . .

—Arnulf of Orleans

TRAGEDY AND COMEDY

Tragedies are poems in which the ancient deeds and crimes of kings were chanted before the watching people in doleful song.[3] Comedies are poems in which the acts, sayings, or deeds of private men were chanted, and which narrated in their fables the rape of virgins or the love of prostitutes. Comedians or comedies are so called either from the place, because the action took place in country districts which the Greeks called *kómas*, or from *comissatio*, "feast." For men used to come to hear them after eating.[4] They were written by the poets in three ways. They might be narratives in which the poet alone speaks, as in Vergil's *Georgics*; or they might be in dramatic form so that the poet never speaks, but only the persons introduced. This method is proper to both tragedies and comedies. The third method is a mixture of the first two, where both the poet and the persons introduced speak, as in *The Aeneid* of Vergil. Thus Vergil in *The Aeneid*, Lucan, and Ovid in the *Metamorphoses* may be called tragic poets because they use tragic material in that they write of the fall of kings and of great men, and of public matters.

—Nicholas Trivet

ON THE MARRIAGE OF PHILOLOGY AND MERCURY

Let us see therefore what Mercury and Philology are and how they are joined together. The name *Mercury* means "discourse," since it is as if to say either *medius currens,* "running in between," or *mercatorum kyrios,* "lord of merchants"; for discourse takes place between men and thrives especially among merchants.[5] Discourse, however, consists of the intelligible voice brought forth by a man, and to it three things are necessary: that it be correct, that it be ornamented, and that it be true. But we speak correctly through grammar, ornately through rhetoric, and truly through dialectic.[6] Moreover, these things should be married to Philology, for Cicero tells us that eloquence without wisdom is extremely injurious while wisdom without eloquence is of little benefit.[7] Since we know, then, what discourse is and how we may use it, let us see now what philology is and how we may acquire it. *Philos* means "love" and *logos* means "reason," whence it appears that philology is the love of reason. . . .

—Alexander Neckam

VENUS

We read that there are two Venuses, a legitimate Venus and a goddess of lechery. We say that the legitimate Venus is world music, or, that is, the equal proportion of worldly things, which others call Astrea,[8] and still others call natural justice. And she is in the sidereal heavens, in times, and in animate things. But the shameless Venus, the goddess of lechery, we call concupiscence of the flesh because she is the mother of all fornication.[9]

—Bernard Silvestris

Venus is pictured nude, either because the crime of libido is hardly to be concealed, or because it is convenient for nude persons, or because it denudes anyone of counsel and does not permit concealment. Roses are ascribed to Venus, for roses redden and prick just as libido causes redness through the opprobrium of shame, and the dart of sin pricks. Moreover, just as roses delight for a short while but are destroyed by the quick passage of time, so also is it with libido. Doves are consecrated to Venus because these birds (in order to

have young frequently) are believed to be especially fervid in coitus. She is depicted floating on the sea because it cannot be doubted that libido brings about the shipwreck of things. Hence Porphyrius says in an epigram,

Nude and needy the shipwrecked of Venus is in the sea.

She is shown to carry a conch shell because that animal being open mingles the whole body in coitus. The myrtle is said to be hers, either because that tree thrives on the shore and Venus is said to have been procreated in the sea, or because, as the physicians say, this tree is useful for various feminine necessities. She is placated by verbena since that herb has no seed. Whence it is said that "the altar is bound with chaste verbenas."[10] From the isle of Cyprus, most fruitful in spices, she is called *Cypris,* which means "mixture."

—The Third Vatican Mythographer

Venus was depicted as a most beautiful girl nude and floating in the sea and holding in her hand a conch shell. She was ornamented with roses and surrounded by flying doves. And she is said to have been married to Vulcan the god of fire, who was an extremely ugly rustic. Before her stood three nude young girls called the three graces, two of whom had their faces turned toward her and the third had hers turned in the other direction. She was accompanied by her blind son Cupid who was shooting at Apollo with his bow and arrows, and when the gods were disturbed by this, the timid boy fled to his mother's lap.

These things are literally attributed to the planet which is called Venus, for this planet is of feminine complexion[11] and is, moreover, pictured as a nude girl. She is also warm and humid,[12] and is thus said to be married to Vulcan, or fire, and exposed or immersed in the sea, for in this way heat and humidity may be seen to be joined. And she is aptly said to give birth to Cupid, the god of love, or concupiscence of the flesh because the warmth and humidity of this planet excite concupiscence of the flesh.

Setting aside the literal exposition, by this goddess we may understand, according to the explanation of Fulgentius, either the life of pleasure or any lecherous person. Such persons are said to be feminine because of their variable inconstancy, and nude because of their inevitable indecency. Venus is said to be floating in the sea because she wishes to be always immersed in delights. She is said to carry a conch shell in her hand into which she is forever singing or chanting because she always wishes to be singing and full of light airs. For truly the pleasure of lechery is feminine because it does not endure and nude because a man hardly conceals it when it comes to light. And it wishes to swim in the sea, or in wealth, always enjoying the conch of empty happiness. Venus is said to be born in the sea because lechery never leaves the flowing tides of wealth and delight. Whence the nude whore is seen to say in the Scriptures [Isa. 23:10, 16], "Pass thy land as a river, O daughter of the sea, thou hast a girdle no more. . . . Take a harp, go about the city, thou harlot that hast been forgotten: sing well, sing many a song, that thou mayst be remembered." She nourishes her pleasant doves, or the lecherous, with roses, which is to say that she loves flowers and courtly airs. She produces Cupid, or concupiscence of the flesh, who occasionally wounds Apollo, a figure for just men, with the arrow of temptation. . . . Or say that Cupid the son of Venus is carnal love, the son of pleasure who is shown winged because love is frequently seen to fly away suddenly. For it happens sometimes that a man is suddenly and without deliberation inflamed by love for some person, and this love may be called winged and volatile. Moreover, this god is portrayed as being blind because when it affects someone he does not seem to be paying attention to anything. Again, it places itself in the poor as well as in the rich, in the ugly as well as in the beautiful, in the religious as well as in laymen. It is blind in yet another way, for through it men become blind too. For nothing is more blind than a man inflamed by love for another person or for another thing. Whence Seneca says that love knows no discernment. Briefly, the poets wish to depict two blind deities, Cupid and Fortune. For Cupid, or love as it is called, is so blind that it sometimes undertakes the impossible, as is clear in the example of Narcissus, who loved his shadow unto death. In the same way we see vile persons love noble persons and vice versa. Fortune is also said to be blind when it provides for the unworthy and deprives the worthy. As St. Paul says [Rom. 11:25], "blindness has happened in Israel."

—Petrus Berchorius

Let us consider first of all the quality of the place [in which the Temple of Venus is located]. The author[13]

Figure 23 *Cupid as the Gothic god of love. Ivory mirror case. Late fourteenth century.*

says that it is on the Mount of Cithaeron. . . . To make these things clear it is necessary to know first of all that just as Mars is said above to represent the irascible appetite, so Venus represents the concupiscible appetite. And this Venus is double. The first one should be understood as the one through whom arises every honest and legitimate desire, like the desire to have a woman in order to have children, and other desires like this one. This Venus is not relevant here. The second Venus is that one through whom every lascivious thing is desired, and who is commonly called the goddess of love. And it is this one for whom the author describes the temple and the things connected with it, as the text shows. Thus the author describes the Temple as being located on Mount Cithaeron for two reasons: first it is located there because of the actions carried out there, for Mount Cithaeron is near Thebes, and upon it the Thebans at certain times of the year made feasts and offered many sacrifices in honor of Venus; and second it is there because of the quality of the place, which is very convenient for Venus, because the region is very temperate with respect to heat and frost. . . . The author says that the place is full of pine trees, the fruits of which when eaten have marvellous force in provoking that appetite. Moreover, he places in the most secret part near Venus the two figures Bacchus and Ceres, which stand for eating and drinking. For these two things, when precious viands and good wines are properly used, revive that appetite wonderfully. Then he tells us that the place is most beautiful to see, and that there one may see conies, deer, sparrows, doves, and, finally, barefoot and ungirdled ladies dancing. These things incite much when seen by the libidinous, some because they show the effects of Venus, like the conies, sparrows, and doves, and some because of their clothing and acts, like the barefoot and ungirdled and dancing ladies. Further, he describes Venus nude, for seeing this sight has a marvellous force. . . .

—Giovanni Boccaccio

VENUS AND MARS

Mars is also said to have lain secretly with Venus, and when the Sun saw this act, he betrayed it to Vulcan. The latter, tying the lovers together with adamantine chains while they were joined, evilly showed them as they lay to the other gods.[14] In revenge Venus ignited the five daughters of the Sun—Pasiphae, Medea, Phaedra, Circe, and Dirce—with detestable love. Thus Mars was polluted by the embrace of Venus; that is, virtue was corrupted by the illicit acts of libido. He was revealed by the witness of the Sun, or, that is, he was known to be guilty by the light of Truth, which showed virtue lured by evil habit chained in the toils of fetters. Thus Venus obscured with her corruption the five daughters of the Sun, or the five human senses dedicated to light and truth and to the perception of the diversity of things, as the philosophers say. For there is no sense which pleasure does not infect with its lures.

—The Third Vatican Mythographer

MARS

The figure of Mars was that of a furious man seated in a chariot with a helmet on his head and a scourge in his hand. Before him was depicted a wolf because that animal was especially consecrated to him among the ancients. He was called *Mavors*, or "devouring males," and was the god of war among the pagans. . . . Or say that Mars signifies the sin of discord which is seated in the chariot of malice supported by the four wheels of four spiritual vices, avarice, pride, detraction, and injury. . . .

—Petrus Berchorius

The author[15] says first of all that the house of Mars was in Thrace, in a cold and cloudy place, full of water, winds, ice, and a forest of unfruitful trees, a place shadowy, sunless, and full of tumult. To understand these things it is necessary to know that in every man there are two principal appetites. First there is the concupiscible appetite that desires and is delighted to possess the things which, according to his judgment, whether reasonable or corrupted, are enjoyable and pleasant to have. The other is called the irascible appetite, by which a man is disturbed either because delightful things are taken away from him, or because he is impeded in his pursuit of them, or because he cannot have them. This irascible appetite is found most promptly in men who are very sanguine, because blood according to its nature is hot, and hot things are kindled by any little motion. And thus it happens that very sanguine persons become suddenly wrathful, so that some of them only with the greatest force of reason control themselves and recover from their ire. And since, as we have shown in another place, men in the colder regions are more sanguine than elsewhere, the author says that the Temple of Mars, or, that is, of this irascible appetite, is in Thrace, which is a northern region and very cold where men are most fierce and warlike and wrathful because of their sanguine nature. The place is said to be cloudy to show that wrath obscures the counsel of reason, an idea developed further on where it is said that the house of Mars is hidden from the rays of the sun. By the ice is understood the coldness in the hearts of the wrathful, who, overcome by an enkindled ire, become cruel and rigid and without any charity. . . . There are two kinds of wrath. . . . First, there is that through which one becomes enraged without reason, and that is the one relevant here. The other may be reasonable, as when one becomes disturbed by some injustice, and this kind receives the counsel of the reason in reproving an evil deed or in causing it to be amended. . . .

—Giovanni Boccaccio

Since it is evident that the poets imitate the philosophers in their fictions, it is relevant to consider what the astrologers have said about Mars, and especially the most distinguished of them, who was called Albumasar. According to his teaching, Mars is by nature suddenly fiery, hot, and dry, desirous of praise and glory, wrathful, iniquitous in judgment, a depradator, crafty, criminal, impious, inconstant, improvident, precipitous, disordered and obscene in speech, quick to respond, ferocious, incontinent, impudent, a lover of ornaments, a scorner of religion, unfaithful, lying, a perjurer, assiduous in evil deeds, a dissipator of goods, unstable, pertinacious and obstinate, shameless, laborious, energetic, a derider, a fornicator and a lover of the filth of coitus. The planet signifies youth, fortitude, fire, arson, war and the society of kings, instruments of war, robberies, ruins, the breaking of roads, tortures, captivities, fears, disputes, those who care for wounds, masters of arms, breakers of graves, strippers of corpses, and the like. It may easily be understood from these things how much the poets agree with the philosophers.

—Giovanni Boccaccio

SATURN

Saturn was depicted and described as an old man, bent, sad, and pale. He had a scythe in one hand and carried in the same hand the image of a dragon gnawing his own tail with his teeth. With his other hand he applied a little child to his mouth and devoured it with his teeth. . . . The sea was pictured before him in which his virile members were seen to be thrown and from which Venus, a most beautiful girl, was born. . . . Just as Saturn was the first of the gods, so also Saturn is the first of all the planets. It is called old because it moves more slowly than the other planets and completes its circuit more slowly. . . . It devours its children because those born under the constellation of Saturn[16] rarely live very long. . . . Or these things may be explained naturally, for Saturn means time. His children are the four elements; that is, Jupiter is fire, Juno air, Neptune

Figure 24 *The ram, the house of Mars. From an astrological treatise by Boccaccio's friend Andalo.*

water, and Pluto earth. Saturn is said to be castrated by fire for the reason that all the powers of time, or all the fruits which time produces, are known to be consumed by fire. And also Saturn or time is said to eat his children because everything born in time is attenuated or consumed by time. . . .

—Petrus Berchorius

DIANA

Diana, who is also called Luna and Proserpina and Hecate, is the seventh of the planets. . . . She was depicted in the appearance of a lady holding a bow and arrows and following timid deer in a hunt. . . . We may understand by this goddess the Glorious Virgin, armed with the flexible bow of mercy and the arrows of devotion and prayer, by whose mediation the horned deer, or the proud devil, is overcome. . . .

—Petrus Berchorius

One must know that Diana among the ancients was the goddess of chastity who did not receive into her company any women except virgins. And the ancients say that their exercise and that of their followers was confined to the woods and consisted of hunting. They say this to show that anyone who wishes to preserve chastity intact must flee as much as possible all human consort, and similarly flee idleness. For these two things . . . are the greatest reasons why people fall into the lascivious acts of Venus.

—Giovanni Boccaccio

PLUTO

Pluto the son of Saturn is called by the ancients the god of the lower kingdoms and of darkness and of the souls of the dying. . . . His image was that of a terrible man seated on a sulphurous throne with a royal scepter in his hand treading the triple dog Cerberus under his feet. And near him he had three Furies and three Harpies and three Parcae. They said that from the sulphurous throne flowed four rivers: Lethe, Cocytus, Phlegethon, and Acheron. And they placed the pool of Styx nearby. Next to Pluto sat the Queen of the Underworld, Proserpina, who acted as Pluto's wife. The three Furies were three horrible old women with serpentine hair called Alecto, Thesiphone, and Megaera. They caused furor in men. The Parcae, or Fates, are named by antiphrasis, since *parcant* "they spare" no one. They were three sisters of the household, of whom one held a distaff, another spun thread, and the third broke off the thread. Their names were Clotho, Lachesis, and Atropos. The Harpies were most rapacious birds with faces of virgins. . . . The first river of Hell, called Lethe, means "oblivion"; Cocytus means "guilt"; Phlegethon means "burning"; and Acheron means "without joy, or health". . . . Styx means "sadness."[17]

We say that allegorically by Pluto is understood the Devil, who is the king of the material Inferno, and also king of the spiritual Inferno, which is the world. He rules with Proserpina, that is, he rules his sulphurous throne with iniquity, who is his queen and wife, which is to say that he rules in a sordid heart and in a fervid breast where his scepter and jurisdiction hold sway in so far as he and his evil suggestions are obeyed there in everything. If, however, it happens that this image of the Devil resides within the human breast, it is necessary that many other images, or other vices, accompany it. For there also are avarice, represented by Cerberus, concupiscence, represented by the Furies, cruelty, represented by the Fates, and rapine, represented by the Harpies. Avarice is understood by insatiable Cerberus, a dog with three heads, for avarice elevates and exalts itself for wealth, for knowledge, and for fame.[18] Or the dog has three heads because avarice ardently acquires, tenaciously holds, and sorrowfully loses. By the Furies, also said to be three, are understood concupiscence, for there are three things chiefly seized upon by men: wealth, the concupiscence for which makes the avaricious furious; delights, concupiscence for which makes the lecherous furious; and eminence, concupiscence for which makes the ambitious furious. . . .

—Petrus Berchorius

MINERVA

Minerva is feigned to be born without a mother because wisdom is without a beginning or an end. Again, she is a virgin because wisdom receives no corruption of vice, but perpetually enjoys uncorrupted habits. Martianus in his fiction[19] shows Pallas descending from a more sublime and more splendid place because wisdom dwells in the highest place and surmounts all vileness of earthly corruption. She herself says [Ecclus 24:7], "I dwelt in the highest places, and my throne is in a pillar of a cloud." The poets feign that Minerva inheres in the head of Jove, for according to the fable she is shown to be born from his head. And by this fiction is signified the fact that she was born from the highest wisdom of God. "I," she says [Ecclus 24:25], "came out of the mouth of the most high." For the fact that Pallas was born without a mother shows that Eternal Wisdom does not proceed from elsewhere, but has its origin from the substance of God. Because she is a virgin and without a mother, the number seven is sacred to her, for that number alone in the series from one to ten, as arithmetic demonstrates, neither generates any other number from itself, nor is generated by any other number save unity alone, which is the mother of all numbers.

—The Third Vatican Mythographer

NARCISSUS

Nor do the poets say without cause that Echo was ignited with love for Narcissus. For by Narcissus is meant "vainglory," which is deceived by its own image. Vainglory is deceived by its own vanity when it admires and commends itself too much. The image of Narcissus by which he was inflamed to become an over-ardent lover of himself was reflected in waters, for when stupefied vainglory admires its own shadowy pomp in transitory things it is ignited with too much love of itself. Then it was turned into a flower, for the glory of the world passes away. Now only the name Narcissus remains.

—Alexander Neckam

ORPHEUS

Orpheus is used to designate any wise and eloquent man, and hence the name Orpheus is as if to say *orea phone*, or "best voice." His wife is Euridice, or, that is, natural concupiscence which is joined to everyone, for no one can live without it, not even a child one day old. Whence the poets feign it to be a god, that is, Genius, who is born with everyone and dies with him. Whence Horace calls him "a god good and bad," who is "in every mortal head."[20] Genius is natural concupiscence. But this natural concupiscence is well called "Euridice," or "judgment of the good," for whatever anyone judges to be good, whether rightly or wrongly, he desires. This concupiscence while it wandered in the meadow was loved by Aristeus. Aristeus is used to represent virtue, for *ares* means "virtue." But this virtue loved that Euridice, or natural concupiscence, as it wandered through the meadow, or through terrestrial things, which like a meadow now flourish and now dry up. That is, virtue follows concupiscence always, because it needs to take it away from earthly things. But Euridice fled from Aristeus, for natural concupiscence contradicts virtue, since it desires its own pleasure, which virtue forbids. But then it dies and descends to Hell, or, that is, to delight in terrestrial things. When his wife dies Orpheus sorrows, because when a wise man sees his effort and delight residing in temporal things he is displeased. But even though he may overcome everything else with his modulations, he cannot overcome the sorrow for his lost wife, because even if a wise man with his eloquence and wisdom can overcome the vices of others, he cannot take away his own concupiscence from temporal things. Hence he sorrows greatly. But Orpheus descends to Hell to take out his wife when a wise man descends to a knowledge of terrestrial things so that, having seen that there is no good in them, he may withdraw his concupiscence from them. But a law is given to him that he must not look back, for [Luke 9:62] "No man putting his hand to the plough, and looking back, is fit for the kingdom of God . . . ." If anyone reading Fulgentius may see this fable explained in another way,[21] let him not condemn our explanation on this account, for concerning the same thing seen in different ways different explanations may be found. The diversity of exposition is not to be a cause of concern but rather of enjoyment. What is important is that there be no contradiction in a single exposition.

—William of Conches

WAYS OF DESCENDING TO HELL

The descent into Hell, however, is quadriform: there is a descent of nature, another of virtue, another of vice, and another of artifice. The natural descent is the birth of man, for in that event the soul naturally begins to be in this fallen region and thus to descend to Hell, to recede from its divinity, and soon to bend toward vices and to consent to sensual pleasures. But this way is common to all. There is another descent of virtue which is made when a wise man descends to worldly things to consider them, not so that he may place his intention in them, but so that their fragility being known, he may cast them aside and hastily return to the realm of invisible things and know the Creator more clearly through a knowledge of the creatures.[22] In this way Orpheus and Hercules, who were called wise men, descended. There is a third descent of vice, which is common, in which one is brought to temporal things in such a way that the whole intention is placed in them and they are served with the whole mind, nor is the soul moved from them any more. In this way we read that Euridice descended to Hell. Moreover, from this descent there is no return. The fourth descent is of artifice, for in necromancy the descent is carried out by artifice.

—Bernard Silvestris

Notes

1   Cf. Horace, *Ars poetica*, 333–334.

2   Arnulf is speaking here literally of events in the poem. Philosophically speaking, it was usual to say that magical metamorphosis is mere illusion and that the most spectacular kind of metamorphosis is spiritual or moral. This is the doctrine of William of Conches in his discussion of Circe as she appears in *The Consolation of Philosophy*. In the discussion which follows here, the motion of the planets is said to be contrary to the motion of the firmament. What is meant is the *apparent* motion of the planets which move more slowly than the firmament in the same direction. The slowness of their movement makes them appear to go the other way. This idea is a commonplace of medieval astronomy.

3   Isidore, *Etymologies*, 18:45.

4   Isidore, *Etymologies*, 8:7, 6.

5   The above definitions are based generally on those of Remigius of Auxerre. On Remigius, see Cora E. Lutz, *Remigii Autissiodorensis commentum in Martianum Capellam*, E. J. Brill, Leiden, 1962, 1965.

6   These are the studies of the trivium. Later in the discussion (not included here) Neckam decides that through the trivium and the quadrivium one is able to marry Mercury and Philology, or combine eloquence and wisdom. The doctrine of William of Conches that eloquence and wisdom embrace all knowledge is not heterodox, as some scholars have maintained.

7   Cf. Cicero, *De inventione*, 1:1, 1.

8   For Astrea (Astraea), see Ovid, *Metamorphoses*, 1:149–150. Natural justice "abandoned the earth," so to speak, at the Fall of man. That is, this justice is the harmony of nature "as it was created from the beginning," to use St. Augustine's phrase.

9   The word *fornication* here means any turning away of the will from God. The "shameless Venus" is thus, as Remigius indicates, original sin, or the malady of that sin.

10   Horace, *Carmina*, 4:11, 6–7. Exactly what plant is meant by *verbena*, a word used by the ancients for laurel, olive, myrtle, and a number of other plants, is not clear.

11   Planets were said by the astrologers to be either masculine or feminine.

12   Each planet was said to be either hot or cold and either moist or dry.

13   By "the author" Boccaccio himself is meant. This selection is from the beginning of Boccaccio's note on his picture of the Temple of Venus in the *Teseida*.

14   For the story, see Ovid, *Metamorphoses*, 4:171ff. In "The Complaint of Mars" Chaucer plays on the traditional mythological and astrological meanings of this story.

15   The author is again Boccaccio himself. This selection is from the opening of Boccaccio's comment on the Temple of Mars in his notes on the *Teseida*.

16   That is, Capricorn or Aquarius.

17   The Latin word is *tristitia*, a sinful sorrow brought about by temporal loss or frustration.

18   The word *avaritia* usually conveyed much more than the love of wealth.

19   That is, his work on the marriage of Philology and Mercury.

20   *Epistles*, 2:2, 188–189.

21   For the interpretation of Fulgentius, see Manfred Bukofzer, "Speculative Thinking in Mediaeval Music," *Speculum*, vol. 17, 1942, pp. 174–175.

22   Cf. Rom. 1:20.

F. The Festival of the Pui

Late medieval song was characteristically functional, often associated with formal social occasions of various kinds. In this respect it differs sharply from the later lyric, which is more personal in its inception and has a more immediate subjective appeal. In songs of a more sophisticated type, moreover, the music did not express any emotional implications that might arise from the words. The following account of the festivals of the London Pui as they were celebrated during the late thirteenth century gives us a good indication of the nature of one social occasion for which songs were employed and, at the same time, furnishes a general idea of the standards demanded of them. Since the subject of the songs is "the becoming pleasance of virtuous ladies," we may assume that many of the songs were love lyrics, but the circumstances of their presentation also make it clear that these were not personal lyrics in the romantic sense of the word.

The Pui was primarily an organization of prosperous merchants which had chapters in various European cities as well as in England. We do not know what the name implies. The lyrics for several "crowned" songs by Jean Froissart survive, although none of them was written for the London group. One is printed in Section VII of this volume.

The character of late medieval song and the change that took place in the lyric at the Reformation are well described by John Stevens, Music and Poetry in the Early Tudor Court, *University of Nebraska Press, Lincoln, 1961. The following extract is reprinted from the London* Liber Customarum, *edited by H. T. Riley, London, 1860.*

From
THE FESTIVAL OF THE PUI

In honor of God, Our Lady Saint Mary, and all Saints, both male and female; and in honor of our Lord the King and all the Barons of the country; and for the increasing of loyal love. And to the end that the city of London may be renowned for all good things in all places; and to the end that mirthfulness, peace, honesty, joyousness, gaiety, and good love, without end, may be maintained. And to the end that all blessings may be set before us, and all evils [cast] behind. The loving companions who are dwelling in and repairing unto the good city of London have ordained, confirmed, and established a festival that is called the "Pui." And to the end that the aforesaid festival may be maintained in peace and in love, each one ought to bind himself by his affiance, firmly, as reputable men, that so long as there shall be five companions, he shall be bound to be the sixth, and shall be bound to obey all the commandments, good and lawful, of the Pui.

And each man ought to give, upon entering into the company, six pence for his entrance, by way of remembrance; and such pence ought to go to the benefit of the Pui. And he who shall wish to enter the brother-

hood of the Pui, is bound to maintain and to promote it to the utmost of his power, loyally, according to his affiance. And after this, each companion, on the day of the sitting, shall pay twelve pence; and as to him who shall have a new song, his song shall acquit him thereof; and upon this the Prince ought to provide the feast, so fairly as befits the Pui. And if the Prince have need of assistance, he ought to take twelve of the companions, of the most sufficient men residing in the city, to aid him in advising upon the day of the feast, and throughout all the year after ensuing. The other prince, after this, upon the [same] day in the year next ensuing, ought to choose eleven other companions, good and sufficient, to do well in all things for the common profit of the company; and all the other princes [the same], from year to year, so long as the Pui shall last. And [if] his expenses are in excess upon that day, the companions shall pay them in common. And if there should be any one to contravene this, he is to be expelled from the company.

And upon the day of the sitting, there ought to be no one in the company, to eat there, or to stay, or to hear the singing, if he be not one of the company. And if any one of the companions there should know any man [to be there] who is not of the Pui, he ought to tell the same unto the Prince, upon his oath; and the Prince ought to make him go away or become one of the company, if he be sufficient thereunto. And if he shall not become one of the brotherhood, they are not to sing so long as he is there. And if so be that the Prince should go out of the city, he ought to leave a sufficient companion in his place, the Sunday before Pentecost in each year. And at each sitting, they ought to have a new Prince; and the old Prince ought to appoint him, and the twelve companions, at most, chosen each year. And the Prince ought to be chosen as being good, and loyal, and sufficient, upon the oath of eleven companions, or of the twelve, to their knowledge, upon their oath, that the Pui may be promoted thereby, and maintained, and upheld. And he who shall be chosen for Prince, may not refuse it, upon his oath. And when the old Prince and his companions shall have to make a new Prince, at the great feast, the old Prince and his companions shall go through the room, from one end to the other, singing; and the old Prince shall carry the crown of the Pui upon his head, and a gilt cup in his hands, full of wine. And when they shall have gone round, the old Prince shall give to drink unto him whom they shall have chosen, and shall give him the crown; and such person shall be Prince.

And the old Prince and the new one ought to decide as to the songs, as also those of the companions who understand it best, to the number of fifteen at the most. And they ought to decide as to the best of the songs, to the utmost of their knowledge, upon their oath that they will not fail, for love, for hate, for gift, for promise, for neighborhood, for kindred, or for any acquaintanceship, old or new; nor yet for any thing that is. And the best of the songs ought to be crowned, and the crown ought to belong to him who shall be crowned. And afterwards, each of the companions who is not with the companions upon the day of the sitting, is bound to pay twelve pence, just as much as if he had been there, if he [then] be in the city. And if he be in the city, he is to send the twelve pence to the Prince; and they shall send him bread, wine, and meat sufficiently. And if there be any companion who, upon the day of the sitting, is out of the city, he ought to pay four pence to the Prince, for that which they shall provide for him. And if there be any companion who departs beyond sea, and remains beyond sea without returning, he is acquitted of his oath and of arrears. And if so be that he returns to London at any time, he is bound upon his oath to pay

the arrears to him who shall at such time be Prince. And if there be any one of the companions who marries in the city of London, or who becomes a clerk-priest, he ought to let the companions know thereof, and each shall be there according to his oath, if he have not a proper excuse. And the married person ought to give them chaplets, all of one kind; and all the companions ought to go with the bridegroom to church, and to make offering, and to return from the church to the house. And if there be any one of the companions of the brotherhood who departs this life and dies, all the companions ought to be there, and to carry the body to church, by leave of the kindred, and to make offering. And if there be any one who is unwilling to be obedient unto the peace of God, and unto the peace of our Lord the King—whom may God preserve—the community of the companions do not wish to have him or his fees, through whom the good company may be accused or defamed. And if there be any one of the companions who is evilly disposed in word or in deed, the Prince and the twelve companions ought to make peace to the utmost of their power, saving the rights of the King and the city of London. . . .

Whereas the company of the honored festival of the Pui is ordained and established in honor of Our Lord Jesus Christ, and in honor of Our Lady Saint Mary, his blessed Mother, for the nurturing and the increasing between people of good love, pleasant mirthfulness, and courteous solace, joy and gladness; and for the annihilating of wrath and rancor, crimes, and all vices; and for the obliterating of afflictions, and for the maintaining of the great honor and wellbeing of this good company and the joyous festival of the Pui unto all time; therefore, the gentle companions of the Pui of London, upon the affiances and loyal assurances whereby they are inter-allied, upon the salvation of their souls, to hold the same to the utmost of their power, while confirming the first Statutes of the Pui— which may the good company never forsake or abandon—have, by way of amendment, devised and established these Articles under-written, to hold the same as Statutes to all time. . . .

And whereas the royal feast of the Pui is maintained and established principally for crowning a royal song; inasmuch as it is by song that it is honored and enhanced, all the gentle companions of the Pui by right reason are bound to exalt royal songs to the utmost of their power, and especially the one that is crowned by assent of the companions upon the day of the great feast of the Pui. Wherefore it is here provided, as concerning such songs, that each new Prince, the day that he shall wear the crown and shall govern the feast of the Pui, and so soon as he shall have had his blazon of his arms hung in the room where the feast of the Pui shall be held, shall forthwith cause to be set up beneath his blazon the song that was crowned on the day that he was chosen as the new Prince, plainly and correctly written, without default. For no singer by right ought to sing any royal song, or to proffer the same, at the feast of the Pui, until he shall have seen the song that was last crowned in the year just past honored according to its right, in the manner aforesaid.

And that, for deciding as to the songs, there be chosen two or three who well understand singing and music, for the purpose of trying and examining the notes and the points of the song, as well as the nature of the words composed thereto. For without singing no one ought to call a composition of words a song, nor ought any royal song to be crowned without the sweet sounds of melody sung.

And although the becoming pleasance of virtuous ladies is a rightful theme and principal occasion for royal singing, and for composing and furnishing royal songs, nevertheless it is hereby provided that no lady or other woman ought to be at the great [sitting] of the Pui, for the reason that the [members] ought hereby to take example, and rightful warning, to honor, cherish, and commend all ladies, at all times in all places, as much in their absence as in their presence. And this breeding requires and all good propriety. . . .

oue seauce comenti
il eſt icy deſſus con
tenu en noſtre hiſ
toire comment le roy de france eſ

VII

FRENCH LITERATURE IN ENGLAND

Beginning in the twelfth century, authors who wrote for the Norman nobility in England produced some of the most significant works of early French literature. For example, Geoffrey Gaimar was a pioneer in the production of vernacular rhymed chronicles. One of the most important romances in any language, the *Tristran* of Thomas, was written in England, and Marie de France, who wrote in England, has few equals on the Continent for short narrative poems. Literature in French continued to flourish on English soil until the late fourteenth century, when John Gower wrote in French, as well as in English and Latin. Only a few examples of this large body of material can be presented here. Two poems by a Provençal troubadour are included, not only because one of them was written in England, but because troubadour poetry influenced

Facing page: Ladies and gentlemen riding to a tournament in London.

the development of the lyric in English and French, not to mention Irish and Welsh. Although Froissart was not, strictly speaking, either French or English, he was for a time the most important poet at the English court, and his *Chronicles* have long been a classic for English readers.

A survey of French literature in England with helpful bibliographical notes has recently been published by M. Dominica Legge, *Anglo-Norman Literature and Its Background*, Clarendon Press, Oxford, 1963.

For the historical background of the period, the relevant volumes in The Oxford History of England are most useful: A. L. Poole, *From Domesday Book to Magna Carta*, Clarendon Press, Oxford, 1951; Sir Maurice Powicke, *The Thirteenth Century*, Clarendon Press, Oxford, 1959; May McKisack, *The Fourteenth Century*, Clarendon Press, Oxford, 1959. On English feudalism, see Sir Frank Stenton, *The First Century of English Feudalism*, Clarendon Press, Oxford, 1932. A pleasant and convenient introduction to the social history of the period from the Conquest to the death of Edward I is Doris May Stenton, *English Society in the Early Middle Ages*, Penguin Books, Inc., Baltimore, 1951. Various aspects of English society are discussed by Sir Maurice Powicke, *Medieval England*, Oxford University Press, London, 1931.

 ## A. Marie de France

Marie de France (fl. ca. 1180–1195) has not been identified with certainty. Various conjectures have associated her with an abbess of Shaftesbury, or with Marie the daughter of Waleran de Meulan, or with certain other ladies. Whoever she was, she had an exceptional education for a medieval woman, and considerable talent. She wrote, in addition to twelve lais, a collection of fables and an Espurgatoire S. Patrice.

The word lai *is probably derived from a Celtic word meaning " song." The Breton jongleurs were famous for their narrative songs, or lais, although none of them has survived. Marie probably derived her plots from such songs, which she heard in French. According to Denis Piramus, who mentions Marie in his twelfth-century* Life of St. Edmund, *Marie's poems were especially popular among the ladies. The verse form of the lais may be illustrated in the first four lines of the original:*

> Ki Deus ad duné escience
> E de parler bon eloquence
> Ne s'en deit taisir ne celer
> Ainz, se deit volunters mustrer.

There is a good annotated edition of the text by A. Ewert, Basil Blackwell & Mott, Ltd., Oxford, 1944.

For discussions of Marie, see Urban T. Holmes, Jr., A History of Old French Literature, *F. S. Crofts & Co., New York, 1938; and, with special reference to her use of Arthurian material, Ernest Hoepffner, " The Breton Lais," in R. S. Loomis,* Arthurian Literature in the Middle Ages, *Clarendon Press, Oxford, 1959. The following selections have been translated by the editor.*

LAIS

Prologue

He to whom God has given knowledge and the eloquence to speak well ought not to remain silent nor conceal what he knows, but should willingly make it known to others.[1] When a great good is heard by many, then it comes into flower for the first time; and when it is praised by many, then its flowers have opened up.

According to the testimony of Priscian,[2] the ancients spoke obscurely in the books that they wrote for those who were to come after them and who were to learn from them, so that they would be able to gloss the

Figure 25 *Bayeux tapestry. Death of Harold.*

letter and to separate the sense from the surplus material.[3] The philosophers knew this, and understood that the more the times changed the more subtle their sense would become, so that men would have to be more careful in order not to misinterpret what they had said in their books. For this reason, he who would defend himself from vice should study, and seek to understand, and apply himself seriously. In this way he can more easily reject vice and deliver himself from great sorrow. Considering these things, I began to think of translating some good history from Latin into romance; but this would not have been of much honor to me because so many others have done the same thing. I thought of the lais that I had heard and did not hesitate, for well I knew that they who had first composed them and sent them forth had done so in order that the events they had heard about might be remembered. I have heard a number of them told, and do not wish them to be neglected or forgotten. I have put them in rhyme and made a poem, frequently sitting awake over them.

In your honor, noble king,[4] who are so worthy and courteous, before whom all joy bows, and in whose heart all good takes root, I undertook to collect lais, put them in rhyme, and retell them. I thought and said in my heart, Sire, that I would present them to you. If it pleases you to receive them, you shall bring me great joy, and I shall be forever happy. Do not think me presumptuous if I make this gift to you. Now, hear the beginning!

Equitan

Very noble are the Bretons, the knights of Brittany. In times gone by, for the sake of prowess, courtesy, and nobility, they were accustomed to make lais of the adventures which befell many men so that they might be remembered and not lost in forgetfulness. They made one which I have heard related, and which should not be forgotten, concerning Equitan, who was a most noble lord of Nantes, just and royal.

Equitan was much esteemed and much loved in his country. He loved pleasure and the love of women and maintained his chivalry on that account. Those who love without sense and measure set their lives at nought, for such is the force of their love that reason does not guide them at all. Equitan had a seneschal, a good knight, worthy and loyal. He administered the land well, maintaining it in justice. But never would the king for any need that arose except war give up his pleasure, his hunting, and his hawking.

The seneschal had married a wife, from whom great evils arose in the land afterward. The dame was irresistably beautiful and of very good breeding. She had a gentle body and a fine figure. Nature labored to form her. Her eyes were bright, and she had a fair face, a good mouth, and a well-shaped nose. There was none in the realm to equal her. The king heard men praise her often and frequently sent her greetings and gifts from his treasure. He desired her without having seen her, and wished to speak with her as quickly as possible. Secretly he went to amuse himself hunting in the country where she resided, and he took lodging for the night when he returned from the hunt in the seneschal's castle. There he could talk with her as much as he wished and show her his heart and his desire. He found her very courteous and wise, beautiful of body and face, pleasant and well-mannered. Love had taken him into his household and loosened an arrow at him which made a great wound when it lodged in his heart, so that there he had no need for sense or understanding. He was so overcome by the lady that he was sorrowful and pensive. Now when he had most need he could not defend himself at all. That night he neither slept nor rested but blamed and scolded himself.

"Alas!" he said, "What destiny has led me into this country? On account of this lady I have seen, an anguish has struck my heart that makes me tremble all over. I thought I had need to love, but if I love her I shall do evil, for she is the wife of the seneschal. I should guard him with love and faith just as I wish him to guard me.[5] If he should learn about this love by any trick, I know it would grieve him much. Nevertheless, it would be enough of an evil if I should be made a fool of by him. It would be a bad thing indeed if such a beautiful lady did not have a lover! What would become of her courtesy if she did not love outside of wedlock? There is no man on earth who would not amend himself vigorously if she loved him. If the seneschal should hear about it, he should not be too grieved. He should not have all that to himself. I'll share it with him."

When he had said this, he sighed. Then he tossed about thinking, and said, "Why am I so uneasy and upset? I do not know yet, nor have I sought to discover, whether she will make me her lover or not. But I shall soon know. If she feels what I feel, I'll lose this sorrow. God! it's a long time until daylight and a long time since I went to bed last night."

The king stayed awake until sunrise, for which he had waited with great pain. He arose and went forth as if to hunt, but soon came back saying that he was not well. He went to his chamber and went to bed. The seneschal was very sorrowful on this account, not knowing what the malady was that gave the king the shivers. His wife was the real occasion for it. He bade her go speak with the king to please and comfort him. When she did so, the king discovered his heart to her,

assuring her that he was about to die on her account. She could either cure him completely, he said, or just as well cause him to die.

"Sir," the lady said to him, "I must have a little time for this, for on this first occasion I am without counsel. You are a king of great nobility, but I am not so wealthy that you should select me to love or to take as your mistress. When you have had your desire, I know truly that your love will not last, but you will leave me at once and I shall be greatly harmed. If it happens that I love you and grant your request, love will not be equally divided between us, for you are a powerful king and my husband is one of your tenants. It seems to me that you would think to have the mastery in such a love, and love is not worthy except between equals. A poor man who is loyal, if he has sense and courage, is more valuable than a prince or king when he does not maintain loyalty, and there is more joy in his love. If anyone sets his love more highly than his wealth justifies, he must be always doubtful about it. On the other hand, the rich man for his part thinks that no one can take his love from him, for he thinks to maintain love through the power of his lordship."

Equitan answered, "Lady, have mercy! Say no more! What you say is not refined and courteous but is the bargain of a merchant, who for the sake of wealth and much land puts his effort in evil dealings. There is no lady under heaven, if she is wise, courteous, and generous, who, provided that she holds her love dear and does not seek novelty, if she had nothing under her mantle but the rich prince of a castle, would not exert herself for him and love him well and loyally. Those who seek novelty in love and descend to trickery are scorned and deceived. We have seen many such. It is no wonder that they lose that which they desert through their own effort. My dear lady, I submit to you! Don't think of me as a king but as your man and your friend! I swear and say to you assuredly that I will do your pleasure! Don't let me die for you! You will be the lady and I the servant; you will be the proud lord and I the suppliant!"

The king had spoken with her in such a way and cried mercy so often that she assured him of her love and gave him her body. They pledged each other with rings and swore fealty to each other. They cherished each other and loved each other greatly. Then they died and came to an end because of it.

Their secret love lasted a long while because it was

unknown to anyone. At the times when they met and spoke together the king had his household informed that he had gone privately to be bled. The doors of the chambers were closed, and you would not have found a man so rash as to enter unless the king had sent for him. Then the seneschal held court to hear the pleas and the petitions. The king loved a long time, for he had no desire for another woman. He had no wish to marry and demanded that no one speak of such a thing. The people disliked this greatly, so that the wife of the seneschal often heard them talking about it. She was very sorrowful and afraid that she would lose the love of the king. When she had an opportunity to speak with him and should have been joyful—kissing him, hugging him, embracing him, and playing with him—she wept copiously and lamented dolefully. The king asked her what was the matter, and she replied, "Sire, I weep for our love, which brings me great sorrow. You will take a wife, the daughter of a king, and so you will leave me. I have often heard talk about it and know it well. And I, alas! What will become of me? I shall die on your account, for I know no other comfort."

The king said to her with great love, "Sweet friend, do not be afraid! Certainly, I shall neither take a wife nor leave you for another. Know that for truth and believe it. If your husband were dead, I would make you my wife and queen. Meanwhile, I shall not leave you in spite of anyone."

The lady thanked him and said that she was much obliged to him, and that since he had said that he would not leave her for another, she would quickly seek to bring about the death of her husband. This, she said, would be easy to accomplish if the king would help her. He said that he would help her, since there was nothing he would not do for her to the best of his ability, whether wise or foolish.

"Sire," she said, "if it pleases you, come to hunt in the country where I live, and lodge in my husband's castle. There have yourself bled, and bathe on the third day. My husband will be bled with you and will bathe with you. I implore you, order him directly, do not forbid that he accompany you! I will have the baths heated and the two tubs brought in. His bath will be so hot and scalding that there is no man living under heaven who would not be scalded and endangered as soon as he sat in it. When he is dead and scalded, call your men and his, and you can show how he suddenly died in the bath."

The king granted that he would do her will in everything.

Three months had not passed when the king went hunting in the country. He had himself bled on account of his sickness, and the seneschal with him. On the third day he said that he would bathe. The seneschal greatly wished a bath also.

"Bathe with me," said the king.

"I grant it," the seneschal replied.

The lady had the baths heated and the two tubs brought in. She had the tubs placed near the beds, with the tub of boiling water where the seneschal would enter. The seneschal had arisen and gone forth for his pleasure. The lady wished to speak with the king, who sat her down beside him. They lay on the bed of the seneschal, playing and amusing themselves there by the fiery tub that was before them. They had stationed a servant girl at the door to hold and guard it. The seneschal returned hastily and knocked on the door, where the servant girl detained him. Angered, he threw open the door and found the king and his wife where they lay embracing each other. The king looked up and saw him come in. To hide his villainy, for he had taken off his clothes and was nude, he jumped into the tub without thinking, his feet together. There he scalded and killed himself. Upon himself his evil trick returned, and the other is safe and free of it. The seneschal had well seen what happened to the king. He straightway seized his wife and pushed her head into the tub. Thus they both died, the king first and the lady with him.

Whoever wishes to listen to reason can take these things as an example: if anyone accomplishes the evil of another, evil will return to him. These events happened as I have told them, and the Bretons have made a lai of them concerning Equitan and how he and the dame he loved so much came to an end.

Lanval

I shall tell you the adventure of another lai as it happened. It was made concerning a very gentle vassal. In Brittany it is called "Lanval."

The worthy and courteous King Arthur was staying at Carlisle because of the Picts and Scots who were destroying the country. They were entering the land of Logres [6] and damaging it very savagely. The king had gone there in the summer at Pentecost. He gave many rich gifts to his knights and barons and to the men of the Round Table—there were not so many like these in all the world. Women and lands he distributed to all, except to one who had served him. That was Lanval. They neither gave him anything nor cared for him. Most of them envied him for his valor, his generosity, his beauty, and his prowess. Such men showed him a semblance of love, but if a misfortune befell the knight, they made no lament over it. He was the son of a king of high lineage, but was far from his heritage. Although he belonged to Arthur's household, he had spent all of his wealth because the king gave him nothing and he would ask for nothing. Now Lanval is in a bad plight, pensive and very sorrowful. Lords, be not astonished. A stranger in another land who is without counsel is very sorrowful because he does not know where to turn for aid.

The knight I have been telling you about who had served the king as I have said mounted his destrier one day to seek amusement. He rode out of town and came to a meadow alone. He rode down to a running stream, but his horse trembled violently and would not cross it. Lanval loosened the saddle girth, let the horse go, and lay down in the meadow. He folded the skirt of his mantle and placed it under his head. He was very pensive because of his uncomfortable situation, and could think of nothing to please him. He looked down along the river and saw two damsels more beautiful than any he had ever seen. They were very richly dressed, laced tightly in long scarlet tunics, and very pleasant to look at. One of them carried a pair of well-made basins of refined gold—I shall tell you the truth of this without fail. The other carried a towel. They were coming straight to where the knight was lying. Lanval, who was very well-mannered, rose to his feet before them. They told him their message:

"Sir Lanval, my lady, who is most wise and beautiful, has sent us to you. Come with us now. We shall conduct you safely. Look, the pavilion is nearby."

The knight went with them, taking no care for his horse, which was grazing nearby in the meadow. They led him to the tent, which was very beautiful and well devised. Neither Queen Semiramis, when she once had much wealth and power and knowledge, nor the Emperor Octavian[7] could pay for the right flap of the tent. It had a golden eagle on top of it. I don't know how to tell you the value of it, nor that of the cords and poles that held up the tent walls. No king under heaven could buy them for any wealth he could give for them. Within this tent was the maiden. She exceeded in beauty the lily and the new rose when it opens in the summer. She lay on a very beautiful bed—the coverlet on it was worth a castle—dressed only in her chemise. Her body was very gentle and shapely. On account of the chill, she had thrown over herself an expensive mantle of white ermine lined with Alexandrine silk. Her side, face, neck, and bosom, which were uncovered, were whiter than hawthorn flowers. The knight approached as she called him and sat down before the bed.

"Lanval," she said, "good friend, for you I have left my country and come from afar to seek you. If you will be prudent and courteous, neither emperor nor count nor king will have such joy and wealth; for I love you above everything."

He looked at her and saw that she was beautiful. Love pricked him with his spark so that his heart was lighted and enkindled. He responded in seemly fashion.

"Fair one," he said, "if it pleases you, and that joy comes to me because you wish to love me, you will not be able to command anything that I will not do to the best of my ability, whether it may lead to folly or to wisdom. I shall fulfill your commandments and abandon everyone else for you. I do not wish to part from you ever. That is what I most desire."

When the maiden heard how he could love her, she gave him her love and her body. Now Lanval is on the right road! She gave him another gift also. He would never more wish anything that he could not have at his desire. He might give and spend generously, and she would find enough for him. Lanval was very well lodged. The more richly he spent, the more gold and silver he had.

"Now, friend," she said, "I warn you, command you, and pray you that you reveal this to no man! I shall tell you what this means. You will have lost me forever if this love is shown; you will never be able to see me again nor to have seisin of my body."

He replied that he would hold her commandment well. She was beside him in the bed. Now Lanval was well lodged! He remained with her all afternoon, almost until Vespers, and would have remained longer if he had been able and his friend had consented.

"Friend," she said, "get up! You may stay no longer. You go forth and I shall stay. But I shall say one thing.

When you wish to speak with me, unless you do so in a place where no man may have his girl without reproach and without villainy, I shall always be with you to fulfill your desire. No man except you should see me or hear my voice."

When he heard this, he was very happy about it. He kissed her and arose. Those who had brought him to the tent clothed him in rich garments. When he was newly dressed, there was not a more attractive youth anywhere, and he was neither foolish nor villainous. They gave him water with which to wash his hands, and a towel to dry them. Then they brought something to eat. He had supper with his friend. He was served very courteously and he ate with great joy. He had plenty of a good appetizer which pleased him much; for he frequently kissed his friend and hugged her tightly.

When they had arisen from supper, the maidens brought him his horse. They put the saddle on neatly; much he found of good service. He took his leave, mounted, and rode toward the city. Frequently he looks back, and now Lanval is in great fear. He rides along thinking of his adventure and feeling doubtful in his heart. He is astonished and does not know what to think. He fears that he will never see his friend again. He comes to his lodging where his men find him very well dressed, and there he lodged very well that night. But no one knew where his wealth came from. There was no poor knight in all the town who had great need of sustenance whom Lanval did not have come to him to be richly and well served. Lanval gave rich gifts. Lanval released prisoners. Lanval clothed the jongleurs. Lanval did great honor to everyone; there was no one either foreign or native to whom Lanval did not give something. Much joy and pleasure he had, and he could see his friend frequently, either by day or by night. She was altogether at his command.

It was, I think, in the same year near the Feast of St. John[8] that about thirty knights went out to enjoy themselves in a garden below the tower where the queen was staying. With them was Gawain and his fair cousin Yvain. And Gawain, the noble and worthy knight who made himself beloved by all, said, "By God, sirs, we do our friend Lanval a disservice by not asking him to come with us, for he is very generous and courteous, and his father is a powerful king."

Then they turned back, went to Lanval's lodging, and prayed him to join them. The queen, who was in the company of three dames, part of the household retinue appointed by the king, was leaning on a window barred with stone lattice. She saw and recognized Lanval. She called one of the dames and through her commanded that some of the most attractive and beautiful of her damsels go with her to take their sport there in the garden with the knights. She took thirty or more with her. In the proper order from the highest down, the knights went to meet them and had great joy of them. They took them by the hands, and their conversation was not villainous. Lanval went apart, far from the others. He was impatient to have his friend, to kiss her, to embrace her, and to feel her close to him. He thought the joy of others little if he did not have his own delight. When the queen saw him alone, she went to him at once. She sat next to him, addressed him, and showed him what was in her heart.

"Lanval, I have honored you much and cherished you and loved you. You can have all my love. Now tell me your will! I give you the love of my body. You should be very glad to have me."

"Dame," he said, "let me be! I have no wish to love you. I have long served the king, and I have no desire to lie against my sworn faith to him. Neither for you nor for your love will I do evil to my lord."

The queen was very annoyed at this reply, and in her wrath she spoke evilly. "Lanval," she said, "they think well who say that you do not love such delight. People have told me often that you have no desire for women. You have well-trained boys with whom you delight yourself. Villainous coward of ill faith, my Sire is badly served to have suffered you to be with him. Indeed, he loses God thereby!"

When he heard this, Lanval was very sorrowful, and he was not slow to respond. He said a thing in ill will that he often repented. "Dame," he said, "I do not know how to aid those of the condition you mention at all. But I love, and am loved by, a woman who deserves precedence over all those whom I know. And I'll tell you something else that you may know well and clearly: any one of the damsels who follows her, even the poorest of her servant maidens, is better than you are, O queen, in body, in face, in beauty, in training, and in goodness."

The queen left immediately and went to her chamber weeping. She was very sorrowful and cross because he had reviled her in that way. She lay ill in her bed, saying that she would not get up until the king had made right that about which she was complaining.

The king returned from the forest, where he had enjoyed a good day, and entered the chamber of the queen. When she saw him, she called out, fell at his feet, and cried mercy, saying that Lanval had shamed her. He had, she said, asked for her body, and when she refused him, he had insulted and reviled her repeatedly. He boasted of a friend who was so attractive and noble and grand that the poorest chambermaid who served her was worth more than the queen. The king was greatly irritated, and he swore an oath: if Lanval could not defend himself in court, he should be burned or hanged. The king went forth from the chamber and called three of his barons. He sent them for Lanval, who was already suffering sorrow and evil enough. He had returned to his lodging knowing well that he had lost his friend because he had revealed their secret love. He was all alone, pensive and anxious in his chamber. He called his friend frequently, but that did not avail him in the least. He lamented and sighed, and from time to time swooned. Then he cried mercy a hundred times, asking that she would speak to her lover. He cursed his heart and his mouth, and it is a wonder that he did not kill himself. He did not know how to cry out or bray or tear himself in such a way that she would have mercy concerning anything she could see there. Alas! How should he behave?

Those sent by the king arrived and said to him that he should go to the court without delay and that the king had sent for him because the queen had accused him. Lanval accompanied them with great sorrow. They would have killed him if they had had their way. He came before the queen, sorrowful, silent, speechless, and with a sad countenance. The king said to him with ill will, "Vassal, you have wronged me greatly! You have begun a villainous undertaking indeed, to shame and revile me and to vilify the queen. You have boasted foolishly. Your friend is very noble indeed when her maiden is more beautiful and worthy than the queen."

Lanval denied any shame and dishonor to his lord, denying word for word the king's accusation that he had asked the queen's love. Concerning that which he had said, he told the truth about the love he had boasted of. He was sorrowful because he had lost it, and he said that he would do whatever the court decreed. The king was very wrathful. He sent his men straightway to decide what he should do so that no one would interpret his action unfavorably. They performed his commandment, whether pleasant or unpleasant. Together they went aside, judged, and decided that Lanval should have a day in court, but that he should find sureties for his lord so that he would await his judgment and return to his presence. Then the court would be strengthened, for there was no one present at the time except the household.[9] The barons returned to the king and revealed their decision. The king demanded sureties. Lanval was alone and forlorn, without relations or friends. Gawain stepped forward and offered surety, and all his companions after him. The king said to them, "I grant it, upon the pledge of whatever you hold of me, lands and fiefs, each one to offer his own."

When Lanval had pleaded his case, he had nothing left. He returned to his lodging, accompanied by the knights. They blamed and reprimanded him for making such sorrow, and they deprecated such a foolish love. They went every day to see him, for they wished to see that he ate and drank because they were afraid that he was going mad.

On the day that they had named the barons were assembled. The king and the queen were there, and the sureties brought Lanval. Everyone was very sorry for him. I think that there were a hundred of them who did everything in their power to free him without trial. They thought that he was accused with great wrong. But the king demanded a verdict according to the claim and the response. Now everything was in the hands of the barons. They went to judgment. Many were pensive and sorrowful concerning a nobleman from another country who had suffered such a misfortune among them. On the other hand, many wished him condemned because of the will of their lord.

The Count of Cornwall said, "As far as we are concerned, there should be no default, for whoever may be pleased or displeased by it, justice should take precedence. The king speaks against his vassal, whom I have heard called Lanval. He accuses him of felony and charges him with a misdeed in which he boasted of his love and angered my lady the queen. No one accuses him except the king. By the faith that I owe you, if anyone wishes to speak truth about this matter, there ought not to be any response to the charge were it not for the principle that a man ought to do honor to his lord in everything. Let Lanval take an oath, and let the king excuse us: And if Lanval can show proof, and his friend comes forward, and it appears that what he said that vexed the queen was true, then he ought to have mercy because he did not vilify her. And if he can not get proof, then we should make this known: he should lose all of his service of the king and depart from him."

They sent to the knight and announced to him that he should make his friend come to defend him and act as warranty for him. He told them that he could not do so, and that he had no one to succor him. They returned to the judges, saying that never from her would he obtain succor. The king pressed them hard on account of the queen, who was waiting for them.

When they were about to depart, they saw two maidens coming on two fine palfreys. They were extremely attractive, dressed in scarlet taffeta which covered their nude flesh. The knights looked at them most willingly. Gawain with three knights went to Lanval and told him, showing him the maidens. Gawain was very happy, and pressed Lanval to tell him whether one of the maidens might be his friend. But Lanval told him that he did not know who they were, or where they came from, or where they were going. The maidens, who came forward mounted, dismounted before the dais where King Arthur was seated. They were very beautiful and spoke very courteously.

"King, make ready some chambers hung with brocade where my lady may stay, for she wishes to lodge with you."

The king granted the request willingly, and called two knights to lead the maidens to the chambers. The knights did not hesitate to do so. The king demanded the judgment and the response from his barons, saying that he was very irritated because they had delayed. "Sire," they said, "we shall deliver judgment. Because of the ladies we saw we neglected it. Now we shall resume the trial." Then they assembled very sorrowfully with enough noise and strife. When they were engaged in this heated discussion, they saw two maidens nobly furnished, dressed in garments of Phrygian silk and mounted on two Spanish mules coming down the street. The knights were very joyful to see them, and said among themselves that Lanval, the noble and hardy knight, now had his warranty. Yvain went to him with his companions.

"Sir," he said, "cheer up! For the love of God, speak to us! Here come two very comely and beautiful damsels. One of them is certainly your friend!" Lanval hastily replied that he did not recognize them, or know them, or love them. They came up and dismounted before the king. Many praised them for their figures, their faces, and their color, saying that none surpassed them, not even the queen. The eldest was courteous and wise, and quickly delivered her message: "King, make ready chambers in which my lady may be lodged. She comes to speak with you."

The king commanded that they be taken with the others who had come before. Even the mules made no complaint. When he was freed of the damsels, the king again commanded his barons that the judgment be rendered. The hour was late, and the queen, who had been waiting for a long time, was angry.

The judges were about to depart when they saw coming through the town on horseback a single maiden. There was none more beautiful in all the world. She rode on a white palfrey which carried her gracefully and safely. It was very well shaped, both neck and head. There was no more beautiful beast beneath the sky. It was richly equipped, and indeed there was no king or count beneath the heavens who could buy the trappings without selling or engaging land. The damsel was dressed in this way. She wore a chemise of white linen laced in two parts which revealed all her sides. Her body was gentle, her hips were low, her neck whiter than snow on a branch, her eyes were bright and her countenance was clear. She had a beautiful mouth and a well-formed nose. Her eyebrows were brown, and she had a fair forehead. Her hair was curly and fair. A thread of gold would not be as brilliant as was her hair in the light. Her mantle, the skirts of which were wrapped about her, was of scarlet. She held a falcon on her wrist, and a hunting dog walked beside her. There was no one in the city, small or large, old or young, who did not run to see her. When they saw her riding along, there were no jests about her beauty. She came riding slowly. When the judges saw her, they were astonished, for not a single one who looked at her failed to be overcome with great joy. Those who loved Lanval went to him and told him of the maiden who was coming, God willing, to deliver him.

"Sir companion, here comes one who is neither yellow nor brown. She is the most beautiful woman among all those who are in the world." Lanval heard them and raised his head. He knew her well, and sighed. The blood rushed to his face, and he was eager to speak. "By my faith," he said, "that is my friend! Now it matters little if someone kills me, for she has had mercy on me. I am healed when I see her."

The lady entered the palace. No one had seen anyone

Figure 26 *Tristram and Iseult. Misericord, Chester Cathedral.*

more beautiful. She descended before the king in such a way that all could see her well, letting her mantle fall so that she might be better seen. The king, who was very well-mannered, advanced to greet her, and all the rest hastened forward to serve her. When they had looked at her well and vigorously praised her beauty, she spoke as follows, for she did not wish to stay:

"King, I have loved one of your vassals. See him here! It is Lanval! He was charged in your court. I do not wish what he said to be used against him. You should know that the queen did wrong, for he never at any time asked her love. If the boast that he made may be vindicated by me, let your barons free him!"

That Lanval might be judged by right, the king granted that it should be so. There was not a one who did not judge that Lanval had been completely defended. He was delivered by their judgment, and the maiden prepared to depart. The king could not detain her, nor could the many men who wished to serve her. Outside the room had been placed a huge stone of dark marble where sorrowful men mounted who went away from the court of the king, and Lanval was mounted upon it. When the maiden went out of the gate on the palfrey, Lanval leaped behind her with a single bound. The Bretons say that he went with her to Avalon, a very beautiful island. There the youth was taken away. No one ever heard any more of him, and I can tell you no more.

The Woodbine

The lai which is called "Chevrefoil"[10] pleases me so much and is so suited to my inclination that I shall tell you the truth of the events for which it was made and presented. Many persons have recounted it to me, and I have found it in writing concerning Tristram and the queen, and their love which was so fine. From it they had many sorrows and died of it on the same day.

King Mark was irritated, very angry with his nephew Tristram, and sent him from his land on account of the queen whom he loved. Tristram went to his own country in South Wales, where he was born, and remained there a whole year. Nor could he go back, so that he exposed himself to death and destruction. You should not marvel at this at all, for he loved very loyally and was very doleful and pensive when he could not have his love. He was so doleful and pensive that he left his country and went straight to Cornwall where the queen was staying. He hid himself alone in a forest,[11] not wishing to be seen by anyone. He came out at night when it was time to find shelter and stayed with peasants and poor people. He asked news of the king and how he was conducting himself. They told him that they had heard that the barons had been summoned to come to Tintagel where the king wished to hold court, and that all would be there at Pentecost. He would have much joy and delight, and the queen would be there.

Tristram was very glad to hear these things. The queen would not be able to go without his seeing her pass by. And Tristram went to the wood, near the road where he knew that the retinue would pass. He cut a hazel[12] stick and split it so that it had four sides. When he had prepared the wand, he wrote his name on it with his knife. Thus the queen would see it, for she would watch very carefully for it since it happened that she had seen the same thing before. She would know how to interpret the wand when she saw it.[13] This was the implication of the writing that he had sent, to inform her that he had long been waiting to know and to discover how he might see her, for he could not live without her. With them it was as with the woodbine wound around the hazel. When the woodbine is interlaced with the hazel and has grown completely over it, the two may survive together. But if anyone then wishes to separate them, the hazel dies quickly and the woodbine

also. "Sweet friend, so it is with us: you may not exist without me, nor I without you."

The queen came riding along the road looking attentively. She saw the wand and perceived it well, recognizing all the letters on it. She commanded all the knights riding with her to stop because she wished to dismount and rest. They obeyed her command. She went far from her retinue with Brangien, her maid, who was of good faith. Going a little aside from the road, she found in the forest him whom she loved more than anyone else alive. Great joy was there between them. She spoke to him at leisure, telling him her will. Afterward, she showed him how he might have peace with the king. She told him how sorrowful she was because he had been banished as a result of the accusations that had been made. Then she took her leave and departed from her friend. But when the time for parting came, they began to weep. Tristram returned to Wales as his uncle had commanded.

Because of the joy he had experienced with his friend when he saw her, and because of what he had written as the queen directed, and because of his desire to remember the words, Tristram, who knew well how to play the harp, made a new lai. Very briefly I shall name it for you: they call it "Goatleaf" in English; the French call it "Chevrefoil." I have told you the truth of the lai which I have here related for you.

Notes

1   This is a reflection of the medieval ideal of combined wisdom and eloquence.

2   The reference is to the beginning of the *Institutions* of the grammarian Priscian. However, what Marie goes on to say is relevant to Priscian only in a very general way.

3   The text reads, *"K'i peussent gloser la lettre/E de lur sen le surplus mettre."* The present translation takes *lettre* as a collective noun forming a plural antecedent for *lur*. The usual translations take "those who were to come after them" as the antecedent of *lur*, yielding something like "so that those who were to come after them might construe their writing and add to it from their own ingenuity." *Letter*, as Hugh of St. Victor tells us, consists of the words or "sounds" of a text and their arrangement. Thus he says (*Didascalicon*, 6:8), "The letter is found in every discourse, for the very sounds are letters."

4   Probably Henry II.

5   This is a reference to the mutual fealty which ideally existed between a vassal and his overlord.

6   That is, England.

7   Augustus.

8   June 24, the nativity of St. John the Baptist.

9   That is, they held in effect a preliminary hearing to determine whether Lanval should be tried before the full court. Marie is meticulous about legal formalities in this tale.

10 That is, goat-leaf, a plant of the genus *capriofolaceae*, now known as *Lonicera periclymenum*, called honeysuckle, because its flowers were sucked for their sweetness, or woodbine, because of its habit of winding around trees. The latter characteristic is relevant here.

11 In medieval contexts, the word *forest* has no romantic associations but suggests "desert," or unpleasant and uninhabited country.

12 The hazel (*Corylus avellana*) is a small tree, the wood of which is close-grained and suitable for carving.

13 There has been much discussion of this passage. However, it may be assumed that the queen would draw the conclusions indicated from (1) the name, (2) the nature of the wood, (3) her present situation, and (4) her previous experience.

 B. Bernart of Ventadour

Bernart is one of the most famous of the troubadours. He was born, legend has it, of humble parents in the Castle of Ventadour in Limousin. Having won a reputation as a poet, he probably came to England for the festivals at the coronation of Henry II in 1154.

The troubadours have suffered much from the modern romantic imagination, which tends to overlook the detachment and humor in many of their songs, as well as the feudal convention that permitted them to address noble ladies in rather forthright amorous language for the sake of a place, not in their bedchambers, but at the dining tables of their household followers. Again, some of their religious pieces, colored by the unblushing language of the biblical Canticle of Canticles, have been very difficult for the post-Reformation mind to comprehend. Some of the troubadours were rough equivalents of news commentators and propagandists in the service of various feudal or ecclesiastical causes.

Troubadour melodies were probably unmeasured, and the accompaniments played on lutes probably avoided chords. The melody given here for one of the songs has been provided with a modern guitar accompaniment. In general, each note corresponds with a syllable of the text, although at times the note may be broken up to make a flourish. The songs should be sung slowly in a high, slightly nasal voice with as little vibrato as possible. The surviving melodies of the troubadours have been collected by Friedrich Gennrich, Der Musikalische Nachlass der Troubadours, in Summa musicae medii aevi, vols. III, IV, Darmstadt, 1958, 1960. Some songs are available as sheet music in modern transcription. Since it is impossible to preserve the syllabic count of the originals in English, it is best to sing the songs in Provençal.

The most reliable book on the troubadours is Alfred Jeanroy, La poésie lyrique des troubadours, Toulouse, 1935. Unfortunately, discussions of the troubadours in English tend to be romantic, sentimental, or marred by modern expressionistic attitudes that would have been out of place in a medieval cultural setting. The poems of Bernart have been edited by Carl Appel, Bernart von Ventadorn, Halle, 1915. The following translations are by the editor.

"LANCAN VEI PER MEI LA LANDA...."

When I see through all the land
Leaves that fall on every hand,
Before the chill and frost expand
And winter makes its cold demand,

It would be good to make a song.   5
Two years' silence is all wrong,
And to me a reprimand.

It's hard to flatter her once more;
She's so proud and such a bore,

She has no single word in store   10
For one whose heart for her is sore.
I'll be killed by fool desire
Which doesn't know it must require
Love, and not what goes before.

With such tricks she can deceive,   15
She almost leads me to believe
Her sweet nothings will relieve,
Not tear my heart and make it grieve.
Dame, be careful what you do:
The evil will all come to you,   20
Not to him whose harm you weave.

May God, who holds the world in place,
Lead me to her close embrace,
For eating brings me now no grace,
And wealth is hardly worth the chase.   25
My lady has me in her sway;
She can either give away
Or sell me, now that I'm so base.

She'll do great wrong to me unless
In her chamber she'll undress,   30
And bring me in; I'll press
Near the bed, kneeling, and address
Myself to taking off her shoes
Humbly, that is, if she won't refuse
To extend her feet for this caress.   35

This song is made up to the end,
Without mistakes that may offend,
Beyond the savage seas that bend
Where Norman lands last extend.
My lady love who draws my heart   40
Like a magnet when we part,
Far away, may God defend!

If the English King and Norman Duke
Wishes it, I'll see her before
Winter comes.   45

For the King I would be English or Norman
If it were not for my Magnet.
I shall remain here until after Christmas.

"CAN VEI LA LAUZETA MOVER...."

When I see the lark fly
Joyfully against the sun
Until, forgetting it must die
In all the sweetness it has won,
It falls, I am filled with spite   5
For those who dwell in joy apart.
I marvel, then, that by right
Longing does not melt my heart.

Oh, I thought myself so wise
In love, but little did I know.   10
No lady have I deigned to prize
But one I thought could well bestow.
She's taken all my heart and me,
Taken herself, and all besides,
And left me nothing for my fee   15
But longing that my heart derides.

Since I looked into her eyes
All my self-control is gone.
That mirror taught me to despise
All the reason I had known.   20
Glass, I die to look once more;
Sorrow makes of me a fool
Like Narcissus, who of yore
Loved his shadow in a pool.

Of all the ladies I despair;   25
No more faith they'll have of me.
I used to love them everywhere,
But now I'll doubt each one I see.
Not one volunteers to plead
My case before the noble dame   30
Whose coldness causes me great need.
For all of me, they're all the same.

She tries so hard to look so good,
My lady, at whose feet I pray,
She'll never do a thing I would,   35
But always works the other way.
I've fallen in a sad disgrace
Like that fool who dared to try
To cross the bridge and lost his place.
I've set my object far too high.   40

Can vei la lauzeta mover   *Bernart of Ventadour*

Can vei la lau-ze-ta mo — ver De joi sas alas contral rai

Que s'o-blid es lais-sa cha — zer Per la dous-sor c'al cor li vai,

Ai! tan grans en-vey a m'en ve De cui qu'eu vey a jau-zi — on,

Me-ra-vil-has ai, car des-se Lo cor de de-zi-rer nom fon.

Pity, I'm afraid, is lost,
And where it's gone I cannot see.
She who ought to have it most
Has none of it. Where can it be?
It seems an evil when she sees   45
A lover lying in despair,
Who from her will gets all his ease,
And lets him die unpitied there.

Since she'll grant no more return
For prayers, pleas, or rights of mine,   50

And doesn't care how much I burn
With love for her, I'll just decline
Both her and love, and sing no more.
She's killed me now; I'm dead I swear,
Since she won't hold a man so poor,   55
An exile, gone I don't know where.

Tristran, you don't have it worse,
For I depart with only woe;
Gone my joy and hushed my verse,
I haven't any place to go.   60

C. *The Anglo-Norman Play of Adam*

The Mystère d'Adam *is significant as one of the earliest examples of a drama containing liturgical elements to be prepared for presentation before the congregation in the vernacular and to be staged, not in the choir, but outside the portal of the church. It furnishes yet another indication of the desire of ecclesiastical authorities of the later twelfth century to appeal to the people in new and striking ways, a desire which underlies many of the characteristics of the Gothic style. The play consists of three parts: (1) a play about Adam, (2) a play about Cain and Abel, and (3) a play about the prophets. Only the first of these is printed here. It was written in a Norman, or Anglo-Norman dialect, presumably in England.*

The play is discussed by Hardin Craig, English Religious Drama of the Middle Ages, *Clarendon Press, Oxford, 1955; and by Grace Frank,* The Medieval French Drama, *Clarendon Press, Oxford, 1963. There is a good edition of the original by Paul Aebischer, Geneva, 1963. The following translation is that of Edward Noble Stone, University of Washington Press, Seattle, 1928, reprinted here by permission.*

ADAM
Order of the Presentation of Adam

Let Paradise be set up in a somewhat lofty place; let there be put about it curtains and silken hangings, of such an height that those persons who shall be in Paradise can be seen from the shoulders upward; let there be planted there sweet-smelling flowers and foliage; let divers trees be therein, and fruits hanging upon them, so that it may seem a most delectable place.

Then let the Savior come, clothed in a dalmatic, and let Adam and Eve be set before him. Let Adam be clothed in a red tunic; Eve, however, in a woman's garment of white, and a white silken wimple; and let them both stand before the Figure;[1] but Adam a little nearer, with composed countenance; Eve, however, with countenance a little more subdued.

And let Adam himself be well instructed when he shall make his answers, lest in answering he be either too swift or too slow. Let not only Adam, but all the persons, be so instructed that they shall speak composedly and shall use such gestures as become the matter whereof they are speaking; and in uttering the verses, let them neither add a syllable nor take away, but let them pronounce all clearly; and let those things that are to be said be said in their due order.

Whoever shall speak the name of Paradise, let him look back at it and point it out with his hand.

Then let the Lesson begin:

"In the beginning God created the heaven and the earth."[2]

And after this is ended let the choir sing: R̶

"And the Lord God formed man."

And when this is ended, let the Figure *say:*
Adam! *And let him answer:* Lord!

FIGURE   Out of earthly clay
> I fashioned thee.

ADAM   I know it, yea!

FIGURE   A living soul to thee I gave,
> In thee my likeness did I grave,
> Mine earthly image making thee.   5
> Never must thou rebellious be.

ADAM   Not I! but I will trust thee aye,
> And my Creator I'll obey.

FIGURE   A fitting fere I've given thee
> (Eve is she hight) thy wife to be—   10
> Thy wife to be and partener,
> And thou must ever cleave to her,
> Do thou love her, let her love thee;
> So shall ye both be blest of me.
> Let her thine own commands obey,   15
> And both be subject to my sway.
> From thy rib-bone her form I wrought:
> No stranger she, but from thee brought.
> Out of thy body I shaped her frame;
> From thee, not from without, she came.   20
> Govern her, then, with counsel wise,
> Nor let dissent betwixt you rise,
> But love and mutual service great.
> Such is the law of wedlock's state.

FIGURE (TO EVE)   Now will I speak to thee, O Eve.   25
> Take heed, nor lightly this receive:
> If thou to do my will art fain,
> Thy heart its goodness will retain;
> Honor and love to me accord,
> Thy Maker and acknowledged Lord;   30
> To serve me be thy heart inclined
> With all thy might and all thy mind.
> Love Adam, hold him dear as life;
> He is thy husband, thou his wife;
> Ever to him submit thy heart   35
> And from his teaching ne'er depart;
> Serve him and love, with willing mind;
> Therein is wedlock's law defined.
> If thou art proved a helper meet,
> I'll set you both in glory's seat.   40

EVE   Lord, I will do what pleaseth thee,
> In nothing will neglectful be;
> To thee, as sovereign, I will bow,
> And him my fere and liege avow.
> To him I will at all times cleave,   45
> From me good counsel he'll receive;
> Thy pleasure and his service aye
> Will I perform, in every way.

Then let the FIGURE *call Adam nearer, and more particularly addressing him, say:*

> Listen! O Adam. Hearken unto me.
> I formed thee; now this gift I add in fee: 50
> Thou mayest live alway—if thou loyal be—
> And hale and sound, from every sickness free.
>   Thou'lt hunger not, nor thirst shall thee
>   annoy,
> Neither shall heat nor cold thine ease destroy,
> Nor weariness thy perfect bliss alloy,   55
> Nor any suffering abate thy joy.
>   All of thy life in pleasance thou shalt spend;
> 'T will not be short—a life withouten end!
> I tell thee this, and will that Eve attend;
> Unless she heed, to folly she will bend.   60
>   Dominion over all the earth ye'll hold;
> Birds, beasts—all creatures—be by you
>   controlled;
> Who grudgeth this, his worth is lightly told,
> For your demesne shall the whole world
>   enfold.
>   Of good and ill I grant you choice to make;   65
> (Who hath such choice is tethered to no stake;)
> Weigh all in the balance fairly, nor mistake;
> Be true to me, my counsel ne'er forsake.
>   Leave thou the evil, choose the good as
>   guide;
> Love thou thy Lord, and keep thee at his side;   70
> None other counsel e'er for mine be tried:
> Do this, so shalt thou without sin abide.

ADAM   Great thanks I give thee for thy kindness,
>   Lord,
> Who madest me and dost such grace accord,
> To place both good and evil in my ward.   75
> Thy service shall my fullest joy afford.
>   Thou art my Lord, and in myself I see
> Thy handiwork, for thou didst fashion me;
> Nor ever shall my will so stubborn be,
> But that my chiefest care be serving thee.   80

Then let the FIGURE *with his hand point out Paradise to Adam, saying:*

> Adam!

ADAM   Lord!

FIGURE   Hear my plan; lift up thine eyes;
> This garden see.

ADAM   Its name?

FIGURE   'Tis Paradise.

ADAM   A place most fair!
FIGURE   Myself did it devise
    And plant. Who here shall dwell as friend I'll
        prize.
    I place it in thy trust, to keep for aye.   85

Then shall he send them into Paradise, saying:

    I set you both herein.
ADAM   And shall we stay?
FIGURE   Through all your life. Nothing shall you
        affray;
    Now ye can neither die nor waste away.

Let the choir sing: ℞

    "And the Lord took the man."

Then shall the FIGURE *stretch forth his hand toward
Paradise, saying:*

        The nature of this garden I'll recite:
    Here shalt thou feel the lack of no delight;   90
    No earthly good, desired of any wight,
    But each may here be found in measure right.
        Here wife from man shall no harsh word
            obtain,
    Nor man from wife have shame or cause to
        plain;
    Begetting, man shall sinless still remain,   95
    And woman bear her children without pain.
        For aye thou'lt live; so blest is this sojourn,
    With passing years thine age no change shall
        learn;
    Nor dread of death shall bring to thee concern;
    I will thy dwelling here to be eterne.   100

Let the choir sing: ℞

    "And the Lord said unto Adam."

*Then let the Figure with his hand point out unto Adam
the trees of Paradise, saying:*

    Of all these fruits thou mayest eat each day.

*And let him shew him the forbidden tree, and its fruits,
saying:*

    This I forbid thee, here make no essay;
    If thou dost eat thereof thou'rt dead
        straightway;
    My love thou'lt lose, thy weal with woe repay.

ADAM   All thy commandments will I keep in
        mind,   105
    Not I nor Eve to break them be inclined;
    If for one fruit such dwelling were resigned,
    Rightly should I be outcast to the wind.
        If for an apple I thy love gainsay,
    Ne'er in my life can I my folly pay;   110
    A traitor should he judgëd be for aye,
    Who doth himself forswear, his lord betray.

*Then let the Figure go to the church,[3] and let Adam and
Eve walk about, innocently delighting themselves in Paradise.
In the mean time, let the demons run to and fro through the
square, making fitting gestures; and let them come, one after
another, alongside of Paradise, shewing Eve the forbidden
fruit, as if entreating her to eat thereof. Then let the Devil
come unto Adam; and he shall say unto him:*

    How liv'st thou, Adam?
ADAM   In felicity.
DEVIL   Is it well with thee?
ADAM   There's nothing vexeth me.
DEVIL   It can be better.   115
ADAM   Nay—I know not how.
DEVIL   Then, wouldst thou know?
ADAM   It recks me little now.
DEVIL   I know, forsooth!
ADAM   What boots it me to learn?
DEVIL   And why not, pray?
ADAM   Naught doth it me concern.
DEVIL   Concern thee 't will!
ADAM   I know not when.
DEVIL   I'll not make haste to tell thee, then.   120
ADAM   Nay, tell me!
DEVIL   No! I'll keep thee waiting
    Till thou art sick of supplicating.
ADAM   To know this thing I have no need.
DEVIL   Thou dost deserve no boon, indeed!
    The boon thou hast thou canst not use.   125
ADAM   Prithee, how's that?
DEVIL   Thou'lt not refuse
    To hear? Well, then—'twixt thee and me—
ADAM   I'll listen, most assuredly!
DEVIL   Now mark me, Adam. I tell thee it
    For thine own good.   130
ADAM   That I'll admit.
DEVIL   Thou'lt trust me, then?
ADAM   Full trust I bring!
DEVIL   In every point?
ADAM   All—save one thing.

DEVIL   What thing is that?
ADAM   This: I'll do naught
    Offensive to my Maker's thought.
DEVIL   Dost fear him so?   135
ADAM   I fear him; yes—
    Both love and fear.
DEVIL   That's foolishness!
    What can he do thee?
ADAM   Good and bale.
DEVIL   Thou'st listened to an idle tale!
    An evil thing befall thee? Why,
    In glory born, thou canst not die!   140
ADAM   God saith I'll die, without redress,
    Whene'er his precepts I transgress.
DEVIL   What is this great transgression, pray?
    I fain would learn without delay.
ADAM   I'll tell thee all in perfect truth.   145
    This the command he gave, forsooth:
    Of all the fruits of Paradise
    I've leave to eat (such his advice)—
        All, save one only, which is banned;
    That I'll not touch, e'en with my hand.   150
DEVIL   Which fruit is that?

*Then let Adam stretch forth his hand and shew him the
forbidden fruit, saying:*

ADAM   See'st yonder tree?
    That fruit hath he forbidden me.
DEVIL   Dost know the reason?
ADAM   Certes, no!
DEVIL   The occasion of this thing I'll show:
    No whit cares he for all the rest;   155
    But yon, that hangeth loftiest,
    —The fruit of Knowledge—can bestow
    The gift all mysteries to know.
    If thou eat'st that, 't will profit thee.
ADAM   In what way, pray?   160
DEVIL   That thou shalt see:
    Thine eyes will straightway be unsealed,
    All future things to thee revealed;
    All that thou will'st thou canst perform;
    'T will bring thee blessings in a swarm.
    Eat, and thou shalt repent it not;   165
    Then thou'lt not fear thy God in aught;
    Instead, thou'lt be in all his peer;
    For this, he filled thy soul with fear.
    Wilt trust me? Then to taste proceed.

ADAM   That will I not!   170
DEVIL   Fine words, indeed!
    Thou wilt not?
ADAM   No!
DEVIL   A fool art thou!
    Thou'lt yet mind what I tell thee now.

*Then let the Devil depart; and he shall go to the other
demons, and he shall make an excursion through the square;
and after some little interval, cheerful and rejoicing, he shall
return to his tempting of Adam, and he shall say unto him:*

    How farest thou, Adam? Wilt change thy
        mind?
    Or still to stubbornness inclined?
    I meant to tell thee recently   175
    God as his almsman keepeth thee.
    He put thee here the fruit to eat,
    Hast other recreation sweet?
ADAM   Here nothing lacks I could desire.
DEVIL   Dost to naught loftier aspire?   180
    Canst boast thyself a man of price!
    —God's gardener of Paradise!
    He made thee keeper of his park;
    Wilt thou not seek a higher mark?
    Filling thy belly!—Surely, he   185
    Had nobler aims in mind for thee!
    Listen now, Adam, and attend
    The honest counsel that I lend.
    Thou couldest from thy Lord be free,
    And thy Creator's equal be.   190
    In brief, I'll this assurance make:
    If of this apple thou partake,
    (Then shall he lift his hand toward Paradise.)
    Then thou shalt reign in majesty!
    In power, God's partner thou canst be!
ADAM   Go! Get thee hence!   195
DEVIL   What! Adam. How!
ADAM   Go! Get thee hence! Satan art thou!
    Ill counsel giv'st thou.
DEVIL   How, pray tell!
ADAM   Thou would'st deliver me to hell!
    Thou would'st me with my Lord embroil,
    Move me from bliss to bale and moil.   200
    I will not trust thee! Get thee hence!
    Nor ever have the impudence
    Again to come before my face!
    Traitor forsworn, withouten grace!

Then shall the Devil, sadly and with downcast countenance, depart from Adam and he shall go even unto the gates of Hell, and he shall hold converse there with the other demons. Thereafter, he shall make an excursion among the people; but presently he shall draw near to Paradise, on the side where Eve is, and approaching Eve with a cheerful countenance and much blandishment, he thus accosteth her:

[DEVIL]   Eve, hither am I come, to thee. 205
EVE   And prithee, Satan, why to me?
DEVIL   Seeking thy weal, thine honor, too.
EVE   God grant it!
DEVIL   Then, thy fears eschew.
   Long since, I've mastered by my pains
   Each secret Paradise contains; 210
   A part of them to thee I'll tell.
EVE   Begin, then, and I'll listen well.
DEVIL   Thou'lt hearken to me?
EVE   Hearken? yea,
   Nor vex thy soul in any way.
DEVIL   Thou'lt keep it hidden? 215
EVE   Yea, in truth.
DEVIL   Not publish it?
EVE   Not I! forsooth.
DEVIL   Then, to this contract I'll agree,
   Nor further pledge require of thee.
EVE   Might'st safely trust my promise, though.
DEVIL   Thou'st been to a good school, I trow! 220
   Adam I've seen—a fool is he.
EVE   A little hard.
DEVIL   He'll softer be;
   But harder now than iron is.
EVE   A noble man!
DEVIL   A churl! I wis.
   Thought for himself he will not take; 225
   Let him have care, e'en for thy sake.
   Thou art a delicate, tender thing,
   Thou'rt fresher than the rose in spring;
   Thou'rt whiter than the crystal pale,
   Than snow that falls in the icy vale. 230
   An ill-matched pair did God create!
   Too tender thou, too hard thy mate.
   But thou'rt the wiser, I confess;
   Thy heart is full of cleverness;
   Therefore 't is good to treat with thee. 235
   To thee I'd speak; have faith in me.
   Let none know of it.
EVE   Who should know?

DEVIL   Not Adam even.
EVE   Be it so.
DEVIL   Now will I speak; do thou give ear.
   None, save us twain, is present here, 240
   (And Adam yon, who hath not heard.)
EVE   Speak up! He'll not perceive a word.
DEVIL   I'll shew thee, then, what crafty plot
   Was 'gainst you in this garden wrought:
   The fruit God gave you to possess 245
   Hath in it little goodliness,
   But in the fruit to you forbidden
   Exceeding virtue lieth hidden;
   Therein is found of life the dower,
   Dominion, mastery, and power, 250
   Knowledge of evil and of good.
EVE   What savor hath 't?
DEVIL   'T is heavenly food!
   To thy fair body, to thy face,
   Most meet it were to add this grace:
   That thou be queen of the world—of this, 255
   Of the firmament, and of the abyss—
   And know all things that shall befall,
   And be the mistress of them all.
EVE   Is such the fruit?
DEVIL   Truly, it is.

Then shall Eve carefully consider the forbidden fruit, and after she hath considered it for a season, she shall say:

   Only to see it brings me bliss! 260
DEVIL   But what, if thou shalt eat it, Eve?
EVE   How should I know?
DEVIL   Wilt not believe?
   First take it, and to Adam bear;
   Heaven's crown will then be yours to wear;
   Ye shall be like your Maker then, 265
   He'll hide no secrets from your ken.
   Soon as ye've eaten of the fruit,
   Your hearts it straightway will transmute;
   With God ye'll be—free from all blight—
   Of equal goodness, equal might. 270
   Come taste it!
EVE   That I'm thinking on.
DEVIL   Trust Adam not!
EVE   I'll taste anon.
DEVIL   But when?
EVE   Let me deferment make
   Till Adam his repose shall take.

DEVIL   But eat it. Put thy fears away.   275
    'Twere childish greatly to delay.

*Then shall the Devil depart from Eve and shall go unto
Hell; but* ADAM *shall come unto Eve, being sore displeased
because the Devil hath spoken with her, and he shall say
unto her:*

Say, wife, what thing of thee inquired
That evil Satan? what desired?
EVE   'T was of our honor he conversed.
ADAM   Believe him not—the traitor curs'd!   280
    That he's a traitor, I've no doubt.
EVE   And wherefore, pray?
ADAM   I've found him out.
EVE   What boots it? See him once—thou'lt find
    Eftsoons he'll make thee change thy mind!
ADAM   Not he! I'll trust him not at all   285
    Till I've made trial of him withal.
    Let him no more come near to thee;
    He's full of foulest perfidy,
    His sovereign Lord he sought to cheat
    And set himself in the highest seat.   290
    A knave that's done such wickedness
    To thee shall never have access.

*Then a serpent, cunningly put together, shall ascend along
the trunk of the forbidden tree, unto which Eve shall approach
her ear, as if harkening unto its counsel. Thereafter, Eve
shall take the apple, and shall offer it unto Adam. But he
shall not yet receive it, and* EVE *shall say unto him:*

    Eat! Adam; thou know'st not what is offered!
    Let's take the gift thus freely proffered.
ADAM   Is it so good?   295
EVE   That thou shalt see;
    But canst not, till it tasted be.
ADAM   I fear!
EVE   Then, leave it!
ADAM   Nay, I'll taste.
EVE   Faint-heart! so long thy time to waste!
ADAM   I'll take the fruit.
EVE   Here, eat it! So
    Thou shalt both good and evil know.   300
    But, first, myself I'll taste it now.
ADAM   And I next?
EVE   Marry! Next shalt thou.

*Then shall Eve eat a part of the apple, and she shall say
unto Adam:*

    I've tasted! Pardi! What a savor!
    I've never known so sweet a flavor!
    With such a savor 't is endued—
ADAM   What savor?   305
EVE   —as no mortal food!
    Now do mine eyes so clearly see
    I seem Almighty God to be!
    All that has been or shall befall
    I know—am mistress of it all!   310
    Eat! Adam, eat! No more abstain;
    Thou'lt do it to thy lasting gain.

*Then shall Adam receive the apple from the hand of Eve,
saying:*

ADAM   I'll trust thy word, thou art my peer.
EVE   Take, eat; thou hast no cause to fear.

*Then shall Adam eat a part of the apple; and having eaten
it, he shall straightway take knowledge of his sin; and he
shall bow himself down so that he cannot be seen of the people,
and shall put off his goodly garments, and shall put on poor
garments of fig-leaves sewn together; and manifesting exceeding great sorrows, he shall begin his lamentation:*

[ADAM]   O! sinful wretch! What have I done?   315
    Now my avoidless death's begun!
    Now, without rescue, am I dead;
    My fortune fair is evil sped;
    My lot, a little time ago
    So happy, now is turned to woe;   320
    I my Creator did forsake
    Through counsel of my evil make.
    O! sinner lost! What shall I do?
    How can I now my Maker view?
      Upon my Maker can I look,   325
    Whom through my folly I forsook?
    Ne'er such ill bargain did I strike!
    Now do I know what sin is like!
    O Death! Why dost thou let me live,
    Nor to the earth clean riddance give?   330
    Why, cumbering earth, do I yet stay?
    The depths of hell must I essay;
    In hell my dwelling aye shall be
    Until one come to succor me.

In hell henceforward I shall fare, 335
And whence shall help come to me there?
Whence shall aid thither come to me?
Who from such pains shall set me free?
Why did I thus my Lord offend?
Now there is none can be my friend; 340
None will there be can me avail;
Lost am I now, withouten fail!
Against my Lord I've done such sin,
No suit with him can I begin,
For right is he, and wrong am I. 345
O God! 'Neath what a curse I lie!
Who, henceforth, will take thought of me,
Who've wronged the King of Majesty?
'Gainst Heaven's own king such wrong I've
    done
That claim upon him have I none. 350
No friend I have, no neighbor near,
Who as my surety might appear;
And whom shall I beseech for aid,
When mine own wife hath me betrayed,
Whom God gave me my fere to be? 355
An evil counsel gave she me!
Alas! O Eve!

Then shall he look upon Eve, his wife, and shall say:

            Insensate wife!
In an ill hour I gave thee life!
O had that rib been burned, alas!
That brought me to this evil pass! 360
Had but the fire that rib consumed,
That me to such confusion doomed!
Why, when from me the rib he drew,
Burned he it not, nor me then slew?
The rib the body hath betrayed, 365
Ill-treated, and all useless made.
I know not what to say or try;
Unless grace reach me from on high,
From pain I cannot be released,
Such malady on me hath seized. 370
Alas! O Eve! Woe worth the day—
Such torment holdeth me in sway—
Thou e'er becamest wife to me!
Now I am lost through heeding thee;
Through heeding thee I'm in this plight, 375
Brought down most low from a great height.
Thence will no mortal rescue me—

None, save the God of Majesty.
What say I? Wretch! Why named I him?
He help! I've gained his anger grim! 380
None will e'er bring me succor—none
Save him who'll come as Mary's son.
From none can I henceforth get aid
Since we our trust with God betrayed.
Then, let all be as God ordains; 385
No course, except to die, remains.

Then let the choir begin: R℣

        " *The voice of the Lord God walking in the
        garden.*"

*After this hath been sung, the Figure shall come, wearing
a stole, and looking about him, as if seeking to know where
Adam is. But Adam and Eve shall be hidden in a corner of
Paradise, as if conscious of their wretchedness; and the
FIGURE shall say:*

    Adam, where art thou?

*Then shall they both arise and stand before the Figure, yet
not fully upright, but through shame for their sin, bending
forward a little, and exceeding sad; and let ADAM make
answer:*

            Lord, I'm here.
    I hid; thine anger did I fear;
    I saw my nakedness revealed,
    Therefore myself have I concealed. 390
FIGURE   What hast thou done? How gone astray?
    Who thee from goodness drew away?
    What hast thou done? Why blushest thou?
    How shall I reckon with thee now?
    Thou hadst, a little while ago, 395
    No reason any shame to show;
    Now see I thee downcast, distraught;
    Small joy thy dwelling here hath brought!
ADAM   So great is my confusion, I
    Do hide me from thee, Lord. 400
FIGURE   And why?
ADAM   Such shame my body doth enlace,
    I dare not look thee in the face.
FIGURE   Why overstept'st thou my decree?
    Hath this brought any gain to thee?
    My servant thou, thy Lord am I. 405
ADAM   This can I in no wise deny.
FIGURE   In mine own likeness thee I wrought;
    Why set'st thou my command at naught?

After mine image formed I thee;
Why hast thou thus affronted me?   410
Thou didst in no wise heed my hest;
Deliberately thou hast transgressed!
That fruit thou atest which I said
I had for thee prohibited.
Didst reckon thus my peer to be?   415
I do not think thou'lt jest with me!

Then shall ADAM *stretch forth his hand toward the
Figure, and thereafter toward Eve, saying:*

The woman that thou gavest me,
She first did this iniquity;
She gave me it, and I did eat;
Now is my life with woe replete.   420
Most rashly meddled I therein;
'T was through my wife that I did sin.
FIGURE   Thy wife thou trustedst more than me,
Didst eat without my warranty;
This recompense to thee I'll make: 425
Curs'd shall the ground be for thy sake,
Where thou shalt wish thy grain to sow,
Nor shall it any fruit bestow;
Curs'd shall it 'neath thy hand remain,
And all thy tillage be in vain.   430
Its fruit to thee it shall not yield,
But thorns and thistles fill thy field;
'T will change whate'er is sown by thee;
Its curse shall be thy penalty.
With grievous toil and bitter pain   435
To eat thy bread shalt thou be fain;
In sweat, in great affliction, aye
Thou'lt live hereafter, night and day.

*Then shall the Figure turn toward Eve, and with a
threatening countenance shall say unto her:*

Thou, too, O Eve, woman of sin,
Didst thy rebellion soon begin   440
And briefly heededst my decree.
EVE   The wicked serpent tempted me.
FIGURE   Didst think through him to be my peer?
Hast learned to make things hidden clear?
Erstwhile thou heldest sovereignty   445
Over all living things that be;
How quickly hast thou lost thy crown!
Now see I thee sad and cast down.

Hast thou thereby got gain, or hurt?
I'll render thee thy just desert;   450
Thy service I will thus repay:
Woe thee shall find in every way;
In sorrow thou'lt thy children bear,
In pain throughout their life they'll fare;
In sorrow they'll be born of thee,   455
And end their days in misery.
To such distress and direful need
Thou'st brought thyself and all thy seed;
All thy descendents ever more
Thy sin shall bitterly deplore.   460

And Eve shall make answer, saying:

EVE   Yea, I have sinned—'t was through my
folly vain;
For one sole apple I have got such bane
As doometh me and mine to bitter pain—
Great toll of wretchedness, with little gain!
If I have sinned, 't was nothing strange, I   465
fear,
Whenas the serpent charmed my silly ear;
Much guile he hath, no lamb doth he appear;
Unhappy he who would his counsel hear!
I took the fruit—' twas folly, now I see;
This wickedness I wrought 'gainst thy decree;   470
I tasted it, and won thine enmity.
For a little fruit, my life must forfeit be!

Then shall the FIGURE *threaten the serpent, saying:*

Thou, too, O Serpent, curs'd shalt be;
I will exact my due of thee:
Upon thy belly shalt thou go   475
Through all the days thy life shall know;
The dust shall be thy daily food,
On moor or heath, or in the wood;
Woman shall bear thee enmity,
An evil neighbor ever be;   480
To strike her heel thou'lt lie in wait,
But she herself shall bruise thy pate;
Thy head with such a Hammer smite
'T will put thee in a sorry plight;
Therefrom shall she such aidance get,   485
She'll be avengèd of thee yet!
Thou sought'st her acquaintance to thy woe;
She yet shall bring thy head full low;

There yet shall spring from her a Root
That all thy cunning shall confute.   490

*Then shall the Figure drive them forth out of Paradise,
saying:*

From Paradise, go! get you hence!
Ye've made ill change of residence.
On earth shall ye your dwelling make;
In Paradise ye have no stake,
No title there, and no concern;   495
Forth shall ye go, without return.
Through judgment ye can claim naught there;
Now find you lodgment otherwise.
Go! From felicity depart!
Hunger shall fail you not, nor smart,   500
But pain and weariness abound
Day after day, the whole week round.
On earth a weary term ye'll spend,
And die thereafter, in the end;
After ye've tasted death, straightway   505
To hell ye'll come without delay.
Here exile shall your bodies quell,
And danger daunt your souls in hell.
Satan shall hold your souls in thrall;
There'll be no helper ye can call,   510
None by whom rescue can be sent,
Unless I pity and relent.

Let the choir sing: ℞

" In the sweat of thy face."

*In the mean time there shall come an angel, clad in white
garments, and bearing a shining sword in his hand, whom the
Figure shall set over against the gate of Paradise, and he
shall say unto him:*

Guard well my Paradise, that ne'er
Again this outlaw enter there—
That him no leave or chance befall   515
To touch the fruit of Life at all;
With this thy sword that flameth aye,
Forever bar for him the way.

*When they shall be clean outside of Paradise, sad and
confounded in appearance, they shall bow themselves to the
ground, even unto their feet, and the Figure shall point to
them with his hand, his face being turned toward Paradise;
and the choir shall begin:* ℞

" Behold Adam is become as one [of us]."

*And when this is ended, the Figure shall go back unto the
church.*

*Then shall Adam have a spade, and Eve a mattock, and
they shall begin to till the ground, and they shall sow wheat
therein. After they shall have finished their sowing, they
shall go and sit for a season in a certain place, as if wearied
with their toil, and with tearful eyes shall they look back
ofttimes at Paradise, beating their breasts. Meanwhile shall
the Devil come and plant thorns and thistles in their tillage,
and then he shall depart. When Adam and Eve shall come to
their tillage, and when they shall have beheld the thorns and
thistles that have sprung up, stricken with grievous sorrow,
they shall cast themselves down upon the ground; and remaining there, they shall beat their breasts and their thighs,
manifesting their grief by their gestures; and Adam shall then
begin his lamentation:*

Woe worth the hour—hateful for ever
     more—
That e'er my sinfulness so whelmed me o'er!   520
That I forsook the Lord whom all adore!
To succor me, whom shall I now implore?

*Here let Adam look back at Paradise; and he shall lift up
both hands toward it; and devoutly bowing his head, he shall
say:*

O Paradise! How sweet to dwell in thee!
Garden of glory! Oh how fair to see!
Thence, for my sin, must I an outcast be;   525
Hope of return is ever lost to me!
   I was therein; but little joy I got;
Through heeding counsel false I thence was
     brought.
Now I repent; scorn earn I, as I ought.
'T is all too late, my sighing boots me naught.   530
   Where was my memory? whither fled my
     wit?
That I, for Satan, glory's King should quit!
Now, sore my grief—no help is there in it;
My sin on history's pages shall be writ.

*Then shall Adam lift up his hand against Eve, who shall
have been set some little distance away, on higher ground,
and moving his head with great indignation, he shall say
unto her:*

O evil woman, full of perfidy!   535
How quickly to perdition brought'st thou me,

When thou mad'st sense and reason both to
    flee!
Now I repent, but can no pardon see.
    To evil how inclined wert thou to cleave!
How quick the serpent's counsel to receive!   540
Through thee I die, through thee my life I
    leave.
Writ in the book thy sin shall be, O Eve!
    Seest thou these tokens of confusion dread?
Earth doth perceive what curse o'erhangs our
    head;
'T was corn we sowed—thistles spring up   545
    instead.
Greatly we've sweat, ill have we profited!
    Thou seest the outset of our evil state;
Great sorrow 't is, but greater doth await;
To hell shall we be brought, without rebate;
Pain shall not fail us, neither torment great.   550
    O wretched Eve! How seemeth it to thee?
This hast thou gained thee as thy dowery:
Ne'er more canst thou bring man felicity,
But aye opposed to reason thou wilt be.
    All they who come hereafter, of our seed,   555
Shall feel the punishment of thy misdeed;
Thou sinnedst; all must bear the doom
    decreed.
Late will he come who shall relieve their need.

Then let EVE *make answer unto Adam:*

Adam, dear lord, much hast thou chidden
    me,
And much reviled and blamed my villainy;   560
If I have sinned, my punishment I dree;
Guilty, I am, of God I'll judgëd be.
    Toward God and thee much evil have I
    wrought;
'Gainst my offense long shall reproach be
    brought;
My fault is great, my sin torments my   565
    thought!
O wretched me! Of good in me is naught!

No ground have I wherewith to make my
    plea,
That God's just doom be not pronounced
    on me;
Forgive me! No atonement can I see,
Else would my sacrifice be offered free.   570
    A miserable sinner, vile within,
Hiding my face from God for my great sin—
Oh, take me, Death! Now let my death begin!
Shipwrecked and lost, the shore I cannot win.
    The serpent fell, the snake of evil fame,   575
Caused me to eat the apple, to my shame;
I gave it thee—to serve thee was mine aim;
For this thy sin thyself I may not blame.
    Oh, why did I my Maker's will defy?
Wherefore, dear lord, thy teachings thus   580
    deny?
Thou sinnedst, but the root thereof am I!
Our sickness doth a long, long cure imply.
    For my great error, my adventure vain,
Our seed, henceforth, will dearly pay again;
The fruit was sweet, bitter will be the pain!   585
In sin we ate, ours will the guilt remain.
    Yet, none the less, my hope in God I base:
Sometime atonement will our guilt efface,
And I shall know God's favor and his grace;
His power will bring us from that evil place.   590

*Then shall the Devil come, and three or four other devils
with him, bearing in their hands chains and iron shackles,
which they shall place on the necks of Adam and Eve.*

*And certain ones shall push them on, others shall drag
them toward hell; other devils, however, shall be close beside
hell, waiting for them as they come, and these shall make a
great dancing and jubilation over their destruction; and other
devils shall, one after another, point to them as they come;
and they shall take them up and thrust them into hell; and
thereupon they shall cause a great smoke to arise, and they
shall shout one to another in hell, greatly rejoicing; and they
shall dash together their pots and kettles, so that they may be
heard without. And after some little interval, the devils shall
go forth, and shall run to and fro in the square; certain of
them, however, shall remain behind in hell.*

Notes

1   The Figure represents the Second Person of the Trinity, the Word which was made Incarnate in
Christ. Paradise was set up probably on one side of the west portal of the church, and a place representing
hell was on the other side. The church itself represented the celestial paradise.

2 The liturgical elements here and elsewhere in this part of the play are from matins on Septuagesima Sunday. The fall of Adam and its consequences were (and still are) the subjects of this service. The play as we have it is incomplete, but it is quite possible that the third part of it, containing the prophecies, was followed by the service of lauds. If this was the arrangement, we should imagine the action taking place quite early in the morning.

3 That is, the celestial paradise. See n. 1.

D. Jean Froissart

Jean Froissart (1337–1404) arrived in England in 1361, where he presented Queen Philippa with a version of his chronicle and became her secretary. He visited Scotland, Dax, and Italy, remaining under the Queen's protection until her death in 1369. After the death of the Queen, Froissart obtained the patronage of Duke Wenceslas of Luxembourg. In 1373 he became curate of Les Estinnes, where he remained until 1382. He was made canon of Chimay and chaplain to Guy de Blois. In 1388 he set out on some extensive travels, which took him to Foix, Avignon, Riom, and Paris. He returned to England in 1395, where he presented a book to King Richard. After about eighteen months, he returned to Hainault, where he died, presumably in 1404.

Froissart is best known for his Chronicles, *which are not only important historically, but have been much admired for their prose style. However, he has left us in addition a considerable body of poetry. In a sense, he was Chaucer's immediate predecessor as the most distinguished poet in the English court between 1361 and 1369.*

A readable but superficial introduction to Froissart is F. S. Shears, Froissart, *Routledge & Kegan Paul, Ltd , London, 1930. The poetry has never received adequate attention. The following selections from the* Chronicles *are from a modernization of the translation by Lord Berners.*

ROYAL SONG CROWNED AT ABBEVILLE[1]

Because they see the ladies at their sport
Showing good cheer to all, and speaking fair
To everyone who passes, tall or short—
And since they greet all humbly and declare
Their hearts with smiles and many a carefree air— 5
Some men there are who presumptuously swear
That all that's needed is an earnest prayer
If mercy isn't theirs at first perusal.
But such as these who suddenly lay bare
Their hearts, are often greeted with refusal. 10

For if a lady's fashioned to desire,
Humane to all, courteous in speech,
And with all this has nothing to require
But a request from one who would beseech
Her mercy, Love has no need to reach 15
Her heart with virtues he alone can preach,

For then neither Shame nor Fear may teach
Restraint in giving what she can bestow.
Love wishes no one to impeach
Her honor, but to make her honor grow. 20

When in a lady Sense and Fear hold sway,
Her honor's strengthened when she can deny.
And when she goes with those who in their play
Think mercy's theirs at once without a sigh,
Hoping, before Love has let his arrow fly, 25
Then Refusal hastens to supply
Sense and Fear, which seek to fortify
The lady, so that all entry now is barred,
And he who sought so foolishly to try
Her honor, now finds all his effort marred. 30

Thought can abuse the thinker in this way,
Promising what it never can bestow.
To trust in it is to be led astray.
For he who builds solidly must go

To Love, must trust his lady, and must grow   35
Faithful in her service, and must know
That if she has real mercy on his woe,
She'll not grant her gift to him too soon,
For Sense and Fear will keep it guarded so
That Love may grant the lover his sweet boon.   40

Lady whom I love, so gay and fair,
The fine delight that only you inspire,
Your gracious manner, and your pleasant air—
All fill me often with a great desire.
Although your bearing burns my heart with fire,   45
Your words refusing me always require
That I consent, however I admire.
For the joy of love will prove to be much greater
When I have so long waited to acquire
The mercy that I hope will be mine later.   50

That man has little knowledge in his head
Who thinks to get a lady to his bed
Because she smiles, or winks, or is well bred.

From the
CHRONICLES
_____

Book I

*Chapter LXXVII   The King of England
Is Engaged in an Amour with the
Duchess of Salisbury* [2]

The same day that the Scots departed from the castle,
king Edward came thither, with all his host, about noon,
and came to the same place the Scots had lodged, and
was much displeased that he found not the Scots there,
for he had proceeded with so much haste, that his horse
and men were greatly fatigued. Then he commanded
them to halt there that night, and said that he would go
to the castle, to visit the noble lady therein, for he had
not seen her since she was married: then every man
took his lodging as he pleased. And so soon as the king
had unarmed, he took ten or twelve knights with him,
and went to the castle, to salute the countess of Salisbury, and to see the nature of the assaults of the Scots,
and the defense that had been made against them. As
soon as the lady knew of the king's approach, she set

open the gates, and came out so richly dressed, that
every man was astonished at her beauty, and could not
cease to regard her nobleness of countenance and
gracious manner of address with admiration! When
she came before the king, she kneeled down to the
earth, thanking him for his succors, and then led him
into the castle, to entertain and do him honor, which
she was well qualified to do. Every man regarded her
marvelously; the king himself could not withhold his
admiration, for he thought he never before saw so
noble and so fair a lady: he was stricken therewith to
the heart, with a sparkle of pure love, that long afterward endured; he supposed no lady in the world so
worthy of being beloved as she. Thus they entered the
castle hand in hand; the countess led him first into the
hall, and then into a chamber richly furnished; the king
so admiring the lady, that she blushed. At last he went
to a window to rest himself, and there fell into a deep
study: the lady proceeded to compliment the lords and
knights that were there, and commanded the hall to be
prepared for dinner. When she had given full directions,
then she came to the king with a cheerful air, who was
still involved in thought, and said "Dear Sir, what can
occupy your thoughts so much? your grace is not displeased? it appertaineth not to you so to do: you should
rather be happy and joyful, seeing you have put your
enemies to flight, who dared not await your arrival: let
other men think of the future." Then the king said,
"Ah! dear lady, be assured, that since I came into the
castle, that there is a theme come into my mind that I
cannot help studying, nor can I tell what will be the
issue, nor can I banish it from my mind." "Ah! Sire,"
quoth the lady, "you ought always to be in good spirits,
to comfort your people therewith: God hath so
favored you, and bestowed on you so many virtues,
that you are the most redoubted and honored prince
in all Christendome; and if the king of Scots have done
you any despite or damage, you may well revenge it
whenever you please, as you have often done before
this: Sire, leave off musing, if it pleaseth thee, your
dinner is all ready." "Ah! fair lady," replied the king,
"other things oppress me, which you know not of; but
truly, the sweet behavior, the perfect wisdom, the
elegant grace, nobleness, and surpassing beauty, that I
see in you, hath so enraptured my soul, that I cannot
but love you; and without your return of love, I am
but as dead." Then the lady said "Ah! most noble
prince, for God's sake, mock not nor tempt me; I can-

not listen to such a declaration, nor that so noble a prince would think to dishonor me, and my lord my husband, who is so valiant a knight, and hath done your grace so much service, and still lieth in prison for your quarrel: certainly, Sire, you would in this case derive but little praise, and no benefit; I had never as yet such a thought in my heart, and, I trust in God, never shall have, for any man living; if I had any such intention, your grace ought not only to blame me, but also to punish my body, yea, and by true justice, to be dismembered": therewith the lady left the king, and went into the hall to hasten the dinner, and upon her return, brought some of the knights with her, and said "Sire, if it please you to come into the hall, your knights remain for you to wash, you have been long fasting." Then the king went into the hall and washed, and sat down among his lords, and the lady also. The king ate but little; he still sat musing, and, as he durst, cast his eyes upon the lady. His knights were surprised at his sadness, for he was not accustomed to be so; some attributing the cause to the circumstance of the Scots having escaped from him. All that day the king tarried there, but knew not what to do: he sometimes imagined that honor and truth forbade him to set his heart on such a project, to dishonor such a lady, and so true a knight as her husband was, who had always so well and faithfully served him. On the other hand, love so constrained him, that the power thereof surmounted honor and truth. Thus the king debated within himself all that day, and all that night: in the morning he dislodged his troops, and drew after the Scots, to drive them out of his realm. Then he took leave of the countess, saying "My dear lady, to God I commend you till I return again, requiring you to prevail upon yourself otherwise than you have said to me." "Most noble prince," replied the lady, "God, the father glorious, direct your conduct, and remove from you all sinful and pernicious thoughts; Sire, I am, and ever shall be ready to do your grace service, to your honor and mine": whereupon the king departed quite abashed; and pursued the Scots till he came to the town of Berwick, and went and encamped within four leagues of Jedburgh, where king David and all his troops were entered, in reliance upon the great barrenness of the country. The king of England tarried there three days, to see if the Scots would march out to fight him. In these three days there were several skirmishes on both sides, and many of the Scots slain, taken, and severely wounded. Sir William Douglas most harassed the English; he bore azure, a comble silver, three stars gules.

Chapter LXXXIX   Of the Feasts and Tournaments that the King of England Made at London, for the Love of the Countess of Salisbury

You have before fully heard that the king of England had great wars in many countries, and had men of arms in garrison, at a great expense, in Picardy, Normandy, Gascony, Xantoinge, Poictou, Brittany and Scotland: you have heard also, that the king had fallen in love with the countess of Salisbury; a love that excited him day and night; her great beauty and elegant demeanor was continually in his memory, though the earl of Salisbury was one of the chiefs of his counsel, and one that had been of great service to him. So it happened that for the love of this lady, and for the desire the king had to see her, he caused a great feast to be proclaimed, and a justing to be held in the city of London, in the middle of August: which proclamation was also made in Flanders, Hainault, Brabant, and France, giving all comers out of every country free liberty to come and go: and had given commands, through his own realm, that all lords, knights, squires, ladies, and damsels, should be there without any excuse, and commanded expressly of the earl of Salisbury, that the lady his wife should be there, and to bring with her all ladies and damsels of that country. The earl obeyed the king, as he suspected no danger; the good lady durst not refuse, although she came much against her will, for she saw clearly how it was; but she dared not discover the matter to her husband; she thought she would act so as to get the king from his opinion.

This was a noble feast; there was the earl William of Hainault, and Sir John of Hainault, his uncle, and a great number of lords and knights of high lineage; they continued dancing and justing for the space of fifteen days; the lord John, eldest son to the viscount Beaumont in England was slain at the justs. All ladies and damsels were handsomely dressed, according to their degrees, except Alice, countess of Salisbury, for she dressed as simply as she could, to the end that the king might not regard her, for she was fully determined to do nothing that should dishonor either her husband or herself. At this feast was Sir Henry with the wry neck, earl of Lancaster, and Sir Henry his son, earl of Derby; Sir Robert d'Artois, earl of Richmond; the earls of Northampton and of Gloucester, the earl of Warwick, the earl of Salisbury, the earl of Pembroke, the earl of Hereford, the earl of Arundel, the earl of Cornwall, the earl of Oxford, the earl of Suffolk, the baron of Stamford, and many other lords and knights of England. And before all these nobles departed, the king received letters from many lords of several countries, out of Gascony, Bayonne, Flanders, from James d'Arteville, and out of Scotland, from the lord Ross, and the lord Percy, and from Sir Edward Bailleul, captain of Berwick, who informed the king that the Scots did not strictly observe the truce concluded the year before, for they again assembled together many people, for what purpose they could not tell. Also the captains in Poictou, Xantoinge, Rochell, and Burdelois, wrote to the king that the Frenchmen made great preparations for the war: for the truce made at Arras was nearly expired, therefore it was time for the king to take counsel and advice; and so he answered the messengers from point to point.

Chapter C   Of the Order of Saint George, That King Edward Established in the Castle of Windsor

At this time it pleased the king to rebuild the castle of Windsor, which was begun by king Arthur; and there first began the table round, whereby sprang the fame of so many noble knights throughout all the world. Then king Edward determined to make an order and brotherhood of a certain number of knights, to be called knights of the blue garter; and a feast to be held yearly, on St. George's day, at Windsor. To begin this order, the king assembled together earls, lords, and knights of his realm, and declared to them his purpose; they all gladly agreed with his desire, because they saw it was a very honorable thing, whereby great amity and love would grow and increase. Then there were selected a certain number of the most valiant men of the realm, and they swore and affixed their seals to maintain the ordinances which were devised. The king dedicated a chapel in the castle of Windsor, to St. George, and established certain canons there, to serve God, and appointed them good livings. Then the king sent to publish this feast, by his heralds, into France, Scotland, Burgundy, Hainault, Flanders, Brabant, and into the

empire of Germany; giving to every knight and squire, that would come to the feast, fifteen days safe conduct before, and the same number of days after it; to commence at Windsor, on St. George's day next after, in the year of our Lord 1344; and the queen to be there, accompanied by three hundred ladies and damsels, all of noble lineage, and apparelled accordingly.

Chapter CXLVI   The town of Calais Is Surrendered to the King of England

After the French king had thus departed from Sangate they within Calais clearly discovered that their succors failed them, which caused them great sorrow. Then they so strongly persuaded their captain, Sir John of Vien, that he went to the walls of the town, and made a signal to speak with some person of the English army. When the king heard thereof, he sent thither Sir Walter of Manny and Sir Basset. Then Sir John of Vien said to them "Sirs, you are very valiant knights in deeds of arms; and you know well that the king my master hath sent me and others to this town, and commanded us to keep it for his advantage, in such a manner that we shall incur no blame, nor do him any injury: and we have done all that lieth in our power. Now our succors have failed us, and we are so short of provisions that we have not sufficient to live upon; we must therefore all die, or else be rendered mad by famine, unless your noble and redoubted king will take mercy on us: we require you to desire him to have pity on us, and permit us to go, and depart as we are, and let him take the town and castle, and all the goods that are therein, of which there is great abundance." Then Sir Walter of Manny said "Sir, we know somewhat of the intention of the king our master, for he hath declared it unto us; be assured that it is not his intention that you, or they within the town, should depart so, for it is his will that you all should put yourselves into his power, to ransom all such as pleaseth him, and to put to death such as he chooses: for they of Calais have been so inveterate against him, and have caused him to expend so much, and to lose so many of his men, that he is much enraged against them." Then the captain said "Sir, this is too hard a matter for us; we who are here within are an inferior rank of knights and squires, who have truly served the king our master, as well as you serve yours: and we have also endured much pain and disquietude; but we will yet endure as much fatigue as ever any knights did, rather than consent that the meanest person in the town should suffer any worse misfortune than the greatest of us all. Therefore, Sir, we pray, that you, of your humility, will yet go and speak to the king of England, and desire him to have pity on us, for we trust that there is so much nobleness in him, that by the grace of God he will change his purpose." Sir Walter of Manny and Sir Basset returned to the king, and related to him all that had been said. The king said he would not swerve from his resolution, but that they should surrender themselves up unconditionally to his pleasure. Then Sir Walter said "Sir, saving your displeasure in this, you may be in the wrong, for you will give by this a bad example. If you send any of us your servants into any fortress, we shall not be very glad to go, if you put any of them in the town to death, after they have surrendered, for they will likewise deal so with us in a similar case": which opinion was supported and maintained by many other lords who were then present. Then the king said "Sirs, I will not maintain my opinion against you all; therefore, Sir Walter of Manny, you shall go and say to the captain, that all the favor which he shall now obtain from me is, that they let six of the chief burgesses of the town come out bare headed, bare footed, and bare legged, and in their shirts, with halters about their necks, with the keys of the town, and castle in their hands, and these six shall yield themselves unconditionally to my will, and the residue I will take to mercy." Then Sir Walter returned, and found Sir John of Vien still on the wall, awaiting an answer. Then Sir Walter related to him all the favor that he could procure from the king. "Well Sir," quoth Sir John, "I require you to remain here for a certain time, till I go into the town, and relate this to the commons of the town, who sent me hither." Then Sir John went into the market place, and rang the common bell; upon which men and women immediately assembled there. Then the captain reported to them all that he had done, and said "Sirs, we shall obtain no other conditions, therefore now take advice, and make a short answer." Then all the people began to weep, and to make such bewailing, that there was not so hard a heart, if they had seen them, but that would have commiserated their case: the captain himself wept piteously. At last the richest burgess of all the town, called Eustace de St. Pierre, rose up and said openly "Sirs, great and small, it would be an infamous thing to suffer such people as are in this town to die, either by famine or otherwise, when there is a means of saving them; I think that he or they would obtain great merit of our Lord God, who would preserve them from such misfortune: as for my part, I have such good faith in our Lord God, that if I were to die in the venture to save the residue, I hope God would pardon me; wherefore to save them I will be the first to put my life to the hazard." When he had thus said, every man worshipped him, and many knelt down at his feet with piteous tears and sighs. Then another honest burgess rose and said "I will keep company with my friend Eustace"; he was called John Dayre. Then rose up James of Wissant, who was rich in goods and inheritance; he said also that he would accompany his two cousins likewise: as did also Peter of Wissant, his brother; and then there rose two others, who said that they would do the same. Then they went and dressed themselves as the king desired. The captain then went with them to the gate: there was great lamentation made by men, women, and children, at their departure. Then the gate was opened, and he issued out with the six burgesses, and closed the gate again, so that they were between the gate and the barriers. Then the captain said to Sir Walter of Manny "Sir, I deliver here to you, as captain of Calais, by the unanimous consent of all the people of the town, these six burgesses; and I swear to you truly, that they are and were to day the most honorable, rich, and notable burgesses of all the town of Calais; wherefore, noble knight, I desire you to entreat the king to have mercy on them, that they may not die." Sir Walter answered "I cannot say what the king will do, but I shall do for them the best that I can." Then the barriers were opened, and the six burgesses went towards the king, while the captain returned again into the town. When Sir Walter presented these burgesses to the king, they knelt down, and held up their hands and said "Noble king, behold here we six, who were burgesses of Calais, and great merchants: we have brought to you the keys of the town and of the castle, and we now submit ourselves unconditionally to your will and pleasure, by that means to save the residue of the people of Calais, who have suffered great privations. Sir, we beseech your grace to have pity on us, through your great nobleness." Upon this, all the earls and barons, and others that were there, wept for pity. The king looked indignantly upon them, for he bore an inveterate hatred against the people of Calais, on account of the numerous injuries and offences they had done him on the sea before. Then he commanded their heads to be struck off; upon which every man entreated the king to have mercy on them; but he would attend to no man who spoke in their behalf. Then Sir Walter of Manny said "Ah, noble king! for God's sake restrain your anger; you have acquired the name of sovereign greatness, therefore do not now commit any thing that would blemish your renown, nor that would give cause to any one to speak ill of you: every man will say it was a great cruelty to put to death such honest persons, who of their own wills have put themselves on your mercy to save their towns-people." Then the king turned away from him, and commanded the hangman to be sent for, and said "The people of Calais have caused many of my men to be slain, wherefore these shall die in like manner." Then the queen, who was at that time pregnant, knelt down, and with much weeping, said "Ah, noble Sir! since I passed the sea in imminent danger, I have not desired any thing of you; therefore now I humbly require of you, for the honor of the son of the Virgin Mary, and for the love of me, that you will receive these six burgesses to mercy." The king beheld the queen, and stood still in a deep study for some time, and then he answered "Ah, dame! I wish you had been at this time in some other place; for you make such a request of me, that I cannot deny you; wherefore I give them to you, that you may do as you please with them." Then the queen commanded them to be brought into her chamber, and she ordered that the halters should be taken from their necks, and then caused them to be newly clothed, and afterward she gave them their dinner at their leisure: and then she presented each of them with six nobles, and caused them to be conducted out of the host in security, and set at their liberty.

Chapter CLXII   Of the Battle of Poictiers between the Prince of Wales and the French King

When the prince saw that he should engage, and that the cardinal was gone, without making any peace or truce, and saw that the French king did not much esteem him, he said to his men "Now Sirs, though we are but a small company, in regard to the puissance of our enemies, let us not be on that account terrified; for the victory is not gained by numbers, but by God's will: if it should happen that the victory be ours, we shall be the most honored people of all the world, and if we die in our just quarrel, I have the king my father, and brethren, and you have also good friends and kinsmen, who will revenge our deaths: therefore Sirs, I require you, for God's sake, to do your duty this day; for if God and St. George be pleased, this day you shall see me a good knight." These words, and such others that the prince spoke, comforted all his people. The lord Sir John Chandos that day never went from the prince, nor did the lord James Audely for a long while: but when he saw that they must fight, he said to the prince "Sir, I have always truly served my lord your father, and you also, and shall do so as long as I live; I say this because I once made a vow, that the first battle that either the king your father, or any of his children should be at, that I would be one of the first to commence the attack, or else die in the task; therefore I require your grace, as a reward for any service I ever did to the king your father, or to you, that you will give me permission to depart from you, and to place myself there, that I may accomplish my vow." The prince assented to his desire, and said "Sir James, God give you grace this day to be the best knight of all others": and so took him by the hand. Then the knight departed from the prince, and went in front of the foremost division, accompanied only by four squires, who promised not to fail him. This lord James was a very sage and valiant knight, and by him was a great part of the host drawn up and governed the day before. Thus Sir James was in front of the army, ready to fight with the host of the marshals of France. The lord Eustace d'Ambreticourt likewise endeavored to be one of the foremost to commence. When Sir James Audely began to set forward against his enemies, it happened to Sir Eustace d'Ambreticourt as you shall hereafter be informed. You have heard before that the Germans in the French host were appointed to remain still on horseback: Sir Eustace being on horseback, put his spear in the rest, and ran into the French army: and then a knight of Germany, called the lord Lois of Coucibras (who bore a silver shield five roses gules, and Sir Eustace bore ermines, two humets gules), who saw the lord Eustace come from his company, rode against him, and they met so violently that both knights fell to the earth: the German was hurt in the shoulder, therefore he rose not so quickly as did Sir Eustace, who, when he was up and had taken his breath, came to the other knight as he lay on the ground: but then five other knights of

Germany came on him all at once, and bore him to the earth, and so by force he was taken prisoner, and brought to the earl of Nassau, who then took no heed of him; nor can I say whether they swore him prisoner or no, but they tied him to a chair, and there permitted him to stand. Then the battle began on all parts, and the divisions of the marshals of France approached, and they set forward who were appointed to break the ranks of the archers; they entered on horseback into the way, where the great hedges were on both sides, set full of archers; as soon as the men of arms entered, the archers began to shoot on both sides, and slew and wounded horses and knights, so that the horses when they felt the sharp arrows, would in no wise go forward, but drew back, and flung and kicked so fiercely, that many of them fell on their masters, so that, on account of the confusion, they could not rise again; insomuch that the marshal's battle could never come at the prince: certain knights and squires that were well horsed passed through the archers, and expected to approach the prince, but they could not. The lord James Audely, with his four squires, was in the front of that division, and there did marvels in arms; and by great prowess he came and fought with Sir Arnold Dandrehen, under his own banner, and there they fought long together, and Sir Arnold was there severely handled. The division of the marshals began to be in disorder, by reason of the shot of the archers, with the aid of the men of arms, who came in among them, and slew them, and did what they chose; and there the lord Arnold Dandrehen was taken prisoner, by other men than Sir James Audely, or his four squires, for on that day he took no prisoners, but always fought and went on his enemies. Also on the French party the lord John Clermont fought under his own banner as long as he was able to hold out, but there he was beaten down, and could not be relieved nor ransomed, but was slain without mercy: it was said to be on account of the words he had the day before with Sir John Chandos. Within a short time the marshal's divisions were discomfited, for they fell one upon another, and could not go forward; and the Frenchmen who were behind, and could not get forward, retreated, and came on the division of the duke of Normandy, which was very numerous, and were on foot: but they soon began to open behind: for when they knew that the marshal's division was discomfited, they took their horses and departed, as fast as possible. They also saw a party of English coming down a little mountain on

horseback, and many archers with them, who broke in on the side of the duke's division. The archers certainly did their company great advantage on that day, for they shot so thick that the French army knew not what part to defend; and by degrees, the Englishmen gained ground on them. And when the men of arms of England saw that the marshal's division was discomfited, and that the duke's began to be in disorder, and to open, they leaped on their horses, which they had ready by them, and assembling together they cried St. George for Guienne! And the lord Chandos said to the prince "Sir, take your horse, and ride forth, the victory is yours; God is this day your protector; let us go to the French king's division, for there lieth the cause of the war: I think verily by his valor that he will not fly, so I trust we shall take him by the grace of God and St. George, if we can meet him: and, Sir, I heard you say that this day I should see you a good knight." The prince said "Let us go forward, you shall not see me this day turn back"; and he said, "advance banner, in the name of God and St. George." The knight who bore his banner obeyed. There was then a desperate and perilous battle, and many a man overthrown; and he that was once down could not be raised without great assistance. As the prince entered among his enemies, he saw on his right, in a little bush, the lord Robert of Duras lying dead, and his banner by him, and ten or twelve of his men about him: then the prince said to two of his squires, and to three archers "Sirs, take the body of this knight on a target, and bear him to Poictiers, and present him from me to the cardinal of Perigord, and say, that I salute him by that token"; and this was done. The prince was informed that the cardinals men were in the field against him, which was not consistent with the law of arms; for men of the church, who come and go to treat for peace, ought not to bear arms nor fight for either party; but should be neutral: and as these men had done so, the prince was displeased with the cardinal, and therefore sent to him the dead body of his nephew, the lord Robert of Duras. And the chatelain of Amposta was taken, and the prince would have had his head struck off, because he belonged to the cardinal, but the lord Chandos said "Sir, for a time attend to greater matters, and peradventure the cardinal will make such an excuse that will content you." Then the prince and his company attacked the division of the duke of Athenes, constable of France; there was many a man slain and cast to the earth. As the French troops fought in companies, they exclaimed, Mountjoy St. Denys! as did the Englishmen St. George for Guienne! In a short time the prince with his company met with the division of Germans, whereof the earl of Saltzburg, the earl of Nassau, and the earl Neydo, were captains; but in a short time they were put to flight: the archers shot so regularly together, that none dared come within their reach; for they slew many men who could not come to ransom; among the rest these three earls were there slain, and many other knights and squires of their company. And there was the lord Eustace d'Ambreticourt rescued by his own men, and set on horseback, and afterwards on that day he performed many great feats of arms, and took a number of prisoners. When the division of the duke of Normandy saw the prince approach, they thought to save themselves, and so the duke and the king's children, the earl of Poictiers, and the earl of Toraine, who were very young, by permission of their governors departed from the field, accompanied by upwards of eight hundred spearmen, who were not engaged during the whole of that day. However, the lord Guiscard de l'Angle, and the lord John of Saintre, who were with the earl of Poictiers, would not fly, but entered into the thickest of the battle. The king's three sons took the way to Chavigny; and the lord John of Landas, and the lord Thybault de Bodenay, who were set to attend the duke of Normandy, when they had brought the duke to the distance of a long league from the field of battle, they took leave of him, and desired the lord of St. Venont not to leave the duke, but to attend him to a place of safety, whereby he would receive more thanks of the king than by remaining still in the field: then they met also the duke of Orleans, and a great company with him, who had also departed from the field without engaging. There were many great knights and squires, who, though their masters had left the field, would rather have died than incur any reproach. Then the king's division attacked the English army; there was a great fight, and many severe wounds given and received. The king and his youngest son met with the division of the English marshals, the earl of Warwick, and the earl of Suffolk, and with them of Gascony, the captal de Buche, the lord of Pumiers, the lord Amery of Charre, the lord of Musident, the lord of Languran, and the lord de la Strade. The lord John of Landas, and the lord de Bodenay, who were of the French party, returned time enough: they alighted, and went into the king's division; and a little on one side fought the duke of Athenes, constable of France, and a little before him the duke of Bourbon, and many noble knights of Bourbon, and of Picardy with him; and a little on one side there were those of Poictou, as the lord de Pons, the lord of Partney, the lord of Dampmare, the lord of Montaboton, the lord of Suggeres, the lord John Saintre, the lord Guiscard de l'Angle, the lord Argenton, the lord of Limiers, the lord of Montaudre, and many others; also the viscount of Rocheuart, and the earl of Aulnoy; and of Burgundy, the lord James of Beauvieu, the lord de la Castell Vilain, and others; in another part, there was the earl of Vantadowre; and of Mounpenser, the lord James of Bourbon, the lord John d'Artois, and also the lord James his brother, the lord Arnaut de Cervole, called the arch-priest, who was armed for the young earl of Alençon: and of Auvergne there were the lord of Marcuell, the lord de la Tour, the lord of Chalenton, the lord of Montague, the lord of Rochfort, the lord de la Chaire, and the lord Dachone; and of Limosin there were the lord de Linal, the lord of Norwell, and the lord Pierre de Buffier; and of Picardy there were the lord William of Merle, the lord Arnold of Renewall, the lord Geoffrey of St. Dygier, the lord of Chauny, the lord of Heley, the lord of Mounsaunt, the lord of Hagnes, and many others. And there was also, in the king's division the earl Douglas of Scotland, who fought for some time very valiantly, but when he discovered the discomfiture, he departed and saved himself, for he would not on any account be taken prisoner by the English army; he would rather have been slain on the field of battle. On the part of the English, the lord James Audely, with the assistance of his four squires, was always fighting in the most dangerous part of the battle, and was severely wounded both in the body and in the face; nevertheless, as long as he could sustain himself, he maintained the combat; at last, when the battle was at an end, his four squires took him and conveyed him out of the field, and laid him under the side of a hedge, that he might refresh himself; and they unarmed him, and bound up his wounds as well as they were able. On the side of the French, king John proved himself on that day to be a most valiant and noble knight; and had the fourth part of his troops done their duty as well as he did, the victory would most probably have been his: however, the whole of those who were then present were either slain or taken, except a few that were with the king, who saved themselves.

There were slain in this engagement the duke Peter of Bourbon, the lord Guiscard of Beauvieu, the lord of Landas, and the duke of Athenes, constable of France; the bishop of Chalons in Champagne, the lord William of Nevil, the lord Eustace of Rybemont, the lord de la Tour, the lord William of Montague, Sir Guyventon of Chambley, Sir Baudrin de la House, and many others, as they fought in companies: and there were taken prisoners, the lord de Bodenay and the lord of Pompador: and the arch-priest was severely wounded, together with the earl of Vaudemont, the earl of Mons, the earl of Genvill, the earl of Vendôme, Sir Lois of Melwall, the lord Pierre de Buffier, and the lord of Senerache. There were in the whole, upwards of two hundred knights slain and taken prisoners in that battle.

Chapter CLXIII   Of Two Frenchmen Who Fled from the Battle of Poictiers, and Two Englishmen Who Followed Them

During the attacks, rencontres, chases, and pursuits that took place on that day in the field, it happened to Sir Edward of Roucy, that when he departed from the field, because he saw the day was lost, beyond all possibility of recovery, he determined not to await the revenge of the Englishmen, and therefore fled alone, and had gone the distance of a league from the field of battle, when he was pursued by an English knight, who continually cried to him, and said "Return again, Sir knight, it is a shame to fly away in this manner": then the knight turned back, and the English knight endeavored to strike him with his spear in the target, but in this he failed, for Sir Edward sprang aside, and thus avoided the stroke; but he was not foiled by the English knight, for he gave him such a stroke on the helmet with his sword, that he was astonished, and fell from his horse to the earth, and lay still; upon this Sir Edward alighted and came to him before he could rise, and said "Surrender, Sir, rescue or no rescue, otherwise I will kill you": and the Englishman yielded and went with him, and was afterwards ransomed.

It also happened that another, a squire of Picardy, called John de Helenes, fled from the field of battle, and met with his page, who delivered to him a fresh horse, whereon he rode away alone; at the same time there was in the field, the lord Berkeley of England, a young and noble knight, who had on that day erected his banner; and he alone pursued the said John of Helenes;

and when he had followed him for the distance of a league, the said John turned again, and placed his sword in the rest instead of a spear, and so came running towards the lord Berkeley, who lifted up his sword to strike the squire; who, when he perceived the stroke aimed against him, turned from it, so that the Englishman lost his stroke, and John struck him on the arm as he passed, so violently, that the lord Berkeley's sword fell to the earth: when he found his sword had fallen, he alighted quickly from his horse, and came to the place where his sword lay, and as he stooped down to take up his sword, the French squire made a thrust at him with his sword, and by chance struck him through both thighs, so that the knight fell to the earth, and could not help himself; and then John alighted from his horse, and took up the knight's sword that lay on the ground, and came to him and demanded whether he would surrender himself or not: the knight then demanded his name. Sir, said he, I am John of Helenes, but what is your name? Certainly, said the knight, my name is Thomas, and I am lord of Berkeley, a fine castle on the river Severn, in the marches of Wales. Well Sir, quoth the squire, then you shall be my prisoner, and I will conduct you in safety, and will take care that you shall be recovered from your wound. Well, said the knight, I am willing to be your prisoner, for you have taken me by the law of arms: and so there he swore to be his prisoner, rescue or no rescue: and then the squire drew forth the sword out of the knight's thighs, and the wound was open; then he wrapped and bound up the wound, and set him on his horse, and so brought him gently and easily to Châtel Herault, where he remained for more than fifteen days for the sake of his prisoner, and procured him a cure for his wounds; and when he was somewhat recovered, he then procured a litter for him, and so brought him without fatigue to his house at Picardy; where he continued for more than a year, till he was perfectly cured of his wound: and when he departed he paid six thousand nobles for his ransom. And so this squire was made a knight, on account of the money that he received from the lord Berkeley.

Chapter CLXIV   How King John Was Taken Prisoner at the Battle of Poictiers

The adventures of amour and war are frequently more fortunate and astonishing than any man can think or wish; this battle truly, which was fought near Poictiers, in the fields of Beauvoir and Maupertuis, was very great and perilous, and many deeds of arms were there done, all of which came not to my knowledge. The combatants on both sides endured much pain: king John with his own hands did that day many great deeds; he had an axe in his hands, wherewith he defended himself, and fought in the midst of the fugitives. Near to the king there was taken the earl of Tancarville, Sir James of Bourbon, the earl of Ponthieu, and the lord John of Artois, earl of Ewe; and a little above that, under the banner of the captal de Buche, was taken Sir Charles of Artois, and many other knights and squires: the pursuit continued to the gates of Poictiers. There were many slain and beaten down, both horses and men, for they of Poictiers closed their gates, and would suffer none to enter; wherefore in the street before the gate there was a horrid massacre, and many wounded and beaten down. The Frenchmen yielded themselves as soon as they could discover an Englishman at a distance. There were many English archers who had four, five, or six prisoners: the lord of Pons, a great baron of Poictou, was there slain, and many other knights and squires also: and there was taken the earl of Rocheuart, the lord of Dampmare, the lord of Partney; and of Xainton, the lord of Montendre, and the lord John of Saintre, who was so severely wounded that he never after recovered his health; he was reputed to be one of the best knights of France. And there was left for dead, among the slain, the lord Guiscard de l'Angle, who fought that day by the king very valiantly; as did also the lord of Charney, on whom was a great number, because he bore the banner of the king: his own banner was also in the field, which was three scutcheons of silver gules. So many Englishmen and Gascoigns came to that part, that by force they opened the king's division, so that the Frenchmen were so mingled among their enemies, that at times there were five men upon one gentleman; the lord of Pompador, and the lord Bartholomew de Brunes were there taken; and Sir Geoffrey of Charney was slain, with the king's banner in his hand[3]; also the lord Reynold Cobham slew the earl of Damartin. Then there was a great crowd to take the king, and such as knew him cried "Sir, yield yourself, or else we shall kill you." There was a knight of St. Omers, retained in pay by the king of England, called Sir Dennis Morbec, who had served the Englishmen five years before, because in his youth he had forfeited the realm of France, for a murder which he committed at St. Omers: it happened fortunately for him that he was next to the king when they were about to take him; he stepped forth into the crowd, and by the strength of his body and arms, came to the French king, and said in good French "Sir, surrender." The king beheld the knight, and said "To whom shall I yield? Where is my cousin, the prince of Wales; if I could see him I would speak with him." Dennis answered and said "Sir, he is not here, but yield to me and I will conduct you to him." "Who are you?" quoth the king. "Sir," answered he, "I am Dennis of Morbec, a knight of Artois, but I serve the king of England, because I am banished the realm of France, and have forfeited all my possessions there." Then the king gave him his right gauntlet, saying "I deliver myself to you." There was a great number about the king, for every man compelled him to say he had taken him, so that the king could not proceed, with his young son the lord Philip, on account of the crowd. The prince of Wales, who was courageous and fierce as a lion, took great pleasure on that day in fighting and pursuing his enemies. The lord John Chandos, who accompanied him, never left him all that day, nor delayed for the purpose of taking any prisoner. At the end of the battle he said to the prince "Sir, it would be advisable for you to rest here, and set your banner on high in this bush, that your people may draw hither, for they are much scattered about. I can see no banners or penons of the French party, wherefore, Sir, rest and refresh yourself, for you are much fatigued." Then the prince's banner was erected on a bush, and trumpets and clarions began to sound: Then the prince took off his basenet, as did the knights of his body; and they of his chamber were ready about him; and a red pavilion was erected: and then drink was brought to the prince, and for such lords as were about him, who increased as they came from the pursuit: there they remained, and their prisoners with them. And when the two marshals were come to the prince, he demanded of them if they knew any tidings of the French king. They answered "Sir, we hear none authentically, but we think he is either dead or taken, for he has not gone out of the battle." Then the prince said to the earl of Warwick, and to Sir Reynold Cobham "Sirs, I desire you to go and obtain what information you can, that you may be able to inform me": these two lords took their horses, and departed from the prince, and rode up a little hill to look about them; then they perceived a number of men of arms coming together much fatigued: there was the French king on foot in great danger, for those of England and Gascony were his masters, and had taken him from Sir Dennis Morbec by force: and such as were most powerful said, "I have taken him": "nay," quoth another, "I have taken him": so they contended who should have him. Then the French king, to avoid that danger, said "Sirs, strive not, lead me and my son courteously to my cousin the prince, and quarrel not about the taking of me, for I am a lord great enough to make you all rich": the king's words somewhat appeased them: nevertheless, as they went they still continued to make a riot, and challenged the taking of the king. When the two aforesaid lords saw and heard that noise and contention among them, they came to them and said "Sirs, what is this you strive for." "Sirs," says one of them, "it is for the French king, who is here taken prisoner, and there are more than ten knights and squires who challenge the taking of him and his son." Then the two lords entered the crowd, and caused every man to retire, and commanded them, in the prince's name, on pain of their lives, to make no more noise, or approach the king nearer, unless they were ordered. Then every man gave room to the lords, and they alighted and did their reverence to the king, and then conveyed him and his son in peace and quietness to the prince of Wales.

Book III

Chapter LXXIV   Sir John Holland and Sir Raynold de Roy Fight Together in Lists before the Duke of Lancaster, in the Town of Betanzos

It was related that Betanzos had made a composition with the duke of Lancaster, and had surrendered to him, because the king of Castile had not assisted them; and how the duchess of Lancaster and her daughter came to the city of Oporto in Portugal, to see the king and queen there, and how the king and the lords there received them joyfully, as it was reason. While the duke of Lancaster sojourned in the town of Betanzos, tidings came thither from Valladolid, by a herald of France, who inquired which was the lodging of Sir John Holland; and he was brought thither: then he knelt down before him, and delivered him a letter, saying "Sir, I am an officer of arms, sent to you from Sir Raynold de Roy, who saluteth you; if it please you to read your letter." "Most willingly," replied Sir John, "and you are welcome." Having read the letter, he found that Sir Raynold du Roy challenged him, by way of amours, and for the love of his lady, to run three courses with a spear, three strokes with a sword, three with a dagger, and three with an axe; and that if it pleased him to come to Valladolid, he would provide passports for him and sixty horse; if not, he would come to Betanzos, with thirty horse, if he would procure a passport from the duke of Lancaster. Sir John Holland smiled as he read the letter, and said to the herald "Friend, thou art welcome; you have brought me tidings that please me well, and I accept his challenge: you shall remain here in my house with my company, and to morrow you shall have answer where our feats shall be accomplished, either in Galicia or Castile." "Sir," said the herald, "as it pleaseth God and you." The herald was there at his ease, and Sir John went to the duke, and found him talking with the marshal: then he shewed them his tidings and the letters. "Well," said the duke, "and have you accepted his challenge?" "Yea, truly," said he; "and I desire nothing so much as deeds of arms, and the knight hath desired me; but now, Sir, where would you wish us to contend." The duke, after musing a little, replied "Let it be in this town; make a passport for him, as it shall please you, and I shall seal it." "In the name of God," said Sir John, "that is well said." The passport was written for him and thirty knights and squires, to come and go safe. Then Sir John Holland delivered it to the herald, and gave him a mantle furred with minever, and twelve angel nobles. The herald took his leave, and returned to Valladolid to his master, and there shewed how he had succeeded, and delivered the passport. On the other part, tidings came to Oporto to the king of Portugal and the ladies there, that these deeds of arms would be done at Betanzos. "Well," said the king, "I will be there, and the queen my wife, with other ladies and damsels": and the duchess of Lancaster, who was then there, thanked the king in that she should at her return be accompanied by the king and queen: and ere long the time approached. Then the king of Portugal, the queen, the duchess, and her other daughter, with other ladies and damsels, rode towards Betanzos in good order; and when the duke of Lancaster knew that the king came thither, he and many other lords took their horses, and issued out of Betanzos, and met the king

te grant amor. et de trop grant na
lor. et grant uolente auoient de
faire chive. et quant ce mcguer
as glaiues brisser. il sentrferir

puignon autdefour. par force cur
meo. sil le peust faire. et il auoiet
la lor afaire ace mene. quil m auo
it nul delo quil neust plaies grat

Figure 27 *A tournament.*

and the ladies: and the king and the duke received each other kindly, and so entered the town together, and their lodging was appointed according to the custom of the country, and that was not so easy nor large as though they had been at Paris.

About three days after the king of Portugal came to Betanzos, Sir Raynold de Roy came thither, accompanied by many knights and squires: he had six score horses, and they were all well lodged, for the duke of Lancaster had prepared their lodging. Next day Sir John Holland and Sir Raynold Roy were armed, and mounted their horses, and so came to a good place, ready sanded, where they were to contend; and scaffolds were made for the king and the ladies, and for the duke and other lords of England, for they had all come thither to see the deeds of arms of these two knights; who came into the field as well mounted and accoutred as could be devised, and there was brought in their spears, axes, and swords: so each of them, at a good distance apart, pranced about briskly, for they knew well they were observed: every thing was ordained at their desire, and all their arms granted, except the fighting at utterance: howbeit, neither of them could be secure of his life, for since they had come thither they

must needs meet at the point of their spears, and then with their swords, axes, and daggers: what danger they were in to exalt their honor! for their lives were hazarded on the mischance of one stroke. They ran together, and met as even as though they had run by a line, and struck each other in the visor of their helmets, so that Sir Raynold broke his spear in four pieces, and the shivers flew high in the air; which course was much praised: Sir John Holland also struck Sir Raynold in the visor, but the stroke was of no force, because the visor of his helmet was tied but with a small lace, which broke with the force of the stroke, and the helmet flew off his head, so that the knight was bare-headed, and so passed forth their course, and Sir John bore his staff freshly; then every man said it was a good course.

Then these knights resumed their places, and Sir Raynold was helmed again, and had a new spear, and so they ran together again: they were both well horsed, and could well guide them: they struck each other on the helmets, so that the fire flew out: the spears broke not, but Sir Raynold's helmet again flew off his head. Ah, said the English, the Frenchman has the advantage. Why is not his helmet as fast buckled as that of Sir John Holland? We think he does wrong: let him set his helmet as his companion does. Hold your peace, Sirs, said the duke of Lancaster, let each gain all the advantage he can: if Sir John thinks his antagonist has the advantage let him take his plan; but for my part, said the duke, were I in their place, I would have my helmet buckled as fast as I could, and I think many here are of my opinion. Then the English said no more: and the ladies and damsels said they had justed well, and the king of Portugal said the same, and said to Sir John Ferant "Sir John, in our country knights just not in this goodly manner." "Sir," said he, "these knights just well: and, Sir, I have heretofore seen Frenchmen just before the king your brother; when we were at Elvas against the king of Castile, I saw like justs there between Sir William Windsor and another French knight; but their helmets were faster tied than this knight's." Then the king looked at the combatants, to see their third course. In this course they regarded each other wisely, to take their advantage, which they could well do, their horses being very tractable; they again struck each other on the helmets, so that their eyes trembled in their heads, and their staves broke, and again Sir Raynold's helmet flew off his head, and they passed on freshly, while every one said they had justed nobly: but the English greatly blamed Sir Raynold de Roy in that his helmet was not faster set on his head: but the duke blamed him not, but said "I think him wise who could gain any lawful advantage; it appears Sir Raynold has not to learn to just, for though Sir John has behaved so well, his adversary has most skill." Then they fought with their axes, with which they gave three great strokes on their helmets; after that with their swords, and then their daggers, and when all was over, neither of them were hurt. The French led Sir Raynold to his lodging, and the English Sir John Holland to his. The same day the duke of Lancaster gave a dinner to all the Frenchmen in his lodging, and the duchess sat at the table by the duke, and Sir Raynold du Roy below her: after dinner they went into a council chamber, and the duchess took Sir Raynold by the hand, and led him in at the same time as herself; and there she communed with him and other of the French knights, till it was time to call for drink; then the duchess said to the French knights "Sirs, I am surprised that you sustain the cause of a bastard; for you know, and so does all the world, that the late king Henry of Castile was a bastard; therefore why do you support that cause, against the right heir of Castile? For I and all the world know that I

and my sister were daughters by lawful marriage, to king Don Pedro; wherefore God knoweth the right we have to the realm of Castile." The good lady wept when she spoke of her father. Then Sir Raynold de Roy made his obeisance and said "Madam, we know that all you have said is true; but the king our master is of a contrary opinion, and we, as his subjects, must make war at his pleasure, and go where he will send us; we cannot say nay." So the duchess went to the duke, and the French knights drank, and then took leave and went to their lodging, where every thing was ready to depart: then they quitted Betanzos, and rode the same day to Noya, and there rested, and then rode on to Valladolid.

Book IV

Chapter XXV   Of a Feast and Justs Made by the King of England in London, While the Christian Knights and Squires Were at the Siege of Africa against the Saracens, Which Feast Was Published in Various Parts[4]

You have heard before in this history that a feast was holden at Paris when queen Isabella of France made her first entry into that city; of which feast tidings spread abroad into every country. King Richard of England and his three uncles, hearing of this famous feast at Paris, by the reports of such knights and squires as had been present at the said feast, ordained a great feast to be holden in the city of London; where there should be for the entertainment of the visitors, justs, and sixty knights, with sixty ladies to keep them company: these knights were to just on the Sunday and the two following days, and the challenge to commence upon the Sunday after the feast of Saint Michael, in the year of our Lord 1390: on which day, at two o'Clock in the afternoon, these sixty knights and sixty ladies were to issue out in procession from the tower of London, and proceed along the city through Cheapside to Smithfield; and that twelve knights should be there ready to receive all knights and strangers who were willing to just. This day was called the Sunday of the Feast of Challenge; and on the following Monday, the said sixty knights were to remain in the same place ready to just, and to receive all those who could courteously run with rockets;[5] and the best performer of the outside should have for his prize a rich crown of gold, and the best of the inside, duly examined by the ladies in the queen's chamber, a rich girdle of gold. On the Tuesday following, the knights were to be again in the same place, and to receive all manner of squires, strangers and others, as would just with rockets; the best juster on the outside was to have for his prize a courser equipped and harnessed; and the victor of the inside, a falcon.

The manner of this feast was thus ordained and devised: and heralds were charged to publish it in England, Scotland, Germany, Flanders, Brabant, Hainault, and France; so the heralds departed, having time sufficient, and proclaimed these tidings in several countries. Knights and squires of different parts prepared to come to the feast; some to see the manners of England, and others to just. When the news reached Hainault, Sir William earl of Ostrevant, in that country, who was young and liberal, and desirous to just, purposed in himself to go to this feast in England, to see and to honor his cousins, king Richard of England, and his uncles, whom he had never yet seen: he greatly desired to be acquainted with them, and desired other knights and squires to accompany him, especially the lord Gomegines, because he was well acquainted with the English, having been several times among them. Then Sir William proposed, while making the necessary arrangements for his departure, to proceed for Holland to consult with his father Aubert, earl of Hainault, Holland, and Zealand, and to take leave of him before he departed for England: he went from Quesnoy in Hainault, and rode till he came to the Hague in Holland, where the earl his father was at that time, and he told him his intention of going to England to see the country and his cousins whom he had never seen. Then the earl his father replied "William, my worthy son, you have no business in England, for you are now by covenant of marriage allied to the realm of France, and your sister is to be married to the duke of Burgundy; wherefore you need seek no other alliance." "Dear father," quoth he, "I will not go to England to make any alliance, but merely to feast and make merry with my cousins, whom I never yet saw; and because the fame of the feast which is to be holden at London is published abroad: wherefore, since I have signified my intention of going, it will be said I am weak and presumptuous were I now to decline it; wherefore, in regard for my honor, I will go thither; therefore dear father, I request you to agree thereto." "Son," quoth he, "do as you please, but I think surely you had better remain at home." When the earl of Ostrevant saw that his words contented not his father, he spoke no more of that matter, but fell into other conversation; but he resolved what he would do, and so daily sent his provisions to Calais. Gomegines the herald was sent to England from the earl of Ostrevant, to inform king Richard and his uncles that he intended to come honorably to his feast at London. The king and his uncles were quite joyful at these tidings, and gave to the herald great gifts, which proved afterwards of great use to him, for towards the end of his days he became blind; I cannot tell whether God was displeased with him or not, for in his healthful days he lived strangely; wherefore in his old age when he had lost his sight, but few shewed any concern for him. Thus the earl of Ostrevant took leave of his father, and returned to Quesnoy in Hainault to the countess his wife.

This noble feast of which I am speaking, being proclaimed in several places, many knights and squires, and others equipped themselves to go thither. The earl Valeran of Saint Poule, who was then married to the sister of king Richard of England, made great preparations to go into England, and so came to Calais: also the earl of Ostrevant departed from Hainault, well accompanied by knights and squires, and passed through the country of Artois to Calais, where he met with the earl of Saint Poule, and the passage vessels for Dover were there ready: and when the ships were charged and the wind fair, these lords put to sea; but I was informed, and I believe it was the case, that the earl of St. Poule arrived in England before the earl of Ostrevant; who when he came to London found the king, and his brother-in-law Sir John Holland, and other lords and knights of England, who received him with great joy, and inquired what news he brought from the realm of France: he answered them well and wisely. The earl of Ostrevant landed on a Thursday, and proceeded to Canterbury, and on the Friday he visited Saint Thomas's shrine, and offered there in the morning, and staid there that day; the next day he proceeded to Rochester; and because he had a great company, he travelled by easy journeys to relieve his horses; on Sunday he rode to Dartford to dinner, and after dinner to London, to be at the feast, which began the same day.

On the first Sunday after the feast of Saint Michael the celebration of this feast and triumph was to begin, when there was to be performed in Smithfield justs called the Challenge: so the same Sunday about three o'clock in the afternoon, there issued out of the tower of London, first, sixty coursers equipped for the justs, on each of which was a squire of honor riding an easy pace: then there came sixty ladies of honor richly apparelled mounted on fair palfreys riding on the one side, every lady led a knight with a chain of silver, which knights were equipped for the justs. In this order they rode along the streets of London with a great band of trumpeters and other musicians, and came to Smithfield, where the king and queen of England and other ladies and damsels were in chambers richly adorned to see the justs. When the ladies that led the knights arrived at the place, they were dismounted from their palfreys, and went into chambers ready prepared for them; then the squires of honor alighted from their coursers, and the knights in good order mounted on them, with their helmets on and fully equipped: then came the earl of St. Poule nobly accompanied with knights and squires all in armor, and immediately began the justs; and there justed all such knights and squires who were willing, and had leisure, for the night came on: thus the justs of challenge commenced, and continued till night; then the knights and ladies retired, and the queen withdrew to the bishop's palace, where the supper was prepared. The same evening the earl of Ostrevant came to the king, and was nobly received.

Now for these justs on the Sunday, of the victor without, the earl Valeran of St. Poule had the prize; and of the challengers the earl of Huntingdon. There was elegant dancing in the queen's apartments, in the presence of the king and his uncles, and other barons of England, with ladies and damsels, continuing till it was day, when every person went to their respective homes, except the king and queen, who remained in the bishop's palace, where they abode during the time of the feasts and justs.

On the following Monday, there was seen in the streets of the city of London, numbers of squires and varlets going about with harness, and doing other business for their masters. In the afternoon king Richard came to the place armed and richly apparelled, accompanied by dukes, earls, lords, and knights; he was one of the inner party. Then the queen, accompanied with ladies and damsels, came to the place appointed for the justs, and mounted into chambers and scaffolds prepared for them. Then came the earl of Ostrevant into the field, well attended by knights of his own country; and then came the earl of St. Poule, with other knights of France who were willing to just. So the justs began: some were struck from their horses, and every man exerted himself to obtain honor. These justs continued till the approach of night; then all the knights and ladies withdrew to their lodgings till the hour for supper, when they repaired to the court; where was a delicious supper elegantly set out. On that day the prize was given to the earl of Ostrevant, as being the best juster of the outer party, and well he deserved it; the prize was given him by the ladies, lords, and heralds, who were ordained to be judges: and of the inner party Sir Hugh Spencer, a knight of England, gained the prize.

The next day, Tuesday, the justs commenced in the same place, between all manner of squires, which continued till night, in the presence of the king, queen, lords, and ladies, when every man returned to his lodging, as they had done the preceding days, and afterwards assembled at the bishop's palace to supper, where the king, the queen, and the ladies, were already met. The repast was elegant and costly, and the dancing continued all night. On the Wednesday, after dinner, all manner of knights and squires, such as chose, justed in the same place, which was keenly supported till night, when the parties withdrew; and at the hour of supper they all resorted to the bishop's palace, as on the preceding evening. The king gave a supper to all the knights and gentlemen, strangers, on the Thursday, as did the queen to all the ladies and damsels. On the Friday the duke of Lancaster made a dinner for all the strange knights and squires, which was a goodly dinner; and on the Saturday the king and all the lords left London for Windsor, whence the earl of Ostrevant, the earl of St. Poule, and all the other foreign knights and squires were invited to accompany them. Then there began again sumptuous entertainments given by the king; and especially great respect and honor was shewn to the earl of Ostrevant, who was desired by the king and his uncles that he would take on him the order of the garter. The earl answered that he would take counsel in that matter; and thereupon consulted the lord of Gomegines and the bastard Fierabras of Vertan, who in no wise would prevent his acceptance of that dignity. He therefore took it upon him, which created much surprise and murmuring among the knights and squires of France, who said "The earl of Ostrevant appears to shew a decided partiality for the English rather than the French, since he accepts the order of the garter, and bears the king of England's device: he evinceth clearly that he regardeth not the house of France, nor the house of Burgundy: the time will come when he will repent himself; all things considered, he knows not what he has done, for he was well beloved of the French king, and of the duke of Touraine his brother, and of all the blood royal, in such a manner, that when he came to Paris or into any other place among them, they always paid more honor to him than the rest of their cousins": thus these Frenchmen accused him of evil without cause; for what he had done was not at all detrimental to the realm of France, nor to his cousins and friends in that kingdom; what he had done was merely from honor and love, and to please his cousins in England; which would tend to unite England and France the closer: and when he thus took upon him the said order of the garter and oath, every man might have understood that he made no alliance whatever to do any prejudice to the realm of France; for what he did was purely from motives of regard and good fellowship: but no man can prevent the envious from speaking evil.

When they had danced and enjoyed themselves a certain space in the castle of Windsor, and the king had given many handsome presents to the knights and squires of honor of the realm of France and Hainault, and especially to the young earl of Ostrevant, then every man took leave of the king and the queen, and of the other ladies and damsels, and of the king's uncles. This ceremony being performed, then the earl of St. Poule and the Frenchmen, and the Hainaulters and Germans, departed. Thus ended this great feast in the city of London, and every man went to his own home. Then it happened, as news spread quickly abroad, that the French king, his brother, and his uncles, were informed by such as had been in England at the said feast, of every thing that had been done and said; nothing was forgotten, but rather more was added in blazing of evil deeds, than in furthering accounts of good ones. It was shewed the king plainly, how the earl of Ostrevant had been in England, and had taken great pains to advance the honor of the English, and to promote the feast holden at London; and how he had the chief prize and honor of the justs above all other strangers: and how he had spoken so fair to the Englishmen, that he was become a favorite with the king, and had made service

and alliance with him; and had taken on him the order of the garter, in the chapel of St. George in Windsor, which order was first established by king Edward III, and his son the prince of Wales; and how that no man could be admitted to that dignity without he made assurance or oath never to bear arms against the crown of England; which promise they said the earl of Ostrevant had made without any reservation. With these tidings the French king, his brother, and his uncles, were much troubled, and grievously displeased with the earl of Ostrevant. Then the French king said "Lo, Sirs, you may perceive how useless it is to oblige him; it is not yet a year since he desired me that his brother might have the bishopric of Cambray; and by what you now report, that gift was rather prejudicial to the realm of France than otherwise: it had been better to have given it to our cousin of St. Poule. The Hainaulters never did any good for us, and never will, for they are proud, presumptuous, and much too fierce. They have always entertained more friendship for the English than for us; but a day will come when they shall repent it. We will send to the earl of Ostrevant, commanding him to come to us, to do us homage for the county of Ostrevant, or else we shall put him from it and annex it to our realm." They of his council answered and said "Sir, you have well devised; let it be done as you have said." It may well be said that the duke of Burgundy, whose daughter the earl of Ostrevant had to his wife, was not pleased with those reports, for he had always recommended his son of Ostrevant to the king and his council. This matter was not forgotten; but the French king immediately wrote sharp letters to the earl of Ostrevant, who was at Quesnoy in Hainault, commanding him to come to Paris to do his homage before the king and the other peers of France, for the county of Ostrevant, or else the king would take it from him and make him war. When the earl had well considered these letters, and perceived that the French king and his council were displeased with him, to make his answer he called his council together, such as the lord of Fontaines, the lord of Gomegines, Sir William of Hermes, the lord of Trassegines, the bailiff of Hainault, the lord of Sancelles, Sir Rafe of Montigny, the abbot of Crispine, John Semart, Jaquemart Barrier of Valenciennes: these wise men consulted together what answer might be made to the king's letters. There were many opinions given; but at last, all things considered, they thought it best to write to the French king, and to his council, requesting a day to be appointed for answering all demands, by the testimony of certain credible persons, and none by writing: and in the interim they sent certain notable personages to his father the earl of Hainault and Holland, to have his advice as to the answer most proper to be made. This done, they wrote courteously to the king and his council, so that they were well satisfied therewith. Then the earl despatched the lord of Trassegines into Holland, accompanied by the lord of Sancelles, John Semart, and Jaquemart Barrier. They rode to the earl of Hainault, and shewed him the state of matters, and the letters that the French king had written to his son the earl of Ostrevant. The earl of Hainault had marvel of that matter, and said "Sirs, I always imagined it would come to this pass; William my son had no business to go into England; I have delivered to him the rule and governance of the county of Hainault; and he might have conducted himself according to the counsel of the country. Sirs, I shall tell you what you must do. Go to my worthy cousin the duke of Burgundy, for it lieth well in his power to reconcile and adjust all these matters with the French king: I can give you no better advice." With this answer they left Holland and came again into Hainault, and there shewed what answer they had, with which the earl and his council were satisfied.

The lord of Trassegines, Sir William of Hermes, Sir Rafe of Montigny, John Semart, and Jaquemart Barrier, were assigned to go into France to the duke of Burgundy, to shew and declare all the circumstances of this affair, which would be too long here to recite. But after the duke of Burgundy had done all in his power, it was finally concluded that the earl of Ostrevant must come personally to Paris, and to know his homage due to the French king for the county of Ostrevant, or otherwise to have war declared against him. The lord of Coucy and Sir Oliver of Clisson took great interest on the part of the earl, but Sir John Mercier and the lord de la River, exerted themselves on the contrary side as much as they could. Now let us return to the siege before Africa.

Chapter LII   Sir John Froissart Arrives in England, and Presents the King with a Book

True it was, that I Sir John Froissart (at that time treasurer and canon of Chimay, in the earldom of Hainault, in the diocese of Liege), had a great desire to go and see the realm of England, when I had been in Abbeville, and saw that peace was concluded between the realms of England and France, and other countries to them conjoined, and their adherents, to endure four years by sea and by land. Many reasons enticed me to make that voyage; one was, because in my youth I had been brought up in the court of the noble king Edward III, and of queen Philippa his wife and among their children, and other barons of England, such as were then alive, in whom I found all nobleness, honor, largess, and courtesy; therefore I desired to see the country, thinking thereby I should live much the longer, for I had not been there for twenty-seven years, and I thought, though I should not see those lords whom I had left alive there, yet at least I should see their heirs, the which would do me much good to see, and also to justify the histories and matters that I had written of them: and before I took my journey, I spoke with duke Aubert of Bavaria, and with the earl of Hainault, Holland, Zealand, and lord of Friezland, and with my lord William earl of Ostrevant, and with my right honorable lady Jane duchess of Brabant and of Luxembourg, and with the lord Engerant, lord of Coucy, and with the gentle knight the lord of Gomegines, who in his youth and mine had been together in England in the king's court; in likewise so had I seen there the lord of Coucy, and several other nobles of France, who held great households in London, when they laid there in hostage for the redemption of king John, as then French king, as it hath been shewed here before in this history.

These said lords, and the duchess of Brabant, advised me to take this journey, and gave me letters of recommendation to the king of England and to his uncles, except the lord of Coucy; he would not write to the king because he was a Frenchman, therefore he durst not, but to his daughter who was then called duchess of Ireland; and I had engrossed in a fair book well enlumined, all the matters of amours and moralities, that in four and twenty years before I had made and compiled, which greatly hastened my desire to go into England to see king Richard, who was son to the noble prince of Wales and of Aquitaine, for I had not seen this king Richard since he was christened in the cathedral church of Bourdeaux, at which time I was there, and thought to have gone with the prince the journey into Galicia in Spain; and when we were in the city of Dax,

Figure 28 *The tomb of the Black Prince, Canterbury Cathedral.*

the prince sent me back into England to the queen his mother.

For these and other reasons I had a great desire to go into England to see the king and his uncles. Also I had this fair book well covered with velvet, garnished with clasps of silver and gilt, thereof to make a present to the king at my first coming into his presence; I had such a desire to go this voyage, that the pain and fatigue availed me little.

Thus provided with horses and other necessaries, I crossed the sea at Calais, and came to Dover, the twelfth day of the month of July; when I came there I found no man who knew me, it was so long since I had been in England, and the houses were all newly built, and young children had become men, and the women knew me not, nor I them; so I stopt half a day and all night at Dover; it was on a Tuesday, and the next day by nine o'clock I came to Canterbury, to Saint

Thomas's shrine, and to the tomb of the noble prince of Wales, who is there interred very magnificently; there I heard mass, and made my offering to the holy saint, and then dined at my lodging; and there I was informed how king Richard would be there the next day on pilgrimage, which was after his return out of Ireland, where he had been the space of nine months or thereabout. The king had a devotion to visit St. Thomas's shrine, and also because the prince his father was there buried: then I thought to stop there till the king came and so I did; and the next day the king came thither with a noble company of lords, ladies, and damsels: and when I was among them, they seemed to me to be all strangers, I knew no person there; the time was greatly changed in twenty-eight years, and with the king as then was none of his uncles; the duke of Lancaster was in Acquitaine, and the dukes of York and Gloucester were in other businesses, so that I was at the first greatly ashamed, for if I had seen any ancient knight that had been with king Edward, or with the prince, I had been much comforted and would have gone to him, but I could see none such. Then I demanded for a knight called Sir Richard Stury, whether he was alive or not? and I was told he was, but he was at London. Then I resolved to go to the lord Thomas Percy, great seneschal of England, who was there with the king; so I obtained acquaintance with him, and found him very generous and affable, and he offered to present my letters to the king, whereof I was very much pleased, for it was reasonable for me to have some person to introduce me to the presence of such a monarch as the king of England. He went to the king's chamber, at which time, he told me the king was gone to rest, and bade me return to my lodging, and come again. Accordingly I complied with his desire, and went to the bishop's palace, where I found the lord Thomas Percy ready to ride to Ospring, who desired me not to make myself known there, but to follow the court; and said he would cause me to be well provided for, till the king should be at the fair castle of Leeds in Kent.

I did according to his advice, and rode forward to Ospring; and by chance I was lodged in a house where was a brave knight of England, called Sir William of Lisle; he was left there behind the king, because he had a pain in his head the night before: he was one of the king's privy chamber; and when he perceived I was a stranger, imagining by my language that I was a native of the country of France, we formed acquaintance with each other; for gentlemen of England are courteous, affable, and desirous of acquaintance. Then he asked me who I was, and what business I had to do in those parts? I told him my principal reasons for coming there, and all that the lord Thomas Percy had said to me, and what he desired me to do. He then replied, that I could not have had a better medium, and told me that on Friday the king was expected at the castle of Leeds; also he informed me that when I went thither, I should find the duke of York, the king's uncle, of which intelligence I was much rejoiced, because I had letters directed to him, and also because he had seen me in his youth, in the court of the noble king Edward his father, and with the queen his mother.

On the morning of Friday, Sir William Lisle and I rode together, and on the way I asked him whether he had been with the king in his expedition to Ireland? He answered my question in the affirmative. Then I inquired of him concerning the hole which is in Ireland, called Saint Patrick's purgatory, whether what was commonly reported of that place was true or false. Then he told me that there was such a hole beyond all doubt, and that he himself and another knight of the realm of England had been there while the king remained at Dublin, and he said that they entered into the hole and were closed in at the time of the setting of the sun, and remained there all night, and issued out again the following morning at sun-rising.

I then asked him if he had any such strange sights or visions as were reported to have been seen there. He told me that when he and his companion were entered and past the gate which was called the purgatory of Saint Patrick, and had gone down three or four paces, descending as into a cellar, a certain hot vapor rose against them, and so affected their heads, that they were overpowered, and were obliged to sit down on the steps which were of stone, and when they had sat there a while, being very drowsy, they fell asleep and slept there all night. Then I inquired if in their sleep they knew where they were, or what visions they had. He answered me, that during their sleep their fancy was worked upon by strange imaginations and marvellous dreams, otherwise than they were used to have in their own habitations; and in the morning they issued out, and in the course of a short time entirely forgot their dreams and visions, for which reason he said he thought all that was reported concerning that place, was merely a fantastic delusion.

Then I discontinued to converse any further concerning that affair, because I was desirous to obtain of him an account of the result of the expedition to Ireland; and I intended to have inquired what the king had done in that enterprise; but then a company of other knights came and fell in conversation with him, so I relinquished my purpose for that time.

Thus we rode to Leeds, and thither came the king and all his company, and there I found his highness Edmund duke of York. Then I went to him and delivered the letters entrusted to my charge from the earl of Hainault his cousin, and from the earl of Ostrevant.

The duke knew me well, and gave me a hearty welcome, and said "Sir John, hold you always near to us, and we will show you great kindness and courtesy: we are bound so to do in remembrance of our love in time past, and likewise for the love of her majesty the old queen my mother, in whose court you were, we have good remembrance of your former services." Then I thanked him, according to the rules of reason and good breeding.

Thus I was advanced by reason of the favor and attention of the duke of York, Sir Thomas Percy, and Sir William Lisle; by means of these persons I was brought into the king's chamber, and introduced into his presence by means of his uncle the duke of York. Then I delivered my letters to the king, and he took and read them deliberately and at leisure. Then he said to me that I was welcome as one that had been formerly a member of the English court, and that I might now also consider myself a member of the same.

On that day I did not shew the king the book which I had to offer for his acceptance, he was so busily occupied in great affairs, that I had no opportunity to present it.

The king was very busily engaged there with important consultations concerning two great and mighty matters. The first was in determining to send sufficient messengers, as the earl of Rutland his cousin-german, the earl Marshall, the archbishop of Dublin, the bishop of Ely, the lord Lois Clifford, the lord Henry Beaumond, the lord Hugh Spencer, and many others, over the sea to Charles, king of France, to treat with him for a marriage, to be had between the king of England and the eldest daughter of the king of France, named Isabella, of the age of eight years.

The second cause of the assembly of this council, was the legation of the lord de la Barde, the lord of Tarride, the lord of Pintherne, the lord of Chateau-neuf, the lord De l'Evesque, the lord of Copane, and the counsellors of Bourdeaux, Bayonne, and of Dax, into England had diligently pursued their business since the king's return out of Ireland, to have an answer of the requests and process that they had put forth to the king, concerning the gift which the king had given to his uncle the duke of Lancaster, of the lands, seigniories, manors, and baronies in Aquitaine, which they proved to appertain to the king and realm of England; they had alleged to the king and his council, that his gift ought not to be disposed of in that manner, because it was unprofitable and of no utility. For they said all those lands belonged of right to the crown of England, wherefore they said they would not disjoin or separate them from the crown. They alleged furthermore many other reasonable causes, as you shall hereafter be informed in this process.

Thus to hold consultation of these two great matters, the king had sent for the greater part of the prelates and lords of England to be at the feast of Maudelintide, at a manor of his own called Eltham, seven English miles distant from London; and when they had tarried at Leeds four days, the king returned through Rochester to Eltham, and so I rode forth in the king's company.

From Chapter LIII

On the Sunday following all such as had been there were departed, and all their counsellors except the duke of York, who abode still about the king; and the lord Thomas Percy and Sir Richard Stury shewed my business to the king. Then the king desired to see the book which I had brought for him; so he saw it in his chamber, for I had laid it there ready on his bed. When the king opened it, it pleased him well, for it was finely illumined and written, and covered with crimson velvet, with ten buttons of silver and gilt, and roses of gold in the middle, with two great clasps gilt, richly wrought. Then the king asked me whereof it treated, and I told him of affairs of love; whereof the king was glad, and looked in it and read many parts of it, for he could speak and read French very well; and he delivered it to a knight of his chamber, named Sir Richard Creadon, to take it into his secret chamber. On the same Sunday I fell in acquaintance with a squire of England, called Henry Castide, a wise honest man, who could speak French fluently; he accompanied with me because he saw I was countenanced by the king and other lords, and also he had seen the book which I gave to the king; also Sir Richard Stury had told him that I was an historian. . . .

Notes

1   Presumably crowned at a festival of the Pui in Abbeville. For information on the Pui, see Section VI. The music for this song, here translated by the editor, has not survived.

2   Jean le Bel, upon whose chronicle Froissart based the first part of his own work, says that King Edward took the Duchess by force during the night. However, in one MS of his chronicle Froissart explicitly denies the truth of this story.

3   Geoffrey de Charney is the author of a treatise on chivalry.

4   The lists for these jousts were prepared under the direction of the Clerk of the King's Works, Geoffrey Chaucer.

5   That is, with blunted lances.

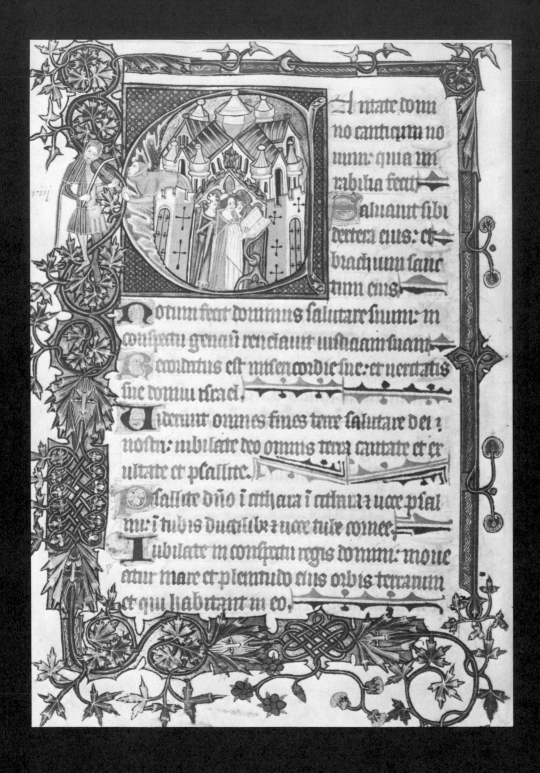

Antate dom
no canticum no
uum: quia mi
rabilia fecit.
Saluauit sibi
dertera eius: et
brachium sanc
tum eius.

Notum fecit dominus salutare suum: in
conspectu gentium reuelauit iusticiam suam.
Recordatus est misericordie sue: et ueritatis
sue domui israel.

Uiderunt omnes fines terre salutare dei ?
nostri: iubilate deo omnis terra cantate et ex
ultate et psallite.

Psallite dño i cithara i cithara ? uoce psal
mi: i tubis ductilibz ? uoce tube cornee.

Iubilate in conspectu regis domini: moue
atur mare et plenitudo eius orbis terrarum
et qui habitant in eo.

VIII

MIDDLE ENGLISH LITERATURE: SONGS AND SHORT POEMS

Middle English began to emerge as a literary language in the course of the twelfth century. Much of the literature of the early period is historical or overtly didactic, inferior in quality to the Latin and French literature contemporary with it. One or two exceptions to this generalization, like *The Owl and the Nightingale* of the early thirteenth century, and a few lyrics, may appear, but it was not until the later thirteenth century that the possibilities of Middle English as a vehicle for literary craftsmanship began to be exploited. Forms popular in French, especially the romance, were produced in English, and as English became the language of the provincial courts, these forms acquired considerable sophistication. There is, however, a large element of truth in the old opinion that Geoffrey Chaucer is the true father of English poetry,

Facing page: The new song and the old song.

345

for it was not until English became the literary language of the royal court in the latter fourteenth century that a demand arose for the same kind of refinement and learning in English that had previously characterized French poetry.

A good account of early Middle English literature and its background appears in R. M. Wilson, *Early Middle English Literature*, Methuen & Co., Ltd., London, 1939. Romances, lyrics, and *Piers the Ploughman* are discussed by George Kane, *Middle English Literature*, Methuen & Co., Ltd, London, 1951. Middle English writings of all kinds are described with full bibliographical annotations in J. E. Wells et al., *A Manual of the Writings in Middle English*, with nine supplements, New Haven, Conn., 1916–1951.

The Middle English song makes its first appearance in our manuscripts in the thirteenth century, long after the troubadours and trouvéres had established the tradition of the vernacular song in Provençal and French. Like their continental contemporaries, English song writers looked for inspiration to the long history of the Latin lyric, which extends unbroken from classical times throughout the Middle Ages. The earlier vernacular tradition in Ireland was virtually unknown to poets in English. Many of their works are translations. After the beginning of the second half of the century, songs and short poems began to be gathered in collections, the most famous of which appears, along with other material, in a manuscript now known as Harley 2253. In the fourteenth century the Franciscans were especially active in collecting and composing poems for use in their sermons to the common people.

Unlike modern lyrics, the songs and short poems of the Middle Ages, many of which were used for private devotion, are frequently conventional in imagery and theme and do not express strong personal feeling. This principle applies to love songs as well as to devotional and moral pieces that rely heavily on the Bible for ideas and figures. The appeal of this poetry thus lies more in the fresh use of the familiar than in the creation of new ideas or the exploitation of new feelings. For example, the idea that divine grace descends like dew (which does not actually descend) is very old, but its use in "I Sing of a Maiden" is nevertheless peculiarly effective. Perhaps it should be emphasized once more that we should not expect in these pieces the spontaneous expression of feeling to be found in romantic and post romantic lyrics; in fact, it is better not to call them lyrics at all except to mean "words for a song" in those instances where the poems were set to music.

Since early Middle English is frequently very difficult, the poems in the first part of this collection have been "modernized" or "translated" by the editor. It has sometimes been necessary to take certain regrettable liberties with the texts in order to preserve something of the original form. When these selections are used in the classroom, the teacher can perform a real service by reading the originals aloud.

For texts of these and other lyrics, see E. K. Chambers and F. Sidgwick, *Early English Lyrics*, Sidgwick and Jackson, Ltd., London, 1921; Carleton Brown, *English Lyrics of the Thirteenth Century*, Clarendon Press, Oxford, 1932; Carleton Brown, *Religious Lyrics of the Fourteenth Century*, Clarendon Press, Oxford, 1924; Carleton Brown, *Religious Lyrics of the Fifteenth Century*, Clarendon Press, Oxford, 1939; R. H. Rollins, *Secular Lyrics of the Fourteenth and Fifteenth Centuries*, Clarendon Press, Oxford, 1952. The poems in MS Harley 2253 have been presented in modern annotated editions by G. L. Brook, *The Harley Lyrics*, second edition, University of Manchester Press, Manchester, 1956, and by Sabino Casieri, *Canti e liriche medioevali inglesi*, La Goliardica, Milan, 1962. The latter edition seeks to emphasize Continental influences on the poetry. For information about the music to which some of these pieces were sung, see J. A. Westrup, "Medieval Song," in *Early Medieval Music*, The New Oxford History of Music, vol. II, Oxford University Press, London, 1955; and Manfred F. Bukofzer, "Popular and Secular Music in England," in *Ars Nova and Renaissance*, The New Oxford History of Music, vol. III, Oxford University Press, London, 1960. There is a very useful study with emphasis on the later part of the period by F. Ll. Harrison, *Music in Medieval Britain*, Routledge & Kegan Paul, Ltd., London, 1958. The standard work on the carol is R. L. Greene, *The Early English Carol*, Clarendon Press, Oxford, 1935. The same author has provided an attractive and useful short anthology, *A Selection of English Carols*, Clarendon Press, Oxford, 1962. The religious lyric is the subject of a magnificent study by Rosemary Woolf, *The English Religious Lyric in the Middle Ages*, Clarendon Press, Oxford, 1968.

"MERRY IT IS . . . . ."[1]

Merry it is while summer lasts
With fowl's song.
But now nears the wind's blast,
And weather strong.
Ai! Ai! but the night is long,   5
And I with much wrong
Sorrow, and mourn, and fast.

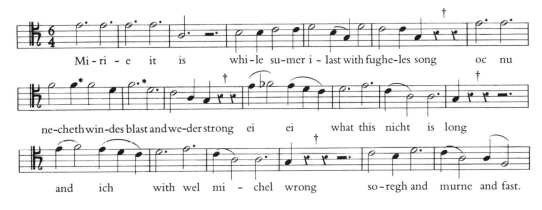

Mi - ri - e it is whi-le su-mer i - last with fughe-les song oc nu ne-chethwin-des blast and we-der strong ei ei what this nicht is long and ich with wel mi - chel wrong so-regh and murne and fast.

Note

    1 This piece, which survives in a manuscript of about 1225, is probably the oldest English song of which we have any record. The musical transcription is from J. F. R. Stainer and C. Stainer, *Early Bodleian Music*, Novello & Co., London, 1901. It is probably not, in spite of modern statements to the contrary, secular, since "summer," "winter," and "night" have very commonplace figurative associations in devotional poetry.

"FOWLS IN THE FRITH"[1]

Fowls in the frith,
The fishes in the flood,
And I must wax wood.
Much sorrow I walk with
For best of bone and blood.

Glossary

1 frith   wood.   **3 wood**   mad.

Note

1   This song probably dates from about 1270. The melody is not popular in character, and the usual view that the text is secular is dubious. The transcription of the music is from Stainer, *Early Bodleian Music*, Novello & Co., London, 1901.

"NOW GOES THE SUN"[1]

Now goes the sun under wood;
I pity, Mary, thy fair rode.
Now goes the sun under tree;
I pity, Mary, thy son and thee.

Glossary

1 wood   probably intended to suggest (*a*) a wood, (*b*) the Cross.   **2 rode**   face or complexion.
3 tree   the Cross.

Note

1   These verses occur in a manuscript of *The Mirror of Holy Church* by St. Edmund Rich in connection with the commitment of the Virgin to St. John at the Cross. After calling attention to the
anguish she must have felt at having lost Christ the Son of God and found for her protector only John
the son of Zebedee, St. Edmund quotes Ruth 1:20, "Call me not Naomi [i.e., 'beautiful'] but call me
Mara [i.e., 'bitter'], for the Almighty has filled me with bitterness." He then cites Cant. 1:5, "Do not
consider that I am brown because the sun hath altered my color." On the basis of this last verse, St.
Edmund says, an Englishman wrote the poem quoted above. The relation between the bride in the
Canticle of Canticles and Mary became well established during the second half of the twelfth century,
and the first seventeen verses are still used in the liturgy in connection with her feasts. The scene envisaged
in the poem is the Descent from the Cross, a subject popular in early Renaissance art, where it was often
associated with lamentation. The poem itself would have made an excellent vehicle for meditation at
Compline, the service for which usually contained a hymn to the Virgin. For the *Mirror* of St. Edmund,
see Eric Colledge, *The Mediaeval Mystics of England*, Charles Scribner's Sons, New York, 1961. The
association between Cant. 1:5 and Mary's sorrow at the Passion is supported by contemporary scriptural
commentary.

"SUMER IS ICUMEN IN"[1]

FOUR EQUAL VOICES

Sum - mer is a - com-ing in, _____ Loud-ly sing cuc - koo,

Original texts { Su - mer is i - cum-en in, _____ Lhu - de sing cuc - cu,
Per - spi - ce Christi - co - la _____ que dig - na - ti - o,

Grow - eth seed, and blow -eth mead, And springeth woods a - new.
Grow - eth sed, and blow -eth med, And springth the wo - de nu.
Ce - li - cus a - gri - co - la pro vi - tis vi - ci - o

Sing cuc - koo, Ewe now bleat-eth af - ter lamb, Lowth
Sing cuc - cu, A - we ble - teth af - ter lomb, Lhouth
Fi - li - o Non par - cens ex - po - su - it Mor -

af - ter calf the cow; Bul - lock start - eth, buck now ver - teth,
af - ter cal - ve cu; Bul - loc ster - teth, buck - e ver - teth
tis ex - i - ci - o. Qui cap - ti - vos se - mi - vi - vos

Mer - ry sing cuc - koo, Cuc - koo, cuc - koo,
Mu - rie sing cuc - cu. Cuc - cu, cuc - cu,
a sup - pli - ci - o Vi - te do - nat,

Well sing - est thou cuc - koo, Nor cease thou ne - ver now.
Wel sin - ges thu cuc - cu, Ne swik thu na - ver nu.
et se - cum co - ro - nat in ce - li so - li - o.

The 2nd, 3rd and 4th voices begin when the preceding voice reaches the ✠.
The piece concludes when the 1st voice has sung the melody through once.

Pes. TWO EQUAL VOICES

Sing cuc - koo, now Sing cuc - koo now.
Sing cuc - cu. nu Sing cuc - cu nu.

Repeat the Pes until the 1st voice has sung the melody through once.

Note

1 This is by far the most famous of Middle English songs. It may have been written by a monk of Reading Abbey around 1240, although efforts have been made by musicologists to fix a later date for the tune (ca. 1310), which is one of the few medieval melodies that are still spontaneously appealing. In l. 10 the translation should read *farteth*, not *verteth*. The music is from Harold Gleason, *Examples of Music before 1400*, Appleton-Century-Crofts, Inc., New York, 1942, and is reproduced here by permission of the publishers.

"FOR ONE THAT IS SO FAIR AND BRIGHT"[1]

For one that is so fair and bright,
 Velut maris stella,
Brighter than the day is light,
 Parens et puella.
I cry thy grace of thee,   5
Lady, pray to thy son for me
 Tam pia,
That I may come to thee,
 Maria.

Lady, best of any thing,   10
 Rosa sine spina,
Thou bore Jesu, Heaven-King,
 Gratia divina.
Of all thou bearest the prize,
High Queen in Paradise   15
 Electa,
Mother mild and maiden too
 Effecta.

In care and counsel thou art best,
 Felix fecundata;   20
To all the weary thou art rest,
 Mater honorata.

Behold thou him with gentle mood
That for us all has shed his blood
 In cruce.   25
Pray that we may come to him
 In luce.

All the world was once forlorn
 Through *Eva peccatrice*
Before Lord Jesus yet was born   30
 Ex te gentrice;
Through *Ave* he turned away
The dark night; then came the day
 Salutis;
Out of thee springs the well   35
 Virtutis.

Well thou knowest he is thy son
 Ventre quem portasti;
He'll not deny to thee thy boon,
 Parvum quem lactasti.   40
So good and so mild he is,
He brings us all into his bliss
 Superni;
He has shut up the foul pit
 Inferni.   45

Glossary

2 maris stella ("Star of the Sea") a common epithet for the Virgin, who was thought of as a guide to mariners on the storm-tossed sea of this world. **4 Parens et puella** a standard paradox used to stimulate contemplation. **11 Rosa sine spina** another common epithet for the Virgin, suggesting that although she was very beautiful, she was without sin. **32** Wordplay on *Eva* and *Ave* (the first word in the Hail Mary) was common in hymns and doctrinal pieces.

Note

1 This song was very popular and was still being sung in the fifteenth century, two hundred years after it was composed.

"ANGELUS AD VIRGINEM"[1]

Gabriel, from Heaven-King
  Sent to the maiden sweet,
Brought her blissful tiding,
  And fair he did her greet:
    "Hail be thou, full of grace aright!   5
    For God's Son, the Heaven's light,
    For man's love—
    Great God above—
    Will take
    Flesh of thee, maiden bright,   10
    Mankind free to make
    Of sin and devil's might."

Mildly she did make reply,
  The mild maiden then,
"In whatever way may I   15
  Have child without a man?"
    The angel said, "Now dread thee nought;
    Through the Holy Ghost shall be brought
    This very thing
    Whereof tiding   20
    I bring.
    All mankind will be bought
    Through thy sweet childing,
    And out of torment brought."

When the maid had understood   25
  And the angel's voice had heard,
Mildly and with gentle mood,
  To the angel, this her word:
    "Our Lord's servant maid, iwis,

I am, that above us is;   30
Concerning me
Fulfilled be
Thy saw—
That I, since His will it is,
A maiden, outside the law   35
Of mothers, have the bliss."

The angel went away then
  All out of sight;
Her womb anon to grow began
  Through Holy Spirit's might.
    In her was Christ enclosed anon,   40
    True God, true man in flesh and bone,
    And of this bride
    At proper tide
    Was born.
    Hence our joy has grown.   45
    When we were all forlorn,
    He died for us alone.

Maiden, mother without peer,
  Fully bound with grace,
Pray to Him that thou didst bear,   50
  Who chose thee for His place,
    That He forgive us sin and wrack,
    And make us whole of every lack,
    With heaven's bliss
    When our time is   55
    To go.
    Grant us now that for your sake
    We may serve Him here below
    So that He our souls will take.

Note

1   This is a translation of a Latin sequence. The song, a favorite of Nicolas in Chaucer's Miller's Tale, could be sung to the same melody in either Latin or English. The music is here reprinted by permission from *Ars Nova and the Renaissance*, The New Oxford History of Music, vol. III, Oxford University Press, London, 1960.

An - ge - lus ad vir - gi - nem sub - in - trans in con - cla - ve,

Ga - bri - el fram ev - ene king sent to the mai - de swe - te,

Vir - gi - nis for - mi - di - nem de - mul - cens, in - quit: 'A - ve, A -

Brou - te hire blis - ful ti - ding and faire he gan hire gre - ten: 'Heil

ve, re - gi - na vir - gi - num, Coe - li ter - ræ - que do - mi - num Con -

be thu ful of grace a - rith, for go - des sone this ev - ene lith for

- ci - pi - es Et pa - ri - es In - ta - cta Sa - lu - tem ho - mi -

ma - nes loven wile man bi - comen and ta - ken fles of the mai - den

- num: Tu por - ta cœ - li fa - cta, Me - de - la cri - mi - num.'

brith, man - ken fre for to ma - ken of senne and deu - les smith'.

"A SONG OF LEWES"[1]

Sit still now and hearken to me!
The King of Allemagne, by my loyalty,
Thirty thousand pounds asked he
  For to make peace in the country,
  And so he did more.   5
Richard, though thou be ever trichard,
  Trick shalt thou nevermore!

Richard of Allemagne, while he was king,
He spent all his treasure upon swyving.
He gets himself not from Wallingford a farthing;   10
Let him have as he brew, sorrow to drink,
  In spite of Windsor.
Richard, etc.

The King of Allemagne thought to do well;   15
He seized upon the mill for a castle.
With their sharp swords they ground the mill;
He thought the sails were mangonel
  To help Windsor.
Richard, etc.   20

The King of Allemagne gathered his host,
Made him a castle of a mill post;
Puffed by his pride and by his great boast,
Brought from Allemagne many a sorry ghost   25
  To store Windsor.
Richard, etc.

By God that is above us, he did much sin
That let pass over sea the Earl of Warenne;   30
He has robbed England, the moor and the fen,
The gold and the silver, and taken them then
  For love of Windsor.
Richard, etc.   35

Sir Simon de Montfort has sworn by his chin,
If he had here now the earl of Warenne,
He should never more come to his inn,
Nor with shield, nor with spear, nor other engine,
  Come to aid Windsor.   40
Richard, etc.

Sir Simon de Montfort has sworn by his top,
Had he now here Sir Hugh de Bigot,
He'd pay him back his twelve-month scot,   45
So he'd never more cast in his lot
  To help Windsor.
Richard, etc.

Be thee lief, be thee loth, Sir Edward,   50
Thou shalt ride spurless on thy lyard
All the right way to Doverward;
Shalt thou nevermore break forward,
  And that reweth sore.
Edward thou didst as a shreward,   55
  Left thine uncle's lore.
Richard, etc.

Glossary

2 King of Allemagne Richard of Cornwall, brother of Henry III, who was elected King of Germany in 1257. **7 trichard** traitor. **9 swyving** sexual intercourse. Richard was accused of an insatiable pursuit of women of all ranks. **10 Wallingford** Richard's castle, where he was imprisoned after the battle. **16 the mill** During the battle Richard took refuge in a mill, where he was captured. **30 the Earl of Warenne** John de Warenne and Hugh Bigod (l. 44) fought against Earl Simon but escaped after the battle and made their way across the Channel. **51 lyard** horse. **52 Doverward** Edward was taken to Dover Castle in 1265. **55 shreward** scoundrel. **56 thine uncle's lore** Earl Simon was Edward's uncle.

Note

1 Simon de Montfort, Earl of Leicester, leader of the baronial opposition to Henry III, was one of the most striking figures in English medieval history. After his death at the Battle of Evesham, he became a popular saint. Legends grew up around his life, and songs were sung in his memory. This song was

made after Simon's victory at Lewes. For an account of the battle by one of the most distinguished historians of our time, see Sir Maurice Powicke, *The Thirteenth Century*, Clarendon Press, Oxford, 1953, pp. 188ff. The Battle of Lewes was fought on May 14, 1264. The song must have been written before Simon's defeat at Evesham in August, 1265. It appears without music in the most famous of Middle English poetic collections, MS Harley 2253.

"ALYSOUN"[1]

Between March and April,
When the spray begins to spring,
The little bird has its will
On its song to sing.
I live in love-longing   5
For the fairest of any thing:
She may my bliss now bring,
For I to her am bound.
   An hendy hap ichabbe yhent,
   Ichot from hevene it is me sent: 10
   From alle wymmen mi love is lent,
   And lyht on Alysoun.

In hue her hair is fair to see,
Her brows are brown, her eyes are black.
With lovesome cheer she looks on me.   15
Her middle small betrays no lack;
Unless she'll take me now, alack,
For hers, without turning back,

I'll suffer death's abrupt attack,
And fated fall a-down.   20

At night, when I turn and wake—
For this my cheeks are growing wan—
Lady, all for your sweet sake
Longing has me quite undone.
Of clever men there now is none   25
Can count her beauties every one;
Her neck is whiter than the swan—
The fairest maid in town!

Wooing keeps me up too late,
Weary as water on the shore;   30
Lest any take from me my mate
I have yearnéd yore.
Better to suffer a little sore
Than mourn forevermore.
Loveliest under gore,   35
Listen to my round.

Glossary

9–12 *An hendy hap*, etc.   The refrain, which has a jaunty rhythm, has been left in Middle English: "I have seized a happy chance, which I thought came to me from heaven. My love has come away from all other women and alighted on Alysoun." **35 gore** clothing. **36 round** secret message.

Note

1 This selection, like the last one, is from MS Harley 2253. The name *Alysoun* or *Alis* seems to have been associated frequently with strong physical attractiveness.

"WINTER SONG"[1]

Winter wakens all my care;
Now these trees are growing bare.
Oft I ponder in despair
   When it comes into my thought
   How this world's joy goes all to nought.   5

Now it's here, and now it's gone,
As though it never yet were won;

One truth is clear, whate'er be done:
   All passes soon but God's own will,
   And we shall die, come good or ill.   10

All the grain men bury green
Soon decays below, unseen.
Jesus, help it to be seen,
   And shield us from the pit of Hell;
   I may not here much longer dwell.   15

Note

1   This lyric, like the last two, is from MS Harley 2253. Winter is a figure for adverse fortune, or the fading away in the mind of those earthly joys associated with summer and good fortune. The last stanza of the poem is based on the imagery of John 12:24–25: "Amen, amen, I say to you, unless the grain of wheat falling into the ground die, itself remaineth alone. But if it die, it bringeth forth much fruit. He that loveth his life shall lose it, and he that hateth his life in this world, keepeth it unto life eternal."

"UNDO THY DOOR"[1]

Undo thy door, my spouse so dear,
Alas! why stand I locked out here?
   I am thy Lord to take.
Look at my locks and at my head,
And all my limbs with blood o'erspread   5
   For thy sake.

Alas! Alas! Ill have I sped,
For since Jesu is from me fled,
   My true love,
Without the gate He stands alone,   10

Sorrowfully makes his moan
   To me above.

Lord, for sin I sorrow sore;
Forgive, and I will do no more.
With all my might I'll sin forsake   15
And open my heart thee in to take.
Thy heart is cloven our love to catch;
Thy love is chosen us all to fetch.
It would pierce my heart if I were just,
Thy sweet love to keep in trust.   20
Pierce my heart with thy loving
That in thee I'll have my dwelling.

Note

1   This song is from a commonplace book compiled by a Franciscan friar, John Grimestone, in 1372. The first fourteen lines constitute a dialogue between Christ, the husband, and the soul which should be His spouse. The imagery is based generally on the Canticle of Canticles, which was frequently read as an epithalamium celebrating the marriage of the human soul to Christ. In ll. 13–22 the soul expresses its resolution to become a fitting bride.

"TEACH TO LOVE AS I LOVE THEE"[1]

Teach to love as I love thee;
On all my limbs thou mayest see
How sore they quake for cold.
For thee I suffer now much woe,
Love me, sweet—the rest forego—   5
To thee I cling and hold.

Jesu, my sweet son so dear,
In humble bed thou liest here,
And that doth grieve me sore;
For thy bed is like a bier.
Ox and ass are with thee here,   10
And I that weep therefore.

Jesu, sweet, be not wroth;
I have neither clout nor cloth
Thee in for to fold.
In my skirt I shall thee wrap.   15
Lay thy feet against my pap,
And keep thee from the cold.

Cold takes thee, I may well see.
For love of man all this must be
That thou must suffer woe.   20
For better it is to suffer this
Than man should lose all heaven's bliss;
Thou must redeem him so.

Since it must be that thou must die
To save men from the devil sly,   25
Thy sweet will be done.
But let me not stay here too long;
After thy death take me along
To be with thee as one.

Figure 29 *Nativity.*

Note

   1   This lyric, like the last one, is from the commonplace book of John Grimestone. The Christ child speaks in the first stanza, and the remainder of the poem constitutes Mary's reply. The scene described is that conventionally represented in late Gothic Nativities. It is best to think of the first stanza as an address to mankind generally rather than as a speech addressed exclusively to Mary.

"A MAIDEN IN THE MOOR LAY"[1]

A maiden in the moor lay,
  In the moor lay,
Seven nights full—
Seven nights full—
A maiden in the moor lay,   5
  In the moor lay,
Seven nights full—
Seven nights full
  And a day.

Well was her meat.   10
  What was her meat?
The primrose and the—
The primrose and the—
Well was her meat.
  What was her meat?   15
The primrose and the—
The primrose and the
  Violet.

Well was her drink.
  What was her drink?   20
The chilled water of the—
The chilled water of the—
Well was her drink.
  What was her drink?
The chilled water of the—   25
The chilled water of the
  Well spring.

Well was her bower.
  What was her bower?
The red rose and the—   30
The red rose and the—
Well was her bower.
  What was her bower?
The red rose and the—
The red rose and the   35
  Lily flower.

Note

1 Richard de Ledrede, a Franciscan who served as Bishop of Ossory, Ireland, between 1317 and 1360, found his clergy singing songs that he regarded as being "theatrical, wicked, and secular." He wrote Latin lyrics to replace them. Among the "wicked" songs replaced was this one, for which the Bishop substituted a Latin lyric beginning "*Peperit virgo.*" Modern scholars disagree about whether Bishop Ledrede's ideas of wickedness should still be maintained. A literal picture of a maiden lying for seven nights and a day in a desert under a bower of lilies and roses where she ate primroses and violets and drank cold water has been taken as a suggestion of witchcraft of some sort. The activity is, to say the least, suspicious and peculiar. On the other hand, the poem may not be literal at all. *Night* and *desert* are figurative commonplaces associated with the world under the Old Law; eight, the number of the day in the poem, is conventionally associated with Christ, whose day is Sunday, or the eighth day (i.e., the octave of Sunday); and the various flowers, as a glance at the Wilton Diptych will show, were conventionally associated with Mary. As for the water, there is still current a folk hymn beginning, "May the waters be chilly, O Lord, when I die." That is, the water of grace is conventionally cold. However, the reader is at liberty to interpret the song for himself, and may, if he wishes, regard it as being "theatrical" or "wicked." However, Franciscans had a reputation for being literal-minded.

"AS I WENT ON YOLE DAY"[1]

Kyrie, so *kyrie*
   Jankin singeth merie,
     With *eleyson.*

As I went on Yole day
   In oure prosession,
Knew I joly Jankyn,
   Be his merie tone.
Jankyn began the offis   5
   On the Yole day;
And yit me thinketh it dos me good,
   So merie gan he say
     Kyrieleyson.

Jankin red the pistil   10
   Full fair and full well,
And yit me thinketh it dos me good,
   As ever have I sel.

Jankin at the *Sanctus*
   Craketh a merie note,   15
And yit me thinketh it dos me good,
   I payed for his cote.
Jankin craketh notes
   An hunderid on a knot,
And yit he hakketh hem smallere   20
   Than wortes to the pot.
     Kyrieleyson.

Jankin at the *Agnus*
   Bereth the *Pax* brede;
He twinkeled, but said nought,   25
   And on mine fote he trede.
Benedicamus Domino,
   Crist from schame me schilde!
Deo gracias thereto.
   Alas, I go with childe.   30
     Kyrieleyson.

Glossary

10 pistil epistle. **13 sel** happiness. **21 wortes** herbs.

Note

1 Since this song is late and not very difficult, it has been left in Middle English. The text is that in E. K. Chambers and F. Sedgwick, *Early English Lyrics*, Sidgwick and Jackson, Ltd., London, 1921. The song is supposed to be sung by one Alysoun, whose name makes a pun with *Eleyson* in the *Kyrie*, and who has been overfamiliar with a clerk named Jankyn. Readers of Chaucer will recall an affair between a clerical Jankyn and an amorous Alysoun. The action of treading on the foot of a member of the opposite sex was a conventional amorous gesture in late medieval iconography.

"TO ROSEMOUNDE"[1]

Madame, ye ben of al beaute shryne
As fer as cercled is the mapemounde,
For as the cristal glorious ye shyne,
And lyke ruby ben your chekes rounde.
Therwith ye ben so mery and so jocounde   5
That at a revel whan that I see you daunce,

It is an oynement unto my wounde,
Thogh ye to me ne do no daliaunce.

For thogh I wepe of teres ful a tyne,
Yet may that wo myn herte nat confounde.   10
Your semly voys, that ye so smal out-twyne,
Maketh my thoght in joy and blis habounde.
So curtaysly I go, with love bounde,

That to my self I sey, in my penaunce,
Suffyseth me to love you, Rosemounde,   15
Though ye to me ne do no daliaunce.

Nas never pyk walwed in galauntyne
As I in love am walwed and ywounde,

For which ful ofte I of myself devyne
That I am trewe Tristam the secounde.   20
My love may not refreyd be nor affounde.
I brenne ay in amorous plesaunce.
Do what you list, I wyl your thral be founde,
Thogh ye to me ne do no daliaunce.

—Geoffrey Chaucer

Glossary

2 mapemounde map of the world. **9 tyne** barrel. **17 walwed in galauntyne** wallowed in sauce. **21 refreyd** cooled; **affounde** benumbed with cold.

Note

1   This humorous and good-natured *balade* is in the typical Chaucerian manner.

"A BALADE OF GOOD COUNSEL" [1]

Flee fro the prees, and dwelle with sothfastnesse.
Suffice to thee thy good, though it be smal;
For hord hath hate, and climbing tikelnesse,
Prees hath envye, and wele blent overal.
Savor no more than thee bihove shal;   5
Reule wel thyself, that other folk canst rede,
And trouthe thee shal delivere, it is no drede.

Tempest thee noght al croked to redresse,
In trust of hir that turneth as a bal.
Gret reste stant in litel besinesse;   10
And eek be war to sporne ageyn an al.
Stryve noght, as doth the crokke with the wal.
Daunte thy self, that dauntest otheres dede,
And trouthe thee shal delivere, it is no drede.

That thee is sent, receyve in buxumnesse.   15
The wrastling for this worlde axeth a fal.
Her nis non hoom, her nis but wildernesse.
Forth, pilgrim, forth! Forth, beste, out of thy stal!
Know thy contree! Look up! thank God of al;
Hold the hye wey, and lat thy gost thee lede,   20
And trouthe the shal delivere, it is no drede.

Envoy

Therefore, thou vache! leve thyn old wrecchednesse.
Unto the world leve now to be thral.
Crye Him mercy, that of His hy goodnesse
Made thee of noght, and in especial   25
Draw unto him, and pray in general
For thee, and eek for other, hevenlich mede,
And trouthe thee shal delivere, it is no drede.

—Geoffrey Chaucer

Glossary

4 blent blinds (deceives). **6 rede** advise. **7 trouthe** Cf. John 8:32. **9 hir that turneth as a bal** Fortune. **11 sporne agayn an al** kick against an awl. **15 buxumnesse** humility. **18 pilgrim** Figuratively, all Christians are pilgrims in this world. **beste** beast, a creature without reason. **19 contree** i.e., heaven; cf. Boethius, *Consolation*, 1:5, 6. **22 vache** cow (unreasoning creature). **27 mede** reward.

Note

1   This poem expresses well the basic philosophical attitude that pervades Chaucer's work. Those who wish to understand Chaucer should therefore study it carefully.

"GENTILESSE"[1]

The firste Stok, fader of gentilesse,
What man that claymeth gentil for to be
Must folowe His trace, and alle his wittes dresse
Vertu to sewe, and vyces for to flee.
For unto vertu longeth dignitee,   5
And noght the revers, saufly dar I deme,
Al were he mytre, croune, or diademe.

This firste Stok was ful of rightwisnesse,
Trewe of his word, sobre, pitous, and fre,
Clene of his goste, and loved besinesse,   10

Ageinst the vyce of slouthe, in honestee;
And but His heir love vertu, as dide He,
He is noght gentil, thogh he riche seme,
Al were he mytre, croune, or diademe.

Vyce may wel be heir to old richesse;   15
But ther may no man, as men may wel see,
Bequethe his heir his vertuous noblesse
That is appropred unto no degree
But to the Firste Fader in megestee,
That maketh him his heir, that can Him queme,   20
Al were he mytre, croune, or diademe.

—Geoffrey Chaucer

Glossary

1 **Stok** stock, i.e., God; **gentilesse** nobility. **4 sewe** pursue. **9 fre** generous. **10–11 besinesse . . . in honestee** useful activity as opposed to sloth, which might include either idleness or fruitless activity. **15 Vyce** a vicious person. **20 queme** please.

Note

1 The doctrine that true nobility rests on virtue is a medieval commonplace. See Boethius, *Consolation*, 3: pr. 6, met. 6. Inherited nobility implied a necessity to honor the virtues of one's ancestors and to emulate them. It was obvious, however, that a nobleman by birth might be villainous or base in action. Chaucer's statement of the doctrine, which probably owes something directly both to Boethius and to Dante, is especially vigorous.

"LAK OF STEDFASTNESSE"[1]

Som tyme this world was so stedfast and stable
That mannes word was obligacioun;
And now it is so fals and deceivable
That word and deed, as in conclusioun,
Ben nothing oon, for turned up-so-doun   5
Is al this world for mede and wilfulnesse,
That al is lost for lak of stedfastnesse.

What maketh this world to be so variable
But lust that folk have in dissensioun?
For among us now a man is holde unable,   10
But if he can, by som collusioun,
Don his neighbor wrong or oppressioun.
What causeth this but wilful wrecchednesse,
That al is lost for lak of stedfastnesse?

Trouthe is put doun, resoun is holden fable;   15
Vertu hath now no dominacioun;
Pitee exyled, no man is merciable;
Through covetyse is blent discrecioun.
The world hath mad a permutacioun
Fro right to wrong, fro truth to fikelnesse,   20
That al is lost for lak of stedfastnesse.

L'envoy to King Richard

O prince, desyre to be honorable,
Cherish thy folk and hate extorcioun!
Suffre no thing that may be reprevable
To thyn estat don in thy regioun.   25
Shew forth thy swerd of castigacioun,
Dred God, do law, love trouthe and worthinesse,
And wed thy folk agayn to stedfastnesse.

—Geoffrey Chaucer

Glossary

2 obligacioun In a feudal society, where the contractual arrangements between lord and vassal were verbal, truth to one's word was extremely important. **4 word and deed** The standard definition of a lie was to have one thing in the heart but to express something else in speech; when word and deed are not "oon," it follows that what was spoken was not in the heart. **5 nothing oon** not at all the same. **6 mede** reward or material profit; **wilfulnesse** wilful action according to selfish desire rather than reasonable action. **15 resoun** the power in man which enables him to control desire in the light of truth. **18 blent** blinded; **discrecioun** the ability to choose reasonably (*not* the ability to choose warily in self-interest).

Note

1 This poem reveals the kind of dissatisfaction with his own age that formed the basis for Chaucer's satire throughout his work. His criticism is usually humorous, but in this poem to King Richard he seeks to make it as explicit as possible.

"I SING OF A MAIDEN"[1]

I sing of a maiden
  That is makeles,
King of all Kinges
  To her son sche ches.
He cam also stille   5
  There his moder was,
As dew in Aprille
  That falleth on the grass.
He cam also stille
  To his moderes bour,   10

As dew in Aprille   15
  That falleth on the flour.
He cam also stille
  There his moder lay,
As dew in Aprille
  That falleth on the spray.   20
Moder and maiden
  Was never non but sche;
Well may swich a lady
  Godes moder be.

Glossary

2 makeles without a mate. **4 ches** chose.

Note

1 This very attractive song to the Virgin has been printed many times. The use of dew as a sign for grace is very old and appears in other poems on the same theme. For an interesting critical analysis, see Leo Spitzer, "*Explication de texte* applied to Three Great Middle English Poems," in *Essays on English and American Literature*, Princeton University Press, Princeton, N.J., 1962. The technique of this analysis, however, has severe limitations.

In a time of a somers day,
  The sune shon full merily that tide,
I took my hawke me for to play,
  My spaniell renning by my side.
A feasaunt henne than gon I see;   5
  My houndes put her sone to flight;
I lett my hawke unto her flee;
  To me it was a deinty sight.

My faucon flewe fast unto her pray;
  My hound gan renne with glad chere.   10
And sone I spurned in my way;
  My leg was hent all in a breer.
This breer forsothe it did me gref,
  I wis it made me to turn aye,
For he bare writing in every leff,   15
  This Latin word *Revertere*.

I kneled and pulled this breer me fro,
  And rede this word ful merily.
My hart fell down unto my toc,
  That was before full likingly.   20
I lett may hawke and feasaunt fare;
  My spaniell fell down unto my knee.
It took me with a sighing farc,
  This new lessun *Revertere*.

Liking is moder of sinnes all,   25
  And norse to every wiked dede;
To much mischefe she maketh men fall,
  And of sorow the daunce she doth lede.
This hawke of youth is high of porte;
  And wildness maketh him wide to flee, 30
And oft to fall in wiked sorte;
  And then is best *Revertere*.

Figure 30 *The hunt of love.*

Glossary

11 spurned stumbled. **15 leff** leaf. **20 likingly** bent on the pursuit of pleasure. **25 Liking** pleasure (cf. Venus). **29 hawke of youth** A frequent medieval iconographic device portrays a lover interested in pleasure as a young man with a hawk. The hawk is sometimes shown being presented to him by the god of love.

Figure 31 *Shepherds.*

"A PASTOURELLE"[1]

"Hey, troly loly lo, maid, whither go you?"
"I go to the meadow to milk my cow."
"Then at the meadow I will you meet,
To gather the flowers both fair and sweet."
"Nay, God forbid! That may not be!   5
I wis my mother then shall us see."

"Now in this meadow fair and green
We may us sport and not be seen;
And if ye will, I shall consent.
How say ye, maid? Be ye content?"   10
"Nay, in good faith, I'll not mell with you!
I pray you, sir, let me go milk my cow."

"Why will ye not give me no comfort,
That now in these fields we may us sport?"
"Nay, God forbid! That may not be!   15
I wis my mother then shall us see."

"Ye be so nice, and so meet of age,
That ye greatly move my courage.
Sith I love you, love me again;
Let us make one, though we be twain."   20
"I pray you, sir, let me go milk my cow."

"Ye have my heart, say what ye will,
Wherefore ye must my mind fulfil,
And grant me here your maidenhead,
Or elles I shall for you be dead."   25
"I pray you, sir, let me go milk my cow."

"Then for this once I shall you spare;
But the next time ye must beware
How in the meadow ye milk your cow.
Adieu, farewell! And kiss me now!"   30
"I pray you, sir, let me go milk my cow."

Glossary

6 wis know. **11 mell** meddle. **17 meet** proper. **18 courage** heart.

Note

1   The MS in which this poem appears is said to have belonged to Henry VIII. The above version follows the arrangement adopted by Chambers and Sidgwick. In the typical *pastourelle* a knight meets a girl of humble birth in the countryside and attempts to seduce her, with results that vary from poem to poem. The earliest surviving example of the type is by the troubadour Marcabru, whose rustic wench succeeds in demonstrating that she is more noble than the knight who approaches her and in turning him away in derision.

IX

MIDDLE ENGLISH
LITERATURE: ROMANCE

The word *romanz* in Old French was first used to mean a work translated from Latin into the vernacular, but was soon applied to any work in Old French. During the thirteenth century, however, it came to mean specifically a fabulous narrative of considerable length and varied incident usually written in octosyllabic verse. It was distinguished from the *lai* or *conte*, which was shorter, confined to a central incident, and more rapid in its narrative development. The first romances were based on classical sources, notably on the epics of Vergil and Statius. Greco-Byzantine and other sources were later used for narrative material in romances, but the most

Facing page: The temptation of Sir Gawain.

famous romances are those centering on King Arthur and Tristran. The first Arthurian romance was the *Erec* of Chrétien de Troyes, probably written between 1150 and 1170. During the late twelfth and thirteenth centuries long romances in prose were composed.

Over forty works usually called romances survive in Middle English, the best of which is *Sir Gawain and the Green Knight*, printed below. Many of the others are inferior imitations of French sources, and still others are properly *lais* or *contes* rather than romances. The most attractive poem of the last type is the fourteenth-century *Sir Orfeo*. The most famous of the romances on English, as distinct from British or Arthurian, themes is *Havelok the Dane*. In England the romance has no strict form and is not a genre in the modern sense of the word.

The most comprehensive collection of verse romances in English is W. H. French and C. B. Hale, *Middle English Metrical Romances*, Prentice-Hall, Inc., Englewood Cliffs, N.J., 1930. A representative selection is available in Donald B. Sands, *Middle English Verse Romances*, Holt, Rinehart and Winston, Inc., New York, 1966. For the development of the romance in France, see the relevant chapters in Urban Tigner Holmes, Jr., *A History of Old French Literature*, F. S. Crofts, Inc., New York, 1938. Arthurian romances are discussed, but from a uniform and somewhat restricted point of view, in R. S. Loomis, ed., *Arthurian Literature in the Middle Ages*, Clarendon Press, Oxford, 1959. For the English romances in particular, see Laura A. Hibbard, *Mediaeval Romance in England*, Oxford University Press, New York, 1924. W. P. Ker's book, *Epic and Romance*, Dover Publications, Inc., New York, 1957, although first published many years ago, is still attractive and stimulating.

 # A. Sir Gawain and the Green Knight

Sir Gawain and the Green Knight, universally acclaimed as the finest romance in Middle English, survives in a manuscript of about 1400 containing three other poems—" Pearl," " Purity," and " Patience"—probably written by the same author. About this author we know nothing except that the poems reveal a good education, probably ecclesiastical, and that they are written in a dialect that suggests Lancashire or Cheshire. The use of alliteration in the poems rather than a type of verse more closely resembling French models also suggests a provincial origin. Among the poems in the manuscript, Gawain and " Pearl" have attracted most attention.

Translations of all the poems are now available in John Gardner, The Complete Works of the Gawain Poet, University of Chicago Press, Chicago, 1965. The Middle English text of Gawain has been well edited by J. R. R. Tolkien and E. V. Gordon, Sir Gawain and the Green Knight, second edition revised by Norman Davis, Clarendon Press, Oxford, 1967. Recent interest in the poem has produced a number of important studies, among which are Henry L. Savage, The Gawain Poet, The University of North Carolina Press, Chapel Hill, 1956; Hans Schnyder, Sir Gawain and the Green Knight, Francke Verlag, Bern, 1961; Marie Borroff, Sir Gawain and the Green Knight, Yale University Press, New Haven, Conn., 1962; Larry D. Benson, Art and Tradition in Sir Gawain and the Green Knight, Rutgers University Press, New Brunswick, N.J., 1965; and J. A. Burrow, A Reading of Sir Gawain and the Green Knight, Routledge & Kegan Paul, Ltd., London, 1965. This translation is by Theodore Howard Banks, Jr.

SIR GAWAIN AND THE GREEN KNIGHT

When the siege and assault ceased at Troy,[1] and
    the city
Was broken, and burned all to brands and to
    ashes,
The warrior who wove there the web of his
    treachery
Tried was for treason, the truest on earth.
'T was Æneas, who later with lords of his lineage
Provinces quelled, and became the possessors
Of well-nigh the whole of the wealth of the
    West Isles.
Then swiftly to Rome rich Romulus journeyed,
And soon with great splendor builded that city,
Named with his own name, as now we still
    know it.   10
Ticius to Tuscany turns for his dwellings;
In Lombardy Langobard lifts up his homes;
And far o'er the French flood fortunate Brutus
With happiness Britain on hillsides full broad
                 Doth found.
        War, waste, and wonder there
        Have dwelt within its bound;
        And bliss has changed to care
        In quick and shifting round.[2]

And after this famous knight founded his
    Britain,   20
Bold lords were bred there, delighting in battle,
Who many times dealt in destruction. More
    marvels
Befell in those fields since the days of their
    finding
Than any where else upon earth that I know of.
Yet of all kings who came there was Arthur most
    comely;
My intention is, therefore, to tell an adventure
Strange and surprising, as some men consider,
A strange thing among all the marvels of Arthur.
And if you will list to the lay for a little,
Forthwith I shall tell it, as I in the town   30
               Heard it told
        As it doth fast endure
        In story brave and bold,
        Whose words are fixed and sure,
        Known in the land of old.

In Camelot Arthur the King[3] lay at Christmas,
With many a peerless lord princely companioned,
The whole noble number of knights of the
    Round Table;
Here right royally held his high revels,
Care-free and mirthful. Now much of the
    company,   40
Knightly born gentlemen, joyously jousted,
Now came to the court to make caroles; so kept
    they
For full fifteen days this fashion of feasting,
All meat and all mirth that a man might devise.
Glorious to hear was the glad-hearted gaiety,
Dancing at night, merry din in the daytime;
So found in the courts and the chambers the
    fortunate
Ladies and lords the delights they best loved.
In greatest well-being abode they together:
The knights whose renown was next to the
    Savior's,   50
The loveliest ladies who ever were living,
And he who held court, the most comely of
    kings.
For these fine folk were yet in their first flush of
    youth
               Seated there,
        The happiest of their kind,
        With a king beyond compare.
        It would be hard to find
        A company so fair.

And now while the New Year was young
    were the nobles
Doubly served as they sat on the dais,   60
When Arthur had come to the hall with his court,
In the chapel had ceased the singing of mass;
Loud shouts were there uttered by priests and by
    others,
Anew praising Noel, naming it often.
Then hastened the lords to give handsel, cried
    loudly
These gifts of the New Year, and gave them in
    person;
Debated about them busily, briskly.
Even though they were losers, the ladies laughed
    loudly,
Nor wroth was the winner, as well ye may know.

All this manner of mirth they made till meat-
time,   70
Then when they had washed, they went to be
seated,
Were placed in the way that appeared most
proper,
The best men above. And Guinevere, beautiful,
Was in the midst of the merriment seated
Upon the rich dais, adorned all about:
Fine silks on all sides, and spread as a canopy
Tapestries treasured of Tars and Toulouse,
Embroidered and set with stones most splendid—
They'd prove of great price if ye pence gave to
buy them
                 Some day.   80
       The comeliest was the Queen,
       With dancing eyes of gray.
       That a fairer he had seen
       No man might truly say.

  But Arthur would eat not till all were attended;
Youthfully mirthful and merry in manner,
He loved well his life, and little it pleased him
Or long to be seated, or long to lie down,
His young blood and wild brain were so busy and
brisk.
Moreover, the King was moved by a custom   90
He once had assumed in a spirit of splendor:
Never to fall to his feast on a festival
Till a strange story of something eventful
Was told him, some marvel that merited
credence
Of kings, or of arms, or all kinds of adventures;
Or some one besought him to send a true knight
To join him in proving the perils of jousting,
Life against life, each leaving the other
To have, as fortune would help him, the fairer
lot.
This, when the King held his court, was his
custom   100
At every fine feast 'mid his followers, freemen,
             In hall.
       And so with countenance clear
       He stands there strong and tall,
       Alert on that New Year,
       And makes much mirth with all.

  At his place the strong King stands in person,
full courtly

Talking of trifles before the high table.
There sat the good Gawain by Guinevere's side,
And Sir Agravain, he of the Hard Hand, also,   110
True knights, and sons of the sister of Arthur.
At the top, Bishop Baldwin the table begins,
And Ywain beside him ate, Urien's son.
On the dais these sat, and were served with dis-
tinction;
Then many a staunch, trusty man at the side
tables.
The first course was served to the sharp sound of
trumpets,
With numerous banners beneath hanging
brightly.
Then newly the kettledrums sounded and noble
pipes;
Wild and loud warbles awakened such echoes
That many a heart leaped on high at their
melody.   120
Came then the choice meats, cates rare and
costly,
Of fair and fresh food such profusion of dishes
'T was hard to find place to put by the people
The silver that carried the various stews
             On the cloth.
       Each to his best loved fare
       Himself helps, nothing loth;
       Each two, twelve dishes share,
       Good beer and bright wine both.[4]

  And now I will say nothing more of their
service,   130
For well one may know that naught there was
wanted.
Now another new noise drew nigh of a sudden,
To let all the folk take their fill of the feast.
And scarcely the music had ceased for a moment,
The first course been suitably served in the court,
When a being most dreadful burst through the
hall-door,
Among the most mighty of men in his measure.
From his throat to his thighs so thick were his
sinews,
His loins and his limbs so large and so long,
That I hold him half-giant, the hugest of men,   140
And the handsomest, too, in his height, upon
horseback.
Though stalwart in breast and in back was his
body,

His waist and his belly were worthily small;
Fashioned fairly he was in his form, and in
     features
               Cut clean.
          Men wondered at the hue
          That in his face was seen.
          A splendid man to view
          He came, entirely green.[5]

All green was the man, and green were his
     garments: 150
A coat, straight and close, that clung to his sides,
A bright mantle on top of this, trimmed on the
     inside
With closely-cut fur, right fair, that showed
     clearly,
The lining with white fur most lovely, and hood
     too,
Caught back from his locks, and laid on his
     shoulders,
Neat stockings that clung to his calves, tightly
     stretched,
Of the same green, and under them spurs of gold
     shining
Brightly on bands of fine silk, richly barred;
And under his legs, where he rides, guards of
     leather.
His vesture was verily color of verdure: 160
Both bars of his belt and other stones, beautiful,
Richly arranged in his splendid array
On himself and his saddle, on silken designs.
'T would be truly too hard to tell half the trifles
Embroidered about it with birds and with flies
In gay, verdant green with gold in the middle;
The bit-studs, the crupper, the breast-trappings'
     pendants,
And everything metal enamelled in emerald.
The stirrups he stood on the same way were
     colored,
His saddle-bows too, and the studded nails
     splendid,   170
That all with green gems ever glimmered and
     glinted.
The horse he bestrode was in hue still the same,
               Indeed;
          Green, thick, and of great height,
          And hard to curb, a steed
          In broidered bridle bright
          That such a man would need.

This hero in green was habited gaily,
And likewise the hair on the head of his good
     horse;
Fair, flowing tresses enfolded his shoulders,   180
And big as a bush a beard hung on his breast.
This, and the hair from his head hanging
     splendid,
Was clipped off evenly over his elbows,
In cut like a king's hood, covering the neck,
So that half of his arms were held underneath it.
The mane of the mighty horse much this re-
     sembled,
Well curled and combed, and with many knots
     covered,
Braided with gold threads about the fair green,
Now a strand made of hair, now a second of
     gold.
The forelock and tail were twined in this fashion, 190
And both of them bound with a band of bright
     green.
For the dock's length the tail was decked with
     stones dearly,
And then was tied with a thong in a tight knot,
Where many bright bells of burnished gold rang.
In the hall not one single man's seen before this
Such a horse here on earth, such a hero as on him
               Goes.
          That his look was lightning bright
          Right certain were all those
          Who saw. It seemed none might   200
          Endure beneath his blows.

Yet the hero carried nor helmet nor hauberk,
But bare was of armor, breastplate or gorget,
Spear-shaft or shield, to thrust or to smite.
But in one hand he bore a bough of bright
     holly,[6]
That grows most greenly when bare are the
     groves,
In the other an axe, gigantic, awful,
A terrible weapon, wondrous to tell of.
Large was the head, in length a whole ell-yard,
The blade of green steel and beaten gold both;   210
The bit had a broad edge, and brightly was
     burnished,
As suitably shaped as sharp razors for shearing.
This steel by its strong shaft the stern hero
     gripped:
With iron it was wound to the end of the wood,

And in work green and graceful was everywhere
    graven.
About it a fair thong was folded, made fast
At the head, and oft looped down the length of
    the handle.
To this were attached many splendid tassels,
On buttons of bright green richly embroidered.
Thus into the hall came the hero, and hastened   220
Direct to the dais, fearing no danger.
He gave no one greeting, but haughtily gazed,
And his first words were, "Where can I find him
    who governs
This goodly assemblage? for gladly that man
I would see and have speech with." So saying,
    from toe

              To crown
        On the knights his look he threw,
        And rolled it up and down;
        He stopped to take note who
        Had there the most renown.   230

There sat all the lords, looking long at the
    stranger,[7]
Each man of them marvelling what it might
    mean
For a horse and a hero to have such a hue.
It seemed to them green as the grown grass, or
    greener,
Gleaming more bright than on gold green
    enamel.
The nobles who stood there, astonished, drew
    nearer,
And deeply they wondered what deed he would
    do.
Since never a marvel they'd met with like this
    one,
The folk all felt it was magic or phantasy.
Many great lords then were loth to give answer,   240
And sat stone-still, at his speaking astounded,
In swooning silence that spread through the hall.
As their speech on a sudden was stilled, fast
    asleep

              They did seem.
        They felt not only fright
        But courtesy, I deem.
        Let him address the knight,
        Him whom they all esteem.

This happening the King, ever keen and
    courageous,
Saw from on high, and saluted the stranger   250
Suitably, saying, "Sir, you are welcome.
I, the head of this household, am Arthur;
In courtesy light, and linger, I pray you,
And later, my lord, we shall learn your desire."
"Nay, so help me He seated on high," quoth the
    hero,
"My mission was not to remain here a moment;
But, sir, since thy name is so nobly renowned,
Since thy city the best is considered, thy barons
The stoutest in steel gear that ride upon steeds,
Of all men in the world the most worthy and
    brave,   260
Right valiant to play with in other pure pastimes,
Since here, I have heard, is the highest of
    courtesy—
Truly, all these things have brought me at this
    time.
Sure ye may be by this branch that I bear
That I pass as in peace, proposing no fight.
If I'd come with comrades, equipped for a quarrel,
I have at my home both hauberk and helmet,
Shield and sharp spear, brightly shining, and
    other
Weapons to wield, full well I know also.
Yet softer my weeds are, since warfare I wished
    not;   270
But art thou as bold as is bruited by all,
Thou wilt graciously grant me the game that I
    ask for

              By right."
        Arthur good answer gave,
        And said, "Sir courteous knight,
        If battle here you crave,
        You shall not lack a fight,"[8]

"Nay, I ask for no fight;[9] in faith, now I tell
    thee
But beardless babes are about on this bench.
Were I hasped in my armor, and high on a horse,   280
Here is no man to match me, your might is so
    feeble.
So I crave but a Christmas game in this court;
Yule and New Year are come, and here men
    have courage;

If one in this house himself holds so hardy,
So bold in his blood, in his brain so unbalanced
To dare stiffly strike one stroke for another,
I give this gisarme, this rich axe, as a gift to him,
Heavy enough, to handle as pleases him;
Bare as I sit, I shall bide the first blow.
If a knight be so tough as to try what I tell,   290
Let him leap to me lightly; I leave him this
    weapon,
Quitclaim it forever, to keep as his own;
And his stroke here, firm on this floor, I shall
    suffer,
This boon if thou grant'st me, the blow with
    another
                    To pay;
            Yet let his respite be
            A twelvemonth and a day.
            Come, let us quickly see
            If one here aught dare say."

    If at first he had startled them, stiller then sat
        there   300
The whole of the court, low and high, in the hall.
The knight on his steed turned himself in his
    saddle,
And fiercely his red eyes he rolled all around,
Bent his bristling brows, with green gleaming
    brightly,
And waved his beard, waiting for one there to
    rise.
And when none of the knights spoke, he coughed
    right noisily,
Straightened up proudly, and started to speak:
"What!" quoth the hero, "Is this Arthur's house-
    hold,
The fame of whose fellowship fills many
    kingdoms?
Now where is your vainglory? Where are your
    victories?   310
Where is your grimness, your great words, your
    anger?
For now the Round Table's renown and its revel
Is worsted by one word of one person's speech,
For all shiver with fear before a stroke's shown."
Then so loudly he laughed that the lord was
    grieved greatly,
And into his fair face his blood shot up fiercely

                    For shame.
            As wroth as wind he grew,
            And all there did the same.
            The King that no fear knew   320
            Then to that stout man came.

    And said, "Sir, by heaven, strange thy request
        is;
As folly thou soughtest, so shouldest thou find it.
I know that not one of the knights is aghast
Of thy great words. Give me thy weapon, for
    God's sake,
And gladly the boon thou hast begged I shall
    grant thee."
He leaped to him quickly, caught at his hand,
And fiercely the other lord lights on his feet.
Now Arthur lays hold of the axe by the handle,
As if he would strike with it, swings it round
    sternly.   330
Before him the strong man stood, in stature
A head and more higher than all in the house.
Stroking his beard, he stood with stern bearing,
And with a calm countenance drew down his
    coat,
No more frightened or stunned by the axe
    Arthur flourished
Than if on the bench some one brought him a
    flagon
                    Of wine.
            Gawain by Guinevere
            Did to the King incline:
            "I pray in accents clear   340
            To let this fray be mine."[10]

    "If you now, honored lord," said this knight
        to King Arthur,
"Would bid me to step from this bench, and to
    stand there
Beside you—so could I with courtesy quit then
The table, unless my liege lady disliked it—
I'd come to your aid before all your great court.
For truly I think it a thing most unseemly
So boldly to beg such a boon in your hall here,
Though you in person are pleased to fulfil it,
While here on the benches such brave ones are
    seated,   350

Than whom under heaven, I think, none are
    higher
In spirit, none better in body for battle.
I am weakest and feeblest in wit, I know well,
And my life, to say truth, would be least loss of
    any.
I only since you are my uncle have honor;
Your blood the sole virtue I bear in my body.
Unfit is this foolish affair for you. Give it
To me who soonest have sought it, and let
All this court if my speech is not seemly, decide
                Without blame."   360
        The nobles gather round,
        And all advise the same:
        To free the King that's crowned,
        And Gawain give the game.

    The King then commanded his kinsman to rise,
And quickly he rose up and came to him
    courteously,
Kneeled by the King, and caught the weapon,
He left it graciously, lifted his hand,
And gave him God's blessing, and gladly bade
    him
Be sure that his heart and his hand both were
    hardy.   370
"Take care," quoth the King, "how you start,
    coz, your cutting,
And truly, I think, if rightly you treat him,
That blow you'll endure that he deals you after."
Weapon in hand, Gawain goes to the hero,
Who boldly remains there, dismayed none the
    more.
Then the knight in the green thus greeted Sir
    Gawain,
"Let us state our agreement again ere proceeding.
And now first, sir knight, what your name is I
    beg
That you truly will tell, so in that I may trust."
"In truth," said the good knight, "I'm called Sir
    Gawain,   380
Who fetch you this blow, whatsoever befalls,
And another will take in return, this time twelve-
    month,
From you, with what weapon you will; with no
    other
              I'll go."
        The other made reply:
        "By my life here below,

        Gawain, right glad am I
        To have you strike this blow.

    By God," said the Green Knight, "Sir Gawain,
    it pleases me—
Here, at thy hand, I shall have what I sought.   390
Thou hast rightly rehearsed to me, truly and
    readily,
All of the covenant asked of King Arthur;
Except that thou shalt, by thy troth, sir, assure
    me
Thyself and none other shalt seek me, wherever
Thou thinkest to find me, and fetch thee what
    wages
Are due for the stroke that to-day thou dost deal
    me
Before all this splendid assembly." "Where
    should I,"
Said Gawain, "go look for the land where thou
    livest?
The realm where thy home is, by Him who
    hath wrought me,
I know not, nor thee, sir, thy court nor thy
    name.   400
Truly tell me thy title, and teach me the road,
And I'll use all my wit to win my way thither.
And so by my sure word truly I swear."
"'T is enough. No more now at New Year is
    needed,"
The knight in the green said to Gawain the
    courteous:
"If truly I tell when I've taken your tap
And softly you've struck me, if swiftly I tell you
My name and my house and my home, you may
    then
Of my conduct make trial, and your covenant
    keep;
And if no speech I speak, you speed all the
    better: 410
No longer need look, but may stay in your land.
              But ho!
        Take your grim tool with speed,
        And let us see your blow."
        Stroking his axe, "Indeed,"
        Said Gawain, "gladly so."

    With speed then the Green Knight took up his
    stand,
Inclined his head forward, uncovering the flesh,

And laid o'er his crown his locks long and lovely,
And bare left the nape of his neck for the
    business.   420
His axe Gawain seized, and swung it on high;
On the floor his left foot he planted before him,
And swiftly the naked flesh smote with his
    weapon.
The sharp edge severed the bones of the stranger,
Cut through the clear flesh and cleft it in twain,
So the blade of the brown steel bit the ground
    deeply.
The fair head fell from the neck to the floor,
So that where it rolled forth with their feet many
    spurned it.[11]
The blood on the green glistened, burst from the
    body;
And yet neither fell nor faltered the hero,   430
But stoutly he started forth, strong in his stride;
Fiercely he rushed 'mid the ranks of the Round
    Table,
Seized and uplifted his lovely head straightway;
Then back to his horse went, laid hold of the
    bridle,
Stepped into the stirrup and strode up aloft,
His head holding fast in his hand by the hair.
And the man as soberly sat in his saddle
As if he unharmed were, although now headless,
                     Instead.
          His trunk around he spun,   440
          That ugly body that bled.
          Frightened was many a one
          When he his words had said.

For upright he holds the head in his hand,
And confronts with the face the fine folk on the
    dais.
It lifted its lids, and looked forth directly,
Speaking this much with its mouth, as ye hear:
"Gawain, look that to go as agreed you are
    ready,
And seek for me faithfully, sir, till you find me,
As, heard by these heroes, you vowed in this hall.   450
To the Green Chapel go you,[12] I charge you, to
    get
Such a stroke as you struck. You are surely
    deserving,
Sir knight, to be promptly repaid at the New
    Year.

As Knight of the Green Chapel many men know
    me;
If therefore to find me you try, you will fail not;
Then come, or be recreant called as befits thee."
With furious wrench of the reins he turned
    round,
And rushed from the hall-door, his head in his
    hands,
So the fire of the flint flew out from the foal's
    hoofs.
Not one of the lords knew the land where he
    went to,   460
No more than the realm whence he rushed in
    among them.
               What then?
        The King and Gawain there
        At the Green Knight laughed again;
        Yet this the name did bear
        Of wonder among men.

Though much in his mind did the courtly
    King marvel,
He let not a semblance be seen, but said loudly
With courteous speech to the Queen, most
    comely:
"To-day, my dear lady, be never alarmed;   470
Such affairs are for Christmas well fitted to sing
    of
And gaily to laugh at when giving an interlude,
'Mid all the company's caroles, most courtly.
None the less I may go now to get my meat;
For I needs must admit I have met with a
    marvel."
He glanced at Sir Gawain, and gladsomely said:
"Now sir, hang up thine axe; enough it has
    hewn."
O'er the dais 't was placed, to hang on the
    dosser,
That men might remark it there as a marvel,
And truly describing, might tell of the wonder.   480
Together these two then turned to the table,
The sovereign and good knight, and swiftly men
    served them
With dainties twofold, as indeed was most fitting,
All manner of meat and of minstrelsy both.
So the whole day in pleasure they passed till night
    fell

O'er the land.
Now take heed Gawain lest,
Fearing the Green Knight's brand,
Thou shrinkest from the quest
That thou hast ta'en in hand.   490

II

This sample had Arthur of strange things right
    early,
When young was the year, for he yearned to
    hear boasts.
Though such words when they went to be seated
    were wanting,
Yet stocked are they now with hand-fulls of
    stern work.
In the hall glad was Gawain those games to
    begin,
But not strange it would seem if sad were the
    ending;
For though men having drunk much are merry
    in mind,
Full swift flies a year, never yielding the same,
The start and the close very seldom according.
So past went this Yule, and the year followed
    after,[13]   500
Each season in turn succeeding the other.
There came after Christmas the crabbed Lenten,
With fish and with plainer food trying the flesh;
But then the world's weather with winter
    contends;
Down to earth shrinks the cold, the clouds are
    uplifted;
In showers full warm descends the bright rain,
And falls on the fair fields. Flowers unfold;
The ground and the groves are green in their
    garments;
Birds hasten to build, blithesomely singing
For soft summer's solace ensuing on slopes   510
        Everywhere.
        The blossoms swell and blow,
        In hedge-rows rich and rare,
        And notes most lovely flow
        From out the forest fair.

After this comes the season of soft winds of
    summer,
When Zephyrus sighs on the seeds and the green
    plants.

The herb that then grows in the ground is right
    happy,
When down from the leaves drops the
    dampening dew
To abide the bright sun that is blissfully shining.   520
But autumn comes speeding, soon grows severe,
And warns it to wax full ripe for the winter.
With drought then the dust is driven to rise,
From the face of the fields to fly to the heaven.
With the sun the wild wind of the welkin is
    struggling;
The leaves from the limbs drop, and light on the
    ground;
And withers the grass that grew once so greenly.
Then all ripens that formerly flourished, and rots;
And thus passes the year in yesterdays many,
And winter, in truth, as the way of the world is,   530
        Draws near,
        Till comes the Michaelmas moon
        With pledge of winter sere.
        Then thinks Sir Gawain soon
        Of his dread voyage drear.

Till the tide of Allhallows with Arthur he
    tarried;
The King made ado on that day for his sake
With rich and rare revel of all of the Round
    Table,
Knights most courteous, comely ladies,
All of them heavy at heart for the hero.   540
Yet nothing but mirth was uttered, though many
Joyless made jests for that gentleman's sake.
After meat, with sorrow he speaks to his uncle,
And openly talks of his travel, saying:
"Liege lord of my life, now I ask of you leave.
You know my case and condition, nor care I
To tell of its troubles even a trifle.
I must, for the blow I am bound to, to-morrow
Go seek as God guides me the man in the green."
Then came there together the best in the castle: 550
Ywain, Eric, and others full many,
Sir Dodinel de Sauvage, the Duke of Clarence,
Lancelot, Lyonel, Lucan the good,
Sir Bors and Sir Bedevere, both of them big
    men,
Mador de la Port, and many more nobles.
All these knights of the court came near to the
    King

With care in their hearts to counsel the hero;
Heavy and deep was the dole in the hall
That one worthy as Gawain should go on that
    errand,
To suffer an onerous stroke, and his own sword   560
              To stay.
       The knight was of good cheer:
       "Why should I shrink away
       From a fate stern and drear?
       A man can but essay."

  He remained there that day; in the morning
    made ready.
Early he asked for his arms; all were brought
    him.
And first a fine carpet was laid on the floor,
And much was the gilt gear that glittered upon it.
Thereon stepped the strong man, and handled the
    steel,   570
Dressed in a doublet of Tars that cost dearly,
A hood made craftily, closed at the top,
And about on the lining bound with a bright
    fur.
Then they set on his feet shoes fashioned of steel,
And with fine greaves of steel encircled his legs.
Knee-pieces to these were connected, well
    polished,
Secured round his knees with knots of gold.
Then came goodly cuisses, with cunning
    enclosing
His thick, brawny thighs; with thongs they
    attached them.
Then the man was encased in a coat of fine mail,   580
With rings of bright steel on a rich stuff woven,
Braces well burnished on both of his arms,
Elbow-pieces gay, good, and gloves of plate,
All the goodliest gear that would give him most
    succor
              That tide:
       Coat armor richly made,
       His gold spurs fixed with pride,
       Girt his unfailing blade
       By a silk sash to his side.

  When in arms he was clasped, his costume was
    costly;   590
The least of the lacings or loops gleamed with
    gold.

And armed in this manner, the man heard mass,
At the altar adored and made offering, and after-
    ward
Came to the King and all of his courtiers,
Gently took leave of the ladies and lords;
Him they kissed and escorted, to Christ him
    commending.
Then was Gringolet ready, girt with a saddle
That gaily with many a gold fringe was
    gleaming,
With nails studded newly, prepared for the
    nonce.
The bridle was bound about, barred with bright
    gold;   600
With the bow of the saddle, the breastplate, the
    splendid skirts,
Crupper, and cloth in adornment accorded,
With gold nails arrayed on a groundwork of red,
That glittered and glinted like gleams of the sun.
Then he caught up his helm, and hastily kissed
    it;
It stoutly was stapled and stuffed well within,
High on his head, and hasped well behind,
With a light linen veil laid over the visor,
Embroidered and bound with the brightest of
    gems
On a silken border; with birds on the seams   610
Like painted parroquets preening; true love-
    knots
As thickly with turtle doves tangled as though
Many women had been at the work seven
    winters
                      In town.
       Great was the circle's price
       Encompassing his crown;
       Of diamonds its device,
       That were both bright and brown.

  Then they showed him his shield, sheer gules,
    whereon shone
The pentangle[14] painted in pure golden hue.   620
On his baldric he caught, and about his neck cast
    it;
And fairly the hero's form it befitted.
And why that great prince the pentangle suited
Intend I to tell, in my tale though I tarry.
'T is a sign that Solomon formerly set
As a token, for so it doth symbol, of truth.

A figure it is that with five points is furnished;
Each line overlaps and locks in another,
Nor comes to an end; and Englishmen call it
Everywhere, hear I, the endless knot.   630
It became then the knight and his noble arms
    also,
In five ways, and five times each way still
    faithful.
Sir Gawain was known as the good, refined gold,
Graced with virtues of castle, of villainy void,
            Made clean.
      So the pentangle new
      On shield and coat was seen,
      As man of speech most true,
      And gentlest knight of mien.

   First, in his five wits he faultless was found;   640
In his five fingers too the man never failed;
And on earth all his faith was fixed on the five
    wounds
That Christ, as the creed tells, endured on the
    cross.
Wheresoever this man was midmost in battle,
His thought above everything else was in this,
To draw all his fire from the fivefold joys[15]
That the fair Queen of Heaven felt in her child.
And because of this fitly he carried her image
Displayed on his shield, on its larger part,
That whenever he saw it his spirit should sink
    not.[16]   650
The fifth five the hero made use of, I find,
More than all were his liberalness, love of his
    fellows,
His courtesy, chasteness, unchangeable ever,
And pity, all further traits passing. These five
In this hero more surely were set than in any.
In truth now, fivefold they were fixed in the
    knight,
Linked each to the other without any end,
And all of them fastened on five points unfailing;
Each side they neither united nor sundered,
Evermore endless at every angle,   660
Where equally either they ended or started.
And so his fair shield was adorned with this
    symbol,
Thus richly with red gold wrought on red gules,
So by people the pentangle perfect 't was called,

            As it ought.
      Gawain in arms is gay;
      Right there his lance he caught,
      And gave them all good-day
      For ever, as he thought.

   He set spurs to his steed, and sprang on his
    way   670
So swiftly that sparks from the stone flew behind
    him.
All who saw him, so seemly, sighed, sad at heart;
The same thing, in sooth, each said to the other,
Concerned for that comely man: "Christ, 't is a
    shame
Thou, sir knight, must be lost whose life is so
    noble!
To find, faith! his equal on earth is not easy.
'T would wiser have been to have acted more
    warily,
Dubbed yonder dear one a duke. He seems
    clearly
To be in the land here a brilliant leader:
So better had been than brought thus to naught,   680
By an elf-man beheaded for haughty boasting.
Who e'er knew any king such counsel to take,
As foolish as one in a Christmas frolic?"
Much was the warm water welling from eyes
When the seemly hero set out from the city
            That day.
      Nowhere he abode,
      But swiftly went his way;
      By devious paths he rode,
      As I the book heard say.   690

   Through the realm of Logres[17] now rides this
    lord,
Sir Gawain, for God's sake, no game though he
    thought it.
Oft alone, uncompanioned he lodges at night
Where he finds not the fare that he likes set
    before him.
Save his foal, he 'd no fellow by forests and hills;
On the way, no soul but the Savior to speak to.
At length he drew nigh unto North Wales, and
    leaving
To left of him all of the islands of Anglesey,
Fared by the forelands and over the fords

Near the Holy Head; hastening hence to the
  mainland,   700
In Wyral he went through the wilderness. There,
Lived but few who loved God or their fellows
  with good heart.
And always he asked of any he met,
As he journeyed, if nearby a giant they knew of,
A green knight, known as the Knight of the
  Green Chapel.
All denied it with nay, in their lives they had
  never
Once seen any hero who had such a hue
          Of green.
      The knight takes roadways strange
      In many a wild terrene;   710
      Often his feelings change
      Before that chapel 's seen.

Over many cliffs climbed he in foreign
  countries;[18]
From friends far sundered, he fared as a stranger;
And wondrous it were, at each water or shore
That he passed, if he found not before him a foe,
So foul too and fell that to fight he could fail not.
The marvels he met with amount to so many
Too tedious were it to tell of the tenth part.
For sometimes with serpents he struggled and
  wolves too,   720
With wood-trolls sometimes in stony steeps
  dwelling,
And sometimes with bulls and with bears and
  with boars;
And giants from high fells hunted and harassed
  him.
If he'd been not enduring and doughty, and
  served God,
These doubtless would often have done him to
  death.
Though warfare was grievous, worse was the
  winter,
When cold, clear water was shed from the clouds
That froze ere it fell to the earth, all faded.
With sleet nearly slain, he slept in his armor
More nights than enough on the naked rocks,   730
Where splashing the cold stream sprang from the
  summit,
And hung in hard icicles high o'er head.
Thus in peril and pain and desperate plights,

Till Christmas Eve wanders this wight through
  the country
          Alone.
      Truly the knight that tide
      To Mary made his moan,
      That she direct his ride
      To where some hearth-fire shone.

By a mount on the morn he merrily rides   740
To a wood dense and deep that was wondrously
  wild;
High hills on each hand, with forests of hoar
  oaks
Beneath them most huge, a hundred together.
Thickly the hazel and hawthorn were tangled,
Everywhere mantled with moss rough and
  ragged,
With many a bird on the bare twigs, mournful,
That piteously piped for pain of the cold.
Sir Gawain on Gringolet goes underneath them
Through many a marsh and many a mire,
Unfriended, fearing to fail in devotion,   750
And see not His service, that Sire's, on that very
  night
Born of a Virgin to vanquish our pain.
And so sighing he said: "Lord, I beseech Thee,
And Mary, the mildest mother so dear,
For some lodging wherein to hear mass full
  lowly,
And matins, meekly I ask it, to-morrow;
So promptly I pray my pater and ave
          And creed."
      Thus rode he as he prayed,
      Lamenting each misdeed;   760
      Often the sign he made,
      And said, " Christ's cross me speed."

He scarcely had signed himself thrice, ere he
  saw
In the wood on a mound a moated mansion,
Above a fair field, enfolded in branches
Of many a huge tree hard by the ditches:
The comeliest castle that knight ever kept.
In a meadow 't was placed, with a park all about,
And a palisade, spiked and pointed, set stoutly
Round many a tree for more than two miles.   770

The lord on that one side looked at the stronghold
That shimmered and shone through the shapely
    oak trees;
Then duly his helm doffed, and gave his thanks
    humbly
To Jesus and Julian, both of them gentle,
For showing him courtesy, hearing his cry.
"Now good lodging," quoth Gawain, "I beg
    you to grant me."
Then with spurs in his gilt heels he Gringolet
    strikes,
Who chooses the chief path by chance that
    conducted
The man to the bridge-end ere many a minute
             Had passed.   780
          The bridge secure was made,
          Upraised; the gates shut fast;
          The walls were well arrayed.
          It feared no tempest's blast.

  The hero abode on his horse by the bank
Of the deep, double ditch that surrounded the
    dwelling.
The wall stood wonderfully deep in the water,
And again to a huge height sprang overhead;
Of hard, hewn rock that reached to the cornices,
Built up with outworks under the battlements   790
Finely; at intervals, turrets fair fashioned,
With many good loopholes that shut tight; this
    lord
Had ne'er looked at a barbican better than this
    one.
Further in he beheld the high hall; here and there
Towers were stationed set thickly with spires,
With finials wondrously long and fair fitting,
Whose points were cunningly carven, and
    craftily.
There numerous chalk-white chimneys he
    noticed
That bright from the tops of the towers were
    gleaming.
Such pinnacles painted, so placed about every-
    where.   800
Clustering so thick 'mid the crenels, the castle
Surely appeared to be shaped to cut paper.[19]
The knight on his foal it fair enough fancies
If into the court he may manage to come,
In that lodging to live while the holiday lasts

          With delight.
          A porter came at call,
          His mission learned, and right
          Civilly from the wall
          Greeted the errant knight.   810

Quoth Gawain: "Good sir, will you go on my
    errand,
Harbor to crave of this house's high lord?"
"Yea, by Peter. I know well, sir knight," said the
    porter,
"You're welcome as long as you list here to
    tarry."
Then went the man quickly, and with him, to
    welcome
The knight to the castle, a courteous company.
Down the great drawbridge they dropped, and
    went eagerly
Forth; on the frozen earth fell on their knees
To welcome this knight in the way they thought
    worthy;
Threw wide the great gate for Gawain to enter.   820
He bid them rise promptly, and rode o'er the
    bridge.
His saddle several seized as he lighted,
And stout men in plenty stabled his steed.
And next there descended knights and esquires
To lead to the hall with delight this hero.
When he raised his helmet, many made haste
From his hand to catch it, to care for the courtly
    man.
Some of them took then his sword and his shield
    both.
Then Gawain graciously greeted each knight;
Many proud men pressing to honor that prince,   830
To the hall they led him, all hasped in his
    harness,[20]
Where fiercely a fair fire flamed on the hearth.
Then came the lord of this land from his
    chamber
To fittingly meet the man on the floor,
And said: "You are welcome to do what your
    will is;
To hold as your own, you have all that is here
           In this place."
          "Thank you," said Gawain then,
          "May Christ reward this grace."
          The two like joyful men   840
          Each other then embrace.

Gawain gazed at the man who so graciously
    greeted him;
Doughty he looked, the lord of that dwelling,
A hero indeed huge, hale, in his prime;
His beard broad and bright, its hue all of beaver;
Stern, and on stalwart shanks steadily standing;
Fell faced as the fire, in speech fair and free.
In sooth, well suited he seemed, thought Gawain,
To govern as prince of a goodly people.
To his steward the lord turned, and strictly
    commanded   850
To send men to Gawain to give him good
    service;
And prompt at his bidding were people in plenty.
To a bright room they brought him, the bed
    nobly decked
With hangings of pure silk with clear golden
    hems.
And curious coverings with comely panels,
Embroidered with bright fur above at the edges;
On cords curtains running with rings of red
    gold;
From Tars and Toulouse were the tapestries
    covering
The walls; under foot on the floor more to
    match.
There he soon, with mirthful speeches, was
    stripped   860
Of his coat of linked mail and his armor; and
    quickly
Men ran, and brought him rich robes, that the
    best
He might pick out and choose as his change of
    apparel.
When lapped was the lord in the one he selected,
That fitted him fairly with flowing skirts,
The fur by his face, in faith it seemed made,
To the company there, entirely of colors,
Glowing and lovely; beneath all his limbs were.
That never made Christ a comelier knight
             They thought.   870
        On earth, or far or near,
        It seemed as if he ought
        To be a prince sans peer
        In fields where fierce men fought.

   A chair by the chimney where charcoal was
    burning
For Gawain was fitted most finely with cloths,

Both cushions and coverlets, cunningly made.
Then a comely mantle was cast on the man,
Of a brown, silken fabric bravely embroidered,
Within fairly furred with the finest of skins,   880
Made lovely with ermine, his hood fashioned
    likewise.
He sat on that settle in clothes rich and seemly;
His mood, when well he was warmed, quickly
    mended.
Soon was set up a table on trestles most fair;
With a clean cloth that showed a clear white it
    was covered,
With top-cloth and salt-cellar, spoons too of
    silver.
When he would the man washed, and went to his
    meat,
And seemly enough men served him with several
Excellent stews in the best manner seasoned,
Twofold as was fitting, and various fishes;   890
In bread some were baked, some broiled on
    the coals,
Some seethed, some in stews that were savored
    with spices;
And ever such subtly made sauces as pleased
    him.
He freely and frequently called it a feast,
Most courtly; the company there all acclaimed
    him
             Well-bred.
        "But now this penance take,
        And soon 't will mend," they said.
        That man much mirth did make,
        As wine went to his head.   900

   They enquired then and queried in guarded
    questions
Tactfully put to the prince himself,
Till he courteously owned he came of the court
The lord Arthur, gracious and goodly, alone
    holds,
Who rich is and royal, the Round Table's King;
And that Gawain himself in that dwelling was
    seated,
For Christmas come, as the case had befallen.
When he learned that he had that hero, the lord
Laughed loudly thereat so delightful he thought
    it.
Much merriment made all the men in that castle   910
By promptly appearing then in his presence;

For all prowess and worth and pure polished
    manners
Pertain to his person. He ever is praised;
Of all heroes on earth his fame is the highest.
Each knight full softly said to his neighbor,
"We now shall see, happily, knightly behavior,
And faultless terms of talking most noble;
What profit's in speech we may learn without
    seeking,
For nurture's fine father has found here a
    welcome;
In truth God has graciously given His grace   920
Who grants us to have such a guest as Gawain
When men for His birth's sake sit merry and
    sing.

                    To each
            Of us this hero now
            Will noble manners teach;
            Who hear him will learn how
            To utter loving speech."

When at length the dinner was done, and the
    lords
Had risen, the night-time nearly was come.
The chaplains went their way to the chapels   930
And rang right joyfully, just as they should do,
For evensong solemn this festival season.
To this goes the lord, and the lady likewise;²¹
She comes in with grace to the pew closed and
    comely,
And straightway Gawain goes thither right gaily;
The lord by his robe took him, led to a seat,
Acknowledged him kindly and called him by
    name,
Saying none in the world was as welcome as he
    was.
He heartily thanked him; the heroes embraced,
And together they soberly sat through the
    service.   940
Then longed the lady to look on the knight,
And emerged from her pew with many fair
    maidens;
In face she was fairest of all, and in figure,
In skin and in color, all bodily qualities;
Lovelier, Gawain thought, even than Guinevere.
He goes through the chancel to greet her, so
    gracious.
By the left hand another was leading her, older

Than she, a lady who looked as if aged,
By heroes around her reverenced highly.
The ladies, however, unlike were to look on: 950
If fresh was the younger, the other was yellow;
Rich red on the one was rioting everywhere,
Rough wrinkled cheeks hung in rolls on the
    other;
One's kerchiefs, with clear pearls covered and
    many,
Displayed both her breast and her bright throat
    all bare,
Shining fairer than snow on the hillsides falling;
The second her neck in a neck-cloth enswathed,
That enveloped in chalk-white veils her black
    chin;
Her forehead in silk was wrapped and enfolded
Adorned and tricked with trifles about it   960
Till nothing was bare but the lady's black brows,
Her two eyes, her nose, and her lips, all naked,
And those were bleared strangely, and ugly to see.
A goodly lady, so men before God
                    Might decide!
            Her body thick and short,
            Her hips were round and wide;
            One of more pleasant sort
            She led there by her side.

When Gawain had gazed on that gay one so
    gracious   970
In look, he took leave of the lord and went
    toward them,
Saluted the elder, bowing full lowly,
The lovelier lapped in his two arms a little,
And knightly and comely greeted and kissed her.
They craved his acquaintance, and quickly he
    asked
To be truly their servant if so they desired it.
They took him between them, and led him with
    talk
To the sitting-room's hearth; then straightway
    for spices
They called, which men sped to unsparingly
    bring,
And with them as well pleasant wine at each
    coming.   980
Up leaped right often the courteous lord,
Urged many a time that the men should make
    merry,

Snatched off his hood, on a spear gaily hung it,
And waved it, that one for a prize might win it
Who caused the most mirth on that Christmas
    season.
"I shall try, by my faith, to contend with the
    finest
Ere hoodless I find myself, helped by my
    friends."
Thus with laughing speeches the lord makes
    merry
That night, to gladden Sir Gawain with games.
             So they spent   990
             The evening in the hall.
             The king for lights then sent,
             And taking leave of all
             To bed Sir Gawain went.

On the morn when the Lord, as men all
    remember,
Was born, who would die for our doom, in
    each dwelling
On earth grows happiness greater for His sake;
So it did on that day there with many a dainty:
With dishes cunningly cooked at meal-times,
With doughty men dressed in their best on the
    dais.   1000
The old lady was seated the highest; beside her
Politely the lord took his place, I believe;
The gay lady and Gawain together sat, mid-most,
Where fitly the food came, and afterward fairly
Was served through the hall as beseemed them
    the best,
Of the company each in accord with his station.
There was meat and mirth, there was much joy,
    too troublous
To tell, though I tried in detail to describe it;
Yet I know both the lovely lady and Gawain
So sweet found each other's society (pleasant   1010
And polished their converse, courtly and private;
Unfailing their courtesy, free from offence)
That surpassing, in truth, any play of a prince
    was
             Their game.
             There trumpets, drums and airs
             Of piping loudly came.
             Each minded his affairs,
             And those two did the same.

Much mirth was that day and the day after
    made,
And the third followed fast, as full of delight.   1020
Sweet was the joy of St. John's day to hear of,
The last, as the folk there believed, of the festival.
Guests were to go in the gray dawn, and there-
    fore
They wondrously late were awake with their
    wine,
And danced delightful, long lasting caroles.
At length when 't was late they took their leave,
Each strong man among them to start on his
    way.
Gawain gave him good-day; then the good man
    laid hold of him,
Led to the hearth in his own room the hero;
There took him aside, and gave suitable thanks   1030
For the gracious distinction that Gawain had
    given
In honoring his house that holiday season,
And gracing his castle with courteous company.
"I'll truly as long as I live be the better
That Gawain at God's own feast was my guest."
"Gramercy," said Gawain, "by God, sir, not
    mine
Is the worth, but your own; may the high King
    reward you.
I am here at your will to work your behest,
As in high and low it behooves me to do
             By right."   1040
             The lord intently tries
             Longer to hold the knight;
             Gawain to him replies
             That he in no way might.

Then the man with courteous question
    enquired
What dark deed that feast time had driven him
    forth,
From the King's court to journey alone with such
    courage,
Ere fully in homes was the festival finished.
"In sooth," said the knight, "sir, ye say but the
    truth;
From these hearths a high and a hasty task took
    me.   1050
Myself, I am summoned to seek such a place
As to find it I know not whither to fare.

I'd not fail to have reached it the first of the
New Year,
So help me our Lord, for the whole land of
Logres;
And therefore, I beg this boon of you here, sir;
Tell me, in truth, if you ever heard tale
Of the Chapel of Green, of the ground where it
stands,
And the knight, green colored, who keeps it. By
solemn
Agreement a tryst was established between us,
That man at that landmark to meet if I lived.   1060
And now there lacks of New Year but little;
I'd look at that lord, if God would but let me,
More gladly than own any good thing, by God's
Son.
And hence, by your leave, it behooves me to go;
I now have but barely three days to be busy.
As fain would I fall dead as fail of my mission."
Then laughing the lord said: "You longer must
stay,
For I'll point out the way to that place ere the
time's end,
The ground of the Green Chapel. Grieve no
further;
For, sir, you shall be in your bed at your ease   1070
Until late, and fare forth the first of the year,
To your meeting place come by mid-morning,
to do there
            Your pleasure.
        Tarry till New Year's day,
        Then rise and go at leisure.
        I'll set you on your way;
        Not two miles is the measure."

Then was Gawain right glad, and gleefully
laughed.
"Now for this more than anything else, sir, I
thank you.
I have come to the end of my quest; at your will   1080
I shall bide, and in all things act as you bid me."
The lord then seized him, and set him beside
him,
And sent for the ladies to better delight him.
Seemly the pleasure among them in private.
So gay were the speeches he spoke, and so
friendly,

The host seemed a man well-nigh mad in
behavior.
He called to the knight there, crying aloud:
"Ye have bound you to do the deed that I bid
you.
Here, and at once, will you hold to your word
sir?"
"Yes, certainly sir," the true hero said;   1090
"While I bide in your house I obey your behest."
"You have toiled," said the lord; "from afar
have travelled,
And here have caroused, nor are wholly
recovered
In sleep or in nourishment, know I for certain.
In your room you shall linger, and lie at your
ease
To-morrow till mass-time, and go to your meat
When you will, and with you my wife to amuse
you
With company, till to the court I return.
            You stay
        And I shall early rise,   1100
        And hunting go my way."
        Bowing in courteous wise,
        Gawain grants all this play.

"And more," said the man, "let us make an
agreement:
Whatever I win in the wood shall be yours;
And what chance you shall meet shall be mine in
exchange.
Sir, let's so strike our bargain and swear to tell
truly
Whate'er fortune brings, whether bad, sir, or
better."
Quoth Gawain the good: "By God, I do grant
it.
What pastime you please appears to me pleasant." 1110
"On the beverage brought us the bargain is
made,"
So the lord of the land said. All of them laughed,
And drank, and light-heartedly revelled and
dallied,
Those ladies and lords, as long as they liked.
Then they rose with elaborate politeness, and
lingered,
With many fair speeches spoke softly together,

Right lovingly kissed, and took leave of each
    other.
Gay troops of attendants with glimmering
    torches
In comfort escorted each man to his couch
              To rest.   1120
        Yet ere they left the board
        Their promise they professed
        Often. That people's lord
        Could well maintain a jest.

III

Betimes rose the folk ere the first of the day;[22]
The guests that were going then summoned their
    grooms,
Who hastily sprang up to saddle their horses,
Packed their bags and prepared all their gear.
The nobles made ready, to ride all arrayed;
And quickly they leaped and caught up their
    bridles,   1130
And started, each wight on the way that well
    pleased him.
The land's beloved lord not last was equipped
For riding, with many a man too. A morsel
He hurriedly ate when mass he had heard,
And promptly with horn to the hunting field
    hastened.
And ere any daylight had dawned upon earth,
Both he and his knights were high on their
    horses.
The dog-grooms, accomplished, the hounds then
    coupled,
The door of the kennel unclosed, called them
    out,
On the bugle mightily blew three single notes;   1140
Whereupon bayed with a wild noise the brachets,
And some they turned back that went straying,
    and punished.
The hunters, I heard, were a hundred. To station
             They go,
        The keepers of the hounds,
        And off the leashes throw.
        With noise the wood resounds
        From the good blasts they blow.

At the first sound of questing, the wild crea-
    tures quaked;

The deer fled, foolish from fright, in the dale,   1150
To the high ground hastened, but quickly were
    halted
By beaters, loud shouting, stationed about
In a circle. The harts were let pass with their high
    heads,
And also the bucks, broad-antlered and bold;
For the generous lord by law had forbidden
All men with the male deer to meddle in close
    season.
The hinds were hemmed in with hey! and ware!
The does to the deep valleys driven with great
    din.
You might see as they loosed them the shafts
    swiftly soar—
At each turn of the forest their feathers went
    flying—   1160
That deep into brown hides bit with their broad
    heads;
Lo! they brayed on the hill-sides, bled there, and
    died,
And hounds, fleet-footed, followed them head-
    long.
And hunters after them hastened with horns
So loud in their sharp burst of sound as to sunder
The cliffs. What creatures escaped from the
    shooters,
Hunted and harried from heights to the waters,
Were pulled down and rent at the places there
    ready;
Such skill the men showed at these low-lying
    stations,
So great were the greyhounds that quickly they
    got them   1170
And dragged them down, fast as the folk there
    might look
             At the sight.
        Carried with bliss away,
        The lord did oft alight,
        Oft gallop; so that day
        He passed till the dark night.

Thus frolicked the lord on the fringe of the
    forest,
And Gawain the good in his gay bed reposed,
Lying snugly, till sunlight shone on the walls,
'Neath a coverlet bright with curtains about it.   1180
As softly he slumbered, a slight sound he heard

At his door, made with caution, and quickly it
    opened.
The hero heaved up his head from the clothes;
By a corner he caught up the curtain a little,
And glanced out with heed to behold what had
    happened.
The lady it was, most lovely to look at,
Who shut the door after her stealthily, slyly,
And turned toward the bed. Then the brave man,
    embarrassed,
Lay down again subtly to seem as if sleeping;
And stilly she stepped, and stole to his bed,   1190
There cast up the curtain, and creeping within it,
Seated herself on the bedside right softly,
And waited a long while to watch when he
    woke.
And the lord too, lurking, lay there a long while,
Wondering at heart what might come of this
    happening,
Or what it might mean—a marvel he thought it.
Yet he said to himself, "'T would be surely more
    seemly
By speaking at once to see what she wishes."
Then roused he from sleep, and stretching turned
    toward her,
His eyelids unlocked, made believe that he
    wondered,   1200
And signed himself so by his prayers to be safer
        From fall.
        Right sweet in chin and cheek,
        Both white and red withal,
        Full fairly did she speak
        With laughing lips and small.

"Good morrow, Sir Gawain," that gay lady
    said,
"You're a sleeper unwary, since so one may
    steal in.
In a trice you are ta'en! If we make not a truce,
In your bed, be you certain of this, I shall bind
    you."   1210
All laughing, the lady delivered those jests.
"Good morrow, fair lady," said Gawain the
    merry,
"You may do what you will, and well it doth
    please me,
For quickly I yield me, crying for mercy;
This method to me seems the best—for I must!"

So the lord in turn jested with laughter right
    joyous.
"But if, lovely lady, you would, give me leave,
Your prisoner release and pray him to rise,
And I'd come from this bed and clothe myself
    better;
So could I converse with you then with more
    comfort."   1220
"Indeed no, fair sir," that sweet lady said,
"You'll not move from your bed; I shall manage
    you better;
For here—and on that side too—I shall hold you,
And next I shall talk with the knight I have
    taken.
For well do I know that your name is Sir
    Gawain,
By everyone honored wherever you ride;
Most highly acclaimed is your courtly behavior
With lords and ladies and all who are living.
And now you're here, truly, and none but we
    two;
My lord and his followers far off have fared;   1230
Other men remain in their beds, and my
    maidens;
The door is closed, and secured with a strong
    hasp;
Since him who delights all I have in my house,
My time, as long as it lasts, I with talking
        Shall fill.
        My body's gladly yours;
        Upon me work your will.
        Your servant I, perforce,
        Am now, and shall be still."

"In faith," quoth Sir Gawain, "a favor I think it,   1240
Although I am now not the knight you speak of;
To reach to such fame as here you set forth,
I am one, as I well know myself, most unworthy.
By God, should you think it were good, I'd
    be glad
If I could or in word or action accomplish
Your ladyship's pleasure—a pure joy 't would
    prove."
"In good faith, Sir Gawain," the gay lady said,
"Ill-bred I should be if I blamed or belittled
The worth and prowess that please all others.
There are ladies enough who'd be now more
    delighted   1250

To have you in thraldom, as here, sir, I have you,
To trifle gaily in talk most engaging,
To give themselves comfort and quiet their cares,
Than have much of the gold and the goods they
    command.
But to Him I give praise that ruleth the heavens,
That wholly I have in my hand what all wish."
          So she
      Gave him good cheer that day,
      She who was fair to see.
      To what she chanced to say   1260
      With pure speech answered he.

  Quoth the merry man, "Madam, Mary reward
    you,
For noble, in faith, I've found you, and generous.
People by others pattern their actions,
But more than I merit to me they give praise;
'T is your courteous self who can show naught
    but kindness."
"By Mary," said she, "to me it seems other!
Were I worth all the host of women now living,
And had I the wealth of the world in my hands,
Should I chaffer and choose to get me a
    champion,   1270
Sir, from the signs I've seen in you here
Of courtesy, merry demeanor, and beauty,
From what I have heard, and hold to be true,
Before you no lord now alive would be chosen."
"A better choice, madam, you truly have made;
Yet I'm proud of the value you put now upon
    me.
Your servant as seemly, I hold you my sovereign,
Become your knight, and Christ give you
    quittance."
Thus of much they talked till mid-morning was
    past.
The lady behaved as if greatly she loved him,   1280
But Gawain, on guard, right gracefully acted.
"Though I were the most lovely of ladies," she
    thought,
"The less would he take with him love." He was
    seeking,
          With speed,
      Grief that must be: the stroke
      That him should stun indeed.
      She then of leaving spoke,
      And promptly he agreed.

Then she gave him good-day, and glanced at
    him, laughing,
And startled him, speaking sharp words as she
    stood: 1290
"He who blesses all words reward this reception!
I doubt if indeed I may dub you Gawain."
"Wherefore?" he queried, quickly enquiring,
Afraid that he'd failed in his fashion of speech.
But the fair lady blessed him, speaking as
    follows:
"One as good as is Gawain the gracious
    considered,
(And courtly behavior 's found wholly in him)
Not lightly so long could remain with a lady
Without, in courtesy, craving a kiss
At some slight subtle hint at the end of a story."   1300
"Let it be as you like, lovely lady," said Gawain;
"As a knight is so bound, I'll kiss at your
    bidding,
And lest he displease you, so plead no longer."
Then closer she comes, and catches the knight
In her arms, and salutes him, leaning down
    affably.
Kindly each other to Christ they commend.
She goes forth at the door without further ado,
And he quickly makes ready to rise, and hastens,
Calls to his chamberlain, chooses his clothes,
And merrily marches, when ready, to mass.   1310
Then he fared to his meat, and fitly he feasted,
Made merry all day with amusements till moon-
    rise.
          None knew
      A knight to better fare
      With dames so worthy, two:
      One old, one younger. There
      Much mirth did then ensure.

  Still was absent the lord of that land on his
    pleasure,
To hunt barren hinds in wood and in heath.
By the set of the sun he had slain such a number   1320
Of does and different deer that 't was wondrous.
Eagerly flocked in the folk at the finish,
And quickly made of the killed deer a quarry;
To this went the nobles with numerous men;
The game whose flesh was the fattest they
    gathered;
With care, as the case required, cut them open.

And some the deer searched at the spot of assay,
And two fingers of fat they found in the poorest.
They slit at the base of the throat, seized the
    stomach,
Scraped it away with a sharp knife and sewed it;   1330
Next slit the four limbs and stripped off the hide;
Then opened the belly and took out the bowels
And flesh of the knot, quickly flinging them out.
They laid hold of the throat, made haste to
    divide, then,
The windpipe and gullet, and tossed out the guts;
With their sharp knives carved out the shoulders
    and carried them
Held through a small hole to have the sides
    perfect.
The breast they sliced, and split it in two;
And then they began once again at the throat,
And quickly as far as its fork they cut it;   1340
Pulled out the pluck, and promptly thereafter
Beside the ribs swiftly severed the fillets,
Cleared them off readily right by the back-bone,
Straight down to the haunch, all hanging
    together.
They heaved it up whole, and hewed it off there,
And the rest by the name of the numbles—and
    rightly—
             They knew.
        Then where divide the thighs,
        The folds behind they hew,
        Hasten to cut the prize   1350
        Along the spine in two.

And next both the head and the neck off they
    hewed;
The sides from the backbone swiftly they
    sundered;
The fee of the ravens[23] they flung in the branches.
They ran through each thick side a hole by the
    ribs,
And hung up both by the hocks of the haunches,
Each fellow to have the fee that was fitting.
On the fair beast's hide, they fed their hounds
With the liver and lights and the paunch's lining,
Among which bread steeped in blood was
    mingled.   1360
They blew boldly the blast for the prize; the
    hounds barked.

Then the venison took they and turned toward
    home,
And stoutly many a shrill note they sounded.
Ere close of the daylight, the company came
To the comely castle where Gawain in comfort
        Sojourned.
        And when he met the knight
        As thither he returned,
        Joy had they and delight,
        Where the fire brightly burned.   1370

  In the hall the lord bade all his household to
    gather,
And both of the dames to come down with their
    damsels.
In the room there before all the folk he ordered
His followers, truly, to fetch him his venison.
Gawain he called with courteous gaiety,
Asked him to notice the number of nimble
    beasts,
Showed him the fairness of flesh on the ribs.
"Are you pleased with this play? Have I won
    your praise?
Have I thoroughly earned your thanks through
    my cunning?"
"In faith," said Sir Gawain, "this game is the
    fairest   1380
I've seen in the season of winter these seven
    years."
"The whole of it, Gawain, I give you," the host
    said;
"Because of our compact, as yours you may
    claim it."
"That is true," the knight said, "and I tell you
    the same:
That this I have worthily won within doors,
And surely to you with as good will I yield it."
With both of his arms his fair neck he embraced,
And the hero as courteously kissed as he could.
"I give you my gains. I got nothing further;
I freely would grant it, although it were greater." 1390
"It is good," said the good man; "I give you my
    thanks.
Yet things so may be that you'd think it better
To tell where you won this same wealth by your
    wit."
"'T was no part of our pact," said he; "press me
    no more;

For trust entirely in this, that you've taken
        Your due."
    With laughing merriment
    And knightly speech and true,
    To supper soon they went
    With store of dainties new.   1400

  In a chamber they sat, by the side of the
    chimney,
Where men right frequently fetched them mulled
    wine.
In their jesting, again they agreed on the morrow
To keep the same compact they came to before:
That whatever should chance, they'd exchange at
    evening,
When greeting again, the new things they had
    gotten.
Before all the court they agreed to the covenant;
Then was the beverage brought forth in jest.
At last they politely took leave of each other,
And quickly each hero made haste to his couch.   1410
When the cock but three times had crowed and
    cackled,
The lord and his men had leaped from their beds.
So that duly their meal was dealt with, and mass,
And ere daylight they'd fared toward the forest,
    on hunting
        Intent.
    The huntsmen with loud horns
    Through level fields soon went,
    Uncoupling 'mid the thorns
    The hounds swift on the scent.

  Soon they cry for a search by the side of a
    swamp.[24]   1420
The huntsmen encourage the hounds that first
    catch there
The scent, and sharp words they shout at them
    loudly;
And thither the hounds that heard them hastened,
And fast to the trail fell, forty at once.
Then such clamor and din from the dogs that
    had come there
Arose that the rocks all around them rang.
With horn and with mouth the hunters heartened
    them;
They gathered together then, all in a group,

'Twixt a pool in that copse and a crag most
    forbidding.
At a stone-heap, beside the swamp, by a cliff,   1430
Where the rough rock had fallen in rugged
    confusion,
They fared to the finding, the folk coming after.
Around both the crag and the rubble-heap
    searched
The hunters, sure that within them was hidden
The beast whose presence was bayed by the
    bloodhounds.
Then they beat on the bushes, and bade him rise
    up,
And wildly he made for the men in his way,
Rushing suddenly forth, of swine the most
    splendid.
Apart from the herd he'd grown hoary with age,
For fierce was the beast, the biggest of boars. 1440
Then many men grieved, full grim when he
    grunted,
For three at his first thrust he threw to the earth,
And then hurtled forth swiftly, no harm doing,
    further.
They shrilly cried hi! and shouted hey! hey!
Put bugles to mouth, loudly blew the recall.
The men and dogs merry in voice were and
    many;
With outcry they all hurry after this boar
        To slay.
    He maims the pack when, fell,
    He often stands at bay.   1450
    Loudly they howl and yell,
    Sore wounded in the fray.

  Then to shoot at him came up the company
    quickly.
Arrows that hit him right often they aimed,
But their sharp points failed that fell on his
    shoulders'
Tough skin, and the barbs would not bite in his
    flesh;
But the smooth-shaven shafts were shivered in
    pieces,
The heads wherever they hit him rebounding.
But when hurt by the strength of the strokes they
    struck,
Then mad for the fray he falls on the men,   1460

And deeply he wounds them as forward he
    dashes.
Then many were frightened, and drew back in
    fear;
But the lord galloped off on a light horse after
    him,
Blew like a huntsman right bold the recall
On his bugle, and rode through the thick of the
    bushes,
Pursuing this swine till the sun shone clearly.
Thus the day they passed in doing these deeds,
While bides our gracious knight Gawain in bed,
With bed-clothes in color right rich, at the castle
                Behind.   1470
        The dame did not forget
        To give him greetings kind.
        She soon upon him set,
        To make him change his mind.

Approaching the curtain, she peeps at the
    prince,
And at once Sir Gawain welcomes her worthily.
Promptly the lady makes her reply.
By his side she seats herself softly, heartily
Laughs, and with lovely look these words
    delivers:
"If you, sir, are Gawain, greatly I wonder   1480
That one so given at all times to goodness
Should be not well versed in social conventions,
Or, made once to know, should dismiss them
    from mind.
You have promptly forgotten what I in the
    plainest
Of talk that I knew of yesterday taught you."
"What is that?" said the knight. "For truly I
    know not;
If it be as you say, I am surely to blame."
"Yet I taught you," quoth the fair lady, "of
    kissing;
When clearly he's favored, quickly to claim one
Becomes each knight who practices courtesy."   1490
"Cease, dear lady, such speech," said the strong
    man;
"I dare not for fear of refusal do that.
'T would be wrong to proffer and then be
    repulsed."
"In faith, you may not be refused," said the fair
    one;

"Sir, if you pleased, you have strength to compel
    it,
Should one be so rude as to wish to deny you."
"By God, yes," said Gawain, "good is your
    speech;
But unlucky is force in the land I live in,
And every gift that with good will's not given.
Your word I await to embrace when you wish;   1500
You may start when you please, and stop at your
    pleasure."
              With grace
        The lady, bending low,
        Most sweetly kissed his face.
        Of joy in love and woe
        They talked for a long space.

"I should like," said the lady, "from you, sir,
    to learn,
If I roused not your anger by asking, the reason
Why you, who are now so young and valiant,
So known far and wide as knightly and courteous 1510
(And principally, picked from all knighthood, is
    praised
The sport of true love and the science of arms;
For to tell of these true knights' toil, it is surely
The title inscribed and the text of their deeds,
How men their lives for their leal love
    adventured,
Endured for their passion doleful days,
Then themselves with valor avenged, and their
    sorrow
Cast off, and brought bliss into bowers by their
    virtues),
Why you, thought the noblest knight of your
    time,
Whose renown and honor are everywhere noted, 1520
Have so let me sit on two separate occasions
Beside you, and hear proceed from your head
Not one word relating to love, less or more.
You so goodly in vowing your service and
    gracious
Ought gladly to give to a young thing your
    guidance,
And show me some sign of the sleights of true
    love.
What! know you nothing, and have all renown?
Or else do you deem me too dull, for your talking

Unfit?
> For shame! Alone I come; 1530
> To learn some sport I sit;
> My lord is far from home;
> Now, teach me by your wit."

"In good faith," said Gawain, "God you
    reward;
For great is the happiness, huge the gladness
That one so worthy should want to come hither,
And pains for so poor a man take, as in play
With your knight with looks of regard; it
    delights me.
But to take up the task of telling of true love,
To touch on those themes, and on tales of arms 1540
To you who've more skill in that art, I am
    certain,
By half than a hundred men have such as I,
Or ever shall have while here upon earth,
By my faith, 't would be, madam, a manifold
    folly.
Your bidding I'll do, as in duty bound,
To the height of my power, and will hold myself
    ever
Your ladyship's servant, so save me the Lord."
Thus the fair lady tempted and tested him often
To make the man sin—whate'er more she'd in
    mind;
But so fair his defence was, no fault was apparent, 1550
Nor evil on either side; each knew but joy
> On that day.
> At last she kissed him lightly,
> After long mirth and play,
> And took her leave politely,
> And went upon her way.

The man bestirs himself, springs up for mass.
Then made ready and splendidly served was their
    dinner;
In sport with the ladies he spent all the day.
But the lord through fields oft dashed as he
    followed 1560
The savage swine, that sped o'er the slopes,
And in two bit the backs of the best of his
    hounds
Where he stood at bay; till 't was broken by
    bowmen,

Who made him, despite himself, move to the
    open,
The shafts flew so thick when the throng had
    assembled.
Yet sometimes he forced the stoutest to flinch,
Till at last too weary he was to run longer,
But came with such haste as he could to a hole
In a mound, by a rock whence the rivulet runs
    out.
He started to scrape the soil, backed by the slope, 1570
While froth from his mouth's ugly corners came
    foaming.
White were the tushes he whetted. The bold men
Who stood round grew tired of trying from far
To annoy him, but dared not for danger draw
    nearer.
> Before,
> So many he did pierce
> That all were loth a boar
> So frenzied and so fierce
> Should tear with tusks once more,

Till the hero himself came, spurring his horse, 1580
Saw him standing at bay, the hunters beside him.
He leaped down right lordly, leaving his courser,
Unsheathed a bright sword and strode forth
    stoutly,
Made haste through the ford where that fierce
    one was waiting.
Aware of the hero with weapon in hand,
So savagely, bristling his back up, he snorted
All feared for the wight lest the worst befall him.
Then rushed out the boar directly upon him,
And man was mingled with beast in the midst
Of the wildest water. The boar had the worse, 1590
For the man aimed a blow at the beast as he met
    him,
And surely with sharp blade struck o'er his breast
    bone,
That smote to the hilt, and his heart cleft asunder.
He squealing gave way, and swift through the
    water
> Went back.
> By a hundred hounds he's caught,
> Who fiercely him attack;
> To open ground he's brought,
> And killed there by the pack.

The blast for the beast's death was blown on
    sharp horns,   1600
And the lords there loudly and clearly hallooed.
At the beast bayed the brachets, as bid by their
    masters,
The chief, in that hard, long chase, of the
    hunters.
Then one who was wise in woodcraft began
To slice up this swine in the seemliest manner.
First he hews off his head, and sets it on high;
Then along the back roughly rends him apart.
He hales out the bowels, and broils them on hot
    coals,
With these mixed with bread, rewarding his
    brachets.
Then slices the flesh in fine, broad slabs,   1610
And pulls out the edible entrails properly.
Whole, though, he gathers the halves together,
And proudly upon a stout pole he places them.
Homeward they now with this very swine
    hasten,
Bearing in front of the hero the boar's head,
Since him at the ford by the force of his strong
    hand
                He slew.
        It seemed long till he met
        In hall Sir Gawain, who
        Hastened, when called, to get   1620
        The payment that was due.

The lord called out loudly, merrily laughed
When Gawain he saw, and gladsomely spoke.
The good ladies were sent for, the household
    assembled;
He shows them the slices of flesh, and the story
He tells of his largeness and length, and how
    fierce
Was the war in the woods where the wild swine
    had fled.
Sir Gawain commended his deeds right
    graciously,
Praised them as giving a proof of great prowess.
Such brawn on a beast, the bold man declared,   1630
And such sides on a swine he had ne'er before
    seen.
Then they handled the huge head; the courteous
    hero
Praised it, horror-struck, honoring his host.

Quoth the good man, "Now Gawain yours is
    this game
By our covenant, fast and firm, you know truly."
"It is so," said the knight; "and as certain and
    sure
All I get I'll give you again as I pledged you."
He about the neck caught, with courtesy kissed
    him,
And soon a second time served him the same
    way.
Said Gawain, "We've fairly fulfilled the
    agreement   1640
This evening we entered on, each to the other
                    Most true."
        "I, by Saint Giles, have met
        None," said the lord, "like you.
        Riches you soon will get,
        If you such business do."

    And then the tables they raised upon trestles,
And laid on them cloths; the light leaped up
    clearly
Along by the walls, where the waxen torches
Were set by the henchmen who served in the
    hall.   1650
A great sound of sport and merriment sprang up
Close by the fire, and on frequent occasions
At supper and afterward, many a splendid song,
Conduits of Christmas, new carols, all kinds
Of mannerly mirth that a man may tell of.
Our seemly knight ever sat at the side
Of the lady, who made so agreeable her manner,
With sly, secret glances to glad him, so stalwart,
That greatly astonished was Gawain, and wroth
With himself; he in courtesy could not refuse
    her,   1660
But acted becomingly, courtly, whatever
The end, good or bad, of his action might be.
                When quite
        Done was their play at last,
        The host called to the knight,
        And to his room they passed
        To where the fire burned bright.

    The men there make merry and drink, and
    once more
The same pact for New Year's Eve is proposed;

But the knight craved permission to mount on
    the morrow: 1670
The appointment approached where he had to
    appear.
But the lord him persuaded to stay and linger,
And said, "On my word as a knight I assure you
You'll get to the Green Chapel, Gawain, on New
    Year's,
And far before prime, to finish your business.
Remain in your room then, and take your rest.
I shall hunt in the wood and exchange with you
    winnings,
As bound by our bargain, when back I return,
For twice I've found you were faithful when
    tried:
In the morning 'best be the third time,'
    remember. 1680
Let's be mindful of mirth while we may, and
    make merry,
For care when one wants it is quickly encoun-
    tered."
At once this was granted, and Gawain is stayed;
Drink blithely was brought him; to bed they
    were lighted.
                The guest
         In quiet and comfort spent
         The night, and took his rest.
         On his affairs intent,
         The host was early dressed.

After mass a morsel he took with his men.[25] 1690
The morning was merry; his mount he
    demanded.
The knights who'd ride in his train were in
    readiness,
Dressed and horsed at the door of the hall.
Wondrous fair were the fields, for the frost was
    clinging;
Bright red in the cloud-rack rises the sun,
And full clear sails close past the clouds in the
    sky.
The hunters unleashed all the hounds by a wood-
    side:
The rocks with the blast of their bugles were
    ringing.
Some dogs there fall on the scent where the fox
    is,
And trail oft a traitoress using her tricks. 1700

A hound gives tongue at it; huntsmen call to
    him;
Hastens the pack to the hound sniffing hard,
And right on his track run off in a rabble,
He scampering before them. They started the
    fox soon;
When finally they saw him, they followed fast,
Denouncing him clearly with clamorous anger.
Through many a dense grove he dodges and
    twists,
Doubling back and harkening at hedges right
    often;
At last by a little ditch leaps o'er a thorn-hedge,
Steals out stealthily, skirting a thicket 1710
In thought from the wood to escape by his wiles
From the hounds; then, unknowing, drew near
    to a hunting-stand.
There hurled themselves, three at once, on him
    strong hounds,
                All gray.
         With quick swerve he doth start
         Afresh without dismay.
         With great grief in his heart
         To the wood he goes away.

   Huge was the joy then to hark to the hounds.
When the pack all met him, mingled together, 1720
Such curses they heaped on his head at the sight
That the clustering cliffs seemed to clatter down
    round them
In heaps. The men, when they met him, hailed
    him,
And loudly with chiding speeches hallooed him;
Threats were oft thrown at him, thief he was
    called;
At his tail were the greyhounds, that tarry he
    might not.
They rushed at him oft when he raced for the
    open,
And ran to the wood again, reynard the wily.
Thus he led them, all muddied, the lord and his
    men,
In this manner along through the hills until
    midday. 1730
At home, the noble knight wholesomely slept
In the cold of the morn within comely curtains.
But the lady, for love, did not let herself sleep,
Or fail in the purpose fixed in her heart;

But quickly she roused herself, came there
    quickly,
Arrayed in a gay robe that reached to the
    ground,
The skins of the splendid fur skillfully trimmed
    close.
On her head no colors save jewels, well-cut,
That were twined in her hair-fret in clusters of
    twenty.
Her fair face was completely exposed, and her
    throat;   1740
In front her breast too was bare, and her back.
She comes through the chamber-door, closes it
    after her,
Swings wide a window, speaks to the wight,
And rallies him soon in speech full of sport
                And good cheer.
        "Ah! man, how can you sleep?
        The morning is so clear."
        He was in sorrow deep,
        Yet her he then did hear.

    In a dream muttered Gawain, deep in its
    gloom,   1750
Like a man by a throng of sad thoughts sorely
    moved
Of how fate was to deal out his destiny to him
That morn, when he met the man at the Green
    Chapel,
Bound to abide his blow, unresisting.
But as soon as that comely one came to his
    senses,
Started from slumber and speedily answered,
The lovely lady came near, sweetly laughing,
Bent down o'er his fair face and daintily kissed
    him.
And well, in a worthy manner, he welcomed her.
Seeing her glorious, gaily attired,   1760
Without fault in her features, most fine in her
    color,
Deep joy came welling up, warming his heart.
With sweet, gentle smiling they straightway
    grew merry;
So passed naught between them but pleasure,
    joy,
                And delight.
        Goodly was their debate,
        Nor was their gladness slight.

        Their peril had been great
        Had Mary quit her knight.

    For that noble princess pressed him so closely,   1770
Brought him so near the last bound, that her love
He was forced to accept, or, offending, refuse
    her:
Concerned for his courtesy not to prove caitiff,
And more for his ruin if wrong he committed,
Betraying the hero, the head of that house.
"God forbid," said the knight; "that never shall
    be";
And lovingly laughing a little, he parried
The words of fondness that fell from her mouth.
She said to him "Sir, you are surely to blame
If you love not the lady beside whom you're
    lying,   1780
Of all the world's women most wounded in
    heart,
Unless you've one dearer, a lover you like more,
Your faith to her plighted, so firmly made fast
You desire not to loosen it—so I believe.
Now tell me truly I pray you; the truth,
By all of the loves that in life are, conceal not
                    Through guile."
        The knight said, "By Saint John,"
        And pleasantly to smile
        Began, "In faith I've none,   1790
        Nor will have for a while."

    "Such words," said the lady, "the worst are of
    all;
But in sooth I am answered, and sad it seems to
    me.
Kiss me now kindly, and quickly I'll go;
I on earth may but mourn, as a much loving
    mortal."
Sighing she stoops down, and kisses him seemly;
Then starting away from him, says as she stands,
"Now, my dear, at parting, do me this pleasure:
Give me some gift, thy glove if it might be,
To bring you to mind, sir, my mourning to
    lessen."   1800
"On my word," quoth the hero, "I would that I
    had here,
For thy sake, the thing that I think the dearest
I own, for in sooth you've deserved very often
A greater reward than one I could give.

But a pledge of love would profit but little;
'T would help not your honor to have at this
    time
For a keepsake a glove, as a gift of Gawain.
I've come on a mission to countries most strange;
I've no servants with splendid things filling their
    sacks:
That displeases me, lady, for love's sake, at
    present;   1810
Yet each man without murmur must do what he
    may

                    Nor repine."
        "Nay, lord of honors high,
        Though I have naught of thine,"
        Quoth the lovely lady, "I
        Shall give you gift of mine."

She offered a rich ring, wrought in red gold,
With a blazing stone that stood out above it,
And shot forth brilliant rays bright as the sun;
Wit you well that wealth right huge it was
    worth.   1820
But promptly the hero replied, refusing it,
"Madam, I care not for gifts now to keep;
I have none to tender and naught will I take."
Thus he ever declined her offer right earnest,
And swore on his word that he would not accept
    it;
And, sad he declined, she thereupon said,
"If my ring you refuse, since it seems too rich,
If you would not so highly to me be beholden,
My girdle, that profits you less, I'll give you."
She swiftly removed the belt circling her sides, 1830
Round her tunic knotted, beneath her bright
    mantle;
'T was fashioned of green silk, and fair made
    with gold,
With gold, too, the borders embellished and
    beautiful.
To Gawain she gave it, and gaily besought him
To take it, although he thought it but trifling.
He swore by no manner of means he'd accept
Either gold or treasure ere God gave him grace
To attain the adventure he'd there undertaken.
"And, therefore, I pray, let it prove not
    displeasing,
But give up your suit, for to grant it I'll never 1840

                    Agree.
        I'm deeply in your debt
        For your kind ways to me.
        In hot and cold I yet
        Will your true servant be."

  "Refuse ye this silk," the lady then said,
"As slight in itself? Truly it seems so.
Lo! it is little, and less is its worth;
But one knowing the nature knit up within it,
Would give it a value more great, peradventure; 1850
For no man girt with this girdle of green,
And bearing it fairly made fast about him,
Might ever be cut down by any on earth,
For his life in no way in the world could be
    taken."
Then mused the man, and it came to his mind
In the peril appointed him precious 't would
    prove,
When he'd found the chapel, to face there his
    fortune.
The device, might he slaying evade, would be
    splendid.
Her suit then he suffered, and let her speak;
And the belt she offered him, earnestly urging it 1860
(And Gawain consented), and gave it with good
    will,
And prayed him for her sake ne'er to display it,
But, true, from her husband to hide it. The hero
Agreed that no one should know of it ever.
                  Then he
        Thanked her with all his might
        Of heart and thought; and she
        By then to this stout knight
        Had given kisses three.

  Then the lady departs, there leaving the lord, 1870
For more pleasure she could not procure from
    that prince.
When she's gone, then quickly Sir Gawain
    clothes himself,
Rises and dresses in noble array,
Lays by the love-lace the lady had left him,
Faithfully hides it where later he'd find it.
At once then went on his way to the chapel,
Approached in private a priest, and prayed him
To make his life purer, more plainly him teach

How his soul, when he had to go hence, should
    be saved.
He declared his faults, confessing them fully,   1880
The more and the less, and mercy besought,
And then of the priest implored absolution.
He surely absolved him, and made him as
    spotless,
Indeed, as if doomsday were due on the morrow.
Then among their fair ladies he made more
    merry
With lovely caroles, all kinds of delights,
That day than before, until darkness fall.
         All there
      Were treated courteously,
      "And never," they declare,   1890
      "Has Gawain shown such glee
      Since hither he did fare."

  In that nook where his lot may be love let him
    linger!
The lord's in the meadow still, leading his men.
He has slain this fox that he followed so long;
As he vaulted a hedge to get view of the villain,
Hearing the hounds that hastened hard after him,
Reynard from out a rough thicket came
    running,
And right at his heels in a rush all the rabble.
He, seeing that wild thing, wary, awaits him,   1900
Unsheaths his bright brand and strikes at the
    beast.
And he swerved from its sharpness and back
    would have started;
A hound, ere he could, came hurrying up to
    him;
All of them fell on him fast by the horse's feet,
Worried that sly one with wrathful sound.
And quickly the lord alights, and catches him,
Takes him in haste from the teeth of the hounds,
And over his head holds him high, loudly
    shouting,
Where brachets, many and fierce, at him barked.
Thither huntsmen made haste with many a horn, 1910
The recall, till they saw him, sounding right
    clearly.
As soon as his splendid troop had assembled,
All bearing a bugle blew them together,
The others having no horns all hallooed.
'T was the merriest baying that man ever heard

That was raised for the soul of reynard with
    sounding
         Din.
      They fondle each dog's head
      Who his reward did win.
      Then take they reynard dead   1920
      And strip him of his skin.

  And now, since near was the night, they turned
    homeward,
Strongly and sturdily sounding their horns.
At last at his loved home the lord alighted,
A fire on the hearth found, the hero beside it,
Sir Gawain the good, who glad was withal,
For he had 'mong the ladies in love much delight.
A blue robe that fell to the floor he was wearing;
His surcoat, that softly was furred, well beseemed
    him;
A hood of the same hue hung on his shoulders,   1930
And both were bordered with white all about.
He, mid-most, met the good man in the hall,
And greeted him gladly, graciously saying:
"Now shall I first fulfil our agreement
We struck to good purpose, when drink was not
    spared."
Then Gawain embraced him, gave him three
    kisses,
The sweetest and soundest a man could bestow.
"By Christ, you'd great happiness," quoth then
    the host,
"In getting these wares, if good were your
    bargains."
"Take no care for the cost," the other said
    quickly,   1940
"Since plainly the debt that is due I have paid."
Said the other, "By Mary, mine's less worth.
The whole of the day I have hunted, and gotten
The skin of this fox—the fiend take its foulness!—
Right poor to pay for things of such price
As you've pressed on me here so heartily, kisses
         So good."
      "Say no more," Gawain saith;
      "I thank you, by the rood!"
      How the fox met his death   1950
      He told him as they stood.

With mirth and minstrelsy, meat at their
    pleasure

They made as merry as any men might
(With ladies' laughter, and launching of jests
Right glad were they both, the good man and
    Gawain)
Unless they had doted or else had been drunken.
Both the man and the company make many
    jokes,
Till the time is come when the two must be
    parted,
When finally the knights are forced to go bed-
    ward.
And first of the lord his respectful leave   1960
This goodly man took, and graciously thanked
    him:
"May God you reward for the welcome you
    gave me
This high feast, the splendid sojourn I've had
    here.
I give you myself, if you'd like it, to serve you.
I must, as you know, on the morrow move on;
Give me some one to show me the path, as you
    said,
To the Green Chapel, there, as God will allow
    me,
On New Year the fate that is fixed to perform."
"With a good will, indeed," said the good man;
    "whatever
I promised to do I deem myself ready."   1970
He a servant assigns on his way to set him,
To take him by hills that no trouble he'd have,
And through grove and wood by the way most
    direct
                Might repair.
            The lord he thanked again
            For the honor done him there.
            The knight his farewell then
            Took of those ladies fair.

   To them with sorrow and kissing he spoke,
And besought them his thanks most sincere to
    accept;   1980
And they, replying, promptly returned them,
With sighings full sore to the Savior commended
    him.
Then he with courtesy quitted the company,
Giving each man that he met his thanks
For kindness, for trouble he'd taken, for care

Whereby each had sought to serve him right
    eagerly.
Pained was each person to part with him then,
As if long they in honor had lived with that
    noble.
With people and lights he was led to his
    chamber,
To bed gaily brought there to be at his rest;   1990
Yet I dare not say whether soundly he slept,
For much, if he would, on the morn to remember
               Had he.
            Let him lie stilly there
            Near what he sought to see.
            What happened I'll declare,
            If you will silent be.

IV

   The New Year draws near, and the nighttime
    now passes;[26]
The day, as the Lord bids, drives on to darkness.
Outside, there sprang up wild storms in the
    world;   2000
The clouds cast keenly the cold to the earth
With enough of the north sting to trouble the
    naked;
Down shivered the snow, nipping sharply the
    wild beasts;
The wind from the heights, shrilly howling,
    came rushing,
And heaped up each dale full of drifts right huge.
Full well the man listened who lay in his bed.
Though he shut tight his lids, he slept but a little;
He knew by each cock that crowed 't was the
    tryst time,
And swiftly ere dawn of the day he arose,
For there shone then the light of a lamp in his
    room;   2010
To his chamberlain called, who answered him
    quickly,
And bade him his saddle to bring and his mail-
    shirt.
The other man roused up and fetched him his
    raiment,
Arrayed then that knight in a fashion right noble.
First he clad him in clothes to ward off the cold,
Then his other equipment, carefully kept:
His pieces of plate armor, polished right cleanly,
The rings of his rich mail burnished from rust.

All was fresh as at first; he was fain to give thanks
                    To the men.   2020
          He had on every piece
          Full brightly burnished then.
          He, gayest from here to Greece,
          Ordered his steed again.

He garbed himself there in the loveliest garments
(His coat had its blazon of beautiful needlework
Stitched upon velvet for show, its rich stones
Set about it and studded, its seams all
          embroidered,
Its lovely fur in the fairest of linings),
Yet he left not the lace, the gift of the lady: 2030
That, Gawain did not, for his own sake, forget.
When the brand on his rounded thighs he had
          belted,
He twisted his love-token two times about him.
That lord round his waist with delight quickly
          wound
The girdle of green silk, that seemed very gay
Upon royal red cloth that was rich to behold.
But Gawain the girdle wore not for its great
          price,
Or pride in its pendants although they were
          polished,
Though glittering gold there gleamed on the
          ends,
But himself to save when he needs must suffer   2040
The death, nor could stroke then of sword or of
          knife
                    Him defend.
          Then was the bold man dressed;
          Quickly his way did wend;
          To all the court expressed
          His great thanks without end.

Then was Gringolet ready that great was and
          huge,
Who had safely, as seemed to him pleasant, been
          stabled;
That proud horse pranced, in the pink of
          condition.
The lord then comes to him, looks at his coat,   2050
And soberly says, and swears on his word,
"In this castle's a company mindful of courtesy,
Led by this hero. Delight may they have;

And may love the dear lady betide all her life-
          time.
If they for charity cherish a guest,
And give so great welcome, may God reward
          them,
Who rules the heaven on high, and the rest of
          you.
Might I for long live my life on the earth,
Some repayment with pleasure I'd make, if
          'twere possible."
He steps in the stirrup, strides into the saddle,   2060
Receives on his shoulder the shield his man
          brings him,
And spurs into Gringolet strikes with his gilt
          heels;
Who leaps on the stones and lingers no longer
                    To prance.
          The knight on his horse sits,
          Who bears his spear and lance,
          The house to Christ commits,
          And wishes it good chance.

Then down the drawbridge they dropped, the
          broad gates
Unbarred, and on both sides bore them wide
          open.   2070
He blessed them quickly, and crossed o'er the
          planks there
(He praises the porter, who knelt by the prince
Begging God to save Gawain, and gave him
          good-day),
And went on his way with but one man attended
To show him the turns to that sorrowful spot
Where he must to that onerous onset submit.
By hillsides where branches were bare they both
          journeyed;
They climbed over cliffs where the cold was
          clinging.
The clouds hung aloft, but 't was lowering
          beneath them.
On the moor dripped the mist, on the mountains
          melted;   2080
Each hill had a hat, a mist-cloak right huge.
The brooks foamed and bubbled on hillsides
          about them,
And brightly broke on their banks as they rushed
          down.

Full wandering the way was they went through
    the wood,
Until soon it was time for the sun to be
    springing.
                Then they
        Were on a hill full high;
        White snow beside them lay.
        The servant who rode nigh
        Then bade his master stay.   2090

"I have led you hither, my lord, at this time,[27]
And not far are you now from that famous place
You have sought for, and asked so especially
    after.
Yet, sir, to you surely I'll say, since I know you,
A man in this world whom I love right well,
If you'd follow my judgment, the better you'd
    fare.
You make haste to a place that is held full of
    peril;
One dwells, the worst in the world, in that waste,
For he's strong and stern, and takes pleasure in
    striking.
No man on the earth can equal his might;   2100
He is bigger in body than four of the best men
In Arthur's own household, Hector or others.
And thus he brings it about at the chapel:
That place no one passes so proud in his arms
That he smites him not dead with a stroke of his
    hand.
He's a man most immoderate, showing no
    mercy;
Be it chaplain or churl that rides by the chapel,
Monk or priest, any manner of man,
Him to slay seems as sweet as to still live himself.
So I say, as sure as you sit in your saddle   2110
You're killed, should the knight so choose, if you
    come here;
That take as the truth, though you twenty lives
    had
                To spend.
        He's lived in this place long
        In battles without end.
        Against his strokes right strong
        You cannot you defend.

"So let him alone, good Sir Gawain, and leave
By a different road, for God's sake, and ride
To some other country where Christ may
    reward you.   2120
And homeward again I will hie me, and promise
To swear by the Lord and all his good saints
(So help me the oaths on God's halidom sworn)
That I'll guard well your secret, and give out no
    story
You hastened to flee any hero I've heard of."
"Thank you," said Gawain, and grudgingly
    added,
"Good fortune go with you for wishing me well.
And truly I think you'd not tell; yet though
    never
So surely you hid it, if hence I should hasten,
Fearful, to fly in the fashion you tell of,   2130
A coward I'd prove, and could not be pardoned.
The chapel I'll find whatsoever befalls,
And talk with that wight the way that I want to,
Let weal or woe follow as fate may wish.
                Though the knave,
        Hard to subdue and fell,
        Should stand there with a stave,
        Yet still the Lord knows well
        His servants how to save."

Quoth the man, "By Mary, you've said now
    this much: 2140
That you wish to bring down your own doom
    on your head.
Since you'd lose your life, I will stay you no
    longer.
Put your helm on your head, take your spear in
    your hand,
And ride down this road by the side of that rock
Till it brings you down to the dale's rugged
    bottom;
Then look at the glade on the left hand a little:
You'll see in the valley that self-same chapel,
And near it the great-limbed knight who is
    guarding it.
Gawain the noble, farewell now, in God's name!
I would not go with thee for all the world's
    wealth,   2150
Nor in fellowship ride one more foot through
    the forest."
The man in the trees there then turns his bridle,
As hard as he can hits his horse with his heels,

And across the fields gallops, there leaving Sir
    Gawain
                Alone.
      "By God," the knight said, "now
      I'll neither weep nor groan.
      Unto God's will I bow,
      And make myself his own."

He strikes spurs into Gringolet, starts on the
    path;   2160
By a bank at the side of a small wood he pushes
    in,
Rides down the rugged slope right to the dale.
Then about him he looks, and the land seems
    wild,
And nowhere he sees any sign of a shelter,
But slopes on each side of him, high and steep,
And rocks, gnarled and rough, and stones right
    rugged.
The clouds there seemed to him scraped by the
    crags.
Then he halted and held back his horse at that
    time,
And spied on all sides in search of the chapel;
Such nowhere he saw, but soon, what seemed
    strange,   2170
In the midst of a glade a mound, as it might be,
A smooth, swelling knoll by the side of the
    water,
The falls of a rivulet running close by;
In its banks the brook bubbled as though it were
    boiling.
The knight urged on Gringolet, came to the
    glade,
There leaped down lightly and tied to the limb
Of a tree, right rugged, the reins of his noble
    steed,
Went to the mound, and walked all about it,
Debating what manner of thing it might be:
On the end and on each side an opening; every-
    where   2180
Over it grass was growing in patches,
All hollow inside, it seemed an old cave
Or a crag's old cleft: which, he could not decide.
              Said the knight,
      "Is this the chapel here?
      Alas, dear Lord! here might

The fiend, when midnight's near,
      His matin prayers recite.

  "Of a truth," said Gawain, "the glade here is
    gloomy;
The Green Chapel's ugly, with herbs overgrown. 2190
It greatly becomes here that hero, green-clad,
To perform in the devil's own fashion his
    worship.
I feel in my five senses this is the fiend
Who has made me come to this meeting to kill
    me.
Destruction fall on this church of ill-fortune!
The cursedest chapel that ever I came to!"
With helm on his head and lance in his hand
He went right to the rock of that rugged abode.
From that high hill he heard, from a hard rock
    over
The stream, on the hillside, a sound wondrous
    loud.   2200
Lo! it clattered on cliffs fit to cleave them, as
    though
A scythe on a grindstone some one were
    grinding.[28]
It whirred, lo! and whizzed like a water-mill's
    wheel;
Lo! it ground and it grated, grievous to hear.
"By God, this thing, as I think," then said
    Gawain,
"Is done now for me, since my due turn to meet
    it
                Is near.
      God's will be done! 'Ah woe!'
      No whit doth aid me here.
      Though I my life forego   2210
      No sound shall make me fear."

  And then the man there commenced to call
    loudly,
"Who here is the master, with me to hold tryst?
For Gawain the good now is going right near.
He who craves aught of me let him come hither
    quickly;
'T is now or never; he needs to make haste."
Said somebody, "Stop," from the slope up above
    him,
"And promptly you'll get what I promised to
    give you."

Yet he kept up the whirring noise quickly a
 while,
Turned to finish his sharpening before he'd
 descend.   2220
Then he came by a crag, from a cavern
 emerging,
Whirled out of a den with a dreadful weapon,
A new Danish axe to answer the blow with:
Its blade right heavy, curved back to the handle,
Sharp filed with the filing tool, four feet in
 length,
'T was no less, by the reach of that lace gleaming
 brightly.
The fellow in green was garbed as at first,
Both his face and his legs, his locks and his beard,
Save that fast o'er the earth on his feet he went
 fairly,
The shaft on the stone set, and stalked on beside
 it.   2230
On reaching the water, he would not wade it;
On his axe he hopped over, and hastily strode,
Very fierce, through the broad field filled all
 about him
              With snow.
        Sir Gawain met the man,
        And bowed by no means low,
        Who said, "Good sir, men can
        Trust you to tryst to go."

    Said the green man, "Gawain, may God you
     guard!
You are welcome indeed, sir knight, at my
 dwelling.   2240
Your travel you've timed as a true man should,
And you know the compact we came to between
 us;
A twelvemonth ago you took what chance gave,
And I promptly at New Year was pledged to
 repay you.
In truth, we are down in this dale all alone;
Though we fight as we please, here there's no
 one to part us.
Put your helm from your head, and have here
 your payment;
Debate no further than I did before,
When you slashed off my head with a single
 stroke."

"Nay," quoth Gawain, "by God who gave me
 my spirit,   2250
I'll harbor no grudge whatever harm happens.
Exceed not one stroke and still I shall stand;
You may do as you please, I'll in no way oppose
              The blow."
        He left the flesh all bare,
        Bending his neck down low
        As if he feared naught there,
        For fear he would not show.

    Then the man in green raiment quickly made
     ready,
Uplifted his grim tool Sir Gawain to smite;   2260
With the whole of his strength he heaved it on
 high,
As threateningly swung it as though he would
 slay him.
Had it fallen again with the force he intended
That lord, ever-brave, from the blow had been
 lifeless.
But Gawain a side glance gave at the weapon
As down it came gliding to do him to death;
With his shoulders shrank from the sharp iron a
 little.[29]
The other with sudden jerk stayed the bright axe,
And reproved then that prince with proud words
 in plenty:
"Not Gawain thou art who so good is
 considered,   2270
Ne'er daunted by host in hill or in dale;
Now in fear, ere thou feelest a hurt, thou art
 flinching;
Such cowardice never I knew of that knight.
When you swung at me, sir, I fled not nor
 started;
No cavil I offered in King Arthur's castle.
My head at my feet fell, yet never I flinched,
And thy heart is afraid ere a hurt thou feelest,
And therefore thy better I'm bound to be thought
              On that score."
        "I shrank once," Gawain said,   2280
        "And I will shrink no more;
        Yet cannot I my head,
        If it fall down, restore.

    "But make ready, sir, quickly, and come to
     the point;

My destiny deal me, and do it forthwith;
For a stroke I will suffer, and start no further
Till hit with thy weapon; have here my pledged
  word."
Quoth the other, heaving it high, "Have at
  thee!"
As fierce in his manner as if he were mad,
He mightily swung but struck not the man,   2290
Withheld on a sudden his hand ere it hurt him.
And firmly he waited and flinched in no
  member,
But stood there as still as a stone or a stump
In rocky ground held by a hundred roots.
Then the Green Knight again began to speak
  gaily:
"It behooves me to hit, now that whole is thy
  heart.
Thy high hood that Arthur once gave you now
  hold back,
Take care that your neck at this cut may
  recover."
And Gawain full fiercely said in a fury,
"Come! lay on, thou dread man; too long thou
  art threatening.   2300
I think that afraid of your own self you feel."
"In sooth," said the other, "thy speech is so
  savage
No more will I hinder thy mission nor have it
                  Delayed."
          With puckered lips and brow
          He stands with ready blade.
          Not strange 't is hateful now
          To him past hope of aid.

    He lifts his axe lightly, and lets it down deftly,
The blade's edge next to the naked neck.   2310
Though he mightily hammered he hurt him no
  more
Than to give him a slight nick that severed the
  skin there.
Through fair skin the keen axe so cut to the flesh
That shining blood shot to the earth o'er his
  shoulders.
As soon as he saw his blood gleam on the snow
He sprang forth in one leap, for more than a
  spear length;
His helm fiercely caught up and clapped on his
  head;

With his shoulders his fair shield shot round in
  front of him,
Pulled out his bright sword, and said in a passion
(And since he was mortal man born of his
  mother   2320
The hero was never so happy by half),
"Cease thy violence, man; no more to me offer,
For here I've received, unresisting, a stroke.
If a second thou strikest I soon will requite thee,
And swiftly and fiercely, be certain of that,
                  Will repay.
          One stroke on me might fall
          By bargain struck that way,
          Arranged in Arthur's hall;
          Therefore, sir knight, now stay!"   2330

    The man turned away, on his weapon rested,
The shaft on the ground set, leaned on the sharp
  edge,
And gazed at Sir Gawain there in the glade;
Saw that bold man, unblenching, standing right
  bravely,
Full-harnessed and gallant; at heart he was glad.
Then gaily the Green Knight spoke in a great
                  voice,
And said to the man in speech that resounded,
"Now be not so savage, bold sir, for towards
  you
None here has acted unhandsomely, save
In accord with the compact arranged in the
  King's court.   2340
I promised the stroke you've received, so hold
  you
Well payed. I free you from all duties further.
If brisk I had been, peradventure a buffet
I'd harshly have dealt that harm would have
  done you.
In mirth, with a feint I menaced you first,
With no direful wound rent you; right was my
  deed,
By the bargain that bound us both on the first
  night,
When, faithful and true, you fulfilled our agree-
  ment,
And gave me your gain as a good man ought to.
The second I struck at you, sir, for the morning 2350
You kissed my fair wife and the kisses accorded
  me.

Two mere feints for both times I made at you,
    man,
                    Without woe.
            True men restore by right,
            One fears no danger so;
            You failed the third time, knight,
            And therefore took that blow.

"'T is my garment you're wearing, that
    woven girdle,
Bestowed by my wife, as in truth I know well.
I know also your kisses and all of your acts   2360
And my wife's advances; myself, I devised them.
I sent her to try you, and truly you seem
The most faultless of men that e'er fared on his
    feet.
As a pearl compared to white peas is more
    precious,
So next to the other gay knights is Sir Gawain.
But a little you lacked, and loyalty wanted,
Yet truly 't was not for intrigue or for wooing,
But love of your life; the less do I blame you."
Sir Gawain stood in a study a great while,
So sunk in disgrace that in spirit he groaned;   2370
To his face all the blood in his body was flowing;
For shame, as the other was talking, he shrank.
And these were the first words that fell from his
    lips:
"Be cowardice cursed, and coveting! In you
Are vice and villainy, virtue destroying."
The lace he then seized, and loosened the strands,
And fiercely the girdle flung at the Green Knight.
"Lo! there is faith-breaking! evil befall it.
To coveting came I, for cowardice caused me
From fear of your stroke to forsake in myself   2380
What belongs to a knight: munificence, loyalty.
I'm faulty and false, who've been ever afraid
Of untruth and treachery; sorrow betide both
                    And care!
            Here I confess my sin;
            All faulty did I fare.
            Your good will let me win,
            And then I will beware."

Then the Green Knight laughed, and right
    graciously said,
"I am sure that the harm is healed that I suffered. 2390
So clean you're confessed, so cleared of your
    faults,

Having had the point of my weapon's plain
    penance,
I hold you now purged of offence, and as
    perfectly
Spotless as though you'd ne'er sinned in your life.
And I give to you, sir, the golden-hemmed
    girdle,
As green as my gown. Sir Gawain, when going
Forth on your way among famous princes,
Think still of our strife and this token right
    splendid,
'Mid chivalrous knights, of the chapel's adventure.
This New Year you'll come to my castle again,   2400
And the rest of this feast in revel most pleasant
                    Will go."
            Then pressed him hard the lord:
            "My wife and you, I know.
            We surely will accord,
            Who was your bitter foe."

"No indeed," quoth the hero, his helm seized
    and doffed it
Graciously, thanking the Green Knight; "I've
    stayed
Long enough. May good fortune befall you;
    may He
Who all fame doth confer give it fully to you,
    sir.   2410
To your lady, gracious and lovely, commend
    me,
To her and that other, my honored ladies,
That so with their sleights deceived their knight
    subtly.
But no marvel it is for a fool to act madly,
Through woman's wiles to be brought to woe.
So for certain was Adam deceived by some
    woman,
By several Solomon, Samson besides;
Delilah dealt him his doom; and David
Was duped by Bath-sheba, enduring much
    sorrow.
Since these were grieved by their guile, 't would
    be great gain   2420
To love them yet never believe them, if knights
    could.
For formerly these were most noble and
    fortunate,
More than all others who lived on the earth;

And these few
By women's wiles were caught
With whom they had to do.
Though I'm beguiled, I ought
To be excused now too.

"But your girdle," said Gawain, "may God
    you reward!
With a good will I'll use it, yet not for the gold,   2430
The sash or the silk, or the sweeping pendants,
Or fame, or its workmanship wondrous, or cost,
But in sign of my sin I shall see it oft.[30]
When in glory I move, with remorse I'll
    remember
The frailty and fault of the stubborn flesh,
How soon 't is infected with stains of defilement;
And thus when I'm proud of my prowess in
    arms,
The sight of this sash shall humble my spirit.
But one thing I pray, if it prove not displeasing;
Because you are lord of the land where I stayed   2440
In your house with great worship (may He now
    reward you
Who sitteth on high and upholdeth the heavens),
What name do you bear? No more would I
    know."
And then. "That truly I'll tell," said the other;
"Bercilak de Hautdesert here am I called.
Through her might who lives with me, Morgan
    le Fay,
Well-versed in the crafts and cunning of magic
(Many of Merlin's arts she has mastered,
For long since she dealt in the dalliance of love
With him whom your heroes at home know,
    that sage   2450
                        Without blame.
            'Morgan the goddess,' so
            She's rightly known by name.
            No one so proud doth go
            That him she cannot tame),

"I was sent in this way to your splendid hall
To make trial of your pride, and to see if the
    people's
Tales were true of the Table's great glory.
This wonder she sent to unsettle your wits,
And to daunt so the Queen as to cause her to die   2460
From fear at the sight of that phantom speaker

Holding his head in his hand at the high table.
Lives she at home there, that ancient lady;
She's even thine aunt, King Arthur's half-sister,
Tyntagel's duchess's daughter, whom Uther
Made later the mother of mighty Lord Arthur.
I beg thee, sir, therefore, come back to thine
    aunt;
In my castle make merry. My company love
    thee,
And I, sir, wish thee as well, on my word,
As any on earth for thy high sense of honor."   2470
He said to him, nay, this he'd never consent to.
The men kiss, embrace, and each other
    commend
To the Prince of Paradise; there they part
                        In the cold.
            Gawain on his fair horse
            To Arthur hastens bold;
            The bright Green Knight his course
            Doth at his pleasure hold.

Through the wood now goes Sir Gawain by
    wild ways
On Gringolet, given by God's grace his life.   2480
Oft in houses, and oft in the open he lodged,
Met many adventures, won many a victory:
These I intend not to tell in this tale.
Now whole was the hurt he had in his neck,
And about it the glimmering belt he was bearing,
Bound to his side like a baldric obliquely,
Tied under his left arm, that lace, with a knot
As a sign that with stain of sin he'd been found.
And thus to the court he comes all securely.
Delight in that dwelling arose when its lord
    knew   2490
That Gawain had come; a good thing he thought
    it.
The King kissed the lord, and the Queen did
    likewise,
And next many knights drew near him to greet
    him
And ask how he'd fared; and he wondrously
    answered,
Confessed all the hardships that him had befallen,
The happenings at chapel, the hero's behavior,
The lady's love, and lastly the lace.
He showed them the nick in his neck all naked
The blow that the Green Knight gave for deceit

Him to blame.   2500
In torment this he owned;
Blood in his face did flame;
With wrath and grief he groaned,
When showing it with shame.

Laying hold of the lace, quoth the hero, "Lo!
    lord!
The band of this fault I bear on my neck;
And this is the scathe and damage I've suffered,
For cowardice caught there, and coveting also,
The badge of untruth in which I was taken.
And this for as long as I live I must wear,   2510
For his fault none may hide without meeting
    misfortune,
For once it is fixed, it can ne'er be unfastened."
To the knight then the King gave comfort;[31] the
    court too
Laughed greatly, and made this gracious
    agreement:

That ladies and lords to the Table belonging,
All of the brotherhood, baldrics should bear
Obliquely about them, bands of bright green,
Thus following suit for the sake of the hero.
For the Round Table's glory was granted that
    lace,
And he held himself honored who had it there-
    after,   2520
As told in the book, the best of romances.
In the days of King Arthur this deed was done
Whereof witness is borne by Brutus's book.
Since Brutus, that bold man, first came here to
    Britain,
When ceased, indeed, had the siege and assault
            At Troy's wall,
        Full many feats ere now
        Like this one did befall.
        May He with thorn-crowned brow
        To His bliss bring us all.   Amen.   2530

Hony soyt qui mal pence.

Notes

1   Brutus, the grandson of Aeneas, was the legendary founder of Britain. It should be remembered that Aeneas was above all *pius* and that his piety consisted in part of a reverence for the best traditions of Troy (which had been neglected as a result of the judgment of Paris and the subsequent rape of Helen) and in part of his steadiness of purpose in establishing the foundations of Roman *pietas*. Moreover, in his quest to found "walls and customs" Aeneas was faced with certain temptations, some, like the affair with Dido, arising from opportunities to abandon his quest in favor of a life of ease and pleasure, and some arising from formidable obstacles like the enmity of Turnus. The Romans were quite aware of the fact that Vergil's narrative is not historically accurate; what was important to them was not fact, but the example set by the protagonist. In the same way, many Englishmen probably understood that the legend of Brutus was not factual; nevertheless, it established a continuity between the *pietas* and chivalry of Aeneas and the *pietas* and chivalry of England. In *Sir Gawain* the function of Gawain is to exemplify the tradition of the piety of Aeneas in a manner consistent with the ideals of Christian chivalry.

2   The alternation of prosperity and adversity in Britain and the dangers to the realm attendant upon each form central thematic concerns in both Gildas and Geoffrey of Monmouth. *Sir Gawain* is primarily concerned with the danger to the realm arising from prosperity.

3   In England after the appearance of Geoffrey of Monmouth's *History*, Arthur became a symbol of the glory of the realm of England. Thus Edward III founded the Order of the Garter, for example, to maintain the traditions of the Round Table. The glory of England might, however, be tarnished, as Geoffrey himself amply demonstrates. Here Arthur should be taken in this symbolic sense, not as a historical figure. The characters in the poem cannot be understood with reference to French romances like those of Chrétien de Troyes, who had no interest in the promotion of English chivalric ideals.

4 The description of the Christmas revels is designed to show the realm of England devoted to pleasure and childlike gaiety, all serious purpose (including the memory of Christ) lost in display, festivity, and dalliance. Part of the description is similar to the account of Baltasar's feast in "Purity," and indeed the festival here has implications similar to those of the biblical festival (Dan. 5). The appearance of the Green Knight has a function similar to that of the handwriting on the wall, but the realm is saved in this instance through the action of Sir Gawain.

5 The color green was frequently associated with the Word of God, which, like "the tree which is planted near running waters" (Ps. 1) or like the palm, does not wither but maintains its vitality and greenness forever. It had other connotations as well, but this one is consistent with (1) the season, (2) the symbolism of the holly, and (3) the action of the Green Knight as a testing agent. There was no special connection in England between the color green and faeries, and fourteenth-century noblemen were entirely unfamiliar with vegetation spirits.

6 Since palm leaves were frequently unavailable in England, other evergreens, including holly, were used in Church services. In l. 265, the Green Knight himself indicates that his holly branch is an obvious sign of peace. It is a reminder, in other words, of the Prince of Peace who is being neglected at His own festival in Arthur's court. The holly has nothing whatsoever to do with pagan rites in this poem. It is unlikely that either the author or the audience knew much about peasant superstitions or that they would have regarded them with anything but contempt if they had known about them.

7 The reaction of the court is a sufficient indication of the state of unreadiness into which the fellowship of Arthur has fallen.

8 The Green Knight has just explained that he has come unarmed and desires nothing but peace. Arthur's answer is patently foolish and another indication of the unhealthy state of the realm.

9 The game proposed is that used to test the bravery of the warriors seeking the hero's portion in *The Feast of Bricriu*. In *Sir Gawain* it presents a singular challenge to the courage of the members of the Round Table that they are markedly reluctant to accept.

10 Gawain's humility is noteworthy.

11 The action of kicking the severed head is hardly courageous.

12 The vague directions indicate that the Green Chapel is not, actually, a place in space and time. This does not mean, of course, that the scenery around the chapel may not have been based in part on an actual location familiar to the poet.

13 The alternation of the seasons again suggests the alternation of good and bad fortune, a theme first stated in ll. 16–19.

14 The symbolism of this device is sufficiently explained in the poem itself. It is designed to show Gawain's qualifications for the quest before him. The quest (to reestablish the *pietas* of the Round Table) is moral, not physical; hence the necessary qualifications are moral also. The explanation of the pentangle should be taken with all seriousness since it is an essential part of the thematic structure of the poem. With reference to the device itself, there is a similar (though curvilinear) figure in the window tracery of the fourteenth-century choir at Lichfield, and it is probable that pentangles were used elsewhere in the decorative arts of the period with implications similar to those developed in the poem.

15 These are usually described as the Annunciation, the Nativity, the Resurrection, the Ascension, and the Assumption.

16 Like Geoffrey of Monmouth's King Arthur, Gawain bears the image of the Blessed Virgin on his shield. Mary was regarded in the fourteenth century as an inspiration to courtesy (good behavior at court) and chivalry.

17 England.

18 The serpents, trolls, bulls, bears, and so on encountered by Gawain should neither be taken literally nor regarded as folkloristic decoration. The cold, wintry wilderness full of monstrous adversaries is indicative of temptations of adversity in the world that impede Gawain in his effort to accomplish his mission. The scenery and its inhabitants are no more literal and no more naïve than the long, empty corridors of the existentialist cinema. Gawain is saved from the trials that confront him because he served God; and he is relieved altogether of this kind of temptation when he prays devoutly to Christ and Mary (ll. 753–762).

19   Paper castles were used as decorations at feasts. The long spires and pinnacles are characteristic of the decorated style of English Gothic architecture, although they appear most clearly on tombs, screens, sedilia, and in manuscript decoration. Their liberal application to larger architectural forms like this castle would have been extremely costly. The impression desired here is one of overwhelming luxury.

20   The luxuriousness of the castle is an appropriate setting for the temptations of prosperity, which Gawain must now face. The rich furnishings, fine clothing, sumptuous food, excellent service, and the company of a beautiful and amorously inclined lady here place Gawain in a position to face alone and in a systematic way the kinds of temptations that have corrupted Arthur's court.

21   The two ladies exemplify the difficulties Gawain must face. That is, the old and ugly Morgan le Fay, who sent the Green Knight to Arthur's court in the first place, represents the trials of adversity, while the young and beautiful lady represents the temptations of prosperity or good fortune. Readers of Boethius will recall that both kinds of fortune are actually useful and are, to the eye of reason, a necessary part of the Providential Order. Again it should be emphasized that the action being described is symbolic action, not action in space and time.

22   The hunt on each day parallels thematically the temptation offered Gawain on the same day. That is, the lord on the first day hunts barren hinds and brings home venison. The lady (ll. 1236–1237) openly offers Gawain her body. The temptations of prosperity are those of gluttony (or lechery), vainglory, and avarice (covetousness or desire for eminence in the world). It was said that Adam was overcome by these temptations in the garden, but that Christ overcame them in the wilderness. Taken together, they were said to represent those aspects of the flesh (or the inherited weakness of the flesh), the devil, and the world which cause man to turn away from God or, in terms of the story before us, to lose his chivalry. Philippe de Mézières, who founded the chivalric Order of the Passion in the late fourteenth century, attributed the decay of chivalry to weakness before these temptations.

23   A piece of gristle from the breastbone.

24   The boar hunt seems to owe some of its details to Ovid's description of the hunt for the Calydonian boar, *Metamorphoses*, 8:260ff. Angered by the failure of King Oenus to offer her a sacrifice, Diana let loose a monstrous boar in his country. A hunt for the boar was organized. Meleager killed it and proudly presented its head to Atalanta, with whom he was in love. This act aroused the anger of his uncles, who took the head for themselves. Angered in turn, Meleager killed them. His mother, Althaea, enraged by the slaughter of her brothers, vengefully threw a piece of wood, with which Meleager's life was bound up, into the fire, killing her son. Later she stabbed herself with a dagger. The baleful consequences of wrath arising from injured pride are here sufficiently plain. In medieval contexts the boar was associated with fierce and vainglorious worldly rulers. On this day the lady appeals to Gawain's pride by calling attention to his reputation and asking him to speak of love. Gawain, however, maintains an attitude of humility. When he is given the boar's head, he praises his host.

25   The traitorous fox suggested the malicious and avaricious. In art, the fox frequently represented evil and avaricious friars. On this day, appropriately, the lady tempts Gawain with gifts, one of which, her green girdle, he accepts when he is made to believe that anyone who wears it may not be killed. Later on (l. 2374), he accuses himself of cowardice for flinching before the Green Knight's feint with the axe and of covetousness for having accepted the girdle. Thus Gawain successfully overcame the temptations of lechery and vainglory but weakened a little before the temptation of avarice. He does not, as he should, give his host the girdle in exchange for the skin of the fox.

26   The cold stormy weather and the forbidding landscape indicate that Gawain must once more face the temptations of adversity. Since he succumbed to a certain extent in prosperity, we should expect him to show some weakness now.

27 Here Gawain is tempted to abandon his quest on the ground that it is too perilous and difficult, but he reasserts his faith in God (ll. 2138–2139) and in Providence (ll. 2158–2159).

28 It has been suggested that the poet remembered an actual location near a fulling mill. However, the noise as it appears in the poem is designed to enhance the fearfulness of the setting, not to remind anyone of an actual place.

29 In spite of the girdle and his faith in God, Gawain flinches once. That is, his weakness before the temptation of avarice has hampered his ability to face the tests of adversity. The slip, however, was not extremely serious.

30 The green girdle here becomes a sign of contrition. Perhaps it was thought of as contrasting with the girdle of Pallas worn by Turnus in pride.

31 The knights of the Round Table (the chivalry of Britain) wear the girdle as a token of honor, although some of them may not regard it very seriously. It is true in a sense that he who wears it and is penitent cannot suffer death. The poem ends as it began by recalling the tradition of *pietas* that the British inherit from Aeneas. They may carry it on, the poem implies, so long as they maintain—as Kipling was to remind them many years later—a humble and a contrite heart. "He with the thorn-crowned brow" has, as it were, proper followers in those who wear the green girdle, not only over their shoulders but in their hearts. If this association between contrition and chivalry seems strange, it may be relevant to point out that the most famous chivalric order of the later Middle Ages was the Order of the Passion of Our Lord.

 # B. Sir Thomas Malory

Thomas Malory of Newbold Revel (ca. 1405–1471) was probably the author of the famous collection of romances known as La Morte d'Arthur, *a work (or series of works) composed in prison, where the author spent the last twenty years of his life. As a young man, Malory served with Richard Beauchamp, Earl of Warwick, who enjoyed an international reputation for chivalry. In 1445 Malory became a member of Parliament, but in 1451 he began a series of actions that involved him in increasing difficulties with the law and that resulted finally in his imprisonment.*

For the most part Malory's sources are French prose romances, which he adapted to suit his own purposes. His treatment of them displays the stylistic tastes of the Renaissance, to which his work properly belongs. In the French sources narratives are broken up into episodes: a story once begun is soon abandoned to be replaced by another; after an interval it is resumed, only to be interrupted by another narrative, and so on. In the originals the primary interest was not so much in narrative for the sake of narrative as it was in certain abstract ideas that could be developed through a series of interwoven narratives. But Malory, who had little conception of the abstractions which governed his source materials, untangled the narratives before him, changed the typifying characters of the originals into crude personalities, and brought the action into focus as though it represented a series of actual events in space and time. As he made the action more literal, he also added touches of sentiment to the speeches of the characters to create still further verisimilitude. Although he rationalized symbolic events frequently to make them literally plausible, many of them were essential to the narrative and could not easily be explained away. Their retention against a background of literal narrative creates a heightened effect of the marvellous in his work.

Had Malory been a writer of more sophistication, he might well have sought to retain more of the thematic values

of his sources; just as, for example, early Netherlandish painters were able to create a remarkable surface verisi-
militude in highly symbolic representations. But Malory lacked both the knowledge and the inclination to develop
the content of his materials in a new style. Instead, he steeped his materials in a superficial and somewhat senti-
mentalized morality characteristic of less well-educated persons of his time. Although this morality evinces no very
great intellectual power, it helps to give Malory's narratives an impression of unity beyond that created by a
general chronological sequence and the persistence of a number of characters whose actions center around the court
of King Arthur. We gain an impression of a great nation whose strength is sapped by the blood lust of the sons
of King Lot and by the adulterous love of the Queen. With reference to the latter theme, however, both Guinevere
and her lover, Sir Lancelot, are treated with considerable sympathy. The resultant ambiguity lends the whole work
a strong appeal to twentieth-century readers.

For Malory's career, see Eugène Vinaver, Malory, Clarendon Press, Oxford, 1929. The whole conception
of Malory's artistry underwent a change with the publication of a newly discovered manuscript of his work by
Eugène Vinaver, The Works of Thomas Malory, Clarendon Press, Oxford, 1947. The new views, however,
have not gone unchallenged, and there has been considerable recent discussion. See the studies in J. A. W. Bennett,
Essays on Malory, *Clarendon Press, Oxford, 1963, and in R. M. Lumiansky, Malory's Originality, The*
Johns Hopkins Press, Baltimore, 1964. A sympathetic account of Malory's work as a unified whole is provided
by Edmund Reiss, Sir Thomas Malory, Twayne Publishers, New York, 1967. The traditionally accepted
identity of Sir Thomas Malory the author has been questioned by William Matthews, The Ill-Framed Knight,
The University of California Press, Berkeley, 1967. This text is from Professor Vinaver's anthology of selections,
King Arthur and His Knights, *Houghton Mifflin Company, Boston, 1956, reprinted by permission.*

"THE FAIR MAID OF ASTOLAT"

Thus it passed until Our Lady Day of the Assumption. Within a fifteen days of that feast the king let cry a great jousts and a tournament that should be at that day at Camelot, otherwise called Winchester. And the king let cry[1] that he and the king of Scots would joust against all the world.

And when this cry was made, thither came many good knights, that is to say the King of North Wales, and King Anguish of Ireland, and the King with the Hundred Knights, and Sir Galahalt the Haut Prince, and the King of Northumberland, and many other noble dukes and earls of others divers countries.

So King Arthur made him ready to depart to his jousts, and would have had the queen with him; but at that time she would not, she said, for she was sick and might not ride.

"That me repenteth," said the king, "for this seven year ye saw not such a noble fellowship together except at the Whitsuntide when Sir Galahad departed from the court."

"Truly," said the queen, "ye must hold me excused, I may not be there."

And many deemed the queen would not be there because of Sir Lancelot, for he would not ride with the king, for he said he was not whole of the play[2] of Sir Mador. Wherefore the king was heavy[3] and passing wroth, and so he departed toward Winchester with his fellowship.

And so by the way the king lodged at a town called Astolat, that is in English Guildford, and there the king lay in the castle. So when the king was departed the queen called Sir Lancelot unto her and said thus:

"Sir, ye are greatly to blame thus to hold you[4] behind my lord. What will your enemies and mine say and deem? 'See how Sir Lancelot holdeth him ever behind the king, and so the queen doth also, for that they would[5] have their pleasure together.' And thus will they say," said the queen.

"Have ye no doubt, madam," said Sir Lancelot. "I allow your wit.[6] It is of late come syn ye were waxen[7] so wise! And therefore, madam, at this time I will be ruled by your counsel, and this night I will take my rest, and to-morrow betime I will take my way toward Winchester. But wit you well," said Sir Lancelot unto the queen, "at that jousts I will be against the king and against all his fellowship."

"Sir, ye may there do as ye list," said the queen, "but by my counsel ye shall not be against your king and your fellowship, for there been full many hardy[8] knights of your blood."

"Madam," said Sir Lancelot, "I shall take the adventure that God will give me."

And so upon the morn early he heard mass and dined, and so he took his leave of the queen and departed. And then he rode so much unto the time [9] he came to Astolat; and there it happened him that in the evening-tide he came to an old baron's place that hight Sir Barnard of Astolat. And as Sir Lancelot entered into his lodging, King Arthur espied him as he did walk in a garden beside the castle: he knew him well enough.

"Well, sirs," said King Arthur unto his knights that were by him beside the castle, "I have now espied one knight," he said, "that will play his play [10] at the jousts, I undertake."

"Who is that?" said the knights.

"At this time ye shall not wit for me," said the king, and smiled, and went to his lodging.

So when Sir Lancelot was in his lodging, and unarmed in his chamber, the old baron, Sir Barnard, came to him and welcomed him in the best manner, but he knew not Sir Lancelot.

"Fair sir," said Sir Lancelot till [11] his host, "I would pray you to lend me a shield that were not openly known, for mine is well known."

"Sir," said his host, "ye shall have your desire, for meseemth ye be one of the likeliest [12] knights that ever I saw, and therefore, sir, I shall show you friendship." And said: "Sir, wit you well I have two sons that were but late made knights. And the eldest hight Sir Tirry, and he was hurt that same day he was made knight, and he may not ride; and his shield ye shall have, for that is not known, I daresay, but here and in no place else." And his younger son hight Sir Lavain. "And if it please you, he shall ride with you unto that jousts, for he is of [13] his age strong and wight. [14] For much my heart giveth unto [15] you, that [16] ye should be a noble knight. And therefore I pray you to tell me your name," said Sir Barnard.

"As for that," said Sir Lancelot, "ye must hold me excused as at this time. And if God give me grace to speed well at the jousts I shall come again and tell you my name. But I pray you in any wise let me have your son, Sir Lavain, with me, and that I may have his brother's shield."

"Sir, all this shall be done," said Sir Barnard.

So this old baron had a daughter that was called that time the Fair Maiden of Astolat, and ever she beheld Sir Lancelot wonderfully. [17] And as the book saith, she cast such a love unto [18] Sir Lancelot that she could never withdraw her love, wherefore she died. And her name was Elaine le Blanke.

So thus as she came to and fro she was so hot in love that she besought Sir Lancelot to wear upon him at the jousts a token of hers.

"Damsel," said Sir Lancelot, "and if I grant you that, ye may say that I do more for your love [19] than ever I did for lady or gentlewoman."

Then he remembered himself that he would go to the jousts disguised, and because he had never aforn [20] borne no manner of token of no [21] damsel, he bethought him to bear a token of hers, that [22] none of his blood thereby might know him. And then he said,

"Fair maiden, I will grant you to wear a token of yours upon mine helmet. And therefore what is it? Show ye it me."

"Sir," she said, "it is a red sleeve of mine, of scarlet, well embroidered with great pearls."

And so she brought it him. So Sir Lancelot received it and said,

"Never did I erst [23] so much for no damsel."

Then Sir Lancelot betook [24] the fair maiden his shield in keeping, and prayed her to keep it until time that he come again. [25] And so that night he had merry rest and great cheer, for this damsel Elaine was ever about Sir Lancelot all the while she might be suffered. [26]

So upon a day, on the morn, King Arthur and all his knights departed, for there the king had tarried three days to abide his noble knights. And so when the king was ridden, Sir Lancelot and Sir Lavain made them ready to ride, and either of them had white shields, and the red sleeve Sir Lancelot let carry with him.

And so they took their leave at Sir Barnard, the old baron, and at his daughter, the fair maiden, and then they rode so long till they came to Camelot, that time called Winchester. And there was great press [27] of kings, dukes, earls and barons, and many noble knights. But Sir Lancelot was lodged privily by the means of Sir Lavain with a rich burgess, that no man in that town was ware what they were. And so they reposed them there till Our Lady Day of the Assumption, that [28] the great jousts should be.

So when trumpets blew unto the field, and King Arthur was set on high upon a chafflet [29] to behold who did best (but, as the French book saith, the king would not suffer Sir Gawain to go from him, for never had Sir Gawain the better an Sir Lancelot were in the field, and many times was Sir Gawain rebuked so when Sir Lancelot was in the field in any jousts disguised), then some of the kings, as King Anguish of Ireland and the King of Scots, were that time turned[30] to be upon the side of King Arthur. And then the other party was the King of North Wales, and the King with the Hundred Knights, and the King of Northumberland, and Sir Galahalt the Haut Prince. But these three kings and this duke was passing[31] weak to hold against Arthur's party, for with him[32] were the noblest knights of the world.

So then they withdrew them either party from other and every man made him ready in his best manner to do what he might. Then Sir Lancelot made him ready and put the red sleeve upon his helmet and fastened it fast. And so Sir Lancelot and Sir Lavain departed out of Winchester privily and rode until[33] a little leaved[34] wood behind the party that held against King Arthur's party. And there they held them[35] still till the parties smote together. And then came in the King of Scots and the King of Ireland on King Arthur's party, and against them came in the King of Northumberland and the King with the Hundred Knights.

And there began a great medley, and there the King of Scots smote down the King of Northumberland, and the King with the Hundred Knights smote down King Anguish of Ireland. Then Sir Palomides, that was on Arthur's party, he encountered with Sir Galahalt, and either of them smote down other, and either party helped their lords on horseback again. So there began a strong assail[36] on both parties.

And then came in Sir Braundiles, Sir Sagramore le Desirous, Sir Dodinas le Savage, Sir Kay le Seneschal, Sir Grifflet le Fyz de Dieu, Sir Lucan de Butler, Sir Bedivere, Sir Agravain, Sir Gaheris, Sir Mordred, Sir Meliot de Logres, Sir Ozanna le Cure Hardy, Sir Safir, Sir Epinogris, Sir Galleron of Galway. All these fifteen knights, that were knights of the Round Table, so these with more other came in together and beat aback the King of Northumberland and the King of North Wales.

When Sir Lancelot saw this, as he hoved[37] in the little leaved wood, then he said unto Sir Lavain,

"See yonder is a company of good knights, and they hold them[38] together as boars that were chased with dogs."

"That is truth," said Sir Lavain.

"Now," said Sir Lancelot, "an ye will help a little,

ye shall see the yonder fellowship that chaseth now these men on our side, that they shall go as fast backward as they went forward."

"Sir, spare ye not for my part,"[39] said Sir Lavain, "for I shall do what I may."

Then Sir Lancelot and Sir Lavain came in at the thickest of the press, and there Sir Lancelot smote down Sir Braundiles, Sir Sagramore, Sir Dodinas, Sir Kay, Sir Grifflet, and all this he did with one spear. And Sir Lavain smote down Sir Lucan de Butler and Sir Bedivere. And then Sir Lancelot gat another great spear, and there he smote down Sir Agravain and Sir Gaheris, Sir Mordred, Sir Meliot de Logres; and Sir Lavain smote down Sir Ozanna le Cure Hardy. And then Sir Lancelot drew his sword, and there he smote on the right hand and on the left hand, and by great force he unhorsed Sir Safir, Sir Epinogris, and Sir Galleron.

And then the knights of the Table Round withdrew them aback, after they had gotten their horses as well as they might.

"Ah, mercy Jesu," said Sir Gawain. "What knight is yonder that doth so marvellous deeds in that field?"

"I wot what he is," said the king, "but as at this time I will not name him."

"Sir," said Sir Gawain, "I would say it were Sir Lancelot by his riding and his buffets[40] that I see him deal. But ever meseemeth it should not be he, for that he beareth the red sleeve upon his helmet; for I wist him never bear token at no jousts of lady ne gentlewoman."

"Let him be," said King Arthur, "for he will be better known and do more or ever he depart."

Then the party that was against King Arthur were well comforted, and then they held them[41] together that beforehand were sore rebuked.[42] Then Sir Bors, Sir Ector de Maris, and Sir Lionel, they called unto them the knights of their blood, as Sir Blamore de Ganis, Sir Bleoberis, Sir Aliduke, Sir Galihud, Sir Eliodin, Sir Bellengere le Beuse. So these nine knights of Sir Lancelot's kin thrust in mightily, for they were all noble knights, and they of great hate and despite[43] thought to rebuke[44] Sir Lancelot and Sir Lavain, for they knew them not.

And so they came hurling together and smote down many knights of North Wales and of Northumberland. And when Sir Lancelot saw them fare so, he gat a great spear in his hand; and there encountered with him all at once, Sir Bors, Sir Ector, and Sir Lionel. And they three smote him at once with their spears, and with force of themself [45] they smote Sir Lancelot's horse revers [46] to the earth. And by misfortune Sir Bors smote Sir Lancelot through the shield into the side, and the spear brake, and the head left still [47] in the side.

When Sir Lavain saw his master lie on the ground he ran to the King of Scots and smote him to the earth; and by great force he took his horse and brought him to Sir Lancelot, and maugre [48] them all he made him to mount upon that horse. And then Sir Lancelot gat a spear in his hand, and there he smote Sir Bors, horse and man, to the earth; and in the same wise he served Sir Ector and Sir Lionel; and Sir Lavain smote down Sir Blamore de Ganis. And then Sir Lancelot drew his sword, for he felt himself so sore hurt that he weened there to have had his death. And then he smote Sir Bleoberis such a buffet on the helmet that he fell down to the earth in a swoon and in the same wise he served Sir Aliduke and Sir Galihud. And Sir Lavain smote down Sir Bellengere that was son to Alisaunder le Orphelin.

And by [49] this was done was Sir Bors horsed again and in came with Sir Ector and Sir Lionel, and all they three smote with their swords upon Sir Lancelot's helmet. And when he felt their buffets, and with that [50] his wound grieved him grievously, then he thought to do what he might while he could endure. And then he gave Sir Bors such a buffet that he made him bow his head passing low; and therewithal he raced off [51] his helm, and might have slain him, but when he saw his visage so pulled him down. And in the same wise he served Sir Ector and Sir Lionel; for, as the book saith, he might have slain them, but when he saw their visages his heart might not serve him thereto, [52] but left them there.

And then afterwards he hurled into the thickest press [53] of them all, and did there the marvelloust [54] deeds of arms that ever man saw, and ever Sir Lavain with him. And there Sir Lancelot with his sword smote down and pulled down, as the French book saith, more than thirty knights, and the most party were [55] of the Table Round. And there Sir Lavain did full well that day, for he smote down ten knights of the Table Round.

"Mercy, Jesu," said Sir Gawain unto King Arthur, "I marvel what knight that he is with the red sleeve."

"Sir," said King Arthur, "he will be known or ever he depart."

And then the king blew unto lodging, [56] and the prize was given by heralds unto the knight with the white shield that bare the red sleeve. Then came the King of North Wales, and the King of Northumberland, and the King with the Hundred Knights, and Sir Galahalt the Haut Prince, and said unto Sir Lancelot:

"Fair knight, God you bless, for much have ye done for us this day. And therefore we pray you that ye will come with us, that ye may receive the honor and the prize as ye have worshipfully [57] deserved it."

"Fair lords," said Sir Lancelot, "wit ye well, if I have deserved thank I have sore [58] bought it, and that me repenteth it, for I am never like [59] to escape with the life. Therefore, my fair lords, I pray you that ye will suffer me to depart where me liketh, for I am sore hurt. And I take none force of none [60] honor, for I had liefer repose me [61] than to be lord of all the world."

And therewithal he groaned piteously, and rode a great wallop [62] awayward from them until he came under a wood's eves. [63] And when he saw that he was from the field nigh a mile, that he was sure he might not be seen, then he said with an high voice and with a great groan,

"Ah, gentle knight, Sir Lavain! help me that this truncheon [64] were out of my side, for it sticketh so sore that it nigh slayeth me."

"Ah, mine own lord," said Sir Lavain, "I would fain do that might please you, but I dread me sore, an I pull out the truncheon, that ye shall be in peril of death."

"I charge [65] you," said Sir Lancelot, "as ye love me, draw it out!"

And therewithal he descended from his horse, and right so did Sir Lavain; and forthwithal he drew the truncheon out of his side, and gave a great shriek and a grisly groan that [66] the blood brast out nigh a pint at once, that at the last [67] he sank down upon his arse and so swooned down, pale and deadly.

"Alas," said Sir Lavain, "what shall I do?"

And then he turned Sir Lancelot into the wind, and so he lay there nigh half-an-hour as he had been dead. And so at the last Sir Lancelot cast up his eyen, and said,

"Ah, Sir Lavain, help me that I were on my horse! For here is fast by, within this two mile, a gentle [68] hermit that sometime was a full noble knight and a great lord of possessions. And for great goodness he hath taken him to wilful [69] poverty, and forsaken mighty lands. And his name is Sir Baudwin of Britain, and he is a full noble surgeon and a good leech. Now let see and help me up that I were there, for ever my heart giveth me[70] that I shall never die of my cousin-germain's[71] hands."

And then with great pain Sir Lavain holp him upon his horse, and then they rode a great wallop[72] together, and ever Sir Lancelot bled, that it[73] ran down to the earth. And so by fortune they came to an hermitage which was under a wood, and a great cliff on the other side, and a fair water[74] running under it. And then Sir Lavain beat on the gate with the butt of his spear and cried fast,[75]

"Let in, for Jesu's sake!"

And anon there came a fair child[76] to them and asked them what they would.

"Fair son," said Sir Lavain, "go and pray thy lord the hermit for God's sake to let in here a knight that is full sore wounded. And this day, tell thy lord, I saw him do more deeds of arms than ever I heard say that any man did."

So the child went in lightly,[77] and then he brought the hermit which was a passing likely[78] man. When Sir Lavain saw him he prayed him for God's sake of succor.

"What knight is he?" said the hermit. "Is he of the house of King Arthur or not?"

"I wot not," said Sir Lavain, "what he is, nother what is his name, but well I wot I saw him do marvellously this day as of deeds of arms."

"On whose party was he?" said the hermit.

"Sir," said Sir Lavain, "he was this day against King Arthur, and there he won the prize of all the knights of the Round Table."

"I have seen the day," said the hermit, "I would have loved him the worse because he was against my lord, King Arthur, for sometime I was one of the fellowship, but now I thank God I am otherwise disposed. But where is he? Let me see him."

Then Sir Lavain brought the hermit to him. And when the hermit beheld him as he sat leaning upon his saddle-bow, ever bleeding spiteously,[79] and ever the knight hermit thought that he should know him; but he could not bring him to knowledge because he was so pale for bleeding.

"What knight are ye," said the hermit, "and where were ye born?"

"My fair lord," said Sir Lancelot, "I am a stranger and a knight adventurous that laboreth throughout many realms for to win worship."

Then the hermit advised him better[80] and saw by a wound on his cheek that he was Sir Lancelot.

"Alas," said the hermit, "mine own lord! Why lain[81] you your name from me? Perdy,[82] I ought to know you of right, for ye are the most noblest knight of the world. For well I know you for Sir Lancelot."

"Sir," said he, "sith ye know me, help me, an ye may, for God's sake! For I would be out of this pain at once, other to death other to life."

"Have ye no doubt," said the hermit, "for ye shall live and fare right well."

And so the hermit called to him two of his servants, and so they bare him into the hermitage, and lightly unarmed him, and laid him in his bed. And then anon the hermit staunched his blood and made him to drink good wine, that he was well revigored and knew himself.[83] For in these days it was not the guise[84] as is nowadays; for there were none hermits in those days but that they had been men of worship and of prowess, and those hermits held great households and refreshed[85] people that were in distress.

Now turn we unto King Arthur, and leave Sir Lancelot in the hermitage. So when the kings were together on both parties, and the great feast should be holden, King Arthur asked the King of North Wales and their fellowship where was that knight that bare the red sleeve.

"Let bring him before me, that he may have his laud and honor and the prize,[86] as it is right."

Then spake Sir Galahalt the Haut Prince and the King with the Hundred Knights, and said,

"We suppose that knight is mischieved[87] so that he is never like to see you nother none of us all. And that is the greatest pity that ever we wist of any knight."

"Alas," said King Arthur, "how may this be? Is he so sore hurt? But what is his name?" said King Arthur.

"Truly," said they all, "we know not his name, nother from whence he came, nother whither he would."

"Alas," said the king, "this is the worst tidings that came to me this seven year! For I would not for all the lands I wield to know and wit it were so that that noble knight were slain."

"Sir, know ye aught of him?" said they all.

"As for that," said King Arthur, "whether I know him other none, ye shall not know for me what man he is but[88] Almighty Jesu send me good tidings of him."

And so said they all.

"By my head," said Sir Gawain, "if it so be that the good knight be so sore hurt, it is great damage[89] and pity to all this land, for he is one of the noblest knights that ever I saw in a field handle spear or sword. And if he may be found I shall find him, for I am sure he is not far from this country."

"Sir, ye bear you well," said King Arthur, "and ye may find him, unless that he be in such a plight that he may not wield himself."[90]

"Jesu defend!" said Sir Gawain. "But wit well I shall know what he is an I may find him."

Right so Sir Gawain took a squire with him upon hackneys[91] and rode all about Camelot within six or seven mile, but soon he came again[92] and could hear no word of him. Then within two days King Arthur and all the fellowship returned unto London again. And so as they rode by the way it happened Sir Gawain at Astolat to lodge with Sir Barnard thereas[93] was Sir Lancelot lodged.

And so as Sir Gawain was in his chamber to repose him Sir Barnard, the old baron, came in to him, and his daughter Elaine, to cheer him and to ask him what tidings, and who did best at the tournament of Winchester.

"So God me help," said Sir Gawain, "there were two knights that bare white shields, but one of them bare a red sleeve upon his head, and certainly he was the best knight that ever I saw joust in field. For I dare say," said Sir Gawain, "that one knight with the red sleeve smote down forty knights of the Round Table, and his fellow did right well and worshipfully."

"Now blessed be God," said this fair maiden of Astolat, "that that knight sped so well! For he is the man in the world that I first loved,[94] and truly he shall be the last that ever I shall love."

"Now, fair maiden," said Sir Gawain, "is that good knight your love?"[95]

"Certainly, sir," said she, "he is my love."[96]

"Then know ye his name?" said Sir Gawain.

"Nay truly, sir," said the damsel, "I know not his name nother from whence he came, but to say that I love him, I promise God and you I love him."

"How had ye knowledge of him first?" said Sir Gawain.

Then she told him, as ye have heard before, and how her father betook[97] him her brother to do him service, and how her father lent him her brother's, Sir Tirry's, shield: "and here with me he left his own shield."

"For what cause did he so?" said Sir Gawain.

"For this cause," said the damsel, "for his shield was full well known among many noble knights."

"Ah, fair damsel," said Sir Gawain, "please it you let me have a sight of that shield?"

"Sir," she said, "it is in my chamber, covered with a case, and if ye will come with me ye shall see it."

"Not so," said Sir Barnard to his daughter, "but send ye for that shield."

So when the shield was come,[98] Sir Gawain took off the case, and when he beheld that shield he knew it anon that it was Sir Lancelot's shield and his own arms.

"Ah, Jesu, mercy!" said Sir Gawain, "now is my heart more heavier than ever it was tofore."

"Why?" said this maid Elaine.

"For I have a great cause," said Sir Gawain. "Is that knight that oweth this shield[99] your love?"

"Yea, truly," she said, "my love[100] is he. God would that I were his love."

"So God me speed," said Sir Gawain, "fair damsel, ye have right,[101] for an he be your love ye love the most honorablest knight of the world and the man of most worship."

"So methought ever," said the damsel, "for never or that time no knight that ever I saw loved I never none erst."[102]

"God grant," said Sir Gawain, "that either of you may rejoice other, but that is in a great adventure.[103] But truly," said Sir Gawain unto the damsel, "ye may say ye have a fair grace,[104] for why I have known that noble knight this four-and-twenty year, and never or that day I nor none other knight, I dare make good, saw never nother heard say that ever he bare token or sign of no lady, gentlewoman, nor maiden at no jousts nother tournament.[105] And therefore, fair maiden, ye are much beholden to him to give him thank. But I dread me," said Sir Gawain, "that ye shall never see him in this world, and that is as great pity as ever was of any earthly man."

"Alas!" said she, "how may this be? Is he slain?"

"I say not so," said Sir Gawain, "but wit you well he is grievously wounded, by all manner of signs, and by means of sight[106] more likelier to be dead than to be on live. And wit you well he is the noble knight Sir Lancelot, for by this shield I know him."

"Alas!" said this fair maiden of Astolat, "how may this be? And what was his hurt?"

"Truly," said Sir Gawain, "the man in the world that loved best him hurt him. And I dare say," said Sir Gawain, "an that knight that hurt him knew the very certainty [107] that he had hurt Sir Lancelot, it were the most sorrow that ever came to his heart."

"Now, fair father," said then Elaine, "I require you give me leave to ride and seek him, other else I wot well I shall go out of my mind. For I shall never stint till that I find him and my brother, Sir Lavain."

"Do ye as it liketh you," said her father, "for me sore repenteth of the hurt of that noble knight."

Right so the maid made her ready and departed before Sir Gawain making great dole. Then on the morn Sir Gawain came to King Arthur and told him all how he had found Sir Lancelot's shield in the keeping of the fair maiden of Astolat.

"All that knew I aforehand," said King Arthur, "and that caused me I would not suffer [108] you to have ado [109] at the great jousts; for I espied him when he came until [110] his lodging, full late in the evening, into Astolat. But great marvel have I," said King Arthur, "that ever he would bear any sign of any damsel, for or now I never heard say nor knew that ever he bare any token of none earthly woman."

"By my head, sir," said Sir Gawain, "the fair maiden of Astolat loveth him marvellously well. What it meaneth I cannot say. And she is ridden after to seek him."

So the king and all came to London, and there Gawain all openly disclosed it to all the court that it was Sir Lancelot that jousted best. And when Sir Bors heard that, wit you well he was an heavy [111] man, and so were all his kinsmen. But when the queen wist that it was Sir Lancelot that bare the red sleeve of the fair maiden of Astolat, she was nigh out of her mind for wrath. And then she sent for Sir Bors de Ganis in all haste that might be. So when Sir Bors was come before the queen she said,

"Ah, Sir Bors! Have ye not heard say how falsely Sir Lancelot hath betrayed me?"

"Alas, madam," said Sir Bors, "I am afeard he hath betrayed himself and us all."

"No force," [112] said the queen, "though he be destroyed, for he is a false traitor-knight."

"Madam," said Sir Bors, "I pray you say ye no more so, for wit you well I may not hear no such language of him."

"Why so, Sir Bors?" said she. "Should I not call him traitor when he bare the red sleeve upon his head at Winchester, at the great jousts?"

"Madam," said Sir Bors, "that sleeve-bearing repenteth me, [113] but I dare say he did bear it to none [114]

evil intent, but for this cause he bare the red sleeve that none of his blood [115] should know him. For or then we nother none of us all never knew that ever he bare token or sign of maiden, lady, nother gentlewoman."

"Fie on him!" said the queen. "Yet for all his pride and bobaunce, [116] there ye proved yourself better man than he."

"Nay, madam, say ye nevermore so, for he beat me and my fellows, and might have slain us an he had would."

"Fie on him!" said the queen. "For I heard Sir Gawain say before my lord Arthur that it were marvel to tell the great love that is between the fair maiden of Astolat and him."

"Madam," said Sir Bors, "I may not warn [117] Sir Gawain to say what it pleaseth him, but I daresay, as for my lord Sir Lancelot, that he loveth no lady, gentlewoman, nother maiden, but as he loveth all inlike much. [118] And therefore, madam," said Sir Bors, "ye may say what ye will, but wit you well I will haste me to seek him and find him wheresomever he be, and God send me good tidings of him!"

And so leave we them there, and speak we of Sir Lancelot that lay in great peril. And so as this fair maiden Elaine came to Winchester she sought there all about, and by fortune Sir Lavain, her brother, was ridden to sport him to enchafe [119] his horse. And anon as this maiden Elaine saw him she knew him, and then she cried on-loud till him, and when he heard her he came to her. And anon with that she asked her brother,

"How doth my lord, Sir Lancelot?"

"Who told you, sister, that my lord's name was Sir Lancelot?"

Then she told him how Sir Gawain by his shield knew him.

So they rode together till that they came to the hermitage, and anon she alight. So Sir Lavain brought her in to Sir Lancelot, and when she saw him lie so sick and pale in his bed she might not speak, but suddenly she fell down to the earth in a swough. And there she lay a great while. And when she was relieved [120] she shricked and said,

"My lord, Sir Lancelot! Alas, why lie ye in this plight?"

And then she swooned again. And then Sir Lancelot prayed Sir Lavain to take her up, "and bring her hither to me."

And when she came to herself Sir Lancelot lift her and said,

"Fair maiden, why fare ye thus? For ye put me to more pain.[121] Wherefore make ye no such cheer, for an ye be come to comfort me ye be right welcome; and of this little hurt that I have I shall be right hastily whole, by the grace of God. But I marvel," said Sir Lancelot, "who told you my name?"

And so this maiden told him all how Sir Gawain was lodged with her father.

"And there by your shield he discovered your name."

"Alas," said Sir Lancelot, "that repenteth me[122] that my name is known, for I am sure it will turn until anger."[123]

And then Sir Lancelot compassed in his mind[124] that Sir Gawain would tell Queen Guinevere how he bare the red sleeve, and for whom, that he wist well would turn unto great anger.[125]

So this maiden Elaine never went from Sir Lancelot, but watched[126] him day and night, and did such attendance to him that the French book saith there was never woman did never more kindlier for man. Then Sir Lancelot prayed Sir Lavain to make espies[127] in Winchester for Sir Bors if he came there, and told him by what tokens he should know him: by a wound in his forehead.

"For I am sure," said Sir Lancelot, "that Sir Bors will seek me, for he is the same good knight that hurt me."

Now turn we unto Sir Bors de Ganis that came until Winchester to seek after his cousin Sir Lancelot. And when he[128] came to Winchester Sir Lavain laid watch[129] for Sir Bors. And anon he had warning of him, and so he found him, and anon he salewed him and told him from whence he came.

"Now, fair knight," said Sir Bors, "ye be welcome, and I require you that ye will bring me to my lord Sir Lancelot."

"Sir," said Sir Lavain, "take your horse, and within this hour ye shall see him."

So they departed and came to the hermitage. And when Sir Bors saw Sir Lancelot lie in his bed, dead pale and discolored, anon Sir Bors lost his countenance, and for kindness and pity he might not speak, but wept tenderly a great while. But then when he might speak he said thus:

"Ah, my lord Sir Lancelot, God you bless, and send you hasty recovering! For full heavy am I of my misfortune and of mine unhappiness. For now I may call myself unhappy, and I dread me that God is greatly displeased with me, that He would suffer me to have such a shame for to hurt you that are all our leader and all our worship;[130] and therefore I call myself unhappy.[131] Alas, that ever such a caitiff[132] knight as I am should have power by unhappiness[133] to hurt the most noblest knight of the world! Where I so shamefully set upon you and overcharged you,[134] and where ye might have slain me, ye saved me; and so did not I, for I and all our blood did to you their utterance.[135] I marvel," said Sir Bors, "that my heart or my blood would serve me. Wherefore, my lord Sir Lancelot, I ask you mercy."

"Fair cousin," said Sir Lancelot, "ye be right welcome; and wit you well, overmuch ye say for the pleasure of me which pleaseth me nothing,[136] for why I have the same isought;[137] for I would with pride have overcome you all. And there in my pride I was near slain, and that was in mine own default;[138] for I might have given you warning of my being there, and then had I had[139] no hurt. For it is an old-said saw, 'there is hard battle thereas[140] kin and friends doth battle either against other,' for there may be no mercy but mortal war. Therefore, fair cousin," said Sir Lancelot, "let this language overpass,[141] and all shall be welcome that God sendeth. And let us leave off this matter and speak of some rejoicing, for this that is done may not be undone; and let us find a remedy how soon that I may be[142] whole."

Then Sir Bors leaned upon his bed's side and told Sir Lancelot how the queen was passing wroth with him, "because ye wore the red sleeve at the great jousts." And there Sir Bors told him all how Sir Gawain discovered it, "by your shield that ye left with the fair maiden of Astolat."

"Then is the queen wroth?" said Sir Lancelot. "Therefore am I right heavy,[143] but I deserved no wrath, for all that I did was because I would not be known."

"Sir, right so excused I you," said Sir Bors, "but all was in vain, for she said more largelier[144] to me than I to you say now. But, sir, is this she," said Sir Bors, "that is so busy about you, that men call the Fair Maiden of Astolat?"

"Forsooth, she it is," said Sir Lancelot, "that by no means I cannot put her from me."[145]

"Why should ye put her from you?" said Sir Bors. "For she is a passing fair damsel, and well beseen[146] and well taught.[147] And God would, fair cousin," said Sir

Bors, "that ye could love her, but as to that I may not nother dare not counsel you. But I see well," said Sir Bors, "by her diligence about you that she loveth you entirely."[148]

"That me repenteth,"[149] said Sir Lancelot.

"Well," said Sir Bors, "she is not the first that hath lost her pain[150] upon you, and that is the more pity."

And so they talked of many more things.

And so within three or four days Sir Lancelot waxed big and light. Then Sir Bors told Sir Lancelot how there was sworn a great tournament betwixt King Arthur and the King of North Wales, that should be upon All Hallowmass Day, besides Winchester.

"Is that truth?" said Sir Lancelot. "Then shall ye abide with me still a little while until that I be whole, for I feel myself reasonably big and strong."

"Blessed be God!" said Sir Bors.

Then were they there nigh a month together, and ever this maiden Elaine did ever her diligence and labor night and day unto Sir Lancelot, that[151] there was never child nother wife more meeker till father and husband than was this fair maiden of Astolat; wherefore Sir Bors was greatly pleased with her.

So upon a day, by the assent of Sir Lavain, Sir Bors and Sir Lancelot, they made the hermit to seek in woods for divers herbs, and so Sir Lancelot made fair Elaine to gather herbs for him to make him a bam.[152] So in the meanwhile Sir Lancelot made Sir Lavain to arm him at all pieces,[153] and there he thought to essay himself upon horseback with a spear, whether he might wield his armor and his spear for his hurt or not.

And so when he was upon his horse he stirred him freshly,[154] and the horse was passing lusty and frick[155] because he was not labored of a month before. And then Sir Lancelot bade Sir Lavain give him that great spear, and so Sir Lancelot couched that spear in the rest. The courser leapt mightily when he felt the spurs, and he that was upon him, which was the noblest horseman of the world, strained him[156] mightily and stably, and kept still the spear in the rest. And therewith Sir Lancelot strained himself so straitly,[157] with so great force, to get the courser forward, that the bottom of his wound brast[158] both within and without, and therewithal the blood came out so fiercely that he felt himself so feeble that he might not sit upon his horse. And then Sir Lancelot cried unto Sir Bors,

"Ah, Sir Bors and Sir Lavain, help! For I am come unto mine end!"

And therewith he fell down on the one side to the earth like a dead corpse. And then Sir Bors and Sir Lavain came unto him with sorrow-making out of measure. And so by fortune this maiden Elaine heard their mourning; and then she came, and when she found Sir Lancelot there armed in that place she cried and wept as she had been wood.[159] And then she kissed him and did what she might to awake him, and then she rebuked her brother and Sir Bors, and called them false traitors, and said,

"Why would ye take him out of his bed? For an he die, I will appeal you of[160] his death."

And so with that came the hermit, Sir Baudwin of Britain, and when he found Sir Lancelot in that plight he said but little, but wit ye well he was wroth. But[161] he said, "Let us have him in," and anon they bore him into the hermitage and unarmed him, and laid him in his bed; and evermore his wound bled spiteously,[162] but he stirred no limb of him. Then the knight-hermit put a thing in his nose and a little deal of water in his mouth, and then Sir Lancelot waked of his swough. And then the hermit staunched his bleeding, and when Sir Lancelot might speak he[163] asked why he put his life so in jeopardy.

"Sir," said Sir Lancelot, "because I weened I had been strong enough, and also Sir Bors told me that there should be at Hallowmass a great jousts betwixt King Arthur and the King of North Wales. And therefore I thought to essay myself, whether I might be there or not."

"Ah, Sir Lancelot," said the hermit, "your heart and your courage will never be done until your last day! But ye shall do now by my counsel: let Sir Bors depart from you, and let him do at that tournament what he may; and, by the grace of God," said the knight-hermit, "by that[164] the tournament be done and he comen hither again, sir, ye shall be whole, so[165] that ye will be governed by me."

Then Sir Bors made him ready to depart from him, and Sir Lancelot said,

"Fair cousin, Sir Bors, recommend me unto all those ye ought recommend me unto, and I pray you, enforce[166] yourself at that jousts that ye may be best, for my love. And here shall I abide you, at the mercy of God, till your again-coming."[167]

And so Sir Bors departed and came to the court of King Arthur, and told them in what place he left Sir Lancelot.

"That me repenteth,"[168] said the king. "But syn he shall have his life, we all may thank God."

And then Sir Bors told the queen what jeopardy Sir Lancelot was in when he would essayed[169] his horse:

"And all that he did was for the love of you, because he would have been at this tournament."

"Fie on him, recreant knight!" said the queen. "For wit you well I am right sorry an he shall have his life."

"Madam, his life shall he have," said Sir Bors, "and who that would otherwise, except you, madam, we that be of his blood would help to shorten their lives! But, madam," said Sir Bors, "ye have been oftentimes displeased with my lord Sir Lancelot, but at all times at the end ye found him a true knight."

And so he departed. And then every knight of the Round Table that were there that time present made them ready to that jousts at All Hallowmass. And thither drew many knights of divers countries. And as Hallowmass drew near, thither came the King of North Wales, and the King with the Hundred Knights, and Sir Galahalt the Haut Prince of Surluse. And thither came King Anguish of Ireland, and the King of Northumberland, and the King of Scots. So these three kings came to King Arthur's party.

And so that day Sir Gawain did great deeds of arms, and began first; and the heralds numbered that Sir Gawain smote down twenty knights. Then Sir Bors de Ganis came in the same time, and he was numbered that he[170] smote down twenty knights; and therefore the prize was given betwixt[171] them both, for they began first and longest endured. Also Sir Gareth, as the book saith, did that day great deeds of arms, for he smote down and pulled down thirty knights: but when he had done that deeds he tarried not but so departed, and therefore he lost his prize. And Sir Palomides did great deeds of arms that day, for he smote down twenty knights; but he departed suddenly, and men deemed that he and Sir Gareth rode together to some manner[172] adventures.

So when this tournament was done Sir Bors departed, and rode till he came to Sir Lancelot, his cousin. And then he found him walking on his feet, and there either made great joy of other.

And so he told Sir Lancelot of all the jousts, like as ye have heard.

"I marvel," said Sir Lancelot, "that Sir Gareth, when he had done such deeds of arms, that he would not tarry."

"Sir, thereof we marvelled all," said Sir Bors, "for but if it were you, other[173] the noble knight Sir Tristram, other the good knight Sir Lamorak de Galis, I saw never knight bear[174] so many knights and smite down in so little a while as did Sir Gareth. And anon as he was gone we all wist not where he became."[175]

"By my head," said Sir Lancelot, "he is a noble knight, and a mighty man and well-breathed;[176] and if he were well essayed," said Sir Lancelot, "I would deem he were good enough for any knight that beareth the life.[177] And he is gentle, courteous and right bounteous, meek and mild, and in him is no manner of mal engine,[178] but plain, faithful, and true."

So then they made them ready to depart from the hermitage. And so upon a morn they took their horses and this Elaine le Blanke with them. And when they came to Astolat there were they well lodged, and had great cheer of Sir Barnard, the old baron, and of Sir Tirry, his son.

And so upon the morn when Sir Lancelot should depart, fair Elaine brought her father with her, and Sir Lavain and Sir Tirry, and then thus she said:

"My lord, Sir Lancelot, now I see ye will depart from me. Now, fair knight and courteous knight," said she, "have mercy upon me, and suffer me not to[179] die for your love."

"Why, what would ye that I did?" said Sir Lancelot.

"Sir, I would have you to my husband," said Elaine.

"Fair damsel, I thank you heartily," said Sir Lancelot, "but truly," said he, "I cast me never[180] to be wedded man."

"Then, fair knight," said she, "will ye be my paramour?"

"Jesu defend me!" said Sir Lancelot. "For then I rewarded your father and your brother full evil for their great goodness."

"Alas! Then," said she, "I must die for your love."

"Ye shall not so," said Sir Lancelot, "for wit you well, fair maiden, I might have been married an I had would,[181] but I never applied me yet to be married. But because, fair damsel, that ye love me as ye say ye do, I will for your good will and kindness show to you some goodness. That is this, that wheresomever ye will beset[182] your heart upon some good knight that will wed you, I shall give you together[183] a thousand pound yearly, to you and to your heirs. This much will I give you, fair maiden, for your kindness, and always while I live to be your own knight."

"Sir, of all this," said the maiden, "I will none, for but if ye will wed me, other to be my paramour at the least, wit you well, Sir Lancelot, my good days are done."

"Fair damsel," said Sir Lancelot, "of these two things ye must pardon[184] me."

Then she shrieked shrilly[185] and fell down in a swough; and then women bare her into her chamber, and there she made overmuch sorrow. And then Sir Lancelot would[186] depart, and there he asked Sir Lavain what he would do.

"Sir, what should I do," said Sir Lavain, "but follow you but if ye drive me from you or command me to go from you?"

Then came Sir Barnard to Sir Lancelot and said to him,

"I cannot see but that my daughter will die for your sake."

"Sir, I may not do withal,"[187] said Sir Lancelot, "for that me sore repenteth. For I report me to yourself[188] that my proffer is fair. And me repenteth," said Sir Lancelot, "that she loveth me as she doth, for I was never the causer of it; for I report me unto your son, I never early nother late proffered her bounty nother fair behests.[189] And as for me," said Sir Lancelot, "I dare do that a knight should do, and say that she is a clean maiden for me, both for deed and will. For I am right heavy of her distress! For she is a full fair maiden, good and gentle, and well itaught."[190]

"Father," said Sir Lavain, "I dare make good she is a clean maiden as for my lord Sir Lancelot; but she doth as I do, for sithen I saw first my lord Sir Lancelot I could never depart from him, nother nought I will, an I may[191] follow him."

Then Sir Lancelot took his leave, and so they departed, and came to Winchester. And when King Arthur wist that Sir Lancelot was come whole and sound, the king made great joy of him; and so did Sir Gawain and all the knights of the Round Table, except Sir Agravain and Sir Mordred. Also Queen Guinevere was wood wroth[192] with Sir Lancelot, and would by no means speak with him, but estranged herself from him. And Sir Lancelot made all the means that he might[193] for to speak with the queen, but it would not be.

Now speak we of the fair maiden of Astolat that made such sorrow day and night that she never slept, ate, nother drank, and ever she made her complaint unto Sir Lancelot. So when she had thus endured a ten days, that she feebled so that she must needs pass out of this world, then she shrove her clean and received her Creator. And ever she complained still upon Sir Lancelot. Then her ghostly[194] father bade her leave such thoughts. Then she said,

"Why should I leave such thoughts? Am I not an earthly woman? And all the while the breath is in my body I may complain me, for my belief is that I do none offense, though I love an earthly man, unto God, for He formed me thereto, and all manner of good love cometh of God. And other than good love loved I never Sir Lancelot du Lake. And I take God to record, I loved never none but him, nor never shall, of earthly creature; and a clean maiden I am for him and for all other. And sithen it is the sufferance[195] of God that I shall die for so noble a knight, I beseech Thee, High Father of Heaven, have mercy upon me and my soul, and upon mine innumerable pains that I suffer may be allegeance[196] of part of my sins. For, Sweet Lord Jesu," said the fair maiden, "I take God to record, I was never to Thee great offencer nother against Thy laws but that I loved this noble knight, Sir Lancelot, out of measure. And of myself, Good Lord, I had no might to withstand the fervent love, wherefore I have my death."

And then she called her father, Sir Barnard, and her brother, Sir Tirry, and heartily she prayed her father that her brother might write a letter like as she did indite,[197] and so her father granted her. And when the letter was written word by word like as she devised it, then she prayed her father that she might be watched until she was dead. "And while my body is hot let this letter be put in my right hand, and my hand bound fast with the letter until that I be cold. And let me be put in a fair bed with all the richest clothes that I have about me, and so let my bed and all my richest clothes be laid with me in a chariot[198] unto the next[199] place where the Thames is; and there let me be put within a barget,[200] and but one man with me, such as ye trust to steer me thither; and that my barget be covered with black samite[201] over and over. And thus, father, I beseech you let it be done."

So her father granted it her faithfully all thing should be done like as she had devised. Then her father and her brother made great dole for her. And when this was done anon she died.

And when she was dead the corpse and the bed all was led the next way unto the Thames, and there a man and the corpse and all things as she had devised was put in the Thames. And so the man steered the barget unto Westminster, and there it rubbed and rolled to and fro a great while or any man espied it.

So by fortune King Arthur and Queen Guinevere were talking together at a window, and so as they looked into the Thames they espied that black barget and had marvel what it meant. Then the king called Sir Kay, and showed it him.

"Sir," said Sir Kay, "wit you well, there is some new tidings."

"Therefore go ye thither," said the king to Sir Kay, "and take with you Sir Braundiles and Sir Agravain, and bring me ready word what is there."

Then these three knights departed and came to the barget and went in. There they found the fairest corpse lying in a rich bed that ever ye saw, and a poor man sitting in the barget's end, and no word would he speak. So these three knights returned unto the king again, and told him what they found.

"That fair corpse will I see," said the king.

And so the king took the queen by the hand and went thither. Then the king made the barget to be held fast, and then the king and the queen went in with certain knights with them, and there he saw the fairest woman lie in a rich bed, covered unto her middle[202] with many rich clothes,[203] and all was of cloth of gold. And she lay as she had smiled.

Then the queen espied the letter in her right hand and told the king. Then the king took it and said,

"Now am I sure this letter will tell us what she was, and why she is come hither."

So then the king and the queen went out of the barget, and so commanded a certain[204] to wait[205] upon the barget. And so when the king was come to his chamber he called many knights about[206] him, and said that he would wit openly[207] what was written within that letter. Then the king brake it, and made a clerk to read it, and this was the intent[208] of the letter.

"Most noble knight, my lord Sir Lancelot, now hath death made us two at debate[209] for your love. And I was your lover, that men called the Fair Maiden of Astolat. Therefore unto all ladies I make my moan,[210] yet for my soul ye pray and bury me at the least and offer ye my mass-penny: this is my last request. And a clean maiden I died, I take God to witness. And pray for my soul, Sir Lancelot, as thou[211] art peerless."

This was all the substance in the letter. And when it was read, the king, the queen and all the knights wept for pity of the doleful complaints. Then was Sir Lancelot sent for, and when he was come King Arthur made the letter to be read to him. And when Sir Lancelot heard it word by word, he said,

"My lord Arthur, wit ye well I am right heavy of the death of this fair lady. And God knoweth I was never causer of her death by my willing, and that will I report me unto[212] her own brother that here he is, Sir Lavain. I will not say nay," said Sir Lancelot, "but that she was both fair and good, and much I was beholden unto her, but she loved me out of measure."

"Sir," said the queen, "ye might have showed her some bounty[213] and gentleness which might have preserved her life."

"Madam," said Sir Lancelot, "she would none otherways be answered but that she would be my wife other else my paramour, and of these two I would not grant her. But I proffered her, for her good love that she showed me, a thousand pound yearly to her and to her heirs, and to wed any manner of knight that she could find best to love in her heart. For, madam," said Sir Lancelot, "I love not to be constrained to love, for love must only arise of the heartself, and not by none constraint."

"That is truth, sir," said the king, "and with many knights, love is free in himself, and never will be bound; for where he is bounden he looseth himself." Then said the king unto Sir Lancelot, "Sir, it will be your worship that ye oversee[214] that she be interred worshipfully."[215]

"Sir," said Sir Lancelot, "that shall be done as I can best devise."

And so many knights yode thither to behold that fair dead maiden, and so upon the morn she was interred richly. And Sir Lancelot offered her mass-penny;[216] and all those knights of the Table Round that were there at that time offered with Sir Lancelot. And then the poor man went again[217] with the barget.

Then the queen sent for Sir Lancelot and prayed him of mercy for why that she had been wroth with him causeless.[218]

"This is not the first time," said Sir Lancelot, "that ye have been displeased with me causeless. But, madam, ever I must suffer you,[219] but what sorrow that I endure, ye take no force."[220]

So this passed on all that winter, with all manner of hunting and hawking, and jousts and tourneys were many betwixt many great lords.

Glossary

1 let it be proclaimed. 2 wound (F: *plaie*). 3 grieved. 4 remain. 5 because they wish to. 6 I commend your judgment. 7 It is not long since you have grown. 8 brave. 9 until. 10 perform valiant deeds. 11 to. 12 handsomest. 13 for. 14 stalwart. 15 I feel drawn to you. 16 because. 17 with admiration. 18 had so great a love for. 19 for your sake. 20 before. 21 for any. 22 so that. 23 hitherto. 24 entrusted to. 25 until he returned. 26 allowed. 27 throng. 28 when. 29 platform. 30 decided. 31 too. 32 with Arthur. 33 to. 34 leafy. 35 remained. 36 attack. 37 stood. 38 keep. 39 do not hold back on my account. 40 blows. 41 pressed the attack. 42 shamefully defeated. 43 angered and resentful. 44 defeat. 45 with their combined strength. 46 with back-handed blows. 47 sticking. 48 in spite of. 49 when. 50 and as. 51 tore off. 52 had no heart to do it. 53 throng. 54 most wonderful. 55 they were mostly. 56 ordered that the fighting should cease for the night. 57 honorably. 58 dearly. 59 unlikely. 60 I do not care for any. 61 I would sooner rest. 62 gallop. 62 the edge of a wood. 64 shaft (of spear). 65 command. 66 as. 67 and presently. 68 noble. 69 voluntary. 70 tells me. 71 first cousin's. 72 at full speed. 73 so that the blood. 74 stream. 75 loudly. 76 handsome young nobleman. 77 quickly. 78 handsome. 79 copiously. 80 thought again. 81 conceal. 82 par Dieu. 83 so that his strength returned and his spirits revived. 84 custom. 85 succored. 86 be praised, honored and rewarded. 87 come to some harm. 88 until. 89 a misfortune. 90 has lost consciousness. 91 hacks. 92 back. 93 where. 94 that was my first love. 95 lover *or* beloved. 96 beloved. 97 entrusted to. 98 brought. 99 to whom this shield belongs. 100 beloved. 101 are right. 102 for never before did I see any knight that I loved. 103 there is little chance of this. 104 you are extremely fortunate. 105 never before that day did I or any other knight . . . see or hear say that he ever carried a token at a tournament. 106 by his looks. 107 for certain. 108 allow. 109 to fight. 110 to. 111 sorrowful. 112 No matter. 113 I regret. 114 with no. 115 kin. 116 boasting. 117 prevent. 118 equally. 119 exercise. 120 recovered. 121 cause me more distress. 122 I regret. 123 cause ill-feeling. 124 realized. 125 unhappiness. 126 sat by. 127 send out searchers. 128 Sir Lavain. 129 lay in wait. 130 leader of us all and the glory of our fellowship. 131 unfortunate. 132 miserable. 133 through mischance. 134 sorely pressed you. 135 their worst. 136 you say all this to please me, but it pleases me not. 137 for my intention was the same as yours. 138 that was my own fault. 139 I should have had. 140 where. 141 do not let us speak thus. 142 that would soon make me. 143 it grieves me. 144 spoke more harshly. 145 send her away. 146 comely. 147 well-behaved. 148 with all her heart. 149 that is a pity. 150 pains. 151 for. 152 bath. 153 fully. 154 urged him on vigorously. 155 frisky. 156 held him. 157 severely. 158 the deepest part of his wound burst. 159 mad. 160 blame you for. 161 And. 162 copiously. 163 the hermit. 164 by the time. 165 provided. 166 exert. 167 your return. 168 That is a pity. 169 wished to try. 170 it was reckoned that he. 171 divided between. 172 kind of. 173 or. 174 strike. 175 went. 176 strong-winded. 177 lives. 178 guile. 179 do not let me. 180 I never intend. 181 wished. 182 bestow. 183 both. 184 excuse. 185 piercingly. 186 was about to. 187 I cannot help it. 188 But you will agree. 189 your son will bear witness that at no time did I show her regard or make her sweet promises. 190 well behaved. 191 and never shall, if I am allowed to. 192 wildly angry. 193 did all he could. 194 spiritual. 195 will. 196 relief. 197 as she would direct. 198 cart. 199 nearest. 200 small boat. 201 rich silk. 202 waist. 203 coverings. 204 someone. 205 keep watch. 206 to. 207 wished to hear in their presence. 208 content. 209 divided us. 210 lament. 211 thou who. 212 as to that I call to witness. 213 favor. 214 take care. 215 with honor. 216 an offering of money made at mass. 217 back. 218 prayed him to forgive her for having been unjustly displeased with him. 219 bear with you. 220 it matters not to you.

MIDDLE ENGLISH LITERATURE: PIERS THE PLOUGHMAN

Piers the Ploughman is a long poem that enjoyed considerable popularity during the fourteenth and fifteenth centuries. It is usually attributed to one "William Langland," although if a man by that name was, in fact, the author, or one of the authors, we know nothing about him. The *persona Will* in the poem is designed to fit into the structure of the poem, not to reveal any literal information about the author. The poem survives in three versions, conventionally described in modern times as the A text, the B text, and the C text. It is now usually assumed that the A text was written about 1370, the B text between 1377 and 1379, and the C text shortly after 1390. Of these versions the B text has received most attention, although the C text is longer and sometimes clearer. There has been a prolonged controversy in modern times about the subject

Facing page: Illustrated psalter from the late fourteenth century. Probably executed in London.

and meaning of the poem. In general, it may be said that the author showed deep concern for the state of the Church in his own day when viewed against a background of the traditional ideals of medieval Christianity. The B text, the first part of which is printed here in translation, contains "The Vision of William concerning Piers the Ploughman" followed by lives of Do-well, Do-better, and Do-best. Modern scholars do not agree about the meaning of the figure of Piers nor about what was meant by the subjects of the various lives.

The poem is written in the alliterative verse popular in the northern and western provinces of England. The following lines from the Prologue constitute a fair sample:

In a somer seson when soft was the sonne,
I shope me in shroudes as I a shepe were,
In habite as an heremite unholy of werkes,
Went wyde in this world wondres to here.

If the verse is read aloud slowly with some expression it has a solemn roll that is quite impressive. In form the work is a complex dream vision ordered around the conventional structure of the pilgrimage.

Some recent studies of the poem are E. Talbot Donaldson, *Piers Plowman: The C-Text and Its Poet*, Yale University Press, New Haven, Conn., 1949; D. W. Robertson, Jr., and B. F. Huppé, *"Piers Plowman" and Scriptural Tradition*, Princeton University Press, Princeton, N.J., 1951; R. W. Frank, Jr., *Piers Plowman and the Scheme of Salvation*, Yale University Press, New Haven, Conn., 1957; David C. Fowler, *Piers the Plowman: Literary Relations of the A and B Text*, The University of Washington Press, Seattle, 1961; M. W. Bloomfield, *Piers Plowman as a Fourteenth-century Apocalypse*, Rutgers University Press, New Brunswick, N.J., 1962. A convenient anthology of studies representing various scholarly attitudes has been provided by Edward Vasta, *Interpretations of Piers Plowman*, University of Notre Dame Press, Notre Dame, Ind., 1968. All three texts of the poem were edited with copious notes by W. W. Skeat, Oxford University Press, London, 1886. A new edition of the A text has been published by George Kane, Athlone Press, London, 1960. The best available translation is that by J. F. Goodridge, *Piers the Ploughman*, Penguin Books, Inc., Baltimore, 1959. Those interested in the poem who do not read Middle English with ease will find this translation of the entire B text most convenient. The first part of it is reprinted here by permission.

PIERS THE PLOUGHMAN

Prologue
The Plain Full of People

One summer season, when the sun was warm, I rigged myself out in shaggy woollen clothes, as if I were a shepherd; and in the garb of an easy-living hermit I set out to roam far and wide through the world, hoping to hear of marvels. But on a morning in May, among the Malvern Hills, a strange thing happened to me, as though by magic. For I was tired out by my wanderings, and as I lay down to rest under a broad bank by the side of a stream, and leaned over gazing into the water, it sounded so pleasant that I fell asleep.

And I dreamt a marvellous dream: I was in a wilderness, I could not tell where, and looking Eastwards[1] I saw a tower high up against the sun, and splendidly built on top of a hill; and far beneath it was a great gulf, with a dungeon in it, surrounded by deep, dark pits, dreadful to see. But between the tower and the gulf I saw a smooth plain, thronged with all kinds of people, high and low together, moving busily about their worldly affairs.[2]

Some labored at ploughing and sowing, with no time for pleasure, sweating to produce food for the gluttons to waste. Others spent their lives in vanity, parading themselves in a show of fine clothes. But many, out of love for our Lord and in the hope of Heaven, led strict lives devoted to prayer and penance —for such are the hermits and anchorites who stay in their cells, and are not forever hankering to roam about, and pamper their bodies with sensual pleasures.

Others chose to live by trade, and were much better off—for in our worldly eyes such men seem to thrive.[3] Then there were the professional entertainers, some of whom, I think, are harmless minstrels, making an honest living by their music; but others, babblers and vulgar jesters,[4] are true Judas' children! They invent fantastic tales about themselves, and pose as half-wits, yet they show wits enough whenever it suits them, and could easily work for a living if they had to! I will not say all that St Paul says about them; it is enough to quote, "He who talks filth is a servant of the Devil."[5]

And there were tramps and beggars hastening on their rounds, with their bellies and their packs crammed full of bread. They lived by their wits, and fought over their ale—for God knows, they go to bed glutted with food and drink, these brigands, and get up with foul language and filthy talk; and all day long, Sleep and shabby Sloth are at their heels.

And I saw pilgrims and palmers banding together to visit the shrines at Rome and Compostella. They went on their way full of clever talk, and took leave to tell fibs about it for the rest of their lives. And some I heard spinning such yarns of the shrines they had visited, you could tell by the way they talked that their tongues were more tuned to lying than telling the truth, no matter what tale they told.[6]

Troops of hermits with their hooked staves were on their way to Walsingham, with their wenches following after. These great, long lubbers, who hated work, were got up in clerical gowns to distinguish them from laymen, and paraded as hermits for the sake of an easy life.

I saw the Friars there too—all four Orders of them—preaching to the people for what they could get. In their greed for fine clothes, they interpreted the Scriptures to suit themselves and their patrons. Many of these Doctors of Divinity can dress as handsomely as they please, for as their trade advances, so their profits increase. And now that Charity has gone into business, and become confessor-in-chief to wealthy lords, many strange things have happened in the last few years; unless the Friars and Holy Church mend their quarrel, the worst evil in the world[7] will soon be upon us.

There was also a Pardoner, preaching like a priest. He produced a document covered with Bishops' seals, and claimed to have power to absolve all the people from broken fasts and vows of every kind. The ignorant folk believed him and were delighted. They came up and knelt to kiss his documents, while he, blinding them with letters of indulgence thrust in their faces, raked in their rings and jewellery with his roll of parchment! So the people give their gold to support these gluttons, and put their trust in dirty-minded scoundrels. If the Bishop were worthy of the name, if he kept his ears open to what went on around him, his seal would not be sent out like this to deceive the people. But it is not by the Bishop's leave that this rogue preaches; for the parish priest is in league with the Pardoner, and they divide the proceeds between them—money which, but for them, would go to the poor of the parish.[8]

Then I heard parish priests complaining to the Bishop that since the Plague their parishes were too poor to live in; so they asked permission to live in London, where they could traffic in Masses,[9] and chime their voices to the sweet jingling of silver. Bishops and novices, Doctors of Divinity and other great divines—to whom Christ has given the charge of men's souls, and whose heads are tonsured to show that they must absolve, teach, and pray for their parishioners, and feed the poor —I saw them all living in London,[10] even in Lent. Some took posts at Court counting the king's money, or in the Courts of Exchequer and Chancery, where they claimed his dues from the wards of the City and his right to unclaimed property. Others went into the service of lords and ladies, sitting like stewards managing household affairs—and gabbled their daily Mass and Office without devotion. Indeed, I fear that there are many whom Christ, in His great Consistory Court,[11] will curse for ever.

Then I understood something of that power which was entrusted to Peter, to "bind and unbind"[12] as the Scripture puts it. Peter, by our Lord's command, left it in the hands of Love, sharing it out among the four greatest virtues,[13] which are called Cardinal. For these are the hinges on which swing the gates of Christ's kingdom, closing against some, and opening on the bliss of Heaven to others. But as to those other Cardinals at Rome who have assumed the same name, taking upon themselves the appointment of a Pope to possess the power of St Peter, I will not call them in question. The election of a Pope requires both love and learning. There is much more I could say about the Papal Court, but it is not for me to say it.

Then there came into the field a king, guided by the knights. The powers of the Commons gave him his throne, and Common Sense provided men of learning to counsel him and to protect the people.

The king, with his nobles and counsellors, decided that the common people should provide them with resources; so the people devised different trades, and engaged ploughmen to labor and till the soil for the good of the whole community, as honest ploughmen should. Then the king and the people, helped by Common Sense, established law and order, so that every man might know his rights and duties.

Whereupon a long, lean, crazy fellow [14] knelt before the king and said gravely: "God save you, your majesty, and protect your kingdom. May He grant you grace to be so just a ruler, that you may win the love of your loyal subjects, and the reward of Heaven hereafter."

And then from the air on high an angel of Heaven [15] stooped down and spoke something in Latin—for the ignorant folk could not speak for themselves, they could only suffer and serve; so the angel said:

Sum rex, sum Princeps, neutrum fortasse deinceps;
O qui iura regis Christi specialia regis,
Hoc quod agas melius iustus es, esto pius!
Nudum ius a te vestiri vult pietate;
Qualia vis metere talia grana sere.
Si ius nudatur nudo de iure metatur;
Si seritur pietas de pietate metas! [16]

A garrulous fellow, with his head full of quotations, took offence at these words, and retorted to the angel:

Dum rex a regere dicatur nomen habere,
Nomen habet sine re nisi studet iura tenere. [17]

Whereupon all the common people, wishing to add their own piece of advice to the king, shouted out a line of Latin—let him make what he could of it—

Precepta regis sunt nobis vincula legis. [18]

Then all at once there ran out a horde of rats, and with them more than a thousand little mice, all coming to hold a Council to discuss their common safety. For a cat from a certain court used to come when he chose, to pounce on them and paw them, toss them about and play with them in the most alarming manner. "We're surrounded with so many dangers," they said, "that we scarcely dare to move. And if we complain of his games, he'll plague us all the more and never let us alone—he'll scratch and claw us and trap us between his paws, till our lives are not worth living! If we could only think of some scheme to stop him, we could be lords in our own domain and live at ease."

Then a certain rat, well known as an eloquent speaker, put forward an excellent plan of his own invention: "I have noticed," he said, "certain liveried men in the City, who wear bright gold chains around their necks, and fancy collars. They behave like dogs off the leash, straying about wherever they like over warrens and commons; and I'm told that they sometimes go wandering off and cause trouble elsewhere.

Now it has often occurred to me, that if they had bells attached to their collars, people could hear them coming and run away!

"So," continued the rat, "I have thought of a good scheme like that for us. We must buy a bell of brass or shining silver, attach it to a collar and hang it round the cat's neck! Then we shall be able to hear what he's up to—whether he's stirring abroad or having a rest or running out to play; and if he's in a pleasant, frisky mood, we can peep out of our holes and just put in an appearance, but if he's in a bad temper, we can take care and keep out of his way."

The whole rat-assembly applauded this scheme. But when the bell was bought and attached to the collar, there was not a rat in the whole company who dared to fix it round the cat's neck—not for the whole realm of England! So they were disgusted with themselves and ashamed of their feeble plan, and felt that all their long labor and planning had been wasted.

Then a mouse who looked very shrewd pushed himself boldly forward, and, standing before them all, spoke like this: "Even if we killed the cat, another like him would come to scratch us—and it would be no use our creeping under the benches! So I advise all commoners to leave him alone: and let's not be so rash as even to show him the bell.

"I heard my father say, several years ago, that when the cat is a kitten the court is a sorry place. And so it says in Holy Scripture: 'Woe to that land whose king is a child.' [19] For then no one can rest for the rats at night. In any case, the cat is not after our blood while he's off catching rabbits; [20] let us give him his due—he's content with his 'venison.' So surely a little trouble now is better than long years of misery and confusion. True, we should be rid of a tyrant, but what would happen?— We mice would be eating up men's malt, and you rats would tear their clothes to shreds. So thank God the cat can outrun you! For if you had your own way, you could never govern yourselves.

"Therefore my counsel is, don't offend the cat or the kitten in any way; for I can foresee all the trouble it would lead to. And let us have no more talk of this collar. Not that I ever gave any money for it myself— though if I had, I must say I should have kept quiet about it. So let them both go, cat and kitten, leashed or unleashed, and catch what they can. Be sensible and mark my words—and let us keep out of what doesn't concern us!"

Now what this dream means you folk must guess for yourselves, for I haven't the courage to tell you—and that's God's truth![21]

Besides all this, a hundred men in silk gowns stood swaying from side to side and making speeches. These were the lawyers who served at the bar, pleading their cases for as much money as they could get. Never once did they open their mouths out of love for our Lord; indeed you could sooner measure the mist on the Malvern Hills, than get a sound out of them without first producing some cash![22]

I saw many more in this great concourse of people, as you shall hear presently: barons, burgesses, and peasants; bakers, brewers, and butchers; linen-weavers and tailors, tinkers and toll-collectors, masons and miners and many other tradesfolk. And all kinds of laborers suddenly appeared—shoddy workmen, who would while away their hours with bawdy songs—like "God help you, Mistress Emma!"—while cooks with their boys cried, "Hot pies! Hot pies! Fat pigs and geese! Come and eat!" and inn-keepers were bawling, "White wine! Red wine! Gascon and Spanish! Wash down your meat with the finest Rhenish!"[23]

All this I saw in my dream, and a great deal more besides.

Notes

1   That is, toward the rising sun, a symbol of the Resurrection. Medieval churches were generally so oriented that the altar stood at the eastern end; the nave opened to the west. Thus one looked eastward toward the celebrant and the Host at mass.

2   The scene embraces the tower of Truth toward the east, the dungeon of hell toward the west, and the field of the world lying in between. This setting, which is symbolic and not literal, persisted into the Renaissance as an artistic motif. One may see a variant of it, for example, in the background of Titian's "Sacred and Profane Love." Here the tower, bathed in the light of the afternoon sun, stands on the viewer's left (but on the right of Amor, or charity, in the center). On the right is the dale, here represented by a lake near a village. Hell, in this instance, is the world. It is true that there is a church in the village, but readers of the Apocalypse will recall that there are no churches in heaven. Before the village Titian represents temporal pursuits in the form of a hunt of Venus (i.e., a hare hunt together with a certain activity on the grass in the far right). For the combined bath and sarcophagus in the center, see Rom. 6:4.

3   The ploughmen, anchorites, and merchants are, like the setting in which they move, symbolic. A ploughman in the "field of folk" is a priest cultivating his church so that it may be fruitful for the Lord. The food he supplies is spiritual food, like the "daily bread" of the Paternoster. The anchorites represent the contemplative life, and the merchants the active life. It was conventional to say that there are three sorts of men in the Church: prelatical, contemplative, and active. The vain men who love fine clothes are probably intended to suggest prelates like the friars described below, who "in their greed for fine clothes interpreted the Scriptures to suit themselves."

4   The minstrels of both types are probably intended to represent men of all the various classes considered in accordance with their modes of speech. The good ones speak truth and praise God in their hearts as well as with their lips. The false ones are mere pretenders, praising in word only. To put this in another way, the true minstrels sing the new song of charity; the false ones actually sing the old song, or the melody of delight in temporal satisfactions.

5   The quotation is not in St. Paul in this form. Having considered the people in general according to their classes (prelatical, contemplative, and active; those who praise God sincerely and those who do not), the poet now turns to literal types, moving from the lowest degrees upward.

6   Pilgrimages, which were supposed to be almost ritualistic reflections of the pilgrimage of the human spirit undertaken in penance, were frequently turned into vacations during which the participants merely enjoyed themselves. Palmers were professional beggars who frequented the pilgrimage routes.

7 That is, the coming of Antichrist. The friars were notorious for their abuse of the administration of penance and generally for seeking nothing but material profit.

8 Compare Chaucer's Pardoner. Pardoners were supposed to collect money for charitable institutions, offering in return for contributions remission of penance. However, they frequently promised miraculous results to their customers and used the money they collected for themselves.

9 That is, sing masses for the dead in chantry chapels. Chaucer's ideal parson of *The Canterbury Tales* refuses to do this.

10 Many bishops had palatial residences in London.

11 At the Day of Judgment.

12 See Matt. 16:9.

13 Prudence, temperance, justice, and fortitude.

14 "a lunatik, a lene thing with-alle." The previous passage is probably intended as a generalized account of the establishment of the social order. Here a "lunatik" who speaks "clergealy," or learnedly, calls attention to the need for justice in the administration of the commonwealth. The learned lunatic probably represents someone wise before God but foolish before the world. Justice, however, is not enough, as an angel proceeds to explain. The subject is still the origin of the social order, so that it is unwise to identify the persons as actual persons.

15 The angel calls attention to the principles of the New Law, which like the angel himself, can come only from heaven.

16 "'I am a king, a prince,' you say, but soon you may be neither. O King, that your laws may reflect the justice of Christ the King, and that what you do may be more just, be merciful! Naked justice wishes to be clothed by you in mercy. Sow seed of the kind that will produce the crops you wish to reap. If justice is denuded of mercy, you will reap naked justice for yourself; if mercy is sown, your harvest will be in mercy!" The Old Law was a law of strict justice. The New Law offers mercy to those who are sincerely penitent for their transgressions, and this law should govern the activity of temporal rulers. The doctrine is well stated by Duke Theseus in Chaucer's Knight's Tale, by Isabella in Shakespeare's *Measure for Measure*, 2:2, and most eloquently, by Portia, *Merchant of Venice*, 4:1.

17 "Since a king (*rex*) is said to have his name from the act of ruling (*regere*), he has the name without the thing unless he seeks to maintain justice." The quotation is from the *Etymologies* of Isidore of Seville (9:3). But our "garrulous fellow" is guilty of partial quotation, for Isidore goes on to say that although the two principal virtues of a king are justice and mercy, mercy is more praiseworthy than strict justice, which is too severe.

18 "The decrees of the king are to us the chains of the law." That is, the nature of the chains will depend upon the king's exercise of mercy.

19 Eccles. 10:16.

20 Pursuing women.

21 The poet turns from a generalized picture of a kingdom to a fable reflecting what he thinks of as the situation in England in his own time. He feels that the king and his court have become rapacious, but that if the king were disposed of, a new tyrant would take his place. Moreover, if the king's powers were restricted, the commons themselves would become lawless and rapacious too. The author of our poem was no revolutionary; what he thought he saw before him was the degeneration of a society based on justice and mercy into a society in which most of the citizens, from the top of the social hierarchy to the bottom, were allowing themselves to be dominated only by greed and self-interest. There is in this poem no special pleading for the commons (who were not, in the fourteenth century, common people in the modern sense) nor for the lower classes in any form.

22 Compare Chaucer's Man of Law, who had amassed considerable holdings in fee simple.

23 The import of this paragraph is that people of all sorts—barons, burgesses, and peasants—are interested only in the satisfaction of their fleshly appetites. Since we have in our own time developed societies whose economies are based on exactly these impulses and whose ethics are founded on "enlightened self-interest," the view of the fourteenth-century poet seems remote. For him, social evils were the result of personal immorality; he had no notion that they might be corrected by reorganization or by revolutionary legislation.

Book I

The Teaching of Holy Church

Now I will show you the meaning of the mountain, the dark valley, and the plain full of people.

A fair lady, clothed in linen, came down from a castle and called me gently, saying, "My son, are you asleep?[1] Do you see these people, moving about in such a turmoil of activity? Most people who pass through this world wish for nothing better than worldly success: the only heaven they think about is on earth."

Lovely as she was, something in her face made me uneasy, and I said, "Forgive me, Lady, but what does it all mean?"

"The tower on the hill," she replied, "is the home of Truth, and He would have you learn to obey His word. For He is the Father of Faith, who created you all, giving you a body and five senses with which to worship Him while you dwell below. And therefore He commanded the earth to provide wool and linen and food, enough for everyone to live in comfort and moderation.

"And of His goodness He ordained three things in common,[2] which are all that your body requires: clothing to protect you from cold, food to keep you from want, and drink when you are thirsty.

"But do not drink too much, so that you're the worse for it when you ought to be at work. Remember the story of Lot,[3] whose fondness for drink drove him to consort with his daughters, to the Devil's great delight—how he revelled in strong drink, and this suited the Devil's purpose, and being consumed with lust, he slept with both his daughters. 'Come,' they said, 'let us make our father drink wine, and we will lie with him, that we may preserve seed of our father.' So Lot was overwhelmed by wine and women, and there, in his gluttony, he begat evil sons. So be guided by me, and avoid strong drinks. Moderation is always wholesome, though you may crave for more. Not all that the belly desires is good for the soul; nor is all that the soul loves, food for the body. Put no trust in your body, for its promptings come from the World, and the World is a liar out to betray you. And the Flesh and the Devil are in league to pursue your soul, and speak evil things to your heart. I give you this good counsel that you may be watchful."

"Pardon me, Lady," I said, "I find your teaching good. But tell me, the money of this world, which men cling to so eagerly—whom does it all belong to?"

"Read the Gospel,"[4] she answered, "and see what Christ said when the people brought Him a penny in the Temple, and asked Him whether or not they should honor Caesar. 'Whose is the image and inscription?' He asked. 'Caesar's,' they answered, 'We can all recognize him!' 'Then render to Caesar,' He said, 'the things that are Caesar's, and to God the things that are God's; otherwise you wrong Him.'

"For Right Reason should rule you in this matter, and Common Sense look after your money for you, giving you some as you need it; for Thrift and these two go hand in hand."

Then I begged her in God's name to tell me the meaning of the fearful dungeon in the dark abyss.

"That is the Castle of Sorrow," she said, "Whoever enters there may well curse the day he was born. In it there lives a creature called Wrong, who begat Falsehood, and first founded the dungeon. It was he who persuaded Adam and Eve to sin, who tempted Cain to murder his brother, and enticed Judas with the Jews' silver and then hanged him on an elder-tree. He thwarts love and deceives everyone: those who trust in his riches are the first to be betrayed."

Then I wondered what woman this could be to quote such wise words of Holy Scripture; and I implored her, in the name of God, before she left me, to tell me who she was that taught me so kindly.

"I am Holy Church," she replied, "You should recognize me, for I received you when you were a child, and first taught you the Faith. You came to me with godparents, who pledged you to love and obey me all your life."

Then I fell on my knees and besought her mercy,

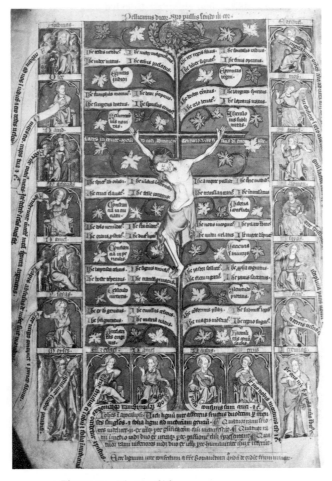

Figure 32 *The tree of life.*

everywhere; for Christians and heathens alike are crying out for it.

"And kings and nobles should be Truth's champions: they should ride to war and put down criminals throughout their realms, and bind them fast till Truth has reached a final verdict on them.[7] That is clearly the proper profession of a knight—not merely to fast one Friday in a hundred years, but to stand by every man and woman who seeks plain truth, and never desert them for love or money.

"King David in his time[8] dubbed knights, making them swear on their swords to serve Truth for ever. And if anyone broke that vow, he was an apostate to the Order.

"And Christ himself, the king of kings, knighted ten Orders of angels:[9] Cherubim and Seraphim and seven like them—and one other, the Order of Lucifer. And God, in His majesty, made them His Archangels, the rulers over His whole household, and they rejoiced in the power which He gave them. And He taught them to understand Truth by the Holy Trinity, and required nothing of them but to obey Him.

"But Lucifer, though he too, with others of his Order, had received this teaching in Heaven, broke the vow of obedience, lost his happiness, and, in the likeness of a fiend, fell from the angelic company into a deep, dark hell where he must abide for ever. And innumerable legions sprang out after him in loathsome shapes, for they believed his lying words—'I will exalt my throne above the stars of God: I will sit in the sides of the North . . . I will be like to the most High.'[10] And all those who put their hope in these words, Heaven could hold no longer. And they fell in the form of devils, for nine days together, till God in His mercy stopped their fall, causing the spaces of Chaos to close and cohere, and bringing them to rest.

"They fell in so strange a way that some remained in the air, some on earth, and some in the depths of hell. But Lucifer, on account of his pride, lies the lowest of all, and his pain will never cease. And all those who do wrong must go after death to dwell with him in the pit; but the righteous who die still honoring Truth may be sure their souls will go to Heaven, where Truth himself, dwelling in the Holy Trinity, will enthrone them.

"So I say again, that when all treasures are tested, Truth is the best; my two texts prove it. Teach this to the ignorant, for the learned know it already: Truth is the most perfect treasure on earth."

begging her to take pity on me and pray for my sins; and I asked her to teach me plainly how to believe in Christ and do the will of Him who created me. "Teach me no more about earthly treasure, O Lady whom men call Holy, but tell me one thing: *How May I Save My Soul?*"

"When all treasures are tested," she said, "Truth is the best. And to prove it and test what is true, I appeal to the text 'God is love'.[5] For Truth is as precious a jewel as our dear Lord himself.

"For he who speaks nothing but the truth, and acts by it, wishing no man ill, is like Christ, a god on earth and in Heaven—those are St Luke's words.[6] Men of learning who know this teaching should proclaim it

"But," I said, "I have no natural gift for grasping Truth. You must teach me better. How does truth grow in me? Is there some special faculty somewhere in my body?"

"You stupid fellow!" she said, "Why are you so dull-witted? You can't have learnt much Latin at school—*Heu mihi, quod sterilem duxi vitam iuvenilem!*[11]

"There is a natural knowledge in your heart, which prompts you to love your Lord better than yourself and to die rather than commit mortal sin. That, surely, is Truth. If anyone else can teach you better, listen, and learn accordingly.

"For this is the testimony of God's word, the word by which you must live: that Love is Heaven's sovereign remedy, and he who takes it has no trace of sin left. By Love, God chose to fashion all His works. He taught Moses[12] that it was the dearest of all things, the virtue closest to Heaven, the plant of Peace[13] whose leaves are most precious for healing.

"Heaven could not hold Love, it was so heavy in itself. But when it had eaten its fill of earth, and taken flesh and blood, then it was lighter than a leaf on a linden-tree, more subtle and piercing than the point of a needle. The strongest armor was not proof against it, the tallest ramparts could not keep it out.

"Therefore Love is first among the company of the Lord of Heaven; He is a mediator between God and man, as a Mayor is between king and people: He alone delivers judgment on man for his misdeeds, and assesses the penalties.

"And so that one can recognize love by natural instinct, it begins by some power whose source and center is in the heart of man. For every virtue springs from a natural knowledge in the heart, implanted there by the Father who created us—He who looked upon us with love and let His Son die for our sins, wishing no evil to those who tortured Him and put Him to death, but praying for their forgiveness.

"From this you may see an example in His own person, that He was mighty yet gentle, and granted mercy to those that hanged Him on the Cross and pierced His heart.

"So I advise you who are rich to have pity on the poor; and though you have power to summon them before the courts, be merciful in what you do. For 'with what measure ye mete'[14]—whether well or ill—you shall be measured with that when you leave this world.

"For though you speak the truth and are honest in your dealings, and as chaste as an innocent child that weeps at its baptism, unless you love men truly, and give to the poor, generously sharing the goods God has given you, you shall have no more merit from your Masses and Hours than old Molly from her maidenhead, that no man wants.

"For the great Apostle James laid down in his Epistle that faith without deeds[15] is worthless—dead as a doornail. So Chastity without Charity shall lie bound in hell; it is no more use than a lamp without a light.

"Many chaplains are chaste, but lack all charity. There are no men more greedy, once they get preferment. Ungrateful to their own relations and to all their fellow-christians, they swallow up everything they are given, and cry out for more. Such a loveless virtue as this shall be fettered in hell.

"And there are parish priests galore who keep their bodies pure, yet are so burdened with avarice that they cannot wrench it off; it is hinged on them like a lid. This is not the truth of the Trinity, but the treachery of hell, and it teaches the layfolk to give less readily of their goods.

"Therefore our Lord says, 'Give and it shall be given to you,[16] since I gave you all that you have. This is the key which unlocks love, and sets free my grace to comfort the sorrowful, heavy-laden with sin.'

"Love is the physician of life, the power nearest to our Lord himself, and the direct way to Heaven. Therefore I repeat from these texts, that when all treasures are tested, Truth is the best. Now I have told you what Truth is, and shown you that no treasure is better, and I can stay with you no longer. May our Lord protect you."

Notes

1 That is, spiritually asleep.

2 Holy Church appropriately bases her opening discourse to explain the activity of the self-seeking people on themes from the Sermon on the Mount. A careful reading of Matt. 6:19–34 will make what she has to say easier to understand.

3 Gen. 19.

4 Matt. 22:21.

5 1 John 4:8, 16. What follows is a sermon based on this theme.

6 Cf. 1 John 4:16–17; Luke 6:35.

7 The chief functions of a medieval ruler were, ideally, to keep the peace at home and to maintain the best interests of the realm abroad.

8 See 2 Kings 23.

9 Seraphim, Cherubim, Thrones, Dominations, Virtues, Powers, Principalities, Archangels, Angels, and the Order of Lucifer.

10 Isa. 14:14–34.

11 "Alas, that I led a fruitless life in youth!"

12 Deut. 6:5; 11:13.

13 Isa. 53:2. The "leaves" of the plant are the verbal teachings of Christ.

14 Matt. 7:2. Cf. Shakespeare's title *Measure for Measure*.

15 James 2:26.

16 Luke 6:38.

Book II

The Marriage of Lady Lucre[1]

But again I fell on my knees and besought her help, saying, "Forgive me, Lady, for the love of Mary Queen of Heaven, who bore the blessed child who died for us—but show me some way by which I can recognize Falsehood."

"Look to your left[2] and see," the Lady said. "There he stands, Falsehood himself, with Flattery and all their companions."

I looked to the left as the Lady told me, and saw a woman, richly dressed, whose robe was trimmed with the finest fur in the land. She was crowned with a coronet like a queen's, and her fingers were prettily adorned[3] with gold filigree rings, set with rubies that glowed like red-hot coals, with priceless diamonds and sapphires, both deep-blue and azure, with amethysts and with beryls to protect her from poisons.[4] Her dress was gorgeously colored with rich scarlet dye, set off with bands of bright gold lace studded with gems. I was dazzled by her magnificence, for I had never seen such riches before; and I wondered who she was, and whose wife she could possibly be.

"Who is this woman," I asked, "that wears such splendid garments?"

"That is Lucre the Maiden," said the Lady. "Many is the time she has injured me, slandering my dear friend Honesty, and denouncing her before the magistrates. She comes and goes in the Pope's palace as familiarly as I do, though Truth objects to this, because she is illegitimate. For her father was Falsehood, who has a deceitful tongue, and has never told the truth since he came into this world. And Lucre has inherited his character, according to the law of nature, for it is written: 'Like father, like son: Every good tree bringeth forth good fruit.'[5] So I ought to take precedence over her, for I came of better stock.

"My father is the great God, the source of all graces—the one God who had no beginning; and I am his good daughter, to whom he has given Mercy as a marriage portion; so that any man who is merciful, and who truly loves me, shall be my lord, and I his lover, in Heaven.[6]

"And I swear by my life, the man who takes Lucre to wife[7] will lose for her sake all his portion of mercy. What does David say in the Psalter about those who take bribes, and about the way of salvation for men in authority?

> Lord, who shall dwell in thy tabernacle:
> or who shall rest upon thy holy hill? . . .
> He who taketh no bribes against the innocent.[8]

"And now this Lucre is to be married to one Fraud Serpent's-tongue, a cursed creature begotten by a devil. Flattery first paved the way for her, enchanting all the folk with his charming speech, but it was Liar who made the match.

"Tomorrow is the Maiden's wedding-feast, where you will be able to meet all their retinue, and learn what sort of people they are. Get to know them all if you can, but hold your tongue and say nothing against them; let them be, till Honesty comes as a Judge with power to punish them; then you may speak out.

"Now I commend you to Christ," she said, "and His spotless Mother. And never let your conscience be burdened through love of lucre."

Thus the Lady left me lying asleep; and dreaming still, I saw the marriage of Lady Lucre. All the rich company who owe their places to Falsehood were invited to the wedding, both by bride and bridegroom. In this vast assembly were men of every status, high and low: knights and clerics, jurors and summoners,[9] sheriffs with their clerks, beadles and bailiffs, business brokers and purveyors, victuallers and advocates—I cannot number the throng that ran at Lucre's heels.

Those who seemed most familiar with her were Father Simony and Lord Civil-Law, with his host of jurymen. But Flattery led the way to her chamber to fetch her out, for he was the agent commissioned to hand her over. And Simony and Civil-Law, when they realized what the couple wanted, had agreed for a certain sum to say whatever they were asked. Then Liar pushed himself forward, saying, "See! Here's a deed of conveyance, that Guile, with his great oaths, has given them both"; and he begged Lord Civil Law to look it over, and Father Simony to read it. Whereupon Simony and Civil, standing up before the guests, unfolded this solemn deed drawn up by Falsehood, and began singing it out at the tops of their voices:

"*Sciant presentes et futuri*[10] . . . Be it known and witnessed by all the world, that the Lady Lucre is married, not for her virtue, beauty, or kindness, but solely for her property. Fraud is glad to have her, because he knows her wealth. And, by this charter, Sir Flattery-of-the-Double-tongue invests them with the following assets: to live as princes, to be proud and despise poverty, to backbite, boast, and bear false witness, to mock, scorn, and slander, and to break the commandments boldly without restraint.

"And he bestows upon them the Earldom of Wrath and Envy, together with the Castles of Strife and Senseless-Chattering; also the County of Covetousness and all the adjacent lands, including the twin towns of Usury and Avarice, both of which I grant them, with all their hagglings and traffickings besides, and furthermore the Borough of Theft. And, moreover, I grant them the whole lordship of Lechery from end to end, with all its appurtenances

of clothes, words, and deeds, of wishing, and eager watching with the eyes, and of idle thoughts that persist when the powers of performance fail."

Besides all this, he gave them the apanage of Gluttony, with its many privileges, viz. to swear great oaths and drink all day in diverse taverns, and gossip and joke there, and judge one's fellow-Christians; to eat before the proper time on fast-days, and then sit gorging till overpowered by sleep; to breed like town-pigs, and wallow luxuriously in bed till their sides were fattened with sloth and sleep; and finally to awake in despair, with no will to amend, and in their last agonies, to believe themselves lost.

"And to have and to hold, and all their heirs, a dwelling with the Devil, and be damned for ever; therewith all the dependencies of Purgatory extending into the pains of Hell; giving in return, at the end of one year, their souls to the Devil, to dwell with him and suffer torment as long as God is in Heaven."

And these were the witnesses: first, Wrong himself; then Piers the Pardoner, of the Pauline Order; Bett, the beadle of Buckinghamshire; Randolph, the reeve of Rutland; Mund the Miller, and many others. It was signed and sealed, in the year of the Devil, in the presence of Simony, by authority of Civil-Law.

Theology, when he heard this recital, could contain himself no longer. "The Devil take you and your weddings!" he said to Sir Civil-Law, "contriving such mockeries in defiance of Truth! I hope you'll be sorry for this affair before it is finished!

"For Lucre is an honest woman,[11] and the daughter of Restitution. God intended her for Honest Work, and you have given her to a rogue—God confound your impudence! Is that how you understand the text 'The laborer is worthy of his hire'?[12] A plague on your Law! You earn your living by lying and pimping, you and all your notaries and your fine friend Simony—you ravage Holy Church and rob the people. By God, you shall pay for it dearly! Fraud, as you well know, you hypocrites, is a faithless, treacherous bastard descended from Beelzebub; and Lucre is a well-born lady, who might kiss the king himself as a true cousin, if she chose.

"So use your intelligence, and take her to London to put the case before the Law, and see if any law will allow such a shocking match. And if by any chance the judges do permit it, yet mind what you're up to, for Truth is no fool, and Sir Conscience, who knows you both, is one of His council. If He finds you guilty of helping

Fraud, it will go hard with your souls on the Day of Judgment."

Sir Civil agreed to go to London, but neither Simony nor the notaries would assent until they had been paid for their services. So Flattery produced a great supply of florins, and bade Guile hand out gold to all and sundry, especially to the notaries, "that none of them fail us"; and he retained False-Witness by means of a large sum, "for he knows how to manage Lucre and put her at my disposal."

Everyone thanked Fraud and Flattery profusely for their splendid gifts, and came along to reassure Fraud, saying, "Never fear, dear sir, we shall not cease from our efforts until, by our combined influence, Lucre is your wedded wife. Already, with a little gentle encouragement, we have persuaded the Lady to come to London and hear what the Law will say; and we feel sure that before long you will both be united for ever."

Then Fraud and Flattery were pleased, and they summoned all the men in the neighboring shires, beggars included, to be ready to accompany them to Westminster [13] and act as witnesses.

Then they wanted some horses to take them there, so Flattery procured a supply: he set Lucre on a newly-shod Sheriff, Fraud on a gently-trotting Juryman, and himself on a finely-harnessed Sycophant.

But the notaries were annoyed because they had no horses, and Civil-Law and Simony were left to go on foot. So Civil and Simony swore they would saddle the Summoners, and have those petty inquisitors harnessed as palfreys. "Father Simony shall bestride them himself," said Sir Civil. "Bring together all the deans, sub-deans, archdeacons, Bishops' Officers, and registrars, and have them saddled with silver bribes, so they'll condone our sins—adultery, divorce, and private usury—and let them carry the bishops about on their visitations. The Paulines will help as well; they know everyone's secrets, and will draw up law-suits for me in the Consistory Courts. And put a bridle on the Commissary too—he shall draw our waggon, and will get us provisions with fines from fornicators.

"And as for all the others still on foot, the friars and rogues and the rest, yoke Liar to a big cart and make him draw them all."

So Fraud and Flattery set out together with Lucre between them, and all these men behind. I haven't the time to describe all the rag-tag that followed them—men of every sort on earth. But Guile was at their head directing them all.

However, Honesty saw him, and although he said nothing, he spurred his palfrey and passed them all by; and coming to the king's court, he told the news to Sir Conscience; and Sir Conscience informed the king.

"By God!" said the king, "if I could catch Fraud or Flattery or any of their crew, I'd teach those wretches to stir up trouble! I shall have them hanged by the neck, and their accomplices along with them! No one shall go bail for them; they shall feel the full force of the Law." And he commanded an Officer, who came forthwith, to arrest them at all costs, and put Fraud in fetters, regardless of bribes. "And strike off Guile's head before he goes a step further. And if you take Liar, hold him fast till you have put him in the pillory, and don't listen to his pleadings. And then bring Lucre here to me."

Dread stood at the door and overheard this decree; so he went quickly and warned Fraud and his followers to scatter.

Then Fraud fled in fear to the Friars.[14] And Guile, in terror of death, was searching round for a way of escape, when some merchants met him and took him in with them, shutting him up in their shop as a salesman; and they rigged him up as an apprentice to serve the customers.

Then Liar nimbly bounded away, to skulk in the alley-ways, and be lugged about by all and sundry. He was nowhere welcome, in spite of his many tales; everywhere he was jeered at and sent packing. But at last the Pardoners took pity on him and pulled him indoors. They washed and wiped him and wrapped him in rags, and sent him on Sundays to the churches with seals, selling pounds-worths of Pardons. Then the doctors were annoyed, and sent him an urgent letter asking him to join them, and help them analyze urine. And the grocers also sought his help for hunting out their wares, for he knew something of their trade, and had all the drugs and spices at his command. But then he fell in with some minstrels and messengers, and they kept him with them for six months and eleven days. And finally the Friars lured him away and disguised him in their own habit so that visitors should not recognize him; but he has leave to come and go at his pleasure, living with them on and off whenever it suits him.

Thus they all fled in terror and went into hiding, except for Lucre the Maiden, who alone made no attempt to escape. And even she trembled with fear when she was arrested, weeping and wringing her hands.

Notes

1 Lady Meed, or "reward," in the original.

2 The left side was associated with evil. Hence, for example, the damned appear on the left hand of Christ in pictorial representations of the Last Judgment.

3 The description of Lady Lucre is based partly on that of the Whore of Babylon in the Apocalypse.

4 She wears precious stones for display and for magical purposes. Properly regarded, such stones were suggestive of various virtues.

5 Cf. Matt. 7:17.

6 The Church is the bride of Christ, and, by transference, the heavenly bride of a good Christian.

7 The fact that marriage implied a hierarchy made it a convenient figure for relationships of many kinds.

8 Ps. 14.

9 On the functions of the summoner, see the opening lines of Chaucer's Friar's Tale.

10 The conventional opening words to a charter.

11 That is, there is a proper use of reward.

12 Luke 10:7.

13 The king's court sat in Westminster Hall.

14 The attitude toward the friars in the poem is consistently hostile and owes much to the traditional criticisms first advanced by William of St. Amour.

Book III

Lady Lucre at Westminster

Lady Lucre, deserted by all her companions, was brought before the king by the beadles and bailiffs. And the king, calling one of his counsellors (I need not mention his name), told him to take her and see that she was properly looked after. "I shall examine her myself," the king said, "and ask her outright which man she would really prefer. If she proves amenable and is willing to do as I tell her, I intend, God willing, to pardon her for this offence."

Then, as the king commanded, this counsellor politely put his arm round Lucre and guided her to her chamber, where music and other entertainments were provided for her amusement.

All those who resided at Westminster treated Lucre with the greatest respect. Some of the judges, with the Clergy's permission, hastened along full of gallantry and good humor, to console her as she sat in her boudoir. "Do not lose heart, Lady Lucre," they said. "You have no cause for distress. We will speak to the king and smooth the way for you. And we can promise you that you will be able to marry whom you wish, in spite of Conscience and all his tricks!"

Lucre thanked them graciously for their great kindness, giving everyone presents of gold and silver vessels, with rings, rubies, and valuables of all kinds, not forgetting a gold piece even for the lowest of their retainers. Then the judges took their leave of her.

Whereupon the Clergy and Counsellors came to comfort her in the same way, saying, "Take heart, Lady, for we will always be at your disposal, for as long as there's life left in you; don't hesitate to make full use of us." Lucre politely returned the compliment, and said that for her part she would always be faithful to them, get them titles, and obtain seats for them in the Bishop's Court. "You needn't worry about your education," she said, "as long as you're friends of mine; I'm well known in places where learning gets you nowhere."

Her next visitor was a Friar, come to hear her confession. Speaking in the dulcet undertones of the confession-box, he said to Lucre, "Don't worry how many men you have had to do with, clerics or laymen, or if Falsehood has hung at your heels for half a century, I will still give you absolution—for a small offering, of course—shall we say one horse-load of wheat? For that I will undertake to be your own beadsman, and spread your influence among the gentry and clergy, undermining Conscience wherever I go."[1]

So Lucre knelt before him and made her confession, shamelessly; and when she had told him a suitable tale or two, she gave him a coin accepting him as her beadsman and personal agent. Then, after gabbling through the form of absolution, he added, "We are having a stained-glass window made for us, and it's proving rather expensive. If you would care to pay for the glazing yourself, and have your name engraved in the window, you may have no doubts of your eternal salvation."

"Ah! If I can be sure of that," the woman said, "I will do anything for you, Father. You can count me your unfailing friend—but never be hard on those lords and ladies who give way to their lusts. Do not blame them for it, for lechery is a frailty of the flesh, a natural instinct, Father—that's what all the books say. We all began that way, so there can't be much harm in it, as long as one avoids a scandal. And it's quite the easiest to forgive of all the Seven Deadlies. So you be kind to them, and then I will roof your church, build you a cloister, whitewash your walls, glaze your windows, have paintings and images made, and pay for everything. People will all be saying I am a lay-sister of your Order."

But God forbids us to blazon our good deeds on walls and windows, lest they become mere monuments of pride and worldly pomp. For all your motives and purposes lie open to God; He sees your natural greed, and knows where the money really belongs.

Therefore I advise you, lords and ladies, have done with such inscriptions, and do not cry out for the notice of men of God when you want to give alms, lest you have your reward on earth,[2] and your Heaven too. And "Let not thy left hand know what thy right hand doeth,"[3] for so the Gospel bids men do good deeds.

And you Mayors and Officers who uphold the Law, and are the chief link between king and people, be sure that you punish all fraudulent tradesmen, the brewers, the bakers, the butchers, and the cooks, in your pillories and ducking-stools. For these are the men who do most harm to the poor, poisoning them with adulterated food, at extortionate prices. They grow rich by selling at retail prices, and invest in properties by robbing the bellies of the poor. For how could they build themselves such tall houses, and buy up lands and tenements, if they were honest dealers? But Lucre has begged the Mayor to accept money from them—or if not money, plate, and gold rings and other valuables—to let them stay in business undisturbed. "For my sake," she says, "leave them all alone, and let them overcharge just a wee bit."

Now hear what Solomon said for the benefit of such Mayors and officials: "Fire shall consume the tabernacles of those who freely take bribes"[4]—that is, all who expect gratuities or New Year boxes because they hold office will have their houses and homes burned to ashes.

The king, coming from his Council, sent for Lucre at once, and a band of his officers, in great high spirits, escorted her to his private chamber.

Then the king spoke graciously to her and said, "This is not the first time, Lady, that you have acted unwisely, but you never did worse than when you accepted Fraud! However, I will forgive you this time —but never do such a thing again, as long as you live.

"Now I have a knight called Conscience, who has recently come from overseas. If he is willing to make you his wife, will you have him?"

"Certainly, my liege," answered the Lady. "God forbid that I should refuse! Why, I'd rather be hanged than shirk any wish of yours."

So Sir Conscience was summoned to appear before the king and Council. He made a low obeisance to the king, and knelt to hear his wishes.

"Are you willing to marry this woman, if I give my consent?" said the king. "She would gladly accept you as a husband."

"God forbid!" said Conscience, "I'd rather be damned than marry such a wife! She is fickle and faithless, and has led countless men into sin. Thousands already have been betrayed by trusting in her riches. She makes wantons of wives and widows, using presents as baits to lure them into sin. She has poisoned Popes and corrupted Holy Church, and your own father[5] she ruined by her false promises. I swear to God you won't find a greater bawd between Heaven and hell, though you search the whole earth! She's as lecherous as a monkey—a tale-bearer too!—and as common as a cart-track to every wayfaring wretch—monks and minstrels and the lepers that lie under the hedges. The only men who treat her with respect are jurors and summoners and suchlike, and County Sheriffs who would be ruined without her; for by bribing them she causes men to lose their lands and their lives. She gives gold to the gaolers to let prisoners loose, and lets criminals wander at large, while honest men, who have done no harm, are seized, cast into irons, and hanged, to satisfy her spite.

"What does she care about threats of excommunication? She keeps the Bishop's men in clothes, and can get absolution whenever she likes. Her purse can do more in a single month than the king's privy seal can do in six.[6] Even the Pope confides in her—as is well known to those who buy livings in Rome; for it is she and Simony who seal her Papal mandates.

"She makes bishops of men who can scarcely read. She provides livings for parsons and for lawless priests to spend their lives with mistresses and concubines, and rear families. Heaven help that land where she wins the king's favor! For she will always smile on falsehood and trample on the truth.

"Christ! How her jewels mow down the magistrates! How she perjures herself in the law-courts, and chokes up the course of justice! Her florins fly so thick, that truth is smothered with them. She bends the Law as she likes, chooses her own days for settling disputes, and makes men lose for her sake what the Law might have won them. A poor man is bewildered and confused: he may plead in the courts for ever, but the Law will not move an inch; it hates to reach a verdict, and without bribes or presents Lucre will satisfy no one.

"So she brings disaster upon barons and burgesses, and all commoners who try to lead honest lives. This, my liege, is her way of life—and may God confound her and all her supporters! For she has coupled Education with Avarice, and she holds such sway over men of property that, no matter how the poor are wronged, there is nothing they can do about it."

Then Lucre looked aggrieved, and whined to the king for a chance to speak and defend herself; and the king willingly allowed her. "Excuse yourself if you can, by all means," he said, "for with all these accusations of Conscience, you are like to be packed off for good."

"Ah, my good lord," said the Lady, "when you know the truth of the matter you will credit him less. In times of trouble, Lucre is very useful.—And you know well enough, Conscience, that I did not come here in pride, to quarrel, or slander you. You know too, you liar, unless you try to gloss it over, that you have come crawling to me many times in the past, and laid your hands on my gold and doled it out as you liked. So why you should be so angry with me now, I can't imagine. For I can still honor you with my favors, if I choose, and bolster up your courage in ways that you never dreamt of.

"But you have foully slandered me before the king here. For I never killed, or planned the death of a king, nor did any of the things that you say—as the king himself will bear me witness. And in the French Wars, I did him no wrong at all—unlike you, who shamed him again and again, creeping into hovels to keep your fingers warm, fearing the winter would last for ever, frightened to death of a few storm-clouds—and then rushing home because your belly was empty!

"And you robbed the poor men without pity, you thief, and carried their money away on your back, to sell at Calais. And meanwhile, I stayed behind with my lord, to protect his life. I cheered his men up and made them forget their miseries, and slapped them on the back to liven up their spirits, till they fairly danced for joy, hoping to have me all to themselves. By God, if I had been Commander of his men, I wager my life I'd have made him master of that whole land, from end to end—and king, too, and what an honor that would have been for his family—the smallest brat among them would now be as good as a baron!

"But then you, Conscience, stepped in with your coward's advice—to give it all up,[7] the richest realm under the sun, for a handful of silver!

"Why, a king, as guardian of the realm, is bound to give lucre to those who serve him, and show courtesy to all men, especially to foreigners, with handsome gifts. Such openhandedness makes people love and respect him. And without me, how could the nobles, or even emperors, retain young men to ride about for them? Even the Pope and the prelates accept offerings, and reward those who uphold their laws. Servants all get fixed wages for services rendered; beggars demand a reward for their begging, and minstrels for entertaining. The king receives money from his men, to keep peace in the land. Schoolmasters get paid for their pupils; skilled workmen take fees for their apprentices; and even priests expect a wage, of food or Mass-offerings, for teaching people virtue; and surely merchants must make a profit, to carry on their trade. There's not a man on earth that can live without lucre!"

"By Heaven!" said the king to Conscience, "Lucre has certainly won her point, it seems to me."

"No," said Conscience, and he knelt down on the ground. "By your leave, my lord, there are two different kinds of payment. The one is the gift of Heaven which God, of His grace, gives to those who do their work well on earth. The Psalmist speaks of this: 'Lord, who shall dwell in thy tabernacle, with thy saints? Who shall dwell in thy holy hill?'[8] And King David answers the question too: 'He that walketh uprightly, and worketh righteousness'—that is, he who is unspotted from the world, and single-minded, who has acted with reason and justice, and sought after truth; who has taught the poor, and has not lived by usury—'Who putteth not out his money to usury, nor taketh rewards against the innocent.'[10] So all who help the innocent and side with the righteous, doing good to them without reward, and maintaining truth, shall have this payment from God in their time of greatest need, when they leave this world.[11]

"But there is another kind of payment, a lucre without measure, which men in authority grasp at—the bribes they get for supporting evil-doers. And of them the Psalter also speaks:

In whose hands is wickedness:
and their right hand is full of gifts.[12]

And even the man who receives money from them shall pay a bitter price for it, unless the Scripture lies! And priests who seek their own pleasure, exacting money for the Masses they sing, gain all their reward on earth, as we read in St Matthew: 'Verily I say unto you, they have their reward.'[13]

"The money, my liege, which laborers receive from their master, is not lucre at all, but a fair wage. Nor is there any lucre in trading with goods: it is simply an exchange, one pennyworth for another.

"Tell me, you shameless Lucre, did you never read the Book of Samuel,[14] nor notice why vengeance fell on Saul and his children? For God sent a message to Saul, by his prophet Samuel, that Agag, king of the Amalekites, and all his people, must die for a deed done by their ancestors. 'Therefore,' said Samuel to Saul, 'God himself commands you to obey Him and do His will, to go with thy host to the land of the Amalekites, and slay all that you find there—men and beasts alike, burn them to death; wives, widows, and children, all their estates and belongings, and everything you find, burn it, and carry nothing away, no matter how valuable. Take no booty; destroy it all; spare nothing, and it will be better for you.'

"And because Saul coveted the booty, and spared the life of the king and of his beasts, against the prophet's warning, God told Samuel that Saul and all his seed should die, and come to a shameful end. This was what lucre did for Saul—such harm that God hated him for

evermore, and all his heirs after him. But I had better draw no conclusions from this, lest anyone should be offended. For this world is so changed now, that the man who tells the truth to those in power is condemned first.

"Yet I am certain of one thing, for Common Sense has taught me to believe it: that Reason shall reign supreme and rule over the nations. And there are many who shall share the fate of Agag; for once more Samuel shall slay him, and Saul shall be condemned, and David shall be crowned king[15] and subdue all kingdoms. Then one Christian king shall rule over the whole world.

"And no more shall Lucre prevail, as she does now; but Love and Meekness and Honesty shall be the rulers of the earth, and the guardians of truth.

"And if any man commits a sin against truth, or takes a bribe to permit a falsehood, he shall have but one judge, and that is Honesty. Lawyers shall no longer plead at the bar with their hoods of silk and cloaks of ermine. For as it is now, Lucre is a law unto herself: she makes lords of criminals, and rules kingdoms over the heads of judges.

"But Natural Love and Conscience shall come together, and turn Law into an honest workman. Such love shall arise, and such peace and perfect truth among the people, that the Jews, amazed that men should be so truthful, will be filled with joy, thinking that Moses or the Messiah has come to earth.

"And any man who carries a sword,[16] a lance, an axe, a dagger, or any kind of weapon, shall be put to death, unless he sends it to the smithy to be turned into a scythe, a sickle, or a ploughshare. 'They shall beat their swords into ploughshares, and their spears into pruning hooks.' And men will pass their time in digging or ploughing, spinning yarn or spreading dung, or else there will be nothing for them to do.

"And the only kind of hunting left to priests will be for the souls of the dead;[17] and they will hammer at their Psalms from morn till night. For if any of them hunt with hawks and hounds, they shall lose their boasted livings.

"No king or knight or officer or Mayor shall tyrannize over the people, or summon them to serve on juries and compel them to take oaths. But each criminal will be punished according to his crime, heavily or lightly as Truth shall decide. And the King's Court, the Common Court, the Church Court, and the

Chapter shall all be one Court, with a single judge, one True-tongue, an honest man who never opposed me. There shall be no more battles, and any blacksmith who forges a weapon shall perish by it.

Nation shall not lift up sword against nation, neither shall they learn war any more.[18]

"But before this comes to pass, men shall see the worst; and the sign of its coming will be six suns in the sky,[19] with a ship and half a sheaf of arrows. And then an Easter full moon shall convert the Jews; and when they see these things, the Saracens shall sing the *Gloria in Excelsis*. But to you, Lucre, and to Mahomet, will come disaster; for it is written,

A good name is rather to be chosen than great riches, and loving favor rather than silver or gold.[20]

Then Lucre suddenly grew as furious as the wind. "I don't know any Latin," she said, "I leave that to the scholars. But you should read what Solomon says in the Book of Proverbs: 'He that giveth gifts winneth the victory, and hath much honor withal.'[21]

"Your quotation is quite correct, Madam," said Conscience. "But you are like a certain lady reading the Scriptures, who, when she came to the words 'Prove all things,' was highly delighted. However, the text broke off at the end of a page, and if she had turned over, she would have found the rest of it—'Hold fast to that which is good.'[22]

"You, my Lady, have done the same as she did. You've discovered half the text, but you could never find the rest, not if you pored over Proverbs all day long: you need a scholar to turn the pages for you! Your version would suit the lords of this world very well, but the sequel is bitter medicine for those who take bribes. For this is the text complete—

He that giveth gifts winneth the victory, and hath much honor withal, *but he taketh away the soul of him that receiveth them.*"

Notes

1 The poet, to whom the basic problems of society are moral, insists repeatedly in various ways that the friars "undermine conscience." Since the New Law offers mercy only to those who are penitent, this is an extremely serious charge.

2 Cf. Matt. 6:2.

3 Matt. 6:3.

4 Job 15:34.

5 Perhaps an allusion to Edward II.

6 That is, to obtain benefices.

7 An allusion to the Treaty of Bretigny (1360) in which Edward agreed to renounce his claim to the French throne and to accept three million gold crowns as ransom for King John.

8 Ps. 14:1.

9 The Douay text reads (Ps. 14:2) "He that walketh without blemish and worketh justice," which explains the poet's phrase "unspotted from the world."

10 Ps. 14:5.

11 The painted chamber of the king's palace at Westminster contained on the side of the entrance a wall painting showing two lions face to face and nearby the motto *KE NE DUNE KE NE TINE NE PRENT KE DESIRE* ("He who does not give of what he has does not take what he desires").

12 Ps. 25:10.

13 Matt. 6:5.

14 That is, 1 Kings (Vulgate).

15 This is probably a veiled reference to the Second Coming.

16 For this passage, see Isa. 2:2–5.

17 Priests were supposed to be hunters for the Lord, as in Jer. 16:16, not hunters of game.

18 Isa. 2:4.

19 These are figurative portents of Antichrist, probably stated with a certain mocking irony.
20 Prov. 22:1.
21 Prov. 22:9.
22 1 Thess. 5:21.

Book IV
The Downfall of Lady Lucre

"Stop!" said the king, "I will not allow this any longer. You must be reconciled and obey me, both of you. Conscience, I command you to kiss her and make it up."

"Good God, no!" said Conscience. "Banish me for ever first! I'd rather die than kiss her unless Reason says so."

"Then I command you to ride quickly and fetch Reason at once. Tell him to come quickly, as I have some news for him. From now onwards, he alone shall direct my kingdom and be my Chief Counsellor. And he shall discuss with you, Conscience, how you teach the people, clerics, lay folk and all."

"I am very glad of this," said Conscience. And he rode directly to Reason, whispered the king's command in his ear, then took his leave.

"Stay and rest for a bit," said Reason, "while I go and get ready." And he called for his servants, Cato Fairspeech and Tom True-tongue-tell-me-no-idle-tales-for-I-don't-find-them-funny, and said, "Set my saddle on Wait-till-I-get-a-chance, gird him with a belly-band of Good Advice, and put on the heavy bridle to hold his head down, for he's sure to start neighing before we get there."

Then Conscience and Reason rode as fast as they could, conferring privately about Lucre and the subtle hold she had on mankind.

But before long, they were pursued by two men, Worldly Wisdom and his friend Cunning, who had certain matters to clear up in the Courts of Exchequer and Chancery, and were galloping hard to catch up with Reason. For they hoped, for a small fee, to get his advice; he might save them a great deal of trouble and embarrassment.

But they were both covetous men, and Conscience, who knew them well, told Reason to ride faster, and take no notice of them. "Their talk is deceptive," he said. "The truth is that they spend their time with Lucre, and make their money out of strife and quarrels; Love and Honesty they avoid like the plague.

Destruction and unhappiness is in their ways,
    and the way of peace they have not known.[1]

They don't give a straw for God—'There is no fear of God before their eyes.' These men, I tell you, would do more for a horse-load of oats or a dozen chickens, than for all the love of our Lord and His blessed Saints. So let them ride by themselves, Reason, and keep their money-bags. Conscience does not acknowledge them, nor I think does Christ."

So, with Conscience to guide him, Reason galloped full tilt along the highway, till he came to Court.

The king courteously came to meet him, and offered him a seat on the dais between himself and his son. And they spoke together very seriously for a long time.

Then a man named Peace came to Parliament bringing in a petition against one Crime. "He has run away with my wife," he said, "and assaulted Rosy, Reg's girl, and had his way with Margaret too, for all her struggling. And besides that, his ruffians have seized my pigs and geese, and I'm too scared of him to argue or put up a fight. He has borrowed my horse and never brought it back, and refused to pay a farthing for it though I begged him for the money. He stands by and eggs his men on to murder my servants, and forestalls my goods and starts a brawl over them at the market. He breaks down my barn doors and carries off my corn, and all I get is a tally-stick for two hundredweight or more of oats.[2] And on top of all this, he beats me up and goes to bed with my daughter, and I live in such terror of him, I daren't lift a finger."

The king was aware that Peace was telling the truth; he knew already from Conscience of the misery that this ruffian caused among his subjects. So Crime began to feel alarmed, and applied to Worldly Wisdom to smooth things over with money. "If only I could get in the king's good books," he said, offering Wisdom a large bag of silver, "Peace and all his gang could howl on for ever and it wouldn't worry me!"

But in view of the terrible sins Crime had committed, Wisdom and Cunning decided to read him a lecture before helping him: "People who act on impulse," they said, "will always be running their heads into trouble. Such is the case with you, my good man, and you'll soon discover how right we are. It looks as though you're in a bad way, unless Lucre can fix things up for you, for the king holds your life and lands at his mercy."

Then Crime began imploring Worldly Wisdom to settle the matter for him—a few coins in his palm and a little juggling, and all would be well! So Wisdom and Cunning, taking Lucre with them, went off together to get Crime a pardon.

Then Peace held forward his blood-stained head to show them, saying, "God knows, I've done nothing to deserve a blow like this. Conscience and all the people will vouch for that." But Wisdom and Cunning set to work quickly, and tried to bowl the king over with solid cash.

The king, however, stood his ground, and swore by God and his crown that Crime should suffer for his offences; and he commanded an officer to cast him in irons at once—"And make sure he never sees his feet for years," he added.

"Good heavens above!" said Worldly Wisdom, "that is surely very ill-advised. If the man is willing to pay compensation, why not let him have bail? And then his surety can pay a ransom for him, and the whole affair will be straightened out. That will be much better for all concerned."

Cunning agreed with him and urged the same course. "There's no sense in making matters worse," he said. "Two wrongs don't make a right."

Then Lucre thought it was her turn, and, begging the king to show mercy, she offered Peace a gift of pure gold. "Accept this from me, my good fellow," she said, "as a little something to make up for your injury. I'll promise you Crime will never do it again."

So now Peace himself, with tears in his eyes, begged the king to have mercy on the man who had done him so many wrongs—"for he has given me good security, as Sir Wisdom advised, and with your consent, I am quite willing to forgive him. For my part, it seems the best way out; Lady Lucre has paid me the damages, and what more could I ask?"

"No!" said the king. "Crime shall not be allowed to escape; I will learn more of this matter first. If he gets off lightly, he will treat the whole affair as a joke, and beat up my servants more boldly than ever. Unless Reason takes pity on him or he is ransomed by Humbleness, he shall sit in my stocks till his dying day!"

Then some of the court pleaded with Reason to take pity on the poor wretch, and persuade the king and Conscience to let Lucre ransom him.

"It's no use asking me to have mercy," answered Reason, "till lords and ladies learn to love the truth, and turn away from filth and ribaldry; and Lady Peacock casts her finery off, and locks her furs away in her clothes-chest; and parents spoil their children only with rods, and jesters become famous for their holy living; till the clergy are greedy to clothe and feed the poor, and men of Religion who wander off to Rome sing Mass in their cloisters instead, as Benedict, Bernard, and Francis ruled that they should; till preachers prove what they preach by their own practice, and the king's Council serves the public good; and bishops sell their horses to buy shelter for beggars, and their hawks and hounds to help poor monks and friars; till St James is sought[3] in a place of my own choosing, and no one goes to Galicia except to stay there; till no more money bearing the king's image, stamped or unstamped, gold or silver, is carried abroad to fill the pockets of Papal robbers; and till all who go running off to Rome or Avignon[4] are searched for money at Dover—except, of course, for all the merchants and their men, the messengers with their letters, the priests, the penitent pilgrims, and those seeking livings from Rome!

"Yet I shall still have no pity," continued Reason, "while Lucre has any hold on this Court. I have seen so much of the havoc she creates, and could give you proof if you wished. If I, for my part, were a king, with a realm to protect, I should leave no wrong unpunished, on peril of my soul. Nor, God willing, would anyone win my favor with gifts, or gain my mercy through Lucre; only their Meekness would influence me.

"For a man named *Nullum Malum* met with one called *Impunitum*, and bade *Nullum Bonum* be *irremuneratum*.[5] Let your confessor, my lord, interpret this riddle for you, without glossing over it. And if you carry it out, I swear that the Law shall turn laborer and drive a muck-cart, and Love shall rule over your land as you have always wished."

Then the king's confessors put their heads together, to see if they could interpret this sentence in the king's interests—though not for the good of his soul or his people's benefit. For I noticed how Lucre, as she sat in the Council-Chamber, made signs to the lawyers, and how they, chuckling to themselves, left Reason's side and skipped across to her. And Worldly Wisdom winked at her and said, "I'm the very man for you, Madam. For however well I may argue when pleading a case, I haven't a word to say once I light on some money!"

But all the just men among them, including most of the Court and many great nobles, declared in favor of Reason; and even Cunning agreed, and praised Reason's speech. And they thought Meekness a true scholar, and Lucre no better than a common slut. Love himself turned against her, and Honesty despised her, and voiced his opinion so loudly that the whole Court heard him. "If anyone marries her for her money," he said, "he'll soon be a fine cuckold!"

But Lucre sat there sullen and crestfallen, branded as a whore by the greater part of the Court. Yet one of the jurors and a summoner still went after her eagerly; and a sheriff's clerk swore at the whole assembly, saying, "Many's the time I've assisted you at the bar, and none of you ever gave me a brass farthing!"

Then the king, calling Reason and Conscience to his side, gave his verdict in favor of Reason. He frowned threateningly on Lucre, and turned angrily to Law— the Law that Lucre had almost overthrown—saying,

"I have you to thank, no doubt, for the loss of half my estates. This Lucre of yours has choked up the truth and trampled on your justice. But Reason will settle with you before I have reigned much longer, and judge you as you deserve, make no mistake. Nor shall Lucre stand bail for you either! From now on I will have honest lawyers, and there's an end of the matter! As for Crime, the majority of this Court have judged him guilty, and he shall be sentenced accordingly."

Then Conscience said to the king, "Unless you win the support of the common people, you will find it very hard to bring all this about, and govern your subjects strictly according to justice."

"I'd rather be drawn alive," exclaimed Reason, "than rule your kingdom in any other way. And you must give me the power to command obedience."

"I swear by our blessed Lady," answered the king, "I will support you in this, once I have called together my Council, the nobles and clerics. I gladly accept you, Reason, and while I live you shall never leave my side."

"And for my part, I am ready to stay with you for ever," said Reason, "but you must let Conscience remain here as our adviser; that is all I ask."

"I grant it," answered the king. "God forbid we should fail! Let us live together for the rest of our lives."[6]

Notes

1 Ps. 13:3.

2 The complaint here is against false purveyors for the Crown, who are among the criminals of various kinds described.

3 The shrine of St. James of Compostella in Spain was a favorite goal of pilgrims.

4 That is, to the papal Curia.

5 This is a reference to Pope Innocent's *De miseria humanae conditionis*, where it is said that "he is a just judge who leaves no evil deed unpunished and no good deed unrewarded."

6 The situation here described is not a reflection of any actual events. What the poet is saying is that a king should seek to rule according to the dictates of reason and the counsel of conscience. The same principle applies to any individual, who should govern himself in the same way. However, if in the community of the realm any such rule is to be effected, the commons must be made to consent; and no such consent will be forthcoming unless they can be persuaded to give up their cupidinous desires and purge themselves of vice. In the same way, any individual must give up his vices if he is to live according to reason and conscience. Hence the confessional theme of the next book.

Book V

The Confession of the Seven Deadly Sins and the Search for Truth

The king and his nobles went to church to hear Mass and Matins for the day. And then I awoke from sleep, disappointed that I had not slept more soundly and seen more. But scarcely had I gone two hundred yards, when I felt so faint and sleepy that I could walk no further. So I sat down quietly and said my Creed, and dropped asleep muttering my Rosary.

Then I saw much more than before. For again I beheld the field full of people, and now Reason, standing before the king with a Cross in his hand, and preparing to preach to the whole kingdom.

He made it plain to them that their sin alone had caused the Plagues, and that the great gale[1] which came from the South-west on Saturday evening was clearly the judgment of God on their excessive pride. "Your pears and plum-trees toppled before the blast," he said, "as a parable to warn you to do better. And beeches and mighty oaks were dashed to the ground, with their roots twisted high in the air, as a terrible sign of the destruction that deadly sin will bring upon you all, on the Day of Doom."

I could preach a long sermon on this myself, but I will speak only of what I saw—how clearly Reason preached before the people.

He told Waster to go and work, at whatever trade he could do best, and so win back the money that he had squandered. He begged Lady Peacock to leave off wearing her furs, and put them by in a chest against time of need. He directed Tom Stowe to take a couple of cudgels, and rescue his wife Felicity from the ducking-stool. He warned Walter that his wife was much to be blamed for wearing a headdress worth five guineas, while his ragged old hood would hardly fetch threepence. And he bade Mr Bett cut himself some birch-rods, and beat his daughter Betty till she was willing to work.

Then he told the merchants to discipline their children. "If you make a lot of money, don't pamper them with it," he said, "and even if the Plague carries off half the neighborhood, still you must never spoil them unreasonably. My mother and father used to say to me, 'The more you love the child, the more you must correct him.' And Solomon, the author of Wisdom, said the same—'He that spareth his rod hateth his son.'"[2]

And then he admonished the priests and Bishops, saying, "Prove by your own lives what you preach to others. This will bring blessing to yourselves, and encourage us to have better faith in your teaching."[3]

Next, he exhorted the monks and friars to keep to their Rule—"lest the king and his Council cut down your supplies, and decide to manage your property for you until you are better governed."

Then he counselled the king to love his people—"for they are your greatest treasure in times of peace, and in times of trouble your chief support." And he begged the Pope to have pity on Holy Church, and govern himself before distributing grace to others.

"And as for you men who maintain the laws," he said, "you must covet Truth, and not gold or gifts if you would please God. For the Gospel tells us that neither God nor His saints in Heaven will acknowledge any man who opposes the truth—'Verily I say unto you, I know you not.'[4]

"And you folk who go on pilgrimages and visit the shrines of St James and the saints in Rome, must seek instead for the blessed Saint Truth,[5] for He alone can save you, who with the Father and the Son liveth and reigneth for ever and ever. And may He bless and save all who follow my teachings."

So ended Reason, and Repentance ran to take up his theme, till William wept bitterly to hear him.[6]

Pride[7]

The Lady Peacock Proud-heart threw herself flat on the ground and lay there for a long time. Then she raised her head, crying "Lord, have mercy," and vowed to God that she would slit her smock and fasten a hair-shirt on the inside, to tame the fierce lusts of her flesh. "Here's an end to all my swaggering airs," she said. "For now I intend to take a humble place and endure insults gladly—that will be something new for me! And I will be meek and beseech God for mercy, for this is the thing my heart has always loathed."

Lechery

Then Lecher cried "Alas!" and besought Our Lady to intercede for his soul, and pray God to have mercy on his sins; and for this he made her a vow, that every Saturday for many years to come, he would drink nothing but water and be content with only one meal.[8]

Envy

Then with a heavy heart Envy asked for penance, and sorrowfully began to say the *Confiteor*. He was as pale as ashes, and shook like a man with the palsy. His clothes were so coarse and shabby, I can scarcely describe them —a rough tunic with a kirtle below, a knife by his side, and foresleeves cut from a Friar's habit. With his shrivelled cheeks, and scowling horribly, he looked like a leek that has been lying too long in the sun. His body was all blistered with wrath, and he went about biting his lips and twisting his fingers, always scheming some vengeance by word or deed, and looking for a chance to carry it out. His tongue was like an adder's: every word he spoke was backbiting and detraction. He made his living by slander and bearing false witness; and in whatever company he shewed his face, his displayed his manners by flinging dirt at everyone.[9]

"I would be shriven, if only I dared," said this creature, "but I am far too ashamed. For I swear I would far rather see Bert, my neighbor, get into trouble, than win half a ton of Essex Cheese tomorrow.

"There's one near neighbor of mine whom I've almost ruined. I've so slandered him to the gentry that he's lost all his money, and my lies have turned even his friends against him. It makes my blood boil to see him in luck, or getting credit for anything.

"I cause such strife among folk with my evil talk, that it sometimes ends in loss of life or limb. Yet when I meet the man I detest most, in the market place, I greet him politely, as if I were his best friend. For I daren't offend him—he's far stronger than I am. But if once I got him in my power, God knows what I'd do to him!

"And when I go to church, and the priest tells us to kneel before the Rood and pray for pilgrims and all the people, then on my knees I call down curses from Heaven on the thieves who've run off with the bowl I use for rubbish, and my tattered sheet! And then I turn my eyes away from the altar, and seeing that Ellen has a new coat, I wish to God it were mine, together with all the cloth from which it was cut.

"I gloat over other men's losses, and bewail their gains. I condemn their actions, while my own are much worse. And if anyone tells me off, I hate him for ever. I could only be happy if everyone were my slave, for it drives me mad to think that anyone else should have more than I have.

"And so I live, without love, like a mangy cur, my whole body swollen with bitter gall. Why, for many years I could scarcely eat, Envy and Ill-will are so hard to digest. Haven't you got some sweet syrup that can soothe my swellings, some gentle linctus of shame or penance, to drive it out of my heart?—or will you have to scour my stomach?"

"Yes, indeed I have," said Repentance, and he advised him what was best—"Sorrow for sin can always save a man's soul."

"But I *am* sorry," said the man, "I am seldom otherwise. That is why I'm so thin—because I can never get my revenge! When I was living in London, among the rich merchants, I would use Backbite as my private agent, to run down other men's wares! And when mine wouldn't sell, and theirs would, then you should see how I scowled and slandered them and their goods! Still, if I can, through the grace of Almighty God, I intend to make amends for all these things."

Anger

Then Anger, with staring eyes, was roused to repentance, and hanging his head came forward snivelling. "I am Anger," he said. "I used to be a friar, and worked at the Friary as a gardener, grafting shoots. So I grafted on to those beggars such lies and tales that they bore great branches of flattering words to please the gentry, and blossomed out into ladies' bowers to hear confessions. And now this tree of mine has borne strange fruit: for the people would rather go to the friars for Confession, than to their parish priests. And the salaried priests, finding they have to share their profits with the friars, denounce them from the pulpits. Then the friars retaliate in kind, and wherever they go on their rounds preaching, I, Anger, walk with them, and teach them from my holy books.[10]

"Both parties will boast of their own spiritual power, and despise each other, till either they all become beggars and live by *my* spiritual power, or else grow rich, and ride about on horseback! So I never rest from pursuing these wicked folk, for I reckon that's my vocation.

"I have an aunt who's a nun—an Abbess in fact. She would rather drop down dead than suffer a moment's pain! For many months I served as a cook in her convent kitchen, and in the monastery too. My chief job was concocting soups for the Prioress, and the other poor ladies. So I brewed them broths of every conceivable slander—that Mother Joanna was an illegitimate child, that Sister Clarice might be a knight's daughter, but her mother was no better than she should be, and that Sister Peacock had an affair with a priest—'She'll never be Prioress,' they said. 'She had a baby last year in cherry-time; it's the talk of the Convent!'

"And I fed them with such a hash of spiteful gossip, that two of them would sometimes burst out 'Liar!' together, and slap each other across the face. Christ! If they'd both had knives, they'd have slaughtered each other!

"St Gregory was a good Pope, with great foresight, for it was he who laid down that no Prioress could hear confessions.[11] Otherwise they would all have been disgraced on the very first day, for women can never keep anything secret.

"I might, of course, live with the monks, but I mostly avoid them. They have too many fierce fellows watching out for men like me, Priors and Sub-Priors and Father Abbots. If I tell any tales there, they hold a special meeting, and make me fast every Friday on bread and water. Then they give me a telling-off in the Chapter-house, as though I were a child, and have me whacked with my trousers down. I am not very fond of living with fellows like that. There's nothing to eat there but stinking fish and watery ale. So that if, once in a while, they get in some good wine and I manage to drink in the evening, it gives me a flux of foul talk for five days after. I repeat all the evil I know about any of our brethren, till the whole house has heard it."

"You must repent," said Repentance, "and never again repeat anyone's secrets, no matter how you came by them. And do not take too much pleasure in drink, or swallow too much, lest it weakens your will and you get another attack of malice. For the Scripture says, 'Be ye sober.'"[12] And then he gave Anger his absolution, bidding him try to be contrite and weep for his sins.

Avarice

And then came Covetousness; no words can describe him, he looked so hungry and hollow, such a crafty old codger! He had beetling brows and thick, puffy lips, and his eyes were as bleary as a blind old hag's. His baggy cheeks sagged down below his chin, flapping about like a leather wallet, and trembling with old age. His beard was all bespattered with grease, like a serf's with bacon fat. He wore a hood on his head with a lousy

cap on top, and a dirty-brown smock at least a dozen years old, torn and filthy and crawling with lice. It was so threadbare that even a louse would have preferred to hop elsewhere.

"I have been covetous," said this old wretch, "I confess it all now. I began as an apprentice under Sim-at-the-Stile, and I had to make his business pay. I learnt to lie in a small way to begin with, and my first lesson was in giving false weights. Then my master would send me to the fairs at Weyhill and Winchester, with all kinds of wares; and God knows they would still be unsold to this day, but for the grace of Guile which crept amongst them!

"Then I went to school with the drapers, and was shown how to stretch the selvedge and make the cloth look longer. My chief lesson was with the best, striped stuff—how to pierce it with pack-needles and join the strips together and lay them in a press, till ten or eleven yards were stretched into thirteen.

"My wife was a weaver of woollen cloth. She employed spinners to spin it out for her, and paid them by the pound. But if truth be known, the pound weight she used weighed a quarter more than my own steel-yard.

"Then I bought her some barley-malt, and she took to brewing beer for retail. She would mix a little good ale with a lot of small beer, and put this brew on one side for poor laborers and common folk. But the best she always hid away in the parlor or in my bedroom; and if anyone took a swig at that, he paid for it through the nose—four bob a pint at least, and that's God's truth. Even so, she would measure it out in cupfuls—she was a crafty old girl! They called her Rose the Racketeer, and she's been a regular huckster all her life.

"But now I swear to break myself of these sins—no more selling short weight or swindling the customers. And I'll make a pilgrimage to Walsingham, with my wife as well, and pray to the Rood of Bromholm[13] to get me out of debt."

"Have you ever repented," said Repentance, "or made any restitution?"[14]

"Yes, indeed I have: I was staying at an inn once, with some merchants, and while they were asleep I got up and burgled their bags."

"That wasn't restitution, that was robbery!" said Repentance. "You ought to be hanged for that, more than for everything else you've told me."

"I thought restitution meant robbery," he said, "I

never learned to read, and the only French I know comes from the wilds of Norfolk!"

"Have you ever in your life practiced usury?"

"No, certainly not, except in my young days. I did pick up a thing or two then, I admit, chiefly from Jews and Lombards. They showed me how to weigh coins with a balance, clip the heavier ones, and then lend them out, all for love of the cross—the one on the back of the gold pieces! The borrower would give me a pledge he was almost certain to lose, and that was worth more to me than the clipped coins. And you should have seen the agreements I used to draw up in case my debtors didn't pay on the nail. I've acquired far more properties through arrears of debt, than I ever could have got by 'showing kindness and lending'[15] Why, I have lent money and goods to lords and ladies before now, and afterwards been their broker, and bought them out for nothing!

"I do a roaring trade in barter and money-lending; people lose the better part of every crown I lend them. And sometimes, when I've carried the Lombards' letters to Rome with their gold, I have taken the money by tally here in London, and counted it out as a good deal less when I got to the other end."

"But did you ever pay noblemen money to connive at your crimes?"

"I have certainly paid out money to noblemen, but they didn't love me for it, I assure you! I've turned many a knight into a mercer or draper[16]—and they never paid me a thing for their apprenticeship, not so much as a pair of gloves!"

"Then are you merciful to poor men who are forced to borrow?"

"I pity them as much as a pedlar pities cats—he'd kill them for their skins if he could only catch them!"

"Well, are you kind at least to your neighbors? Do you invite them in for a meal?"

"My neighbors think I'm as kind as a dog in a kitchen," he said.

"Then you had better repent soon," said Repentance, "or the only prayer I can say for you is this: that you may never live to make good use of your riches, that your children after you may never enjoy them, nor your executors put them to any good purpose; but that all you have wickedly gained may be spent by the wicked.

"For if I were a Friar, and belonged to an honest, charitable House, I should never consent to spend money of yours on vestments or church repairs. Nor would I accept an extra penny on my allowance, if I knew, or had any suspicion, that it came from a man like you—not if you were to give me the best manuscript in the Friary, with leaves of burnished gold! For it is written, 'Thou art the slave of another, when thou seekest after dainty dishes; feed rather upon bread of thine own, and thou shalt be free.'[17]

"You are a vile wretch, and I cannot give you absolution. You must first settle accounts with all the people you have robbed. I have no power to pardon you till all their losses are made good, and Reason has entered it in the register of Heaven. For it is written, 'The sin is not remitted unless restitution be made.'[18] And all who have received any part of your wealth are bound before God to help you pay it back. If you doubt it, read what is written in the Psalter Commentary, under the verse, 'Behold, Thou desirest truth in the inward parts.'[19] For no man who uses your ill-gotten gains can ever prosper.

With the merciful Thou wilt show thyself merciful:
and with the froward Thou wilt show thyself
froward.[20]

Then this scoundrel fell into despair, and would have hanged himself, had not Repentance offered him comfort at once, saying, "Think of God's mercy, and pray aloud for it. For it is written, 'God's tender mercies are above all His works,'[21] and again, 'Compared with the mercy of God, all the evil that man can do or think in this world, is as a spark quenched in the ocean.'[22]

"So fill your heart with thoughts of mercy. And as for your business, give it up. You have no right to buy yourself so much as a roll of bread, unless you can earn the money with your own hands, or beg it. All your wealth sprang from deceit, so you cannot live by it; and if you do, you are not paying for what you buy, but living on credit. And in case you are not sure whom to repay, take your money to the Bishop, and ask him to dispose of it for you, in whatever way is best for your soul. He shall answer for you before the Judgment of God—for you, and many more besides. For believe me, every bishop will render an account to God, both of what he taught you in Lent, and what he gave you from the riches of God's grace, to guard and keep you from sin."

Gluttony

And then Gluttony set out to go to Confession. But as he sauntered along to the church, he was hailed by Betty, the ale-wife, who asked him where he was going.

"To Holy Church," he replied, "to hear Mass and go to Confession; then I shan't commit any more sins."

"I've got some good ale here, Glutton," she said. "Why don't you come and try it, ducky?"

"Have you got hot spices in your bag?"

"Yes, I've got pepper, and peony-seeds, and a pound of garlic—or would you rather have a ha'porth of fennel-seed, as it's a fish-day?"

So Glutton entered the pub, and Great Oaths followed him. He found Cissie the shoemaker sitting on the bench, and Wat the gamekeeper with his wife, and Tim the tinker with two of his apprentices, and Hick the hackneyman, and Hugh the haberdasher, and Clarice, the whore of Cock Lane, with the parish clerk, and Davy the ditcher, and Father Peter of Prie-Dieu Abbey, with Peacock the Flemish wench,[23] and a dozen others, not to mention a fiddler, and a rat-catcher, and a Cheapside scavenger, a rope-maker and a trooper. Then there was Rose the pewterer, Godfrey of Garlick-hithe, Griffiths the Welshman, and a crew of auctioneers. Well, there they all were, early in the morning, ready to give Glutton a good welcome and start him off with a pint of the best.

Then Clement the cobbler pulled off his cloak and flung it down for a game of handicap. So Hick the hackneyman threw down his hood and asked Bett the butcher to take his part, and they chose dealers to price the articles and decide on the odds.

Then the two dealers jumped up quickly, went off into a corner, and began in whispers to value these rubbishy garments. But as they had scruples about it and couldn't agree, they asked Robin the ropemaker to join them as an umpire, and so they settled the business between the three of them.

As it turned out, Hick the hostler got the cloak, while Clement had to fill the cup and content himself with Hick's hood. And the first man to go back on his word was to do the honors, and stand Glutton a gallon of ale.

Then there were scowls and roars of laughter and cries of "Pass round the cup!" And so they sat shouting and singing till time for vespers. By that time, Glutton had put down more than a gallon of ale, and his guts were beginning to rumble like a couple of greedy sows. Then, before you had time to say the Our Father, he

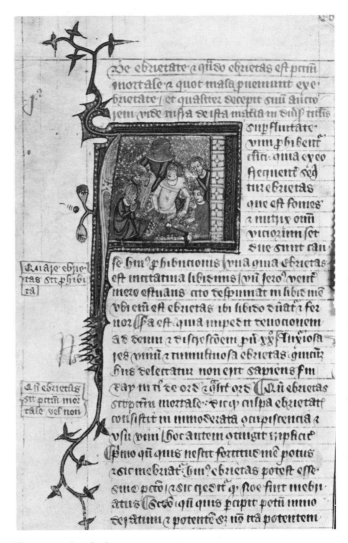

Figure 33   *Drunkards.*

had pissed a couple of quarts, and blown such a blast on the round horn of his rump, that all who heard it had to hold their noses, and wished to God he would plug it with a bunch of gorse!

He could neither walk nor stand without his stick. And once he got going, he moved like a blind minstrel's bitch, or like a fowler laying his lines, sometimes sideways, sometimes backwards. And when he drew near to the door, his eyes grew glazed, and he stumbled on the threshold and fell flat on the ground. Then Clement the cobbler seized him round the middle to lift him up, and got him on to his knees. But Glutton was a big fellow, and he took some lifting; and to make matters worse, he was sick in Clement's lap, and his vomit smelt so foul that the hungriest hound in Hertfordshire would never have lapped it up.

At last, with endless trouble, his wife and daughter managed to carry him home and get him into bed. And after all this dissipation, he fell into a stupor, and slept throughout Saturday and Sunday. Then at sunset on Sunday he woke up, and as he wiped his bleary eyes, the first words he uttered were, "Who's had the tankard?"

Then his wife scolded him for his wicked life, and Repentance joined in, saying, "You know that you have sinned in word and deed, so confess yourself, and show some shame and make an act of contrition."

"I, Glutton, confess that I am guilty," said the man, "I have sinned by word of mouth more often than I can remember: I have sworn by 'God's Soul' and said 'God and the saints help me' hundreds of times when there was no need to.

"And I have let myself go at supper, and sometimes dinner too, so badly that I have thrown it all up again before I have gone a mile, and wasted food that might have been saved for the hungry. On fast-days I have eaten the tastiest foods I could get, and drunk the best wines, and sometimes sat so long at my meals that I've slept and eaten both at the same time. And to get more drink and hear some gossip, I've had my dinner at the pub on fast-days too, and rushed off to a meal before midday."

"God will reward you for this good confession," said Repentance.

Then Glutton began to weep and bewail his vicious life; and he made a vow of fasting, saying, "Every Friday from now on, I shan't give my belly a morsel of anything, not even fish, no matter how hungry and thirsty I get—not till my Aunt Abstinence gives me permission—though up to now I have always loathed her!"

Sloth

Then came Sloth, all beslobbered, with his gummy eyes. "I shall have to sit down," he said, "or I'll fall asleep. I cannot stand or prop myself up all the time, and you can't expect me to kneel without a hassock. If I had been put to bed now, you'd never get me up before dinner was ready, not for all your bell-ringing—not unless nature called."

Then, with a loud belch, he started his "Bless me, father," and beat his breast, but as he stopped to stretch, he yawned, grunted, and finally started to snore.

"Hey! Wake up, man!" shouted Repentance. "Get a move on, and make your confession."

"If this were my dying day," said Sloth, "I still couldn't be bothered to keep awake. I don't even know the Paternoster perfectly, not as a priest should really sing it. I know plenty of ballads about Robin Hood and Randolph Earl of Chester,[24] but I don't know a verse about our Lord or our Lady.

"I have made hundreds of vows, and forgotten them the next morning. I have never yet managed to do the penance the priest has given me, or felt really sorry for my sins. And when I'm saying my Rosary, my heart is miles away from the words, except when I say them in a fit of temper. I spend every day, holydays and all, gossiping idly at the pub—sometimes even in church—and I never give a thought to the Passion of Christ.

"Nor have I ever once visited the sick or the prisoners chained in the dungeons. For I enjoy a bawdy joke, or a riotous day at the village wake, or a juicy bit of scandal about some neighbor, more than all that Matthew, Mark, Luke, and John ever penned. I don't keep account of vigils or fast-days—they just seem to slip by. And in Lent, I am lying in bed with my mistress in my arms till long after Mass and Matins are over, then I go to the Friary for a late Mass. And once I get to the 'Ite, Missa est,' I've had enough! Why, unless illness drives me to it, I sometimes go a whole year without making a confession, and then I do it by guesswork.

"I have been a parish priest for more than thirty years, yet I can neither sing my notes right, nor read a Lesson. I can start a hare in a ploughed field better than I can construe a single verse in the Psalms, or expound it to the parish. I'm good at presiding at Settlement Days, and auditing Reeves' accounts, but I can't read a line of Canon Law. And if I take anything on credit, it goes clean out of my mind unless it is marked on a tally. The man can ask for it six or seven times over, but I'll swear blind I know nothing about it. That's the way I ill-use honest men, day in and day out.

"It is a grim day for all concerned when I have to read the accounts of my servants' wages, and find how far behind I am with them. So I pay them off—with arrears of spite and resentment.

"And if someone does me a good turn, or helps me in need, I pay him back with rudeness; for I can never understand courtesy. My manners have always been like those of a hawk: you can't lure me by love alone, you must always hold a tit-bit under your thumb. My fellow-Christians must have done me hundreds of favors in times past, but I have forgotten them all. And I have wasted good foodstuffs, deliberately or through carelessness—meat, fish, bread, butter, cheese, and ale—all gone to waste till they weren't fit to eat.

"When I was a boy I never got down to my studies, but I trotted about from place to place instead; and this vile sloth has made me a beggar ever since. 'Heu mihi, quod sterilem duxi iuvenilem!' [25]

"Do you repent?" said Repentance—but at that moment Sloth dozed off again.

Then the Watcher, whose name is *Vigilate*,[26] threw some cold water over his face and dashed it into his eyes, shouting earnestly, "Look out! For Despair is out to betray you! Say to yourself 'I am sorry for my sins,' and beat your breast and beseech God for grace. For His goodness is greater than all the guilt in the world."

Then Sloth sat up, blessed himself hastily, and made a vow before God to fight against his foul sloth, saying, "Not a single Sunday shall pass from now on—unless sickness prevent me—but I will go to holy church before dawn, and hear Mass and Matins like a monk. And I will never again sit over my ale after dinner, but go to church and hear Evensong instead. I make this vow before the Holy Rood. Moreover I intend, if I can find the means, to pay back all that I have wrongfully acquired since I was a boy. I will not stint anyone, even if I go without myself; every man shall have what is his, before I leave this world. And with whatever is left, I swear by the Rood of Chester, I will turn pilgrim, and seek Truth first, even if I never see Rome!"

Then Robert the Robber began weeping bitterly, for he remembered the text, "Render to all men their dues," [27] and had no means of making restitution. And yet this wretched sinner was praying under his breath, "O Jesus, who died on the Cross of Calvary, and took pity even on Dismas my brother,[28] because he said, 'Remember me, Lord, when thou comest into thy kingdom,' [29] have mercy now on this robber who has not wherewith to repay.[30] For I can never earn enough with my hands to repay all that I owe. Yet I beseech You, out of Your great mercy, to accept what little I can do. Do not condemn me at Doomsday for doing so ill."

I cannot tell for sure what happened to this robber. But I know that he wept bitter tears, and acknowledged his guilt to Christ again and again. And he promised to polish afresh his pikestaff of penance, and tramp the world with it for the rest of his life—because he had slept with Latro, Lucifer's Aunt.

Then Repentance had pity on all the penitents, and bidding them kneel, he said, "And now I will beg our Savior's grace for all sinners, that He may have mercy on us all and help us to do better—

"O God, who in Your goodness [31] created the world, and fashioned all things out of nothing, making man the closest to Your image—and yet allowed him to sin, and so bring a sickness upon us all—and all for the best, for so I believe, whatever the Scriptures say—

O felix culpa, O necessarium peccatum Adae! [32]

—for through that sin, Your Son was sent to this earth, and became man, and was born of a Virgin to save mankind; and in the Person of Your Son, O God, You made yourself like us sinful men, for it is written, 'Let us make man in our own image, after our likeness,' [33] and again, 'He that dwelleth in love, dwelleth in God, and God in him.' [34]

"So You, O God, robed in our flesh with Your Son, died for our sake on that Good Friday, at high noon—though neither You nor Your Son felt any sorrow in death, for the anguish was felt only in our human flesh, and Your Son overcame it—'He led captivity captive'; [35] yet on account of the weakness of the flesh, Your Son closed His eyes for a while, at about midday when the light is greatest which is the meal-time of Your saints; [36] and then You fed with Your fresh Blood our forefathers who dwelt in darkness—

The people that walked in darkness, have seen a great light [37]

—and by the Light which leapt forth from you then, Lucifer was blinded, and with Your dying breath You swept all those blessed souls into the bliss of Paradise.

"And the third day after, You walked again in our flesh, and the first to see You was not Mary Your Mother, but a sinful Mary; and You allowed it to be so, in order to comfort the sinful, for it is written, 'I came not to call the righteous, but sinners to repentance.' [38]

"And since Your most mighty deeds, all that Matthew, Mark, Luke, and John recorded, were done in our human coat-armor (for 'The Word was made flesh and dwelt among us'[39]), so I believe we may confidently pray and beseech You, who art our Father and our Brother, to have mercy on us, and, if it be Your will, to take pity on these wretched sinners here, who repent so sorely that they ever offended You, in thought, word, or deed."

Then Hope seized a horn of *Yet-didst-thou-turn-and-refresh-me*,[40] and blew it to the tune of *Blessed-is-he-whose-sins-are-forgiven*,[41] till all the saints in Heaven took up the song—

"Thou, Lord, shalt save both man and beast; How excellent is thy mercy, O God:

and the children of men shall put their trust under the shadow of thy wings."[42]

Then a thousand men thronged together, crying aloft to Christ and His Virgin Mother, that Grace might go with them in their search for Truth.

But not one of them had the wisdom to know the way. So they blundered on like beasts,[43] over humps and hills, till at last, late in the day and far from home, they met a man dressed like a strange Saracen, as pilgrims are. He carried a staff, with a broad strip of cloth twisted round it like bindweed. By his side were slung a bag and begging-bowl, and souvenirs were pinned all round his hat—dozens of phials of holy oil, scallop-shells from Galicia, and emblems from Sinai. His cloak was sewn all over with devices—Holy Land crosses, cross-keys from Rome, and a St Veronica handkerchief across the front—to let everyone know how many shrines he had seen.

"Where have you come from?" the people asked.

"From Sinai," he said, "and from Our Lord's Sepulchre. I have also visited Bethlehem, Babylon, Armenia, Alexandria, and many more holy places. You can see by the signs in my hat how widely I've travelled—on foot and in all weathers, seeking out shrines of the saints for the good of my soul."

"Do you know anything about a saint called Truth?" they said. "Can you tell us where to find him?"

"Good Heavens, no!" said the man. "I've met plenty of palmers with their staffs and scrips, but no one ever asked for a saint by that name."

"By St Peter!"[44] said a ploughman, pushing his way through the crowd, "I know Him, as well as a scholar knows his books. Conscience and Common Sense showed me the way to His place, and they made me swear to serve Him for ever, and do His sowing and planting for as long as I can work. I've been His man for the last fifty years;[45] I've sown His seed and herded His beasts, and looked after all His affairs, indoors and out. I ditch and dig, sow and thresh, and do whatever Truth tells me—tailoring and tinkering, spinning and weaving —I put my hand to anything He bids me.

"And Truth is pleased with my work, though I say it myself.[46] He pays me well, and sometimes gives me extra; for He's as ready with His wages as any poor man could wish, and never fails to pay His men each night. Besides, He's as mild as a lamb, and always speaks to you kindly. So if you would like to know where He lives, I'll put you on the track in no time."[47]

"Thank you, Piers old fellow," the pilgrims said; and they offered him money to guide them to Truth's castle.

"No, by my soul!" swore Piers, "I wouldn't take a farthing, not for all the riches in St Thomas's shrine! Truth would find it hard to forgive me for that! But if you want to go the right way, listen now, while I set you on Truth's path.

"You must all set out through *Meekness*, men and women alike, and continue till you come to *Conscience*; for Christ may know by this that you love God above all things,[48] and your neighbor next, and treat others as you would like them to treat you.

"Then turn down by the stream *Be-gentle-in-speech*, till you come to a ford, *Honor-thy-father-and-mother*. There you must wade into the water and wash yourselves thoroughly, then you'll step more lightly for the rest of your life. Next, you will see a place called *Swear-not-without-necessity-and-above-all-take-not-the-name-of-the-Lord-thy-God-in-vain*.

"After that, you will pass by a farm where you must not trespass on any account, for its name is *Thou-shalt-not-covet-thy-neighbor's-cattle-nor-his-wives-nor-any-of-his-servants-lest-you-do-him-an-injury*. So take care not to break any branches there, unless they are your own property.

"You will also see there two pairs of stocks; but do not stop, for they are *Steal-not* and *Kill-not*. Go round and leave them on your left, and don't look back at them. And remember to observe Holy Days, and keep them holy from morning till nightfall.

"Then you will come to a hill, *Bear-no-false-witness*. Turn right away from it, for it is thickly wooded with bribes, and bristling with florins. At all costs gather no blossoms there, or you will lose your soul. And so you will arrive at a place called *Speak-the-truth-and-mean-it-and-never-swerve-from-the-truth-for-any-man.*

"From there you will see a mansion[49] as bright as the sun, surrounded by a moat of *Mercy*, with walls of *Wisdom*, to keep out passion. It has battlements of *Christendom* to save mankind, and is buttressed with *Believe-or-you-cannot-be-saved.*

"And all the buildings, halls, and chambers are roofed, not with lead, but with *Love*, and are covered with the *Lowly-speech-of-brothers*. The drawbridge is of *Ask-and-you-shall-receive*, and each pillar is built of penance and prayers to the saints, and all the gates are hung on hinges of almsdeeds.

"The doorkeeper's name is Grace, a good man, who has a servant, Amendment, well known among men. And this is the password you must give him so that Truth may know you are honest: 'I have done the penance which the priest gave me; I am very sorry for my sins, I always shall be whenever I think of them, and still should be even if I were Pope!'

"Then you must ask Amendment to beg his Master to open the wicket-gate that Eve shut in the beginning, when she and Adam ate the sour apples. For 'Through Eve the door was closed to all men, and through the Virgin Mary it was opened again.'[50] So Mary always has the key, even when the King is sleeping.

"And if Grace gives you leave to enter by this gate, you will find Truth dwelling in your heart, hung on a chain of charity. And you will submit to Him as a child to its father, never opposing His will.

"But then beware of the villain Wrath, who envies Him who dwells in your heart. For he will push Pride in your way and make you feel so pleased with yourself that you are blinded by the glory of your own good deeds. So you will be driven out 'as the early dew,'[51] the door will be locked and bolted against you, and it may be a hundred years before you enter again. Thus by thinking too much of yourself, you may lose God's love, and enter His courts no more, unless His grace intervenes.

"But there are also seven sisters, the eternal servants of Truth, who keep the postern-gates of the castle. These are Abstinence and Humility, Chastity and Charity, His chief maidens, Patience and Peace, who help many people, and the Lady Bountiful, who opens the gates to still more, and has helped thousands out of the Devil's pound.

"Anyone related to these seven is wonderfully welcome there, and received with honor. But if you are kin to none of them, it is very hard for you to get in at all, except by the special mercy of God."

"Christ!" said a cutpurse, "I've got no relatives there!"

"Nor me, as far as I know," said a juggler with a monkey.

"Lord 'a mercy!" said a market woman, "if it's as bad as that, I'm not going a step further—not for no Friar's preaching!"

"Yes, but listen," said Piers, still trying to spur them on, "Mercy[52] herself is a maiden there, with power over all the others. She and her Son are akin to all sinners. So if you will put your trust in them, you may still find grace—but you must go quickly."

"By St Paul!" said a Pardoner. "It may be that they don't know me there. I'll go and fetch my box of indulgences and my Bishops' Letters."

"By Jesus, I'll go with you!" said a prostitute. "You can say I'm your sister." But what became of these two I cannot tell.

Notes

1   Perhaps a reference to a violent storm in January, 1362. However, this contemporary allusion is exemplary. As Boethius explains in *The Consolation of Philosophy*, evil fortune of whatever kind serves as a warning that one should not place one's trust in temporal things.

2   Prov. 13:24.

3   Cf. the ideal parson of the General prologue to *The Canterbury Tales*.

4   Matt. 25:12.

5   These lines are frequently so read as to make St. Truth the Holy Spirit. However, it may be that

St. Truth is Christ (frequently called *Veritas* in medieval texts) and that "He alone" refers to the Holy Spirit, sent by Christ for the salvation of humanity.

6   For *William* the text has *Will*. What is meant is that when Repentance preaches, Will (the human will) weeps in contrition. The speaker in the poem may be one Will Langland, the author, but he is made to represent the human will seeking grace.

7   The seven principal vices speak in turn. A vice is a habit of the soul that may lead to sins of various kinds. Thus a person who is habitually proud may show this fact in various ways: dress, speech, demeanor, criminal action, and so on. If one of these manifestations involves the consent of the reason and is thus deliberate, it is a deadly sin which must be revealed at the confessional in true contrition if the sinner is to be saved. Since the New Law offers mercy only to those who are repentant for their sins (and all men are sinful, or, in medieval terms, unreasonable, from time to time), confession in the proper spirit was thought to be extremely important. Penance was thus called "the second raft after shipwreck" in the world, the first "raft" being baptism. That is, the Christian is cleansed at baptism and given, so to speak, a white robe which is his wedding garment for his marriage with Christ. He buries the "old man," or the inherited evil habit of the flesh, crucifying it so that the "new man," or the spirit, may live. Thus he is for the time being on a kind of ark which prevents him from drowning in the sea of the world and is ready to begin his voyage, or pilgrimage, to Christ. But all men who live beyond the age of reason lapse after baptism, soiling and tearing their white garments, and falling, as it were, by the wayside, or into the sea. Penance (sometimes called a laundry) gives the Christian an opportunity to cleanse and repair his robes and to escape from the waves so that he may resume his voyage or pilgrimage toward Truth. Hence the nature of true penance, which consists of three parts (contrition of heart, confession of mouth, and satisfaction of works), is a major concern in this poem as well as in *The Canterbury Tales*, which ends with a sermon on the subject. For an example of true repentance, see Shakespeare, *Measure for Measure*, 2:3. We may compare the false repentance of Othello, who offers excuses and is unwilling to bear the shame of his act. In our poem the vices are personified to make them more vivid.

8   The emphasis on food and drink here is due to a principle best known in the Middle Ages in a maxim from Terence, which was frequently repeated: "Without Ceres and Bacchus, Venus grows cold." Langland ignores the details of the vice itself, perhaps because they were well enough known already.

9   The description of Envy is based on Ovid, *Metamorphoses*, 2:770ff., although the poet may have found the details in some derivative of this source, which was widely imitated. Ovid is largely responsible for the late medieval taste for personified abstractions adorned with significant details.

10   Compare the angry friar of Chaucer's Summoner's Tale.

11   The reference is to a decree of Pope Gregory IX.

12   1 Peter 4:7; 5:8.

13   A cross at the priory of Bromholm (Norfolk) was said to be made of fragments of the True Cross.

14   The reason for this question is that no real absolution was possible unless restitution of goods wrongfully held (or their equivalent) was made first. Cf. the observations of King Claudius as he seeks to pray in *Hamlet*, 3:3.

15   Ps. 111:5.

16   That is, by buying cloth from him at a low rate.

17   The exact source of this quotation is unknown.

18   A widely quoted statement by St. Augustine.

19   The Psalter Gloss referred to is probably Peter Lombard's commentary on the Psalms, which was a standard work of reference. The original quotes parts of Ps. 50:3, 8, the fourth penitential psalm. (The phrase "in the inward parts" is neither in the poem nor in the Latin Bible.) The import of the comment is that recognition of one's sin and contrition for it are necessary.

20   Ps. 17:26.

21   Ps. 144:9.

22 A common saying of uncertain origin.

23 That is, a whore. Flemish girls frequently served as prostitutes in late medieval England.

24 This is the earliest reference to Robin Hood. The early Robin Hood ballads inculcate an admiration for violence against established authority and are hardly to be commended on any grounds.

25 "Alas, that I led a fruitless life in youth!"

26 See Mark 13:27.

27 Rom. 13:7.

28 The penitent thief on the cross.

29 Luke 23:42.

30 Cf. Luke 7:42.

31 The prayer of Repentance is an elaboration of the Apostles' Creed.

32 The quotation is from the liturgy for Holy Saturday.

33 Gen. 1:26.

34 I John 4:16.

35 Eph. 4:8. This is a reference to the rescue of the damned corresponding with *Descendit ad inferna* in the Creed.

36 That is, at the ninth hour. The "meal-time" corresponds with the phrase *sanctorum communionem* in the Creed.

37 Isa. 9:2.

38 Matt. 9:13. This corresponds with the phrase *remissionem peccatorem* in the Creed.

39 John 1:14.

40 Ps. 70:20. The text continues, ". . . and hast brought me back again from the depths of the earth." The Psalter Gloss explains that the Lord has led the speaker back in hope from the subversion of sin.

41 Ps. 31:1.

42 Ps. 35:7.

43 Cf. Matt. 9:36ff.

44 The reference to the first of the Apostles, the "rock" on which the Church is founded (see Matt. 10:2; 16:18–19), suggests something of the nature of the personification Piers (or Peter) the Ploughman, which now appears. The true priesthood of God begins with Melchisedech (Gen. 14:18). It became known as the "order of Melchisedech" (Ps. 109:4), to which Christ as God Incarnate belonged (see Heb. 5). After the establishment of the Church, however, the true priesthood was carried on by St. Peter and by those who came after him in the apostolic succession. The work of the priest in sowing the seed of the virtues in the human heart, extirpating the weeds of the vices, manuring the soil with penance, etc., to prepare a fruitful harvest for the Lord and the influence of figurative passages like Luke 9:62 and 17:7; 1 Cor. 9:10; and Ecclus 38:26 produced the convention of referring to priests as ploughmen. Thus in commenting on the first of the scriptural passages mentioned, St. Jerome says that the ploughman is one who works with the Gospels, his ploughshare is charity, and his four oxen are the four Evangelists. The imagery was considerably developed in other comments, so that by the fourteenth century it was commonplace. Piers the Ploughman in the poem is the true priesthood of God on earth. Our poet sharply distinguishes between this priesthood and individual priests who may not represent it well. Indeed, at the end of the poem he implies that the Church has become so corrupted, especially by the activities of the friars in destroying true contrition, that the true priesthood of God cannot be found. Conscience says that he will become a pilgrim "and walk as wide as the world lasts to seek Piers the Ploughman" and grace or charity, which he finds unavailable among the priests he has seen. The character of Piers does not develop or change in the poem; the action in which he takes part serves to reveal his nature, not to indicate changes in it in space and time. Moreover, the character has nothing whatever to do with actual ploughmen, the poor, or the simple rustic virtuous, who did not attract sentimental regard to any great extent until the second half of the eighteenth century.

45 That is, always.

46 Cf. Matt. 10:10.

47 It is the function of the priesthood to lead men in their pilgrimage. Thus, for example, Chaucer's Parson offers to "show the way, in this journey, of that perfect glorious pilgrimage that is called the celestial Jerusalem," and his sermon is about one of the "spiritual roads that lead folk to Our Lord Jesus Christ."

48 Piers begins with the New Law (Matt. 22:37–40) and proceeds with a generalized account of the Commandments.

49 The human heart. See 1 Cor. 3:16.

50 A common saying, frequently stated poetically in devotional songs.

51 Osee 13:3.

52 That is, the Blessed Virgin.

Book VI
Piers Sets the World to Work [1]

Then the people complained to Piers and said, "This is a grim way you've described to us. We should need a guide for every step of the road."

"Now look," said Piers the Ploughman, "I have half an acre of land here by the highway. Once I can get it ploughed and sown, I will go with you and show you the way myself." [2]

"We should have a long time to wait," said a veiled lady. "What work could we women be doing to pass the time?"

"Why, some of you can sew up the sacks," [3] said Piers, "to keep the seed from spilling. And you fair ladies with slender fingers—you have plenty of silks and fine stuffs to sew. Make some vestments for priests, while you've got the time, and lend a hand in beautifying the churches. And those of you who are married or widows can spin flax and make some cloth, and teach your daughters to do it too. For Truth commands us to take care of the needy and clothe the naked. I'll give them food myself, so long as the harvest doesn't fail. For I don't mind working all my life for the love of God, to provide meat and bread for rich and poor. [4]

"So come along now, all you men who live by food and drink—lend a hand to the man who provides you with it, and we will finish the job quickly."

"By Heavens!" said a knight, "this fellow knows what's good for us! But to tell the truth, I've never handled a team of oxen. Give me a lesson, Piers, and I'll do my best, by God!"

"That's a fair offer," said Piers. "And for my part, I'll sweat and toil for us both as long as I live, and gladly do any job you want. But you must promise in return to guard over Holy Church, and protect me from the thieves and wasters who ruin the world. And you'll have to hunt down all the hares and foxes and boars and badgers that break down my hedges, and tame falcons to kill the wild birds that crop my wheat."

Then the knight answered courteously and said, "I give you my word, Piers, as I am a true knight; and I'll keep this promise through thick and thin and protect you to the end of my days."

"Ah, but there's one thing more I must ask you," said Piers. "Never ill-treat your tenants, and see that you punish them only when Truth compels you to—even then, let Mercy assess the fine, and be ruled by Meekness, and at all costs have no truck with Lucre. And if poor men offer you gifts, don't ever accept them—it may be that you do not deserve them, and will have to pay them all back at the year's end, in a perilous place called Purgatory!

"And take care also that you never ill-use your serfs. It will be better for you in the long run, for though they are your underlings here on earth, they may be above you in Heaven, in greater happiness, unless you lead a better life than they do. For Our Lord said: 'When thou art bidden, go and sit down in the lowest room; that when he that bade thee cometh, he may say unto thee, Friend, go up higher.' [5] And it is very hard to tell a knight from a serf when he comes to lie in the church-vaults—so lay that to heart.

"And you must always speak the truth, and show contempt for all tales that are told you, except such as are wise, and apt for rebuking your workmen. Have nothing to do with jesters and don't listen to their tattle, least of all when you sit at meals in your hall. For believe me, they are the Devil's minstrels!"

"Now, by St James," the knight answered, "I'll abide by your words for ever."

"Then I will dress as a pilgrim," said Piers, "and go

with you till we find Truth. I will put on my working clothes, all darned and patched, my leggings, and my old gloves to keep my fingers warm; and I'll hang my hopper around my neck for a scrip, with a bushel of rye inside. And then, when I have sown my seed, I will turn palmer, and go on a pilgrimage to gain a pardon.

"And those who help me to plough and sow before I set out, shall have leave to glean here in harvest-time, and make merry with what they can get, no matter what people say. And I will provide food for men of all trades, so long as they are faithful and honest.—But there'll be none for Jack the juggler or Janet from the stews, none for Daniel the dice-player or Doll the whore, nor Friar Rogue nor any of his Order, nor Robin the ribald with his bawdy jokes. For Truth once told me to have no dealings with such men—'Let them be blotted out of the book of the living'[6]—and so He bade me tell others. Holy Church is forbidden so much as to take tithes from them, for the Scripture says: 'Let them not be written with the righteous.' And they get off lightly at that, God help them!"

Now Piers' wife was called Dame *Work-while-you've-got-a-chance*, his daughter was called *Do-as-you're-told-or-you'll-get-a-good-hiding*, and his son's name was *Always-give-way-to-your-elders-and-don't-contradict-or-maybe-you'll-wish-you-hadn't*.

Then Piers turned to his wife and children, saying, "May God be with you all, as His word teaches. For now that I am old and gray, and have enough to live on, I am going away with these folk on a pilgrimage, to do penance. So before I go, I will have my will written:

Piers' Will

"In the name of God, Amen. I, Piers, make this will myself. My soul shall go to Him who has best deserved it, and He shall, I trust, defend it from the Devil till I come to the day of reckoning, as my Creed tells me. And then I shall have a release and a remission from all the rent I owe on it.

"The Church shall have my flesh and shall keep my bones. For the parish priest took his tithe of my corn and earnings, and for my soul's sake I always paid it promptly; so he is bound, I hope, to remember me in his Mass, when he prays for all Christians.

"My wife shall have what I've earned by honest toil alone; and she shall share it among my daughters and my dear children. For though I should die this very day, my debts are all paid, and I've always returned what I've borrowed, before going to bed.

"And now I swear by the Holy Rood of Lucca to devote all that is left to the worship of Truth, and to serve Him for the rest of my life. And I will be His pilgrim, following the plough for poor men's sake; and my plough-shoe shall be my pikestaff, to cleave through the roots, and help my coulter to cut and cleanse the furrows."

And now Piers and his pilgrims have gone to the plough, and many folk are helping him to till his half acre. Ditchers and diggers are turning up the headlands, and others, to please Peter, are hoeing up the weeds, while he is delighted with their labors and quick to praise them. They are all eager to work, and every man finds something useful to do.

Then at nine o'clock in the morning Piers left his plough in order to see how things were going, and pick out the best workers to hire again at harvest-time. At this, some of them sat down to drink their ale and sing songs—thinking to plough his field with a "*Hey-nonny-nonny*"!

"By the Lord!" said Piers, bursting with rage. "Get up and go back to your work at once—or you'll get no bread to sing about when famine comes. You can starve to death, and to hell with the lot of you!"

Then the shirkers were scared, and pretended to be blind, or twisted their legs askew, as these beggars can, moaning and whining to Piers to have pity on them. "We're sorry, master, but we've no limbs to work with. But we'll pray for you, Piers—God bless you, sir, and may God in His goodness multiply your grain, and reward you for the charity you give us here. For we're so racked with pain, we can't lift a finger."

"I shall soon see if what you say is true," said Piers. "But I know quite well you are shirking—you can't get away from Truth. I'm an old servant of His, and I've promised to keep an eye open for folk in the world who wrong His workmen, and warn Him about them. You are the men who waste the food that others sweat for. Still, Truth will soon teach you to drive His oxen— or you'll be eating barley-bread and drinking from the stream!

"If anyone is really blind or crippled, or has his limbs bolted with irons, he shall eat wheaten bread and drink at my table, till God in His goodness sends him better days. But as for you, you could work for Truth well enough if you wanted: you could earn your food and wages by herding cattle or keeping the beasts from the corn, or ditch or dig or thresh away at the sheaves; or you could help mix mortar or cart muck to the field. The fact is you would rather have a life of lechery, lying, and sloth, and it is only through God's mercy that you go unpunished.

"No, I would rather give my earnings to hermits and anchorites, who eat nothing from one noon to the next; and those who have cloisters and churches to maintain—I'm quite willing to keep them in clothes. But Robert Runabout will get nothing from me, nor the wandering preachers, unless they know how to preach, and have the Bishop's license. And if that is so, they can make themselves at home, and I'll give them bread and soup—for even an Apostle can't live on air!"[7]

Then one of the vagabonds lost his temper with Piers, flung out a challenge and squared up for a fight. And a blustering Frenchman shouted out, "Go and stuff your plough, you stingy old scoundrel! We'll do as we please—you can take it or leave it. We shall fetch as much of your flour and meat as we want, and make a feast with it—so you go and hang yourself!"

Then Piers the Ploughman begged the knight to keep his promise, and protect him from these damned villains, the wolves who rob the world of its food. "For while they devour it all," he said, "and produce nothing themselves, there will never be plenty for the people. And meanwhile my plough lies idle."

So the knight, who was courteous by nature, spoke kindly to Waster, and warned him to mend his ways—"or, by my Order of Knighthood," he said, "I shall bring you to justice."

"I have never worked yet," said Waster, "and I don't intend to start now"—and he began to jeer at the Law and rail at the knight, and told Piers to go and piddle with his plough, for he'd beat him up if ever they met again.

"By God!" said Piers, "I'll teach you all a lesson!" And with that he holloed out for Hunger; and Hunger heard him at once and started up. "Avenge me on these wretches who eat up the world," cried Piers.[8]

Then Hunger leapt at Waster and seized him by the belly, wringing his guts till the water ran from his eyes. And he gave the Frenchman such a drubbing that he looked as lean as a rake for the rest of his life. He pasted them so soundly that he almost broke their ribs; and if Piers hadn't offered Hunger a pease-loaf and besought him to leave off, by now they'd both be pushing up the

daisies! "Spare their lives," said Piers, "and let them eat with the hogs and have bean and bran swill, or milk and thin ale."[9]

Then these rogues fled in terror to the barns, and threshed away with their flails from morning till night; and Hunger did not dare to molest them, because Piers had made them a pot of pease-pudding. And a crowd of hermits, cutting their cloaks to make jerkins and seizing some tools, went to work with spades and shovels, and dug and ditched like mad to stave off Hunger. Then thousands of blind and bed-ridden folk suddenly recovered, and men who used to sit begging for silver were miraculously cured! And the starving people appeased their hunger with bran-mash, and beggars and poor men worked gladly with peas for wages, pouncing like sparrowhawks on any work that Piers gave them. And Piers was proud of his success, and he set them all to work, giving them a fair wage and as much food as he could spare.

Then Piers took pity on the people, and begged Hunger to go home and stay in his own country. "For thanks to you," he said, "I am well avenged on these wastrels. But before you go, there's one thing I would like to ask you. What is the best thing to do with beggars and loafers? Once you've gone, I know quite well they will start slacking again. It is only their misery that makes them so submissive, and famine which has put them in my power. Yet they are truly my blood-brothers," said Piers, "for Christ redeemed us all, and Truth once taught me to love all men alike and give freely to everyone in need. So I should like you to tell me what would be best, and advise me as to how to control them and make them work."

"Listen then," said Hunger, "and mark my words. The big tough beggars who are capable of hard work, you can keep alive with horse-bread and dog-biscuits, and bring their weight down with a diet of beans—that will flatten their bellies! And if they grumble, tell them to go and work, and they'll get tastier suppers when they've earned them.

"But if you find a man who has fallen on evil days or been ruined by swindlers, for the love of Christ do your best to relieve him. You must seek out such folk and give them alms, and love them, as the law of God teaches—'Bear ye one another's burdens, and so ye shall fulfil the law of Christ.'[10] So give all you can spare to those who are penniless—show them charity and do not reproach them; leave God to punish them if they have done wrong—'Vengeance is mine; I will repay, said the Lord.'[11] For if you wish to find favor with God, you must obey the Gospel, and make yourself beloved among humble folk—'Make to yourselves friends of the mammon of unrighteousness'[12]—and then God will reward you."

"I would not offend God for all the world," said Piers. "Are you sure I can treat the shirkers as you say, without committing a sin?"

"Yes, I assure you," said Hunger, "or else the Bible is wrong. Ask the giant Genesis, the begetter of all men: 'In the sweat of thy brow,' he says, 'shalt thou eat bread'[13]—that is God's command. It says the same in the Book of Proverbs—

The sluggard will not plow by reason of the cold: therefore shall he beg in harvest, and have nothing.[14]

And St Matthew, whose sign has a man's face,[15] tells this parable:[16] There was a worthless servant who had only one talent; and because he would not work and trade with it, he lost his master's favor for evermore. And his master took his talent away from him, and gave it to the one who had ten, saying: 'He that hath shall receive, and find help when he needs it; but he that hath not shall receive nothing, and no one shall help him; and I shall take away from him even that which he thinks he hath.'

"It is common sense that every man must work, either by ditching and digging, or by travailing in prayer—the active or the contemplative life—for such is God's will. And according to Psalm 128,[17] a man who lives by his own honest labor is blessed in body and soul—

For thou shalt eat the labors of thine hands: O well is thee, and happy shalt thou be."

"Thank you," said Piers, "and now, friend Hunger, if you have any knowledge of medicine, I pray you, teach me it, for the love of God. For I and a number of my servants have got such a belly-ache, that we've been off work now for a whole week."[18]

"Ah! I know what's wrong with you," said Hunger; "you've been eating too much—no wonder you are in such agonies. If you want to get better, follow these instructions: never drink on an empty stomach, and never eat till hunger pinches you and sends you some of his sharp sauce to whet your appetite. And don't sit too long over dinner and spoil your supper; always get up before you've eaten your fill. What is more, never allow Sir Surfeit at your table—don't trust him, he's a great gourmand and his guts are always crying out for more dishes.[19]

"If you follow these instructions, I'll bet you the doctors will soon be selling their ermine hoods and their fine cloaks of Calabrian fur with gold tassels, to get themselves a square meal; and you'll see them gladly giving up their medicine for farmwork to avoid starvation. For these doctors are mostly murderers, God help them! their medicines kill thousands before their time."

"By heaven!" said Piers. "This is the best advice I've heard. And now, Hunger, I know you must be anxious to go—so the best of luck, old man, and God reward you for all you have done for me."

"Good gracious!" said Hunger, "I'm not going yet —not until I've had a square meal and something to drink."[20]

"I haven't a penny left," said Piers, "so I can't buy you pullets or geese or pigs. All I've got is a couple of fresh cheeses, a little curds and cream, an oat-cake, and two loaves of beans and bran which I baked for my children. Upon my soul, I haven't a scrap of bacon, and I haven't a cook to fry you steak and onions. But I've some parsley and shallots and plenty of cabbages, and a cow and a calf, and a mare to cart my dung, till the drought is over. And with these few things we must live till Lammas time, when I hope to reap a harvest in my fields. Then I can spread you a feast, as I'd really like to."

Then all the poor folk came with peas-cods, and brought beans and baked apples by the lapful, and spring onions and chervils and hundreds of ripe cherries, and offered these gifts to Piers, to satisfy Hunger.

Hunger soon gobbled it all up and asked for more. So the poor folk were afraid, and quickly brought up supplies of green leeks and peas, and would gladly have poisoned him. But by that time the harvest was approaching, and new corn came to market. So the people took comfort, and fed Hunger royally—Glutton himself couldn't wish for better ale. And so they put him to sleep.

And then Waster would not work any more, but set out as a tramp. And the beggars refused the bread that had beans in it, demanding milk loaves and fine white wheaten bread. And they would not drink cheap beer at any price, but only the best brown ale that is sold in the towns.

And the day-laborers, who have no land to live on but their shovels, would not deign to eat yesterday's vegetables. And draught-ale was not good enough for them, nor a hunk of bacon, but they must have fresh meat or fish, fried or baked and hot from the oven at that, lest they catch a chill on their stomachs![21]

And so it is nowadays—the laborer is angry unless he gets high wages, and he curses the day that he was ever born a workman. And he won't listen to wise Cato's advice—"Bear the burden of poverty patiently." But he blames God, and murmurs against Reason, and curses the king and his Council for making Statutes on purpose to plague the workmen![22] Yet none of them ever complained while Hunger was their master, nor quarrelled with *his* Statutes, he had such a fierce look about him.

But I warn you laborers, work while you have the chance,[23] for Hunger is coming fast, and shall awake with the floods to deal justice on wastrels. And before five years have passed, a famine shall arise, and floods and tempests shall destroy the fruits of the earth. For so Saturn has predicted, and has sent you this warning: *When you see the sun awry and two monks' heads in the Heavens—when a Maiden has magical power, then multiply by eight—the Black Death shall withdraw, and Famine shall judge the world, and Davy the ditcher shall die of hunger—unless God, in His mercy, grants us all a truce.*

Notes

1 The imagery of this book is probably based on Prov. 24:27–34: "Prepare thy work without, and diligently till thy ground: that afterward thou mayst build thy house. Be not witness without cause against thy neighbor: and deceive not any man with thy lips. Say not: I will do to him as he hath done to me: I will render to every one according to his work. I passed by the field of the slothful man, and by the vineyard of the foolish man: And behold it was all filled with nettles, and thorns had covered the face thereof, and the stone wall was broken down. Which when I had seen, I laid it up in my heart, and by the example I received instruction. Thou wilt sleep a little, said I, thou wilt slumber a little, thou wilt fold thy hands a little to rest: And poverty [i.e., hunger] will come to thee as a runner, and beggary as an armed man." Bede explains in his commentary (which was standard) that he begins to erect his house who weeds out vices and cultivates good deeds. In the poem, it is the function of Piers to assist the folk in these tasks so that they may erect a proper temple for Truth.

2 That is, the human heart must be prepared before Truth may be found in it.

3 The various actions described here and elsewhere in the instructions of Piers typify good deeds.

4 The food provided by Piers is, of course, spiritual food; he is not promising to furnish literal "meat and bread" for "the rich."

5 Luke 14:10.

6 Ps. 68:29. That is, those who refuse to cooperate in the work of Christian society are excommunicated.

7 The friars are meant here.

8 This book is concerned with two kinds of hunger: hunger for spiritual food to appease that persistent uneasiness of spirit which all men feel and hunger for food to nourish the flesh. When Piers, whose function is to supply spiritual food, calls upon Hunger, he is in effect, excommunicating the wasters so that they may have no access to the grace of the sacraments and what was conventionally referred to as "the refreshment of the Word of God."

9 Piers supplies them only with the bare rudiments.

10 The quotation is from Gal. 6:2. The whole passage, however, is relevant: "Brethren, if a man be overtaken in any fault, you who are spiritual, instruct such a one in the spirit of meekness, considering thyself, lest thou also be tempted. Bear ye one another's burdens; and so you shall fulfil the law of

Christ. . . . And let him that is instructed in the word, communicate to him that instructeth him, in all good things."

11 Rom. 12:19; Heb. 10:30.

12 Luke 16:9.

13 Gen. 3:19. As one commentator explains, the "bread" is Christ, who cannot be reached without labor.

14 Prov. 20:4. The text reads "in summer," not "in harvest." Bede tells us that this means that he who refuses to do the work of God in this world will have nothing in the realm of God.

15 In the visual arts, Matthew was represented as a man, Mark as a lion, Luke as a bull, and John as an eagle.

16 The Parable of the Talents, Matt. 25:14–30. In effect, he who refuses to engage in spiritual labor will lose that spiritual good which he has, while he who works will be fully rewarded.

17 Ps. 127 (Vulgate). V. 2 is quoted in the text following.

18 The discussion here turns from the subject of spiritual food to that of temporal food, or, that is, to the proper use of temporal things.

19 This passage echoes the doctrine of moderation stated by Holy Church in book I.

20 Hunger cannot leave until the folk labor as they should to prepare the fields of their hearts spiritually and learn to use temporal things in moderation.

21 Many of the people seek to placate spiritual hunger through a surfeit of physical satisfactions. Put in a somewhat different way, this is still a literary theme in some existentialist novels.

22 The scene shifts once more from a generalized account to the fourteenth-century world, full of people lusting after "hot pies" and complaining about the result of their own failure to work as they should.

23 The Hunger here threatened is that which will come to the wastrels on the Day of Judgment, of which the lines following are an ironic prediction.

Book VII

Piers the Ploughman's Pardon

When Truth heard of these things, He sent a message to Piers telling him to take his team of oxen[1] and till the earth, and He granted him a Pardon from guilt and punishment,[2] both for himself and for his heirs for ever. And He said that Piers must stay at home[3] and plough the fields, and whoever helped him to plough or plant or sow, or did any useful work for him, would be included with him in the Pardon.

All kings and knights who defend Holy Church and rule their people justly, have a pardon to pass lightly through Purgatory, and enjoy the company of the patriarchs and prophets in Heaven.

And all truly consecrated Bishops who live up to their calling, so long as they are well versed in both the Laws[4] and preach them to the laity, and do all in their power to convert sinners, are equal with the Apostles (as Piers' Pardon shows), and will sit with them at the high table on Judgment Day.

In the margin of the Bull, the merchants too had many years' indulgence, but none from guilt as well as punishment—the Pope would never grant them that, for they will not keep Holy Days as the Church requires, and they swear "By my soul!" and "God help me!" against their conscience, in order to sell their wares.

But Truth sent the merchants a letter under His secret seal, telling them to buy up boldly all the best goods they could get, then sell them again, and use the profits to repair the hospitals and to help folk in trouble—to get the bad roads mended quickly and rebuild the broken bridges—to enable poor girls to marry or to enter nunneries—to feed the poor and the men in prisons—to send boys to school or apprentice them to a trade, and to assist Religious Orders and give them better endowments.—"And if you will do these things," said Truth, "I myself will send you St Michael my Archangel when you die, so that no devil shall harm your souls or make you afraid; and he will ward off despair, and lead your souls in safety to meet my saints in Heaven."

The merchants were pleased with this, and many of them wept for joy, praising Piers for gaining them such an indulgence.

But the men of Law who plead at the bar were to receive the least pardon of all. For the Psalm denies salvation to those who take bribes, especially from innocent folk who suspect no guile—"He who taketh no bribes against the innocent."[5] An advocate should do his utmost to help and to plead for such poor folk, and princes and prelates should pay him for it—"Their wages shall be from kings and rulers."[6] But I assure you, many of these Judges and jurymen would do more for their friend John than for the love of God himself. Yet if an advocate uses his eloquence on behalf of the poor, and pleads for the innocent and the needy, comforting them in their misfortunes without seeking gifts—if he explains the Law to them as he has learnt it, for the love of God, and does no man injury—he shall take no harm from the Devil when he dies, and his soul shall be safe. This is proved by the Psalm, "Lord, who shall dwell in Thy tabernacle."[7]

For human intelligence is like water, air, and fire—it cannot be bought or sold. These four things the Father of Heaven made to be shared on earth in common. They are Truth's treasures, free for the use of all honest men, and no one can add to them or diminish them without God's will. So when, at the approach of death, the men of Law seek for indulgences, there is very little pardon for them if they have ever taken money from the poor for their counsel. You lawyers and advocates can be sure of this—blame St Matthew if I lie, for he gave me this proverb for you: "All things whatsoever ye would that men should do to you, do ye even so unto them."[8]

But every laborer on earth who lives by his hands, who earns his own wages and gets them honestly, living in charity and obeying the Law, shall have for his humility the same absolution that was sent to Piers.

But beggars and tramps have no place in the Bull, unless they have an honest reason for begging. A man who begs without need is a swindler, and like the Devil, for he defrauds others who are really in need, and deceives men into giving against their will. For if the almsgiver knew the beggar was not in need, he would give his alms to someone who deserved it more, and help the most needy. Cato teaches this, and so does the author of the Scholastic Histories. "Take care whom you give alms to"—"so Cato[9] says. And this is Peter Comestor's[10] advice: "Keep your alms in your hand until you have made sure whom you are giving them to."

Yet Gregory the Great, who was a holy man, bade us give alms to all that ask, for the love of Him who gave us all things. "Do not choose whom you pity," he said, "and be sure not to pass over by mistake one who deserves to receive your gifts; for you never know for whose sake you are more pleasing to God."[11] Nor do you ever know who is really in need—only God can know that. If there is any treachery, it is on the beggar's side, not on the giver's. For the giver is repaying God's gifts, and so preparing himself for death; but the beggar is borrowing, and running into debt, a debt which he can never repay, and for which Almighty God is his security; for only God can pay back the creditor, and pay him with interest. "Wherefore then gavest thou not my money into the bank, that at my coming I might have required mine own with usury."[12]

So except in dire need, you tramps should avoid begging, for it is written that whoever has enough to buy bread, has all he needs, even if that is all he possesses. "He is rich enough who does not lack bread."[13] Comfort yourselves, therefore, by reading the lives of the Saints, and profit by their example. The Scriptures strictly forbid begging, and condemn you in these words:

"I have been young, and now am old:
And yet saw I never the righteous forsaken, nor his seed begging bread."[14]

For your lives are bereft of charity, and you keep no law. Many of you do not marry the women you consort with; you mount and set to work, braying like wild beasts, and bring forth children who are branded bastards. Then you break their backs or their bones in childhood, and go begging with your offspring for ever after. There are more misshapen creatures among you beggars, than in all other professions put together! But be warned that on the day of your death, you will curse the time you were ever created men.

Not so the old men with white hair, who are weak and helpless, nor the women with child who cannot work, nor the blind and bedridden whose limbs are broken, nor the lepers, nor any such folk who bear their afflictions meekly: these shall have as full a pardon as the Ploughman himself. For out of love for their humility, our Lord has given them their purgatory and penance here on earth.

Then a priest[15] spoke to Piers and said: "Let me read your Pardon, Piers. I will construe each article for you and explain it to you in English."

So Piers, at the priest's request, opened his Pardon, and I, who was standing behind them both, could see the whole Bull. It was contained entirely in two lines, and these were the words, attested by Truth:

*And they that have done good shall go into life everlasting:
And they that have done evil into everlasting fire.*[16]

"By St Peter!" the priest said, "I cannot find any Pardon here. All it says is, 'Do well and earn well, and God shall have your soul: do ill and earn ill and the Devil will certainly have it after you die.'"[17]

Then Piers, in sheer rage, tore the Pardon in two,[18] and said:

Yea, though I walk through the valley of the shadow of death, I will fear no evil:
For Thou art with me.[19]

I shall give up my sowing, and cease from all this hard labor.[20] Why should I work so hard, merely to fill my stomach? From now on, prayers and penance shall be my plough, and at night, when I should be asleep, I shall weep instead for my sins. What does it matter if I have no wheaten bread! The prophet ate his bread in penance and sorrow, and the Psalter tells of many who did the same. If a man sincerely loves God, his livelihood is easy enough to get, for it is written, 'My tears have been my meat day and night'.[21] And St Luke teaches us to live like the birds, and take no thought for the pleasures of the world, 'nor be solicitous, saying What shall we drink?'[22]—showing us, by such examples, how to govern our lives. Who is it that gives the birds in the fields their food in winter time? They have no barns to go to, yet God provides for them all."

"What!" said the priest to Perkin. "It sounds to me as if you can read, Peter! Who taught you your letters?"

"Abstinence the Abbess," answered Piers. "She taught me my ABC—then Conscience came and taught me a good deal more."

"Why, Piers, if only you were a priest, you would make a real theologian, then you could preach on the text 'The fool hath spoken.'"[23]

"You ignorant good-for-nothing!" said Piers. "It is

seldom you ever look at the Bible! When did you last read the Proverbs of Solomon? 'Cast out the scorner, and contention shall go out; yea, strife and reproach shall cease.'"[24]

So the priest and Perkin argued, and their noise awoke me. And I looked about, and saw the sun to the southwards, and found myself on the Malvern Hills, starving and penniless. So I went on my way, puzzling over my dream.

Since then, I have thought many times about this dream, and wondered if what I saw in my sleep were really true. And I have often felt anxious for Piers, and asked myself what sort of pardon it was with which he consoled the people, and how it was that the priest gainsaid it with a few clever words. But I have no relish for interpreting dreams, I see how often it fails. Cato, and men skilled in Canon Law, advise us to put no faith in such divination—"Pay no heed to dreams,"[25] says Cato.

Yet it is related in the Bible how Daniel expounded the dreams of a monarch whom the scholars call Nebuchadnezzar.[26] "Your dream means, your Majesty," he said, "that strange warriors will come and divide your kingdom, and all your land will be parcelled out among petty princes." And afterward it fell out just as Daniel had foreseen. Nebuchadnezzar lost his kingdom, and it was seized by lesser lords.

Joseph also had a wonderful dream,[27] in which the sun and the moon and the eleven stars all made obeisance to him. And Jacob his father interpreted it, saying, "This means, my son, that I and your eleven brothers will come and seek you and ask for your help in time of famine." And it happened just as his father had said; for when Joseph was Lord Chief Justice of Egypt in Pharoah's time, his father and brothers came to him for food.

All this makes me reflect on my dream—how the priest proved that no pardon could compare with Do-well, and thought Do-well surpassed indulgences, biennials, triennials, and Bishops' Letters—and how, on Judgment Day, Do-well will be received with honor, and exceed all the pardons of St Peter's Church.[28]

Yet the Pope has the power to grant men pardon, so that they may pass into Heaven without doing any penance. This is our belief; the theologians teach it— "And whatsoever thou shalt bind on earth shall be bound in Heaven: and whatsoever thou shalt loose on earth shall be loosed in Heaven."[29] And so I firmly believe (God forbid otherwise!)—that pardons, penances, and prayers do save souls, even if they have committed deadly sin seven times over. But I certainly think that to put one's trust in these Masses is not so sure for the soul as is Do-well.

So I warn all you rich men who trust in your wealth to have triennials said for you after your death, not to be bolder therefore to break the Ten Commandments. And especially you men in authority, Mayors and Judges—no doubt you are thought wise, and possess enough of the world's wealth to buy yourselves pardons and papal Bulls—but on that dreadful day when the dead shall rise and all men shall come before Christ to render up their accounts, then the sentence shall state openly how you led your lives, how well you kept God's laws, and everything that you have practised day by day. Then, you may have pardons or provincials' letters by the sackful, and belong to the Fraternity of all the Four Orders, and possess double or treble indulgences, but unless Do-well helps you, I would not give a peascod for all your pardons and certificates!

So I advise all Christians to pray to God, and to His Mother Mary, our mediator, for grace[30] to do such works in this life, that after our death and on the Day of Judgment, Do-well may declare that we did as he commanded.

Here Ends William's Vision of Piers the Ploughman

Notes

1 The four evangelists. See Mark 16:15.

2 An ordinary pardon granted a remission of penance, but no remission of guilt. This pardon, however, implies grace through the Redemption of Christ. See Rom. 3:20–26. It is, in effect, the New Law, which brings peace to men of goodwill on earth and enables them to look forward to union with Truth.

3 That is, Piers cannot go at once to heaven; he must first labor. The significance of this statement will emerge from a reading of the Acts of the Apostles.

4 The Old Law and the New Law which fulfils it.

5 Ps. 14:5.

6 Not identified.

7 Ps. 14.

8 Matt. 7:12.

9 This is one of the *sententiae* in Cato's Distichs.

10 The reference is to the *Historia scholastica*, a favorite school text.

11 The authority is actually St. Jerome. Our author probably quoted often from memory and made occasional slips.

12 Luke 19:23.

13 The authority is probably St. Jerome.

14 Ps. 36:25.

15 This, of course, is a piece of downright presumption on the part of a man who does not recognize the ideal that he himself is supposed to represent. The priest is meant to typify the priesthood of the poet's own time.

16 The last two lines of the Athanasian Creed. See Matt. 25:31–46; John 5:19–29. Those who have "done good" are those who have been merciful and loved God and their neighbors. The texts refer to the Day of Judgment, when Christ will preside as Judge and the charitable will, so to speak, have their pardon confirmed. Most medieval readers would have been familiar with the implications of the Crèed, which was recited daily in Church services; and the hopeful implications of the Day of Judgment were commonplace, since pictorial representations of it were common in wall paintings over chancel arches, and many churches on the Continent bore sculptured representations of the scene over their west

Figure 34 *The Wilton Diptych. King Richard III, under guidance of his patron saint, about to depart for paradise.*

portals. The modern eye, looking upon these visual representations, is inclined to linger on the torments of the damned, which seem inhumane and superstitious; but medieval men remembered that it was only the New Law which kept everyone from being on the left side of the Judge.

17 The priest sees only the Old Law, which is the obvious literal import of the lines outside their context. Moreover, his subsequent behavior shows that this is what he believes in.

18 The action is probably a reflection of the action of Moses in Exod. 32:17–19: "And Josue hearing the noise of the people shouting, said to Moses: The noise of battle is heard in the camp. But he answered: It is not the cry of men encouraging to fight, nor the shout of men compelling to flee: but I hear the voice of singers. And when he came nigh to the camp, he saw the calf [i.e., an idol], and the dances: and being very angry, he threw the tables [of the Law] out of his hand, and broke them at the foot of the mount." Patristic and medieval comments on this passage say that it signifies spiritually the necessity for fulfilling the Old Law of the Decalogue with the New Law of charity. This is exactly what the priest (or the priesthood of the English Church in the fourteenth century) needs to learn.

19 Ps. 22:4. Moses broke the tables when he saw the idolatry of his people. The action of walking through the valley of the shadow of death meant, as we learn from the Psalter Gloss, the action of associating with those ignorant of God. Here Piers finds, so to speak, that his own representatives on earth are ignorant of the implications of the New Dispensation.

20 These resolutions may be intended as exemplary actions, since the priest has spent too little time in contemplation and penance and too much time with merely external concerns. However, they also imply that Piers, or the true priesthood of God, abandons its "sowing," or labors, on earth. We should remember that Piers is neither a person nor a personality capable of anger or exasperation in any literal sense. The author is not saying that the true priesthood of God deliberately abandons its assigned tasks in the world; what he does say is that the world, including its ecclesiastical hierarchy, so arranges matters that, to quote a famous remark in a chronicle, "Christ and His saints sleep."

21 Ps. 41:4. The context is relevant: "As the hart panteth after the fountains of water; so my soul panteth after thee, O God. . . . My tears have been my bread day and night, whilst it is said to me daily: Where is thy God? . . . I shall go over into the place of the wonderful tabernacle, even to the house of God: with the voice of joy and praise. . . . With me is prayer to the God of my life. I will say to God: Thou art my support. Why hast thou forgotten me?"

22 Luke 12:22. This admonition is, in terms of the poem, a command to avoid the temptations of Lady Lucre.

23 This is the first verse of Pss. 13 and 52, which are quite similar. The subject was taken to be the general corruption of men before the Redemption of Christ, or by transference, the corruption of any unredeemed man. Ps. 13 begins: "The fool hath said in his heart: There is no God. They are corrupt and are become abominable in their ways: there is none that doth good, no not one. The Lord hath looked down from heaven upon the children of men, to see if there be any that understand and seek God. They are all gone aside, they are become unprofitable together: there is none that doth good, no not one." The implication is clear: to do good requires the grace of the Redemption, or charity. The priest speaks to Piers in derision, implying that he is a fool, but his quotation is actually a comment on himself.

24 Prov. 22:10.

25 From the Distichs of Cato.

26 See Daniel 2:29, 5. The observations about dreams are intended to encourage the reader to study the allegorical implications of the poem.

27 Gen. 37:9–10.

28 The priest says that Do-well is better than indulgences, masses for the dead, and so on, and, further, that it will be rewarded on the Day of Judgment. So far as it goes, what he says is true, except that when Do-well is regarded as an end in itself, the result is a return to the Old Law of justice on the one hand and the introduction of a kind of Pelagianism on the other. As Will learns in later portions of the poem, man is saved neither by faith nor by works, but by the grace of Christ which vivifies both. This grace is the essence or spirit of the pardon given Piers, not the literal implication of the words, which is all the priest can understand.

29 Matt. 16:9.

30 This grace is what Will (the human will) must discover if he is to learn to do well.

XI

MIDDLE ENGLISH LITERATURE: CHAUCER

Geoffrey Chaucer (ca. 1345–1400) was the son of a prosperous London wine merchant. We know nothing of his boyhood, but he may well have gone to school at St. Paul's, which was not far from his father's house in Thames Street, next to Walbrook. Our first record of Geoffrey indicates that in 1357 he was in the household of Lionel, Duke of Clarence, probably as a page. In 1359 and 1360 young Chaucer was among Lionel's men in the siege of Reims. He was taken prisoner but ransomed by King Edward for £16.[1] A year later Prince Lionel was appointed Lieutenant of Ireland, and Chaucer must have left his service, although we do not know exactly how he occupied himself. It is possible that he studied for a time at the Inner Temple.

Whatever he may have been doing in the intervening years, in 1366 Chaucer married

Facing page: Très riches heures de Jean de France. *The sun entering Taurus in April.*

Philippa (d. 1387), a daughter of Sir Payne Roet.[2] A record for the following year shows that Chaucer was a valet in the royal household with an annual salary of twenty marks. Two years later, in 1369, we find him again in military service, campaigning in France as a squire. But he was back in England in August when he and Philippa were granted an allowance for clothing to wear in mourning for the Queen, who died of the plague. On September 12, Blanche, Duchess of Lancaster, died of the same malady.

The year 1369 proved to be an important one for both political and literary history. If England may be said to have had a court poet in that year, it was Jean Froissart, secretary to Queen Philippa. Both the Queen and King Edward spoke French as the language of their childhood, and Froissart wrote in French. If the death of the Queen meant that England lost Froissart, the death of Blanche a month later provided the subject for the first important poem by Chaucer, an English elegy. Perhaps this poem, "The Book of the Duchess," was read at one of the annual memorial services for Blanche maintained by John of Gaunt at St. Paul's Cathedral. In any event, from this time forward England's most eminent poet wrote in English under the patronage of the King and of the country's most powerful nobleman, John of Gaunt.

If Froissart was the poet and chronicler of the late flowering of English chivalry, Chaucer was the poet of its decline. In the sixties England was the center of European chivalry. Edward's spectacular victory at Crécy (1346), his taking of Calais (1347), and his successes in the consolidation of Gascony were crowned by the victory of the Black Prince at Poitiers (1356), where King John of France was taken prisoner. For the next ten years knights from all over Europe went to England to attend a court unequalled anywhere for splendor and pageantry. It was in this atmosphere that young Chaucer grew to maturity, in close association with the royal household. But when the war with France reopened in 1369, England had a new enemy, the astute and crafty Charles V. For the remainder of the century English prestige abroad declined steadily, while at home dissension, political intrigue, and even open revolt replaced the vigorous confidence of Edward's best days. Edward fell under the domination of an unscrupulous mistress, Alice Perrers, and John of Gaunt was never able to equal the military prowess of his brother, Prince Edward. Although young King Richard showed courage and dignity when he faced the peasants at Mile End and Smithfield in 1381, his reign became a history of failure and disintegration.

During the years from 1370 to 1380 Chaucer was employed on a number of diplomatic missions for the King. These included visits to Italy in 1373 and 1378, where he may have come to know the work of the great Italian poets, Dante, Petrarch, and Boccaccio. In 1374 he was granted a daily pitcher of wine by the King, a house above Aldgate by the corporation of London (which he held until 1386), an annuity of £10 by John of Gaunt, and he was made Comptroller of the Customs and Subsidy of Wools, Skins, and Hides in the Port of London. The further post of Comptroller of the Petty Customs for the Port of London, with the privilege of appointing a deputy, was granted him in 1382. Three years later he was allowed to exercise his duties at the Wool Quay by deputy, and we find him acting as Knight of the Shire from Kent, in which capacity he attended the "Wonderful Parliament" of 1386.

The proceedings of the Parliament, which were directed toward reform, were dominated by John of Gaunt's most powerful enemy, the Duke of Gloucester. The fear of invasion from France was acute, unemployed mercenary soldiers were plundering the countryside, and there was widespread uneasiness. A council was set up, with Gloucester at its head, to control the extravagance of the King. John of Gaunt, who might have been able to exercise a moderating influence, had departed for Spain. Probably as a result of action by Gloucester's faction, Chaucer was deprived of his comptrollerships and left with no income other than that from his annuities. He took up residence in Greenwich. Philippa died in 1387, and Chaucer, now deprived of her income, did nothing of an official nature until after 1389, when King Richard reasserted his powers. Meanwhile the "Merciless Parliament" of 1388 achieved, among its judicial murders, the execution of Chaucer's old associate at the Customs House, Nicholas Brembre, and that of his literary admirer, Thomas Usk.

Although Chaucer probably had small sympathy for Richard's personal weaknesses, there is every reason to suppose that he was on principle loyal to the Crown, and that his attitude toward political affairs and toward society in general resembled, with somewhat more sophistication, that of John of Gaunt. The Duke of

Lancaster had for a time been a staunch supporter of Wyclif, not because he shared any of Wyclif's extreme theological views, but because Wyclif had vigorously and courageously attacked abuses in the Church. There was in England during the 1370s and 1380s a kind of "Lollardy" that had little to do either with theological speculation or with the inspiration of semiliterate preaching. It was, on the contrary, frequently orthodox, looking to the past for its inspiration. It sought to infuse new spirit into the existing hierarchies of Church and society, which were, in many ways glaringly corrupt. Some of Chaucer's closest associates at court were, in this sense, Lollards, not to mention a number of prominent bishops. The same desire for spiritual reform inspired new chivalric orders throughout Europe, the most important of which was the Order of the Passion of Our Lord. Its founder was Philippe de Mézières, for a time Chancellor to Pierre de Lusignan, tutor to Charles VI, and a distinguished crusader and poet, whose "apostle" in England was Oton de Grandson, a courtier and poet whom Chaucer admired greatly. Those who had seen the glories of Edward's best days naturally looked with misgivings at the society around them. The devastating attacks on exemplars of English social groups, both lay and ecclesiastical, in *The Canterbury Tales*, although they are usually glossed over by modern sentimental criticism, represent a biting comment on the society of Chaucer's later years.

On May 3, 1389, King Richard declared himself of age, dismissed Gloucester and his council, and hastened to recall John of Gaunt. In July Chaucer was given his most important office, that of Clerk of the King's Works. He held this office until June 17, 1391, with the then substantial salary of 2s. a day. In the fourteenth century this was not an unusually short term for this position, which was usually a stepping-stone to preferment if the clerk were an ecclesiastic or to a pension if he were a layman. The clerk had an office at Westminster near the Hall. He was responsible for the impressment of workmen, the purchase of stone, timber, and other materials, and the requisition of horses and carts, all used in the maintenance of the royal buildings and estates. A pension of £20 was granted Chaucer in 1394. For the next few years he was apparently in somewhat straitened circumstances and not always in good health. But Henry was crowned in October, 1399, and shortly thereafter, perhaps in response to Chaucer's "Complaint to His Empty Purse," granted the poet a renewal of his old pension and a new one of 40 marks as well. Having achieved financial security, Chaucer leased a house in the garden of the Chapel of St. Mary, Westminster, where he remained until his death in 1400.

The most useful edition of Chaucer's works is still W. W. Skeat, *The Works of Geoffrey Chaucer*, Clarendon Press, Oxford, 1894–1897. The text here included is reprinted by permission from this edition. A convenient and more modern edition with textual improvements is F. N. Robinson, *The Works of Geoffrey Chaucer*, second edition, Houghton Mifflin Company, Boston, 1961. There are numerous editions of separate works, among which the edition of *Troilus* by R. K. Root, Princeton University Press, Princeton, N.J., 1945, is especially noteworthy. The standard bibliographies are Eleanor P. Hammond, *Chaucer: A Bibliographical Manual*, The Macmillan Company, New York, 1908; D. D. Griffiths, *Bibliography of Chaucer 1908–1953*, University of Washington Press, Seattle, 1953; and William R. Crawford, *Bibliography of Chaucer 1954–1963*, University of Washington Press, Seattle, 1967. The surviving documents concerning Chaucer's life have been edited by Martin M. Crow and Clair C. Olson, *Chaucer Life-Records*, Clarendon Press, Oxford, 1966. Documents illustrating fourteenth-century daily life are collected in Edith Rickert, *Chaucer's World*, revised edition, Columbia University Press, New York, 1948. Early references to Chaucer have been collected by C. F. E. Spurgeon, *Five Hundred Years of Chaucer Criticism and Allusion*, Cambridge University Press, London, 1925.

There have been many books about Chaucer or about special aspects of his work, only a few of which can be mentioned here. A good anthology of articles reviewing recent criticism and bibliography is provided by Beryl Rowland, *Companion to Chaucer Studies*, Oxford University Press, New York, 1968. Among collections of essays on Chaucer two deserve special mention: R. J. Schoeck and Jerome Taylor, *Chaucer Criticism*, 2 vols., Notre Dame Press, Notre Dame, Ind., 1960, 1961; and Derek Brewer, *Chaucer and Chaucerians*, University of Alabama Press, University, 1966. Useful factual information concerning the Canterbury pilgrims and their background is provided in Muriel Bowden, *A Commentary on the General Prologue to the Canterbury Tales*, The Macmillan Company, New York, 1949. Stimulating new perspectives are brought to bear on Chaucer's work by Charles Muscatine, *Chaucer and the French Tradition*, University of California Press, Berkeley, 1957. More controversial attitudes are developed in D. W. Robertson, Jr., *A* *Preface to Chaucer*, Princeton University Press, Princeton, N.J., 1962, and in the same author's *Chaucer's London*, John Wiley and Sons, Inc., New York, 1968.

Notes

1 It is difficult to estimate the value of fourteenth-century money in modern times, especially since all modern currencies have been enormously inflated. However, it was possible to have a substantial house built in the latter fourteenth century for £14. The ordinary workman earned about sixpence or sevenpence a day. There are twelve pence to the shilling, and twenty shillings to the pound. In 1378 one could purchase ten eggs for a penny in London.

2 At the time of her marriage Philippa was a lady in waiting to the Queen; she later entered the service of the second Duchess of Lancaster. There is no evidence to support the allegation that relations between John and Philippa were improper, and the likelihood that they were is very slight. However, in 1372 Philippa's sister Katherine became John of Gaunt's mistress. She had been the wife of Sir Hugh Swynford, who died in Aquitaine in 1372, and the guardian of the children of Blanche of Lancaster. John of Gaunt married Katherine in 1396.

 *Chaucer's Language*

Chaucer wrote in the London dialect of late Middle English, somewhat modified, perhaps, by the fact that he was addressing a court audience strongly influenced by French fashions. His poetry, which was intended for oral presentation, is generally informal and conversational, with much of the raciness and vigor once characteristic of ordinary speech. Those who wish to enjoy it should learn to read it aloud, although for this purpose a strict attention to accuracy is not necessary. When Chaucer's verse is read aloud, sentence rhythm should be respected and every effort made to avoid literary airs.

The following simplified guide to pronunciation may be helpful. The problems are not so formidable as this summary may make them appear, and it is no substitute for an opportunity to listen to someone who reads with ease and assurance.

a (long); spelled *a*, *aa*; pronounced like *a* in *father*.

a (short); spelled *a*; pronounced the same, but shorter (not like *a* in *hat*, which is almost *e*).

e (long); spelled *e*, *ee*; may be pronounced either as an open sound approaching the *a* in *hat* or as a close sound like *a* in *date* (really *e* plus *i* in Modern English. To get the Middle English sound, try to omit the *i* glide after the *e*). The open sound appears frequently in words now spelled *ea*: *heeth*, now *heath*; *breeth*, now *breath*.

e (short); spelled *e*; pronounced like *e* in *let*.

e (final); spelled *e*. The pronunciation of final *e* in Chaucer's work is now in dispute, some authorities maintaining that it was silent. In accordance with the traditional view, final *e* should be pronounced except where the next word following immediately without pause begins with a vowel. The sound recommended is a neutral vowel somewhat like final *a* in *papa*.

i (long); spelled *i*, *y*; pronounced like *i* in *machine*.

i (short); spelled *i*, *y*; pronounced the same, but shorter.

o (long); spelled *o, oo*; may be pronounced either as an open sound like *oa* in *broad* or as a close sound like German long *o* (i.e., like *o* in *note* without the *u* glide which usually follows long *o* in Modern English).

u (long); spelled *ow, ou, o* before *gh*; pronounced like *oo* in *loot*.

u (short); spelled *u* and frequently *o*, especially before *n* or *m*; pronounced the same, but shorter. The spelling *o* is due to the peculiar character of Gothic script, in which *u* and *n* are frequently indistinguishable, and *m* looks like a *u* or *n* with an extra stroke. Thus the combination *num* spelled "properly" consists of seven very similar vertical strokes in a row. If *o* is substituted for the third and fourth of these strokes, the situation becomes much clearer.

iu; spelled *u, eu, ew*; pronounced like *u* in *mute*.

ei; spelled *ai, ay, ei, ey*; pronounced either like the exaggerated long *i* in *die* with the two parts (*a* plus *i*) distinct or like the exaggerated long *a* in *day* with the two parts (*e* plus *i*) distinct.

au; spelled *au, aw*; pronounced like *ou* in *mouse*.

eu (long); spelled *eu, ew*; may be pronounced either as a long, open *e* or as a long, close *e* plus *u* (*w*).

oi; spelled *oi, oy*; pronounced like *oy* in *boy*.

ou (long); spelled *ou, ow*; may be pronounced either as a long, close *o* or as a long, open *o* plus *u* (*w*)

ch; spelled *ch*; pronounced like *ch* in *church*, not *chemise*.

gg; may be pronounced either like *dg* in *judge* or like *gg* in *bigger*.

gh; represents a sound like German *ch* in *ich* or *ach*.

kn; was pronounced with the *k* retained.

l; was retained in combinations like *half, folk*.

Words were sometimes accented as in French. Here the meter should be used as a guide.

A more complete account of these matters with strict attention to philological accuracy may be found in H. Kökeritz, *A Guide to Chaucer's Pronunciation*, Stockholm and New Haven, 1954. Those interested in Chaucer's grammar should consult the editions of Skeat and Robinson mentioned in the Introduction to Chaucer.

Chaucer's poetry is oral poetry—a musical score for the human voice. The versification in these selections is fairly simple: the verse usually consists of roughly decasyllabic lines rhyming in couplets. Whether one retains the final *e* or not, the lines should not be scanned so as to make them sound as though they were written

in iambic pentameter with "felicitous variation." In fact, the student will do more justice to Chaucer's line if he thinks of it as having four major stresses. But a systematic pursuit of a four-stress pattern will interfere with a proper appreciation of Chaucer's rhythms.

In the oral rendition of poetry a number of types of variation are involved: variation in stress, pitch, vowel length, sonority, and speed, not to mention variation in tonal quality, which can express cheerfulness, politeness, sarcasm, bitterness, sorrow, and so on. In other words, such things as aspiration, nasalization, the muscle tone of the throat and lips, and the positioning of the voice in the mouth can and do affect both the meaning and the affective quality of what is being said. Variation in speed affects pauses, or intervals of silence, which are just as much a part of the verse as are the sounds. With reference to pitch (the only kind of variation indicated by punctuation in medieval manuscripts) and vowel length, Modern American English is a relatively colorless language, in which short vowels have degenerated into neutral sounds pronounced near the center of the vowel ellipse, and long vowels are distinguished not so much by their length as by the fact that they have become diphthongs or glides. A few minutes in conversation with a group of uneducated men from the south of England will convince the most skeptical of the poverty of American English in pitch variation. Semantic distinctions once conveyed by such variation are now achieved by circumlocution. In reading Chaucer's verse aloud, therefore, the modern student will do well to exaggerate variation in pitch and vowel length.

Latin rhetoric—the kind of rhetoric taught in medieval schools and heard in medieval churches—was largely concerned with sentence rhythm. Such rhythms may be either formal, like that in the opening lines of the General Prologue, which form an elaborate "period," or informal, like that in colloquial speech. Chaucer usually maintains a colloquial tone, although this tone is sometimes achieved through the use of colloquial diction rather deceptively ensconced in fairly sophisticated rhythmic patterns. It should not be forgotten that Chaucer's audience was aristocratic, a fact that implied a taste for a certain disciplined grace and elegance combined with a strong distaste for false airs.

The simple facts of versification mentioned above are of far less importance to the student than is a proper appreciation for the rhythms of Chaucer's sentences.

The lines of verse themselves will maintain a fairly even length (1) if the student pronounces final *e* as suggested in the guide to pronunciation or (2) if he abandons final *e* altogether (except in words ending with *ee*) but pays attention to vowel length, exaggerating it slightly in words bearing a heavy stress. Usually, but not always, there is a natural pause somewhere within the line; and usually, but not always, there is another at the end of the line. The latter pause should not be exaggerated for its own sake.

Since variations in pitch, stress, and so on within a sentence cannot be determined except on the basis of an understanding of what the sentence means, it follows that except for the roughly decasyllabic line and the rhyme Chaucer's poetry has no real versification independent of its meaning. It is therefore of utmost importance to determine as closely as possible the meaning of each sentence, its tonal variations, and the manner in which what is said is conveyed. It is impossible to consider all the possible variations of stress, pitch, speed, vowel length, and so on separately and to produce on the basis of calculation a satisfactory result. It is possible, on the other hand, to exploit the possibilities for emphasis provided by Chaucer's sentences, to be alert for ironic intonation, humorous anticlimax, mock solemnity, and other similar devices so frequently suggested by both meaning and rhythm, and finally, through experiment and practice to achieve a vigorous and effective delivery. Chaucer has provided an excellent score. The goal is a lively music produced by what is potentially the most versatile and beautiful of all instruments.

 *The Canterbury Tales*

THE GENERAL PROLOGUE TO THE CANTERBURY TALES

The General Prologue to The Canterbury Tales *can be read most profitably if we seek to understand first the way in which Chaucer wished to mirror the society around him. Medieval society was much more thoroughly organized into tightly knit small groups than is modern society. People thought of themselves and their problems more or less spontaneously in terms of these groups rather than in terms of individual psychology or personality. A man's identity was not so much an identity in isolation, with the whole world of men forming the "others," as it was an identity with relation to a group in which each member had a more or less natural place. Efforts to move from one group to another had been regarded with suspicion ever since antiquity, and efforts to establish a false place within the hierarchy of any single group were resented and frequently satirized. Finally, it was felt that the integrity of each of the small groups was essential to the welfare of the community of the realm as a whole. One further fact is of supreme importance. The groups we have mentioned, whether they were trade guilds or orders of chivalry, had a religious basis. Their integrity was essentially a spiritual integrity, and deviations from it were described in terms of morality. Thus medieval man was occupied with moral problems in situations that we should regard as being psychological or personal.*

What Chaucer has done in the Prologue is to present a few figures who exemplify the ideals he thought proper to the groups to which they belong—the Knight, the Clerk, and the Parson (together with his brother, the Plowman)—and a further series of characters, much more numerous, who, through pride, avarice, or the lusts of the flesh, exemplify deviations from the ideals of their various groups. The resultant characters are thus neither typical nor realistic. And they do not represent personalities, a concept for which Chaucer had no word, for the simple reason that in his society there was no need for it.

For example, Chaucer tells us, several times in fact, that the Knight was worthy; that he loved the abstract virtues of chivalry (fidelity, honor, generosity, and courtesy); that, as evidence of this worth and love, he had fought in many great enterprises; that he was wise; and finally, that he was humble and, by implication, penitent. The resultant figure is not a typical knight of the latter fourteenth century, and he has, moreover, none of the complexities we have come to think of as making up a personality. Instead, he exemplifies the ideals of chivalry which Chaucer held in veneration and which he thought were being improperly fulfilled by many of the armed knights of his time. The battles in which the Knight had fought recall the chivalric splendor of England in the days of Chaucer's youth and suggest, by implication, the shortcomings of chivalric enterprise in the later fourteenth century, shortcomings made explicit in the portrait of the Knight's son, the Squire.

Similarly, the portraits of the Prioress, the Monk, and the Friar reveal various abuses characteristic of those who devote themselves to the contemplative life. The Prioress, who wishes to be thought of as a noble lady rather than as a prioress, puts on courtly airs with amusingly small success and, in this endeavor, substitutes sentimental tenderness for conscience. The Monk is flagrantly inconstant in his profession and seeks to become a prosperous man of the world. In studying these portraits we should remember that nuns and monks were voluntarily widowed from worldly concern, that their chief duty was attendance at the daily services (matins, lauds, prime, tierce, mass, sext, none, vespers, and compline), and that they were bound by vows to a life of contemplation and abstinence. Friars also lived by a rule, but in addition they were allowed to preach and to administer the sacraments. The Friar in the Prologue is an arrant hypocrite who abuses his office for the sake of his own gluttony, vainglory, and avarice. The shortcomings of these characters were probably common enough, but the implication is not that they were typical. Their various weaknesses were typical of the groups to which they belonged, but not necessarily combined all together in the extreme forms represented in any particular individuals. Just as the Knight exemplifies certain group ideals, in the same way the less noble characters in the Prologue exemplify various forms of neglect of the ideals proper to their stations.

Although Chaucer's audience must have been amused and delighted by the verisimilitude of some of his more elaborate sketches, they are not realistic. As an artistic movement, realism developed during the nineteenth century in France, partly as a result of a kind of romantic disillusionment with the middle-class society that had triumphed in the French Revolution. It sought social reforms, not in the name of traditional morality, which realists deliberately if not altogether successfully avoided, but on the basis of a sentimental, humanitarian outlook that sometimes manifested itself in specific social or political philosophies. Realistic literature is characteristically serious-minded, sentimentally appealing, and absorbed with the problems of human isolation, and in consequence, with psychology. Chaucer, on the other hand, is thoroughly and conventionally moral in his criticisms, and his chief weapons are irony, sarcasm, and humor. If he sometimes names his characters, makes them resemble to a certain extent actual historical personages, and sometimes specifies

their geographic origins, he is merely giving to "airy nothings," which are, in this instance, ideas, a "local habitation and a name." His prevailingly humorous tone, moreover, is consistent with an intellectual rather than an emotional appeal. Chaucer probably witnessed riot and bloodshed of the Peasant's Revolt in London in 1381; but his only reference to it is a jocular allusion in the Nun's Priest's Tale. A realistic writer would have dwelt on the plight of the peasants and supplied shocking details of the uprising, either stating or implying some kind of social doctrine. Chaucer's criticism of society is moral and has nothing in common with the social criticism of modern realists.

Much of the material in Chaucer's descriptions is conventional either in substance or in detail. Thus the friars were widely accused of seducing women, of giving easy penances for their own profit, and of being generally vain and hypocritical. Chaucer makes these accusations vivid by exemplifying their validity in a single person, recognizable because many unworthy friars shared one or more of his characteristics and given a certain life and vigor by the lively wit and humorous indirection used to describe him. The Friar's "daliaunce and fair langage" become purposeful with the revelation that he had

maad ful many a mariage
Of yonge women, at his owene cost.

This means, of course, that he charged nothing for performing the marriage ceremony when the brides had become urgently marriageable through his ministrations. The observation is followed by the tongue-in-cheek (and somewhat obscene) remark,

Unto his ordre he was a noble post.

The humorous indirection of these lines is far more biting than a simple accusation of lechery could be, and it makes the Friar seem to come alive before our eyes. But we should not be misled into thinking that the basic accusation is any less serious because the surface effect is amusing and productive of the illusion of verisimilitude. Chaucer had no sentimental regard for vice on the ground that it is typically human.

More specific material is also frequently conventional in one way or another. Details like the Miller's wart or the Pardoner's hair are used with their conventional significations in medieval physiognomy. The Wife's deafness and the Pardoner's eunuchry both carry connotations derived from the Bible and its commentaries. Generally, the details function in much the same way that attributes function in the medieval visual arts. And the actions described, like the table manners of the Prioress, which are derived from the worldly wise advice of the unscrupulous Old Woman in the Roman de la rose, have a symbolic rather than a literal force. Thus Chaucer can mingle general description of character, details of costume and appearance, and traits of behavior in-

Figure 35 *The murder of Thomas Becket.*

*discriminately without destroying the coherence of his dis-
course. For the coherence arises from the significance of the
concrete materials, not from their superficial appearances.*

*It should be emphasized that to Chaucer abstractions like
"fidelity, honor, generosity," on the one hand, or "gluttony,
vainglory, and avarice" (which typify all of the sins), on the
other, were very real indeed. Medieval Christianity generally,
in spite of the arguments of a few scholastics, carried with it a
considerable platonic emphasis on the reality of the intelligible.
Where we should use the techniques of psychology for the
analysis of character, Chaucer used the moral philosophy of
his day, which described conduct in terms of virtues and vices
regarded as manifestations of love. Love, whether for some
ideal virtue or for some sort of physical satisfaction, was
thought of as the wellspring of conduct, without which life
could not exist. Love, although it cannot be touched with the
hand nor recorded, except by implication, on a photographic
plate, has its own reality. The vividness of Chaucer's*

*characters is in part a tribute to his understanding of the ways
in which this reality operates. We shall not go far astray if
we seek to evaluate these characters by considering how and
what they love.*

Here biginneth the Book of the Tales of Caunterbury.

Whan that Aprille with his shoures sote
The droghte of Marche hath perced to the rote,
And bathed every veyne in swich licour,
Of which vertu engendred is the flour;
Whan Zephirus eek with his swete breeth   5
Inspired hath in every holt and heeth
The tendre croppes, and the yonge sonne
Hath in the Ram his halfe cours y-ronne,
And smale fowles maken melodye,
That slepen al the night with open yë,   10
(So priketh hem nature in hir corages):
Than longen folk to goon on pilgrimages
(And palmers for to seken straunge strondes)
To ferne halwes, couthe in sondry londes;
And specially, from every shires ende   15
Of Engelond, to Caunterbury they wende,
The holy blisful martir for to seke,
That hem hath holpen, whan that they were seke.
  Bifel that, in that seson on a day,
In Southwerk at the Tabard as I lay   20
Redy to wenden on my pilgrimage
To Caunterbury with ful devout corage,
At night was come in-to that hostelrye
Wel nyne and twenty in a companye,
Of sondry folk, by aventure y-falle   25
In felawshipe, and pilgrims were they alle,
That toward Caunterbury wolden ryde;
The chambres and the stables weren wyde,
And wel we weren esed atte beste.
And shortly, whan the sonne was to reste,   30
So hadde I spoken with hem everichon,
That I was of hir felawshipe anon,
And made forward erly for to ryse,
To take our wey, ther as I yow devyse.
  But natheles, whyl I have tyme and space,   35
Er that I ferther in this tale pace,
Me thinketh it acordaunt to resoun,
To telle yow al the condicioun
Of ech of hem, so as it semed me,
And whiche they weren, and of what degree;   40
And eek in what array that they were inne:

And at a knight than wol I first biginne.

A KNIGHT ther was, and that a worthy man,
That fro the tyme that he first bigan
To ryden out, he loved chivalrye,   45
Trouthe and honour, fredom and curteisye.
Ful worthy was he in his lordes werre,
And therto hadde he riden (no man ferre)
As wel in Cristendom as hethenesse,
And ever honoured for his worthinesse.   50
At Alisaundre he was, whan it was wonne;
Ful ofte tyme he hadde the bord bigonne
Aboven alle naciouns in Pruce.
In Lettow hadde he reysed and in Ruce,
No Cristen man so ofte of his degree.   55
In Gernade at the sege eek hadde he be
Of Algezir, and riden in Belmarye.
At Lyeys was he, and at Satalye,
Whan they were wonne; and in the Grete See
At many a noble aryve hadde he be.   60
At mortal batailles hadde he been fiftene,
And foughten for our feith at Tramissene
In listes thryes, and ay slayn his foo.
This ilke worthy knight had been also
Somtyme with the lord of Palatye,   65
Ageyn another hethen in Turkye:
And evermore he hadde a sovereyn prys.
And though that he were worthy, he was wys,
And of his port as meke as is a mayde.
He never yet no vileinye ne sayde   70
In al his lyf, un-to no maner wight.
He was a verray parfit gentil knight.
But for to tellen yow of his array,
His hors were gode, but he was nat gay.
Of fustian he wered a gipoun   75
Al bismotered with his habergeoun;
For he was late y-come from his viage,
And wente for to doon his pilgrimage.

With him ther was his sone, a yong SQUYER,
A lovyere, and a lusty bacheler,   80
With lokkes crulle, as they were leyd in presse.
Of twenty yeer of age he was, I gesse.
Of his stature he was of evene lengthe,
And wonderly deliver, and greet of strengthe.
And he had been somtyme in chivachye,   85
In Flaundres, in Artoys, and Picardye,
And born him wel, as of so litel space,
In hope to stonden in his lady grace.

Embrouded was he, as it were a mede
Al ful of fresshe floures, whyte and rede.   90
Singinge he was, or floytinge, al the day;
He was as fresh as is the month of May.
Short was his goune, with sleves longe and wyde.
Wel coude he sitte on hors, and faire ryde.
He coude songes make and wel endyte,   95
Iuste and eek daunce, and wel purtreye and wryte.
So hote he lovede, that by nightertale
He sleep namore than dooth a nightingale.
Curteys he was, lowly, and servisable,
And carf biforn his fader at the table.   100

A Yeman hadde he, and servaunts namo
At that tyme, for him liste ryde so;
And he was clad in cote and hood of grene;
A sheef of pecok-arwes brighte and kene
Under his belt he bar ful thriftily;   105
(Wel coude he dresse his takel yemanly:
His arwes drouped noght with fetheres lowe),
And in his hand he bar a mighty bowe.
A not-heed hadde he, with a broun visage.
Of wode-craft wel coude he al the usage.   110
Upon his arm he bar a gay bracer,
And by his syde a swerd and a bokeler,
And on that other syde a gay daggere,
Harneised wel, and sharp as point of spere;
A Cristofre on his brest of silver shene.   115
An horn he bar, the bawdrik was of grene;
A forster was he, soothly, as I gesse.

Ther was also a Nonne, a PRIORESSE,
That of hir smyling was ful simple and coy;
Hir gretteste ooth was but by sëynt Loy;   120
And she was cleped madame Eglentyne.
Ful wel she song the service divyne,
Entuned in hir nose ful semely;
And Frensh she spak ful faire and fetisly,
After the scole of Stratford atte Bowe,   125
For Frensh of Paris was to hir unknowe.
At mete wel y-taught was she with-alle;
She leet no morsel from hir lippes falle,
Ne wette hir fingres in hir sauce depe.
Wel coude she carie a morsel, and wel kepe,   130
That no drope ne fille up-on hir brest.
In curteisye was set ful muche hir lest.
Hir over lippe wyped she so clene,
That in hir coppe was no ferthing sene
Of grece, whan she dronken hadde hir draughte.   135

Ful semely after hir mete she raughte,
And sikerly she was of greet disport,
And ful plesaunt, and amiable of port,
And peyned hir to countrefete chere
Of court, and been estatlich of manere,   140
And to ben holden digne of reverence.
But, for to speken of hir conscience,
She was so charitable and so pitous,
She wolde wepe, if that she sawe a mous
Caught in a trappe, if it were deed or bledde.   145
Of smale houndes had she, that she fedde
With rosted flesh, or milk and wastel-breed.
But sore weep she if oon of hem were deed,
Or if men smoot it with a yerde smerte:
And al was conscience and tendre herte.   150
Ful semely hir wimpel pinched was;
His nose tretys; hir eyen greye as glas;
Hir mouth ful smal, and ther-to softe and reed;
But sikerly she hadde a fair forheed;
It was almost a spanne brood, I trowe;   155
For, hardily, she was nat undergrowe.
Ful fetis was hir cloke, as I was war.
Of smal coral aboute hir arm she bar
A peire of bedes, gauded al with grene;
And ther-on heng a broche of gold ful shene,   160
On which ther was first write a crowned A,
And after, *Amor vincit omnia.*

    Another NONNE with hir hadde she,
That was hir chapeleyne, and PREESTES three.

    A MONK ther was, a fair for the maistrye,   165
An out-rydere, that lovede venerye;
A manly man, to been an abbot able.
Ful many a deyntee hors hadde he in stable:
And, whan he rood, men mighte his brydel here
Ginglen in a whistling wind as clere,   170
And eek as loude as dooth the chapel-belle,
Ther as this lord was keper of the celle.
The reule of seint Maure or of seint Beneit,
By-cause that it was old and som-del streit,
This ilke monk leet olde thinges pace,   175
And held after the newe world the space.
He yaf nat of that text a pulled hen,
That seith, that hunters been nat holy men;
Ne that a monk, whan he is cloisterlees,
Is lykned til a fish that is waterlees;   180
This is to seyn, a monk out of his cloistre.
But thilke text held he nat worth an oistre;
And I seyde, his opinioun was good.

What sholde he studie, and make him-selven
    wood,
Upon a book in cloistre alwey to poure,   185
Or swinken with his handes, and laboure,
As Austin bit? How shal the world be served?
Lat Austin have his swink to him reserved.
Therfore he was a pricasour aright;
Grehoundes he hadde, as swifte as fowel in flight; 190
Of priking and of hunting for the hare
Was al his lust, for no cost wolde he spare.
I seigh his sleves purfiled at the hond
With grys, and that the fyneste of a lond;
And, for to festne his hood under his chin,   195
He hadde of gold y-wroght a curious pin:
A love-knotte in the gretter ende ther was.
His heed was balled, that shoon as any glas,
And eek his face, as he had been anoint.
He was a lord ful fat and in good point;   200
His eyen stepe, and rollinge in his heed,
That stemed as a forneys of a leed;
His botes souple, his hors in greet estat.
Now certeinly he was a fair prelat;
He was nat pale as a for-pyned goost.   205
A fat swan loved he best of any roost.
His palfrey was as broun as is a berye.

    A FRERE ther was, a wantown and a merye,
A limitour, a ful solempne man.
In alle the ordres foure is noon that can   210
So muche of daliaunce and fair langage.
He hadde maad ful many a mariage
Of yonge wommen, at his owne cost.
Un-to his ordre he was a noble post.
Ful wel biloved and famulier was he   215
With frankeleyns over-al in his contree,
And eek with worthy wommen of the toun:
For he had power of confessioun,
As seyde him-self, more than a curat,
For of his ordre he was licentiat.   220
Ful swetely herde he confessioun,
And pleasaunt was his absolucioun;
He was an esy man to yeve penaunce
Ther as he wiste to han a good pitaunce;
For unto a povre ordre for to yive   225
Is signe that a man is wel y-shrive.
For if he yaf, he dorste make avaunt,
He wiste that a man was repentaunt.
For many a man so hard is of his herte,
He may nat wepe al-thogh him sore smerte.   230

Therfore, in stede of weping and preyeres,
Men moot yeve silver to the povre freres.
His tipet was ay farsed ful of knyves
And pinnes, for to yeven faire wyves.
And certeinly he hadde a mery note;   235
Wel coude he singe and pleyen on a rote.
Of yeddinges he bar utterly the prys.
His nekke whyt was as the flour-de-lys;
Ther-to he strong was as a champioun.
He knew the tavernes wel in every toun,   240
And everich hostiler and tappestere
Bet than a lazar or a beggestere;
For un-to swich a worthy man as he
Acorded nat, as by his facultee,
To have with seke lazars aqueyntaunce.   245
It is nat honest, it may nat avaunce
For to delen with no swich poraille,
But al with riche and sellers of vitaille.
And over-al, ther as profit sholde aryse,
Curteys he was, and lowly of servyse.   250
Ther nas no man no-wher so vertuous.
He was the beste beggere in his hous;
And yaf a certeyn ferme for the graunt;
Noon of his brethren cam ther in his haunt;
For thogh a widwe hadde noght a sho,   255
So pleasant was his " In principio,"
Yet wolde he have a ferthing, er he wente.
His purchas was wel bettre than his rente.
And rage he coude, as it were right a whelpe.
In love-dayes ther coude he muchel helpe.   260
For there he was nat lyk a cloisterer,
With a thredbar cope, as is a povre scoler,
But he was lyk a maister or a pope.
Of double worsted was his semi-cope,
That rounded as a belle out of the presse.   265
Somwhat he lipsed, for his wantownesse,
To make his English swete up-on his tonge;
And in his harping, whan that he had songe,
His eyen twinkled in his heed aright,
As doon the sterres in the frosty night.   270
This worthy limitour was cleped Huberd.

    A MARCHANT was ther with a forked berd,
In mottelee, and hye on horse he sat,
Up-on his heed a Flaundrish bever hat;
His botes clasped faire and fetisly.   275
His resons he spak ful solempnely,
Souninge alway thencrees of his winning.
He wolde the see were kept for any thing

Figure 36 *The false fox: illustration for Psalm 58: 15. Here the "dogs" of the psalm are exemplified by a "false dog" or fox, frequently used in the late Middle Ages to represent a friar. Compare Chaucer's Nun's Priest's Tale.*

Bitwixe Middelburgh and Orewelle.
Wel coude he in eschaunge sheeldes selle.   280
This worthy man ful wel his wit bisette;
Ther wiste no wight that he was in dette,
So estatly was he of his governaunce,
With his bargaynes, and with his chevisaunce.
For sothe he was a worthy man with-alle,   285
But sooth to seyn, I noot how men him calle.
    A CLERK ther was of Oxenford also,
That un-to logik hadde longe y-go.
As lene was his hors as is a rake,
And he nas nat right fat, I undertake;   290
But loked holwe, and ther-to soberly.
Ful thredbar was his overest courtepy;
For he had geten him yet no benefyce,
Ne was so worldly for to have offyce.
For him was lever have at his beddes heed   295
Twenty bokes, clad in blak or reed,
Of Aristotle and his philosophye,
Than robes riche, or fithele, or gay sautrye.
But al be that he was a philosophre,
Yet hadde he but litel gold in cofre;   300
But al that he mighte of his freendes hente,
On bokes and on lerninge he it spente,
And bisily gan for the soules preye
Of hem that yaf him wher-with to scoleye.

Of studie took he most cure and most hede.   305
Noght o word spak he more than was nede,
And that was seyd in forme and reverence,
And short and quik, and ful of hy sentence.
Souninge in moral vertu was his speche,
And gladly wolde he lerne, and gladly teche.   310
    A Sergeant of the Lawe, war and wys,
That often hadde been at the parvys,
Ther was also, ful riche of excellence.
Discreet he was, and of greet reverence:
He semed swich, his wordes weren so wyse.   315
Iustyce he was ful often in assyse,
By patente, and by pleyn commissioun;
For his science, and for his heigh renoun
Of fees and robes hadde he many oon.
So greet a purchasour was no-wher noon.   320
Al was fee simple to him in effect,
His purchasing mighte nat been infect.
No-wher so bisy a man as he ther nas,
And yet he semed bisier than he was.
In termes hadde he caas and domes alle,   325
That from the tyme of king William were falle.
Therto he coude endyte, and make a thing,
Ther coude no wight pinche at his wryting;
And every statut coude he pleyn by rote.
He rood but hoomly in a medlee cote   330
Girt with a ceint of silk, with barres smale;
Of his array telle I no lenger tale.
    A Frankeleyn was in his companye;
Whyt was his berd, as is the dayesye.
Of his complexioun he was sangwyn.   335
Wel loved he by the morwe a sop in wyn.
To liven in delyt was ever his wone,
For he was Epicurus owne sone,
That heeld opinioun, that pleyn delyt
Was verraily felicitee parfyt.   340
An housholdere, and that a greet, was he;
Seint Iulian he was in his contree.
His breed, his ale, was alwey after oon;
A bettre envyned man was no-wher noon.
With-oute bake mete was never his hous,   345
Of fish and flesh, and that so plenteous,
It snewed in his hous of mete and drinke,
Of alle deyntees that men coude thinke.
After the sondry sesons of the yeer,
So chaunged he his mete and his soper.   350
Ful many a fat partrich hadde he in mewe,
And many a breem and many a luce in stewe.

Wo was his cook, but-if his sauce were
Poynaunt and sharp, and redy al his gere.
His table dormant in his halle alway   355
Stood redy covered al the longe day.
At sessiouns ther was he lord and sire;
Ful ofte tyme he was knight of the shire.
An anlas and a gipser al of silk
Heng at his girdel, whyt as morne milk.   360
A shirreve hadde he been, and a countour;
Was no-wher such a worthy vavasour.
    An Haberdassher and a Carpenter,
A Webbe, a Dyere, and a Tapicer,
Were with us eek, clothed in o liveree,   365
Of a solempne and greet fraternitee.
Ful fresh and newe hir gere apyked was;
Hir knyves were y-chaped noght with bras,
But al with silver, wroght ful clene and weel,
His girdles and hir pouches every-deel.   370
Wel semed ech of hem a fair burgeys,
To sitten in a yeldhalle on a deys.
Everich, for the wisdom that he can,
Was shaply for to been an alderman.
For catel hadde they y-nogh and rente,   375
And eek hir wyves wolde it wel assente;
And elles certein were they to blame.
It is ful fair to been y-clept "ma dame,"
And goon to vigilyës al bifore,
And have a mantel royalliche y-bore.   380
    A Cook they hadde with hem for the nones,
To boille the chiknes with the mary-bones,
And poudre-marchant tart, and galingale.
Wel coude he knowe a draughte of London ale.
He coude roste, and sethe, and broille, and frye,   385
Maken mortreux, and wel bake a pye.
But greet harm was it, as it thoughte me,
That on his shine a mormal hadde he;
For blankmanger, that made he with the beste.
    A Shipman was ther, woning fer by weste: 390
For aught I woot, he was of Dertemouthe.
He rood up-on a rouncy, as he couthe,
In a gowne of falding to the knee.
A daggere hanging on a laas hadde he
Aboute his nekke under his arm adoun.   395
The hote somer had maad his hewe al broun;
And, certeinly, he was a good felawe.
Ful many a draughte of wyn had he y-drawe
From Burdeux-ward, whyl that the chapman
    sleep.

Of nyce conscience took he no keep.   400
If that he faught, and hadde the hyer hond,
By water he sente hem hoom to every lond.
But of his craft to rekene wel his tydes,
His stremes and his daungers him bisydes,
His herberwe and his mone, his lodemenage,   405
Ther nas noon swich from Hulle to Cartage.
Hardy he was, and wys to undertake;
With many a tempest hadde his berd been shake.
He knew wel alle the havenes, as they were,
From Gootlond to the cape of Finistere,   410
And every cryke in Britayne and in Spayne;
His barge y-cleped was the Maudelayne.

　　With us ther was a Doctour of Phisyk,
In al this world ne was ther noon him lyk
To speke of phisik and of surgerye;   415
For he was grounded in astronomye.
He kepte his pacient a ful greet del
In houres, by his magik naturel.
Wel coude he fortunen the ascendent
Of his images for his pacient.   420
He knew the cause of everich maladye,
Were it of hoot or cold, or moiste, or drye,
And where engendred, and of what humour;
He was a verrey parfit practisour.
The cause y-knowe, and of his harm the rote,   425
Anon he yaf the seke man his bote.
Ful redy hadde he his apothecaries,
To sende him drogges and his letuaries,
For ech of hem made other for to winne;
Hir frendschipe nas nat newe to biginne.   430
Wel knew he the olde Esculapius,
And Deiscorides, and eek Rufus,
Old Ypocras, Haly, and Galien;
Serapion, Razis, and Avicen;
Averrois, Damascien, and Constantyn;   435
Bernard, and Gatesden, and Gilbertyn.
Of his diete mesurable was he,
For it was of no superfluitee,
But of greet norissing and digestible.
His studie was but litel on the Bible.   440
In sangwin and in pers he clad was al,
Lyned with taffata and with sendal;
And yet he was but esy of dispence;
He kepte that he wan in pestilence.
For gold in phisik is a cordial,   445
Therfore he lovede gold in special.

　　A good Wyf was ther of bisyde Bathe,

Figure 37 *"The Jealous Husband," an illustration for the* Roman de la Rose. *The wife is here obviously "gat-tothed" like Chaucer's Wyf of Bath. On the* Roman de la Rose, *one of Chaucer's favorite books, see John V. Fleming,* The Roman de la Rose, *Princeton University Press, Princeton, N.J., 1969.*

But she was som-del deef, and that was scathe.
Of clooth making she hadde swiche an haunt,
She passed hem of Ypres and of Gaunt.   450
In al the parisshe wyf ne was ther noon
That to the offring bifore hir sholde goon;
And if ther dide, certeyn, so wrooth was she,
That she was out of alle charitee.
Hir coverchiefs ful fyne were of ground;   455
I dorste swere they weyeden ten pound
That on a Sonday were upon hir heed.
Hir hosen weren of fyn scarlet reed,
Ful streite y-teyd, and shoos ful moiste and newe.
Bold was hir face, and fair, and reed of hewe.   460
She was a worthy womman al hir lyve,
Housbondes at chirche-dore she hadde fyve,
Withouten other companye in youthe;
But therof nedeth nat to speke as nouthe.
And thryes hadde she been at Ierusalem;   465
She hadde passed many a straunge streem;
At Rome she hadde been, and at Boloigne,
In Galice at seint Iame, and at Coloigne.
She coude muche of wandring by the weye.
Gat-tothed was she, soothly for to seye.   470
Up-on an amblere esily she sat,

Y-wimpled wel, and on hir heed an hat
As brood as is a bokeler or a targe;
A foot-mantel aboute hir hipes large,
And on hir feet a paire of spores sharpe.   475
In felawschip wel coude she laughe and carpe.
Of remedyes of love she knew per-chaunce,
For she coude of that art the olde daunce.

   A good man was ther of religioun,
And was a povre PERSOUN of a toun;   480
But riche he was of holy thoght and werk.
He was also a lerned man, a clerk,
That Cristes gospel trewely wolde preche;
His parisshens devoutly wolde he teche.
Benigne he was, and wonder diligent,   485
And in adversitee ful pacient;
And swich he was y-preved ofte sythes.
Ful looth were him to cursen for his tythes,
But rather wolde he yeven, out of doute,
Un-to his povre parisshens aboute   490
Of his offring, and eek of his substaunce.
He coude in litel thing han suffisaunce.
Wyd was his parisshe, and houses fer a-sonder,
But he ne lafte nat, for reyn ne thonder,
In siknes nor in meschief, to visyte   495
The ferreste in his parisshe, muche and lyte,
Up-on his feet, and in his hand a staf.
This noble ensample to his sheep he yaf,
That first he wroghte, and afterward he taughte;
Out of the gospel he tho wordes caughte;   500
And this figure he added eek ther-to,
That if gold ruste, what shal iren do?
For if a preest be foul, on whom we truste,
No wonder is a lewed man to ruste;
And shame it is, if a preest take keep,   505
A shiten shepherde and a clene sheep.
Wel oghte a preest ensample for to yive,
By his clennesse, how that his sheep shold live.
He sette nat his benefice to hyre,
And leet his sheep encombred in the myre,   510
And ran to London, un-to sëynt Poules,
To seken him a chaunterie for soules,
Or with a bretherhed to been withholde;
But dwelte at hoom, and kepte wel his folde,
So that the wolf ne made it nat miscarie;   515
He was a shepherde and no mercenarie.
And though he holy were, and vertuous,
He was to sinful man nat despitous,
Ne of his speche daungerous ne digne,

But in his teching discreet and benigne.   520
To drawen folk to heven by fairnesse
By good ensample, was his bisinesse:
But it were any persone obstinat,
What-so he were, of heigh or lowe estat,
Him wolde he snibben sharply for the nones.   525
A bettre preest, I trowe that nowhere noon is.
He wayted after no pompe and reverence,
Ne maked him a spyced conscience,
But Cristes lore, and his apostles twelve,
He taughte, and first he folwed it him-selve.   530
   With him ther was a PLOWMAN, was his
        brother,
That hadde y-lad of dong ful many a fother,
A trewe swinker and a good was he,
Living in pees and parfit charitee.
God loved he best with al his hole herte   535
At alle tymes, thogh him gamed or smerte,
And thanne his neighebour right as him-selve.
He wolde thresshe, and ther-to dyke and delve,
For Cristes sake, for every povre wight,
Withouten hyre, if it lay in his might.   540
His tythes payed he ful faire and wel,
Bothe of his propre swink and his catel.
In a tabard he rood upon a mere.

   Ther was also a Reve and a Millere,
A Somnour and a Pardoner also,   545
A Maunciple, and my-self; ther were namo.
   The MILLER was a stout carl, for the nones,
Ful big he was of braun, and eek of bones;
That proved wel, for over-al ther he cam,
At wrastling he wolde have alwey the ram.   550
He was short-sholdred, brood, a thikke knarre,
Ther nas no dore that he nolde heve of harre,
Or breke it, at a renning, with his heed.
His berd as any sowe or fox was reed,
And ther-to brood, as though it were a spade.   555
Up-on the cop right of his nose he hade
A werte, and ther-on stood a tuft of heres,
Reed as the bristles of a sowes eres;
His nose-thirles blake were and wyde.
A swerd and bokeler bar he by his syde;   560
His mouth as greet was as a greet forneys.
He was a Ianglere and a goliardeys,
And that was most of sinne and harlotryes.
Wel coude he stelen corn, and tollen thryes;
And yet he hadde a thombe of gold, pardee.   565
A whyt cote and a blew hood wered he.

A baggepype wel coude he blowe and sowne,
And ther-with-al he broghte us out of towne.
　　A gentil MAUNCIPLE was ther of a temple,
Of which achatours mighte take exemple　　　570
For to be wyse in bying of vitaille.
For whether that he payde, or took by taille,
Algate he wayted so in his achat,
That he was ay biforn and in good stat.
Now is nat that of God a ful fair grace,　　　575
That swich a lewed mannes wit shal pace
The wisdom of an heep of lerned men?
Of maistres hadde he mo than thryes ten,
That were of lawe expert and curious;
Of which ther were a doseyn in that hous,　　　580
Worthy to been stiwardes of rente and lond
Of any lord that is in Engelond,
To make him live by his propre good,
In honour dettelees, but he were wood,
Or live as scarsly as him list desire;　　　585
And able for to helpen al a shire
In any cas that mighte falle or happe;
And yit this maunciple sette hir aller cappe.
　　The REVE was a sclendre colerik man,
His berd was shave as ny as ever he can.　　　590
His heer was by his eres round y-shorn.
His top was dokked lyk a preest biforn.
Ful longe were his legges, and ful lene,
Y-lyk a staf, ther was no calf y-sene.
Wel coude he kepe a gerner and a binne;　　　595
Ther was noon auditour coude on him winne.
Wel wiste he, by the droghte, and by the reyn,
The yelding of his seed, and of his greyn.
His lordes sheep, his neet, his dayerye,
His swyn, his hors, his stoor, and his pultrye,　　　600
Was hoolly in this reves governing,
And by his covenaunt yaf the rekening,
Sin that his lord was twenty yeer of age;
Ther coude no man bringe him in arrerage.
Ther nas baillif, ne herde, ne other hyne,　　　605
That he ne knew his sleighte and his covyne;
They were adrad of him, as of the deeth.
His woning was ful fair up-on an heeth,
With grene treës shadwed was his place.
He coude bettre than his lord purchace.　　　610
Ful riche he was astored prively,
His lord wel coude he plesen subtilly,
To yeve and lene him of his owne good,
And have a thank, and yet a cote and hood.

In youthe he lerned hadde a good mister;　　　615
He was a wel good wrighte, a carpenter.
This reve sat up-on a ful good stot,
That was al pomely grey, and highte Scot.
A long surcote of pers up-on he hade,
And by his syde he bar a rusty blade.　　　620
Of Northfolk was this reve, of which I telle,
Bisyde a toun men clepen Baldeswelle.
Tukked he was, as is a frere, aboute,
And ever he rood the hindreste of our route.
　　A SOMNOUR was ther with us in that place,　　　625
That hadde a fyr-reed cherubinnes face,
For sawcefleem he was, with eyen narwe.
As hoot he was, and lecherous, as a sparwe;
With scalled browes blake, and piled berd;
Of his visage children were aferd.　　　630
Ther nas quik-silver, litarge, ne brimstoon,
Boras, ceruce, ne oille of tartre noon,
Ne oynement that wolde clense and byte,
That him mighte helpen of his whelkes whyte,
Nor of the knobbes sitting on his chekes.　　　635
Wel loved he garleek, oynons, and eek lekes,
And for to drinken strong wyn, reed as blood.
Thanne wolde he speke, and crye as he were
　　　wood.
And whan that he wel dronken hadde the wyn,
Than wolde he speke no word but Latyn.　　　640
A fewe termes hadde he, two or three,
That he had lerned out of som decree;
No wonder is, he herde it al the day;
And eek ye knowen wel, how that a Iay
Can clepen "Watte," as well as can the pope.　　　645
But who-so coude in other thing him grope,
Thanne hadde he spent al his philosophye;
Ay "Questio quid iuris" wolde he crye.
He was a gentil harlot and a kinde;
A bettre felawe sholde men noght finde.　　　650
He wolde suffre, for a quart of wyn,
A good felawe to have his concubyn
A twelf-month, and excuse him atte fulle:
Ful prively a finch eek coude he pulle.
And if he fond o-wher a good felawe,　　　655
He wolde techen him to have non awe,
In swich cas, of the erchedeknes curs,
But-if a mannes soule were in his purs;
For in his purs he sholde y-punisshed be.
"Purs is the erchedeknes helle," seyde he.　　　660
But wel I woot he lyed right in dede;

Of cursing oghte ech gilty man him drede—
For curs wol slee, right as assoilling saveth—
And also war him of a *significavit*.
In daunger hadde he at his owne gyse   665
The yonge girles of the diocyse,
And knew hir counseil, and was al hir reed.
A gerland hadde he set up-on his heed,
As greet as it were for an ale-stake;
A bokeler hadde he maad him of a cake.   670

   With him ther rood a gentil PARDONER
Of Rouncival, his freend and his compeer,
That streight was comen fro the court of Rome.
Ful loude he song, "Com hider, love, to me."
This somnour bar to him a stif burdoun,   675
Was never trompe of half so greet a soun.
This pardoner hadde heer as yelow as wex,
But smothe it heng, as dooth a strike of flex;
By ounces henge his lokkes that he hadde,
And ther-with he his shuldres overspradde;   680
But thinne it lay, by colpons oon and oon;
But hood, for Iolitee, ne wered he noon,
For it was trussed up in his walet.
Him thoughte, he rood al of the newe Iet;
Dischevele, save his cappe, he rood al bare.   685
Swiche glaringe eyen hadde he as an hare.
A vernicle hadde he sowed on his cappe.
His walet lay biforn him in his lappe,
Bret-ful of pardoun come from Rome al hoot.
A voys he hadde as smal as hath a goot.   690
No berd hadde he, ne never sholde have,
As smothe it was as it were late y-shave;
I trowe he were a gelding or a mare.
But of his craft, fro Berwik into Ware,
Ne was ther swich another pardoner.   695
For in his male he hadde a pilwe-beer,
Which that, he seyde, was our lady veyl:
He seyde, he hadde a gobet of the seyl
That sëynt Peter hadde, whan that he wente
Up-on the see, til Iesu Crist him hente.   700
He hadde a croys of latoun, ful of stones,
And in a glas he hadde pigges bones.
But with thise relikes, whan that he fond
A povre person dwelling up-on lond,
Up-on a day he gat him more moneye   705
Than that the person gat in monthes tweye.
And thus, with feyned flaterye and Iapes,
He made the person and the peple his apes.
But trewely to tellen, atte laste,

He was in chirche a noble ecclesiaste.   710
Wel coude he rede a lessoun or a storie,
But alderbest he song an offertorie;
For wel he wiste, whan that song was songe,
He moste preche, and wel affyle his tonge,
To winne silver, as he ful wel coude;   715
Therefore he song so meriely and loude.

   Now have I told you shortly, in a clause,
Thestat, tharray, the nombre, and eek the cause
Why that assembled was this companye
In Southwerk, at this gentil hostelrye,   720
That highte the Tabard, faste by the Belle.
But now is tyme to yow for to telle
How that we baren us that ilke night,
Whan we were in that hostelrye alight.
And after wol I telle of our viage,   725
And al the remenaunt of our pilgrimage.
But first I pray yow, of your curteisye,
That ye narette it nat my vileinye,
Thogh that I pleynly speke in this matere,
To telle yow hir wordes and hir chere;   730
Ne thogh I speke hir wordes properly.
For this ye knowen al-so wel as I,
Who-so shal telle a tale after a man,
He moot reherce, as ny as ever he can,
Everich a word, if it be in his charge,   735
Al speke he never so rudeliche and large;
Or elles he moot telle his tale untrewe,
Or feyne thing, or finde wordes newe.
He may nat spare, al-thogh he were his brother;
He moot as wel seye o word as another.   740
Crist spak him-self ful brode in holy writ,
And wel ye woot, no vileinye is it.
Eek Plato seith, who-so that can him rede,
The wordes mote be cosin to the dede.
Also I prey yow to foryeve it me,   745
Al have I nat set folk in hir degree
Here in this tale, as that they sholde stonde;
My wit is short, ye may wel understonde.

   Greet chere made our hoste us everichon,
And to the soper sette he us anon;   750
And served us with vitaille at the beste.
Strong was the wyn, and wel to drinke us leste.
A semely man our hoste was with-alle
For to han been a marshal in an halle;
A large man he was with eyen stepe,   755
A fairer burgeys is ther noon in Chepe:
Bold of his speche, and wys, and wel y-taught,

And of manhod him lakkede right naught.
Eek therto he was right a mery man,
And after soper pleyen he bigan, 760
And spak of mirthe amonges othere thinges,
Whan that we hadde maad our rekeninges;
And seyde thus: "Now, lordinges, trewely,
Ye been to me right welcome hertely:
For by my trouthe, if that I shal nat lye, 765
I ne saugh this yeer so mery a companye
At ones in this herberwe as is now.
Fayn wolde I doon yow mirthe, wiste I how.
And of a mirthe I am right now bithoght,
To doon yow ese, and it shal coste noght. 770

Ye goon to Caunterbury; God yow spede,
The blisful martir quyte yow your mede.
And wel I woot, as ye goon by the weye,
Ye shapen yow to talen and to pleye;
For trewely, confort ne mirthe is noon 775
To ryde by the weye doumb as a stoon;
And therfore wol I maken yow disport,
As I seyde erst, and doon yow som confort.
And if yow lyketh alle, by oon assent,
Now for to stonden at my Iugement, 780
And for to werken as I shal yow seye,
To-morwe, whan ye ryden by the weye,
Now, by my fader soule, that is deed,
But ye be merye, I wol yeve yow myn heed.
Hold up your hond, withouten more speche." 785

Our counseil was nat longe for to seche;
Us thoughte it was noght worth to make it wys,
And graunted him withouten more avys,
And bad him seye his verdit, as him leste.

"Lordinges," quod he, "now herkneth for the
beste; 790
But tak it not, I prey yow, in desdeyn;
This is the poynt, to speken short and pleyn,
That ech of yow, to shorte with your weye,
In this viage, shal telle tales tweye,
To Caunterbury-ward, I mene it so, 795
And hom-ward he shal tellen othere two,
Of aventures that whylom han bifalle.
And which of yow that bereth him best of alle,
That is to seyn, that telleth in this cas
Tales of best sentence and most solas, 800
Shal have a soper at our aller cost
Here in this place, sitting by this post,
Whan that we come agayn fro Caunterbury.
And for to make yow the more mery,

I wol my-selven gladly with yow ryde, 805
Right at myn owne cost, and be your gyde.
And who-so wol my Iugement withseye
Shal paye al that we spenden by the weye.
And if ye vouche-sauf that it be so,
Tel me anon, with-outen wordes mo, 810
And I wol erly shape me therfore."

This thing was graunted, and our othes swore
With ful glad herte, and preyden him also
That he wold vouche-sauf for to do so,
And that he wolde been our governour, 815
And of our tales Iuge and reportour,
And sette a soper at a certeyn prys;
And we wold reuled been at his devys,
In heigh and lowe; and thus, by oon assent,
We been acorded to his Iugement. 820
And ther-up-on the wyn was fet anon;
We dronken, and to reste wente echon,
With-outen any lenger taryinge.

A-morwe, whan that day bigan to springe,
Up roos our host, and was our aller cok, 825
And gadrede us togidre, alle in a flok,
And forth we riden, a litel more than pas,
Un-to the watering of seint Thomas.
And there our host bigan his hors areste,
And seyde; "Lordinges, herkneth, if yow leste. 830
Ye woot your forward, and I it yow recorde.
If even-song and morwe-song acorde,
Lat se now who shal telle the firste tale.
As ever mote I drinke wyn or ale,
Who-so be rebel to my Iugement 835
Shal paye for al that by the weye is spent.
Now draweth cut, er that we ferrer twinne;
He which that hath the shortest shal biginne.
Sire knight," quod he, "my maister and my lord,
Now draweth cut, for that is myn acord. 840
Cometh neer," quod he, "my lady prioresse;
And ye, sir clerk, lat be your shamfastnesse,
Ne studieth noght; ley hond to, every man."

Anon to drawen every wight bigan,
And shortly for to tellen, as it was, 845
Were it by aventure, or sort, or cas,
The sothe is this, the cut fil to the knight,
Of which ful blythe and glad was every wight;
And telle he moste his tale, as was resoun,
By forward and by composicioun, 850
As ye han herd; what nedeth wordes mo?
And whan this gode man saugh it was so,

As he that wys was and obedient
To kepe his forward by his free assent,
He seyde: "Sin I shal biginne the game,   855
What, welcome be the cut, a Goddes name!
Now lat us ryde, and herkneth what I seye."
    And with that word we riden forth our weye;

And he bigan with right a mery chere
His tale anon, and seyde in this manere.   860

*Here endeth the prolog of this book; and here biginneth
the first tale, which is the Knightes Tale.*

Glossary

1 Aprille   April (the final *e* in this word was probably silent); **shoures**   showers; **sote**   sweet.
2 droghte   drought; **rote**   root.   **3 veyne**   vein (sap vessel of a plant).   **4 vertu**   power.   **5
Zephirus**   the west wind.   **6 holt**   wood; **heeth**   meadow.   **7 croppes**   shoots; **yonge sonne**
young sun (i.e., the sun which has just begun its northward motion).   **8 Ram**   the constellation Aries,
the first sign of the Zodiac; **halfe cours**   half course (the last part of its course, or its course in early
April, so that by implication the sun now enters Taurus, the house of Venus, goddess of love).   **9 fowles**
birds (which appear in medieval iconography in association either with lustful love or with fruitful love
enjoyed after an escape from the trials of winter, or bad fortune, and the snares of the fowler, Satan).
10 yë   eye.   **11 priketh**   spurs; **corages**   hearts.   **12 goon**   go; **pilgrimages**   journeys taken
ostensibly in a spirit of penance to a holy place as a reminder of the pilgrimage of the soul toward the
celestial Jerusalem. Both actual pilgrimages and the inner pilgrimage were theoretically motivated by
love. The imagery in this passage suggests the Resurrection, a promise of the Resurrection of the Just,
and love, which may inspire either a true pilgrimage or, if it is misdirected, various kinds of wandering
from the way. For a similar thematic configuration in the visual arts, see Botticelli's *Birth of Venus*, which
contains Zephyrus, Flora, Venus, and a figure representing spring.   **13 palmers**   beggars on pilgrimage routes; **strondes**   strands (shores).   **14 ferne**   distant; **halwes**   hallowed places; **couthe**
known.   **17 blisful martir**   St. Thomas à Becket, whose shrine was in Canterbury Cathedral.   **18
holpen**   helped.   **20 Southwerk**   Southwark, a suburb of London, immediately across London
Bridge from the city; **Tabard**   an inn identified by a sign shaped like a tabard, or coat. The inn mentioned was a part of the Abbot of Hyde's Inn or town residence .   **21 wenden**   go .   **22 corage**   heart.
25 aventure   chance; **y-falle**   fallen.   **27 wolden ryde**   wished to ride.   **29 atte beste**   at the
best (in the best manner).   **31 everichon**   every one.   **33 made forward**   made ready.   **34 devyse**
describe.   **36 Er**   before.   **37 me thinketh**   it seems to me; **acordaunt to resoun**   reasonable.
39 semed me   seemed to me.   **41 eek**   also; **array**   dress, costume.   **46 Trouthe**   fidelity; **fredom**
generosity.   **47 werre**   war.   **48 ferre**   farther.   **49 hethenesse**   heathen territory.   **51 Alisaundre**
Alexandria, won in a celebrated victory by Pierre de Lusignan in 1365.   **52 the bord bigonne**   occupied
the place of honor at a ceremonial banquet among the Teutonic Knights; **Pruce**   Prussia.   **54 Lettow**
Lithuania; **reysed**   raided; **Ruce**   Russia.   **56 Gernade**   the province of Granada in Spain.   **57
Algezir**   Algeciras, taken from the Moors by Alfonso of Castile in 1344; **Belmarye**   Morocco.
58 Lyeys   Ayas in Armenia, taken by Pierre de Lusignan in 1367; **Satalye**   Attalia in Turkey, taken
by Pierre de Lusignan in 1361.   **59 Grete See**   Mediterranean.   **60 aryve**   disembarkation.   **62
Tramissene**   Tlemcen, Algeria.   **65 Palatye**   Balat (evidently a campaign under a pagan ruler).
67 prys   excellence.   **68 worthy**   of great competence in his profession; **wys**   wise (i.e., having the
virtue of *sapientia*, or wisdom, much admired in persons of rank during the Middle Ages. On the
difference between wisdom and prudence, see Cicero, *Offices*, 1.43.153).   **69 port**   demeanor.   **72
verray**   true; **parfit**   perfect.   **75 fustian**   coarse, unbleached cloth; **gypoun**   sleeveless tunic.
76 bismotered   stained; **habergeoun**   a sleeveless coat of mail.   **77 viage**   expedition.   **80 bachelor**
youthful beginner (i.e., accomplishments like singing and dancing were sometimes said to be character-

istic of *bachelerie*, used as a term of contempt for false chivalry). **81 crulle** curled. **83 evene lengthe** well-proportioned. **84 deliver** agile. **85 in chivachye** on cavalry raids. **86 Flaundres . . . Artoys . . . Picardye** area of the disastrous and disgraceful crusade led by the Bishop of Norwich in 1383. **88 in his lady grace** in his lady's grace (cf. l. 48. The Squire is interested in amorous satisfaction rather than in the virtues proper to his office). **89 Embrouded** embroidered; **mede** meadow (cf. ll. 75–76). **91 floytinge** playing the flute. **95 endyte** compose lyrics for the songs. **96 purtreye** draw. **97 by nightertale** at night. **99 Curteys** courteous (in a manner. Cf. l. 46). **101 Yeman** yeoman (in this instance a very humble retainer for a man of such distinction as the Knight); **namo** no more. **102 him liste** it pleased him (i.e., the Knight). **109 not-heed** short haircut (indicative of low estate). **110 coude** knew. **111 bracer** armguard. **115 Cristofre** medal of St. Christopher, patron of foresters. **116 bawdrik** baldric (belt worn diagonally across the shoulder). **120 sëynt Loy** probably St. Eligius, patron of goldsmiths, noted for his physical beauty. **121 cleped** named; **Eglentyne** Sweetbriar (an amusingly elegant name for a nun). **123 entuned in hir nose** i.e., properly without vibrato. **124 fetisly** elegantly. **125 Stratford atte Bowe** probably a reference to the nunnery of St. Leonard's at Bromley, near Stratford-Bow, Middlesex. **127 At mete** at meat (i.e., in her demeanor at table). **129 sauce depe** deep sauce (i.e., it was customary at more elegant dinners to serve several varieties of sauce in small, deep vessels into which morsels could be dipped; however, the Prioress could not have learned to use such vessels at the simple meals of a well-regulated nunnery). **132 curteisye** courtesy (courtly manners. This word and its cognates frequently carry ironic overtones. Cf. ll. 46, 99, 250); **lest** desire, aspiration. **134 ferthing** farthing (here a small, round spot of floating grease). **136 raughte** reached. **138 port** demeanor. **139 countrefete** imitate; **chere** mannerisms. **140 estatlich** as if of high estate. **141 digne** worthy (with connotations of haughtiness). **142 conscience** awareness of one's own moral state. **143 charitable** possessing the virtue of charity, or the love of God and of one's neighbor for the sake of God (cf. ll. 532–535); **pitous** merciful, with connotations of both *pity* and *piety*. **147 wastel-breed** the best white bread. **151 wimpel** wimple (a headdress which covered the cheeks and chin). **152 tretys** well-shaped. **154 sikerly** surely. **155 spanne** span, the distance between the end of the little finger and the end of the thumb with the hand outstretched, or about nine inches. **156 hardily** certainly. **157 fetis** elegant. **159 bedes** beads (i.e., a rosary); **gauded** containing decorated large beads to indicate pauses for rejoicing. **161 crowned A** the letter *A* (for *Amor*) with an inscribed crown of victory. **162 Amor vincit omnia** ("Love conquers all"), properly the love of God, but with the implication here that the Prioress's love is consistent with her courtly airs. **165 a fair for the maistrye** an excellent one. **166 out-rydere** outrider, a monk whose function it was to visit the monastic estates; **venerye** venery (still an ambiguous word). **168 deyntee** fine. **170 Ginglen** jingle. **171 eek** also. **172 lord** (ironic); **keper of the celle** prior of a subordinate monastery. **173 reule of seint Maure or of seint Beneit** the Benedictine Rule. **174 streit** rigorous. **175 ilke** same; **leet olde thinges pace** neglected old things (of traditional value). **176 And held after the newe world the space** "and seized upon the opportunity for less restraint offered by new fashions." **177 pulled hen** plucked hen (a thing of very little worth). **178 hunters been nat holy men** perhaps a reference to the Decretals of Gratian (canon law), but the idea, which was commonplace, has figurative overtones based on Ps. 90:3 and on the character of Esau. **179 cloisterlees** out of the cloister. **183 good** (ironic). **184 wood** insane. **186 swinken** work. **187 Austin** St. Augustine, whose *De opera monachorum* was frequently adduced in criticism of slack contemplatives; **the world** worldly as distinct from spiritual interests, with a probable ironic allusion to 1 John 2:15–17. **189 pricasour** hunter on horseback (with obscene overtones). **191 priking** tracking (with obscene overtones). **192 lust** desire. **193 seigh** saw; **purfiled** trimmed. **194 grys** fur of the gray squirrel, which monks were forbidden to wear. **200 in good point** in good condition. **201 stepe** large (a sign of lechery). **202 stemed** gleamed; **forneys of a leed** furnace under a cauldron. **205 for-pyned** wasted (away). **209 limitour** a friar who purchased the privilege of begging within certain limits; **solempne** pompous (i.e., the friar was actually wanton but maintained a pious exterior). **210 ordres foure** Franciscans, Dominicans, Carmelites, and Augustinians. **213 at his owne cost** i.e., he performed the marriage ceremony without a fee after the "yonge wommen" had become pregnant as a result of his ministrations. **214 post** post (cf. "pillar of the Church"), with obscene overtones. **216 frankeleyns** wealthy landowners in the country. **217 worthy wommen** wealthy ladies (worthy in their own estimation). **219 curat** priest with a cure of souls, a parish priest. **220 licentiat** licensed to hear confessions. **221 swetely** sweetly (cheerfully). **224 pitaunce** pittance (i.e., monetary satisfaction from the penitent which the friar eagerly accepted and in return for which he gave absolution). **226 is wel y-shrive** has confessed well (ironic). **227 make avaunt** boast. **230 wepe** weep (for one's sins at confession; such weeping was customarily expected of the truly contrite). **232 yeve** give. **233 tipet** a long strip of cloth fastened to the sleeve at one end. **236 rote** a round or oval stringed instrument without a neck played by plucking (here "play on a rote" probably has obscene overtones). **237 yeddinges** songs. **241 tappestere** barmaid. **242 lazar** leper; **beggestere** female beggar (friars were supposed to offer spiritual assistance to the sick and needy). **247 poraille** poor folk. **248 vitaille** victuals. **250 curteys** cf. l. 99, of which this is an echo. **251 vertuous** (ironic). **253 ferme** fee (for the privilege of begging in a certain area). **256 In principio** the opening of the Gospel of St. John—"In the beginning [was the Word]"—the first fourteen lines of which were used by the friars as a devotional recital, or abused to impress their illiterate victims. **257 ferthing** farthing (becomes a pun in the Summoner's Tale). **258 purchas** personal gain (which was greater than the amount returned to the friary). **260 love-dayes** days appointed to settle disputes out of court. The implication is that the friar liked to act as arbiter on such occasions and accepted bribes from the litigants. **261 cloisterer** contemplative who remained in his cloister. **262 cope** a cape made in the form of a semicircle. England was famous in the latter fourteenth century for the production of elaborately embroidered copes, and the friars were notorious, in spite of their voluntary poverty, for wearing very expensive ones. **263 maister** master (at the university), with a reference to Matt. 23:10 (and the surrounding context), frequently used in the antifraternal literature of the period. **266 lipsed** lisped (as an affectation). **273 mottelee** particolored cloth, or cloth with a figured design used for liveries, especially on state occasions, probably here a sign of ostentation. **275 fetisly** elegantly. **276 solempnely** pompously. **277 Souninge** calling attention to. **278 see were kept** (free of hostile ships). **279 Middleburgh** a port on the coast (across from Orwell) where the wool staple was located between 1384 and 1388. **280 sheeldes** French *écus*; the Merchant was illegally making a profit in foreign exchange. **283 estatly** of high estate (i.e., the Merchant feigned prosperity). **284 chevisaunce** usury. **285 worthy** (ironic. Cf. ll. 43, 47, 50, 64, 68). **288** "Who had studied logic a long time." **292 courtepy** coat. **293 benefyce** benefice (i.e., the Clerk had not obtained a parish, placed it in the hands of a vicar, and used the income to study. Cf. l. 507). **294 offyce** secular office. **295 him was lever** he had rather. **296 Twenty bokes** a large number of books. **298 robes** Cf. ll. 262–265; **fithele** fiddle; **sautrye** psaltery, a stringed instrument somewhat resembling a zither. **299 philosophre** in this context a lover of wisdom, with a pun involved because alchemists, who were lovers of gold, were also called philosophers. **301 hente** gain. **308 hy sentence** elevated doctrine. **309 Souninge in** pointing the way toward. **311 Sergeant of the Lawe** a barrister especially selected for royal service because of distinction in his profession; **war and wys** wary and wise (in a worldly sense). **312 parvys** the nave and courtyard of St. Paul's Cathedral, London, where a number of notaries did a flourishing business and where lawyers resorted in the afternoon. **315 wyse** The implication is that the Sergeant was not so wise as his words. **316 in assyse** sessions held by justices acting under special commission. **317 By patente** by royal letters patent making a special appointment; **by pleyn comissioun** by general commission. **319 fees and robes** money and suits of clothing donated by grateful clients. **320 purchasour** buyer of land (indicating that the administration of justice was not only lucrative but offered opportunities to obtain land). **321 fee simple** without encumbrance. **322 infect** invalidated (i.e., he had clear title to his holdings). **325 In termes** in formal language; **caas and domes** cases and judgments. **326 king William** William the Conqueror (a satirical exaggeration calling attention to the Sergeant's assumed knowledge). **327** i.e., draw up legal documents. **329 pleyn by rote** fully word for word. **330 hoomly** in homely attire (ironic); **medlee** particolored cloth. **331 ceint** girdle; **barres** metal ornaments. **333 Frankeleyn** wealthy landowner (cf. the later *country squire*). **335 sangwyn** sanguine (i.e., dominated by the sanguine humor, a condition that implied a desire for feminine companionship, good food, and gaiety). **336 morwe** morning; **sop** white bread in a sauce of wine, almond paste, and spices. **337 wone** custom. **338 Epicurus** Greek philosopher, castigated by Cicero, Boethius, and by medieval authorities for his doctrine that pleasure is the highest good; **sone** son (disciple). **342 Seint Iulian** St. Julian, said to have abandoned his wealth and station to feed the poor and thus invited Christ to dinner. The application to the Franklin is ironic. **343 after oon** of uniform high quality. **344 envyned** possessing a good wine cellar. **347 snewed** snowed. **352 breem** bream; **luce** luce or pike; **stewe** fishpond. **355 table dormant** a table set up permanently instead of the usual medieval board placed on trestles and taken down after meals. **357 sessiouns** sessions (of the justice of the peace. In 1388 there were by statute six justices of the peace in every county. Their competence was properly regarded with suspicion by the government in the latter fourteenth century). **358 knight of the shire** member of Parliament from his district. **359 anlas** broad, double-edged hunting knife; **gipser** an ornamental purse. **361 shirreve** sheriff (whose chief functions were to empanel juries, to authorize bailiffs to make arrests, and to issue summonses); **countour** accountant (with the implication that the Franklin knew how to make his office profitable for himself). **362 vavasour** originally a knight of inferior status but used loosely for substantial landowners. Cf. use of *worthy* in ll. 43, 47, 50, 64, 68. **364 Webbe** weaver; **tapicer** maker of tapestries. **365 liveree** here the livery of a parish fraternity. Since the occupations mentioned were of minor civic importance in the late fourteenth century in London, the general impression created by these fraternal brethren would have been one of ridiculous pretentiousness. **367 apyked** adorned. **368 y-chaped** ornamented at the top of the sheath, here ostentatiously with silver. **371 burgeys** burgess. **372 yeldhalle** guildhall; **deys** dias (position of honor). No member of the occupations here mentioned became an alderman in London between 1370 and 1400. Chaucer is satirizing minor tradesmen for pretentiousness and the whole passage is humorous. **373 wisdom** (ironic, since the "wisdom" consisted of property and income). **375 catel** property; **rente** income. **378 ma dame** ironic reference to the pride of the wives. **379 vigilyës** vigils (festivals of the fraternity). **381 for the nones** at that time. **382 mary-bones** marrow bones (for stock). **383 poudre-marchant** powdered spices; **galingale** galangal (the powdered roots of *alpinia officinarum* or *a. calcarata*, once widely used for medicine and for flavoring). **386 mortreaux** puddings of highly seasoned fish or meat; **pye** mixture of highly seasoned meats and eggs baked in a heavy crust. **388 mormal** ulcer. **389 blankmanger** white sauce. **390 woning** dwelling. **391 Dertemouthe** Dartmouth. **392 rouncy** probably a large, awkward horse; **as he couthe** as best he could (i.e., he was a poor rider). **393 falding** coarse wool. **394 laas** a cord worn as a baldric. **396** i.e., he was well tanned. **397 good felawe** good companion (ironic. Cf. ll. 650, 652, 655). **398–399** i.e., he knew how to steal wine from the casks on board ship while the merchant (chapman) who was importing them from Bordeaux was unwary. **400 nyce conscience** what he regarded as foolish conscience (cf. l. 142). **402 by water** i.e., he threw his victims into the sea. **403 craft** skill. **404 stremes** currents. **406 herberwe** harbor, safe anchorage; **mone** moon (as it was useful for calculating tides); **lodemenage** piloting. **406 Hulle to Cartage** i.e., from England to Spain. **407 hardy . . . and wys to undertake** daring and crafty to make a venture. **410** i.e., between Scandinavia and Spain. **411 cryke** creek mouth (for surreptitious landings). **412 barge** small sailing vessel. **416 astronomye** astronomy, i.e., astrology, the use of which in medicine was ridiculed by the best opinion of the time. **418 In houres** i.e., treated him with reference to the planetary influences for each hour of the day; **magik naturel** "natural" as distinguished from "black," or malevolent, magic. **419 fortunen** determine the good or bad fortune of; **ascendent** the constellation rising at the time of the calculation. **420 images** images of the signs of the zodiac, which were used by some physicians, but which were said by one distinguished and well-known fourteenth-century authority to "have no other value than that which they have by virtue of the material from which they are made." **421** i.e., he professed to know. **422 hoot . . . drye** the four qualities; each humor was thought to combine two of them. **423 humour** humor (i.e., blood, hot and moist; phlegm, cold and moist; choler, hot and dry; melancholy, cold and dry). **426 bote** remedy. **428 letuaries** lectuaries (syrups containing powdered medicines). **429 winne** win (gain profit). **431 Esculapius** legendary father of medicine, venerated throughout the antique world in a widespread cult. **432 Deiscorides** Dioscorides, ancient authority on pharmacology; **Rufus** (of Ephesus), authority on the parts of the body. **433 Ypocras** Hippocrates; **Haly** probably the Persian Hali ibn el Abbas; **Galien** Galen. **434 Serapion** probably an Arabic medical writer; **Razis** Arabic medical authority; **Avicen** Avicenna. **435 Averrois** Averroes; **Damascien** not identified with certainty; **Constantyn** translator of Arabic medical books. **436 Bernard** Bernard of Gordon, a French medical author of the fourteenth century, widely known in Chaucer's time; **Gatesden** John Gaddesden, physician to Edward II; **Gilbertyn** Gilbertus Anglicus, English physician of the thirteenth century. **440 litel on the Bibel** Physicians were famous neither for piety nor for sound ethical practice. **441 sangwin** red; **pers** blue. **442 sendal** silk. **443 esy of dispence** loth to spend money. **446 lovede gold** (ironic. Cf. l. 299). **447 Wyf** woman, here a woman of the working class; **bisyde Bath** perhaps the parish of St. Michael-without-the-walls, adjoining Bath on the north. **448 som-del** somewhat; **deef** deaf (cf. Matt. 11:15; 13:9, 43; Mark 4:9, 23; Luke 8:8; 14:35; Matt. 13:15; Isa. 6:9–10, the applicability of which is clear in the Wyf's Prologue). **449 haunt** skill. **450** Ypres and Ghent were centers of clothmaking, but the cloth of Bath was inferior; what is meant is that the Wife was very good in her own estimation. **452 offring** offering (the desire to be first at the offering in Church was conventionally regarded as a manifestation of pride). **455 coverchiefs** cloths worn over the head; in this instance their quality and weight (exaggerated) indicate ostentation; **fyne . . . of grounde** finely textured. **458 hosen** coverings for the feet and legs. **461 worthy** cf. ll. 43, etc. **462 at chirche-dore** at the door of the church, where marriage ceremonies were customarily held during the Middle Ages; **fyve** five (cf. John 4:1–19). **463 Withouten** aside from. **464 as nouthe** at present. **465 thryes** thrice. **467 Boloigne** Boulogne-sur-mer, where there was a shrine to the Blessed Virgin. **468 Galice** Galicia in Spain; **seint Iame** the shrine of St. James at Compostella; **Coloigne** Cologne, where the tomb of the Magi was said to be located. **469 coude** knew. **470 Gat-tothed** having the front teeth set wide apart, a characteristic regarded as a sign of boldness and lechery. **471 amblere** pacer. **472 Y-wimpled** wearing a wimple, a headdress covering the cheeks and chin. **473 bokeler . . . targe** small shield. **474 foot-mantel** outer skirt. **476 carpe** talk boldly. **477 remedyes of love** cures for love as described by Ovid in the *Remedia amoris* (with the implication, made explicit in the next line, that she also knew the techniques of the *Ars amatoria*, and so had need of the remedies). **478 olde daunce** old dance (i.e., sexual intercourse for delight together with its various preliminaries). **487 y-preved** proved; **ofte sythes** many times. **488 cursen** excommunicate (for failure to pay tithes). **489 yeven** give. **490 parisshens** parishioners. **494 lafte** ceased. **496 ferreste** farthest; **muche and lyte** whether of high or low estate. **499 wroghte** performed (good deeds). **500 gospel** Cf. Matt. 5:19. **502 gold** i.e., the wise; **iren** iron (i.e., the ignorant). **504 lewed** unlearned. **506 shiten** Figurative language involving excrement was frequently used to describe sin. **508 clennesse** innocence, or freedom from sin. **509** i.e., he did not turn his benefice over to a vicar for a small part of its income and go elsewhere to increase his earnings. Cf. l. 293. Chaucer shared with Wiclif a distaste for pluralism. **510 sheep** parishioners. **511 sëynt Poules** St. Paul's Cathedral, London. **512 chaunterie** chantry, an office for which the priest said mass daily for the souls of the dead. There were thirty-five chantries at St. Paul's in 1380, each celebrant receiving about seven marks a year. **513** i.e., to be retained as chaplain by a gild. **514 folde** sheepfold (parish). **515 wolf** i.e., the devil. **516 mercenarie** hireling (cf. John 10:11–17). **518 despitous** merciless. **519 daungerous** severe (in lordly fashion); **digne** haughty. **525 snibben** reprimand; **for the nones** for the time being. **527 wayted after** demanded. **528 spyced conscience** affected scrupulousness with reference to trivialities. **529 lore** teaching. **531 Plowman** here probably intended to suggest a figure typifying the apostolic succession, frequently described in terms of "plowmen" and "plowing" in commentaries on Scripture. **532 y-lad** carried; **fother** load. **533 swinker** worker. **535–537** Cf. Matt. 22:37–39. **536 thogh him gamed or smerte** i.e., whether the consequences were pleasant or unpleasant to him. **538 dyke** dig ditches; **delve** dig for cultivation. **542 catel** property. **543 tabard** coat; **mere** mare, used as a riding horse only by the humble. **544 Reve** reeve, a manorial official, in this instance with the functions of a steward. **545 Sumnour** summoner, a kind of police officer for the ecclesiastical courts; **Pardoner** a priest licensed to collect funds for charitable purposes in return for remission of penance. **546 Maunciple** purchaser of provisions for a college, in this instance for the Inner or Middle Temple, London; **namo** no more. **547 stout** strong; **carl** fellow (with connotations of low station and lack of refinement); **for the nones** for the occasion (here used as an intensive; i.e., he was very strong). **548 braun** brawn; **eek** also. **550 ram** the prize awarded for victory in wrestling matches (suggestive of the vice of discord, represented in the visual arts by showing a wrestling match). **551 thikke knarre** a thick knot (in wood; hence a tough, unyielding, and troublesome person). **552 harre** hinge. **555 spade** The red spade beard was suggestive of treachery. **556 cop** tip. **557 werte** wart (suggestive in medieval physiognomy of a violent fornicator). **559 nose-thirles** nostrils (here wide and black to indicate lust and anger). **561 forneys** furnace (the large mouth being indicative of the boasting and swearing described in the next line). **562 Ianglere** jangler, a person given to irreverent talk; **goliardeys** a follower of Goliath (Golias) known for vain speech (Ps. 143:8, 11) and boasting (Ecclus. 47:5), **563 harlotryes** base and villainous acts. **564 tollen thryes** take three times the toll due him for his service (the toll being a percentage of the grain he processed for his customers). **565 thombe of gold** from the proverb, "An honest miller has a thumb of gold"; i.e., there are no honest millers. **567 baggepype** bagpipe, suggestive of discord and (because of its shape) lechery. **568 out of towne** The fact that the Miller leads the pilgrims on their way to the tune of a bagpipe has, in view of the nature and function of the pilgrimage, strong ironic implications. **569 temple** either the Inner Temple or the Middle Temple, London. **570 achatours** buyers. **571 vitaille** victuals. **572 by taille** by recording his indebtedness on tally sticks (i.e., a stick was split lengthwise to form two, one for the lender and one for the debtor. Notches were made to show indebtedness with the two sticks together in their original position. When the two parts were later brought together and shown to tally, the amount of the indebtedness could be verified). **573 Algate** either way; **wayted** watched carefully; **achat** purchasing. **574 ay biforn** always financially ahead. **576 pace** outdo. **584 wood** insane. **585 scarsly** abstemiously; **as him list desire** as he wished. **587 cas** case. **588 sette hir aller cappe** made fools of them all (by arranging his transactions in such a way as to make money for himself on the side). **589 colerik** bilious (i.e., irascible. Cf. l. 423). **590–592** The close shave and the fashion of wearing the hair suggest low station. **593–594** Thin legs were suggestive of lust and intemperance. **596** i.e., no auditor could find fault with his accounts. **599 neet** cattle. **604 arrerage** arrears. **605 herde** herdsman; **hyne** hind. **606 covyne** deceitfulness. **608 woning** dwelling. **610 purchace** deal. **615 mister** mystery (craft). **616 wrighte** workman. **617 stot** workhorse. **618 Scot** common name for a horse. **619 pers** blue. **622 Baldeswelle** a small village. **623 Tukked** i.e., with his surcoat tucked up (an indication of low status). **626 cherubinnes face** like the cherubim in color (dark red). **627 sawcefleem** i.e., his face was red, pimply, and swollen about the eyes, a condition indicative of an extreme sanguine complexion implying lechery and a bad diet. The eyebrows and beard described below are in keeping with this condition. **628 sparwe** sparrow, a bird traditionally used to typify lecherousness. **629 scalled** scabbed; **piled** scanty. **631 litarge** litharge (lead monoxide); **brimstoon** sulphur. **632 Boras** borax; **ceruce** white lead. **636 garleek, oynons, and eek lekes** i.e., a diet indicative of carnality (cf. Num. 11:5). **645 Watte** a name taught to jays (cf. *Polly* taught to parrots). **646 him grope** test him. **648 Questio quid juris?** ["The question is, what part of the law (is relevant)?"], a phrase heard frequently at the archdeacon's court. **649 gentil** noble (ironic); **harlot** low fellow. **650 bettre felawe** better companion (ironic). **654 prively** secretly; **a finch eek coude he pulle** either "he could love a wench carnally," or "he could part a fool from his money." **657 erchedeknes curs** archdeacon's excommunication (the punishment meted out to the unrepentant in the ecclesiastical court, presided over by the archdeacon). **663 curs wol slay** excommunication will slay spiritually; **assoilling** absolution (i.e., properly administered excommunication and absolution are efficacious, but the Summoner's threats of excommunication are made for the wrong reason, so that they do not promote contrition, just as the friar's easy absolutions tend to destroy contrition. It should be remembered that the mercy of the New Law is available only to the contrite and that, to the medieval mind, a society without "humble and contrite" hearts is a society where tyranny, oppression, and injustice flourish). **664 significavit** first word of a writ remanding an excommunicated person to prison under civil authority. **665 daunger** dominion (i.e., under his power); **at his owne gyse** at his will. **666 girles** probably here women. **667 al hir reed** adviser to all of them. **668 gerland** garland (suggestive of idolatry). **669 ale-stake** sign for an alehouse (conventionally a branch or bush). **670 bokeler** shield (a grotesque attribute, probably intended to suggest conceptions like those in Rom. 16:18 and Phil. 3:18–19). **672 Rouncival** the hospital of the Blessed Mary of Rouncivalle, Westminster; **compeer** companion. **673 court of Rome** the papal court, where the Pardoner claims to have obtained his pardons. **675 burdoun** burden of a song, but also a staff, the latter meaning forming a humorous (and obscene) suggestion. **677 yelow as wex** The thin yellow hair was thought to be indicative of effeminacy. **678 strike** hank. **679 ounces** bunches. **681 colpons** strips. **684 Him thoughte** it seemed to him; **newe Iet** new fashion (i.e., without a hood. The canons of St. Mary of Rouncivalle wore black hoods to show that they were dead to the world; the Pardoner is dead to anything else). **685 Dischevele** with hair hanging loose, another indication of worldliness. **686 glaringe eyen** glaring eyes, regarded as a sign of eunuchry. **687 vernicle** small copy of a kerchief, the original of which was in Rome, said to have been lent to Christ by St. Veronica as He was bearing the Cross and to show the imprint of His face. The Pardoner wears it to show that he had been to Rome, but since the Pardoner consistently refuses to "bear the Cross," his vernicle has strong ironic overtones. **689 Bret-ful** brimful. **690** The goatish voice is consistent with the other physical characteristics that indicate eunuchry. **691** The lack of a beard indicated eunuchry and presumption. **692 gelding or a mare** i.e., either a *castratus* or a eunuch from birth. For the significance of this condition (which is an attribute), see Deut. 23:1, which the Gloss explains as an admonition against those "who live softly, nor perfect any virile [i.e., virtuous] work." For the reverse of this eunuchry, see the third type described in Matt. 19:12, who, as the Gloss explains, "are continent for the sake of Christ." The general implication is that the Pardoner is spiritually sterile. **694 fro Berwick into Ware** i.e., in all England north of London. **696 male** sack; **pilwe-beer** pillowcase. **697 our lady** Our Lady's. **698 gobet** piece. **700 hente** seized (cf. Matt. 14:29–31). **701 croys** cross; **latoun** latten, a mixture of copper and zinc hammered thin. **703 relikes** remains of holy persons used for purposes of veneration (ironic). **704 up-on lond** in the country. **707 Iapes** tricks. **708 apes** fools. **710 noble ecclesiaste** noble ecclesiastic (in appearance). **711 rede a lessoun or a storie** read a lesson (from the Old Testament) or the Gospel narrative for the day (with the implication that the Pardoner was a good narrator). **712 alderbest** best of all; **offertorie** the offertory in the mass, which followed the sermon and which the Pardoner would read when he was celebrant and in a position to preach. **714 affyle** make smooth. **718 Thestat tharray** the estate, the array; **eek** also. **720 gentil** noble (ironic). **721 faste by the Belle** right next to the Bell, probably a tavern, possibly a house of ill repute. **723 baren us** conducted ourselves. **728 narette it nat** do not attribute it. **729 pleynly** openly (for the implications of this passage, see Cicero, *Offices*, 1.28.97). **734 moot** should. **741–742** squeamishness about language was associated with hypocrisy. **743 Plato** i.e., *Timaeus*, 29, where it is said that words should describe the intelligible rather than the tangible. **752 us leste** it pleased us. **754 marshal in an halle** an official in a nobleman's retinue whose duties included the assignment of rooms and provisions to guests, the supervision of meals, and the keeping of good order (humorous exaggeration). **755 eyen stepe** Cf. l. 201. **756 Chepe** the Ward of Cheap, London. **757 wys . . . and wel y-taught** (in his own estimation; the Host consistently misunderstands the tales he hears). **760** i.e., after the bills had been paid. **767 herberwe** lodging. **772 blisful martir** Cf. l. 17. **779 yow lyketh** it pleases you. **786 seche** seek. **787 make it wys** to deliberate. **794 viage** voyage (journey); **tales tweye** two tales (but Chaucer decided later to include only one tale by each pilgrim on the way to Canterbury). **800 sentence** implied doctrine; **solas** pleasing surface (cf. Horace, *Ars poetica*, l. 343). **801 our aller cost** at the expense of all of us. **822 echon** each one. **825 our aller cok** cock (ruler) of all of us. **827 a litel more than pas** a short distance. **828 watering of seint Thomas** a brook about two miles down the road to Kent. **831 forward** promise; **it yow recorde** recall it to you. **838 draweth cut** draw straws; **ferrer twinne** depart farther. **846 aventure, or sort, or cas** all words for chance, which, as Boethius informs us, is a mere word without a referent. **850 forward and . . . composicioun** promise and agreement. **856 a Goddes name** in God's name.

THE KNIGHT'S TALE

In medieval books it was customary to place the most important materials at the beginning and at the end. The Knight's Tale, which opens The Canterbury Tales, sets the main themes of the collection, themes which are intertwined in various ways in the subsequent tales and brought to a logical conclusion in the last tale, which is not a tale at all in the usual sense of the word, but a sermon delivered by the Parson on the subject of penance. This fact, however, is not immediately apparent and hence requires some explanation.

In the first place, as a general rule, narratives written before the middle of the eighteenth century, whether poetic or dramatic, even though their apparent subjects may seem remote, are always translatable, so to speak, in terms of everyday life. Chaucer's tale is not actually about events that took place once years ago in ancient Athens. He did not believe in Venus, Mars, Saturn, and so on; nor did he think that Palamon and Arcite were ever historical personages. Although he probably regarded some details of his narrative— like the elaborate funeral of Arcite—as being reflections of ancient practice, he was not, basically, interested in history. Instead, his tale is about principles which he regarded as being of the utmost importance in his own life and in the lives of his contemporaries. The classical setting, the characters, and the patterns of the narrative are all figurative devices used

to make ideas attractive and vital. That is, they are used as means to an end. This does not imply, however, that these means are not important. Traditional ideas tend to lose their significance and impact when they are expressed abstractly. They become empty and commonplace. To make them meaningful they must be conveyed in a vehicle which is in itself striking, attractive, and interesting.

During the latter part of the fourteenth century there was an increasing interest in classical materials among noblemen and ecclesiastics. The vehicle Chaucer selected, therefore, was one particularly suited to his courtly audience. It lent authority, as well as interest, to what he had to say. At the same time that classical materials were becoming more popular, there was a renewed interest in The Consolation of Philosophy of Boethius, a work that expressed orthodox principles of Christian philosophy in a language easily made harmonious with a classical setting. When Chaucer combined philosophical materials from Boethius and the trappings of classical narrative, he was making a deliberate appeal to the most advanced and cultivated tastes of his day.

The basic problem of the Knight's Tale is not very different from that of the Oresteia of Aeschylus. In that trilogy the wrathful furies which have devastated the house of Atreus are transformed into Eumenides, or beneficial contributors to civil peace, by the wisdom of Athena. Chaucer could not have known the Oresteia, but in his tale the misdirected concupiscible and irascible passions that have devastated the lineage of Thebes are transformed into constructive impulses by the wisdom of Theseus. In the tale, the concupiscible passions are exemplified in Palamon, a devotee of Venus, or the pleasures of the flesh. The irascible passions, which were thought to arise when concupiscence is frustrated and which were said to destroy those whom they infected, are exemplified in Arcite, a devotee of Mars, or unreasonable wrath. The difference between Palamon and Arcite is one of degree. Concupiscence checked may lead to wrath, and if it is strong enough, to mania and death. Where concupiscence is sufficiently amenable to reason, however, it may be controlled so that the fatal consequences of selfish wrath do not follow. In the tale both alternatives are presented. The wrathful Arcite is destroyed, but Palamon is directed by Theseus and his wisdom to a reasonable solution, marriage. In Christian terms, marriage is the first of the sacraments to be established as a remedy against the inborn concupiscence inherited from the Fall.

The wisdom of Theseus is, of course, expressed in Christian terms, or that is, in terms of the New Law. Under the Old Law men were doomed to suffer strict justice for their transgressions. A rigorous code of righteousness made peace of mind and hope for salvation extremely difficult. The New Law, brought by Christ, or as He was frequently called, the Wisdom of the Father, offers mercy to all those who are penitent. Chaucer's Theseus is a kind of chivalric exemplification of this kind of wisdom. Since its efficacy depends on the penitence of the transgressor, the concluding sermon of the Parson establishes in a detailed way the conditions for transferring one's place in the order of justice to a place in the order of mercy. That is, if there are to be wise men in the sense that Theseus is wise and if we expect to enjoy the kind of mercy offered to Palamon, it behooves us to listen to the Parson.

Meanwhile, we should recall that in Christian terms marriage is a sacrament by virtue of the fact that it reflects the hierarchical relationship between Christ and the Church. This relationship is analogous with that between the spirit and the flesh, or again, with that between wisdom and the passions. This basic hierarchy is suggested in various ways in the tale: in the marriage of Theseus at the beginning, in the marriage of Palamon and Emily, and in the hierarchical relationship finally established between the city of Athens, representing wisdom, and the city of Thebes, representing discord and passion. The wisdom of the New Law, like the wisdom of Athena in Aeschylus, offers a solution to the problems of discord, both in society and within the human heart.

Although his themes are serious, the Knight tells his story with good-natured detachment, and the behavior of his characters is frequently comic. Palamon and Arcite are often ridiculous, and the ladies in the tale are amusingly feminine. Chaucer's seriousness is intellectual, not emotional.

Chaucer's immediate source for this tale was the Teseida of Boccaccio, used in conjunction with a glossed text of the Thebaid of Statius. Whether or not he read the explanatory notes Boccaccio wrote for his poem is not certain, but in any event, their content would have been obvious to him.

Iamque domos patrias, Scithice post aspera gentis Prelia, laurigero, &c.

[Statius, *Theb.* xii. 519.]

Whylom, as olde stories tellen us,
Ther was a duk that highte Theseus;
Of Athenes he was lord and governour,
And in his tyme swich a conquerour,
That gretter was ther noon under the sonne. 5
Ful many a riche contree hadde he wonne;
What with his wisdom and his chivalrye,
He conquered al the regne of Femenye,
That whylom was y-cleped Scithia;
And weddede the quene Ipolita, 10
And broghte hir hoom with him in his contree
With muchel glorie and greet solempnitee,
And eek hir yonge suster Emelye.
And thus with victorie and with melodye
Lete I this noble duk to Athenes ryde, 15
And al his hoost, in armes, him bisyde.

And certes, if it nere to long to here,
I wolde han told yow fully the manere,
How wonnen was the regne of Femenye
By Theseus, and by his chivalrye; 20
And of the grete bataille for the nones
Bitwixen Athenës and Amazones;
And how asseged was Ipolita,
The faire hardy quene of Scithia;
And of the feste that was at hir weddinge, 25
And of the tempest at hir hoom-cominge;
But al that thing I moot as now forbere.
I have, God woot, a large feeld to ere,
And wayke been the oxen in my plough.
The remenant of the tale is long y-nough. 30
I wol nat letten eek noon of this route;
Lat every felawe telle his tale aboute,
And lat see now who shal the soper winne;
And ther I lefte, I wol ageyn biginne.

This duk, of whom I make mencioun, 35
When he was come almost unto the toun,
In al his wele and in his moste pryde,
He was war, as he caste his eye asyde,

Wher that ther kneled in the hye weye
A companye of ladies, tweye and tweye,   40
Ech after other, clad in clothes blake;
But swich a cry and swich a wo they make,
That in this world nis creature livinge,
That herde swich another weymentinge;
And of this cry they nolde never stenten,   45
Til they the reynes of his brydel henten.
"What folk ben ye, that at myn hoom-cominge
Perturben so my feste with cryinge?"
Quod Theseus, "have ye so greet envye
Of myn honour, that thus compleyne and crye?   50
Or who hath yow misboden, or offended?
And telleth me if it may been amended;
And why that ye ben clothed thus in blak?"
    The eldest lady of hem alle spak,
When she hadde swowned with a deedly chere,   55
That it was routhe for to seen and here,
And seyde: "Lord, to whom Fortune hath yiven
Victorie, and as a conquerour to liven,
Noght greveth us your glorie and your honour;
But we biseken mercy and socour.   60
Have mercy on our wo and our distresse.
Som drope of pitee, thurgh thy gentillesse,
Up-on us wrecched wommen lat thou falle.
For certes, lord, ther nis noon of us alle,
That she nath been a duchesse or a quene;   65
Now be we caitifs, as it is wel sene:
Thanked be Fortune, and hir false wheel,
That noon estat assureth to be weel.
And certes, lord, to abyden your presence,
Here in the temple of the goddesse Clemence   70
We han ben waytinge al this fourtenight;
Now help us, lord, sith it is in thy might.
    I wrecche, which that wepe and waille thus,
Was whylom wyf to king Capaneus,
That starf at Thebes, cursed be that day!   75
And alle we, that been in this array,
And maken al this lamentacioun,
We losten alle our housbondes at that toun,
Whyl that the sege ther-aboute lay.
And yet now the olde Creon, weylaway!   80
That lord is now of Thebes the citee,
Fulfild of ire and of iniquitee,
He, for despyt, and for his tirannye,
To do the dede bodyes vileinye,
Of alle our lordes, whiche that ben slawe,   85
Hath alle the bodyes on an heep y-drawe,

And wol nat suffren hem, by noon assent,
Neither to been y-buried nor y-brent,
But maketh houndes ete hem in despyt."
And with that word, with-outen more respyt,   90
They fillen gruf, and cryden pitously,
"Have on us wrecched wommen som mercy,
And lat our sorwe sinken in thyn herte."
    This gentil duk doun from his courser sterte
With herte pitous, whan he herde hem speke.   95
Him thoughte that his herte wolde breke,
Whan he saugh hem so pitous and so mat,
That whylom weren of so greet estat.
And in his armes he hem alle up hente,
And hem conforteth in ful good entente;   100
And swoor his ooth, as he was trewe knight,
He wolde doon so ferforthly his might
Up-on the tyraunt Creon hem to wreke,
That al the peple of Grece sholde speke
How Creon was of Theseus y-served,   105
As he that hadde his deeth ful wel deserved.
And right anoon, with-outen more abood,
His baner he desplayeth, and forth rood
To Thebes-ward, and al his host bisyde;
No neer Athenës wolde he go ne ryde,   110
Ne take his ese fully half a day,
But onward on his wey that night he lay;
And sente anoon Ipolita the quene,
And Emelye hir yonge suster shene,
Un-to the toun of Athenës to dwelle;   115
And forth he rit; ther nis namore to telle.
    The rede statue of Mars, with spere and targe,
So shyneth in his whyte baner large,
That alle the feeldes gliteren up and doun;
And by his baner born is his penoun   120
Of gold ful riche, in which ther was y-bete
The Minotaur, which that he slough in Crete.
Thus rit this duk, thus rit this conquerour,
And in his host of chivalrye the flour,
Til that he cam to Thebes, and alighte   125
Faire in a feeld, ther as he thoghte fighte.
But shortly for to speken of this thing,
With Creon, which that was of Thebes king,
He faught, and slough him manly as a knight
In pleyn bataille, and putte the folk to flight;   130
And by assault he wan the citee after,
And rente adoun bothe wal, and sparre, and
    rafter;
And to the ladyes he restored agayn

The bones of hir housbondes that were slayn,
To doon obsequies, as was tho the gyse. 135
But it were al to long for to devyse
The grete clamour and the waymentinge
That the ladyes made at the brenninge
Of the bodyes, and the grete honour
That Theseus, the noble conquerour, 140
Doth to the ladyes, whan they from him wente;
But shortly for to telle is myn entente.
Whan that this worthy duk, this Theseus,
Hath Creon slayn, and wonne Thebes thus,
Stille in that feeld he took al night his reste, 145
And dide with al the contree as him leste.
   To ransake in the tas of bodyes dede,
Hem for to strepe of harneys and of wede,
The pilours diden bisinesse and cure,
After the bataille and disconfiture. 150
And so bifel, that in the tas they founde,
Thurgh-girt with many a grevous blody wounde,
Two yonge knightes ligging by and by,
Bothe in oon armes, wroght ful richely,
Of whiche two, Arcita hight that oon, 155
And that other knight hight Palamon.
Nat fully quike, ne fully dede they were,
But by hir cote-armures, and by hir gere,
The heraudes knewe hem best in special,
As they that weren of the blood royal 160
Of Thebes, and of sustren two y-born.
Out of the tas the pilours han hem torn,
And han hem caried softe un-to the tente
Of Theseus, and he ful sone hem sente
To Athenës, to dwellen in prisoun 165
Perpetuelly, he nolde no raunsoun.
And whan this worthy duk hath thus y-don,
He took his host, and hoom he rood anon
With laurer crowned as a conquerour;
And there he liveth, in Ioye and in honour, 170
Terme of his lyf; what nedeth wordes mo?
And in a tour, in angwish and in wo,
Dwellen this Palamoun and eek Arcite,
For evermore, ther may no gold hem quyte.
   This passeth yeer by yeer, and day by day, 175
Til it fil ones, in a morwe of May,
That Emelye, that fairer was to sene
Than is the lilie upon his stalke grene,
And fresshher than the May with floures newe—
For with the rose colour stroof hir hewe, 180
I noot which was the fairer of hem two—

Er it were day, as was hir wone to do,
She was arisen, and al redy dight;
For May wol have no slogardye a-night.
The sesoun priketh every gentil herte, 185
And maketh him out of his sleep to sterte,
And seith "Arys, and do thyn observaunce."
This maked Emelye have remembraunce
To doon honour to May, and for to ryse.
Y-clothed was she fresh, for to devyse; 190
Hir yelow heer was broyded in a tresse,
Bihinde hir bak, a yerde long, I gesse.
And in the gardin, at the sonne up-riste,
She walketh up and doun, and as hir liste
She gadereth floures, party whyte and rede, 195
To make a sotil gerland for hir hede,
And as an aungel hevenly she song.
The grete tour, that was so thikke and strong,
Which of the castel was the chief dongeoun,
(Ther-as the knightes weren in prisoun, 200
Of whiche I tolde yow, and tellen shal)
Was evene Ioynant to the gardin-wal,
Ther as this Emelye hadde hir pleyinge.
Bright was the sonne, and cleer that morweninge,
And Palamon, this woful prisoner, 205
As was his wone, by leve of his gayler,
Was risen, and romed in a chambre on heigh,
In which he al the noble citee seigh,
And eek the gardin, ful of braunches grene,
Ther-as this fresshe Emelye the shene 210
Was in hir walk, and romed up and doun.
This sorweful prisoner, this Palamoun,
Goth in the chambre, roming to and fro,
And to him-self compleyning of his wo;
That he was born, ful ofte he seyde, "alas!" 215
And so bifel, by aventure or cas,
That thurgh a window, thikke of many a barre
Of yren greet, and square as any sparre,
He caste his eye upon Emelya,
And ther-with-al he bleynte, and cryde "a!" 220
As though he stongen were un-to the herte.
And with that cry Arcite anon up-sterte,
And seyde, "Cosin myn, what eyleth thee,
That art so pale and deedly on to see?
Why crydestow? who hath thee doon offence? 225
For Goddes love, tak al in pacience
Our prisoun, for it may non other be;
Fortune hath yeven us this adversitee.
Som wikke aspect or disposicioun

Of Saturne, by sum constellacioun, 230
Hath yeven us this, al-though we hadde it sworn;
So stood the heven whan that we were born;
We moste endure it: this is the short and pleyn."
    This Palamon answerde, and seyde ageyn,
"Cosyn, for sothe, of this opinioun 235
Thou hast a veyn imaginacioun.
This prison caused me nat for to crye.
But I was hurt right now thurgh-out myn yë
In-to myn herte, that wol my bane be.
The fairnesse of that lady that I see 240
Yond in the gardin romen to and fro,
Is cause of al my crying and my wo.
I noot wher she be womman or goddesse;
But Venus is it, soothly, as I gesse."
And ther-with-al on kneës doun he fil, 245
And seyde: "Venus, if it be thy wil
Yow in this gardin thus to transfigure
Bifore me, sorweful wrecche creature,
Out of this prisoun help that we may scapen.
And if so be my destinee be shapen 250
By eterne word to dyen in prisoun,
Of our linage have som compassioun,
That is so lowe y-broght by tirannye."
And with that word Arcite gan espye
Wher-as this lady romed to and fro. 255
And with that sighte hir beautee hurte him so,
That, if that Palamon was wounded sore,
Arcite is hurt as muche as he, or more.
And with a sigh he seyde pitously:
"The fresshe beautee sleeth me sodeynly 260
Of hir that rometh in the yonder place;
And, but I have hir mercy and hir grace,
That I may seen hir atte leeste weye,
I nam but deed; ther nis namore to seye."
    This Palamon, whan he tho wordes herde, 265
Dispitously he loked, and answerde:
"Whether seistow this in ernest or in pley?"
    "Nay," quod Arcite, "in ernest, by my fey!
God help me so, me list ful yvele pleye."
    This Palamon gan knitte his browes tweye: 270
"It nere," quod he, "to thee no greet honour
For to be fals, ne for to be traytour
To me, that am thy cosin and thy brother
Y-sworn ful depe, and ech of us til other,
That never, for to dyen in the peyne, 275
Til that the deeth departe shal us tweyne,
Neither of us in love to hindren other,

Figure 38 *The god of love shoots his arrow. The first arrow of love is beauty. See lines 240, 260.*

Ne in non other cas, my leve brother;
But that thou sholdest trewely forthren me
In every cas, and I shal forthren thee. 280
This was thyn ooth, and myn also, certeyn;
I wot right wel, thou darst it nat withseyn.
Thus artow of my counseil, out of doute.
And now thou woldest falsly been aboute
To love my lady, whom I love and serve, 285
And ever shal, til that myn herte sterve.
Now certes, fals Arcite, thou shalt nat so.
I loved hir first, and tolde thee my wo
As to my counseil, and my brother sworn
To forthre me, as I have told biforn. 290
For which thou art y-bounden as a knight
To helpen me, if it lay in thy might,
Or elles artow fals, I dar wel seyn."
    This Arcitë ful proudly spak ageyn,
"Thou shalt," quod he, "be rather fals than I; 295
But thou art fals, I telle thee utterly;
For *par amour* I loved hir first er thow.
What wiltow seyn? thou wistest nat yet now
Whether she be a womman or goddesse!
Thyn is affeccioun of holinesse, 300
And myn is love, as to a creature;
For which I tolde thee myn aventure
As to my cosin, and my brother sworn.
I pose, that thou lovedest hir biforn;

Wostow nat wel the olde clerkes sawe, 305
That "who shal yeve a lover any lawe?"
Love is a gretter lawe, by my pan,
Than may be yeve to any erthly man.
And therefore positif lawe and swich decree
Is broke al-day for love, in ech degree. 310
A man moot nedes love, maugree his heed.
He may nat fleen it, thogh he sholde be deed,
Al be she mayde, or widwe, or elles wyf.
And eek it is nat lykly, al thy lyf,
To stonden in hir grace; namore shal I; 315
For wel thou woost thy-selven, verraily,
That thou and I be dampned to prisoun
Perpetuelly; us gayneth no raunsoun.
We stryve as dide the houndes for the boon,
They foughte al day, and yet hir part was noon; 320
Ther cam a kyte, whyl that they were wrothe,
And bar awey the boon bitwixe hem bothe.
And therfore, at the kinges court, my brother,
Ech man for him-self, ther is non other.
Love if thee list; for I love and ay shal; 325
And soothly, leve brother, this is al.
Here in this prisoun mote we endure,
And everich of us take his aventure."
    Greet was the stryf and long bitwixe hem
        tweye,
If that I hadde leyser for to seye; 330
But to theffect. It happed on a day,
(To telle it yow as shortly as I may)
A worthy duk that highte Perotheus,
That felawe was un-to duk Theseus
Sin thilke day that they were children lyte, 335
Was come to Athenes, his felawe to visyte,
And for to pleye, as he was wont to do,
For in this world he loved no man so:
And he loved him as tendrely ageyn.
So wel they loved, as olde bokes seyn, 340
That whan that oon was deed, sothly to telle,
His felawe wente and soghte him doun in helle;
But of that story list me nat to wryte.
Duk Perotheus loved wel Arcite,
And hadde him knowe at Thebes yeer by yere; 345
And fynally, at requeste and preyere
Of Perotheus, with-oute any raunsoun,
Duk Theseus him leet out of prisoun,
Freely to goon, wher that him liste over-al,
In swich a gyse, as I you tellen shal. 350

This was the forward, pleynly for tendyte,
Bitwixen Theseus and him Arcite:
That if so were, that Arcite were y-founde
Ever in his lyf, by day or night or stounde
In any contree of this Theseus, 355
And he were caught, it was acorded thus,
That with a swerd he sholde lese his heed;
Ther nas non other remedye ne reed,
But taketh his leve, and homward he him spedde;
Let him be war, his nekke lyth to wedde! 360
    How greet a sorwe suffreth now Arcite!
The deeth he feleth thurgh his herte smyte;
He wepeth, wayleth, cryeth pitously;
To sleen him-self he wayteth prively.
He seyde, "Allas that day that I was born! 365
Now is my prison worse than biforn;
Now is me shape eternally to dwelle
Noght in purgatorie, but in helle.
Allas! that ever knew I Perotheus!
For elles hadde I dwelled with Theseus 370
Y-fetered in his prisoun ever-mo.
Than hadde I been in blisse, and nat in wo.
Only the sighte of hir, whom that I serve,
Though that I never hir grace may deserve,
Wolde han suffised right y-nough for me. 375
O dere cosin Palamon," quod he,
"Thyn is the victorie of this aventure,
Ful blisfully in prison maistow dure;
In prison? certes nay, but in paradys!
Wel hath fortune y-turned thee the dys, 380
That hast the sighte of hir, and I thabsence.
For possible is, sin thou hast hir presence,
And art a knight, a worthy and an able,
That by som cas, sin fortune is chaungeable,
Thou mayst to thy desyr som-tyme atteyne. 385
But I, that am exyled, and bareyne
Of alle grace, and in so greet despeir,
That ther nis erthe, water, fyr, ne eir,
Ne creature, that of hem maked is,
That may me helpe or doon confort in this. 390
Wel oughte I sterve in wanhope and distresse;
Farwel my lyf, my lust, and my gladnesse!
    Allas, why pleynen folk so in commune
Of purveyaunce of God, or of fortune,
That yeveth hem ful often in many a gyse 395
Wel bettre than they can hem-self devyse?
Som man desyreth for to han richesse,

That cause is of his mordre or greet siknesse.
And som man wolde out of his prison fayn,
That in his hous is of his meynee slayn.   400
Infinite harmes been in this matere;
We witen nat what thing we preyen here.
We faren as he that dronke is as a mous;
A dronke man wot wel he hath an hous,
But he noot which the righte wey is thider;   405
And to a dronke man the wey is slider.
And certes, in this world so faren we;
We seken faste after felicitee,
But we goon wrong ful often, trewely.
Thus may we seyen alle, and namely I,   410
That wende and hadde a greet opinioun,
That, if I mighte escapen from prisoun,
Than hadde I been in Ioye and perfit hele,
Ther now I am exyled fro my wele.
Sin that I may nat seen yow, Emelye,   415
I nam but deed; ther nis no remedye."
    Up-on that other syde Palamon,
Whan that he wiste Arcite was agon,
Swich sorwe he maketh, that the grete tour
Resouneth of his youling and clamour.   420
The pure fettres on his shines grete
Weren of his bittre salte teres wete.
"Allas!" quod he, "Arcita, cosin myn,
Of al our stryf, God woot, the fruyt is thyn.
Thow walkest now in Thebes at thy large,   425
And of my wo thou yevest litel charge.
Thou mayst, sin thou hast wisdom and manhede,
Assemblen alle the folk of our kinrede,
And make a werre so sharp on this citee,
That by som aventure, or som tretee,   430
Thou mayst have hir to lady and to wyf,
For whom that I mot nedes lese my lyf.
For, as by wey of possibilitee,
Sith thou art at thy large, of prison free,
And art a lord, greet is thyn avauntage,   435
More than is myn, that sterve here in a cage.
For I mot wepe and wayle, whyl I live,
With al the wo that prison may me yive,
And eek with peyne that love me yiveth also,
That doubleth al my torment and my wo."   440
Ther-with the fyr of Ielousye up-sterte
With-inne his brest, and hente him by the herte
So woodly, that he lyk was to biholde
The box-tree, or the asshen dede and colde.

Tho seyde he; "O cruel goddes, that governe   445
This world with binding of your word eterne,
And wryten in the table of athamaunt
Your parlement, and your eterne graunt,
What is mankinde more un-to yow holde
Than is the sheep, that rouketh in the folde?   450
For slayn is man right as another beste,
And dwelleth eek in prison and areste,
And hath siknesse, and greet adversitee,
And ofte tymes giltelees, pardee!
    What governaunce is in this prescience,   455
That giltelees tormenteth innocence?
And yet encreseth this al my penaunce,
That man is bounden to his observaunce,
For Goddes sake, to letten of his wille,
Ther as a beest may al his lust fulfille.   460
And whan a beest is deed, he hath no peyne;
But man after his deeth moot wepe and pleyne,
Though in this world he have care and wo:
With-outen doute it may stonden so.
The answere of this I lete to divynis,   465
But wel I woot, that in this world gret pyne is.
Allas! I see a serpent or a theef,
That many a trewe man hath doon mescheef,
Goon at his large, and wher him list may turne.
But I mot been in prison thurgh Saturne,   470
And eek thurgh Iuno, Ialous and eek wood,
That hath destroyed wel ny al the blood
Of Thebes, with his waste walles wyde.
And Venus sleeth me on that other syde
For Ielousye, and fere of him Arcite."   475
    Now wol I stinte of Palamon a lyte,
And lete him in his prison stille dwelle,
And of Arcita forth I wol yow telle.
    The somer passeth, and the nightes longe
Encresen double wyse the peynes stronge   480
Bothe of the lovere and the prisoner.
I noot which hath the wofullere mester.
For shortly for to seyn, this Palamoun
Perpetuelly is dampned to prisoun,
In cheynes and in fettres to ben deed;   485
And Arcite is exyled upon his heed
For ever-mo as out of that contree,
Ne never-mo he shal his lady see.
    Yow loveres axe I now this questioun,
Who hath the worse, Arcite or Palamoun?   490
That oon may seen his lady day by day,

But in prison he moot dwelle alway.
That other wher him list may ryde or go,
But seen his lady shal he never-mo.
Now demeth as yow liste, ye that can,   495
For I wol telle forth as I bigan.

Explicit prima pars. Sequitur pars secunda.
Whan that Arcite to Thebes comen was,
Ful ofte a day he swelte and seyde "allas,"
For seen his lady shal he never-mo.
And shortly to concluden al his wo,   500
So muche sorwe had never creature
That is, or shal, whyl that the world may dure.
His sleep, his mete, his drink is him biraft,
That lene he wex, and drye as is a shaft,
His eyen holwe, and grisly to biholde;   505
His hewe falwe, and pale as asshen colde,
And solitarie he was, and ever allone,
And wailling al the night, making his mone.
And if he herde song or instrument,
Then wolde he wepe, he mighte nat be stent;   510
So feble eek were his spirits, and so lowe,
And chaunged so, that no man coude knowe
His speche nor his vois, though men it herde.
And in his gere, for al the world he ferde
Nat oonly lyk the loveres maladye   515
Of Hereos, but rather lyk manye
Engendred of humour malencolyk,
Biforen, in his celle fantastyk.
And shortly, turned was al up-so-doun
Bothe habit and eek disposicioun   520
Of him, this woful lovere daun Arcite.
    What sholde I al-day of his wo endyte?
Whan he endured hadde a yeer or two
This cruel torment, and this peyne and wo,
At Thebes, in his contree, as I seyde,   525
Up-on a night, in sleep as he him leyde,
Him thoughte how that the winged god Mercurie
Biforn him stood, and bad him to be murye.
His slepy yerde in hond he bar uprighte;
An hat he werede up-on his heres brighte.   530
Arrayed was this god (as he took keep)
As he was whan that Argus took his sleep;
And seyde him thus: "To Athenes shaltou wende;
Ther is thee shapen of thy wo an ende."
And with that word Arcite wook and sterte.   535
"Now trewely, how sore that me smerte,"
Quod he, "to Athenes right now wol I fare;

Ne for the drede of deeth shal I nat spare
To see my lady, that I love and serve;
In hir presence I recche nat to sterve."   540
    And with that word he caughte a greet mirour,
And saugh that chaunged was al his colour,
And saugh his visage al in another kinde.
And right anoon it ran him in his minde,
That, sith his face was so disfigured   545
Of maladye, the which he hadde endured,
He mighte wel, if that he bar him lowe,
Live in Athenes ever-more unknowe,
And seen his lady wel ny day by day.
And right anon he chaunged his array,   550
And cladde him as a povre laborer,
And al allone, save oonly a squyer,
That knew his privetee and al his cas,
Which was disgysed povrely, as he was,
To Athenes is he goon the nexte way.   555
And to the court he wente up-on a day,
And at the gate he profreth his servyse,
To drugge and drawe, what so men wol devyse.
And shortly of this matere for to seyn,
He fil in office with a chamberleyn,   560
The which that dwelling was with Emelye.
For he was wys, and coude soon aspye
Of every servaunt, which that serveth here.
Wel coude he hewen wode, and water bere,
For he was yong and mighty for the nones,   565
And ther-to he was strong and big of bones
To doon that any wight can him devyse.
A yeer or two he was in this servyse,
Page of the chambre of Emelye the brighte;
And "Philostrate" he seide that he highte.   570
But half so wel biloved a man as he
Ne was ther never in court, of his degree;
He was so gentil of condicioun,
That thurghout al the court was his renoun.
They seyden, that it were a charitee   575
That Theseus wolde enhauncen his degree,
And putten him in worshipful servyse,
Ther as he mighte his vertu excercyse.
And thus, with-inne a whyle, his name is spronge
Bothe of his dedes, and his goode tonge,   580
That Theseus hath taken him so neer
That of his chambre he made him a squyer,
And yaf him gold to mayntene his degree;
And eek men broghte him out of his contree
From yeer to yeer, ful prively, his rente;   585

But honestly and slyly he it spente,
That no man wondred how that he it hadde.
And three yeer in this wyse his lyf he ladde,
And bar him so in pees and eek in werre,
Ther nas no man that Theseus hath derre. 590
And in this blisse lete I now Arcite,
And speke I wol of Palamon a lyte.

In derknesse and horrible and strong prisoun
This seven yeer hath seten Palamoun,
Forpyned, what for wo and for distresse; 595
Who feleth double soor and hevinesse
But Palamon? that love destreyncth so,
That wood out of his wit he gooth for wo;
And eek therto he is a prisoner
Perpetuelly, noght oonly for a yeer. 600
Who coude ryme in English proprely
His martirdom? for sothe, it am nat I;
Therefore I passe as lightly as I may.

It fel that in the seventhe yeer, in May,
The thridde night, (as olde bokes seyn, 605
That al this storie tellen more pleyn,)
Were it by aventure or destinee,
(As, whan a thing is shapen, it shal be,)
That, sone after the midnight, Palamoun,
By helping of a freend, brak his prisoun, 610
And fleeth the citee, faste as he may go;
For he had yive his gayler drinke so
Of a clarree, maad of a certeyn wyn,
With nercotikes and opie of Thebes fyn,
That al that night, thogh that men wolde him
    shake, 615
The gayler sleep, he mighte nat awake;
And thus he fleeth as faste as ever he may.
The night was short, and faste by the day,
That nedes-cost he moste him-selven hyde,
And til a grove, faste ther besyde, 620
With dredful foot than stalketh Palamoun.
For shortly, this was his opinioun,
That in that grove he wolde him hyde al day,
And in the night than wolde he take his way
To Thebes-ward, his freendes for to preye 625
On Theseus to helpe him to werreye;
And shortly, outher he wolde lese his lyf,
Or winnen Emelye un-to his wyf;
This is theffect and his entente pleyn.

Now wol I torne un-to Arcite ageyn, 630
That litel wiste how ny that was his care,
Til that fortune had broght him in the snare.

The bisy larke, messager of day,
Saluëth in hir song the morwe gray;
And fyry Phebus ryseth up so brighte, 635
That al the orient laugheth of the lighte,
And with his stremes dryeth in the greves
The silver dropes, hanging on the leves.
And Arcite, that is in the court royal
With Theseus, his squyer principal, 640
Is risen, and loketh on the myrie day.
And, for to doon his observaunce to May,
Remembring on the poynt of his desyr,
He on a courser, sterting as the fyr,
Is riden in-to the feeldes, him to pleye, 645
Out of the court, were it a myle or tweye;
And to the grove, of which that I yow tolde,
By aventure, his wey he gan to holde,
To maken him a gerland of the greves,
Were it of wodebinde or hawethorn-leves, 650
And loude he song ageyn the sonne shene:
"May, with alle thy floures and thy grene,
Wel-come be thou, faire fresshe May,
I hope that I som grene gete may."
And from his courser, with a lusty herte, 655
In-to the grove ful hastily he sterte,
And in a path he rometh up and doun,
Ther-as, by aventure, this Palamoun
Was in a bush, that no man mighte him see,
For sore afered of his deeth was he. 660
No-thing ne knew he that it was Arcite:
God wot he wolde have trowed it ful lyte.
But sooth is seyd, gon sithen many yeres,
That "feeld hath eyen, and the wode hath eres."
It is ful fair a man to bere him evene, 665
For al-day meteth men at unset stevene.
Ful litel woot Arcite of his felawe,
That was so ny to herknen al his sawe,
For in the bush he sitteth now ful stille.

Whan that Arcite had romed al his fille, 670
And songen al the roundel lustily,
In-to a studie he fil sodeynly,
As doon thise loveres in hir queynte geres,
Now in the croppe, now doun in the breres,
Now up, now doun, as boket in a welle. 675
Right as the Friday, soothly for to telle,
Now it shyneth, now it reyneth faste,
Right so can gery Venus overcaste
The hertes of hir folk; right as hir day
Is gerful, right so chaungeth she array. 680

Selde is the Friday al the wyke y-lyke.
  Whan that Arcite had songe, he gan to syke,
And sette him doun with-outen any more:
"Alas!" quod he, "that day that I was bore!
How longe, Iuno, thurgh thy crueltee,   685
Woltow werreyen Thebes the citee?
Allas! y-broght is to confusioun
The blood royal of Cadme and Amphioun;
Of Cadmus, which that was the firste man
That Thebes bulte, or first the toun bigan,   690
And of the citee first was crouned king,
Of his linage am I, and his of-spring
By verray ligne, as of the stok royal:
And now I am so caitif and so thral,
That he, that is my mortal enemy,   695
I serve him as his squyer povrely.
And yet doth Iuno me wel more shame,
For I dar noght biknowe myn owne name;
But ther-as I was wont to highte Arcite,
Now highte I Philostrate, noght worth a myte.   700
Allas! thou felle Mars, allas! Iuno,
Thus hath your ire our kinrede al fordo,
Save only me, and wrecched Palamoun,
That Theseus martyreth in prisoun.
And over al this, to sleen me utterly,   705
Love hath his fyry dart so brenningly
Y-striked thurgh my trewe careful herte,
That shapen was my deeth erst than my sherte.
Ye sleen me with your eyen, Emelye;
Ye been the cause wherfor that I dye.   710
Of al the remenant of myn other care
Ne sette I nat the mountaunce of a tare,
So that I coude don aught to your plesaunce!"
And with that word he fil doun in a traunce
A longe tyme; and after he up-sterte.   715
  This Palamoun, that thoughte that thurgh his
      herte
He felte a cold swerd sodeynliche glyde,
For ire he quook, no lenger wolde he byde.
And whan that he had herd Arcites tale,
As he were wood, with face deed and pale,   720
He sterte him up out of the buskes thikke,
And seyde: "Arcite, false traitour wikke,
Now artow hent, that lovest my lady so,
For whom that I have al this peyne and wo,
And art my blood, and to my counseil sworn,   725
As I ful ofte have told thee heer-biforn,
And hast by-iaped here duk Theseus,

And falsly chaunged hast thy name thus;
I wol be deed, or elles thou shalt dye.
Thou shalt nat love my lady Emelye,   730
But I wol love hir only, and namo;
For I am Palamoun, thy mortal fo.
And though that I no wepne have in this place,
But out of prison am astert by grace,
I drede noght that outher thou shalt dye,   735
Or thou ne shalt nat loven Emelye.
Chees which thou wilt, for thou shalt nat asterte."
  This Arcitë, with ful despitous herte,
Whan he him knew, and hadde his tale herd,
As fiers as leoun, pulled out a swerd,   740
And seyde thus: "by God that sit above,
Nere it that thou art sik, and wood for love,
And eek that thou no wepne hast in this place,
Thou sholdest never out of this grove pace,
That thou ne sholdest dyen of myn hond.   745
For I defye the seurtee and the bond
Which that thou seyst that I have maad to thee.
What, verray fool, think wel that love is free,
And I wol love hir, maugre al thy might!
But, for as muche thou art a worthy knight,   750
And wilnest to darreyne hir by batayle,
Have heer my trouthe, to-morwe I wol nat fayle,
With-outen witing of any other wight,
That here I wol be founden as a knight,
And bringen harneys right y-nough for thee;   755
And chees the beste, and leve the worste for me.
And mete and drinke this night wol I bringe
Y-nough for thee, and clothes for thy beddinge.
And, if so be that thou my lady winne,
And slee me in this wode ther I am inne,   760
Thou mayst wel have thy lady, as for me."
This Palamon answerde: "I graunte it thee."
And thus they been departed til a-morwe,
When ech of hem had leyd his feith to borwe.
  O Cupide, out of alle charitee!   765
O regne, that wolt no felawe have with thee!
Ful sooth is seyd, that love ne lordshipe
Wol noght, his thankes, have no felaweshipe;
Wel finden that Arcite and Palamoun.
Arcite is riden anon un-to the toun,   770
And on the morwe, er it were dayes light,
Ful prively two harneys hath he dight,
Bothe suffisaunt and mete to darreyne
The bataille in the feeld bitwix hem tweyne.
And on his hors, allone as he was born,   775

He carieth al this harneys him biforn;
And in the grove, at tyme and place y-set,
This Arcite and this Palamon ben met.
Tho chaungen gan the colour in hir face;
Right as the hunter in the regne of Trace,   780
That stondeth at the gappe with a spere,
Whan hunted is the leoun or the bere,
And hereth him come russhing in the greves,
And breketh bothe bowes and the leves,
And thinketh, "heer cometh my mortel enemy,   785
With-oute faile, he moot be deed, or I;
For outher I mot sleen him at the gappe,
Or he mot sleen me, if that me mishappe;"
So ferden they, in chaunging of hir hewe,
As fer as everich of hem other knewe.   790
Ther nas no good day, ne no saluing;
But streight, with-outen word or rehersing,
Everich of hem halp for to armen other,
As freendly as he were his owne brother;
And after that, with sharpe speres stronge   795
They foynen ech at other wonder longe.
Thou mightest wene that this Palamoun
In his fighting were a wood leoun,
And as a cruel tygre was Arcite:
As wilde bores gonne they to smyte,   800
That frothen whyte as foom for ire wood.
Up to the ancle foghte they in hir blood.
And in this wyse I lete hem fighting dwelle;
And forth I wol of Theseus yow telle.

    The destinee, ministre general,   805
That executeth in the world over-al
The purveyaunce, that God hath seyn biforn,
So strong it is, that, though the world had sworn
The contrarie of a thing, by ye or nay,
Yet somtyme it shal fallen on a day   810
That falleth nat eft with-inne a thousand yere.
For certeinly, our appetytes here,
Be it of werre, or pees, or hate, or love,
Al is this reuled by the sighte above.
This mene I now by mighty Theseus,   815
That for to honten is so desirous,
And namely at the grete hert in May,
That in his bed ther daweth him no day,
That he nis clad, and redy for to ryde
With hunte and horn, and houndes him bisyde.   820
For in his hunting hath he swich delyt,
That it is al his Ioye and appetyt
To been him-self the grete hertes bane;

For after Mars he serveth now Diane.
    Cleer was the day, as I have told er this,   825
And Theseus, with alle Ioye and blis,
With his Ipolita, the fayre quene,
And Emelye, clothed al in grene,
On hunting be they riden royally.
And to the grove, that stood ful faste by,   830
In which ther was an hert, as men him tolde,
Duk Theseus the streighte wey hath holde.
And to the launde he rydeth him ful right,
For thider was the hert wont have his flight,
And over a brook, and so forth on his weye.   835
This duk wol han a cours at him, or tweye,
With houndes, swiche as that him list comaunde.

    And whan this duk was come un-to the launde,
Under the sonne he loketh, and anon
He was war of Arcite and Palamon,   840
That foughten breme, as it were bores two;
The brighte swerdes wenten to and fro
So hidously, that with the leeste strook
It seemed as it wolde felle an ook;
But what they were, no-thing he ne woot.   845
This duk his courser with his spores smoot,
And at a stert he was bitwix hem two,
And pulled out a swerd and cryed, "ho!
Namore, up peyne of lesing of your heed.
By mighty Mars, he shal anon be deed,   850
That smyteth any strook, that I may seen!
But telleth me what mister men ye been,
That been so hardy for to fighten here
With-outen Iuge or other officere,
As it were in a listes royally?"   855
    This Palamon answerde hastily,
And seyde: "sire, what nedeth wordes mo?
We have the deeth deserved bothe two.
Two woful wrecches been we, two caytyves,
That been encombred of our owne lyves;   860
And as thou art a rightful lord and Iuge,
Ne yeve us neither mercy ne refuge,
But slee me first, for seynte charitee;
But slee my felawe eek as wel as me.
Or slee him first; for, though thou knowe it lyte,   865
This is thy mortal fo, this is Arcite,
That fro thy lond is banished on his heed,
For which he hath deserved to be deed.
For this is he that cam un-to thy gate,
And seyde, that he highte Philostrate.   870
Thus hath he Iaped thee ful many a yeer,

And thou has maked him thy chief squyer;
And this is he that loveth Emelye.
For sith the day is come that I shal dye,
I make pleynly my confessioun, 875
That I am thilke woful Palamoun,
That hath thy prison broken wikkedly.
I am thy mortal fo, and it am I
That loveth so hote Emelyë the brighte,
That I wol dye present in hir sighte. 880
Therfore I axe deeth and my Iuwyse;
But slee my felawe in the same wyse,
For bothe han we deserved to be slayn."

    This worthy duk answerde anon agayn,
And seyde, "This is a short conclusioun: 885
Youre owne mouth, by your confessioun,
Hath dampned you, and I wol it recorde,
It nedeth noght to pyne yow with the corde.
Ye shul be deed, by mighty Mars the rede!"

    The quene anon, for verray wommanhede, 890
Gan for to wepe, and so dide Emelye,
And alle the ladies in the companye.
Gret pitee was it, as it thoughte hem alle,
That ever swich a chaunce sholde falle;
For gentil men they were, of greet estat, 895
And no-thing but for love was this debat;
And sawe hir blody woundes wyde and sore;
And alle cryden, bothe lasse and more,
"Have mercy, lord, up-on us wommen alle!"
And on hir bare knees adoun they falle, 900
And wolde have kist his feet ther-as he stood,
Til at the laste aslaked was his mood;
For pitee renneth sone in gentil herte.
And though he first for ire quook and sterte,
He hath considered shortly, in a clause, 905
The trespas of hem bothe, and eek the cause:
And al-though that his ire hir gilt accused,
Yet in his reson he hem bothe excused;
As thus: he thoghte wel, that every man
Wol helpe him-self in love, if that he can, 910
And eek delivere him-self out of prisoun;
And eek his herte had compassioun
Of wommen, for they wepen ever in oon;
And in his gentil herte he thoghte anoon,
And softe un-to himself he seyde: "fy 915
Up-on a lord that wol have no mercy,
But been a leoun, bothe in word and dede,
To hem that been in repentaunce and drede
As wel as to a proud despitous man

That wol maynteyne that he first bigan! 920
That lord hath litel of discrecioun,
That in swich cas can no divisioun,
But weyeth pryde and humblesse after oon."
And shortly, whan his ire is thus agoon,
He gan to loken up with eyen lighte, 925
And spak thise same wordes al on highte:—
"The god of love, a! *benedicite*,
How mighty and how greet a lord is he!
Ayeins his might ther gayneth none obstacles,
He may be cleped a god for his miracles; 930
For he can maken at his owne gyse
Of everich herte, as that him list devyse.
Lo heer, this Arcite and this Palamoun,
That quitly weren out of my prisoun,
And mighte han lived in Thebes royally, 935
And witen I am hir mortal enemy,
And that hir deeth lyth in my might also,
And yet hath love, maugree hir eyen two,
Y-broght hem hider bothe for to dye!
Now loketh, is nat that an heigh folye? 940
Who may been a fool, but-if he love?
Bihold, for Goddes sake that sit above,
Se how they blede! be they noght wel arrayed?
Thus hath hir lord, the god of love, y-payed
Hir wages and hir fees for hir servyse! 945
And yet they wenen for to been ful wyse
That serven love, for aught that may bifalle!
But this is yet the beste game of alle,
That she, for whom they han this Iolitee,
Can hem ther-for as muche thank as me; 950
She woot namore of al this hote fare,
By God, than woot a cokkow or an hare!
But al mot been assayed, hoot and cold;
A man mot been a fool, or yong or old;
I woot it by my-self ful yore agoon: 955
For in my tyme a servant was I oon.
And therfore, sin I knowe of loves peyne,
And woot how sore it can a man distreyne,
As he that hath ben caught ofte in his las,
I yow foryeve al hoolly this trespas, 960
At requeste of the quene that kneleth here,
And eek of Emelye, my suster dere.
And ye shul bothe anon un-to me swere,
That never-mo ye shul my contree dere,
Ne make werre up-on me night ne day, 965
But been my freendes in al that ye may;
I yow foryeve this trespas every del."

And they him swore his axing fayre and wel,
And him of lordshipe and of mercy preyde,
And he hem graunteth grace, and thus he seyde: 970
    "To speke of royal linage and richesse,
Though that she were a quene or a princesse,
Ech of yow bothe is worthy, doutelees,
To wedden whan tyme is, but nathelees
I speke as for my suster Emelye,   975
For whom ye have this stryf and Ielousye;
Ye woot your-self, she may not wedden two
At ones, though ye fighten ever-mo:
That oon of yow, al be him looth or leef,
He moot go pypen in an ivy-leef;   980
This is to seyn, she may nat now han bothe,
Al be ye never so Ielous, ne so wrothe.
And for-thy I yow putte in this degree,
That ech of yow shal have his destinee
As him is shape; and herkneth in what wyse;   985
Lo, heer your ende of that I shal devyse.
    My wil is this, for plat conclusioun,
With-outen any replicacioun,
If that yow lyketh, tak it for the beste,
That everich of yow shal gon wher him leste   990
Frely, with-outen raunson or daunger;
And this day fifty wykes, fer ne ner,
Everich of yow shal bringe an hundred knightes,
Armed for listes up at alle rightes,
Al redy to darreyne hir by bataille.   995
And this bihote I yow, with-outen faille,
Up-on my trouthe, and as I am a knight,
That whether of yow bothe that hath might,
This is to seyn, that whether he or thou
May with his hundred, as I spak of now,   1000
Sleen his contrarie, or out of listes dryve,
Him shal I yeve Emelya to wyve,
To whom that fortune yeveth so fair a grace.
The listes shal I maken in this place,
And God so wisly on my soule rewe,   1005
As I shal even Iuge been and trewe.
Ye shul non other ende with me maken,
That oon of yow ne shal be deed or taken.
And if yow thinketh this is wel y-sayd,
Seyeth your avys, and holdeth yow apayd.   1010
This is your ende and your conclusioun."
    Who loketh lightly now but Palamoun?
Who springeth up for Ioye but Arcite?
Who couthe telle, or who couthe it endyte,
The Ioye that is maked in the place   1015

Whan Theseus hath doon so fair a grace?
But doun on knees wente every maner wight,
And thanked him with al her herte and might,
And namely the Thebans ofte sythe.
And thus with good hope and with herte blythe   1020
They take hir leve, and hom-ward gonne they
    ryde
To Thebes, with his olde walles wyde.

Explicit secunda pars. Sequitur pars tercia.
I trowe men wolde deme it necligence,
If I foryete to tellen the dispence
Of Theseus, that goth so bisily   1025
To maken up the listes royally;
That swich a noble theatre as it was,
I dar wel seyn that in this world ther nas.
The circuit a myle was aboute,
Walled of stoon, and diched al with-oute.   1030
Round was the shap, in maner of compas,
Ful of degrees, the heighte of sixty pas,
That, whan a man was set on o degree,
He letted nat his felawe for to see.
    Est-ward ther stood a gate of marbel whyt,   1035
West-ward, right swich another in the opposit.
And shortly to concluden, swich a place
Was noon in erthe, as in so litel space;
For in the lond ther nas no crafty man,
That geometrie or ars-metrik can,   1040
Ne purtreyour, ne kerver of images,
That Theseus ne yaf him mete and wages
The theatre for to maken and devyse.
And for to doon his ryte and sacrifyse,
He est-ward hath, up-on the gate above,   1045
In worship of Venus, goddesse of love,
Don make an auter and an oratorie;
And west-ward, in the minde and in memorie
Of Mars, he maked hath right swich another,
That coste largely of gold a fother.   1050
And north-ward, in a touret on the wal,
Of alabastre whyt and reed coral
An oratorie riche for to see,
In worship of Dyane of chastitee,
Hath Theseus don wroght in noble wyse.   1055
    But yet hadde I foryeten to devyse
The noble kerving, and the portreitures,
The shap, the countenaunce, and the figures,
That weren in thise oratories three.
    First in the temple of Venus maystow see   1060

Wroght on the wal, ful pitous to biholde,
The broken slepes, and the sykes colde;
The sacred teres, and the waymenting;
The fyry strokes of the desiring,
That loves servaunts in this lyf enduren;　　　　1065
The othes, that hir covenants assuren;
Plesaunce and hope, desyr, fool-hardinesse,
Beautee and youthe, bauderie, richesse,
Charmes and force, lesinges, flaterye,
Dispense, bisynesse, and Ielousye,　　　　1070
That wered of yelwe goldes a gerland,
And a cokkow sitting on hir hand;
Festes, instruments, caroles, daunces,
Lust and array, and alle the circumstaunces
Of love, whiche that I rekne and rekne shal,　　　　1075
By ordre weren peynted on the wal,
And mo than I can make of mencioun.
For soothly, al the mount of Citheroun,
Ther Venus hath hir principal dwelling,
Was shewed on the wal in portreying,　　　　1080
With al the gardin, and the lustinesse.
Nat was foryeten the porter Ydelnesse,
Ne Narcisus the faire of yore agon,
Ne yet the folye of king Salamon,
Ne yet the grete strengthe of Hercules—　　　　1085
Thenchauntements of Medea and Circes—
Ne of Turnus, with the hardy fiers corage,
The riche Cresus, caytif in servage.
Thus may ye seen that wisdom ne richesse,
Beautee ne sleighte, strengthe, ne hardinesse,　　　　1090
Ne may with Venus holde champartye;
For as hir list the world than may she gye.
Lo, alle thise folk so caught were in hir las,
Til they for wo ful ofte seyde "allas!"
Suffyceth heer ensamples oon or two,　　　　1095
And though I coude rekne a thousand mo.
　　The statue of Venus, glorious for to see,
Was naked fleting in the large see,
And fro the navele doun all covered was
With wawes grene, and brighte as any glas.　　　　1100
A citole in hir right hand hadde she,
And on hir heed, ful semely for to see,
A rose gerland, fresh and wel smellinge;
Above hir heed hir dowves flikeringe.
Biforn hir stood hir sone Cupido,　　　　1105
Up-on his shuldres winges hadde he two;
And blind he was, as it is ofte sene;
A bowe he bar and arwes brighte and kene.

Why sholde I noght as wel eek telle yow al
The portreiture, that was up-on the wal　　　　1110
With-inne the temple of mighty Mars the rede?
Al peynted was the wal, in lengthe and brede,
Lyk to the estres of the grisly place,
That highte the grete temple of Mars in Trace,　　　　1115
In thilke colde frosty regioun,
Ther-as Mars hath his sovereyn mansioun.
　　First on the wal was peynted a foreste,
In which ther dwelleth neither man ne beste,
With knotty knarry bareyn treës olde　　　　1120
Of stubbes sharpe and hidous to biholde;
In which ther ran a rumbel and a swough,
As though a storm sholde bresten every bough:
And downward from an hille, under a bente,
Ther stood the temple of Mars armipotente,　　　　1125
Wroght al of burned steel, of which thentree
Was long and streit, and gastly for to see.
And ther-out cam a rage and such a vese,
That it made al the gates for to rese.
The northren light in at the dores shoon,
For windowe on the wal ne was ther noon,　　　　1130
Thurgh which men mighten any light discerne.
The dores were alle of adamant eterne,
Y-clenched overthwart and endelong
With iren tough; and, for to make it strong,
Every piler, the temple to sustene,　　　　1135
Was tonne-greet, of iren bright and shene.
　　Ther saugh I first the derke imagining
Of felonye, and al the compassing;
The cruel ire, reed as any glede;
The pykepurs, and eek the pale drede;　　　　1140
The smyler with the knyf under the cloke;
The shepne brenning with the blake smoke;
The treson of the mordring in the bedde;
The open werre, with woundes al bi-bledde;
Contek, with blody knyf and sharp manace;　　　　1145
Al ful of chirking was that sory place.
The sleere of him-self yet saugh I ther,
His herte-blood hath bathed al his heer;
The nayl y-driven in the shode a-night;
The colde deeth, with mouth gaping up-right.　　　　1150
Amiddes of the temple sat meschaunce,
With disconfort and sory contenaunce.
Yet saugh I woodnesse laughing in his rage;
Armed compleint, out-hees, and fiers outrage.
The careyne in the bush, with throte y-corve;　　　　1155
A thousand slayn, and nat of qualm y-storve;

The tiraunt, with the prey by force y-raft;
The toun destroyed, ther was no-thing laft.
Yet saugh I brent the shippes hoppesteres;
The hunte strangled with the wilde beres: 1160
The sowe freten the child right in the cradel;
The cook y-scalded, for al his longe ladel.
Noght was foryeten by the infortune of Marte;
The carter over-riden with his carte,
Under the wheel ful lowe he lay adoun. 1165
Ther were also, of Martes divisioun,
The barbour, and the bocher, and the smith
That forgeth sharpe swerdes on his stith.
And al above, depeynted in a tour,
Saw I conquest sitting in greet honour, 1170
With the sharpe swerde over his heed
Hanginge by a sotil twynes threed.
Depeynted was the slaughtre of Iulius,
Of grete Nero, and of Antonius;
Al be that thilke tyme they were unborn, 1175
Yet was hir deeth depeynted ther-biforn,
By manasinge of Mars, right by figure;
So was it shewed in that portreiture
As is depeynted in the sterres above,
Who shal be slayn or elles deed for love. 1180
Suffyceth oon ensample in stories olde,
I may not rekne hem alle, thogh I wolde.
    The statue of Mars up-on a carte stood,
Armed, and loked grim as he were wood;
And over his heed ther shynen two figures 1185
Of sterres, that been cleped in scriptures,
That oon Puella, that other Rubeus.
This god of armes was arrayed thus:
A wolf ther stood biforn him at his feet
With eyen rede, and of a man he eet; 1190
With sotil pencel was depeynt this storie,
In redoutinge of Mars and of his glorie.
    Now to the temple of Diane the chaste
As shortly as I can I wol me haste,
To telle yow al the descripcioun. 1195
Depeynted been the walles up and doun
Of hunting and of shamfast chastitee.
Ther saugh I how woful Calistopee,
Whan that Diane agreved was with here,
Was turned from a womman til a bere, 1200
And after was she maad the lode-sterre;
Thus was it peynt, I can say yow no ferre;
Hir sone is eek a sterre, as men may see.
Ther saugh I Dane, y-turned til a tree,

I mene nat the goddesse Diane, 1205
But Penneus doughter, which that highte Dane.
Ther saugh I Attheon an hert y-maked,
For vengeaunce that he saugh Diane al naked;
I saugh how that his houndes have him caught,
And freten him, for that they knewe him naught. 1210
Yet peynted was a litel forther-moor,
How Atthalante hunted the wilde boor,
And Meleagre, and many another mo,
For which Diane wroghte him care and wo.
Ther saugh I many another wonder storie, 1215
The whiche me list nat drawen to memorie.
This goddesse on an hert ful hye seet,
With smale houndes al aboute hir feet;
And undernethe hir feet she hadde a mone,
Wexing it was, and sholde wanie sone. 1220
In gaude grene hir statue clothed was,
With bowe in honde, and arwes in a cas.
Hir eyen caste she ful lowe adoun,
Ther Pluto hath his derke regioun.
A womman travailinge was hir biforn, 1225
But, for hir child so longe was unborn,
Ful pitously Lucyna gan she calle,
And seyde, "help, for thou mayst best of alle."
Wel couthe he peynten lyfly that it wroghte,
With many a florin he the hewes boghte. 1230
    Now been thise listes maad, and Theseus,
That at his grete cost arrayed thus
The temples and the theatre every del,
Whan it was doon, him lyked wonder wel.
But stinte I wol of Theseus a lyte, 1235
And speke of Palamon and of Arcite.
    The day approcheth of hir retourninge,
That everich sholde an hundred knightes bringe,
The bataille to darreyne, as I yow tolde;
And til Athenes, hir covenant for to holde, 1240
Hath everich of hem broght an hundred knightes
Wel armed for the werre at alle rightes.
And sikerly, ther trowed many a man
That never, sithen that the world bigan,
As for to speke of knighthod of hir hond, 1245
As fer as God hath maked see or lond,
Nas, of so fewe, so noble a companye.
For every wight that lovede chivalrye,
And wolde, his thankes, han a passant name,
Hath preyed that he mighte ben of that game; 1250
And wel was him, that ther-to chosen was.
For if ther fille to-morwe swich a cas,

Ye knowen wel, that every lusty knight,
That loveth paramours, and hath his might,
Were it in Engelond, or elles-where,   1255
They wolde, hir thankes, wilnen to be there.
To fighte for a lady, *benedicite!*
It were a lusty sighte for to see.

   And right so ferden they with Palamon.
With him ther wenten knightes many oon;   1260
Som wol ben armed in an habergeoun,
In a brest-plat and in a light gipoun;
And somme woln have a peyre plates large;
And somme woln have a Pruce sheld, or a targe;
Somme woln ben armed on hir legges weel,   1265
And have an ax, and somme a mace of steel.
Ther nis no newe gyse, that it nas old.
Armed were they, as I have you told,
Everich after his opinioun.

   Ther maistow seen coming with Palamoun   1270
Ligurge him-self, the grete king of Trace;
Blak was his herd, and manly was his face.
The cercles of his eyen in his heed,
They gloweden bitwixe yelow and reed;
And lyk a griffon loked he aboute,   1275
With kempe heres on his browes stoute;
His limes grete, his braunes harde and stronge,
His shuldres brode, his armes rounde and longe.
And as the gyse was in his contree,
Ful hye up-on a char of gold stood he,   1280
With foure whyte boles in the trays.
In-stede of cote-armure over his harnays,
With nayles yelwe and brighte as any gold,
He hadde a beres skin, col-blak, for-old.
His longe heer was kembd bihinde his bak,   1285
As any ravenes fether it shoon for-blak:
A wrethe of gold arm-greet, of huge wighte,
Upon his heed, set ful of stones brighte,
Of fyne rubies and of dyamaunts.
Aboute his char ther wenten whyte alaunts,   1290
Twenty and mo, as grete as any steer,
To hunten at the leoun or the deer,
And folwed him, with mosel faste y-bounde,
Colers of gold, and torets fyled rounde.
An hundred lordes hadde he in his route   1295
Armed ful wel, with hertes sterne and stoute.

   With Arcita, in stories as men finde,
The grete Emetreus, the king of Inde,
Up-on a stede bay, trapped in steel,
Covered in cloth of gold diapred weel,   1300

Cam ryding lyk the god of armes, Mars.
His cote-armure was of cloth of Tars,
Couched with perles whyte and rounde and grete.
His sadel was of brend gold newe y-bete;
A mantelet upon his shuldre hanginge   1305
Bret-ful of rubies rede, as fyr sparklinge.
His crispe heer lyk ringes was y-ronne,
And that was yelow, and glitered as the sonne.
His nose was heigh, his eyen bright citryn,
His lippes rounde, his colour was sangwyn,   1310
A fewe fraknes in his face y-spreynd,
Betwixen yelow and somdel blak y-meynd,
And as a leoun he his loking caste.
Of fyve and twenty yeer his age I caste.
His berd was wel bigonne for to springe;   1315
His voys was as a trompe thunderinge.
Up-on his heed he wered of laurer grene
A gerland fresh and lusty for to sene.
Up-on his hand he bar, for his deduyt,
An egle tame, as eny lilie whyt.   1320
An hundred lordes hadde he with him there,
Al armed, sauf hir heddes, in al hir gere,
Ful richely in alle maner thinges.
For trusteth wel, that dukes, erles, kinges,
Were gadered in this noble companye,   1325
For love and for encrees of chivalrye.
Aboute this king ther ran on every part
Ful many a tame leoun and lepart.
And in this wyse thise lordes, alle and some,
Ben on the Sonday to the citee come   1330
About pryme, and in the toun alight.

   This Theseus, this duk, this worthy knight,
Whan he had broght hem in-to his citee,
And inned hem, everich in his degree,
He festeth hem, and dooth so greet labour   1335
To esen hem, and doon hem al honour,
That yet men weneth that no mannes wit
Of noon estat ne coude amenden it.
The minstralcye, the service at the feste,
The grete yiftes to the moste and leste,   1340
The riche array of Theseus paleys,
Ne who sat first ne last up-on the deys,
What ladies fairest been or best daunsinge,
Or which of hem can dauncen best and singe,
Ne who most felingly speketh of love: 1345
What haukes sitten on the perche above,
What houndes liggen on the floor adoun:
Of al this make I now no mencioun;

But al theffect, that thinketh me the beste;
Now comth the poynt, and herkneth if yow leste. 1350
The Sonday night, er day bigan to springe,
When Palamon the larke herde singe,
Although it nere nat day by houres two,
Yet song the larke, and Palamon also.
With holy herte, and with an heigh corage 1355
He roos, to wenden on his pilgrimage
Un-to the blisful Citherea benigne,
I mene Venus, honurable and digne.
And in hir houre he walketh forth a pas
Un-to the listes, ther hir temple was, 1360
And doun he kneleth, and with humble chere
And herte soor, he seyde as ye shul here.
"Faireste of faire, o lady myn, Venus,
Doughter to Iove and spouse of Vulcanus,
Thou glader of the mount of Citheroun, 1365
For thilke love thou haddest to Adoun,
Have pitee of my bittre teres smerte,
And tak myn humble preyer at thyn herte.
Allas! I ne have no langage to telle
Theffectes ne the torments of myn helle; 1370
Myn herte may myne harmes nat biwreye;
I am so confus, that I can noght seye.
But mercy, lady bright, that knowest weel
My thought, and seest what harmes that I feel,
Considere al this, and rewe up-on my sore, 1375
As wisly as I shal for evermore,
Emforth my might, thy trewe servant be,
And holden werre alwey with chastitee;
That make I myn avow, so ye me helpe.
I kepe noght of armes for to yelpe, 1380
Ne I ne axe nat to-morwe to have victorie,
Ne renoun in this cas, ne veyne glorie
Of pris of armes blowen up and doun,
But I wolde have fully possessioun
Of Emelye, and dye in thy servyse; 1385
Find thou the maner how, and in what wyse.
I recche nat, but it may bettre be,
To have victorie of hem, or they of me,
So that I have my lady in myne armes.
For though so be that Mars is god of armes, 1390
Your vertu is so greet in hevene above,
That, if yow list, I shal wel have my love.
Thy temple wol I worshipe evermo,
And on thyn auter, wher I ryde or go,
I wol don sacrifice, and fyres bete. 1395
And if ye wol nat so, my lady swete,

Than preye I thee, to-morwe with a spere
That Arcita me thurgh the herte bere.
Thanne rekke I noght, whan I have lost my lyf,
Though that Arcita winne hir to his wyf. 1400
This is theffect and ende of my preyere,
Yif me my love, thou blisful lady dere."
Whan thorisoun was doon of Palamon,
His sacrifice he dide, and that anon
Ful pitously, with alle circumstaunces, 1405
Al telle I noght as now his observaunces.
But atte laste the statue of Venus shook,
And made a signe, wher-by that he took
That his preyere accepted was that day.
For thogh the signe shewed a delay, 1410
Yet wiste he wel that graunted was his bone;
And with glad herte he wente him hoom ful sone.
The thridde houre inequal that Palamon
Bigan to Venus temple for to goon,
Up roos the sonne, and up roos Emelye, 1415
And to the temple of Diane gan hye.
Hir maydens, that she thider with hir ladde,
Ful redily with hem the fyr they hadde,
Thencens, the clothes, and the remenant al
That to the sacrifyce longen shal; 1420
The hornes fulle of meth, as was the gyse;
Ther lakked noght to doon hir sacrifyse.
Smoking the temple, ful of clothes faire,
This Emelye, with herte debonaire,
Hir body wessh with water of a welle; 1425
But how she dide hir ryte I dar nat telle,
But it be any thing in general;
And yet it were a game to heren al;
To him that meneth wel, it were no charge:
But it is good a man ben at his large. 1430
Hir brighte heer was kempt, untressed al;
A coroune of a grene ook cerial
Up-on hir heed was set ful fair and mete.
Two fyres on the auter gan she bete,
And dide hir thinges, as men may biholde 1435
In Stace of Thebes, and thise bokes olde.
Whan kindled was the fyr, with pitous chere
Un-to Diane she spak, as ye may here.
"O chaste goddesse of the wodes grene,
To whom bothe hevene and erthe and see is sene, 1440
Quene of the regne of Pluto derk and lowe,
Goddesse of maydens, that myn herte hast knowe
Ful many a yeer, and woost what I desire,
As keep me fro thy vengeaunce and thyn ire,

That Attheon aboughte cruelly.   1445
Chaste goddesse, wel wostow that I
Desire to been a mayden al my lyf,
Ne never wol I be no love ne wyf.
I am, thou woost, yet of thy companye,
A mayde, and love hunting and venerye,   1450
And for to walken in the wodes wilde,
And noght to been a wyf, and be with childe.
Noght wol I knowe companye of man.
Now help me, lady, sith ye may and can,
For tho thre formes that thou hast in thee.   1455
And Palamon, that hath swich love to me,
And eek Arcite, that loveth me so sore,
This grace I preye thee with-oute more,
As sende love and pees bitwixe hem two;
And fro me turne awey hir hertes so,   1460
That al hir hote love, and hir desyr,
And al hir bisy torment, and hir fyr
Be queynt, or turned in another place;
And if so be thou wolt not do me grace,
Or if my destinee be shapen so,   1465
That I shal nedes have oon of hem two,
As sende me him that most desireth me.
Bihold, goddesse of clene chastitee,
The bittre teres that on my chekes falle.
Sin thou are mayde, and keper of us alle,   1470
My maydenhede thou kepe and wel conserve,
And whyl I live a mayde, I wol thee serve."

    The fyres brenne up-on the auter clere,
Whyl Emelye was thus in hir preyere;
But sodeinly she saugh a sighte queynte,   1475
For right anon oon of the fyres queynte,
And quiked agayn, and after that anon
That other fyr was queynt, and al agon;
And as it queynte, it made a whistelinge,
As doon thise wete brondes in hir brenninge,   1480
And at the brondes ende out-ran anoon
As it were blody dropes many oon;
For which so sore agast was Emelye,
That she was wel ny mad, and gan to crye,
For she ne wiste what it signifyed;   1485
But only for the fere thus hath she cryed,
And weep, that it was pitee for to here.
And ther-with-al Diane gan appere,
With bowe in hond, right as an hunteresse,
And seyde: "Doghter, stint thyn hevinesse.   1490
Among the goddes hye it is affermed,
And by eterne word write and conformed,

Thou shalt ben wedded un-to oon of tho
That han for thee so muchel care and wo;
But un-to which of hem I may nat telle.   1495
Farwel, for I ne may no lenger dwelle.
The fyres which that on myn auter brenne
Shul thee declaren, er that thou go henne,
Thyn aventure of love, as in this cas."
And with that word, the arwes in the cas   1500
Of the goddesse clateren faste and ringe,
And forth she wente, and made a vanisshinge;
For which this Emelye astoned was,
And seyde, "What amounteth this, allas!
I putte me in thy proteccioun,   1505
Diane, and in thy disposicioun."
And hoom she gooth anon the nexte weye.
This is theffect, ther is namore to seye.

    The nexte houre of Mars folwinge this,
Arcite un-to the temple walked is   1510
Of fierse Mars, to doon his sacrifyse,
With alle the rytes of his payen wyse.
With pitous herte and heigh devocioun,
Right thus to Mars he seyde his orisoun:
    "O stronge god, that in the regnes colde   1515
Of Trace honoured art, and lord y-holde,
And hast in every regne and every lond
Of armes al the brydel in thyn hond,
And hem fortunest as thee list devyse,
Accept of me my pitous sacrifyse.   1520
If so be that my youthe may deserve,
And that my might be worthy for to serve
Thy godhede, that I may been oon of thyne,
Than preye I thee to rewe up-on my pyne.
For thilke peyne, and thilke hote fyr,   1525
In which thou whylom brendest for desyr,
Whan that thou usedest the grete beautee
Of fayre yonge fresshe Venus free,
And haddest hir in armes at thy wille,
Al-though thee ones on a tyme misfille   1530
Whan Vulcanus had caught thee in his las,
And fond thee ligging by his wyf, allas!
For thilke sorwe that was in thyn herte,
Have routhe as wel up-on my peynes smerte.
I am yong and unkonning, as thou wost,   1535
And, as I trowe, with love offended most,
That ever was any lyves creature;
For she, that dooth me al this wo endure,
Ne reccheth never wher I sinke or flete.
And wel I woot, er she me mercy hete,   1540

I moot with strengthe winne hir in the place;
And wel I woot, withouten help or grace
Of thee, ne may my strengthe noght availle.
Than help me, lord, to-morwe in my bataille,
For thilke fyr that whylom brente thee,   1545
As wel as thilke fyr now brenneth me;
And do that I to-morwe have victorie.
Myn be the travaille, and thyn be the glorie!
Thy soverein temple wol I most honouren
Of any place, and alwey most labouren   1550
In thy plesaunce and in thy craftes stronge,
And in thy temple I wol my baner honge,
And alle the armes of my companye;
And evere-mo, un-to that day I dye,
Eterne fyr I wol biforn thee finde.   1555
And eek to this avow I wol me binde:
My berd, myn heer that hongeth long adoun,
That never yet ne felte offensioun
Of rasour nor of shere, I wol thee yive,
And ben thy trewe servant whyl I live.   1560
Now lord, have routhe up-on my sorwes sore,
Yif me victorie, I aske thee namore."
    The preyere stinte of Arcita the stronge,
The ringes on the temple-dore that honge,
And eek the dores, clatereden ful faste,   1565
Of which Arcita som what him agaste.
The fyres brende up-on the auter brighte,
That it gan al the temple for to lighte;
And swete smel the ground anon up-yaf,
And Arcita anon his hand up-haf,   1570
And more encens in-to the fyr he caste,
With othere rytes mo; and atte laste
The statue of Mars bigan his hauberk ringe.
And with that soun he herde a murmuringe
Ful lowe and dim, that sayde thus, "Victorie:"   1575
For which he yaf to Mars honour and glorie.
And thus with Ioye, and hope wel to fare,
Arcite anon un-to his inne is fare,
As fayn as fowel is of the brighte sonne.
    And right anon swich stryf ther is bigonne   1580
For thilke graunting, in the hevene above,
Bitwixe Venus, the goddesse of love,
And Mars, the sterne god armipotente,
That Iupiter was bisy it to stente;
Til that the pale Saturnus the colde,   1585
That knew so manye of aventures olde,
Fond in his olde experience an art,
That he ful sone hath plesed every part.

As sooth is sayd, elde hath greet avantage;
In elde is bothe wisdom and usage;   1590
Men may the olde at-renne, and noght at-rede.
Saturne anon, to stinten stryf and drede,
Al be it that it is agayn his kynde,
Of al this stryf he gan remedie fynde.
    "My dere doghter Venus," quod Saturne,   1595
"My cours, that hath so wyde for to turne,
Hath more power than wot any man.
Myn is the drenching in the see so wan;
Myn is the prison in the derke cote;
Myn is the strangling and hanging by the throte;   1600
The murmure, and the cherles rebelling,
The groyning, and the pryvee empoysoning:
I do vengeance and pleyn correccioun
Whyl I dwelle in the signe of the leoun.
Myn is the ruine of the hye halles,   1605
The falling of the toures and of the walles
Up-on the mynour or the carpenter.
I slow Sampsoun in shaking the piler;
And myne be the maladyes colde,
The derke tresons, and the castes olde;   1610
My loking is the fader of pestilence.
Now weep namore, I shal doon diligence
That Palamon, that is thyn owne knight,
Shal have his lady, as thou hast him hight.
Though Mars shal helpe his knight, yet nathelees   1615
Bitwixe yow ther moot be som tyme pees,
Al be ye noght of o complexioun,
That causeth al day swich divisioun.
I am thin ayel, redy at thy wille;
Weep thou namore, I wol thy lust fulfille."   1620
    Now wol I stinten of the goddes above,
Of Mars, and of Venus, goddesse of love,
And telle yow, as pleynly as I can,
The grete effect, for which that I bigan.

Explicit tercia pars. Sequitur pars quarta.

Greet was the feste in Athenes that day,   1625
And eek the lusty seson of that May
Made every wight to been in swich plesaunce,
That al that Monday Iusten they and daunce,
And spenden it in Venus heigh servyse.
But by the cause that they sholde ryse   1630
Erly, for to seen the grete fight,
Unto hir reste wente they at night.
And on the morwe, whan that day gan springe,
Of hors and harneys, noyse and clateringe

Ther was in hostelryes al aboute;   1635
And to the paleys rood ther many a route
Of lordes, up-on stedes and palfreys.
Ther maystow seen devysing of herneys
So uncouth and so riche, and wroght so weel
Of goldsmithrie, of browding, and of steel;   1640
The sheeldes brighte, testers, and trappures;
Gold-hewen helmes, hauberks, cote-armures;
Lordes in paraments on hir courseres,
Knightes of retenue, and eek squyeres
Nailinge the speres, and helmes bokelinge,   1645
Gigginge of sheeldes, with layneres lacinge;
Ther as need is, they weren no-thing ydel;
The fomy stedes on the golden brydel
Gnawinge, and faste the armurers also
With fyle and hamer prikinge to and fro;   1650
Yemen on fote, and communes many oon
With shorte staves, thikke as they may goon;
Pypes, trompes, nakers, clariounes,
That in the bataille blowen blody sounes;
The paleys ful of peples up and doun,   1655
Heer three, ther ten, holding hir questioun,
Divyninge of thise Thebane knightes two.
Somme seyden thus, somme seyde it shal be so;
Somme helden with him with the blake berd,
Somme with the balled, somme with the thikke-
    herd;   1660
Somme sayde, he loked grim and he wolde fighte;
He hath a sparth of twenty pound of wighte.
Thus was the halle ful of divyninge,
Longe after that the sonne gan to springe.
   The grete Theseus, that of his sleep awaked   1665
With minstralcye and noyse that was maked,
Held yet the chambre of his paleys riche,
Til that the Thebane knightes, bothe y-liche
Honoured, were into the paleys fet.
Duk Theseus was at a window set,   1670
Arrayed right as he were a god in trone.
The peple preesseth thider-ward ful sone
Him for to seen, and doon heigh reverence,
And eek to herkne his hest and his sentence.
   An heraud on a scaffold made an ho,   1675
Til al the noyse of the peple was y-do;
And whan he saugh the peple of noyse al stille,
Tho showed he the mighty dukes wille.
   "The lord hath of his heigh discrecioun
Considered, that it were destruccioun   1680
To gentil blood, to fighten in the gyse

Of mortal bataille now in this empryse;
Wherfore, to shapen that they shul not dye,
He wol his firste purpos modifye.
No man therfor, up peyne of los of lyf,   1685
No maner shot, ne pollax, ne short knyf
Into the listes sende, or thider bringe;
Ne short swerd for to stoke, with poynt bytinge,
No man ne drawe, ne bere it by his syde.
Ne no man shal un-to his felawe ryde   1690
But o cours, with a sharp y-grounde spere;
Foyne, if him list, on fote, him-self to were.
And he that is at meschief, shal be take,
And noght slayn, but be broght un-to the stake
That shal ben ordeyned on either syde;   1695
But thider he shal by force, and ther abyde.
And if so falle, the chieftayn be take
On either syde, or elles slee his make,
No lenger shal the turneyinge laste.
God spede yow; goth forth, and ley on faste. 1700
With long swerd and with maces fight your fille.
Goth now your wey; this is the lordes wille."
   The voys of peple touchede the hevene,
So loude cryden they with mery stevene:
"God save swich a lord, that is so good,   1705
He wilneth no destruccioun of blood!"
Up goon the trompes and the melodye.
And to the listes rit the companye
By ordinaunce, thurgh-out the citee large,
Hanged with cloth of gold, and nat with sarge. 1710
Ful lyk a lord this noble duk gan ryde,
Thise two Thebanes up-on either syde;
And after rood the quene, and Emelye,
And after that another companye
Of oon and other, after hir degree.   1715
And thus they passen thurgh-out the citee,
And to the listes come they by tyme.
It nas not of the day yet fully pryme,
Whan set was Theseus ful riche and hye,
Ipolita the quene and Emelye,   1720
And other ladies in degrees aboute.
Un-to the seetes preesseth al the route.
And west-ward, thurgh the gates under Marte,
Arcite, and eek the hundred of his parte,
With baner reed is entred right anon;   1725
And in that selve moment Palamon
Is under Venus, est-ward in the place,
With baner whyt, and hardy chere and face.
In al the world, to seken up and doun,

So even with-outen variacioun,   1730
Ther nere swiche companyes tweye.
For ther nas noon so wys that coude seye,
That any hadde of other avauntage
Of worthinesse, ne of estaat, ne age,
So even were they chosen, for to gesse.   1735
And in two renges faire they hem dresse.
Whan that hir names rad were everichoon,
That in hir nombre gyle were ther noon,
Tho were the gates shet, and cryed was loude:
"Do now your devoir, yonge knightes proude!"   1740
    The heraudes lefte hir priking up and doun;
Now ringen trompes loude and clarioun;
Ther is namore to seyn, but west and est
In goon the speres ful sadly in arest;
In goth the sharpe spore in-to the syde.   1745
Ther seen men who can Iuste, and who can ryde;
Ther shiveren shaftes up-on sheeldes thikke;
He feleth thurgh the herte-spoon the prikke.
Up springen speres twenty foot on highte;
Out goon the swerdes as the silver brighte.   1750
The helmes they to-hewen and to-shrede;
Out brest the blood, with sterne stremes rede.
With mighty maces the bones they to-breste.
He thurgh the thikkeste of the throng gan threste.
Ther stomblen stedes stronge, and doun goth al.   1755
He rolleth under foot as dooth a bal.
He foyneth on his feet with his tronchoun,
And he him hurtleth with his hors adoun.
He thurgh the body is hurt, and sithen y-take,
Maugree his heed, and broght un-to the stake,   1760
As forward was, right ther he moste abyde;
Another lad is on that other syde.
And som tyme dooth hem Theseus to reste,
Hem to refresshe, and drinken if hem leste.
Ful ofte a-day han thise Thebanes two   1765
Togidre y-met, and wroght his felawe wo;
Unhorsed hath ech other of hem tweye.
Ther nas no tygre in the vale of Galgopheye,
Whan that hir whelp is stole, whan it is lyte,
So cruel on the hunte, as is Arcite   1770
For Ielous herte upon this Palamoun:
Ne in Belmarye ther nis so fel leoun,
That hunted is, or for his hunger wood,
Ne of his praye desireth so the blood,
As Palamon to sleen his fo Arcite.   1775
The Ielous strokes on hir helmes byte;
Out renneth blood on bothe hir sydes rede.

Som tyme an ende ther is of every dede;
For er the sonne un-to the reste wente,
The stronge king Emetreus gan hente   1780
This Palamon, as he faught with Arcite,
And made his swerd depe in his flesh to byte;
And by the force of twenty is he take
Unyolden, and y-drawe unto the stake.
And in the rescous of this Palamoun   1785
The stronge king Ligurge is born adoun;
And king Emetreus, for al his strengthe,
Is born out of his sadel a swerdes lengthe,
So hitte him Palamon er he were take;
But al for noght, he was broght to the stake.   1790
His hardy herte mighte him helpe naught;
He moste abyde, whan that he was caught
By force, and eek by composicioun.
    Who sorweth now but woful Palamoun,
That moot namore goon agayn to fighte?   1795
And whan that Theseus had seyn this sighte,
Un-to the folk that foghten thus echoon
He cryde, "Ho! namore, for it is doon!
I wol be trewe Iuge, and no partye.
Arcite of Thebes shal have Emelye,   1800
That by his fortune hath hir faire y-wonne."
Anon ther is a noyse of peple bigonne
For Ioye of this, so loude and heigh with-alle,
It semed that the listes sholde falle.
    What can now faire Venus doon above?   1805
What seith she now? what dooth this quene of
    love?
But wepeth so, for wanting of hir wille,
Til that hir teres in the listes fille;
She seyde: "I am ashamed, doutelees."
Saturnus seyde: "Doghter, hold thy pees.   1810
Mars hath his wille, his knight hath al his bone,
And, by myn heed, thou shalt ben esed sone."
    The trompes, with the loude minstralcye,
The heraudes, that ful loude yolle and crye,
Been in hir wele for Ioye of daun Arcite.   1815
But herkneth me, and stinteth now a lyte,
Which a miracle ther bifel anon.
    This fierce Arcite hath of his helm y-don,
And on a courser, for to shewe his face,
He priketh endelong the large place,   1820
Loking upward up-on this Emelye;
And she agayn him caste a freendlich yë,
(For wommen, as to speken in comune,
They folwen al the favour of fortune),

THE KNIGHT'S TALE 511

And she was al his chere, as in his herte.   1825
Out of the ground a furie infernal sterte,
From Pluto sent, at requeste of Saturne,
For which his hors for fere gan to turne,
And leep asyde, and foundred as he leep;
And, er that Arcite may taken keep,   1830
He pighte him on the pomel of his heed,
That in the place he lay as he were deed,
His brest to-brosten with his sadel-bowe.
As blak he lay as any cole or crowe,
So was the blood y-ronnen in his face.   1835
Anon he was y-born out of the place
With herte soor, to Theseus paleys.
Tho was he corven out of his harneys,
And in a bed y-brought ful faire and blyve,
For he was yet in memorie and alyve,   1840
And alway crying after Emelye.
    Duk Theseus, with al his companye,
Is comen hoom to Athenes his citee,
With alle blisse and greet solempnitee.
Al be it that this aventure was falle,   1845
He nolde noght disconforten hem alle.
Men seyde eek, that Arcite shal nat dye;
He shal ben heled of his maladye.
And of another thing they were as fayn,
That of hem alle was ther noon y-slayn,   1850
Al were they sore y-hurt, and namely oon,
That with a spere was thirled his brest-boon.
To othere woundes, and to broken armes,
Some hadden salves, and some hadden charmes;
Fermacies of herbes, and eek save   1855
They dronken, for they wolde hir limes have.
For which this noble duk, as he wel can,
Conforteth and honoureth every man,
And made revel al the longe night,
Un-to the straunge lordes, as was right.   1860
Ne ther was holden no disconfitinge,
But as a Iustes or a tourneyinge;
For soothly ther was no disconfiture,
For falling nis nat but an aventure;
Ne to be lad with fors un-to the stake   1865
Unyolden, and with twenty knightes take,
O persone allone, with-outen mo,
And haried forth by arme, foot, and to,
And eek his stede driven forth with staves,
With footmen, bothe yemen and eek knaves,   1870
It nas aretted him no vileinye,
Ther may no man clepen it cowardye.

For which anon duk Theseus leet crye,
To stinten alle rancour and envye,
The gree as wel of o syde as of other,   1875
And either syde y-lyk, as otheres brother;
And yaf hem yiftes after hir degree,
And fully heeld a feste dayes three;
And conveyed the kinges worthily
Out of his toun a Iournee largely.   1880
And hoom wente every man the righte way.
Ther was namore, but "far wel, have good day!"
Of this bataille I wol namore endyte,
But speke of Palamon and of Arcite.
    Swelleth the brest of Arcite, and the sore   1885
Encreesseth at his herte more and more.
The clothered blood, for any lechecraft,
Corrupteth, and is in his bouk y-laft,
That neither veyne-blood, ne ventusinge,
Ne drinke of herbes may ben his helpinge.   1890
The vertu expulsif, or animal,
Fro thilke vertu cleped natural
Ne may the venim voyden, ne expelle.
The pypes of his longes gonne to swelle,
And every lacerte in his brest adoun   1895
Is shent with venim and corrupcioun.
Him gayneth neither, for to gete his lyf,
Vomyt upward, ne dounward laxatif;
Al is to-brosten thilke regioun,
Nature hath now no dominacioun.   1900
And certeinly, ther nature wol nat wirche,
Far-wel, phisyk! go ber the man to chirche!
This al and som, that Arcita mot dye,
For which he sendeth after Emelye,
And Palamon, that was his cosin dere;   1905
Than seyde he thus, as ye shul after here.
    "Naught may the woful spirit in myn herte
Declare o poynt of alle my sorwes smerte
To yow, my lady, that I love most;
But I biquethe the service of my gost   1910
To yow aboven every creature,
Sin that my lyf may no lenger dure.
Allas, the wo! allas, the peynes stronge,
That I for yow have suffred, and so longe!
Allas, the deeth! allas, myn Emelye!   1915
Allas, departing of our companye!
Allas, myn hertes quene! allas, my wyf!
Myn hertes lady, endere of my lyf!
What is this world? what asketh men to have?
Now with his love, now in his colde grave   1920

Allone, with-outen any companye.
Far-wel, my swete fo! myn Emelye!
And softe tak me in your armes tweye,
For love of God, and herkneth what I seye.

I have heer with my cosin Palamon   1925
Had stryf and rancour, many a day a-gon,
For love of yow, and for my Ielousye.
And Iupiter so wis my soule gye,
To speken of a servant proprely,
With alle circumstaunces trewely,   1930
That is to seyn, trouthe, honour, and knighthede,
Wisdom, humblesse, estaat, and heigh kinrede,
Fredom, and al that longeth to that art,
So Iupiter have of my soule part,
As in this world right now ne knowe I non   1935
So worthy to ben loved as Palamon,
That serveth yow, and wol don al his lyf.
And if that ever ye shul been a wyf,
Foryet nat Palamon, the gentil man."
And with that word his speche faille gan,   1940
For from his feet up to his brest was come
The cold of deeth, that hadde him overcome.
And yet more-over, in his armes two
The vital strengthe is lost, and al ago.
Only the intellect, with-outen more,   1945
That dwelled in his herte syk and sore,
Gan faillen, when the herte felte deeth,
Dusked his eyen two, and failled breeth.
But on his lady yet caste he his yë;
His laste word was, "mercy, Emelye!"   1950
His spirit chaunged hous, and wente ther,
As I cam never, I can nat tellen wher.
Therfor I stinte, I nam no divinistre;
Of soules finde I nat in this registre,
Ne me ne list thilke opiniouns to telle   1955
Of hem, though that they wryten wher they
      dwelle.
Arcite is cold, ther Mars his soule gye;
Now wol I speken forth of Emelye.

Shrighte Emelye, and howleth Palamon,
And Theseus his suster took anon   1960
Swowninge, and bar hir fro the corps away.
What helpeth it to tarien forth the day,
To tellen how she weep, both eve and morwe?
For in swich cas wommen have swich sorwe,
Whan that hir housbonds been from hem ago,   1965
That for the more part they sorwen so,
Or elles fallen in swich maladye,

That at the laste certeinly they dye.
Infinite been the sorwes and the teres
Of olde folk, and folk of tendre yeres,   1970
In al the toun, for deeth of this Theban;
For him ther wepeth bothe child and man;
So greet a weping was ther noon, certayn,
Whan Ector was y-broght, al fresh y-slayn,
To Troye; allas! the pitee that was ther,   1975
Cracching of chekes, rending eek of heer.
"Why woldestow be deed," thise wommen crye,
"And haddest gold y-nough, and Emelye?"
No man mighte gladen Theseus,
Savinge his olde fader Egeus,   1980
That knew this worldes transmutacioun,
As he had seyn it chaungen up and doun,
Ioye after wo, and wo after gladnesse:
And shewed hem ensamples and lyknesse.

"Right as ther deyed never man," quod he,   1985
"That he ne livede in erthe in som degree,
Right so ther livede never man," he seyde,
"In al this world, that som tyme he ne deyde.
This world nis but a thurghfare ful of wo,
And we ben pilgrimes, passinge to and fro;   1990
Deeth is an ende of every worldly sore."
And over al this yet seyde he muchel more
To this effect, ful wysly to enhorte
The peple, that they sholde hem reconforte.

Duk Theseus, with al his bisy cure,   1995
Caste now wher that the sepulture
Of good Arcite may best y-maked be,
And eek most honurable in his degree.
And at the laste he took conclusioun,
That ther as first Arcite and Palamoun   2000
Hadden for love the bataille hem bitwene,
That in that selve grove, swote and grene,
Ther as he hadde his amorous desires,
His compleynt, and for love his hote fires,
He wolde make a fyr, in which thoffice   2005
Funeral he mighte al accomplice;
And leet comaunde anon to hakke and hewe
The okes olde, and leye hem on a rewe
In colpons wel arrayed for to brenne;
His officers with swifte feet they renne   2010
And ryde anon at his comaundement.
And after this, Theseus hath y-sent
After a bere, and it al over-spradde
With cloth of gold, the richest that he hadde.
And of the same suyte he cladde Arcite;   2015

Upon his hondes hadde he gloves whyte;
Eek on his heed a croune of laurer grene,
And in his hond a swerd ful bright and kene.
He leyde him bare the visage on the bere,
Therwith he weep that pitee was to here.   2020
And for the peple sholde seen him alle,
Whan it was day, he broghte him to the halle,
That roreth of the crying and the soun.

   Tho cam this woful Theban Palamoun,
With flotery berd, and ruggy asshy heres,   2025
In clothes blake, y-dropped al with teres;
And, passing othere of weping, Emelye,
The rewfulleste of al the companye.
In as muche as the service sholde be
The more noble and riche in his degree,   2030
Duk Theseus leet forth three stedes bringe,
That trapped were in steel al gliteringe,
And covered with the armes of daun Arcite.
Up-on thise stedes, that weren grete and whyte,
Ther seten folk, of which oon bar his sheeld,   2035
Another his spere up in his hondes heeld;
The thridde bar with him his bowe Turkeys,
Of brend gold was the cas, and eek the harneys;
And riden forth a pas with sorweful chere
Toward the grove, as ye shul after here.   2040
The nobleste of the Grekes that ther were
Upon his shuldres carieden the bere,
With slakke pas, and eyen rede and wete,
Thurgh-out the citee, by the maister-strete,
That sprad was al with blak, and wonder hye   2045
Right of the same is al the strete y-wrye.
Up-on the right hond wente old Egeus,
And on that other syde duk Theseus,
With vessels in hir hand of gold ful fyn,
Al ful of hony, milk, and blood, and wyn;   2050
Eek Palamon, with ful greet companye;
And after that cam woful Emelye,
With fyr in honde, as was that tyme the gyse,
To do thoffice of funeral servyse.

   Heigh labour, and ful greet apparaillinge   2055
Was at the service and the fyr-makinge,
That with his grene top the heven raughte,
And twenty fadme of brede the armes straughte;
This is to seyn, the bowes were so brode.
Of stree first ther was leyd ful many a lode.   2060
But how the fyr was maked up on highte,
And eek the names how the trës highte,
As ook, firre, birch, asp, alder, holm, popler,

Wilow, elm, plane, ash, box, chasteyn, lind, laurer,
Mapul, thorn, beech, hasel, ew, whippeltree,   2065
How they weren feld, shal nat be told for me;
Ne how the goddes ronnen up and doun,
Disherited of hir habitacioun,
In which they woneden in reste and pees,
Nymphes, Faunes, and Amadrides;   2070
Ne how the bestes and the briddes alle
Fledden for fere, whan the wode was falle;
Ne how the ground agast was of the light,
That was nat wont to seen the sonne bright;
Ne how the fyr was couched first with stree,   2075
And than with drye stokkes cloven a three,
And than with grene wode and spycerye,
And than with cloth of gold and with perrye,
And gerlandes hanging with ful many a flour,
The mirre, thencens, with al so greet odour;   2080
Ne how Arcite lay among al this,
Ne what richesse aboute his body is;
Ne how that Emelye, as was the gyse,
Putte in the fyr of funeral servyse;
Ne how she swowned whan men made the fyr,   2085
Ne what she spak, ne what was hir desyr;
Ne what Ieweles men in the fyr tho caste,
Whan that the fyr was greet and brente faste;
Ne how som caste hir sheeld, and som hir spere,
And of hir vestiments, whiche that they were,   2090
And cuppes ful of wyn, and milk, and blood,
Into the fyr, that brente as it were wood;
Ne how the Grekes with an huge route
Thryës riden al the fyr aboute
Up-on the left hand, with a loud shoutinge,   2095
And thryës with hir speres clateringe;
And thryës how the ladies gonne crye;
Ne how that lad was hom-ward Emelye;
Ne how Arcite is brent to asshen colde;
Ne how that liche-wake was y-holde   2100
Al thilke night, ne how the Grekes pleye
The wake-pleyes, ne kepe I nat to seye;
Who wrastleth best naked, with oille enoynt,
Ne who that bar him best, in no disioynt.
I wol nat tellen eek how that they goon   2105
Hoom til Athenes, whan the pley is doon;
But shortly to the poynt than wol I wende,
And maken of my longe tale an ende.

   By processe and by lengthe of certeyn yeres
Al stinted is the moorning and the teres   2110
Of Grekes, by oon general assent.

Than semed me ther was a parlement
At Athenes, up-on certeyn poynts and cas;
Among the whiche poynts y-spoken was
To have with certeyn contrees alliaunce,   2115
And have fully of Thebans obeisaunce.
For which this noble Theseus anon
Leet senden after gentil Palamon,
Unwist of him what was the cause and why;
But in his blake clothes sorwefully   2120
He cam at his comaundement in hye.
Tho sente Theseus for Emelye.
Whan they were set, and hust was al the place,
And Theseus abiden hadde a space
Er any word cam from his wyse brest,   2125
His eyen sette he ther as was his lest,
And with a sad visage he syked stille,
And after that right thus he seyde his wille.
   "The firste moevere of the cause above,
Whan he first made the faire cheyne of love,   2130
Greet was theffect, and heigh was his entente;
Wel wiste he why, and what ther-of he mente;
For with that faire cheyne of love he bond
The fyr, the eyr, the water, and the lond
In certeyn boundes, that they may nat flee;   2135
That same prince and that moevere," quod he,
"Hath stablissed, in this wrecched world adoun,
Certeyne dayes and duracioun
To al that is engendred in this place,
Over the whiche day they may nat pace,   2140
Al mowe they yet tho dayes wel abregge;
Ther needeth non auctoritee allegge,
For it is preved by experience,
But that me list declaren my sentence.
Than may men by this ordre wel discerne,   2145
That thilke moevere stable is and eterne.
Wel may men knowe, but it be a fool,
That every part deryveth from his hool.
For nature hath nat take his beginning
Of no partye ne cantel of a thing,   2150
But of a thing that parfit is and stable,
Descending so, til it be corrumpable.
And therfore, of his wyse purveyaunce,
He hath so wel biset his ordinaunce,
That speces of thinges and progressiouns   2155
Shullen enduren by successiouns,
And nat eterne be, with-oute lye:
This maistow understonde and seen at eye.
   "Lo the ook, that hath so long a norisshinge

From tyme that it first biginneth springe,   2160
And hath so long a lyf, as we may see,
Yet at the laste wasted is the tree.
   "Considereth eek, how that the harde stoon
Under our feet, on which we trede and goon,
Yit wasteth it, as it lyth by the weye.   2165
The brode river somtyme wexeth dreye.
The grete tounes see we wane and wende.
Than may ye see that al this thing hath ende.
   "Of man and womman seen we wel also,
That nedeth, in oon of thise termes two,   2170
This is to seyn, in youthe or elles age,
He moot ben deed, the king as shal a page;
Som in his bed, som in the depe see,
Som in the large feeld, as men may se;
Ther helpeth noght, al goth that ilke weye.   2175
Thanne may I seyn that al this thing moot deye.
What maketh this but Iupiter the king?
The which is prince and cause of alle thing,
Converting al un-to his propre welle,
From which it is deryved, sooth to telle.   2180
And here-agayns no creature on lyve
Of no degree availleth for to stryve.
   "Thanne is it wisdom, as it thinketh me,
To maken vertu of necessitee,
And take it wel, that we may nat eschue,   2185
And namely that to us alle is due.
And who-so gruccheth ought, he dooth folye,
And rebel is to him that al may gye.
And certeinly a man hath most honour
To dyen in his excellence and flour,   2190
Whan he is siker of his gode name;
Than hath he doon his freend, ne him, no shame.
And gladder oghte his freend ben of his deeth,
Whan with honour up-yolden is his breeth,
Than whan his name apalled is for age;   2195
For al forgeten is his vasselage.
Than is it best, as for a worthy fame,
To dyen whan that he is best of name.
The contrarie of al this is wilfulnesse.
Why grucchen we? why have we hevinesse,   2200
That good Arcite, of chivalrye flour
Departed is, with duetee and honour,
Out of this foule prison of this lyf?
Why grucchen heer his cosin and his wyf
Of his wel-fare that loved hem so weel?   2205
Can he hem thank? nay, God wot, never a deel,
That bothe his soule and eek hem-self offende,

And yet they mowe hir lustes nat amende.
  "What may I conclude of this longe serie,
But, after wo, I rede us to be merie,   2210
And thanken Iupiter of al his grace?
And, er that we departen from this place,
I rede that we make, of sorwes two,
O parfyt Ioye, lasting ever-mo;
And loketh now, wher most sorwe is her-inne,   2215
Ther wol we first amenden and biginne.
  "Suster," quod he, "this is my fulle assent,
With al thavys heer of my parlement,
That gentil Palamon, your owne knight,
That serveth yow with wille, herte, and might,   2220
And ever hath doon, sin that ye first him knewe,
That ye shul, of your grace, up-on him rewe,
And taken him for housbonde and for lord:
Leen me your hond, for this is our acord.
Lat see now of your wommanly pitee.   2225
He is a kinges brother sone, pardee;
And, though he were a povre bacheler,
Sin he hath served yow so many a yeer,
And had for yow so greet adversitee,

It moste been considered, leveth me;   2230
For gentil mercy oghte to passen right."
  Than seyde he thus to Palamon ful right;
"I trowe ther nedeth litel sermoning
To make yow assente to this thing.
Com neer, and tak your lady by the hond."   2235
Bitwixen hem was maad anon the bond,
That highte matrimoine or mariage,
By al the counseil and the baronage.
And thus with alle blisse and melodye
Hath Palamon y-wedded Emelye.   2240
And God, that al this wyde world hath wroght,
Sende him his love, that hath it dere a-boght.
For now is Palamon in alle wele,
Living in blisse, in richesse, and in hele;
And Emelye him loveth so tendrely,   2245
And he hir serveth al-so gentilly,
That never was ther no word hem bitwene
Of Ielousye, or any other tene.
Thus endeth Palamon and Emelye;
And God save al this faire companye! Amen.   2250

Here is ended the Knightes Tale.

Glossary

  Quotation "And now [Theseus, approaching] his native land, after sharp battle with the Scythian people [i.e., the Amazons], in his chariot decked with laurel. . . ." These lines herald the approach of the conquering hero, Theseus, who resolves the action in the last book of the *Thebaid*. **1 Whylom** once. **2 Theseus** ruler (here called duke for Latin *dux*) of Athens, who had a well-established reputation during the Middle Ages as an exemplar of wisdom (*sapientia*, a "knowledge of things human and divine") and chivalry, the virtues mentioned in l. 7. **3 Athenes** Athens, conventionally associated with Athena or Minerva (wisdom). Boccaccio explains that Minerva was the patron saint of Athens much in the same way that John the Baptist was the patron saint of Florence. **8 Femenye** the country of the Amazons. As legend had it, the Scythian women, tired of being dominated by their husbands, killed all the men in their dominions and then proceeded to kill all male intruders also. Theseus put an end to this "evil custom" and married the Amazonian Queen, Hippolyte. In effect, his "wisdom and chivalry" established a hierarchical ascendancy over the rampant "effeminacy" of the Amazons, setting their realm right side up again. **9 y-cleped** called. **10** This line begins the theme of marriage in *The Canterbury Tales*. Here marriage serves as it should, to preserve or restore the natural order in which effeminacy (sensuality) becomes subject to virility (wise virtue). **14 melodye** harmony, here not only the audible harmony of Theseus' triumph but also, in terms of medieval music, a moral harmony. **17 certes** certainly; **nere** were not. **27 moot** must. **29 wayke** weak. **31 letten** prevent (from telling his tale); **eek** also; **route** company. **32 aboute** in turn. **34 ther** in the place where. **37 wele** success. **38 war** aware. **44 weymentinge** lamentation. **45 nolde** would not; **stenten** cease. **46 henten** seized. **51 misboden** injured. **55 deedly chere** deathly appearance. **62 gentillesse** nobility. **65 nath** has not. **66 caitifs** wretches. **68** "That assures no (single) estate of prosperity." **69 certes** certainly; **abyden** await. **70 the godesse Clemence** i.e., the abstraction of clemency venerated as a goddess. In Statius she has an altar in Athens surrounded by a grove of trees. It contains no image, for Clemency "delights to dwell in minds and hearts." There the wretched from all lands find sanctuary. To the medieval mind the temple suggested the New Law of mercy, which was associated appropriately with Athens, the city of wisdom. **74 Capaneus** one of the seven leaders who attacked Thebes. In his wrath he scaled the walls of the city, challenged Jupiter, and was killed by a thunderbolt. **76 array** condition. **80 Creon** King of Thebes, gave his kingdom to Oedipus for solving the riddle of the Sphinx. When the sons of Oedipus, Eteocles and Polynices, killed each other, Creon took the kingdom back and refused burial to the Argives and to Polynices. **81 Thebes** a city associated with discord and with devotion to Bacchus and Venus (drunkenness and lechery). **84 vileinye** any kind of ignoble behavior. **86 y-drawe** drawn together. **88 y-brent** burned. **89 houndes** dogs; **in despyt** without pity. **90 respyt** delay. **91 gruf** face down. **94 gentil** noble; **sterte** leaped. **96 Him thoughte** it seemed to him. **97 saugh** saw; **mat** defeated. **99 hente** seized. **102 ferforthly** thoroughly. **103 wreke** avenge. **107 abood** delay. **113 Ipolita** Hippolyte, Queen of the Amazons. **114 shene** fair. **117 Mars** god of wrath (here just wrath against evil); **targe** shield. **118 feeldes** fields (in the line of march). **121 y-bete** beaten (so as to form an image). **122 Minotaur** monstrous half bull, half man, the son of Pasiphae (typifying lechery and pride overcome by Theseus). **123 rit** rode. **135 tho** then; **gyse** manner. **147 tas** heap. **148 harneys** equipment; **wede** clothing. **149 pilours** despoilers. **152 Thurgh-girt** pierced through. **153 ligging** lying; **by and by** side by side. **154 oon armes** bearing the same heraldic markings. **155 Arcita** a name, like *Palamon*, derived from Boccaccio's *Teseida*; **hight** was called. **157 quike** quick (alive). **161 sustren** sisters. **166 nolde** did not desire; **raunsoun** ransom (it was customary to hold prisoners for ransom, a very profitable business in the late fourteenth century. Theseus, however, desires no monetary reward for his victory, his interest being in the just punishment of the royal house of Thebes. His action here should be regarded in this light, not in the light of modern humanitarian considerations) **169 laurer** laurel (cf. the quotation at the beginning of the tale). **170 Ioye** joy. **174 quyte** ransom. **176 morwe** morning; **May** The subsequent actions of the tale take place in early May. Boccaccio explains in a note to the *Teseida* at this point that he places the sun in Taurus and Jupiter in Pisces and that this configuration disposes persons to be amorous. In medieval contexts the season of May was also said to be characteristic of paradise before the Fall. **181 noot** know not. **182 Er** before; **wone** custom. **183 dight** arrayed. **185 priketh** spurs. **187 observaunce** observance (i.e., it was customary to go out to gather flowers and to make garlands in early May). **190 for to devyse** for the purpose. **193 gardin** garden (i.e., the setting is a walled garden, suggestive of paradise, adjacent to the tower. A paradise is a "garden of delights" which may be either physical or spiritual. Gardens of this kind are conventional settings in medieval literature used for their overtones of meaning rather than for emotional atmosphere). **193 at the sonne up-riste** at sunrise. **194 as hir liste** as it pleased her. **206 wone** custom. **208 seigh** saw. **210 shene** fair. **216 cas** chance. **220 bleynte** blenched. **225 crydestow** did you cry. **230 Saturne** cf. l. 1599. **231** "although we had sworn it not to be true." **238 thurgh-out myn yë** through my eye (i.e., conventionally the "arrow of Cupid" [beauty or **fairnesse**] enters the eye and lodges as a phantasy in the heart. What follows is an elaboration of a conventional pattern of action based on medieval discussions of Matt. 5:28. The lady's eyes are not specifically involved here). **243 noot wher** do not know whether. **244 Venus** goddess of love. **252 linage** lineage (i.e., the lineage of Thebes, which was notoriously unfortunate. The city was founded by Cadmus, who sowed the teeth of a serpent in the earth. When these sprang up as men, they fought among themselves until only five were left. The subsequent history of the city founded by Cadmus and these men is characterized by discord and misery. In their quarrel Palamon and Arcite fulfill the tradition of their lineage). **256 hir beautee hurte him so** i.e., her beauty entered his eye, lodged in his heart, and provoked a painful cupidity.   **264 I nam but deed**   i.e., "I am only a dead man." The threat to die of frustration if a beautiful object once seen were not enjoyed to the full was universally regarded with ridicule. Cf. Shakespeare, *Henry V*, 5:2, 98ff. Chaucer does not, in medieval terms, make the behavior of the two brothers here either sentimentally or intellectually appealing.   **266 Dispitously**   pitilessly.   **267**   i.e., "Do you say this seriously or jokingly?"   **269 me list ful yvele**   it would please me not at all.   **274**   i.e., Palamon and Arcite are not only cousins but sworn brothers.   **275 for to dyen in the peyne**   even though one of us should die by torture.   **284 woldest . . . been aboute**   wish to make preparations.   **285 serve**   Palamon's service has been purely imaginary.   **286 sterve**   die.   **289 As to my conseil**   i.e., "as if to one obliged to counsel me." The importance of reliable counsel in a feudal society should not be overlooked.   **291 y-bounden as a knight**   i.e., by the virtue of fidelity.   **297 par amour**   for the sake of love (not with a view to marriage).   **298 wistest nat yet now**   did not know a moment ago.   **304 I pose**   I grant the proposition conditionally for the sake of argument.   **306**   The quotation is from Boethius, *Consolation*, 3:12, where the question is asked despairingly in view of the foolish behavior of Orpheus in looking back at (and so losing) Euridice.   **309 positif law**   man-made law as distinct from natural or divine law. Arcite is, in this passage, deliberately recommending criminal behavior.   **310 al-day**   all the time; **in ech degree**   in every social rank.   **311 maugree his heed**   no matter what the consequences to himself.   **313**   i.e., it makes no difference whether the source of pleasurable satisfaction envisaged is a virgin, a widow, or a married woman.   **314–315**   i.e., "it is unlikely that you will enjoy a reciprocal affection while you live, and I shall not do so either." This, of course, is an excellent reason for both young men to forget their enmity, but Arcite deliberately spurns this implication.   **316 thou woost**   you know.   **318 us gayneth no raunsoun**   i.e., no ransom will free us.   **319 houndes**   dogs (The same fable is used by Deschamps to show the foolishness of lovers striving for the same woman).   **323–324**   It is obvious that this conclusion does not follow from the fable. It is designed to emphasize Arcite's foolishness.   **325 ay shal**   always shall.   **327 mote we**   we must.   **331 theffect**   the effect (subsequent events).   **333 Perotheus**   Pirithous, King of the Lapithae. The friendship between Theseus and Pirithous was widely celebrated.   **335 lyte**   little.   **350 In swich a gyse**   in such a manner.   **351 forward**   agreement; **tendyte**   to describe it.   **354 stounde**   hour.   **358 reed**   counsel.   **360 to wedde**   as a pledge.   **364 wayteth**   expects.   **367 is me shape**   I am destined.   **368 in helle**   i.e., deprived of the sight of Emily.   **376ff.**   Note that these lines constitute a soliloquy and are not addressed to Palamon in person.   **380 y-turned thee the dys**   turned the dice in your favor.   **386 bareyne**   barren.   **388**   i.e., any of the four elements.   **391 wanhope**   despair.   **392 lust**   pleasure.   **394 purveyaunce**   Providence (the following argument takes up some principles from *The Consolation of Philosophy* of Boethius and concludes by avoiding, in an amusing way, their logical implications).   **395 in many a gyse**   in many ways.   **396 devyse**   devise (i.e., people frequently find themselves better situated than they might have been if allowed to devise their own fates).   **399**   i.e., would gladly be free of prison.   **400 meynee**   household (cf. Lat. *familia*).   **402 witen**   know.   **406 slider**   slippery.   **411 wende**   thought.   **416**   Cf. l. 264. Here Arcite comes to a conclusion directly contrary to that which logically follows from the doctrine he has expounded.   **418 wiste**   knew.   **421 pure**   very (i.e., his tears streamed down below his knees, a humorous exaggeration).   **423ff.**   Note that this speech, like Arcite's just concluded, is a soliloquy, the purpose of which is to reveal something about the speaker, not something about the subject of his discourse.   **426 charge**   care.   **429 make a werre**   make war (under feudal custom, the only legal and honorable course Arcite may take to win Emily).   **432 mot nedes**   must of necessity.   **443 woodly**   insanely.   **443–444 lyk . . . the box-tree**   i.e., pale (with a humorous allusion to Thisbe's condition on finding Pyramus dead. See Ovid, *Metamorphoses*, 4:134–135).   **447 athamaunt**   adamant.   **450 rouketh**   cowers.   **455ff.**   This passage, like that beginning in l. 394, recalls principles in *The Consolation of Philosophy* but disregards Philosophy's teaching, so that it is a patently foolish complaint.   **458 observaunce**   duty.   **459 to letten of his wille**   to restrain his desire.   **470 Saturne**   Cf. l. 1599.

471 Iuno Juno, whom Boccaccio calls the goddess of matrimony (i.e., matrimony venerated as an ideal), was angry with the Thebans because Jupiter had loved Semele, daughter of Cadmus and mother of Bacchus, and Theban Alcmena, mother of Hercules. **482 mester** occupation. **486 upon his head** i.e., on pain of losing his head. **495 demeth** judge (the answer implied being that they are both prisoners of their own passions). **498 swelte** fainted. **504 wex** became. **506 hewe** color; **falwe** yellow. **514 gere** erratic behavior. **515–516 loveres maladye Of Hereos** the lover's malady, treated at length in medical writings by Arnaldus of Villanova and Bernard of Gordon. When a phantasy of a beautiful woman enters the eye (or is otherwise perceived), is lodged in the memory, and is venerated, the result is a disease which may lead to mania and death. The general medieval attitude toward this condition was not respectful, and there is nothing romantic or sentimentally attractive in the present description. **517 humour malencolyk** melancholy, or black bile. **518 celle fantastyk** the anterior of the three cells of the brain as described by medieval writers. The second cell controlled reason, and the third (posterior) cell controlled memory. When the first was disturbed, the other two were thrown out of order. **519 up-so-doun** i.e., the reign of his mind was inverted, so that reason no longer controlled his passions. **527 Him thoughte how** it seemed to him that; **Mercurie** Mercury, god of eloquence (which might be either constructive or destructive. Here the advice of Mercury is a figure for evil counsel). **529 slepy yerde** sleep-producing rod, the caduceus (now used as a symbol by physicians), employed by Mercury to put Argus (i.e., as Boccaccio explains, reason) to sleep. **532 Argus** put to sleep by Mercury while he was guarding Io at the behest of Juno (see Ovid, *Metamorphoses*, 1:568ff.). **536 how sore that me smerte** no matter how much I suffer for it. **553 privitee** secret. **558 drugge** drudge; **drawe** haul (cf. Isa. 5:18). **560 fil in office with a chamberleyn** obtained employment with a chamberlain (household attendant). **564 hewen wode, and water bere** a reminiscence of Josue 9, where the Gabaonites who came in servile disguise before Josue were condemned to perpetual servitude hewing wood and drawing water. This servile condition was thought to indicate a servitude of the spirit. The implication here is that Arcite had placed himself in spiritual servitude through his passion. **570 Philostrate** a name from Boccaccio's *Filostrato*, where it is said to mean "vanquished by love." **581 so neer** i.e., so near to his person. **585 prively** secretly; **rente** his income from holdings in Thebes. **586 honestly and slyly** i.e., deceitfully, but with an honest or virtuous appearance. The pejorative implications of these words should not be glossed over. **590 derre** dearer. **592 a lyte** a little. **595 Forpyned** wasted away. **598 wood** insane. **602–603** The attitude toward the lovers is here and elsewhere witty and derisive, not romantic and serious. The Knight was not an arrested adolescent. **605** The date of Palamon's escape is May 3, unfortunate astrologically, because the sun entered the "face" of Saturn at about that time, and also unfortunate for lovers in the ecclesiastical calendar as the Feast of the Discovery of the Holy Cross. According to legend, a statue of Venus was thrown down that the Cross might be raised. **607 aventure or destinee** chance or fate (i.e., since Boethius explains that chance is a mere word and that destiny is the operation of Providence in particular instances, what ll. 607–608 imply is that the escape was Providential. Cf. ll. 805–814). **613 clarree** mixture of wine, honey, and spices. **614 opie of Thebes** opium from Thebes, properly Thebes in Egypt, but perhaps here with pejorative overtones concerning Palamon's country. **616 sleep** slept. **619 nedes-cost** of necessity. **621 dredful** fearful. **626 werreye** make war (cf. l. 429; here Palamon proposes to behave honorably). **635–636** perhaps an echo of Dante, *Purgatorio*, 1:20, with the deliberate substitution of Phoebus, the sun, for Venus, the morning star. **637 greves** branches. **644 sterting** leaping. **650 wodebinde** woodbine (European honeysuckle). **651 shene** bright. **656 sterte** leaped. **662 trowed** expected. **665– 666** i.e., it is good for a man to observe restraint, for people frequently meet at unexpected times. **667 woot** knew. **668 herknen** listen to; **sawe** discourse. **671 roundel** rondeau, a song with a refrain repeated within the stanza of a type sung frequently by young people at festivals during the Middle Ages. In this one, the first three lines of which appear as ll. 652–654 the first two lines may be thought to constitute the refrain. **673 queynte geres** curious kinds of erratic behavior, with the possibility of a humorous suggestion in *queynte* (cf. Modern English "cunt"), common in Chaucer's later poetry. **674 in the croppe** in the tree top (i.e., with elevated spirits). **675 boket in a welle** typifying the ups and downs of fortune, to which a lover of this kind subjects himself. **676 Friday** Venus's day, proverbially inconstant in terms of the rest of the week. **678 gery** erratic. **680 gerful** erratic; **array** i.e., aspect. **681** i.e., Friday is seldom like the rest of the week. **685 Iuno** Juno (cf. l. 471). **688 blood royal of Cadme and Amphioun** Cf. l. 252 and n. Amphion was the son of Jupiter and Antiope. He was King of Thebes, whose walls he built with the music of his lyre. He stabbed himself in grief at the death of his sons, thus making a typical Theban ill ending. **692 linage** lineage (cf. l. 252 and n. Arcite behaves as though he venerated the examples set by Cadmus and his successors). **694 so caitif and so thral** so wretched and so enslaved. **696** Cf. l. 564. **698** i.e., he is attempting an extramarital liaison of the kind exemplified by Jupiter's Theban affairs, and he is violating the principles of matrimony secretly. **701 felle Mars** i.e., wrath, which if uncontrolled, leads to self-destruction. **706 fyry dart** fiery arrow (cf. l. 238). **712 mountaunce of a tare** value of a tare (weed). **714 traunce** trance (i.e., Arcite's reason is so disturbed by passion that he loses his senses. This kind of behavior was thought to be effeminate). **718 byde** wait. **721 sterte him** leaped. **727 by-iaped** thoroughly tricked. **734 am astert** have escaped. **738 despitous** piti- less. **742 Nere it** were it not. **746 seurtee** surety. **748 verray** true. **749 maugre** in spite of. **751 darreyne hir** decide the right to her. **753 witing** knowledge. **756 chees** choose. **764 to borwe** as a pledge. **765 Cupide** the god of love, son of Venus. A distinction was sometimes made between Cupid, the stimulus to love or the desire to love, and Venus, the pleasure of love; **out of alle charitee** without any love for another (i.e., the desire inspired by Cupid is entirely selfish). **766** It is a commonplace that cupidinous love is always accompanied by jealousy. **767–768** Cf. Ovid, *Ars amatoria*, 3:564. **768 his thankes** willingly. **772 harneys** suits of armor; **dight** prepared. **773 mete** fitting; **darreyne** decide. **780 Trace** Thrace, associated with Mars (cf. l. 1972). **783 greves** brush. **791 good day** "good morning"; **saluing** salutation. **796 foynen** thrust and parry. **797 wene** think. **802 Up to the ancle** up to the ankle (a phrase used in romances, but here humorous exaggeration). **805–814** i.e., the subsequent discovery of Palamon and Arcite by Theseus should not be thought of as being fortuitous. The narrative logic here and elsewhere is the logic of the Providential order, not the logic of events. **817 namely** especially; **grete herte** the hart, regarded in medieval hunting poems as noble game. The hunt for the hart, here associated with Diana, suggested virtuous pursuits. **824 Diane** Diana, who hunted ferocious wild beasts. Her hunt is contrasted with that of Venus, who recommended hunting small, furry creatures that turn their backs. See Ovid, *Metamorphoses*, 10:553ff., and 705–707. The hunt of Venus, most frequently represented in terms of hare or rabbit hunt- ing, but also with falconry, is a figure for the pursuit of pleasure. **839 Under the sonne** i.e., in this instance eastward, below the morning sun. **841 breme** furiously. **847 stert** bound. **852 what mister men** men of what office. **859 caytyves** wretches. **867 on his heed** on pain of losing his head. **871 Iaped** tricked. **881 Iuwyse** sentence. **888 pyne** torture. **890ff.** In one of the most famous chivalric gestures of the period, King Edward spared the burghers of Calais at the behest of Queen Philippa, who wept for them. The reaction of Theseus here is in the best chivalric tradition. **893 it thoughte hem** it seemed to them. **903** a favorite expression of Chaucer's, sometimes (al- though not here) ironic, when either the pity or the nobility involved is questionable. Cf. Ovid, *Tristia*, 3:5, 31–32. **904 quook** quaked. **913 ever in oon** continually. **915–923** The principle expressed here is that of the New Law, where justice is tempered with mercy to those who are repentant. Cf. Shakespeare, *Merchant of Venice*, 4:1, 184–189. **927 The god of love** Cupid; **benedicite** a common expression of astonishment. **931 at his owne gyse** according to his own plan. **934 quitly** entirely. **946 wenen** think. **949 Iolitee** jollity (ironic). **950** i.e., is no more responsible for their plight than I am. **959 las** noose. **964 dere** injure. **980** Cf. the current expression "fly a kite." **983 in**

this degree in this position. **987 plat** plain. **988 replicacioun** appeal. **992 fer ne ner** neither more nor less. **994 at alle rightes** in all respects. **995 by bataille** Resort to trial by battle was customary in the fourteenth century when sufficient proofs could not be obtained to establish the right of either litigant. **996 bihote** promise. **1006 even** just. **1010 avys** counsel. **1019 namely** especially; **ofte sythe** many times. **1022** Cf. l. 473. **1032 degrees** seats arranged stepwise. **1040 ars-metrik** arithmetic. **1042 mete** food. **1050 fother** load. **1060ff.** The description of the Temple of Venus, who is here the goddess of lustful love, is based on that in Boccaccio's *Teseida*, but contains additions from other sources. Chaucer used materials from Boccaccio neglected here in the description of the Temple of Venus in *The Parliament of Fowls*. **1070 Ielousye** jealousy, said to be an inevitable attribute of lecherous love. **1071 goldes** marigolds, probably the corn marigold of England (not, in any event, one of the various types of *Tagetes* now widely cultivated), associated with jealousy because of its yellow color. **1072 cokkow** the cuckoo, which lays its eggs in the nests of other birds and was hence associated with cuckoldry and jealousy. **1073 caroles** dances in which the participants join hands and sing. **1078 Citheroun** according to Boccaccio a mountain near Thebes where sacrifices were offered to Venus and where the climate was temperate and conducive to the act of Venus. **1082 Ydelnesse** idleness, conventionally the porter to the garden of sensual delights; that is, idleness is conducive to the contemplation of venereal pleasures. **1084** The folly of Solomon in allowing himself to be dominated by women was proverbial. See 3 Kings (Vulgate) 11:1–9. **1085 Hercules** Boccaccio adduces here the hero's unfortunate passion for Iole, which aroused the jealousy of his wife, which in turn provoked the gift of the poisonous shirt. **1086 Medea** notorious as an enchantress who committed many crimes because of her unrequited passion for Jason; **Circes** Circe, who attempted to ensnare Ulysses with her cup. **1087 Turnus** a warrior, the unsuccessful lover of Lavinia in *The Aeneid*. **1088 Cresus** Croesus, who failed to heed the warnings of his daughter to rule mercifully and was hanged. **1091 champartye** successful rivalry (i.e., as the previous examples show, Venus has the power to overcome anyone, no matter how wise, wealthy, beautiful, crafty, strong, or hardy, and to bring about his destruction. The examples should serve as a warning to any suppliant in this temple). **1097–1100** The description here is derived ultimately from Fulgentius and was thought to mean that Venus leads her followers to poverty and denudes them of counsel. **1101 citole** a stringed instrument, here used to suggest the "melody" or delightful modulation of sexual love. **1103 rose gerland** conventionally associated with Venus to show that libido causes blushes of shame and pricks with the awareness of sin. **1104 dowves** doves, associated with Venus because of their alleged lecherousness. **1105 Cupido** Cupid (cf. l. 765. The wings of Cupid were taken to mean that love is light and impermanent; his blindness indicated unreasonableness and lack of discrimination. The arrows either provoke or discourage love). **1111ff.** The description of the Temple of Mars is based on that in the *Teseida* with some additions, frequently humorous, of Chaucer's own. Mars generally represents wrath, which may be either reasonable or unreasonable. The present temple is that of unreasonable wrath. **1114 estres** interior walls. **1115 highte** is called; **Trace** Thrace. Boccaccio explains that Thrace is cold, cloudy, wet, windy, icy, savage, full of unfruitful trees, dark, inimical to the sun, and full of tumult. The place is suited, he says, to very irascible people. **1116 colde frosty regioun** i.e., as Boccaccio explains, because the wrathful are cold, or cruel and rigid, through lack of charity. **1117–1120** The forest, Boccaccio says, indicates the secret malice of the wrathful. It is empty of men and beasts because the wrathful rule neither themselves nor others. The trees are barren to show that wrath destroys and lays waste the fruits of human action. **1121 rumbel and a swough** thunder and the noise of the wind, presaging storms of wrathful passion. **1122 bresten** break. **1123 bente** hillside. **1124 armipotente** powerful in arms. **1125 burned steel** i.e., to indicate the hardness and obstinacy of the wrathful; **thentree** the entry. **1126 streit** narrow; **gastly** terrible. **1127 vese** blast. **1128 rese** shake. **1129 northren light** dim light; the darkness of the temple indicates that the light of grace is excluded. **1132 adamant** a very hard substance, which, Boccaccio says, excludes human counsel. **1133** i.e., bound crosswise and lengthwise. **1136 tonne-greet** weighing a ton. **1139 glede** coal. **1142 shepne** stable or fold. **1145 Contek** strife. **1146 chirking** harsh, shrill sound. **1147 sleere of him-self** slayer of himself (in the visual arts the vice of wrath was frequently represented as a man thrusting a knife into his own breast). **1149 shode** temples (cf. Judges 4:21). **1150 up-right** face up. **1153 woodnesse** madness. **1154 out-hees** alarm. **1156 qualm** pestilence, the business of Saturn rather than Mars. **1159 shippes hoppesteres** bobbing ships. **1161 freten** devour. **1168 stith** stithy (anvil). **1172 sotil** thin. **1173 Iulius** Julius Caesar. **1174 Antonius** Antony. **1187 Puella . . . Rubeus** figures in geomancy representing Mars direct and Mars retrograde. **1189 wolf** a conventional attribute of Mars used to indicate that he was a devourer of men. In some manuals of mythography, the wolf is also said to represent a prostitute. **1192 redoutinge** reverence. **1193 temple of Diane** not in the *Teseida*. Chaucer wittily borrows some details from Boccaccio's Temple of Venus, which illustrate offenses against Diana as she represents chastity. **1198 Calistopee** Callisto, a beautiful virgin of Arcady in the train of Diana. When Jupiter saw her, he could not restrain himself. As a ruse, he disguised himself as Diana. Callisto, thinking him to be Diana, ran to embrace him. When she later became unmistakably pregnant, Diana cast her out. She gave birth to a son, Arcas. In anger Juno turned Callisto into a bear. One day when he was hunting, Arcas killed her by mistake. Jupiter took pity on both of them, turned Arcas into a bear, and placed both in heaven, where one is Ursa Major and the other Ursa Minor. The tail of the latter contains the lodestar. **1201 lode-sterre** i.e., the group of stars of which the most prominent is the lodestar. **1202 ferre** further. **1203 sterre** i.e., the group of stars making up Ursa Major. **1204 Dane** Daphne, who while fleeing from the amorous pursuit of Apollo, was turned into a laurel tree (see Ovid, *Metamorphoses*, 1:548ff.). **1207 Attheon** Actaeon, who saw Diana naked in a pool. Angered, she turned him into a stag, and he was torn to pieces by his own dogs (see Ovid, *Metamorphoses*, 3:198ff.). The fierce dogs of Actaeon are sometimes said to represent his own passions. **1212 Atthalanta** Atalanta of Arcadia, first to strike the Calydonian boar in the famous hunt. The boar had been loosed by Diana. When Meleager, who loved Atalanta, presented the trophy of the hunt to her, his uncles resented the gift. In the ensuing dispute, he killed them both. Later his mother killed him to avenge the deaths of her brothers. **1219 mone** the moon. Diana was a triple goddess, representing (1) the moon, (2) chastity, and (3) Lucina, or Proserpina, queen of the underworld (i.e., the devil's wife). **1224 Pluto** King of Hades (i.e., Satan). **1227 Lucyna** Lucina, Queen of Hades, supposed to be helpful to women in childbirth. **1229 lyfly** with verisimilitude. **1230 florin** a coin worth six shillings; **hewes** colors. **1234 him lyked** pleased him. **1239 darreyne** decide. **1245 of hir hond** based on deeds performed with the hand. **1249 his thankes** willingly; **passant** well-known. **1251 wel was him** i.e., he was well off. **1254 paramours** for the sake of love (i.e., not with a view to marriage). **1261 habergeoun** sleeveless coat of mail. **1262 gipoun** tunic. **1264 Pruce sheld** Prussian shield; **targe** small shield. **1271 Ligurge** Lycurgus, called King of Thrace in a gloss to the *Thebaid*, is not, in this description, a recognizable figure from traditional sources. Neither is Emetreus (l. 2156). The attributes of the two figures have never been satisfactorily explained, but in any event, they suggest, in somewhat exaggerated terms, the fierceness of the impending battle. **1275 griffon** a lionlike monster with wings of an eagle. **1276 kempe** combed. **1280 char** chariot. **1281 trays** trace. **1284 beres-skin** bearskin. Bears and lions were associated with fierce, worldly tyrants on the basis of Prov. 28:15 and were sometimes represented in the visual arts with this significance (cf. ll. 917, 1313); **for-old** very old. **1286 for-blak** very black. **1290 alaunts** wolfhounds. **1293 mosel** muzzle. **1294 torets fyled rounde** rings for attaching a leash. **1302 cloth of Tars** probably silk. **1309 citryn** greenish yellow. **1310 sangwyn** ruddy. **1311 fraknes** freckles. **1312 y-meynd** mixed. **1319 deduyt** diversion. **1331 pryme** the first hour of the natural day (the day from dawn to sunset). **1334 inned hem** given them lodgings. **1335 festeth** prepares a feast for. **1337 weneth** thinks. **1342 deys** dias (the place of honor). **1355 holy** pious; **heigh corage** high hopes. **1358 digne** worthy.

1359 hir houre Each hour of the day (divided into twelve hours from sunrise to sunset and twelve hours from sunset to sunrise) was said to be governed by a separate planet. The planets were arranged in the following order: Saturn, Jupiter, Mars, sun, Venus, Mercury, moon. The first hour after dawn on Sunday was that of the sun, the second that of Venus, and so on. If the remainder of the hours are filled by repeating the series, the first hour on Monday is that of the moon, the second that of Saturn, and so on. Palamon went to the temple during the twenty-third hour of Sunday, an hour of Venus. He went, however, on the day of the sun. **1365 mount of Citheroun** See l. 1078. There may be in this line a humorous suggestion based on the usual meaning of *mons Veneris*. **1366 Adoun** Adonis (the mention of Adonis in this prayer is not especially tactful, since Venus could not persuade Adonis to hunt the small fearful creatures dear to her and he was killed by a boar. See Ovid, *Metamorphoses*, 10:519ff.). **1367 smerte** painful. **1377–1378** The true servant of Venus must make perpetual war on chastity. This vow is entirely inconsistent with any desire to marry Emily; what Palamon wants is to use Emily as an instrument to assist him in the service of Venus (pleasure). **1380 kepe noght** care not; **yelpe** boast. Palamon renounces all interest in chivalry. **1387 recche** care. **1394 ryde or go** ride or walk. **1403 thorisoun** the orison (prayer). **1413 The thridde houre inequal** i.e., the first hour of Monday, or the hour of Diana on Diana's day. **1419 Thencens** the incense. **1421 meth** mead (here carried in drinking horns). **1428 a game** an amusing experience. **1429 charge** burden (for the sense of this line, see Titus 1:15; Rom. 14:13–14). **1430 at his large** free (i.e., without the burden of hearing something which might be unclean to him, or, in St. Paul's words, a "stumbling block." Chaucer was probably thinking of sacrifices of living beasts like those described by Statius, *Thebaid* 4:443ff.). **1432 ook cerial** according to Boccaccio, acorn-bearing oak worn in honor of Diana as goddess of forests. **1436 Stace** Statius (see l. 1430n.). **1440 is sene** to be seen. **1442 maydens** virgins. It should be remembered that chastity is only a virtue when its end is charity. Thus St. Gregory says that chastity for the sake of reputation is "fornication of the spirit." **1445 Atheon** See l. 1207n. **1446 wostow** you know. **1450 hunting and venerye** an expression made somewhat amusing by the double meaning of *venery*. **1455 thre formes** See l. 1219n. **1475 queynte** curious. **1476 queynte** quenched. **1478 queynt** quenched. **1479 queynte** was quenched (by this time the repetition of this word has become humorous. See l. 673n.). **1490 stint** cease. **1500 cas** quiver. **1509 houre of Mars** i.e., the fourth hour on Diana's day. **1516 Trace** Thrace (see l. 1115n.). **1518 brydel** bridle (i.e., control). **1531 Vulcanus** Vulcan, husband of Venus. These lines refer to the story of Vulcan's trap in which Mars and Venus were caught naked in bed together committing adultery. Their amour had been revealed by Apollo, the sun (see Ovid, *Metamorphoses*, 4:167ff.; *Ars amatoria*, 2:561ff.). Arcite's reference to this story is in somewhat dubious taste, since Mars did not fare very well. Ovid distinctly ridicules him in this connection, and the story was frequently applied in such a way as to show how military virtue may be chained and debilitated by lust. **1539 flete** float (i.e., swim). **1540 hete** promise. **1545 fyr** the fire of lust, a common figure which may be found in the Bible, in classical sources, and in medieval poetry. **1547 do that** make it so that. **1560** In view of the nature of the temple, what Arcite is promising is to be perpetually wrathful, a promise consistent with the lineage of Thebes. **1579 fowel** bird. **1585 Saturnus** Saturn, a cold, old planet associated with time and with misfortune. The attributes of the gods and the planets mingle freely, both in the manuals of the mythographers and in poetry. Saturn was said to consume his children. That is, time destroys those who pursue temporal ends. **1588 plesed every part** i.e., satisfied all the celestial disputants. **1590 wisdom** As a representative of wisdom, Saturn personifies the Providential working out of the wrath, or punitive justice, of God typified in the Old Law. **1591 at-renne** outrun; **at-rede** outwit. **1592 stinten** bring an end to. **1595 doghter Venus** Venus could be called, with almost equal propriety, "daughter of Jove" (as in l. 1364), "daughter of Caelus," or, as here, "daughter of Saturn." The last relationship exists by virtue of the fact that in one account the goddess was born from the sea when it became impregnated by the virile members of Saturn, cut off and thrown there by Jupiter. The curious will find a sufficient explanation of these relationships in Boccaccio's *Genealogie deorum gentilium*. Meanwhile, Venus is appropriately associated with Jupiter, a benevolent astrological influence, in l. 1364, and with Saturn, a malevolent influence, in the present line. **1596 cours** course in the heavens. Saturn was regarded as the outermost and slowest of the planets. **1598 drenching** drowning. **1599 cote** dungeon. **1604 signe of the leon** the constellation Leo. **1610 castes** contrivances. **1611 loking** influence. **1617 complexioun** complexion; i.e., Venus was said to be hot and moist (sanguine) while Mars was hot and dry (choleric). **1618 divisioun** dissension. When the influences of Venus and Mars were combined, as they are in the Wife of Bath, the result was a lecherous and contentious person, bold and shameless. **1628 Monday** the day before the tournament, which took place on Tuesday, the day of Mars. **1629 in Venus heigh servyse** i.e., in making love in the manner suggested by the description of the Temple of Venus. **1638 herneys** equipment. **1639 uncouth** strange. **1640 browding** embroidery. **1641 testers** head armor for horses; **trappures** trappings for horses. **1643 paraments** rich clothing. **1644 Nailinge** fastening on the heads. **1646 Gigginge** fitting with an arm strap; **layneres** straps. **1650 prikinge** spurring (riding hastily). **1653 nakers** kettledrums; **clariounes** trumpets. **1656 holding hir questioun** discussing the probable outcome of the battle. **1662 sparth** battle-axe. **1669 fet** brought. **1674 his hest and his sentence** his command and his decision. **1675 an ho** a call to order. **1692 Foyne** thrust and parry; **were** defend. **1710 sarge** serge. **1717 by tyme** soon. **1721 degrees** seats. **1736 renges** ranks. **1745ff.** The alliteration in these lines is used for humorous effect. **1748 herte-spoon** the end of the breastbone. **1757 tronchoun** truncheon of a spear. **1761 forward** the agreement. **1768 Galgopheye** perhaps the vale of Gargaphie, sacred to Diana, although the significance of the reference, if it is one, is not clear. **1772 Belmarye** Benmarin, Morocco. **1780 hente** seize. **1784 Unyolden** without having yielded. **1811 bone** boon. **1820 priketh** rides. **1823 in comune** generally. The observation about women is in keeping with the behavior of Emily, who has no real knowledge of either Palamon or Arcite. **1825** i.e., insofar as his heart was concerned, he had no joy other than Emily. **1826 furie** Fury. The three Furies were said to represent passions which cause men to forget their true interest and expose themselves to perils. They are Alecto, Tisiphone, and Megara, usually associated in one way or another with cupidity, lust, and wrath. In the narrative, Saturn, or time, had this fury sent by Pluto, or Satan, to cause a wound in Arcite's breast. This arrangement was probably intended to suggest that Arcite was a victim of his own wrathful passion. When he seeks to turn from Mars to Venus, the dissension of the two (cf. l. 1618) within him destroys him. Mars, it will be remembered, is a "devourer of men." **1831 pighte** pitched; **pomel** top. **1839 blyve** quickly. **1849 fayn** glad. **1852 thirled** pierced. **1855 Fermacies** medicines; **save** a decoction of herbs. **1859 revel** feasting. **1871 nas aretted him** was not attributed to him. **1872 clepen** call. **1874 stinten** stop. **1875 gree** rank in the combat (i.e., neither side was to be considered overcome). **1888 bouk** trunk of the body. **1889 veyne-blood** drawing off venous blood (an ancient remedy, practiced until recent times); **ventusinge** use of a cupping-glass for blood-letting. **1891 vertu expulsif** the "animal virtue," said to be of force in expelling poisons. **1895 lacerte** muscle. **1896 shent** destroyed. **1897 Him gayneth** i.e., it helps him. **1899 to-brosten** broken in pieces. **1893 al and som** inevitable conclusion. **1921** Cf. Eccles. 4:10. **1933 Fredom** generosity. **1953 divinistre** theologian. **1957 Mars** (not a very trustworthy guide). **1976 Cracching** scratching (with the nails in grief). **1977–1978** The very materialistic concern of the women is intended to be amusing. It is consistent in tone with the remainder of this passage, which is not pathetic, but full of humorous exaggeration. **1984 lyknesse** similitude. **1990 pilgrimes** The pilgrimage of the spirit forms the basic thematic framework of *The Canterbury Tales.* **1992 muchel** much. **1993 enhorte** exhort. **2002 selve** same. **2008 rewe** row. **2009 colpons** long strips (here logs split lengthwise). **2013 bere** bier. **2025 flotery** uncombed (fluttery); **ruggy** rough. **2043 slakke** slow. **2046 y-wrye** draped. **2057 grene top** i.e., of the pyre; **raughte** reached. **2058 armes straughte** sides of the pyre stretched. **2059 bowes** boughs. **2060 stree** straw. **2064 chasteyn** chestnut. **2065 whippeltree** cornelian cherry. **2066 feld** felled. **2075 couched** laid (couched). **2076 stokkes** logs. **2078 perrye** jewelry. **2080 mirre** myrrh. **2100 liche-wake** wake. **2102 wake-pleyes** funeral games. **2104 disioynt** evil plight. **2109 certeyn yeres** several years, time enough for Palamon's passion and the sorrow of the Athenians to cool. **2116 of Thebans obeisaunce** i.e., to make Thebes, the city of discord and passion, subject to Athens, the city of wisdom. **2129ff.** The long speech of Theseus is based on *The Consolation of Philosophy* of Boethius (especially 2:met. 8; 4: pr. 6, met. 6; 3:pr. 10). It furnishes, together with ll. 915–922, the basic philosophical doctrine of the tale. **2129 firste moevere** God. **2130 faire cheyne of love** the bond of celestial love responsible for the intelligible harmony of creation. This love is, in classical terms, the celestial Venus; in Christian terms, it is the Holy Spirit, which is everywhere. **2138 dayes and duracioun** i.e., every living creature has a life cycle of a certain duration. **2141 abregge** abridge. **2153 purveyaunce** Providence. **2175 ilke** same. **2177 Iupiter** here a figure for God. **2179 welle** will. **2186 that** that which. **2187 gruccheth** complains (against the Providential Order). For examples, see ll. 365–416, 445–475. **2188 gye** govern. **2196 vasselage** the qualities of a good vassal, or chivalric virtue. **2209 serie** argument. **2213 rede** advise. **2217 parlement** The establishment of harmonious relations between countries, here the concern of the Athenian Parliament, was accounted one of the virtuous motives for marriage. **2218 thavys** the counsel. **2231** Cf. ll. 915–923. **2237 matrimoine** matrimony (cf. l. 10n.). The marriage is in no sense an answer to Palamon's prayer, except insofar as it is made under the auspices of the celestial Venus (cf. l. 2130n.). It establishes a proper relationship between Athens and Thebes and is, at the same time, a reasonable solution to Palamon's difficulties. One of the functions of marriage is to put down concupiscence. **2239 melodye** Cf. l. 14n. **2244 hele** well-being. We may assume that the wrath of Juno against Thebes is appeased by this marriage, so that the lineage of Thebes here loses its traditional character through the domination of Athens, or wisdom. **2248 Ielousye** Cf. ll. 766, 1070. There is a sense in which Diana triumphs in the end, since the implication here is that the marriage was chaste (i.e., faithful); **tene** vexation.

THE MILLER'S TALE

The Miller's Tale is one of the finest of Chaucer's stories, both for its "solas," which is still appealing, and for its "sentence," which is inadvertent insofar as the Miller himself is concerned. Most of the figures on Chaucer's pilgrimage tell tales that are unwitting revelations of their own weaknesses. Idealized characters like the Knight or the Clerk may be said in a sense to represent the author, or to exemplify his ideals, but the less savory characters express dubious views of one kind or another, only to reveal to the discerning audience that such views are foolish.

At the outset the drunken Miller offers to do the Knight one better with a story of how a clerk deceived a carpenter. The Reeve objects, feeling that the proposed story may be a reflection on him. Medieval men had a strong sense of the community of their trades and professions, and they were likely to regard unsavory implications about other members of the same trades or professions as personal affronts. But for his pains the Reeve is made to hear a little sermon to the effect that a man should not be curious about the secret things of God, on the one hand, nor about the secret things of his wife, on the other. This theme is indeed elaborated in the tale, where the references to "privitee" of one sort or another are amusingly appropriate.

However, the tale suggests another, more profound theme at the same time. Nicholas, an expert in "derne love" and "solas," is obviously intensely interested in the pleasures of the flesh. His approach to Alysoun is direct and unmistakable. Absolon, with his elaborate coiffure and costume, peculiar sensitivity, and heroic efforts at playing Herod, is clearly vain. And the old carpenter John, with his "keping," his "Ialousye," and his reaction to the prospect of being lord "of al the world," suggests the traditional portrait of the avaricious man. Meanwhile, Alysoun is carefully described in such a way as to appeal to all the senses.

These features of the story as well as the references to the Flood would have suggested certain ideas to Chaucer's audience. In the Gospel story of the temptations in the wilderness, Satan approaches Jesus with three propositions. As they are related in Matthew (4.1ff.), he says first, "command that these stones be made bread"; then, "cast thyself down"; and finally, "all these [kingdoms of the world] will I give thee." In Patristic and later medieval accounts, these temptations were said to represent appeals to gluttony (or the desires of the flesh generally), vainglory (or self-glorification), and avarice (or elation over worldly things). Further, they were equated with the temptations in the garden that led to the Fall, so that they came to represent the three basic weaknesses of humanity that led to the downfall of man before Christ. But Christ overcame them, so that those who love Him might overcome them also.

The downfall of man before Christ is most vividly represented in the story of the Flood, which was thought of as a general purification of the world brought about chiefly as a result of man's submission to lechery, or the desires of the flesh, which lead in a sort of progression to the further weaknesses of vainglory and avarice.

Bearing these facts in mind, it is easy to see that the Miller's Tale is in a way a local echo of the Flood and that John is a false Noah. Like Noah, he is a carpenter. Noah's Ark is a conventional figure of the Church, and John is engaged in work on the priory church in Osney. But John's chief concern is an avaricious passion for his wife. The pursuit of Alysoun by the lecherous Nicholas and the vainglorious Absolon, as well as John's "keping," are all appropriately and amusingly rewarded at the close of the story. Thus what might have been merely a "merry tale" or a joke becomes high comedy. The Miller speaks better than he knows, and his tale is a reflection on exactly the kinds of weakness that he himself displays. In effect, the wisdom of Theseus can hardly be obscured by a drunken Miller, who will inadvertently reflect it even when he intends a simple lesson for the worldly wise.

Here folwen the wordes bitwene the Host and the Millere.

Whan that the Knight had thus his tale y-told,
In al the route nas ther yong ne old
That he ne seyde it was a noble storie,
And worthy for to drawen to memorie;
And namely the gentils everichoon.   5
Our Hoste lough and swoor, "so moot I goon,
This gooth aright; unbokeled is the male;
Lat see now who shal telle another tale:
For trewely, the game is wel bigonne.
Now telleth ye, sir Monk, if that ye conne,   10
Sumwhat, to quyte with the Knightes tale."
The Miller, that for-dronken was al pale,
So that unnethe up-on his hors he sat,
He nolde avalen neither hood ne hat,
Ne abyde no man for his curteisye,   15
But in Pilates vois he gan to crye,

And swoor by armes and by blood and bones,
"I can a noble tale for the nones,
With which I wol now quyte the Knightes tale."
Our Hoste saugh that he was dronke of ale,   20
And seyde: "abyd, Robin, my leve brother,
Som bettre man shal telle us first another:
Abyd, and lat us werken thriftily."
"By goddes soul," quod he, "that wol nat I;
For I wol speke, or elles go my wey."   25
Our Hoste answerde: "tel on, a devel wey!
Thou art a fool, thy wit is overcome."
"Now herkneth," quod the Miller, "alle and some!
But first I make a protestacioun
That I am dronke, I knowe it by my soun;   30
And therfore, if that I misspeke or seye,
Wyte it the ale of Southwerk, I yow preye;
For I wol telle a legende and a lyf
Bothe of a Carpenter, and of his wyf,
How that a clerk hath set the wrightes cappe."   35
The Reve answerde and seyde, "stint thy clappe,
Lat be thy lewed dronken harlotrye.
It is a sinne and eek a greet folye
To apeiren any man, or him diffame,
And eek to bringen wyves in swich fame.   40
Thou mayst y-nogh of othere thinges seyn."
This dronken Miller spak ful sone ageyn,
And seyde, "leve brother Osewold,
Who hath no wyf, he is no cokewold.
But I sey nat therfore that thou art oon;   45
Ther been ful gode wyves many oon,
And ever a thousand gode ayeyns oon badde,
That knowestow wel thy-self, but-if thou madde.
Why artow angry with my tale now?
I have a wyf, pardee, as well as thou,   50
Yet nolde I, for the oxen in my plogh,
Taken up-on me more than y-nogh,
As demen of my-self that I were oon;
I wol beleve wel that I am noon.
An housbond shal nat been inquisitif   55
Of goddes privetee, nor of his wyf.
So he may finde goddes foyson there,
Of the remenant nedeth nat enquere."
What sholde I more seyn, but this Millere
He nolde his wordes for no man forbere,   60
But tolde his cherles tale in his manere;
Me thinketh that I shal reherce it here.

And ther-fore every gentil wight I preye,
For goddes love, demeth nat that I seye
Of evel entente, but that I moot reherce 65
Hir tales alle, be they bettre or werse,
Or elles falsen som of my matere.
And therfore, who-so list it nat y-here,
Turne over the leef, and chese another tale;
For he shal finde y-nowe, grete and smale, 70
Of storial thing that toucheth gentillesse,
And eek moralitee and holinesse;
Blameth nat me if that ye chese amis.
The Miller is a cherl, ye knowe wel this;
So was the Reve, and othere many mo, 75
And harlotrye they tolden bothe two.
Avyseth yow and putte me out of blame;
And eek men shal nat make ernest of game.

Here endeth the prologe.

Here biginneth the Millere his tale.

Whylom ther was dwellinge at Oxenford
A riche gnof, that gestes heeld to bord,
And of his craft he was a Carpenter.
With him ther was dwellinge a povre scoler,
Had lerned art, but al his fantasye 5
Was turned for to lerne astrologye,
And coude a certeyn of conclusiouns
To demen by interrogaciouns,
If that men axed him in certein houres,
Whan that men sholde have droghte or elles
    shoures, 10
Or if men axed him what sholde bifalle
Of every thing, I may nat rekene hem alle.
   This clerk was cleped hende Nicholas;
Of derne love he coude and of solas;
And ther-to he was sleigh and ful privee, 15
And lyk a mayden meke for to see.
A chambre hadde he in that hostelrye
Allone, with-outen any companye,
Ful fetisly y-dight with herbes swote;
And he him-self as swete as is the rote 20
Of licorys, or any cetewale.
His Almageste and bokes grete and smale,
His astrelabie, longinge for his art,
His augrim-stones layen faire a-part
On shelves couched at his beddes heed: 25
His presse y-covered with a falding reed.
And al above ther lay a gay sautrye,

On which he made a nightes melodye
So swetely, that al the chambre rong;
And *Angelus ad virginem* he song; 30
And after that he song the kinges note;
Ful often blessed was his mery throte.
And thus this swete clerk his tyme spente
After his freendes finding and his rente.
   This Carpenter had wedded newe a wyf 35
Which that he lovede more than his lyf;
Of eightetene yeer she was of age.
Ialous he was, and heeld hir narwe in cage,
For she was wilde and yong, and he was old,
And demed him-self ben lyk a cokewold. 40
He knew nat Catoun, for his wit was rude,
That bad man sholde wedde his similitude.
Men sholde wedden after hir estaat,
For youthe and elde is often at debaat.
But sith that he was fallen in the snare, 45
He moste endure, as other folk, his care.
   Fair was this yonge wyf, and ther-with-al
As any wesele hir body gent and smal.
A ceynt she werede barred al of silk,
A barmclooth eek as whyt as morne milk 50
Up-on hir lendes, ful of many a gore.
Whyt was hir smok, and brouded al bifore
And eek bihinde, on hir coler aboute,
Of col-blak silk, with-inne and eek with-oute.
The tapes of hir whyte voluper 55
Were of the same suyte of hir coler;
Hir filet brood of silk, and set ful hye:
And sikerly she hadde a likerous yë.
Ful smale y-pulled were hir browes two,
And tho were bent, and blake as any sloo. 60
She was ful more blisful on to see
Than is the newe pere-ionette tree;
And softer than the wolle is of a wether.
And by hir girdel heeng a purs of lether
Tasseld with silk, and perled with latoun. 65
In al this world, to seken up and doun,
There nis no man so wys, that coude thenche
So gay a popelote, or swich a wenche.
Ful brighter was the shyning of hir hewe
Than in the tour the noble y-forged newe. 70
But of hir song, it was as loude and yerne
As any swalwe sittinge on a berne.
Ther-to she coude skippe and make game,
As any kide or calf folwinge his dame.
Hir mouth was swete as bragot or the meeth, 75

Figure 39 *The sin of lechery, from a devotional manual. The gesture here, imitated by Nicholas, was used conventionally in the visual arts to illustrate lechery. In the Miller's Tale it serves as an "attribute" for Nicholas, who is an exemplification of an idea, not a "personality." On the right stands an ale house with its "bush."*

Or hord of apples leyd in hey or heeth.
Winsinge she was, as is a Ioly colt,
Long as a mast, and upright as a bolt.
A brooch she baar up-on hir lowe coler,
As brood as is the bos of a bocler.   80
Hir shoes were laced on hir legges hye;
She was a prymerole, a pigges-nye
For any lord to leggen in his bedde,
Or yet for any good yeman to wedde.
    Now sire, and eft sire, so bifel the cas,   85
That on a day this hende Nicholas
Fil with this yonge wyf to rage and pleye,
Whyl that hir housbond was at Oseneye,
As clerkes ben ful subtile and ful queynte;
And prively he caughte hir by the queynte,   90
And seyde, "y-wis, but if ich have my wille,
For derne love of thee, lemman, I spille."
And heeld hir harde by the haunche-bones,
And seyde, "lemman, love me al at-ones,
Or I wol dyen, also god me save!"   95

And she sprong as a colt doth in the trave,
And with hir heed she wryed faste awey,
And seyde, "I wol nat kisse thee, by my fey,
Why, lat be," quod she, "lat be, Nicholas,
Or I wol crye out 'harrow' and 'allas.'   100
Do wey your handes for your curteisye!"
    This Nicholas gan mercy for to crye,
And spak so faire, and profred hir so faste,
That she hir love him graunted atte laste,
And swoor hir ooth, by seint Thomas of Kent,   105
That she wol been at his comandement,
Whan that she may hir leyser wel espye.
"Myn housbond is so ful of Ialousye,
That but ye wayte wel and been privee,
I woot right wel I nam but deed," quod she.   110
"Ye moste been ful derne, as in this cas."
    "Nay ther-of care thee noght," quod Nicholas,
"A clerk had litherly biset his whyle,
But-if he coude a Carpenter bigyle."
And thus they been acorded and y-sworn   115
To wayte a tyme, as I have told biforn.
Whan Nicholas had doon thus everydeel,
And thakked hir aboute the lendes weel,
He kist hir swete, and taketh his sautrye,
And pleyeth faste, and maketh melodye.   120
    Than fil it thus, that to the parish-chirche,
Cristes owne werkes for to wirche,
This gode wyf wente on an haliday;
Hir forheed shoon as bright as any day,
So was it wasshen whan she leet hir werk.   125
    Now was ther of that chirche a parish-clerk,
The which that was y-cleped Absolon.
Crul was his heer, and as the gold it shoon,
And strouted as a fanne large and brode;
Ful streight and even lay his Ioly shode.   130
His rode was reed, his eyen greye as goos;
With Powles window corven on his shoos,
In hoses rede he wente fetisly.
Y-clad he was ful smal and proprely,
Al in a kirtel of a light wachet;   135
Ful faire and thikke been the poyntes set.
And ther-up-on he hadde a gay surplys
As whyt as is the blosme up-on the rys.
A mery child he was, so god me save,
Wel coude he laten blood and clippe and shave,   140
And make a chartre of lond or acquitaunce.
In twenty manere coude he trippe and daunce
After the scole of Oxenforde tho,

And with his legges casten to and fro,
And pleyen songes on a small rubible;   145
Ther-to he song som-tyme a loud quinible;
And as wel coude he pleye on his giterne.
In al the toun nas brewhous ne taverne
That he ne visited with his solas,
Ther any gaylard tappestere was.   150
But sooth to seyn, he was somdel squaymous
Of farting, and of speche daungerous.
    This Absolon, that Iolif was and gay,
Gooth with a sencer on the haliday,
Sensinge the wyves of the parish faste;   155
And many a lovely look on hem he caste,
And namely on this carpenteres wyf.
To loke on hir him thoughte a mery lyf,
She was so propre and swete and likerous.
I dar wel seyn, if she had been a mous,   160
And he a cat, he wolde hir hente anon.
    This parish-clerk, this Ioly Absolon,
Hath in his herte swich a love-longinge,
That of no wyf ne took he noon offringe;
For curteisye, he seyde, he wolde noon.   165
The mone, whan it was night, ful brighte shoon,
And Absolon his giterne hath y-take,
For paramours, he thoghte for to wake.
And forth he gooth, Iolif and amorous,
Til he cam to the carpenteres hous   170
A litel after cokkes hadde y-crowe;
And dressed him up by a shot-windowe
That was up-on the carpenteres wal.
He singeth in his vois gentil and smal,
"Now, dere lady, if thy wille be,   175
I preye yow that ye wol rewe on me,"
Ful wel acordaunt to his giterninge.
This carpenter awook, and herde him singe,
And spak un-to his wyf, and seyde anon,
'What! Alison! herestow nat Absolon   180
That chaunteth thus under our boures wal?"
And she answerde hir housbond ther-with-al,
"Yis, god wot, Iohn, I here it every-del."
    This passeth forth; what wol ye bet than wel?
Fro day to day this Ioly Absolon   185
So woweth hir, that him is wo bigon.
He waketh al the night and al the day;
He kempte hise lokkes brode, and made him gay;
He woweth hir by menes and brocage,
And swoor he wolde been hir owne page;   190
He singeth, brokkinge as a nightingale;

He sente hir piment, meeth, and spyced ale,
And wafres, pyping hote out of the glede;
And for she was of toune, he profred mede.
For som folk wol ben wonnen for richesse,   195
And som for strokes, and som for gentillesse.
    Somtyme, to shewe his lightnesse and maistrye,
He pleyeth Herodes on a scaffold hye.
But what availleth him as in this cas?
She loveth so this hende Nicholas,   200
That Absolon may blowe the bukkes horn;
He ne hadde for his labour but a scorn;
And thus she maketh Absolon hir ape,
And al his ernest turneth til a Iape.
Ful sooth is this proverbe, it is no lye,   205
Men seyn right thus, "alwey the nye slye
Maketh the ferre leve to be looth."
For though that Absolon be wood or wrooth,
By-cause that he fer was from hir sighte,
This nye Nicholas stood in his lighte.   210
    Now bere thee wel, thou hende Nicholas!
For Absolon may waille and singe "allas."
And so bifel it on a Saterday,
This carpenter was goon til Osenay;
And hende Nicholas and Alisoun   215
Acorded been to this conclusioun,
That Nicholas shal shapen him a wyle
This sely Ialous housbond to bigyle,
And if so be the game wente aright,
She sholde slepen in his arm al night,   220
For this was his desyr and hir also.
And right anon, with-outen wordes mo,
This Nicholas no lenger wolde tarie,
But doth ful softe un-to his chambre carie
Bothe mete and drinke for a day or tweye,   225
And to hir housbonde bad hir for to seye,
If that he axed after Nicholas,
She sholde seye she niste where he was,
Of al that day she saugh him nat with yë;
She trowed that he was in maladye,   230
For, for no cry, hir mayde coude him calle;
He nolde answere, for no-thing that mighte falle.
    This passeth forth al thilke Saterday,
That Nicholas stille in his chambre lay,
And eet and sleep, or dide what him leste,   235
Til Sonday, that the sonne gooth to reste.
    This sely carpenter hath greet merveyle
Of Nicholas, or what thing mighte him eyle,
And seyde, "I am adrad, by seint Thomas,

It stondeth nat aright with Nicholas.   240
God shilde that he deyde sodeynly!
This world is now ful tikel, sikerly;
I saugh to-day a cors y-born to chirche
That now, on Monday last, I saugh him wirche.
    Go up," quod he un-to his knave anoon,   245
"Clepe at his dore, or knokke with a stoon,
Loke how it is, and tel me boldely."
    This knave gooth him up ful sturdily,
And at the chambre-dore, whyl that he stood,
He cryde and knokked as that he were wood: 250
"What! how! what do ye, maister Nicholay?
How may ye slepen al the longe day?"
    But al for noght, he herde nat a word;
An hole he fond, ful lowe up-on a bord,
Ther as the cat was wont in for to crepe;   255
And at that hole he looked in ful depe,
And at the laste he hadde of him a sighte.
This Nicholas sat gaping ever up-righte,
As he had kyked on the newe mone.
Adoun he gooth, and tolde his maister sone   260
In what array he saugh this ilke man.
    This carpenter to blessen him bigan,
And seyde, "help us, seinte Frideswyde!
A man woot litel what him shal bityde.
This man is falle, with his astromye,   265
In som woodnesse or in som agonye;
I thoghte ay wel how that it sholde be!
Men sholde nat knowe of goddes privetee.
Ye, blessed be alwey a lewed man,
That noght but oonly his bileve can!   270
So ferde another clerk with astromye;
He walked in the feeldes for to prye
Up-on the sterres, what ther sholde bifalle,
Til he was in a marle-pit y-falle;
He saugh nat that. But yet, by seint Thomas,   275
Me reweth sore of hende Nicholas.
He shal be rated of his studying,
If that I may, by Iesus, hevene king!
    Get me a staf, that I may underspore,
Whyl that thou, Robin, hevest up the dore.   280
He shal out of his studying, as I gesse"—
And to the chambre-dore he gan him dresse.
His knave was a strong carl for the nones,
And by the haspe he haf it up atones;
In-to the floor the dore fil anon.   285
This Nicholas sat ay as stille as stoon,
And ever gaped upward in-to the eir.

This carpenter wende he were in despeir,
And hente him by the sholdres mightily,
And shook him harde, and cryde spitously,   290
"What! Nicholay! what, how! what! loke adoun!
Awake, and thenk on Cristes passioun;
I crouche thee from elves and fro wightes!"
Ther-with the night-spel seyde he anon-rightes
On foure halves of the hous aboute,   295
And on the threshfold of the dore with-oute:
"Iesu Crist, and seynt Benedight,
Blesse this hous from every wikked wight,
For nightes verye, the white pater-noster!
Where wentestow, seynt Petres soster?"   300
    And atte laste this hende Nicholas
Gan for to syke sore, and seyde, "allas!
Shal al the world be lost eftsones now?"
    This carpenter answerde, "what seystow?
What! thenk on god, as we don, men that
    swinke."   305
    This Nicholas answerde, "fecche me drinke;
And after wol I speke in privetee
Of certeyn thing that toucheth me and thee;
I wol telle it non other man, certeyn."
    This carpenter goth doun, and comth ageyn,   310
And broghte of mighty ale a large quart;
And whan that ech of hem had dronke his part,
This Nicholas his dore faste shette,
And doun the carpenter by him he sette.
    He seyde, "Iohn, myn hoste lief and dere,   315
Thou shalt up-on thy trouthe swere me here,
That to no wight thou shalt this conseil wreye;
For it is Cristes conseil that I seye,
And if thou telle it man, thou are forlore;
For this vengaunce thou shalt han therfore,   320
That if thou wreye me, thou shalt be wood!"
"Nay, Crist forbede it, for his holy blood!"
Quod tho this sely man, "I nam no labbe,
Ne, though I seye, I nam nat lief to gabbe.
Sey what thou wolt, I shal it never telle   325
To child ne wyf, by him that harwed helle!"
    "Now John," quod Nicholas, "I wol nat lye;
I have y-founde in myn astrologye,
As I have loked in the mone bright,
That now, a Monday next, at quarter-night,   330
Shal falle a reyn and that so wilde and wood,
That half so greet was never Noës flood.
This world," he seyde, "in lasse than in an hour
Shal al be dreynt, so hidous is the shour;

Thus shal mankynde drenche and lese hir lyf."   335
  This carpenter answerde, "allas, my wyf!
And shal she drenche? allas! myn Alisoun!"
For sorwe of this he fil almost adoun,
And seyde, "is ther no remedie in this cas?"
  "Why, yis, for gode," quod hende Nicholas,   340
"If thou wolt werken after lore and reed;
Thou mayst nat werken after thyn owene heed.
For thus seith Salomon, that was ful trewe,
'Werk al by conseil, and thou shalt nat rewe.'
And if thou werken wolt by good conseil,   345
I undertake, with-outen mast and seyl,
Yet shal I saven hir and thee and me.
Hastow nat herd how saved was Noë,
Whan that our lord had warned him biforn
That al the world with water sholde be lorn?"   350
  "Yis," quod this carpenter, "ful yore ago."
  "Hastow nat herd," quod Nicholas, "also
The sorwe of Noë with his felawshipe,
Er that he mighte gete his wyf to shipe?
Him had be lever, I dar wel undertake,   355
At thilke tyme, than alle hise wetheres blake,
That she hadde had a ship hir-self allone.
And ther-fore, wostou what is best to done?
This asketh haste, and of an hastif thing
Men may nat preche or maken tarying.   360
  Anon go gete us faste in-to this in
A kneding-trogh, or elles a kimelin,
For ech of us, but loke that they be large,
In whiche we mowe swimme as in a barge,
And han ther-inne vitaille suffisant   365
But for a day; fy on the remenant!
The water shal aslake and goon away
Aboute pryme up-on the nexte day.
But Robin may nat wite of this, thy knave,
Ne eek thy mayde Gille I may nat save;   370
Axe nat why, for though thou aske me,
I wol nat tellen goddes privetee.
Suffiseth thee, but if thy wittes madde,
To han as greet a grace as Noë hadde.
Thy wyf shal I wel saven, out of doute,   375
Go now thy wey, and speed thee heer-aboute.
  But whan thou hast, for hir and thee and me,
Y-geten us thise kneding-tubbes three,
Than shaltow hange hem in the roof ful hye,
That no man of our purveyaunce spye.   380
And whan thou thus hast doon as I have seyd,
And hast our vitaille faire in hem y-leyd,

And eek an ax, to smyte the corde atwo
When that the water comth, that we may go,
And broke an hole an heigh, up-on the gable,   385
Unto the gardin-ward, over the stable,
That we may frely passen forth our way
Whan that the grete shour is goon away—
Than shaltow swimme as myrie, I undertake,
As doth the whyte doke after hir drake.   390
Than wol I clepe, 'how! Alison! how! John!
Be myrie, for the flood wol passe anon.'
And thou wolt seyn, 'hayl, maister Nicholay!
Good morwe, I se thee wel, for it is day.'
And than shul we be lordes al our lyf   395
Of al the world, as Noë and his wyf.
  But of o thyng I warne thee ful right,
Be wel avysed, on that ilke night
That we ben entred in-to shippes bord,
That noon of us ne speke nat a word,   400
Ne clepe, ne crye, but been in his preyere;
For it is goddes owne heste dere.
  Thy wyf and thou mote hange fer a-twinne,
For that bitwixe yow shal be no sinne
No more in looking than ther shal in dede;   405
This ordinance is seyd, go, god thee spede!
Tomorwe at night, whan men ben alle aslepe,
In-to our kneding-tubbes wol we crepe,
And sitten ther, abyding goddes grace.
Go now thy wey, I have no lenger space   410
To make of this no lenger sermoning.
Men seyn thus, 'send the wyse, and sey no-thing';
Thou art so wys, it nedeth thee nat teche;
Go, save our lyf, and that I thee biseche."
  This sely carpenter goth forth his wey.   415
Ful ofte he seith "allas" and "weylawey,"
And to his wyf he tolde his privetee;
And she was war, and knew it bet than he,
What al this queynte cast was for to seye.
But nathelees she ferde as she wolde deye,   420
And seyde, "allas! go forth thy wey anon,
Help us to scape, or we ben lost echon;
I am thy trewe verray wedded wyf;
Go, dere spouse, and help to save our lyf."
  Lo! which a greet thyng is affeccioun!   425
Men may dye of imaginacioun,
So depe may impressioun be take.
This sely carpenter biginneth quake;
Him thinketh verraily that he may see
Noës flood come walwing as the see   430

To drenchen Alisoun, his hony dere.
He wepeth, weyleth, maketh sory chere,
He syketh with ful many a sory swogh.
He gooth and geteth him a kneding-trogh,
And after that a tubbe and a kimelin,   435
And prively he sente hem to his in,
And heng hem in the roof in privetee.
His owne hand he made laddres three,
To climben by the ronges and the stalkes
Un-to the tubbes hanginge in the balkes,   440
And hem vitailled, bothe trogh and tubbe,
With breed and chese, and good ale in a Iubbe,
Suffysinge right y-nogh as for a day.
But er that he had maad al this array,
He sente his knave, and eek his wenche also,   445
Up-on his nede to London for to go.
And on the Monday, whan it drow to night,
He shette his dore with-oute candel-light,
And dressed al thing as it sholde be.
And shortly, up they clomben alle three;   450
They sitten stille wel a furlong-way.
    "Now, *Pater-noster*, clom!" seyde Nicholay,
And "clom," quod Iohn, and "clom," seyde
        Alisoun.
This carpenter seyde his devocioun,
And stille he sit, and biddeth his preyere,   455
Awaytinge on the reyn, if he it here.
    The dede sleep, for wery bisinesse,
Fil on this carpenter right, as I gesse,
Aboute corfew-tyme, or litel more;
For travail of his goost he groneth sore,   460
And eft he routeth, for his heed mislay.
Doun of the laddre stalketh Nicholay,
And Alisoun, ful softe adoun she spedde;
With-outen wordes mo, they goon to bedde
Ther-as the carpenter is wont to lye.   465
Ther was the revel and the melodye;
And thus lyth Alison and Nicholas,
In bisinesse of mirthe and of solas,
Til that the belle of laudes gan to ringe,
And freres in the chauncel gonne singe.   470
    This parish-clerk, this amorous Absolon,
That is for love alwey so wo bigon,
Up-on the Monday was at Oseneye
With companye, him to disporte and pleye,
And axed up-on cas a cloisterer   475
Ful prively after Iohn the carpenter;
And he drough him a-part out of the chirche,
And seyde, "I noot, I saugh him here nat wirche
Sin Saterday; I trow that he be went
For timber, ther our abbot hath him sent;   480
For he is wont for timber for to go,
And dwellen at the grange a day or two;
Or elles he is at his hous, certeyn;
Wher that he be, I can nat sothly seyn."
    This Absolon ful Ioly was and light,   485
And thoghte, "now is tyme wake al night;
For sikirly I saugh him nat stiringe
Aboute his dore sin day bigan to springe.
So moot I thryve, I shal, at cokkes crowe,
Ful prively knokken at his windowe   490
That stant ful lowe up-on his boures wal.
To Alison now wol I tellen al
My love-longing, for yet I shal nat misse
That at the leste wey I shal hir kisse.
Som maner confort shal I have, parfay,   495
My mouth hath icched al this longe day;
That is a signe of kissing atte leste.
Al night me mette eek, I was at a feste.
Therfor I wol gon slepe an houre or tweye,
And al the night than wol I wake and pleye."   500
    Whan that the firste cok hath crowe, anon
Up rist this Ioly lover Absolon,
And him arrayeth gay, at point-devys.
But first he cheweth greyn and lycorys,
To smellen swete, er he had kembd his heer.   505
Under his tonge a trewe love he beer,
For ther-by wende he to ben gracious.
He rometh to the carpenteres hous,
And stille he stant under the shot-windowe;
Un-to his brest it raughte, it was so lowe;   510
And softe he cogheth with a semi-soun—
"What do ye, hony-comb, swete Alisoun?
My faire brid, my swete cinamome,
Awaketh, lemman myn, and speketh to me!
Wel litel thenken ye up-on my wo,   515
That for your love I swete ther I go.
No wonder is thogh that I swelte and swete;
I moorne as doth a lamb after the tete.
Y-wis, lemman, I have swich love-longinge,
That lyk a turtel trewe is my moorninge;   520
I may nat ete na more than a mayde."
    "Go fro the window, Iakke fool," she sayde,
"As help me god, it wol nat be 'com ba me,'
I love another, and elles I were to blame,
Wel bet than thee, by Iesu, Absolon!   525

Go forth thy wey, or I wol caste a ston,
And lat me slepe, a twenty devel wey!"
   "Allas," quod Absolon, "and weylawey!
That trewe love was ever so yvel biset!
Than kisse me, sin it may be no bet,   530
For Iesus love and for the love of me."
   "Wiltow than go thy wey ther-with?" quod
      she.
   "Ye, certes, lemman," quod this Absolon.
   "Thanne make thee redy," quod she, "I come
      anon";
And un-to Nicholas she seyde stille,   535
"Now hust, and thou shalt laughen al thy fille."
   This Absolon doun sette him on his knees,
And seyde, "I am a lord at alle degrees;
For after this I hope ther cometh more!
Lemman, thy grace, and swete brid, thyn ore!"   540
   The window she undoth, and that in haste,
"Have do," quod she, "com of, and speed thee
      faste,
Lest that our neighebores thee espye."
   This Absolon gan wype his mouth ful drye;
Derk was the night as pich, or as the cole,   545
And at the window out she putte hir hole,
And Absolon, him fil no bet ne wers,
But with his mouth he kiste hir naked ers
Ful savourly, er he was war of this.
   Abak he sterte, and thoghte it was amis,   550
For wel he wiste a womman hath no berd;
He felte a thing al rough and long y-herd,
And seyde, "fy! allas! what have I do?"
"Tehee!" quod she, and clapte the window to;
And Absolon goth forth a sory pas.   555
   "A berd, a berd!" quod hende Nicholas,
"By goddes *corpus*, this goth faire and weel!"
   This sely Absolon herde every deel,
And on his lippe he gan for anger byte;
And to him-self he seyde, "I shal thee quyte!"   560
   Who rubbeth now, who froteth now his lippes
With dust, with sond, with straw, with clooth,
      with chippes,
But Absolon, that seith ful ofte, "allas!
My soule bitake I un-to Sathanas,
But me wer lever than al this toun," quod he,   565
"Of this despyt awroken for to be!
Allas!" quod he, "allas! I ne hadde y-bleynt!"
His hote love was cold and al y-queynt;
For fro that tyme that he had kiste hir ers,

Of paramours he sette nat a kers,   570
For he was heled of his maladye;
Ful ofte paramours he gan deffye,
And weep as dooth a child that is y-bete.
A softe paas he wente over the strete
Un-til a smith men cleped daun Gerveys,   575
That in his forge smithed plough-harneys;
He sharpeth shaar and culter bisily.
This Absolon knokketh al esily,
And seyde, "undo, Gerveys, and that anon."
   "What, who artow?" "It am I, Absolon."   580
"What, Absolon! for Cristes swete tree,
Why ryse ye so rathe, ey, *benedicite!*
What eyleth yow? som gay gerl, god it woot,
Hath broght yow thus up-on the viritoot;
By sëynt Note, ye woot wel what I mene."   585
   This Absolon ne roghte nat a bene
Of al his pley, no word agayn he yaf;
He hadde more tow on his distaf
Than Gerveys knew, and seyde, "freend so dere,
That hote culter in the chimenee here,   590
As lene it me, I have ther-with to done,
And I wol bringe it thee agayn ful sone."
   Gerveys answerde, "certes, were it gold,
Or in a poke nobles alle untold,
Thou sholdest have, as I am trewe smith;   595
Ey, Cristes foo! what wol ye do ther-with?"
   "Ther-of," quod Absolon, "be as be may;
I shal wel telle it thee to-morwe day"—
And caughte the culter by the colde stele.
Ful softe out at the dore he gan to stele,   600
And wente un-to the carpenteres wal.
He cogheth first, and knokketh ther-with-al
Upon the windowe, right as he dide er.
   This Alison answerde, "Who is ther
That knokketh so? I warante it a theef."   605
   "Why, nay," quod he, "god woot, my swete
      leef,
I am thyn Absolon, my dereling!
Of gold," quod he, "I have thee broght a ring;
My moder yaf it me, so god me save,
Ful fyn it is, and ther-to wel y-grave;   610
This wol I yeve thee, if thou me kisse!"
   This Nicholas was risen for to pisse,
And thoghte he wolde amenden al the Iape,
He sholde kisse his ers er that he scape.
And up the windowe dide he hastily,   615
And out his ers he putteth prively

Over the buttok, to the haunche-bon;
And ther-with spak this clerk, this Absolon,
"Spek, swete brid, I noot nat wher thou art."

This Nicholas anon leet flee a fart,   620
As greet as it had been a thonder-dent,
That with the strook he was almost y-blent;
And he was redy with his iren hoot,
And Nicholas amidde the ers he smoot.

Of gooth the skin an hande-brede aboute,   625
The hote culter brende so his toute,
And for the smert he wende for to dye.
As he were wood, for wo he gan to crye—
"Help! water! water! help, for goddes herte!"

This carpenter out of his slomber sterte,   630
And herde oon cryen "water" as he were wood,
And thoghte, "Allas! now comth Nowelis flood!"
He sit him up with-outen wordes mo,
And with his ax he smoot the corde a-two,
And doun goth al; he fond neither to selle,   635
Ne breed ne ale, til he cam to the celle
Up-on the floor; and ther aswowne he lay.

Up sterte hir Alison, and Nicholay,
And cryden "out" and "harrow" in the strete.
The neighebores, bothe smale and grete,   640
In ronnen, for to gauren on this man,
That yet aswowne he lay, bothe pale and wan;
For with the fal he brosten hadde his arm;

But stonde he moste un-to his owne harm.
For whan he spak, he was anon bore doun   645
With hende Nicholas and Alisoun.
They tolden every man that he was wood,
He was agast so of "Nowelis flood"
Thurgh fantasye, that of his vanitee
He hadde y-boght him kneding-tubbes three,   650
And hadde hem hanged in the roof above;
And that he preyed hem, for goddes love,
To sitten in the roof, *par companye.*

The folk gan laughen at his fantasye;
In-to the roof they kyken and they gape,   655
And turned al his harm un-to a Iape.
For what so that this carpenter answerde,
It was for noght, no man his reson herde;
With othes grete he was so sworn adoun,
That he was holden wood in al the toun;   660
For every clerk anon-right heeld with other.
They seyde, "the man is wood, my leve brother";
And every wight gan laughen of this stryf.

Thus swyved was the carpenteres wyf,
For al his keping and his Ialousye;   665
And Absolon hath kist hir nether yë;
And Nicholas is scalded in the toute.
This tale is doon, and god save al the route!

Here endeth the Millere his tale.

Glossary

2 route company. **5 namely** especially; **everichoon** everyone. **6 so moot I goon** as I may walk (cf. "as I live"). **7 gooth aright** goes well; **unbokeled is the male** the bag is unbuckled (i.e., the contents are beginning to be displayed). **11 quyte with** compare with. **12 for-dronken** in an advanced stage of drunkenness. **13 unnethe** hardly. **14** "He would not doff either hood or hat" (i.e., in courtesy before his superiors). **15 abyde** wait for. **16 Pilates vois** perhaps a high, shrill voice, but the expression has unsavory implications illustrated in the next line. **17** i.e., by the arms, blood, and bones of Christ. Medieval men were much more sensitive to this kind of profanity than they were to exclamatory references to excretion or to the sexual organs. The Miller here reveals himself as a crude, bold, and malicious character. **19 quyte** repay. **23 thriftily** profitably. **24 by goddes soul!** a very terrible oath. **26 a devel way** an exclamation. **30 soun** sound. **32 Wyte it**

attribute it to. Chaucer is here at some pains to show that the tale that follows is of a kind that might be expected from a drunken miller. **35 set the wrightes cappe** made a fool of the wright (carpenter). **36 Reve** The Reeve is a carpenter. **37 lewed** vulgar; **harlotrye** villainous behavior. **39 apeiren** injure. **40 eek** also. **44ff.** The following sarcastic little speech shows what the Miller hopes to demonstrate in his tale. **43 leve** beloved. **44 Who** he who; **cokewold** cuckold. **47** an inversion of Eccles. 7:29. **50 pardee** by God. **51 nolde** would not. **53 demen** deem; **oon** i.e., a cuckold. **56 goddes privitee** the secret things of God; **of his wyf** i.e., with the idea "secret things" implied (for the meaning of this line see the Wife's Prologue, ll. 331ff.). **57 goddes foyson there** God's plenty there (i.e., in the secret things of his wife). **58 remanent** remnant (i.e., of these things as they are bestowed elsewhere). **62 Me thinketh** it seems to me, here an expression of intention. The lines following actually serve, by indirection, to alert the reader to the significance of the tale. That is, the argument that Chaucer must say exactly what each pilgrim said is an obvious fiction, and the warning to turn the leaf is a clear temptation to read on. **69 chese** choose. **70 y-nowe** enough. **71 storial thing** historical matter; **toucheth** has a bearing on. **77 Avyseth yow** take care. **78 make ernest of game** i.e., take the surface matter of a joke seriously.

1 whylom once. **2 gnof** lout; **gestes heeld to bord** took in boarders. **5 lerned art** studied the arts; **fantasye** imagination (pejorative, contrasted with reason). **7 coude** knew; **a certeyn** a certain number; **conclusiouns** astrological propositions. **8 demen** judge; **interrogaciouns** determinations of the positions of the planets. **13 cleped** called; **hende** handy; **Nicholas** a name suggestive of (1) St. Nicholas, the patron saint of clerks, and (2) the Nicolait heretics, who were said to be ardent pursuers of the pleasures of the flesh. The latter suggestion is strengthened in the next line. **14 derne** secret (i.e., illicit); **solas** pleasure. **15 sleigh** sly; **privee** secret. **16 meke for to see** i.e., he gave the impression of innocence. **18** Cf. the Knight's Tale, l. 1921. **19 fetisly** neatly; **y-dight** decorated; **swote** sweet. **20 rote** root. **21 cetewale** zedoary (turmeric). **22 Almageste** either the *Almagest* of Ptolemy or some treatise on astrology loosely so-called. **23 astrelabie** astrolabe, an instrument whose use is described by Chaucer in a special treatise. **24 augrim-stones** counters for use on an abacus. **25 couched** set. **26 presse** clothes closet; **falding** coarse cloth. **27 sautrye** psaltery, a stringed instrument. **30 Angelus ad virginem** a hymn celebrating the Annunciation. See Sect. VIII. **31 the kinges note** an unidentified song, but probably something contrasting in spirit with the hymn mentioned above. **34 finding** upkeep provided for study. **35 newe** recently. **38 Ialous** jealous (the old jealous husband was often a type of the avaricious man); **in cage** under close supervision (i.e., like a caged bird). **40 demed** deemed; **cokewold** cuckold. **41 Catoun** Dionysius Cato, to whom a famous collection of proverbs and maxims was attributed. **42 similitude** i.e., should marry a person like himself in age and station. **45 sith** since. **47ff.** Note that in the following passage Alysoun is made to appeal to the five senses and to the acquisitive desires. **48 wesele** weasel. **49 ceynt** girdle; **barred** striped. **50 barmcloth** apron; **morne milk** i.e., milk from a cow milked in the morning. **51 lendes** loins. **52 brouded** embroidered. **53 coler** collar. **55 voluper** cap. **57 filet** headband. **58 sikerly** surely; **likerous yë** lecherous eye (i.e., an inviting glance). **59 smale** narrow; **y-pulled** plucked (for shape). **60 sloo** sloe (a small, bitter, wild plum). **62 pere-ionette** Jeanette pear, i.e., a pear that bears about St. John's Day (June 24); cf. "John Apple." The "newe" tree is the tree in flower. In medieval literature pears and pear trees often have sexual associations. **64 purs** purse, frequently an attribute of avarice in the visual arts. **65 perled with latoun** decorated with hollow, round buttons made from thin metal, or latten. **67 thenche** imagine. **68 popelote** little puppet or doll (with which to play), **wenche** sexually promising girl. **69 hewe** complexion. **70 tour** the Tower of London; **noble** a coin worth 6s. 8d. In 1344 Edward III issued an especially fine gold noble. **71 yerne** shrill. **72 swalwe** the swallow arrives in England in April, nesting frequently in barns and outbuildings. **73 skippe and make game** skip and play. **75 bragot** a mixture of ale and honey; **meeth** mead.

76 heeth heather. **77 Winsinge** skittish; **Ioly** jolly (lively). **78 Long** tall and straight; **bolt** a short arrow used in crossbows. **80 bos** boss; **bocler** buckler (small shield). **82 prymerole** primrose (used loosely for an early flower, like the daisy); **pigges-nye** *pig's eye*, a term of endearment for a wench; also a flower. **83 leggen** lay. **85 eft** later. **87 rage** dally. **89 queynte** sly. **90 queynte** Cf. Modern English "cunt." The gesture here appears in the visual arts to indicate the vice of lechery. **91 y-wis** truly; **but if** unless. **92 derne** secret; **lemman** sweetheart; **spille** die. **96 trave** a frame used to hold a horse while shoes are applied. **97 wryed** wrenched. **100 harrow** a cry of alarm. **103 profred** propositioned. **105 seint Thomas of Kent** St. Thomas of Canterbury. **113 litherly biset his whyle** wasted his time. **114 But-if** unless. **118 thakked** stroked; **lendes** thighs. **119 sautrye** psaltery. **125 leet** left. **127 Absolon** The name, as well as some of the attributes of this figure were suggested by the biblical Absalom. For the story, see 2 Kings 13ff. (Douay). During the Middle Ages, Absalom was noted for his physical beauty and was associated with the vice of vainglory (as well as lechery). **128 Crul** curled. **129 strouted** spread wide. **130 shode** hair part. **131 rode** complexion. **132 Powles window** Paul's window; i.e., a design resembling that of the great window of St. Paul's, London, was carved in his shoes. **133 hoses** stockings; **fetisly** properly (ironic). **135 kirtel** kirtle (tunic); **wachet** light blue. **136 poyntes** laces. **137 surplys** robe. **138 rys** twig. **139 child** young man. **140 laten blood** let blood (bloodletting was a common remedy, often administered by barbers); **clippe** cut hair. **141 acquitaunce** release. **143 scole of Oxenforde** manner of Oxford (probably ironic). **145 rubible** fiddle. **146 quinible** a very high voice. **147 giterne** gittern, a stringed instrument with a flat back. A specimen (falsely restored) survives in the British Museum as the only extant wooden instrument of the fourteenth century. **150 gaylard** gay and amiable; **tappestere** barmaid. **151 squaymous** squeamish (i.e., about the farting of other people, here an indication of affected sensitivity). **152 daungerous** disdainful. **154 sencer** censer. **156 lovely** amorous. **157 namely** especially. **158 him thoughte** seemed to him. **159 likerous** lecherous (sexually inviting). **161 hente** seized. **168 paramours** amorous play for its own sake. **171 cokkes hadde y-crowe** i.e., a little after first cockcrow, or around midnight. **172 shot-windowe** bolted window. **180 herestow nat** don't you hear. **183 every-del** every bit. **189 menes** intermediaries; **brocage** bargaining. **191 brokkinge** trilling. **192 piment** sweet wine; **meeth** mead. **193 glede** oven. **194 for** because; **mede** tangible gifts. **196 gentillesse** high estate. **198 pleyeth Herodes** plays the part of Herod in a mystery play. Herod was associated with vainglory. **201 blowe the bukkes horn** i.e., his efforts are wasted. **203 ape** fool. **204 ernest** ardor; **til a Iape** to a joke. **206 nye slye** the sly one near at hand. **207 ferre leve** the lover farther away. **208 wood** mad; **wrooth** angry. **214 Osenay** Osney, a village adjoining Oxford. **217 shapen** contrive. **228 niste** did not know. **230 trowed** thought. **235 what him leste** what he pleased. **241 shilde** forbid. **242 tikel** precarious. **243 cors** corpse. **246 Clepe** call. **258 up-righte** flat on his back. **259 kyked** gaped. **263 Frideswyde** St. Frideswide, patron of a priory at Oxford. **264 woot** knows. **265 astromye** astrology. **266 woodnesse** madness. **267 thoghte ay wel** always believed. **268 goddes privitee** the secret things of God (cf. Prologue, ll. 55–56). **269 lewed** unlearned. **270 bileve** the Apostles Creed; **can** knows. **271 ferde** fared. **271–275 another clerk** the story was told of Thales of Miletus and used as an exemplum illustrating the folly of belief in judicial astrology. Note that John, in the subsequent action, disregards the implications of his own exemplum. **274 marle-pit** lime pit. **276 Me reweth sore of** I am sorry for. **277 rated of** berated for. **279 underspore** pry up. **282 gan him dresse** applied himself. **283 for the nones** for the occasion. **284 haf** heaved; **atones** at once. **286 ay** ever. **288 wende** thought. **289 hente** seized. **290 spitously** without pity. **293 crouche** cross; **wightes** creatures. **294 night-spel** the popular prayer in ll. 297–300. **297 seynt Benedight** St. Benedict. **299–300** The meaning of these lines is not clear. **302 syke** sigh. **303 eftsones** soon. **305 swinke** work. The workingman's self-righteousness is here satirized. **315 lief** beloved. **316 trouthe** honor. **317 wreye** betray. **318** Cf. Prologue, ll. 55–56. **319 forlore** lost completely. **321 wood** insane (cf. ll. 661–663). **323 labbe** tale-teller. **324** i.e., I talk but do not gossip. **326 child ne wyf** man nor woman. **330 quarter-night** at the time halfway between sunset and midnight. **334 dreynt** drowned. **335 drenche** drown; **lese** lose. **336–339** Note that John cares nothing for mankind in general and thinks only of his wife. **340 for gode** by God. **341 lore and reed** learning and counsel. **347** Cf. Ecclus. 32:24. **351 ful yore ago** a long time ago (note that John seems to have forgotten the promise of Gen. 9:9–17). **354 wyf** in the mystery plays Noah's wife (a figure for the flesh) is often recalcitrant and does not want to board the Ark. In this instance, Alisoun, for reasons of her own, is anxious to get aboard. **359 asketh** requires. **361 in** dwelling. **362 kneding-trogh** a large trough or tub used for kneading dough in commercial baking; **kimelin** a brewer's tub. **364 swimme** float. **367 aslake** recede. **368 pryme** the first of the daylight hours. **369 wite** know. **370 eek** also. **372** Cf. Prologue, ll. 55–56. **373 but if thy wittes madde** unless you are crazy. **380 purveyaunce** preparations. **395–396** the temptation of avarice (cf. Matt. 4:8–10). **402 heste** commandment. **403 a-twinne** apart. **409 goddes grace** note the humorous contrast between this and what the clerk actually awaits. **419 queynte cast** clever device (with humorous wordplay); **was for to seye** implied. **420 ferde** fared. **422 echon** each one. **423 verray** real. **426 imaginacioun** imagination regarded as a misleading (not a creative) faculty. **427 impressioun** the impression of a fantasy on the memory, the nature of which in this instance is revealed in the next lines. **429 Him thinketh** it seems to him. **430 walwing** rolling. **433 swogh** sigh. **436 prively** secretly; **in** dwelling. **439 stalkes** uprights. **440 balkes** beams. **442 Iubbe** jug. **444 array** arrangement. **445 knave** servant boy. **451 furlong-way** a furrow's length apart (exaggeration). **452 clom!** an exclamation enjoining quiet (cf. "sh!"). **454 devocioun** prayer. **455 biddeth** prays. **461 routeth** snores. **466 the revel and the melodye** the feast and the music (the line should probably be followed by an exclamation point). **469 belle of laudes** the bell for the service of lauds, which followed the first service of the day (matins) and took place at sunrise. **475 cloisterer** a monk. **478 I noot** I do not know. **479 trow** believe. **489 So moot I thryve** Cf. "as I live"; **cokkes crowe** There were three cockcrows during the night: at about midnight, at about midway between midnight and dawn, and just before dawn. Absolon proposes to approach Alisoun at first cockcrow, or around midnight. Cf. ll. 171, 501. **491 his boures wal** the wall of his bedchamber. **497 signe** Note that this sign has, in the ensuing action, implications of which Absolon is not aware. **498 me mette** I dreamed; **feste** feast (cf. l. 466). **503 at point-devys** meticulously (note the implication of vainglory again). **504 greyn** probably a cardomom seed. **506 trewe love** not certainly identified, but probably a superstitious aid to eloquence. **507 wende he** he thought. **510 raughte** reached. **511 semi-soun** whisper. **514 lemman** sweetheart. **517 swelte** faint. **518 tete** tit. **519 Y-wis** certainly; **swich** such. **520 turtel** turtle dove, noted in popular lore for its faithfulness to a single mate. **522 Iakke** Cf. "jackass" as an epithet of contempt. **523 com ba me** come kiss me. **526 cast a ston** Cf. John 8:1–7. **527 a twenty devel wey!** an exclamation. **536 hust** hush. **540 ore** favor. **552 y-herd** haired. **555 a sory pas** with sorrowful step. **557 corpus** (Lat.), body. **560 quyte** repay. **561 froteth** rubs. **566 despyt** pitiless action of contempt. Absolon's vanity is deeply injured. **567 I ne hadde y-bleynt!** that I did not turn aside (before the kiss). **568 y-queynt** quenched, with humorous wordplay. **574 paas** step. **576 plough-harneys** plow irons. **577 shaar** plowshare; **culter** colter, a long-pointed, iron bar affixed to the front of the plowframe. The colter on a medieval plow entered the earth deeply, while the share, fixed at the rear of the frame, turned over the sod. **581 swete tree** i.e., the Cross. **582 rathe** early; **benedicite!** a common exclamation. **583 gerl** possibly girl, or, perhaps, young man. **584 viritoot** a word of uncertain meaning. **585 sëynt Note** St. Neot. **586 roghte** cared. **588 tow on his distaf** i.e., more to do. **591 As lene it me** lend it to me. **599 stele** handle. **603 er** before. **606 swete leef** sweet love. **610**

y-grave engraved. **625 hande-brede** hand's breadth. **626 toute** rump. **632 Nowelis** Noah's. **636 celle** floorboards. **641 gauren** gaze. **643 brosten** broken. **649 vanitee** foolishness. **653 par companye** for company. **655 kyken** stare. **660 wood** crazy. **664 swyved** Cf. Modern English "fucked," but the word was not quite so shocking in the fourteenth century.

THE WIFE OF BATH'S TALE

Because of her spirited attack on conventional authority and her vigorous assertion of the attractions of physical pleasure, the Wife of Bath has gained more modern admirers than any of Chaucer's other characters. Modern taste, as T. Gautier long ago observed, does not sincerely relish virtuous women; the other kind offer more alluring prospects, so that the "whore with the heart of gold" has become an astonishingly popular type. But the Wife of Bath is not, actually, a woman of this persuasion. The admiration for her is largely the product of a post romantic spirit of rebelliousness and a sentimental humanitarianism that are essentially alien to fourteenth-century attitudes. In Chaucer's time, she probably had little sentimental or human appeal. Her portrait was, on the other hand, highly comic. Humor arises from a foolish departure from an accepted scale of values, and it becomes comic when the departure is of such a nature that it reflects weaknesses common to a large segment of humanity. In those rare instances where a comic effect is successfully achieved, the underlying positive values are vivified and rendered more meaningful. That is, what Chaucer has to say through the Wife is basically philosophical and serious. If this were not true, the comic effect would be impossible. But the seriousness is philosophical, not emotional; and the humor arises from the play of a brilliant intellect confronted by a peculiarly fundamental aspect of human weakness. Alisoun of Bath is in a sense a manifestation of what the nineteenth century thought of as the Eternal Feminine, an abstraction most vividly exemplified in women, but by no means confined to them. But she does not, in Chaucer's narrative, behave as she does in the works of Goethe and his nineteenth-century followers. That is, instead of drawing us upward and on, she leads us, in spite of reason and learning, to wander haplessly "by the weye."

Historically speaking, the Wife is a late English variant of a traditional classical and medieval type, perhaps best described as the Old Whore. Her antecedents include Eve, Ovid's Dipsas, the Synagogue (the Old Law personified), Héloïse in Abelard's Historia calamitatum, *La Vieille in the* Roman de la rose, *the wench who seduces Aristotle in the* Lai of Aristotle, *and a number of other related figures. In general, this type is made to suggest disobedience in various forms: the fall of Eve, the shameful Venus, worldly wisdom, the "letter" as contrasted with the "spirit," the rampant flesh as contrasted with reason, the revolt of the Church against Christ, and so on. These and related ideas are implied in the sources Chaucer drew upon for his description, which, in substance, is highly conventional. But he is able to make his materials especially vivid by giving them a "local habitation and a name" that has considerable verisimilitude. We see the Wife both as a young woman and as an old one, a fact that considerably enlarges the possibilities of implication. Her triumphs over her husbands are described in some detail. The first three "good" husbands are, it is true, treated together, but the last two are individualized. This arrangement permits a climactic treatment in which the triumph over the fifth husband, who is young and wise, acts as a resounding echo of the fall of Adam and of all those after him who have struggled unsuccessfully, as most of us do, to keep a firm rein on effeminacy.*

The same themes are echoed in the tale as in the others, but this time with an added flourish that is only suggested at the close of the Prologue. If a man allows himself to be dominated by his effeminate inclinations, then he will have access to a fool's paradise in which everything will seem fair. The joys of this paradise are elaborated further in the Merchant's Tale. But Chaucer left it to the Clerk to demonstrate the rewards of true obedience, which are neither transitory nor illusory.

The Prologe of the Wyves Tale of Bathe.

"Experience, though noon auctoritee
Were in this world, were right y-nough to me
To speke of wo that is in mariage;
For, lordinges, sith I twelf yeer was of age,
Thonked be god that is eterne on lyve,   5
Housbondes at chirche-dore I have had fyve;
For I so ofte have y-wedded be;
And alle were worthy men in hir degree.
But me was told certeyn, nat longe agon is,
That sith that Crist ne wente never but onis   10
To wedding in the Cane of Galilee,
That by the same ensample taughte he me
That I ne sholde wedded be but ones.
Herke eek, lo! which a sharp word for the nones
Besyde a welle Iesus, god and man,   15
Spak in repreve of the Samaritan:
'Thou hast y-had fyve housbondes,' quod he,

'And thilke man, the which that hath now thee,
Is noght thyn housbond'; thus seyde he certeyn;
What that he mente ther-by, I can nat seyn;   20
But that I axe, why that the fifthe man
Was noon housbond to the Samaritan?
How manye mighte she have in mariage?
Yet herde I never tellen in myn age
Upon this nombre diffinicioun;   25
Men may devyne and glosen up and doun.
But wel I woot expres, with-oute lye,
God bad us for to wexe and multiplye;
That gentil text can I wel understonde.
Eek wel I woot he seyde, myn housbonde   30
Sholde lete fader and moder, and take me;
But of no nombre mencioun made he,
Of bigamye or of octogamye;
Why sholde men speke of it vileinye?
    Lo, here the wyse king, dan Salomon;   35
I trowe he hadde wyves mo than oon;
As, wolde god, it leveful were to me
To be refresshed half so ofte as he!
Which yifte of god hadde he for alle his wyvis!
No man hath swich, that in this world alyve is.   40
God woot, this noble king, as to my wit,
The firste night had many a mery fit
With ech of hem, so wel was him on lyve!
Blessed be god that I have wedded fyve!
Welcome the sixte, whan that ever he shal.   45
For sothe, I wol nat kepe me chast in al;
Whan myn housbond is fro the world y-gon,
Som Cristen man shal wedde me anon;
For thanne thapostle seith, that I am free
To wedde, a goddes half, wher it lyketh me.   50
He seith that to be wedded is no sinne;
Bet is to be wedded than to brinne.
What rekketh me, thogh folk seye vileinye
Of shrewd Lameth and his bigamye?
I woot wel Abraham was an holy man,   55
And Iacob eek, as ferforth as I can;
And ech of hem hadde wyves mo than two;
And many another holy man also.
Whan saugh ye ever, in any maner age,
That hye god defended mariage   60
By expres word? I pray you, telleth me;
Or wher comanded he virginitee?
I woot as wel as ye, it is no drede,
Thapostel, whan he speketh of maydenhede;
He seyde, that precept ther-of hadde he noon.   65

Men may conseille a womman to been oon,
But conseilling is no comandement;
He putte it in our owene Iugement.
For hadde god comanded maydenhede,
Thanne hadde he dampned wedding with the
            dede;   70
And certes, if ther were no seed y-sowe,
Virginitee, wher-of than sholde it growe?
Poul dorste nat comanden atte leste
A thing of which his maister yaf noon heste.
The dart is set up for virginitee;   75
Cacche who so may, who renneth best lat see.
    But this word is nat take of every wight,
But ther as god list give it of his might.
I woot wel, that thapostel was a mayde;
But natheless, thogh that he wroot and sayde,   80
He wolde that every wight were swich as he,
Al nis but conseil to virginitee;
And for to been a wyf, he yaf me leve
Of indulgence; so it is no repreve
To wedde me, if that my make dye,   85
With-oute excepcioun of bigamye.
Al were it good no womman for to touche,
He mente as in his bed or in his couche;
For peril is bothe fyr and tow tassemble;
Ye knowe what this ensample may resemble.   90
This is al and som, he heeld virginitee
More parfit than wedding in freletee.
Freeltee clepe I, but-if that he and she
Wolde leden al hir lyf in chastitee.
    I graunte it wel, I have noon envye,   95
Thogh maydenhede preferre bigamye;
Hem lyketh to be clene, body and goost,
Of myn estaat I nil nat make no boost.
For wel y knowe, a lord in his houshold,
He hath nat every vessel al of gold;   100
Somme been of tree, and doon hir lord servyse.
God clepeth folk to him in sondry wyse,
And everich hath of god a propre yifte,
Som this, som that—as him lyketh shifte.
    Virginitee is greet perfeccioun,   105
And continence eek with devocioun.
But Crist, that of perfeccioun is welle,
Bad nat every wight he sholde go selle
All that he hadde, and give it to the pore,
And in swich wyse folwe him and his fore.   110
He spak to hem that wolde live parfitly;
And lordinges, by your leve, that am nat I.

I wol bistowe the flour of al myn age
In the actes and in fruit of mariage.

Telle me also, to what conclusioun   115
Were membres maad of generacioun,
And for what profit was a wight y-wroght?
Trusteth right wel, they wer nat maad for noght.
Glose who-so wole, and seye bothe up and doun,
That they were maked for purgacioun   120
Of urine, and our bothe thinges smale
Were eek to knowe a femele from a male,
And for noon other cause: sey ye no?
The experience woot wel it is noght so;
So that the clerkes be nat with me wrothe,   125
I sey this, that they maked been for bothe,
This is to seye, for office, and for ese
Of engendrure, ther we nat god displese.
Why sholde men elles in hir bokes sette,
That man shal yelde to his wyf hir dette?   130
Now wher-with sholde he make his payement,
If he ne used his sely instrument?
Than were they maad up-on a creature,
To purge uryne, and eek for engendrure.

But I seye noght that every wight is holde,   135
That hath swich harneys as I to yow tolde,
To goon and usen hem in engendrure;
Than sholde men take of chastitee no cure.
Crist was a mayde, and shapen as a man,
And many a seint, sith that the world bigan,   140
Yet lived they ever in parfit chastitee.
I nil envye no virginitee;
Lat hem be breed of pured whete-seed,
And lat us wyves hoten barly-breed;
And yet with barly-breed, Mark telle can,   145
Our lord Iesu refresshed many a man.
In swich estaat as god hath cleped us
I wol persevere, I nam nat precious.
In wyfhode I wol use myn instrument
As frely as my maker hath it sent.   150
If I be daungerous, god yeve me sorwe!
Myn housbond shal it have bothe eve and morwe,
Whan that him list com forth and paye his dette.
An housbonde I wol have, I nil nat lette,
Which shal be bothe my dettour and my thral,   155
And have his tribulacioun with-al
Up-on his flessh, whyl that I am his wyf.
I have the power duringe al my lyf
Up-on his propre body, and noght he.
Right thus the apostel tolde it un-to me;   160

And bad our housbondes for to love us weel.
Al this sentence me lyketh every-deel"—
Up sterte the Pardoner, and that anon,
"Now dame," quod he, "by god and by seint
    Iohn,
Ye been a noble prechour in this cas!   165
I was aboute to wedde a wyf; allas!
What sholde I bye it on my flesh so dere?
Yet hadde I lever wedde no wyf to-yere!"
    "Abyde!" quod she, "my tale is nat bigonne;
Nay, thou shalt drinken of another tonne   170
Er that I go, shal savoure wors than ale.
And whan that I have told thee forth my tale
Of tribulacioun in mariage,
Of which I am expert in al myn age,
This to seyn, my-self have been the whippe;   175
Than maystow chese whether thou wolt sippe
Of thilke tonne that I shal abroche.
Be war of it, er thou to ny approche;
For I shal telle ensamples mo than ten.
Who-so that nil be war by othere men,   180
By him shul othere men corrected be.
The same wordes wryteth Ptholomee;
Rede in his Almageste, and take it there."
    "Dame, I wolde praye yow, if your wil it
    were,"
Seyde this Pardoner, "as ye bigan,   185
Telle forth your tale, spareth for no man,
And teche us yonge men of your praktike."
    "Gladly," quod she, "sith it may yow lyke.
But yet I praye to al this companye,
If that I speke after my fantasye,   190
As taketh not a-grief of that I seye;
For myn entente nis but for to pleye.

    Now sires, now wol I telle forth my tale.
As ever mote I drinken wyn or ale,
I shal seye sooth, tho housbondes that I hadde,   195
As three of hem were gode and two were badde.
The three men were gode, and riche, and olde;
Unnethe mighte they the statut holde
In which that they were bounden un-to me.
Ye woot wel what I mene of this, pardee!   200
As help me god, I laughe whan I thinke
How pitously a-night I made hem swinke;
And by my fey, I tolde of it no stoor.
They had me yeven hir gold and hir tresoor;
Me neded nat do lenger diligence   205
To winne hir love, or doon hem reverence.

They loved me so wel, by god above,
That I ne tolde no deyntee of hir love!
A wys womman wol sette hir ever in oon
To gete hir love, ther as she hath noon. 210
But sith I hadde hem hoolly in myn hond,
And sith they hadde me yeven al hir lond,
What sholde I taken hede hem for to plese,
But it were for my profit and myn ese?
I sette hem so a-werke, by my fey, 215
That many a night they songen 'weilawey!'
The bacoun was nat fet for hem, I trowe,
That som men han in Essex at Dunmowe.
I governed hem so wel, after my lawe,
That ech of hem ful blisful was and fawe 220
To bringe me gaye thinges fro the fayre.
They were ful glad whan I spak to hem fayre;
For god it woot, I chidde hem spitously.

   Now herkneth, how I bar me proprely,
Ye wyse wyves, that can understonde. 225

   Thus shul ye speke and bere hem wrong on
      honde;
For half so boldely can ther no man
Swere and lyen as a womman can.
I sey nat this by wyves that ben wyse,
But-if it be whan they hem misavyse. 230
A wys wif, if that she can hir good,
Shal beren him on hond the cow is wood,
And take witnesse of hir owene mayde
Of hir assent; but herkneth how I sayde.

   "Sir olde kaynard, is this thyn array? 235
Why is my neighebores wyf so gay?
She is honoured over-al ther she goth;
I sitte at hoom, I have no thrifty cloth.
What dostow at my neighebores hous?
Is she so fair? artow so amorous? 240
What rowne ye with our mayde? benedicite!
Sir olde lechour, lat thy Iapes be!
And if I have a gossib or a freend,
With-outen gilt, thou chydest as a feend,
If that I walke or pleye un-to his hous! 245
Thou comest hoom as dronken as a mous,
And prechest on thy bench, with yvel preef!
Thou seist to me, it is a greet meschief
To wedde a povre womman, for costage;
And if that she be riche, of heigh parage, 250
Than seistow that it is a tormentrye
To suffre hir pryde and hir malencolye.
And if that she be fair, thou verray knave,

Thou seyst that every holour wol hir have;
She may no whyle in chastitee abyde, 255
That is assailled up-on ech a syde.

   Thou seyst, som folk desyre us for richesse,
Somme for our shap, and somme for our
      fairnesse;
And som, for she can outher singe or daunce,
And som, for gentillesse and daliaunce; 260
Som, for hir handes and hir armes smale;
Thus goth al to the devel by thy tale.
Thou seyst, men may nat kepe a castel-wal;
It may so longe assailled been over-al.

   And if that she be foul, thou seist that she 265
Coveiteth every man that she may se;
For as a spaynel she wol on him lepe,
Til that she finde som man hir to chepe;
Ne noon so grey goos goth ther in the lake,
As, seistow, that wol been with-oute make. 270
And seyst, it is an hard thing for to welde
A thing that no man wol, his thankes, helde.
Thus seistow, lorel, whan thow goost to bedde;
And that no wys man nedeth for to wedde,
Ne no man that entendeth un-to hevene. 275
With wilde thonder-dint and firy levene
Mote thy welked nekke be to-broke!

   Thow seyst that dropping houses, and eek
      smoke,
And chyding wyves, maken men to flee
Out of hir owene hous; a! benedicite! 280
What eyleth swich an old man for to chyde?

   Thow seyst, we wyves wol our vyces hyde
Til we be fast, and than we wol hem shewe;
Wel may that be a proverbe of a shrewe!

   Thou seist, that oxen, asses, hors, and houndes, 285
They been assayed at diverse stoundes;
Bacins, lavours, er that men hem bye,
Spones and stoles, and al swich housbondrye,
And so been pottes, clothes, and array;
But folk of wyves maken noon assay 290
Til they be wedded; olde dotard shrewe!
And than, seistow, we wol oure vices shewe.

   Thou seist also, that it displeseth me
But-if that thou wolt preyse my beautee,
And but thou poure alwey up-on my face, 295
And clepe me "faire dame" in every place;
And but thou make a feste on thilke day
That I was born, and make me fresh and gay,
And but thou do to my norice honour,

And to my chamberere with-inne my bour,   300
And to my fadres folk and his allyes;
Thus seistow, olde barel ful of lyes!
   And yet of our apprentice Ianekyn,
For his crisp heer, shyninge as gold so fyn,
And for he squiereth me bothe up and doun,   305
Yet hastow caught a fals suspecioun;
I wol hym noght, thogh thou were deed
      to-morwe.
   But tel me this, why hydestow, with sorwe,
The keyes of thy cheste awey fro me?
It is my good as wel as thyn, pardee.   310
What wenestow make an idiot of our dame?
Now by that lord, that called is seint Iame,
Thou shalt nat bothe, thogh that thou were wood,
Be maister of my body and of my good;
That oon thou shalt forgo, maugree thyne yën;   315
What nedeth thee of me to enquere or spyën?
I trowe, thou woldest loke me in thy chiste!
Thou sholdest seye, 'wyf, go wher thee liste,
Tak your disport, I wol nat leve no talis;
I knowe yow for a trewe wyf, dame Alis.'   320
We love no man that taketh kepe or charge
Wher that we goon, we wol ben at our large.
   Of alle men y-blessed moot he be,
The wyse astrologien Dan Ptholome,
That seith this proverbe in his Almageste,   325
'Of alle men his wisdom is the hyeste,
That rekketh never who hath the world in
      honde.'
By this proverbe thou shalt understonde,
Have thou y-nogh, what thar thee recche or care
How merily that othere folkes fare?   330
For certeyn, olde dotard, by your leve,
Ye shul have queynte right y-nough at eve.
He is to greet a nigard that wol werne
A man to lighte his candle at his lanterne;
He shal have never the lasse light, pardee;   335
Have thou y-nough, thee thar nat pleyne thee.
   Thou seyst also, that if we make us gay
With clothing and with precious array,
That it is peril of our chastitee;
And yet, with sorwe, thou most enforce thee,   340
And seye thise wordes in the apostles name,
'In habit, maad with chastitee and shame,
Ye wommen shul apparaille yow,' quod he,
'And noght in tressed heer and gay perree,
As perles, ne with gold, ne clothes riche';   345

After thy text, ne after thy rubriche
I wol nat wirche as muchel as a gnat.
Thou seydest this, that I was lyk a cat;
For who-so wolde senge a cattes skin,
Thanne wolde the cat wel dwellen in his in;   350
And if the cattes skin be slyk and gay,
She wol nat dwelle in house half a day,
But forth she wole, er any day be dawed,
To shewe hir skin, and goon a-caterwawed;
This is to seye, if I be gay, sir shrewe,   355
I wol renne out, my borel for to shewe.
   Sire olde fool, what eyleth thee to spyën?
Thogh thou preye Argus, with his hundred yën,
To be my warde-cors, as he can best,
In feith, he shal nat kepe me but me lest;   360
Yet coude I make his berd, so moot I thee.
   Thou seydest eek, that ther ben thinges three,
The whiche thinges troublen al this erthe,
And that no wight ne may endure the ferthe;
O leve sir shrewe, Iesu shorte thy lyf!   365
Yet prechestow, and seyst, an hateful wyf
Y-rekened is for oon of thise meschances.
Been ther none othere maner resemblances
That ye may lykne your parables to,
But-if a sely wyf be oon of tho?   370
   Thou lykenest wommanes love to helle,
To bareyne lond, ther water may not dwelle.
Thou lyknest it also to wilde fyr;
The more it brenneth, the more it hath desyr
To consume every thing that brent wol be.   375
Thou seyst, that right as wormes shende a tree,
Right so a wyf destroyeth hir housbonde;
This knowe they that been to wyves bonde."
   Lordinges, right thus, as ye have understonde,
Bar I stiffly myne olde housbondes on honde,   380
That thus they seyden in hir dronkenesse;
And al was fals, but that I took witnesse
On Ianekin and on my nece also.
O lord, the peyne I dide hem and the wo,
Ful giltelees, by goddes swete pyne!   385
For as an hors I coude byte and whyne.
I coude pleyne, thogh I were in the gilt,
Or elles often tyme hadde I ben spilt.
Who-so that first to mille comth, first grint;
I pleyned first, so was our werre y-stint.   390
They were ful glad to excusen hem ful blyve
Of thing of which they never agilte hir lyve.
   Of wenches wolde I beren him on honde,

Whan that for syk unnethes mighte he stonde.
Yet tikled it his herte, for that he 395
Wende that I hadde of him so greet chiertee.
I swoor that al my walkinge out by nighte
Was for tespye wenches that he dighte;
Under that colour hadde I many a mirthe.
For al swich wit is yeven us in our birthe; 400
Deceite, weping, spinning god hath yive
To wommen kindely, whyl they may live.
And thus of o thing I avaunte me,
Atte ende I hadde the bettre in ech degree,
By sleighte, or force, or by som maner thing, 405
As by continuel murmur or grucching;
Namely a-bedde hadden they meschaunce,
Ther wolde I chyde and do hem no plesaunce;
I wolde no lenger in the bed abyde,
If that I felte his arm over my syde, 410
Til he had maad his raunson un-to me;
Than wolde I suffre him do his nycetee.
And ther-fore every man this tale I telle,
Winne who-so may, for al is for to selle.
With empty hand men may none haukes lure; 415
For winning wolde I al his lust endure,
And make me a feyned appetyt;
And yet in bacon hadde I never delyt;
That made me that ever I wolde hem chyde.
For thogh the pope had seten hem biside, 420
I wolde nat spare hem at hir owene bord.
For by my trouthe, I quitte hem word for word.
As help me verray god omnipotent,
Thogh I right now sholde make my testament,
I ne owe hem nat a word that it nis quit. 425
I broghte it so aboute by my wit,
That they moste yeve it up, as for the beste;
Or elles hadde we never been in reste.
For thogh he loked as a wood leoun,
Yet sholde he faille of his conclusioun. 430

   Thanne wolde I seye, "gode lief, tak keep
How mekely loketh Wilkin oure sheep;
Com neer, my spouse, lat me ba thy cheke!
Ye sholde been al pacient and meke,
And han a swete spyced conscience, 435
Sith ye so preche of Iobes pacience.
Suffreth alwey, sin ye so wel can preche;
And but ye do, certein we shal yow teche
That it is fair to have a wyf in pees.
Oon of us two moste bowen, doutelees; 440
And sith a man is more resonable

Than womman is, ye moste been suffrable.
What eyleth yow to grucche thus and grone?
Is it for ye wolde have my queynte allone?
Why taak it al, lo, have it every-deel; 445
Peter! I shrewe yow but ye love it weel!
For if I wolde selle my *bele chose*,
I coude walke as fresh as is a rose;
But I wol kepe it for your owene tooth.
Ye be to blame, by god, I sey yow sooth." 450
   Swiche maner wordes hadde we on honde.
Now wol I speken of my fourthe housbonde.

   My fourthe housbonde was a revelour,
This is to seyn, he hadde a paramour;
And I was yong and ful of ragerye, 455
Stiborn and strong, and Ioly as a pye.
Wel coude I daunce to an harpe smale,
And singe, y-wis, as any nightingale,
Whan I had dronke a draughte of swete wyn.
Metellius, the foule cherl, the swyn, 460
That with a staf birafte his wyf hir lyf,
For she drank wyn, thogh I hadde been his wyf,
He sholde nat han daunted me fro drinke;
And, after wyn, on Venus moste I thinke:
For al so siker as cold engendreth hayl, 465
A likerous mouth moste han a likerous tayl.
In womman vinolent is no defence,
This knowen lechours by experience.

   But, lord Crist! whan that it remembreth me
Up-on my yowthe, and on my Iolitee, 470
It tikleth me aboute myn herte rote.
Unto this day it dooth myn herte bote
That I have had my world as in my tyme.
But age, allas! that al wol envenyme,
Hath me biraft my beautee and my pith; 475
Lat go, fare-wel, the devel go therwith!
The flour is goon, ther is na-more to telle,
The bren, as I best can, now moste I selle;
But yet to be right mery wol I fonde.
Now wol I tellen of my fourthe housbonde. 480

   I seye, I hadde in herte greet despyt
That he of any other had delyt.
But he was quit, by god and by seint Ioce!
I made him of the same wode a croce;
Nat of my body in no foul manere, 485
But certeinly, I made folk swich chere,
That in his owene grece I made him frye
For angre, and for verray Ialousye.
By god, in erthe I was his purgatorie,

For which I hope his soule be in glorie. 490
For god it woot, he sat ful ofte and song
Whan that his shoo ful bitterly him wrong.
Ther was no wight, save god and he, that wiste,
In many wyse, how sore I him twiste.
He deyde whan I cam fro Ierusalem, 495
And lyth y-grave under the rode-beem,
Al is his tombe noght so curious
As was the sepulcre of him, Darius,
Which that Appelles wroghte subtilly;
It nis but wast to burie him preciously. 500
Lat him fare-wel, god yeve his soule reste,
He is now in the grave and in his cheste.
     Now of my fifthe housbond wol I telle.
God lete his soule never come in helle!
And yet was he to me the moste shrewe; 505
That fele I on my ribbes al by rewe,
And ever shal, un-to myn ending-day.
But in our bed he was so fresh and gay,
And ther-with-al so wel coude he me glose,
Whan that he wolde han my *bele chose*, 510
That thogh he hadde me bet on every boon,
He coude winne agayn my love anoon.
I trowe I loved him beste, for that he
Was of his love daungerous to me.
We wommen han, if that I shal nat lye, 515
In this matere a queynte fantasye;
Wayte what thing we may nat lightly have,
Ther-after wol we crye al-day and crave.
Forbede us thing, and that desyren we;
Prees on us faste, and thanne wol we flee. 520
With daunger oute we al our chaffare;
Greet prees at market maketh dere ware,
And to greet cheep is holde at litel prys;
This knoweth every womman that is wys.
     My fifthe housbonde, god his soule blesse! 525
Which that I took for love and no richesse,
He som-tyme was a clerk of Oxenford,
And had left scole, and wente at hoom to bord
With my gossib, dwellinge in oure toun,
God have hir soule! hir name was Alisoun. 530
She knew myn herte and eek my privetee
Bet than our parisshe-preest, so moot I thee!
To hir biwreyed I my conseil al.
For had myn housbonde pissed on a wal,
Or doon a thing that sholde han cost his lyf, 535
To hir, and to another worthy wyf,
And to my nece, which that I loved weel,

I wolde han told his conseil every-deel.
And so I dide ful often, god it woot,
That made his face ful often reed and hoot 540
For verray shame, and blamed him-self for he
Had told to me so greet a privetee.
     And so bifel that ones, in a Lente,
(So often tymes I to my gossib wente,
For ever yet I lovede to be gay, 545
And for to walke, in March, Averille, and May,
Fro hous to hous, to here sondry talis),
That Iankin clerk, and my gossib dame Alis,
And I my-self, in-to the feldes wente.
Myn housbond was at London al that Lente; 550
I hadde the bettre leyser for to pleye,
And for to see, and eek for to be seye
Of lusty folk; what wiste I wher my grace
Was shapen for to be, or in what place?
Therefore I made my visitaciouns, 555
To vigilies and to processiouns,
To preching eek and to thise pilgrimages,
To pleyes of miracles and mariages,
And wered upon my gaye scarlet gytes.
Thise wormes, ne thise motthes, ne thise mytes, 560
Upon my peril, frete hem never a deel;
And wostow why? for they were used weel.
     Now wol I tellen forth what happed me.
I seye, that in the feeldes walked we,
Til trewely we hadde swich daliance, 565
This clerk and I, that of my purveyance
I spak to him, and seyde him, how that he,
If I were widwe, sholde wedde me.
For certeinly, I sey for no bobance,
Yet was I never with-outen purveyance 570
Of mariage, nof othere thinges eek.
I holde a mouses herte nat worth a leek,
That hath but oon hole for to sterte to,
And if that faille, thanne is al y-do.
     I bar him on honde, he hadde enchanted me; 575
My dame taughte me that soutiltee.
And eek I seyde, I mette of him al night;
He wolde han slayn me as I lay up-right,
And al my bed was ful of verray blood,
But yet I hope that he shal do me good; 580
For blood bitokeneth gold, as me was taught.
And al was fals, I dremed of it right naught,
But as I folwed ay my dames lore,
As wel of this as of other thinges more.
     But now sir, lat me see, what I shal seyn? 585

A! ha! by god, I have my tale ageyn.

Whan that my fourthe housbond was on bere
I weep algate, and made sory chere,
As wyves moten, for it is usage,
And with my coverchief covered my visage; 590
But for that I was purveyed of a make,
I weep but smal, and that I undertake.

To chirche was myn housbond born a-morwe
With neighebores, that for him maden sorwe;
And Iankin oure clerk was oon of tho. 595
As help me god, whan that I saugh him go
After the bere, me thoughte he hadde a paire
Of legges and of feet so clene and faire,
That al myn herte I yaf un-to his hold.
He was, I trowe, a twenty winter old, 600
And I was fourty, if I shal seye sooth;
But yet I hadde alwey a coltes tooth.
Gat-tothed I was, and that bicam me weel;
I hadde the prente of sëynt Venus seel.
As help me god, I was a lusty oon, 605
And faire and riche, and yong, and wel bigoon;
And trewely, as myne housbondes tolde me,
I had the beste *quoniam* mighte be.
For certes, I am al Venerien
In felinge, and myn herte is Marcien. 610
Venus me yaf my lust, my likerousnesse,
And Mars yaf me my sturdy hardinesse.
Myn ascendent was Taur, and Mars ther-inne.
Allas! allas! that ever love was sinne!
I folwed ay myn inclinacioun 615
By vertu of my constellacioun;
That made me I coude noght withdrawe
My chambre of Venus from a good felawe.
Yet have I Martes mark up-on my face,
And also in another privee place. 620
For, god so wis be my savacioun,
I ne loved never by no discrecioun,
But ever folwede myn appetyt,
Al were he short or long, or blak or whyt;
I took no kepe, so that he lyked me, 625
How pore he was, ne eek of what degree.

What sholde I seye, but, at the monthes ende,
This Ioly clerk Iankin, that was so hende,
Hath wedded me with greet solempnitee,
And to him yaf I al the lond and fee 630
That ever was me yeven ther-bifore;
But afterward repented me ful sore.
Ne nolde suffre nothing of my list.

By god, he smoot me ones on the list,
For that I rente out of his book a leef, 635
That of the strook myn ere wex al deef.
Stiborn I was as is a leonesse,
And of my tonge a verray Iangleresse,
And walke I wolde, as I had doon biforn,
From hous to hous, al-though he had it sworn. 640
For which he often tymes wolde preche,
And me of olde Romayn gestes teche,
How he, Simplicius Gallus, lefte his wyf,
And hir forsook for terme of al his lyf,
Noght but for open-heeded he hir say 645
Lokinge out at his dore upon a day.

Another Romayn tolde he me by name,
That, for his wyf was at a someres game
With-oute his witing, he forsook hir eke.
And than wolde he up-on his Bible seke 650
That ilke proverbe of Ecclesiaste,
Wher he comandeth and forbedeth faste,
Man shal nat suffre his wyf go roule aboute;
Than wolde he seye right thus, with-outen doute,

Who-so that buildeth his hous al of salwes, 655
And priketh his blinde hors over the falwes,
And suffreth his wyf to go seken halwes,
Is worthy to been hanged on the galwes!

But al for noght, I sette noght an hawe
Of his proverbes nof his olde sawe, 660
Ne I wolde nat of him corrected be.
I hate him that my vices telleth me,
And so do mo, god woot! of us than I.
This made him with me wood al outrely;
I nolde noght forbere him in no cas. 665

Now wol I seye yow sooth, by seint Thomas,
Why that I rente out of his book a leef,
For which he smoot me so that I was deef.

He hadde a book that gladly, night and day,
For his desport he wolde rede alway. 670
He cleped it Valerie and Theofraste,
At whiche book he lough alwey ful faste.
And eek ther was som-tyme a clerk at Rome,
A cardinal, that highte Seint Ierome,
That made a book agayn Iovinian; 675
In whiche book eek ther was Tertulan,
Crisippus, Trotula, and Helowys,
That was abbesse nat fer fro Parys;
And eek the Parables of Salomon,
Ovydes Art, and bokes many on, 680

And alle thise wer bounden in o volume.
And every night and day was his custume,
Whan he had leyser and vacacioun
From other worldly occupacioun,
To reden on this book of wikked wyves. 685
He knew of hem mo legendes and lyves
Than been of gode wyves in the Bible.
For trusteth wel, it is an impossible
That any clerk wol speke good of wyves,
But-if it be of holy seintes lyves, 690
Ne of noon other womman never the mo.
Who peyntede the leoun, tel me who?
By god, if wommen hadde writen stories,
As clerkes han with-inne hir oratories,
They wolde han writen of men more wikkednesse 695
Than all the mark of Adam may redresse.
The children of Mercurie and of Venus
Been in hir wirking ful contrarious;
Mercurie loveth wisdom and science,
And Venus loveth ryot and dispence. 700
And, for hir diverse disposicioun,
Ech falleth in otheres exaltacioun;
And thus, god woot! Mercurie is desolat
In Pisces, wher Venus is exaltat;
And Venus falleth ther Mercurie is reysed; 705
Therfore no womman of no clerk is preysed.
The clerk, whan he is old, and may noght do
Of Venus werkes worth his olde sho,
Than sit he doun, and writ in his dotage
That wommen can nat kepe hir mariage! 710
    But now to purpos, why I tolde thee
That I was beten for a book, pardee.
Up-on a night Iankin, that was our syre,
Redde on his book, as he sat by the fyre,
Of Eva first, that, for hir wikkednesse, 715
Was al mankinde broght to wrecchednesse,
For which that Iesu Crist him-self was slayn,
That boghte us with his herte-blood agayn.
Lo, here expres of womman may ye finde,
That womman was the los of al mankinde. 720
    Tho redde he me how Sampson loste his heres,
Slepinge, his lemman kitte hem with hir sheres;
Thurgh whiche tresoun loste he bothe his yën.
    Tho redde he me, if that I shal nat lyen,
Of Hercules and of his Dianyre, 725
That caused him to sette himself a-fyre.
    No-thing forgat he the penaunce and wo
That Socrates had with hise wyves two;

How Xantippa caste pisse up-on his heed;
This sely man sat stille, as he were deed; 730
He wyped his heed, namore dorste he seyn
But 'er that thonder stinte, comth a reyn.'
    Of Phasipha, that was the quene of Crete,
For shrewednesse, him thoughte the tale swete;
Fy! spek na-more—it is a grisly thing— 735
Of hir horrible lust and hir lyking.
    Of Clitemistra, for hir lecherye,
That falsly made hir housbond for to dye,
He redde it with ful good devocioun.
    He tolde me eek for what occasioun 740
Amphiorax at Thebes loste his lyf;
Myn housbond hadde a legende of his wyf,
Eriphilem, that for an ouche of gold
Hath prively un-to the Grekes told
Wher that hir housbonde hidde him in a place, 745
For which he hadde at Thebes sory grace.
    Of Lyma tolde he me, and of Lucye,
They bothe made hir housbondes for to dye;
That oon for love, that other was for hate;
Lyma hir housbond, on an even late, 750
Empoysoned hath, for that she was his fo.
Lucya, likerous, loved hir housbond so,
That, for he sholde alwey up-on hir thinke,
She yaf him swich a maner love-drinke,
That he was deed, er it were by the morwe; 755
And thus algates housbondes han sorwe.
    Than tolde he me, how oon Latumius
Compleyned to his felawe Arrius,
That in his gardin growed swich a tree,
On which, he seyde, how that his wyves three 760
Hanged hem-self for herte despitous.
'O leve brother,' quod this Arrius,
'Yif me a plante of thilke blissed tree,
And in my gardin planted shal it be!'
    Of latter date, of wyves hath he red, 765
That somme han slayn hir housbondes in hir bed,
And lete hir lechour dighte hir al the night
Whyl that the corps lay in the floor up-right.
And somme han drive nayles in hir brayn
Whyl that they slepte, and thus they han hem
    slayn. 770
Somme han hem yeve poysoun in hir drinke.
He spak more harm than herte may bithinke.
And ther-with-al, he knew of mo proverbes
Than in this world ther growen gras or herbes.
'Bet is,' quod he, 'thyn habitacioun 775

Be with a leoun or a foul dragoun,
Than with a womman usinge for to chyde.
Bet is,' quod he, 'hye in the roof abyde
Than with an angry wyf doun in the hous;
They been so wikked and contrarious; 780
They haten that hir housbondes loveth ay.'
He seyde, 'a womman cast hir shame away,
Whan she cast of hir smok;' and forther-mo,
'A fair womman, but she be chaast also,
Is lyk a gold ring in a sowes nose.' 785
Who wolde wenen, or who wolde suppose
The wo that in myn herte was, and pyne?

    And whan I saugh he wolde never fyne
To reden on this cursed book al night,
Al sodeynly three leves have I plight 790
Out of his book, right as he radde, and eke,
I with my fist so took him on the cheke,
That in our fyr he fil backward adoun.
And he up-stirte as dooth a wood leoun,
And with his fist he smoot me on the heed, 795
That in the floor I lay as I were deed.
And when he saugh how stille that I lay,
He was agast, and wolde han fled his way,
Til atte laste out of my swogh I breyde:
'O! hastow slayn me, false theef?' I seyde, 800
'And for my land thus hastow mordred me?
Er I be deed, yet wol I kisse thee.'
    And neer he cam, and kneled faire adoun,
And seyde, 'dere suster Alisoun,
As help me god, I shal thee never smyte; 805
That I have doon, it is thy-self to wyte.
Foryeve it me, and that I thee biseke'—
And yet eft-sones I hitte him on the cheke,
And seyde, 'theef, thus muchel am I wreke;
Now wol I dye, I may no lenger speke.' 810
But atte laste, with muchel care and wo,
We fille acorded, by us selven two.
He yaf me al the brydel in myn hond
To han the governance of hous and lond,
And of his tonge and of his hond also, 815
And made him brenne his book anon right tho.
And whan that I hadde geten un-to me,
By maistrie, al the soveraynetee,
And that he seyde, 'myn owene trewe wyf,
Do as thee lust the terme of al thy lyf, 820
Keep thyn honour, and keep eek myn estaat'—
After that day we hadden never debaat.
God help me so, I was to him as kinde

As any wyf from Denmark un-to Inde,
And also trewe, and so was he to me. 825
I prey to god that sit in magestee,
So blesse his soule, for his mercy dere!
Now wol I seye my tale, if ye wol here."

Biholde the wordes bitween the Somonour and the Frere.

The Frere lough, whan he hadde herd al this,
"Now, dame," quod he, "so have I ioye or blis, 830
This is a long preamble of a tale!"
And whan the Somnour herde the Frere gale,
"Lo!" quod the Somnour, "goddes armes two!
A frere wol entremette him ever-mo.
Lo, gode men, a flye and eek a frere 835
Wol falle in every dish and eek matere.
What spekestow of preambulacioun?
What! amble, or trotte, or pees, or go sit doun;
Thou lettest our disport in this manere."
    "Ye, woltow so, sir Somnour?" quod the
        Frere, 840
"Now, by my feith, I shal, er that I go,
Telle of a Somnour swich a tale or two,
That alle the folk shal laughen in this place."
    "Now elles, Frere, I bishrewe thy face,"
Quod this Somnour, "and I bishrewe me, 845
But if I telle tales two or thre
Of freres er I come to Sidingborne,
That I shal make thyn herte for to morne;
For wel I woot thy pacience is goon."
    Our hoste cryde "pees! and that anoon!" 850
And seyde, "lat the womman telle hir tale.
Ye fare as folk that dronken been of ale.
Do, dame, tel forth your tale, and that is best."
    "Al redy, sir," quod she, "right as yow lest,
If I have licence of this worthy Frere." 855
    "Yis, dame," quod he, "tel forth, and I wol
here."

Here endeth the Wyfe of Bathe hir Prologe.

Here biginneth the Tale of the Wyf of Bathe.

In tholde days of the king Arthour,
Of which that Britons speken greet honour,
All was this land fulfild of fayerye.
The elf-queen, with hir ioly companye, 5
Daunced ful often in many a grene mede;
This was the olde opinion, as I rede.

I speke of manye hundred yeres ago;
But now can no man see none elves mo.
For now the grete charitee and prayeres   10
Of limitours and othere holy freres,
That serchen every lond and every streem,
As thikke as motes in the sonne-beem,
Blessinge halles, chambres, kichenes, boures,
Citees, burghes, castels, hye toures,   15
Thropes, bernes, shipnes, dayeryes,
This maketh that ther been no fayeryes.
For ther as wont to walken was an elf,
Ther walketh now the limitour him-self
In undermeles and in morweninges,   20
And seyth his matins and his holy thinges
As he goth in his limitacioun.
Wommen may go saufly up and doun,
In every bush, or under every tree;
Ther is noon other incubus but he,   25
And he ne wol doon hem but dishonour.

    And so bifel it, that this king Arthour
Hadde in his hous a lusty bacheler,
That on a day cam rydinge fro river;
And happed that, allone as she was born,   30
He saughe a mayde walkinge him biforn,
Of whiche mayde anon, maugree hir heed,
By verray force he rafte hir maydenheed;
For which oppressioun was swich clamour
And swich pursute un-to the king Arthour,   35
That dampned was this knight for to be deed
By cours of lawe, and sholde han lost his heed
Paraventure, swich was the statut tho;
But that the quene and othere ladies mo
So longe preyeden the king of grace,   40
Til he his lyf him graunted in the place,
And yaf him to the quene al at hir wille,
To chese, whether she wolde him save or spille.

    The quene thanketh the king with al hir might,
And after this thus spak she to the knight,   45
Whan that she saugh hir tyme, up-on a day:
"Thou standest yet," quod she, "in swich array,
That of thy lyf yet hastow no suretee.
I grante thee lyf, if thou canst tellen me
What thing is it that wommen most desyren?   50
Be war, and keep thy nekke-boon from yren.
And if thou canst nat tellen it anon,
Yet wol I yeve thee leve for to gon
A twelf-month and a day, to seche and lere
An answere suffisant in this matere.   55

And suretee wol I han, er that thou pace,
Thy body for to yelden in this place."
    Wo was this knight and sorwefully he syketh;
But what! he may nat do al as him lyketh.
And at the laste, he chees him for to wende,   60
And come agayn, right at the yeres ende,
With swich answere as god wolde him purveye;
And taketh his leve, and wendeth forth his weye.
    He seketh every hous and every place,
Wher-as he hopeth for to finde grace,   65
To lerne, what thing wommen loven most;
But he ne coude arryven in no cost,
Wher-as he mighte finde in this matere
Two creatures accordinge in-fere.
    Somme seyde, wommen loven best richesse,   70
Somme seyde, honour, somme seyde, Iolynesse;
Somme, riche array, somme seyden, lust abedde,
And ofte tyme to be widwe and wedde.
    Somme seyde, that our hertes been most esed,
Whan that we been y-flatered and y-plesed.   75
He gooth ful ny the sothe, I wol nat lye;
A man shal winne us best with flaterye;
And with attendance, and with bisinesse,
Been we y-lymed, bothe more and lesse.
    And somme seyn, how that we loven best   80
For to be free, and do right as us lest,
And that no man repreve us of our vyce,
But seye that we be wyse, and no-thing nyce.
For trewely, ther is noon of us alle,
If any wight wol clawe us on the galle,   85
That we nil kike, for he seith us sooth;
Assay, and he shal finde it that so dooth.
For be we never so vicious with-inne,
We wol been holden wyse, and clene of sinne.
    And somme seyn, that greet delyt han we   90
For to ben holden stable and eek secree,
And in o purpos stedefastly to dwelle,
And nat biwreye thing that men us telle.
But that tale is nat worth a rake-stele;
Pardee, we wommen conne no-thing hele;   95
Witnesse on Myda; wol ye here the tale?
    Ovyde, amonges othere thinges smale,
Seyde, Myda hadde, under his longe heres,
Growinge up-on his heed two asses eres,
The which vyce he hidde, as he best mighte,   100
Ful subtilly from every mannes sighte,
That, save his wyf, ther wiste of it na-mo.
He loved hir most, and trusted hir also;

He preyede hir, that to no creature
She sholde tellen of his disfigure.   105
   She swoor him "nay, for al this world to winne,
She nolde do that vileinye or sinne,
To make hir housbond han so foul a name;
She nolde nat telle it for hir owene shame."
But nathelees, hir thoughte that she dyde,   110
That she so longe sholde a conseil hyde;
Hir thoughte it swal so sore aboute hir herte,
That nedely som word hir moste asterte;
And sith she dorste telle it to no man,
Doun to a mareys faste by she ran;   115
Til she came there, hir herte was a-fyre,
And, as a bitore bombleth in the myre,
She leyde hir mouth un-to the water doun:
"Biwreye me nat, thou water, with thy soun,"
Quod she, "to thee I telle it, and namo;   120
Myn housbond hath longe asses eres two!
Now is myn herte all hool, now is it oute;
I mighte no lenger kepe it, out of doute."
Heer may ye se, thogh we a tyme abyde,
Yet out it moot, we can no conseil hyde;   125
The remenant of the tale if ye wol here,
Redeth Ovyde, and ther ye may it lere.
   This knight, of which my tale is specially,
Whan that he saugh he mighte nat come therby,
This is to seye, what wommen loven moost,   130
With-inne his brest ful sorweful was the goost;
But hoom he gooth, he mighte nat soiourne.
The day was come, that hoomward moste he
      tourne,
And in his wey it happed him to ryde,
In al this care, under a forest-syde,   135
Wher-as he saugh up-on a daunce go
Of ladies foure and twenty, and yet mo;
Toward the whiche daunce he drow ful yerne,
In hope that som wisdom sholde he lerne.
But certeinly, er he came fully there,   140
Vanisshed was this daunce, he niste where.
No creature saugh he that bar lyf,
Save on the grene he saugh sittinge a wyf;
A fouler wight ther may no man devyse.
Agayn the knight this olde wyf gan ryse,   145
And seyde, "sir knight, heer-forth ne lyth no wey.
Tel me, what that ye seken, by your fey?
Paraventure it may the bettre be;
Thise olde folk can muchel thing," quod she.
   "My leve mooder," quod this knight certeyn,   150

"I nam but deed, but-if that I can seyn
What thing it is that wommen most desyre;
Coude ye me wisse, I wolde wel quyte your hyre."
   "Plighte me thy trouthe, heer in myn hand,"
      quod she,
"The nexte thing that I requere thee,   155
Thou shalt it do, if it lye in thy might;
And I wol telle it yow er it be night."
"Have heer my trouthe," quod the knight, "I
      grante."
   "Thanne," quod she, "I dar me wel avante,
Thy lyf is sauf, for I wol stonde therby,   160
Up-on my lyf, the queen wol seye as I.
Lat see which is the proudeste of hem alle,
That wereth on a coverchief or a calle,
That dar seye nay, of that I shal thee teche;
Lat us go forth with-outen lenger speche."   165
Tho rounded she a pistel in his ere,
And bad him to be glad, and have no fere.
   Whan they be comen to the court, this knight
Seyde, "he had holde his day, as he hadde hight,
And redy was his answere," as he sayde.   170
Ful many a noble wyf, and many a mayde,
And many a widwe, for that they ben wyse,
The quene hir-self sittinge as a Iustyse,
Assembled been, his answere for to here;
And afterward this knight was bode appere.   175
   To every wight comanded was silence,
And that the knight sholde telle in audience,
What thing that worldly wommen loven best.
This knight ne stood nat stille as doth a best,
But to his questioun anon answerde   180
With manly voys, that al the court it herde:
   "My lige lady, generally," quod he,
"Wommen desyren to have sovereyntee
As wel over hir housbond as hir love,
And for to been in maistrie him above;   185
This is your moste desyr, thogh ye me kille,
Doth as yow list, I am heer at your wille."
   In al the court ne was ther wyf ne mayde,
Ne widwe, that contraried that he sayde,
But seyden, "he was worthy han his lyf."   190
   And with that word up stirte the olde wyf,
Which that the knight saugh sittinge in the grene:
"Mercy," quod she, "my sovereyn lady quene!
Er that your court departe, do me right.
I taughte this answere un-to the knight;   195
For which he plighte me his trouthe there,

The firste thing I wolde of him requere,
He wolde it do, if it lay in his might.
Bifore the court than preye I thee, sir knight,"
Quod she, "that thou me take un-to thy wyf;   200
For wel thou wost that I have kept thy lyf.
If I sey fals, sey nay, up-on thy fey!"
   This knight answerde, "allas! and weylawey!
I woot right wel that swich was my biheste.
For goddes love, as chees a newe requeste;   205
Tak al my good, and lat my body go."
   "Nay than," quod she, "I shrewe us bothe
      two!
For thogh that I be foul, and old, and pore,
I nolde for al the metal, ne for ore,
That under erthe is grave, or lyth above,   210
But-if thy wyf I were, and eek thy love."
"My love?" quod he; "nay, my dampnacioun!
Allas! that any of my nacioun
Sholde ever so foule disparaged be!"
But al for noght, the ende is this, that he   215
Constreyned was, he nedes moste hir wedde;
And taketh his olde wyf, and gooth to bedde.
   Now wolden som men seye, paraventure,
That, for my necligence, I do no cure
To tellen yow the Ioye and al tharray   220
That at the feste was that ilke day.
To whiche thing shortly answere I shal;
I seye, ther nas no Ioye ne feste at al,
Ther nas but hevinesse and muche sorwe;
For prively he wedded hir on a morwe,   225
And al day after hidde him as an oule;
So wo was him, his wyf looked so foule.
   Greet was the wo the knight hadde in his
      thoght,
Whan he was with his wyf a-bedde y-broght;
He walweth, and he turneth to and fro.   230
His olde wyf lay smylinge evermo,
And seyde, "o dere housbond, *benedicite!*
Fareth every knight thus with his wyf as ye?
Is this the lawe of king Arthures hous?
Is every knight of his so dangerous?   235
I am your owene love and eek your wyf;
I am she, which that saved hath your lyf;
And certes, yet dide I yow never unright;
Why fare ye thus with me this firste night?
Ye faren lyk a man had lost his wit;   240
What is my gilt? for goddes love, tel me it,
And it shal been amended, if I may."

"Amended?" quod this knight, "allas! nay,
      nay!
It wol nat been amended never mo!
Thou art so loothly, and so old also,   245
And ther-to comen of so lowe a kinde,
That litel wonder is, thogh I walwe and winde.
So wolde god myn herte wolde breste!"
   "Is this," quod she, "the cause of your
      unreste?"
"Ye, certainly," quod he, "no wonder is."   250
"Now, sire," quod she, "I coude amende al
      this,
If that me liste, er it were dayes three,
So wel ye mighte bere yow un-to me.
   But for ye speken of swich gentillesse
As is descended out of old richesse,   255
That therfore sholden ye be gentil men,
Swich arrogance is nat worth an hen.
Loke who that is most vertuous alway,
Privee and apert, and most entendeth ay
To do the gentil dedes that he can,   260
And tak him for the grettest gentil man.
Crist wol, we clayme of him our gentillesse,
Nat of our eldres for hir old richesse.
For thogh they yeve us al hir heritage,
For which we clayme to been of heigh parage,   265
Yet may they nat biquethe, for no-thing,
To noon of us hir vertuous living,
That made hem gentil men y-called be;
And bad us folwen hem in swich degree.
   Wel can the wyse poete of Florence,   270
That highte Dant, speken in this sentence;
Lo in swich maner rym is Dantes tale:
'Ful selde up ryseth by his branches smale
Prowesse of man, for god, of his goodnesse,
Wol that of him we clayme our gentillesse';   275
For of our eldres may we no-thing clayme
But temporel thing, that man may hurte and
      mayme.
   Eek every wight wot this as wel as I,
If gentillesse were planted naturelly
Un-to a certeyn linage, doun the lyne,   280
Privee ne apert, than wolde they never fyne
To doon of gentillesse the faire offyce;
They mighte do no vileinye or vyce.
   Tak fyr, and ber it in the derkeste hous
Bitwix this and the mount of Caucasus,   285
And lat men shette the dores and go thenne;

Yet wol the fyr as faire lye and brenne,
As twenty thousand men mighte it biholde;
His office naturel ay wol it holde,
Up peril of my lyf, til that it dye. 290

Heer may ye see wel, how that genterye
Is nat annexed to possessioun,
Sith folk ne doon hir operacioun
Alwey, as dooth the fyr, lo! in his kinde.
For, god it woot, men may wel often finde 295
A lordes sone do shame and vileinye;
And he that wol han prys of his gentrye
For he was boren of a gentil hous,
And hadde hise eldres noble and vertuous,
And nil him-selven do no gentil dedis, 300
Ne folwe his gentil auncestre that deed is,
He nis nat gentil, be he duk or erl;
For vileyns sinful dedes make a cherl.
For gentillesse nis but renomee
Of thyne auncestres, for hir heigh bountee, 305
Which is a strange thing to thy persone.
Thy gentillesse cometh fro god allone;
Than comth our verray gentillesse of grace,
It was no-thing biquethe us with our place.

Thenketh how noble, as seith Valerius, 310
Was thilke Tullius Hostilius,
That out of povert roos to heigh noblesse.
Redeth Senek, and redeth eek Boëce,
Ther shul ye seen expres that it no drede is,
That he is gentil that doth gentil dedis; 315
And therfore, leve housbond, I thus conclude,
Al were it that myne auncestres were rude,
Yet may the hye god, and so hope I,
Grante me grace to liven vertuously.
Thanne am I gentil, whan that I biginne 320
To liven vertuously and weyve sinne.

And ther-as ye of povert me repreve,
The hye god, on whom that we bileve,
In wilful povert chees to live his lyf.
And certes every man, mayden, or wyf, 325
May understonde that Iesus, hevene king,
Ne wolde nat chese a vicious living.
Glad povert is an honest thing, certeyn;
This wol Senek and othere clerkes seyn.
Who-so that halt him payd of his poverte, 330
I holde him riche, al hadde he nat a sherte.
He that coveyteth is a povre wight,
For he wolde han that is nat in his might.
But he that noght hath, ne coveyteth have,

Is riche, al-though ye holde him but a knave. 335
Verray povert, it singeth proprely;
Iuvenal seith of povert merily:
'The povre man, whan he goth by the weye,
Bifore the theves he may singe and pleye.'
Povert is hateful good, and, as I gesse, 340
A ful greet bringer out of bisinesse;
A greet amender eek of sapience
To him that taketh it in pacience.
Povert is this, al-though it seme elenge:
Possessioun, that no wight wol chalenge. 345
Povert ful ofte, whan a man is lowe,
Maketh his god and eek him-self to knowe.
Povert a spectacle is, as thinketh me,
Thurgh which he may his verray frendes see.
And therfore, sire, sin that I noght yow greve, 350
Of my povert na-more ye me repreve.

Now, sire, of elde ye repreve me;
And certes, sire, thogh noon auctoritee
Were in no book, ye gentils of honour
Seyn that men sholde an old wight doon favour, 355
And clepe him fader, for your gentillesse;
And auctours shal I finden, as I gesse.

Now ther ye seye, that I am foul and old,
Than drede you noght to been a cokewold;
For filthe and elde, al-so moot I thee, 360
Been grete wardeyns up-on chastitee.
But natheles, sin I knowe your delyt,
I shal fulfille your worldly appetyt.

Chese now," quod she, "oon of thise thinges tweye,
To han me foul and old til that I deye, 365
And be to yow a trewe humble wyf,
And never yow displese in al my lyf,
Or elles ye wol han me yong and fair,
And take your aventure of the repair
That shal be to your hous, by-cause of me, 370
Or in som other place, may wel be.
Now chese your-selven, whether that yow lyketh."

This knight avyseth him and sore syketh,
But atte laste he seyde in this manere,
"My lady and my love, and wyf so dere, 375
I put me in your wyse governance;
Cheseth your-self, which may be most plesance,
And most honour to yow and me also.
I do no fors the whether of the two;
For as yow lyketh, it suffiseth me." 380

"Thanne have I gete of yow maistrye," quod
  she,
"Sin I may chese, and governe as me lest?"
    "Ye, certes, wyf," quod he, "I holde it best."
    "Kis me," quod she, "we be no lenger wrothe;
For, by my trouthe, I wol be to yow bothe,   385
This is to seyn, ye, bothe fair and good.
I prey to god that I mot sterven wood,
But I to yow be al-so good and trewe
As ever was wyf, sin that the world was newe.
And, but I be to-morn as fair to sene   390
As any lady, emperyce, or quene,
That is bitwixe the est and eke the west,
Doth with my lyf and deeth right as yow lest.
Cast up the curtin, loke how that it is."
    And whan the knight saugh verraily al this,   395

That she so fair was, and so yong ther-to,
For Ioye he hente hir in his armes two,
His herte bathed in a bath of blisse;
A thousand tyme a-rewe he gan hir kisse.
And she obeyed him in every thing   400
That mighte doon him plesance or lyking.
    And thus they live, un-to hir lyves ende,
In parfit Ioye; and Iesu Crist us sende
Housbondes meke, yonge, and fresshe a-bedde,
And grace toverbyde hem that we wedde.   405
And eek I preye Iesu shorte hir lyves
That wol nat be governed by hir wyves;
And olde and angry nigardes of dispence,
God sende hem sone verray pestilence.

Here endeth the Wyves Tale of Bathe.

Glossary

1 auctoritee written authority. The Wife is here paraphrasing La Vieille, the worldly wise old woman of the *Roman de la rose*. **3 wo** woe (suffering). Note that this is the subject under discussion. **4 lordinges** Cf. "ladies and gentlemen," here in a somewhat vulgar form. **6 chirche-dore** church door. Marriage ceremonies in the Middle Ages were performed outside the church, although newly married couples might enter the church after the ceremony to attend mass; **fyve** The five husbands suggest a parallel with the Samaritan women, mentioned in l. 16. **9 certeyn** certainly. **10 Cane of Galilee** See John 2:1–11. The transformation of water into wine at this wedding was conventionally interpreted to represent the transformation of the Old Law into the New Law. At the same time the sacrament of marriage (by virtue of which the union of husband and wife is a reflection of the union of Christ and the Church) was established here. See Eph. 5:28–32. **13** This argument is advanced by St. Jerome in his treatise *Against Jovinian*, one of the principal sources for the first part of the Wife's Prologue. In actual fourteenth-century practice, widows might remarry, but second and subsequent marriages were not celebrated as solemnly as first marriages by virtue of the fact that they do not precisely reflect the union of Christ and the Church. **14 eek** also; **for the nones** for the occasion. **15** See John 4:1–19. The *welle* in the story was taken by medieval commentators to represent the source of the waters of sensual delight, as contrasted with the "living water" of vv. 10, 13, 14. Christ says that he who drinks of the water of the well shall "thirst again." That is, the senses are insatiable. **17 fyve housbondes** Medieval authorities interpreted this to mean that the Samaritan had always been governed by the five senses and had never subjected herself to reason, or spiritual understanding. **20** Cf. John 4:17, 19ff. The Samaritan (as contrasted with the Wife) does come to understand. The Wife goes on, in effect, to argue against the position taken by Christ. **21 axe** ask. **26 devyne** declare; **glosen** compose glosses on the text. **27 woot** know; **expres** clearly. **28 wexe and multiplye** increase and multiply (see Gen. 1:28). This was regarded as a command under the Old Law but as permissive under the New. Interpreting it spiritually, medieval commentators said that it was an injunction to multiply the number of the truly faithful in the Church and the number of virtues within oneself. The Wife, however, takes it neither literally (as though it meant to have children) nor spiritually, but simply as an injunction to engage in frequent sexual intercourse. This misinterpretation was a current joke, still circulating in the eighteenth century. See Steele, *Tatler*, no. 20. Commentators made a generalized figure of *multiplying*, so that one might be said to perform this act in various ways either spiritually or physically.   **30–31 he seyde**   i.e., in Matt. 19:5–12, where Christ quotes Gen. 2:24, explaining the implication "What . . . God hath joined together, let no man put asunder," and the further advisability of becoming (figuratively) a "eunuch for the kingdom of heaven." The Wife brazenly disregards the spirit of the passage.   **33 octogamye**   the state of having eight wives or husbands.   **35 here**   hear. An exclamation point should probably follow this word. **dan Salomon** lord Solomon (see 3 Kings 11:1–9, where Solomon is said to have had seven hundred wives and three hundred concubines, who "turned away his heart" so that he "followed strange gods." The foolishness of Solomon in his old age was almost a proverbial commonplace).   **39 yifte of God**   gift of God (cf. 1 Cor. 7:7, etc.). But the gifts of God are matters of grace, unlike the pleasures of Solomon, which were gifts of fortune.   **40 swich**   such.   **43 on lyve**   in living.   **44**   A number of MSS contain the following lines here:

> Of whiche I have pyked out the beste,
> Both of here nether purs and of here cheste.
> Divers scoles maken parfyt clerkes,
> And diverse practyk in many sondry werkes
> Maketh the werkman parfyt sekirly.
> Of fyve husbondes scoleiyng am I—

The Wife is clearly proud of her experimental "learning."   **45 sixte**   sixth, with an ironic reference to Christ, who came to the Samaritan's well in the sixth hour, in the sixth age, and became, in effect, her sixth husband.   **49 thapostle**   the apostle, i.e., in 1 Cor. 7:39; but the Wife neglects the implications of the phrase "only in the lord" ("a goddes half") as well as the advice which follows to the effect that widows should not remarry. See also Rom. 7:2–6.   **51–52**   See 1 Cor. 7:9, 28, 39. Although St. Paul does say this, he does not recommend marriage as a means of keeping the fire hot.   **52 brinne**   burn. **53 What rekketh me**   what do I care.   **54 Lameth**   Lamech, last of the literal generation of Cain, famous as an adulterer. See Gen. 4.   **55–56 Abraham . . . Iacob**   Under the Old Law it was permissible to have more than one wife. Readers of Scripture were repeatedly cautioned against using the customs of the Old Dispensation as excuses for vices and crimes under the New.   **60 defended**   forbade. **62**   Literal virginity was a matter of counsel, not precept (see 1 Cor. 7:25ff., the first verse of which is quoted in l. 65).   **71–72**   This argument, which became conventional, was advanced by St. Jerome. **74 heste**   commandment.   **75 dart**   prize in a race (see 1 Cor. 9:24).   **77**   Cf. Matt. 19:11–12. **79–84**   Cf. 1 Cor. 7:6–7.   **85 make**   mate.   **87**   Cf. 1 Cor. 7:1.   **89–90**   "Lechery," said the fourteenth-century scholar Pierre Bersuire, "is light and impetuous. For it is like fire in tow, since it suddenly and without warning burns vigorously. Human members are the tow suddenly thus ignited by lechery."   **96 preferre**   outrank.   **97 body and goost**   body and spirit. Virginity of the spirit (freedom from the stain of sin, or innocence) was held to be far more important than virginity of the flesh.   **98 estaat**   spiritual estate. The Church was said to be made up of three spiritual types: "Married Folk," deeply concerned with the world; "Widows," who, whether actually monks or nuns, were "widowed" from the world; and "Virgins," unconcerned with the world and ready to sacrifice themselves for others.   **99–101**   See 2 Timothy 2:20ff.   **101 tree**   wood. The wooden vessels are vessels "unto dishonor" used to clean the precious vessels.   **103**   See 1 Cor. 7:7.   **105**   See Apoc. 14:1–4. The virginity here in question is spiritual (not literal) virginity. Spiritual virginity (or innocence) was thought to be necessary for salvation.   **106 continence . . . with devocioun**   the spiritual state of widowhood.   **107–110**   i.e., in Matt. 19:21–25. The implication of the passage was thought to be that those who put their trust in the world shall not enter the kingdom of heaven.   **110 fore**   steps.   **114 fruit**   The "fruit" of marriage, as the Parson explains in his sermon to the pilgrims, are the progeny; but the Wife displays no interest in children. The word *fruit* also means "enjoyment," and this, in a crude sense, is what interests the Wife. **116 maad** made. **128 engendrure** engendering (children), an activity in which the Wife shows no interest. **129–130** See 1 Cor. 7:1–5. The Wife overlooks the fact that the "marriage debt" was instituted as a safeguard against unfaithfulness, not as a means of cultivating concupiscence. **135 wight** person; **holde** obliged. **136 harneys** equipment. **144–145** The imagery is from St. Jerome, who says that it is better to marry (eat barley bread) than to commit fornication (eat cow manure), but even better to remain a virgin (eat wheaten bread). **143 pured** refined. **144 hoten** be called. **145 Mark** The Wife (not Chaucer) here cites the wrong Evangelist. The account of the multiplication of the loaves and fishes is in John 6:1–15, a narrative traditionally taken to mean that Christ transformed and multiplied the Old Law (barley bread), which had previously been hard and bitter, feeding the multitude with the New Law. In effect once again the Wife associates herself with the Old Law. **147 cleped** called (see 1 Cor. 7:20). **148 precious** fastidious. **151 daungerous** disdainful; **yeve** give. **153 him list** he desired to. **154 lette** delay. **155 thral** servant. **156 tribulacioun** See 1 Cor. 7:28. **158–160** 1 Cor. 7:4, the first part of which the Wife omits: "The wife hath not power of her own body, but the husband." **161 love us weel** from the discussion in Eph. 5. The Wife, as usual, omits the context: "Let women be subject to their husbands, as to the Lord, as Christ is the head of the Church. Therefore as the Church is subject to Christ, so also let wives be to their husbands in all things. Husbands, love your wives, as Christ also loved the Church. . . ." **162 sentence** doctrine; **me lyketh** pleases me; **every-deel** every bit. **163 sterte** jumped. **166–167** The Pardoner is not actually capable of marriage, and he is unwilling to undergo physical discomfort on any account. **168 to-yere** this year. **171 savoure** taste. **176 chese** choose. **180–181** i.e., he who does not profit by the example of others will himself become an example to correct others. Note that the lesson applies with especial aptness to that "wooden vessel" the speaker. **182 Ptholomee** Ptolemy (the quotation is from a saying ascribed to Ptolemy, although it is not in the *Almagest* proper). **188 sith** since; **lyke** please. **191 a-grief** amiss. **198 Unnethe** hardly; **statut** statute, i.e., the obligation of the marriage debt. **200 pardee** by God. **202 swinke** work. **203 tolde of it no stoor** valued it not at all. **204 yeven** given. **208** i.e., I cared nothing for their love. **209 ever in oon** steadfastly. **217–218 bacoun . . . at Dunmowe** At Dunmow a flitch of bacon was awarded annually to the married couple who had neither quarrelled nor regretted their union during the year. **219 after my lawe** i.e., by bearing them down. **220 fawe** eager. **223 spitously** without pity. **226 hem** i.e., your husbands; **wrong on honde** i.e., keep them subdued and in the wrong. **230 But-if** unless; **misavyse** act without discretion. **232 beren him on honde** convince him (contrary to the actual circumstances); **the cow is wood** the chough (crow) is crazy; i.e., that anyone who accuses her of infidelity is crazy. **235 kaynard** dotard; **array** i.e., the clothing provided for me. **238 thrifty cloth** decent clothing, i.e., "I have nothing to wear." **341 rowne** whisper; **benedicite** an exclamation (cf. "Bless you!"). **242 Iapes** tricks. **243 gossib** close friend. **247 with yvel preef** with malicious themes. **249 costage** expense. **250 parage** birth. **254 holour** lecher. **260 gentillesse** high birth or bearing; **daliaunce** social amiability. **261 smale** slender. **268 chepe** buy. **271 welde** control. **272 his thankes** voluntarily; **helde** hold. **273 lorel** wretch. **277 welked** wrinkled. **278 dropping houses** etc., a common saying, the imagery of which is derived from the Book of Proverbs. See *Piers the Plowman* (B), 17:315ff. **283 fast** i.e., safely married. **286 assayed** tested; **stoundes** times. **300 chamberere** chambermaid. **309 cheste** chest (for keeping wealth). **311 wenestow** do you think to; **oure dame** the mistress of the house. **315 maugree** in spite of. **319 leve no talis** believe any tales. **324 Ptholome** Ptolemy. **329 thar** need; **recche** concern yourself. **332 queynte** Cf. Modern English "cunt." **333 werne** prevent. **340 enforce thee** strengthen your position. **342–345** See 1 Tim. 2:9ff.; 1 Peter 3:1–4. **346 rubriche** rubric, the title of a section written in red, in this instance probably "Women are not to teach." **350 in** house or dwelling. **353 dawed** dawned. **354 a-caterwawed** caterwauling. **356 borel** coarse woolen cloth, here used in contempt of the husband's furnishings for his wife. **358**

Argus set to guard Io from Jupiter's attentions by Juno, but the eloquence of Mercury (with which that of the Wife may be compared) put Argus to sleep. **359 warde-cors** bodyguard. **360 but me lest** unless it pleases me. **361 make his berd** i.e., overcome him. **362–364** Cf. Prov. 30:21–23. **371–375** Cf. Prov. 30:15–16. **376 shende** destroy. **378 bonde** bound. **388 spilt** killed. **390 werre y-stint** war stopped. **391 blyve** quickly. **392 agilte hir lyve** were guilty during their lives. **393 beren him on honde** accuse him. **394 syk** illness. **396 chiertee** concern. **398 dighte** lay with. **400 swich** such; **us** i.e., women. **402 kindely** naturally. **403 avaunte me** boast. **404 in ech degree** in every way. **406 grucching** complaining. **407 Namely** especially. **411 raunson** ransom, i.e., reward or promise. **412 nycetee** frivolous behavior (frivolous because of age). **414 al is for to selle** everything (including sexual favors) is for sale. **416 winning** profit. **418 bacon** Cf. ll. 217–218. **421 bord** dining table. **422 quitte** repay. **429 wood leoun** mad lion. **430 conclusioun** argument. **431 gode lief** sweetheart. **433 ba** kiss. **435 spyced conscience** scrupulous conscience. **443 grucche** complain. **447 bele chose** pretty thing. **448 fresh** i.e., in new clothing. **453 revelour** person addicted to festivities. **455 ragerye** passion. **456 pye** magpie. **460 Metellius** character in a narrative by Valerius Maximus. **464 Venus** sexual pleasure. **474 envenyme** poison. **481 despyt** anger. **483 St. Ioce** St. Jodocus. **484 croce** cross. **489** The idea that marriage may become a purgatory for the husband was commonplace. **492** an old saying (cf. "with his shoe on the wrong foot"). **494 twiste** tortured. **505 moste shrewe** greatest scoundrel. **506 by rewe** in a row. **509 glose** explain my text, or, in this instance, exploit my potentialities. **511 bet on every boon** beaten on every bone. **516 queynte** curious (with wordplay). **517 Wayte** withhold. **521 chaffare** merchandise, i.e., "we show our hand." **530 Alisoun** name of the Wife, of the young wife in the Miller's Tale, and of the present lady. The name connoted a lusty wench. **531 privitee** secrets. **534 pissed on a wal** i.e., done a trivial thing (cf. 3 Kings 16:11). **548 Iankin** i.e., Johnny. Cf. the carol "Kyrie, so kyrie," no. 98 in R. L. Greene, *A Selection of English Carols*, Clarendon Press, Oxford, 1962. **551 leyser** leisure. **552 seye** seen. **553–554** i.e., "How did I know where my good fortune was destined to be, or in what place?" **555–559** Cf. Ovid, *Ars amatoria*, 67ff., where there is a lengthy description of places for good hunting. **556 vigilies** vigils. **559 gytes** gowns. **560 562** Cf. Matt. 6:19–21. **561 frete** ate. **566 purveyance** planning and foresight. **569 bobance** boasting. **571 nof** nor of. **573 sterte** jump. **575 bar him on honde** convinced him. **576 My dame** probably a reference to La Vieille in the *Roman de la rose* and generally to the Old Whore, who, in one guise or another, is a conventional character in medieval literature. **577 mette** dreamed. **578 bere** bier. **589 moten** must; **usage** custom. **591 for that** because; **purveyed of** i.e., had made arrangements for. **593 a-morwe** in the morning. **596 go** walk. **599 hold** possession. **602 coltes tooth** i.e., a lusty sexual appetite. **603 Gat-tothed** i.e., with the upper front incisors spaced wide (an indication of a lecherous disposition). **604** i.e., a birthmark attributable to the influence of "St." Venus (lechery). **606 wel bigon** well provided. **608 quoniam** Cf. *queynte*, for which this is a slang expression. **610 Mercien** under the domination of Mars (wrath). **613** i.e., Taurus, the house of Venus, was in the ascendent and Mars was in it at the time of her birth. This arrangement indicates a wrathful and lecherous nature with a weakness for fornication, adultery, etc. The astrology here (like the mythology and astrology in the Knight's Tale) is used iconographically, not literally. It is impossible to construct a horoscope from the information given here. **614** For *love* understand *lust*. **616** Whatever influence the planets might have, they were thought to have no effect on the reason, so that statements of this kind were not regarded as valid excuses. **619 Martes mark** the mark of Mars. The Wife here attributes her lack of restraint to Mars. **626 degree** social rank. **628 hende** handy. **633 list** pleasure. **634 on the list** should probably read, with some MSS, **with his fist** **636** The Wife, as she has amply demonstrated, "has ears and hears not" (Rom. 11:8ff.). In this instance, she fails to listen to the wisdom of her husband's book. **638 Iangleresse** a woman whose speech is loud, contentious, and irrepressible. **640 al-though he had it sworn** i.e., although he had sworn that she should not be a gadabout. **642 gestes** stories. **643** The story is told by Valerius Maximus. **645 open-headed** bareheaded; **say** saw. **649 witing** knowing. **651 Ecclesiaste** Ecclesiasticus (25:35). **655 salwes** willow twigs; the quotation is proverbial. **656 priketh** spurs; **falwes** fallow ground. **657 halwes** holy places. **658 galwes** gallows. **659 hawe** haw (fruit of the hawthorn). **660 nof** nor of; **sawe** saying. **663 mo** more. **664 outrely** openly. **666 seint Thomas** i.e., Thomas à Becket. **671 Valerie** the *Epistle of Valerius* by Walter Map; **Theofraste** the "Golden Book of Theophrastus" quoted in St. Jerome's *Against Jovinian*. **676 Tertulan** Tertullian, who wrote treatises on chastity, monogamy, and shame. **677 Crisippus** Chrysippus, but the reference is not certainly identified; **Trotula** name given the author or authors of certain treatises on the diseases of women, the passions of women, and cosmetics; **Helowys** Abelard's *Historia calamitatum*, here regarded properly, not as a record of romantic passion, but as a satirical attack on effeminacy. **679 Parables of Salomon** the Book of Proverbs. **680 Ovydes Art** i.e., the *Ars amatoria*, here regarded properly as a witty satire on amorous pursuits. **692** See Aesop's fable of the Man and the Lion. **696 mark** likeness. **697 children of Mercurie** In astrology those most influenced by a single planet are called the children of the planet. Here, the "children of Mercury" are wise and eloquent men, or clerks. **Venus** lechery. Study was regarded as a means of discouraging Venus. **700 dispence** extravagance. **702** i.e., astrologically, but this is a figurative way of saying that those devoted to lechery are foolish, and those devoted to wisdom are not lecherous. **703–705** Venus has her "exaltation" in Pisces, but Mercury has his "fall" in this house; on the other hand, Mercury has his exaltation in Scorpio, but Venus has her fall there. **707–710** A common accusation, still frequently made by members of the sect of the Wife of Bath against St. Paul and St. Augustine. **720** Cf. Ecclus. 25:33. **721–723** For the story of Samson, see Judges 16. **724–726** See Ovid, *Metamorphoses*, 9:159ff. **733–736** See Ovid, *Metamorphoses*, 8:132–137, 169; 9:735–740; *Ars amatoria*, 1:295ff. Pasiphae became passionate for a bull, which she deceived by having Dedalus make a hollow wooden cow for her to take a stance in. **737–739** The story runs that in return for "the brooch of Thebes," a beautiful but ill-starred ornament fashioned by Vulcan that had the power to induce sexual passion, Eriphyle, wife of Amphiarus, revealed the hiding place of her husband so that he was forced to accompany the Greeks attacking Thebes. During the attack, the earth opened and Amphiarus was swallowed into Hades alive. This incident is mentioned near the beginning of the third book of Chaucer's *Troilus*, and the brooch, or "ouche of gold," plays a prominent part in "The Complaint of Mars." Here the deceit and lust of Eriphyle make the point of Jankyn's exemplum. **743 ouche** jewelled ornament. This one is described by Statius, *Thebaid*, 2:269–305. **747–756** These incidents are described by Map in the *Epistle of Valerius*. **755 morwe** morning. **756 algates** in every way. **757–764** a popular story used frequently as an exemplum. **767 dighte** lie with. **768 up-right** flat on its back. **775** Cf. Ecclus. 25:23. **778–781** Cf. Prov. 21:9; 25:24. **784–785** Prov. 11:22. **788 fyne** finish. **790 plight** plucked. **799 swogh** swoon; **breyde** awoke. **806 wyte** blame. **809 wreke** avenged. **813 brydel** bridle, i.e., control. The image would have recalled the popular and frequently illustrated story of how Aristotle foolishly submitted himself to a woman and allowed her to ride him, saddled and bridled. **818 soveraynetee** i.e., the Wife has refused to submit her will to the sovereignty of her husband and thus inverted the traditional hierarchy. **832 gale** cry out. **833 goddes armes two** a very malicious oath. **834 entremette** meddle, or thrust himself forward. **837 preambulacioun** literally "walking before," but a play on "preamble" in l. 831. The implication is that the friar is always getting in the way of others. **838 pees** i.e., stand still. **839 Thou lettest** you hinder. **847 Sidingbourne** Sittingbourne, a village about forty miles from London on the road to Canterbury. **850** The fact that a tavernkeeper here must pacify two ecclesiastics is a humorous indication of disorder.

2 tholde the old; **Arthour** King Arthur, i.e., in the realm of fable. Chaucer apparently regards Arthur, in the manner of the French romances, as a figure used to indicate the presence of what was technically called a "fabulous narrative," a fable with a philosophical import. Any overtones involving British *pietas* are here used satirically. **3 fayerye** fairies, i.e., agents of the devil. **4 elf-queen** fairy queen, here a sort of feminine counterpart of the devil, like Proserpine; not a personification of British sovereignty except by satirical implication. **11 limitours** friars licensed to beg in specified areas. **15 burghes** boroughs. **16 Thropes** villages; **shipnes** sheds. **20 undermeles and in morweninges** probably at various times of the day before the midday dinner. **25 incubus** a male demon said to impregnate women at night (often used as a weak excuse). **26** i.e., "The friar will do nothing but dishonor them" (through sexual ministrations). **28 lusty bacheler** Cf. the description of the Squire in the General Prologue. **29 fro river** idiomatically "from hawking," and figuratively, "in quest of sexual gratification." **33** The penalty for rape under English law was quite severe. **38 tho** then. **39–43** The queen, in effect, gains sovereignty in this matter. **43 spille** kill. **47 array** condition. **54 seche** seek; **lere** learn. **58 syketh** sighs; **60 wende** go. **67 cost** coast (region). **69 in-fere** together. **78 attendance** attention. **79 y-lymed** caught in a bird snare (captured); **more and lesse** great (in rank) and lowly. **81 us lest** it pleases us. **82 repreve** reprove. **83 nyce** having curious tastes. **85 clawe us on the galle** rub the sore spot (probably a reference to galls on horses. Conventionally, a woman is like a horse, the man like the rider, both spiritually and physically. Cf. the inversion of this order in l. 813). **91 stable** trustworthy; **secree** quiet about secret matters. **94 rake-stele** handle of a rake. **96 Myda** Midas. For the story, see Ovid, *Metamorphoses*, 11:146–193. In the original tale (that the Wife asks us to read in ll. 981–982) Midas acquired the ears of an ass by judging the music of the pipes of Pan to be superior to that of the lyre of Apollo (i.e., he preferred passion to truth). In other words, like the Wife herself, he had ears and heard not, or, in Boethian language, was "like an ass to the harp." He was betrayed, not by his wife, but by his barber, who whispered the secret to a hole in the ground and covered it up. But the sly reeds that grew there revealed it in their whispering. Once the similarity between the Wife and Midas is understood, it is apparent that what she says here is that a woman will reveal her own iniquity. **113** i.e., "It seemed to her that some word must spring from her." **131 goost** spirit. **138 yerne** eagerly. **141–143** i.e., what appeared to be a large group of women turned out to be a single old woman representing, like the Wife herself, a sort of essence of femininity in the larger sense. As we might expect this personification is unable to keep the great secret of her sex. **144 wight** person. **146** i.e., There is no use going further (since what you are seeking is here). **153 wisse** guide; **quyte** pay. **159 avante** boast. **163 calle** headdress. **166 rounded** whispered (cf. the barber in Ovid's story of Midas, or, as the Wife would have it, the wife); **pistel** message. **169 hight** promised. **172 wyse** i.e., wise like the Wife herself, through "experience." **175 bode** commanded. **207 shrewe us** curse us. **209 nolde** should not wish. **210 grave** buried. **211 But-if** unless. **213 nacioun** descent. **214 disparaged** here with the sense "degraded from the status of one's peers or equals." **221 ilke** same. **226 oule** owl. **235 dangerous** disdainful. **246 kinde** nature (descent). Actually, the Old Woman, like La Vieille in the *Roman de la rose*, belongs to the type of the Old Whore. This figure appears young and luscious to the lustful but is actually (or spiritually) old and foul as she appears here. That is, in effect, the Old Woman is another manifestation of the type represented by the Wife of Bath. **254 gentillesse** nobility. What follows is the conventional medieval doctrine of true nobility, here derived largely from Dante. It was maintained that outward nobility of lineage entails an obligation to virtue. The difficulty with the lady's argument is that her virtue is purely verbal. **256 therefore** i.e., on account of inherited (feudal) wealth. **259 Privee and apert** both inwardly and outwardly. **265 parage** peerage (estate). **271 Dant** Dante, in *Convivio*, 4. **281 fyne** cease. **284–300** The argument is commonplace. **304 renomee** renown. **306 strange thing** i.e., not an inborn attribute. **310 Valerius** Valerius Maximus. **313 Senek** Seneca; **Boëce** Boethius. The idea that nobility is a matter of virtue and not of descent is classical as well as Christian. **320–321** It is clear that the speaker, like the Wife, has not yet begun. **322 povert** poverty. The idea that voluntary poverty is a great good was a medieval commonplace. Although the Wife has her heroine become quite eloquent about it, it is evident that neither is actually very much interested in it personally. **331 halt him payd** considers himself well rewarded. **332** It was widely held that true wealth lies in the absence of covetousness and avarice. **337 singeth** expresses joy. **342 bisinesse** agitated concern. **343 sapience** wisdom. **345 elenge** miserable. **349 spectacle** eyeglass. **350 verray** true. **353 elde** old age. Respect for the wisdom of the elderly, in whom the demands of sensuality had died down, was a habit ingrained by medieval law and custom. **364 worldly appetyt** i.e., sensual appetite. This promise is, of course, a denial of the wisdom of the arguments just advanced. That is, it is neither virtuous, consistent with voluntary self-denial, nor wise. **368 displese** i.e., through unfaithfulness and desire for money. **369 repair** the concourse of interested people. **379** i.e., "I do not care which of the two." **387 sterven wood** die insane. **390 to-morn** tomorrow. **395-401** The Wife here proposes a miracle of Venus. However, the actual point is that the Old Whore becomes attractive once one has submitted to her and hence become blind to her foulness and deceit. **397 hente** seized. **399 a-rewe** in succession. **400-401** i.e., she satisfies his "worldly appetyt," in defiance of the good doctrine expressed earlier. **405 toverbyde** overcome.

THE PARDONER'S TALE

The Pardoner is by far the most unsavory character among Chaucer's pilgrims. His eunuchry is not a realistic detail, but an indication of his spiritual sterility, a sterility amply demonstrated in his prologue and tale.

The tale itself is extremely well told and has won a lasting reputation as a story, without reference to its meaning. Nevertheless, its structure is apparent only if we have some understanding of its content. At the outset the Pardoner tells us that the theme of all his preaching is that cupidity is the root of all evils and that, moreover, his own motivation in preaching is always cupidity. He cleverly uses a condemnation of cupidity to appeal to the cupidity of his audience and thus to satisfy his own cupidity.

In elaborating the idea of cupidity, the Pardoner discusses three sins: gluttony, gambling, and false swearing. These sins reflect (although the Pardoner does not tell us so) a kind of road to spiritual death through submission to the flesh, the world, and the devil successively. In the story, the rioters take exactly this road through drunkenness, lust for gold, and forswearing. In the end it is apparent that the Pardoner has run the same course, so that the deaths of the rioters constitute a kind of paradigm of his own fate and the fates of all those whom he successfully tempts to follow him. At the close of The Canterbury Tales, the Parson offers to show his fellow pilgrims the "weye" of that "parfit glorious pilgrimage" called "Jerusalem celestial" through penance. The Pardoner demonstrates the way to spiritual death through impenitence.

The wordes of the Host to the Phisicien and the Pardoner.

Our Hoste gan to swere as he were wood,
"Harrow!" quod he, "by nayles and by blood!

This was a fals cherl and a fals Iustyse!
As shamful deeth as herte may devyse
Come to thise Iuges and hir advocats!   5
Algate this sely mayde is slayn, allas!
Allas! to dere boghte she beautee!
Wherfore I seye al day, as men may see,
That yiftes of fortune or of nature
Ben cause of deeth to many a creature.   10
Hir beautee was hir deeth, I dar wel sayn;
Allas! so pitously as she was slayn!
Of bothe yiftes that I speke of now
Men han ful ofte more harm than prow.
But trewely, myn owene mayster dere,   15
This is a pitous tale for to here.
But natheles, passe over, is no fors;
I prey to god, so save thy gentil cors,
And eek thyne urinals and thy Iordanes,
Thyn Ypocras, and eek thy Galianes,   20
And every boist ful of thy letuarie;
God blesse hem, and our lady seinte Marie!
So mot I theen, thou art a propre man,
And lyk a prelat, by seint Ronyan!
Seyde I nat wel? I can nat speke in terme;   25
But wel I woot, thou doost my herte to erme,
That I almost have caught a cardiacle.
By corpus bones! but I have triacle,
Or elles a draught of moyste and corny ale,
Or but I here anon a mery tale,   30
Myn herte is lost for pitee of this mayde.
Thou bel amy, thou Pardoner," he seyde,
"Tel us som mirthe or Iapes right anon."

"It shall be doon," quod he, "by seint Ronyon!
But first," quod he, "heer at this ale-stake   35
I wol both drinke, and eten of a cake."
    But right anon thise gentils gonne to crye,
"Nay! lat him telle us of no ribaudye;
Tel us som moral thing, that we may lere
Som wit, and thanne wol we gladly here."   40
"I graunte, y-wis," quod he, "but I mot thinke
Up-on som honest thing, whyl that I drinke.

Here folweth the Prologe of the Pardoners Tale.

    Radix malorum est Cupiditas: Ad Thimotheum, sexto.

"Lordings," quod he, "in chirches whan I preche,
I peyne me to han an hauteyn speche,
And ringe it out as round as gooth a belle,
For I can al by rote that I telle.
My theme is alwey oon, and ever was—   5
'Radix malorum est Cupiditas.'
    First I pronounce whennes that I come,
And than my bulles shewe I, alle and somme.
Our lige lordes seel on my patente,
That shewe I first, my body to warente,   10
That no man be so bold, ne preest ne clerk,
Me to destourbe of Cristes holy werk;
And after that than telle I forth my tales,
Bulles of popes and of cardinales,
Of patriarkes, and bishoppes I shewe;   15
And in Latyn I speke a wordes fewe,
To saffron with my predicacioun,
And for to stire men to devocioun.
Than shewe I forth my longe cristal stones,
Y-crammed ful of cloutes and of bones;   20
Reliks been they, as wenen they echoon.
Than have I in latoun a sholder-boon
Which that was of an holy Iewes shepe.
'Good men,' seye I, 'tak of my wordes kepe;
If that this boon be wasshe in any welle,   25
If cow, or calf, or sheep, or oxe swelle
That any worm hath ete, or worm y-stonge,
Tak water of that welle, and wash his tonge,
And it is hool anon; and forthermore,
Of pokkes and of scabbe, and every sore   30
Shal every sheep be hool, that of this welle
Drinketh a draughte; tak kepe eek what I telle.
If that the good-man, that the bestes oweth,
Wol every wike, er that the cok him croweth,
Fastinge, drinken of this welle a draughte,   35

As thilke holy Iewe our eldres taughte,
His bestes and his stoor shal multiplye.
And, sirs, also it heleth Ialousye;
For, though a man be falle in Ialous rage,
Let maken with this water his potage,   40
And never shal he more his wyf mistriste,
Though he the sooth of his defaute wiste;
Al had she taken preestes two or three.
    Heer is a miteyn eek, that ye may see.
He that his hond wol putte in this miteyn,   45
He shal have multiplying of his greyn,
Whan he hath sowen, be it whete or otes,
So that he offre pens, or elles grotes.
    Good men and wommen, o thing warne I yow,
If any wight be in this chirche now,   50
That hath doon sinne horrible, that he
Dar nat, for shame, of it y-shriven be,
Or any womman, be she yong or old,
That hath y-maad hir housbond cokewold,
Swich folk shul have no power ne no grace   55
To offren to my reliks in this place.
And who-so findeth him out of swich blame,
He wol com up and offre in goddes name,
And I assoille him by the auctoritee
Which that by bulle y-graunted was to me.'   60
    By this gaude have I wonne, yeer by yeer,
An hundred mark sith I was Pardoner.
I stonde lyk a clerk in my pulpet,
And whan the lewed peple is doun y-set,
I preche, so as ye han herd bifore,   65
And telle an hundred false Iapes more.
Than peyne I me to strecche forth the nekke,
And est and west upon the peple I bekke,
As doth a dowve sitting on a berne.
Myn hondes and my tonge goon so yerne,   70
That it is Ioye to see my bisinesse.
Of avaryce and of swich cursednesse
Is al my preching, for to make hem free
To yeve her pens, and namely un-to me.
For my entente is nat but for to winne,   75
And no-thing for correccioun of sinne.
I rekke never, whan that they ben beried,
Though that her soules goon a-blakeberied!
For certes, many a predicacioun
Comth ofte tyme of yvel entencioun;   80
Som for plesaunce of folk and flaterye,
To been avaunced by ipocrisye,
And som for veyne glorie, and som for hate.

For, whan I dar non other weyes debate,
Than wol I stinge him with my tonge smerte 85
In preching, so that he shal nat asterte
To been defamed falsly, if that he
Hath trespased to my brethren or to me.
For, though I telle noght his propre name,
Men shal wel knowe that it is the same 90
By signes and by othere circumstances.
Thus quyte I folk that doon us displesances;
Thus spitte I out my venim under hewe
Of holynesse, to seme holy and trewe.
    But shortly myn entente I wol devyse; 95
I preche of no-thing but for coveityse.
Therfor my theme is yet, and ever was—
'Radix malorum est cupiditas.'
Thus can I preche agayn that same vyce
Which that I use, and that is avaryce. 100
But, though my-self be gilty in that sinne,
Yet can I maken other folk to twinne
From avaryce, and sore to repente.
But that is nat my principal entente.
I preche no-thing but for coveityse; 105
Of this matere it oughte y-nogh suffyse.
    Than telle I hem ensamples many oon
Of olde stories, longe tyme agoon:
For lewed peple loven tales olde;
Swich thinges can they wel reporte and holde. 110
What? trowe ye, the whyles I may preche,
And winne gold and silver for I teche,
That I wol live in povert wilfully?
Nay, nay, I thoghte it never trewely!
For I wol preche and begge in sondry londes; 115
I wol not do no labour with myn hondes,
Ne make baskettes, and live therby,
Because I wol nat beggen ydelly.
I wol non of the apostles counterfete;
I wol have money, wolle, chese, and whete, 120
Al were it yeven of the povrest page,
Or of the povrest widwe in a village,
Al sholde hir children sterve for famyne.
Nay! I wol drinke licour of the vyne,
And have a Ioly wenche in every toun. 125
But herkneth, lordings, in conclusioun;
Your lyking is that I shal telle a tale.
Now, have I dronke a draughte of corny ale,
By god, I hope I shal yow telle a thing
That shal, by resoun, been at your lyking. 130
For, though myself be a ful vicious man,

A moral tale yet I yow telle can,
Which I am wont to preche, for to winne.
Now holde your pees, my tale I wol beginne.

Here biginneth the Pardoners Tale.

In Flaundres whylom was a companye 135
Of yonge folk, that haunteden folye,
As ryot, hasard, stewes, and tavernes,
Wher-as, with harpes, lutes, and giternes,
They daunce and pleye at dees bothe day and
    night,
And ete also and drinken over hir might, 140
Thurgh which they doon the devel sacrifyse
With-in that develes temple, in cursed wyse,
By superfluitee abhominable;
Hir othes been so grete and so dampnable,
That it is grisly for to here hem swere; 145
Our blissed lordes body they to-tere;
Hem thoughte Iewes rente him noght y-nough;
And ech of hem at otheres sinne lough.
And right anon than comen tombesteres
Fetys and smale, and yonge fruytesteres, 150
Singers with harpes, baudes, wafereres,
Whiche been the verray develes officeres
To kindle and blowe the fyr of lecherye,
That is annexed un-to glotonye;
The holy writ take I to my witnesse, 155
That luxurie is in wyn and dronkenesse.
    Lo, how that dronken Loth, unkindely,
Lay by his doghtres two, unwitingly;
So dronke he was, he niste what he wroghte.
    Herodes, (who-so wel the stories soghte), 160
Whan he of wyn was replet at his feste,
Right at his owene table he yaf his heste
To sleen the Baptist Iohn ful giltelees.
    Senek seith eek a good word doutelees;
He seith, he can no difference finde 165
Bitwix a man that is out of his minde
And a man which that is dronkelewe,
But that woodnesse, y-fallen in a shrewe,
Persevereth lenger than doth dronkenesse.
O glotonye, ful of cursednesse, 170
O cause first of our confusioun,
O original of our dampnacioun,
Til Crist had boght us with his blood agayn!
Lo, how dere, shortly for to sayn,
Aboght was thilke cursed vileinye; 175

Corrupt was al this world for glotonye!
  Adam our fader, and his wyf also,
Fro Paradys to labour and to wo
Were driven for that vyce, it is no drede;
For whyl that Adam fasted, as I rede,   180
He was in Paradys; and whan that he
Eet of the fruyt defended on the tree,
Anon he was out-cast to wo and peyne.
O glotonye, on thee wel oghte us pleyne!
O, wiste a man how many maladyes   185
Folwen of excesse and of glotonyes,
He wolde been the more mesurable
Of his diete, sittinge at his table.
Allas! the shorte throte, the tendre mouth,
Maketh that, Est and West, and North and South, 190
In erthe, in eir, in water men to-swinke
To gete a glotoun deyntee mete and drinke!
Of this matere, o Paul, wel canstow trete,
"Mete un-to wombe, and wombe eek un-to
      mete,
Shal god destroyen bothe," as Paulus seith.   195
Allas! a foul thing is it, by my feith,
To seye this word, and fouler is the dede,
Whan man so drinketh of the whyte and rede,
That of his throte he maketh his privee,
Thurgh thilke cursed superfluitee.   200
  The apostel weping seith ful pitously,
"Ther walken many of whiche yow told have I,
I seye it now weping with pitous voys,
That they been enemys of Cristes croys,
Of whiche the ende is deeth, wombe is her god."   205
O wombe! O bely! O stinking cod,
Fulfild of donge and of corrupcioun!
At either ende of thee foul is the soun.
How greet labour and cost is thee to finde!
Thise cokes, how they stampe, and streyne, and
      grinde,   210
And turnen substaunce in-to accident,
To fulfille al thy likerous talent!
Out of the harde bones knokke they
The mary, for they caste noght a-wey
That may go thurgh the golet softe and swote;   215
Of spicerye, of leef, and bark, and rote
Shal been his sauce y-maked by delyt,
To make him yet a newer appetyt.
But certes, he that haunteth swich delyces
Is deed, whyl that he liveth in tho vyces.   220
  A lecherous thing is wyn, and dronkenesse

Is ful of stryving and of wrecchednesse.
O dronke man, disfigured is thy face,
Sour is thy breeth, foul artow to embrace,
And thurgh thy dronke nose semeth the soun   225
As though thou seydest ay "Sampsoun,
      Sampsoun;"
And yet, god wot, Sampsoun drank never no
      wyn.
Thou fallest, as it were a stiked swyn;
Thy tonge is lost, and al thyn honest cure;
For dronkenesse is verray sepulture   230
Of mannes wit and his discrecioun.
In whom that drinke hath dominacioun,
He can no conseil kepe, it is no drede.
Now kepe yow fro the whyte and fro the rede,
And namely fro the whyte wyn of Lepe,   235
That is to selle in Fish-strete or in Chepe.
This wyn of Spayne crepeth subtilly
In othere wynes, growing faste by,
Of which ther ryseth swich fumositee,
That whan a man hath dronken draughtes three,   240
And weneth that he be at hoom in Chepe,
He is in Spayne, right at the toune of Lepe,
Nat at the Rochel, ne at Burdeux toun;
And thanne wol he seye, "Sampsoun,
      Sampsoun."
  But herkneth, lordings, o word, I yow preye,   245
That alle the sovereyn actes, dar I seye,
Of victories in the olde testament,
Thurgh verray god, that is omnipotent,
Were doon in abstinence and in preyere;
Loketh the Bible, and ther ye may it lere   250
  Loke, Attila, the grete conquerour,
Deyde in his sleep, with shame and dishonour,
Bledinge ay at his nose in dronkenesse;
A capitayn sholde live in sobrenesse.
And over al this, avyseth yow right wel   255
What was comaunded un-to Lamuel—
Nat Samuel, but Lamuel, seye I—
Redeth the Bible, and finde it expresly
Of wyn-yeving to hem that han Iustyse.
Na-more of this, for it may wel suffyse.   260
  And now that I have spoke of glotonye,
Now wol I yow defenden hasardrye.
Hasard is verray moder of lesinges,
And of deceite, and cursed forsweringes,
Blaspheme of Crist, manslaughtre, and wast also   265
Of catel and of tyme; and forthermo,

Figure 40 *Dice players.*

It is repreve and contrarie of honour
For to ben holde a commune hasardour.
And ever the hyër he is of estaat,
The more is he holden desolaat.   270
If that a prince useth hasardrye,
In alle governaunce and policye
He is, as by commune opinoun,
Y-holde the lasse in reputacioun.
    Stilbon, that was a wys embassadour,   275
Was sent to Corinthe, in ful greet honour,
Fro Lacidomie, to make hir alliaunce.
And whan he cam, him happede, par chaunce,
That alle the grettest that were of that lond,
Pleyinge atte hasard he hem fond.   280
For which, as sone as it mighte be,
He stal him hoom agayn to his contree,
And seyde, "ther wol I nat lese my name;
Ne I wol nat take on me so greet defame,
Yow for to allye un-to none hasardours.   285
Sendeth othere wyse embassadours;
For, by my trouthe, me were lever dye,
Than I yow sholde to hasardours allye.
For ye that been so glorious in honours
Shul nat allyen yow with hasardours   290
As by my wil, ne as by my tretee."
This wyse philosophre thus seyde he.
    Loke eek that, to the king Demetrius
The king of Parthes, as the book seith us,

Sente him a paire of dees of gold in scorn,   295
For he hadde used hasard ther-biforn;
For which he heeld his glorie or his renoun
At no value or reputacioun.
Lordes may finden other maner pley
Honeste y-nough to dryve the day awey.   300
    Now wol I speke of othes false and grete
A word or two, as olde bokes trete.
Gret swering is a thing abhominable,
And false swering is yet more reprevable.
The heighe god forbad swering at al,   305
Witnesse on Mathew; but in special
Of swering seith the holy Ieremye,
"Thou shalt seye sooth thyn othes, and nat lye,
And swere in dome, and eek in rightwisnesse";
But ydel swering is a cursednesse.   310
Bihold and see, that in the firste table
Of heighe goddes hestes honurable,
How that the seconde heste of him is this—
"Tak nat my name in ydel or amis."
Lo, rather he forbedeth swich swering   315
Than homicyde or many a cursed thing;
I seye that, as by ordre, thus it stondeth;
This knowen, that his hestes understondeth,
How that the second heste of god is that.
And forther over, I wol thee telle al plat,   320
That vengeance shal nat parten from his hous,
That of his othes is to outrageous.
"By goddes precious herte, and by his nayles,
And by the blode of Crist, that it is in Hayles,
Seven is my chaunce, and thyn is cink and treye;   325
By goddes armes, if thou falsly pleye,
This dagger shal thurgh-out thyn herte go"—
This fruyt cometh of the bicched bones two,
Forswering, ire, falsnesse, homicyde.
Now, for the love of Crist that for us dyde,   330
Leveth your othes, bothe grete and smale;
But, sirs, now wol I telle forth my tale.
Thise ryotoures three, of whiche I telle,
Longe erst er pryme rong of any belle,
Were set hem in a taverne for to drinke;   335
And as they satte, they herde a belle clinke
Biforn a cors, was caried to his grave;
That oon of hem gan callen to his knave,
"Go bet," quod he, "and axe redily,
What cors is this that passeth heer forby;   340
And look that thou reporte his name wel."
    "Sir," quod this boy, "it nedeth never-a-del.

It was me told, er ye cam heer, two houres;
He was, pardee, an old felawe of youres;
And sodeynly he was y-slayn to-night,   345
For-dronke, as he sat on his bench upright;
Ther cam a privee theef, men clepeth Deeth,
That in this contree al the peple sleeth,
And with his spere he smoot his herte a-two,
And wente his wey with-outen wordes mo.   350
He hath a thousand slayn this pestilence:
And, maister, er ye come in his presence,
Me thinketh that it were necessarie
For to be war of swich an adversarie:
Beth redy for to mete him evermore.   355
Thus taughte me my dame, I sey na-more."
"By seinte Marie," seyde this taverner,
"The child seith sooth, for he hath slayn this yeer,
Henne over a myle, with-in a greet village,
Both man and womman, child and hyne, and
        page.   360
I trowe his habitacioun be there;
To been avysed greet wisdom it were,
Er that he dide a man a dishonour."
"Ye, goddes armes," quod this ryotour,
"Is it swich peril with him for to mete?   365
I shal him seke by wey and eek by strete,
I make avow to goddes digne bones!
Herkneth, felawes, we three been al ones,
Lat ech of us holde up his hond til other,
And ech of us bicomen otheres brother,   370
And we wol sleen this false traytour Deeth;
He shal be slayn, which that so many sleeth,
By goddes dignitee, er it be night."
    Togidres han thise three her trouthes plight,
To live and dyen ech of hem for other,   375
As though he were his owene y-boren brother.
And up they sterte al dronken, in this rage,
And forth they goon towardes that village,
Of which the taverner had spoke biforn,
And many a grisly ooth than han they sworn,   380
And Cristes blessed body they to-rente—
"Deeth shal be deed, if that they may him hente."
    Whan they han goon nat fully half a myle,
Right as they wolde han troden over a style,
An old man and a povre with hem mette.   385
This olde man ful mekely hem grette,
And seyde thus, "now, lordes, god yow see!"
    The proudest of thise ryotoures three
Answerde agayn, "what? carl, with sory grace,

Why artow al forwrapped save thy face?   390
Why livestow so longe in so greet age?"
    This olde man gan loke in his visage,
And seyde thus, "for I ne can nat finde
A man, though that I walked in-to Inde,
Neither in citee nor in no village,   395
That wolde chaunge his youthe for myn age;
And therfore moot I han myn age stille,
As longe time as it is goddes wille.
    Ne deeth, allas! ne wol nat han my lyf;
Thus walke I, lyk a restelees caityf,   400
And on the ground, which is my modres gate,
I knokke with my staf, bothe erly and late,
And seye, 'leve moder, leet me in!
Lo, how I vanish, flesh, and blood, and skin!
Allas! whan shul my bones been at reste?   405
Moder, with yow wolde I chaunge my cheste,
That in my chambre longe tyme hath be,
Ye! for an heyre clout to wrappe me!'
But yet to me she wol nat do that grace,
For which ful pale and welked is my face.   410
    But, sirs, to yow it is no curteisye
To speken to an old man vileinye,
But he trespasse in worde, or elles in dede.
In holy writ ye may your-self wel rede,
'Agayns an old man, hoor upon his heed,   415
Ye sholde aryse'; wherfor I yeve yow reed,
Ne dooth un-to an old man noon harm now,
Na-more than ye wolde men dide to yow
In age, if that ye so longe abyde;
And god be with yow, wher ye go or ryde.   420
I moot go thider as I have to go."
    "Nay, olde cherl, by god, thou shalt nat so,"
Seyde this other hasardour anon;
"Thou partest nat so lightly, by seint Iohn!
Thou spak right now of thilke traitour Deeth,   425
That in this contree alle our frendes sleeth.
Have heer my trouthe, as thou art his aspye,
Tel wher he is, or thou shalt it abye,
By god, and by the holy sacrament!
For soothly thou art oon of his assent,   430
To sleen us yonge folk, thou false theef!"
    "Now, sirs," quod he, "if that yow be so leef
To finde Deeth, turne up this croked wey,
For in that grove I lafte him, by my fey,
Under a tree, and ther he wol abyde;   435
Nat for your boost he wol him no-thing hyde.
See ye that ook? right ther ye shul him finde.

God save yow, that boghte agayn mankinde,
And yow amende!"—thus seyde this olde man.
And everich of thise ryotoures ran,   440
Til he cam to that tree, and ther they founde
Of florins fyne of golde y-coyned rounde
Wel ny an eighte busshels, as hem thoughte.
No lenger thanne after Deeth they soughte,
But ech of hem so glad was of that sighte,   445
For that the florins been so faire and brighte,
That doun they sette hem by this precious hord.
The worste of hem he spake the firste word.

    "Brethren," quod he, "tak kepe what I seye;
My wit is greet, though that I bourde and pleye.   450
This tresor hath fortune un-to us yiven,
In mirthe and Iolitee our lyf to liven,
And lightly as it comth, so wol we spende.
Ey! goddes precious dignitee! who wende
To-day, that we sholde han so fair a grace?   455
But mighte this gold be caried fro this place
Hoom to myn hous, or elles un-to youres—
For wel ye woot that al this gold is oures—
Than were we in heigh felicitee.
But trewely, by daye it may nat be;   460
Men wolde seyn that we were theves stronge,
And for our owene tresor doon us honge.
This tresor moste y-caried be by nighte
As wysly and as slyly as it mighte.
Wherfore I rede that cut among us alle   465
Be drawe, and lat se wher the cut wol falle;
And he that hath the cut with herte blythe
Shal renne to the toune, and that ful swythe,
And bringe us breed and wyn ful prively.
And two of us shul kepen subtilly   470
This tresor wel; and, if he wol nat tarie,
Whan it is night, we wol this tresor carie
By oon assent, wher-as us thinketh best."
That oon of hem the cut broughte in his fest,
And bad hem drawe, and loke wher it wol falle;   475
And it fil on the yongeste of hem alle;
And forth toward the toun he wente anon.
And al-so sone as that he was gon,
That oon of hem spak thus un-to that other,
"Thou knowest wel thou art my sworne brother,   480
Thy profit wol I telle thee anon.
Thou woost wel that our felawe is agon;
And heer is gold, and that ful greet plentee,
That shal departed been among us three.
But natheles, if I can shape it so   485

That it departed were among us two,
Hadde I nat doon a freendes torn to thee?"
    That other answerde, "I noot how that may be;
He woot how that the gold is with us tweye,
What shal we doon, what shal we to him seye?"   490
    "Shal it be conseil?" seyde the firste shrewe,
"And I shal tellen thee, in wordes fewe,
What we shal doon, and bringe it wel aboute."
    "I graunte," quod that other, "out of doute,
That, by my trouthe, I wol thee nat biwreye."   495
    "Now," quod the firste, "thou woost wel we
        be tweye,
And two of us shul strenger be than oon.
Look whan that he is set, and right anoon
Arys, as though thou woldest with him pleye;
And I shal ryve him thurgh the sydes tweye   500
Whyl that thou strogelest with him as in game,
And with thy dagger look thou do the same;
And than shal al this gold departed be,
My dere freend, bitwixen me and thee;
Than may we bothe our lustes al fulfille,   505
And pleye at dees right at our owene wille."
And thus acorded been thise shrewes tweye
To sleen the thridde, as ye han herd me seye.
    This yongest, which that wente un-to the toun,
Ful ofte in herte he rolleth up and doun   510
The beautee of thise florins newe and brighte.
"O lord!" quod he, "if so were that I mighte
Have al this tresor to my-self allone,
Ther is no man that liveth under the trone
Of god, that sholde live so mery as I!"   515
And atte laste the feend, our enemy,
Putte in his thought that he shold poyson beye,
With which he mighte sleen his felawes tweye;
For-why the feend fond him in swich lyvinge,
That he had leve him to sorwe bringe,   520
For this was outrely his fulle entente
To sleen hem bothe, and never to repente.
And forth he gooth, no lenger wolde he tarie,
Into the toun, un-to a pothecarie,
And preyed him, that he him wolde selle   525
Som poyson, that he mighte his rattes quelle;
And eek ther was a polcat in his hawe,
That, as he seyde, his capouns hadde y-slawe,
And fayn he wolde wreke him, if he mighte,
On vermin, that destroyed him by nighte.   530
    The pothecarie answerde, "and thou shalt have
A thing that, al-so god my soule save,

In al this world ther nis no creature,
That ete or dronke hath of this confiture
Noght but the mountance of a corn of whete,   535
That he ne shal his lyf anon forlete;
Ye, sterve he shal, and that in lasse whyle
Than thou wolt goon a paas nat but a myle;
This poyson is so strong and violent."
    This cursed man hath in his hond y-hent   540
This poyson in a box, and sith he ran
In-to the nexte strete, un-to a man,
And borwed [of] him large botels three;
And in the two his poyson poured he;
The thridde he kepte clene for his drinke   545
For al the night he shoop him for to swinke
In caryinge of the gold out of that place.
And whan this ryotour, with sory grace,
Had filled with wyn his grete botels three,
To his felawes agayn repaireth he.   550
    What nedeth it to sermone of it more?
For right as they had cast his deeth bifore,
Right so they han him slayn, and that anon.
And whan that this was doon, thus spak that oon,
"Now lat us sitte and drinke, and make us merie,   555
And afterward we wol his body berie."
And with that word it happed him, par cas,
To take the botel ther the poyson was,
And drank, and yaf his felawe drinke also,
For which anon they storven bothe two.   560
    But, certes, I suppose that Avicen
Wroot never in no canon, ne in no fen,
Mo wonder signes of empoisoning
Than hadde thise wrecches two, er hir ending.
Thus ended been thise homicydes two,   565
And eek the false empoysoner also.
    O cursed sinne, ful of cursednesse!
O traytours homicyde, o wikkednesse!
O glotonye, luxurie, and hasardrye!
Thou blasphemour of Crist with vileinye   570
And othes grete, of usage and of pryde!
Allas! mankinde, how may it bityde,
That to thy creatour which that thee wroghte,
And with his precious herte-blood thee boghte,
Thou art so fals and so unkinde, allas!   575
    Now, goode men, god forgeve yow your
        trespas,
And ware yow fro the sinne of avaryce.
Myn holy pardoun may yow alle waryce,
So that ye offre nobles or sterlinges,

Figure 41 *The wheel of fortune.*

Or elles silver broches, spones, ringes.   580
Boweth your heed under this holy bulle!
Cometh up, ye wyves, offreth of your wolle!
Your name I entre heer in my rolle anon;
In-to the blisse of hevene shul ye gon;
I yow assoile, by myn heigh power,   585
Yow that wol offre, as clene and eek as cleer
As ye were born; and, lo, sirs, thus I preche.
And Iesu Crist, that is our soules leche,
So graunte yow his pardon to receyve;
For that is best; I wol yow nat deceyve.   590
    But sirs, o word forgat I in my tale,
I have relikes and pardon in my male,
As faire as any man in Engelond,
Whiche were me yeven by the popes hond.
If any of yow wol, of devocioun,   595
Offren, and han myn absolucioun,
Cometh forth anon, and kneleth heer adoun,
And mekely receyveth my pardoun:
Or elles, taketh pardon as ye wende,
Al newe and fresh, at every tounes ende,   600
So that ye offren alwey newe and newe
Nobles and pens, which that be gode and trewe.
It is an honour to everich that is heer,
That ye mowe have a suffisant pardoneer
Tassoille yow, in contree as ye ryde,   605
For aventures which that may bityde.
Peraventure ther may falle oon or two
Doun of his hors, and breke his nekke atwo.

Look which a seuretee is it to yow alle
That I am in your felaweship y-falle,   610
That may assoille yow, bothe more and lasse,
Whan that the soule shal fro the body passe.
I rede that our hoste heer shal biginne,
For he is most envoluped in sinne.
Com forth, sir hoste, and offre first anon,   615
And thou shalt kisse the reliks everichon,
Ye, for a grote! unbokel anon thy purs."
    "Nay, nay," quod he, "than have I Cristes curs!
Lat be," quod he, "it shal nat be, so theech!
Thou woldest make me kisse thyn old breech,   620
And swere it were a relik of a seint,
Thogh it were with thy fundement depeint!
But by the croys which that seint Eleyne fond,
I wolde I hadde thy coillons in myn hond

In stede of relikes or of seintuarie;   625
Lat cutte hem of, I wol thee helpe hem carie;
Thay shul be shryned in an hogges tord."
    This pardoner answerde nat a word;
So wrooth he was, no word ne wolde he seye.
    "Now," quod our host, "I wol no lenger pleye   630
With thee, ne with noon other angry man."
But right anon the worthy knight bigan,
Whan that he saugh that al the peple lough,
"Na-more of this, for it is right y-nough;
Sir pardoner, be glad and mery of chere;   635
And ye, sir host, that been to me so dere,
I prey yow that ye kisse the pardoner.
And pardoner, I prey thee, drawe thee neer,
And, as we diden, lat us laughe and pleye."
Anon they kiste, and riden forth hir weye.   640

Here is ended the Pardoners Tale.

Glossary

Heading   The Physician has just completed a version of the story of Appius and Virginia. The Pardoner was licensed to preach and to sell indulgences for remission of penance. See the General Prologue.   **1 wood**   insane.   **2 by nayles . . . blood**   i.e., by the nails and blood of Christ (a malicious and vicious oath).   **6 algate**   nevertheless; **sely**   unfortunate.   **9 yiftes of fortune or of nature** gifts of fortune (rank, wealth, etc.) or of nature (strength, beauty, wit, etc.).   **14 prow**   profit.   **18 cors** body.   **19 urinals and . . . Iordanes**   urinals and chamberpots to contain specimens for diagnosis. **20 Ypocras**   Hippocras, a sweetened and spiced red wine; **Galianes**   a word of unknown meaning. **21 boist**   box; **letuarie**   electuary (sweet medicated paste).   **23 theen**   thrive (cf. "as I live").   **24 prelat**   prelate, i.e., a man of authority; **Ronyan**   properly St. Ninian, but here probably with word-play to produce a vulgar allusion to the scrotum. The remarks of the Host are blasphemous and full of blustery sarcasm directed toward the Physician. Chaucer's audience had a keen sense of social hierarchy and would have found the tavernkeeper's remarks amusing. The Physician seems to suffer this abuse with some justification.   **25 in terme**   in technical language.   **26 erme**   grieve.   **27 cardiacle**   a pain in the heart.   **28 corpus bones**   the bones of the body of Christ; **triacle**   a remedy.   **29 corny** grainy, i.e., full-bodied and tasting of malt.   **32 bel amy** (Fr.), good friend, used with the same irreverent tone used to address the Physician.   **33 Iapes**   jokes.   **34 Ronyon**   See l. 24n. The Pardoner's oath has a curious irony in view of his physical condition.   **35 ale-stake**   a sign of an alehouse, or, by exten-sion, an alehouse.   **37 gentils**   the pilgrims of higher rank.   **38 ribaudye**   ribaldry.   **39 lere**   learn. **40 wit**   reasonable doctrine, as contrasted with wiful desire.   **41 y-wis**   indeed.   **42 honest thing** something conducive to virtue.

Motto: Radix malorum . . .   The Douay version of 1 Tim. 6:10 reads "Desire of money is the root of all evils."   *Cupiditas* does indeed mean desire of money, but it was also used commonly in a much broader sense to mean lust for any created thing as distinct from love of God. Both senses should be kept in mind. Technically, the Pardoner's Prologue and Tale constitute a sermon, or, more accurately, a description and illustration of a sermon. The text above is its theme, from which the principal ideas are developed, and the narrative is an exemplum. Our present sermon is delivered in an alehouse ("the devil's temple") rather than in a church. **1 Lordings** Cf. "Ladies and Gentlemen." **2 hauteyn** haughty. **5 oon** the same. **7 whennes that I come** i.e., from Rome. **8 bulles** i.e., papal bulls granting the Pardoner his powers. **9 lige lordes seal** the seal of the local bishop, who has granted the Pardoner permission to preach in his diocese; **patente** open letter or license. **10 warente** protect. **12 Cristes holy werk** a profoundly ironic expression in view of what the Pardoner is actually doing. **17 saffron** spice. The unlearned were impressed by Latin, which was a sign of learning. **19 stones** cases. **20 cloutes** rags. **21 reliks** relics of saints; **wenen they** they (the members of the audience) think. **22 latoun** latten. **23 holy Iewes shepe** i.e., a relic of Old Testament antiquity (to which are here attributed effects proper to the Old Law). **27 ete** eaten (cattle were thought to suffer diseases caused by eating worms). **29 hool** whole (well). **32 eek** also. **33 oweth** owns. **34 wike** week. **37 multiplye** The theme of multiplication in various senses is prominent in the Tales. One might multiply either physically or spiritually. The Pardoner's eunuchry is an indication of spiritual sterility, since he can multiply only in a physical sense and urges others to do likewise. That is, he multiplies his own wealth, tempts others to do the same, and thus multiplies the number of eunuchs like himself in the Church. **40 let maken** let be made. **41 mistriste** mistrust. **42 sooth** truth. **43 taken preestes** i.e., to bed with her. **44 miteyn** mitten. **48 grotes** groats (silver coins worth 4d.). **49 o** one. **52 y-shriven** shriven. **55 Swich** such. **57 out of** free from. **61 gaude** trick. **62 mark** marcs (coins worth 14s. 4d. apiece). **63 lyk a clerk** like a learned man. **68 bekke** beckon. **70 yerne** eagerly. **73 free** generous. **74 namely** especially. **78 a-blakeberied** to pick blackberries (i.e., wandering at will toward Hell). **86 asterte** be astonished. **92 quyte** requite. **96 coveityse** covetousness, the desire to gain possessions, as distinct from avarice, the desire to retain them. However, the two are related and are used interchangeably, as l. 100 indicates. **102 twinne** separate themselves (i.e., by giving to the Pardoner through covetousness). **107 ensamples** *exempla*, or exemplary narratives used in sermons and doctrinal treatises. **109 lewed** illiterate. It was widely held that while literate persons might listen with interest to doctrinal exposition, the unlearned were best taught by exemplary narratives, to which they would pay attention. **113 povert** poverty. **117 make baskettes** i.e., like Paul the Hermit. **125 Ioly wenche** a thing of small use to the Pardoner, who is here boasting. **127 lyking** pleasure. **135 whylom** once. **137 hasard** gambling; **stewes** houses of prostitution. **138 giternes** gitterns. **142 develes temple** i.e., the tavern. It should be recalled that the Host is an innkeeper and that the present "sermon" is being delivered in an alehouse. **146 to-tere** tear apart; that is, they swear by the parts of the Lord's body. Cf. l. 2 of "The Words of the Host." **147 Hem thoghte** it seemed to them that; **Iewes** Jews (at the Crucifixion). **149 tombesteres** dancing girls. **150 Fetys and smale** neat and slender; **fruytesteres** girls selling fruit. **151 wafereres** vendors of cakes. **153 fyr of lecherye** Sexual passion was frequently described as a fire. **154 glotonye** gluttony. Food and drink were often said to be stimulants to lechery. **155 holy writ** i.e., Eph. 5:18. **157 Loth** Lot (see Gen. 19:30–38); **unkindely** unnaturally. **159 niste** did not know; **wroghte** did. **160 Herodes** Herod (see Matt. 14:1–11; Mark 6:21–28). **162 heste** command. **164 Senek** See Seneca, *Epist.* 83:18. **167 dronkelewe** drunk. **168 woodnesse** insanity; **shrewe** person. **171 cause first** Eve's appetite for the forbidden fruit was frequently attributed to gluttony. **175 thilke** that same. **182 defended** forbidden. **184 pleyne** complain. **185 wiste** knew (cf. Ecclus. 37:32–34. However, the idea is a commonplace of medieval doctrine). **189 shorte throte** i.e., the brief pleasure of swallowing. **191 to-swinke** work hard. **193 Paul** i.e., in 1 Cor. 6:13. **198 whyte and red** white and red wine. **199 maketh his privee** i.e., vomits. **201 the apostel** i.e., Paul in Phil. 3:18–19. The verses well characterize the Pardoner himself. **205 wombe** belly. **206 cod** bag. **209 finde** maintain. **211** In Aristotelian metaphysics the "substance" is the real essence of something, the "accident" embraces its outward or accidental qualities. Chaucer derived this remark about cooks, who had been scorned as ministers to the flesh at least since the time of Plato's *Gorgias*, from Innocent III. **212 talent** desire. **219–220** An echo of the discussion of widowhood in I Tim. 5. V. 6 reads "For she that liveth in pleasures, is dead while she is living." **221** Cf. Prov. 20:1. **224 artow** art thou. **226 ay** always. **228 stiked swyn** stuck pig. **229 honest cure** virtuous discipline. **235 Lepe** village in Spain between Ayamonte and Huelva once famous for its strong white wine. **236 Fish-strete** a street in London near London Bridge; **Chepe** Cheapside, London. **237 crepeth subtilly** i.e., it was used to adulterate other more costly wines. **241 weneth** thinks. **243 Rochel** La Rochelle, a seaport north of Bordeaux. **248 verray** true. **256 Lamuel** who receives instructions from his mother in Prov. 31; see especially vv. 4–5. **259 han Iustyse** have the administration of justice. **262 defenden** prohibit; **hasardrye** gambling. The Pardoner turns from the weakness of the flesh, the beginning of the way to death, to the second step, immersion in the world through subjection to fortune. **263 verray moder** true source. That is, gambling, taken in a larger sense, is the source of lying, deceit, forswearing, and blasphemy, all of which are aspects of the third topic to be taken up, swearing. **263 lesinges** lies. **265 wast** waste. **266 repreve** reproof. **270 desolaat** empty of honor. **275 Stilbon** The story is told of one *Chilon* by John of Salisbury. **284 defame** defamation. **295 dees** dice. **306 Mathew** See Matt. 5:33–37. **307 Ieremye** See Jer. 4:2. **312 hestes** commandments. **315 rather** earlier. The Second Commandment was said to forbid, in a spiritual sense, the denial of Christ. This, in effect, is what the devil seeks in his pursuit of man. The Pardoner here completes his discussion of the influence of the flesh (gluttony), the world (gambling), and the devil (swearing). The following tale well illustrates a progression involving these three stages on the way to death. **321** Cf. Ecclus. 23:12. **324 Hayles** a village in Gloucestershire where a portion of Christ's blood was said to be preserved in a vial. **325 chaunce** i.e., at dice; **cink and treye** five and three. The "chance" was the winning number for the player involved. **328 bicched bones** "bitchy" dice. **333 ryotoures** i.e., members of the "companye" of ll. 135–136, exemplifying all those who give themselves up to the flesh, the world, and the devil. That is, what happens to the "ryotoures" is a paradigm of what happens, in one way or another, to all persons who seek to overcome death through cupidity. **334 Longe erst er** much earlier than; **pryme** the end of the "hour" marked by one sixth of the time between sunrise and midday. **338 knave** servant. **339 Go bet** go quickly (a command for hunting dogs). **344 felawe** companion. **345 to-night** last night. **346 For-dronke** dead drunk. **347** Cf. I Thess. 5:2–10. The indirect reference to this famous passage is unmistakable, and its lesson is forcefully implied. **351 this pestilence** i.e., during the current pestilence. **356 my dame** my mother, probably with overtones suggesting the Church and the Blessed Virgin, invoked by the taverner in the next line. The boy has appropriately reflected the doctrines of the "new," or "young," man, as contrasted with those of the "old" man later on, who serves as a guide to the death of the spirit. See Rom. 6:3–13; Eph. 4:22–24; Coloss. 3:5–10. *Youth* and *age* were frequently used to suggest ideas related to these in medieval art and literature; they still echo in Shakespeare, *Henry IV*, where Falstaff is an "old" man. **362 avysed** prepared in advance. **372** Cf. Osee 13:14; I Cor. 15:51–58; Heb. 2:14. All men seek to conquer death; but from a Christian point of view, youth can be renewed and death conquered only through Christ. The rioters engage on their quest "al dronken" in the weakness of the flesh. Through the Old Man they are led to the temptation of the world, which leads them to draw lots for life. And, finally, their denial of the fidelity they owe one another leads them to death. **378 sterte** jump. **381** Cf. ll. 146–147. **385 old man** a figure for St. Paul's "old man." See the references given for l. 356. Parts of the description reflect Boethius, *Consolation*, 1: met. 1, and the elegies of Maximian, but these sources are not literal. **387 god yow see** a common greeting. **389 with sory grace** with bad grace. **390 forwrapped** all wrapped up (as if for burial). **394 Inde** India (i.e., a very long way). **396** In Pauline terms, only Christ exchanges his youth for one's age. Figuratively, the Old Man walks just so long as men refuse to "bury" him so that the "New Man" may live. See the references given for l. 356. **400 caityf** wretched captive. **401 my modres gate** my mother's gate, i.e., the Old Man is "of the earth earthy." See I Cor. 15:42–50. This line, as well as certain other details, makes no sense if the Old Man is taken to represent literal old age. **406 cheste** clothes chest. **408 heyre clout** hair shirt (i.e., the Old Man achieves death through penance). **410 welked** withered. **414 holy writ** i.e., Lev. 19:32, but the speaker omits the concluding admonition of the verse: "and fear the Lord thy God." **416 reed** advice. **417–418** Cf. Ecclus. 8:7. **420 go** walk. **421 moot** must. **427 trouthe** troth; **aspye** spy. **428 abye** pay for. **430 assent** i.e., in agreement with him. **431 yonge folk** ironic in the context; cf. Falstaff's "we youth." **432 leef** desirous. **433 croked wey** Cf. Ecclus. 2:16; Isa. 59:8; Prov. 4:26; 15:21ff. **442 florins** coins worth 6s. 8d. each. The gold constitutes an exemplification of the *radix malorum* in the Pardoner's theme. **443 Wel ny an** Cf. "well nigh on" (coll.); **hem thoughte** it seemed to them. **450 bourde** joke. **451 fortune** Fortune, a personification representing the apparently fortuitous alternation of worldly prosperity and adversity, which, as Boethius explains, is actually Providential. **462 doon us honge** cause us to be hanged. **465 rede** advise; **cut be drawe** i.e., that straws be drawn (so that the decision is in the hands of Fortune). **468 swythe** quickly. **469 breed and wyn** bread and wine, suggestive of the sacrament of the altar. The three men are now critically in need of Christ. **480 sworne brother** a logical premise that neglects the fact that the youngest, who is absent, is also a sworn brother. **491 shrewe** sinner. **496 quod** said; **woost** knowest. **514 trone** throne. **516 feend** the devil (or enemy) who is God's testing agent. That is, the actual temptation arises from within the sinner, although the devil may test him. See James 1:12–15, a text to which Chaucer refers toward the close of the Clerk's Tale. **519–520 in swich lyvinge / That he had leeve** i.e., in a spiritual condition (the contemplation of murder through covetousness) of such a nature that the devil could bring him to destruction. **527 hawe** yard. **529 wreke** avenge. **534 confiture** compound. **535 mountance** amount; **corn** grain. **536 forlete** give up. **537 sterve** die. **538 paas** step (short distance). **546 shoop him** planned; **swinke** work. **560 storven** died. **561 Avicen** Avicenna, an Arabic medical authority, author of a book known as the *Canon* or "Rule"; **fen** a subdivision of Avicenna's book. **563 wonder** strange. **566 eek** also. **569–570** The Pardoner returns to the three subdivisions of his sermon, illustrated in his story. **571 usage** habit. **575 unkinde** unnatural (i.e., in swearing). Note that swearing here is not merely a vice of speech, but falsehood to Christ. **576ff** Here the Pardoner illustrates the appeal he customarily makes in his sermons. **577 avaryce** i.e., cupidity. **578 waryce** cure. **579 nobles** coins worth 6s. 8d.; **sterlinges** silver pennies. **582 wolle** will. **586–587 as clene . . . born** The Pardoner here exaggerates his powers. **588 leche** physician. The concept of Christ the Physician of souls is a commonplace. In ll. 588–590 the Pardoner acknowledges that the pardon of Christ, or the New Law, which offers grace to those who are sincerely repentent, is best. **591ff.** Here the Pardoner denies the acknowledgment of ll. 588–590, revealing his own impenitence through presumption. In effect, the Pardoner has taken the same way that the three sinners take in his tale, and he wishes to lead the pilgrims along it with him. **592 male** sack, the "walet" that "lay biforn him in his lappe" described in the General Prologue. This constitutes, in effect, the Pardoner's "coillons" or instrument of "multiplication." **605 Tassoille** to absolve. **606 aventures** chance misfortunes. **613 rede** advise. **619 so theech** so may I thrive. **622 fundement** excretion; **depeint** stained. **623 croys** Cross; **seint Eleyne** St. Helen. **624 coillons** testicles, appendages that the Pardoner lacks. **625 seintuarie** sacred object. **626 Lat cutte hem of** let them be cut off. **627 tord** turd. **637 kisse** The kiss was a common sign of peace and friendship, often used in the Middle Ages to seal contracts. The kiss in the modern marriage ceremony is a survival of a contractual kiss of this kind.

XII

MIDDLE ENGLISH LITERATURE: EARLY DRAMA IN ENGLAND

It is now conventional to divide early plays in English into three types: mystery plays, morality plays, and miracle plays. The last type, which is rare in English (or at least in our surviving manuscripts), uses narrative materials from the lives of the saints or from miraculous events concerning the sacraments. The morality plays, of which the most famous is *Everyman*, derived from a Dutch source, did not begin to be popular until the late fourteenth century. In these plays the principal characters are personified abstractions, and the interaction of these characters directly illustrates what was considered to be some salubrious point of doctrine. In this respect they are much simpler and less sophisticated than the mystery plays, in which the doctrines arising from the narrative were frequently implied rather than stated directly.

Facing page: Shepherds and a thief.

During the last quarter of the fourteenth century, mystery plays, or plays based on scriptural narrative, began to gain popularity, and they continued to flourish well into the sixteenth century. They were customarily presented in "cycles," or groups of plays covering the high points of scriptural narrative from the Creation to Doomsday. Each play or "pageant" was presented by a local guild or, at times, by a group of local guilds which cooperated in financing and presenting the play assigned to them. In the fourteenth century "craft" guilds and "religious" guilds were not always sharply distinguished, but in England the craft guilds were assuming increasing importance. Many craft guilds liked to perform pageants or processional demonstrations to express and to strengthen their community spirit. The plays offered the craft guilds an opportunity to present their pageants together under the supervision of the municipality in an organized and systematic fashion on the festival of Corpus Christi.

Typically, each play in a cycle was staged on a pageant wagon, or on the wagon and in the immediate area surrounding it. The wagons moved in procession around the city, pausing at certain specified stations for their performances. Groups of people were assembled at each station, where they could watch each play in sequence as the pageant wagons made their round. The whole performance thus had an air of festivity and symbolic pageantry. Men and women of all degrees, from the lowest to the highest, constituted the audience, and it was probably not difficult for many of them to recognize their neighbors among the performers. The pageant as a whole was a community venture, and a community spirit probably helped as much as the official warnings of the municipal authorities to keep the crowds orderly. It should be remembered, however, that the message of the Gospels, which dominated even Old Testament narratives by implication, is essentially joyful, and that religious observances in the Middle Ages could accommodate a considerable amount of hilarity without seeming offensive.

Of the craft plays only four cycles and a few fragments remain. We have no plays from London, where the parish clerks and other clerks of the city had charge of the performances and the plays were all presented in one location. Among the surviving dramatic pieces, the plays of the Wakefield Master in the Towneley Cycle (named after a family who once owned the manuscript)

are the most attractive. These were probably written at some time during the first half of the fifteenth century.

For general bibliography, see Carl J. Stratman, C.S.V., *Bibliography of Medieval Drama*, University of California Press, Berkeley, 1954. The standard authority on the English plays is E. K. Chambers, *The Medieval Stage*, Clarendon Press, Oxford, 1903, although the nonfactual material in this work is now largely outdated. A briefer account by the same author appears in *English Literature at the Close of the Middle Ages*, Clarendon Press, Oxford, 1945. Significant advances in approach are made by Hardin Craig, *English Religious Drama in the Middle Ages*, Clarendon Press, Oxford, 1951. A less technical approach is provided by Arnold Williams, *The Drama of Medieval England*, The Michigan State University Press, East Lansing, 1961. There have been a number of recent studies, among which M. D. Anderson, *Drama and Imagery in English Medieval Churches*, Cambridge University Press, London, 1963, demonstrates interesting connections between the drama and the visual arts; and V. A. Kolve, *The Play Called Corpus Christi*, Stanford University Press, Stanford, Calif., 1966, presents some new views about the rationale of the cycles. A good selective anthology of the plays is John Quincy Adams, *Chief Pre-Shakespearean Dramas*, Houghton Mifflin Company, Boston, 1924, from which the text of *Everyman* is here printed. The Wakefield texts here included are from A. C. Cawley, *The Wakefield Pageants in the Towneley Plays*, Manchester University Press, Manchester, 1958.

MACTACIO ABEL

Dramatis Personae

    Garcio (Pikeharnes)   Cayn   Abell   Deus

Enter Garcio, Cain's servant.

GARCIO   All hayll, all hayll, both blithe and glad,
      For here com I, a mery lad!
      Be peasse youre dyn, my master bad,
      Or els the dwill you spede.
      Wote ye not I com before?   5
      Bot who that ianglis any more,
      He must blaw my blak hoill bore,
      Both behynd and before,

Till his tethe blede.
Felows, here I you forbede   10
To make nother nose ne cry;
Whoso is so hardy to do that dede,
The dwill hang hym vp to dry!

Gedlyngys, I am a full grete wat.
A good yoman my master hat: 15
Full well ye all hym ken.
Begyn he with you for to stryfe,
Certys, then mon ye neurer thryfe;
Bot I trow, bi God on life,
Som of you ar his men.[1]   20
Bot let youre lippis couer youre ten,
Harlottys euerichon!
For if my master com, welcom hym then.
Farewell, for I am gone. [*Exit.*]

Enter Cain, driving his plough-team.[2]
CAYN   Io furth, Greynhorne! and war oute,
           Gryme!   25
       Drawes on! God gif you ill to tyme!
       Ye stand as ye were fallen in swyme.
       What, will ye no forther, mare?
       War! let me se how Down will draw;
       Yit, shrew, yit, pull on a thraw!   30
       What, it semys for me ye stand none aw!
       I say, Donnyng, go fare!
       Aha! God gif the soro and care!
       Lo, now hard she what I saide;
       Now yit art thou the warst mare   35
       In plogh that euer I haide.

       How, Pikeharnes, how! com heder belife!

Re-enter Garcio.
GARCIO   I fend, Godys forbot, that euer thou
             thrife!
CAYN   What, boy, shal I both hold and drife?
         Heris thou not how I cry?   40
GARCIO   Say, Mall and Stott, will ye not go?
         [*Calls to the team.*]
         Lemyng, Morell, Whitehorn, io!
         Now will ye not se how thay hy?
CAYN   Gog gif the sorow, boy. Want of mete it
             gars.
GARCIO   Thare prouand, syr, forthi, I lay behynd
             thare ars,   45

And tyes them fast bi the nekys,
With many stanys in thare hekys.
CAYN   That shall bi thi fals chekys! [*Strikes him.*]
GARCIO   And haue agane as right! [*Strikes back.*]
CAYN   I am thi master. Wilt thou fight?   50
GARCIO   Yai, with the same mesure and weght
         That I boro will I qwite.
CAYN   We! now nothyng bot call on tyte,
         That we had ployde this land.
GARCIO   Harrer, Morell! io furth, hyte!   55
         And let the plogh stand. [*Aside.*]

Enter Abel.[3]
ABELL   God, as he both may and can,
         Spede the, brother, and thi man.
CAYN   Com kis myne ars![4] Me list not ban;
         As welcom standys theroute.   60
         Thou shuld haue bide til thou were cald;
         Com nar, and other drife or hald—
         And kys the dwillis toute!
         Go gresc thi shepe vnder the toute,
         For that is the moste lefe.   65
ABELL   Broder, ther is none hereaboute
         That wold the any grefe.

         Bot, leif brother, here my sawe:
         It is the custom of oure law,
         All that wyrk as the wise   70
         Shall worship God with sacrifice.
         Oure fader vs bad, oure fader vs kend,
         That oure tend shuld be brend.
         Com furth, brothere, and let vs gang
         To worship God; we dwell full lang.   75
         Gif we hym parte of oure fee,
         Corn or catall wheder it be.

         And therfor, brother, let vs weynd,
         And first clens vs from the feynd
         Or we make sacrifice;   80
         Then blis withoutten end
         Get we for oure seruyce,

         Of hym that is oure saulis leche.[5]
CAYN   How! let furth youre geyse; the fox will
             preche.[6]
         How long wilt thou me appech   85
         With thi sermonyng?
         Hold thi tong, yit I say,

Euen ther the good wife strokid the hay;
Or sit downe in the dwill way,
With thi vayn carpyng.   90

Shuld I leife my plogh and all thyng,
And go with the to make offeryng?
Nay, thou fyndys me not so mad!
Go to the dwill, and say I bad!
What gifys God the to rose hym so?   95
Me gifys he noght bot soro and wo.

ABELL   Caym, leife this vayn carpyng,
For God giffys the all thi lifyng.
CAYN   Yit boroed I neuer a farthyng
Of hym—here my hand.   100
ABELL   Brother, as elders haue vs kend,
First shuld we tend with oure hend,
And to his lofyng sithen be brend.
CAYN   My farthyng is in the preest hand[7]
Syn last tyme I offyrd.   105
ABELL   Leif brother, let vs be walkand;
I wold oure tend were profyrd.

CAYN   We! wherof shuld I tend, leif brothere?
For I am ich yere wars then othere—
Here my trouth, it is none othere.   110
My wynnyngys ar bot meyn:
No wonder if that I be leyn.
Full long till hym I may me meyn,
For bi hym that me dere boght,[8]
I traw that he will leyn me noght.   115
ABELL   Yis, all the good thou has in wone
Of Godys grace is bot a lone.
CAYN   Lenys he me? As com thrift apon the so!
For he has euer yit beyn my fo;
For had he my freynd beyn,   120
Othergatys it had beyn seyn.
When all mens corn was fayre in feld,
Then was myne not worth a neld.
When I shuld saw, and wantyd seyde,
And of corn had full grete neyde,   125
Then gaf he me none of his;
No more will I gif hym of this.
Hardely hold me to blame
Bot if I serue hym of the same.
ABELL   Leif brother, say not so,   130
Bot let vs furth togeder go.
Good brother, let vs weynd sone;
No longer here, I rede, we hone.

CAYN   Yei, yei, thou iangyls waste!
The dwill me spede if I haue hast,   135
As long as I may lif,
To dele my good or gif,
Ather to God or yit to man,
Of any good that euer I wan.
For had I giffen away my goode,   140
Then myght I go with a ryffen hood;
And it is better hold that I haue
Then go from doore to doore and craue.
ABELL   Brother, com furth, in Godys name;
I am full ferd that we get blame.   145
Hy we fast, that we were thore.
CAYN   We! ryn on, in the dwills nayme, before!
Wemay, man, I hold the mad!
Wenys thou now that I list gad
To gif away my warldys aght?   150
The dwill hym spede that me so taght!
What nede had I my trauell to lose,
To were my shoyn and ryfe my hose?
ABELL   Dere brother, hit were grete wonder
That I and thou shuld go in sonder;   155
Then wold oure fader haue grete ferly.
Ar we not brether, thou and I?
CAYN   No, bot cry on, cry, whyls the thynk
good!
Here my trowth, I hold the woode.
Wheder that he be blithe or wroth,   160
To dele my good is me full lothe.
I haue gone oft on softer wise
Ther I trowed som prow wold rise.
Bot well I se go must I nede;
Now weynd before—ill myght thou
spede!—   165
Syn that we shall algatys go.
ABELL   Leif brother, whi sais thou so?
Bot go we furth both togeder.
Blissid be God, we haue fare weder.
[They go to the place of sacrifice.]

CAYN   Lay downe thi trussell apon this hill.   170
ABELL   Forsoth, broder, so I will;
Gog of heuen take it to good.
CAYN   Thou shall tend first, if thou were wood.
ABELL   God that shope both erth and heuen,
I pray to the thou here my steven,
[Kneels to make his offering.]   175
And take in thank, if thi will be,
The tend that I offre here to the;

For I gif it in good entent
To the, my Lord, that all has sent.
I bren it now with stedfast thoght,   180
   [*Burns his tithe.*]
In worship of hym that all has wroght.
CAYN   Ryse! Let me now, syn thou has done.
   Lord of heuen, thou here my boyne!
   And ouer Godys forbot be to the
   Thank or thew to kun me;   185
   For, as browke I thise two shankys,
   It is full sore myne vnthankys
   The teynd that I here gif to the
   Of corn or thyng that newys me.
   Bot now begyn will I then,   190
   Syn I must nede my tend to bren.
      [*Begins to count the first ten sheaves, reserving
      the best for himself.*]

   Oone shefe, oone, and this makys two;
   Bot nawder of thise may I forgo.
   Two, two, now this is thre:
   Yei, this also shall leif with me,   195
   For I will chose and best haue—
   This hold I thrift—of all this thrafe.
   Wemo, wemo! foure, lo, here!
   Better groved me no this yere.
   At yere tyme I sew fayre corn,   200
   Yit was it sich when it was shorne:
   Thystyls and brerys⁹—yei, grete plenté—
   And all kyn wedys that myght be.
   Foure shefys, foure, lo, this makys fyfe:
   Deyll I fast thus, long or I thrife!   205
   Fyfe and sex, now this is sevyn;
   Bot this gettys neuer God of heuen.
   Nor none of thise foure, at my myght,
   Shall neuer com in Godys sight.
   Sevyn, sevyn, now this is aght—   210
ABELL   Cam, brother, thou art not God betaght.
CAYN   We! therfor is it that I say
   I will not deyle my good away.
   Bot had I gyffen hym this to teynd,
   Then wold thou say he were my freynd;   215
   Bot I thynk not, bi my hode,
   To departe so lightly fro my goode.
   We! aght, aght, and neyn, and ten is this:
   We! this may we best mys. [*Chooses the first
      tithe-sheaf.*]
   Gif hym that that ligys thore?   220
   It goyse agans myn hart full sore.

ABELL   Cam! teynd right of all bedeyn.
CAYN   We lo! xij, xv, and xvj— [*Begins counting
      the second ten sheaves.*]

ABELL   Caym, thou tendys wrang, and of the
      warst.
CAYN   We! com nar, and hide myne een!   225
   In the wenyand, wist ye now at last!
   Or els will thou that I wynk?
   Then shall I doy no wrong, me thynk.¹⁰
      [*Finishes counting with his eyes closed.*]

   Let me se now how it is— [*Opens his eyes.*]
   Lo, yit I hold me paide;   230
   I teyndyd wonder well bi ges,
   And so euen I laide.

ABELL   Came, of God me thynke thou has no
      drede.
CAYN   Now and he get more, the dwill me
      spede!—
   As mych as oone reepe—   235
   For that cam hym full light chepe;
   Not as mekill, grete ne small,
   As he myght wipe his ars withall.
   For that, and this that lyys here,
   Haue cost me full dere;   240
   Or it was shorne, and broght in stak,
   Had I many a wery bak.
   Therfor aske me no more of this,
   For I haue giffen that my will is.
ABELL   Cam, I rede thou tend right,   245
   For drede of hym that sittys on hight.
CAYN   How that I tend, rek the neuer a deill,
   Bot tend thi skabbid shepe wele;
   For if thou to my teynd tent take,
   It bese the wars for thi sake.   250
   Thou wold I gaf hym this shefe? or this
      sheyfe?
   Na, nawder of thise ij wil I leife.
   Bot take this. Now has he two,
      [*Chooses the second tithe-sheaf.*]
   And for my saull now mot it go;
   Bot it gos sore agans my will,   255
   And shal he like full ill.
ABELL   Cam, I reyde thou so teynd
   That God of heuen be thi freynd.
CAYN   My freynd?—na, not bot if he will!
   I did hym neuer yit bot skill.   260

If he be neuer so my fo,
I am avisid gif hym no mo.
Bot chaunge thi conscience, as I do myn.
Yit teynd thou not thi mesel swyne?

ABELL   If thou teynd right thou mon it fynde.   265

CAYN   Yei, kys the dwills ars behynde!
The dwill hang the bi the nek!
How that I teynd, neuer thou rek.
Will thou not yit hold thi peasse?
Of this ianglyng I reyde thou seasse;   270
And teynd I well or tend I ill,
Bere the euen and speke bot skill.
Bot now, syn thou has teyndid thyne,
Now will I set fyr on myne. [*Tries to burn
his tithe.*]
We! out, haro! help to blaw!   275
It will not bren for me, I traw.
Puf! this smoke dos me mych shame—
[*Blows on it.*]
Now bren in the dwillys name!
A! what dwill of hell is it?
Almost had myne breth beyn dit;   280
Had I blawen oone blast more,
I had beyn choked right thore.
It stank like the dwill in hell,
That longer ther myght I not dwell.

ABELL   Cam, this is not worth oone leke;   285
Thy tend shuld bren withoutten smeke.

CAYN   Com kys the dwill right in the ars!
For the it brens bot the wars.
I wold that it were in thi throte,
Fyr, and shefe, and ich a sprote.   290

God speaks from above:

DEUS   Cam, whi art thou so rebell
Agans thi brother Abell?
Thar thou nowther flyte ne chyde.
If thou tend right thou gettys thi mede;
And be thou sekir, if thou teynd fals,   295
Thou bese alowed therafter als.[11]

CAYN   Whi, who is that hob ouer the wall?
We! who was that that piped so small?
Com, go we hens, for parels all;
God is out of hys wit!   300
Com furth, Abell, and let vs weynd.
Me thynk that God is not my freynd;
On land then will I flyt.

ABELL   A, Caym, brother, that is ill done.

CAYN   No, bot go we hens sone;   305
And if I may, I shall be
Ther as God shall not me see.

ABELL   Dere brother, I will fayre
On feld ther oure bestys ar,
To looke if thay be holgh or full.   310

CAYN   Na, na, abide! We haue a craw to pull.
Hark, speke with me or thou go.
What, wenys thou to skape so?
We! na! I aght the a fowll dispyte,
And now is tyme that I hit qwite.   315

ABEL   Brother, whi art thou so to me in ire?

CAYN   We! theyf, whi brend thi tend so shyre,
Ther myne did bot smoked,
Right as it wold vs both haue choked?

ABEL   Godys will I trow it were   320
That myn brened so clere;
If thyne smoked am I to wite?

CAYN   We! yei! that shal thou sore abite;
With cheke-bon, or that I blyn,
Shal I the and thi life twyn. [*Strikes Abel
down with a jaw-bone.*]   325
So, lig down ther and take thi rest;
Thus shall shrewes be chastysed best.

ABELL   Veniance, veniance, Lord, I cry!
For I am slayn, and not gilty. [*Dies.*]

CAYN   Yei, ly ther, old shrew! ly ther, ly!   330
And if any of you thynk I did amys,
[*To the audience.*]
I shal it amend wars then it is,
That all men may it se:
Well wars then it is,
Right so shall it be.   335

Bot now, syn he is broght on slepe,
Into som hole fayn wold I crepe.
For ferd I qwake, and can no rede;
For be I taken, I be bot dede.
Here will I lig this fourty dayes,   340
And I shrew hym that me fyrst rayse.

God speaks from above:

DEUS   Caym, Caym!

CAYN   Who is that that callis me?
I am yonder, may thou not se?

DEUS   Caym, where is thi brother Abell?

CAYN   What askys thou me? I trow at hell,   345
    At hell I trow he be—
    Whoso were ther then myght he se—
    Or somwhere fallen on slepyng.
    When was he in my kepyng?
DEUS   Caym, Caym, thou was wode.   350
    The voyce of thi brotherys blode,
    That thou has slayn on fals wise,
    From erth to heuen venyance cryse.
    And, for thou has broght thi brother downe,
    Here I gif the my malison.   355
CAYN   Yei, dele aboute the, for I will none,
    Or take it the when I am gone.
    Syn I haue done so mekill syn
    That I may not thi mercy wyn,
    And thou thus dos me from thi grace,   360
    I shall hyde me fro thi face.
    And whereso any man may fynd me,
    Let hym slo me hardely;
    And whereso any man may me meyte,
    Ayther bi sty or yit bi strete;   365
    And hardely, when I am dede,
    Bery me in Gudeboure at the quarell hede[12];
    For, may I pas this place in quarte,
    Bi all men set I not a fart.
DEUS   Nay, Caym, it besc not so;   370
    I will that no man other slo,
    For he that sloys the, yong or old,
    It shall be punyshid sevenfold.[13]
CAYN   No force! I wote wheder I shall:
    In hell, I wote, mon be my stall.   375
    It is no boyte mercy to craue,
    For if I do I mon none haue.

    Bot this cors I wold were hid,
    For som man myght com at vngayn:
    "Fle, fals shrew!" wold he bid,   380
    And weyn I had my brother slayn.

    Bot were Pikeharnes, my knafe, here,
    We shuld bery hym both in fere.
    How, Pykeharnes! scapethryft! how,
      Pikeharnes, how!

    Re-enter Garcio.

GARCIO   Master, master!   385

CAYN   Harstow, boy? Ther is a podyng in the pot.
    Take the that, boy, take the that! [*Strikes him.*]

GARCIO   I shrew thi ball vnder thi hode,
    If thou were my syre of flesh and blode!
    All the day to ryn and trott,   390
    And euer amang thou strykeand;
    Thus am I comen bofettys to fott.
CAYN   Peas, man! I did it bot to vse my hand.

    Bot harke, boy, I haue a counsell to the to
      say—
    I slogh my brother this same day;   395
    I pray the, good boy, and thou may,
    To ryn away with the bayn.
GARCIO   We! out apon the, thefe!
    Has thou thi brother slayn?
CAYN   Peasse, man, for Godys payn!   400

    I saide it for a skaunce.
GARCIO   Yey, bot for ferde of grevance,
    Here I the forsake;
    We mon haue a mekill myschaunce
    And the bayles vs take.   405

CAYN   A, syr, I cry you mercy! Seasse,
    And I shall make you a releasse.
GARCIO   What, wilt thou cry my peasse
    Throughout this land?

CAYN   Yey, that I gif God avow, belife.   410
GARCIO   How will thou do, long or thou thrife?
CAYN   Stand vp, my good boy, belife,
    And thaym peasse, both man and wife;
    And whoso will do after me,
    Full slape of thrift then shal he be.   415
    Bot thou must be my good boy,
    And cry "oyes, oyes, oy!"
GARCIO   Browes, browes to thi boy!

    [*Cain proclaims the king's peace for himself
    and Pikeharnes, who echoes him in mocking
    asides addressed to the audience.*

CAYN   I commaund you in the kyngys nayme,
GARCIO   And in my masteres, fals Cayme,   420
CAYN   That no man at thame fynd fawt ne blame,
GARCIO   Yey, cold rost is at my masteres hame.
CAYN   Nowther with hym nor with his knafe,
GARCIO   What! I hope my master rafe.
CAYN   For thay ar trew full manyfold.   425
GARCIO   My master suppys no coyle bot cold.

CAYN   The kyng wrytys you vntill.
GARCIO   Yit ete I neuer half my fill.
CAYN   The kyng will that thay be safe.
GARCIO   Yey, a draght of drynke fayne wold I
            hayfe.   430
CAYN   At thare awne will let tham wafe.
GARCIO   My stomak is redy to receyfe.
CAYN   Loke no man say to theym, on nor other—
GARCIO   This same is he that slo his brother.
CAYN   Byd euery man thaym luf and lowt.   435
GARCIO   Yey, ill-spon weft ay comes foule out.
CAYN   Long or thou get thi hoyse, and thou go
            thus aboute!

            Byd euery man theym pleasse to pay.

GARCIO   Yey, gif Don, thyne hors, a wisp of hay!
            [*Saves himself from Cain's wrath by climbing
            out of his reach.*]
CAYN   We! com downe in twenty dwill way!   440
            The dwill I the betake;
            For bot it were Abell, my brothere,
            Yit knew I neuer thi make.

GARCIO   [*Garcio addresses the audience:*]
            Now old and yong, or that ye weynd,
            The same blissyng withoutten end,   445
            All sam then shall ye haue,
            That God of heuen my master has giffen.

Browke it well, whils that ye liffen;
He vowche it full well safe.

CAYN   Com downe yit, in the dwillys way,   450
            And angre me no more! [*Garcio descends.*]
            And take yond plogh, I say,
            And weynd the furth fast before;
            And I shall, if I may,
            Tech the another lore.   455
            I warn the, lad, for ay,
            Fro now furth euermore,
            That thou greue me noght;
            For, bi Codys sydys, if thou do,
            I shall hang the apon this plo,   460
            With this rope, lo, lad, lo,
            By hym that me dere boght! [*Exit Garcio.
            Cain addresses the audience:*]
            Now fayre well, felows all,[14] for I must
            nedys weynd,
            And to the dwill be thrall, warld withoutten
            end:
            Ordand ther is my stall, with Sathanas the
            feynd.   465
            Euer ill myght hym befall that theder me
            commend
            This tyde.
            Fare well les, and fare well more!
            For now and euermore
            I will go me to hyde. [*Exit.*]   470
Explicit Mactacio Abell. Sequitur Noe.

Glossary

3 peasse silence. **4 dwill** devil. **6 ianglis** talks idly. **11 nose** noise. **14 Gedlyngys** fellows; **wat** man. **15 hat** is called. **21 ten** teeth. **27 swyme** swoon. **30 thraw** little while. **37 belife** quickly. **44 it gars** causes it. **47 stanys** stones; **hekys** hayracks. **53 call on tyte** call the team on quickly. **59 ban** curse. **64 toute** tail. **72 kend** taught. **73 tend** tithe; **brend** burnt. **78 weynd** wend. **84 geyse** geese, i.e., "let your geese out and the fox will preach" or "the fox will get one by his guile." **85 appech** accuse. **88** "where the good wife stroked the hay." The obscene reference is fairly clear. **89 in the dwill way** Cf. "in the devil's name." **90 vayn carpyng** empty gabble. **95 rose** praise. **100 here my hand** here is my hand on it. **102 tend** tithe. **103 lofyng** praise; **sithen** afterward. **104** Cf. Chaucer's Summoner's Tale. **109** "each year worse than the one before." **113 meyn** complain. **118** "Does he give me anything? May you have the same fare." **121 Othergatys** otherwise. **123 neld** needle. **133 hone** delay. **134 iangyls waste** waste words. **141 ryffen** riven. **145 ferd** afraid. **148 Wemay!** an exclamation. **149 Wenys** do you think. **150 warldys aght** worldly goods. **153 ryfe** rive. **156 ferly** marvel. **163 prow** profit. **166 algatys** anyhow. **170 trussell** bundle. **175 steven**

voice. **183 boyne** prayer. **184–185** "And God forbid that you should give me any thanks for it." **186** "As I use these two legs." **187 vnthankys** unwillingness. **189 newys me** "newly grows for me." **195 leif** stay. **197 thrafe** sheaf. **199 groved** grew. **200 At yere tyme** at the proper season. **222 bedeyn** quickly. **226 wenyand** waning of the moon (an unlucky time). **235 reepe** sheaf. **247 neuer a deill** never a deal, or, not at all. **249 tent take** take account. **250 bese the wars** will be the worse. **260 bot skill** but what is reasonable. **264 mesel** measly. **265 mon it fynde** will find out about it. **280 dit** stopped. **290 ich a** every. **293** "You need neither quarrel nor chide." **296 als** accordingly. **314 aght** owe. **315 qwite** quit. **317 shyre** clear. **322 to wite** to blame. **338 can no rede** do not know what to do. **341 rayse** to raise (game) from a lair. **355 malison** curse. **367 Gudeboure** Goodybower near the quarry in Wakefield, renamed Brook Street in the last century. **368 quarte** good health (safely). **376 boyte** use. **379 vngayn** unexpectedly. **381 weyn** know. **391** "And you are always hitting me." **392 fott** fetch. **397 bayn** the bones of the corpse. **401 skaunce** jest. **405 bayles** bailiffs. **408 peasse** pardon. **413 thaym** to them. **415 slape** crafty. **418 browes** broth. **426 coyle** pottage. **431 wafe** wander. **435 lowt** respect. **436** "May it be long before you get your hose," or, that is, prosper. **448 Browke** enjoy.

Notes

1 It was customary to think of all men as belonging either to the "generation of Cain," or to the "generation of Abel (or Seth)" in a spiritual sense. The word *Cain* was said to mean possession, and the sons of Cain are the inhabitants of the world who seek to make it (rather than the celestial city) their home. When Pikeharnes says, "Some of you are his men," he means that some of the spectators of the play are spiritual descendants of Cain.

2 The failure of Cain to control his horses and his man is probably intended to suggest the failure of the wicked to maintain the kind of dominion God gave to Adam (Gen. 1:26). It was said that to control others it is necessary to control one's own passions first. Cain's rebelliousness from God's dominion implies a concomitant rebelliousness of everything under Cain's dominion.

3 There has been some tendency among modern critics to belittle Abel in this play, but the author obviously had no intention of making him a pious hypocrite. The name *Abel* was said to mean grief, and the suffering of Abel looks forward to the suffering of Christ and hence to the sufferings of the virtuous in the world. The action in this play typifies the Crucifixion and, concomitantly, all the implications of that act. The reader will begin to do some justice to this play, and to others like it, when he learns to view the characters not as personalities, but as typifying figures.

4 The obscene language of Cain suggests the malice of his generation. Neither the author nor his audience would have been shocked by it, since such language was (and still is) common among malicious persons, although the better-educated have means of disguising it.

5 The offerings of the play represent the self-sacrifice that anyone who "bears the cross" is supposed to make.

6 The fox preaching to the geese, a common theme in the medieval visual arts, represents the hypocrite deceiving the innocent for his own worldly profit. The irony of the accusation arises from the fact that Cain is hardly innocent and Abel is far from being a seeker of worldly profit. Cain's remark is a reflection on himself. This device of having a speaker point to his own weakness while seeming to denounce someone else is common in both Chaucer and Shakespeare.

7 If one reads the play literally, this is an anachronism due to the quaint naïveté of the old author. But the play is not about an event which took place once long ago at a fixed point in space and time. It is, rather, about a perennial event, which takes place again and again wherever there are Christian

societies. This also accounts for the fact that the characters look and speak like contemporaries. The author was not interested in history except as a key to the behavior of the Cains, Abels, and Pikeharnesses of his own society.

8   An anachronistic reference to Christ and the Redemption. See n. 7.

9   See Gen. 3:18. In terms of *Piers the Ploughman* (and these terms are conventional), Cain has not kept his field free of the weeds of the vices.

10   Cain tithes blindly. His winking is an indication of his lack of spiritual insight. Cf. the close of Chaucer's Nun's Priest's Tale and, for similar themes in the visual arts, Erwin Panofsky, *Studies in Iconology*, Harper & Row, Publishers, Incorporated, New York, 1962, ch. IV.

11   On the contrast between the two sacrifices and the deficiency of Cain's in particular, see St. Augustine, *The City of God* 15:7, in Whitney J. Oates (ed.), *Basic Writings of Saint Augustine*, Random House, Inc., New York, 1948, vol. II, pp. 281–284. The dramatist has handled the various possibilities suggested by the Fathers and the exegetes with great skill.

12   The action is appropriately located in the immediate vicinity of Wakefield, where this play was presented. See n. 7.

13   See Gen. 4:15.

14   Cain bids farewell to his fellows, or to the "descendants of Cain" in the audience, pointing out to them what their fate will be.

SECUNDA PASTORUM[1]

Incipit Alia eorundem

Primus Pastor (Coll)	Vxor eius (Gyll)
Secundus Pastor (Gyb)	Angelus
Tercius Pastor (Daw)[2]	Maria
Mak	Christ-child

Open fields near a town.[3] Enter the First Shepherd.

ɪ PASTOR   Lord, what these weders ar cold![4]
    And I am yll happyd.
I am nerehande dold, so long haue I nappyd;
My legys thay fold, my fyngers ar chappyd.
It is not as I wold, for I am al lappyd
In sorrow.   5
In stormes and tempest,
Now in the eest, now in the west,
Wo is hym has neuer rest
Mydday nor morow!

Bot we sely husbandys that walkys on the
    moore,   10
In fayth we ar nerehandys outt of the doore.
No wonder, as it standys, if we be poore,
For the tylthe of oure landys lyys falow as
    the floore,
As ye ken.

We ar so hamyd,   15
Fortaxed and ramyd,
We ar mayde handtamyd
With thyse gentlery-men.[5]

Thus thay refe vs oure rest, oure Lady theym
    wary!
These men that ar lord-fest, thay cause the
    ploghe tary.   20
That men say is for the best, we fynde it
    contrary.
Thus ar husbandys opprest, in ponte to
    myscary
On lyfe;
Thus hold thay vs hunder,
Thus thay bryng vs in blonder;   25
It were greatte wonder
And euer shuld we thryfe.

For may he gett a paynt slefe or a broche
    now-on-dayes,
Wo is hym that hym grefe or onys agane
    says!
Dar noman hym reprefe, what mastry he
    mays;   30
And yit may noman lefe oone word that he
    says—
No letter.
He can make purveance

With boste and bragance,
And all is thrugh mantenance   35
Of men that ar gretter.

Ther shall com a swane as prowde as a po;
He must borow my wane, my ploghe also;
Then I am full fane to graunt or he go.
Thus lyf we in payne, anger, and wo,   40
By nyght and day.
He must haue if he langyd,
If I shuld forgang it;
I were better be hangyd
Then oones say hym nay.   45

It dos me good, as I walk thus by myn oone,
Of this warld for to talk in maner of mone.
To my shepe wyll I stalk, and herkyn anone,
Ther abyde on a balk, or sytt on a stone
Full soyne;   50
For I trowe, perdé,
Trew men if thay be,
We gett more compané
Or it be noyne.

Enter the Second Shepherd, who does not see
the First Shepherd.

2 PASTOR   Bensté and Dominus, what may this
                bemeyne?   55
            Why fares this warld thus? Oft haue we not
                sene.
            Lord, thyse weders ar spytus, and the
                wyndys full kene,
            And the frostys so hydus thay water myn
                eeyne—
            No ly.
            Now in dry, now in wete,   60
            Now in snaw, now in slete,
            When my shone freys to my fete
            It is not all esy.

            Bot as far as I ken, or yit as I go,
            We sely wedmen[6] dre mekyll wo: 65
            We haue sorow then and then; it fallys oft so.
            Sely Copyle, oure hen, both to and fro
            She kakyls;
            Bot begyn she to crok,
            To groyne or to clok,   70

Wo is hym is oure cok,
For he is in the shakyls.[7]

These men that ar wed haue not all thare
    wyll;
When they ar full hard sted, thay sygh full
    styll.
God wayte thay ar led full hard and full yll;   75
In bowere nor in bed thay say noght thertyll.
This tyde
My parte haue I fun,
I know my lesson:
Wo is hym that is bun,   80
For he must abyde.

Bot now late in oure lyfys—a meruell to me,
That I thynk my hart ryfys sich wonders to
    see;
What that destany dryfys it shuld so be—
Som men wyll haue two wyfys, and som
    men thre   85
In store;
Som ar wo that has any.
Bot so far can I:
Wo is hym that has many,
For he felys sore.   90

[Admonishes the young men in the audience:]

Bot, yong men, of wowyng, for God that
    you boght,
Be well war of wedyng, and thynk in youre
    thoght:
"Had-I-wyst" is a thyng that seruys of
    noght.
Mekyll styll mowrnyng has wedyng home
    broght,
And grefys,   95
With many a sharp showre;
For thou may cach in an owre
That shall sow the full sowre
As long as thou lyffys.

For, as euer rede I pystyll,[8] I haue oone to
    my fere   100
As sharp as thystyll, as rugh as a brere;
She is browyd lyke a brystyll, with a sowre-
    loten chere;

Had she oones wett hyr whystyll, she couth
    syng full clere
Hyr Paternoster.
She is as greatt as a whall,   105
She has a galon of gall;
By hym that dyed for vs all,
I wald I had ryn to I had lost hir!

[First Shepherd interrupts him:]

1 PASTOR   God looke ouer the raw! Full defly ye
    stand.
2 PASTOR   Yee, the dewill in thi maw, so tariand!   110
    Sagh thou awre of Daw?
1 PASTOR   Yee, on a ley-land
    Hard I hym blaw. He commys here at hand,
    Not far.
    Stand styll.
2 PASTOR   Qwhy?
1 PASTOR   For he commys, hope I.   115
2 PASTOR   He wyll make vs both a ly
    Bot if we be war.

Enter the Third Shepherd, a boy.

3 PASTOR   Crystys crosse me spede, and Sant
    Nycholas!
    Thereof had I nede; it is wars then it was.
    Whoso couthe take hede and lett the warld
    pas,   120
    It is euer in drede and brekyll as glas,
    And slythys.
    This warld fowre neuer so,
    With meruels mo and mo—
    Now in weyll, now in wo,   125
    And all thyng wrythys.

    Was neuer syn Noe floode sich floodys seyn,[9]
    Wyndys and ranys so rude, and stormes so
    keyn—
    Som stamerd, som stod in dowte, as I weyn.
    Now God turne all to good! I say as I mene, 130
    For ponder:
    These floodys so thay drowne,
    Both in feyldys and in towne,
    And berys all downe;
    And that is a wonder. *[Catches sight of the*
    other shepherds.]   135
    We that walk on the nyghtys, oure catell to
    kepe,

We se sodan syghtys when othere men slepe.
Yit me thynk my hart lyghtys; I se shrewys
    pepe.
Ye ar two all-wyghtys—I wyll gyf my
    shepe
A turne.   140
Bot full yll haue I ment;
As I walk on this bent,
I may lyghtly repent,
My toes if I spurne.

[Greets them:]

A, syr, God you saue, and master myne!   145
A drynk fayn wold I haue, and somwhat to
    dyne.
1 PASTOR   Crystys curs, my knaue, thou art a
    ledyr hyne!
2 PASTOR   What, the boy lyst raue! Abyde vnto
    syne;
    We haue mayde it.
    Yll thryft on thy pate!   150
    Though the shrew cam late,
    Yit is he in state
    To dyne—if he had it.[10]

3 PASTOR   Sich seruandys as I, that swettys and
    swynkys,
    Etys oure brede full dry, and that me
    forthynkys.   155
    We ar oft weytt and wery when master-men
    wynkys;
    Yit commys full lately both dyners and
    drynkys.
    Bot nately
    Both oure dame and oure syre,
    When we haue ryn in the myre,   160
    Thay can nyp at oure hyre,
    And pay vs full lately.

    Bot here my trouth, master: for the fayr that
    ye make,
    I shall do therafter—wyrk as I take.
    I shall do a lytyll, syr, and emang euer lake, 165
    For yit lay my soper neuer on my stomake
    In feyldys.
    Wherto shuld I threpe?
    With my staf can I lepe;

And men say, "Lyght chepe   170
    Letherly foryeldys."

1 PASTOR   Thou were an yll lad to ryde on
                wowyng
           With a man that had bot lytyll of spendyng.
2 PASTOR   Peasse, boy, I bad. No more ianglyng,
           Or I shall make the full rad, by the heuens
                kyng!   175
           With thy gawdys—
           Where ar oure shepe, boy?—we skorne.
3 PASTOR   Sir, this same day at morne
           I thaym left in the corne,
           When thay rang lawdys.   180
           Thay haue pasture good, thay can not go
                wrong.
1 PASTOR   That is right. By the roode, thyse
                nyghtys ar long!
           Yit I wold, or we yode, oone gaf vs a song.
2 PASTOR   So I thoght as I stode, to myrth vs
                emong.
3 PASTOR   I grauntt.   185
1 PASTOR   Lett me syng the tenory.
2 PASTOR   And I the tryble so hye.
3 PASTOR   Then the meyne fallys to me.
           Lett se how ye chauntt. [*They sing*.]

Tunc intrat Mak in clamide se super togam vestitus.[11]

MAK   Now, Lord, for thy naymes vij, that made
                both moyn and starnes   190
           Well mo then I can neuen, thi will, Lorde,
                of me tharnys.
           I am all vneuen; that moves oft my harnes.
           Now wold God I were in heuen, for ther
                wepe no barnes
           So styll.
1 PASTOR   Who is that pypys so poore?   195
MAK   Wold God ye wyst how I foore!
           Lo, a man that walkys on the moore,
           And has not all his wyll.

2 PASTOR   Mak, where has thou gone? Tell vs
                tythyng.
3 PASTOR   Is he commen? Then ylkon take hede
                to his thyng. [*Et accipit clamidem ab ipso*.]   200
MAK   What! ich be a yoman, I tell you, of the
                kyng,

The self and the some, sond from a greatt
    lordyng,
And sich.
Fy on you! Goyth hence
Out of my presence!   205
I must haue reuerence.
Why, who be ich?

1 PASTOR   Why make ye it so qwaynt? Mak, ye
                do wrang.
2 PASTOR   Bot, Mak, lyst ye saynt? I trow that
                ye lang.
3 PASTOR   I trow the shrew can paynt, the
                dewyll myght hym hang!   210
MAK   Ich shall make complaynt, and make you
                all to thwang
           At a worde,
           And tell euyn how ye doth.
1 PASTOR   Bot, Mak, is that sothe?
           Now take outt that Sothren tothe,   215
           And sett in a torde!
2 PASTOR   Mak, the dewill in youre ee! A stroke
                wold I leyne you.
3 PASTOR   Mak, know ye not me? By God, I
                couthe teyn you. [*They threaten him, and
                Mak hastily becomes himself again*.]
MAK.   God looke you all thre! Me thoght I had
                sene you.
           Ye ar a fare compané.   220
1 PASTOR   Can ye now mene
                you?
2 PASTOR   Shrew, pepe!
           Thus late as thou goys,
           What wyll men suppos?
           And thou has an yll noys
           Of stelyng of shepe.[12]   225

MAK   And I am trew as steyll, all men waytt;
           Bot a sekenes I feyll that haldys me full
                haytt:
           My belly farys not weyll; it is out of astate.
3 PASTOR   Seldom lyys the dewyll dede by the
                gate.
MAK   Therfor   230
           Full sore am I and yll,
           If I stande stone-styll.
           I ete not an nedyll
           Thys moneth and more.

1 PASTOR	How farys thi wyff? By thi hoode,	
	how farys she?	235
MAK	Lyys walteryng—by the roode—by the	
	fyere, lo!	
	And a howse full of brude. She drynkys	
	well, to;	
	Yll spede othere good that she wyll do!	
	Bot sho	
	Etys as fast as she can,	240
	And ilk yere that commys to man	
	She bryngys furth a lakan—	
	And, som yeres, two.	

	Bot were I now more gracyus and rychere	
	be far,	
	I were eten outt of howse and of harbar.	245
	Yis is she a fowll dowse, if ye com nar;	
	Ther is none that trowse nor knowys a war	
	Then ken I.	
	Now wyll ye se what I profer?—	
	To gyf all in my cofer	250
	To-morne at next to offer	
	Hyr hed-maspenny.	
2 PASTOR	I wote so forwakyd is none in this	
	shyre;	
	I wold slepe, if I takyd les to my hyere.	
3 PASTOR	I am cold and nakyd, and wold haue a	
	fyere.	255
1 PASTOR	I am wery, forrakyd, and run in the	
	myre—	
	Wake thou! [Lies down.]	
2 PASTOR	Nay, I wyll lyg downe by,	
	For I must slepe, truly. [Lies down beside him.]	
3 PASTOR	As good a mans son was I	260
	As any of you. [Lies down, and makes Mak	
	join them.]	
	Bot, Mak, com heder! Betwene shall thou	
	lyg downe.	
MAK	Then myght I lett you bedene of that ye	
	wold rowne,	
	No drede.	
	Fro my top to my too,	265
	Manus tuas commendo,	
	Poncio Pilato;	
	Cryst-crosse me spede! [Tunc surgit,	
	pastoribus dormientibus, et dicit:]	
	Now were tyme for a man that lakkys what	
	he wold	

	To stalk preuely than vnto a fold,	270
	And neemly to wyrk than, and be not to	
	bold,	
	For he myght aby the bargan, if it were told	
	At the endyng.	
	Now were tyme for to reyll;	
	Bot he nedys good counsell	275
	That fayn wold fare weyll,	
	And has bot lytyll spendyng. [Casts a spell	
	on the sleeping shepherds.]	
	Bot abowte you a serkyll, as rownde as a	
	moyn,	
	To I haue done that I wyll, tyll that it be	
	noyn,	
	That ye lyg stone-styll to that I haue doyne;	280
	And I shall say thertyll of good wordys a	
	foyne:	
	"On hight,	
	Ouer youre heydys, my hand I lyft.	
	Outt go youre een! Fordo youre syght!" [13]	
	Bot yit I must make better shyft	285
	And it be right. [The shepherds begin to snore.]	
	Lord, what thay slepe hard! That may ye all	
	here.	
	Was I neuer a shepard, bot now wyll I lere.	
	If the flok be skard, yit shall I nyp nere.	
	How! drawes hederward! Now mendys	
	oure chere	290
	From sorow	
	A fatt shepe, I dar say,	
	A good flese, dar I lay.	
	Eft-whyte when I may,	
	Bot this will I borow. [Goes off home with	
	the sheep.]	295
	How, Gyll, art thou in? Gett vs som lyght.	
VXOR EIUS	Who makys sich dyn this tyme of	
	the nyght?	
	I am sett for to spyn; I hope not I myght	
	Ryse a penny to wyn, I shrew them on	
	hight!	
	So farys	300
	A huswyff that has bene	
	To be rasyd thus betwene.	
	Here may no note be sene	
	For sich small charys.	

MAK	Good wyff, open the hek! Seys thou not	
	what I bryng?	305

VXOR   I may thole the dray the snek. A, com in,
    my swetyng!

MAK   Yee, thou thar not rek of my long
    standyng.

VXOR   By the nakyd nek art thou lyke for to
    hyng.

MAK   Do way!
    I am worthy my mete,   310
    For in a strate can I gett
    More then thay that swynke and swette
    All the long day. [*Shows her the sheep.*]
    Thus it fell to my lott, Gyll; I had sich grace.

VXOR   It were a fowll blott to be hanged for the
    case.   315

MAK   I haue skapyd, Ielott, oft as hard a glase.

VXOR   "Bot so long goys the pott to the water,"
    men says,
    "At last
    Comys it home broken."

MAK   Well knowe I the token,   320
    Bot let it neuer be spoken!
    Bot com and help fast.

    I wold he were flayn; I lyst well ete.
    This twelmothe was I not so fayn of oone
    shepe-mete.

VXOR   Com thay or he be slayn, and here the
    shepe blete—   325

MAK   Then myght I be tane. That were a cold
    swette!
    Go spar
    The gaytt-doore.

VXOR   Yis, Mak,
    For and thay com at thy bak—

MAK   Then myght I by, for all the pak,   330
    The dewill of the war!

VXOR   A good bowrde haue I spied, syn thou
    can none:
    Here shall we hym hyde, to thay be gone,
    In my credyll. Abyde! Lett me alone,
    And I shall lyg besyde in chylbed, and grone. 335

MAK   Thou red,
    And I shall say thou was lyght
    Of a knaue-childe this nyght.

VXOR   Now well is me day bright
    That euer was I bred!   340

    This is a good gyse and a far-cast;
    Yit a woman avyse helpys at the last.

    I wote neuer who spyse; agane go thou fast.

MAK   Bot I com or thay ryse, els blawes a
    cold blast!
    I wyll go slepe. [*Returns to the shepherds.*]   345
    Yit slepys all this meneye;
    And I shall go stalk preuely,
    As it had neuer bene I
    That caryed thare shepe. [*Lies down between
    them.*]

[*The First and Second Shepherds awake; the
Second Shepherd helps the First to stand up.*]

I PASTOR   *Resurrex a mortruus!* Haue hold my
    hand.   350
    Iudas carnas dominus! I may not well stand;
    My foytt slepys, by Iesus, and I water
    fastand.
    I thoght that we layd vs full nere Yngland.

2 PASTOR   A, ye?
    Lord, what I haue slept weyll!   355
    As fresh as an eyll,
    As lyght I me feyll
    As leyfe on a tre.

[*The Third Shepherd awakes from a nightmare.*]

3 PASTOR   Bensté be herein! So me qwakys,
    My hart is outt of skyn, whatso it makys.   360
    Who makys all this dyn? So my browes
    blakys,
    To the dowore wyll I wyn. Harke, felows,
    wakys!
    We were fowre—
    Se ye awre of Mak now?[14]

I PASTOR   We were vp or thou.   365

2 PASTOR   Man, I gyf God avowe,
    Yit yede he nawre.

3 PASTOR   Me thoght he was lapt in a wolfe-
    skyn.[15]

I PASTOR   So ar many hapt now, namely
    within.[16]

3 PASTOR   When we had long napt, me thoght
    with a gyn   370
    A fatt shepe he trapt; bot he mayde no dyn.

2 PASTOR   Be styll!
    Thi dreme makys the woode;
    It is bot fantom, by the roode.[17]

I PASTOR   Now God turne all to good,   375
    If it be his wyll.

[*They rouse Mak, who pretends to have been fast asleep.*]

2 PASTOR Ryse, Mak, for shame! Thou lygys right lang.
MAK Now Crystys holy name be vs emang!
    What is this? For Sant Iame, I may not well gang!
    I trow I be the same. A! my nek has lygen wrang   380
    Enoghe. [*They pull him up from the ground.*]
    Mekill thank! Syn yister-euen,
    Now by Sant Stevyn,
    I was flayd with a swevyn—
    My hart out of sloghe!   385

    I thoght Gyll began to crok and trauell full sad,
    Wel-ner at the fyrst cok, of a yong lad
    For to mend oure flok. Then be I neuer glad;
    I haue tow on my rok more then euer I had.
    A, my heede!   390
    A house full of yong tharmes,
    The dewill knok outt thare harnes!
    Wo is hym has many barnes,
    And therto lytyll brede.

    I must go home, by youre lefe, to Gyll, as I thoght.   395
    I pray you looke my slefe, that I steyll noght;
    I am loth you to grefe, or from you take oght. [*Goes off home.*]
3 PASTOR Go furth, yll myght thou chefe! Now wold I we soght,
    This morne,
    That we had all oure store.   400
1 PASTOR Bot I will go before;
    Let vs mete.
2 PASTOR   Whore?
3 PASTOR At the crokyd thorne. [*Exeunt.*]

Mak is seen standing outside the door of his cottage.

MAK Vndo this doore! Who is here? How long shall I stand?
VXOR EIUS Who makys sich a bere? Now walk in the wenyand!   405
MAK A, Gyll, what chere? It is I, Mak, youre husbande.

VXOR Then may we se here the dewill in a bande,
    Syr Gyle!
    Lo, he commys with a lote,
    As he were holden in the throte.   410
    I may not syt at my note
    A handlang while.

MAK Wyll ye here what fare she makys to gett hir a glose?
    And dos noght bot lakys, and clowse hir toose.
VXOR Why, who wanders, who wakys? Who commys, who gose?   415
    Who brewys, who bakys? What makys me thus hose?
    And than
    It is rewthe to beholde—
    Now in hote, now in colde,
    Full wofull is the householde   420
    That wantys a woman.

    Bot what ende has thou mayde with the hyrdys, Mak?
MAK The last worde that thay sayde when I turnyd my bak,
    Thay wold looke that thay hade thare shepe, all the pak.
    I hope thay wyll nott be well payde when thay thare shepe lak,   425
    Perdé!
    Bot howso the gam gose,
    To me thay wyll suppose,
    And make a fowll noyse,
    And cry outt apon me.   430

    Bot thou must do as thou hyght.
VXOR   I accorde me thertyll;
    I shall swedyll hym right in my credyll.
    [*She muffles up the sheep and puts it in the cradle.*]
    If it were a gretter slyght, yit couthe I help tyll.
    I wyll lyg downe stright. Com hap me.
MAK   I wyll. [*Covers her.*]
VXOR Behynde!   435
    Com Coll and his maroo,
    Thay will nyp vs full naroo.

MAK   Bot I may cry "out, haroo!"
       The shepe if thay fynde.

VXOR   Harken ay when thay call; thay will com
            onone.   440
        Com and make redy all, and syng by thyn
            oone;
        Syng "lullay" thou shall, for I must grone,
        And cry outt by the wall on Mary and Iohn,
        For sore.
        Syng "lullay" on fast   445
        When thou heris at the last;
        And bot I play a fals cast,
        Trust me no more.

        The shepherds meet at the crooked thorn.

3 PASTOR   A, Coll, goode morne! Why slepys
                thou nott?
1 PASTOR   Alas, that euer was I borne! We haue
                a fowll blott—   450
        A fat wedir haue we lorne.
3 PASTOR   Mary, Godys forbott!
2 PASTOR   Who shuld do vs that skorne? That
                were a fowll spott.
1 PASTOR   Som shrewe.
        I haue soght with my dogys
        All Horbery shrogys,   455
        And of xv hogys
        Fond I bot oone ewe.

3 PASTOR   Now trow me, if ye will—by Sant
                Thomas of Kent,
        Ayther Mak or Gyll was at that assent.[18]
1 PASTOR   Peasse, man, be still! I sagh when he
                went.   460
        Thou sklanders hym yll; thou aght to repent
        Goode spede.
2 PASTOR   Now as euer myght I the,
        If I shuld euyn here de,
        I wold say it were he   465
        That dyd that same dede.

3 PASTOR   Go we theder, I rede, and ryn on oure
                feete.
        Shall I neuer ete brede, the sothe to I wytt.
1 PASTOR   Nor drynk in my heede, with hym
                tyll I mete.

2 PASTOR   I wyll rest in no stede tyll that I hym
                grete,   470
        My brothere.
        Oone I will hight:
        Tyll I se hym in sight,
        Shall I neuer slepe one nyght
        Ther I do anothere.   475

[*As the shepherds draw near to Mak's cottage, they
        hear Gyll groaning and Mak singing a tuneless
        lullaby.*]

3 PASTOR   Will ye here how thay hak? Oure
                syre lyst croyne.
1 PASTOR   Hard I neuer none crak so clere out of
                toyne.
        Call on hym.
2 PASTOR   Mak, vndo youre doore soyne!
MAK   Who is that spak, as it were noyne,
       On loft?   480
       Who is that, I say?
3 PASTOR   Goode felowse, were it day.
MAK   As far as ye may, [*Opens the door.*]
       Good, spekys soft,

       Ouer a seke womans heede that is at
           mayllcasse;   485
       I had leuer be dede or she had any dyseasse.
VXOR   Go to anothere stede! I may not well
            qweasse;
        Ich fote that ye trede goys thorow my nese
        So hee.
1 PASTOR   Tell vs, Mak, if ye may,   490
        How fare ye, I say?
MAK   Bot ar ye in this towne to-day?
       Now how fare ye?

       Ye haue ryn in the myre, and ar weytt yit;
       I shall make you a fyre, if ye will sytt.   495
       A nores wold I hyre. Thynk ye on yit?
       Well qwytt is my hyre—my dreme, this is
           itt—
       A seson. [*Points to the cradle.*]
       I haue barnes, if ye knew,
       Well mo then enewe;   500
       Bot we must drynk as we brew,
       And that is bot reson.

I wold ye dynyd or ye yode. Me thynk that
        ye swette.
2 PASTOR   Nay, nawther mendys oure mode
        drynke nor mette.
MAK   Why, syr, alys you oght bot goode?   505
3 PASTOR   Yee, oure shepe that we gett
    Ar stollyn as thay yode. Oure los is grette.
MAK   Syrs, drynkys!
    Had I bene thore,
    Som shuld haue boght it full sore.
1 PASTOR   Mary, som men trowes that ye wore,   510
    And that vs forthynkys.
2 PASTOR   Mak, som men trowys that it shuld
        be ye.
3 PASTOR   Ayther ye or youre spouse, so say we.
MAK   Now if ye haue suspowse to Gill or to me,
    Com and rype oure howse, and then may
        ye se   515
    Who had hir.
    If I any shepe fott,
    Ayther cow or stott—
    And Gyll, my wyfe, rose nott
    Here syn she lade hir—   520

    As I am true and lele, to God here I pray
    That this be the fyrst mele that I shall ete
        this day. [Points to the cradle.]
1 PASTOR   Mak, as haue I ceyll, avyse the, I say:
    He lernyd tymely to steyll that couth not say
        nay.
VXOR   I swelt!   525
    Outt, thefys, fro my wonys!
    Ye com to rob vs for the nonys.
MAK   Here ye not how she gronys?
    Youre hartys shuld melt. [The shepherds
        approach the cradle.]
VXOR   Outt, thefys, fro my barne! Negh hym
        not thor!   530
MAK   Wyst ye how she had farne, youre hartys
        wold be sore.
    Ye do wrang, I you warne, that thus
        commys before
    To a woman that has farne—bot I say no
        more.
VXOR   A, my medyll!
    I pray to God so mylde,   535
    If euer I you begyld,
    That I ete this chylde
    That lygys in this credyll.

MAK   Peasse, woman, for Godys payn, and cry
        not so!
    Thou spyllys thy brane, and makys me
        full wo.   540
2 PASTOR   I trow oure shepe be slayn. What
        fynde ye two?
3 PASTOR   All wyrk we in vayn; as well may
        we go.
    Bot hatters!
    I can fynde no flesh,
    Hard nor nesh,   545
    Salt nor fresh—
    Bot two tome platers.

    Whik catell bot this, tame nor wylde,
    None, as haue I blys, as lowde as he smylde.
VXOR   No, so God me blys, and gyf me ioy of
        my chylde!   550
1 PASTOR   We haue merkyd amys; I hold vs
        begyld.
2 PASTOR   Syr, don.
    Syr—oure Lady hym saue!—[To Mak.]
    Is you're chyld a knaue?
MAK   Any lord mygth hym haue,   555
    This chyld, to his son.

    When he wakyns he kyppys, that ioy is to se.
3 PASTOR   In good tyme to hys hyppys, and in
        celé!
    Bot who was his gossyppys so sone redé?
MAK   So fare fall thare lyppys!   560
1 PASTOR   Hark now, a le. [Aside.]
MAK   So God thaym thank,
    Parkyn, and Gybon Waller, I say,
    And gentill Iohn Horne, in good fay—
    He made all the garray—
    With the greatt shank.   565

2 PASTOR   Mak, freyndys will we be, for we ar
        all oone.
MAK   We? Now I hald for me, for mendys gett
        I none.
    Fare well all thre! All glad were ye gone.
        [Aside.]
3 PASTOR   Fare wordys may ther be, bot luf is
        ther none
    This yere. [Exeunt shepherds.]   570
1 PASTOR   Gaf ye the chyld any thyng?
2 PASTOR   I trow not oone farthyng.

3 PASTOR Fast agane will I flyng;
Abyde ye me there. [*Runs back.*]

Mak, take it to no grefe if I come to thi
barne. 575
MAK Nay, thou dos me greatt reprefe, and
fowll has thou farne.
3 PASTOR The child will it not grefe, that lytyll
day-starne.
Mak, with youre leyfe, let me gyf youre
barne
Bot vj pence.[19]
MAK Nay, do way! He slepys. 580
3 PASTOR Me thynk he pepys.
MAK When he wakyns he wepys.
I pray you go hence!

[*The First and Second Shepherds return.*]

3 PASTOR Gyf me lefe hym to kys, and lyft vp
the clowtt. [*Takes a peep.*]
What the dewill is this? He has a long
snowte! 585
I PASTOR He is merkyd amys. We wate ill
abowte.
2 PASTOR Ill-spon weft, iwys, ay commys foull
owte.
Ay, so! [*Recognizes the sheep.*]
He is lyke to oure shepe!
3 PASTOR How, Gyb, may I pepe? 590
I PASTOR I trow kynde will crepe
Where it may not go.

2 PASTOR This was a qwantt gawde and a far-
cast:
It was a hee frawde.
3 PASTOR Yee, syrs, wast.
Lett bren this bawde and bynd hir fast. 595
A fals skawde hang at the last;
So shall thou.
Wyll ye se how thay swedyll
His foure feytt in the medyll?
Sagh I neuer in a credyll 600
A hornyd lad or now.

MAK Peasse, byd I. What, lett be youre fare!
I am he that hym gatt, and yond woman
hym bare.
I PASTOR What dewill shall he hatt, Mak? Lo,
God, Makys ayre!

2 PASTOR Lett be all that! Now God gyf hym
care, 605
I sagh.
VXOR A pratty child is he
As syttys on a wamans kne;
A dyllydowne, perdé,
To gar a man laghe. 610

3 PASTOR I know hym by the eere-marke; that
is a good tokyn.
MAK I tell you, syrs, hark!—hys noyse was
brokyn.
Sythen told me a clerk that he was forspokyn.
I PASTOR This is a fals wark; I wold fayn be
wrokyn.
Gett wepyn! 615
VXOR He was takyn with an elfe,
I saw it myself;
When the clok stroke twelf
Was he forshapyn.

2 PASTOR Ye two ar well feft sam in a stede. 620
I PASTOR Syn thay manteyn thare theft, let do
thaym to dede.
MAK If I trespas eft, gyrd of my heede.[20]
With you will I be left.
3 PASTOR Syrs, do my reede:
For this trespas
We will nawther ban ne flyte, 625
Fyght nor chyte,
Bot haue done as tyte,
And cast hym in canvas.[21] [*They toss Mak.*]

I PASTOR Lord, what I am sore, in poynt for to
bryst!
In fayth, I may no more; therfor wyll I ryst. 630
2 PASTOR As a shepe of vij skore he weyd in my
fyst.
For to slepe aywhore me thynk that I lyst.
3 PASTOR Now I pray you
Lyg downe on this grene.
I PASTOR On these thefys yit I mene. 635
3 PASTOR Wherto shuld ye tene?
Do as I say you. [*They lie down and sleep*]

Angelus cantat "Gloria in exelsis"; postea dicat:[22]

ANGELUS Ryse, hyrd-men heynd, for now is he
borne

That shall take fro the feynd that Adam had
    lorne;
That warloo to sheynd, this nyght is he
    borne.   640
God is made youre freynd now at this morne,
He behestys.
At Bedlem go se
Ther lygys that fre
In a cryb full poorely,   645
Betwyx two bestys. [*The angel withdraws.*]

1 PASTOR   This was a qwant stevyn that euer yit
    I hard.
    It is a meruell to neuyn, thus to be skard.
2 PASTOR   Of Godys son of heuyn he spak
    vpward.
    All the wod on a leuyn me thoght that he
    gard   650
    Appere.
3 PASTOR   He spake of a barne
    In Bedlem, I you warne.
1 PASTOR   That betokyns yond starne;
    [*Points to the sky.*]
    Let vs seke hym there.   655

2 PASTOR   Say, what was his song? Hard ye not
    how he crakyd it,
    Thre brefes to a long?
3 PASTOR   Yee, Mary, he hakt it:
    Was no crochett wrong, nor nothyng that
    lakt it.
1 PASTOR   For to syng vs emong, right as he
    knakt it,
    I can.   660
2 PASTOR   Let se how ye croyne!
    Can ye bark at the mone?
3 PASTOR   Hold youre tonges! Haue done!
1 PASTOR   Hark after, than. [*He sings, and the
    others join in.*]

2 PASTOR   To Bedlem he bad that we shuld gang;   665
    I am full fard that we tary to lang.
3 PASTOR   Be mery and not sad—of myrth is
    oure sang!
    Euerlastyng glad to mede may we fang,
    Withoutt noyse.
1 PASTOR   Hy we theder forthy,   670
    If we be wete and wery,

To that chyld and that lady;
We haue it not to lose.

[*Tries to sing again, but is interrupted by the Second
Shepherd:*]

2 PASTOR   We fynde by the prophecy—let be
    youre dyn!—
    Of Dauid and Isay and mo then I myn—   675
    Thay prophecyed by clergy—that in a
    vyrgyn
    Shuld he lyght and ly, to slokyn oure syn,
    And slake it,
    Oure kynde, from wo;
    For Isay sayd so: 680
    Ecce virgo
    Concipiet a chylde that is nakyd.[23]

3 PASTOR   Full glad may we be, and abyde that
    day
    That lufly to se, that all myghtys may.
    Lord, well were me for ones and for ay,   685
    Myght I knele on my kne, som word for to
    say
    To that chylde.
    Bot the angell sayd
    In a cryb was he layde;
    He was poorly arayd,   690
    Both mener and mylde.

1 PASTOR   Patryarkes that has bene, and
    prophetys beforne,
    Thay desyryd to haue sene this chylde that
    is borne.
    Thay ar gone full clene; that haue thay lorne.
    We shall se hym, I weyn, or it be morne,[24]   695
    To tokyn.
    When I se hym and fele,
    Then wote I full weyll
    It is true as steyll
    That prophetys haue spokyn: 700

    To so poore as we ar that he wold appere,
    Fyrst fynd, and declare by his messyngere.
2 PASTOR   Go we now, let vs fare; the place is vs
    nere.
3 PASTOR   I am redy and yare; go we in fere
    To that bright. [*They go to Bethlehem.*]   705
    Lord, if thi wylles be—

We ar lewde all thre—
Thou grauntt vs somkyns gle
To comforth thi wight. [*They enter the stable.*]

1 PASTOR   Hayll, comly and clene! Hayll, yong
    child!   710
    Hayll, maker, as I meyne, of a madyn so
    mylde!
    Thou has waryd, I weyne, the warlo so
    wylde:
    The fals gyler of teyn, now goys he begylde.
    Lo, he merys,
    Lo, he laghys, my swetyng!   715
    A wel fare metyng!
    I haue holden my hetyng:
    Haue a bob of cherys.²⁵

2 PASTOR   Hayll, sufferan sauyoure, for thou has
    vs soght!
    Hayll, frely foyde and floure, that all thyng
    has wroght!   720
    Hayll, full of fauoure, that made all of noght!
    Hayll! I kneyll and I cowre. A byrd haue I
    broght
    To my barne.
    Hayll, lytyll tyne mop!
    Of oure crede thou art crop;   725
    I wold drynk on thy cop,
    Lytyll day-starne.

3 PASTOR   Hayll, derlyng dere, full of Godhede!
    I pray the be nere when that I haue nede.

Hayll, swete is thy chere! My hart wold blede   730
To se the sytt here in so poore wede,
With no pennys.
Hayll! Put furth thy dall!
I bryng the bot a ball:
Haue and play the withall,   735
And go to the tenys.

MARIA   The fader of heuen, God omnypotent,
    That sett all on seuen, his son has he sent.
    My name couth he neuen, and lyght or he
    went.
    I conceyuyd hym full euen thrugh myght, as
    he ment;   740
    And now is he borne.
    He kepe you fro wo!
    I shall pray hym so.
    Tell furth as ye go,
    And myn on this morne.   745

1 PASTOR   Fare well, lady, so fare to beholde,
    With thy childe on thi kne.
2 PASTOR   Bot he lygys full cold.
    Lord, well is me! Now we go, thou behold.
3 PASTOR   Forsothe, allredy it semys to be told
    Full oft.   750
1 PASTOR   What grace we haue fun!
2 PASTOR   Com furth; now ar we won!
3 PASTOR   To syng ar we bun—
    Let take on loft! [*They go out singing.*]

Explicit pagina Pastorum.

Glossary

1 **happyd** clothed. 2 **dold** numb. 10 **husbandys** husbandmen. 15 **hamyd** hamstrung. 16 **ramyd** crushed. 19 **refe** take away. 20 **lord-fest** bound to a lord. 22 **ponte** point. 25 **blonder** blunder, misfortune. 28 **paynt slefe or a broche** decorated sleeve or brooch, indicating the protection of a great man. 30 **mastry** mastery, force; **mays** makes use of. 33 **purveance** purchases at his own price in the name of his master. 37 **po** peacock. 38 **wane** waggon. 43 **langyd** longed (wished). 43 **forgang** forego. 49 **balk** a strip of untilled land separating two fields. 55 **Bensté** benedicite. 57 **spytus** spiteful. 62 **shone** shoes. 65 **wedmen** married men; **dre mekyll** suffer much. 67 **Copyle** Crested. 75 **wayte** knows. 80 **bun** bound. 83 **ryfys** rives. 96 **showre** attack (of a painful variety). 98 **sow** follow. 108 **ryn to** run until. 109 **raw** row (furrow). 111 **awre** aught (anything). 112 **ley-land** fallow land. 122 **slythys** slips away. 123 **fowre** fared. 126 **wrythys** writhes (turns aside). 131 **ponder** think. 139 **all-wyghtys** meaning uncertain, perhaps "real men" (ironic). 141 **ment** thought. 142 **bent**

field. **147 ledyr hyne** worthless hind. **148 unto syne** until later. **149 mayde** eaten. **155 forthynkys** displeases. **156 wynkys** sleep. **158 nately** thoroughly. **161 nyp at** reduce. **163 fayre** fare (food). **165 emang ever lake** meanwhile always take my sport. **168 threpe** argue. **170** "A small investment yields badly." **175 rad** afraid. **176 gawdys** gauds. **180 lawdys** lauds (dawn). **182 roode** rood (Cross). **183 yode** went away. **191 neuen** name; **tharnys** is lacking. **192 vneuen** uneven (at odds); **harnes** brains. **201** Mak has come disguised as a man in livery. A yeoman ranked just below a squire. Mak speaks in a mock southern dialect. **202 sond** messenger. **208 qwaynt** knowing ("Why do you pretend to be more knowing than you actually are?"). **209 saynt** play the saint; **lang** want to do so. **211 thwang** be flogged. **218 teyn** annoy. **221 mene** behave. **224 noys** reputation. **226 waytt** know. **227 haytt** hot. **236 walteryng** wallowing. **237 brude** brood. **242 lakan** baby. **246 dowse** female companion of easy virtue. **247 war** worse. **252 hed-maspenny** the reference is to a mass for the dead. **253 forwakyd** sleepy from staying awake too long. **254** "even if I was paid less." **256 forrakyd** worn out. **263 rowne** whisper. **266** "I commend my spirit to your hands, Pontius Pilate." This is a comic perversion of Ps. 30:6 (and Luke 23:46) which was used in the liturgy at Compline. **270 preuely** secretly. **271 neemly** nimbly. **274 reyll** hasten. **281 foyne** few. **288 lere** learn. **289 skard** scared; **nyp nere** grab tightly. **294 Eft-whyte** pay back. **302 rasyd** aroused. **303 note** need. **304 charys** chores. **305 hek** door. **306 thole** suffer; **snek** latch. **307 thar not rek** need take no thought. **311 strate** strait, difficulty. **312 swynke** work. **316 glase** blow. **325 or** before. **330–331** "Then I might get from the whole pack the devil of the worse!" **332 bowrde** trick. **335 lyg** lie. **336 red** get ready. **341 gyse** underhand way to go about it; **far-cast** good trick. **344** "If I don't get back before they get up, an ill wind will blow!" **346 meneye** company. **350** a corruption of a phrase in the Creed. **351** The Latin words are probably a corruption of a liturgical tag so far not identified; however, this expression together with the one in l. 350 should be considered as an admonition to the shepherd's sleeping foot. He is trying to say something like "Waken from the dead, O treacherous flesh, by God!" **352 water fastand** totter from fasting. **361 blakys** darken. **362 dowore** door. **364 awre** anything; cf. "ary" (Amer. dial.). **367** "He's gone nowhere yet." **369 hapt** clothed. **373 woode** insane. **385** "My heart was out of my skin" (I was so frightened). **386 trauell** travail. **389 rok** distaff. **391 tharmes** bellies (to feed). **392 harnes** brains. **396 slefe** sleeve (of his "disguise" coat). **398 chefe** fare. **404 crokyd thorne** a place near Horbury in the neighborhood of Wakefield. **405 bere** noise; **walk in the wenyand** walk in the waning (of the moon); i.e., "Bad luck to you!" **409 lote** noise. **410** "As if he were held by the throat," i.e., about to be hanged. **412 handlang** hand-long (little). **413 glose** excuse. **414 lakys** plays; **clowse hir toose** scratches her toes. **416 hose** stockings. **426 Perdé** by God. **434 hap** cover. **436 maroo** mate. **440 onone** anon. **455 Horbery shrogys** Horbury underbrush. Horbury was near Wakefield. **463 the** thrive. **464 de** die. **476 hak** sing; **croyne** croon. **477 crak** song. **485 maylleasse** unwell (malaise). **487 stede** place; **qweasse** breath. **503 yode** went away. **504 mendys oure mode** makes us feel better. **505** "ails you aught but good?" **510 trowes** think. **511 forthynkys** troubles. **517 fott** fetched. **523 ceyll** bliss. **543 hatters!** (interjection). **547 tome** empty. **549 smylde** smelled. **557 kyppys** snatches. **558 hyppys** hips; **celé** happiness. **559 gossyppys** sponsors at baptism; **561 le** lie. **564 garray** commotion. **567 mendys** amends. **586** "We pry about wrongfully." **591 kynde** nature. **595 bren** burn. **596 skawde** scold. **613 Sythen** afterward; **forspokyn** bewitched. **619 forshapyn** misshapen. **624 reede** advice. **625 ban ne flyte** curse nor contend. **626 chyte** chide. **627 tyte** quickly. **631 skore** score (twenty). **635 mene** think. **636 tene** sorrow. **638 heynd** gracious. **640 warloo** warlock; **sheynd** destroy. **644 lygys** lies. **647 stevyn** voice. **648 neuyn** name. **650 leuyn** lightning. **658 crochett** crotchet (mus.). **666 fard** afraid. **668 fang** take. **670 forthy** at once. **677 slokyn** quench. **684 that all myghtys**

may who may do all great things. **691 mener** poorer. **712 waryd** cursed. **713 of teyn** malicious. **717 hetyng** command. **720 frely foyde** noble child. **726 cop** cup (chalice). **733 dall** hand. **739 lyght** alighted (in me). **745 myn** think. **751 fun** found. **753 bun** bound. **754** "Let us sing out!"

Notes

1 There are two plays about the shepherds in this cycle; this is the second.

2 Coll and Gyb are fellow shepherds; Daw, who is younger, is Coll's servant.

3 The scene is laid in the cultivated fields near Wakefield, as the reference to Horbury in l. 455 indicates. The time is the time of the presentation of the play, not the historical time of the Nativity, for the author was interested here, as in the *Mactacio Abel*, not in an event isolated in space and time, but in an event (the birth of Christ) which may come to any man. He was, however, especially interested in how it might come to those in his immediate audience at Wakefield.

4 The first two shepherds complain about the cold, stormy weather. See ll. 55–63. The third considers the weather in terms of the mutability of the world (ll. 118–126) and finds the floods especially a cause of wonder (ll. 127–135). The harsh weather is used to indicate tribulation under the Old Law before the coming of Christ. It should be emphasized that according to Christian teaching people are by nature "children of wrath" and live under a kind of perpetual Old Law until they learn, through Christ, to embrace the New Law. Under the Old Dispensation the world, which was created good (Gen. 1:10) seems unreasonable. The young shepherd who finds the weather a source of wonder is more perceptive than his elders and retains this characteristic throughout the play. Like the tempest referred to in Reason's sermon in *Piers the Ploughman*, the floods may be seen, like the Flood itself (see n. 13), as manifestations of the wrath of God (His strict justice) as compared with His mercy manifested in the coming of Christ.

5 The first shepherd complains at length about the oppressions of liverymen and purveyors. Cf. the character of Crime in *Piers the Ploughman*, Book II. The activities of these men were a just cause for complaint in late medieval England, but again the author would have us think of tyranny under the Old Law before rulers and their representatives had access to grace which would enable them to be merciful.

6 The second shepherd's complaint stresses the theme of inversion exemplified in marriage, where the rule of the wife suggested the rule of the passions over the reason. Again, this is a condition requiring the grace of the New Law as a remedy. Cf. Chaucer's Wife of Bath's Prologue and, earlier, Walter Map's epistle of Valerius.

7 Cf. the condition of Chanticleer under the domination of Pertelote in the Nun's Priest's Tale.

8 This reference to the Epistles is, like the reference to a priest in the *Mactacio Abel*, an anachronism if the play is read literally. But see n. 3. There are many similar anachronisms in the play before us (ll. 9, 10, 11, 12, 15, 182, 209, 266–268, etc.).

9 Noah's Flood was a cleansing of the world from the generation of Cain, which, unfortunately, sprang up again afterward. From the point of view of the individual, the Flood had its analogy in baptism, which cleansed the soul of sin.

10 This speech and the response to it indicate that the elder shepherds treat Daw much in the same way that they are treated by their superiors. It should be emphasized that the author has no interest in the class struggle, which rests on a nineteenth-century formulation of history; he wishes to show a general lack of charity and its implications before the (perennial) birth of Christ.

11 Mak enters with a cloak over his tunic. Cf. Mark 6:9.

12 Mak is known as a thief. In the subsequent action he leads the shepherds to a false Nativity. Figuratively, shepherds are pastors of the people; considered in this light, Mak is a false prophet.

13 Mak wishes to make the shepherds blind. Since they have not yet learned to be vigilant as they "watch their flocks by night," he succeeds.

14 The third shepherd, Daw, who is again more perceptive than his elders, has an inkling of what has happened.

15 Cf. Matt. 7:15.

16 Cf. John 10:11–13.

17 Cf. the attitude taken by Pertelote in the Nun's Priest's Tale or by Mercutio in Shakespeare's *Romeo and Juliet*.

18 It is significant that it is the young shepherd Daw who insists on the true identity of the thief. He is, figuratively, "newer" than the other shepherds.

19 Six pence was a fair day's wage for skilled labor. The charitable inclination of Daw, not the blustering of the other shepherds, reveals the sheep.

20 Mak at last admits his crime and promises not to repeat it.

21 Daw suggests a jocular punishment much less severe than strict justice, and the other shepherds agree. What they have done is, in effect, an act of mercy, and it is this that prepares them to hear the message of the angel.

22 "The angel sings Gloria in excelsis and then says":

23 Isa. 7:14.

24 There is no spatial distance between Wakefield and Bethlehem on the road that these shepherds (and the audience of the play) may travel.

25 Cherries are, of course, out of season, except for the fact that the events described can take place at any time of the year. In any event, the gifts are probably intended to be symbolic. Various interpretations are possible and, indeed, in the kind of meditation the author wished to inspire, desirable.

EVERYMAN

Dramatis Personæ

GOD	CONFESSION
EVERYMAN	BEAUTY
DEATH	STRENGTH
GOOD FELLOWSHIP	DISCRETION
KINDRED	FIVE WITS
COUSIN	MESSENGER
GOODS	ANGEL
GOOD DEEDS	DOCTOR
KNOWLEDGE	

Here Begynneth a Treatyse How Ye Hye Fader of Heuen sendeth Dethe to Somon Euery Creature to come and gyue Acounte of theyr Lyues in this Worlde, and is in Maner of a Morall Playe.

[*Enter a Messenger as a Prologue.*]

MESSENGER   I pray you all gyue your audyence,
    And here this mater with reuerence,
    By fygure a morall playe.
    "The Somonynge of Eueryman" called it is,
    That of our lyues and endynge shewes   5
    How transytory we be all daye.
    This mater is wonder[ou]s precyous;
    But the entent of it is more gracyous,
    And swete to bere awaye.
    The story sayth: Man, in the begynnynge   10
    Loke well, and take good heed to the endynge,
    Be you neuer so gay!
    Ye thynke synne in the begynnynge full swete,
    Whiche in the ende causeth the soule to wepe
    Whan the body lyeth in claye.   15
    Here shall you se how Falawshyp, and Iolyte,
    Bothe Strengthe, Pleasure, and Beaute,
    Wyll fade from the as floure in Maye;
    For ye shall here how our Heuen Kynge
    Calleth Eueryman to a generall rekenynge.   20
    Gyue audyence, and here what he doth saye.
    [*Exit.*]

God speketh [from above].

GOD   I perceyue, here in my maieste,
    How that all creatures be to me vnkynde,

Lyuynge without drede in worldely
    prosperyte.
Of ghostly syght the people be so blynde,   25
Drowned in synne, they know me not for
    theyr God.
In worldely ryches is all theyr mynde;
They fere not my ryghtwysnes, the sharpe
    rod;
My lowe that I shewed whan I for them dyed
They forgete clene, and shedynge of my
    blode rede;   30
I hanged bytwene two, it can not be denyed;
To gete them lyfe I suffred to be deed;
I heled theyr fete, with thornes hurt was my
    heed.
I coude do no more than I dyde, truely;
And nowe I se the people do clene forsake me.   35
They vse the seuen deedly synnes dampnable.
As pryde, coueytyse, wrathe, and lechery
Now in the worlde be made commendable;
And thus they leue of aungelles, ye heuenly
    company.
Euery man lyueth so after his owne pleasure,   40
And yet of theyr lyfe they be nothynge sure.
I se the more that I them forbere
The worse they be fro yere to yere;
All that lyueth appayreth faste.
Therefore I wyll, in all the haste,   45
Haue a rekenynge of euery mannes persone;
For, and I leue the people thus alone
In theyr lyfe and wycked tempestes,
Veryly they wyll become moche worse than
    beestes;
For now one wolde by enuy another vp ete;   50
Charyte they do all clene forgete.
I hoped well that euery man
In my glory shulde make his mansyon;
And thereto I had them all electe.
But now I se, lyke traytours deiecte,   55
They thanke me not for ye pleasure that I
    to them ment,
Nor yet for theyr beynge that I them haue
    lent.
I profered the people grete multytude of
    mercy,
And fewe there be that asketh it hertly.
They be so combred with worldly ryches   60
That nedes on them I must do iustyce,

On euery man lyuynge, without fere.
Where art thou Deth, thou myghty
    messengere?

[*Enter Death.*]

DEATH   Almyghty God, I am here at your wyll,
    Your commaundement to fulfyll.   65
GOD   Go thou to Eueryman,
    And shewe hym, in my name,
    A pylgrymage he must on hym take,
    Which he in no wyse may escape;
    And that he brynge with hym a sure
        rekenynge,   70
    Without delay or ony taryenge.

[*God withdraws.*]

DEATH   Lorde, I wyll in the worlde go renne
        ouer all,
    And cruelly out-serche bothe grete and
        small.
    Euery man wyll I beset that lyueth beestly
    Out of Goddes lawes, and dredeth not foly.   75
    He that loueth rychesse I wyll stryke with
        my darte,
    His syght to blynde, and fro heuen to
        departe—
    Excepte that almes be his good frende[1]—
    In hell for to dwell, worlde without ende.

[*Enter Everyman at a distance.*]

    Loo, yonder I se Eueryman walkynge.   80
    Full lytell he thynketh on my comynge;
    His mynde is on flesshely lustes, and his
        treasure;
    And grete payne it shall cause hym to endure
    Before the Lorde, heuen['s] Kynge.

[*Death halts Everyman.*]

    Eueryman, stande styll! Whyder arte thou
        goynge   85
    Thus gayly? Hast thou thy maker forgete?
EVERYMAN   Why askest thou?
    Woldest thou wete?
DEATH   Ye, syr; I wyll shewe you:
    In grete hast I am sende to the   90
    Fro God out of his Mageste.
EVERYMAN   What! sente to me?

DEATH   Ye, certaynly.
    Thoughe thou haue forgete hym here,
    He thynketh on the in the heuenly spere,   95
    As, or we departe, thou shalte knowe!
EVERYMAN   What desyreth God of me?
DEATH   That shall I shewe thee:
    A rekenynge he wyll nedes haue
    Without ony lenger respyte.   100
EVERYMAN   To gyue a rekenynge longer layser
    I craue.
    This blynde mater troubleth my wytte.
DEATH   On the thou must take a longe iourney;[2]
    Therfore thy boke of counte with the thou
      brynge,
    For turne agayne thou can not by no waye.   105
    And loke thou be sure of thy rekenynge,
    For before God thou shalte answere and
      shewe
    Thy many badde dedes, and good but a
      fewe,
    How thou hast spente thy lyfe, and in what
      wyse,
    Before the Chefe Lorde of paradyse.   110
    Haue ado that we were in that waye,
    For wete thou well thou shalte make none
      attournay.
EVERYMAN   Full vnredy I am suche rekenynge to
    gyue.
    I knowe the not. What messenger arte thou?
DEATH   I am Dethe, that no man dredeth;   115
    For euery man I rest, and no man spareth;
    For it is Goddes commaundement
    That all to me sholde be obedyent.
EVERYMAN   O Deth! thou comest whan I had ye
    leest in mynde!
    In thy power it lyeth me to saue;   120
    Yet of my good wyl I gyue ye, yf thou wyl
      be kynde;
    Ye, a thousande pounde shalte thou haue,
    And [thou] dyfferre this mater tyll an other
      daye.
DEATH   Eueryman, it may not be, by no waye!
    I set not by golde, syluer, nor rychesse,   125
    Ne by pope, emperour, kynge, duke, ne
      prynces;
    For, and I wolde receyue gyftes grete,
    All the worlde I myght gete;
    But my custome is clene contrary.

    I gyue the no respyte. Come hens, and not
    tary!   130
EVERYMAN   Alas! shall I haue no lenger respyte?
    I may saye Deth geueth no warnynge!
    To thynke on the it maketh my herte seke,
    For all vnredy is my boke of rekenynge.
    But twelve yere and I myght haue abydynge,   135
    My countynge-boke I wolde make so clere
    That my rekenynge I sholde not nede to fere.
    Wherfore, Deth, I praye the, for Goddes
      mercy,
    Spare me tyll I be prouyded of remedy!
DEATH   The auayleth not to crye, wepe, and
    praye;   140
    But hast the lyghtly that thou wert gone
      that iournaye!
    And preue thy frendes, yf thou can;
    For wete thou well the tyde abydeth no man;
    And in the worlde eche lyuynge creature
    For Adams synne must dye of nature.   145
EVERYMAN   Dethe, yf I sholde this pylgrymage
    take,
    And my rekenynge suerly make,
    Shewe me, for Saynt Charyte,
    Sholde I not come agayne shortly?
DEATH   No, Eueryman; and thou be ones there,   150
    Thou mayst neuer more come here,
    Trust me veryly.
EVERYMAN   O gracyous God in the hye sete
    celestyall,
    Haue mercy on me in this moost nede!
    Shall I haue no company fro this vale
      terestryall   155
    Of myne acqueyn[taun]ce that way me to
      lede?
DEATH   Ye, yf ony be so hardy
    That wolde go with the and bere the
      company.
    Hye the that thou wert gone to Goddes
      magnyfycence,
    Thy rekenynge to gyue before his presence.   160
    What! wenest thou thy lyue is gyuen the,
    And thy worldely gooddes also?
EVERYMAN   I had wende so, veryle.
DEATH   Nay, nay; it was but lende the;
    For, as soone as thou arte go,   165
    Another a whyle shall haue it, and than go
      therfro,

Euen as thou hast done.

Eueryman, thou arte mad! Thou hast thy
  wyttes fyue,

And here on erthe wyll not amende thy lyue;

For sodeynly I do come.   170

EVERYMAN   O wretched caytyfe! wheder shall I
  flee

That I myght scape this endles sorowe?

Now, gentyll Deth, spare me tyll
  to-morowe,

That I may amende me

With good aduysement.   175

DEATH   Naye; therto I wyll not consent,

Nor no man wyll I respyte;

But to the herte sodeynly I shall smyte

Without ony aduysement.

And now out of thy syght I wyll me hy.   180

Se thou make the redy shortely,

For thou mayst saye this is the daye

That no man lyuynge may scape awaye.

    [*Exit Death.*]

EVERYMAN   Alas! I may well wepe with syghes
  depe!

Now haue I no maner of company   185

To helpe me in my iourney and me to kepe;

And also my wrytynge is full vnredy.

How shall I do now for to excuse me?

I wolde to God I had neuer be gete!

To my soule a full grete profyte it had be; 190

For now I fere paynes huge and grete.

The tyme passeth. Lorde, helpe, that all
  wrought!

For though I mourne it auayleth nought;

The day passeth, and is almoost ago.

I wote not well what for to do.   195

To whome were I best my complaynt to
  make?

What and I to Felawshyp therof spake,

And shewed hym of this sodeyne chaunce?

For in hym is all myne affyaunce,

We haue in the worlde so many a daye 200

Be good frendes in sporte and playe.

I se hym yonder certaynely.

I trust that he wyll bere me company,

Therfore to hym wyll I speke to ese my
  sorowe.

Well mette, Good Felawshyp! and good
  morowe!   205

Felawshyp speketh.

FELLOWSHIP   Eueryman, good morowe, by this
  daye!

Syr, why lokest thou so pyteously?

If ony thynge be amysse, I praye the me
  saye,

That I may helpe to remedy.

EVERYMAN   Ye, Good Felawshyp, ye; I am in
  greate ieoparde.   210

FELLOWSHIP   My true frende, shewe to me your
  mynde;

I wyll not forsake the to my lyues ende

In the waye of good company.

EVERYMAN   That was well spoken, and louyngly! 215

FELLOWSHIP   Syr, I must nedes knowe your
  heuynesse;

I haue pyte to se you in ony dystresse.

If ony haue you wronged, ye shall reuenged
  be,

Thoughe I on the grounde be slayne for the,

Though that I knowe before that I sholde
  dye!   220

EVERYMAN   Veryly, Felawshyp, gramercy.

FELLOWSHIP   Tusshe! by thy thankes I set not a
  strawe!

Shewe me your grefe, and saye no more.

EVERYMAN   If I my herte sholde to you breke,

And than you to tourne your mynde fro me 225

And wolde not me comforte whan ye here
  me speke,

Than sholde I ten tymes soryer be.

FELLOWSHIP   Syr, I saye as I wyll do, indede.

EVERYMAN   Than be you a good frende at nede!

I haue founde you true here before.   230

FELLOWSHIP   And so ye shall euermore;

For, in fayth, and thou go to hell

I wyll not forsake the by the waye.

EVERYMAN   Ye speke lyke a good frende! I
  byleue you well.

I shall deserue it, and I may.   235

FELLOWSHIP   I speke of no deseruynge, by this
  daye!

For he that wyll saye, and nothynge do,

Is not worthy with good company to go.

Therfore shewe me the grefe of your mynde,

As to your frende mooste louynge and
    kynde.   240
EVERYMAN   I shall shewe you how it is:
    Commaunded I am to go a iournaye—
    A longe waye, harde, and daungerous—
    And gyue a strayte counte, without delaye,
    Before the hye Iuge, Adonay.   245
    Wherfore, I pray you, bere me company,
    As ye haue promysed, in this iournaye.
FELLOWSHIP   That is mater indede! Promyse is
    duty;
    But, and I sholde take suche a vyage on me,
    I knowe it well, it shulde be to my payne,   250
    Also it make[th] me aferde, certayne.
    But let vs take counsell here, as well as we
    can;
    For your wordes wolde fere a stronge man.
EVERYMAN   Why, ye sayd yf I had nede
    Ye wolde me neuer forsake, quycke ne deed,   255
    Thoughe it were to hell, truely.
FELLOWSHIP   So I sayd, certaynely!
    But suche pleasures be set asyde, the sothe to
    saye.
    And also, yf we toke suche a iournaye,
    Whan sholde we come agayne?   260
EVERYMAN   Naye, neuer agayne, tyll the daye of
    dome!
FELLOWSHIP   In fayth! than wyll not I come
    there!
    Who hath you these tydynges brought?
EVERYMAN   Indede, Deth was with me here.
FELLOWSHIP   Now, by God, that all hathe bought,   265
    If Dethe were the messenger,
    For no man that is lyuynge to-daye
    I wyll not go that lothe iournaye—
    Not for the fader that bygate me!
EVERYMAN   Ye promysed otherwyse, parde.   270
FELLOWSHIP   I wote well I sayd so, truely.
    And yet, yf thou wylte ete, and drynke, and
    make good chere,
    Or haunt to women the lusty company,
    I wolde not forsake you whyle the daye is
    clere,
    Truste me, veryly.   275
EVERYMAN   Ye, therto ye wolde be redy!
    To go to myrthe, solas, and playe,
    Your mynde wyll soner apply,
    Than to bere me company in my longe
    iournaye.

FELLOWSHIP   Now, in good fayth, I wyll not that
    waye.   280
    But and thou wylte murder, or ony man kyll,
    In that I wyll helpe the with a good wyll.
EVERYMAN   O, that is a symple aduyse, indede.
    Gentyll Felaw[ship]e, helpe me in my
    necessyte!
    We haue loued longe, and now I nede;   285
    And now, gentyll Felawshyp, remenbre me!
FELLOWSHIP   Wheder ye haue loued me or no,
    By Saynt Iohan, I wyll not with the go!
EVERYMAN   Yet, I pray the, take ye labour, and
    do so moche for me
    To brynge me forwarde, for Saynt Charyte,   290
    And comforte me tyll I come without the
    towne.
FELLOWSHIP   Nay, and thou wolde gyue me a
    newe gowne,
    I wyll not a fote with the go!
    But, and thou had taryed, I wolde not haue
    lefte the so.
    And as now God spede the in thy iournaye!   295
    For from the I wyll departe as fast as I maye.
EVERYMAN   Wheder awaye, Felawshyp? Wyll
    you forsake me?
FELLOWSHIP   Ye, by my faye! To God I betake
    the.
EVERYMAN   Farewell, Good Felawshyp! for ye
    my herte is sore.
    Adewe for euer! I shall se the no more!   300
FELLOWSHIP   In fayth, Eueryman, fare well now
    at the ende!
    For you I wyll remembre that partynge is
    mournynge. [*Exit Fellowship.*]

EVERYMAN   Alacke! shall we thus departe indede
    (A, Lady helpe!) without ony more
    comforte?
    Lo, Felawshyp forsaketh me in my moost
    nede.   305
    For helpe in this worlde wheder shall I
    resorte?
    Felawshyp here before with me wolde mery
    make,
    And now lytell sorowe for me dooth he take.
    It is sayd, "In prosperyte men frendes may
    fynde,
    Whiche in aduersyte be full vnkynde."   310
    Now wheder for socoure shall I flee,

Syth that Felawshyp hath forsaken me?
To my kynnesmen I wyll, truely,
Prayenge them to helpe me in my necessyte.
I byleue that they wyll do so,   315
For "kynde wyll crepe where it may not go."
I wyll go saye, for yonder I se them go.
Where be ye now, my frendes and
    kynnesmen?

[Enter Kindred and Cousin.]

KINDRED   Here be we now, at your
    commaundement.
Cosyn, I praye you shewe vs your entent
In ony wyse, and do not spare.   320
COUSIN   Ye, Eueryman, and to vs declare
Yf ye be dysposed to go ony whyder;
For, wete you well, we wyll lyue and dye
    togyder.
KINDRED   In welth and wo we wyll with you
    holde,   325
For ouer his kynne a man may be bolde.
EVERYMAN   Gramercy, my frendes and
    kynnesmen kynde.
Now shall I shewe you the grefe of my
    mynde.
I was commaunded by a messenger
That is a hye kynges chefe offycer;   330
He bad me go a pylgrymage, to my payne;
And I knowe well I shall neuer come agayne:
Also I must gyue a rekenynge strayte,
For I haue a grete enemy that hath me in
    wayte,
Whiche entendeth me for to hynder.   335
KINDRED   What a[c]counte is that whiche ye
    must render?
That wolde I knowe.
EVERYMAN   Of all my workes I must shewe
How I haue lyued, and my dayes spent;
Also of yll dedes that I haue vsed   340
In my tyme syth lyfe was me lent,
And of all vertues that I haue refused.
Therfore, I praye you, go thyder with me
To helpe to make myn accounte, for Saynt
    Charyte.
COUSIN   What! to go thydr? Is that the mater?   345
Nay, Eueryman, I had leuer fast brede and
    water
All this fyue yere and more.
EVERYMAN   Alas, that euer I was bore!

For now shall I neuer be mery,
If that you forsake me.   350
KINDRED   A, syr, what! ye be a mery man!
Take good herte to you, and make no mone.
But one thynge, I warne you, by Saynt
    Anne—
As for me, ye shall go alone!
EVERYMAN   My Cosyn, wyll you not with me go? 355
COUSIN   No, by Our Lady! I haue the crampe in
    my to[e].
Trust not to me; for, so God me spede,
I wyll deccyue you in your moost nede.
KINDRED   It auayleth not vs to tyse.
Ye shall haue my mayde with all my herte;   360
She loueth to go to feestes, there to be nyse,
And to daunce, and abrode to sterte:
I wyll gyue her leue to helpe you in that
    iourney,
If that you and she may agree.
EVERYMAN   Now, shewe me the very effecte of
    your mynde;   365
Wyll you go with me, or abyde behynde?
KINDRED   Abyde behynde? ye, that wyll I, and
    I maye!
Therfore farewell tyll another daye. [*Exit
    Kindred.*]

EVERYMAN   Howe sholde I be mery or gladde?
For fayre promyses men to me make,   370
But whan I haue moost nede they me
    forsake.
I am deceyued; that maketh me sadde.
COUSIN   Cosyn Eueryman, farewell now;
For veryly I wyll not go with you.
Also of myne owne lyfe an vnredy rekenynge 375
I haue to accounte; therfore I make taryenge.
Now God kepe the, for now I go. [*Exit
    Cousin.*]

EVERYMAN   A Iesus! is all come hereto?
Lo, fayre wordes maketh fooles fayne;
They promyse, and nothynge wyll do
    certayne.   380
My kynnesmen promysed me faythfully
For to abyde with me stedfastly;
And now fast awaye do they flee.
Euen so Felawshyp promysed me.
What frende were best me of to prouyde?   385
I lose my tyme here longer to abyde;

Yet in my mynde a thynge there is:
All my lyfe I haue loued ryches;
If that my Good now helpe me myght
He wolde make my herte full lyght.   390
I wyll speke to hym in this dystresse.
Where arte thou, my Gooddes and ryches?

GOODS [*within*]   Who calleth me? Eueryman?
        What! hast thou haste?
    I lye here in corners, trussed and pyled so hye,
    And in chestes I am locked so fast,   395
    Also sacked in bagges—thou mayst se with
        thyn eye—
    I can not styre. In packes, lowe, I lye.
    What wolde ye haue? lyghtly me saye.

EVERYMAN   Come hyder, Good, in al the hast
        thou may;
    For of counseyll I must desyre the.   400

[*Enter Goods.*]

GOODS   Syr, and ye in the worlde haue sorowe
        or aduersyte,
    That can I helpe you to remedy shortly.

EVERYMAN   It is another dysease that greueth me;
    In this worlde it is not, I tell the so;
    I am sent for an other way to go,   405
    To gyue a strayte counte generall
    Before the hyest Iupyter of all;
    And all my lyfe I haue had ioye and pleasure
        in the,
    Therfore, I pray the, go with me;
    For, parauenture, thou mayst before God
        Almyghty   410
    My rekenynge helpe to clene and puryfye;
    For it is sayd euer amonge
    That "money maketh all ryght that is
        wronge." [3]

GOODS   Nay, Eueryman; I synge an other songe!
    I folowe no man in suche vyages;   415
    For, and I wente with the,
    Thou sholdes fare much the worse for me;
    For bycause on me thou dyd set thy mynde,
    Thy rekenynge I haue made blotted and
        blynde,
    That thyne accounte thou can not make
        truly—   420
    And that hast thou for the loue of me!

EVERYMAN   That wolde greue me full sere,

Whan I sholde come to that ferefull answere.
Vp, let vs go thyder to gyder.

GOODS   Nay, not so! I am to brytell; I may not
        endure.   425
    I wyll folowe no man one fote, be ye sure.

EVERYMAN   Alas! I haue the loued, and had grete
        pleasure
    All my lyfe-dayes on good and treasure.

GOODS   That is to thy dampnacyon without
        lesynge!
    For my loue is contrary to the loue
        euerlastynge.   430
    But yf thou had me loued moderately
        durynge
    As to the poore to gyue parte of me,
    Than sholdest thou not in this dolour be,
    Nor in this grete sorowe and care.

EVERYMAN   Lo! now was I deceyued or I was
        ware;   435
    And all, I may wyte, my[s]spendynge of
        tyme.

GOODS   What! wenest thou that I am thyne?

EVERYMAN   I had went so.

GOODS   Naye, Eueryman; I saye no.
    As for a whyle I was lente the;   440
    A season thou hast had me in prosperyte.
    My condycyon is mannes soule to kyll;
    Yf I saue one, a thousande I do spyll.
    Wenest thou that I wyll folowe the
    From this worlde? nay, veryle.   445

EVERYMAN   I had wende otherwyse.

GOODS   Therfore to thy soule Good is a thefe;
    For whan thou arte deed, this is my gyse—
    Another to deceyue in this same wyse
    As I haue done the, and all to his soules
        reprefe.   450

EVERYMAN   O false Good! cursed may thou be,
    Thou traytour to God, that hast deceyued me
    And caugh[t] me in thy snare!

GOODS   Mary! thou brought thy selfe in care!
    Whereof I am right gladde.   455
    I must nedes laugh; I can not be sadde.

EVERYMAN   A, Good! thou hast had longe my
        hertely loue;
    I gaue the that which sholde be the Lordes
        aboue.
    But wylte thou not go with me indede?
    I praye the trouth to saye.   460

GOODS   No, so God me spede!
    Therfore farewell, and haue good daye!
    [*Exit Goods.*]

EVERYMAN   O, to whome shall I make my mone
    For to go with me in that heuy iournaye?
    Fyrst Felawshyp sayd he wolde with me
       gone—   465
    His wordes were very plesaunte and gaye;
    But afterwarde he lefte me alone.
    Than spake I to my kynnesmen, all in
       despayre,
    An[d] also they gaue me wordes fayre—
    They lacked no fayre spekynge!   470
    But all forsoke me in the endynge.
    Than wente I to my Goodes, that I loued
       best,
    In hope to haue comforte; but there had I
       leest,
    For my Goodes sharpely dyd me tell
    That he bryngeth many into hell.   475
    Than of my selfe I was ashamed;
    And so I am worthy to be blamed.
    Thus may I well my selfe hate.
    Of whom shall I now counseyll take?
    I thynke that I shall neuer spede   480
    Tyll that I go to my Good Dede.
    But, alas! she is so weke
    That she can nother go nor speke.
    Yet wyll I venter on her now.
    My Good Dedes, where be you?   485

[*Good Deeds speaks up from the ground.*]

GOOD DEEDS   Here I lye, colde in the grounde.
    Thy synnes hath me sore bounde,
    That I can not stere.
EVERYMAN   O Good Dedes! I stande in fere!
    I must you pray of counseyll,   490
    For helpe now sholde come ryght well.
GOOD DEEDS   Eueryman, I haue vnderstandynge
    That ye be somoned a[c]counte to make
    Before Myssyas, of Iherusalem Kynge;
    And you do by me, that iournay with you
       wyll I take.   495
EVERYMAN   Therfore I come to you my moone
    to make.
    I praye you that ye wyll go with me.

GOOD DEEDS   I wolde full fayne, but I can not
    stande, veryly.
EVERYMAN   Why, is there ony thynge on you
    fall?
GOOD DEEDS   Ye, syr, I may thanke you of all!   500
    Yf ye had parfytely chered me,
    Your boke of counte full redy had be.

[*Good Deeds shows him his Book of Account.*]

    Loke, the bokes of your workes and dedes
       eke!
    Behold how they lye vnder the fete
    To your soules heuynes.   505
EVERYMAN   Our Lorde Iesus helpe me!
    For one letter here I can not se.
GOOD DEEDS   There is a blynde rekenynge in
    tyme of dystres!
EVERYMAN   Good Dedes, I praye you helpe me
    in this nede,
    Or elles I am for euer dampned indede!   510
    Therfore helpe me to make my rekenynge
    Before the Redemer of all thynge,
    That Kynge is, and was, and euer shall.
GOOD DEEDS   Eueryman, I am sory of your fall;
    And fayne wolde I helpe you, and I were able. 515
EVERYMAN   Good Dedes, your counseyll I pray
    you gyue me.
GOOD DEEDS   That shall I do veryly.
    Thoughe that on my fete I may not go,
    I haue a syster that shall with you also,
    Called Knowlege, whiche shall with you
       abyde   520
    To helpe you to make that dredefull
       rekenynge.

[*Enter Knowledge.*]

KNOWLEDGE   Eueryman, I wyll go with the, and
    be thy gyde,
    In thy moost nede to go by thy syde.
EVERYMAN   In good condycyon I am now in
    euery thynge,
    And am hole content with this good thynge, 525
    Thanked be God my createre!
GOOD DEEDS   And whan he hath brought you
    there
    Where thou shalte hele the of thy smarte,
    Than go you with your rekenynge and your
       Good Dedes togyder

For to make you ioyfull at herte 530
Before the Blessyd Trynyte.

EVERYMAN My Good Dedes, gramercy!
I am well content, certaynly,
With your wordes swete.

KNOWLEDGE Now go we togyder louyngly 535
To Confessyon, that clensyng ryuere.

EVERYMAN For ioy I wepe! I wolde we were
there!
But, I pray you, gyue me cognycyon
Where dwelleth that holy man, Confessyon?

KNOWLEDGE In the house of saluacyon; 540
We shall fynde hym in that place,
That shall vs comforte, by Goddes grace.

[*Knowledge leads Everyman to Confession.*]

Lo, this is Confessyon. Knele downe, and
aske mercy;
For he is in good conceyte with God
Almyghty.

EVERYMAN [*kneeling*] O gloryous fountayne, that
all vnclennes doth claryfy, 545
Wasshe fro me the spottes of vyce vnclene,
That on me no synne may be sene.
I come, with Knowlege, for my redempcyon,
Redempte with herte and full contrycyon;
For I am commaunded a pylgrymage to take, 550
And grete accountes before God to make.
Now I praye you, Shryfte, moder of
saluacyon,
Helpe my Good Dedes for my pyteous
exclamacyon.

CONFESSION I knowe your sorowe well,
Eueryman.
Bycause with Knowlege ye come to me, 555
I wyll you comforte as well as I can;
And a precyous iewell I wyll gyue the,
Called penaunce, voyder of aduersyte;
Therwith shall your body chastysed be
With abstynence, and perseueraunce in
Goddes seruyce. 560

[*Gives Everyman a scourge.*]

Here shall you receyue that scourge[4] of me,
Whiche is penaunce stronge that ye must
endure
To remembre thy Sauyour was scourged for
the

With sharpe scourges, and suffred it
pacyently;
So must thou, or thou scape that paynful
pylgrymage. 565
Knowlege, kepe hym in this vyage,
And by that tyme Good Dedes wyll be with
the.
But in ony wyse be seker of mercy,
For your tyme draweth fast; and ye wyll
saued be,
Aske God mercy, and he wyll graunte truely. 570
Whan with the scourge of penaunce man
doth hym bynde,
The oyle of forgyuenes than shall he fynde.

EVERYMAN Thanked be God for his gracyous
werke!
For now I wyll my penaunce begyn;
This hath reioysed and lyghted my herte, 575
Though the knottes be paynfull and harde
within.

KNOWLEDGE Eueryman, loke your penaunce
that ye fulfyll,
What payne that euer it to you be;
And Knowlege shall gyue you counseyll at
wyll
How your accounte ye shall make clerely. 580

[*Everyman kneels in Prayer.*]

EVERYMAN O eternal God! O heuenly fygure!
O way of ryghtwysnes! O goodly vysyon!
Whiche descended downe in a vyrgyn pure
Because he wolde euery man redeme,
Whiche Adam forfayted by his
dysobedyence! 585
O blessyd Godheed! electe and hye deuyne!
Forgyue me my greuous offence.
Here I crye the mercy in this presence.
O ghostly treasure! O raunsomer and
redemer!
Of all the worlde hope and conduyter! 590
Myrrour of ioye! foundatour of mercy,
Whiche enlumyneth heuen and erth therby!
Here my clamorous complaynt, though it
late be.
Receyue my prayers, vnworthy of thy
benygnytye.
Though I be a synner moost abhomynable, 595
Yet let my name be wryten in Moyses table.

O Mary! praye to the Maker of all thynge
Me for to helpe at my endynge,
And saue me fro the power of my enemy;
For Deth assayleth me strongly.   600
And, Lady, that I may by meane of thy
    prayer
Of your Sones glory to be partynere
By the meanes of his passyon, I it craue.
I beseche you helpe my soule to saue.

[*He rises.*]

Knowlege, gyue me the scourge of
    penaunce.   605
My fleshe therwith shall gyue aquytaunce.
I wyll now begyn, yf God gyue me grace.
KNOWLEDGE   Eueryman, God gyue you tyme
    and space!
Thus I bequeth you in ye handes of our
    Sauyour.
Now may you make your rekenynge sure.   610
EVERYMAN   In the name of the Holy Trynyte
My body sore punysshyd shall be.

[*He begins to scourge himself.*]

Take this, body, for the synne of the flesshe!
Also thou delytest to go gay and fresshe,
And in the way of dampnacyon thou dyd
    me brynge;   615
Therfore suffre now strokes of punysshynge!
Now of penaunce I wyll wade the water
    clere,
To saue me from purgatory, that sharpe fyre.

[*Good Deeds rises from the floor.*]

GOOD DEEDS   I thanke God, now I can walke
    and go,
And am delyuered of my sykenesse and wo.   620
Therfore with Eueryman I wyll go, and not
    spare;
His good workes I wyll helpe hym to
    declare.5
KNOWLEDGE   Now, Eueryman, be mery and
    glad!
Your Good Dedes cometh now, ye may not
    be sad.
Now is your Good Dedes hole and sounde,   625
Goynge vpryght vpon the grounde.

EVERYMAN   My herte is lyght, and shalbe
    euermore.
Now wyll I smyte faster than I dyde before.
GOOD DEEDS   Eueryman, pylgryme, my specyall
    frende,
Blessyd be thou without ende!   630
For the is preparate the eternall glory!
Ye haue me made hole and sounde,
Therfore I wyll byde by the in euery stounde.
EVERYMAN   Welcome, my Good Dedes! Now I
    here thy voyce
I wepe for very swetenes of loue.   635
KNOWLEDGE   Be no more sad, but euer reioyce;
God seeth thy lyuynge in his trone aboue.
Put on this garment to thy behoue,
Whiche is wette with your teres,
Or elles before God you may it mysse,   640
Whan ye to your iourneys ende come shall.
EVERYMAN   Gentyll Knowlege, what do ye it call?
KNOWLEDGE   It is the garmente of sorowe;
Fro payne it wyll you borowe;
Contrycyon it is   645
That getteth forgyuenes,
It pleaseth God passynge well.
GOOD DEEDS   Eueryman, wyll you were it for
    your hele?

[*Everyman puts on the robe of contrition.*]

EVERYMAN   Now blessyd be Iesu, Maryes sone,
For now haue I on true contrycyon.   650
And lette vs go now without taryenge.
Good Dedes, haue we clere our rekenynge?
GOOD DEEDS   Ye, indede, I haue here.
EVERYMAN   Than I trust we nede not fere.
Now, frendes, let vs not parte in twayne.   655
KNOWLEDGE   Nay, Eueryman, that wyll we not,
    certayne.
GOOD DEEDS   Yet must thou le[a]d with the
Thre persones of grete myght.
EVERYMAN   Who sholde they be?
GOOD DEEDS   Dyscrecyon and Strength they
    hyght,   660
And thy Beaute may not abyde behynde.
KNOWLEDGE   Also ye must call to mynde
Your Fyue Wyttes as for your counseylours.
GOOD DEEDS   You must haue them redy at all
    houres.
EVERYMAN   Howe shall I gette them hyder?   665

KNOWLEDGE   You must call them all togyder,
And they wyll here you incontynent.
EVERYMAN   My frendes, come hyder and be
present,
Dyscrecyon, Strengthe, my Fyue Wyttes,
and Beaute!

[*Enter Discretion, Strength, Five Wits, and Beauty.*]

BEAUTY   Here at your wyll we be all redy.   670
What wyll ye that we sholde do?
GOOD DEEDS   That ye wolde with Eueryman go
And helpe hym in his pylgrymage.
Aduyse you; wyll ye with him or not in that
vyage?
STRENGTH   We wyll brynge hym all thyder,   675
To his helpe and comforte, ye may beleue
me.
DISCRETION   So wyll we go with hym all togyder.
EVERYMAN   Almyghty God, loued may thou be!
I gyue the laude that I haue hyder brought
Strength, Dyscrecyon, Beaute and Five
Wyttes. Lacke I nought.   680
And my Good Dedes, with Knowlege clere,
All be in company at my wyll here.
I desyre no more to my besynes.
STRENGTH   And I, Strength, wyll by you stande
in dystres,
Though thou wolde in batayle fyght on the
grounde.   685
FIVE WITS   And though it were thrugh the
worlde rounde,
We wyll not departe for swete ne soure.
BEAUTY   No more wyll I, vnto dethes houre,
What so euer therof befall.
DISCRETION   Eueryman, aduyse you fyrst of all;   690
Go with a good aduysement and
delyberacyon.
We all gyue you vertuous monycyon
That all shall be well.
EVERYMAN   My frendes, harken what I wyll tell—
I praye God rewarde you in his heuenly
spere—   695
Now herken all that be here,
For I wyll make my testament
Here before you all present:
In almes halfe my good I wyll gyue with my
handes twayne

In the way of charyte with good entent,   700
And the other halfe styll shall remayne,
In queth to be retourned there it ought to be.
This I do in despyte of the fende of hell,
To go quyte out of his perell
Euer after and this daye.   705
KNOWLEDGE   Eueryman, herken what I saye:
Go to Presthode, I you aduyse,
And receyue of hym, in ony wyse,
The holy sacrament and oyntement togyder;
Than shortly se ye tourne agayne hyder;   710
We wyll all abyde you here.
FIVE WITS   Ye, Eueryman, hye you that ye redy
were.
There is no emperour, kinge, duke, ne baron,
That of God hath commycyon
As hath the leest preest in the worlde beynge;   715
For of the blessyd sacramentes pure and
benygne
He bereth the keyes, and therof hath the cure
For mannes redempcyon—it is euer sure—
Whiche God for our soules medycyne
Gaue vs out of his herte with grete payne,   720
Here in this transytory lyfe for the and me.
The blessyd sacramentes seven there be—
Baptym, confyrmacyon, with preesthode
good,
And ye sacrament of Goddes precyous flesshe
and blod,
Maryage, the holy extreme vnccyon, and
penaunce.   725
These seuen be good to haue in
remembraunce,
Gracyous sacramentes of hye deuynyte.
EVERYMAN   Fayne wolde I receyue that holy
body,
And mekely to my ghostly fader I wyll go.
FIVE WITS   Eueryman, that is the best that ye
can do.   730
God wyll you to saluacyon brynge,
For preesthode excedeth all other thynge:
To vs holy scrypture they do teche,
And conuerteth man fro synne heuen to
reche;
God hath to them more power gyuen   735
Than to ony aungell that is in heuen.
With five wordes he may consecrate
Goddes body in flesshe and blode to make,

And handeleth his Maker bytwene his
  hande[s].
The preest byndeth and vnbyndeth all
  bandes,   740
Both in erthe and in heuen.
Thou mynystres all the sacramentes seuen;
Though we kyst thy fete, thou wert worthy;
Thou arte the surgyon that cureth synne
  deedly;
No remedy we fynde vnder God   745
But all onely preesthode.
Eueryman, God gaue preest[s] that dygnyte
And setteth them in his stede amonge vs to be.
Thus be they aboue aungelles in degree.

[*Exit Everyman to receive from the priest the
Sacrament and extreme unction. Knowledge and
the rest remain.*]

KNOWLEDGE   If preestes be good, it is so, suerly.   750
  But whan Iesu hanged on ye crosse with
    grete smarte,
  There he gaue out of his blessyd herte
  The same sacrament in grete tourment.
  He solde them not to vs, that Lorde
    omnypotent;
  Therefore Saynt Peter the Apostell dothe
    saye   755
  That Iesus curse hath all they
  Whiche God theyr Sauyour do by or sell,
  Or they for ony money do take or tell.
  Synfull preests gyueth the synners example
    bad;
  Theyr chyldren sytteth by other mennes
    fyres, I haue harde;   760
  And some haunteth womens company
  With vnclen lyfe, as lustes of lechery.
  These be with synne made blynde.[6]
FIVE WITS   I trust to God no suche may we fynde.
  Therfore let vs preesthode honour,   765
  And folowe theyr doctryne for our soules
    socoure.
  We be theyr shepe, and they shepeherdes be,
  By whome we all be kepte in suerte.
  Peas! for yonder I se Eueryman come,
  Whiche hath made true satysfaccyon.   770
GOOD DEEDS   Methynke it is he indede.

[*Re-enter Everyman.*]

EVERYMAN   Now Iesu be your alder spede!
  I haue receyued the sacrament for my
    redempcyon,
  And than myne extreme vnccyon.
  Blessyd be all they that counseyled me to
    take it!   775
  And now, frendes, let vs go without longer
    respyte.
  I thanke God that ye haue taryed so longe.
  Now set eche of you on this rodde your
    honde,
  An shortely folowe me.
  I go before there I wolde be. God be our
    gyde!   780
STRENGTH   Eueryman, we wyll not fro you go
  Tyll ye haue done this vyage longe.
DISCRETION   I, Dyscrecyon, wyll byde by you
    also.
KNOWLEDGE   And though this pylgrymage be
    neuer so stronge,
  I wyll neuer parte you fro.   785
  Eueryman, I wyll be as sure by the
  As euer I dyde by Iudas Machabee.

[*They proceed together to the grave.*]

EVERYMAN   Alas! I am so faynt I may not stande!
  My lymmes vnder me doth folde!
  Frendes, let vs not tourne agayne to this
    lande,   790
  Not for all the worldes golde;
  For into this caue must I crepe
  And tourne to erth, and there to slepe.
BEAUTY   What! into this graue? Alas!
EVERYMAN   Ye, there shall ye consume, more
    and lesse.   795
BEAUTY   And what! sholde I smoder here?
EVERYMAN   Ye, by my fayth, and neuer more
    appere.
  In this worlde lyue no more we shall,
  But in heuen before the hyest Lorde of all.
BEAUTY   I crosse out all this! Adewe, by Saynt
    Iohan!   800
  I take my cap in my lappe, and am gone.
EVERYMAN   What, Beaute! whyder wyll ye?
BEAUTY   Peas! I am defe. I loke not behynde me,
    Not and thou woldest gyue me all ye golde
    in thy chest! [*Exit Beauty.*]

EVERYMAN   Alas! wherto may I truste?   805
    Beaute gothe fast awaye fro me!
    She promysed with me to lyue and dye.
STRENGTH   Eueryman, I wyll the also forsake and
    denye.
    Thy game lyketh me not at all.
EVERYMAN   Why than, ye wyll forsake me all?   810
    Swete Strength, tary a lytell space.
STRENGTH   Nay, syr, by the rode of grace!
    I wyll hye me from the fast,
    Though thou wepe tyll thy herte tobrast.
EVERYMAN   Ye wolde euer byde by me, ye sayd.   815
STRENGTH   Ye, I haue you ferre ynoughe
    conueyde!
    Ye be olde ynoughe, I vnderstande,
    Your pylgrymage to take on hande.
    I repent me that I hyder came.
EVERYMAN   Strength, you to dysplease I am to
    blame,   820
    Yet promise is dette, this ye well wot.
STRENGTH   In fayth, I care not!
    Thou arte but a foole to complayne.
    You spende your speche, and wast your
    brayne.
    Go, thryst the into the grounde! [Exit
    Strength.]   825

EVERYMAN   I had wende surer I shulde you haue
    founde.
    He that trusteth in his Strength
    She hym deceyueth at the length.
    Bothe Strength and Beaute forsaketh me;
    Yet they promysed me fayre and louyngly.   830
DISCRETION   Eueryman, I will after Strength be
    gone.
    As for me, I will leue you alone.
EVERYMAN   Why Dyscrecyon! wyll ye forsake
    me?
DISCRETION   Ye, in fayth, I wyll go fro the;
    For whan Strength goth before   835
    I folowe after euer more.
EVERYMAN   Yet, I pray the, for the loue of the
    Trynyte,
    Loke in my graue ones pyteously.
DISCRETION   Nay, so nye wyll I not come.
    Fare well euerychone! [Exit Discretion.]   840

EVERYMAN   O, all thynge fayleth, saue God
    alone—

    Beaute, Strength, and Dyscrecyon;
    For whan Deth bloweth his blast
    They all renne fro me full fast.
FIVE WITS   Eueryman, my leue now of the I take.   845
    I wyll folowe the other, for here I the
    forsake.
EVERYMAN   Alas! than may I wayle and wepe,
    For I toke you for my best frende.
FIVE WITS   I wyll no lenger the kepe.
    Now farewell, and there an ende! [Exit Five
    Wits.]   850

EVERYMAN   O Iesu, helpe! All hath forsaken me!
GOOD DEEDS   Nay, Eueryman; I wyll byde with
    the.
    I wyll not forsake the indede;
    Thou shalte fynde me a good frende at nede.
EVERYMAN   Gramercy, Good Dedes! Now may
    I true frendes se.   855
    They haue forsaken me, euerychone;
    I loued them better than my Good Dedes
    alone.
    Knowlege, wyll ye forsake me also?
KNOWLEDGE   Ye, Eueryman, whan ye to Deth
    shall go;
    But not yet, for no maner of daunger.   860
EVERYMAN   Gramercy, Knowlege, with all my
    herte!
KNOWLEDGE   Nay, yet I wyll not from hens
    departe
    Tyll I se where ye shall be come.
EVERYMAN   Methynke, alas, that I must be gone
    To make my rekenynge, and my dettes
    paye;   865
    For I se my tyme is nye spent awaye.
    Take example, all ye that this do here or se,
    How they that I loued best do forsake me,
    Excepte my Good Dedes that bydeth truely.
GOOD DEEDS   All erthly thynges is but vanyte.   870
    Beaute, Strength, and Dyscrecyon do man
    forsake,
    Folysshe frendes, and kynnesmen, that fayre
    spake—
    All fleeth saue Good Dedes, and that am I.
EVERYMAN   Haue mercy on me, God moost
    myghty,
    And stande by me, thou moder and mayde,
    Holy Mary!   875
GOOD DEEDS   Fere not; I wyll speke for the.

EVERYMAN   Here I crye God mercy!

GOOD DEEDS   Shorte oure ende, and mynysshe
    our payne.
    Let vs go, and neuer come agayne.

EVERYMAN   Into thy handes, Lorde, my soule I
    commende.   880
    Receyue it, Lorde, that it be not lost.
    As thou me boughtest, so me defende,
    And saue me from the fendes boost,
    That I may appere with that blessyd hoost
    That shall be saued at the day of dome.   885
    In manus tuas, of myghtes moost
    For euer, *commendo spiritum meum!*[7]

[*Everyman and Good Deeds descend into the grave.*]

KNOWLEDGE   Now hath he suffred that we all
    shall endure.
    The Good Dedes shall make all sure.
    Now hath he made endynge.   890
    Methynketh that I here aungelles synge,
    And make grete ioy and melody
    Where Euerymannes soule receyued shall be.

ANGEL [*within*]   Come, excellente electe spouse
    to Iesu!
    Here aboue thou shalte go,   895
    Bycause of thy synguler vertue.
    Now the soule is taken the body fro,
    Thy rekenynge is crystall clere.
    Now shalte thou in to the heuenly spere;
    Vnto the whiche all ye shall come   900

    That lyueth well before the daye of dome.
    [*Exit Knowledge.*]

[*Enter the Doctor as an Epilogue.*]

DOCTOR   This morall men may haue in mynde.
    Ye herers, take it of worth, olde and yonge!
    And forsake Pryde, for he deceyueth you in
    the ende.
    And remember Beaute, Five Wyttes,
    Strength, and Dy[s]crecyon,   905
    They all at the last do euery man forsake,
    Saue his Good Dedes there dothe he take—
    But beware, and they be small
    Before God he hath no helpe at all.
    None excuse may be there for euery man.   910
    Alas, how shall he do, than?
    For, after dethe, amendes may no man make;
    For than mercy and pyte doth hym forsake.
    If his rekenynge be not clere whan he doth
    come
    God wyll saye: " *Ite, maledicti, in ignem
    eternum!* "   915
    And he that hath his accounte hole and
    sounde,
    Hye in heuen he shall be crounde.
    Vnto whiche place God brynge vs all thyder,
    That we may lyue body and soule togyder.
    Therto helpe, the Trynyte!   920
    Amen, saye ye, for Saynt Charyte.

Finis.

Glossary

3 **By fygure**   by a figurative representation.   8 **entent**   sentence, or lesson.   25 **ghostly syght** spiritual understanding.   29 **lowe**   love.   44 **appayreth**   grows worse.   72 **renne**   run.   88 **wete** know.   95 **spere**   sphere.   101 **layser**   leisure.   116 **rest**   arrest.   121 **good**   possession.   189 **gete** begotten.   197 **and**   if.   253 **fere**   frighten.   306 **wheder**   whither.   317 **saye**   assay.   358 **tyse** entice.   422 **sere**   sore.   503 **eke**   also.   525 **hole**   wholly.   566 **vyage**   voyage.   590 **conduytor** establisher.   633 **euery stounde**   always.   679 **laude**   praise.   692 **monycyon**   instruction.   702 **queth**   bequest.   772 **your alder spede**   prosperity to you all.   878 **mynysshe**   diminish.

Notes

1   The play is directed especially against the avaricious for whom the giving of alms was a traditional penance.

2   The use of terms like "account book" (see also l. 502) and Everyman's fondness for Goods suggest

a town audience to whom charity is most readily explainable in terms of almsgiving, and who are prone to put their trust in money and property. In this respect the play has a distinctly postfeudal or modern air, which accounts in part for its continued popularity as a suitable medium for church entertainments.

3 Everyman's confidence in money as a remedy for all difficulties is again an indication that the audience addressed was probably made up largely of merchants.

4 The scourge is a traditional symbol for penance in the visual arts. Cf. the Irish poem, "I would have for King of Kings," on p. 38.

5 Underlying this action is the traditional doctrine that mercy is available only to the penitent. Penance enables Everyman to have the assistance of Good Deeds and to wear his robe of Contrition, which is a sign of grace. It is noteworthy that the play is not Pelagian; Good Deeds without penance and grace are of no use to Everyman.

6 This is a manifestation of the traditional theme of spiritual blindness (see *Mactacio Abel*, n. 10).

7 Ps. 30:6 (and Luke 23:46), used in the office of Compline.

INDEX